THE BOOK
OF THE STATES
1984-1985

VOLUME 25

THE COUNCIL OF
STATE GOVERNMENTS

THE COUNCIL OF STATE GOVERNMENTS

LEXINGTON, KENTUCKY

Manufactured in the United States of America

THE COUNCIL OF STATE GOVERNMENTS

The Council is a joint agency of all state governments—created, supported and directed by them. It conducts research on state programs and problems; maintains an information service available to state agencies, officials and legislators; issues a variety of publications; assists in state-federal liaison; promotes regional and state-local cooperation; and provides staff for affiliated organizations.

HEADQUARTERS OFFICE
Iron Works Pike
P.O. Box 11910
Lexington, Kentucky 40578

EASTERN OFFICE
1500 Broadway
18th Floor
New York, New York 10036

MIDWESTERN OFFICE
203 North Wabash Avenue
Chicago, Illinois 60601

SOUTHERN OFFICE
3384 Peachtree Road, NE
Atlanta, Georgia 30326

WESTERN OFFICE
720 Sacramento Street
Third Floor
San Francisco, California 94108

WASHINGTON, D.C. OFFICE
Hall of the States
444 North Capitol Street, NW
Washington, D.C. 20001

Staff

Editing
L. Edward Purcell, Editor
Susan Morrisette, Editorial Associate
Beth Ann Murray, Editorial Assistant
Martha Copeland, Administrative Assistant
David Burg, Editorial Consultant

Typesetting
Karen Pinches, Compositor

Proofreading
Rosemary Staley
Beth Ann Murray
Elaine S. Knapp
Susan Mohler
Susan Morrisette

Production
Beth Ann Murray
Charles Haspel

Research and Information Development
Deborah Gona, Information Coordinator
Sandra Schneider, Information Assistant

A Note on Use

Symbols: Unless otherwise noted, all tables in *The Book of the States* use the following scheme:

. . .—no data
blank cell—not applicable
0—zero quantity.

Sources: Unless otherwise noted, the sources of data for tables are surveys and research by The Council of State Governments.

CONTENTS

Section I
INTERGOVERNMENTAL
AFFAIRS

1. **Interstate Organizations**
The Council of State Governments 1
Officers and Executive Committee 4
Regional Conferences 5
National Secretariat Organizations 6
Offices and Directors. 7
Selected Organizations Serving State
 and Local Government Officials 8
Interstate Compacts. 11

2. **Intergovernmental Relations**
Intergovernmental Relations 15
Federal-State Relations 18
State-Local Relations 21
General Revenue Sharing 24
State Aid to Local Government 30

Section II THE GOVERNORS
AND THE EXECUTIVE BRANCH

The Governors, 1982-83 39
Governors and Legislatures 42
The Executive Branch: Elective
 Officials and Organizations 44
The Executive Branch: Issues. 47

Section III THE LEGISLATURES

The State Legislatures 79

Section IV THE JUDICIARY

State of the Judiciary. 142

Section V LEGISLATION, ELECTIONS
AND CONSTITUTIONS

1. **Legislation**
Trends in State Legislation: 1982-83 165
Uniform State Laws. 173

2. **Elections**
Election Legislation 180

3. **Constitutions**
State Constitutions: 1982-83. 211
State Constitutional Changes. 214
Sources on State Constitutions 218

Section VI ADMINISTRATION

1. **Financial Administration**
State Financial Administration 231

2. **Budgeting**
Budgeting in the 1980s. 242

3. **Purchasing**
Procurement Challenges 251

4. **Information Systems**
State Information Management. 253
State Information Systems 261
State Library Agencies 265

5. **Employment**
State Government Employment 271
Finances of State-Administered Public
 Employee Retirement Systems. 279
Developments in State Personnel
 Systems 288

Section VII FINANCES

1. **Revenue, Expenditure and Debt**
State and Local Government Finances
 in 1981-82 299
State Finances in 1982 314

2. **Taxation**
Recent Trends in State Taxation 327
State Tax Collections in 1983 341

Section VIII MAJOR STATE SERVICES

1. **Education**
Education, 1982-1983 353
Elementary-Secondary Education
 Issues 357
Postsecondary Education 359

2. **Transportation**
Transportation in the 1980s 376

3. **Health and Human Services**
Public Welfare 390
Food Stamps, Medicaid, Social
 Services and Aging. 392
State Health Agency Programs 403

4. Safety and Public Protection
Corrections, Courts and Criminal
    Justice 415
State Regulation of Occupations
    and Professions 420
State Police and Highway Patrols 424
Developments in Public Utilities
    Regulation..........................427

5. Development and Housing
State Economic Development 434
Housing and Community Development 436
Business and Industrial Development 440

6. Natural Resources
Environmental Management:
    Emerging Issues 450
State Parks and Outdoor Recreation 458
State Agriculture 463
State Forestry Administration and
    Management........................472
Soil and Water Conservation 482

7. Labor Relations
Labor Legislation: 1982-1983 488

Section IX   THE STATE PAGES 506

Index 541

LIST OF TABLES

Section I   INTERGOVERNMENTAL AFFAIRS

1. Interstate Organizations
Participation in selected interstate compacts 12

2. Intergovernmental Relations
Total federal aid to states: fiscal 1978-82 20
Entitlement periods and authorized distri-
bution amounts (general revenue sharing) 24
General revenue sharing payments to state gov-
ernments, by state, by entitlement period 26
General revenue sharing payments to local gov-
ernments, by state, by entitlement period 28
Direct state aid to local governments 30
State payments to local governments and re-
ceipts from federal government: fiscal 1982 31
Summary of state intergovernmental
payments: 1942 to 1982 33
State intergovernmental expenditure, by
state: 1976 to 1982 34
Per capita state intergovernmental expendi-
ture, by function and by state: 1982 35
State intergovernmental expenditure, by
function and by state: 1982 36
State intergovernmental expenditure, by type
of receiving government and by state: 1982 37

Section II   THE GOVERNORS
AND THE EXECUTIVE BRANCH

Separately elected state officials: 1965 and 1984 45
The governors 49
The governors: qualifications for office 51
The governors: compensation 52
The governors: powers 53
The governors: provisions and procedures for
transition 54
Gubernatorial executive orders: authorization,
provisions, procedures 55
Lieutenant governors: qualifications and terms 57
Lieutenant governors: powers and duties 58
Attorneys general and secretaries of state:
qualifications for office 59
Secretaries of state: election and registration
duties 60
Secretaries of state: custodial, publication
and legislative duties 61
Attorneys general: prosecutorial and advisory
duties 62
Attorneys general: consumer protection activ-
ities and subpoena and antitrust powers 63
Attorneys general: duties to administrative
agencies and miscellaneous duties 64
State cabinet systems 65
State administrative officials: annual salaries 66
Constitutional and statutory provisions for
length and number of terms of elected state
officials 72
State administrative officials: methods of
selection 74

Section III   THE LEGISLATURES

Names of state legislative bodies and
convening place 84
The legislators: numbers, terms and party
affiliations 85
The legislators: qualifications for office 86
Senate leadership positions: methods
of selection 88
House leadership positions: methods
of selection 90
Legislative compensation: regular and special
sessions 92
Additional compensation for senate leaders 95
Additional compensation for house leaders 97
Legislative compensation: interim payments
and other direct payments 100
Membership turnover in the legislatures: 1982 103
Introductions and enactments: regular sessions,
1981 and 1982 sessions 104
Introductions and enactments: special sessions,
1981 and 1982 sessions 106
Legislative sessions: legal provisions 108
Enacting legislation: veto, veto override
and effective date 112
Legislative procedure: time limits on bill
introduction 114
Legislative procedure: bill introduction and
reference 117
Legislative procedure: standing committees 118
Legislative procedure: standing committee
action 120
Staff for legislative standing committees 121
Legislative appropriations process: budget
documents and bills 122
Staff for individual legislators 124
Fiscal notes: content and distribution 125
Legislative review of administrative regula-
tions: powers 127
Legislative review of administrative regula-
tion: structures and procedures 128
Summary of sunset legislation 130
Legislative applications of electronic data
processing 134
Lobbyists: as defined in state statutes 136
Lobbyists: registration and reporting 138

Section IV   THE JUDICIARY

State courts of last resort 146
Number of judges and terms for intermediate
and appellate courts and major trial courts 148
Compensation of judges of appellate courts
and major trial courts 150
Qualifications of judges of state appellate
courts and trial courts of general
jurisdiction 152
Selection and retention of judges 154
Methods for removal of judges and filling of
vacancies 156
Selected data on court administrative offices 163

Section V LEGISLATION, ELECTIONS AND CONSTITUTIONS

1. Legislation
Initiative provisions for state legislation 167
Provisions for referendum on state legislation 168
Provisions for recall of state officials 170
Minimum age for specified activities 171
Legalized gaming in the states 172
Record of passage of uniform and model acts 175

2. Elections
Campaign finance laws: filing requirements 183
Campaign finance laws: limitations on con-
tributions by organizations 188
Campaign finance laws: limitations on con-
tributions by individuals 192
Funding of state elections: tax provisions
and public financing 197
Voter registration information 199
Polling hours: general elections 200
State officers to be elected: 1984 and 1985 202
Methods of nomination for state officials 204
Primary elections for state officers 206
Voter turnout for presidential elections:
1972, 1976 and 1980 208
Voter turnout in non-presidential election
years: 1974, 1978 and 1982 209
Voting statistics for gubernatorial
elections 210

3. Constitutions
State constitutional changes by method of
initiation, 1970-71, 1980-81 and 1982-83 212
Substantive changes in state constitutions:
proposed and adopted, 1970-71, 1980-81,
1982-83 216
General information on state constitutions 221
Constitutional amendment procedure: by the
legislature 223
Constitutional amendment procedure: by
initiative 225
Procedures for calling constitutional
conventions 226
State constitutional commissions 228
Constitutional conventions 229

Section VI ADMINISTRATION

1. Financial Administration
State cash management 233
State accounting and reporting 236
State auditing 238

2. Budgeting
State budgetary practices 244
Budget agency functions 246
Budget: officials or agencies responsible for
preparation, review and controls 248

4. Information Systems
State statistical activities 256
State interagency statistical coordination 258
Rank order of statistical functions performed 260
Availability of official state projections 260
State information systems: external problems 263
State information systems: internal problems 263
State information systems: security 264
State library agencies 267
Functions and responsibilities of state library
agencies 268

5. Employment
Government employment and payrolls,
1970-1982 271
State employment by major functions,
1970-1982 272
State full-time equivalent employment per
10,000 population, October 1980 272
State government average full-time pay,
October 1982 272
Summary of state government employment:
1952-1982 274
Employment and payrolls of state and local
governments, by function: October 1982 274
State and local government employment, by
state: October 1982 275
State and local government payrolls and
average earnings of full-time employees,
by state: October 1982 276
State government employment (full-time
equivalent), total and for selected func-
tions, by state: October 1982 277
State government payrolls, total and for se-
lected functions, by state: October 1982 278
Percentage distribution of total receipts,
selected years: 1962 to 1982 280
Number, membership and benefits of state-
administered employee retirement systems,
by system characteristics: 1981-82 281
National summary of finances of state-administered employee retirement systems, se-
lected years: 1972-1982 281
Membership and benefit operations of state-
administered employee retirement systems:
last month of fiscal 1982 282
Finances of state-administered employee
retirement systems, by state: 1981-82 284
Comparative statistics for state-ad-
ministered public employee retirement
systems: 1981-82 286
State employees: personnel system organiza-
tion and collective bargaining 291
State employees: compensation provisions
and selected benefits 293
State employees: paid holidays 294
State employees evaluation systems 296

Section VII FINANCES

1. Revenue, Expenditure and Debt

Indebtedness of state and local governments
at end of fiscal 1982, by state 303
Summary of governmental finances, by level
of government: 1981-82 304
Summary of state and local government
finances: 1977-78 to 1981-82................306
General revenue of state and local governments by source and by state: 1981-82 308
Per capita general revenue of state and local
governments by source and by state:
1981-82 309
Origin and allocation, by level of government, of general revenue of state and local
governments: 1981-82 310
Direct general expenditure of state and local
governments, for selected items, by state:
1981-82 311
Per capita direct general expenditure of state
and local governments, for selected items,
by state: 1981-82..........................312
Relation of selected items of state and local
government finances to personal income:
1981-82 313
Summary financial aggregates, by state: 1982 317
National totals of state government finances,
selected years: 1960-82 318
State general revenue, by source and by state:
1982 320
State government expenditure, by characteristic and object and by state: 1982..........322
State general expenditure in total and for
selected functions, by state: 1982.............324
State debt outstanding at end of fiscal year,
by state: 1982 326

2. Taxation

Agencies administering major state taxes 329
Food and drug sales tax exemptions 331
State excise rates.............................332
State individual income taxes 334
State severance taxes: 1983 336
Range of state corporate income tax rates 339
Percentage distribution of state tax col-
lections, by major tax category, selected
years 1957-1983 342
National summary of state government tax
revenue, by type of tax: 1981 to 1983 344
Summary of state government tax revenue,
by state: 1981 to 1983 345
State government tax revenue, by type of
tax: 1983 346
State government sales and gross receipts
tax revenue: 1983 348
State government license tax revenue: 1983 350
Fiscal year, population and personal income,
by state 352

Section VIII MAJOR STATE SERVICES

1. Education

Changes in total state support for education,
1980-81 to 1982-83 362
Changes in enrollments in public education,
1980-81 to 1982-83 363
Changes in per student state support for
education, 1980-81 to 1982-83 364
Total revenues for elementary/secondary
education and percentage share of total revenues by source, 1980-81 and 1982-83.........365
Changes in number of teachers and average
teacher salary, 1980-81 to 1982-83 366
State course requirements for high school
graduation 367
State minimum competency testing for pupils 368
Total enrollments in higher education: 1982 369
Appropriations of state tax funds for operating
expenses of higher education 370
Programs of student financial aid, based
upon need, for state residents to attend
either public or non-public colleges or universities: 1981-82 to 1983-84 371
Number of institutions of higher education
and branches: 1980-81 and 1982-83 372
Number of postsecondary schools with occupational programs, by state and type of
school: 1982 373
Average salaries of full-time instructional faculty on 9-month contracts,
in institutional units of higher education: 1982-83 374
Average salaries of full-time instructional
faculty on 12-month contracts, in institutional units of higher education: 1982-83 375

2. Transportation

Total road and street mileage: 1982 378
State receipts for highways: 1982 379
State disbursements for highways: 1982 380
Apportionment of federal-aid highway funds:
fiscal 1983 381
Motor vehicle laws 382
State no-fault motor vehicle insurance laws 384
State motor vehicle registrations: 1982 387
Motor vehicle operators and chauffeurs li-
censes: 1982 388

3. Health and Human Services

Aid to families with dependent children:
recipients of cash payments and amount
by state 395
Food stamp program 396
Supplemental security income, by state: 1982 397
Supplemental security income for aged,
blind and disabled (May 1983) 398
Medicaid expenditures: fiscal 1981 400
Child enforcement: fiscal 1982..................401
Federal allotments to states for Title XX
social services: fiscal 1981-84 402

Selected public health responsibilities
delegated to state health agencies:
fiscal 1982 407
Persons receiving selected personal health
services from state health agencies:
fiscal 1982 408
Public health program expenditures of state
health agencies, by program: fiscal 1982. 411
Public health expenditures of state health
agencies, by source of funds: fiscal 1982 412

4. Safety and Public Protection
State death penalty 418
Trends in state prison population 419
Status of mandatory continuing education
for selected professions 423
Number of state law enforcement personnel:
1982 426
State public utility commissions. 430
Certain regulatory functions of state
public utilities commissions 431
Average monthly bills, by customer class,
for electricity and gas: 1981 432

5. Development and Housing
State housing finance agencies 439
Financial assistance for industry 442
Tax incentives for industry and other
pertinent laws 444
Special services for industrial development 447

6. Natural Resources
State environmental organizations 454
Hazardous waste facility siting. 455
Waste disposal sites 457
State park statistics 460
Farm income: 1982 465
Farm acreage and income per farm: 1982 466
Production of major grains, by state:
1982 467
Livestock on U.S. farms, by state: 1982 468
Agricultural production, by commodity,
for selected items, by state: 1982 469
U.S. agricultural landholdings of foreign
owners, by state, December 1982. 470
Farm real estate values: 1982 471
Forest resources: 1982 475
Rural fire prevention and control program 476
Summary of forestry incentive programs
and rural forestry assistance expenditures 477
Insect and disease management expenditures,
urban and community expenditures, profes-
sional forestry personnel, and state
nursery programs 478
Administration of state forest agencies 479
Types of death tax incentives applied to
forestland: 1982 480
Types of property taxes applied to standing
or severed timber: 1982 .481
Growth of state and local government funds in
soil conservation district programs, 1957-
1983, in actual dollars 483

Major state soil and water conservation
programs 485
Conservation districts 486
Conservation district employees 487

7. Labor Relations
Maximum benefits for temporary total
disability provided by workers' compen-
sation statutes. 492
Preliminary estimates for workers' com-
pensation payments: 1980 and 1981 494
Status of state plans developed in accordance
with the federal occupational safety and
health act. 496
Selected state child labor standards affect-
ing minors under 18 498
Changes in basic minimum wages in non-farm
employment under state law: selected years
1965 to 1984 502
Selected data on state unemployment insurance
operations, by state: calendar 1982 504
Total unemployment and unemployment rates,
by state annual averages: 1976-1981 505

Section IX   THE STATE PAGES

Official names of states and jurisdictions,
capitols, zip codes and central switch-
boards 507
The states of the union—historical data 508
State statistics 510

FOREWORD

Published as it is on a biennial schedule, *The Book of the States* provides an unusual perspective on the states—longer than the familiar annual summaries, but shorter than grand five or 10-year evaluations. The dominant themes of this 25th edition are, for the most part, positive. Authors have found the states emerging from the encounters with New Federalism and financial hard times with a revived sense of mission and accomplishment. The tone, despite major reservations in some areas, is decidedly more optimistic than two years ago.

This edition of the *Book* is noticeably more compact than recent volumes, but the slimming down results more from changes in format than a reduction in comparative data. We made efforts to shorten the essays, asking authors to focus sharply on their topics.

As usual, many have contributed to this volume. Dozens of experts wrote essays and gathered data for the tables from diverse sources. The staff of The Council of State Governments conducted independent surveys and made countless inquiries in order to once again present this unique reference on the American states.

The Council is grateful for the help of all who contributed to this book.

April 1984

Carl W. Stenberg
Executive Director

Section I INTERGOVERNMENTAL AFFAIRS
1. Interstate Organizations

THE COUNCIL OF STATE GOVERNMENTS

The Council of State Governments is a non-profit, state-supported and directed service organization of all 50 states. Formally organized in 1933, the Council collects and distributes information, promotes interstate cooperation, and works to improve state administration and management. The mission of the Council is to strengthen the operations of states and the role of state government in the American federal system.

In 1983, the Council celebrated its 50th anniversary at a special governing board meeting in Lexington, Kentucky, location of the Council's headquarters office. The Council remains uniquely dedicated to addressing the needs of all branches of state government—executive, legislative and judicial.

Governance and Funding

Overall direction of the Council's staff and activities comes from a governing board consisting of all the nation's governors and, typically, two legislators from each state and jurisdiction. By tradition, the president of the Council is a governor, and the chairman is a state legislator. Members of the governing board include representatives from the national organizations of lieutenant governors, attorneys general, chief justices, secretaries of state, and state auditors, comptrollers and treasurers. An annual governing board meeting directs Council activities and provides a forum for discussion of substantive state issues.

From this broadly based governing body of approximately 175 elected state officials, an executive committee of about one-fifth that number is selected to manage the business affairs of the Council between annual governing board meetings. State officials also serve on several standing committees which advise the executive committee.

In 1979, the governing board of The Council of State Governments adopted amendments to its articles of organization which were designed to further enhance the regional concept. These changes provided a stronger role for regional state officials in the operation of the Council's regional offices and activities.

The states, U.S. territories and jurisdictions contribute to the Council's financial support. In addition, the Council administers federal and private-foundation grants that support research and information projects that align with the states' interests. The Council also generates revenue from the sale of its publications.

Offices of the Council

From its earliest years, directors of The Council of State Governments have understood the need for regional operations in coordination with a central office. When the Council's first national headquarters opened in Chicago in the early 1930s, a regional director was selected to work with the Council's executive director and charged with the specific duty of serving the Midwestern states.

Three more regional offices have been added during the intervening years. In 1935, the New York office was created to serve the Northeastern states. Soon after, an office was established in San Francisco for Western states, and in 1959, the Atlanta office began to serve Southern states. When the Council's headquarters office moved to Lexington, Kentucky, in 1969, the Chicago office became the regional center for the Midwest.

In 1938, the Council opened a state-federal relations office in Washington, D.C. to serve as a liaison with the federal government and public interest groups.

Activities and Services

The Council of State Governments is based on the premise that the states themselves are the best sources of innovations, ideas and information, and its activities reflect this belief. The Council's headquarters, four regional offices, and the Washington Office collect, analyze and distribute information on and for state governments nationwide. Reports, surveys, newsletters and services are available to state officials through regional and national conferences, training and management programs, research projects, and a variety of publications.

In Lexington, the States Information Center (SIC), a personal, direct-access inquiry and referral service, fields questions from state officials. By quickly locating statistical information, providing in-depth information through documents available for loan, and identifying appropriate experts on a given issue, the SIC unit replies to over 6,000 requests a year. In addition, the SIC library maintains 20,000 documents including Council and other organizational studies and an extensive collection of state legislative and agency reports.

The Council's commitment to keeping the states informed and aware of innovations in state programs, improvements in state administration and solutions to state problems is the impetus behind the development of a range of policy and management services to state governments. The Council's focus is dynamic, with specific priorities established to meet the changing needs of state officials. A few of the Council's policy and management activities are:

• The Innovations Transfer Program reports on innovative solutions to specific state problems. Since 1975, over 70 programs have been selected for study.

• The Interstate Consulting Service offers a quick, low-cost method for a state to obtain expert assistance from sister states.

• The Environmental and Natural Resources program conducts policy research and provides information services in order to improve the states' capacity to manage and develop their natural resources.

• The Committee on Suggested State Legislation collects, analyzes and reviews draft legislation for publication in an annual volume.

• The Legal Affairs staff work on interstate compacts and legislation affecting such state programs as emergency management, election procedures and export trade.

• The Fiscal Affairs unit studies economic development activities and fiscal issues in the states, including infrastructure finance and funding for mass transportation.

• The Financial Management program compiles information on state accounting practices, functions of state treasurers and deferred compensation programs.

• The Licensure and Regulation staff provide information on licensure examinations, administration, disciplinary processes, member training and sunset activities.

• The State Auditor Training program offers on-site training seminars for state employees and prepares auditor training materials for use by individual states.

Regional Office Activities

The Council's four regional offices foster regional cooperation through their work with regional organizations of legislators, governors, attorneys general and other organizations associated with the Council. Regional office staff assist in substantive and logistical support for regional task force and committee meetings on a wide range of specific issue areas, including, for example, environmental protection, transportation, federal preemption, economic development, energy, corrections and human resources. The issues and activities of each regional office are selected by a regional executive committee, comprised of state officials from that region. Regional offices of the Council produce newsletters and substantive issue reports for state officials in their region. In addition, annual conferences of regional organizations of state officials are staffed by the Council's regional offices.

The status of federal regulations, legislation, policies and programs is monitored by the Council's Washington, D.C. office. CSG staff are advocates of the states' interests and CSG policy positions at the federal level and, in addition, assist other CSG offices in substantive and logistical support for conferences and seminars held in Washington.

The Council is a major partner in the Hall of the States and its management entity, the States Services Organization, which provides the central office facilities and administrative support services for most of the states' offices and state associations located in Washington, D.C.

Publications

The Council publishes a variety of materials about state government, including reference works, directories, periodicals, research reports, information briefs and newsletters. The Council's major publications include:

• *The Book of the States* is a biennial reference guide to all major aspects of state government containing quantitative and comparative data and essays written by experts in state operations.

• *State Elective Officials and the Legislatures; State Legislative Leadership, Committees and Staff;* and *State Administrative Officials Classified by Function* are the three supplementary directories which include names, addresses and telephone numbers of state leaders.

• *Suggested State Legislation* is an annual volume of draft legislation and legislative ideas selected by a committee of state officials.

• *State Government News* is the Council's monthly magazine on state developments, innovations and issues which is distributed to over

12,000 state officials, including all elected state officials.

• *State Government* is a quarterly journal providing a forum for the discussion of government problems and solutions.

• *State Government Research Checklist* is a bimonthly inventory of state government reports and current information sources.

• *The Conference Calendar* is a monthly listing of meetings involving the Council and various organizations of state officials.

• The *Backgrounder Series* offers brief special issue reports covering current state actions and trends.

• Research reports provide in-depth, topical information on state programs and policies.

• Newsletters are produced regularly for several national organizations of state officials.

The Council also develops, produces and distributes audio-visual training and informational materials. Packages are presented in a variety of forms including slides, audiotapes, videotapes and films. These training packages are oriented to state government and can be modified to match an agency's needs and methods of operation.

Affiliated and Cooperating Organizations

The Articles of Organization of the Council recognize two forms of association—affiliate and cooperating. In 1983, the Council added two national organizations of state officials to its list of affiliates. The National Association of Secretaries of State (NASS) and the National Conference of State General Service Officers (NCSGSO) joined the National Conference of State Legislatures (NCSL), the Conference of Chief Justices, the National Association of Attorneys General (NAAG), the National Conference of Lieutenant Governors (NCLG), the National Association of State Purchasing Officials (NASPO), the Conference of State Court Administrators, and the National Association of State Auditors, Comptrollers and Treasurers (NASACT) as affiliated organizations of the Council, bringing the total to nine.

Many national organizations of state officials receive staff and secretariat services from the Council, including the production and distribution of newsletters, conference arrangements, research and inquiry response. The Council provides staff support to several of its 27 cooperating organizations, including the National Clearinghouse on Licensure, Enforcement and Regulation (CLEAR) and the National Associa-

tion for State Information Systems (NASIS). The Council maintains a reciprocal information exchange agreement with the majority of its cooperating organizations.

THE COUNCIL OF STATE GOVERNMENTS
Officers and Executive Committee
1983-84

Chairman
Representative Roy Hausauer, North Dakota

President
Governor James R. Thompson, Illinois

Vice-Chairman
Senator James I. Gibson, Nevada

Vice President
Governor George Nigh, Oklahoma

Other Members
Governor George R. Ariyoshi, Hawaii
Governor Victor Atiyeh, Oregon
Attorney General Paul Bardacke, New Mexico
Treasurer Harlan E. Boyles, North Carolina
Representative John T. Bragg, Tennessee
Governor Joseph E. Brennan, Maine
Secretary of State Jack H. Brier, Kansas
Senator James B. Dunn, South Dakota
Representative Harold P. Dyck, Kansas
Representative T.W. Edwards, South Carolina
Chief Justice Ralph J. Erickstad, North Dakota
Governor John V. Evans, Idaho
Senator Hugh T. Farley, New York
Senate President Miles "Cap" Ferry, Utah
Governor Robert Graham, Florida
Senator Sam C. Guess, Washington
Senator Grant Jones, Texas
Senator John J. Marchi, New York
Governor Scott M. Matheson, Utah
Representative Timothy J. Moynihan, Connecticut
Senator David E. Nething, North Dakota
Senator Oliver Ocasek, Ohio
Governor Allen I. Olson, North Dakota
Governor William A. O'Neill, Connecticut
Speaker Pro Tem William F. Passannante, New York
Governor Rudy Perpich, Minnesota
Senator Cary Peterson, Utah
Senate President Fred A. Risser, Wisconsin
Senator Kenneth C. Royall Jr., North Carolina
Lieutenant Governor William W. Scranton III, Pennsylvania
Governor Richard A. Snelling, Vermont
Governor John Spellman, Washington
Representative John J. Thomas, Indiana
Representative W. Paul White, Massachusetts
Senate President Pro Tem Edward E. Willey, Virginia

The Council of State Governments
Regional Conferences
1983-84

EAST

Eastern Regional Conference
Senator Hugh T. Farley, New York, Chairman

Eastern Association of Attorneys General
Attorney General Leroy S. Zimmerman, Pennsylvania, Chairman

MIDWEST

Midwestern Governors' Conference
Governor Rudy S. Perpich, Minnesota, Chairman

Midwestern Conference
Senator James B. Dunn, South Dakota, Chairman

Midwestern Conference of Attorneys General
Attorney General Neil Hartigan, Illinois, Chairman

SOUTH

Southern Governors' Association
Governor Charles S. Robb, Virginia, Chairman

Southern Legislative Conference
Senate President Pro Tem Edward E. Willey, Virginia, Chairman

Southern Conference of Attorneys General
Attorney General John Steven Clark, Arkansas, Chairman

Southern Regional Conference, National Association of State Budget Officers
Stuart W. Connock, Assistant Secretary for Financial Policy, Office of
Administration and Finance, Virginia, Chairman

Southern Council of State Planning Agencies
John T. Herndon, Director, Office of Planning and Budgeting,
Office of the Governor, Florida, Chairman

Southern Environmental Resources Conference
Dr. Joan K. Leavitt, Commissioner, Department of Health,
Oklahoma, Chair

WEST

Western Legislative Conference
Senator Sam Guess, Washington, Chairman

Conference of Western Attorneys General
Attorney General Kenneth O. Eikenberry, Washington, Chairman

The Council of State Governments
National Secretariat Organizations
1983-84

Committee on Suggested State Legislation (SSL)
Senator Thomas A. Casey, Louisiana, Chairman

National Association of Secretaries of State (NASS)
Secretary of State Jack H. Brier, Kansas, President

National Association of State Auditors, Comptrollers and Treasurers (NASACT)
Treasurer Harlan E. Boyles, North Carolina, President

National Association of State Comptrollers (NASC)
Comptroller Edward J. Mazur, Virginia, President

National Association of State Purchasing Officials (NASPO)
Purchasing Director John F. Spath, New York, President

National Association of State Treasurers (NAST)
Treasurer Julian Ridlen, Indiana, President

National Clearinghouse on Licensure, Enforcement and Regulation (CLEAR)
Secretary of State James Douglas, Vermont, Chairman

National Conference of Lieutenant Governors (NCLG)
Lieutenant Governor William W. Scranton III, Pennsylvania, Chairman

National Conference of State General Services Officers (NCSGSO)
Secretary Walter Baran, Department of General Services,
Pennsylvania, President

National State Auditors Association (NSAA)
Auditor General Anthony Piccirilli, Rhode Island, President

The Council of State Governments
Offices and Directors

Headquarters Office

Carl W. Stenberg, Executive Director
Darrell D. Perry, Director
Finance and Administration
R. Douglas Roederer, Director
Research and State Services
William G. Schneider, Director
Communications
P.O. Box 11910
Iron Works Pike
Lexington, Kentucky 40578
(606) 252-2291

Eastern Office

Alan V. Sokolow, Director
1500 Broadway, 18th Floor
New York, New York 10036
(212) 221-3630

Midwestern Office

James H. Bowhay, Director
203 North Wabash Avenue
Chicago, Illinois 60601
(312) 236-4011

Southern Office

Tom E. Richter, Director
3384 Peachtree Road, N.E., Suite 830
Atlanta, Georgia 30326
(404) 266-1271

Western Office

Daniel M. Sprague, Director
720 Sacramento Street, 3rd Floor
San Francisco, California 94108
(415) 986-3760

Washington Office

Norman Beckman, Director
Hall of the States
444 North Capitol Street
Washington, D.C. 20001
(202) 624-5450

SELECTED ORGANIZATIONS
SERVING STATE AND LOCAL
GOVERNMENT OFFICIALS

Academy for State and Local Government, 400 North Capitol Street, NW, Suite 349, Washington, D.C. 20001. (202) 638-1445

Advisory Commission on Intergovernmental Relations, 1111-20th Street, NW, Suite 2000, Washington, D.C. 20575. (202) 653-5640

American Association of Port Authorities, 1612 K Street, NW, Suite 900, Washington, D.C. 20006. (202) 331-1263

American Association of School Administrators, 1801 North Moore Street, Arlington, Virginia 22209. (703) 528-0700

American Association of State Highway and Transportation Officials, 444 North Capitol Street, NW, Suite 225, Washington, D.C. 20001. (202) 624-5810

American Judicature Society, 200 West Monroe, Suite 1606, Chicago, Illinois 60606. (312) 558-6900

American Planning Association, 1313 East 60th Street, Chicago, Illinois 60637. (312) 955-9100

American Public Health Association, 1015-15th Street, NW, Washington, D.C. 20005. (202) 789-5600

American Public Power Association, 2301 M Street, NW, 3rd Floor, Washington, D.C. 20037. (202) 775-8300

American Public Transit Association, 1225 Connecticut Avenue, NW, Suite 200, Washington, D.C. 20036. (202) 828-2800

American Public Welfare Association, 1125-15th Street, NW, Suite 300, Washington, D.C. 20005. (202) 293-7550

American Public Works Association, 1313 East 60th Street, Chicago, Illinois 60637. (312) 667-2200

American Society for Public Administration, 1120 G Street, NW, Suite 500, Washington, D.C. 20005. (202) 393-7878

American Water Works Association, 6666 West Quincy Avenue, Denver, Colorado 80235. (303) 794-7711

Association of Government Accountants, 727 South 23rd Street, Suite 100, Arlington, Virginia 22202. (703) 684-6931

Association of State and Interstate Water Pollution Control Administrators, 444 N. Capitol Street, NW, Suite 330, Washington, D.C. 20001. (202) 624-7782

Association of State and Territorial Health Officials, 1311A Dolly Madison Blvd., Suite 3A, McLean, Virginia 22101. (703) 556-9222

Association of State and Territorial Solid Waste Management Officials, 444 N. Capitol Street, NW, Suite 343, Washington, D.C. 20001. (202) 624-5828

Building Officials and Code Administrators International, 17926 South Halsted Street, Homewood, Illinois 60430. (312) 799-2300

Conference of Chief Justices, 300 Newport Avenue, Williamsburg, Virginia 23185. (804) 253-2000

Conference of State Court Administrators, 300 Newport Avenue, Williamsburg, Virginia 23185. (804) 253-2000

Council for International Urban Liaison, 818 18th Street, NW, Suite 840, Washington, D.C. 20006. (202) 223-1434

Council for Urban Economic Development, 1730 K Street, NW, Suite 1009, Washington, D.C. 20006. (202) 223-4735

Council of State Community Affairs Agencies, 444 North Capitol Street, NW, Suite 251, Washington, D.C. 20001. (202) 393-6435

Council of State Governments, Iron Works Pike, P.O. Box 11910, Lexington, Kentucky 40578. (606) 252-2291

Council of State Housing Agencies, 400 N. Capitol Street, NW, Suite 295, Washington, D.C. 20001. (202) 628-8880

Council of State Planning Agencies, 400 N. Capitol Street, NW, Suite 291, Washington, D.C. 20001. (202) 624-7726

Council on Governmental Ethics Laws, Iron Works Pike, P. O. Box 11910, Lexington, Kentucky 40578. (606) 252-2291

Education Commission of the States, 300 Lincoln Tower Building, 1860 Lincoln Street, Denver, Colorado 80295. (303) 861-4917

Federation of Tax Administrators, 444 North Capitol Street, NW, Suite 334, Washington, D.C. 20001. (202) 624-5890

Institute of Transportation Engineers, 525 School Street, SW, Suite 410, Washington, D.C. 20024. (202) 554-8050

International Association of Assessing Officers, 1313 East 60th Street, Chicago, Illinois 60637. (312) 947-2064

International Association of Chiefs of Police, 13 Firstfield Road, Gaithersburg, Maryland 20878. (301) 948-0922

International Association of Fire Chiefs, 1329 18th Street, NW, Washington, D.C. 20036. (202) 833-3420

International Bridge, Tunnel & Turnpike Association, 2120 L Street, NW, Suite 305, Washington, D.C. 20037. (202) 659-4620

International City Management Association, 1120 G Street, NW, Suite 300, Washington, D.C. 20005. (202) 626-4610

International Institute of Municipal Clerks, 160 N. Altadena Drive, Pasadena, California 91107. (213) 795-6153

International Personnel Management Association, 1850 K Street, NW, Suite 870, Washington, D.C. 20006. (202) 833-5860

Interstate Conference of Employment Security Agencies, 444 North Capitol Street, NW, Suite 126, Washington, D.C. 20001. (202) 628-5588

Municipal Finance Officers Association of U.S. and Canada, 180 North Michigan Avenue, Chicago, Illinois 60601. (312) 977-9700

National Academy of Public Administration, 1120 G Street, NW, 5th Floor, Washington, D.C. 20005. (202) 347-3190

National Association of State Alcohol and Drug-Abuse Directors, 444 North Capitol Street, NW, Suite 530, Washington, D.C. 20001. (202) 783-6868

National Association for State Information Systems, Iron Works Pike, P.O. Box 11910, Lexington, Kentucky 40578. (606) 252-2291

National Association of Attorneys General, 444 North Capitol Street, NW, Suite 403, Washington, D.C. 20001. (202) 628-0431

National Association of Conservation Districts, 1025 Vermont Avenue, NW, Washington, D.C. 20005. (202) 347-5995

National Association of Counties, 440-1st Street, NW, 8th Floor, Washington, D.C. 20001. (202) 393-6226

National Association of Development Organizations, 400 N. Capitol Street, NW, Suite 372, Washington, D.C. 20001. (202) 624-7806

National Association of Housing & Redevelopment Officials, 2600 Virginia Avenue, NW, Suite 404, Washington, D.C. 20037. (202) 333-2020

National Association of Insurance Commissioners, 350 Bishops Way, Brookfield, Wisconsin 53005. (614) 784-9540

National Association of Regional Councils, 1700 K Street, NW, 13th Floor, Washington, D.C. 20006. (202) 457-0710

National Association of Regulatory Utility Commissioners, 1102 ICC Building, P.O. Box 684, Washington, D.C. 20044. (202) 628-7324

National Association of Schools of Public Affairs & Administration, 1120 G Street, NW, 5th Floor, Washington, D.C. 20005. (202) 628-8965

National Association of Secretaries of State, Iron Works Pike, P.O. Box 11910, Lexington, Kentucky 40578. (606) 252-2291

National Association of State Auditors, Comptrollers, and Treasurers, Iron Works Pike, P.O. Box 11910, Lexington, Kentucky 40578. (606) 252-2291

National Association of State Boards of Education, 444 North Capitol Street, NW, Suite 526, Washington, D.C. 20001 (202) 624-5844

National Association of State Budget Officers, 444 North Capitol Street, NW, Suite 328, Washington, D.C. 20001. (202) 624-5382

National Association of State Comptrollers, Iron Works Pike, P.O. Box 11910, Lexington, Kentucky 40578. (606) 252-2291

National Association of State Departments of Agriculture, 1616 H Street, NW, Washington, D.C. 20006. (202) 628-1566

National Association of State Mental Health Program Directors, 1001 Third Street, SW, Suite 114, Washington, D.C. 20024. (202) 554-7807

National Association of State Purchasing Officials, Iron Works Pike, P.O. Box 11910, Lexington, Kentucky 40578. (606) 252-2291

National Association of State Treasurers, Iron Works Pike, P.O. Box 11910, Lexington, Kentucky 40578. (606) 252-2291

National Association of Tax Administrators, 444 North Capitol Street, NW, Suite 334, Washington, D.C. 20001. (202) 624-5890

National Association of Towns & Townships, 1522 K Street, NW, Suite 730, Washington, D.C. 20005. (202) 737-5200

National Center for State Courts, 300 Newport Avenue, Williamsburg, Virginia 23185. (804) 253-2000

National Clearinghouse on Licensure, Enforcement and Regulation, Iron Works Pike, P.O. Box 11910, Lexington, Kentucky 40578. (606) 252-2291

National Conference of Commissioners on Uniform State Laws, 645 North Michigan Avenue, Chicago, Illinois 60611. (312) 321-9710

National Conference of Lieutenant Governors, Iron Works Pike, P.O. Box 11910, Lexington, Kentucky 40578. (606) 252-2291

National Conference of State General Service Officers, Iron Works Pike, P.O. Box 11910, Lexington, Kentucky 40578. (606) 252-2291

National Conference of State Legislatures, 1125 17th Street, 15th Floor, Denver, Colorado 80202. (303) 623-6600

National Council on Governmental Accounting, 180 North Michigan Avenue, Suite 800, Chicago, Illinois 60601. (312) 977-9700

National Criminal Justice Association, 444 North Capitol Street, Suite 305, Washington, D.C. 20001. (202) 347-4900

National Governors' Association, 400 North Capitol Street, NW, Suite 250, Washington, D.C. 20001. (202) 624-5300

National Institute of Governmental Purchasing, 1735 Jefferson Davis Highway, Suite 101, Arlington, Virginia 22202. (703) 920-4020

National Institute of Municipal Law Officers, 1000 Connecticut Avenue, NW, Suite 800, Washington, D.C. 20036. (202) 466-5424

National Institute of Public Affairs, 1120 G Street, NW, 5th Floor, Washington, D.C. 20005. (202) 347-3190

National Intergovernmental Audit Forum, 441 G Street, NW, Washington, D.C. 20548. (202) 275-5200

National League of Cities, 1301 Pennsylvania Avenue, NW, Washington, D.C. 20004. (202) 626-3010

National Municipal League, 55 West 44th Street, New York, New York 10036. (212) 730-7930

National Recreation and Park Association, 3101 Park Center Drive, Alexandria, Virginia 22302. (703) 820-4940

National School Boards Association, 1055 Thomas Jefferson Street, Suite 600, Washington, D.C. 20007. (202) 337-7666

National State Auditors Association, Iron Works Pike, P.O. Box 11910, Lexington, Kentucky 40578. (606) 252-2291

Police Executive Research Forum, 1909 K Street, NW, Suite 400, Washington, D.C. 20006. (202) 466-7820

Public Administration Service, 1497 Chain Bridge Road, McLean, Virginia 22101. (703) 734-8970

State and Territorial Air Pollution Program Administrators, 444 North Capitol Street, NW, Suite 306, Washington, D.C. 20001. (202) 624-7864

State Auditor Coordinating Council, Iron Works Pike, P.O. Box 11910, Lexington, Kentucky 40578. (606) 252-2291

Urban Institute, 2100 M Street, NW, Washington, D.C. 20037. (202) 233-1950

U.S. Conference of Mayors, 1620 Eye Street, NW, Washington, D.C. 20006. (202) 293-6796.

Water Pollution Control Federation, 2626 Pennsylvania Avenue, NW, 3rd Floor, Washington, D.C. 20037. (202) 337-2500

INTERSTATE COMPACTS

Interstate compacts are provided for in the U.S. Constitution to establish permanent arrangements among the states. A compact is a statute in each state and a contract between states subject to the Constitutional endorsement of contracts. When a state adopts a compact, it cannot impair the obligation of the contract or unilaterally renounce the interstate compact except when the party states agree. As contracts, interstate compacts take precedence over state laws that conflict with their provisions. These characteristics make interstate compacts the most binding legal instruments to establish formal cooperation among states.

Although compacts have been used by the states since the Articles of Confederation, until this century such agreements were few in number and usually were agreements dealing with the definition of a border. The growth of compact use in this century, however, has been striking. Over 100 have been negotiated since World War II. The key to this compact growth has almost certainly been the increasing complexity of society, and the demand for creative governmental approaches to its problems.

Since 1970, the growth in the number of interstate compacts has slowed. Emphasis during this period has been on more states joining existing agreements, and working toward improvement. Nevertheless, some new compacts have been created during the last dozen years in important areas. Agreements on hazardous waste control, as well as several on natural resources management, are relevant examples.

There have been several landmarks in interstate compact developments. In 1921, interstate compacts were used to create the first intergovernmental agency on behalf of two states and to alleviate regional problems. In the 1930s, functional compacts were developed, compacts became national in scope, and they were used to establish regulatory machinery. Since the close of World War II, other major trends have been manifest in compact developments. The proportion of regional and national compacts in relation to bi-state agreements has increased greatly.

Compact use over the last few decades demonstrates that these agreements have now been accepted as appropriate devices for dealing with state government problems. They now are seen as unique devices for solving a problem lying somewhere between the state and federal levels. Interstate compacts are increasingly a means of securing the cooperation of governments in functional areas such as nuclear energy, natural resources, health, education, transportation and other areas.

Although many interstate compacts create interstate agencies or commissions, their flexibility is often extremely useful even when no agency is created. This occurs most frequently when compacts are used to obtain intergovernmental action by establishing a legal channel or joint basis of law for the member states. Examples include compacts dealing with driver licensing, detainers, fire and pest control, placement of children, and many others.

Two compacts now in effect are worthy of special note. The Delaware River Basin Compact and the Susquehanna River Basin Compact are leading examples of the very recent development of compacts to which the federal government is actually a party, with binding status similar to that of the member states. This use of compacts offers a new option within the federal system for interstate cooperation.

The use of compacts is likely to continue. As new problems and concerns develop, many approaches will be used. Increasingly complex and interrelated problems will ensure that the demand for such flexible and creative solutions as those offered by interstate compacts will not cease.

This article is adapted from *Interstate Compacts and Agencies* (The Council of State Governments, 1983).

PARTICIPATION IN SELECTED INTERSTATE COMPACTS AND AGREEMENTS

State or other jurisdiction	Agreement on detainers	Agreement on qualification of educational personnel	Atlantic States Marine Fisheries Compact	Bus Taxation Proration & Reciprocity Agreement	Civil Defense & Disaster Compact	Colorado River Compact	Compact for Education	Compact on Mental Health	Compact on Motor Fuels Consumed by Interstate Buses	Delaware River & Bay Authority Compact	Delaware River Basin Compact	Delaware River Port Authority Compact	Driver License Compact	Great Lakes Basin Compact	Gulf States Marine Fisheries Compact	Interpleader Compact	Interstate Compact for Supervision of Parolees & Probationers	Interstate Compact on Juveniles
Alabama		★					★	★					★		★		★	★
Alaska		★					★	★									★	★
Arizona	★					★	★	★					★				★	★
Arkansas	★				★		★	★	★				★				★	★
California	★	★			★	★	★						★				★	★
Colorado	★				★	★	★	★					★				★	
Connecticut	★	★	★	★			★	★					★				★	★
Delaware	★	★	★				★	★		★	★		★				★	★
Florida	★	★			★		★	★							★		★	★
Georgia	★				★		★	★									★	★
Hawaii	★	★					★	★					★				★	★
Idaho	★				★	★	★	★					★				★	★
Illinois	★				★		★	★					★				★	★
Indiana	★	★			★		★	★					★	★			★	★
Iowa	★				★		★	★					★				★	★
Kansas	★				★		★	★					★				★	★
Kentucky	★	★			★		★	★					★				★	★
Louisiana					★		★	★							★		★	★
Maine	★	★	★				★	★					★		★		★	★
Maryland	★	★	★		★		★	★								★	★	★
Massachusetts	★	★	★	★			★	★	★								★	★
Michigan	★	★			★		★	★						★			★	★
Minnesota	★						★	★									★	★
Mississippi							★						★		★		★	★
Missouri	★						★	★					★		★		★	★
Montana	★						★	★					★				★	★
Nebraska	★	★			★	★	★	★					★				★	★
Nevada	★					★							★				★	★
New Hampshire	★	★	★	★			★	★	★				★				★	★
New Jersey	★						★			★	★	★	★				★	★
New Mexico	★					★	★	★					★				★	★
New York	★	★	★				★	★			★		★				★	★
North Carolina	★	★	★		★		★	★					★				★	★
North Dakota	★				★		★	★						★			★	★
Ohio	★	★		★			★	★	★					★			★	★
Oklahoma	★	★					★	★					★				★	★
Oregon	★				★		★	★					★				★	★
Pennsylvania	★		★	★	★		★	★		★	★	★	★				★	★
Rhode Island	★		★	★	★		★	★	★		★		★		★		★	★
South Carolina	★		★				★	★									★	★
South Dakota	★	★					★	★					★				★	★
Tennessee	★						★	★					★				★	★
Texas	★				★	★	★	★					★				★	★
Utah	★					★	★						★		★		★	★
Vermont	★	★		★			★										★	★
Virginia	★	★	★		★		★						★				★	★
Washington	★	★			★		★	★					★				★	★
West Virginia	★	★			★		★	★					★				★	★
Wisconsin	★	★					★	★						★			★	★
Wyoming	★					★	★	★							★		★	★
Dist. of Col.	★	★		★			★	★										★
American Samoa							★											★
Guam																	★	
Puerto Rico	★						★										★	★
Virgin Islands							★											
U.S. govt.	★								★								★	

Note: This is only a partial listing of the compacts and agreements in The Council of State Governments' *Interstate Compacts and Agencies* (1983 edition).

Key:
★—Member.
. . .—Not a member.

State or other jurisdiction	Interstate Compact on Placement of Children	Interstate Corrections Compact	Interstate Library Compact	Interstate Mining Compact	Interstate Oil & Gas Compact	Kansas City Area Transportation Compact	Mentally Disordered Offender Compact	Middle Atlantic Forest Fire Protection Compact	Multistate Highway Transportation Agreement	Multistate Tax Compact	New England Corrections Compact	Non-resident Violator Compact of 1977	Northeastern Forest Fire Protection Compact	Pacific Marine Fisheries Compact	Potomac River Compact of 1958	Potomac Valley Compact	Red River Compact	Republican River Compact
Alabama			★	★	★					★				★				
Alaska	★				★					★				★				
Arizona	★	★	★		★					★							★	
Arkansas	★	★	★		★					★				★				
California	★	★			★				★	★				★				
Colorado	★	★	★		★					★								★
Connecticut	★	★	★								★	★	★					
Delaware	★	★	★				★	★						★				
Florida	★	★	★		★									★				
Georgia	★	★	★											★				
Hawaii										★								
Idaho	★	★	★						★					★				
Illinois	★	★	★	★	★		★											
Indiana	★	★	★	★	★									★				
Iowa	★	★	★															
Kansas	★	★	★		★	★				★		★						★
Kentucky	★	★	★	★	★							★					★	
Louisiana	★		★									★	★					
Maine	★		★					★					★			★	★	
Maryland	★	★	★	★	★			★					★			★		
Massachusetts	★		★								★			★				
Michigan					★					★				★				
Minnesota	★	★	★										★					
Mississippi	★		★							★			★					
Missouri	★	★				★				★								
Montana	★	★	★		★					★								
Nebraska	★	★	★		★					★								★
Nevada		★	★		★				★					★				
New Hampshire	★		★					★			★	★						
New Jersey		★						★										
New Mexico	★		★	★	★		★			★								
New York	★		★	★	★							★	★					
North Carolina	★		★	★														
North Dakota	★		★		★		★			★		★						
Ohio	★	★	★	★	★													
Oklahoma	★		★	★	★					★				★				
Oregon	★		★							★								
Pennsylvania	★	★	★	★	★			★					★				★	
Rhode Island	★		★				★			★	★	★	★					
South Carolina		★		★									★					
South Dakota	★	★	★		★					★			★					
Tennessee	★	★	★	★						★								
Texas	★				★					★								
Utah	★	★	★		★					★		★		★				
Vermont	★	★	★															
Virginia	★	★	★	★	★			★		★		★		★		★	★	
Washington	★		★							★		★					★	
West Virginia	★		★	★	★		★	★		★		★						
Wisconsin	★		★															
Wyoming	★		★		★													
Dist. of Col.										★			★			★		
American Samoa																		
Guam																		
Puerto Rico																		
Virgin Islands																		
U.S. govt.																		

13

State or other jurisdiction	Rio Grande Interstate Compact	South Central Forest Fire Protection Compact	Southeastern Forest Fire Protection Compact	Southern Growth Policies Compact	Southern Interstate Energy Compact	Southern Regional Education Compact	Susquehanna River Basin Compact	Tahoe Regional Planning Compact	Thames River Flood Control Compact	Tri-State Sanitation Compact	Unclaimed Property Compact	Uniform Vehicle Registration Proration & Reciprocity Agreement	Vehicle Equipment Safety Compact	Washington Metropolitan Area Transit Regulation Compact	Waterfront Compact	Western Corrections Compact	Yellowstone River Compact
Alabama			★	★	★	★						★					
Alaska																★	
Arizona												★	★			★	
Arkansas		★		★	★	★						★	★			★	
California								★				★	★			★	
Colorado	★															★	
Connecticut									★	★			★				
Delaware					★								★				
Florida			★	★	★	★							★				
Georgia			★	★	★	★							★				
Hawaii													★			★	
Idaho													★				
Illinois												★	★				
Indiana													★				
Iowa											★		★				
Kansas												★	★				
Kentucky			★	★	★	★											
Louisiana		★		★	★	★							★				
Maine													★				
Maryland					★								★	★			
Massachusetts									★				★				
Michigan													★				
Minnesota												★					
Mississippi		★	★	★	★	★											
Missouri					★								★				
Montana												★	★			★	★
Nebraska												★	★				
Nevada								★				★					
New Hampshire													★			★	
New Jersey										★			★		★		
New Mexico	★												★				
New York							★			★			★		★	★	
North Carolina			★	★	★	★							★				
North Dakota												★	★				★
Ohio													★				
Oklahoma		★		★	★								★				
Oregon											★	★	★			★	
Pennsylvania						★							★				
Rhode Island													★				
South Carolina			★	★	★	★											
South Dakota												★	★				
Tennessee			★	★	★	★							★				
Texas	★	★			★	★							★				
Utah													★			★	
Vermont													★				
Virginia			★	★	★	★						★	★	★			
Washington												★	★	★			
West Virginia			★		★											★	
Wisconsin											★		★				
Wyoming												★	★			★	★
Dist. of Col.													★	★			
American Samoa																	
Guam																	
Puerto Rico				★	★											★	
Virgin Islands																	
U.S. govt.							★										

2. Intergovernmental Relations

INTERGOVERNMENTAL RELATIONS

By Carl W. Stenberg

Intergovernmental relations have been in a period of dramatic and rapid change, unparalleled in recent history. As the pendulum swung over the past few years from a national to a more state and local-oriented federal system, the powers and responsibilities of all three levels of government were—and continue to be—"rebalanced."

The nature and effects of these shifts are not well understood, widely recognized or generally accepted. This article attempts to sort out some of the reality from the rhetoric surrounding the federalism debate of the 1980s. Key events and developments at each level are put into perspective and their longer-term significance is assessed.

The Federal Role in Flux

The federal budget has been the chief instrument for rebalancing intergovernmental relationships. The domestic program-cutting concerns of the early 1980s have been superseded by deficit-financing fears. The "guns versus butter" debate of an earlier decade has been reopened and recast. Questions have been raised not only about the amount and pace of the defense build-up, but also now about the entitlement build-up, especially in the areas of income support and medical care.

Intergovernmental fiscal positions have shifted as well. The rate of state and local spending, which since the Korean War had grown faster than that of the federal government, was braked sharply in the late 1970s by the recession, Proposition 13-type fiscal limits and federal aid cuts. Austerity measures, tax hikes and the national economic recovery have improved the fiscal condition of many states and turned budget deficits into surpluses. In contrast, the federal government has become the big spender as well as the big borrower in the public sector. Mounting federal deficits have bolstered efforts to discipline federal fiscal decision-making through a balanced budget amendment to the Constitution and other means.

The intergovernmental significance of these developments is at least four-fold:

• First, the role of federal grant programs in state and local affairs will not be as great as during the last two decades. The growth rate of federal aid as a percentage of state and local expenditures began to taper off during the Carter administration. The pressures from the deficit, defense and entitlement sides of the federal budget and the presence of surpluses in several states make substantial reversal of this trend unlikely.

• Second, despite these changes, congressional entrepreneurs will not refrain from launching new program initiatives aimed toward essentially state or local matters. Quite the contrary, as underscored by recently enacted surface transportation, drunk driving, and employment and training laws, national responses to highly visible subnational problems will continue; however, they will be more difficult to pass. Moreover, while federal budget constraints may make Congress less inclined to play the role of city council or county board of supervisors, there may well be a strong temptation to demonstrate its concern by mandating state and local action without providing compensatory funding.

• Third, even though there has been a 25 percent reduction in the number of categorical programs, the basic shape of the federal aid system has not changed much. Despite the enactment of 10 block grants since 1980 and the renewal of general revenue sharing, approximately four-fifths of all federal aid is delivered through categorical programs—about the same percentage as in the late 1970s. As a result, while in certain programs recipient flexibility has increased, the system overall has not become more discretionary.

• Fourth, the drive to reduce federal deficits through such revenue enhancing strategies as raising tax rates, closing loopholes or levying new taxes will have major intergovernmental implications. For example, proposals calling for the federal government to dip into state or local tax wells, such as consumption levies, or to end preferred fiscal positions, such as the tax-exempt status of state and local bonds, will create tension and conflict.

Given these developments, in the years ahead we can expect to see greater congressional reluc-

Carl W. Stenberg is Executive Director of The Council of State Governments.

tance to shoulder financial responsibilities for activities considered to be basically state or local, more willingness to enact mandates without providing money, and continued desire to hold on to the categorical program reins. One by-product of these responses, noted by the Advisory Commission on Intergovernmental Relations, might well be movement toward a *de facto* sorting out of responsibilities. The federal domestic role may focus increasingly on national issues or problems that clearly transcend state boundaries, require a nationwide minimum level of effort, call for substantial expenditures, and involve equity between states. Many entitlement programs would qualify under these standards.

The failure of President Reagan's plan to trade federalization of Medicaid and food stamps for state assumption of welfare as well as takeover of a number of smaller programs has been viewed by some observers as a rare historic opportunity that was missed. Yet the aborted "great swap" of 1982 did put federalism on the front pages of the nation's newspapers and did cause public officials to think much more seriously about who does what. If nothing else, the attempt helped sow the seeds for a sorting out effort driven by fiscal pragmatism rather than political philosophy.

States Under the Spotlight

The prospects of a state and local-oriented federalism, with the states in particular being expected to assume previously federal or federally assisted responsibilities, have caused some consternation among members of Congress, the federal bureaucracy, interest groups and the private sector. Often these individuals believe the states to be incapable and insensitive, and they doubt that the states will move to compensate for cuts in federal domestic programs or to assume leadership in meeting citizen needs.

Recent research suggests a different conclusion—that the states are more capable now than ever before of effective and equitable governance. The reformers' checklist has been achieved in most states: constitutions have been simplified; governors and legislatures have been strengthened; executive branches have been streamlined; and court systems have been modernized.

At the same time, it remains to be seen if the states' institutional capacity will be translated into a commitment to take action. There are, however, encouraging signs:

• Most states have taken painful austerity measures and have bitten the fiscal bullet to raise suf-

ficient revenues to maintain service levels and meet new needs. A significant amount of these funds has been used for state aid to local governments and school districts.

• The states have taken the initiative in a number of high priority areas—industrial policy, job creation, drunk driving, enterprise zones, educational quality—well in advance of congressional interest or action.

• The states have compiled an impressive record in managing the recently enacted block grant programs.

Despite these examples, the jury will be out for some time on the states' response to the intergovernmental issues of the 1980s. Stereotypes are not easily overcome, and the philosophical, political and practical reasons for doing business in Washington rather than 50 state capitols cannot be overlooked. Therefore, while the states' early performances have been impressive, they will continue to be under the spotlight.

Greater Grassroots Government

Some observers of the recent decentralizing thrust of intergovernmental relations have noted that the units of government closest to people and their problems—localities—will have greater latitude over and more autonomy in determining priorities and finding ways to meet them. Certainly the Reagan administration and the Congress have taken significant steps in this direction through block grants and regulatory relief. However, at least three obstacles lie in the path of greater grassroots government:

• The often overlooked members of the intergovernmental partnership—the courts—have done much in recent years to call attention to their role and powers. Federal courts have been particularly active in the grant law, anti-trust and official immunity areas. Decisions often have had the effect of reducing local autonomy and discouraging the exercise of discretionary authority. The *Boulder* decision and other franchising cases, for instance, have reaffirmed that local governments are creatures of their states and derive their authority and protection from the legislature. Similarly, the courts have widened the authority of federal regulators to preempt local decisions, such as wage, hour and working conditions in non-traditional functions. And, policy-makers and program administrators have become gun-shy after judicial narrowing of the scope of public official immunity and widening of the circumstances under which officials may be held personally liable for their own or their subordinates' actions or inactions.

• A second factor to be considered here is the "intergovernmentalization" and "privatization" of functions below the state level. Austerity conditions have put pressure on localities to contract for the provision of services with their neighboring jurisdictions or private firms. While these actions may well save money, sharing means a loss of control and independence.

• The third grassroots government consideration has to do with the states. As noted above, recent court decisions have underscored the historic position of local governments *vis-a-vis* the states, as well as the need for state authority to act on a day-to-day basis in some areas. Legal and fiscal constraints are coupled. While the states' fiscal picture has brightened, this has not been the case in localities heavily dependent on property taxes. State aid has risen overall, but much of the increase goes to school districts rather than general purpose units.

So, a number of localities are squeezed in a fiscal vise. Their existing revenues are inadequate to meet citizen needs and service demands. Local governments must go to the state for more money or more authority to tap new sources or raise existing rates. The states' response to requests for local revenue diversification and enhancement will be a litmus test of their readiness to play a significant role in the rebalanced federalism of the 1980s.

To sum up, the federal system will be in a state of flux for some time to come. Shifts in functional and financial responsibilities will be accompanied by friction and uncertainty. For state governments in particular, the developments that have occurred or are underway provide excellent opportunities and real challenges for states to demonstrate that they can serve as "laboratories for democracy," and to take the lead in forging a genuine intergovernmental partnership for the years ahead.

FEDERAL-STATE RELATIONS

By Jane F. Roberts

In his January 1983 State of the Union Message, President Reagan reaffirmed his commitment "to continue efforts to restore to state and local governments their roles as dynamic laboratories of change in a creative society." Yet, the administration's $21 billion legislative package, consolidating 34 programs into four "mega-blocks," was never reported out of committee, and a consensus on the major swap of health care and welfare responsibilities was never achieved. Although the New Federalism legislative package was sidetracked, a number of other legislative, administrative and judicial actions did occur that have significance for federal-state relations and the rebalancing of the federal system.

The intergovernmental legislative agenda contained a mixture of budget battles and program debates, but was quickly eclipsed by concerns about the mounting federal deficit and international issues. Congress failed to approve major new spending programs for industrial revitalization, education and public physical infrastructure repair. It also rejected most proposals calling for further cuts in domestic aid programs. The net result of these actions was to authorize intergovernmental grant outlays at a level 4 percent higher than for fiscal 1983 and 8 percent over fiscal 1982. However, when an inflation factor is applied, the estimated $98.7 billion available in fiscal 1984 federal aid dollars actually falls slightly below the fiscal 1982 level.

Three major federal assistance programs—General Revenue Sharing, urban development action grants and community development block grants—were slated to expire in 1983, and despite some obstacles, all were reauthorized for three years. The Congress also enacted an emergency jobs bill, reauthorized housing assistance programs and created a new housing production program. In addition, supplemental unemployment assistance was extended for 18 months, the vocational rehabilitation program was continued, the Jobs Training Partnership Act received advance funding and the budget authority for the wastewater treatment plants program was continued.

Despite these actions, Congress failed to complete action in several important areas that pose serious fiscal consequences for state and local governments. For example, action was not completed on universal telephone service proposals in response to the break-up of AT & T and the deregulation of the telephone industry. The treatment of governmental units as business customers could result in significant cost increases next year and beyond unless rate structures are revised. Congress also failed to agree on a cable television measure. At issue here are establishing explicit regulatory responsibilities, franchise fee limitations and renewal procedures, phasing out rate regulation where competitive alternatives exist, and grandfathering existing facilities and service requirements.

Proposals to clarify whether and when local governments are liable for antitrust violations also remain on the legislative agenda. Local (and to a lesser extent state) exposure to antitrust litigation, resulting from recent U.S. Supreme Court decisions, is a major intergovernmental concern and could leave government officials and their jurisdictions open to years of protracted litigation and millions of dollars in costs.

On the administrative front, the Task Force on Regulatory Reform, chaired by Vice President Bush, completed its work. Created in early 1981, the Cabinet-level panel reviewed hundreds of regulations and presented its findings on potential cost-saving actions which would benefit both the public and private sectors.

In late 1983, a new executive order took effect, replacing OMB Circular A-95. Under provisions of the new order, the states—in conjunction with their localities—may develop and implement their own consultation processes and procedures involving federal grant decisions, changes at federal installations and other federal actions affecting their jurisdictions. While still in the formative stages, the order offers a potentially important tool to influence federal decision-making in many areas.

Jane F. Roberts is State-Local Relations Associate for the U.S. Advisory Commission on Intergovernmental Relations.

In a related area, the Office of Management and Budget also launched a major effort to review and revise Circular A-102 that governs administrative requirements attached to federal grants. The goal is to simplify and standardize the requirements and to provide greater flexibility to state and local governments where possible.

In response to earlier deregulatory actions, the states demonstrated their adaptability, for the most part, to the new administrative roles and program responsibilities presented by one of the most visible New Federalism initiatives—the nine federal block grants authorized in 1981. Implementation of the Jobs Training Partnership Act also began during 1983.

From a state perspective, the great concern continues to be about funding levels—a legitimate worry when all but a handful of states faced revenue shortfalls and potential budget deficits during the past year. However, states have coped with their new responsibilities and financial cutbacks in a number of ways.

During this second year of implementation, states appeared to move away from *status quo* administration. And, the block grants that have evoked the most changes, understandably, are the ones in which the states were not previously involved, such as the Community Development Small Cities Block Grant and the Community Services Block Grant. For example, state changes in the small cities program include less emphasis on housing and rehabilitation and more on economic development, broader grant competition among a greater number of communities, and a willingness to approve applications from areas not previously funded. The states' ability to shoulder administrative and program responsibility for the small cities program also was clearly apparent—all but four states opted to take over the program for the U.S. Department of Housing and Urban Development by the second year of operation.

There also are indications that states are issuing their own regulations to fill the gaps left by the relative lack of federal restrictions in the block grant programs. For example, several states—particularly in the South—have developed detailed regulations for program performance and fiscal audits.

The record for the states was mixed in the decisions rendered by the U.S. Supreme Court during the 1983 term. While victories were registered in the areas of taxation, preemption, church-state relations and some police powers, the states lost ground on civil rights suits, redistricting, abortion and pensions. No clear trend emerged, and the Court frequently split its votes.

A major victory for the states was won in mid-1983 when the Court upheld the validity of California's unitary method of taxing multinational corporations. The Court concluded that states could include the worldwide income of American-based multinational corporations when determining state tax liability. In upholding the unitary tax method, the Court not only validated this approach for the dozen states currently employing it, but provided an incentive for other states to adopt it.

In a unanimous ruling that could cost state and local governments millions of dollars, the Court determined that federal agencies may seek repayment of misspent grant funds. Actual repayment disputes will be resolved by the lower courts on a case-by-case basis.

While the Court's ruling to eliminate the legislative veto power of the Congress does not apply directly to state legislatures, the reasoning presented in the decision likely will be used in state court challenges. Currently, 32 state legislatures have the authority to suspend, amend or veto executive agency rules and regulations. In light of the concern about the constitutionality of the veto power, several state legislatures are using alternative methods to exercise oversight, including sunset procedures and veto through statute or constitutional amendment.

Federal-state relations will continue to face major challenges and opportunities in the months ahead. The seeds have been sown for greater devolution and decentralization of program and servicing responsibilities. Indeed, as the noted national columnist David Broder has observed: "More and more of the critical decisions in our domestic government are being made in state capitols."

The ability of state policy-makers—and their local counterparts—to respond to the ever-changing economic environment and these rebalancing forces are critical issues for intergovernmental relations for the remainder of this decade and beyond.

TOTAL FEDERAL AID TO STATES: FISCAL 1978-1982
(In thousands of dollars)

State or other jurisdiction	1982	1981	1980	1979	1978
Total	$88,221,369	$94,806,164	$91,365,284	$82,853,441	$77,900,897
Alabama	1,429,024	1,493,313	1,583,543	1,367,631	1,240,569
Alaska	421,922	447,917	451,170	388,580	408,211
Arizona	799,223	864,322	837,882	809,479	763,318
Arkansas	843,779	886,840	940,352	846,856	779,074
California	9,015,844	10,007,616	8,804,443	8,251,050	8,012,965
Colorado	966,730	1,021,503	995,230	942,865	825,855
Connecticut........	1,120,139	1,180,030	1,156,824	1,074,780	1,052,697
Delaware	279,369	313,613	275,358	232,500	225,033
Florida	2,859,149	2,867,706	2,854,439	2,397,511	2,364,186
Georgia	2,185,305	2,169,244	2,373,419	2,181,048	2,036,993
Hawaii	407,598	442,955	463,258	407,881	413,391
Idaho	349,847	361,130	393,079	337,183	336,315
Illinois	4,102,545	4,610,352	4,476,964	3,782,934	3,467,151
Indiana............	1,558,397	1,728,750	1,608,494	1,391,558	1,259,679
Iowa	893,175	961,018	994,733	877,823	796,893
Kansas	706,359	773,800	818,463	722,878	615,820
Kentucky	1,424,407	1,433,417	1,471,228	1,349,703	1,133,308
Louisiana..........	1,591,449	1,729,516	1,567,591	1,513,376	1,358,360
Maine	526,788	535,999	522,546	508,122	470,379
Maryland	1,792,714	1,889,555	1,843,192	1,577,979	1,318,423
Massachusetts	2,745,416	2,888,996	2,886,740	2,726,189	2,581,488
Michigan	3,634,110	4,107,594	3,928,527	3,568,596	3,280,231
Minnesota	1,769,271	1,773,557	1,667,347	1,515,431	1,350,915
Mississippi	1,090,755	1,098,354	1,190,010	1,045,969	915,855
Missouri...........	1,651,796	1,662,812	1,702,897	1,514,482	1,278,467
Montana	381,641	448,779	486,363	434,433	397,300
Nebraska	523,785	517,337	546,513	474,570	458,783
Nevada............	346,200	350,592	335,469	276,828	268,909
New Hampshire	317,026	306,355	345,912	292,753	289,298
New Jersey	2,718,474	2,891,042	2,833,075	2,716,267	2,552,215
New Mexico	727,234	715,855	668,500	617,016	608,411
New York	9,287,674	10,374,341	9,569,624	8,872,407	8,372,465
North Carolina	1,852,428	1,908,847	1,929,241	1,788,832	1,655,955
North Dakota	301,489	317,578	347,200	295,243	259,138
Ohio	3,611,567	3,725,226	3,433,736	3,071,195	2,904,685
Oklahoma	991,209	1,043,326	1,061,483	949,388	937,180
Oregon	1,167,622	1,174,601	1,237,294	1,070,598	1,075,400
Pennsylvania.......	4,629,305	4,886,585	4,515,615	4,099,060	3,912,086
Rhode Island	470,960	481,978	477,446	412,418	388,000
South Carolina	1,042,943	1,009,353	1,067,706	987,215	903,414
South Dakota	324,773	355,544	443,253	316,487	288,446
Tennessee	1,607,375	1,909,665	1,695,667	1,506,920	1,330,860
Texas	3,725,332	4,146,183	3,964,357	3,592,345	3,295,287
Utah	604,617	593,277	571,693	455,561	434,261
Vermont	270,662	279,382	355,597	241,813	240,659
Virginia	1,623,108	1,861,670	1,775,472	1,700,559	1,468,126
Washington.........	1,579,965	1,771,273	1,674,116	1,417,104	1,311,062
West Virginia	771,613	940,997	950,423	771,522	707,622
Wisconsin	1,894,379	2,298,782	2,024,519	1,725,467	1,607,427
Wyoming...........	348,521	320,876	294,386	242,518	235,707
Dist. of Col.	1,295,321	1,417,140	1,336,361	1,138,639	1,105,199
Puerto Rico........	1,397,295	1,351,763	1,430,471	1,308,739	1,156,550
Virgin Islands	116,427	153,557	295,798	228,784	237,699
Other(a)...........	270,008	277,515	215,163	281,269	269,315
Adjustments or undistributed to states....	-142,695	-273,164	-324,898	235,087	943,862

Source: U.S. Department of the Treasury, *Federal Aid to States, Fiscal Year 1982* (rev. ed.).

(a) Includes American Samoa, Guam, Northern Mariana Islands, Tokelau Islands, Trust Territory of the Pacific and Saipan.

STATE-LOCAL RELATIONS

By Jane F. Roberts

State and local governments have been experiencing distress, and in fact, entered 1983 in the worst fiscal shape in at least a decade. Records were set for tax increases, spending cuts and program deferrals. Yet, by year's end, the fiscal picture began to improve as the effects of the national economic recovery and these austerity measures began to take hold.

Despite the understandable preoccupation with budget balancing during the year, state and local officials also placed a renewed emphasis on many traditional programs and servicing responsibilities, took the lead in a range of new entrepreneurial activities, and showed progress in building stronger state-local partnerships. When viewed together, these developments provide hopeful signs that state and local governments are responding to the challenges posed by a decentralizing federal system and new economic realities. Significant developments in at least three areas—education, public physical infrastructure and economic development—provide examples of the diversity and wealth of approaches employed by states and localities during the year.

After years of being eclipsed by a host of other issues, education moved close to the top of the nation's domestic agenda in 1983. The states now provide over half of the total spending for elementary and secondary schools. Their role in shaping education policy and in equalizing educational opportunity is, and will continue to be, crucial. In just the past two years, 130 task forces in 48 states have assumed an active lead in examining education trends and proposing major policy shifts.

Perhaps some of the most significant initiatives and results in education reform occurred in the Southern states. Nearly every state launched—or is about to do so—a major effort to improve its educational system. For example, during a special session, the Florida Legislature approved over $230 million in new taxes to pay for a merit pay plan for teachers, additional math and science programs, longer school days and tougher graduation requirements.

In Tennessee, Governor Lamar Alexander proposed the broadest package of education reform legislation in the country. Although un-successful the first year, the governor's proposals will be re-introduced in some form during the 1984 legislative session.

In Arkansas, where the state courts struck down the school finance system, Governor Bill Clinton named a special commission not only to respond to the court's ruling but to recommend a comprehensive package of reforms for that state's educational system. In November 1983, the legislature approved a series of changes based on the commission's recommendations that among other items include mandatory competency tests for teachers, high school entrance exams, scholarships for students who attend Arkansas colleges and a tax increase to underwrite the $154 million to fund the mandated improvements. To help meet the new requirements, nearly 2,700 classrooms must be built and over 3,700 teachers hired during the next three years. In Mississippi, where a sweeping overhaul of the education system was approved in late 1982, nearly half of last year's budget increase of $170 million will be dedicated to education.

The "infrastructure crisis," publicized by *America in Ruins* in 1981, continued to receive a great deal of intergovernmental attention in 1983. Concerns rested on three issues: an aggregate decline in new investment; deferred, or otherwise inadequate, maintenance of existing capital stock; and arguments that a crumbling physical infrastructure will hurt the national economy.

There are no hard estimates of the extent or cost of the physical infrastructure problem, although it is thought to be a far greater problem in central cities than in suburban areas. In April 1983, the National League of Cities and the U.S. Conference of Mayors released a survey of over 800 city officials that offered a glimmer of hope, concluding that while the public physical infrastructure problem is serious, it nevertheless is "manageable."

Current plans and actions of state and local governments have the greatest consequences of all for infrastructure financing. For example,

Jane F. Roberts is State-Local Relations Associate for the U.S. Advisory Commission on Intergovernmental Relations.

21

Governor Thomas Kean's proposal for a New Jersey Infrastructure Bank would establish a state-subsidized revolving loan fund, based in part on existing federal infrastructure grants, to be repaid as loans. The November 1983 results on major bond issues also may reflect a greater public willingness to finance large capital projects. Nearly 90 percent of the $3.85 billion in bond issues on state and local ballots were approved—the highest approval rate since 1960.

States and localities also have significantly expanded both the level and nature of their development efforts, and two trends have emerged in recent years. First, public officials have begun to confront such traditional issues as health, welfare and unemployment in fundamentally different ways. Rather than concentrating efforts on after-the-fact remedies, lawmakers are examining root causes and devising and implementing prevention strategies. Secondly, state and local governments are assuming entrepreneurial roles in their economies. They are examining such things as barriers to business formation, private investment, and job markets, and devising research and development strategies to maintain a competitive edge. Massachusetts Governor Michael Dukakis recently described this trend: "While the national debate rages on whether we ought to have an industrial policy, there isn't a state that doesn't have one, or isn't putting one together . . . ."

The record of achievement for state and local experimentation with less traditional alternatives and entrepreneurial investments is fairly impressive. For example, in the high-tech field alone, several states now offer financial incentives to attract new companies. Hawaii's Venture Development Fund contains a special inventor's fund to finance and develop new product lines, and the Pennsylvania Ben Franklin Partnership Fund provides seed money for research and development in advanced technology industry.

States also have recognized the need to help ensure that their workforces are trained and likely will need retraining as high technology industries come into their communities. Idaho coordinates technical and electronic programs financed by private industry. And the Colorado Advanced Technology Institute develops training programs for universities and community colleges.

Public and private entrepreneurs have been very active in the transportation field. Shared-ride taxi services, jitneys, vanpools, light rail links and shuttle services are among the service alternatives underwritten by cities of all sizes.

State enterprise zone programs are another example of experimentation in which states have provided leadership. A federal enterprise zone proposal has received scant attention in Congress, but in 1983 the number of state programs grew to 19 with the addition of Arkansas, Georgia, Indiana, Michigan, Mississippi and Texas.

State regulatory activities also continued to be a major intergovernmental issue during the year. While no new state mandate reimbursement programs were enacted, there was appreciable progress in the willingness of state officials to study reimbursement policy and to assess their actions affecting local government budgets, policies and programs. For example, studies of state mandates were initiated in several states such as California, Iowa, New York and Minnesota. In several other states, including Louisiana, Missouri and Michigan, state courts ruled on challenges by local governments on the implementation of various statutory and constitutional provisions. And in Massachusetts, the Division of Local Mandates was organized within the Department of the State Auditor to monitor and analyze proposed and existing legislation, rules and regulations imposing costs on cities and towns, and to determine what those costs are and whether they have been duly reimbursed by the state. The office is a self-described "municipal advocate on the state level" that also will provide a variety of services to localities.

Several states began to grapple with the troublesome results of recent U.S. Supreme Court decisions opening local governments to antitrust liability. North Dakota has adopted the most comprehensive measure thus far, and Maryland has acted to share much of the state's immunity with its localities. Several other states, including Louisiana, Pennsylvania and Virginia, moved to protect jurisdictions in selected areas of activity, while still others—such as Iowa—are studying antitrust immunity within the broader context of tort liability.

State ACIRs and comparable organizations also have become increasingly important vehicles for discussing and studying state-local issues and for proposing solutions to statewide problems. Currently, 20 states have a functioning intergovernmental advisory group, 11 of which are patterned after the national ACIR model. In addition, at least 15 other states considered the creation of a state ACIR during 1983.

During the past year, the litany of issues affecting intergovernmental relations grew. State and local officials initiated a number of innovative efforts, but the basic elements of their part-nership—consultation, cooperation and fiscal and discretionary authority—require constant attention.

Decentralizing and devolutionary trends, coupled with precarious fiscal conditions, pose major challenges to state and local policy-makers. It is a period of transition and adjust-ment for the intergovernmental system, un-paralleled for many years in scope and significance. When the dust settles, state and local governments likely will have substantial new responsibilities for financing and providing services and programs. The ability, capacity and willingness of state and local officials to respond to these challenges are the intergovernmental issues of the 1980s.

GENERAL REVENUE SHARING

By Kent A. Peterson

The revenue sharing program was first enacted with the passage of the State and Local Fiscal Assistance Act of 1972, reauthorized under the State and Local Fiscal Assistance Amendments of 1976, and renewed again with the passage of the State and Local Fiscal Assistance Amendments of 1980. The revenue sharing legislation provided for the distribution of approximately $69 billion to more than 39,000 units of state and local government over a period of 11 years and nine months. According to the 1980 amendments, state governments were not eligible for fiscal 1981 funding but were authorized for fiscal years 1982 and 1983 funding which was not appropriated. In addition, state government funding depended upon the return or non-acceptance of federal categorical funds equal to the revenue sharing allocations. The Revenue Sharing Act, as amended, expired on September 30, 1983. However, the Congress is considering proposals for the renewal of the program.

The revenue sharing program is an "entitlement" program, so no application is necessary to receive funds. Based upon data furnished by the Census Bureau and other federal agencies, funds are distributed to eligible general-purpose governments through formulas prescribed in the act. Special purpose districts, such as school districts, utility districts and library districts, are not eligible to receive funds. To receive funds, eligible governments must execute a simple form, assuring that funds will be spent in accordance with the law.

Payments to eligible governments are made quarterly, based on each unit's entitlement for the period. Each of the first three entitlement periods was of six-month duration, followed by three 12-month periods beginning July 1973. Another six-month period began in 1976. Renewal in 1976 added a nine-month period starting January 1977 (to align the program with the new October-September federal fiscal year) and three 12-month entitlement periods. Renewal in 1980 authorized three more one-year entitlement periods. The amounts authorized for distribution for each entitlement period are shown in Table A.

Under the revenue sharing program until September 30, 1980, one-third of the total appropriation was distributed to the state governments, with the remaining two-thirds distributed to local governments—counties, municipalities, townships, Indian tribes and Alaskan native villages. Payments made to the state and local governments since the beginning of the program are summarized in Tables 1 and 2 following this article.

Table A
ENTITLEMENT PERIODS AND AUTHORIZED DISTRIBUTION AMOUNTS

Entitlement period	Start	End	Amount (in millions)
1	January 1972	June 1972	$2,650.0
2	July 1972	December 1972	2,650.0
3	January 1973	June 1973	2,987.5
4	July 1973	June 1974	6,050.0
5	July 1974	June 1975	6,200.0
6	July 1975	June 1976	6,350.0
7	July 1976	December 1976	3,325.0
8	January 1977	September 1977	4,987.5
9	October 1977	September 1978	6,850.0
10	October 1978	September 1979	6,850.0
11	October 1979	September 1980	6,850.0
12	October 1980	September 1981	4,566.7*
13	October 1981	September 1982	4,566.7*
14	October 1982	September 1983	4,566.7*

*For local governments only; funds for state governments were not appropriated for these entitlement periods.

Table 1 contains payments to state governments for Entitlement Periods 1 through 11. Data on payments to local governments for Entitlement Periods 1 through 13 along with the payments and projected payments for Entitlement Period 14 are exhibited in Table 2. The payments reflected in these tables apply to the entitlement periods in which the funds are credited, not the entitlement periods in which they are paid. Payments for state and local governments for each period displayed in Tables 1 and 2 are different from those previously reported. This is because these payments include accounting and special adjustments for each entitlement after initial payments were made.

The allocation amount for each government is determined by a mathematical formula using data as prescribed by the revenue sharing law.

Kent A. Peterson is Deputy Director, Office of Revenue Sharing, U.S. Department of the Treasury.

The data used to determine allocation amounts for local governments include per capita income, tax effort, population and intergovernmental transfers. Interstate data are population, urbanized population, income, state individual income tax, federal individual income tax, state and local taxes, aggregate personal income and general tax effort factor. The data are supplied by various federal agencies, including the Bureau of the Census, the Bureau of Economic Analysis, the Internal Revenue Service and the Bureau of Indian Affairs.

According to the revenue sharing formula, each government competes with all other eligible governments for a portion of the total revenue sharing amount that is to be allocated. Because of the complexity of the formula and its relative nature, each government's share is computed simultaneously with all other governments. After allocations for local governments have been determined, the amount is then checked to assure that it does not exceed 50 percent of the total of the combined adjusted taxes and intergovernmental transfers of funds for the particular government. An allocation exceeding that amount is reduced to the 50 percent level, with the balance being transferred to the next higher level of government. Excess funds to county governments affected by this rule are redistributed among all governments in the state. The allocation amount for each government must also fall between the minimum and the maximum per capita entitlement permitted under the act. The minimum per capita allocation is 20 percent of the per capita amount allocated to all governments in the state. The maximum amount allocated is 145 percent.

The revenue sharing program was originally conceived as a way of sharing the relatively more progressive federal tax revenue, especially income tax revenue, with state and local governments which traditionally have had to rely on more regressive taxes and revenue sources. Its major goal was to disburse federal funds with minimum restrictions on use, permitting the local decision-making process to determine the programs and activities where the money is most needed.

Under the 1976 and 1980 amendments, revenue sharing funds may be used for any purpose that is a legal use of the government's own funds under state and local laws. The priority expenditure categories which restricted revenue sharing expenditures by governments were eliminated. Furthermore, the prohibition against recipients' use of funds for federal grant matching purposes was also repealed. However, recipients must spend, appropriate or obligate revenue sharing funds within 24 months from the end of the entitlement period for which the funds are received. Although there are no restrictions as to the uses of revenue sharing funds, recipient governments must comply with the public participation, audit and non-discrimination requirements specified by the revenue sharing law.

Table 1
GENERAL REVENUE SHARING PAYMENTS TO STATE GOVERNMENTS, BY STATE, BY ENTITLEMENT PERIOD
(In thousands of dollars)

State or other jurisdiction	Total(a) 1/72-9/83	10/79-9/80	10/78-9/79	10/77-9/78	1/77-9/77
Total	$18,805,950.2	$2,317,738.2	$2,301,240.8	$2,291,638.0	$1,669,754.9
Alabama	303,579.6	36,228.4	36,288.6	36,734.9	26,744.7
Alaska	39,211.0(b)	7,624.1	7,938.1	6,051.1	3,568.6
Arizona	195,165.6	27,011.5	26,466.6	24,890.2	16,143.3
Arkansas	194,363.7	23,027.3	22,666.5	21,768.6	17,598.0
California	2,025,709.6	269,730.2	259,045.5	253,520.0	176,552.6
Colorado	201,555.9	25,760.3	25,425.3	24,993.7	18,265.6
Connecticut	236,477.7(b)	28,959.3	28,658.8	28,395.2	21,066.6
Delaware	59,871.6	6,978.9	7,069.9	7,092.1	5,241.6
Florida	555,949.3	69,002.8	68,007.6	67,670.3	51,109.3
Georgia..................	396,258.6	50,833.4	50,450.6	48,967.2	35,260.4
Hawaii	85,915.4	10,835.6	11,129.7	11,334.5	8,170.6
Idaho	71,524.7	8,730.1	8,692.5	7,787.2	6,327.5
Illinois...................	942,047.6	114,474.9	113,629.2	115,846.8	84,665.4
Indiana...................	386,273.1	45,501.5	46,043.2	48,224.8	35,281.0
Iowa	241,756.1	28,731.2	28,485.1	26,463.1	20,231.1
Kansas	169,946.7	20,570.8	20,118.6	19,425.0	14,927.5
Kentucky	325,265.4	37,396.1	38,022.8	37,617.6	28,175.4
Louisiana.................	395,600.1	42,225.1	44,081.1	46,889.9	33,260.6
Maine	114,693.5	13,204.1	15,277.3	13,920.6	10,273.4
Maryland	368,460.9	44,810.5	45,435.1	45,516.8	33,084.3
Massachusetts	590,981.6	72,323.8	72,475.5	74,141.3	52,374.2
Michigan	781,960.6	99,454.7	95,734.1	94,114.6	67,827.5
Minnesota	372,383.4	46,020.1	45,660.4	45,441.4	33,312.4
Mississippi	289,798.4	32,118.2	33,310.8	33,333.8	25,259.8
Missouri..................	348,178.1	41,721.8	42,133.4	43,246.5	31,151.7
Montana	70,917.9	8,928.1	8,682.6	7,999.0	6,071.9
Nebraska	124,469.4	15,919.7	14,277.1	13,841.2	10,441.1
Nevada...................	43,909.5	5,843.1	5,675.9	5,698.1	4,006.1
New Hampshire	60,891.6	7,862.2	7,786.5	7,680.1	5,318.8
New Jersey................	590,974.6	76,530.2	75,198.7	71,814.6	51,856.2
New Mexico...............	119,951.8	13,663.9	14,345.4	15,735.5	11,051.5
New York.................	2,076,129.0	252,034.8	255,048.4	257,403.1	186,369.0
North Carolina	465,248.9	57,178.7	56,334.5	55,937.2	41,133.1
North Dakota	58,565.8	6,559.1	6,324.3	4,992.8	4,161.8
Ohio	748,418.6	91,407.3	92,500.9	91,884.1	66,717.1
Oklahoma	206,430.6	25,902.2	24,798.4	25,151.5	18,450.9
Oregon	196,276.2	26,248.6	25,338.9	24,765.6	17,879.6
Pennsylvania	955,289.5	112,615.9	111,121.9	114,656.6	86,974.6
Rhode Island	81,410.8	9,979.3	9,798.2	9,863.0	7,109.0
South Carolina	255,840.8	30,953.4	30,705.9	29,985.1	23,303.7
South Dakota	69,991.1	7,868.1	7,665.3	6,890.6	5,384.3
Tennessee.................	347,702.6	44,554.0	42,164.7	41,245.8	30,624.8
Texas	902,818.9	112,113.7	112,528.6	112,470.2	83,332.8
Utah	109,399.9	14,136.4	14,083.5	12,929.5	9,253.2
Vermont..................	54,415.6(b)	6,907.3	6,981.4	6,911.3	4,900.2
Virginia...................	375,661.9	47,494.2	47,478.9	46,569.8	33,487.4
Washington	267,851.0	32,180.4	30,766.0	33,866.4	24,639.5
West Virginia..............	208,004.2	20,531.0	22,466.9	25,285.3	17,622.3
Wisconsin	452,583.4	53,693.9	53,634.7	52,744.4	40,331.5
Wyoming	33,525.7	4,748.8	4,428.9	3,902.8	2,673.1
Dist. of Col................	238,340.7	28,609.2	28,857.8	28,027.2	20,788.3

(a) Total payments include $49 million of revenue sharing reserve funds allocated for distribution to state governments and the District of Columbia. Payments were made on June 30, 1983 to all states and the District of Columbia, except for Montana ($190,500) and Ohio ($1,951,900). Payments to these two states are projected for a later date.

(b) Total payments also include prior period local funds waived to these states for Entitlement Period 12: Alaska—$16,300, Connecticut—$46,300 and Vermont—$7,000.

State or other jurisdiction	Total 1/72-12/76	7/76-12/76	7/75-6/76	7/74-6/75	7/73-6/74	1/73-6/73	7/72-12/72	1/72-6/72
Total	$10,227,366.3	$1,154,919.6	$2,141,089.1	$2,085,768.3	$2,043,336.8	$1,013,029.8	$894,603.6	$894,619.1
Alabama	167,583.0	18,498.2	33,857.0	34,322.0	34,061.3	16,814.5	15,015.0	15,015.0
Alaska	14,012.8	2,087.3	3,089.1	2,735.7	2,609.2	1,291.9	1,100.9	1,098.7
Arizona	100,653.8	11,158.7	21,347.8	21,144.9	20,312.6	10,030.4	8,329.7	8,329.7
Arkansas	109,303.3	12,151.1	22,268.8	22,357.5	21,844.0	11,470.3	9,605.8	9,605.8
California	1,066,861.3	121,936.4	219,922.2	216,051.9	216,338.8	106,828.4	92,891.8	92,891.8
Colorado	107,111.0	12,597.6	23,010.9	21,939.0	21,076.5	10,407.6	9,039.7	9,039.7
Connecticut	129,351.5	14,547.6	28,486.8	26,577.6	25,061.6	12,379.3	11,150.0	11,148.6
Delaware	33,489.1	3,614.5	6,834.2	6,518.0	6,490.1	3,638.3	3,197.0	3,197.0
Florida	300,159.3	35,246.3	65,439.2	64,458.5	57,803.0	28,575.7	24,318.3	24,318.3
Georgia	210,747.0	24,340.5	43,940.1	44,040.0	41,565.5	20,528.7	18,166.1	18,166.1
Hawaii	44,445.0	5,139.0	9,274.8	8,932.6	8,859.9	4,379.1	3,929.8	3,929.8
Idaho	39,987.4	4,377.4	8,163.7	7,963.2	8,318.7	4,107.8	3,528.3	3,528.3
Illinois	513,431.3	58,472.1	107,742.7	103,580.1	102,270.5	50,501.3	45,432.3	45,432.3
Indiana	211,222.6	24,364.8	42,891.5	42,436.7	42,713.4	21,092.0	18,862.1	18,862.1
Iowa	137,845.6	14,035.9	28,138.0	28,221.2	28,397.4	14,022.7	12,515.2	12,515.2
Kansas	94,906.8	10,329.0	19,435.8	18,766.2	19,405.8	9,582.6	8,693.7	8,693.7
Kentucky	184,053.5	19,491.4	36,780.9	35,699.9	37,913.7	20,062.1	17,052.1	17,053.4
Louisiana	229,143.4	25,400.2	45,657.6	46,418.3	46,835.7	23,546.0	20,642.6	20,643.0
Maine	62,018.1	7,092.4	13,325.6	12,752.4	12,211.3	6,030.0	5,303.2	5,303.2
Maryland	199,614.2	22,843.8	42,099.8	40,116.6	39,521.7	19,515.9	17,758.2	17,758.2
Massachusetts	319,666.8	36,170.3	68,847.8	64,879.8	63,604.4	31,407.9	27,378.3	27,378.3
Michigan	424,829.7	46,896.8	89,145.2	87,213.1	85,115.7	42,030.3	37,214.3	37,214.3
Minnesota	201,949.1	22,996.3	44,334.8	40,891.9	39,113.8	19,314.5	17,648.9	17,648.9
Mississippi	165,775.8	17,499.0	31,491.7	34,344.1	35,688.0	16,996.6	14,878.2	14,878.2
Missouri	189,924.7	21,512.9	40,778.4	39,254.5	37,293.9	18,462.0	16,311.5	16,311.5
Montana	39,045.8	4,204.0	7,835.7	8,526.5	7,822.2	3,862.6	3,397.4	3,397.4
Nebraska	69,990.3	7,240.1	14,128.2	13,761.6	14,710.1	7,263.9	6,443.2	6,443.2
Nevada	22,686.3	2,759.2	4,987.3	4,494.5	4,436.4	2,190.7	1,909.1	1,909.1
New Hampshire	32,244.0	3,673.0	6,807.4	6,716.3	6,391.3	3,156.0	2,750.0	2,750.0
New Jersey	315,574.9	35,816.4	66,450.4	64,410.1	62,683.4	30,953.2	27,630.7	27,630.7
New Mexico	65,155.5	7,622.9	13,402.5	13,085.6	13,104.6	6,616.7	5,661.6	5,661.6
New York	1,127,273.7	128,681.1	240,242.7	229,902.3	222,936.7	110,086.5	97,712.2	97,712.2
North Carolina	254,665.4	28,436.7	51,720.6	52,588.9	51,411.7	25,407.5	22,550.0	22,550.0
North Dakota	36,527.8	2,923.1	6,825.3	6,935.6	8,362.3	4,129.3	3,676.1	3,676.1
Ohio	403,957.3	46,065.4	86,486.3	82,198.6	79,165.8	39,092.2	35,474.5	35,474.5
Oklahoma.........	112,127.6	12,745.5	23,151.7	23,300.8	22,354.2	11,038.6	9,768.4	9,768.4
Oregon	102,043.5	12,318.8	22,224.8	20,597.7	19,628.2	9,692.4	8,790.8	8,790.8
Pennsylvania	529,920.5	60,068.0	112,931.1	108,542.1	104,568.6	51,636.1	46,087.3	46,087.3
Rhode Island	44,661.3	4,916.6	9,175.5	9,047.4	9,043.5	4,465.7	4,006.2	4,006.2
South Carolina	140,892.7	16,084.2	29,592.3	28,639.7	27,756.6	14,264.5	12,269.0	12,286.4
South Dakota	42,182.8	3,758.6	8,384.6	8,507.7	9,061.0	4,474.3	3,998.3	3,998.3
Tennessee	189,113.3	21,164.0	39,622.2	39,670.4	37,411.2	18,473.7	16,385.9	16,385.9
Texas	482,373.6	57,455.1	101,911.5	98,365.4	95,175.0	47,178.2	41,144.2	41,144.2
Utah	58,997.3	6,401.0	12,537.4	12,005.1	11,983.1	5,929.3	5,070.7	5,070.7
Vermont	28,708.4	3,382.8	6,188.7	5,823.6	5,644.5	2,787.6	2,440.6	2,440.6
Virginia	200,631.6	23,114.8	42,661.0	40,798.2	39,357.6	19,434.8	17,632.6	17,632.6
Washington	146,398.7	17,002.0	31,277.1	28,935.3	29,002.7	14,321.6	12,930.0	12,930.0
West Virginia	122,098.7	12,167.1	22,427.0	25,810.3	25,683.3	13,453.8	11,278.6	11,278.6
Wisconsin	252,178.9	27,880.2	53,667.8	51,387.3	50,252.6	24,814.8	22,088.1	22,088.1
Wyoming	17,772.1	1,854.1	3,359.1	3,557.3	3,813.6	1,883.2	1,652.4	1,652.4
Dist. of Col.	132,058.2	14,385.2	26,786.5	26,544.3	27,150.1	13,406.7	11,892.7	11,892.7

Source: Office of Revenue Sharing, U.S. Department of the Treasury.

Table 2
GENERAL REVENUE SHARING PAYMENTS TO LOCAL GOVERNMENTS, BY STATE, BY ENTITLEMENT PERIOD
(In thousands of dollars)

State or other jurisdiction	Total 1/72-9/83	Paid/proj. 10/82-9/83	10/81-9/82	10/80-9/81	10/79-9/80	10/78-9/79	10/77-9/78	1/77-9/77
Total...................	$50,613,272.4	$4,565,906.4	$4,567,018.4	$4,571,339.4	$4,536,073.3	$4,556,460.7	$4,530,313.5	$3,297,511.7
Alabama....................	834,223.7	79,075.7	75,128.6	74,116.0	71,464.0	72,589.4	73,512.6	53,481.8
Alaska......................	148,251.1	36,788.0	21,374.5	13,116.0	14,813.5	15,286.3	11,758.5	6,963.6
Arizona	569,659.9	55,051.2	62,084.0	61,911.4	53,347.2	52,948.5	49,772.3	32,343.2
Arkansas	511,967.0	45,801.9	47,773.3	44,569.0	45,428.0	45,460.5	43,833.4	34,869.6
California	5,582,823.4	511,270.9	532,348.3	496,056.1	534,527.5	518,288.1	507,045.8	353,216.1
Colorado	562,385.9	51,547.1	54,321.2	53,707.6	51,423.4	50,871.1	49,983.6	36,531.0
Connecticut	636,317.7	54,095.7	54,165.8	56,318.2	57,083.0	57,317.6	56,786.0	42,129.0
Delaware	151,503.8	13,413.6	13,714.1	14,106.2	13,747.3	14,140.6	14,190.9	10,489.1
Florida	1,595,478.8	164,130.5	161,516.8	160,034.0	136,121.0	136,116.7	135,412.2	102,261.9
Georgia...................	1,118,707.8	111,005.6	109,472.2	107,851.3	100,365.8	100,885.2	97,909.4	70,498.5
Hawaii	238,625.9	22,478.8	23,310.3	21,406.2	21,391.7	22,259.5	22,668.9	16,341.2
Idaho	198,411.7	18,559.2	18,235.5	18,937.8	17,232.3	17,384.8	15,573.9	12,653.5
Illinois....................	2,537,371.0	215,143.4	218,862.8	223,795.6	226,059.5	227,329.1	231,692.5	169,432.1
Indiana	1,025,666.6	85,396.1	82,219.9	87,694.4	89,669.2	92,155.2	96,431.8	70,258.9
Iowa	648,775.5	54,387.0	55,919.5	56,189.9	56,708.4	56,976.8	52,926.0	40,456.3
Kansas	456,875.7	39,326.4	38,056.9	40,475.7	40,638.4	40,284.7	38,835.2	29,809.7
Kentucky	812,692.5	76,016.9	73,995.4	76,752.5	73,684.8	75,425.7	73,860.9	54,261.3
Louisiana	1,117,669.7	93,451.0	96,151.3	94,419.5	96,068.4	101,996.6	108,207.1	76,957.9
Maine	313,667.3	28,207.7	28,741.0	27,826.7	26,043.5	30,554.8	27,826.3	20,546.8
Maryland	1,000,841.6	87,724.0	89,201.3	88,814.6	88,389.9	90,870.7	91,032.7	66,344.5
Massachusetts	1,598,600.6	137,070.8	138,311.1	143,222.1	142,710.3	145,018.0	148,281.2	104,748.5
Michigan	2,107,387.8	175,328.3	179,475.9	191,488.4	196,271.7	191,866.6	188,275.9	136,084.1
Minnesota	1,006,706.0	84,558.5	86,086.4	92,229.0	91,032.8	91,324.1	90,886.8	66,636.4
Mississippi	748,675.2	63,622.9	62,639.2	61,835.5	63,535.1	66,612.8	66,483.6	49,754.7
Missouri	935,995.2	78,791.1	79,996.5	82,870.4	82,273.7	84,291.4	86,495.1	62,300.5
Montana...................	195,695.0	18,613.4	18,181.3	17,395.5	18,006.5	17,365.4	16,017.1	12,173.8
Nebraska	339,480.0	28,505.8	30,764.2	31,992.3	31,409.8	28,565.3	27,675.3	20,865.9
Nevada	128,900.1	13,851.8	13,621.3	13,798.0	11,530.1	11,353.1	11,398.6	8,013.6
New Hampshire	165,752.8	14,085.7	14,887.5	15,259.3	15,516.3	15,574.9	15,358.0	10,662.1
New Jersey................	1,618,880.5	144,289.1	145,513.0	149,959.9	151,057.0	150,397.8	143,682.6	103,731.4
New Mexico................	330,925.0	36,734.3	30,929.0	30,082.7	26,928.2	28,704.2	30,821.4	21,278.7
New York..................	5,550,397.1	464,500.2	463,816.7	476,272.4	497,292.5	510,245.8	514,789.7	372,829.3
North Carolina	1,286,603.9	120,655.4	120,765.3	116,397.5	112,847.1	112,673.7	111,880.9	82,265.2
North Dakota	155,992.0	13,929.8	12,976.1	12,294.9	12,951.7	12,648.5	9,986.3	8,329.2
Ohio	2,022,400.5	172,829.7	174,317.8	181,747.6	184,214.6	185,269.6	184,014.6	133,395.6
Oklahoma	581,690.4	60,063.9	55,060.4	54,781.1	51,121.5	49,601.2	50,303.1	36,907.6
Oregon	553,656.3	54,325.1	53,834.6	53,796.8	51,806.2	50,677.9	49,541.5	35,770.2
Pennsylvania	2,585,941.4	221,316.3	230,057.5	228,338.6	222,071.6	222,258.7	229,291.9	173,950.2
Rhode Island	221,374.1	19,572.8	19,249.8	20,191.8	19,689.1	19,568.2	19,726.0	14,218.0
South Carolina	707,491.4	69,325.5	67,912.8	66,044.2	61,086.0	61,410.6	59,986.0	46,493.5
South Dakota	186,436.3	15,733.3	15,226.7	15,586.5	15,534.4	15,328.8	13,767.3	10,766.4
Tennessee.................	952,326.7	85,700.0	83,689.5	86,806.1	87,954.5	84,339.2	82,502.7	61,264.9
Texas.....................	2,506,214.9	248,650.1	232,252.4	225,379.2	221,222.6	225,142.6	224,985.9	166,706.7
Utah	319,051.4	34,410.3	33,313.8	32,228.7	27,950.6	28,971.5	25,877.2	18,504.7
Vermont...................	147,517.6	12,700.2	12,884.6	13,417.0	13,600.7	13,945.4	13,795.5	9,780.3
Virginia...................	1,058,294.1	98,510.9	98,285.6	95,545.4	93,714.9	94,959.4	93,156.2	66,961.6
Washington	738,848.1	66,902.0	67,790.2	69,802.6	63,454.2	61,530.8	67,731.8	49,302.4
West Virginia..............	443,955.0	41,106.0	42,488.2	42,969.4	39,774.6	41,536.3	40,957.5	27,968.9
Wisconsin.................	1,201,307.7	97,374.3	98,447.9	102,259.3	105,913.0	107,279.2	105,480.0	80,653.1
Wyoming	99,007.8	11,584.1	10,078.5	10,363.6	9,395.0	8,857.8	7,903.8	5,346.2
Dist. of Col.................	54,850.9	18,394.1	17,571.9	18,884.9	0.0	0.0	0.0	0.0

State or other jurisdiction	Total 1/72-12/76	7/76-12/76	7/75-6/76	7/74-6/75	7/73-6/74	1/73-6/73	7/72-12/72	1/72-6/72
Total	$19,988,649.0	$2,238,881.6	$4,209,071.3	$4,088,976.1	$3,987,804.3	$1,967,959.4	$1,747,994.6	$1,747,961.7
Alabama	334,855.6	36,385.4	67,716.9	68,645.3	68,007.1	33,754.6	30,173.1	30,173.2
Alaska	28,150.7	4,096.1	6,061.4	5,859.8	5,219.7	2,542.7	2,183.2	2,187.8
Arizona	202,202.1	21,983.4	42,723.3	42,289.8	41,184.1	20,273.5	16,874.0	16,874.0
Arkansas	204,231.3	23,550.4	43,885.6	42,409.7	40,187.0	19,160.8	17,518.9	17,518.9
California	2,130,070.6	240,148.3	439,848.7	432,177.7	432,671.3	213,657.0	185,783.8	185,783.8
Colorado	214,000.9	24,844.7	46,021.9	43,882.1	42,277.7	20,815.3	18,079.6	18,079.6
Connecticut	258,422.4	28,655.5	56,969.7	53,155.3	50,123.1	24,820.1	22,348.6	22,350.1
Delaware	57,702.0	7,129.8	12,400.8	12,079.2	11,336.7	5,165.5	4,795.0	4,795.0
Florida	599,885.7	69,517.5	130,880.9	128,917.1	115,862.4	57,194.8	48,756.5	48,756.5
Georgia	420,719.8	48,056.4	87,879.3	87,950.9	83,077.7	41,055.5	36,350.0	36,350.0
Hawaii	88,769.3	10,157.2	18,549.6	17,865.2	17,719.9	8,758.2	7,859.6	7,859.6
Idaho	79,834.7	8,606.8	16,331.5	15,923.1	16,635.1	8,219.2	7,059.5	7,059.5
Illinois	1,025,056.0	115,212.0	215,487.2	207,073.9	204,537.0	101,007.7	90,869.1	90,869.1
Indiana	421,841.1	48,047.6	85,755.6	84,961.9	85,420.0	42,191.3	37,732.3	37,732.4
Iowa	275,209.6	27,517.5	56,276.9	56,444.2	56,794.2	28,071.2	25,052.8	25,052.8
Kansas	189,448.7	20,322.1	38,856.3	37,579.1	38,773.9	19,169.4	17,383.5	17,364.4
Kentucky	308,695.0	36,968.4	67,071.0	62,320.7	60,667.5	28,843.6	26,412.6	26,411.2
Louisiana	450,417.9	50,015.7	91,313.8	92,098.0	91,545.8	44,809.6	40,317.8	40,317.2
Maine	123,920.5	13,997.4	26,677.2	25,536.1	24,430.4	12,062.2	10,608.6	10,608.6
Maryland	398,463.9	44,922.8	84,199.6	80,233.5	79,043.2	39,031.8	35,516.5	35,516.5
Massachusetts	639,238.6	71,237.9	137,695.5	129,759.5	127,613.3	63,017.8	54,957.3	54.957.3
Michigan	848,596.9	92,523.9	178,289.2	174,434.5	170,203.2	84,076.5	74,532.9	74,536.7
Minnesota	403,952.0	45,289.8	88,695.0	81,781.8	78,236.6	39,105.6	35,424.8	35,418.4
Mississippi	315,191.4	33,744.4	62,195.3	64,560.5	64,148.2	32,315.2	29,113.9	29,113.9
Missouri	378,976.5	42,446.2	81,511.4	78,463.5	74,506.9	36,784.9	32,631.8	32,631.8
Montana	77,942.0	8,258.8	15,671.3	17,053.0	15,644.3	7,725.2	6,794.7	6,794.7
Nebraska	139,701.4	14,199.5	28,270.0	27,530.3	29,395.0	14,528.2	12,886.5	12,891.9
Nevada	45,333.6	5,452.6	9,969.0	9,021.2	8,872.8	4,381.4	3,818.3	3,818.3
New Hampshire	64,409.0	7,237.8	13,606.7	13,442.3	12,782.2	6,320.4	5,509.8	5,509.8
New Jersey	630,249.7	70,533.2	132,900.8	128,820.7	125,366.3	61,978.3	55,325.2	55,325.2
New Mexico	125,446.5	14,492.0	26,236.9	25,416.5	25,219.9	12,365.2	10,858.0	10,858.0
New York	2,250,650.5	253,497.4	480,494.3	459,753.4	445,873.4	220,176.8	195,427.6	195,427.6
North Carolina	509,118.8	55,951.2	103,450.7	105,177.3	102,826.9	51,038.3	45,337.2	45,337.2
North Dakota	72,875.5	5,657.2	13,649.0	13,872.1	16,723.1	8,262.5	7,355.7	7,355.9
Ohio	806,610.8	90,760.5	172,980.0	164,384.9	158,367.2	78,197.6	70,960.3	70,960.3
Oklahoma	223,851.6	25,091.2	46,301.9	46,599.1	44,707.7	22,077.5	19,537.1	19,537.1
Oregon	203,904.0	24,342.4	44,452.1	41,308.4	39,253.1	19,384.8	17,581.6	17,581.6
Pennsylvania	1,058,656.6	118,304.2	225,925.5	217,030.3	209,246.9	103,459.0	92,345.3	92,345.4
Rhode Island	89,158.4	9,669.5	18,350.9	18,094.8	18,087.0	8,931.4	8,012.4	8,012.4
South Carolina	275,232.8	31,625.8	59,182.1	56,752.6	54,269.2	26,241.7	23,590.7	23,570.7
South Dakota	84,492.9	7,324.4	16,772.2	17,011.8	18,255.5	9,016.4	8,056.3	8,056.3
Tennessee	380,069.8	41,653.1	79,376.1	79,342.3	74,822.3	37,824.2	33,526.6	33,525.2
Texas	961,875.4	113,450.3	203,826.6	196,545.9	190,056.2	93,676.1	82,159.9	82,160.4
Utah	117,794.6	12,586.8	25,071.5	24,010.2	23,990.1	11,834.8	10,150.8	10,150.4
Vermont	57,393.9	6,651.3	12,371.2	11,673.9	11,250.4	5,606.9	4,920.1	4,920.1
Virginia	417,160.1	45,766.8	85,181.3	86,538.8	83,473.2	41,299.1	37,450.4	37,450.5
Washington	292,334.1	33,508.3	62,578.8	57,887.3	57,993.6	28,644.3	25,860.9	25,860.9
West Virginia	167,154.1	18,986.1	35,096.2	35,428.7	32,973.6	15,528.7	14,570.4	14,570.4
Wisconsin	503,900.9	54,861.4	107,344.4	102,763.2	100,505.2	49,790.3	44,318.2	44,318.2
Wyoming	35,478.8	3,642.6	6,718.2	7,114.7	7,627.2	3,766.3	3,304.9	3,304.9
Dist. of Col.	0.0	0.0	0.0	0.0	0.0	0.0	0.0	0.0

Source: Office of Revenue Sharing, U.S. Department of the Treasury.

STATE AID TO LOCAL GOVERNMENT

By Maurice Criz

The financial condition of state governments in fiscal 1982 was extremely weak: grants-in-aid from the federal government dropped for the first time in 40 years, revenue growth slowed because of the economic recession and earlier tax decreases, and general fund balances were depleted in almost all states. Nevertheless, the states attempted to continue to maintain their central role in the federal structure, providing substantial fiscal assistance to local governments to educate the young, to provide necessities of life to the poor, sick and aged, to maintain highways and streets necessary for transporting commodities and people, and for many other governmental services.

Rate of Growth Slows Down

During fiscal 1982, state intergovernmental expenditures totaled $98.7 billion, or $436 per capita. Of this amount, $1.8 billion constituted payments to the federal government for services provided to the states and Supplemental Security Income aid. State payments to local governments totaled $97 billion, comprising 62.7 percent for schools, 12.3 percent for public welfare, 10.4 percent for general local government support, 5.2 percent for highways and streets, and 9.5 percent for all other purposes. It should be noted that these payments include federal funds which pass through the states to local governments, since these are frequently intermingled in state accounts and are not reported separately. In general, the Bureau of the Census defines state payments to local governments as consisting of grants-in-aid, payments in lieu of taxes, reimbursements for services performed, state-collected locally shared taxes, and the extension of contingent loans or advances (where repayment is on a conditional basis).

The rate of growth in state intergovernmental expenditure slowed during 1982, increasing by 6 percent in 1982 as against a 10.3 percent increase in 1981 and 11.2 percent in 1980. This slowdown is comparable to a similar trend for state government direct general expenditure for purchase of goods and services, which grew by 6.4 percent during 1982 as compared with increases of 11.7 percent in 1981 and 15.4 percent in 1980.

State payments to local governments in 1982 remained static as a portion of state general expenditure at 36 percent, but was two percentage points lower than the peak in 1974 (see Table A).

Table A
**DIRECT STATE AID
TO LOCAL GOVERNMENTS
AS A PERCENTAGE OF
STATE GENERAL EXPENDITURE**

Fiscal year	Percent
1964	34.8
1966	36.7
1968	36.3
1970	37.2
1972	37.2
1974	38.0
1976	36.9
1978	36.6
1979	37.1
1980	36.3
1981	36.0
1982	36.0

Approaching the significance of local governments' revenue from state governments in terms of major revenue sources, we find that in fiscal 1982 local governments received 34 percent of their total general revenue from the states. This compares to 7.5 percent received directly from the federal government, and 58.5 percent obtained from taxes, charges and other local revenue sources.

The slowdown in growth of state aid, while by no means universal, has been widespread among the states. Table 2 shows the percentage of change in per capita amounts of state intergovernmental expenditure, the major portion of which is local grants-in-aid, by biennial periods since 1976. Overall, there was an increase of 14.5 percent from 1976 to 1978, a further increase of 20.9 percent from 1978 to 1980, but a decline to 16.5 percent between 1980 and 1982. The breadth of the cutbacks is evidenced by the fact that 12 states showed increases of less than 10 percent in the 1980-82 period as compared with five states in 1978-80, 16 states with increases of 10-20 percent in the most recent period as against 22 states in 1978-80, and six states in the 20-30 percent group compared with 13 states in 1978-80.

Maurice Criz is Senior Advisor, Governments Division, U.S. Bureau of the Census.

The amount of aid to local governments for particular functions reflects the varying governmental structures in the individual states, the distribution of responsibilities as between the state government and local governments, and public policies determining the level of support for competing services. Financial support received by the states from the federal government, on the other hand, reflects national policies that differ from those of the states. Thus, as is shown in Table B, state aid to local governments is distributed primarily for education, followed by public welfare, general support and highways. Federal aid to the states, however, is primarily for public welfare, followed by education and highways, and a separate grant is made to local governments for general support under the general revenue sharing program.

Table B
STATE PAYMENTS TO LOCAL GOVERNMENTS
AND RECEIPTS FROM FEDERAL GOVERNMENT:
FISCAL 1982
(In millions)

Function	To local governments	From federal government
Total	$96,950	$66,026
Education	60,684	13,149
Public Welfare	11,951	31,510
General Support	10,044	(a)
Highways	5,028	8,304
Miscellaneous and Other	9,243	13,063

(a) State participation in the federal general revenue sharing program ended September 30, 1980.

State Aid by Function

In fiscal 1982, the annual increase in local aid from states slowed. The largest drop was in public welfare, which fell to an 8.6 percent increase compared to 19.1 percent in 1981. General support decreased from 10.7 to 5 percent, education from 8.7 to 6 percent, and highways from 8.4 to 5.8 percent.

Aid in different categories varies considerably among the states depending upon whether the service is state or locally administered and the comparative levels of support. Table 3 shows that 20 states had total intergovernmental expenditures of $300 to $400 per capita in 1982, 10 had between $200 and $300, and 11 had $500 or more. For education, the predominant group was between $200 and $300, 26 states; eight states were between $100 and $200; 10 states between $300 and $400; and four states were in the $400 and over class. For general local government support, 31 states provided aid of less than $50 per capita; 11 states were between $50 and $100; and eight states provided $100 or more per capita. As to public welfare, 38 states provided

local aid of less than $25; six were in the $25 to $50 group; and six provided $50 or more. For highways, the largest group was under $25, 30 states; 15 states provided $25 to $50 per capita; and five states were in the $50 to $100 group.

State Aid by Type of Receiving Government

Even though there was a slowdown in fiscal 1982 in the rate of increase of state aid to local governments in total amount and in a number of states, the dollar amount in total increased 6.2 percent to $97 billion from $91.3 billion in 1981. The largest share went to school districts, $48.8 billion or an increase of 5.3 percent over 1981. Counties received $22.7 billion, an increase of 6.8 percent. Municipalities received $15.1 billion, 8.5 percent more than in 1981. The amount of aid to townships remained approximately the same as in 1981, while aid to special districts decreased by 4.5 percent.

Other Types of State Aid

In addition to providing direct monetary assistance to local governments, some state governments help raise funds through the sale of bonds or notes. The North Carolina Local Government Commission sells bonds or notes for counties, municipalities and special districts. Hawaii sells state general obligation bonds from which funds are made available to the counties for capital improvements and withholds payment for debt service from the state-administered real property tax. In Florida, county school districts may authorize the state to sell bonds secured by the county's portion of state motor vehicle license funds, and counties may authorize the state to sell bonds for capital projects with payments to be made from the county's allocation of a special statewide motor fuels tax.

Municipal bond banks have been established in Alaska, Maine, New Hampshire, New York and Vermont. In essence, local governments sell their securities to a state bond bank, which in turn sells securities to the public. Local governments retain the right to sell their bonds independently, but there are advantages to selling through the state. States have better credit ratings and their bond issues get better interest rates in the market. Larger bond issues sell more easily than smaller ones. The state of New York brought New York City through a crisis period in the 1970s by selling bonds secured by certain revenues of the city.

The Alaska Municipal Bond Bank has sold several bond issues since 1976, with varying types of assistance for the local governments. In one series, a state legislative appropriation funded an additional bond reserve (10 percent), and if a municipality fails to meet debt service, the state of Alaska must pay to the bank funds due the municipality from the state in order to clear the default. In a second series, state appropriations subsidize interest rates paid by municipalities. A third series of bonds provides for loans to local governments which qualify for aid under the Federal Coastal Energy Impact Program.

The other state bond banks follow the general principle that they are independent authorities and the credit and taxing power of the state is not pledged to payment of principal and interest on the bonds, although the Maine and Vermont statutes require the state to appropriate funds, if necessary, to maintain the general reserve fund at a level sufficient to meet debt service requirements. The New Hampshire statute provides that the state legislature may make such appropriations if it so desires.

Some states have established authorities to assist local governments in financing public school construction. In Pennsylvania, for example, the state sells bonds to secure funds, builds the schools and leases them to the local school districts. The Virginia Public School Authority operates similarly to a bond bank, selling its own bonds and buying the bonds of the school districts. Other states that have similar authorities to facilitate school construction include Alabama, Georgia, Kentucky and Maine. Hawaii provides the ultimate in state assistance for education—all public education is provided by the state government, and there are no locally administered public schools. In Alaska, public schools located outside borough or city school systems are administered by regional area boards that are financed by state appropriations. In Maine, public schools in unorganized territory and Indian schools are operated and maintained by the State Department of Education.

Other types of state aid to local governments that are not included in intergovernmental payments listed above are the following: (1) Nonfiscal assistance to local governments in the form of advisory services or aid-in-kind; (2) Contributions by a state to trust funds it administers for the financing of retirement benefits to local government employees; (3) Shares of state-imposed taxes which are collected and retained by local governments; (4) Proceeds of state interest-bearing loans to local governments which, unlike contingent loans, are repayable over a specified time. Such loans are treated as debt and investment transactions; (5) Expenditure for the purchase of property, commodities and utility services to other governments; (6) State economic or industrial development agencies' attempts to stimulate business investment, such as creating jobs and boosting local economies and revenues.

Table 1
SUMMARY OF STATE INTERGOVERNMENTAL PAYMENTS: 1942 to 1982
(In millions, except per capita)

| Fiscal year | Total | To federal government | For general local government support | To local governments | | | | | Per capita |
| | | | | For specified purposes | | | | | |
				Total	Education	Public welfare	Highways	All other	
1942	$ 1,780	...	$ 224	$ 1,556	$ 790	$ 390	$ 344	$ 32	$ 13.37
1944	1,842	...	274	1,568	861	368	298	41	13.95
1946	2,092	...	357	1,735	953	376	339	67	15.05
1948	3,283	...	428	2,855	1,554	648	507	146	22.64
1950	4,217	...	482	3,735	2,054	792	610	279	28.11
1951	4,678	...	513	4,165	2,248	974	667	276	30.78
1952	5,044	...	549	4,495	2,525	976	728	268	32.55
1953	5,384	...	592	4,971	2,740	981	803	267	34.19
1954	5,679	...	600	5,079	2,934	1,004	871	269	35.42
1955	5,986	...	591	5,395	3,154	1,046	911	284	36.62
1956	6,538	...	631	5,907	3,541	1,069	984	313	39.28
1957	7,439	...	668	6,771	4,212	1,136	1,083	340	43.86
1958	8,089	...	687	7,402	4,598	1,247	1,167	390	46.76
1959	8,689	...	725	7,964	4,957	1,409	1,207	391	49.37
1960	9,443	...	806	8,637	5,461	1,483	1,247	446	52.75
1961	10,114	...	821	9,293	5,963	1,602	1,266	462	55.51
1962	10,906	...	844	10,062	6,474	1,777	1,326	485	58.94
1963	11,885	...	1,012	10,873	6,993	1,919	1,416	545	63.31
1964	12,968	...	1,053	11,915	7,664	2,104	1,524	623	68.06
1965	14,174	...	1,102	13,072	8,351	2,436	1,630	655	73.43
1966	16,928	...	1,361	15,567	10,177	2,882	1,725	783	86.79
1967	19,056	...	1,585	17,471	11,845	2,897	1,861	868	96.70
1968	21,950	...	1,993	19,957	13,321	3,527	2,029	1,079	110.27
1969	24,779	...	2,135	22,644	14,858	4,402	2,109	1,275	123.20
1970	28,892	...	2,958	25,934	17,085	5,003	2,439	1,407	142.73
1971	32,640	...	3,258	29,382	19,292	5,760	2,507	1,823	158.82
1972	36,759	...	3,752	33,007	21,195	6,944	2,633	2,235	177.16
1973	40,822	...	4,280	36,542	23,316	7,532	2,953	2,741	195.22
1974	45,941	$ 341	4,804	40,796	27,107	7,028	3,211	3,450	218.07
1975	51,978	975	5,129	45,874	31,110	7,127	3,225	4,412	244.71
1976	57,858	1,180	5,674	51,004	34,084	8,296	3,241	5,383	270.42
1977	62,460	1,386	6,373	54,701	36,964	8,756	3,631	5,350	288.65
1978	67,287	1,472	6,819	58,995	40,125	8,586	3,821	6,463	309.52
1979	75,975	1,493	8,224	66,258	46,206	8,667	4,149	7,236	346.18
1980	84,504	1,746	8,644	74,114	52,688	9,242	4,383	7,801	374.13
1981	93,180	1,873	9,570	81,735	57,257	11,009	4,751	8,718	412.47
1982	98,743	1,793	10,044	86,905	60,684	11,951	5,028	9,243	435.86

Source: U.S. Bureau of the Census, *State Payments to Local Governments* (vol. 6, no. 3, of the 1977 census of governments) and annual reports of *State Government Finances.*

Table 2
STATE INTERGOVERNMENTAL EXPENDITURE, BY STATE:
1976 TO 1982

State	Amount (in thousands)				Per capita amounts				Percentage change in per capita amounts		
									1980 to 1982	1978 to 1980	1976 to 1978
	1982	1980	1978	1976	1982	1980	1978	1976	1982	1980	1978
All states	$98,742,976	$84,504,451	$67,287,260	$57,858,241	$435.86	$374.13	$309.52	$270.42	16.5	20.9	14.5
Alabama	1,136,158	1,036,721	856,355	700,064	291.77	266.51	228.85	191.01	9.5	16.5	19.8
Alaska	992,519	340,319	265,975	207,088	2,468.95	850.80	659.99	542.12	190.2	28.9	21.7
Arizona	1,192,237	1,040,614	814,662	694,268	438.63	382.86	346.08	305.84	14.6	10.6	13.2
Arkansas	667,184	624,261	505,103	418,197	291.86	273.20	231.06	198.29	6.8	18.2	16.5
California	17,625,121	15,360,365	9,905,969	8,135,469	744.68	648.97	444.33	378.04	14.7	46.1	17.5
Colorado	1,200,839	947,692	746,746	675,431	415.52	328.03	279.68	261.49	26.7	17.3	7.0
Connecticut.........	760,415	671,287	593,857	525,225	244.66	215.99	191.63	168.50	13.3	12.7	13.7
Delaware	214,619	189,577	183,973	188,428	361.31	318.62	315.56	323.75	13.4	1.0	-2.5
Florida	3,512,218	2,925,889	2,235,987	1,834,215	360.38	300.40	260.18	217.81	20.0	15.5	19.5
Georgia	1,781,763	1,613,179	1,177,775	845,591	326.15	295.24	231.66	170.14	10.5	27.4	36.2
Hawaii	27,875	35,530	49,711	222,772	28.89	36.82	55.42	25.67	-27.5	-33.6	115.9
Idaho	353,787	309,341	225,063	187,358	374.77	327.69	256.34	225.46	14.4	27.8	13.7
Illinois	3,725,170	3,817,128	2,869,480	2,652,553	326.00	334.31	255.22	236.22	-2.5	31.0	8.0
Indiana.............	2,045,228	1,805,564	1,481,065	1,253,233	372.54	328.88	275.60	236.37	13.3	19.3	16.6
Iowa	1,262,391	1,148,360	969,801	797,891	433.22	394.22	334.88	278.01	9.9	17.7	20.5
Kansas	711,548	601,939	474,426	404,805	300.99	254.74	202.06	175.24	18.2	26.1	15.3
Kentucky...........	1,107,357	1,006,756	774,679	510,160	302.56	274.99	221.46	148.82	10.0	24.2	48.8
Louisiana...........	1,599,993	1,315,201	1,116,896	998,899	380.41	312.85	281.62	260.06	21.6	11.1	8.3
Maine	297,274	303,746	274,718	320,491	264.24	270.00	251.80	299.52	-2.1	7.2	-15.9
Maryland	1,708,142	1,431,805	1,199,885	1,460,454	405.06	339.61	289.62	352.43	19.3	17.3	-17.8
Massachusetts........	2,315,564	2,116,477	1,577,703	1,429,110	403.62	368.92	273.24	246.02	9.4	35.0	11.1
Michigan	3,824,824	3,578,343	3,071,384	2,306,268	412.96	386.51	334.25	253.32	6.8	15.6	32.0
Minnesota...........	3,016,693	2,237,164	1,960,373	1,602,859	740.11	548.73	489.12	404.25	34.9	12.2	21.0
Mississippi..........	948,128	856,350	691,567	582,224	376.09	339.69	287.67	247.33	10.7	18.1	16.3
Missouri............	1,167,399	1,088,886	812,678	693,542	237.42	221.45	167.22	145.15	7.2	32.4	15.2
Montana	243,384	230,463	215,838	147,181	309.26	292.84	274.95	195.46	5.6	6.5	40.7
Nebraska	482,635	412,081	347,780	257,768	307.41	262.47	222.22	165.98	17.1	18.1	33.9
Nevada.............	456,728	265,956	197,202	143,910	570.91	332.86	298.79	235.92	71.5	11.4	26.7
New Hampshire	139,824	137,723	105,117	87,832	151.82	149.54	120.69	106.85	1.5	23.9	13.0
New Jersey	4,030,065	3,056,970	2,162,892	1,634,972	547.19	415.12	295.19	222.87	31.8	40.6	32.5
New Mexico	829,899	595,464	461,088	363,060	636.91	458.05	380.44	310.84	39.0	20.4	22.4
New York	11,849,950	10,252,802	10,075,469	9,977,102	674.90	583.97	567.70	551.71	15.6	2.9	2.9
North Carolina	2,440,069	2,028,170	1,960,984	1,652,666	414.84	345.28	351.62	302.19	20.1	-1.8	16.4
North Dakota	355,610	216,844	177,804	148,253	544.58	332.07	272.71	230.56	64.0	21.8	18.3
Ohio	3,561,699	3,249,696	2,610,757	2,095,547	329.85	300.98	242.88	196.03	9.6	23.9	23.9
Oklahoma	1,160,761	800,260	631,479	491,460	383.72	264.55	219.26	177.68	45.0	20.7	23.4
Oregon	1,014,603	879,899	608,505	421,079	385.34	334.18	248.98	180.80	15.3	34.2	37.7
Pennsylvania.........	4,014,697	3,541,237	3,054,225	2,762,409	338.39	298.41	259.93	232.88	13.4	14.8	11.6
Rhode Island	235,816	217,255	170,414	148,660	249.01	229.41	182.26	160.37	8.5	25.9	13.7
South Carolina	1,024,500	781,643	650,372	530,983	328.16	250.61	222.88	186.44	30.9	12.5	20.0
South Dakota	160,201	121,758	85,935	68,306	231.84	176.46	124.54	99.57	31.4	41.7	25.1
Tennessee	1,067,709	974,485	798,272	657,567	232.57	212.26	183.22	156.04	9.6	15.8	17.4
Texas	4,252,176	3,458,969	2,724,758	2,161,147	298.84	243.11	209.37	173.07	22.9	16.1	21.0
Utah	525,165	459,404	369,324	288,129	359.46	314.44	282.57	234.63	14.3	11.3	20.4
Vermont	110,722	110,786	97,068	81,941	216.68	216.80	199.32	172.14	0	8.8	15.8
Virginia	1,658,077	1,268,683	1,045,710	1,010,572	310.09	237.31	203.13	200.83	30.7	16.8	1.2
Washington	2,128,066	1,601,814	1,138,795	947,921	515.02	387.85	301.75	262.44	32.8	28.5	15.0
West Virginia	674,956	533,286	461,282	356,823	346.13	273.48	248.00	195.95	26.6	10.3	26.6
Wisconsin	2,761,315	2,643,133	2,149,735	1,868,145	586.76	561.77	459.44	405.33	4.4	22.3	13.4
Wyoming............	369,903	263,176	150,624	108,213	787.03	558.76	355.25	277.47	40.9	57.1	28.0

Source: U.S. Bureau of the Census, *State Government Finances in 1982*, and previous annual reports.

Table 3
PER CAPITA STATE INTERGOVERNMENTAL EXPENDITURE,
BY FUNCTION AND BY STATE: 1982

State	Total	General local govern- ment support	Specified functions			
			Education	Public welfare	Highways	Miscellaneous and unallocable
All states..................	$435.86	$ 44.34	$267.86	$ 60.67	$22.19	$ 40.80
Alabama.................	291.77	14.85	226.19	0.89	28.72	21.11
Alaska....................	2,468.95	371.91	1,002.11	17.90	82.35	994.68
Arizona	438.63	108.30	281.26	1.21	31.92	15.95
Arkansas	291.86	17.71	217.85	0.42	31.66	24.22
California................	744.68	56.01	382.25	223.01	20.61	62.81
Colorado	415.52	6.22	247.29	85.48	24.23	52.31
Connecticut..............	244.66	29.18	167.74	11.81	7.79	28.14
Delaware	361.31	...	304.31	0.80	7.01	49.19
Florida	360.38	31.95	290.22	...	15.35	22.85
Georgia..................	326.15	2.95	273.47	0.70	13.02	36.02
Hawaii	28.89	18.94	...	4.52	0.36	5.07
Idaho	374.77	24.54	297.99	...	37.05	15.20
Illinois	326.00	36.31	238.73	10.99	23.22	16.76
Indiana..................	372.54	81.78	209.73	31.81	30.93	18.28
Iowa	433.22	44.40	301.17	7.84	53.35	26.46
Kansas	300.99	18.73	249.95	0.08	18.90	13.33
Kentucky	302.56	0.48	252.53	0.67	13.79	35.09
Louisiana................	380.41	53.09	280.16	0.13	16.53	30.49
Maine	264.24	21.75	216.58	7.55	1.71	16.66
Maryland	405.06	35.27	215.43	3.74	78.78	71.84
Massachusetts	403.62	65.99	203.08	21.78	11.27	101.51
Michigan	412.96	57.79	202.73	42.27	51.37	58.79
Minnesota	740.11	121.38	444.88	96.08	40.50	37.28
Mississippi	376.09	57.69	276.04	0.18	30.53	11.66
Missouri	237.42	1.31	197.80	2.02	15.25	21.04
Montana.................	309.26	31.09	232.65	4.03	10.17	31.33
Nebraska	307.41	78.94	126.64	13.79	48.81	39.24
Nevada	570.91	198.22	337.13	7.25	14.64	13.67
New Hampshire	151.82	46.40	75.19	...	7.98	22.25
New Jersey...............	547.19	158.19	242.02	101.11	10.63	35.23
New Mexico...............	636.91	134.15	475.74	...	9.54	17.49
New York................	674.90	51.99	298.20	242.68	9.23	72.81
North Carolina	414.84	22.78	319.49	20.08	7.10	45.38
North Dakota	544.58	60.69	391.77	14.67	57.51	19.94
Ohio	329.85	33.52	196.48	41.03	36.03	22.78
Oklahoma	383.72	4.00	307.63	3.29	47.29	21.51
Oregon	385.34	73.75	235.67	1.56	46.64	27.72
Pennsylvania.............	338.39	5.10	217.74	33.74	17.95	63.86
Rhode Island	249.01	17.61	175.12	28.82	0.41	27.05
South Carolina	328.16	29.01	260.14	2.57	26.95	9.49
South Dakota	231.84	66.69	142.04	0.06	9.51	13.54
Tennessee................	232.57	25.57	167.94	1.59	26.69	10.78
Texas....................	298.84	2.80	288.02	...	2.16	5.86
Utah	359.46	0.68	310.56	2.95	13.57	31.69
Vermont..................	216.68	0.34	167.87	10.28	21.09	17.10
Virginia..................	310.09	4.18	216.45	31.32	12.51	45.63
Washington	515.02	15.15	430.10	4.79	23.57	41.41
West Virginia.............	346.13	7.09	326.51	...	...	12.53
Wisconsin................	586.76	161.28	203.99	133.68	38.00	49.81
Wyoming	787.03	273.62	375.60	0.06	28.25	109.50

Source: U.S. Bureau of the Census, *State Government Finances in 1982.*

Table 4
STATE INTERGOVERNMENTAL EXPENDITURE, BY FUNCTION AND BY STATE: 1982
(In thousands)

State	Total	General local government support	Specified functions			
			Education	Public welfare	Highways	Miscellaneous and combined
All states..................	$98,742,976	$10,044,372	$60,683,583	$13,744,417	$5,028,072	$9,242,543
Alabama...................	1,136,158	57,826	880,794	3,466	111,855	82,217
Alaska....................	992,519	149,507	402,848	7,197	33,106	399,861
Arizona	1,192,237	294,349	764,503	3,276	86,745	43,364
Arkansas	667,184	40,493	498,013	949	72,370	55,369
California.................	17,625,121	1,325,612	9,047,054	5,278,177	487,684	1,486,594 (a)
Colorado	1,200,839	17,964	714,655	247,024	70,015	151,181
Connecticut	760,415	90,679	521,348	36,716	24,208	87,464
Delaware	214,619	. . .	180,760	478	4,165	29,216
Florida	3,512,218	311,429	2,828,459	. . .	149,592	222,738
Georgia...................	1,781,763	16,117	1,493,944	3,811	71,135	196,756
Hawaii	27,875	18,273	. . .	4,357	348	4,897
Idaho	353,787	23,169	281,299	. . .	34,971	14,348
Illinois...................	3,725,170	414,877	2,727,941	125,566	265,298	191,488
Indiana...................	2,045,228	448,990	1,151,430	174,612	169,815	100,381
Iowa	1,262,391	129,370	877,610	22,856	155,459	77,096
Kansas	711,548	44,281	590,879	186	44,687	31,515
Kentucky	1,107,357	1,755	924,251	2,434	50,477	128,440
Louisiana	1,599,993	223,285	1,178,351	562	69,537	128,258
Maine	297,274	24,469	243,648	8,493	1,924	18,740
Maryland	1,708,142	148,736	908,454	15,783	332,220	302,949
Massachusetts	2,315,564	378,565	1,165,049	124,939	64,632	582,379 (b)
Michigan	3,824,824	535,232	1,877,717	391,502	475,826	544,547 (c)
Minnesota	3,016,693	494,744	1,813,330	391,617	165,066	151,936
Mississippi	948,128	145,432	695,897	442	76,972	29,385
Missouri	1,167,399	6,449	972,570	9,956	74,969	103,455
Montana..................	243,384	24,465	183,095	3,169	8,001	24,654
Nebraska	482,635	123,932	198,822	21,651	76,627	61,603
Nevada	456,728	158,577	269,703	5,799	11,711	10,938
New Hampshire	139,824	42,731	69,253	. . .	7,352	20,488
New Jersey	4,030,065	1,165,078	1,782,494	744,711	78,306	259,476
New Mexico...............	829,899	174,794	619,887	. . .	12,425	22,793
New York.................	11,849,950	912,861	5,235,845	4,260,931	161,974	1,278,339 (d)
North Carolina	2,440,069	134,001	1,879,236	118,116	41,777	266,939
North Dakota	355,610	39,628	255,824	9,579	37,556	13,023
Ohio	3,561,699	361,923	2,121,642	443,067	389,063	246,004
Oklahoma	1,160,761	12,108	930,577	9,957	143,061	65,058
Oregon	1,014,603	194,192	620,526	4,102	122,803	72,980
Pennsylvania	4,014,697	60,450	2,583,289	400,311	212,955	757,692
Rhode Island	235,816	16,676	165,837	27,297	390	25,616
South Carolina	1,024,500	90,566	812,154	8,027	84,130	29,623
South Dakota	160,201	46,081	98,150	44	6,573	9,353
Tennessee.................	1,067,709	117,392	770,995	7,309	122,542	49,471
Texas.....................	4,252,176	39,781	4,098,189	. . .	30,765	83,441
Utah	525,165	1,000	453,734	4,305	19,829	46,297
Vermont..................	110,722	173	85,782	5,251	10,778	8,738
Virginia...................	1,658,077	22,354	1,157,355	167,482	66,884	244,002
Washington	2,128,066	62,601	1,777,181	19,796	97,371	171,117
West Virginia	674,956	13,823	636,692	. . .	. . .	24,441
Wisconsin.................	2,761,315	758,982	959,983	629,088	178,847	234,415
Wyoming	369,903	128,600	176,534	26	13,276	51,468

Source: U.S. Bureau of the Census, *State Government Finances in 1982.*

(a) Includes $801,754,000 health aids.

(b) Includes $253,204,000 transit subsidies, $85,586,000 distribution of net lottery profits.

(c) Includes $335,844,000 health aids and $76,245,000 transit subsidies.

(d) Includes $297,127,000 transit subsidies, $290,220,000 health aids, and $90,768,000 for services to the aging.

Table 5
STATE INTERGOVERNMENTAL EXPENDITURE, BY TYPE OF RECEIVING GOVERNMENT AND BY STATE: 1982
(In thousands of dollars)

State	Total intergovern- mental expenditure	Federal	School districts	Counties	Municipali- ties	Townships and New England "towns"	Special districts	Combined and un- allocable
All states	$98,742,976	$1,793,284(a)	$48,793,951	$22,650,495	$15,054,986	$1,051,245	$1,195,296	$8,203,719
Alabama	1,136,158	...	880,794	185,134	66,131	...	...	4,099
Alaska	992,519	2,439	...	392,309	453,381	...	...	144,390
Arizona	1,192,237	1,020	764,466	181,508	241,050	...	82	4,111
Arkansas	667,184	273	497,072	89,794	53,458	...	3,768	22,819
California..............	17,625,121	1,220,678	8,444,673	6,422,873	1,036,891	...	446,734	53,272
Colorado	1,200,839	391	714,655	339,638	103,499	...	42,258	398
Connecticut.............	760,415	1,373	16,144	...	375,253	307,673	2,257	57,715
Delaware	214,619	478	180,760	13,255	14,927	...	...	5,199
Florida	3,512,218	4,541	2,828,459	344,291	292,138	...	...	42,789
Georgia	1,781,763	...	1,493,944	210,623	30,756	...	3,136	43,304
Hawaii	27,875	4,357	...	13,613	9,905	...	...	...
Idaho	353,787	1,541	281,299	36,640	13,212	...	6,116	14,979
Illinois	3,725,170	10,401	2,727,941	287,552	479,862	51,125	95,607	72,682
Indiana	2,045,228	4,164	1,151,430	244,511	172,761	...	6,981	465,381 (b)
Iowa	1,262,391	11,434	877,610	175,982	139,255	...	5,748	52,362
Kansas	711,548	752	590,879	58,953	41,829	1,450	2,421	15,264
Kentucky	1,107,357	...	924,251	143,153	29,419	...	449	10,085
Louisiana	1,599,993	562	1,178,351	221,945	67,068	...	7,985	124,082
Maine	297,274	6,591	...	4,408	...	...	...	286,275
Maryland	1,708,142	171	...	978,648	590,127	...	135	139,061
Massachusetts	2,315,564	117,179	42,700	892	5,075	...	237,527	1,912,191 (c)
Michigan	3,824,824	58,740	1,877,717	1,008,396	527,353	109,951	918	241,749
Minnesota	3,016,693	...	1,801,239	736,443	397,950	27,157	3,736	50,168
Mississippi	948,128	82	695,478	130,658	121,910	...	...	...
Missouri	1,167,399	...	972,570	57,224	69,455	...	2,595	65,555
Montana	243,384	719	182,189	45,859	14,085	...	297	235
Nebraska	482,519	919	198,822	70,986	61,105	...	6,075	144,728
Nevada.................	456,728	2,646	269,703	161,035	18,614	...	370	4,360
New Hampshire	139,824	...	22,718	2,135	26,493	29,547	284	58,647
New Jersey.............	4,030,065	22,697	2,119	836,171	121,877	243	1,714	3,045,244 (d)
New Mexico.............	829,899	...	619,887	24,917	183,149	...	707	1,239
New York	11,849,950	193,761	2,986,185	2,115,750	6,363,786	141,659	7,692	41,117
North Carolina	2,440,069	...	...	2,224,910	196,150	...	15,651	3,358
North Dakota	355,610	...	255,824	55,739	28,177	...	925	14,945
Ohio	3,561,699	...	2,072,728	918,842	143,802	33,426	5,876	387,025 (e)
Oklahoma	1,160,761	...	930,577	157,331	22,601	...	2,005	48,247
Oregon	1,014,603	...	620,526	205,007	73,667	...	6,108	109,295
Pennsylvania............	4,014,697	56,400	2,583,289	690,288	309,832	114,177	203,763	56,948
Rhode Island	235,816	7,056	3,669	...	121,795	86,219	...	17,077
South Carolina	1,024,500	56	812,154	186,635	20,981	...	656	4,018
South Dakota	160,201	44	98,150	51,353	3,772	279	579	6,024
Tennessee..............	1,067,709	...	14,240	634,481	412,918	...	77	5,993
Texas	4,252,176	...	4,098,123	68,562	54,402	...	4,395	26,694
Utah	525,165	422	453,734	46,544	17,979	...	1,394	5,092
Vermont................	110,722	5,251	85,782	...	3,095	13,004	399	3,191
Virginia	1,658,077	...	...	884,682	625,427	...	3,667	144,301
Washington	2,128,066	17,347	1,777,181	127,904	130,822	...	59,474	15,338
West Virginia...........	674,956	...	635,415	18,266	3,287	...	...	17,988
Wisconsin	2,761,315	38,773	951,970	784,450	644,820	135,335	474	205,493
Wyoming	369,903	26	176,534	60,205	119,685	...	4,261	9,192

Source: U.S. Bureau of the Census, *State Government Finances in 1982.*
   (a) Includes $1,779,294,000 Supplemental Security Income payments (additional transfers not separately identified by other states may not be included).
   (b) Includes $403,064,000 property tax replacement distribution to local governments.
   (c) Includes $1,165,049,000 education subsidies, $132,660,000 housing subsidies, $85,586,000 distribution of net lottery profits, and $29,506,000 redistribution of Federal C.E.T.A. aid.
   (d) Includes $1,711,336,000 education subsidies and $1,150,899 property tax relief and shared revenues.
   (e) Includes $350,195,000 tax relief payments.

Section II THE GOVERNORS AND THE EXECUTIVE BRANCH

THE GOVERNORS, 1982-83

By Thad L. Beyle

The main concern of governors and state legislators over the last two years was finances. State revenues declined along with the national economy. Budgets could not be met as revenues fell short of projections, and in some states estimates had to be revised downward several times during one fiscal year. This meant the worst of all worlds to elected state officials—taxes had to be increased, while at the same time budget cutbacks, often severe, reduced state government services to citizens.

During 1982 alone, taxes were raised in 31 states while 41 states cut or limited spending. For state employees in 19 states it meant no cost of living raise; in 23 states there were cutbacks in the workforce. And a number of states spent less in their 1983 budgets than in prior years. Over the biennium, 49 of the 50 states enacted some measure of fiscal austerity.[1]

Activities of state officials in the biennium must be cast within this context of fiscal problems, plus the continuation of the Reagan administration's attempt to shift priorities from domestic programs to defense and responsibility from the federal to the state and local levels.

Governors

Thirty-nine governors were up for election during the two-year period; in 26 of these contests the incumbent stood for an additional term, with 19 being reelected. Of the seven defeated governors, one was unseated in his party's primary (Massachusetts), and six were beaten in the general election (Arkansas, Louisiana, Nebraska, Nevada, New Hampshire and Texas).

Five former governors recaptured their chairs after either being unable to seek earlier reelection due to constitutional restrictions (Alabama, Louisiana) or having been unseated previously (Arkansas, Massachusetts and Minnesota). Two other former governors were unsuccessful in their quests, one being beaten in his party's primary by the eventual winner (Wisconsin), the other losing in the general election while running as an independent but indicating he was not entirely serious (New Hampshire).[2]

The cost of becoming governor continues to grow as measured by these elections. In 1982, the 36 campaigns cost the various candidates over $192 million as officially reported, led by the three campaigns in which expenditures were well over $20 million each (California at $23.4 million, New York at $23.6 million and Texas at $22.4 million). This is an average of $5.3 million per gubernatorial chair, with the average dropping to $3.7 million when the three most expensive campaigns are deleted.

Despite their obvious advantage in position, name recognition and known public record, the incumbent or former governors who were running in 28 of the 36 campaigns spent considerable money. Of the $192 million, approximately $58 million (30 percent) was spent by these governors and former governors—16 of whom were the top spenders in their contests.

The Democrats were most successful in holding and gaining gubernatorial chairs as they won 30 of the 39 races over the two-year period, giving them a 35-to-15 ratio in seats held as of 1984. The 20 new governors inaugurated in 1983-84 included four current or former lieutenant governors (Iowa, Kentucky, New York and Ohio), five current or former attorneys' general (California, Mississippi, Nevada, New Mexico and Texas) and as noted earlier five former governors. Thus the importance of previously holding an elective statewide office is clearly demonstrated as 14 of the 20 new governors used their previous statewide run for and holding of a penultimate statewide office as springboards to the governorship.[3]

The 20 retiring governors—12 Republicans and eight Democrats—had served as governors for a combined total of 129 years with James Rhodes of Ohio (16 years), Robert Ray of Iowa (14 years) and William Milliken of Michigan (14 years) having held the longest tenures. Twelve others were one-term governors, three due to constitutional limitation.

Gubernatorial Transitions

The handing over of the reins of government from one gubernatorial administration to

---

Thad L. Beyle is Professor of Political Science at the University of North Carolina at Chapel Hill and Senior Fellow for Research at the Governors Center at Duke University.

another in recent years has been the subject of more attention both in state governments and among academics.

Since 1968, the National Governors' Association, at first in cooperation with The Council of State Governments but since 1974 in its own right, has conducted a "Seminar for New Governors" within two weeks of the general elections in the even numbered years. Incumbent governors teach the seminars and discuss: organizing the governor's office; press and public relations; management of the executive branch; executive-legislative relations; intergovernmental relations; the governorship as a partnership (spouses involved); and the transition period.[4] Both organizations have also developed materials on the transition and assuming office which are made available to the new governors and their staffs and which can be taken back to the states for use.[5]

But the problems in a gubernatorial transition are as much political as they are administrative. For example, in the 20 transitions following the 1982 and 1983 gubernatorial elections, seven incumbent governors had lost their seats in either the party's primary or general election; six other incumbent governors, who declined or were constitutionally unable to seek reelection, backed the losing candidate either in their party's primary or in the general election. In these 13 states, the personal politics of the campaigns, be they primaries or general elections, had the potential of setting significant roadblocks to the transition.

Party shifts occurred in 12 of the 20 states with Democrats gaining control of 10 formerly Republican-held states, while Republicans returned the favor in two states. Further, in four other states where the same party maintained control there were factional shifts so a different faction of the party gained control, which in many states can mean as much or more potential change and turmoil than if there were a party shift. Therefore in 16 of the 20 transition states there was either a party or a factional shift, meaning that substantial changes in the politics, coalitions and agendas of the governorships were due as the new administrations took office.

In summary, the transitions that followed the 1982-83 gubernatorial elections probably occurred under fairly normal conditions: outgoing governors, some defeated, turning the office over to those who beat them, or to a member of the opposite party or a leader of an opposition faction within their own party, often after a very competitive campaign in which the outgoing

governor, his performance and administration were major issues. Not the best of conditions for an orderly transition—but in our form of democracy this is too often how we transfer power at the state level.[6]

The Governors and the Lieutenant Governor

Compared to the previous biennium there was considerably less controversy between the holders of these two offices in 1982-83. Most of the interest focused on the functions of the lieutenant governor's office. In Illinois, the governor reassigned the functions of the office by executive order when the incumbent resigned because of insufficient responsibilities, and in South Carolina, the legislature designated the office as a half-time position (1981). California rejected a constitutional amendment to remove the lieutenant governor as president of the senate (1982), while the Kansas Legislature passed legislation allowing the governor to appoint the lieutenant governor to head a state department if the qualifications for office are met (1982). He has been directed to organize, direct and chair the state tax review commission and to select the members of the commission who will serve at his pleasure.[7] The governor of North Dakota (1982) also assigned executive branch duties to his lieutenant governor even though the latter retains his legislative responsibilities. These assignments were termed "extensive" and several were full-time such as chairing several boards and commissions which the governor formerly headed.[8] The governor of Wisconsin appointed his lieutenant governor as the secretary of the department of development, and Ohio's governor named the lieutenant governor director of the department of natural resources (1983).

Team election of these two offices continues to grow slowly with Utah to be added to the list of 22 states which do so as of the 1984 elections. However, this trend seems to have abated since Utah is the only state to adopt the change in the 1980s, and Rhode Island voters (1982) rejected team election. And there were indications that while this is an administrative reform to be sought, it may have its political drawbacks as only four of the eight lieutenant governors seeking the governor's chair in 1982-83 were successful. The argument would be that these number two offices in the states lose their importance and visibility when linked so closely to the governor, yet may retain the negatives of the governor's record as they seek the office themselves. Further, in at least one state the joint selection and election of these two officials did not mean compatibility of views or on policy between them.[9]

So in summary, there are no obvious conclusions that can be drawn with just how effective team election of governors and lieutenant governors is as there are both pluses and minuses. It is clear that team election does shift the lieutenant governor's responsibilities toward the executive branch. Of the 22 states in which a team election occurs only nine lieutenant governors retain legislative responsibilities, while 19 of the 20 non-team elected governors have some to considerable legislative powers. But there is no indication that shifting the lieutenant governors' responsibilities into the executive branch is bringing about any permanent changes in the lieutenant governors' role. In fact there is still a sense of impermanence to such shifts that vary by gubernatorial administration.[10]

Notes

1. *Governors Bulletin*, December 2, 1983; June 24, 1983.
2. Richard Winter, "The New Hampshire Gubernatorial Election and Transition," in Thad L. Beyle, ed., *Gubernatorial Transitions: The 1982 Elections* (forthcoming).
3. For a discussion of the concept of penultimate office, see Larry Sabato, *Goodbye to Good-Time Charlie* (Washington, D.C.: Congressional Quarterly Press, 1983), 33-45.
4. See Thad L. Beyle and Robert Huefner, "Quips and Quotes from Old Governors to New," *Public Administration Review* 43 (May/June 1983): 268-70 for an indication of the types of advice given.
5. The Council of State Governments, *Gubernatorial Transition in the States* (1968 and 1974) and *New Governors: Questions They Should Ask Immediately*; National Governors' Association, *The Critical Hundred Days: A Handbook for New Governors* (1975), *The Governor's Office* (1976), *Governing the American States: A Handbook for New Governors* (1978), *Transition and the New Governor: A Critical Overview* (1982).
6. For more detail on these transitions, see Beyle, *Gubernatorial Transitions*.
7. Deborah A. Gona, *The Lieutenant Governor: The Office and Its Powers* (Lexington, Ky.: The Council of State Governments and the National Conference of Lieutenant Governors, 1983), p. 12.
8. Lloyd Omdahl, "North Dakota," *American Review of Public Administration* 16, 2-3 (1982): 241.
9. M. Margaret Conway, "Joint Election of the Governor and Lieutenant Governor in Maryland," *Comparative State Politics Newsletter* 4,6 (December 1983): 22.

10. Gona, *Lieutenant Governor*, 13, 15; "A Survey of Electoral Tickets for Governor and Lieutenant Governor," *Comparative State Politics Newsletter* 4, 3 (May 1983): 17-26.

GOVERNORS AND LEGISLATURES

By Thad L. Beyle

As state governments have increased the capacities of both their executive and legislative branches the potential for conflict has increased.

These conflicts tend to focus on several specifics. First is the area of vetoes. On the gubernatorial use of veto power, Oregon voters (1981) rejected a constitutional amendment to allow the governor more time, 30 rather than 20 days, to veto bills presented close to the session's end, while Montana voters (1982) ratified an amendment to allow a mail poll of legislators by the secretary of state to override a post-session veto. The New Jersey Supreme Court upheld the governor's pocket veto power in 1981, only to have the voters approve a constitutional amendment eliminating it in the November elections.

Conversely, the legislative veto over executive branch activities has had considerable action across the states. The Kentucky Legislature (1982) overrode a gubernatorial veto of legislation granting the legislature veto power over administrative regulations, as did the West Virginia (1982) Legislature which was replacing a law struck down by the courts, and the Alaska (1982) Legislature overrode the veto of a law granting legislative review of administrative regulations and state budgeting by agencies. However, the Kentucky Supreme Court in early 1984 struck down this and other recent legislative efforts to increase its oversight of the executive branch.[1]

Connecticut voters (1982) passed a constitutional amendment authorizing the legislative branch to delegate regulatory power to the executive branch, subject to the review of the legislative branch, and Iowa voters (1984) will be given the opportunity to vote on an amendment allowing the legislature to void a state agency rule.

Several other states enacted laws regarding review of administrative rulemaking procedures, devices which fall short of a veto but involve the legislature in the administrative responsibilities of the executive branch. By mid-1982, 41 states had some formal means of reviewing agency regulations, and 29 had the power to veto, suspend, disapprove or prevent the implementation of agency regulations.[2]

However, some legislatures did not gain this power. Missouri voters (1981) rejected an amendment to authorize the legislature to invalidate a state agency regulation, and the New Jersey state Supreme Court (1982) called the legislative oversight act an unconstitutional violation of the separation of powers concept, as had courts in Alaska, Connecticut, Montana, New Hampshire and West Virginia.[3]

These state court edicts presaged a monumental U.S. Supreme Court decision (1983) which struck down the increasing use of a congressional veto provision in federal legislation as a violation of the separation of powers doctrine in the U.S. Constitution.[4] It is too early to forecast the impact of this decision, since it affects the U.S. Congress only, but clearly the decision will be a landmark in the area of legislative vetoes and can be part of legal challenges in the states. Thus, it is possible that much of what has been established by the state legislatures regarding the use of a legislative veto as an oversight vehicle or "the-gun-behind-the-door" to keep agencies in line will have to be changed if not discarded if the *Chadha* decision is applied to the state governments.[5]

The second major area of conflict concerns appointments to various boards, commissions and heads of departments and agencies. The most notable was in Alaska where the governor needed to call a joint session of the legislature to confirm his major appointments. He had to use state troopers to bring in four representatives to make a quorum in order for the legislature to act.

But, the major problem in appointments is the separation of powers doctrine and whether legislators can serve on executive boards and commissions. A recent study indicates that only four states strictly ban legislators from serving on boards and commissions, while 11 others allow service only on advisory bodies. However, 20 states allow legislators to sit on boards and commissions that exercise management responsibilities.[6]

The North Carolina Supreme Court issued an advisory opinion against such a procedure in 1982 in the instance of one specific board, and the state attorney general ruled it applied to 36 other boards.[7] The attorney general of Mississippi (1982) announced that the practice violated the state's constitution. Kentucky's Supreme Court handed down a similar decision in early 1984.[8] Here again the fallout from the U.S. Supreme Court decision in the *Chadha* case (1983) on the validity of mixed legislative-executive boards as a violation of the separation of power doctrine is hard to predict, but the arguments and a landmark decision are there to follow should interested parties in the states seek to challenge such arrangements. If there are successful challenges to legislators serving on boards in the executive branches, the contours of state policy-making will change significantly in many of the 50 states.

The third area concerns the handling of federal block grant monies by the states. At one level, joint legislative-executive entities have been established to review, plan and coordinate these block grants. As noted previously, some of these entities have been challenged as a violation of the separation of powers doctrine, as in North Carolina. At another level has come a call for legislative review of federal block grants and their implementation, for example, in Maryland (1982) where the governor is to consult with the legislative policy committee on federal grants. West Virginia (1982) will henceforward appropriate federal grants; Florida now requires that any additional block grants for new programs must be included in the governor's budget and approved by the legislature; and Colorado (1982) appropriated the block grants despite no clear authority to do so.[9]

In Kentucky (1982) there was conflict as the legislature overrode a veto of a law authorizing the legislative research commission to rule on applications for federal block grants at the same time as the governor "publicly eschewed" his traditional involvement in the budget process in the legislative session. This, too, was overruled by the Kentucky Supreme Court in early 1984.[10] In a related fiscal action, the Maryland Legislature (1982) created a legislative affordability committee to report on state fiscal matters in each November.

Finally, Colorado (1982) voters adopted an amendment abolishing the "Governor's call" which allowed the governor to determine the agenda, other than fiscal issues, which the state legislature could consider in even-number years. This removed a point of contention between the two branches.[11]

Notes

1. Malcolm E. Jewell, "Court Curbs Legislative Oversight in Kentucky," *Comparative State Politics Newsletter* (February 1984): 13-14.

2. Rich Jones, "Legislative Review of Regulations: How Well Is It Working?" *State Legislatures* (September 1982) as reported in *State Policy Reports*, July 1, 1983, p. 20.

3. Alan Rosenthal, "Legislative Oversight and the Balance of Power in State Government," *State Government* 56, 3 (1983): 94.

4. *Immigration and Naturalization Service v. Jagdish Rai Chandha* (1983).

5. Stephen F. Johnson, "The Legislative Veto in the States," *State Government* 56, 3 (1983): 99-102.

6. "Legislators Serving on Boards and Commissions," *State Legislative Report* (Denver, Colo.: National Conference on State Legislatures, 1983).

7. *State ex. rel. Wallace v. Bone*, 304 N.C. 591, 286 S.E. 2nd 79 (1982).

8. Jewell, "Court Curbs Legislative Oversight in Kentucky."

9. Jerry Fensterman, Susan Szaniszlo and Carl Stenberg, "Coping With Cutbacks: States, Localities 'Make Do' in 1982," *Intergovernmental Perspective* 9, 1 (Winter 1983): 35.

10. Jewell, "Court Curbs Legislative Oversight in Kentucky."

11. Rodney Hero, "The Lamm Landslide in Colorado: Incumbent Popularity and a Divided Opposition," in Thad L. Beyle, ed., *Re-electing The Governor: 1982* (forthcoming, 1984).

THE EXECUTIVE BRANCH:
ELECTIVE OFFICIALS AND ORGANIZATION

By Thad L. Beyle

Elective Officials

As in the previous biennium, there were relatively few changes in the states' elective offices during 1982-83, and most efforts to seek change failed—all occurring in 1982. Voters rejected a constitutional amendment to increase the governor's term from two to four years with a limitation of two consecutive terms in New Hampshire, and for four-year terms for elected officials starting in 1984 in Rhode Island. In a more positive vein, Georgia voters rejected a constitutional amendment that would have prohibited governors from succeeding themselves. Succession in Georgia had been adopted in 1976. North Dakota voters rejected an amendment to move their gubernatorial and lieutenant gubernatorial elections from the presidential election years to the off-year elections beginning in 1990.

Michigan and Ohio voters rejected amendments that would have made their public utilities commissions elective rather than appointive. Finally, Wyoming voters agreed to allow their treasurer to succeed himself; South Carolina voters made the elective commissioner of agriculture a constitutional rather than statutory office; and Mississippi voted to make the superintendency of public institutions appointive rather than elective. In a unique approach the Colorado governor (1983) named the separately elected state treasurer as his chief of staff.[1]

Over the 10 years from 1974 through 1983, there were approximately 56 separate constitutional amendments or constitutional revisions concerning elected executive officials voted upon in the states. Thirty-five were ratified and 21 rejected. In the 1970s, 17 of 27 passed, a 63 percent win ratio, but in the 1980s only eight of 19 have passed, a 42 percent ratio. Most of the amendments focused on governors—their terms, succession, and team election with the lieutenant governor, or appointment power—or on lieutenant governors—their terms, succession, team election and whether they should have the power to be president of the senate.

From a 20-year perspective on the elective officials several trends are apparent in the data in Table A. The number of states having and electing a lieutenant governor has increased, which coincides with the rise in governor-lieutenant governor team elections: seven in 1965, 22 in 1984. Overall, in education 29 states, still a majority, elect their educational leaders, either a board or a superintendent, as opposed to 31 in 1965. Two of the three increases in elected boards of education were due to a switch from an elected superintendent to an elected board; and conversely two of the changes in the elected superintendents are due to a switch from an elected board. The trend seen in the reduction of the number of elected auditors "reflects a trend toward the federal model of having the post audit function handled by someone appointed by the legislature," who serves for a term of five, seven or more years.[2]

Over a broad time span, between 1955 and 1984, the number of state agencies directed by elected officials dropped from 385 to 329 (14.5 percent) and elected executive officials in the states decreased from 709 to 557 (21.4 percent).[3] While all these data indicate a trend to fewer offices being held by fewer elected executive officials, this is not a landslide and indicates just how strong the tie to representative democracy is in our states' executive branches.

State Government Organization

The interest in major reorganization remains low, with governors proposing changes here and there in their state governmental structures to answer particular problems, enhance a function or to ease their role as managers. There were few discernable patterns in the changes called for and adopted except that they tended to be in a few selected functional areas such as economic development and employment, the environment and corrections. Some of the changes were:

Corrections: Iowa (1983) created a separate Department of Corrections; Louisiana (1983) merged the Department of Public Safety and Department of Corrections to create a slot for a new department as only 20 are allowed by the state constitution; Mississippi (1981) "renewed" its Department of Corrections; and, Washington (1981) established a separate Department of Corrections.

Economic Development: South Dakota (1981)

eliminated the Department of Economic and Tourist Development and replaced it with a Bureau of Industrial and Agriculture Development which was moved into the Office of Executive Management,[4] and in 1982 created a Department of Tourism and Commerce; Minnesota (1983) created a Department of Energy and Economic Development and established a Department of Commerce; Montana (1983) created an Economic Development Board to implement a statewide economic development program as required by a 1983 voter initiative; and Oregon (1983) expanded the duties of the Economic Development Department, doubled its funding and created a tourism division within the department. In a slightly different vein Indiana (1982) created a Corporation for Science and Technology, and Minnesota created the Governor's Office of Science and Technology. North Carolina (1983) established a Technological Development Authority Board to assist existing and new small businesses.

Education: Iowa (1982) created a Higher Education Loan Authority to issue revenue bonds; and Mississippi (1982) established a Board of Vocational and Technical Education.

Employment and Labor: Indiana (1982) created an Employment and Development Commission with the power to issue bonds in order to lend money and possibly create jobs; Maryland (1983) created a cabinet-level Department of Employment and Training for various labor related issues; and Massachusetts (1982) created a cabinet-level office of Secretary of Labor.

Environment: Alabama (1982) consolidated seven of the state's environment functions into an umbrella Department of Environmental Management, which will allow for a one-stop permitting process; Idaho (1982) moved its Office of Energy into the Department of Water Resources;[5] Iowa (1982) created a new Department of Water, Air and Waste Management by a reorganization of various water responsibilities; Kentucky (1982) created a state board to pick a site for disposal of hazardous waste; and Louisiana (1983) created a cabinet-level Department of Quality. North Carolina (1983) established an Energy Development Authority to serve as the vehicle for cogeneration projects in which units of government—state and local—may require wastes to be burned with the heat generated used to warm public buildings.

Human Services: As of 1982, the states had four different configurations for their organization of human services programs—integrated central agency (four states), consolidated central

Table A

SEPARATELY ELECTED STATE OFFICIALS: 1965 and 1984

Office	1965	1984	Change 1965-1984
Lieutenant Governor	38	42	+4
Board of Education	9	12	+3
Attorney General	42	43	+1
Controller	9	10	+1
Governor	50	50	0
Agriculture	13	12	-1
Land Commissioner	7	5	-2
Treasurer	40	38	-2
Insurance	10	8	-2
Labor	6	4	-2
Secretary of State	39	36	-3
Mines	4	1	-3
Public Utilities Commission	14	11	-3
Auditor	29	25	-4
Superintendent of Education	22	17	-5

agency (22), confederated central agency (four), and no comprehensive central agency (21).[6] There was a minimum of change as Iowa (1983) renamed the Department of Social Services to the Department of Human Services, Montana (1983) created a Health Facility Authority which may issue project financing bonds or lend money for construction or renovation of health facilities; and South Carolina (1983) established a Health and Human Services Commission to coordinate various human services programs. The commission will be setting policy for spending Medicaid and social service block grant programs.

Finally, at the administrative level, the governor of Illinois (1982) created a Department of Central Management Services by consolidating the departments of Personnel and Administrative Services. The A-95 review process in Idaho (1982) was moved into the Division of Financial Management in the governor's office from the Department of Economics and Community Affairs; and in New Mexico (1983) the Department of Finance and Administration was divided into a General Services Department and a Department of Finance and Administration. North Carolina repealed its Administrative Procedures Act in 1983, effective as of July 1, 1985.

Notes

1. Rodney Hero, "The Lamm Landslide in Colorado: Incumbent Popularity and a Divided Opposition," in Thad L. Beyle, ed. *Re-electing The Governor: 1982* (forthcoming, 1984).

2. *State Policy Reports,* August 8,1983, p. 4.

3. Advisory Commission on Intergovernmental Relations, *State and Local Roles in the Federal System* (Washington, D.C.: 1982), p. 107; *The Book of the States, 1982-83* (Lexington, Ky.: The Council of State Governments, 1982), pp. 168-69.

4. Mitchell J. Beville Jr., "South Dakota," *American Review of Public Administration* 16, 2-3 (1982): 245-46.

5. Sydney Duncombe, "Idaho," *American Review of Public Administration* 16, 2-3 (1982): 232.

6. Thad L. Beyle and Patricia J. Dusenbury, "Health and Human Services Block Grants," *State Government* 55, 1 (1982): 7.

THE EXECUTIVE BRANCH: ISSUES

By Thad L. Beyle

Policy Management

Three of the newly elected governors took quick steps to enhance their policy management capabilities: Alaska (1983) created an Office of Management and Budget by combining the divisions of policy development and planning, budget and management, and internal audit; Minnesota (1983) restored planning as a separate agency; and New Mexico (1983) established an Office of Policy and Planning in the governor's office.

Some states changed the budgetary process, one of the keys in any policy management system. In a survey of the states on trends since 1970, 13 states have changed their budget cycle—eight moving from biennial to annual, two going the other direction to biennial, and two reverting to biennial after the annual budget experiment and one the opposite. Four other states reported they were considering a change, three to biennial and one to annual. Interestingly, respondents were equally divided on their preference for either cycle.

Governors continued to seek assistance in handling the changing picture of federal block grants under the Reagan administration. The governor of Illinois (1981) created two advisory groups to help implement federal block grants: one to work for local government grants and one for human service block grants. Kentucky's governor (1981) established an advisory committee to advise him on federal block grants for education. By the beginning of 1982, at least 21 states had formed interagency task forces or commissions to assist in the decision-making process related to these federal grants.[1]

Appointments

The governor's power to appoint remains an important tool in his or her managerial arsenal. For example, in a recent study of the 320 executive branch boards, commissions and councils in North Carolina, the governor was found to have 2,882 separate appointments. The other 130 appointments were dispersed across other officials of the state. While a majority of these units are advisory (190 or 59 percent) many do have policy-making powers.[2]

Another analysis suggests that the power to make extensive and even excessive appointments in the executive branch can be counter-productive for a governor.[3] However, this power across the states is a shared power with the legislature being part of the process in confirming or rejecting some of these gubernatorial appointments. In a 1981 study several patterns were delineated in this relationship. The most common pattern found in 29 states is for the state senate to confirm appointments to both policy and advisory positions. In nine others only policy positions are confirmed by the senate, and in two states policy appointments must be approved by the whole legislature. In only three states is there no legislative confirmation required.[4]

Some specific recent changes came in Massachusetts (1981), which called for placing students on the five boards of trustees that control the commonwealth's colleges and universities. Washington (1981) modified the provisions for confirmation of gubernatorial appointees. Arizona voters (1982) rejected a constitutional amendment to increase the number of members, whom the governor appoints, of the state board of education, and Minnesota (1983) called on the governor to appoint the commissioner of education who had previously been a board appointee.

Personnel

There were several actions in the area of personnel, especially in salary structures. The Kentucky Committee for Program Review and Investigation reported there was a "gender gap" among state employees as men were paid more on the average than women, but this was due to "occupational segregation" because women held mostly lower paying clerical jobs. Oregon (1983) passed a comparable worth law creating a commission to study the state's compensation and classification plan. Minnesota (1983) added a pay equity provision in an omnibus appropriations bill, which will start bringing the pay of female-dominated classes into line with male-dominated classes where pay inequity on comparable work exists. Washington (1983) also adopted a comparable worth law. A study of state administrators indicated slow progress in the states in the proportion of women and

47

minorities holding office.[5]

In a major decision a federal district court (1983) found a "gender gap" in Washington state pay scales to be "direct, overt and institutionalized" discrimination against its female employees under the Civil Rights Act. The concept of comparable worth was the key, as evidence showed that women were paid less than men in comparable jobs.[6] In a later decision the federal judge ordered the state to take immediate steps to raise the pay of 15,000 female state employees retroactive to September 1979. Similar cases are pending in Connecticut, Hawaii and Wisconsin.

Protection of state personnel was also at issue in several states as Maryland (1982) modified its merit system to further protect "whistle blowers" and provide layoff procedures. Arizona (1982) amended its open meeting law to give 24 hours notice of an executive session to an employee subject to possible dismissal and giving the employee the right to determine whether the discussion should be public. Oregon (1983) passed a "whistle blower" law prohibiting agencies from firing or disciplining an employee who exposes waste or abuse, but Iowa (1982) took a softer approach by setting up a state employee suggestion system.

Open Government

The trend in the states continues toward more open government. During this biennium, Georgia (1982) legislation made it a misdemeanor for officials to willfully obstruct release of public records or information and required 24-hour notice before any public hearing is to be held. Rhode Island (1982) closed loopholes in the state's open meeting law, and Arizona (1982) strengthened its law with the requirement there be the recording or taking of written minutes for executive sessions and notice of an agenda for executive sessions. The Illinois (1982) attorney general ruled that meetings of public bodies can be held by phone only if the press and public are given full access to the discussion in accordance with the Illinois Open Meetings Act and that a conference call involving a quorum of a public body to discuss public business is considered a public meeting. Further, the 1983 Illinois Legislature passed a freedom of information act covering state and local records becoming the 50th state to do so.[7] New York (1982) legislation permitted a court to award attorney's fees to a person who challenges an agency's denial of access to public records if the records sought are clearly of significant public interest and there is no reasonable legal basis for denial.[8] Indiana

(1983) passed an open records law specifying which state records and documents are open, closed or discretionary and placed the burden of proof on the state for refusing access to a public document. Florida's state Supreme Court (1982) removed an initiative from the general election ballot calling its wording ambiguous and misleading. The initiative would have gutted the state's landmark sunshine law.[9]

One approach to making state governments more open is to compile and publish some sort of state register so the public will be able to obtain notice of hearings proposed and adopted rules can be printed. Thirty-three states publish some sort of a register.[10]

Only Virginia (1982) weakened its Freedom of Information Act by allowing public bodies to close additional meetings or records to the public.

Notes

1. Florida Advisory Commission on Intergovernmental Relations, *The Federal Block Grants: A Guide for State and Local Officials* (Tallahassee, 1981).

2. North Carolina Center for Public Policy Research, "Boards, Commissions, and Councils in the Executive Branch of North Carolina State Government" (Raleigh, 1984).

3. Diane Kincaid Blair, "The Gubernatorial Appointment Power: Too Much of a Good Thing?" *State Government* 55, 3 (1982): 91.

4. Kansas Legislative Research Department, *Senate Confirmation Procedures for Gubernatorial Appointments* (Topeka, 1981) reported in *Comparative State Politics Newsletter* 3, 3 (June 1982): 9.

5. F. Ted Hebert and Deil S. Wright, "State Administrators: How Representative? How Professional?," *State Government* 55, 1 (1982): 27.

6. *American Federation of State, County and Municipal Employees et al v. State of Washington et al* (1983).

7. *Common Cause Magazine* 9, 4 (July/August 1983): 37.

8. Thomas W. Carroll, "Public Access Fares Well on New York State," *National Civic Review* 72, 3 (March 1983): 164.

9. *Common Cause Magazine* 9, 1 (January/February 1983): 38.

10. "State Regulatory Reform," *State Policy Reports*, July 1, 1983, 16.

Table 1
THE GOVERNORS
1984

State or other jurisdiction	Name and party	Length of regular term in years	Date of first service	Present term ends	Number of previous terms	Maximum consecutive terms allowed by constitution	Immediate past public position	Profession	Birthdate	State of birth
Alabama	George C. Wallace (D)	4	1/63	1/87	3(a)	2	G	Atty.	8/25/19	Ala.
Alaska	Bill Sheffield (D)	4	12/82	12/86		2		Bus.	6/26/28	Wash.
Arizona	Bruce Babbitt (D)	4	3/78	1/87	1(b)		AG	Atty.	6/27/38	Calif.
Arkansas	Bill Clinton (D)	2	1/79	1/85	1(c)		G	Atty.	8/19/46	Ark.
California	George Deukmejian (R)	4	1/83	1/87			AG	Atty.	6/6/28	N.Y.
Colorado	Richard D. Lamm (D)	4	1/75	1/87	2		SR	Atty.	8/3/35	Wis.
Connecticut	William A. O'Neill (D)	4	12/80	1/87	(d)		LG	Bus.	8/11/30	Conn.
Delaware	Pierre S. du Pont IV (R)	4	1/77	1/85	1	2(e)	C	Bus.	6/22/35	Del.
Florida	Bob Graham (D)	4	1/79	1/87	1	2	S	Atty.	11/9/36	Fla.
Georgia	Joe Frank Harris (D)	4	1/83	1/87			SR	Bus.	2/26/36	Ga.
Hawaii	George R. Ariyoshi (D)	4	10/73	12/86	2	2(f)	LG	Atty.	3/12/26	Hawaii
Idaho	John V. Evans (D)	4	1/77	1/87	1(g)		LG	Bus.	1/18/25	Idaho
Illinois	James R. Thompson (R)	4	1/77	1/87	2(h)		U	Atty.	5/8/36	Ill.
Indiana	Robert D. Orr (R)	4	1/81	1/85		2	LG	Bus.	11/17/17	Ind.
Iowa	Terry Branstad (R)	4	1/83	1/87			LG	Atty.	11/17/46	Iowa
Kansas	John Carlin (D)	4	1/79	1/87	1	2	SH	Farm.	8/3/40	Kan.
Kentucky	Martha Layne Collins (D)	4	12/83	12/87		(i)	LG	Ed.	12/7/36	Ky.
Louisiana	Edwin W. Edwards (D)	4	1/72	3/88	2(j)	2	G	Atty.	8/7/27	La.
Maine	Joseph E. Brennan (D)	4	1/79	1/87	1	2	AG	Atty.	11/2/34	Maine
Maryland	Harry R. Hughes (D)	4	1/79	1/87	1	2	J	Atty.	11/13/26	Md.
Massachusetts	Michael S. Dukakis (D)	4	1/75	1/87	1(k)		G	Atty.	11/3/33	Mass.
Michigan	James J. Blanchard (D)	4	1/83	1/87			C	Atty.	8/8/42	Mich.
Minnesota	Rudy Perpich (DFL)	4	1/76	1/87	(l)		G	Dent.	6/27/28	Minn.
Mississippi	William A. Allain (D)	4	1/84	1/88		(i)	AG	Atty.	2/14/28	Miss.
Missouri	Christopher S. Bond (R)	4	1/73	1/85	1(m)	2(e)	SA	Atty.	3/6/39	Mo.
Montana	Ted Schwinden (D)	4	1/81	1/85		2	LG	Farm.	8/31/25	Mont.
Nebraska	Robert Kerrey (D)	4	1/83	1/87		2		Bus.	8/27/43	Neb.
Nevada	Richard H. Bryan (D)	4	1/83	1/87			AG	Atty.	6/16/37	D.C.
New Hampshire	John H. Sununu (R)	2	1/83	1/85		2		Bus./Ed.	7/2/39	Cuba
New Jersey	Thomas H. Kean (R)	4	1/82	1/86				Bus.	4/21/35	N.Y.
New Mexico	Toney Anaya (D)	4	1/83	1/87		(i)	AG	Atty.	4/29/41	N.M.
New York	Mario M. Cuomo (D)	4	1/83	1/87			LG	Atty.	6/15/32	N.Y.
North Carolina	James B. Hunt Jr. (D)	4	1/77	1/85	1	2(e)	LG	Atty.	5/16/37	N.C.
North Dakota	Allen I. Olson (R)	4	1/81	1/85			AG	Atty.	11/5/38	N.D.
Ohio	Richard F. Celeste (D)	4	1/83	1/87		2	LG	Pub. Ser.	11/11/37	Ohio

THE GOVERNORS—Continued

State or other jurisdiction	Name and party	Length of regular term in years	Date of first service	Present term ends	Number of previous terms	Maximum consecutive terms allowed by constitution	Immediate past public position	Profession	Birthdate	State of birth
Oklahoma	George Nigh (D)	4	1/63	1/87	1(n)	2	LG	Bus.	6/9/27	Okla.
Oregon	Victor G. Atiyeh (R)	4	1/79	1/87	1	2	S	Bus.	2/20/23	Ore.
Pennsylvania	Richard L. Thornburgh (R)	4	1/79	1/87	1	2	I(o)	Atty.	7/16/32	Pa.
Rhode Island	J. Joseph Garrahy (D)	2	1/77	1/85	3		LG	...	11/26/30	R.I.
South Carolina	Richard W. Riley (D)	4	1/79	1/87	1	2	S	Atty.	1/2/33	S.C.
South Dakota	William J. Janklow (R)	4	1/79	1/87	1	2	AG	Atty.	9/13/39	Ill.
Tennessee	Lamar Alexander (R)	4	1/79	1/87	1	2	I(p)	Atty.	7/3/40	Tenn.
Texas	Mark White (D)	4	1/83	1/87			AG	Atty.	3/17/40	Texas
Utah	Scott M. Matheson (D)	4	1/77	1/85	1			Atty.	1/8/29	Ill.
Vermont	Richard A. Snelling (R)	2	1/77	1/85	3		SL	Bus.	2/18/27	Pa.
Virginia	Charles S. Robb (D)	4	1/82	1/86		(i)	LG	Atty.	6/26/39	Ariz.
Washington	John Spellman (R)	4	1/81	1/85			(q)	Atty.	12/29/26	Wash.
West Virginia	John D. Rockefeller IV (D)	4	1/77	1/85	1	2	SS	Pub. Ser.	6/18/37	N.Y.
Wisconsin	Anthony S. Earl (D)	4	1/83	1/87			J	Atty.	4/12/36	Mich.
Wyoming	Ed Herschler (D)	4	1/75	1/87	2		SR	Atty.	10/27/18	Wyo.
American Samoa	Peter T. Coleman (r)	4	1/56	1/85	1(s)	2(t)	G	Atty.	12/8/19	A.S.
Guam	Ricardo J. Bordallo (D)	4	1/75	1/87	1(u)	2	SR	Bus.	12/11/27	Guam
No. Mariana Is.	Pedro P. Tenorio (R)	4	1/82	1/86		3(v)	SL	...	4/18/34	Saipan
Puerto Rico	Carlos Romero-Barcelo (NP)	4	1/77	1/85	1		M	Atty.	9/4/32	P.R.
Virgin Islands	Juan F. Luis (I)	4	1/78	1/87	1(w)	2	LG	Bus.	7/10/40	P.R.

Sources: The Governors Center at Duke University and The Council of State Governments.

Key:
D—Democrat
DFL—Democrat-Farmer-Labor
I—Independent Citizens Movement
NP—New Progressive
R—Republican
G—Governor
LG—Lieutenant governor
AG—Attorney general
C—U.S. Congressman
S—State senator
U—U.S. Attorney
SH—State speaker of the house
J—State administrator
M—Mayor or local government leader
SL—State legislative leader
SS—Secretary of state
I—Federal official
N—None
SA—State auditor
(a) Served 1963-67, 1971-75, 1975-79.
(b) Succeeded to governor's office March 1978. Elected to first full term November 1978.

(c) Served 1979-81.
(d) Succeeded to governor's office December 1980. Elected to first full term November 1982.
(e) Absolute two-term limit, but not necessarily consecutive.
(f) Became acting governor when former governor became ill. Elected to full term November 1974 and may serve three consecutive terms.
(g) Succeeded to governor's office on former governor's resignation, January 1977. Elected to first full term November 1978.
(h) First term was for two years, four years thereafter.
(i) Successive terms forbidden.
(j) Served 1972-76, 1976-80.
(k) Served 1975-79.
(l) Succeeded to governor's office December 1976 on former governor's resignation.
(m) Served 1973-77.
(n) Filled two unexpired terms of former governors. Elected to first full term November 1978.
(o) Assistant U.S. Attorney General.
(p) White House Counsel.
(q) County executive.
(r) American Samoa has no political party system.
(s) Presidentially appointed governor 1956-61. Elected to full three-year term 1978 and to four-year term November 1980.
(t) Limit is statutory.
(u) Served 1975-79.
(v) Absolute three-term limitation, but not necessarily consecutive.
(w) Succeed to governor's office January 1978. Elected to first full term in November 1978.

Table 2
THE GOVERNORS: QUALIFICATIONS FOR OFFICE

State or other jurisdiction	Minimum age (years)	State citizen (years)	U.S. citizen (years)	State resident (years)	Qualified voter (years)
Alabama	30	7	10	7	...
Alaska	30	...	7	7	★
Arizona	25	5	10	...	...
Arkansas	30	...	★	7	★
California	18	...	5	5	★
Colorado	30	...	★	2	...
Connecticut	30	...	...	...	★
Delaware	30	...	12	6	...
Florida	30	...	...	7	★
Georgia	30	6	15	6	...
Hawaii	30	...	★	5	★
Idaho	30	...	★	2	...
Illinois	25	...	★	3	...
Indiana	30	...	5	5	...
Iowa	30	...	★	2	...
Kansas	...	...	...	...	...
Kentucky	30	6	★	6	...
Louisiana	25	5	5	...	★
Maine	30	...	15	5	...
Maryland	30	...	(a)	5	5
Massachusetts	...	...	...	7	...
Michigan(b)	30	...	...	...	4
Minnesota	25	...	★	1	...
Mississippi	30	...	20	5	...
Missouri	30	...	15	10	...
Montana(c)	25	★	★	2	...
Nebraska	30	5	5	5	...
Nevada	25	2	...	2	★
New Hampshire	30	...	...	7	...
New Jersey	30	...	20	7	...
New Mexico	30	...	★	5	★
New York	30	...	★	5	...
North Carolina	30	...	5	2	...
North Dakota	30	...	★	5	★
Ohio(d)	...	...	...	...	★
Oklahoma	31	...	★	...	10
Oregon	30	...	★	3	...
Pennsylvania	30	...	★	7	...
Rhode Island(e)	...	...	...	...	★
South Carolina	30	5	★	5	...
South Dakota	...	...	2	2	...
Tennessee	30	7	★	...	...
Texas	30	...	★	5	...
Utah	30	5	...	5	★
Vermont	...	...	...	4	...
Virginia	30	...	★	5	5
Washington	18	...	★	...	★
West Virginia	30	5	★	★	★
Wisconsin	...	...	★	...	★
Wyoming	30	...	★	5	★
American Samoa	35	...	★(f)	5	...
Guam	30	...	5	5	★
No. Marianas	30	...	...	7	...
Puerto Rico	35	5	5	5	...
Virgin Islands	30	...	5	5	★

Note: This table includes constitutional and statutory qualifications.
Key:
★—Formal provision; number of years not specified.
. . . .—No formal provision.
(a) *Crosse v. Board of Supervisors of Elections* 243 Md. 555, 221A.2d431 (1966)—opinion rendered indicated that U.S. citizenship was, by necessity, a requirement for office.
(b) A person convicted of felony or breach of public trust is not eligible to the office for a period of 20 years after conviction.
(c) A person convicted of a felony is not eligible to hold office until his final discharge from state supervision.
(d) A person convicted of embezzlement of public funds is not eligible to hold office.
(e) A person convicted of bribery is not eligible to hold office.
(f) U.S. citizen or U.S. national.

Table 3
THE GOVERNORS: COMPENSATION

State or other jurisdiction	Salary	Governor's office staff(a)	Access to state transportation			Travel allowance	Official residence
			Automobile	Airplane	Helicopter		
Alabama	$63,839	30	★	★	. . .	(b)	★
Alaska	81,648	79	★	. . .	. . .	(c)	★
Arizona	56,000	26	★	★	. . .	(c)	. . .
Arkansas	35,000	42	★	. . .	. . .	(d)	★
California	49,100	80(e)	★	. . .	. . .	(d)	. . .
Colorado	60,000	40	★	★	. . .	(b)	★
Connecticut	65,000	38	★	. . .	. . .	(b)	★
Delaware	35,000	22	★	. . .	★	$17,800(d)	★
Florida	69,550	304(f)	. . .	★	. . .	(c)	★
Georgia	71,314	40(g)	★	★	★	(b)	★
Hawaii	59,400	33	★	. . .	. . .	45,000 (d)	★
Idaho	50,000	15(h)	★	★	. . .	(b)	★
Illinois	58,000	125	★	★	★	162,300(d)	★
Indiana	66,000	32	★	. . .	★	0	★
Iowa	60,000	19	★	★	. . .	(b)	★
Kansas	47,925	28	★	★	★	(b)	★
Kentucky	60,000	42	★	★	★	(c)	★
Louisiana	73,400	40	★	★	★	48,372 (d)	★
Maine	35,000	11	★	★	. . .	(b)	★
Maryland	75,000	102	★	★	★	(b)	★
Massachusetts	75,000	100	★	. . .	★	(c)	. . .
Michigan	78,000	57	★	★	★	N.A.	★
Minnesota	75,000	26	★	★	★	(b)	★
Mississippi	63,000	24	★	★	★	21,926 (d)	★
Missouri	55,000	34	★	★	. . .	(d)	★
Montana	47,968	20.5	★	★	. . .	(c)	★
Nebraska	40,000	15	★	★	★	(c)	★
Nevada	65,000	16	★	. . .	. . .	(d)	★
New Hampshire	56,495	25	★	★	. . .	(d)	★ (i)
New Jersey	85,000	60	★	. . .	★	(j)	★ (i)
New Mexico	60,000	46	★	★	★	(d)	★
New York	100,000	216	★	★	★	(c)	★
North Carolina	60,768	41	★	★	★	(b)	★
North Dakota	60,862	15.25	★	★	. . .	(b)	★ (i)
Ohio	65,000	21	★	★	. . .	0	★
Oklahoma	70,000	39	★	★	. . .	(b)	★
Oregon	55,423	27	★	. . .	. . .	0	(k)
Pennsylvania	75,000	55	★	★	. . .	(c)	★
Rhode Island	42,500	47	★	★	★	8,500 (d)	★ (i)
South Carolina	60,000	25	★	★	. . .	17,000	★
South Dakota	50,981	N.A.	★	★	. . .	N.A.	★
Tennessee	68,220	35	★	★	★	140,000(d)	★
Texas	88,900	215	. . .	★	★	(c)	★
Utah	51,984	18	★	★	★	16,000	★
Vermont	50,000	9	★	. . .	. . .	(b)	. . .
Virginia	75,000	27	★	★	★	(c)	★
Washington	63,000	35	★	★	. . .	N.A.	★
West Virginia	72,000	39	★	★	★	(j)	★
Wisconsin	75,337	33.5	★	★	. . .	(l)	★
Wyoming	70,000	7	★	★	. . .	(d)	★
American Samoa	50,000	N.A.	★	. . .	. . .	N.A.	★
Guam	50,000	N.A.	★	. . .	. . .	N.A.	★
Puerto Rico	35,000	N.A.	★	. . .	★	N.A.	★
Virgin Islands	52,395	N.A.	★	. . .	. . .	N.A.	★

Key:
★ —Yes
. . .—No
N.A.—Not available
(a) Definitions of "governor's office staff" vary across the states—from general office support to staffing for various operations within the executive office.
(b) Travel allowance included in office budget.
(c) Reimbursed for travel expenses. Alaska—governor is reimbursed per diem. Arizona—reimbursed for actual expenses to a maximum of $40/d in state and $75/d out-of-state. Florida—reimbursed at same rate as other state officials: in state, choice between per diem or actual expenses; out-of-state, actual expenses. Kentucky—mileage at same rate as other state employees. Massachusetts—reimbursed at same rate as other state employees: $13.50/d for meals when overnight travel is involved, and actual and necessary living expenses. Montana—reimbursed for actual and necessary expenses in state up to $55/d, and actual lodging plus meal allowance up to $30/d out-of-state (no annual limit). Nebraska—reasonable and necessary expenses. New York—reimbursed for actual and necessary expenses. Pennsylvania—reimbursed for reasonable ex-

penses.
(d) Amount includes travel allowance for entire staff. Arkansas, Missouri—amount not available. California—$144,000 in state; $24,000 out-of-state. Nevada—$21,500 in state, $7,750 out-of-state. New Hampshire—$6,700 in state, $5,000 out-of-state. New Mexico—$10,000 in state, $22,000 out-of-state. Wyoming—$45,968 in state, $49,502 out-of-state (includes some other executive officials, along with representatives of governor).
(e) Statutorily authorized to have 87.6.
(f) Includes general office and mansion staff and staffing for the Governor's Council for the Prosecution of Organized Crime.
(g) The Office of Planning and Budget (staff of 70) is a statutory component of the governor's office, although it functions as a separate operation.
(h) Number on staff varies from 12 to 20 during the year.
(i) Governor does not occupy residence.
(j) Included in general expense account.
(k) A residence owned by the state is rented to the governor. Rent is deducted from governor's monthly housing allowance.
(l) Averages $32,000/y.

Table 4
THE GOVERNORS: POWERS

State or other jurisdiction	Joint election of governor & lieutenant governor	Official who succeeds governor	Budget making power	Veto power	Reorganization power through executive order	Other statewide elected officials (No. of agencies)(a)	
Alabama	No	LG	F	B	...	17	(8)
Alaska	Yes	LG	F	A	Cn	1	(0) (b)
Arizona	(c)	SS	F	A	...	8	(6)
Arkansas	No	LG	F	B	...	6	(6)
California	No	LG	F	A	St	10	(7)
Colorado	Yes	LG	F	A	...	18	(6)
Connecticut	Yes	LG	F	A	...	5	(5)
Delaware	No	LG	F	A	...	5	(5)
Florida	Yes	LG	F	A	...	7	(7)
Georgia	No	LG	F	A	...	12	(8)
Hawaii	Yes	LG	F	A	...	15	(2)
Idaho	No	LG	F	A	...	6	(6)
Illinois	Yes	LG	F	A	Cn	14	(6)
Indiana	Yes	LG	F	E	...	6	(6)
Iowa	No	LG	F	A	...	6	(6)
Kansas	Yes	LG	S	A	Cn	15	(6)
Kentucky	No	LG	F	B	St	10	(8)
Louisiana	No	LG	S	A	St	21	(10)
Maine	(c)	PS	F	D	...	0	(0)
Maryland	Yes	LG	F	A	Cn	3	(3)
Massachusetts	Yes	LG	F	C	...	13	(6)
Michigan	Yes	LG	F	A	Cn	35	(7)
Minnesota	Yes	LG	F	A	...	5	(5)
Mississippi	No	LG	W	A	St	11	(9)
Missouri	No	LG	F	A	Cn	5	(5)
Montana	Yes	LG	F	C	St	10	(6)
Nebraska	Yes	LG	F	A	...	26	(8)
Nevada	No	LG	F	D	...	23	(7)
New Hampshire	(c)	PS	F	D	...	5	(1)
New Jersey	(c)	PS	F	A	...	0	(0)
New Mexico	Yes	LG	F	C	...	19	(8)
New York	Yes	LG	F	A	...	3	(3)
North Carolina	No	LG	L	N	Cn	9	(9)
North Dakota	Yes	LG	F	A	...	13	(11)
Ohio	Yes	LG	F	A	...	28	(6)
Oklahoma	No	LG	F	A	St	9	(7)
Oregon	(c)	SS	F	C	...	5	(5)
Pennsylvania	Yes	LG	F	A	...	4	(4)
Rhode Island	No	LG	F	D	...	4	(4)
South Carolina	No	LG	W	C	...	8	(8)
South Dakota	Yes	LG	F	A	Cn	9	(7)
Tennessee	No	SpS(d)	F	B	...	3	(1)
Texas	No	LG	W	C	...	33	(8)
Utah	Yes(e)	LG	F	A	...	14	(4)
Vermont	No	LG	F	D	St	5	(5)
Virginia	No	LG	F	C	St	2	(2)
Washington	No	LG	F	C	...	8	(8)
West Virginia	(c)	PS	F	B	St	5	(5)
Wisconsin	Yes	LG	F	C	...	5	(5)
Wyoming	(c)	SS	F	A	...	4	(4)
American Samoa	Yes	LG			...	1	(1)
Guam	Yes	LG			...	36	(3)
No. Mariana Is.	Yes	LG			Cn		
Puerto Rico	(f)	SS			...	0	(0)
Virgin Islands	Yes	LG			...	1	(1)

Sources: The Governors Center at Duke University and The Council of State Governments.
Key:
LG—Lieutenant governor
SS—Secretary of state
PS—President of the senate
SpS—Speaker of the senate
F—Full responsibility
S—Shares responsibility with civil servant or a person appointed by someone else.
L—Shares responsibility with the legislature.
W—Shares responsibility with several others.
A—Item veto with at least two-thirds of legislature needed to override.
B—Item veto with at least two-thirds of legislature needed to override.
C—Item veto with a majority of legislators present needed to override.

D—No item veto but special majority of legislature required to override.
E—No item veto and simple majority of legislature needed to override.
N—No veto
Cn—Constitutional
St—Statutory
(a) Includes only officials who are popularly elected either on constitutional or statutory basis; number of agencies involving these officials in parenthesis.
(b) Lieutenant governor's office is part of governor's office.
(c) No lieutenant governor.
(d) This official bears the additional statutory title of lieutenant governor.
(e) Effective with the 1984 election.
(f) Resident commissioner runs jointly with the governor.

Table 5
THE GOVERNORS: PROVISIONS AND PROCEDURES FOR TRANSITION

State or other jurisdiction	Legislation pertaining to gubernatorial transition	Appropriations available to gov-elect	Gov-elect participation in state budget for coming fiscal year	Gov-elect hires staff to assist during transition	State personnel made available to assist gov-elect	Office space in buildings available to gov-elect	Provisions for acquainting gov-elect staff with office procedures and routine office functions	Provision for transfer of information (files, records etc.)
Alabama	...	...	•	•(a)	•	•	•	...
Alaska	...	...	...	...	•	•	...	•
Arizona	...	...	•	...	•	•	...	•
Arkansas	★	60,000	•	...	•	•	•	•
California	★	288,000(b)	★	★	★	★	...	...
Colorado	★	10,000(c)	★	★	★	★	★	★
Connecticut	★	25,000	•	★	•	★	...	★
Delaware	★	49,000(d)	...	•	•	★	•	•
Florida	•	75,000	...	•	•	★	•	•
Georgia	★	★	•	•	•	★	•	•
Hawaii	★	50,000	★	★	★	★	•	★
Idaho	★	15,000	★	★	•	★	...	•
Illinois	★	...	★	★(e)	★	★	★	★
Indiana	★	40,000	★	★	★	★	★	★
Iowa	★(f)	10,000	★	★	•(g)	•	•	★(h)
Kansas	★	100,000	★	★	★	★	★	★
Kentucky	★	Unspecified	★	★	★	★	★	★
Louisiana	★	10,000	★	★	...	★	•	★
Maine	★	5,000	★	★	★(i)	...	•	★
Maryland	★	50,000	★	★	★	★	★	★
Massachusetts	...	★	•	★	•	★	•	•
Michigan	★	1,000,000(b)	•	...	...	•	...	•
Minnesota	★	29,600	...	...	•	•	...	•
Mississippi	★	25,000	★	★	★	★	★	★
Missouri	★	100,000	★	•	•	★	...	...
Montana	★	30,000	★(j)	★	•	•	•	★
Nebraska	...	30,000(k)	•	•	•	•	•	★
Nevada	...	5,000(l)	★	...	•	•	•	•
New Hampshire	★	5,000	★	★	•	★	★	•
New Jersey	★	150,000	★	★	★	★	•	...
New Mexico	★	25,000	★	★	•	★	•	•
New York	...	...	...	•	•	•	...	•
North Carolina	★	51,000(d)	•(m)	★	★	★	•	•
North Dakota	...	★	...	•	•	•	...	★
Ohio	★	(n)	...	★	★	★	...	•
Oklahoma	★	10,000	•	★	•	★	•	•
Oregon	★	20,000	★	★	★	★	★	★
Pennsylvania	★	100,000	...	★	•	★	★	•
Rhode Island	...	...	★	•	•	•	...	...
South Carolina	★	50,000	★	★	...	★	...	★
South Dakota	★	10,000(j)	...	★	•	★	•	★
Tennessee	★	(o)	•	★	★	★	•	★
Texas	...	...	★	★	★	•	•	•
Utah	...	...	...	...	...	...	...	...
Vermont	...	18,000(p)	★	★	★	★	★	(q)
Virginia	...	52,000	...	★	★	★	★	★
Washington	★	80,000	•	•	•	•	•	...
West Virginia	...	...	...	...	...	•	•	...
Wisconsin	★	Unspecified	★	★	★	★	★	...
Wyoming	...	10,000(r)	★	★	★	•	★	★
American Samoa	...	Unspecified	★(s)	•	•	•	•	•
Guam	...	...	...	...	...	...	...	...
No. Mariana Is.	...	...	...	...	...	...	...	...
Puerto Rico	...	250,000(d)	...	...	...	•	...	...
Virgin Islands	...	...	...	...	...	...	...	...

Source: The Governors Center at Duke University.

Key:

. . .—No provisions or procedures
★—Formal provisions or procedures
•—No formal provisions, occurs informally

(a) Governor usually hires several of incoming key people during transition.
(b) Made available in 1982.
(c) Minimum.
(d) Inaugural expenses are paid from this amount.
(e) On a contractual basis.
(f) Pertains only to funds.
(g) Provided on irregular basis.
(h) Arrangement for transfer of criminal files.

(i) Budget personnel.
(j) Made available in 1978.
(k) Determined prior to each election by legislature.
(l) Is not adequate and is augmented by legislature.
(m) New governor can submit supplemental budget.
(n) Legislature required to make an appropriation, no dollar amount stated.
(o) Money made available from emergency and contingency funds.
(p) Responsible for the preparation of the budget; staff made available.
(q) Not transferred but use may be authorized.
(r) Made available in 1979.
(s) Can submit reprogramming or supplemental appropriation measure for current fiscal year.

Table 6
GUBERNATORIAL EXECUTIVE ORDERS: AUTHORIZATION, PROVISIONS, PROCEDURES

State or other jurisdiction	Authorization	Provisions — Civil defense disasters, public emergencies	Energy emergencies and conservation	Other emergencies	Executive branch reorganization plans and agency creation	Create advisory, coordinating, study or investigative committees/commissions	Respond to federal programs and requirements	State personnel administration	Other administration	Procedures — Filing and publication procedures	Subject to administrative procedure act	Subject to legislative review
Alabama	S,I(a)			★(b)	★					★(c,d)		
Alaska	C				★					★		★
Arizona	I				★							
Arkansas	I				★							
California	S	★		★(e)	★							
Colorado	S		★		★	★	★			★		
Connecticut	C	★★	★		★	★	★	★	★(f,g)	★	★	
Delaware	C,S	★★		★(h)	★	★	★	★	★(i)	★	★	
Florida	C,S	★★	★	★	★	★	★	★		★		
Georgia	S,I(i)				★							
Hawaii	I(a)								★(g,j)			
Idaho	S				★	★				★(c)		
Illinois	C				★	★				★(c)	★	
Indiana	I		★		★							
Iowa	S				★							
Kansas	S	★★	★	★(m)	★	★	★	★	★(k) (n,k,o,p)	★(c,l,d)		
Kentucky	S	★★	★		★	★				★(c)	★	★(r,s)
Louisiana	S(q)			★(t,u)	★	★	★	★	★(j,r,s)	★(l)	★	
Maine	S	★★	★		★					★(d)		
Maryland	C,S	★★	★		★	★	★	★	★(v)		★	★(w)
Massachusetts	C,I	★	★	★(e,t)	★	★	★	★		★(l)		★(x)
Michigan	C,S	★★★			★	★	★	★	★(p)	★(c)	★	★(w)
Minnesota	S	★★			★	★			★(y)	★(c,l)	★	★(w)
Mississippi	S	★★	★		★	★			★(aa,bb)	★(c)		
Missouri	S				★	★	★	★	★	★(w,cc)		★(w,cc)
Montana	S	★★			★				★(p)	★(dd,c)		
Nebraska	S	★			★							
Nevada	I											
New Hampshire	S		★		★				★(p)			
New Jersey	S			★(ee)					★(bb)			

Sources: Massachusetts, Legislative Research Council, "Report Relative to Gubernatorial Executive Orders," House Document No. 6557, April 3, 1981, pp. 89-94; E. Lee Burnick, Department of Political Science, University of North Carolina at Greensboro; The Governors Center at Duke University (Survey, March 1984).

Key:
C—Constitutional
S—Statutory
I—Implied power
★—Formal provision
—Formal provision
. . .—No formal provision

(a) Broad interpretation of gubernatorial authority.
(b) To activate or veto environmental improvement authorities.
(c) Must be filed with secretary of state or other designated officer.
(d) Governor required to keep record in office.
(e) To regulate distribution of necessities during shortages.
(f) To reassign state attorneys and public defenders.
(g) To suspend certain officials and/or other civil actions.
(h) To declare water, crop and refugee emergencies.
(i) Statutory for certain purposes, others implied from constitution.
(j) To designate game and wildlife areas or other public areas.

GUBERNATORIAL EXECUTIVE ORDERS—Continued

State or other jurisdiction	Authorization	Civil defense disasters, public emergencies	Energy emergencies and conservation	Other emergencies	Executive branch reorganization plans and agency creation	Create advisory, coordinating, study or investigative committees/commissions	Respond to federal programs and requirements	State personnel administration	Other administration	Filing and publication procedures	Subject to administrative procedure act	Subject to legislative review
New Mexico	S	★	★		★							
New York	I				★					★	★	★(w)
North Carolina	S,I				★		★		★(s,r)		★	★(w)
North Dakota	C								★(bb)			
Ohio	S				★		★			★(ff)	★	★
Oklahoma	S	★			★				★(gg)	★(c)		★(w)
Oregon	S	★		★(t)								
Pennsylvania		★	★(h,m,t,v)						★(hh)	★(c,l)		
Rhode Island	S(a)	★	★						★(k)	★(ii)		
South Carolina	I	★							★			
South Dakota	C	★			★							
Tennessee	S	★					★		★(r)	★(c)	★	★
Texas	S	★	★						★(r)			★
Utah	S		★									
Vermont	S	★	★		★					★		
Virginia	I	★	★	★(q)	★		★	★	★(kk,jj,g)	★(l)		★
Washington	S	★						★	★(ll)	★(l)		
West Virginia	S	★	★		★		★	★		★(c)	★	★
Wisconsin	I					★(i)		★	★(bb,jj,o)	★(c)		
Wyoming		★				★(i)						
American Samoa	C,S	★	★		★			★		★(mm)	★(mm)	★
No. Mariana Is.	C											

(k) To transfer allocated funds.
(l) Included in state register or code.
(m) To give immediate effect to state regulations in emergencies.
(n) To control administration of state contracts and procedures.
(o) To impound or freeze certain state matching funds.
(p) To reduce state expenditures in revenue shortfall.
(q) Broad grant of authority.
(r) Appointive powers.
(s) To suspend rules and regulations of the bureaucracy.
(t) For fire emergencies.
(u) For financial institution emergencies.
(v) To control procedures for dealing with public.
(w) Reorganization plans only.
(x) Legislative appropriations committees must approve orders issued to handle a revenue shortfall.

(y) To assign duties to lieutenant governor, issue writ of special election.
(aa) To control prison and pardon administration.
(bb) To administer and govern the armed forces of the state.
(cc) For meeting federal program requirements.
(dd) Filed with legislature.
(ee) To declare air pollution emergencies.
(ff) Included as appendix to sessions law volume.
(gg) Relating to local governments.
(hh) To transfer funds in an emergency.
(ii) Must be published in register if they have general applicability and legal effect.
(jj) To transfer functions between agencies.
(kk) To control state-owned motor vehicles.
(ll) To control state agencies.
(mm) If executive order fits definition of rule.

Table 7
LIEUTENANT GOVERNORS: QUALIFICATIONS AND TERMS
(In years)

State or other jurisdiction	Minimum age	State citizen	U.S. citizen	State resident	Qualified voter	Length of term	Maximum consecutive terms allowed
Alabama	30	7	10	7	...	4	2
Alaska	30	...	7	7	★	4	2
Arizona				(a)			
Arkansas	30	...	★	7	★	2	...
California	18	...	5	5	★	4	...
Colorado	30	...	★	2	...	4	...
Connecticut	30	...	...	...	★	4	...
Delaware	30	...	12	6	...	4	...
Florida	30	...	...	7	★	4	...
Georgia	30	6	15	6	...	4	...
Hawaii	30	...	★	5	★	4	2
Idaho	30	...	★	2	...	4	...
Illinois	25	...	★	3	...	4	...
Indiana	30	...	5	5	...	4	...
Iowa	30	...	★	2	...	4	...
Kansas	...	...	...	...	...	4	2
Kentucky	30	6	★	6	...	4	(b)
Louisiana	25	5	5	...	★	4	...
Maine				(a)			
Maryland	30	...	(c)	5	5	4	...
Massachusetts	...	...	...	7	...	4	...
Michigan(d)	30	...	...	...	4	4	...
Minnesota	25	...	★	1	5	4	...
Mississippi	30	...	20	5	...	4	...
Missouri	30	...	15	10	...	4	...
Montana	25	...	★	2	...	4	...
Nebraska	30	5	5	5	...	4	...
Nevada	25	2	...	2	★	4	...
New Hampshire				(a)			
New Jersey				(a)			
New Mexico	30	...	★	5	★	4	(b)
New York	30	...	★	5	...	4	2
North Carolina	30	...	5	2	...	4	...
North Dakota	30	...	★	5	★	4	...
Ohio	...	...	...	...	★	4	...
Oklahoma	31	...	★	...	10	4	...
Oregon				(a)			
Pennsylvania	30	...	★	7	...	4	2
Rhode Island	...	...	...	...	★	2	...
South Carolina	30	5	★	5	...	4	...
South Dakota	...	...	2	2	...	4	2
Tennessee				(a)			
Texas	30	...	★	5	...	4	...
Utah	30	5	...	5	★	4	...
Vermont	...	...	...	4	...	2	...
Virginia	30	...	★	5	5	4	...
Washington	...	...	★	...	★	4	...
West Virginia				(a)			
Wisconsin	...	...	★	...	★	4	...
Wyoming				(a)			
American Samoa	35	...	★	5	...	4	2
Guam	30	...	5	★	★	4	...
No. Marianas	30	...	...	7	★	4	...
Puerto Rico				(a)			
Virgin Islands	30	...	5	★	★	4	...

Note: This table includes constitutional and statutory qualifications.
Key:
★—Formal provision; number of years not specified.
. . .—No formal provision.
(a) No lieutenant governor. In Tennessee, the senate president, elected from senate membership, has statutory title of "Lieutenant Governor."
(b) Successive terms forbidden.
(c) *Crosse v. Board of Supervisors of Elections* 243 Md.555, 221 A.2d431 (1966)—opinion rendered indicated that U.S. citizenship was, by necessity, a requirement for office.
(d) A person who has been convicted of felony or breach of public trust is not eligible to the office for a period of 20 years after conviction.

Table 8

LIEUTENANT GOVERNORS: POWERS AND DUTIES

State or other jurisdiction	Presides over senate	Appoints committees	Breaks roll-call ties	Assigns bills	Authority for governor to assign duties	Member of governor's cabinet or advisory body	Serves when governor out of state
Alabama	★	★	★	★	...	...	★(a)
Alaska	...	...	...	...	★	★	★(b)
Arizona					(c)		
Arkansas	★	...	★	...	...	...	★
California	★	...	★	...	★	...	★
Colorado	...	...	...	...	★	★	★
Connecticut	★	...	★	★	★	★	★
Delaware	★	...	★	★	★	★	...
Florida	...	...	...	...	★	★	...
Georgia	★	★	...	★	★	...	...
Hawaii	...	...	...	...	★	★	★
Idaho	★	★(d)	...	★	★	...	★
Illinois	...	...	...	...	★	...	...
Indiana	★	...	★	...	★	★	...
Iowa	★	★	(e)	★	...	...	(f)
Kansas	...	...	...	...	★	(g)	(f)
Kentucky	★	(h)	★	(h)	★	★	★
Louisiana	...	...	...	...	★	...	★
Maine					(c)		
Maryland	...	...	...	...	★	★	★
Massachusetts	...	...	...	...	★	★	★
Michigan	★	...	★	...	★	★	★
Minnesota	...	...	...	...	★	...	...
Mississippi	★	★	★	★	...	...	★
Missouri	★	...	★	...	★	...	★
Montana	...	...	...	...	★	★	★(a)
Nebraska	★(i)	...	★(j)	...	★	...	★
Nevada	★	(k)	(l)	...	...	...	★
New Hampshire					(c)		
New Jersey					(c)		
New Mexico	★	(m)	★	...	★	★	★
New York	★	...	★	...	★	★	★
North Carolina	★	★	★	★	★	★	★
North Dakota	★	...	★	★	★	...	★
Ohio	...	...	...	...	(n)	★	(o)
Oklahoma	★	...	★	...	★	★	★
Oregon					(c)		
Pennsylvania	★	...	★(j)	★	★	★	...
Rhode Island	★	...	★	★	★	...	★
South Carolina	★	...	★	...	...	...	(f)
South Dakota	★	(p)	★	★	★	...	(q)
Tennessee					(c)		
Texas	★	★	★	★	...	...	★
Utah	...	...	...	...	★	...	...
Vermont	★	★	★	★	...	★	★
Virginia	★	...	★	...	★	★	...
Washington	★	(r)	★(j)	...	★	...	★
West Virginia					(c)		
Wisconsin	...	...	...	...	★	★	(s)
Wyoming					(c)		
American Samoa	...	...	...	...	★	...	★
Guam	...	...	...	...	...	★	★
No. Marianas	...	...	...	...	★	★	★
Puerto Rico					(c)		
Virgin Islands	...	...	...	...	★	★	★

Key:
★—Provision for responsibility.
...—No provision for responsibility.
(a) After 20 days absence. In Montana, after 45 days.
(b) Alaska constitution identifies two types of absence from state: (1) temporary absence during which the lieutenant serves as acting governor; and (2) continuous absence for a period of six months, after which the governor's office is declared vacant and lieutenant governor succeeds to the office.
(c) No lieutenant governor. In Tennessee, speaker of the senate bears the additional statutory title of "Lieutenant Governor."
(d) Select and special purpose committees in consultation with majority/minority leadership.
(e) Only on amendments.
(f) Only in emergency situations.
(g) Governor's cabinet is made up of heads of the state departments; since the state's statutes provide that the lieutenant governor may be assigned to serve as head of a department, the officeholder could become part of the official cabinet at some point during the tenure.

(h) As a member of senate committee responsible for activity.
(i) Unicameral legislative body.
(j) Except on final enactments.
(k) Temporary committees to carry out duties in formal legislative ceremonies.
(l) Constitution provides that lieutenant governor ". . . shall be President of the Senate, but shall only have a casting vote therein." However, interpretation of clause regarding casting vote is currently in dispute.
(m) Special committees only for joint sessions to inform the house and the governor.
(n) Presides over cabinet meetings in absence of governor.
(o) Only if governor asks the lieutenant to serve in that capacity, in the former's absence.
(p) Conference committees.
(q) Only in event of governor's continuous absence from state.
(r) In theory, lieutenant governor is responsible; in practice, appointments are made by majority caucus.
(s) Only in situations of an absence which prevents governor from discharging duties which need to be undertaken prior to his return.

Table 9
ATTORNEYS GENERAL AND SECRETARIES OF STATE: QUALIFICATIONS FOR OFFICE

State or other jurisdiction	Attorneys General						Secretaries of State			
	Minimum age	U.S. citizen (years)	State resident (years)	Qualified voter	Licensed attorney (years)	Membership in the state bar (years)	Minimum age	U.S. citizen (years)	State resident (years)	Qualified voter
Alabama	25	7	5	...	...	...	25	7	5	★
Alaska	...	★	...	...	...	...	(a)	(a)	(a)	(a)
Arizona	25	10	5	...	...	...	25	10	5	★
Arkansas	...	★	★	★	...	...	18	★	★	★
California	18	...	...	...	(b)	(b)	18	★	★	★
Colorado	25	★	2	...	★	...	25	★	★	...
Connecticut	18	★	★	★	10	10	18	★	★	★
Delaware	...	...	...	...	...	...	...	...	...	...
Florida	30	...	7	★	5	5	30	...	7	★
Georgia	25	10	4	...	7	7	25	10	4	...
Hawaii	...	★	1	...	...	...	(a)	(a)	(a)	(a)
Idaho	30	★	2	...	★	★	25	★	2	...
Illinois	25	★	3	...	...	...	25	★	3	...
Indiana	...	...	(c)	...	★	...	...	...	...	...
Iowa	...	...	...	...	...	...	...	...	★	...
Kansas	...	★	...	...	★	★	...	...	...	...
Kentucky	30	2	2(c)	...	8	2	30	2	2(c)	...
Louisiana	25	5	(c)	★	5	5	25	5	(c)	★
Maine	...	...	...	...	...	...	...	...	...	...
Maryland	...	★(d)	10(c)	★	10	10(e)	...	...	...	...
Massachusetts	...	...	5	...	...	★	...	...	5	...
Michigan(f)	...	...	...	★	...	...	...	...	...	★
Minnesota	21	...	30 days	★	...	...	21	★	★	★
Mississippi	26	...	5(c)	...	5	5	25	★	5(c)	★
Missouri	...	...	...	...	...	...	18	★	★	★
Montana(g)	25	★	2	...	5	★	25	★	2	...
Nebraska(h)	21(e)	...	(e)	...	(e)	...	18	★	...	...
Nevada	25	★	2(c)	★	...	...	25	★	2	★
New Hampshire	...	...	...	...	★	★	18	★	★	★
New Jersey	18(e)	...	★	...	★	★	...	...	...	...
New Mexico	30	★	5	...	★	★	30	★	★	★
New York	30	★	5	...	(e)	...	18	★	★	...
North Carolina	21	...	...	★	...	...	21	...	...	...
North Dakota	25	★	★	★	...	...	25	★	...	...
Ohio	18	★	★	★	...	...	18	★	★	★
Oklahoma	31	★	10	10	...	...	31	★	10	10
Oregon	...	...	...	★	...	...	18	★	...	★
Pennsylvania	30	★	7	...	★	★	...	...	...	...
Rhode Island	18	★	★	★	...	...	18	★	★	★
South Carolina	...	...	★	★	...	...	21	...	★	★
South Dakota	...	★	★	★	★	★	18	★	★	...
Tennessee	...	...	...	...	...	...	21	★	★	★
Texas	...	...	...	...	★	★	...	...	...	...
Utah	25	...	5(c)	★	★	★	(a)	(a)	(a)	(a)
Vermont	...	...	...	...	...	...	...	...	...	...
Virginia	30	★	(i)	...	...	(i)	...	...	...	...
Washington	...	★	30 days	★	★	★	18	★	30 days	★
West Virginia	25	★	(c)	★	...	...	18	★	★	★
Wisconsin	...	...	...	...	...	...	18	...	10 days	...
Wyoming	...	...	★	★	4	4	25	★	★	★
Northern Mariana Is.	...	...	...	...	5	...	(a)	(a)	(a)	(a)
Puerto Rico	21(e)	...	...	...	(e)	(e)	35	★	★	★
Virgin Islands	...	★	...	...	(j)	...	(a)	(a)	(a)	(a)

Note: This table contains constitutional and statutory provisions. "Qualified voter" provision may infer additional residency and citizenship requirements.

Key:
★—Formal provision; number of years not specified.
. . .—No formal provision.
(a) No secretary of state.
(b) No statute specifically requires this, but the State Bar act can be interpreted as making this a qualification.
(c) Additional state citizenship requirement. Kentucky, Nevada—two years. Louisiana, Mississippi, Utah, West Virginia—five years.
(d) *Crosse v. Board of Supervisors of Elections* 243 Md. 555, 221A.2d431 (1966)—opinion rendered indicated that U.S. citizenship was, by necessity, a requirement for office.
(e) Implied.
(f) A person convicted of a felony or breach of public trust is not eligible to the office for a period of 20 years after conviction.
(g) No person convicted of felony is eligible to hold public office until final discharge from state supervision.
(h) No person in default as collector and custodian of public money or property shall be eligible to public office; no person convicted of felony shall be eligible unless restored to civil rights.
(i) Must have qualifications of a judge of a court of records—state resident and a member of the state bar for five years.

Table 10
SECRETARIES OF STATE: ELECTION AND REGISTRATION DUTIES

State or other jurisdiction	Election									Registration			
	Chief election officer	Determines ballot eligibility of political parties	Receives initiative and/or referendum petition	Files certificate of nomination or election	Supplies election ballots or material to local officials	Files candidates' expense papers	Files other campaign reports	Conducts voter education programs	Prepares extradition papers or warrants of arrest	Registers corporations (a)	Processes and/or commissions notaries public	Registers securities	Registers trade names/marks
Alabama	★	★	★	★	★	★	★	★	★	★	★	★	★
Alaska(b)	★	...	★	★	...	...	...	...	(c)	...	★	...	★
Arizona	★	★	★	★	★	★	★	★	(c)	...	★	...	★
Arkansas	★	★	★	★	★	★	★	★	(c)	★	★	...	★
California	★	★	★	★	★	★	★	★	(c)	★	★	...	★
Colorado	★	★	★	★	★	★	★	★	...	...	★	★	★
Connecticut	★	★	...	★	★	★	★	★	★	★	★	★	★
Delaware	...	...	...	★	...	★	★	...	...	★	★	★	★
Florida	★	★	★	★	★	★	★	★	...	...	★	★	★
Georgia	★	★	★	★	★	★	★	★	...	★	★	★	★
Hawaii(b)	★	★	...	★	★	★	★	★	...	...	...	★	★
Idaho	★	★	★	★	★	★	★	★	...	★	★	★	★
Illinois	...	...	★	★	...	...	...	...	★	★	★	★	★
Indiana	...	★	...	★	★	...	★	...	★	★	★	★	★
Iowa	★	★	...	★	★	...	...	...	...	★	★	★	★
Kansas	★	★	...	★	★	★	★	...	★	★	★	...	★
Kentucky	★	...	★	★	★	★	...	★	★	★	★	...	★
Louisiana	★	★	★	★	★	...	★	★	★	★	★	...	★
Maine	★	★	★	★	★	...	★	★	...	★	★	...	★
Maryland	...	...	★	...	...	...	...	...	★	★(d)	★	...	★
Massachusetts	★	★	★	★	★	...	...	★	...	★	★	★	★
Michigan	★	★	★	★	★	★	★	★	★	...	★	...	★
Minnesota	★	★	...	★	★	...	★	★	...	★	★	...	★
Mississippi	(e)	★	★	★	★	★	★	...	...	★	★	★	★
Missouri	★	★	★	★	★	★	★	★	★	★	★	★	★
Montana	★	★	★	★	★	...	...	★	★	★	★	...	★
Nebraska	★	★	★	★	★	...	...	★	(c)	★	★	★	★
Nevada	★	★	★	★	★	★	★	★	...	★	★	★	★
New Hampshire	★	★	★	★	★	★	...	★	★	★	★	...	★
New Jersey	★	★	...	★	★	★	★	★	(c)	★	★	...	★
New Mexico	★	★	★	★	★	★	★	★	(c)	...	★	...	★
New York	...	...	...	...	★	...	...	...	...	★	★	...	★
North Carolina	...	...	...	...	★	...	...	...	...	★	★	★	★
North Dakota	★	★	★	★	★	★	★	★	...	★	★	...	★
Ohio	★	★	★	★	★	★	★	★	(c)	★	...	★	★
Oklahoma	...	...	★	...	...	★	...	★	...	★	...	★	★
Oregon	★	★	★	★	★	★	★	★	★	...	★	...	...
Pennsylvania	★	★	...	★	★	★	...	★	★	★	★	★	★
Rhode Island	★	★	★	★	★	...	...	★	...	★	★	...	★
South Carolina	...	...	...	...	...	...	...	...	...	★	★	★	★
South Dakota	★	★	★	★	★	★	★	★	★	★	★	...	★
Tennessee	(f)	...	...	★	★	★	★	★	...	★	★	★	★
Texas	★	★	...	★	★	★	★	★	...	★	★	★	★
Utah(b)	★	★	★	★	...	★	★	★	★	★	★	...	★
Vermont	★	★	...	★	★	★	★	★	...	★	...	...	★
Virginia	...	...	(g)	...	...	...	...	...	...	★	...	★	★
Washington	★	...	★	★	★	★	★	★	★	...	★	...	...
West Virginia	★	★	★	★	★	★	★	★	★	★	★	...	★
Wisconsin	...	...	...	...	...	...	...	...	(c)	★	★	...	★
Wyoming	★	★	★	(h)	★	★	★	★	(c)	★	★	★	★
Puerto Rico	...	...	...	...	...	...	...	...	...	★	...	...	★

Key:
★—Responsible for activity.
...—Not responsible for activity.
(a) Unless otherwise indicated, office registers domestic, foreign and non-profit corporations.
(b) No secretary of state. Duties indicated are performed by lieutenant governor.
(c) Attests to governor's signature on extradition papers or warrants of arrest. In Arizona and Nebraska, signs and places state seal on document; New Jersey, commissions prepared by governor's counsel's office, but signed by secretary; Ohio, certifies papers; Wisconsin, retains copies after affixing seal.
(d) Non-profit only.
(e) State Election Commission composed of governor, secretary of state and attorney general.
(f) Secretary appoints state coordinator of elections.
(g) Certificates of election for U.S. House and Senate; writs of election for special state legislative races.
(h) Files applications for nomination and issues certificates of nomination; governor issues certificates of election.

Table 11
SECRETARIES OF STATE: CUSTODIAL, PUBLICATION AND LEGISLATIVE DUTIES

State or other jurisdiction	Custodial				Publication				Legislative				
	Archives state records and documents	Files state agency rules and regulations	Administers uniform commercial code provisions	Files other corporate documents	State manual or directory	Session laws	State constitution	Statutes	Administrative rules and regulations	Opens legislative sessions(a)	Enrolls and engrosses bills	Retains copies of acts	Registers lobbyists
Alabama	...	...	★	★	...	★	★	★	...	...	★	★	...
Alaska(b)	...	★	...	...	...	...	★	...	★	★	...	★	★
Arizona	...	★	★	★	★	...	★	★	★	...	...	★	★
Arkansas	...	★	★	...	★	★	★	...	★	...	...	★	...
California	★	★	★	★	★	...	...	...	...	...	...	★	★
Colorado	...	★	★	★	...	★	...	...	★	...	...	★	★
Connecticut	★	★	★	★	★	...	★	...	...	(c)	...	★	...
Delaware	★	★	★	★	...	★	...	...	...	...	...	...	...
Florida	★	★	★	★	★	★	★	★	★	...	...	★	...
Georgia	★	★	...	...	★	★	★	★	★	...	...	★	★
Hawaii(b)	(d)	★	...	...	★	(e)	...	(e)	(e)	...	...	...	...
Idaho	...	...	★	★	★	★	★	...	...	...	...	★	★
Illinois	★	...	★	★	★	★	★	...	...	★	H	★	★
Indiana	★	★	★	...	★	...	...	...	...	★	...	★	★
Iowa	(f)	...	★	★	★	...	...	...	...	...	★	...	...
Kansas	★	...	★	★	★	★	★	...	★	★	...	★	★
Kentucky	★	★	★	★	...	★	...	...	...	...	...	★	...
Louisiana	★	...	...	...	★	★	★	...	...	...	...	...	...
Maine	★	★	★	★	...	...	★	...	...	...	★	★	...
Maryland	★(g)	★	...	...	...	...	...	...	★	...	...	★	...
Massachusetts	★	★	★	★	★	★	★	★	★	...	...	...	★
Michigan	★	★	★	...	★	...	...	...	...	...	★	...	★
Minnesota	★	★	★	...	★	...	...	...	...	H	...	★	★
Mississippi	...	★	★	★	...	★	...	...	...	H	★	...	★
Missouri	★	...	★	...	...	...	...	...	★	H	...	...	...
Montana	★(g)	★	★	★	★	...	★	...	★	H	...	★	...
Nebraska	★	★	★	★	★	★	★	...	...	(h)	...	★	...
Nevada	...	★	★	★	★	...	★	...	...	H	★	★	...
New Hampshire	★	★	★	★	★	...	★	...	...	(i)	★	...	★
New Jersey	★	...	★	★	...	★	...	...	...	...	...	★	...
New Mexico	★	★	★	...	★	★	★	★	★	H	...	★	★
New York	★	★	★	★	...	★	...	...	...	...	...	★	★
North Carolina	★	...	★	★	...	...	★	...	...	H(j)	...	★	★
North Dakota	...	...	★	★	★	★	...	...	...	...	...	★	★
Ohio	★	★	★	★	★	★	★	★	★	...	...	...	★
Oklahoma	...	★	...	...	...	...	...	...	...	...	...	★	...
Oregon	★	★	★	★	...	...	...	...	★	...	...	★	...
Pennsylvania	...	...	★	★	...	...	...	...	...	...	...	★	(k)
Rhode Island	★	★	★	★	★	★	★	★	★	...	★	★	★
South Carolina	★	...	★	★	...	...	...	...	...	...	...	...	★
South Dakota	★	★	★	...	★	...	★	...	(l)	H	...	★	★
Tennessee	★	★	★	★	★	★	★	★	★	...	...	★	★
Texas	★	★	★	★	★	★	...	★	★	H	...	★	★
Utah(b)	(d)	...	★	★	...	...	...	...	★	S	★	★	★
Vermont	★	★	★	★	★	★	★	...	★	H(j)	★	★	★
Virginia	...	...	...	...	★	...	...	...	...	...	...	...	★
Washington	★	...	...	★	...	...	...	...	...	...	...	(m)	...
West Virginia	★	★	...	...	...	...	...	...	...	...	...	★	...
Wisconsin	★	★	★	...	★	★	...	...	...	...	...	★	★
Wyoming	...	★	★	...	★	...	...	★	...	H	...	★	...
Puerto Rico	★	★	...	★	...	★	★	★	...	...	...	...	...

Key:
★—Responsible for activity.
. . .—Not responsible for activity.
(a) In this column only: ★—Both houses; H—House; S—Senate.
(b) No secretary of state. Duties indicated are performed by lieutenant governor.
(c) Both houses during trailer sessions (to act on vetoed bills only).
(d) Limited responsibility.
(e) Distributes and sells session laws, statutes and administrative rules and regulations.

(f) Serves as chair of State Records Commission.
(g) As specified by law. In Maryland, Hall of Records is the archivist.
(h) Certifies and seats members of unicameral legislature.
(i) Convenes both houses during special sessions of the legislature.
(j) Until speaker is elected.
(k) Only those making political contributions to candidates or their committees.
(l) Board of Elections and Finance only.
(m) Files session laws.

Table 12
ATTORNEYS GENERAL: PROSECUTORIAL AND ADVISORY DUTIES

State or other jurisdiction	Authority in local prosecutions:				Issues advisory opinions					Reviews legislation	
	Authority to initiate local prosecutions	May intervene in local prosecutions	May assist local prosecutor	May supersede local prosecutor	To state executive officials	To legislators	To local prosecutors	On the interpretation of statutes	On the constitutionality of bills or ordinances	Prior to passage	Before signing
Alabama	A	A,D	A,D	A	★	★	★	★	★	★	...
Alaska	(a)	(a)	(a)	(a)	★	★	...	★	★	★	...
Arizona	A,B,C,D,F	B,D	B,D	B	★	★	★	★	★	★	...
Arkansas	...	D	D	...	★	★	★	★	★	★	★
California	A, E	A,D,E	A,B,D	A	★	★	★	★	★	★	★
Colorado	B,F	B	D,F(b)	B	★	★	★	★	★	★	★
Connecticut	...	...	...	...	★	...	★	★	★	★	★
Delaware					★	★	★	★	★	★	★
Florida	F	D	D	...	★	★	★	★	★	★	★
Georgia	A,B,F	A,B,D,G	A,B,D,F	B	★	★	★	★	★	...	★
Hawaii	E	A,D,G	A,D	A,G	★	★	★	★	★	★	★
Idaho	A,D,F	A	A,D	A	★	★	★	★	...	★	★
Illinois	A,D,E,F,G	A,D,E	A,D,E,F	F	★	★	★	★	★	(c)	(c)
Indiana	F(b)	...	A,D,E,F	G	★	★	★	...	★	★	★
Iowa	D,F	D	D	...	★	★	★	★	★	★	★
Kansas	B,C,D,F	D	D	A,F	★	★	★	★	★	★	★
Kentucky	A,B	B,D	B,D,F	G	★	★	★	★	★	★	★
Louisiana	G	G	D	G	★	★	★	★	★	★	...
Maine	A	A	A	A	★	★	...	★	★	★	★
Maryland	B,C,F	B,C,D	B,C,D	B,C	★	★	★	★	★	★	★
Massachusetts	A,B,C,D,E,F,G	A,B,C,D,E,G	A,B,C,D,E	A,B,C,E	★	★	...	★	★	★	★
Michigan	A	A	A	A	★	★	★	★	★	★	★
Minnesota	B	B,D,G	A,B,D	B	★	★	★	★	★	...	(c)
Mississippi	B,E,F	...	B,F	...	★	★	★	★	★	(c)	(c)
Missouri	F	...	B	...	★	★	★	★	★	★	★
Montana	C,F	A,B,C,D	A,B,C,D,F	A,C	★	★(d)	★	★	★	...	...
Nebraska	A	A	A,D	A	★	★	★	★	★	...	...
Nevada	D,F,G(e)	D(e)	(e,f)	G,F	★	...	★	★	★	...	...
New Hampshire	A	A	A	A	★	★	...	★	★	★	★
New Jersey	A	A,B,D,G	A,D	A,B,D,G	★	★	★	★	★	★	★
New Mexico	A,B,E,F,G	B,D,G	D	B	★	★	★	★	★	★	★
New York	B,F	B	D	B	★	★	★	★	★	★	★
North Carolina	...	D	D	...	★	★	★	★	★	★	...
North Dakota	A,G	A,D	A,D	A	★	★	★	...	★	...	(c)
Ohio	B,C,F	B,F	F	B,C	★	★(g)	★	★	★	...	...
Oklahoma	B,C	B,C	B,C	B,C	★	★	★	★	★	★	★
Oregon	B,F	B,D	B,D	B	★	★	★	★	★	(c)	(c)
Pennsylvania	A,D,G	D,G	D	G	★	★	...	★	...	★	★
Rhode Island	A	D	D	...	★	★	...	★	...	★	★
South Carolina	A	A,D	A,D	A	★	★	★	★	★	★	★
South Dakota	A(h)	A	A	A	★	★	★	★	...	...	★
Tennessee	D,F,G(b)	D,G(b)	D	F	★	★	★	★	★	(c)	(c)
Texas	F	...	D	...	★	★	★	★	★	★	★
Utah	A,B,D,E,F,G	E,G	D,E	E	★	...	★	★	★	(c)	(c)
Vermont	A	A	A	A	★	★	★	★	★	★	★
Virginia	B,F	A,B,D,F	B,D,F	B	★	★	★	★	★	★	★
Washington	B,D,G	B,D,G	D	B	★	★	★	★	★	★	★
West Virginia	...	...	D	...	★	★	★	★	★	(i)	(i)
Wisconsin	B,C,F	B,C,D	D	B,C(j)	★	★	★	★	★	(i)	(i)
Wyoming	B,D(e)	B,D	B,D	...	★	★	★	★	...	★	★
American Samoa	A,E	A,E	A,E	A,E	★	★	...	★	★	★	★
No. Mariana Is.	A	...	...	...	★	★	...	★	★	★	★
Puerto Rico	A,B,E	A,B,E	A,E	A,B,E	★	★	...	★	★	★	★
Virgin Islands	A	...	...	...	★	★	...	★	★	★	★

Key:
A—On own initiative.
B—On request of governor.
C—On request of legislature.
D—On request of local prosecutor.
E—When in state's interest.
F—Under certain statutes for specific crimes.
G—On authorization of court or other body.
★—Has authority in area.
. . .—Does not have authority in area.
(a) Local prosecutors serve at pleasure of attorney general.
(b) Certain statutes provide for concurrent jurisdiction with local prosecutors.

(c) Only when requested by governor or legislature.
(d) To legislative leadership.
(e) In connection with grand jury cases.
(f) Will prosecute as a matter of practice when requested.
(g) To legislature as a whole not individual legislators.
(h) Has concurrent jurisdiction with states' attorneys.
(i) No legal authority, but sometimes informally reviews laws at request of legislature.
(j) If the governor removes the district attorney for cause.

Table 13
ATTORNEYS GENERAL: CONSUMER PROTECTION ACTIVITIES AND SUBPOENA AND ANTITRUST POWERS

State or other jurisdiction	May commence civil proceedings	May commence criminal proceedings	Represents the state before regulatory agencies	Administers consumer protection programs	Handles consumer complaints	Subpoena powers (a)	Antitrust duties
Alabama	★	★	. . .	★	★	•	A, B
Alaska	★	★	★	★	★	★	B, C
Arizona	★	. . .	. . .	★	★	★	A, B, D
Arkansas	★	. . .	★	★	★	★	B, C, D
California	★	. . .	. . .	. . .	★	★	B, C, D
Colorado	★	★	★	★	. . .	•	B, C, D(b)
Connecticut	★	. . .	★	★	. . .	•	A, B, D
Delaware	★	★	★	★	. . .	★	A, B, C
Florida	★	★	. . .	★	★	★	A, B, C, D
Georgia	★	★	★	. . .	. . .	★	B, C, D
Hawaii	★	★	★	. . .	. . .	★	A, B, C, D
Idaho	★	. . .	★	★	★	•	D
Illinois	★	★	★	★	★	•	A, B, D
Indiana	★	. . .	. . .	★	★	. . .	B, C, D
Iowa	★	★	★	★	★	•	A, B, C, D
Kansas	★	★	★	★	★	★	B, C, D
Kentucky	★	★	★	★	★	(c)	A, B, D
Louisiana	★	. . .	★	. . .	★	★	B, C
Maine	★	★	★	★	★	•	B, C
Maryland	★	★	★	★	★	★	B, C, D
Massachusetts	★	★	★	★	★	•	A, B, C, D
Michigan	★	★	★	★	★	•	A, B, C, D
Minnesota	★	. . .	★	★	★	•	B, D
Mississippi	★	. . .	★	★	★	•	B, C
Missouri	★	. . .	. . .	. . .	★	•	A, B, C, D
Montana	★	★	★	. . .	. . .	★	B, C, D
Nebraska	★	. . .	★	★	★	•	A, B, C(d), D
Nevada	★	★	. . .	★	★	★	A, B, D
New Hampshire	★	★	★	. . .	★	•	B, C, D
New Jersey	★	★	★	★	★	•	A, B, C, D
New Mexico	★	★	★	★	★	•	A, C
New York	★	. . .	. . .	. . .	★	★	A, B, C, D
North Carolina	★	. . .	★	★	★	•	A, B, C, D
North Dakota	★	★	. . .	★	★	★	C, D
Ohio	★	★	★	★	★	•	B, C, D
Oklahoma	★	. . .	(e)	★	★	•	B, D
Oregon	★	★	(c)	★	★	•	A, B, C, D
Pennsylvania	★	. . .	★	★	★	•	D
Rhode Island	★	★	★	★	★	•	A, B, C, D
South Carolina	★	★	★	. . .	. . .	•	A, B, C, D
South Dakota	★	★	. . .	★	★	•	A, B, C, D
Tennessee	★	★	★(c)	★	★	•	A, B, C, D
Texas	★	. . .	. . .	★	★	•	B, D
Utah	★(d)	. . .	★(d,f)	. . .	★(f)	★	A(g), B, C, D(g)
Vermont	★	★	. . .	★	★	•	A, B, C, D
Virginia	★	(e)	★	★(f)	★(f)	•	A, B, C, D
Washington	★	. . .	★	★	★	•	A, B, D
West Virginia	★	. . .	★	★	★	★	A, B, D
Wisconsin	★	. . .	★	★	★	•	A, B, C, D
Wyoming	★	. . .	. . .	★	★	. . .	. . .
American Samoa	★	★	★	. . .	. . .	★	. . .
Northern Mariana Is.	★	★	★	★	★	★	B, C, D
Puerto Rico	★	★	★	★(e)	★(e)	★	A, B, C
Virgin Islands	★	★(h)	★	. . .	. . .	★	A, B(i), C, D

Key:
A—Has *parens patriae* authority to commence suits on behalf of consumers in state antitrust damage actions in state courts.
B—May initiate damage actions on behalf of state in state courts.
C—May commence criminal proceedings.
D—May represent cities, counties and other governmental entities in recovering civil damages under federal or state law.
★—Has authority in area.
. . .—Does not have authority in area.
(a) In this column only: ★ broad powers and • limited powers.
(b) Only under Rule 23 of the Rules of Civil Procedure.

(c) When permitted to intervene.
(d) Attorney general has exclusive authority.
(e) To a limited extent.
(f) Attorney general handles legal matters only with no administrative handling of complaints.
(g) Opinion only, since there are no controlling precedents.
(h) May prosecute in inferior courts. May prosecute in district court only by request or consent of U.S. Attorney General.
(i) May initiate damage actions on behalf of jurisdiction in district court.

Table 14
ATTORNEYS GENERAL: DUTIES TO ADMINISTRATIVE AGENCIES AND MISCELLANEOUS DUTIES

State or other jurisdiction	Serves as counsel for state	Appears for state in criminal appeals	Duties to administrative agencies							
					Conducts litigation					
			Issues official advice	Interprets statutes or regulations	In behalf of agency	Against agency	Prepares or reviews legal documents	Represents the public before the agency	Involved in rule-making	Reviews rules for legality
Alabama	A, B, C	★(a)	★	★	★	★	★	(b)	...	★
Alaska	A, B, C	★	★	★	★	★	★	...	★	★
Arizona	A, B, C	(c,d)	★	★	★	★	★	...	★	★
Arkansas	A, B, C	★(a)	★	★	★	...	★	★	★	★
California	A, B, C	★(a)	★	★	★	★	★	...	...	...
Colorado	A, B, C	★(a)	★	★	★	★	★	...	★	★
Connecticut	A, B, C	...	★	★	★	...	★	...	★	★
Delaware	A, B, C	★(a)	★	★	★	★	★	★	★	★
Florida	A, B, C	★(a)	★	★	★	...	★	★	★	★
Georgia	A, B, C	(b,c)	★	★	★	★	★	...	★	★
Hawaii	A, B	(b,c)	★	★	★	★	★	★	★	★
Idaho	A, B, C	★(a)	★	★	★	★	★	...	★	★
Illinois	A, B,* C	(b,c,e)	★	★	★	★	★	★	...	...
Indiana	A, B, C	★(a)	★	★	★	...	★	...	★	★
Iowa	A, B, C	★(a)	★	★	★	★	★	...	...	★
Kansas	A, B, C	★(a)	★	★	★	★	★	...	...	★
Kentucky	A, B*, C	★	★	★	★	★	★	...	★	★
Louisiana	A, B, C	(c)	★	★	★	★	★	...	★	★
Maine	A, B, C	(b,d)	★	★	★	...	★	...	★	★
Maryland	A, B, C	★	★	★	★	(b)	★	★	★	★
Massachusetts	A, B, C	(b,c,d)	★	★	★	★	★	★	★	★
Michigan	A, B, C	(b,c,d)	★	★	★	...	★	★	★	★
Minnesota	A, B, C	(c)	★	★	★	★	★	★	...	★
Mississippi	A, B, C	★	★	★	★	...	★	...	★	★
Missouri	A, B, C	★	★	★	★	...	★	...	★	★
Montana	A, B, C	★	★	★	★	...	★	...	★	★
Nebraska	A, B, C	★	★	★	★	★	★	...	★	★
Nevada	A, B, C	★(d)	★	★	★	...	★	★	★	★
New Hampshire	A, B, C	★(a)	★	★	★	★	★	★	★	★
New Jersey	A, B, C	★(d)	★	★	★	★	★	...	★	★
New Mexico	A, B, C	★(a)	★	★	★	★	★	★	★	★
New York	A, B, C	(b)	★	★	★	★	...	★	...	...
North Carolina	A, B, C	★	★	★	★	★	★	(b)	...	★
North Dakota	A, B, C	(b)	★	★	★	...	★	★	★	★
Ohio	A, B, C	...	★	★	★	★	★	★	★	...
Oklahoma	A, B, C	(b)	★	★	★	★	★	★	★	★
Oregon	A, B, C	★	★	★	★	...	★	...	★	★
Pennsylvania	A, B, C	(c)	★	★	★	★	★	...	★	★
Rhode Island	A, B, C	★(a)	★	★	★	...	★	★	★	★
South Carolina	A, B, C	★(d)	★	★	★	...	★	...	★	★
South Dakota	A, B, C	★(a)	★	★	★	...	★	...	★	★
Tennessee	A, B, C	★(a)	★	★	★	...	★	(b)	★	★
Texas	A, B, C	(c)	★	★	★	★	★	...	★	★
Utah	A, B, C	★(a)	★	★	★	★	★	...	★	★
Vermont	A, B, C	(b)	★	★	★	★	★	(b)	...	★
Virginia	A, B, C	★(a)	★	★	★	★	★	★	★	★
Washington	A, B, C	(c,f)	★	★	★	★	★	★	★	★
West Virginia	A, B, C	★(a)	★	★	★	(f)	★	★	★	...
Wisconsin	A, B, C	(b)	★	★	★	★	★	(b)	★	...
Wyoming	A, B, C	★(a)	★	★	★	...	★	...	★	...
American Samoa	A, B, C	★(a)	★	★	★	...	★	...	★	★
Northern Mariana Is.	A, B, C	★	★	★	★	...	★	...	★	★
Puerto Rico	A, B, C	★	★	★	★	...	★	...	★	★
Virgin Islands	A, B, C(g)	★	★	★	★	...	★	...	★	★

Key: A—Defend state law when challenged on federal constitutional grounds.
B—Conduct litigation on behalf of state in federal and other states' courts.
C—Prosecute actions against another state in U.S. Supreme Court.
*Only in federal courts.
★—Has authority in area.
...—Does not have authority in area.

(a) Attorney general has exclusive jurisdiction.
(b) In certain cases only.
(c) When assisting local prosecutor in the appeal.
(d) Can appear on own discretion.
(e) In certain courts only.
(f) If authorized by the governor.
(g) Except in cases in which the U.S. Attorney is representing the Government of the Virgin Islands.

Table 15
STATE CABINET SYSTEMS

State	Authorization for cabinet system				Criteria for membership			Number of members in cabinet (including governor)	Frequency of cabinet meetings	Open cabinet meetings
	Statute	Constitution	Governor	Tradition	Appointed to specified office	Elected to specified office	Gubernatorial appointment regardless of office			
Alabama				★			★	24	Gov.'s discretion	★
Alaska			★		★			17	Regularly	★(a)
Arizona			★		★			15	Every two weeks	...
Arkansas	★				★		★	17	Monthly	...
California			★		★		★	11	Every two weeks	...
Colorado		★			★			20	Monthly	★
Connecticut	★				★			15	Gov.'s discretion	★(a)
Delaware	★						★(b)	16	Gov.'s discretion	★
Florida		★				★		7	Every two weeks	★
Georgia						(c)				
Hawaii	★				★			18	Gov.'s discretion	...
Idaho						(c)				
Illinois				★	★(b)			21	Gov.'s discretion(d)	★
Indiana						(c)				
Iowa	★					★		5	Weekly	★
Kansas			★				★	14	Monthly	★
Kentucky	★				★			18	Weekly	...
Louisiana						(c)				
Maine			★				★(b)	22	Monthly	(e)
Maryland	★				★(b)			23	Gov.'s discretion	...
Massachusetts	★				★			13	Twice monthly	...
Michigan			★					25	Monthly	(f)
Minnesota			★		★			24(g)	Every two weeks	★
Mississippi						(c)				
Missouri						(c)				
Montana			★		★			15	4-6 times a year	★
Nebraska			★		★			27	Weekly	...
Nevada						(c)				
New Hampshire						(c)				
New Jersey		★			★			21	Once or twice monthly	(h)
New Mexico	★				★			12	Monthly	★
New York			★		★			22	Gov.'s discretion	...
North Carolina(i)			★				★	11	Weekly	...
North Dakota						(c)				
Ohio	★				★		★	27	Every two weeks	(e)
Oklahoma			★				★	8(j)	Gov.'s discretion	...
Oregon			★		★			11	Weekly	...
Pennsylvania	★				★			19	Gov.'s discretion	★
Rhode Island						(c)				
South Carolina						(c)				
South Dakota			★		★		★	23	Gov.'s discretion	...
Tennessee				★	★			21	Gov.'s discretion(k)	(f)
Texas						(c)				
Utah				(l)	(l)			(l)	(l)	★
Vermont			★				★	19	Gov.'s discretion	...
Virginia	★						★	8	Gov.'s discretion(k)	...
Washington			★				★	26	Every 6-8 weeks	★(f)
West Virginia						(c)				
Wisconsin						(c)				
Wyoming						(c)				

Key:
★—Yes
...—No
(a) Except when in executive session.
(b) With the consent of Senate.
(c) No formal cabinet system. In Idaho, however, sub-cabinets have been formed, by executive order; the chairmen report to the governor when requested.
(d) Sub-cabinets meet monthly.
(e) In practice, the media and others do not attend, but cabinet meetings have not been formally designated closed.
(f) In Michigan and Tennessee closed, with some exceptions. In Washington, open with some exceptions.
(g) Five sub-cabinets have been formed.
(h) Closed to press, open to staff.
(i) Constitution provides for a Council of State made up of elective state administrative officials, which makes policy decisions for the state while the cabinet acts more in an advisory capacity.
(j) Each cabinet member is chair of a sub-cabinet (each state agency). These sub-cabinets meet quarterly.
(k) More often during legislative sessions. Tennessee—weekly.
(l) State Planning Advisory Committee, composed of all department heads serves as an informal cabinet. Committee meets at discretion of state planning coordinator.

Table 16
STATE ADMINISTRATIVE OFFICIALS: ANNUAL SALARIES

State or other jurisdiction	Governor	Lieutenant governor	Secretary of state	Attorney general	Treasurer	Adjutant general(a)	Adminis- tration	Agri- culture	Banking	Budget
Alabama	$63,839	$35,985	$32,940	$58,000	$45,000	$48,037	. . .	$44,687	$48,037	$36,478
Alaska	81,648	76,188	(b-1)	73,620	73,620	73,620	73,620	59,532	59,532	76,188
Arizona	56,000	. . .	31,500	50,500	34,000	39,554	57,012	39,554	39,554	43,325
Arkansas	35,000	14,000	22,500	26,500	22,500	37,837	53,473	. . .	36,000	24,206
California	49,100	42,500	42,500	47,500	42,500	65,999	. . .	67,446	57,829	(b-19)
Colorado	60,000	32,500	32,500	40,000	32,500	54,632	57,828	58,364	45,816	58,620
Connecticut	65,000	40,000	35,000	50,000	35,000	44,575	58,639	44,575	47,183	44,575
Delaware	35,000	16,600	44,800	39,600	25,700	34,600	37,800	32,000	42,100	44,800
Florida	69,550	60,455	59,385	59,385	59,385	62,878	53,467	59,385	(b-12)	55,642
Georgia	71,314	41,496	51,896	57,672	41,310	72,913	51,896	51,896	51,896	54,310
Hawaii	59,400	53,460	(b-1)	50,490	(b-9)	67,051	. . .	50,490	31,680	50,490
Idaho	50,000	14,000	37,500	42,000	37,500	58,947	46,176	47,341	41,746	45,053
Illinois	58,000	45,500	50,500	50,500	48,000	32,500	52,000	43,000	42,500	62,000
Indiana	66,000	51,000	46,000	51,000	46,000	35,282	42,432	(b-1)	38,662	42,432
Iowa	60,000	20,500	38,500	50,700	38,500	52,442	44,616	38,500	40,400	(b-12)
Kansas	47,925	14,378	29,288	42,600	29,288	39,012	58,080	47,376	25,116	50,412
Kentucky	60,000	51,010	51,010	51,010	51,010	54,875	59,500	51,010	49,500	(b-19)
Louisiana	73,400	63,367	60,169	60,168	60,168	64,934	66,492	60,168	47,495	52,908
Maine	35,000	. . .	30,000	44,431	30,000	32,469	. . .	36,670	34,570	32,469
Maryland	75,000	62,500	45,000	62,500	62,500	45,533	56,900	56,900	44,500	60,200
Massachusetts	75,000	60,000	60,000	65,000	60,000	65,394	70,047	37,203	40,445	43,971
Michigan	78,000	53,500	75,000	75,000	58,000	60,544 (m)	58,400	49,100	45,200	(b-6)
Minnesota	75,000	44,000	44,000	62,500	44,000	48,191	57,500	50,000	43,284	(b-19)
Mississippi	63,000	34,000	45,000	51,000	45,000	42,000	. . .	45,000	41,000	49,883
Missouri	55,000	30,000	42,500	45,000	42,500	34,000	40,000	40,000	34,000	34,000
Montana	47,968	34,344	31,692	43,745	29,438	47,498	47,500	47,500	35,391	47,500
Nebraska	40,000	32,000	32,000	39,500	32,000	41,194	40,426	36,151	47,500	39,165
Nevada	65,000	10,500	42,500	52,500	41,000	35,100	46,827	38,212	35,751	(b-6)
New Hampshire	56,495	. . .	30,938	39,007	30,938	24,214	50,434	29,596	30,938	(b-12)
New Jersey	85,000	. . .	66,000	70,000	70,000	29,195	. . .	66,000	70,000	(b-12)
New Mexico	60,000	38,500	38,496	44,000	38,500	44,340	(b-21)	50,004	44,340	44,340
New York	100,000	85,000	65,700	85,000	. . .	59,800	. . .	65,700	65,700	75,000
North Carolina	60,768	50,328	50,328	53,976	50,328	48,180	53,880	50,328	48,408	55,740
North Dakota	60,862	48,800	43,380	49,206	43,380	62,447	26,256	43,380	38,004	(s)
Ohio	65,000	35,000	50,000	50,000	50,000	50,003	58,802	45,926	41,350	52,936
Oklahoma	70,000	40,000	37,500	55,000	50,000	57,500	. . .	45,000	53,000	48,000
Oregon	55,423	. . .	45,619	53,308	45,619	47,904	58,236	52,776	47,904	52,776
Pennsylvania	75,000	57,500	48,000	55,000	48,000	48,000	51,500	48,000	48,000	55,000
Rhode Island	42,500	35,500	35,500	35,500	41,875	31,331	53,596	31,331	27,271	42,739
South Carolina	60,000	30,000	55,000	55,000	55,000	55,000	(b-9)	55,000	(b-4)	59,017
South Dakota	50,981	52,562	34,611	43,285	34,611	44,720	54,995	42,494	37,378	(b-19)
Tennessee	68,220	(aa)	51,510	65,650	51,510	46,526	51,510	46,526	46,526	26,364
Texas	88,900	7,200	61,200	69,000	69,000	52,600	. . .	69,000	72,288	55,500
Utah	51,984	35,640	(b-1)	41,004	35,616	32,197	43,180	32,197	34,076	38,169
Vermont	50,000	22,000	30,000	40,000	30,000	26,600	35,450	26,600	26,600	29,000
Virginia	75,000	20,000	30,368	56,000	55,120	36,920	61,360	46,176	59,350	61,360
Washington	63,000	28,600	31,000	47,100	37,200	62,878	57,800	57,800	(cc)	71,500
West Virginia(dd)	72,000	. . .	43,200	50,400	50,400	34,000	36,500	46,800	36,500	(ee)
Wisconsin	75,337	41,390	37,334	58,139	37,334	42,246	63,000	58,241	52,000	52,000
Wyoming	70,000	. . .	52,500	46,296	52,500	49,957	47,460	37,968	36,132	40,908
Dist. of Col.	78,630 (hh)	. . .	. . .	63,700	51,058	N.A.	63,700	. . .	. . .	63,700
American Samoa	50,000	45,000	(b-1)	35,000	(b-6)	. . .	35,000	25,000	(b-25)	33,000
Guam	50,000	45,000	. . .	40,838	26,858	N.A.	36,838	34,838	(b-35)	36,838
No. Mariana Is.	20,000	18,000	. . .	36,000	21,095	. . .	36,000	(b-27)	(b-10)	35,000
Puerto Rico	35,000	. . .	42,000	N.A.	40,000	39,500	39,500	40,000	N.A.	40,000
Virgin Islands	52,395	47,000	. . .	43,500	. . .	38,640	. . .	34,865	(b-1)	38,640

STATE ADMINISTRATIVE OFFICIALS: ANNUAL SALARIES

State or other jurisdiction	Civil rights	Commerce	Community affairs	Comp-troller	Consumer affairs	Correc-tions	Data processing	Disaster prepared-ness	Education (chief school officer)	Educa-tion (higher)
Alabama	. . .	48,037	47,500	36,478	. . .	48,037	36,478	48,037	65,000	62,894
Alaska	59,532	73,620	73,620	53,568	57,384	73,620	59,532	53,568	73,620	59,532
Arizona	47,473	(c)	(d)	(b-19)	(b-3)	57,012	39,554	32,899	40,500	69,127
Arkansas	. . .	(f)	29,200	(b-6)	29,370	49,000	48,388	29,100	52,720	54,200
California	52,979	57,829	44,496	42,500	52,979	57,829	56,160	48,176	42,500	77,628
Colorado	45,816	48,108	39,576	53,028	45,816	59,667	55,680	43,632	71,349	67,500
Connecticut	47,183	50,539	38,790	35,000	50,539	54,215	44,575	33,150	54,215	72,000
Delaware	. . .	. . .	40,000	48,935	29,500	49,300	. . .	24,400	69,000	36,900
Florida	28,507	(b-1)	51,684	59,385	41,328	54,356	(b-9)	39,904	53,779	93,133
Georgia	. . .	55,500	53,000	51,896	42,500	51,896	47,904	(b-5)	58,429	89,239
Hawaii	. . .	50,490	(b-30)	50,490	44,550	31,680	33,216	38,040	50,490	53,460
Idaho	25,064	37,066	(b-10)	(i)	(b-3)	40,061	(b-6)	33,742	37,500	52,000
Illinois	44,000	46,000	(b-10)	48,000	(b-3)	46,000	(b-6)	32,500	69,347	76,500
Indiana	29,094	(b-1)	29,094	(i)	29,094	42,432	35,282	25,610	50,000	67,500
Iowa	31,500	43,900	38,646	52,000	43,410	51,501	44,699	30,000	52,100	52,000
Kansas	34,152	47,928	38,004	52,764	38,268	54,528	50,736	31,584	61,000	54,000
Kentucky	47,724	59,500	32,916	55,000	(b-3)	59,500	(b-6)	32,916	51,010	69,694
Louisiana	(b-3)	53,353	52,366	(b-6)	34,099	52,243	46,033	35,955	60,168	76,193
Maine	24,315	36,670	. . .	32,469	34,570	36,800	30,347	26,083	36,670	0 (l)
Maryland	46,300	40,900	43,000	62,500	45,200	48,000	45,600	32,700	62,000	55,900
Massachusetts	37,203	37,203	57,312	47,800	53,040	51,959	47,800	34,528	51,959	65,000
Michigan	49,000	53,500	45,200	(b-4)	48,900	58,400	36,560	33,930	58,400	36,561
Minnesota	43,125	55,000	41,614	(b-19)	42,500	55,000	53,223	37,605	60,625	55,000
Mississippi	. . .	57,083	(b-30)	(b-31)	31,852	40,000	44,936	28,000	50,000	59,960
Missouri	34,000	34,000	34,000	(b-6)	40,000	40,000	34,000	34,000	34,000	49,000
Montana	29,438	47,500	30,511	(b-6)	26,973	47,500	41,315	33,288	37,718	68,309
Nebraska	42,065	39,966	27,300	(b-6)	. . .	45,780	40,479	33,468	60,000	0
Nevada	30,240	43,200	31,320	41,000	28,060	47,520	41,580	27,137	37,597	43,750
New Hampshire	18,603	29,596	25,600	39,007	26,900	29,596	30,938	25,500	50,434	30,938
New Jersey	45,290	70,000	66,000	60,694	47,555	70,000	52,430	49,932	70,000	70,000
New Mexico	34,776	50,004	. . .	(b-4)	41,472	55,550	46,848	18,816	55,000	(b-15)
New York	59,800	65,700	(b-2)	85,000	55,300	69,200	(b-21)	(b-5)	76,100	(b-15)
North Carolina	28,560	51,636	28,560	. . .	34,500	51,636	60,384	25,968	56,676	89,250
North Dakota	(b-26)	42,000	26,256	(t)	31,920	33,504	31,920	33,096	44,028	69,160
Ohio	27,622	(v)	41,350	(b-4)	49,317	50,648	41,350	31,200	61,796	83,408
Oklahoma	30,000	45,000	42,500	37,401	37,500	55,000	40,200	32,500	55,000	86,580
Oregon	29,364	52,776	47,904	47,904	37,524	52,776	47,904	35,736	45,619	75,005
Pennsylvania	36,792	48,000	48,000	49,700	36,792	41,761	36,792	35,247	55,000	51,440
Rhode Island	24,351	46,359	33,692	35,504	22,545	43,334	33,692	(b-5)	60,000	60,000
South Carolina	43,708	59,686	32,101	55,000	46,984	52,766	50,718	27,191	55,000	58,099
South Dakota	(b-3)	42,494	40,498	34,611	25,374	43,410	(b-6)	27,061	44,990	50,980
Tennessee	24,024	51,510	(b-10)	51,510	46,526	46,526	28,896	24,024	51,510	65,376
Texas	45,000	55,500	49,200	69,000	55,400	64,400	52,000	36,480	63,500	62,200 (bb)
Utah	32,197	38,169	(b-10)	(b-19)	34,076	38,169	38,169	38,169	43,180	78,500
Vermont	37,648	32,500	23,000	29,000	37,648	29,000	36,525	29,141	32,500	. . .
Virginia	. . .	(b-24)	46,176	49,816	(b-7)	52,104	48,756	41,600	61,880	58,448
Washington	48,700	50,500	(b-10)	(b-4)	26,040	60,300	54,700	38,600	42,800	59,928
West Virginia (dd)	33,270	54,425	34,868	46,800	44,200	36,500	39,035	30,500	60,475	64,692
Wisconsin	45,437	(gg)	36,598	51,237	(b-7)	55,000	(b-19)	35,000	58,139	65,799
Wyoming	. . .	34,392	(b-10)	(b-31)	27,528	40,908	40,908	28,212	52,500	28,212
Dist. of Col.	59,883	63,700	51,058	61,879	44,856	63,700	63,700	63,700	. . .	25,327
American Samoa	. . .	27,000	(b-10)	(b-6)	16,497	31,595	31,595	16,617	33,000	(jj)
Guam	. . .	34,838	45,000	39,124	36,838	34,838	37,175	34,838	36,838	N.A.
No. Mariana Is.	36,000	36,000	30,000	(b-19)	(b-10)	16,530	30,000	26,500	30,000	30,000
Puerto Rico	N.A.	40,000	35,000	42,000	40,000	38,000	(b-21)	33,000	40,000	N.A.
Virgin Islands	18,500	43,500	N.A.	. . .	34,778	34,776	. . .	27,674	38,640	. . .

STATE ADMINISTRATIVE OFFICIALS: ANNUAL SALARIES

State or other jurisdiction	Elections adminis- tration	Employ- ment services	Energy resources	Environ- mental conser- vation	Finance	Fish & game	General services	Health	Highway patrol	Highways	Historic preser- vation
Alabama	(b-2)	33,826	40,515	48,037	48,037	(b-27)	(b-19)	87,414	48,037	48,037	37,740
Alaska	59,532	47,544	...	73,620	73,620	73,620	59,532	73,620	59,532	(b-36)	59,532
Arizona	(b-2)	47,473	33,000	47,473	47,473	43,325	(b-6)	62,474	54,227	(b-36)	32,899
Arkansas	28,320	50,485	35,936	37,405	(b-6)	43,186	...	54,220	36,560	58,470	17,654
California	(b-2)	57,829	57,829	66,483	67,446	52,979	57,829	62,624	67,446	40,284	52,979
Colorado	38,724	50,508	N.A.	58,464	40,656	53,028	(b-6)	70,000	53,028	58,620	46,500
Connecticut	37,291	47,183	44,575	54,215	58,639	30,647	58,639	59,968	50,359	47,183	30,647
Delaware	27,800	43,600	23,325	44,800	49,400	32,700	(b-6)	47,600	40,700	46,200	36,700
Florida	44,300	44,881	48,404	55,165	37,947	52,917	54,436	37,000	43,138	(b-36)	32,000
Georgia	44,823	55,548	42,500	55,479	41,310	46,293	(b-6)	67,980	53,688	71,225	34,668
Hawaii	27,492	31,680	31,680	44,550	(b-9)	30,228	(b-12)	50,490	...	44,550	(h)
Idaho	(b-2)	49,691	60,424	46,490	45,053	50,918	(b-6)	51,854	45,427	(b-36)	37,981
Illinois	47,508	...	43,000	43,000	(b-12)	40,000	(b-6)	52,000	37,000	(b-36)	(b-20)
Indiana	25,610	38,662	32,058	(k)	(b-9)	42,432	(b-6)	42,432	42,432	42,432	19,500
Iowa	28,912	40,000	38,900	42,000	42,598	(b-18)	40,000	42,400	39,562	50,454	32,000
Kansas	(b-2)	43,428	33,192	45,000	(b-6)	36,060	(b-6)	54,528	41,940	50,616	40,236
Kentucky	(b-2)	(b-29)	59,500	59,500	59,500	41,500	(b-19)	49,500	49,500	59,500	39,984
Louisiana	60,168	43,836	53,584	53,584	(b-6)	52,366	(b-6)	63,327	48,469	49,931	52,359
Maine	(b-2)	30,347	32,469	36,670	36,670	36,670	(b-19)	31,866	32,469	(b-36)	26,083
Maryland	44,700	60,200	42,300	53,000	(b-12)	44,200	60,200	62,000	48,000	52,600	35,800
Massachusetts	31,000	29,647	53,040	60,496	(b-6)	40,445	(b-33)	51,959	45,550	51,959	...
Michigan	28,940	39,609	23,114	23,114	(b-6)	(b-27)	(b-6)	69,300	53,500	(b-36)	32,865
Minnesota	25,077	48,252	55,000	40,152	63,750	47,004	(b-6)	50,000	(o)	53,280	70,000
Mississippi	(b-2)	43,000	40,000	41,910	...	29,116	36,087	67,290	40,000	45,000	37,000
Missouri	26,412	37,000	34,000	34,000	(b-6)	55,128	(b-6)	60,000	51,606	60,000	(b-28)
Montana	26,500	37,088	34,182	44,222	...	47,500	(b-6)	40,485	39,669	47,500	36,566
Nebraska	(b-2)	35,972	33,946	39,900	(p)	54,443	(b-6)	56,292	40,027	49,500	22,092
Nevada	(b-2)	41,289	...	39,135	(b-12)	35,751	(b-33)	42,000	28,319	(b-36)	27,137
New Hampshire	...	34,967	26,000	...	(b-12)	29,596	30,938	39,007	50,434	50,434	(b-27)
New Jersey	32,188	43,134	66,000	70,000	(b-4)	43,134	49,932	70,000	49,932	(b-36)	29,195
New Mexico	30,048	50,004	50,004	44,340	50,004	44,340	50,004	50,004	46,848	50,004	N.A.
New York	56,500	65,700	65,700	65,700	(b-12)	(b-18)	65,700	69,300	65,700	(b-36)	(b-28)
North Carolina	53,100	48,408	28,560	32,856	53,869	41,748	34,500	58,500	34,500	50,556	23,616
North Dakota	(b-2)	45,576	(b-11)	N.A.	(b-9)	39,000	41,904	68,000	36,000	51,000	19,596
Ohio	(b-2)	45,947	33,010	50,440	(b-6)	34,798	(b-6)	63,502	39,998	(b-36)	N.A. (g)
Oklahoma	48,400	50,000	36,000	35,000	55,000	52,500	36,000	77,500	37,400	(b-36)	32,500
Oregon	37,524	52,776	52,776	52,776	(b-6)	50,268	52,776	47,904	52,776	52,776	20,856
Pennsylvania	28,362	35,247	38,416	(b-27)	51,500	(w)	51,500	51,500	51,500	(b-36)	36,792
Rhode Island	23,743	39,122	37,831	39,122	40,930	27,271	31,331	44,549	44,167	(b-36)	25,313
South Carolina	41,384	56,500	...	40,249	(b-9)	55,520	51,396	67,914	33,083	62,555	22,349
South Dakota	(b-2)	29,994	...	34,632	49,005	41,600	(b-6)	40,560	38,750	41,475	25,917
Tennessee	26,364	46,526	40,440	28,896	(b-6)	45,924	46,526	31,668	28,896	(b-36)	20,100
Texas	(b-2)	52,300	...	...	...	57,000	53,600	62,800	62,800	64,800	44,300
Utah	(b-1)	40,382	30,485	36,060	38,169	34,076	(b-6)	38,169	36,060	(b-36)	30,485
Vermont	(b-2)	29,000	32,500	32,500	29,000	26,600	...	38,000	...	35,450	26,478
Virginia	39,416	44,928	(b-14)	44,928	...	40,768	49,816	61,880	44,928	56,264	32,552
Washington	26,040	32,520	43,100	57,800	(b-9)	57,800	(b-6)	71,500	57,800	(b-36)	38,600
West Virginia (dd)	(b-2)	(ff)	20,860	45,500	45,500	30,289	23,955	54,500	42,500	47,500	26,432
Wisconsin	38,275	57,720	41,000	46,548	51,237	44,117	41,000	64,800	54,200	57,203	34,586
Wyoming	(b-2)	37,044	25,560	39,900	(b-31)	46,296	(b-6)	52,380	36,132	48,636	(b-28)
Dist. of Col.	(ii)	63,700	N.A.	63,700	...	...	63,700	63,700	63,700	56,164	63,700
American Samoa	(b-3)	...	25,000	21,759	(b-6)	28,000	28,000	35,000	15,377	35,000	(b-28)
Guam	29,910	34,838	34,838	34,838	(b-6)	29,976	(b-6)	36,838	36,838	36,838	(b-28)
No. Mariana Is.	17,800	(b-29)	36,000	36,000	30,000	27,000	(b-6)	44,000	5,700	30,000	25,000
Puerto Rico	42,000	N.A.	N.A.	38,000	(b-9)	(b-27)	38,000	40,000	N.A.	37,992	35,000
Virgin Islands	25,000	30,452	36,000	...	36,646	29,020	36,000	43,058	...	...	29,019

STATE ADMINISTRATIVE OFFICIALS: ANNUAL SALARIES

State or other jurisdiction	Industrial develop-ment	Insurance	Labor & industrial relations	Licensing	Mental health	Natural resources	Parks & recreation	Personnel	Planning	Post audit
Alabama	(b-10)	48,037	48,037	...	48,037	48,037	31,408	61,050	...	44,400
Alaska	73,620	59,532	73,620	59,532	59,532	73,620	59,532	59,532	61,548	73,584
Arizona	43,325	39,554	43,325	(e)	47,473	52,043	36,070	47,473	(d)	58,809
Arkansas	45,258	41,272	44,019	...	67,266	32,564	24,206	24,206	...	50,173
California	57,829	57,829	67,446	(b-13)	62,624	52,979	52,979	47,760	52,032	(b-19)
Colorado	43,632	50,508	61,604	48,108	72,804	57,574	48,108	57,574	39,576	54,400
Connecticut	34,475	47,183	50,359	40,333	59,968	54,215	33,150	47,183	38,790	49,075
Delaware	52,000	25,700	39,900	25,400	47,500	44,800	33,200	33,600	...	25,700
Florida	44,000	(b-4)	49,755	51,928	46,776	53,909	40,878	48,438	(b-9)	39,096
Georgia	36,198	(b-12)	55,600	44,823	71,634	55,803	46,777	48,477	47,008	51,937
Hawaii	(b-30)	30,288	50,490	30,288	47,174	50,490	31,680	50,490	31,680	31,680
Idaho	(b-10)	37,066	39,874	33,613	35,433	...	45,074	48,485	(b-10)	43,971
Illinois	(b-10)	43,000	43,000(j)	44,000	52,000	(b-17)	(b-20)	(b-6)	...	48,000
Indiana	32,058	38,662	32,058	...	42,432	23,660	25,610	42,432	29,094	42,432
Iowa	38,000	35,000	37,200	...	49,442	(b-18)	31,844	27,602	42,500	38,500
Kansas	42,120	40,775	43,428	...	50,412	45,000	40,488	48,648	(b-9)	46,368
Kentucky	(b-10)	49,500	59,500	32,916	32,916	(b-18)	49,500	49,500	(b-6)	49,143
Louisiana	(b-10)	60,168	56,021	...	74,196	58,451	43,842	46,968	40,067	(b-9)
Maine	36,670	34,570	36,670	16,806	27,643	36,670	30,306	36,670	32,469	30,000
Maryland	39,500	52,200	48,700	56,900	51,875	56,900	44,200	56,900	56,900	50,700
Massachusetts	(b-10)	40,445	37,203	34,528	47,800	40,445	51,959	43,971	(b-11)	60,000
Michigan	45,200	45,200	53,500	49,000	69,300	39,609	39,609	23,114	...	64,800
Minnesota	(b-11)	43,284	50,000	(b-26)	53,748	55,000	48,000	55,000	57,500	48,000
Mississippi	(b-10)	45,000	...	34,000	54,000	42,119	38,299	43,600	37,172	45,000
Missouri	(b-10)	34,000	40,000	34,000	71,496	40,000	34,000	34,000	(b-9)	42,500
Montana	(b-11)	30,322	47,500	30,511	42,787	47,500	34,182	38,088	(b-11)	41,340
Nebraska	26,940	37,781	35,682	29,016	35,700	39,900	(b-20)	37,057	35,900	32,000
Nevada	38,817	36,982	31,445	...	64,800	42,060	33,290	41,289	...	41,600
New Hampshire	29,596	50,434	29,596	...	39,007	50,434	29,596	34,967	(b-11)	39,007
New Jersey	...	70,000	66,000	47,555	55,050	70,000	45,290	70,000	...	63,000
New Mexico	48,156	36,516	36,516	50,004	39,876	50,004	41,472	46,848	...	38,496
New York	(b-10)	65,700	65,700	(b-2)	69,200	(b-18)	65,700	(q)	(r)	(b-12)
North Carolina	31,380	50,328	50,328	...	61,404	51,636	28,560	51,636	...	50,328
North Dakota	(b-10)	43,380	43,380	...	26,256	...	36,000	26,256	26,256	(u)
Ohio	47,008	49,317	45,926	...	47,424	(b-1)	33,300	43,971	37,877	50,000
Oklahoma	(b-10)	50,000	37,500	...	74,500	43,000	45,000	45,000	...	50,000
Oregon	34,044	47,904	45,619	(b-10)	55,464	35,736	47,904	47,904	...	37,524
Pennsylvania	(b-10)	48,000	51,500	30,963	N.A.(x)	55,000	35,247	36,792	41,761	48,000
Rhode Island	(b-10)	24,351	32,925	22,545	51,786	(b-18)	28,268	33,692	31,331	32,476
South Carolina	(b-10)	56,219	46,122	(z)	65,965	...	46,121	49,614	...	54,455
South Dakota	(b-11)	28,995	47,008	...	31,907	47,008	29,432	39,499	37,502	15,995
Tennessee	(b-10)	46,526	46,526	...	56,339	46,526	26,364	46,526	28,896	(b-12)
Texas	44,300	57,400	51,800	...	68,400	...	(b-20)	...	55,500	65,000
Utah	30,485	32,197	32,197	34,076	36,060	38,169	34,076	38,169	38,169	35,496
Vermont	(b-10)	(b-8)	26,600	(b-2)	34,000	32,500	26,600	29,000	41,600	30,000
Virginia	59,800	(b-32)	43,732	38,168	62,400	46,176	31,039	49,816	(b-9)	53,280
Washington	47,200	37,200	57,800	31,728	63,348	42,800	54,700	57,800	(b-9)	37,200
West Virginia(dd)	37,475	34,000	34,000	...	44,195	45,500	30,289	(b-6)	(b-10)	19,918
Wisconsin	(b-1)	45,000	64,000	41,000	53,115	65,289	45,596	54,002	52,000	54,868
Wyoming	(b-10)	33,552	31,932	...	36,132	...	32,724	40,908	34,392	52,500
Dist. of Col.	(b-10)	56,164	(b-16)	46,302	53,532	...	63,700	63,700	63,700	63,700
American Samoa	(b-10)	7,500	(b-29)	...	17,245	...	33,000	33,000	(b-10)	25,377
Guam	(b-11)	(b-8)	34,838	(b-35)	34,838	34,838	34,838	(b-6)	34,838	...
No. Mariana Is.	(b-10)	...	(b-10)	(b-10)	(b-22)	30,000	18,223	36,000	(b-9)	36,000
Puerto Rico	N.A.	38,000	...	N.A.	25,800	40,000	40,000	(b-6)	40,000	(b-12)
Virgin Islands	34,799	...	...	26,560	30,000	31,911	21,339	34,776	36,000	N.A.

STATE ADMINISTRATIVE OFFICIALS: ANNUAL SALARIES

State or other jurisdiction	Pre audit	Public library	Public utility regulation	Purchasing	Social services	Solid waste	Taxation	Tourism	Transportation	Welfare
Alabama	(b-12)	46,089	40,500	29,198	48,037	48,037	48,037	48,037	48,540	(b-34)
Alaska	41,628	59,532	63,636	41,628	(b-22)	47,544	(b-19)	59,532	73,620	59,532
Arizona	39,554	36,070	39,554	39,554	47,473	(b-18)	57,012	36,070	62,474	62,474
Arkansas	18,824	36,998	40,776	24,206	43,146	18,824	41,317	40,778	(b-23)	53,473
California	(b-12)	33,336	60,700	48,924	57,829	57,829	63,659	36,828	57,829	(b-34)
Colorado	(b-12)	48,747	40,000	50,508	61,605	45,816	60,504	(b-10)	. . .	(b-34)
Connecticut	(b-12)	33,150	55,202	44,575	50,359	35,857	47,183	31,874	58,639	50,359
Delaware	(b-31)	28,900	31,700	33,200	39,300	N.A.(g)	46,800	32,541	46,200	39,300
Florida	41,200	41,000	56,710	43,104	51,355	38,003	58,965	44,520	63,742	46,776
Georgia	(b-31)	43,044	51,896	45,900	51,720	37,818	51,896	34,668	71,225	(b-34)
Hawaii	27,492	44,550	47,520	27,492	50,490	(b-18)	50,490	27,492	50,490	31,680
Idaho	37,500	37,357	36,500	34,577	41,029	44,140	34,500	(b-10)	56,160	42,682
Illinois	(b-12)	. . .	47,500	(b-6)	46,000	. . .	46,000	(b-10)	52,000	52,000
Indiana	46,000	29,094	42,432	(b-6)	42,432	29,094	42,432	(b-24)	38,662	(b-6)
Iowa	. . .	. . .	(b-10)	33,030	52,500	(b-18)	47,500	30,618	50,800	30,493
Kansas	(b-12)	25,236	48,458	37,488	58,080	(b-27)	50,724	31,032	54,024	37,524
Kentucky	47,484	40,788	49,620	32,916	49,500	32,916	59,500	59,500	59,500	49,500
Louisiana	(b-9)	48,713	59,748	(b-6)	48,713	(b-18)	52,366	43,841	58,454	42,624
Maine	(b-12)	30,306	45,236	30,306	25,334	(b-18)	34,570	(b-10)	36,670	(b-34)
Maryland	45,600	33,623	49,500	28,823	60,200	44,200	(b-12)	37,100	62,000	(b-34)
Massachusetts	(b-12)	29,647	37,203	43,971	70,047	34,528	51,959	31,970	40,445	47,800
Michigan	(b-31)	. . .	48,900	39,609	58,400	(b-18)	(n)	39,609	58,400	(b-34)
Minnesota	52,179	46,812	40,000	42,178	53,745	46,400	57,500	48,900	63,750	53,745
Mississippi	(b-31)	37,000	40,000	36,984	45,000	28,114	50,000	35,544	(b-17)	(b-34)
Missouri	34,000	34,344	40,000	34,000	40,000	28,884	40,000	34,000	(b-23)	34,000
Montana	. . .	34,887	35,544	32,614	47,500	29,893	47,500	31,788	35,675	(b-34)
Nebraska	(b-6)	38,863	25,000	34,002	33,600	29,820	43,575	25,536	(b-23)	40,210
Nevada	(b-6)	27,090	45,924	43,459	51,570	(b-18)	41,289	47,500	51,300	44,360
New Hampshire	(b-12)	29,596	50,434	29,596	30,938	21,950	50,434	18,833	(b-23)	(b-34)
New Jersey	(b-12)	51,843	66,000	49,932	70,000	37,262	55,050	37,262	70,000	52,430
New Mexico	45,576	34,776	48,156	39,876	38,340	(b-18)	50,004	41,472	50,004	38,340
New York	(b-12)	. . .	69,200	(b-21)	69,200	(b-18)	65,700	62,500	69,200	(b-34)
North Carolina	(b-31)	31,380	51,328	31,380	36,192	22,500	51,636	29,928	51,636	(b-34)
North Dakota	(s)	28,956	43,380	26,256	63,000	28,956	43,380	23,820	28,956	(b-34)
Ohio	(b-31)	41,350	58,011	27,622	35,880	43,514	44,013	41,350	58,822	53,851
Oklahoma	(b-19)	35,000	46,500	42,400	69,500	37,400	47,600	(b-28)	55,000	(b-34)
Oregon	. . .	43,428	58,236	47,904	58,236	34,044	52,776	29,364	58,236	52,776
Pennsylvania	(b-4)	29,653	42,500	(b-21)	(y)	33,858	(b-19)	(b-10)	55,000	55,000
Rhode Island	(b-12)	31,331	23,429	39,122	42,739	34,321	40,930	26,272	39,667	33,692
South Carolina	(b-12)	37,138	41,604	51,396	59,151	30,586	48,991	30,586	(b-23)	(b-34)
South Dakota	. . .	28,038	26,998	28,454	49,005	33,134	42,494	30,014	50,003	36,264
Tennessee	28,896	17,568	46,526	21,972	28,896	26,364	46,526	46,526	51,510	46,526
Texas	(b-12)	45,600	49,500	(b-21)	64,400	45,480	(b-12)	43,100	(b-23)	(b-34)
Utah	(b-19)	30,485	36,060	30,485	38,169	. . .	34,076	30,485	40,382	30,485
Vermont	(b-19)	24,400	45,953	24,400	32,500	37,398	29,000	40,477	35,450	32,500
Virginia	(b-12)	44,928	59,350	37,092	49,816	0	51,584	31,039	61,360	(b-34)
Washington	. . .	54,500	54,700	(b-6)	(b-22)	33,336	57,800	34,176	71,500	(b-22)
West Virginia (dd)	(b-19)	53,483	43,000	26,316	23,955	26,316	47,500	19,918	19,918	45,500
Wisconsin	38,910	32,228	56,000	53,198	(b-22)	35,124	58,000	40,001	60,000	(b-22)
Wyoming	(b-31)	31,152	41,940	38,928	39,900	29,640	44,064	31,152	. . .	(b-34)
Dist. of Col.	. . .	63,700	63,700	56,164	63,700	54,462	63,700	(b-10)	63,700	59,883
American Samoa	. . .	16,299	. . .	(b-21)	. . .	28,377	28,085	(b-10)	30,000	. . .
Guam	(b-9)	34,838	36,838	21,398	(b-22)	(b-23)	36,838	40,838	30,838	36,838
No. Mariana Is.	(b-31)	13,601	(b-23)	23,256	. . .	(b-23)	20,093	36,000	(b-23)	30,000
Puerto Rico	40,000	N.A.	38,000	N.A.	40,000	35,000	25,800	N.A.	40,000	(b-34)
Virgin Islands	. . .	. . .	25,000	(b-21)	36,000	. . .	38,640	34,776	. . .	(b-34)

Note: The chief administrative officials responsible for each function were determined from information given by the states for the same function as listed in *State Administrative Officials Classifed by Function 1983-84*, published by The Council of State Governments. Salary figures (as of February 1984) are presented as submitted by the states for these same officials except when ranges were given. In those instances, the minimum figure was chosen. When necessary, figures have been rounded to the nearest dollar.

Source: The Council of State Governments' survey of state personnel agencies, 1984.

Key:

N.A.—Not available

. . .—No specific chief administrative official or agency in charge of function.

(a) Salary listed may be of military grade.

(b) Chief administrative official or agency in charge of function:

(b-1) Lieutenant governor
(b-2) Secretary of state
(b-3) Attorney general
(b-4) Treasurer
(b-5) Adjutant general
(b-6) Administration
(b-7) Agriculture
(b-8) Banking
(b-9) Budget
(b-10) Commerce
(b-11) Community affairs
(b-12) Comptroller
(b-13) Consumer affairs
(b-14) Disaster preparedness
(b-15) Education (chief state school officer)
(b-16) Employment services
(b-17) Energy resources
(b-18) Environmental conservation
(b-19) Finance
(b-20) Fish and game
(b-21) General services
(b-22) Health
(b-23) Highways
(b-24) Industrial development
(b-25) Insurance
(b-26) Labor and industrial relations
(b-27) Natural resources
(b-28) Parks and recreation
(b-29) Personnel
(b-30) Planning
(b-31) Post audit
(b-32) Public utility regulation
(b-33) Purchasing
(b-34) Social services
(b-35) Taxation
(b-36) Transportation

(c) Responsibilities shared by Director of the Development Division within the Office of Economic Planning and Development, $36,070, and chief administrative official listed under Industrial Development.

(d) Responsibilities shared by Director of the Planning Division within the Office of Economic Planning and Development, $39,554, and Director of the Development Division within the same office, listed under Commerce. The Director of the Planning Division is also responsible for the function Planning.

(e) Numerous boards and commissions responsible for function.

(f) Responsibilities shared by the chief administrative officials listed under the following functions: Industrial Development and Tourism.

(g) Not a state employee.

(h) Receives only per diem, plane fare and/or mileage allowances.

(i) Responsibility of official listed under function Pre Audit.

(j) Due to reorganization, commencing July 1984, the responsibilities for this function will be shared by the chairperson of the Illinois Educational Labor Relations Board, $50,000, the chairperson of the Illinois Labor Relations Board, $50,000, and the Director of the Department of Labor, $43,000.

(k) Responsibilities shared by chief administrative officials listed under the following functions: Health and Natural Resources.

(l) Expenses only.

(m) Figure given is total income paid by state. The base salary, before federal duty deduction and non-taxable military allowances, is $65,394.

(n) Responsibilities shared by Deputy Treasurer of the Bureau of Collections within the Department of Treasury, $41,900, and Director of Local Government Services within the same department, $41,900.

(o) Responsibilities shared by Commissioner of the Department of Public Safety, $55,000, and Chief of State Patrol Division within the same department, $43,116.

(p) Responsibilities shared by the following administrative officials: Director of Accounting Division within the Department of Administrative Services, $38,002; State Budget Administrator of the Budget Division within the same department, listed under Budget; Auditor of Public Accounts, listed under Post Audit; and State Tax Commissioner of the Department of Revenue, listed under Taxation.

(q) Responsibilities shared by Director of Employee Relations, $69,200, and President of the Civil Service Commission, $65,700.

(r) No central planning agency. Responsibilities shared among the Departments of Commerce, State and Transportation, the State Energy Office, and the Tri-State Planning Commission, whose department heads' salaries range from the mid-$50,000s to the high $60,000s.

(s) Responsibilities shared by Director of the Office of Management and Budget, $55,000, and Executive Budget Analyst of the same office, $36,936. The Director of Management and Budget is also responsible for the function Pre Audit.

(t) Responsibilities shared by chief administrative officials listed under Budget and by the Director of the Accounting Operations Office, $30,384.

(u) Responsibilities shared by the Legislative Budget Analyst and Auditor, $46,896, and the State Auditor, $43,380.

(v) Responsibilities shared by Director of Department of Development, $63,502, and Director of Department of Commerce, $49,317.

(w) Responsibilities shared by Executive Director of the Fish Commission, $36,792, and Executive Director of the Game Commission, $30,963.

(x) Federal government employee, paid by the federal government. Salary information not available from state personnel office.

(y) Responsibilities shared by the Director of Blindness and Visual Services within the Department of Public Welfare, $29,653, and the Director of Children and Youth Services within the same department, $36,792.

(z) Each profession has its own licensing board.

(aa) Speaker of the Senate has the statutory title of lieutenant governor.

(bb) Plus supplement from private sources.

(cc) Responsibilities shared by Supervisor of Banking, $35,028, and Supervisor of Savings and Loan, $35,028.

(dd) Effective July 1, 1984.

(ee) Responsibilities shared by Commissioner of the Department of Finance and Adminstration, listed under Finance, and the Budget Division Director within the same department, $23,955.

(ff) Responsibilities shared by Commissioner of the Department of Employment Security, $34,000, and Director of the Employment Services Division within the same department, $25,168.

(gg) Temporarily occupied by lieutenant governor. Minimum salary for position when permanently filled is $47,406.

(hh) Mayor.

(ii) $12.50/hour (part-time).

(jj) Responsibilities shared by President of the Community College $33,000, and Chairman of the Board of Higher Education, no salary.

Table 17
CONSTITUTIONAL AND STATUTORY PROVISIONS FOR LENGTH AND NUMBER OF TERMS OF ELECTED STATE OFFICIALS

State or other jurisdiction	Governor	Lt. governor	Secretary of state	Attorney general	Treasurer	Auditor	Comptroller	Education	Agriculture	Labor	Insurance	Other
Alabama	4/2	4/2	4/2	4/2	4/2	4/2	...	...	4/2(a)	...	...	Bd. of Education—4/U; Public Service Commn.—4/U
Alaska	4/2(b)	4/2	(c)	...	...	...	...	...	...	...	...	
Arizona	4/U		4/U	4/U	4/2	...	...	4/U	...	...	...	Corporation Commn.—6/U; Mine inspector—2/U
Arkansas	2/U	2/U	2/U	2/U	2/U	2/U	(d)	...	...			Land Commr.—2/U
California	4/U	4/U	4/U	4/U	4/U	(d)	4/U	4/U	...	...	...	Bd. of Equalization—4/U
Colorado	4/U	4/U	4/U	4/U	4/U	...	...	...	...			Regents of Univ. of CO—6/U; Bd. of Education—6/U
Connecticut	4/U	4/U	4/U	4/U	4/U	...	4/U	...	...	...	...	
Delaware	4/2(e)	4/U	...	4/U	4/U	4/U	...	...	...	...	4/U	
Florida	4/2	4/U	4/U	4/U	4/U	...	4/U	4/U	4/U	...	(f)	
Georgia	4/2	4/U	4/U	4/U	...	...	4/U	4/U	4/U	4/U	(g)	Public Service Commn.—6/U
Hawaii	4/2	4/2	(c)	...	...	...	...	...	...			Bd. of Education—4/I
Idaho	4/U	4/U	4/U	4/U	4/U	4/U	(h)	4/U	...	...	...	
Illinois	4/U	4/U	4/U	4/U	4/U	...	4/U	...	...	...	...	Bd. of Trustees, Univ. of IL—6/U
Indiana	4/2(i)	4/U	4/2(i)	4/U	4/2(i)	4/2(i)	...	4/U	(c)	...	...	
Iowa	4/I	4/I	4/I	4/I	4/I	4/I	...	...	4/I	...		
Kansas	4/2	4/2	4/U	4/U	4/U	...	...	...	...		4/U	Bd. of Education—4/U
Kentucky	4/O	4/O	4/O	4/O	4/O	4/O	(d)	4/O	4/O	...	...	Railroad Commn.—4/U
Louisiana	4/2	4/U	4/U	4/U	4/U	...	(j)	4/U	4/U	...	4/U	Bd. of Education—4/U; Public Service Commn.—6/U; Elections Commr.—4/U
Maine	4/2		...	...	...	...	...	...	...	...	...	
Maryland	4/2(b)	4/U	...	4/I	...	...	4/U	...	...	...	...	
Massachusetts	4/U	4/U	4/U	4/U	4/U	4/U	...	...	...			Exec. Council—2/U
Michigan	4/U	4/U	4/U	4/U	...	...	...	...	...			Univ. Regents—8/U; Bd. of Education—8/U
Minnesota	4/U	4/U	4/U	4/U	4/U	4/U	...	...				
Mississippi	4/O	4/U	4/U	4/O	4/U	4/U	(h)	4/U	4/U		4/U	Public Service Commn.—4/U; Highway Commn.—4/U
Missouri	4/2(e)	4/U	4/U	4/U	4/2(e)	4/I	...	...	...	...	...	
Montana	4/U	4/U	4/U	4/U	...	4/U	...	4/U	...	...	(h)	Public Service Commn.—4/U
Nebraska	4/2(b)	4/U	4/U	4/U	4/2(k)	4/U	...	...	...	...	...	Regents of Univ. of NE—6/U; Bd. of Education—4/U; Public Service Commn.—6/U

	Governor	Lt. governor	Secretary of state	Attorney general	Treasurer	Auditor	Comptroller	Education	Agriculture	Labor	Insurance	Other
Nevada	4/2	4/U	4/U	4/U	4/U	...	4/U	...	...	...	...	Bd. of Regents—6/U; Bd. of Education—4/3
New Hampshire	2/U		...	...	...	...	...	...	...	...	...	Exec. Council—2/U
New Jersey	4/2		...	...	...	...	...	...	...	...	...	
New Mexico	4/O(l)	4/O(l)	4/O(l)	4/O(l)	4/O(l)	4/O(l)	...	...	...	...	...	Commr. of Public Lands—4/O(l); Bd. of Education—6/U; Corporation Commn.—6/U
New York	4/U	4/U	...	4/U	...	(m)	4/U	...	4/U	4/U	...	
North Carolina	4/2(e)	4/2(e)	4/U	4/U	4/U	4/U	(n)	4/U	4/U	4/U	4/U	
North Dakota	4/U	4/U	4/U	4/U	4/2	4/U	...	4/U	4/U(o)	4/U(o)	4/U	Public Service Commn.—6/U; Tax Commr.—4/U
Ohio	4/2	4/U	4/U	4/U	4/U	4/U	(p)	...	...	...	...	Bd. of Education—6/U
Oklahoma	4/2	4/I	...	4/I	4/I	4/I	...	4/I	...	...	4/U	Corporation Commn.—6/U
Oregon	4/2(i)		4/2(i)	4/U	4/2(i)	(q)	...	4/U	...	4/U	...	
Pennsylvania	4/2	4/2	...	4/2	4/2(r)	4/2	...	...	...	...	...	
Rhode Island	2/U	2/U	2/U	2/U	2/U	...	...	...	...	...	...	
South Carolina	4/2	4/U	4/U	4/U	4/U	...	4/U	4/U	4/U	...	...	Adjutant General—4/U
South Dakota	4/2	4/2	4/U	4/U	4/U	4/U	(h)	...	...	...	...	Commr. of School & Public Lands—4/U; Public Utilities Commn.—6/U
Tennessee	4/2	(s)	...	...	...	(m)	...	...	...	...	...	Public Service Commn.—6/U
Texas	4/U	4/U	...	4/U	4/U	...	4/U	...	4/U	...	...	Commr. of General Land Off.—6/U; Bd. of Education—6/U; Railroad Commn.—6/U
Utah	4/U	4/U	(c)	4/U	4/U	4/U	4/U	...	...	...	...	Bd. of Education—4/U
Vermont	2/U	2/U	2/U	2/U	2/U	2/U	...	...	...	...	...	
Virginia	4/O	4/I	...	4/I	...	...	...	...	...	...	...	
Washington	4/U	4/U	4/U	4/U	4/U	4/U	(p)	4/U	...	...	4/U	Commr. of Public Lands—4/U
West Virginia	4/2		4/U	4/U	4/U	4/U	(h)	...	4/U	...	...	
Wisconsin	4/U	4/U	4/U	4/U	4/U	...	(d)	4/U	...	...	...	
Wyoming	4/U		4/U	...	4/U	4/U	...	4/U	...	...	...	
Dist. of Col.												Mayor—4/I; Chrmn. of Council—4/I
American Samoa	4/2	4/2	...	(j)	...	(j)	...	...	...	...	...	
Guam	4/2(b)	4/U	...	...	...	...	...	...	...	...	(t)	Bd. of Education—4/U; Village Commr.—4/I
No. Mariana	4/3	4/U	...	...	...	...	(d)	...	(u)	...		
Puerto Rico	4/U		...	...	...	...	...	...	...	...	...	
Virgin Islands	4/2(b)	4/U	...	...	...	...	...	...	...	...	(c)	

Note: First entry in a column refers to number of years per term. Entry following the slash refers to the maximum number of consecutive terms allowed. This table reflects a literal reading of the state constitutions and statutes.

Key:

U—No provision specifying number of terms allowed.
O—Provision specifying officeholder may not succeed self.
I—Provision specifying individual may hold office for an unlimited number of terms.
. . .—Position is appointed or elected by governmental entity (not chosen by electorate).
(a) Commissioner of agriculture and industry.
(b) After two consecutive terms, must wait four years before being eligible again.
(c) Lieutenant governor performs function.
(d) Finance administrator performs function.
(e) Absolute two-term limitation, but not necessarily consecutive.
(f) State treasurer also serves as insurance commissioner.
(g) Comptroller general is ex-officio insurance commissioner.
(h) State auditor performs function.
(i) Eligible for eight out of 12 years.

(j) Head of administration services performs function.
(k) After two consecutive terms, must wait two years before being eligible again.
(l) Must wait four years before being eligible to any office, with the exception of the lieutenant governor who is immediately eligible for the office of governor.
(m) Comptroller performs function.
(n) Budget administrator performs function.
(o) Constitution provides for a secretary of agriculture and labor. However, the legislature was given constitutional authority to provide for (and has provided for) a department of labor distinct from agriculture, and a commissioner of labor distinct from the commissioner of agriculture.
(p) State treasurer performs function.
(q) Secretary of state's office performs function.
(r) Treasurer must wait four years before being eligible to the office of auditor general.
(s) Speaker of the senate has the statutory title "Lieutenant Governor."
(t) Taxation administrator performs function.
(u) Natural resources administrator performs function.

Table 18
STATE ADMINISTRATIVE OFFICIALS: METHODS OF SELECTION

State	Governor	Lt. governor	Secretary of state	Attorney general	Treasurer	Adjutant general	Administration	Agriculture	Banking	Budget	Civil rights	Commerce	Community affairs	Comptroller	Consumer affairs	Corrections	Data processing
Alabama	CE	CE	CE	CE	CE	G	...	CE	G	CS	...	G	G	AG	...	G	CS
Alaska	CE	CE	(a-1)	GB	GB	GB	A	A	A	A	G	GB	GB	GB	AT	GB	A
Arizona	CE	...	CE	CE	CE	G	GS	B	GS	G	A	(b)	(c)	(a-19)	(a-3)	GS	AG
Arkansas	CE	CE	CE	CE	CE	G	G	...	AG	AG	...	(e)	G	(a-6)	AT	GS	GS
California	CE	CE	CE	CE	CE	GS	...	GS	GS	(a-19)	G	GS	GS	CE	GS	GS	G
Colorado	CE	CE	CE	CE	CE	G	GS	GS	A	GS	A	A	A	A	AT	GS	A
Connecticut	CE	CE	CE	CE	CE	G	GE	GE	GE	A	B	GE	A	CE	GE	GE	A
Delaware	CE	CE	GS	CE	CE	GS	GS	GS	GS	GS	...	...	AG	L	AG	GS	...
Florida	CE	CE	CE	CE	CE	GS	GS	GS	CE	(a-12)	A	A	(a-1)	GS	CE	A	(a-9)
Georgia	CE	CE	CE	CE	A	G	GS	CE	GS	G	...	B	G	CE	G	GD	A
Hawaii	CE	CE	(a-1)	GS	(a-9)	GS	...	GS	AG	GS	...	GS	(a-30)	GS	G	A	A
Idaho	CE	CE	CE	CE	CE	G	GS	GS	GS	GS	G	BGS	G	(a-10)	(h)	(a-3)	(a-6)
Illinois	CE	CE	CE	CE	CE	G	GS	GS	GS	GS	GS	GS	GS	(a-10)	CE	(a-3)	(a-6)
Indiana	CE	CE	CE	SE	CE	G	G	(a-1)	G	G	G	(a-1)	A	(h)	AT	G	A
Iowa	CE	CE	CE	CE	CE	GS	A	SE	GS	(a-12)	GS	GS	A	GS	AT	GS	CS
Kansas	CE	CE	CE	CE	SE	GS	GS	B	GS	CS	B	GS	A	A	AT	GS	A
Kentucky	CE	CE	CE	CE	CE	G	G	CE	G	(a-19)	B	G	G	G	(a-3)	AG	(a-6)
Louisiana	CE	CE	CE	CE	CE	GS	G	CE	GS	GS	(a-3)	GS	GS	(a-6)	GS	GS	A
Maine	CE	...	CL	CL	CL	G	...	GLS	GLS	AG	B	GS	...	AG	GLS	AG	CS
Maryland	CE	CE	GS	CE	CL	GS	GS	GS	AGS	GS	GS	A	AG	CE	AT	AGS	A
Massachusetts	CE	CE	CE	CE	CE	G	G	G	G	AG	AT	G	G	G	G	G	A
Michigan	CE	CE	CE	CE	GS	GS	GS	B	GS	(a-6)	B	GS	GS	A	(a-4)	B	A
Minnesota	CE	CE	CE	CE	CE	G	GS	GS	BS	(a-19)	GS	GS	A	(a-19)	GS	GS	A
Mississippi	CE	CE	CE	CE	CE	GS	...	SE	GS	B	...	B	(a-30)	(a-31)	AT	B	B
Missouri	CE	CE	CE	CE	CE	GS	GS	GS	AS	A	B	A	A	(a-6)	GS	GS	A
Montana	CE	CE	CE	CE	A	G	GS	A	G	G	A	G	A	(a-6)	G	A	A
Nebraska	CE	CE	CE	CE	CE	G	GS	GS	GS	A	B	GS	A	(a-6)	...	GS	A
Nevada	CE	CE	CE	CE	CE	G	G	G	BG	A	(a-6)	G	G	CE	A	G	A
New Hampshire	CE	...	CL	GC	CL	GC	GC	GC	GC	(a-12)	B	GOC	GOC	GOC	AT	GOC	B
New Jersey	CE	...	GS	GS	GS	GS	...	BG	GS	(a-12)	A	GS	GS	GS	GS	GS	A
New Mexico	CE	CE	CE	CE	CE	GS	(a-21)	BG	GS	G	G	GS	...	(a-4)	AT	A	A
New York	CE	CE	GS	CE	...	G	...	GS	G	G	G	GS	(a-2)	CE	GS	GS	(a-21)
North Carolina	CE	CE	CE	CE	CE	G	G	CE	GS	AG	A	G	...		AT	A	AG
North Dakota	CE	CE	CE	CE	CE	G	A	CE	GS	(q)	(a-26)	G	A	(r)	AT	GS	A
Ohio	CE	CE	CE	CE	CE	G	GS	GS	A	GS	GS	(t)	G	(a-4)	B	GS	A
Oklahoma	CE	CE	GS	CE	CE	GS	...	GS	GS	G	B	G	G	AG	B	B	A
Oregon	CE	...	CE	SE	CE	G	GS	GS	AG	A	CS	GS	A	A	A	AG	A
Pennsylvania	CE	CE	GS	CE	CE	GS	G	GS	GS	G	GS	GS	GS	A	AG	AG	A
Rhode Island	CE	CE	CE	CE	CE	G	GS	A	G	CS	B	GS	GS	A	BS	GS	A
South Carolina	CE	CE	CE	CE	CE	CE	(a-9)	SE	(a-4)	B	B	G	A	CE	B	B	G
South Dakota	CE	CE	CE	CE	CE	GS	G	GS	A	(a-19)	(a-3)	GS	GS	CE	AG	A	(a-6)
Tennessee	CE	(y)	CL	SC	CL	G	G	G	G	A	B	G	(a-10)	CL	A	G	A
Texas	CE	CE	GS	CE	CE	GS	...	SE	BS	G	B	B	GS	(a-10)	CE	AT	B
Utah	CE	CE	(a-1)	CE	CE	G	GS	GS	GS	G	B	GS	(a-10)	(a-19)	AG	BA	AG
Vermont	CE	CE	CE	SE	CE	SL	GS	GS	GS	GS	AT	A	GS	AGS	AT	GS	CS
Virginia	CE	CE	GB	CE	GB	GB	GB	GB	B	GB	...	(a-24)	A	GB	(a-7)	GB	GB
Washington	CE	CE	CE	CE	CE	GS	GS	GS	(aa)	B	GS	GS	(a-10)	(a-4)	AT	GS	B
West Virginia	CE	...	CE	CE	CE	GS	A	CE	GS	(bb)	GS	GS	A	CE	AT	GS	A
Wisconsin	CE	CE	CE	CE	CE	G	GS	B	GS	A	A	(dd)	A	A	(a-7)	A	(a-19)
Wyoming	CE	...	CE	GS	CE	G	G	B	GS	G	...	G	(a-10)	(a-31)	AT	BG	A

Note: The chief administrative officials responsible for each function were determined from information given by the states for the same function as listed in *State Administrative Officials Classified by Function 1983-84,* published by The Council of State Governments.

STATE ADMINISTRATIVE OFFICIALS: METHODS OF SELECTION

State	Disaster preparedness	Education (chief state school officer)	Education—higher	Elections administration	Employment services	Energy resources	Environmental conservation	Finance	Fish & game	General services	Health	Highway patrol	Highways	Historic preservation	Industrial development	Insurance	Labor & industrial relations
Alabama	CS	B	B	(a-2)	A	CS	G	G	(a-27)	(a-19)	B	G	G	B	(a-10)	G	G
Alaska	A	BG	BG	LG	A	...	GB	GB	GB	A	A	A	(a-36)	A	A	A	GB
Arizona	G	CE	B	(a-2)	GS	GS	GS	AG	B	(a-6)	GS	A	(a-36)	B	G	GS	B
Arkansas	AG	BG	BG	SS	G	GS	G	(a-6)	B	...	GS	AG	G	GS	AG	GS	GS
California	GS	CE	B	(a-2)	GS	B	GS	GS	GS	GS	GS	GS	A	G	GS	GS	GS
Colorado	A	B	B	SS	A	G	A	GS	BA	(a-6)	GS	A	GS	GD	A	A	A
Connecticut	GE	GE	B	GE	AG	A	GE	GE	GE	G	GE	GE	A	G	GE	GE	GE
Delaware	AG	B	B	GS	GS	A	G	A	A	(a-6)	AG	A	GS	AG	AG	CE	GS
Florida	A	CE	B	SS	A	A	GS	A	GS	GOC	A	G	(a-36)	A	A	(a-4)	A
Georgia	(a-5)	CE	B	SS	A	A	A	A	A	A	A	BG	BG	A	A	GD	CE
Hawaii	A	B	B	LG	A	A	AG	(a-9)	AB	(a-12)	GS	...	AG	B	(a-30)	AG	GS
Idaho	A	CE	BGS	(a-2)	GS	G	GS	G	GS	(a-6)	A	A	(a-36)	B	(a-10)	GS	GS
Illinois	GS	B	B	(i)	...	GS	GS	(a-12)	A	(a-6)	GS	GS	(a-36)	(a-20)	(a-10)	GS	(j)
Indiana	GC	SE	B	B	G	G	(k)	(a-9)	A	(a-6)	G	G	G	B	LG	G	G
Iowa	A	GS	GS	SS	GS	GS	GS	A	(a-18)	GS	GS	GS	A	B	GS	GS	GS
Kansas	A	B	B	(a-2)	GS	GS	A	(a-6)	B	(a-6)	GS	GS	A	B	A	SE	GS
Kentucky	G	CE	B	(a-2)	(a-29)	G	G	G	B	(a-19)	AG	GS	G	GS	(a-10)	G	G
Louisiana	GS	CE	B	CE	GS	GS	GS	(a-6)	GS	(a-6)	GS	GS	G	GS	(a-10)	CE	GS
Maine	AG	GLS	GLS	(a-2)	GLS	G	GLS	GLS	GLS	(a-19)	A	AG	(a-36)	B	G	GLS	A
Maryland	G	B	B	G	AG	A	AG	(a-12)	G	GS	GS	GS	AG	A	AG	GS	GS
Massachusetts	G	B	B	SS	G	G	G	(a-6)	G	(a-33)	G	G	G	...	(a-10)	G	G
Michigan	A	B	CS	A	B	G	A	(a-6)	(a-27)	(a-6)	GS	GS	(a-36)	CS	CS	GS	GS
Minnesota	G	BG	GS	SS	GS	GS	GS	GS	A	(a-6)	GS	(m)	A	B	(a-11)	BS	GS
Mississippi	G	CE	B	(a-2)	G	G	B	...	B	B	B	GS	SE	B	(a-10)	SE	...
Missouri	GS	B	B	SS	A	A	A	(a-6)	B	(a-6)	A	GS	B	(a-28)	(a-10)	AS	GS
Montana	A	CE	GS	SS	A	G	A	...	GS	(a-6)	GS	AT	GS	B	(a-11)	A	GS
Nebraska	A	B	B	(a-2)	A	GS	GS	(n)	B	(a-6)	GS	G	GS	A	GS	A	GS
Nevada	G	B	B	(a-2)	G	...	A	(a-12)	A	(a-33)	A	A	(a-36)	A	A	A	G
New Hampshire	G	B	A	(a-2)	GC	G	...	(a-12)	B	AGC	GC	GC	GC	GC	(a-27)	GC	GC
New Jersey	A	GS	BG	A	A	GS	GS	(a-4)	AGC	A	GS	GS	(a-36)	A	...	GS	GS
New Mexico	A	B	(a-15)	SS	GS	GS	A	GS	A	GS	GS	GD	GS	A	A	B	GS
New York	(a-5)	B	(a-15)	A	A	GS	G	(a-12)	(a-18)	GS	GS	GS	(a-36)	(a-28)	(a-10)	GS	GS
North Carolina	G	CE	BG	G	G	AG	A	A	A	A	G	G	AG	G	A	CE	CE
North Dakota	A	CE	B	(a-2)	G	(a-11)	A	(a-9)	G	GS	G	G	G	B	(a-10)	CE	SE
Ohio	AG	B	BG	(a-2)	GS	GS	GS	(a-6)	A	(a-6)	GS	AG	(a-36)	(g)	A	GS	GS
Oklahoma	GS	CE	B	L	B	B	B	G	AB	A	B	GS	(a-36)	B	(a-10)	CE	GS
Oregon	CS	CE	B	SS	AG	GS	B	(a-6)	B	GS	AG	GS	AB	A	A	AG	SE
Pennsylvania	B	GS	AG	G	CS	GS	(a-27)	GS	(u)	GS	GS	GS	(a-36)	BG	(a-10)	GS	GS
Rhode Island	(a-5)	B	B	B	G	G	GS	G	B	A	GB	G	(a-36)	B	(a-10)	G	G
South Carolina	A	CE	B	B	B	...	AG	(a-9)	B	AG	B	B	B	B	(a-10)	B	GS
South Dakota	A	GS	B	(a-2)	A	...	A	A	G	(a-6)	GS	AG	A	GS	(a-11)	A	GS
Tennessee	A	G	B	SS	G	BG	A	(a-6)	B	G	G	A	(a-36)	AB	(a-10)	G	G
Texas	G	BS	B	(a-2)	B	...	...	B	B	B	B	B	B	B	B	B	G
Utah	BG	B	B	(a-1)	AG	A	B	AG	BA	(a-6)	GS	AG	(a-36)	AB	A	GS	GS
Vermont	G	BG	...	(a-2)	GS	G	GS	AGS	AS	...	GS	...	GS	A	(a-10)	(a-8)	GS
Virginia	GB	GB	GB	GB	GB	(a-14)	GB	...	B	GB	GB	GB	GB	GB	GB	(a-32)	GB
Washington	GS	CE	B	SS	GS	GS	GS	(a-9)	B	(a-6)	A	GS	(a-36)	GS	A	SE	GS
West Virginia	G	B	B	(a-2)	(cc)	B	B	GS	A	CS	GS	GS	A	A	A	GS	GS
Wisconsin	GS	CE	BG	BA	A	A	A	A	A	A	GS	GS	A	G	(a-1)	GS	GS
Wyoming	G	CE	G	(a-2)	G	G	G	(a-31)	G	(a-6)	G	AB	B	(a-28)	(a-10)	B	GS

STATE ADMINISTRATIVE OFFICIALS: METHODS OF SELECTION

State	Licensing	Mental health	Natural resources	Parks & recreation	Personnel	Planning	Post audit	Pre audit	Public library	Public utility regulation	Purchasing	Social services	Solid waste	Taxation	Tourism	Transportation	Welfare
Alabama	...	B	G	G	B	...	L	(a-12)	B	SE	CS	G	A	G	G	G	(a-34)
Alaska	A	A	GB	A	A	G	L	A	A	GB	A	(a-22)	GB	(a-19)	A	GB	AG
Arizona	(d)	A	GS	B	AG	(c)	L	AG	B	CE	AG	GS	(a-18)	GS	GS	GS	GS
Arkansas	...	AG	GS	GS	AG	...	L	A	B	GS	AG	AG	AG	AG	AG	(a-23)	G
California	(a-13)	GS	GS	GS	G	G	(a-19)	(a-12)	GS	GS	GS	GS	(f)	BS	G	GS	(a-34)
Colorado	GS	A	GS	BA	GS	A	ACB	(a-12)	A	GS	A	GS	A	GS	(a-10)	...	(a-34)
Connecticut	G	GE	G	CS	A	A	L	(a-12)	B	GS	A	GE	CS	GE	CS	GE	GE
Delaware	AG	AG	AG	AG	GS	...	CE	(a-31)	AG	GS	AG	AG	(g)	AG	AG	GS	GS
Florida	GS	A	GOC	A	A	(a-9)	L	A	A	G	A	A	GS	GOC	A	GS	A
Georgia	SS	BG	G	A	GD	A	SL	(a-31)	A	CE	A	A	A	GS	A	B	(a-34)
Hawaii	GS	A	GS	AB	GS	GS	A	A	B	GS	A	GS	(a-18)	GS	A	GS	A
Idaho	G	A	...	GS	BGS	(a-10)	L	CE	B	GS	A	GS	A	GS	(a-10)	BGS	GB
Illinois	GS	GS	(a-17)	(a-20)	(a-6)	...	L	(a-12)	...	G	(a-6)	A	...	GS	(a-10)	GS	GS
Indiana	...	G	G	A	G	LG	G	CE	B	G	(a-6)	G	A	G	(a-24)	G	(a-6)
Iowa	...	A	(a-18)	GD	BG	G	CE	...	...	(a-10)	CS	GB	(a-18)	GS	GS	GD	A
Kansas	...	AS	AG	BG	A	(a-9)	L	(a-12)	GS	GS	A	GS	(a-27)	GS	A	GS	GS
Kentucky	G	G	(a-18)	G	G	(a-6)	CE	AG	G	G	A	AG	AG	G	G	G	AG
Louisiana	...	GS	GS	GS	B	GS	(a-9)	(a-9)	B	CE	(a-6)	GS	(a-18)	GS	GS	GS	GS
Maine	A	AG	GLS	B	GLS	G	SL	(a-12)	BG	GS	AGS	GLS	(a-18)	AG	(a-10)	GLS	(a-34)
Maryland	GS	A	GS	A	GS	GS	ASH	A	A	GS	CS	AG	A	(a-12)	G	GS	(a-34)
Massachusetts	G	G	G	A	A	(a-11)	CE	(a-12)	A	G	A	G	A	G	A	G	G
Michigan	GS	GS	B	CS	CS	...	CL	(a-31)	...	GS	CS	GS	(a-18)	(l)	CS	GS	(a-34)
Minnesota	(a-26)	GS	GS	A	GS	G	CE	GS	A	GS	A	GS	A	GS	A	GS	GS
Mississippi	...	GS	B	AB	G	G	CE	(a-31)	B	SE	A	B	A	GS	A	(a-17)	(a-34)
Missouri	A	B	GS	A	A	(a-9)	CE	A	B	GS	A	GS	A	GS	B	(a-23)	A
Montana	A	GS	GS	A	AG	(a-11)	L	...	B	SE	A	GS	A	GS	A	B	(a-34)
Nebraska	A	A	B	(a-20)	GS	G	CE	(a-6)	B	CE	A	A	A	GS	A	(a-23)	GS
Nevada	...	A	G	A	A	...	L	(a-6)	G	G	A	G	(a-18)	G	GC	B	A
New Hampshire	...	GC	GC	GC	BGC	(a-11)	L	(a-12)	B	GC	AGC	GC	A	GC	A	(a-23)	(a-34)
New Jersey	A	A	GS	A	A	...	L	(a-12)	A	GS	A	GS	A	GS	A	GS	AB
New Mexico	G	B	GS	A	G	...	CE	A	A	GS	GS	G	(a-18)	G	A	GS	(a-34)
New York	(a-2)	GS	(a-18)	G	(o)	(p)	(a-12)	(a-12)	...	GS	(a-21)	GS	(a-18)	GS	G	GS	(a-34)
North Carolina	...	G	G	G	AG	...	CE	(a-31)	G	GB	AG	G	G	G	A	G	(a-34)
North Dakota	...	A	...	G	AB	A	(s)	(q)	A	CE	A	G	A	CE	B	A	(a-34)
Ohio	...	GS	(a-1)	A	A	A	CE	(a-31)	B	GS	A	GS	GS	GS	A	GS	GS
Oklahoma	...	A	GS	A	B	...	CE	(a-19)	B	CE	A	GS	A	GS	(a-28)	B	(a-34)
Oregon	(a-10)	AG	G	AB	A	...	A	...	B	G	A	GS	A	GS	A	BS	AG
Pennsylvania	G	(v)	GS	CS	AG	G	CE	(a-4)	A	GS	(a-21)	(w)	CS	(a-19)	(a-10)	GS	A
Rhode Island	G	GS	(a-18)	A	GS	CS	A	(a-12)	GS	GS	CS	GS	B	CS	A	GS	A
South Carolina	(x)	B	...	B	B	...	B	(a-12)	B	L	B	B	B	GS	A	(a-23)	(a-34)
South Dakota	...	A	GS	GS	GS	G	L	...	B	SE	A	GS	GS	GS	A	GS	AG
Tennessee	...	G	G	A	G	G	(a-12)	A	A	SE	A	A	G	G	G	G	G
Texas	...	B	...	(a-20)	...	...	L	(a-12)	B	GS	(a-21)	BS	A	(a-12)	B	(a-23)	(a-34)
Utah	AG	AB	GS	BA	AG	G	CE	(a-19)	AB	GS	AG	GS	...	GS	AB	GS	GS
Vermont	(a-2)	GS	GS	A	GS	G	CE	(a-19)	G	GS	G	GS	A	GS	A	GS	GS
Virginia	GB	GB	GB	A	GB	(a-9)	GB	(a-12)	GB	L	A	GB	(z)	GB	A	GB	(a-34)
Washington	GS	A	CE	B	G	(a-9)	CE	...	B	GS	(a-6)	(a-22)	A	GS	A	B	(a-22)
West Virginia	...	A	GS	A	(a-6)	(a-10)	CE	(a-19)	B	GS	A	A	B	GS	A	A	GS
Wisconsin	GS	A	B	A	GS	A	L	A	A	GS	A	(a-22)	A	GS	A	GS	(a-22)
Wyoming	...	A	...	G	G	G	CE	(a-31)	B	GS	A	G	G	G	A	...	(a-34)

Key:
... —No specific chief administrative official or agency in charge of function.
CL —Constitutional, elected by legislature
SE —Statutory, elected
SL —Statutory, elected by legislature
L —Selected by legislature or one of its organs
SC —Statutory, elected by state supreme court

Appointed by:		Approved by:
G	—Governor	
GS	—Governor	Senate
GB	—Governor	Both houses
GE	—Governor	Either house
GC	—Governor	Council
GD	—Governor	Departmental board
GLS	—Governor	Appropriate legislative committee & senate
GLG	—Governor & Lt. governor	
GOC	—Governor & council or cabinet	
LG	—Lieutenant governor	
AT	—Attorney general	
SS	—Secretary of state	

Appointed by:		Approved by:
AT	—Attorney general	
A	—Agency head	
AB	—Agency head	Board
AG	—Agency head	Governor
AGC	—Agency head	Governor & council
AS	—Agency head	Senate
ALS	—Agency head	Appropriate legislative committee & senate
AGS	—Agency head	Governor & senate
ASH	—Agency head	Senate president & house speaker
B	—Board or commission	
BG	—Board	Governor
BGC	—Board	Governor & council
BGS	—Board	Governor & senate
BS	—Board or commission	Senate
BA	—Board or commission	Agency head
CS	—Civil Service	
ACB	—Nominated by audit committee	Both houses

(a) Chief administrative official or agency in charge of function:
(a-1) Lieutenant Governor
(a-2) Secretary of State
(a-3) Attorney General
(a-4) Treasurer
(a-5) Adjutant General
(a-6) Administration
(a-7) Agriculture
(a-8) Banking
(a-9) Budget
(a-10) Commerce
(a-11) Community Affairs
(a-12) Comptroller
(a-13) Consumer Affairs
(a-14) Disaster Preparedness
(a-15) Education (chief state school officer)
(a-16) Employment Services
(a-17) Energy Resources
(a-18) Environmental Conservation
(a-19) Finance
(a-20) Fish and Game
(a-21) General Services
(a-22) Health
(a-23) Highways
(a-24) Industrial Development
(a-25) Insurance
(a-26) Labor and Industrial Relations
(a-27) Natural Resources
(a-28) Parks and Recreation
(a-29) Personnel
(a-30) Planning
(a-31) Post Audit
(a-32) Public Utility Regulation
(a-33) Purchasing
(a-34) Social Services
(a-35) Taxation
(a-36) Transportation

(b) Responsibilities shared by Director of the Development Division within the Office of Economic Planning and Development and chief administrative official listed under Industrial Development.
(c) Responsibilities shared by Director of the Planning Division within the Office of Economic Planning and Development and Director of the Development Division within the same office, listed under Commerce. The Director of the Planning Division is also responsible for the function Planning.
(d) Numerous boards and commissions responsible for function.
(e) Responsibilities shared by the chief administrative officials listed under the following functions: Industrial Development and Tourism.
(f) Solid Waste Management Board is composed of nine voting members: seven appointed by the governor subject to Senate confirmation; one each appointed by the speaker of the Assembly and the Senate Committee on Rules.
(g) Not a state employee.
(h) See entry under Pre-Audit.
(i) Function performed by eight-member board (GS). Four members are nominated by governor and four are nominated by highest ranking constitutional officer of the political party opposite that of the governor. Executive director of the board is chosen by the board.
(j) Due to reorganization, beginning July 1984 the responsibilities for this function will be shared by the chairperson of the Illinois Educational Labor Relations Board, the chairperson of the Illinois Labor Relations Board, and the Director of the Department of Labor.
(k) Responsibilities shared by chief administrative officials listed under the following functions: Health and Natural Resources.
(l) Responsibilities shared by Deputy Treasurer of the Bureau of Collections within the Department of Treasury, and Director of Local Government Services within the same department.
(m) Responsibilities shared by Commissioner of the Department of Public Safety, and Chief of State Patrol Division within the same department.
(n) Responsibilities shared by the following administrative officials: Director of Accounting Division within the Department of Administrative Services; State Budget Administrator of the Budget Division within the same department, listed under Budget; Auditor of Public Accounts, listed under Post Audit; and State Tax Commissioner of the Department of Revenue, listed under Taxation.
(o) Responsibilities shared by Director of Employee Relations, and President of the Civil Service Commission.
(p) No central planning agency. Responsibilities shared among the Departments of Commerce, State and Transportation, the State Energy Office, and the Tri-State Regional Planning Commission.
(q) Responsibilities shared by Director of the Office of Management and Budget and Executive Budget Analyst of the same office. The Director of Management and Budget is also responsible for the function Pre-Audit.
(r) Responsibilities shared by chief administrative officials listed under Budget and by the Director of the Accounting Operations Office.
(s) Responsibilities shared by the legislative budget analyst and auditor (L) and the state auditor (CE).
(t) Responsibilities shared by Director of Department of Development and Director of Department of Commerce.
(u) Responsibilities shared by Executive Director of the Fish Commission and Executive Director of the Game Commission.
(v) Federal government employee.
(w) Responsibilities shared by the Director of Blindness and Visual Services within the Department of Public Welfare, and the Director of Children and Youth Services within the same department.
(x) Each profession has its own licensing board.
(y) Speaker of the Senate has the statutory title of lieutenant governor and is elected by the Senate from among its membership.
(z) Solid Waste Commission is composed of 15 members: four appointed by the speaker (from among the delegates); two appointed by the Senate; and nine appointed by the governor (with the chairman selected from the group).
(aa) Responsibilities shared by Supervisor of Banking and Supervisor of Savings and Loan.
(bb) Responsibilities shared by Commissioner of the Department of Finance and Administration, listed under Finance, and the Budget Division Director within the same department.
(cc) Responsibilities shared by Commissioner of the Department of Employment Security and Director of the Employment Services Division within the same department.

A Note on Use

Symbols: Unless otherwise noted, all tables in *The Book of the States* use the following scheme:

   . . .—no data

   blank cell—not applicable

   0—zero quantity.

Sources: Unless otherwise noted, the sources of data for tables are surveys and research by The Council of State Governments.

Section III THE LEGISLATURES

THE STATE LEGISLATURES

By William T. Pound

American state legislatures have become the focus of increased attention during the past two decades. The process of legislative reform and revitalization which characterized the years following the U.S. Supreme Court decisions on legislative districting (*Baker v. Carr, 1963* and *Reynolds v. Sims, 1965*) had major impact on the structure and operations of most state legislatures. This process of reform slowed between 1977 and 1983, and change took on a somewhat different character. This can be seen in the consolidation and integration of the reforms of the previous period and was influenced by the changing relationships between governors and legislatures and between levels of government in the American federal system.

The initial period of change and reform in state legislatures was characterized by modification of constitutional restrictions and expansion of institutional resources. The modification or removal of constitutional restrictions resulted from a variety of factors, many of which began before the legislative reapportionment decisions. On both the national and state levels, citizen groups had evaluated the legislative process and recommended improvement and modernization. Legislatures themselves sought an increased role in order to become a more effective part of expanded state governments.

Restrictions on legislative sessions were among the earliest areas of change. At the beginning of World War II, only four states held annual legislative sessions. By 1970, a majority of the state legislatures were meeting annually, and in 1984 only seven state constitutions still restrict the legislature to biennial sessions. Legislative sessions not only became more frequent, but longer, as the limitations on the number of days per year a legislature could meet were relaxed in many states. However, the movement toward expanded session length has slowed, if not been reversed, in recent years. There has been no constitutional change formally expanding legislative session time since 1979, when Washington adopted annual sessions.

Legislatures in several states have recently attempted to limit the time spent in session by either legislative rule or statute. Arizona and Iowa, both with constitutionally unlimited sessions, established session ending dates and adhered closely to them. North Dakota, whose constitutional session limit was expanded from 60 to 80 days in the late 1970s, has yet to use all its session days in a biennium. Colorado removed in 1982 the constitutional provision that limited the legislative agenda during the second year of the biennium to budget issues or items referred by the governor, but adopted a second-year session limitation of 140 days. Washington included session limitations when it moved from biennial to annual sessions in 1981. Attempts to further limit legislative sessions are currently underway in several states, either through legislative action or the initiative process.

All of the legislatures mentioned above and several others have developed extensive deadline and scheduling systems to facilitate workflow. Cut-off dates for bill introduction, in some cases limits placed on the number of bills an individual legislator may introduce, and committee hearing and floor action deadlines all demonstrate the legislative desire to use time more efficiently.

Placing limits on session length and activity is part of a larger concern about whether legislatures should be full time or part time. In many states, session limits have been adopted or maintained as a way to preserve the legislature as a body in which the predominant occupation of the members is not that of legislator, but some other vocation. On the other hand, several states have acceded to the increasing demands on state government and legislative activity by adopting a session schedule that extends throughout the year and by providing a commensurate level of compensation and support for legislators. The general tests of a full-time legislature are time in session, level of compensation and occupational self-definition of the members. The legislatures of California, Illinois, Massachusetts, Michigan, New Jersey, New York, Ohio, Pennsylvania and Wisconsin have long sessions, relatively high legislator salaries and many members who consider their occupation to be primarily that of legislator. However, several of the medium-size states

William T. Pound is Director of State Services for the National Conference of State Legislatures, Denver, Colorado.

actually spend as many days in session as do the largest states.

The argument as to time spent in session and the appropriate function of legislative bodies is a continuing one. In recent years, many legislators have struggled to find accommodation between the demands of the legislature, with its increased emphasis on program oversight and legislative budget activity, and the preservation of the individual legislator as other than a full-time governmental official. Even in those states with very limited sessions, the demands on legislative leadership require major commitments of time. Also, many legislatures have expanded their interim activity, and a majority now maintain their regular standing committees during the interim.

Effective use of the legislative interim period can contribute to the effectiveness of limited sessions. The Florida legislature, with 60-day annual sessions, extensively uses the interim, as do a number of other states that schedule committee weeks or weekends.

The past 20 years have seen constitutional restrictions on legislatures modified in other ways. Only six states still limit legislative consideration of issues that are not budget or fiscal (Connecticut, Indiana, Maine, New Mexico, Utah and Wyoming). Several legislatures (Kansas, Illinois, Virginia and Wisconsin) now regularly hold veto sessions to consider bills vetoed by the governor. States which had gone decades without the legislative override of a gubernatorial veto now consider and accomplish such overrides regularly.

Other reflections of the reduction in constitutional restrictions and the changing operating environment of state legislatures are found in the ability of 29 legislatures to call themselves into special session, the increased frequency with which special sessions have been held, and the emerging practice in some states without constitutionally limited sessions of the legislature not adjourning *sine die*, but recessing subject to the call of the leadership. This latter practice allows the legislature to act at any time and respond immediately to changing situations, rather than forfeiting interim authority entirely to the executive branch.

The budgetary problems which characterized state government in 1981-83 contributed to the increased number of special sessions and the practice of maintaining the legislature's ability to take formal, immediate action during the interim. States found it necessary to adjust revenue estimates, reduce budgets and increase taxes several times during a year. Legislatures are increasingly reluctant to cede the authority to make such budget adjustments and their consequent policy implications to the governor and administrators. This is particularly true in states with a legislature controlled by one party and a governor from the opposite party. The number of special legislative sessions in 1981-83 was greater than in any recent year, with at least 36 states having one or more special sessions during this three-year period. State fiscal problems and reapportionment were the primary subjects of these special sessions.

Legislative compensation provisions have gradually been made more flexible. Many states have made legislator compensation a provision of statutory law rather than rigid constitutional definition. There is an observable trend toward more frequent adjustments in legislative salaries, caused by the advent of compensation commissions and the tying of legislator salaries to those of other public officials or state employees. The result is fairer compensation for state legislators.

Wide disparities, however, still exist in legislative salaries, which range from the $200 per biennium paid in New Hampshire to $93,600 per biennium paid in Alaska. Biennial salaries in 15 states are still less than $10,000, while 11 states pay more than $40,000 every two years. In addition to salary, most state legislators receive expense payments which may reflect actual expenses or be a legally specified per diem. The variation in legislative practices in this area makes it difficult to accurately determine or compare the total level of legislator compensation.

The expansion of institutional resources which accompanied legislative modernization is still taking place. This can be seen primarily in increased legislative staff and greater staff specialization, improved and expanded facilities, and greater informational resources.

Permanent legislative research and library reference staff began to develop in the early 20th century. Legislative staff in the early years were part-time, few in number, and dedicated to the recording and administration of the legislative process. The office of the legislative clerk and secretary can be traced to our English parliamentary heritage. (The American Society of Legislative Clerks and Secretaries was the first legislative staff group to develop a professional organization and remains among the most active in training and professional development.)

The legislative council movement began in Kansas in 1933 and had been adopted in a majority of states by the mid-1960s. The legislative council was the method by which legislatures organized during the interim period when not in formal session. Legislative councils directed the interim study committees of the legislature and became the vehicle for the development of a permanent research staff. Permanent staff for bill drafting and legal services had also begun to appear in the early years of this century. Research and legal services staff developed as separate staff units in some states and under the umbrella of a single staff agency, usually called a legislative council or services agency, in others. By the 1950s, several states had begun to build their own fiscal and budget staffs rather than relying solely on executive budget assistance. This trend toward independent budget analysis and information had reached all 50 states by 1975. Post audit and program evaluation had also become important legislative functions in a majority of states by the late 1970s, with such agencies often characterized by large professional staffs. By the 1980s, American state legislatures had more than 16,000 full-time employees, with an additional part-time complement of about 9,000.

Several features characterize the changing nature of legislative staffing. Recent growth had been in personal staff to legislators. Since 1970, legislative councils have been gradually disbanded in favor of more decentralized and specialized staff arrangements, most recently in Louisiana and Oklahoma. Until the 1960s, legislative staff tended to be centralized in agencies which worked for the entire legislature. More recent patterns show increasing decentralization and specialization, with the growth of staff who respond to individual legislators, or one house or committee of the legislature, rather than the institution as a whole. California, Florida, Pennsylvania and New York provide examples.

During recent years, there has also been a growth in partisan staff. Until the 1960s, nearly all permanent legislative staff were nonpartisan, but with the increase in leadership staff, staff who work for caucuses, and the partisan staffing of committees in some states, there are now several states with sizeable partisan staff, including New York, New Jersey, Pennsylvania, Michigan, Illinois, Minnesota, California and Washington.

Accompanying this staff expansion has been an improvement in legislative facilities in most states. In a majority of states, legislators now are provided office space, and no longer have to depend solely on their desks on the floor of the legislature. Several states have built legislative office buildings to house legislators and their expanded staffs. Modern, functional space for committees is frequently found in these facilities or in the many state capitol buildings which have been modernized and restored in the past decade. These new facilities affect the legislature in several ways: the public has better access to legislators and the work of the legislative process, and the legislature works under much better conditions, but the interaction among legislators may suffer.

An institutional sense that accompanied the centralized, more confined working conditions of earlier years is no longer as strong in today's more decentralized working environment where legislators no longer spend as much time with each other. There is greater emphasis on the individual legislator, who has greater resources at his command. Reapportionment and the increasing time spent in session have also affected the character of the legislature in many states. Most legislative bodies today have fewer lawyers than at any recent time and greater representations of persons who are "government professionals." Considerable differences exist between a state legislature which has a very limited session, spends five or six days a week in session, and meets in a capitol city whose location requires most of the members to reside during the session away from their homes, and a legislature which meets throughout the year, spends only two or three days per week in session, and is heavily populated with members who commute daily from their homes.

The expansion of information resources and systems available to legislatures has also had considerable impact on the legislative process. The legislative process, with its emphasis on record keeping and information handling, is a natural area for computerization. Legislatures began to use computers in the 1960s, primarily for bill drafting and statutory retrieval tasks. Most legislatures relied on centralized data processing systems operated by the executive branch. Bill status tracking soon became a second major area of legislative computerization.

With the advent of microcomputers and sophisticated word processing systems, state legislatures entered a new era of computerization. A number of states have undertaken extensive studies of their information needs and developed legislative computer systems. Among these are word processing systems which allow faster, more efficient, and less expensive production of legislative journals, modern bill drafting and status systems, and very detailed fiscal analysis and tracking systems. Washington, Colorado and Louisiana developed systems that effectively monitor in detail governmental expenditures, and Michigan has pioneered sophisticated fiscal analysis programs.

These legislative information systems bring much more information to the legislature, and in most cases, make it available more widely within the legislature. Individual legislators and legislative committees are now able to demand and analyze much more information about government programs and activities. Where word processing is available to individual legislators, it improves ability to communicate with constituents and the ways and frequency with which such communication takes place. Several legislatures now provide computer terminals in the office of every legislator. Such developments contribute to the independence of the individual legislator and the decentralization of the legislative process.

Even with this modernization and institutional reform of state legislatures and the consequent expansion of legislative activity in many areas, legislatures still spend no more than half of one percent of state general fund expenditures on their own operations.

Several trends are discernible in legislatures. One is a greater assertion of legislative authority in such areas as budgeting, program oversight and review of administrative rules. As noted previously, the tools and capacity of legislatures in the field of fiscal analysis have improved dramatically. This has led many legislatures to take more active roles in budget development, expenditure oversight and revenue estimation.

Legislatures, since the mid-1970s, have become actively involved in the review and approval of federal funds. Federal aid has comprised approximately 25 percent of state budgets. The decision to accept federal aid programs and the manner in which they are used often commit a state to a specific future course of action and budgets. A majority of states now require that all federal funds be reviewed and appropriated through the normal legislative budget process. This has restricted executive discretion in some program areas and has met with resistance from governors in many states. There has been considerable litigation between the legislature and the executive over the authority to review federal aid funds to the states, with mixed results. Courts have held that the U.S. Constitution does not preclude such legislative review, but some state constitutions have been interpreted as prohibit-

ing such appropriation. The development under the Reagan administration of federal block grant programs with the wider discretion allowed states has had a mixed legislative response. A few legislatures have been heavily involved in detailed block grant review, while others have deferred to the executive. Decisions on federal programs and fund applications in the states will continue to be an area of legislative-executive confrontation in many states.

The legislative budget process has been strengthened in almost every state. Legislative budget power ranges on the one extreme from the limited power to review and make reductions in the executive budget in Maryland, to actual legislative development of the state budget in Colorado, New Mexico and Texas. In many states, legislatures have attempted to involve more legislators in budget decisions, either through expanding the size of appropriations committees or by bringing other standing committees into the appropriations process.

The past biennium has seen more emphasis on fiscal issues than in any recent period, due to falling state revenues, reduced federal aid, and increasing demand by many groups for services from state government to replace federal reductions. Many states found that the issue of annual or biennial budget cycles had little meaning at a time when major budget adjustments were required every few months. A majority of legislatures enacted significant tax increases during the last three years to respond to their fiscal situation. These included increases in gasoline and excise taxes and increases in the major tax sources of income and sales. In 1984, the state budget situation appeared to have stabilized, and several legislatures were removing temporary taxes and rebating surpluses to taxpayers.

Program evaluation has been used effectively by many legislatures, which adopted several ways of integrating program evaluation into the legislative process. Connecticut, Mississippi, New York and Virginia have separate staff agencies for program evaluation. Other states have placed this function in an existing legislative audit agency, fiscal or research staff. Program evaluation seems to be most effective when closely tied to the budget process or standing committee review.

Sunset review, which places a termination date on programs or agencies and requires their specific reauthorization by the legislature, has had very mixed results. Legislatures have had great difficulty applying sunset to programs or agencies with vocal supporters. Some legislatures have felt that the time and effort expended on sunset have had relatively little effect on state government. However, if sunset has created a greater understanding and use of program evaluation in legislatures, it will have had a positive effect.

The most rapidly growing area of legislative oversight is the review of administrative rules. Forty-one states have established some type of rules review process. These vary widely in their procedures and authority: rules review may be comprehensive or selective; it may be done through a special committee or regular standing committees; it may be advisory or binding; suspension or veto of proposed rules may be by resolution or may require a bill; and such power may be vested in a committee or exercised only by the full legislature. A 1983 U.S. Supreme Court decision in the *Chadha* case, holding the legislative veto exercised by Congress to be unconstitutional as a violation of separation of powers, casts doubt on state legislative activity in this area. Several state constitutional challenges to legislative rules review as a violation of separation of powers have had similar results, but not all such challenges have been successful. It appears that legislative review of administrative rules may have its greatest success when done on an advisory basis backed up by the power of the legislature to amend the law if compliance is not forthcoming.

The most recent biennium, though characterized by fiscal problems and fewer legislative structural and procedural changes than in recent periods, did have other developments. The number of state legislators was 7,438 in 1983-84 and will be 7,461 in 1984-85, as the Maine Senate and both houses of the Idaho Legislature are increased in size. Maine, Idaho, Nevada, New York, North Dakota and Wyoming increased the size of one or both houses to facilitate reapportionment. The Illinois House was reduced by 59 members with the 1982 election, as the result of citizen initiative.

Democrats gained strength in state legislatures at the 1982 election, reversing a trend of gradual Republican gains since 1976. Approximately two-thirds of state legislators are elected as Democrats. The Virginia House held elections in three consecutive years and the Alabama Legislature in two to comply with judicial orders on redistricting. In January 1984, voter recall of two Michigan state senators and subsequent election of opposition party candidates to their vacant seats changed control of the Michigan Senate from Democratic to Republican. Democrats have a majority in both houses in 33 states. Republicans in 11, with five split between the two parties. The Nebraska Unicameral is elected on a nonpartisan basis. There were nearly 1,000 women and more than 300 blacks serving in state legislatures in 1983-84.

The biennium can be seen as one of increased legislative-executive conflict, consistent with trends of recent years and the growing assertions of legislative power which are a natural growth of the legislative modernization movement. Within legislatures, there is a growing tendency toward more independence by the individual legislator, greater strength and activity in legislative committees, and a consequent increase in the power of committee chairmen in some states. These trends indicate a decline in the power of legislative leadership.

Table 1
NAMES OF STATE LEGISLATIVE BODIES AND CONVENING PLACE

State or other jurisdiction	Both bodies	Upper house	Lower house	Convening place
Alabama	Legislature	Senate	House of Representatives	State Capitol
Alaska	Legislature	Senate	House of Representatives	State Capitol
Arizona	Legislature	Senate	House of Representatives	State Capitol(a)
Arkansas	General Assembly	Senate	House of Representatives	State Capitol
California	Legislature	Senate	Assembly	State Capitol
Colorado	General Assembly	Senate	House of Representatives	State Capitol
Connecticut	General Assembly	Senate	House of Representatives	State Capitol
Delaware	General Assembly	Senate	House of Representatives	Legislative Hall
Florida	Legislature	Senate	House of Representatives	State Capitol(b)
Georgia	General Assembly	Senate	House of Representatives	State Capitol
Hawaii	Legislature	Senate	House of Representatives	State Capitol
Idaho	Legislature	Senate	House of Representatives	State Capitol
Illinois	General Assembly	Senate	House of Representatives	State House
Indiana	General Assembly	Senate	House of Representatives	State House/State Capitol
Iowa	General Assembly	Senate	House of Representatives	State Capitol
Kansas	Legislature	Senate	House of Representatives	State House
Kentucky	General Assembly	Senate	House of Representatives	State Capitol
Louisiana	Legislature	Senate	House of Representatives	State Capitol
Maine	Legislature	Senate	House of Representatives	State House
Maryland	General Assembly	Senate	House of Delegates	State House
Massachusetts	General Court	Senate	House of Representatives	State House
Michigan	Legislature	Senate	House of Representatives	State Capitol
Minnesota	Legislature	Senate	House of Representatives	State Capitol
Mississippi	Legislature	Senate	House of Representatives	New Capitol(c)
Missouri	General Assembly	Senate	House of Representatives	State Capitol
Montana	Legislature	Senate	House of Representatives	State Capitol
Nebraska	Legislature	(d)		State Capitol
Nevada	Legislature	Senate	Assembly	Legislative Building
New Hampshire	General Court	Senate	House of Representatives	State House
New Jersey	Legislature	Senate	General Assembly	State House
New Mexico	Legislature	Senate	House of Representatives	State Capitol
New York	Legislature	Senate	Assembly	State Capitol
North Carolina	General Assembly	Senate	House of Representatives	State Legislative Building
North Dakota	Legislative Assembly	Senate	House of Representatives	State Capitol
Ohio	General Assembly	Senate	House of Representatives	State House
Oklahoma	Legislature	Senate	House of Representatives	State Capitol
Oregon	Legislative Assembly	Senate	House of Representatives	State Capitol
Pennsylvania	General Assembly	Senate	House of Representatives	Main Capitol
Rhode Island	General Assembly	Senate	House of Representatives	State House
South Carolina	General Assembly	Senate	House of Representatives	State House
South Dakota	Legislature	Senate	House of Representatives	State Capitol
Tennessee	General Assembly	Senate	House of Representatives	State Capitol
Texas	Legislature	Senate	House of Representatives	State Capitol
Utah	Legislature	Senate	House of Representatives	State Capitol
Vermont	General Assembly	Senate	House of Representatives	State House
Virginia	General Assembly	Senate	House of Delegates	State Capitol(e)
Washington	Legislature	Senate	House of Representatives	Legislative Building
West Virginia	Legislature	Senate	House of Delegates	State Capitol
Wisconsin	Legislature	Senate	Assembly(f)	State Capitol
Wyoming	Legislature	Senate	House of Representatives	State Capitol
Dist. of Col.	Council of the District of Columbia	(d)		District Building
American Samoa	Legislature	Senate	House of Representatives	Maota Fono
Guam	Legislature	(d)		Congress Building
Northern Mariana Is.	Legislature	Senate	House of Representatives	Civic Center
Puerto Rico	Legislative Assembly	Senate	House of Representatives	Capitol
Federated States of Micronesia	Congress	(d)		Congress Office Building
Virgin Islands	Legislature	(d)		Government House

(a) Senate Wing, House Wing.
(b) Senate: Capitol South Wing. House: Capitol North Wing.
(c) New Capitol Senate Chamber; New Capitol House Chamber.
(d) Unicameral legislature. Except in Dist. of Col., members go by the title Senator.
(e) Senate addition; House addition.
(f) Members of the lower house go by the title Representative.

Table 2
THE LEGISLATORS
Numbers, Terms, and Party Affiliations

State or other jurisdiction	Senate Demo-crats	Repub-licans	Other	Vacan-cies	Total	Term	House Demo-crats	Repub-licans	Other	Vacan-cies	Total	Term	Senate and house totals
All States	1,210	725	1	1	1,986	...	3,429	2,006	6	11	5,452	...	7,438
Alabama	32	3	...	...	35	4	97	8	...	...	105	4	140
Alaska	9	11	...	...	20	4	19	21	...	...	40	2	60
Arizona	12	18	...	...	30	2	21	39	...	...	60	2	90
Arkansas	32	3	...	...	35	4	93	7	...	...	100	2	135
California	25	14	1(a)	...	40	4	48	32	...	...	80	2	120
Colorado	14	21	...	...	35	4	25	40	...	...	65	2	100
Connecticut	23	13	...	...	36	2	87	64	...	...	151	2	187
Delaware	13	8	...	...	21	4	24	17	...	...	41	2	62
Florida	32	8	...	...	40	4	84	36	...	...	120	2	160
Georgia	49	7	...	...	56	2	156	24	...	...	180	2	236
Hawaii	20	5	...	...	25	4	43	8	...	...	51	2	76
Idaho	14	21	...	...	35	2	19	51	...	...	70	2	105
Illinois	33	26	...	...	59	4(b)	70	48	...	...	118	2	177
Indiana.............	18	32	...	...	50	4	43	57	...	...	100	2	150
Iowa	28	22	...	...	50	4	60	40	...	...	100	2	150
Kansas	16	24	...	...	40	4	53	72	...	...	125	2	165
Kentucky	28	10	...	...	38	4	76	24	...	...	100	2	138
Louisiana...........	38	1	...	...	39	4	93	11	1(a)	...	105	4	144
Maine	23	10	...	...	33	2	92	59	...	...	151	2	184
Maryland	41	6	...	...	47	4	124	17	...	...	141	4	188
Massachusetts	33	7	...	...	40	2	129	29	...	2	160	2	200
Michigan	20	18	...	...	38	4	63	47	...	...	110	2	148
Minnesota	42(c)	25(d)	...	...	67	4	77(c)	57(d)	...	...	134	2	201
Mississippi	49	3	...	...	52	4	116	5	...	1	122	4	174
Missouri	22	12	...	...	34	4	110	53	...	...	163	2	197
Montana	24	26	...	...	50	4(e)	55	45	...	...	100	2	150
Nebraska	—— Nonpartisan election ——				49	4	————Unicameral————						49
Nevada	17	4	...	...	21	4	23	19	...	...	42	2	63
New Hampshire	9	15	...	...	24	2	158	237	2(a)	3	400	2	424
New Jersey	23	17	...	...	40	4(f)	44	36	...	...	80	2	120
New Mexico	23	19	...	...	42	4	46	24	...	...	70	2	112
New York	26	35	...	...	61	2	97	52	...	1	150	2	211
North Carolina	44	6	...	...	50	2	102	18	...	...	120	2	170
North Dakota	21	32	...	...	53	4	55	51	...	...	106	2	159
Ohio	17	16	...	...	33	4	62	37	...	...	99	2	132
Oklahoma	34	14	...	...	48	4	76	25	...	...	101	2	149
Oregon.............	21	9	...	...	30	4	36	24	...	...	60	2	90
Pennsylvania	23	27	...	...	50	4	103	100	...	...	203	2	253
Rhode Island	29	21	...	...	50	2	85	15	...	...	100	2	150
South Carolina	39	6	...	1	46	4	103	20	...	1	124	2	170
South Dakota	9	26	...	...	35	2	16	54	...	...	70	2	105
Tennessee	22	11	...	...	33	4	60	37	1(a)	1	99	2	132
Texas	26	5	...	...	31	4	114	36	...	...	150	2	181
Utah	5	24	...	...	29	4	17	58	...	...	75	2	104
Vermont	13	17	...	...	30	2	65	83	...	2	150	2	180
Virginia	32	8	...	...	40	4	65	34	1(a)	...	100	2	140
Washington..........	26	23	...	...	49	4	54	44	...	...	98	2	147
West Virginia	31	3	...	...	34	4	87	13	...	...	100	2	134
Wisconsin	19	14	...	...	33	4	59	40	...	...	99	2	132
Wyoming	11	19	...	...	30	4	25	38	1(a)	...	64	2	94
Dist. of Col.(g)	11	1	1(h)	...	13	4	————Unicameral————						13
American Samoa	—— Nonpartisan election ——				18	4	———Nonpartisan election———				21	2	39
Guam	14	7	...	...	21	2	————Unicameral————						21
No. Mariana Is.	1(i)	8(i)	...	...	9	4	8(i)	7(i)	...	...	15	2	24
Puerto Rico	15(j)	12(k)	...	...	27	4	26(j)	25(k)	...	...	51	4	78
Virgin Islands	8	7(l)	...	...	15	2	————Unicameral————						15

Note: Table reflects the legislatures as of August 1983, except for Kentucky, Louisiana, Mississippi, New Jersey, Virginia and the Northern Mariana Islands; information for those jurisdictions is as of January 1984.

(a) Independent.
(b) The entire senate is up for election every ten years, beginning in 1972. Senate districts are divided into three groups. One group elects senators for terms of four years, four years and two years, the second group for terms of four years, two years and four years, the third group for terms of two years, four years and four years.
(c) Democratic-Farmer-Labor.
(d) Independent-Republican.

(e) After each decennial reapportionment, lots will be drawn for half of the senators to serve an initial two year term. Subsequent elections will be for four year terms.
(f) Senate terms beginning in January of second year following the U.S. decennial census are for two years only.
(g) Council of the District of Columbia.
(h) Statehood Party.
(i) The Democratic and Republican parties are not affiliated with the national parties.
(j) Popular Democratic Party.
(k) New Progressive Party.
(l) Independent Citizens Movement.

Table 3
THE LEGISLATORS: QUALIFICATIONS FOR ELECTION

State or other jurisdiction	House					Senate				
	Minimum age (years)	U.S. Citizen (years)	State resident (years)	District resident (years)	Qualified Voter (years)	Minimum age (years)	U.S. Citizen (years)	State resident (years)	District resident (years)	Qualified Voter (years)
Alabama	21	...	3(a)	1	...	25	...	3(a)	1	★
Alaska	21	...	3	1	★	25	...	3	1	★
Arizona	25	★	3	1	...	25	★	3	1	...
Arkansas	21	★	2	1	★	25	★	2	1	★
California	18	3	3	...	★	18	3	3	...	★
Colorado	25	★	...	1	...	25	★	...	1	★
Connecticut	18	...	3(a)	★	★	18	...	3(a)	★	★
Delaware	24	...	2	1	...	27	...	2	1	...
Florida	21	...	(a)	★	★	21	...	(a)	★	★
Georgia	21	★	(a)	1	★	25	★	(a)	1	★
Hawaii	18	...	3	(b)	...	18	...	3	(b)	★
Idaho	18	★	...	1	★	18	★	...	1	★
Illinois	21	★	...	2(c)	...	21	★	...	2(c)	...
Indiana	21	★	2	1	...	25	★	2	1	...
Iowa	21	★	1	60 da.	★	25	★	1	60 da.	★
Kansas	18	...	2(a)	★	...	18	...	6(a)	★	★
Kentucky	24	...	2	1	★	30	...	2	1	★
Louisiana	18	...	1	1	...	18	...	1	1	...
Maine	21	5	1(a)	3 mo.	...	25	5	1(a)	3 mo.	...
Maryland	21	...	1(a)	6 mo.(d)	★	25	...	1(a)	6 mo.(d)	★
Massachusetts	18	...	...	1	...	18	...	5	★	...
Michigan(e)	21	★	...	(b)	★	21	★	...	(b)	★
Minnesota	21	...	1	6 mo.	★	21	...	1	6 mo.	★
Mississippi	21	...	4(a)	2	★	25	...	4	2	4
Missouri	24	...	...	1(f)	2	30	...	...	1(f)	3
Montana(g)	18	...	1(a)	6 mo.(h)	★	18	...	1(a)	6 mo.(h)	★
Nebraska	U	U	U	U	U	21	...	1(a)	(b)	★
Nevada	21	...	1(a)	(b)	★	21	...	7(a)	(b)	★
New Hampshire	18	...	2	★	...	30	...	4(a)	★	...
New Jersey	21	...	2(a)	1	★	30	...	4(a)	1	★
New Mexico	21	...	...	★	...	25	...	5	★	...
New York	18	★	5	1(i)	★	18	★	5	1(i)	★
North Carolina	(j)	★	1	1	★	25	★	2(a)	1	★
North Dakota	18	...	1	(b)	★	18	...	1	(b)	★
Ohio(k)	18	...	...	1	★	18	...	...	1	★

	Senate				House			
	Min. age	U.S. citizen	State residency	District residency	Min. age	U.S. citizen	State residency	District residency
Oklahoma	21	...	...	(b)	25	★	...	(b)
Oregon	21	★	...	1	21	★	...	1
Pennsylvania	21	...	4(a)	...	25	...	4(a)	...
Rhode Island(f)	18	...	...	(b)	18	★	...	(b)
South Carolina	21	★	...	...	25	★	...	...
South Dakota(k,l)	25	★	2	(b)	25	★	2	(b)
Tennessee	21	★	(a)	1(b)	30	★	3	1(b)
Texas	21	★	3	—	26	★	5	—
Utah	25	...	2	6 mo.(b)	25	...	3	6 mo.(b)
Vermont	18	...	...	1	18	...	2	1
Virginia	21	★	...	★	21	★	...	★
Washington	18	★	(a)	(b)	18	★	(a)	(b)
West Virginia(l)	18	...	1	(b)	25	★	1	(b)
Wisconsin	18	★	(a)	1	18	...	(a)	1
Wyoming	21	★	...	...	25	★	...	...
Dist. of Col.	U	U	U	U	18	...	1	1
American Samoa(l)	25	★(m)	5	1	30(n)	★(m)	5	1
Guam(o)	U	U	3	U	25	...	5	—
No. Marianas	21	★	...	★	25	★	2(a)	—
Puerto Rico(p)	25	★	2(a)	1(q)	30	★	2(a)	1(q)
Virgin Islands(o)	U	U	U	U	21	...	3	1(q)

Note: This table includes constitutional and statutory provisions.

Key:

U—Unicameral legislature; members are called senators, except in District of Columbia.

★—Formal provision; number of years not specified.

...—No formal provision.

(a) Additional state citizenship requirement. Alabama, Delaware—three years. Georgia, New Jersey-House, two years; Senate, four years. Mississippi—four years. New Hampshire. New Hampshire—seven years. North Carolina—two years. Pennsylvania—four years. West Virginia—five years.

(b) Must be a qualified voter of the district; number of years not specified.

(c) Following redistricting, a candidate may be elected from any district that contains a part of the district in which he resided at the time of redistricting, and reelected if a resident of the new district he represents for 18 months prior to reelection.

(d) If the district was established for less than six months, residency is length of establishment of district.

(e) No person convicted of felony or convicted of subversion shall be eligible. preceding 20 years or convicted of subversion shall be eligible.

(f) Only if the district has been in existence for one year; if not, then legislator must have been a one year resident of the district(s) from which the new district was created.

(g) No person convicted of felony is eligible to hold office until final discharge from state supervision.

(h) Shall be a resident of the county if it contains one or more districts or of the district if it contains all or parts of more than one county.

(i) After redistricting, must have been a resident of the county in which the district is contained for one year immediately preceding election.

(j) A conflict exists between two articles of the constitution, one specifying age for House members (i.e., "qualified voter of the state") and the other related to general eligibility for elective office (i.e., "every qualified voter ... who is 21 years of age ... shall be eligible for election").

(k) No person convicted of embezzlement of public funds shall hold any office.

(l) Disqualification for bribery. In South Dakota and West Virginia, disqualification also for perjury or other infamous crimes. In American Samoa, also for felony.

(m) Or U.S. national.

(n) Must be registered matai.

(o) Disqualification for felony or crime involving moral turpitude unless person received pardon restoring civil rights.

(p) Read and write the Spanish or English language.

(q) When there is more than one representative district in a municipality, residence in the municipality shall satisfy this requirement.

Table 4
SENATE LEADERSHIP POSITIONS—METHODS OF SELECTION

State or other jurisdiction	President	President pro tem	Majority leader	Assistant majority leader	Majority floor leader	Assistant majority floor leader	Majority whip	Majority caucus chairman	Minority leader	Assistant minority leader	Minority floor leader	Assistant minority floor leader	Minority whip	Minority caucus chairman
Alabama	(a)	ES	EC						EC	EC				
Alaska	ES	(b)	EC						EC	EC			EC	EC
Arizona	ES	ES			EC		EC	EC			EC		EC	EC
Arkansas	(a)	ES												
California	(a)	ES			EC		EC	EC			EC		EC	EC
Colorado	ES	ES	EC	EC					EC	EC				EC
Connecticut	(a)	ES	AT	AT/8(c)			AT/2		EC	AL/4(c)			AL	
Delaware	(a)	ES	EC	EC(d)			EC		EC	EC(d)			EC	
Florida	ES	ES	EC				EC		EC				EC	
Georgia	(a)	ES	EC				EC	EC	EC				EC	EC
Hawaii	ES	ES(e)	EC	EC/3	EC	EC/3	(f)	EC	EC	EC	EC			EC
Idaho	(a)	ES	EC	EC	AT	AT		AP	EC	AL/3	EC			AL
Illinois	ES(g)	ES	(g)	AP/4				EC	EC					EC
Indiana	(a)	ES		EC/2			AT		EC	EC/3				
Iowa	(a)	ES	EC	EC/2			AT							
Kansas	ES	ES(e)	EC	EC	EC		EC	EC	EC	EC	EC		EC	EC
Kentucky	(a)	ES		EC									EC	EC
Louisiana	ES	ES			EC				EC		EC			
Maine	ES	ES			AP									
Maryland	ES	ES	AP	AP(h)		EC	AP(h)		EC				EC	
Massachusetts	ES	ES	EC		EC	AP/2	AP	EC	EC	EC	EC	AL/3	AL	
Michigan	(a)	ES	EC	EC	EC	EC	EC		EC	EC/5	EC	EC	EC	
Minnesota	ES	ES		EC	EC		EC							
Mississippi	(a)	ES												
Missouri	(a)	ES			EC				EC					
Montana	ES	ES			EC		EC	EC	EC		AP	EC(i)	EC	
Nebraska(U)	(a)	ES(j)												
Nevada	(a)	ES	AP	AP					AP	AL			AL	
New Hampshire	ES	AP	AP				AP		EC	EC			EC	
New Jersey	ES	ES	EC	EC/3			AP		EC					
New Mexico	(a)	ES	(k)	AT	EC		EC	EC	EC				EC	EC
New York	(a)	ES(k)	EC	AT			AT	AT	EC				AL	(i)
North Carolina	(a)	ES	EC						EC	AL			AL	EC
North Dakota	(a)	ES	(g)	EC				EC	EC	EC			EC	AL
Ohio	ES(g)	ES	(g)	EC			ES		ES	ES			ES	EC

	(1)	(2)	(3)	(4)	(5)	(6)	(7)	(8)	(9)	(10)	(11)
Oklahoma	(a)	ES			EC/2		EC	EC	EC	EC	EC	EC
Oregon	(a)	ES	EC	EC/2			EC	EC		EC	EC	EC
Pennsylvania	(a)	ES	EC	EC/8		EC/2	EC	EC		EC	EC	EC
Rhode Island	(a)	ES	EC				EC					
South Carolina	(a)	ES										EC
South Dakota	(a)	ES	EC	EC	EC	EC/5	EC		EC		EC	EC
Tennessee	ES(j)	ES	EC	EC/2		EC/2	EC		EC		EC	EC
Texas	(a)	ES	EC			EC	EC				EC	EC
Vermont	(a)	ES	EC			EC	EC		EC		EC	EC
Virginia	(a)	ES	EC	EC	EC	EC	EC	EC	EC	EC	EC	EC
Washington	(a)	AP	EC	EC	AP	AP	EC		EC		EC	EC
West Virginia	ES	AP	AP			AP	EC	EC	EC			
Wisconsin	ES	ES	EC	EC	EC	EC	EC	EC	EC	EC	EC(l)	EC(l)
Wyoming	ES(e)	ES(e)					(p)				EC(l)	(l)
Dist. of Col.	(m)	(n)	ES									
American Samoa	ES	ES	EC			EC	EC		EC		EC	EC
Guam(U)	ES(j)	ES(e)	EC	EC		EC	EC				EC	EC
Puerto Rico	ES	EC(e)	EC	EC		EC	EC		EC		EC	EC
Virgin Islands(U)	ES	ES(e)	ES(o)	EC		(p)					EC(l)	(l)

Note: In some states, the leadership positions in the Senate are not empowered by the law or by the rules of the chamber, but rather by the party members themselves.
Entry following slash indicates number of individuals holding specified position.

Key:
ES—Elected or confirmed by all members of the Senate.
EC—Elected by party caucus.
AP—Appointed by president.
AT—Appointed by president pro tempore.
AL—Appointed by party leader.
U—Unicameral legislature.
...—Position does not exist or is not selected on a regular basis.

(a) Lieutenant governor is president of the Senate by virtue of the office.
(b) President *may* name any member as president pro tempore to serve during the former's absence. The appointment may extend throughout the session unless terminated by the Senate.
(c) Assistant majority leader: deputy majority leader, two assistant majority leaders at-large and five assistant majority leaders. Assistant minority leader: deputy minority leader and three assistant minority leaders.
(d) Official titles are majority leader pro tempore and minority leader pro tempore.
(e) Official title is vice president. In Guam, vice speaker.
(f) Majority policy leader.
(g) President is also majority leader.
(h) Joint appointment by president and the majority leader.
(i) Assistant minority floor leader is also caucus chairman.
(j) Official title is speaker of the Senate. In Tennessee, officer has the statutory title of "lieutenant governor."
(k) President pro tempore is also majority leader.
(l) Minority whip is also majority leader.
(m) Chairman of the Council.
(n) Appointed by the chairman.
(o) Officer designated by a majority of the members.
(p) Any three or more senators may meet in order to select the minority leader (not an officer of the Senate).

Table 5
HOUSE LEADERSHIP POSITIONS—METHODS OF SELECTION

State or other jurisdiction	Speaker	Speaker pro tem	Majority leader	Assistant majority leader	Majority floor leader	Assistant majority floor leader	Majority whip	Majority caucus chairman	Minority leader	Assistant minority leader	Minority floor leader	Assistant minority floor leader	Minority whip	Minority caucus chairman
Alabama	EH	EH	EH						EC					
Alaska	EH		EC				EC		EC	EC	EC		EC	
Arizona	EH	EH	EC				EC		EC				EC/2	
Arkansas	EH	EH	(a)											
California	EH	AS(c)	EC		AS(b)	EC	EC	EC	EC	EC	EC	EC		EC
Colorado	EH	EH	EC	EC			(d)		EC	EC			(d)	EC
Connecticut	EH	EH	EC	AL/13(d)			EC	EC	EC	AL/9(d)	EC		EC	
Delaware	EH		AS				AS	AS	EC	EC(e)			AL/2	AL
Florida	EH	EH	EC		AS/2		AS	AS	EC		EC		EC	EC
Georgia	EH	EH					EC	EC	EC					
Hawaii	EH	EH(f)	EC	EC	EC	EC/5		EC	EC	EC	EC	EC/2		
Idaho	EH		EC	AS/4			AS/2	EC	EC	AL/4			AL/2	EC
Illinois	EH	AS	AS		EC	AS	AS	AS	EC		EC	EC	EC	AL
Indiana	EH	EH	EC	EC/4				EC	EC	EC/4				EC
Iowa	EH	EH												
Kansas	EH	EH	EC	EC	EC		EC	EC	EC	EC	EC		EC	EC
Kentucky	EH	EH											EC	EC
Louisiana	EH	EH			EC	EC	EC	EC	EC	EC	EC			
Maine	EH		EC	EC									EC	
Maryland	EH	EH						EC	EC		EC			
Massachusetts	EH		AS	AS/2	EC	EC/3	AS EC/22		EC	AL/3		EC	AL	EC
Michigan	EH	EH		EC/4				EC	EC	EC	EC		EC	EC
Minnesota	EH		EC		EC	EC	EC			EC/3		EC		
Mississippi	EH	EH						EC					EC	EC
Missouri	EH						EC				EC			
Montana	EH	EH			EC	EC			AS			EC		
Nebraska(g)														
Nevada	EH	EH	AS	AS/2	EC	EC	AS/2		EC	AL/7(h)	EC	EC	EC	EC
New Hampshire	EH	AS		EC/4						EC				
New Jersey	EH	EH	EC				EC/3		EC		EC		AL EC	

State											
New Mexico	EH	AS	AS/2(i)	EC	EC	EC	AL/4(i)	EC	…	…	EC
New York	EH	AS	…	…	AS	AS	…	…	EC	AL	EC
North Carolina	EH	EH(i)	EC	EC	EC	EC	EC	EC	…	EC	EC
North Dakota	EH	EC	…	EH	EH	EH	EH	EH	EH	EH	EC
Ohio	EH	…	…	EH	EH	EH	EH	EH	…	EH	EC
Oklahoma	EH	EH	EC	AS	AS/5(k)	AS	EC	EC	EC	EC	EC
Oregon	EH	EC	EC	(l)	EC(l)	EC	EC	(m)	…	EC	EC
Pennsylvania	EH	AS	EC	…	EC	EC	EC	…	EC	EC	…
Rhode Island	EH	AS	EC/10	…	EC	EC/4	EC	…	EC	EC	…
South Carolina	EH	EH	EC(n)	…	EC	EC	EC	…	EC	EC	…
South Dakota	EH	EH	EC	EC	EC/6	EC	EC	EC	EC	EC	EC
Tennessee	EH	EH	EC	EC	EC	EC	EC	EC	…	EC	…
Texas	EH	AS	EC	EC	EC	EC	EC	EC	EC	EC	EC
Utah	EH	AS	EC	EC	EC	EC	EC	EC	EC	EC	EC
Vermont	EH	…	EC	EC	EC	EC	EC	EC	…	EC	EC
Virginia	EH	EH	EC	EC	EC	EC	EC	EC	EC/2	EC	EC
Washington	EH	AS	EC	AS	AS	AS	AS	AS	…	AL	AL
West Virginia	EH	AS	AS	EC	AS	AS	AS	AS	…	EC	EC
Wisconsin	EH	EH	EC	EC	EC	EC	EC	EC	…	EC(o)	EC
Wyoming	EH	EH	EC	…	EC	EC	EC	…	…	…	(o)
Dist. of Col.(g)	EH										
American Samoa	EH										
Guam(g)											
Puerto Rico	EH	EC(p)									
Virgin Islands(g)											

Note: In some states, the leadership positions in the House are not empowered by the law or by the rules of the chamber, but rather by the party members themselves.

Entry following slash indicates number of individuals holding specified position.

Key:
EH—Elected or confirmed by all members of the House.
EC—Elected by party caucus.
AS—Appointed by speaker.
AL—Appointed by party leader.
…—Position does not exist or is not selected on a regular basis.

(a) Outgoing speaker, by agreement of the House.
(b) Appointed by speaker, after consultation with members of supporting majority.
(c) Official title is deputy speaker.
(d) Assistant majority leader: deputy majority leader (appointed by majority leader), assistant majority leader for fiscal affairs (also serves as majority whip), 11 assistant majority floor leaders (two also serve as majority whips), Assistant minority leader: deputy minority leader (appointed by minority leader), eight assistant minority leaders (two also serve as minority whips).

(e) Minority leader pro tempore.
(f) Official title is vice speaker.
(g) Unicameral legislature; see entries in table on Senate leadership positions.
(h) Assistant minority leader: deputy minority leader, six assistant minority leaders.
(i) Assistant majority leader: deputy majority leader, assistant majority leader. Assistant minority leader: minority leader pro tempore, deputy minority leader, two assistant minority leaders.
(j) Speaker pro tempore is also majority leader.
(k) Assistant majority floor leader: first assistant floor leader, four assistant floor leaders.
(l) Majority floor leader is also majority whip.
(m) Assistant minority leaders are also minority floor leaders.
(n) Majority leader is also majority caucus chairman.
(o) Minority whip is also caucus chairman.
(p) Official title is vice president.

Table 6
LEGISLATIVE COMPENSATION: REGULAR AND SPECIAL SESSIONS

State	Regular sessions		Salaries	Special sessions		Travel allowance		Per diem living expenses
	Per diem salary	Limit on days	Annual salaries	Per diem salary	Limit on days	Cents per mile	Round trips home to capital during session	
Alabama	...	...	$4,800	...	...	20	One	$65 for 105C of regular session and 30C of special session
Alaska	...	...	$48,000	...	...	0	One(a)	None
Arizona	...	...	$15,000	...	...	20.5	Unlimited	$40 ($20 for those living inside Maricopa County) for first 120C of regular and all of special session; $20 ($10 for those living inside county) after 120C of regular session. (U)
Arkansas	(b)	(b)	$7,500(b)	...	...	23	Weekly	Up to $308/w. (V)
California	...	...	$28,110	...	...	(c)	One(d)	$62
Colorado	...	...	$14,000	...	...	20 (24/4-wheel drive)	Weekly(e)	$40 for those who do not live in Denver metro area. (U)
Connecticut	...	...	$10,500	...	...	20	Unlimited	None
Delaware	...	...	$12,255	...	...	15	Unlimited	None
Florida	...	...	$12,000	...	...	20	Weekly	$50 for 60C of regular session and all of special session. (U)
Georgia	...	...	$7,200	...	...	20	Weekly	$59, limited to 40L of regular session and 40L of special session(f)
Hawaii	...	...	$13,650	...	...	(g)	Unlimited	$20 for neighbor island legislators. (U)
Idaho	...	...	$4,200(h)	...	...	18	Five	$44 out-of-town members, $25 Boise members. (U)
Illinois	...	...	$28,000	...	...	20	Weekly	$36 (U)
Indiana	...	...	$9,600	...	...	24	Weekly	$65 (U)
Iowa	...	...	$13,700(i)	(i)	(i)	22	Weekly	$30 for 120C in odd-numbered years and 100C in even-numbered years
Kansas	$47	None	...	$47	None	22	Weekly	$50 (U)
Kentucky(j)	$100	(k)		$100	(l)	20.5	Weekly	$75/C (U)
Louisiana	$75(m)	85C	(m)	$75(m)	None	21 or coach air fare if lives more than 100 miles away from capitol.	Weekly	(m)
Maine	...	...	(n)	$35	None	22		$45 for meals and lodging or $21 for meals only. (U)
Maryland	...	...	$21,000	...	...	19	One(o) if no lodging expense was incurred that day	$68 for lodging and meals. (V)
Massachusetts	...	...	$30,000	...	...	Included in living expense allowance	See living expense allowance	Amount covering mileage, meals and lodging ranges from $5 to $50, depending on distance legislator's district is from Boston.
Michigan	...	...	$33,200	...	...	29.5	Unlimited	$6,700/y. (V)
Minnesota	...	...	$18,500	...	...	26(p)	Weekly	$36 outstate; $23 metro. (U)
Mississippi	...	...	$8,100	$50	None	20	Weekly	$44 actual daily attendance. (U)
Missouri	...	...	$15,000	...	...	17	Weekly	$35
Montana	$49.21	90L	...	$49.21	None	20.5	Four	$45 (U)
Nebraska	...	...	$4,800	...	...	21	One	None
Nevada	$104	(q)	...	$104	(q)	20	(t)	$56 (V)
New Hampshire	...	...	$100(s)	(s)	(s)	38/first 45 miles; 19 thereafter	Unlimited	None

State	Per diem salary	Session day limit	Annual salary	Living expense per diem	Limit	Mileage (¢)	Travel	Living expense allowance
New Jersey	$75	...	$25,000	...	...	0	...	None
New Mexico	...	60C (odd) 30C (even)	...	$75	30C	25	One	None
New York	...	...	$32,960	...	...	0	Weekly	$55 (V)
North Carolina	...	...	$6,936(t)	...	...	25	Weekly	$50/C (U)
North Dakota	...	(v)	...	(u)	None	20	...	(u)
Ohio	...	...	$22,500	...	...	20	Weekly	None
Oklahoma	...	...	$20,000	...	...	22	Weekly(w)	$35 for each night away from home on state business during regular and special sessions. Legislators are only compensated for 90L during regular session, and as per governor's call order for special session.(w)
Oregon	...	...	$8,400	...	...	0	Weekly	$44/C (U)
Pennsylvania	...	...	$35,000(x)	...	...	20	Unlimited	Up to $75/d (U)
Rhode Island	$5	60L	...	...	...	8	...	None
South Carolina	...	...	$10,000(y) $3,200/odd(z) $2,800/even(z)	...	...	23	Weekly	$50/L (V)
South Dakota	...	...	...	...	...	21	Each weekend legislature is in session	$50 (U) for up to 35L in even-numbered years and up to 40L in odd-numbered years. After Jan. 1, 1985, $75 for the same.
Tennessee	(aa)	(aa)	$8,308.08	(aa)	(aa)	19.96	Weekly	$66.47 (U)
Texas	$25	...	$7,200(aa)	...	30C	(bb)	(cc)	None
Utah 1984	...	60C (odd) 20C (even)	...	$25	...	23	One	$25 subsistence. Everyone who lives outside of Salt Lake or Davis receives $35 or mileage but not both.
1985	$65	60C (odd) 20C (even)	...	$65	...	...	...	
Vermont	$55/L(ee)	(ee)	...	$55/L(ee)	25(dd)	20.5	Weekly if room rented in Montpelier or vicinity; otherwise per diem	$27.50 for room and $22.50 for meals if renting room in Montpelier or vicinity; $18.75 if living in Montpelier or vicinity. (U)
Virginia	...	...	$11,000	...	...	20.5	Weekly	$75/C (U)
Washington	...	...	$13,750	...	...	10	One	$44 (U)
West Virginia	...	...	$5,136(ff)	(ff)	(ff)	17	Weekly	$20/d for meals. (U); $30/d lodging. (V)
Wisconsin	...	...	$22,631.04	...	...	21.5(gg)	Weekly	$41.63/L when legislator must establish temporary residence at state capital. Otherwise, $20.81. (U)
Wyoming	$30	40L (odd) 20L (even)	...	$30	None	20	One	$60 (U)

Note: In many states, legislators who receive an annual salary or per diem salary also receive an additional per diem amount for living expenses. Consult appropriate columns for a more complete picture of legislative compensation during sessions. For information on interim compensation and other direct payments and services to legislators, see table on Legislative Compensation: Interim Compensation and Other Direct Payments.

Key:
...—Not applicable
C—Calendar day
L—Legislative day
U—Unvouchered
V—Vouchered
d—day
m—month
y—year
w—week

LEGISLATIVE COMPENSATION: REGULAR AND SPECIAL SESSIONS—Continued

(a) Legislators are reimbursed for whatever expenses are incurred in coming to and from the capital one time. This includes any moving expenses. (V)

(b) In addition to the annual salary of $7,500, legislators receive per diem salary of $20/L.

(c) Legislators are provided a leased state car up to $265/m and gasoline credit card.

(d) Legislators are compensated for one round trip per two-year session if using other than leased car. (V)

(e) Paid only to those who do not live in the Denver metro area.

(f) Unless special session is extended by 3/5 vote of each house and approved by governor.

(g) Travel allowance to neighbor islands during a session on official legislative business, (excluding attendance at a legislative session for neighbor island legislators) to be equal to the maximum allowance for such expenses payable to any public officer or employee. Presently, this equals $45/d inter-island, $60/d out-of-state. (U)

(h) Legislators are paid $800/m for January, February and March; $200/m for April through December; plus $35/d for interim business.

(i) In addition, legislators receive $40/L during special sessions.

(j) Member's organizational session per diem and expense allowance are identical to such compensation for regular or extraordinary sessions, except payment is based on meeting days rather than calendar days. An organizational session may continue for not more than 10 legislative, or meeting, days.

(k) While regular sessions are limited to 60L every other year, per diem amount is paid for every calendar day of the session.

(l) Per diem amount is paid for every calendar day of the session, which is unlimited in duration.

(m) In addition, the legislators receive a monthly expense allowance totaling $16,800/y.

(n) $6,500 first year of biennial session, $3,500 second year.

(o) Legislators automatically receive one round trip mileage per week. They may claim additional trips (to a maximum of one per day) in lieu of lodging for each session day.

(p) The travel allowance is available only to outstate legislators who must move to St. Paul.

(q) While there is no limitation on the number of days the legislature may be in session, the constitution limits the number of days for which legislators may receive compensation. Beyond the 60th day of the regular session and the 20th day of the special session, salaries cease and legislators may only draw upon their expense allowance.

(r) Legislators have a supplemental travel allowance of up to $3,500 for a regular session and $1,000 for

a special session. (V)

(s) In addition to the annual salary of $100, a legislator receives $3/d for up to 15 legislative days of the special session.

(t) Plus $2,064/y expense allowance.

(u) Legislators whose tax home is in Bismarck receive $90/d and no expenses. Others receive $40/d plus $50 expenses. (U)

(v) There is a constitutional limit on legislative sessions of 80 natural days during a biennium. The per diem is payable each calendar day during a session.

(w) Legislators may elect mileage in lieu of per diem, limited to four round trips per week and the per diem amount.

(x) Effective December 1, 1984.

(y) Legislators are also paid $35/d on a non-session day for a committee meeting.

(z) When the legislator is unable to attend a session, his salary is reduced accordingly.

(aa) In addition to an annual salary of $7,200/y, the legislators receive a per diem salary of $30 for 140C of the regular session and 30C of the special session.

(bb) Travel mileage reimbursement is 23 cents per mile in personally-owned automobiles, 40 cents per highway mile when traveling in a personally-owned or leased single engine aircraft, and 65 cents per highway mile when traveling in a personally-owned or leased twin engine aircraft. Reimbursement for commercial air transportation may not exceed the next lowest airline fare below first class unless such is not available.

(cc) Senators are reimbursed for all round trips home to capital during session from funds appropriated for that purpose. Representatives are reimbursed for their first four trips per month from funds appropriated for that purpose; thereafter, reimbursement for round trips is taken from the member's operating account.

(dd) The 25-day limit includes each day the legislator attends veto-override and special sessions and authorized legislative meetings.

(ee) Legislators may receive a maximum of $9,500 during the regular session, and $2,000 during the special session.

(ff) In addition to the annual salary of $5,136, legislators receive $35/d in special sessions.

(gg) As an alternative, any legislator may use any public transportation and be reimbursed for no more than one round trip weekly.

Table 7
ADDITIONAL COMPENSATION FOR SENATE LEADERS

State	President	President pro tem	Majority leader	Minority leader	Other
Alabama	$2/d(a)	0	...	...	
Alaska	$500/y	...	0	0	
Arizona	0	...	0	0	
Arkansas	(a)	$2,500/y(b)	...	...	
California	(a)	0	0	0	
Colorado	$50/d to max. $5,000/y	$50/d to max. $5,000/y	$50/d to max. $5,000/y	$50/d to max. $5,000/y	
Connecticut	(a)	$5,000/y	$4,000/y	$4,000/y	Dep. Maj. Ldr., Dep. Min. Ldr.: $3,000/y; Asst. Maj. Ldrs., Asst. Min. Ldrs.: $2,000/y; Cmte. Chmn.: $1,000/y
Delaware	(a)	$193.50/m	$161.30/m	$161.30/m	Maj. Whip, Min. Whip: $129/m; Chmn., Joint Finance Cmte.: $161.30/m(c); Mbrs. Joint Finance Cmte.: $64.60/m
Florida	$13,000/y	0	0	0	
Georgia	(a)	$2,800/y	$2,400/y(d)	$2,400/y(d)	Admin. Flr. Ldr.: $2,400/y(d); Asst. Admin. Flr. Ldr.: $1,200/y(d)
Hawaii	(a)	0(e)	0	0	
Idaho	(a)	0	0	0	
Illinois	$10,000/y(f)	...	(f)	$10,000/y	Asst. Maj. Ldrs., Asst. Min. Ldrs.: $6,000/y; Maj. Caucus Chmn., Min. Caucus Chmn.: $5,000/y
Indiana	(a)	$3,000/y	$1,500/y	$2,000/y	Maj. Caucus Chmn., Min. Caucus Chmn., Finance Cmte. Chmn., Min. Asst. Flr. Ldr.: $1,500/y
Iowa	$6,800/y(a)	0	$2,300/y	$2,300/y	
Kansas	$4,200/y	$1,800/y(e)	$3,240/y	$3,240/y	Ways & Means Cmte. Chmn.: $3,240/y
Kentucky	$25/d(a)	$25/d	$20/d	$20/d	Asst. Pres. Pro Tem, Maj. Caucus Chmn., Min. Caucus Chmn., Maj. Whip, Min. Whip: $15/d; Standing and Interim Cmte. Chmn.: $10/meeting chaired; LRC Mbrs.: same as per diem in-session per meeting attended, plus necessary expenses.
Louisiana	(g)	0	...	...	
Maine	(h)	...	(h)	(h)	Asst. Maj. Ldr., Asst. Min. Ldr.: (h)
Maryland	$5,000/y(i)	(i)	(i)	(i)	Major Cmte. Chmn.: (i)
Massachusetts	$35,000/y	...	$22,500/y	$22,500/y	Asst. Maj. Flr. Ldrs., Asst. Min. Flr. Ldrs.: $15,000/y
Michigan	(a)	0	$16,000/y	$8,600/y	Chmn. Appropriations Cmte.: $2,000/y
Minnesota	$7,400/y	...	$7,400/y	$7,400/y	Tax Cmte. Chmn., Finance Cmte. Chmn: $3,700/y
Mississippi	(a)	0	...	...	
Missouri	(a)	$2,500/y	$1,500/y	$1,500/y	
Montana	$5/d	0	0	0	
Nebraska	(a)	0(j)	...	...	
Nevada	(a)	(k)	(k)	(k)	(k)
New Hampshire	$50/b	0	0	0	
New Jersey	$8,333.33/y(l)	0	0	0	
New Mexico	(a)	0	0	0	
New York	(a)	$30,000/y(f)	(f)	$25,000/y	Dep. Maj. Ldr.: $24,500/y; Dep. Min. Ldr. $15,000/y; Maj. Whip: $13,000/y; Min. Whip: $3,000/y; Maj. Conf. Chmn.: $18,000/y; Min. Conf. Chmn.: $10,500/y; Maj. Conf. Secy.: $7,000/y; Min. Conf. Secy.: $3,000/y; Cmte. Chmn. & Ranking Min. Mbrs.: Finance: $24,500/y & $15,000/y; Education, Judiciary, Codes: $13,000/y & $8,000/y; Banks, Health, Cities, Corp.: $11,000/y & $7,000/y; All other cmtes.: $9,000/y & $6,500/y
North Carolina	(a)	$1,728/y(m)	$1,728/y(m)	$1,728/y(m)	Chmn., Standing & Interim Cmtes.: $3/d; Chmn., Legislative Council: $5/d during interim
North Dakota	(a)	0	$5/d	$5/d	Asst. Min. Ldr.: $6,500/y; Asst. Pres. Pro Tem: $7,500/y; Min. Whip: $4,500/y; Chmn., Standing Cmtes.: $1,500/y; Chmn., Standing Sub-Cmtes.: $750/y
Ohio	$12,500/y(f)	$9,500/y	(f)	$8,500/y	
Oklahoma	(a)	$9,330/y	$6,440/y	$6,440/y	
Oregon	$700/m	0	0	0	
Pennsylvania(n)	(a)	$19,600/y	$15,680/y	$15,680/y	Maj. Whip, Min. Whip: $11,900/y; Maj. Caucus Chmn., Min. Caucus Chmn.: $7,420/y; Maj. Caucus Secy., Min. Caucus Secy., Maj. Policy Chmn., Min. Policy Chmn., Maj. Caucus Admin., Min. Caucus Admin.: $4,900/y

ADDITIONAL COMPENSATION FOR SENATE LEADERS—Continued

State	President	President pro tem	Majority leader	Minority leader	Other
Rhode Island	(a)	0	0	0	
South Carolina	$1,575/y(a)	$3,600/y	. . .	. . .	
South Dakota	(a)	0	0	0	
Tennessee	(a)	. . .	0	0	
Texas	(a)	0	. . .	. . .	
Utah	(o)	. . .	(o)	(o)	
Vermont	(a)	(p)	0	0	
Virginia	(a)	0	0	0	
Washington	(a)	0	0	0	
West Virginia	$35/d	0	$15/d	$15/d	
Wisconsin	0	0	0	0	
Wyoming	$3/d	0(e)	0	0	

Note: This table reflects the amount paid the leadership in addition to their regular legislative compensation.

Key:
d—day
y—year
b—biennium
m—month
. . .—Position does not exist or is not selected on a regular basis

(a) Lieutenant governor is president of the Senate. Additional compensation noted is that which the lieutenant governor receives for services as president of the Senate. In Georgia, receives extra $20/d for expenses. In Mississippi, constitution states that the salary of the lieutenant governor must be the same as that of the speaker of the House ($34,000), and that the lieutenant governor also receive the same per diem and expenses as members while in session. In Tennessee, lieutenant governor is a statutory title only, and person holding position receives $5,700/y allowance for office in home district, $4,154.01/y allowance for services as speaker, and $750/y for ex-officio services as speaker. In Texas, lieutenant governor is furnished postage, telegraph, telephone, express, and all other expenses incident to the office. In Virginia, lieutenant governor also receives additional expense allowance.

(b) Receives a special public relations expense allowance of $6,450/y.

(c) The positions of chairman and vice-chairman of the Joint Finance Committee alternate between the House and Senate every other year. The vice-chairman also receives $161.30/m.

(d) This amount is provided by resolution of the Senate and cannot be greater than the additional amount provided by law for the speaker pro tempore of the House of Representatives.

(e) Official title is vice-president.

(f) In Illinois and Ohio, president also serves as majority leader. In New York, president pro tempore also serves as majority leader.

(g) Receives $32,000 annual salary and up to $10,000/y in reimbursement for actual expenses, which replaces all per diems and allowances paid to other legislators.

(h) Additional compensation for Senate leaders is calculated according to the following percentages of the base salaries during sessions: president, 50 percent; majority and minority leaders, 25 percent; and assistant majority and minority leaders, 12.5 percent. No additional compensation is given during interim.

(i) Each receives an additional $600/y for district office expenses.

(j) Official title is speaker of the Senate.

(k) Supplemental allowance for postage and telephone not to exceed $300 during regular session or $40 for special session. Chairmen of standing committees also eligible to receive allowance.

(l) Equal to one-third of regular annual salary.

(m) Each receives additional $648/y expense allowance.

(n) Compensation shown effective December 1, 1984.

(o) Beginning January 1, 1985, president of the Senate will receive additional compensation of $1,000/y, and the majority and minority leaders will each receive $500/y.

(p) Receives $325/week during regular and adjourned sessions, $65/d during special sessions and $65/d during interim (when engaged in official duties).

Table 8
ADDITIONAL COMPENSATION FOR HOUSE LEADERS

State	Speaker	Speaker pro tem	Majority leader	Minority leader	Other
Alabama	$2/d	0	...	...	
Alaska	$500/y	...	0	0	
Arizona	0	0	0	0	
Arkansas	$2,500/y(a)	0	0	0	
California	0	0	0	0	
Colorado	$50/d to max. $5,000/y	$50/d to max. $5,000/y	$50/d to max. $5,000/y	$50/d to max. $5,000/y	
Connecticut	$5,000/y	$3,000/y(b)	$4,000/y	$4,000/y	Dep. Maj. Ldr., Dep. Min. Ldr.: $3,000/y; Asst. Maj. Ldrs., Asst. Min. Ldrs.: $2,000/y; Cmte. Chmn.: $1,000/y
Delaware	$193.50/m	...	$161.30/m	$161.30/m	Maj. Whip, Min. Whip: $129/m; Joint Finance Cmte. Mbrs.: $64.40/m; V-Chmn., Joint Finance Committee: $161.30/m(c)
Florida	$13,000/y	0	0	0	
Georgia	(d)	$2,800/y	$2,400/y(e)	$2,400/y(e)	Admin. Flr. Ldr.: $2,400/y(e)
Hawaii	0	0(f)	0	0	
Idaho	0	...	0	0	
Illinois	$10,000/y	...	$7,500/y	$10,000/y	Asst. Maj. Ldrs., Asst. Min. Ldrs.: $6,000/y; Maj. Whips, Min. Whips, Maj. Conf. Chmn., Min. Conf. Chmn.: $5,000/y
Indiana	$3,000/y	$1,500/y	$1,500/y	$2,000/y	Maj. Whip, Maj. Caucus Chmn., Min. Caucus Chmn., Ways & Means Cmte. Chmn., Asst. Min. Flr. Ldr.: $1,500/y
Iowa	$6,800/y(g)	0	$2,300/y	$2,300/y	
Kansas	$4,200/y	$1,800/y	$3,240/y	$3,240/y	Ways & Means Cmte. Chmn.: $3,240/y
Kentucky	$25/d	$15/d	$20/d	$20/d	Maj. Caucus Chmn., Min. Caucus Chmn., Maj. Whip, Min. Whip: $15/d; Standing & Interim Cmte. Chmn.: $10/meeting chaired; Mbrs., LRS, same as per diem in-session per meeting attended, plus necessary expenses.
Louisiana	(h)	0	...	...	
Maine	(i)	...	(i)	(i)	Asst. Maj. Ldr., Asst. Min. Ldr.: (i)
Maryland	$5,000/y(j)	(j)	(j)	(j)	Major Cmte. Chmn.: (j); Major Delegations Chmn.: (j)
Massachusetts	$35,000/y	...	$22,500/y	$22,500/y	Asst. Maj. Flr. Ldrs., Asst. Min. Flr. Ldrs.: $15,000/y
Michigan	$18,000/y	0	0	$8,600/y(k)	Appropriations Cmte. Chmn.: $2,000/y
Minnesota	$7,400/y	...	$7,400/y	$7,400/y	
Mississippi	$25,900/y(l)	...	...	...	
Missouri	$2,500/y	$1,500/y	$1,500/y	$1,500/y	
Montana	$5/d	0	0	0	
Nebraska	-----------------------------Unicameral Legislature-----------------------------				
Nevada	$2/d(m)	(m)	(m)	(m)	(m)
New Hampshire	$50/b	0	0	0	
New Jersey	$8,333.33/y(n)	0	0	0	
New Mexico	0	...	0	0	
New York	$30,000/y	$18,000/y	$25,000/y	$25,000/y	Dep. Spkr.: $18,000/y; Min. Ldr. Pro Tem.: $15,000/y; Chmn., Cmte. on Cmtes.: $18,000/y; Dep. Maj. Ldr., Asst. Maj. Ldr.: $14,000/y; Asst. Min. Ldr., Dep. Min. Ldr., Ranking Min. Mbr., Cmte. on Cmtes., Maj. Whip: $13,000/y; Min. Whip, Maj. Conf. Chmn.: $12,000/y; Min. Conf. Chmn.: $11,000/y; Maj. Conf. V-Chmn.: $9,000/y; Min. Conf. V-Chmn.: $8,000/y; Cmte. Chmn. & Ranking Min. Mbrs.: Ways & Means: $24,500/y & $15,000/y; Education, Judiciary, Codes: $13,000/y & $8,000/y; Banks, Cities, Health, Local Govt., Corp.: $11,000/y & $7,000/y; Labor: $10,000/y & $6,500/y; All other cmtes.: $9,000/y & $6,500/y
North Carolina	$6,924/y(o)	$1,728/y(o,p)	(p)	$1,728/y(o)	Chmn., Standing & Interim Cmtes.: $3/d; Chmn., Legislative Council: $5/d during interim
North Dakota	$5/d	...	$5/d	$5/d	
Ohio	$12,500/y	$9,500/y	$7,500/y	$8,500/y	Asst. Maj. Flr. Ldr.: $4,500/y; Maj. Whip, Min. Whip: $2,500/y; Asst. Min. Ldr.: $6,500/y; Chmn., Standing Cmtes.: $1,500/yr; Chmn., Standing Sub-Cmtes.: $750/y
Oklahoma	$9,330/y	0	$6,440/y	$6,440/y	
Oregon	$700/m	0	0	0	
Pennsylvania(q)	$19,600/y	...	$15,680/y	$15,680/y	Maj. Whip, Min. Whip: $11,900/y; Maj. Caucus Chmn., Min. Caucus Chmn.: $7,420/y; Maj. Caucus Secy., Min. Caucus Secy., Maj. Policy Chmn., Min. Policy Chmn., Maj. Caucus Admin., Min. Caucus Admin.: $4,900/y

ADDITIONAL COMPENSATION FOR HOUSE LEADERS—Continued

State	Speaker	Speaker pro tem	Majority leader	Minority leader	Other
Rhode Island	$5/d	0	0	0	
South Carolina	$11,000/y	$3,600/y	0	0	Speaker Emeritus: $1,500/y
South Dakota	0	0	0	0	
Tennessee	(r)	0	0	0	
Texas	0	0	. . .	. . .	
Utah	0(s)	. . .	0(s)	0(s)	
Vermont	(t)	. . .	0	0	
Virginia	$17,000/y(u)	. . .	0	0	
Washington	0	0	0	0	
West Virginia	$35/d	0	$15/d	$15/d	
Wisconsin	$25/m	0	0	0	
Wyoming	$3/d	0	0	0	

Note: This table reflects the amount paid the leadership in addition to their regular legislative compensation.

Key:
d—day
y—year
b—biennium
m—month
. . .—Position does not exist or is not selected on a regular basis

(a) Receives a special public relations expense allowance of $6,450/y.

(b) Official title is deputy speaker.

(c) The positions of chairman and vice-chairman of the Joint Finance Committee alternate between the House and Senate every other year. The chairman also receives $161.30/m.

(d) Receives an annual salary of $22,800 plus a sum equal to the amount of salary over $30,000 per annum which is received by the lieutenant governor.

(e) This amount is provided by resolution of the House and cannot be greater than the additional amount provided by law for the speaker pro tempore of the House of Representatives.

(f) Official title is vice speaker.

(g) Receives additional $20/d for expenses.

(h) Receives $32,000 annual salary and up to $10,000/y in reimbursement for actual expenses, which replaces all per diems and allowances paid to other legislators.

(i) Additional compensation for House leaders is calculated according to the following percentages of the base salaries during sessions: speaker, 50 percent; majority and minority leaders, 25 percent; and assistant majority and minority leaders, 12.5 percent. No additional compensation is given during interim.

(j) Speaker, speaker pro tempore, majority leader, minority leader and major committee chairmen receive an additional $1,150/y for district office expenses. Chairmen of major delegations receive an addtional $700/y for district office expenses.

(k) Compensation indicated is for minority leaders. The minority floor leader receives no additional compensation.

(l) Total salary is $34,000/y.

(m) Supplemental allowance for postage and telephone, not to exceed $300 during a regular session or $40 during a special session. Chairmen of standing committees also eligible to receive allowance.

(n) Equal to one-third of regular annual salary.

(o) Speaker receives $2,028/y additional expense allowance; speaker pro tempore and minority leader each receive additional $648/y expense allowance.

(p) Speaker pro tempore is also majority leader.

(q) Compensation shown is effective December 1, 1984.

(r) Receives $5,700/y allowance for office in home district, $4,154.01/y allowance for services as speaker, and $750/y for ex-officio services as speaker.

(s) Beginning January 1, 1985, the speaker of the House will receive an additional $1,000/y, and the majority and minority leaders will each receive an additional $500/y.

(t) Receives compensation of $5,850/y, $325/week during regular and adjourned sessions, $65/d during special sessions, plus actual expenses.

(u) Speaker's office is allotted additional $28,500 for one or two aides and $17,500 for one or two clerical staff persons.

Table 9
LEGISLATIVE COMPENSATION: INTERIM PAYMENTS AND OTHER DIRECT PAYMENTS

State	Compensation for committee or official business during interim			Other direct payments or services to legislators
	Per diem compensation for committee or official business	Travel allowance (cents per mile)	Per diem living expenses	
Alabama		20		
Alaska	$20	0	$65 per meeting day	
Arizona	$50	20.5	Actual expenses if legislator travels. (V)	
Arkansas		23		
California	$50/d to max. $2,500	(a)	$62	Max. $420/m for "home office" expenses during interim (V)
Colorado		20 (24/4-wheel drive)	Actual and necessary (V)	
Connecticut		20		$2,500/y expense allowance (U)
Delaware		15		$2,500/y expense allotment (U)
Florida		20	$50 (V)	$1,000/m for district office expenses
Georgia		20	$59	$4,800/y expense allowance limited to the following purposes: rents, district office(s), office supplies and materials, office equipment, secretarial assistance, utilities, postage (which shall not be for a political newsletter), communications, stationery, lodging, meals, travel and per diem differential. (V)
Hawaii	$35	0	$10 on island of residence; $45 inter-island travel; $60 out-of-state	$2,500/y allowance for incidental expenses (U)
Idaho		0	Actual expenses (V)	
Illinois		20	(b)	
Indiana		24	$65 (V)	
Iowa	$40	22	Actual expenses (V)	$15/d, six days a week, for postage and miscellaneous items year-round (U)
Kansas	$47	22	$50 (U)	
Kentucky	$75	20.5	Actual (V)	
Louisiana	$75	21 or coach airfare if lives more than 100 miles from capitol		$400/m April through December to defray expenses $50/session stationery allowance; $950/m interim expense allowance Allowance for reimbursement of travel expenses for attendance at conferences, seminars and other official business approved by the presiding officer, including $40/d, reimbursement of lodging at single occupancy rate, reimbursement for airline ticket at coach fare, and reimbursement for registration fees (V). $325/m allowance to cover rent, utilities and/or expenses for a district office (V). Also, $1,000 initial furniture allowance, plus an additional $250 for each four-year term (title to furniture remains with state).

Compensation for committee or official business during interim

State	Per diem compensation for committee or official business	Travel allowance (cents per mile)	Per diem living expenses	Other direct payments or services to legislators
Maine	$35	22	$45 for meals and lodging or $21 for meals only (V)	
Maryland		19	$68 for lodging and meals (V)	Senators receive $7,050/y, delegates $10,850/y as district office expense account for maintaining offices in legislative districts
Massachusetts		Included in living expense allowance	Amount for mileage, meals and lodging, ranging from $5 to $50 depending on distance legislator's district is from Boston	$2,400/y general expense allowance
Michigan	$48	0		
Minnesota		26	Max. $45/night for lodging, and actual single rates out-of-state	Interim district travel allowance, based on size of district: mileage reimbursement is $.15/sq mile, with a $45/m base rate and $250/m maximum (V)
Mississippi	$40	20	Actual expenses: room, registration fee must be vouchered; meals, tips, etc. unvouchered(c)	$210/m for months when legislature is not in session over 15 days
Missouri		17	Lodging and meals (V)	
Montana	$49.21	20.5	$38.50 (V)	
Nebraska		21	Actual and necessary expenses (V)	$1,000 telephone allowance/regular session, $200/special session (U);
Nevada	$104	24	$47.50 in-state; $21 plus "reasonable room rate" out-of-state (V)	postage allowance of $60/regular session (U)
New Hampshire		38 first 45 miles, 19 thereafter	Actual and necessary (V)	
New Jersey		0		
New Mexico	$75	25	$50 (U)	Stationery, postage, telephone and telegraph (U)
New York		0		$2,064/y expense allowance. Use of telephone in state legislative office for local calls
North Carolina		25	$30 lodging (V); $17 meals (U)	$180/m for uncompensated expenses, paid every six months (U)
North Dakota	$62.50	20	$11 in-state and $18 out-of-state meal allowance	
Ohio		(d)	(V); other actual and necessary traveling expenses. (V)(d)	
Oklahoma	$25	22(e)	$44. Actual and necessary out-of-state expenses (V)	$600 telephone credit card allowance; five rolls of 1st class postage stamps
Oregon		20		$300/m interim expenses (U); where technically possible, state centrex line—rental not to exceed $70/m; $10/m for toll charge calls to max. $180 (V). Where centrex would cost more than $70/m, receives a phone credit card and may charge up to $75/m (V). $10,000/y expense allowance (V) and district office allowance
Pennsylvania		20	Max. $75 (U)	
Rhode Island		0		
South Carolina	$35	23	$50 for committee subsistence (V)	Data and word processing; $400/y postage allowance (V)
South Dakota		21	$18/night for room (V); $14.50/d for meals	$250/m home office allowance (U)
Tennessee	$50	19.96	$66.47 (U)	

LEGISLATIVE COMPENSATION: INTERIM PAYMENTS AND OTHER DIRECT PAYMENTS—Continued

State	Compensation for committee or official business during interim			Other direct payments or services to legislators
	Per diem compensation for committee or official business	Travel allowance (cents per mile)	Per diem living expenses	
Texas		(f)	Max. $55 lodging and actual cost of meals (V)	Senate: all reasonable and necessary office expenses during interim; $13,500/m max. staff payroll in session, $12,500/m max. staff payroll during interim. House: $6,500/m operating account in session, $5,500/m during interim
Utah	$65(g)	23	$25 subsistence. Everyone who lives outside of Salt Lake or Davis receives $35 lodging allowance or mileage but not both	
Vermont	$55	20.5	$27.50 for lodging; $22.50 for meals if renting room in Montpelier or vicinity; $18.75 for meals otherwise (U)	
Virginia	$100	20.5	Actual expenses $50 (V)	$3,000/y for office supplies and expenses; $9,000/y for aides $200/m for actual expenses, travel, subsistence, use of private materials, facilities and personnel, in performance of duties not otherwise entitled to reimbursement during interim (V)
Washington		20.5		
West Virginia ...	$35	17	$20 meals (U); $30 lodging (V)	$25 (for representatives), $75 (for senators) for interim postage and clerical expenses for full calendar months in which legislature is in actual session 3 days or less Telephone credit cards, stationery
Wisconsin		20.5(h)	$41.63 when legislator must establish temporary residence at state capitol	
Wyoming	$30	20	$60 (U) or actual expenses for out-of-state travel (V)	

Note: For more information on legislative compensation, see Legislative Compensation: Regular and Special Sessions.

Key:
U—Unvouchered
V—Vouchered
d—day
m—month
y—year

(a) Legislators are provided a leased state car up to $265 per month and gasoline credit card.
(b) When not in session (i.e. not any day in a calendar week) legislators are permitted two round trips a month with one $36/d allowance for each trip (V).
(c) Legislative Management Committee has authority to set limits.
(d) Business trips must be approved by the speaker of the House or the president of the Senate. To be reimbursed for expenses other than meals, the legislators must fill out an expense report and provide receipts.
(e) Reimbursement limited to 20 round trips during interim.
(f) Travel mileage reimbursement is 23 cents per mile in personally-owned automobiles, 40 cents per highway mile in a personally-owned or leased single engine aircraft, and 65 cents per mile when traveling in a personally-owned or leased twin engine aircraft. Reimbursement for commercial air transportation may not exceed the next lowest airline fare below first class unless such is not available.
(g) Legislators receive this amount each day they attend veto-override and special sessions and authorized legislative interim meetings, not to exceed 25 days per calendar year.
(h) Legislators are entitled to a transportation allowance of one round trip weekly to the capitol.

Table 10
MEMBERSHIP TURNOVER IN THE LEGISLATURES: 1982

	Senate			House		
State	*Total number of members*	*Number of membership changes*	*Percentage change of total*	*Total number of members*	*Number of membership changes*	*Percentage change of total*
Alabama	35	16	46	105	43	41
Alaska	20 (a)	6	30	40	22	55
Arizona	30	9	30	60	20	33
Arkansas	35	11	31	100	18	18
California	40 (a)	9	22	80	25	31
Colorado	35 (a)	11	31	65	27	42
Connecticut	36	10	28	151	42	28
Delaware	21	2	10	41	13	32
Florida	40 (a)	14	35	120	46	38
Georgia	56	12	21	180	48	27
Hawaii	25 (a)	7	28	51	18	35
Idaho	35	10	28	70	22	31
Illinois	59	18	30	118 (b)		
Indiana...............	50 (a)	9	18	100	26	26
Iowa	50 (a)	12	24	100	42	42
Kansas	40 (c)			125	33	26
Kentucky	38 (c)			100 (c)		
Louisiana	39 (c)			105 (c)		
Maine	33	9	27	151	38	25
Maryland	47	19	40	141	50	35
Massachusetts	40	6	15	160	23	14
Michigan	38	16	42	110	46	42
Minnesota	67	22	33	134	43	32
Mississippi	52 (c)			122 (c)		
Missouri..............	34 (a)	7	20	163	47	29
Montana	50 (a)	12	24	100	34	34
Nebraska	49 (a)	10	20	Unicameral		
Nevada...............	21 (d)			42 (d)		
New Hampshire	24	7	29	400	161	40
New Jersey............	40 (c)			80 (c)		
New Mexico	42 (a)	1	2	70	23	33
New York	61 (d)			150	41	27
North Carolina	50	18	36	120	35	29
North Dakota	53 (d)			106 (d)		
Ohio	33 (a)	8	24	99	33	33
Oklahoma	48 (a)	8	17	101	24	24
Oregon...............	30 (a)	9	30	60	15	25
Pennsylvania	50 (a)	6	12	203	39	19
Rhode Island	50 (c)			100	22	22
South Carolina	46 (c)			124	25	20
South Dakota	35	10	28	70	19	27
Tennessee	33 (a)	6	18	99	16	16
Texas	31 (a)	10	32	150	46	31
Utah	29 (a)	6	21	75	30	40
Vermont..............	30	11	37	150	55	37
Virginia	40 (c)			100	34	34
Washington	49 (a)	8	16	98	45	46
West Virginia	34 (a)	14	41	100	40	40
Wisconsin	33 (a)	9	27	99	36	36
Wyoming..............	30 (a)	8	27	64 (d)		

Note: Turnover calculated after 1982 legislative elections. Data was obtained by comparing the 1981-82 and 1983-84 editions of *State Elective Officials and the Legislatures*, published by The Council of State Governments.

(a) Entire Senate membership not up for reelection in 1982.
(b) Voters approved a constitutional amendment in 1980 to reduce the size of the House from 177 to 118. Turnover cannot be determined using method employed here.
(c) No election held in 1982. In Rhode Island, Senate elections were held in 1983 instead of 1982 as a result of court-ordered redistricting.
(d) Total number of seats changed due to redistricting. Turnover cannot be determined using method employed here.

Table 11
INTRODUCTIONS AND ENACTMENTS:
REGULAR SESSIONS, 1981 AND 1982 SESSIONS

State or other jurisdiction	Duration of session*	Introductions		Enactments		Measures vetoed by governor	Length of session
		Bills	Resolu-tions	Bills	Resolu-tions		
Alabama	Feb. 3-May 18, 1981	1,798	334	868	334	N.A.	105C
	Jan. 12-April 26, 1982	1,371	265	628	265	N.A.	105C
Alaska	Jan. 12-June 25, 1981	1,226	N.A.	120	N.A.	5	165L
	Jan. 11-June 3, 1982	567	N.A.	144	N.A.	14	144L
Arizona	Jan. 12-April 25, 1981	906	26	321	3	15	103C
	Jan. 11-April 24, 1982	918	46	338	12	4	103C
Arkansas	Jan. 12-March 18, 1981	1,647	263	1,041	N.A.	47	66C
California	Dec. 1, 1980-Nov. 30, 1982	5,910	582	2,831	365	70	(a)
Colorado	Jan. 7-Nov. 30, 1981	1,146	133	515	80	23(b)	328C
	Jan. 6-May 24, 1982	437	80	173	55	2	139C
Connecticut	Jan. 7-June 3, 1981	3,573	N.A.	473	N.A.	15	95L
	Feb. 3-May 5, 1982	1,653	N.A.	472	N.A.	5	63L
Delaware	Jan. 13-June 30, 1981	870	370	193	N.A.	11	169C
	Jan. 12-June 30, 1982	600	419	270	N.A.	24	170C
Florida	April 7-June 5, 1981	2,210	83	513	55	19	60C
	Jan. 18-March 25, 1982	2,022	100	355	56	7	67C
Georgia	Jan. 12-March 25, 1981	1,598	717	839	562	12	40L
	Jan. 11-March 26, 1982	1,159	689	753(c)	586	12	40L
Hawaii	Jan. 21-April 30, 1981	4,073	1,462(d)	243	646(d)	33	101C
	Jan. 20-April 28, 1982	2,136	883	308	420	0	99C
Idaho	Jan. 12-March 27, 1981	701	61	381	24	16	75C
	Jan. 11-March 24, 1982	617	54	381	23	11	73C
Illinois	Jan. 14-Oct. 30, 1981	3,285	1,185	740	866	89	82L
	Jan. 13, 1982-Jan. 12, 1983	1,098	1,270	319	1,162	11	65L
Indiana	Nov. 18, 1980-April 30, 1981	1,628	265	332	88	7	61L
	Nov. 17, 1981-Feb. 20, 1982	886	191	230	104	5	30L
Iowa	Jan. 12-May 22, 1981	1,457	167	206	N.A.	0	131C
	Jan. 11-April 24, 1982	813	129	270	N.A.	5	104C
Kansas	Jan. 12-May 29, 1981	1,092	72	398	30	12	69L
	Jan. 11-May 14, 1982	988(e)	68	438	27	16	68L
Kentucky	Jan. 5-April 15, 1982	1,229	233	432	28	10(b)	60L
Louisiana	April 20-July 13, 1981	3,049	634	1,027	457	83	(a)
	April 19-July 12, 1982	2,946	416	952	308	69	(a)
Maine	Dec. 3, 1980-June 19, 1981	1,692	2	1,805	2	4	100L
	Jan. 6-April 13, 1982	447	3	163	N.A.	0	50L
Maryland	Jan. 14-April 13, 1981	3,041	176	814	30	95	90C
	Jan. 13-April 12, 1982	3,052	173	916	30	124	90C
Massachusetts	Jan. 7, 1981-Jan. 5, 1982	9,588	N.A.	809	9	8	364C
	Jan. 6, 1982-Jan. 5, 1983	8,858	N.A.	669	12	8	364C
Michigan	Jan. 14-Dec. 30, 1981	1,980	1,669	232	N.A.	2	351C
	Jan. 13-Dec. 29, 1982	1,214	1,762	541	N.A.	8	351C
Minnesota	Jan. 6-May 18, 1981	3,018	N.A.	386	3	7	57L
	Jan. 12-March 19, 1982	1,484	N.A.	286	5	10	34L
Mississippi	Jan. 6-April 8, 1981	2,637	306	636	186	7	93C
	Jan. 5-April 10, 1982	2,326	368	544	187	4	96C
Missouri	Jan. 7-June 30, 1981	1,361	21	156	5	5	(a)
	Jan. 6-May 14, 1982	1,290	82	133	10	5	(a)
Montana	Jan. 5-April 23, 1981	1,362	119	652	75	9	90L
Nebraska	Jan. 7-May 29, 1981	612(f)	196	290	75	14(b)	90L
	Jan. 6-April 16, 1982	409(f)	389	186	71	7(b)	60L
Nevada	Jan. 19-June 4, 1981	1,427	282	782	203	12	101L
New Hampshire	Dec. 3, 1980-Sept. 28, 1981	1,269	102	575	78	16	49L
New Jersey	Jan. 13, 1981-Jan. 12, 1982	1,428	192	570(g)	59	109	61L
	Jan. 12, 1982-Jan. 11, 1983	4,400	505	234	57	63	76L
New Mexico	Jan. 20-March 21, 1981	1,211	37	445	7	65	60C
	Jan. 19-Feb. 18, 1982	413	28	118	4	4	30C
New York	Jan. 7, 1981-Jan. 6, 1982	16,440	2,559	1,054	2,552	123	(h)
	Jan. 6-Dec. 31, 1982	19,363	2,643	414	2,597	311	(h)
North Carolina	Jan. 14-July 10, 1981	2,156	N.A.	970	78	0	127L
	June 2-June 23, 1982	329	N.A.	270	29	0	16L
North Dakota	Jan. 6-March 31, 1981	1,098	179	648	137	2	60L
Ohio	Jan. 5-Dec. 29, 1981(i)	1,206	1,138	140	1,053	2	(a)
	Jan. 4-Dec. 31, 1982(i)	410	1,228	162	1,204	2	(a)
Oklahoma	Jan. 6-July 20, 1981	840	136	354	76	5(b)	90L
	Jan. 5-July 12, 1982	758	144	377(j)	86	3	86L
Oregon	Jan. 12-Aug. 2, 1981	2,394	139	918	55	17	203C
Pennsylvania	Jan. 6, 1981-Jan. 5, 1982	2,153	236	233	83	3	(a)
	Jan. 5-Nov. 30, 1982	579	131	387	51	3	(a)

State or other jurisdiction	Duration of session*	Introductions Bills	Introductions Resolu-tions	Enactments Bills	Enactments Resolu-tions	Measures vetoed by governor	Length of session
Rhode Island	Jan. 6-May 15, 1981	(k)	(k)	625	485	33	65L
	Jan. 5-May 18, 1982	(k)	(k)	657	414	28	66L
South Carolina	Jan. 13-Oct. 1, 1981	1,300	869	275	N.A.	13	(a)
	Jan. 12-June 16, 1982	856	957	312	N.A.	8	(a)
South Dakota	Jan. 6-March 13, 1981	631	9	391	0	20	40L
	Jan. 5-Feb. 27, 1982	578	7	381	4	11	35L
Tennessee	Jan. 28-July 23, 1981	2,882	128(l)	730	(m)	4	(a)
	Jan. 18-May 6, 1982	1,985	102(l)	611	(m)	18	(a)
Texas	Jan. 13-June 1, 1981	3,696	1,775	902	1,385	27	140C
Utah	Jan. 12-March 12, 1981	714	80	290	25	19	60C
	Jan. 11-Jan. 30, 1982	248	66	86	25	4	20C
Vermont	Jan. 7-May 1, 1981	682	82	117	59	1(b)	72L
	Jan. 5-April 22, 1982	346	145	71	50	1	66L
Virginia	Jan. 14-Apr. 2, 1981(n)	1,399	271	638	184	29	41C
	Jan. 13-Apr. 21, 1982(n)	1,411	332	684	239	22	61C
Washington	Jan. 12-March 11, 1981	2,119	76	349	5	7	90C
	Jan. 11-April 10, 1982	942	47	232	5	3	90C
West Virginia	Jan. 14-April 14, 1981(o)	1,820	168	228	57	5	64C
	Jan. 13-March 13, 1982	1,715	60	143	56	9	60C
Wisconsin	Jan. 5, 1981-Jan. 3, 1983	1,987	246	381	98	11(b)	(a)
Wyoming	Jan. 13-Feb. 28, 1981	775	31	176	6	5	40L
	Feb. 9-March 3, 1982	229	11	75	2	4	20L

*Actual adjournment dates are listed regardless of constitutional or statutory limitations. For more information on provisions, see table on Legislative Sessions: Legal Provisions.

Key:
C—Calendar day
L—Legislative day
N.A.—Not available

(a) California: Senate = 257L, Assembly = 248L; Louisiana: 1981 Senate = 60L, House = 57L and 1982 Senate = 60L, House = 56L; Missouri: 1981 Senate = 97L, House = 90L and 1982 Senate = 70L, House = 67L; Ohio: 1981 Senate = 116L, House = 125L and 1982 Senate = 101L; House = 108L; Pennsylvania: 1981 Senate = 75L, House = 81L and 1982 Senate = 59L, House = 64L; South Carolina: 1981 Senate = 130L, House = 123L and 1982 Senate = 90L, House = 89L; Tennessee: 1981 Senate = 58L, House = 60L and 1982 Senate = 32L; House = 30L; Wisconsin: Senate = 122L, Assembly = 130L.

(b) Number of vetoes overridden. Colorado, 1981—three; Kentucky, 1982—seven bills and one resolution; Nebraska, 1981—eight and 1982—one; Oklahoma, 1981—two; Vermont, 1981—one; Wisconsin—two.

(c) 87 were bills carried over from 1981.

(d) Includes both single house and concurrent bills.

(e) In addition, 565 bills were carried over from the 1981 session.

(f) Number of bills introduced in 1981 includes 50 "A" bills; number introduced in 1982 includes 41 "A" bills.

(g) Because legislature has a two-year session, number is based on bills introduced in 1980 and 1981.

(h) In New York, the session is divided into "workdays," during which the Legislature is actually meeting in session, and "legislative days," in which only one or two legislators perfunctorily open and adjourn for the day in order to speed up the bill consideration progress. In 1981, the Senate met for 79 workdays, and the Assembly for 84 workdays. In 1982, the Senate met for 71 workdays, and the Assembly for 73 workdays.

(i) In 1981, adjournment date for the Senate was December 29, and for the House, December 31. In 1982, the convening date for the Senate was January 4, and for the House, January 5.

(j) 35 of these were bills carried over from 1981.

(k) The total number of bills and resolutions introduced in 1981 and 1982 was 2,614 and 2,069, respectively. Separate totals for bills introduced and resolutions introduced were not available.

(l) In 1981 and 1982, there were 468 and 322 joint resolutions introduced, respectively.

(m) 206 House or Senate resolutions and 654 joint resolutions were adopted during the 1981 and 1982 sessions.

(n) In 1981, legislature met from January 14 to February 21, then recessed until April 1. In 1982, from January 13 to March 13, then recessed until April 21.

(o) Legislature met in organizational session on January 14, then recessed until February 11.

Table 12
INTRODUCTIONS AND ENACTMENTS: SPECIAL SESSIONS,
1981 and 1982 SESSIONS

State	Duration of session*	Introductions Bills	Introductions Resolutions	Enactments Bills	Enactments Resolutions	Measures vetoed by governor	Length of session
Alabama	Aug. 4-Aug. 18, 1981	230	N.A.	21	N.A.	N.A.	15C
	Sept. 29-Oct. 21, 1981	206	N.A.	92	N.A.	N.A.	23C
	Nov. 1-Nov. 30, 1981	182	N.A.	128	N.A.	N.A.	31C
	May 24-June 1, 1982	168	31	24	31	N.A.	9C
	June 21-July 5, 1982	259	47	109	47	N.A.	15C
	Aug. 9-Aug. 13, 1982	257	49	62	49	N.A.	5C
Alaska	July 13-July 15, 1981	0	0	1	0	0	3C
Arizona	July 7-Sept. 4, 1981	3	1	1	0	0	60C
	July 8-July 25, 1981	9	4	1	0	0	18C
	Sept. 1-Sept. 3, 1981	1	2	0	0	0	3C
	Nov. 9-Nov. 9, 1981	1	3	1	0	0	1C
	Dec. 1, 1981-May 19, 1982	1	0	0	0	0	170C
	Dec. 1, 1981-May 19, 1982	4	0	4	0	0	170C
	Dec. 1-Dec. 7, 1981	4	0	3	0	0	7C
Arkansas	Nov. 16-Nov. 25, 1981	100	18	45	N.A.	5	10C
California	Nov. 9, 1981-Feb. 25, 1982	15	6	5	6	0	(a)
Colorado	No special sessions						
Connecticut	Nov. 19, 1981-Jan. 25, 1982	104	N.A.	21	N.A.	2	32L
	June 28-June 30, 1982	3	N.A.	3	N.A.	0	2L
Delaware	July 1-July 1, 1981	N.A.	N.A.	N.A.	N.A.	N.A.	1C
	July 7-July 7, 1981	N.A.	N.A.	N.A.	N.A.	N.A.	1C
	July 24-July 24, 1981	N.A.	N.A.	N.A.	N.A.	N.A.	1C
	Oct. 1-Oct. 1, 1981	N.A.	N.A.	N.A.	N.A.	N.A.	1C
	Oct. 9-Oct. 9, 1981	N.A.	N.A.	N.A.	N.A.	N.A.	1C
	July 1-July 1, 1982	N.A.	N.A.	N.A.	N.A.	N.A.	1C
Florida	June 5-June 17, 1981	32	2	6	2	0	13C
	March 26-March 29, 1982	0	1(b)	0	1(b)	0	4C
	March 29-April 7, 1982	40	6(b)	28	6(b)	1	10C
	April 7-April 7, 1982	0	0	0	0	0	1C
	April 7-April 7, 1982	8	0	7	0	0	1C
	May 21-May 21, 1982	16	3	7	3	0	1C
	June 21-June 22, 1982	49	13(b)	28	9(b)	0	2C
Georgia	Aug. 24-Sept. 18, 1981	6	66	5	63	0	18L
	Aug. 3-Aug. 8, 1982	3	25	1	25	0	6L
Hawaii	June 22-June 29, 1981	24	0	22	0	0	6C
	May 5-May 16, 1982	0	0	0	0	0	2C
Idaho	July 7-July 21, 1981	16	3	2	0	1	14C
Illinois	No special sessions						
Indiana	May 27-May 29, 1981	1	0	1	0	0	3L
Iowa	June 24-June 26, 1981 and Aug. 12-Aug. 14, 1981(c)	3	0	N.A.	0	0	6C
Kansas	No special sessions						
Kentucky	No special sessions						
Louisiana	Nov. 2-Nov. 13, 1981	68	60	43	47	1	(a)
Maine	Aug. 3-Aug. 3, 1981	1	1	1	1	0	1L
	Sept. 25-Sept. 25, 1981	4	0	4	0	0	1L
	Dec. 9-Dec. 9, 1981	2	0	2	0	0	1L
	April 28-April 29, 1982	7	2	7	2	0	2L
	May 13-May 13, 1982	5	0	5	0	0	1L
Maryland	Aug. 6-Aug. 6, 1982	6	1	1	0	0	1C
Massachusetts	No special sessions						
Michigan	No special sessions						
Minnesota	June 6-June 6, 1981	6	0	5	0	0	1L
	July 1-July 2, 1981	20	1	6	1	0	2L
	Dec. 1, 1981-Jan. 18, 1982	52	0	4	0	1	17L
	March 30-March 30, 1982	7	0	3	0	0	1L
	July 9-July 9, 1982	8	0	2	0	0	1L
	Dec. 7-Dec. 10, 1982	6	0	1	0	0	4L
Mississippi	Aug. 25-Aug. 27, 1981	15	11	10	10	0	3L
	Dec. 6-Dec. 21, 1982	29	18	3	13	0	16L
Missouri	Nov. 6-Dec. 17, 1981	5	0	0	0	0	(a)
	Aug. 16-Sept. 21, 1982	14	0	8	0	0	(a)
Montana	Nov. 16-Nov. 24, 1981	23	0	13	0	0	8L
	June 21-June 26, 1982	31	5	12	1	(d)	6L
Nebraska	Oct. 30-Nov. 7, 1981	8	7	2	3	0	7L
	Nov. 5-Nov. 13, 1982	3	2	2	2	0	7L
Nevada	No special sessions						
New Hampshire	Nov. 17, 1981-Sept. 16, 1982	77	23	45	21	7	13L

State	Duration of session*	Introductions Bills	Introductions Resolutions	Enactments Bills	Enactments Resolutions	Measures vetoed by governor	Length of session
New Jersey	Jan. 11-Jan. 11, 1982(e)	0	0	4	0	0	1L
New Mexico	March 22-March 26, 1981	25	0	11	0	11	5C
	Jan. 9-Jan. 19, 1982	11	0	4	0	0	11C
	June 14-June 21, 1982	8	0	4	0	0	8C
New York	April 4-May 14, 1981	19	2	0	2	0	(f)
	Sept. 16-Sept. 16, 1981	19	2	0	2	0	(f)
	Dec. 13-Dec. 22, 1982	51	76	17	76	0	(f)
North Carolina	Oct. 5-Oct. 10, 1981 and Oct. 29-Oct. 30, 1981(c)	63	N.A.	160	15	0	8C
	Feb. 9-Feb. 11, 1982 and April 26-April 27, 1982(c)	17	N.A.	10	4	0	5C
North Dakota	Nov. 16-Nov. 19, 1981(g)	19	5	6	5	0	4C
Ohio	No special sessions						
Oklahoma	Aug. 31-Sept. 4, 1981	6	10	3	8	0	5L
Oregon	Oct. 24-Oct. 24, 1981	4	2	3	1	0	1C
	Jan. 18-March 1, 1982	50	6	36	4	0	37C
	June 14-June 14, 1982	4	1	4	0	0	1C
	Sept. 3-Sept. 3, 1982	4	1	4	1	0	1C
Pennsylvania	No special sessions						
Rhode Island	June 12-June 12, 1981	2	2	2	2	0	1L
	July 8-July 29, 1982	5	3	4	2	0	3L
South Carolina	No special sessions						
South Dakota	May 18-May 18, 1981	4	1	2	0	0	1L
	Sept. 23-Sept. 24, 1981	4	0	4	0	0	2L
Tennessee	No special sessions						
Texas	July 13-Aug. 11, 1981	202	380	26	324	1	30C
	May 24-May 28, 1982	30	237	2	204	0	5C
	Sept. 7-Sept. 9, 1982	12	81	2	80	0	3C
Utah	Oct. 28-Nov. 20, 1981	27	8	12	7	2	5C
	June 17-June 19, 1982	22	6	10	5	1	3C
	Dec. 15-Dec. 16, 1982	20	2	11	2	0	2C
Vermont	July 15-July 16, 1981	6	0	2	0	0	2L
Virginia	(h)	27	63	16	56	2	24C
	Apr. 1-Apr. 1, 1982(e)	1	5	1	5	0	1C
Washington	March 12-April 26, 1981	21	0	55	0	3	44C
	April 28-April 28, 1981	N.A.	N.A.	1	N.A.	N.A.	1C
	Nov. 9-Dec. 2, 1981	N.A.	N.A.	14	N.A.	N.A.	24C
	June 26-July 2, 1982	N.A.	N.A.	15	N.A.	N.A.	7C
West Virginia	May 4-May 14, 1981	34	11	10	5	0	11C
	May 27-May 27, 1981	11	7	2	7	0	1C
	April 2-April 3, 1982	10	9	5	7	0	2C
Wisconsin	Nov. 4-Nov. 17, 1981 and Dec. 15-Dec. 17, 1981(i)	6	5	3	5	0	17C
	Apr. 6-Apr. 30, 1982, May 5-May 20, 1982 and May 26-May 28, 1982(j)	17	13	10	12	1	43C
Wyoming	March 2-March 3, 1981	31	0	26	0	3	2L

*Actual adjournment dates are listed regardless of constitutional or statutory limitations. For more information on provisions, see table on Legislative Sessions: Legal Provisions.

Key:
C—Calendar day
L—Legislative day
N.A.—Not available

(a) California: Senate = 23L, Assembly = 29L; Louisiana: Senate = 12L; House = 10L; Missouri: 1981 Senate = 12L, House = 7L and 1982 Senate = 19L; House = 15L.
(b) During these special sessions in 1982, eight joint resolutions were introduced, four were enacted.
(c) These dates comprise one special session.
(d) Governor used line item veto on one bill enacted by legislature.
(e) Veto provisions.

(f) In New York, the session is divided into "workdays," during which the legislature is actually meeting in session, and "legislative days," in which only one or two legislators perfunctorily open and adjourn for the day in order to speed up the bill consideration progress. In the first 1981 special session, the Senate met for four workdays, and the Assembly for three workdays. In the second 1981 special session, the Senate and Assembly each met for one workday. In the 1982 special session, the Senate met for one workday, and the Assembly for five workdays.
(g) Reconvened session called pursuant to a concurrent resolution passed during the regular session.
(h) Legislature came into special session on March 30 and met for a total of 24 days in the period between March 30, 1981 and January 1982.
(i) Legislature met in special session between November 4 and November 17. In that session, the legislature scheduled the December dates as a veto review period.
(j) Legislature met concurrently in the two April sessions and the May session.

Table 13
LEGISLATIVE SESSIONS: LEGAL PROVISIONS

State or other jurisdiction	Regular sessions				Special sessions		
	Year	Legislature convenes Month	Day	Limitation on length of session(a)	Legislature may call	Legislature may determine subject	Limitation on length of session
Alabama	Annual	Jan.	2nd Tues.(b)	30 L in 105 C	No	Yes(f)	12 L in 30 C
		Apr.	3rd Tues.(c,d)				
		Feb.	1st Tues.(e)				
Alaska	Annual	Jan.	3rd Mon.(c)	None	By 2/3 vote of members	Yes(g)	30 C
Arizona	Annual	Jan.	2nd Mon.(e)	(h)	By petition, 2/3 members, each house	Yes(g)	None
Arkansas	Biennial-odd year	Jan.	2nd Mon.	60 C(i)	No	(j)	(j)
California	Annual (k)	Jan.	1st Mon.(d)	None	No	No	None
Colorado	Annual	Jan.	Wed. after 1st Tues.	(l)	By request, 2/3 members, each house	Yes(g)	None
Connecticut	Annual(m)	Jan.	Wed. after 1st Mon.(n)	(p)	Yes(q)	(q)	None(r)
		Feb.	Wed. after 1st Mon.(o)				
Delaware	Annual	Jan.	2nd Tues.	June 30	Joint call, presiding officers, both houses	Yes	None
Florida	Annual	Apr.	Tues. after 1st Mon.(d)	60 C(i)	Joint call, presiding officers, both houses	Yes	20 C(i)
Georgia	Annual	Jan.	2nd. Mon.(d)	40 L	By petition, 3/5 members, each house	Yes(g)	(s)
Hawaii	Annual	Jan.	3rd Wed.	60 L(i)	By petition, 2/3 members, each house	Yes	30 L(i)
Idaho	Annual	Jan.	Mon. on or nearest 9th day	None	No	No	20 C
Illinois	Annual	Jan.	2nd Wed.	None	Joint call, presiding officers, both houses	Yes	20 C
Indiana	Annual	Jan.	2nd Mon.(d,t)	odd-61 L or Apr. 30; even-30 L or Mar. 15	No	Yes	30 L in 40 C
Iowa	Annual	Jan.	2nd. Mon.	(u)	By petition, 2/3 members, both houses	Yes	None
Kansas	Annual	Jan.	2nd Mon.	odd-None; even-90 C(i)	Petition to governor of 2/3 members, each house	Yes	None
Kentucky	Biennial-even yr.	Jan.	Tues. after 1st Mon.(d)	60 L(v)	No	No	None
Louisiana	Annual (k,m)	Apr.	3rd Mon.	60 L in 85 C	By petition, majority, each house	Yes(g)	30 C
Maine	Annual	Dec.	1st Wed.(b)	100 L	Joint call, presiding officers, with consent of majority of members of each political party, each house	Yes(g)	None
		Jan.	Wed. after 1st Tues.(o)	50 L			
Maryland	Annual	Jan.	2nd Wed.	90 C(i)	By petition, majority, each house	Yes	30 C

State	Frequency	Month	Convening day	Limitation on length of session	Who may call special session	Legislator may call	Limit on length
Massachusetts	Annual	Jan.	1st Wed.	None	By petition(w)	Yes	None
Michigan	Annual	Jan.	2nd Wed.(d)	None	No	No	None
Minnesota	(x)	Jan.	Tues. after 1st Mon.(n)	120 L or 1st Mon. after 3rd Sat. in May(x)	No	Yes	None
Mississippi	Annual	Jan.	Tues. after 1st Mon.	125 C(i,y); 90 C(i,y)	No	No	None
Missouri	Annual	Jan.	Wed. after 1st Mon.	odd-June 30; even-May 15	No	No	60 C
Montana	Biennial-odd yr.	Jan.	1st Mon.	90 L	By petition, majority, each house	Yes	None
Nebraska	Annual	Jan.	Wed. after 1st Mon.	odd-90 L(i); even-60 L(i)	By petition, 2/3 members, each house	No	None
Nevada	Biennial-odd yr.	Jan.	3rd Mon.	60 C(u)	No	No	20 C(u)
New Hampshire	Biennial-odd yr.	Jan.	Wed. after 1st Tues.(d)	90 L or July 1(u)	By 2/3 vote of members	Yes	(u)
New Jersey	Annual	Jan.	2nd Tues.	None	By petition, majority, each house	Yes	None
New Mexico	Annual(m)	Jan.	3rd Tues.	odd-60 C; even-30 C	By petition, 3/5 members, each house	Yes(g)	30 C
New York	Annual	Jan.	Wed. after 1st Mon.	None	By petition, 2/3 members, each house	Yes(g)	None
North Carolina	(x)	Jan.	Wed. after 2nd Mon.(n)	None(x)	By petition, 3/5 members, each house	Yes	None
North Dakota	Biennial-odd yr.	Jan.	Tues. after Jan. 3, but not later than Jan. 11(d)	80 L(z)	No	Yes	None
Ohio	Annual	Jan.	1st Mon.	None	Joint call, presiding officers, both houses	Yes	None
Oklahoma	Annual	Jan.	Tues. after 1st Mon.	90 L	By 2/3 vote of members	Yes	None
Oregon	Biennial-odd yr.	Jan.	2nd Mon.	None	By petition, majority, each house	Yes	None
Pennsylvania	Annual	Jan.	1st Tues.	None	By petition, majority, each house	No	None
Rhode Island	Annual	Jan.	1st Tues.	60 L(u)	No	No	None
South Carolina	Annual	Jan.	2nd Tues.(d)	1st Thurs. in June(i)	No	Yes	None
South Dakota	Annual	Jan.	Tues. after 1st Mon. (aa)	odd-40 L; even-35 L	No	No	None
Tennessee	(x)	Jan.	2nd Tues.	90 L(u)	By petition, 2/3 members, each house	Yes	30 L(u)
Texas	Biennial-odd yr.	Jan.		140 C	No	No	30 C
Utah	Annual(m)	Jan.	2nd Mon.	odd-60 C; even-20 C	No	No	30 C
Vermont	(x)	Jan.	Wed. after 1st Mon.(n)	(u)	No	Yes	None
Virginia	Annual	Jan.	2nd Wed.	odd-30 C(i); even-60 C(i)	By petition, 2/3 members, each house	Yes	None
Washington	Annual	Jan.	2nd Mon.	odd-105 C; even-60 C	By petition, 2/3 members, each house	Yes	30 C
West Virginia	Annual	Feb.	2nd Wed.(c,d)	60 C(i)	By petition, 3/5 members, each house	Yes(bb)	None
Wisconsin	Annual(cc)	Jan.	1st Tues. after Jan. 8(d,n)	None	No	No	None

LEGISLATIVE SESSIONS: LEGAL PROVISIONS—Continued

State or other jurisdiction	Regular sessions				Special sessions		
	Legislature convenes			Limitation on length of session(a)	Legislature may call	Legislature may determine subject of session	Limitation on length of session
	Year	Month	Day				
Wyoming	Annual(m)	Jan.	2nd Tues.(n)	odd-40 L; even-20 L	No	Yes	None
		Feb.	2nd Tues.(o)				
Dist. of Col.	(dd)	Jan.	2nd day	None	No	No	None
American Samoa	Annual	Jan.	2nd Mon.	45 L		No	None
		July	2nd Mon.	45 L			None
Guam	Annual	Jan.	1st Mon. (ee)	None	No	No	None
Puerto Rico	Annual	Jan.	2nd Mon.	Apr. 30(i)	No	No	20 C
Virgin Islands	Annual	Jan.	2nd Mon.	75 L	No	No	15 C

Note: Some legislatures will also reconvene after normal session to consider bills vetoed by governor. Connecticut—if governor vetoes any bill, secretary of state must reconvene General Assembly on second Monday after the last day on which governor is either authorized to transmit or has transmitted every bill with his objections, whichever occurs first; General Assembly must adjourn *sine die* not later than three days after its reconvening. Hawaii—legislature may reconvene on 45th day after adjournment *sine die*, in special session, without call. Louisiana—legislature meets in a maximum five-day veto session on the 40th day after final adjournment. Missouri—if governor returns any bill on or after the fifth day before the last day on which legislature may consider bills (in even-numbered years), legislature automatically reconvenes on first Monday in September for a maximum 10 C session. New Jersey—legislature meets in special session (without call or petition) to act on bills returned by governor on 45th day after *sine die* adjournment of the first year of a two-year legislature; a special session may not be convened if the 45th day falls on or after the last day of the legislative year in which the second session occurs. Virginia—legislature reconvenes on sixth Wednesday after adjournment *sine die* for a maximum three-day session (may be extended to seven days upon vote of majority of members elected to each house). Utah—if 2/3 of the members of each house favor reconvening to consider vetoed bills, a maximum five-day session is set by the presiding officers. Washington—upon petition of 2/3 of the members of each house, legislature meets 45 days after adjournment for a maximum five-day session.

Key:

C—Calendar day
L—Legislative day (in some states, called a session day or workday; definition may vary slightly, however, generally refers to any day on which either house of the legislature is in session)

(a) Applies to each year unless otherwise indicated.
(b) General election year (quadrennial election).
(c) Year after quadrennial election.
(d) Meets in organizational session prior to stated convening date. Alabama—in the year after quadrennial election, on the second Tuesday in January for 10 C. California—in the even-numbered, general election year, on first Monday in December for an organizational session, recess until the first Monday in January of the odd-numbered year. Florida—in general election year, 14th day after election. Georgia—in odd-numbered year. Indiana—third Tuesday after first Monday in November. Kentucky—in odd-numbered year, Tuesday after first Monday in January for 10 L. Michigan—held in odd-numbered year. New Hampshire—in even-numbered year, first Wednesday in December. North Dakota—in even-numbered year, Tuesday after certification of election of its members for a maximum three-day session. South Carolina—in even-numbered year, Tuesday after general election, on second Wednesday in January.
(e) Other years.
(f) By 2/3 vote each house.
(g) Only if legislature convenes itself. Special sessions called by the legislature are unlimited in scope in Arizona, Georgia, Maine and New Mexico.
(h) No constitutional or statutory provision; however, legislative rules require that regular sessions adjourn no later than Saturday of the week during which the 100th day of the session falls.
(i) Session may be extended by vote of members in both houses. Arkansas: 2/3 vote. Florida: 3/5 vote. Hawaii: petition of 2/3 membership for maximum 15-day extension. Kansas: 2/3 vote. Maryland: 3/5 vote for maximum 30 C. Mississippi: 2/3 vote for 30-day extension, no limit on number of extensions. Nebraska: 4/5 vote. South Carolina: 2/3 vote. Virginia: 2/3 vote for 30-day extension. West Virginia: 2/3 vote (or if budget bill has not been acted upon three days before session ends, governor issues proclamation extending session). Puerto Rico: joint resolution.

(j) After governor's business has been disposed of, members may remain in session up to 15 C by a 2/3 vote of both houses.
(k) Regular sessions begin after general election, in December of even-numbered year. In California, legislature meets in December for an organizational session, recesses until the first Monday in January of the odd-numbered year and continues in session until Nov. 30 of next even-numbered year. In Maine, session which begins in December of general election year runs into the following year (odd-numbered); second session begins in next even-numbered year.
(l) A 1982 constitutional amendment imposed a time limit of 140 C on regular sessions convening in even-numbered years.
(m) Second session limited to consideration of specific types of legislation. Connecticut—individual legislators may only introduce bills of a fiscal nature. Maine—budgetary matters; legislation in the governor's call; emergency legislation; legislation referred to committees for study. New Mexico—budgets, appropriations and revenue bills; bills drawn pursuant to governor's message; vetoed bills. Utah, Wyoming—budget bills (however, in Utah, by vote of 2/3 members, may consider non-budgetary bills).
(n) Odd-numbered years.
(o) Even-numbered years.
(p) Odd-numbered years—not later than Wednesday after first Monday in June; even-numbered years—not later than Wednesday after first Monday in May.
(q) Constitution provides for regular session convening dates and allows that sessions may also be held "... at such other times as the General Assembly shall judge necessary." Call by majority of legislators is implied.
(r) Upon completion of business.
(s) Limited to 70 days if called by governor and 30 days if called by petition of the legislature, except in cases of impeachment proceedings.
(t) Legislators may reconvene at any time after organizational meeting; however, second Monday in January is the final date by which regular session must be in process.
(u) Indirect limitation. Restrictions on legislators' pay, per diem or daily allowance.
(v) May not extend beyond April 15.
(w) Joint rules provide for the submission of a written statement requesting special session by a specified number of members of each chamber.
(x) Legal provision for session in odd-numbered year; however, legislature may divide, and in practice has divided, to meet in even-numbered years as well.
(y) A 1968 constitutional amendment calls for 90 C sessions every year, except the first year of a gubernatorial administration during which the legislative session runs for 125 C.
(z) No legislative day is shorter than a natural day.
(aa) Commencement of regular session depends on concluding date of organizational session. Legislature meets, in odd-numbered year, on second Tuesday in January for a maximum 15 C organizational session, then returns on the Tuesday following the conclusion of the organizational session.
(bb) According to a 1955 attorney general's opinion, when the legislature has petitioned to the governor to be called into session, it may then act on any matter.
(cc) The legislature, by joint resolution, establishes the session schedule of activity for the remainder of the biennium at the beginning of the odd-numbered year.
(dd) Each Council period begins on January 2 of each odd-numbered year and ends on January 1 of the following odd-numbered year.
(ee) Legislature meets on the first Monday of each month following its initial session in January.

Table 14
ENACTING LEGISLATION: VETO, VETO OVERRIDE AND EFFECTIVE DATE

| State or other jurisdiction | Governor may item veto appropriation bills | | Days allowed governor to consider bill(a) | | | Votes required in each house to pass bills or items over veto(c) | Effective date of enacted legislation(d) |
	Amount	Other(b)	During session: Bill becomes law unless vetoed	After session: Bill becomes law unless vetoed	Bill dies unless signed		
Alabama	★		6		10A	Majority elected	Immediately(e)
Alaska	★(f)		15	20P		2/3 elected(g)	90 days after enactment
Arizona	★		5	10A		2/3 elected	90 days after adjournment(g)
Arkansas	★		5	20A(h)		Majority elected	90 days after adjournment
California	★(f)		12(h,i)	(i)		2/3 elected	(j)
Colorado	★		10(h)	30A(h)		2/3 elected	Immediately(k)
Connecticut		★	5	15P(h)		2/3 elected	Oct. 1
Delaware	★		10		30A(h)	3/5 elected	Immediately
Florida	★	★	7(h)	15P(h)		2/3 elected	60 days after adjournment
Georgia(l)	★		5	30A(m)		2/3 elected	July 1(n)
Hawaii(l)	★(f)		10(o,p)	45A(o,p)		2/3 elected	Immediately
Idaho	★		5	10A		2/3 elected	July 1(n)
Illinois	★(f)		60(h)	60P(h)		3/5 elected(g)	Jan. 1(n)
Indiana		★	7	7A		Majority elected	(q)
Iowa		★	3	(r)		2/3 elected	July 1(n)
Kansas	★		10	10P		2/3 elected	Upon publication
Kentucky	★		10	10A		Majority elected	90 days after adjournment
Louisiana(l)	★	★	10(h)	20P(h)		2/3 elected	60 days after adjournment
Maine		★	10	(m)		2/3 present	90 days after adjournment
Maryland(l)	(s)		6	30P(m)		3/5 elected	June 1(t)
Massachusetts	★(f)	★	10(o)		10P	2/3 present	90 days after enactment
Michigan	★(f)	★	14(h)		14P(h)	2/3 elected and serving	90 days after adjournment
Minnesota	★		3		14P	2/3 elected	Aug. 1(u)
Mississippi	★		5	15P(m)		2/3 elected	60 days after enactment
Missouri	★(f)		15(r)	45P(m,r)		2/3 elected	90 days after adjournment(u,v)
Montana	★(w)	★	5(h)	25A(h)		2/3 present	July 1
Nebraska		★	5	5A		3/5 elected	3 mo. after adjournment
Nevada			5	10A	5P	2/3 elected	July 1
New Hampshire			5		(x)	2/3 present	60 days after enactment
New Jersey	★(f)		(x)	(x)		2/3 present	July 4
New Mexico	★		3		20A	2/3 elected	90 days after adjournment(u)
New York	★		10		30A	2/3 elected	20 days after enactment
North Carolina			(y)				30 days after adjournment
North Dakota	★(f)		3	15A		2/3 elected	July 1
Ohio	★	★	10	10A		3/5 elected	91 days after filed with secretary of state(z)
Oklahoma	★		5	20A		2/3 elected(g)	90 days after adjournment
Oregon	★	★	5	30A(h)		2/3 present	90 days after adjournment
Pennsylvania	★(f)		10(h)	10A(h)		2/3 elected	60 days after enactment
Rhode Island			6	(m)		3/5 present	10 days after enactment
South Carolina		★	5		15A	2/3 present	20 days after enactment
South Dakota	★	★	5	15A		2/3 elected	July 1(n)
Tennessee	★(f)		10	10A		Majority elected	40 days after enactment
Texas	★		10	20A		2/3 present	90 days after adjournment
Utah	★		10(h)	20A(h)		2/3 elected	60 days after adjournment
Vermont			5		3A	2/3 present	July 1

State									
Virginia	7(h)	★	★		30A(h)		2/3 present(aa)		July 1(u,bb)
Washington	5	★	★	★			2/3 present		90 days after adjournment
West Virginia	5	★	★	★ (f)		6P	Majority elected(g)		90 days after enactment
Wisconsin	6	★					2/3 present		Day after publication
Wyoming	3	★			15A(h)		2/3 elected		Immediately
American Samoa	10	★ (f)			20A(cc)	30P	2/3 elected		60 days after adjournment(dd)
Guam	10	(f)			15A(cc)	30P	14 members		Immediately(ee)
No. Marianas	40(ff)	★ (f)					2/3 elected		Immediately
Puerto Rico	10	(f)				30P(h)	2/3 elected		Specified in act
Virgin Islands	10	★				30P(h)	2/3 elected		Immediately

Note: Some legislatures will actually reconvene after normal session to consider bills vetoed by governor. Connecticut—if governor vetoes any bill, secretary of state must reconvene General Assembly on second Monday after the last day on which governor is either authorized to transmit or has transmitted every bill with his objections, whichever occurs first; General Assembly must adjourn *sine die* no later than three days after its reconvening. Hawaii—legislature may reconvene on 45th day after adjournment *sine die*, in special session, without call. Louisiana—legislature meets in a maximum five-day veto session on the 40th day after final adjournment. Missouri—if governor returns any bill on or after the fifth day before the last day on which legislature may consider bills (in even-numbered years), legislature automatically reconvenes on first Monday in September for a maximum 10C session. New Jersey—legislature meets in special session (without call or petition) to act on bills after *sine die* adjournment of the 45th day falls on or after the first year of a two-year legislature; a special session may not be convened if the 45th day of the legislative year in which the second session occurs. Virginia—legislature reconvenes on sixth Wednesday after adjournment for a maximum three-day session (may be extended to seven days upon vote of majority of members elected to each house). Utah—if 2/3 of the members of each house favor reconvening upon petition of 2/3 of the members of each house, legislature meets 45 days after adjournment for a maximum five-day session.

Key:

★—Yes

...—No

A—days after adjournment of legislature

P—days after presentation to governor

(a) Sundays excluded, unless otherwise indicated.

(b) Includes language in appropriations bill.

(c) Bill returned to house of origin with governor's objections.

(d) Effective date may be established by the law itself or may be otherwise changed by vote of the legislature. Special or emergency acts are usually effective immediately.

(e) Penal acts, 60 days.

(f) Governor can also reduce amounts in appropriations bills. In Hawaii, governor can reduce items in executive appropriations measures, but cannot reduce nor item veto amounts appropriated for the judicial or legislative branches.

(g) Different number of votes required for revenue and appropriations bills. Alaska—3/4 elected. Illinois—appropriations reductions, majority elected. Oklahoma—emergency bills, 2/3 vote. West Virginia—budget and supplemental appropriations, 2/3 elected.

(h) Sundays included.

(i) A bill presented to the governor that is not returned within 12 days becomes a law; provided that any bill passed before Sept. 1 of the second calendar year of the biennium of the legislative session and in the possession of the governor on or after Sept. 1 that is not returned by the governor on or before Sept. 30 of that year becomes law. The legislature may not present to the governor any bill after Nov. 15 of the second calendar year of the biennium of the session. If the legislature, by adjournment of a special session prevents the return of a bill with the veto message, the bill becomes law unless the governor vetoes within 12 days by depositing it and the veto message in the office of the secretary of state.

(j) For legislation enacted in regular sessions: January 1 next following 90-day period from date of enactment. For legislation enacted in special sessions: 91 days after adjournment. Does not apply to statutes calling elections, statutes providing for tax levies or appropriations for the usual current state expenses or urgency statutes, all of which take effect immediately.

(k) An act takes effect on the date stated in the act, or if no date is stated in the act, then on its passage.

(m) Bills vetoed after adjournment shall be returned to the legislature for reconsideration. Georgia: returned within 35 days from the date of adjournment for reconsideration within the first 10 days of the next session. Maine: returned within three days after the next meeting of the same legislature which enacted the bill or resolution. Maryland: reconsidered at the next meeting of the same General Assembly.

Mississippi: returned within three days after the beginning of the next session. Missouri: bills returned within four days of adjournment or later in first session are considered at beginning of second session; bills returned in second session are considered in automatic veto session. South Carolina: within two days after the next meeting.

(n) Effective date for bills which become law on or after July 1. Georgia—Jan. 1, unless a specific date has been provided for in legislation. Idaho—special sessions, 60 days after adjournment. Illinois—a bill passed after June 30 does not become effective prior to July 1 of the next calendar year unless legislature, by a 3/5 vote provided for an earlier effective date. Iowa—if governor signs bills after July 1, bill becomes law on Aug. 15; for special sessions, 90 days after adjournment. South Dakota—91 days after adjournment.

(o) Except Sundays and legal holidays. In Hawaii, except Saturdays, Sundays, holidays and any days in which the legislature is in recess prior to its adjournment.

(p) The governor must notify the legislature 10 days before the 45th day of his intent to veto a measure on that day. The legislature may convene on the 45th day after adjournment to consider the vetoed measures. If the legislature fails to reconvene, the bill does not become law. If the legislature reconvenes, it may pass the measure over the governor's veto or it may amend the law to meet the governor's objections. If the law is amended, the governor must sign the bill within 10 days after it is presented to him in order for it to become law.

(q) No act takes effect until it has been published and circulated in the counties, by authority, except in cases of emergency.

(r) Governor must sign or veto all bills presented to him. Iowa—any bill submitted to the governor for his approval during the last three days of a session must be deposited by him in the secretary of state's office within 30 days after adjournment with his approval or objections. Missouri—otherwise, legislature, by joint resolution, reciting fact of such failure, may direct the secretary of state to enroll the bill as an authentic act and it becomes law.

(s) Item veto on supplementary appropriations bills and capital construction bills only.

(t) Bills passed over governor's veto are effective in 30 days or on date specified in bill, whichever is later.

(u) Different date for appropriations acts. Minnesota—July 1. Missouri, New Mexico—immediately.

(v) In event of a recess of 30 days or more, legislature may prescribe, by joint resolution, that laws previously passed and not effective shall take effect 90 days from beginning of recess.

(w) No appropriation can be made in excess of the recommendations contained in the governor's budget unless by a 2/3 vote. The excess is not subject to veto by the governor.

(x) If a bill is not returned by the governor within 10 days after it is presented to him (excluding Sundays), it becomes law, unless the house of origin is in adjournment. In that case, the bill becomes law on the day the house of origin reconvenes. If on the 10th day, the legislature is in adjournment *sine die*, the bill becomes law if the governor signs it within 45 days (excluding Sundays) after the adjournment. On the 45th day, the bill becomes law unless he returns it with his objections (1) on the 45th day if the house of origin has convened in regular or special session of the same two-year legislature; (2) on the 45th day (if the house is in adjournment *sine die*) at the special session which convenes on that day (without petition or call) for the sole purpose of acting on returned bills.

(y) Governor has no approval or veto power.

(z) Ninety days required to permit filing of any referendum petition.

(aa) Must include majority of elected members.

(bb) Special sessions—first day of fourth month after adjournment.

(cc) Five days for appropriations bills.

(dd) Laws required to be approved only by the governor. An act required to be approved by the U.S. Secretary of the Interior only after it is vetoed by the governor and so approved takes effect 40 days after it is returned to the legislature by the Secretary.

(ee) U.S. Congress may annul.

(ff) Twenty days for appropriations bills.

Table 15
LEGISLATIVE PROCEDURE: TIME LIMITS ON
BILL INTRODUCTION

State or other jurisdiction	*Time limit on introduction of bills*	*Procedure for granting exception to time limits*
Alabama	24th L day of regular session(a).	House: 4/5 vote of quorum present and voting. Senate: majority vote after consideration by Rules Committee
Alaska	35th C day of 2nd regular session(b)	2/3 vote of membership (concurrent resolution).
Arizona	29th day of regular session; 10th day of special session.	Permission of Rules Committee.
Arkansas	55th day of regular session (50th day for appropriations bills).	2/3 vote of membership.
California	March 4 of 1st year of regular session; Feb. 17 of 2nd year of regular session(c)	(c)
Colorado	60th L day in odd year session; 30th L day in even year session(d)	House, Senate Committees on Delayed Bills may extend deadline.
Connecticut	Depends on schedule set out by joint rules adopted for biennium(e)	
Delaware	At the discretion of each chamber.	
Florida	House: noon 1st day of regular session(b); Senate: 11th L day of regular session(d,f).	House, Senate committees on Rules and Calendar determine whether existence of emergency compels bill's consideration.
Georgia	House: 30th L day of regular session; Senate: 33rd L day of regular session	House: 3/5 of members present (provided quorum exists); Senate: 2/3 vote of membership.
Hawaii	Actual dates established during session. Deadline must fall after 19th day of session and before the mandatory max. 5-day recess which occurs in the period between the 20th and 40th days of the regular session.	2/3 vote of membership.
Idaho	House: 20th day of session(b); 45th day of session(g); Senate: 12th day of session(b); 35th day of session(g).	
Illinois	House: April 15 of odd year of session(h); Senate: April 15 of odd year of session.	House: rules governing limitations may not be suspended; Senate: rules may be suspended by affirmative vote of majority of members; suspensions approved by Rules Committee, adopted by majority of members present.
Indiana	House: 16th day of odd year of session; 4th day of even year. Senate: 12th day of odd year of session; 4th day of even year.	House: 2/3 vote of membership; Senate: consent of Rules and Legislative Procedures Committee.
Iowa	House: Friday of 7th week of 1st regular session; Friday of 3rd week of 2nd regular session(i). Senate: Friday of 7th week of 1st regular session(i,j); Friday of 2nd week of 2nd regular session(b,i).	
Kansas	31st C day of regular session for individuals(k); 45th day of regular session for committees(l).	Resolution adopted by majority of members of either house may make specific exceptions to deadlines.
Kentucky	House: 38th L day of regular session; Senate: no introductions during last 20 days of session.	Majority vote of membership each house.
Louisiana	15th C day of regular session(m).	2/3 vote of elected members of each house.
Maine	Last Friday in January of 1st regular session; deadlines for 2nd regular session established by Legislative Council(b,n).	Approval of majority of members of Legislative Council.
Maryland	No introductions during last 35 C days of regular session.	2/3 vote of elected members of each house.
Massachusetts	1st Wednesday in December(o).	4/5 vote of members of each house.
Michigan	No limit.	
Minnesota	No limit.	
Mississippi	16th C day of 90-day session; 51st C day of 125-day session(d,p).	2/3 vote of members present and voting.
Missouri	60th L day of odd year of session; 30th L day of even year of session(d).	Majority elected members each house; governor's request for consideration of bill by special message.
Montana	Individual introductions: 14th L day; revenue bills: 21st L day; committee bills: 40th L day; committee revenue bills: 66th L day(d,q).	2/3 vote of members.
Nebraska	10th L day of any session(d,r).	3/5 vote of elected membership(s).
Nevada	20th C day of regular session(t).	2/3 vote of members present; also standing committee of a house if request is approved by 2/3 members of committee. Consent to suspend rule may be given only by affirmative vote of majority members elected.

State or other jurisdiction	Time limit on introduction of bills	Procedure for granting exception to time limits
New Hampshire	House: money bills/resolutions, March 1; other bills: April 5; Senate: deadline established by Joint Rules Committee for transfer of bills out of originating house.	2/3 vote of members present or approval of majority of Rules Committee.
New Jersey	No limit.	
New Mexico	House: 30th L day of regular session(d,u); appropriations bills: 50th L day of regular session.	
New York	Assembly: for unlimited introduction of bills, 1st Tuesday in March; for introduction of 10 or fewer bills, last Tuesday in March(v). Senate: temporary president may designate final date which is not prior to the 1st Tuesday of March(w).	Assembly only: unanimous vote(x).
North Carolina	House: April 1 for local bill or bills prepared to be introduced for departments, agencies or state institutions; Senate: same as House plus resolutions(y).	House: 2/3 of members present and voting; Senate: 2/3 vote of membership, except in case of deadline for local bills which may be suspended by 4/5 of senators present and voting.
North Dakota	15th L day(z); resolutions: 18th L day(aa); bills requested by executive agency or Supreme Court: Dec. 15 prior to regular session.	2/3 vote or approval of majority of Committee on Delayed Bills.
Ohio	After Mar. 15 of 2nd regular session, either house by majority vote of its members may end bill introductions.	Majority vote on recommendation of bill by Reference Committee.
Oklahoma	27th L day for house of origin in 1st session(bb); 19th L day of 2nd session(cc).	2/3 vote of membership.
Oregon	House: 29th C day of session(dd); Senate: 36th C day following election of Senate president(ee).	
Pennsylvania	No limit(ff).	
Rhode Island	House: 35th L day of session(gg); Senate: 40th L day of session.	House: 2/3 vote of members present; Senate: majority vote of members present and voting.
South Carolina	House: Apr. 15 of regular session; May 1 for bills first introduced in Senate(d,hh). Senate: May 1 of regular session for bills originating in House.	House: 2/3 vote of members present and voting; Senate: 2/3 vote of membership.
South Dakota	40-day session: 14th L day; committee bills and joint resolutions, 15th L day. 35-day session: 10th L day; committee bills and joint resolutions, 11th L day; bills introduced at request of department, board, commission or state agency: 4th L day(ii).	2/3 vote of membership.
Tennessee	House: general bills, 10th L day of regular session(jj). Senate: general bills, 10th L day of regular session; resolutions, 30th L day.	House: 2/3 vote of members; Senate: 2/3 vote of members or unanimous consent of Committee on Delayed Bills.
Texas	60th C day of regular session(kk).	4/5 vote of members present and voting.
Utah	30th C day of session.	House: 2/3 vote of members present; Senate: majority of membership.
Vermont	House, Individual introductions: 1st session, March 1; 2nd session, Feb. 1. Committees: 10 days after 1st Tuesday in March(ll). Senate, Individual and committee: 1st session, 53rd C day; 2nd session, sponsor requests bill drafting 25 days before session and all bills are introduced on 1st day(mm).	Approval by Rules Committee.
Virginia	Deadlines may be set during session.	
Washington	(Constitutional limit) No introductions during final 10 days of regular session(d,nn).	2/3 vote of elected members of each house.
West Virginia	House: 50th day of regular session(b,d); Senate: 41st day of regular session(d).	2/3 vote of members present.
Wisconsin	No limit.	
Wyoming	18th L day of odd year of session(d).	2/3 of elected members of either house.
American Samoa ...	15th L day.	2/3 vote of elected members.
Guam	No limit.	
Puerto Rico	60th day.	Majority vote of membership.
Virgin Islands	No limit.	

Table 15—Notes

Key:
C—Calendar day.
L—Legislative day.

(a) Not applicable to local bills that have been advertised or general bills of local application.

(b) Not applicable to bills sponsored by standing committees. In Florida, also does not apply to short-form bills.

(c) Not applicable to constitutional amendments, committee bills introduced pursuant to Assembly Rule 47 or Senate Rule 23, bills introduced in Assembly with permission of speaker or bills introduced in Senate with permission of Senate Rules Committee. Subject to these deadlines, bills may be introduced at any time, except when the houses are in joint summer, interim or final recess.

(d) Not applicable to appropriations bills. In West Virginia, supplementary appropriations bills.

(e) Not applicable to (1) bills providing for current government expenditures; (2) bills the presiding officers certify are of an emergency nature; (3) bills the governor requests because of emergency or necessity; and (4) the legislative commissioners' revisor's bill and omnibus validating act.

(f) Not applicable to local bills and joint resolutions.

(g) Not applicable to House State Affairs, Appropriations, Revenue and Taxation or Ways and Means committees, nor to Senate State Affairs, Finance or Judiciary and Rules committees.

(h) Not applicable to Senate bills, which must be introduced in the House by June 1; appropriations bills (introduced between 2nd Wednesday in January and 1st Friday in April of even year); certain standing committee bills (dependent on introduction date in house of origin); bills determined by Rules Committee to be an emergency; a bill carried over from the odd-numbered year on the interim study calendar of a standing committee on which public hearings have been conducted (during spring session of even-numbered year); a bill transferred from daily calendar of spring session of odd-numbered year by motion adopted by affirmative vote of 60 members prior to the applicable deadline for consideration on final passage (during spring session of even-numbered year).

(i) Unless written request for drafting bill had been filed before deadline.

(j) Not applicable to bills co-sponsored by majority and minority floor leaders.

(k) Deadline for introduction by individual members may be changed to an earlier date in either house by resolution adopted by majority of members.

(l) Not applicable to Ways and Means and Federal and State Affairs committees, the select committees of either house or the House Committee on Calendar and Printing.

(m) Not applicable to concurrent resolutions proposing suspension of law and bills reported by substitute.

(n) Not applicable to bills intended to facilitate legislative business.

(o) Not applicable to messages from governor, reports required or authorized to be made to legislature, petitions filed or approved by voters of cities or towns (or by mayors and city councils) for enactment of special legislation and which do not affect the powers and duties of state departments, boards or commissions.

(p) Not applicable to revenue, local and private bills.

(q) Not applicable to interim study resolutions or joint resolutions concerning administration.

(r) Not applicable to "A" bills and those introduced at the request of the governor.

(s) For standing or special committee to introduce bill after 10th L day.

(t) Requests submitted to legislative counsel for bill drafting. Does not apply to standing committees or to member who had requested bill drafting before 21st C day.

(u) Not applicable to bills to provide for current government expenses; bills referred to legislature by governor by special message setting forth emergency necessitating legislation.

(v) Does not apply to bills introduced by Rules Committee, by message from the Senate, with consent of the speaker or by members elected at special election who take office on or after the first Tuesday of March.

(w) Bills recommended by state department or agency must be submitted to office of temporary president not later than March 1. Bills proposed by governor, attorney general, comptroller, department of education or office of court administration must be submitted to office of temporary president no later than first Tuesday in April.

(x) In no case may a bill be introduced on Fridays, unless submitted by governor or introduced by Rules Committee or by message from Senate.

(y) Not applicable to those honoring memory of the deceased.

(z) No member may introduce more than three bills as prime sponsor after 10th L day.

(aa) Not applicable to resolutions proposing amendments to U.S. Constitution or directing Legislative Council to carry out a study (deadline, 33rd L day).

(bb) Final date for consideration on floor in house of origin during first session. Bills introduced after date are not placed on calendar for consideration until second session.

(cc) Not applicable to reapportionment bills.

(dd) Not applicable to measures approved by Committee on Legislative Rules and Operations or by speaker; appropriation or fiscal measures sponsored by Joint Committee on Ways and Means; true substitute measures sponsored by standing, special or joint committees, or measures drafted by legislative counsel.

(ee) Not applicable to measures approved by Rules Committee, appropriation or fiscal measures sponsored by Joint Committee on Ways and Means; measures requested for drafting by legislative counsel.

(ff) Resolutions fixing the last day for introduction of bills in the House are referred to the Rules Committee before consideration by the full House.

(gg) Not applicable to resolutions of condolence or congratulations, corporate charter renewals, claims bills or city and town bills.

(hh) Not applicable to joint resolutions approving or disapproving agency regulations.

(ii) Not applicable to governor's bills.

(jj) Not applicable to certain local bills or a bill correcting a typographical error or an earlier enactment of the Committee on Delayed Bills.

(kk) Not applicable to local bills, resolutions, emergency appropriations, all emergency matters submitted by governor in special messages to the legislature.

(ll) Not applicable to Appropriations or Ways and Means committees.

(mm) Not applicable to Appropriations or Finance committees.

(nn) Not applicable to substitute bills reported by standing committees for bills pending before such committees.

Table 16
LEGISLATIVE PROCEDURE: BILL INTRODUCTION AND REFERENCE

State or other jurisdiction	Pre-filing of bills allowed(a)	Bills referred to committee by: Senate	House	Bill referral restricted by rule: Senate	House	Bill carryover allowed(b)
Alabama	★(c)	President(d)	Speaker			...
Alaska	★(e)	President	Speaker	★	★	★
Arizona	★	President	Speaker			...
Arkansas	★	Rules Cmte.	Speaker	★	★	
California	(f)	Rules Cmte.	Rules Cmte.	★		★(g)
Colorado	★	President	Speaker			...
Connecticut	★	President(d)	Speaker	★	★	...
Delaware	★	President(d)	Speaker		★	...
Florida	★	President	Speaker	★	★	★
Georgia	...	President(d)	Speaker			★
Hawaii	(h)	President	Speaker	★	★	★
Idaho	...	President(d)	Speaker			...
Illinois	★	Cmte. on Assignment	Cmte. on Assignment			★
Indiana	★	Pres. Pro Tempore	Speaker			...
Iowa	★	President(d)	Speaker	★		★
Kansas	★	President	Speaker	★	★	★
Kentucky	★	Cmte. on Cmtes.(i)	Cmte. on Cmtes.	★	★	
Louisiana	★	President(j)	Speaker(j)	★	★	...
Maine	★(k)	———Secy. of Senate and Clerk of House(l)———				...
Maryland	★	President	Speaker	(m)	(m)	...
Massachusetts	★	Clerk(j)	Clerk(j)	★	★	...
Michigan	...	Majority Ldr.	Speaker			★
Minnesota	★(n)	President	Speaker	(m)	(m)	★
Mississippi	★	President(d)	Speaker			...
Missouri	★	Pres. Pro Tempore	Speaker	★	★	★
Montana	★	President	Speaker			
Nebraska(U)	★	Reference Cmte.		★		★
Nevada	★	Majority Ldr.	Speaker	★		
New Hampshire	★	President	Speaker	★	★	
New Jersey	★(k)	President	Speaker			★
New Mexico	...	Pres. Pro Tempore	Speaker	(m)	(m)	...
New York	★	Pres. Pro Tempore(o)	Speaker			★
North Carolina	...	President(d)	Speaker	(m)	(m)	★
North Dakota	★	President(d)	Speaker	★	★	★
Ohio	★	Reference Cmte.	Reference Cmte.			★
Oklahoma	★	Pres. Pro Tempore	Speaker			★
Oregon	★	President	Speaker		★	★
Pennsylvania	★	President(d)	Speaker			★
Rhode Island	★	President(d)	Speaker			★
South Carolina	★	Pres. Pro Tempore	Speaker			★
South Dakota	★	President(d)	Speaker			...
Tennessee	★	Speaker	Speaker	★	★	★
Texas	★	President(d)	Speaker		★	★
Utah	★	President	Speaker			...
Vermont	★	President(d)	Speaker	★		★
Virginia	★	Clerk	Speaker	★	★	★
Washington	★	President	Speaker			★
West Virginia	★	President	Speaker			...
Wisconsin	★	Presiding Offr.	Presiding Offr.			★
Wyoming	★(k)	President	Speaker			...
American Samoa	★	President	Speaker	★	★	★
Guam(U)	★	Rules Cmte.		★		★
Puerto Rico	★	President	President	★	★	★
Virgin Islands(U)	★	President		★	★	★

Key:
. . .—Procedure not allowed.
(U)—Unicameral legislature.
(a) Unless otherwise indicated by footnote, bills may be introduced prior to convening each session of the legislature. In this column only: ★ —pre-filing is allowed in both chambers (or in the case of Nebraska, Guam and the Virgin Islands, in the unicameral legislature); . . .—pre-filing is not allowed in either chamber.
(b) Bills carry over from the first year of a legislature to the second (does not apply to legislatures meeting in session once every two years). Bills generally do not carry over after an intervening legislative election.
(c) Except between the end of the last regular session of the legislature in any quadrennium and the organizational session following the general election.
(d) Lieutenant governor is the president of the Senate.
(e) Maximum 10 bills.
(f) California has a continuous legislature. Members may introduce bills at any time during the biennium.
(g) Bills introduced in the first year of the regular session and passed by the house of origin on or before January 30 of the second year are "carryover bills."
(h) House only in even-numbered years.

(i) Lieutenant governor as president of the Senate is a member of committee.
(j) Subject to approval or disapproval. Louisiana—majority of members present. Massachusetts—by presiding officer.
(k) Prior to convening of first regular session only.
(l) For the joint standing committee system. Secretary of Senate and clerk of House, after conferring, suggest an appropriate committee reference for every bill, resolve and petition offered in either house. If they are unable to agree, the question of reference is referred to a conference of the president of the Senate and speaker of the House. If the presiding officers cannot agree, the question is resolved by the Legislative Council.
(m) Not restricted, except: Maryland—in House, local bills; in Senate, local bills and bills creating judgeships. Minnesota—bills on government structure and bills appropriating funds which are referred to Finance Committee. New Mexico—in House, bills referred to Appropriations and Finance Committee; in Senate, bills referred to Finance Committee. North Carolina—bills referred to Appropriations, Finance and Ways and Means Committees.
(n) Prior to convening of second regular session only.
(o) Also serves as majority leader.

117

Table 17
LEGISLATIVE PROCEDURE: STANDING COMMITTEES

State or other jurisdiction	Committee members appointed by:		Committee chairpersons appointed by:		Number of standing committees during regular 1983 session(a)	
	Senate	House	Senate	House	Senate	House
Alabama	P(b)	S	P(b)	S	21	23
Alaska	CC(c)	CC(c)	CC(c)	CC(c)	9	9
Arizona	P	S	P	S	11	17
Arkansas	CC	S	CC	S	10(d)	10(d)
California	CR	S	CR	S	20	23
Colorado	MjL,MnL(e)	S,MnL(e)	MjL	S	10	12
Connecticut	PT	S	PT	S	(f)	(f)
Delaware	PT	S	PT	S	19(d)	12(d)
Florida	P	S	P	S	16	22
Georgia	P(b)	S	P(b)	S	24	29
Hawaii	P(g)	(h)	P(g)	(h)	19	19
Idaho	PT(i)	S	PT	S	9	13
Illinois	CC	S,MnL	P	S	18	21
Indiana	PT	S	PT	S	18	25
Iowa	P(b)	S	P(b)	S	16	15
Kansas	CC	S	CC	S	18(d)	21(d)
Kentucky	CC	CC	CC	CC	18	18
Louisiana	P	S	P	S	15	15
Maine	P	S	P	S	(f)	(f)
Maryland	P	S	P	S	8	8
Massachusetts	P	S	P	S	5(d)	5(d)
Michigan	MjL	S	MjL	S	16	33
Minnesota	(j)	S	(j)	S	16	17
Mississippi	P(b)	S	P(b)	S	28(d)	27(d)
Missouri	PT	S	PT	S	27	56
Montana	CC	S	CC	S	17	15
Nebraska(U)	CC		(k)		14	
Nevada	(l)	S(m)	MjL	S	9	13
New Hampshire	P	S	P	S	16	23
New Jersey	P	S	P	S	15	19
New Mexico	CC	S	CC	S	9	15
New York	PT(n)	S	PT(n)	S	30	31
North Carolina	P(b)	S	P(b)	S	34	58
North Dakota	CC	S	CC	S	11(d)	11(d)
Ohio	CC	S	CC	S	12	24
Oklahoma	PT(o)	S	PT	S	14	25
Oregon	P	S	P	S	15	16
Pennsylvania	PT	CC(p)	PT	S	21	24
Rhode Island	MjL	S	MjL	S	6(d)	6(d)
South Carolina	E(q)	S	E	E	15	11
South Dakota	(r)	S	(r)	S	14	14
Tennessee	S	S	S	S	9	12
Texas	P(b)	S(s)	P(b)	S	9	33
Utah	P	S	P	S	11(d)	10(d)
Vermont	P(b)	S	P(b)	S	12	16
Virginia	E	S	(t)	S	11	20
Washington	P(b,u)	S(u)	(u)	S(u)	15	17
West Virginia	P	S	P	S	19(d)	13(d)
Wisconsin	(v)	S	(v)	S	9(d)	29(d)
Wyoming	P(w)	S(w)	P(w)	S(w)	12	12
Dist. of Col.(U)	(x)		(x)		10	
American Samoa	P,E	S,E	P	S	17	17
Guam(U)	(y)		E		10	
Puerto Rico	P	S	P	S	15	23
Virgin Islands(U)	P		P		8	

Note: Standing committees are those which regularly consider legislation during the legislative session.

Key:
CC—Committee on Committees
CR—Committee on Rules
E—Election
MjL—Majority leader
MnL—Minority leader
P—President
PT—President pro tempore
S—Speaker
U—Unicameral legislature

(a) If legislature had no regular session in 1983, then number of standing committees is for 1982.

(b) Lieutenant governor is president of the senate.

(c) Report of Committees on Committees is subject to approval by majority vote of chamber's membership.

(d) Also, joint standing committees. Arkansas, 3; Delaware, 1; Kansas, 4; Massachusetts, 21; Mississippi, 4; North Dakota, 1; Rhode Island, 10; Utah, 10 (joint appropriations); West Virginia, 2; Wisconsin, 8.

(e) Minority leader appoints committee members from minority party.

(f) Substantive standing committees are joint committees. Connecticut, 20; Maine, 19.

(g) President appoints committee members and chairpersons; minority members on committees are nominated by minority party caucus.

(h) By resolution, with members of majority party designating the chairmen, vice-chairmen and majority party members of committees, and members of minority party designating minority party members.

(i) Committee members appointed by the Senate leadership under the direction of the president pro tempore, by and with the Senate's advice.

(j) Subcommittee on Committees of the Committee on Rules and Administration.

(k) Secret ballot by legislature as a whole.

(l) Committee composition and leadership usually determined by party caucus.

(m) For Committee on Ethics, minority leader appoints one member of minority party.

(n) President pro tempore is also majority leader.

(o) Minority floor leader appoints minority members of committees (subject to Senate approval).

(p) Committee on Committees recommends to House for approval the names of committee members.

(q) Seniority system is retained in process.

(r) Presiding officer announces committee membership after selection by president pro tempore, majority and minority leaders.

(s) A maximum of one-half of the membership on each standing committee, exclusive of the chair and vice chair, is determined by seniority; the remaining membership is appointed by the speaker.

(t) Senior member of the majority party on the committee is the chair.

(u) With majority caucus.

(v) Committee on Senate Organization.

(w) With the advice and consent of the Rules and Procedure Committee.

(x) Chairman of the Council.

(y) Chairman of each committee.

Table 18
LEGISLATIVE PROCEDURE: STANDING COMMITTEE ACTION

| State or other jurisdiction | Uniform rules of committee procedure | | | Public access to committee meetings | | | | Recorded roll call on vote to report bill to floor | |
| | Senate | House | Joint | Open to public | | Advance notice required (in days) | | | |
				Senate	House	Senate	House	Senate	House
Alabama	...	★		★	★	...	...	Al	Nv
Alaska	...	...		★	★	...	...	Sm	Sm
Arizona	...	★		★	★	5	(a)	Nv	Nv
Arkansas	★	★	★	★	★	2	2	Sm	Sm
California	★	★	★	★	★	4	4	Al	Al
Colorado	★	★		★	★	...	...	Al	Al
Connecticut	...	...	★	★(b)	★(b)	1	1	Al	Al
Delaware	★	★	...	★	★	(c)	(c)	Al	Al
Florida	★	★		★	★	7	2(d)	Al	Al
Georgia	...	...		★	★	...	...	Nv	Nv
Hawaii	★	★		★	★	2	2	Al	Al
Idaho	★	★		★	★	...	...	Us	Us
Illinois	★	★	...	★	★	6	6.5	Al	Al
Indiana	...	...		★	★	3	1	Al	Al
Iowa	★	★		★	★	...	...	Al	Al
Kansas	★	★		★	★	...	(c)	Sm	Sm
Kentucky	...	...		★	★	...	3	Al	Al
Louisiana	★	★		★	★	1(e)	1(e)	Sm	Al
Maine	...	...	★	★	★	(c)	(c)	Sm	Sm
Maryland	★	★		★	★	(c)	(c)	Al	Al
Massachusetts	...	...		★	★	...	...	Nv	Nv
Michigan	★	★		★	★	(f)	(f)	Al	Al
Minnesota	★	★	★	★	★	3	3	Sm	Sm
Mississippi	...	...		★	★	...	...	Sm	Sm
Missouri	★	★	★	★	★	1	1	Al	Al
Montana	...	...		★	★	(g)	(g)	Al	Al
Nebraska(U)	★			★		5-7		Al	
Nevada	★	★		★	★	(c)	5(h)	Al	Al
New Hampshire	...	...		★	★	3	3	Al	Al
New Jersey	★	★		★	★	5	5	Al	Al
New Mexico	...	...		★	★	...	...	Sm	Al
New York	★	★		★	★	7	7	Al	Al
North Carolina	...	...	...	★(b)	★(b)	(c)	(c)	Sm	Sm
North Dakota	...	...		★	★	(i)	(i)	Al	Al
Ohio	★	★		★	★	5	(c)	Al	Al
Oklahoma	★	★		★	★	(c)	(c)	Sm	Sm
Oregon	★	★		★	★	1(j)	1(k)	Al	Al
Pennsylvania	...	...		★	★	3	3	Al	Al
Rhode Island	★	★	★	★	★	...	...	Sm	Sm
South Carolina	★	★	★	★	★	1	1	Sm	Sm
South Dakota	★	★		★	★	2	2	Al	Al
Tennessee	★	★		★	★	(l)	(l)	Al	Sm
Texas	...	★		★	★	1	5	Sm	Al
Utah	★	★	★	★	★	1	1	Al	Sm
Vermont	★	★	★	★	★	...	...	Sm	Sm
Virginia	★	★		★	★(m)	(c)	(c)	Al	Al
Washington	★	★		★	★	5	5	Sm	Sm
West Virginia	...	...		★	★	...	...	Sm	Sm
Wisconsin	★	★	★	★	★	7	7	Al	Al
Wyoming	...	...	...	★	★	...	...	Sm	Sm
American Samoa	...	...	...	★	★	(d)	1.5	Nv	Nv
Guam(U)	★			★(b)		7		Al	
Puerto Rico	★	★		★	★	...	...	Nv	Nv
Virgin Islands(U)	★			★		7(n)		Us	

Key: ★—Yes
... —No
Al—Always
Us—Usually
Sm—Sometimes
Nv—Never
(U)—Unicameral legislative body

(a) Rules: Thursday of previous week. Statute: 24 hours.
(b) Certain matters specified by statute can be discussed in executive session. Connecticut: upon a 2/3 vote of committee members present and voting and stating the reason for such executive session. North Carolina: appropriations committees are required to sit jointly in open session. Guam: hearings are open to the public but meetings may be closed.
(c) No specified time. Kansas: "due notice" required by House rules. Maine: usually seven days notice given. Maryland: "from time to time," usually seven days. Nevada: "adequate notice." North Carolina: notice must be given in the House or Senate; two methods to waive notice in the Senate. Ohio: "due notice," usually seven days. Virginia: notice published in the daily calendar.
(d) During session: two days notice for first 45 days, two hours thereafter.
(e) One day during session, five days during interim.
(f) Committees meet on regular schedule during sessions. Eighteen-hour notice for rescheduled or special meetings unless legislature is adjourned or recessed for less than 18 hours.
(g) There is an informal agreement to give three days notice.
(h) Public hearings on bills or resolutions of "high public importance" must receive five calendar days notice. All other committee meetings must have 24 hours notice.
(i) Rules require posting of bills and resolutions to be considered at each meeting and provide deadlines for such posting depending upon the schedules for particular committees.
(j) Except in case of meeting to resolve conflicts or inconsistencies among two or more measures, in which case posting and notice to the public shall be given immediately upon call of the meeting, and notice of the meeting shall be announced on the floor if the Senate is in session.
(k) In case of actual emergency, a meeting may be held upon such notice as is appropriate to the circumstances.
(l) Committees meet on a fixed schedule during sessions. Five days notice required during interim.
(m) Committee meetings are required to be open for final vote on bill.
(n) Advance notice may be waived if the committee determines there is cause to conduct a meeting sooner. In that case, notice must be given at least 48 hours in advance. Items on the agenda may be considered by unanimous consent.

Table 19
STAFF FOR LEGISLATIVE STANDING COMMITTEES

State or other jurisdiction	Committee staff assistance				Organizational source of staff services†							
	Senate		House		Joint central agency(a)		Chamber agency(b)		Caucus or leadership		Committee or committee chairman	
	Prof.	Cler.	Prof.	Cler.	Prof.	Cler.	Prof.	Cler.	Prof.	Cler.	Prof.	Cler.
Alabama	(c)	★	(c)	★	B						B	B
Alaska	★	★	★	★	B			B	B	B	B	B
Arizona	★	★	★	★	(d)		B	B	B		B	
Arkansas	★	★	★	★	B	B		B				
California	★	★	★	★			B	B				
Colorado	★	...	★	...	B							
Connecticut	★(e)	★(e)	★(e)	★(e)	(e)	(e)						
Delaware	(c)	★(f)	(c)	★(f)	B	B			B	B		
Florida	★	★	★	★							B	B
Georgia	★	★(f)	★	★(f)	B		S			B	H	
Hawaii	(g)	★	(g)	★	B	B	B	B	B	B	B	B
Idaho	(c)	★	(c)	★	B							B
Illinois	★	★	★	★					B	B		
Indiana	★	★	★	...	B					S		
Iowa	★	★	★	★	B			B(h)	B			B(h)
Kansas	★	★	★	★	B	B		B	B			B
Kentucky	★	★	★	★	B	B						
Louisiana	★	★	★	★				B			B	B
Maine	★(e)	★(e)	★(e)	★(e)	(e)							(e)
Maryland	★	★	★	★	B							B
Massachusetts	★	★	★	★	B		B		B	B	B	B
Michigan	★	★	★	★				H	B		B	B
Minnesota	★	★	★	★							B	B
Mississippi	•	★	★		B	B						
Missouri	(c,f)	★	(c,f)	★					B	B	B	B
Montana	★	★	★		B	B						B
Nebraska(U)	★	★					(i)	(i)			(i)	(i)
Nevada	(c)	★	(c)	★	B			B				
New Hampshire	•	★(f)	•	★(f)	B	B				H		
New Jersey	★	★	★	★	B	B						
New Mexico	•	★	•	★	B			B				
New York	★	★	★	★	B	B	B	B	B	B	B	B
North Carolina	•	★	•	★	B		B	B	B			
North Dakota	(c)	★	(c)	★	B			B				
Ohio	★	★	★	★	B				B	B		
Oklahoma	•	★	•	★			B	B			B	B
Oregon	★	★	★	★							B	B
Pennsylvania	★	★	★	★			B	B			B	B
Rhode Island	★	★	★	★							B	B
South Carolina	•	★	•	★	B	B	B	B		B	B	B
South Dakota	★	★	★	★	B					B		
Tennessee	★	★	★	★	B				B	B	S	B
Texas	★	★	★	★	B	B		B(f)			B	B
Utah	★	★	★	★	B					B		
Vermont	★	★	★	★	B	B						
Virginia	★	★	★	★	B			B				B(h)
Washington	★	★	★	★			B	B	B	B	B	
West Virginia	★	★	★	★	B	B	B	B			B	B
Wisconsin	★	★	★	★	B		B				B	B
Wyoming	★(f)	★	★(f)	★	B			B				
American Samoa	★(f)	...	★(f)	...	B							
Guam(U)	★	★			(i)	(i)			(i)	(i)	(i)	(i)
Puerto Rico	★	★	★	★	B						B	B
Virgin Islands(U)	★	★			(i)	(i)						(i)

†Multiple entries reflect a combination of organizational location of services.

Key:
★—All committees
•—Some committees
. . .—No committees
B—Both chambers
H—House
S—Senate
U—Unicameral

(a) Includes legislative council or service agency, central management agency.

(b) Includes chamber management agency, office of clerk or secretary and House or Senate research office.

(c) Money committees only.

(d) Joint Legislative Budget Committee provides staff assistance to the money committees of both houses.

(e) Standing committees are joint House and Senate committees.

(f) Provided on a pool basis.

(g) All professional committee staff (except Finance committees) during session only. During interim, assistance provided by year-round majority and minority research offices.

(h) The Senate secretary and House clerk maintain supervision of committee clerks. Iowa: during the session each committee selects its own clerk.

(i) Unicameral legislative body.

Table 20
LEGISLATIVE APPROPRIATIONS PROCESS: BUDGET DOCUMENTS AND BILLS

| State or other jurisdiction | Budget document submission | | | | | | | Budget bill introduction | | |
| | Legal source of deadline | | Submission date relative to convening | | | | | | | |
	Consti-tutional	Statutory	Prior to session	Within one week	Within two weeks	Within one month	Over one month	Same time as budget document	Another time	Not until cmte. review of budget document
Alabama	...	★	...	2nd da.	...	...	...	★	...	...
Alaska	...	★	...	★	...	...	...	★	...	...
Arizona	...	★	...	★	...	...	...	...	...	(a)
Arkansas	...	...	...	...	(b)	...	...	...	...	★
California	★	...	...	...	...	...	(c)	★	...	...
Colorado	...	★	...	...	★(d)	...	...	...	...	★
Connecticut	...	★	...	...	...	★(e)	...	★	...	...
Delaware	...	★	...	...	...	Feb. 1	...	★(f)	...	...
Florida	...	★	30 da.	...	...	...	...	★	...	★(g)
Georgia	★	...	...	★	...	...	...	★	...	...
Hawaii	...	★	20 da.	...	...	...	...	...	★	...
Idaho	...	★	...	★	...	...	...	...	...	★
Illinois	...	★	...	...	...	...	★	...	★	...
Indiana	...	★	7 da.(h)	...	...	...	...	★	...	...
Iowa	...	★	...	...	...	★	...	...	...	★(g)
Kansas	...	★	...	...	...	★(e)	...	...	★(i)	...
Kentucky	...	...	...	...	...	...	(j)	★	...	...
Louisiana	...	★	...	1st da.	...	...	...	...	(k)	...
Maine	...	★	...	...	★(l)	...	...	★	...	...
Maryland	★	...	...	★(l)	...	...	...	★(m)	...	...
Massachusetts	★	...	...	...	...	★(l)	...	★(a)	...	...
Michigan	...	★	...	...	★(n)	...	...	★	...	...
Minnesota	...	★	...	...	...	★	...	...	...	★
Mississippi	...	★	Dec. 15	...	...	...	...	...	...	★
Missouri	★	...	...	...	...	★	...	★	...	...
Montana	...	★	...	1st da.	...	...	...	...	★	...
Nebraska	...	★	...	...	★	...	...	...	...	★(f)
Nevada	...	★	...	...	★	...	...	...	...	★
New Hampshire	...	★	...	...	...	...	★	...	...	★
New Jersey	...	★	...	...	...	★(l)	...	...	...	★
New Mexico	...	★	...	(o)	...	...	...	★	...	...
New York	★	...	...	...	★(l)	...	...	★(p)	...	...
North Carolina	...	...	...	(b)	...	...	...	★	...	...
North Dakota	...	★	...	3rd da.(q)	...	...	...	★	...	...
Ohio	...	★	...	...	...	★(l)	...	★	...	...
Oklahoma	...	★	...	★	...	...	...	★	...	...
Oregon	...	★	Dec. 1(l)	...	...	...	...	★	...	...
Pennsylvania	...	★	...	...	...	...	★(l,r)	...	...	★
Rhode Island	...	★	...	...	...	...	★(s)	★	...	...
South Carolina	...	★	1st Tues. in Jan.	...	...	...	...	...	...	★
South Dakota	...	★	Dec. 1	...	...	...	...	...	...	★
Tennessee	...	★	...	...	★(l)	...	...	★	...	...
Texas	...	★	...	★	...	...	...	★	...	...
Utah	...	★	(t)	...	★(e)	...	...	...	...	★
Vermont	...	★	...	...	...	★	...	...	...	★
Virginia	...	★	...	★	...	...	...	★	...	...
Washington	...	★	Dec. 20	...	...	...	...	...	★	...
West Virginia	★	...	...	1st da.(l)	...	...	...	★	...	...
Wisconsin	...	★	...	...	...	★(u)	...	★	...	...
Wyoming	...	★	Jan. 1	...	...	...	...	...	...	★
American Samoa	...	...	(b)	...	...	...	...	...	★	...
Guam	...	★	...	...	...	★	...	★	...	...
Puerto Rico	★	...	...	...	...	★	...	...	...	★
Virgin Islands	...	★	...	...	...	★(v)	...	★	...	...

Key:
★—Yes
...—No

(a) General appropriations bill only.

(b) By custom only. No statutory or constitutional provisions.

(c) Session begins in December. Within the first 10 days of each calendar year.

(d) Copies of agency budgets to be presented to the legislature by November 1. Governor's budget usually is presented in January.

(e) Even year. Connecticut—first day; Kansas—second day; Utah—first day.

(f) Executive budget bill is introduced and used as working tool for committee. Delaware: after hearings on executive bill, a new bill is then introduced. The committee bill is considered by the legislature.

(g) Executive submits bill, but it is not introduced; used as a working tool by committee.

(h) Budget document submitted prior to session does not necessarily reflect budget message which is given sometime during the first three weeks of session.

(i) Within one month for most bills; however, some are introduced later.

(j) No set time.

(k) Subject to same 15-day constitutional limit as other bills.

(l) Later for first session of a new governor. Maine—six weeks; Maryland—10 days; Massachusetts—two months; New Jersey—February 15; New York—February 1; Ohio—March 16; Oregon—February 1; Pennsylvania—first full week in March; Tennessee—March 1; West Virginia—one month.

(m) Appropriations bills other than the budget bill (supplementary) may be introduced at any time. They must provide their own tax source and may not be enacted until the budget bill is enacted.

(n) Long-range capital budget: 30 days.

(o) Statutes provide for submission by 25th legislative day; however, the executive budget is usually presented by the first day of the session. The legislative budget is usually presented on the first day or at the pre-legislative session conference of the standing finance committees.

(p) Governor has 30 days to amend or complete submission bills which enact the recommendations contained in this executive budget, computed from the designated submission date for the budget.

(q) For whole legislature. The Legislative Council only receives budget on December 1.

(r) Submitted by governor as soon as possible after General Assembly organizes, but not later than the first full week in February.

(s) Twenty-fourth legislative day. Legislature normally meets for four legislative days per week.

(t) Must submit confidential copy to fiscal analyst 30 days prior to session.

(u) Last Tuesday in January. A later submission date may be requested by the governor.

(v) Organic Act specifies at opening of each regular session; statute specifies on or before May 30.

Table 21
STAFF FOR INDIVIDUAL LEGISLATORS

	Senate			House		
	Capitol			Capitol		
State	Personal	Shared	District	Personal	Shared	District
Alabama	(a)	YR	(b)	(a)	YR	(b)
Alaska	YR	...	...	YR	...	...
Arizona	YR	...	...	...	IO	...
Arkansas	...	SO	(c)	...	SO	(c)
California	YR	...	YR	YR	...	YR
Colorado	(a)	YR	...	(a)	YR	...
Connecticut	(a)	YR/2	...	(a)	YR/6	...
Delaware	SO	SO/3(d)	...	SO	SO/8	...
Florida	YR(e)	...	(e)	YR(e)	...	(e)
Georgia	...	(f)	...	...	(f)	...
Hawaii	SO	YR	...	SO	YR	...
Idaho	...	YR	...	...	YR	...
Illinois	YR	...	YR	...	YR/2	YR
Indiana	(a)	YR/4	...	...	YR/4	...
Iowa	SO	YR	...	SO	YR	...
Kansas	SO(g)	...	...	(g)	SO/1-3	...
Kentucky	...	YR	...	...	YR	...
Louisiana	SO	...	YR	...	...	YR
Maine	(a)	SO	...	(a)	SO	...
Maryland	YR	...	(c)	...	YR	(c)
Massachusetts	YR	...	...	YR	YR/3	...
Michigan	YR	YR	...	YR	YR	...
Minnesota	SO	...	...	...	YR	...
Mississippi	...	YR	...	...	SO	...
Missouri	YR	(d)	YR	YR	IO	...
Montana	...	SO	...	...	SO	...
Nebraska	YR	...	...	--------Unicameral--------		
Nevada	(a)	YR	...	(a)	YR	...
New Hampshire	...	(a)	...	...	(a)	...
New Jersey	YR(e)	...	(e)	YR(e)	...	(e)
New Mexico	...	SO/2-10	...	...	SO/2-10	...
New York	YR	...	YR	YR	...	YR
North Carolina	SO	...	...	SO	...	...
North Dakota	(a)	SO/10	...	(a)	SO/12	...
Ohio	YR	YR/3	...	(h)	YR/2	...
Oklahoma	SO(g)	IO/4	...	SO	YR	...
Oregon	SO	...	...	(c)	...	...
Pennsylvania	YR	...	YR	YR	YR	YR
Rhode Island	...	YR	...	...	YR	...
South Carolina	...	YR/2	(i)	...	...	(i)
South Dakota	...	SO	...	...	SO	...
Tennessee	YR	...	...	(a)	YR/2.5	...
Texas(c)	YR	...	YR	YR	...	YR
Utah	...	YR(j)	...	...	YR(j)	...
Vermont	...	...	...	...	...	...
Virginia	(c)	SO/2	(c)	(c)	SO/2	(c)
Washington	YR	...	YR	SO	YR/8	...
West Virginia	SO	...	...	...	(k)	...
Wisconsin	YR	...	...	YR	...	...
Wyoming	...	SO	...	...	SO	...

Note: For entries under column heading "Shared," figure after slash indicates approximate number of legislators per staff person, where available.

Key:
...—Staff not provided.
YR—Year-round.
SO—Session only.
IO—Interim only.

(a) Staff provided to leadership only (may include specific committee chairmen). Alabama—provided to lieutenant governor (as president), president pro tempore, and chairmen of the Rules, Finance and Taxation committees in the Senate, and the speaker and chairmen of the Ways and Means and Rules committees in the House. Connecticut—year-round personal staff. Nevada—staff provided during session only.

(b) Some of the larger delegations have year-round district staff.

(c) Expense allowance used for staffing. Arkansas—legislators may use "home office" expense allowance to employ special staff assistance. Maryland—legislators may employ staff from district office expense funds. Oregon—may be used for session and/or interim staffing.

Virginia—legislators receive allowance for one or two staff persons; may be employed at capitol or in district.

(d) Upon member's request, secretarial staff may be provided at any time.

(e) Personal and district staff are the same. Florida—two staff persons per legislator.

(f) Centralized staffing only through Legislative Counsel, Budget and Fiscal offices.

(g) Year-round staffing for leadership. In Kansas, two or three per member.

(h) Based on seniority or position in House leadership.

(i) Although legislators are not provided with district staffing, a legislative delegation office (with staff) is present in most county court houses.

(j) In Senate, eight clerical assistants also available during session; three during interim. In House, 12 clerical assistants during session; two during interim.

(k) During the session and during monthly interim meetings.

Table 22
FISCAL NOTES: CONTENT AND DISTRIBUTION

State or other jurisdiction	Intent or purpose of bill	Cost involved	Projected future cost	Proposed source of revenue	Fiscal impact on local government	Other	All	Available on request	Bill sponsor	Members	Chairman only	Fiscal staff	Executive budget staff
Alabama	...	★	...	★	★(a)		★(b)	...	...	...	...	...	...
Alaska	...	★	★	★(c)	...		★(d)	...	...	...	...	...	...
Arizona	...	★	★	★	★		★	...	...	...	...	★	★
Arkansas	(e)	(e)	(e)	...	(e)		(e)	...	...	...	...	...	...
California	★	★	★	★	★		★	...	...	...	...	★	★
Colorado	★	★	★	★	★		★	...	...	...	...	★	★
Connecticut	...	★	★	...	★		★	...	...	...	...	★	★
Delaware	...	★	★	...	...	★(f)	...	★	...	★	...	★	★
Florida	★	★	★	★	★	★(g)	★	...	...	...	...	★	★
Georgia	...	★	★	★	★		...	★	...	...	...	...	...
Hawaii													
Idaho	★	★	★	★(h)	★		★	...	...	...	...	...	...
Illinois	...	★	★	★	★	(i)	...	★(j)	★(j)	...	...	...	...
Indiana	★	★	★	★	★		★	...	...	...	...	★	★
Iowa	...	★	★	★	★		★	...	...	...	...	...	...
Kansas	★	★	★	★	★		...	★	★	...	★(k)	★	★
Kentucky	★	★	★	★	...		...	★	★	★	...	★	★
Louisiana	...	★	★	...	★		...	★	★	...	...	★(l)	...
Maine	...	★	★	...	...		★	★	...	...	...	★	...
Maryland	★	★	★	★	★		...	★	★	★(k)	...	★	★
Massachusetts	...	★(m)	...		...		★	★	...	...	...	★	...
Michigan	★	★	★	★	★	★(n)	★(o)	★	...	...	...	★	...
Minnesota	★	★	★	★	...		...	★	★	★	...	★	...
Mississippi	★	★	★	...	★		...	★	...	...	★	...	...
Missouri	...	★	★	★	★		★	...	...	...	...	...	...
Montana	★(p)	★	★	★	★	★(g)	★	...	...	...	...	...	...
Nebraska	...	★	★	★	★		★	...	...	...	...	★	★
Nevada	★	★	★	★	★		★	...	...	...	...	★	★
New Hampshire	★	★	★	★	★		★	...	...	...	...	★	★
New Jersey	★	★	★	...	★	★	★(q)	...	...	...	...	★	★
New Mexico	★	★	★	...	(h)	★(r)	...	(s)	...	...	★(s)	★	...
New York	★	★(t)	...	...	★		...	★	★	★	★	★	...
North Carolina	★	★	★	...	★	★(u)	...	★	★	...	★	★	...
North Dakota	★	★	★(v)	★	...		...	★	...	...	★	★	...
Ohio	★	★	★	★	★		★(w)	★	★	★	...	...	...
Oklahoma													
Oregon	...	★	★	★	★		★	...	...	...	...	★	★
Pennsylvania	...	★	★	★	★	★(i)	★	...	...	...	...	★	★
Rhode Island	...	★	★	...	★	★(x)	...	★	...	...	★	★	★
South Carolina	...	★	★	...	...		...	★	★	...	...	...	...
South Dakota	...	★	★	★	★		...	★	...	...	...	...	...
Tennessee	★	★	★	★	★	★(y)	★	...	...	...	...	★	★
Texas	...	★	★	★	★		...	★	★	★(k)	...	...	★
Utah	...	★	★	★	★		★	...	...	...	...	...	...
Vermont	★	★	★	★	...		...	★	...	...	★	...	...
Virginia	★	★	★	★(z)	...	★	...	★	★	★	...	...	...
Washington	★	★	★	★	★		...	★	★	...	...	★	★
West Virginia	★	★	★	★	★(aa)		★	...	...	...	...	...	...
Wisconsin	...	★	★	★	★		★	...	...	...	...	...	...
Wyoming	...	★	★	★	★		★	...	...	...	...	...	...
American Samoa													
Guam	★	★	★	★	★		★	...	...	...	...	★	★
Puerto Rico	...	★	...	...	★		★	...	...	...	...	...	...
Virgin Islands	★	★	...	★	...		★	...	...	...	...	...	...

FISCAL NOTES: CONTENT AND DISTRIBUTION
Notes

Key:
★—Yes
. . .—No
(a) Senate only.
(b) Fiscal notes are included in bills for final passage calendar.
(c) Contained in the bill, not in the fiscal note.
(d) Fiscal notes are attached to the bill before it is reported to the Rules Committee. Governor's bills must have fiscal note before introduction.
(e) Required on retirement and local government bills and distributed to all legislators.
(f) Relevant data and prior fiscal year cost information.
(g) Mechanical defects in bill and effective date.
(h) Occasionally.
(i) Bill proposing changes in retirement system of state or local government must have an actuarial note.
(j) A summary of the fiscal note is attached to the summary of the relevant bill in the Legislative Synopsis and Digest. Fiscal notes are prepared for the sponsor of the bill and are attached to the bill on file in either the office of the clerk of the House or the secretary of the Senate.
(k) Or to committee to which referred.
(l) Prepared by Legislative Fiscal Office; copies sent to House and Senate staff offices respectively.
(m) Fiscal notes are prepared only if cost exceeds $100,000 or matter has not been acted upon by the Joint Committee on Ways and Means.
(n) Other relevant data.

(o) Analyses prepared by Senate Fiscal Agency, distributed to Senate members only; analyses prepared by House Fiscal Agency, distributed to House members only.
(p) Comment or opinion on the merits of the bill is prohibited.
(q) Sponsor may disapprove fiscal note; if disapproved, fiscal note is not printed or distributed.
(r) Impact of revenue bills reviewed by Legislative Council Service and executive agencies.
(s) Legislative Finance Committee staff prepares fiscal notes for Appropriations Committee chairman; other fiscal impact statements prepared by Legislative Council Service and executive agencies are available to anyone upon request.
(t) Rules of the Assembly require sponsors' memoranda to include estimate of cost to state and/or local government. Fiscal note required by law to be included on all pension bills.
(u) Fiscal note required in Senate. In House, staff prepares a summary.
(v) A two-year projection.
(w) If a bill comes up for floor consideration.
(x) Technical or mechanical defects may be noted.
(y) Effects of revenue bills.
(z) The Department of Taxation prepares revenue impact notes including the intent and revenue impact.
(aa) House of Delegates only.

Table 23
LEGISLATIVE REVIEW OF ADMINISTRATIVE REGULATIONS: POWERS

State	Reviewing committee's powers:				Legislative powers:		
	Review of proposed rules	Review of existing rules	No objection constitutes approval of proposed rule	Committee may suspend rule	Legislature must sustain committee action	Time limit for legislative action	Legislature can amend or modify rule
Alabama	★	★	★	★	★	End of regular session	...
Alaska	★	★	★	★	★	30 days after convening of regular session	...
Arizona	...	★	...	...	★	1 year	★
Arkansas	★	★	...	...	...		...
California				------(a)------			
Colorado	...	★	...	...	★	Next regular session	★
Connecticut	★	★	★	★	(b)	(b)	★(c)
Delaware				------(a)------			
Florida	★	★	★	...	...		★
Georgia	★	...	★	...	★	30 days after convening of regular session	
Hawaii	(d)	...	...	...	...		...
Idaho	★	★	★	...	★	End of regular session	★
Illinois	★	★	★	★	★	150 days	★
Indiana				------(a)------			
Iowa	★	★	★	★	★	45 session days	...
Kansas	★	★	★	...	★	End of regular session	★
Kentucky	★	★	★	(e)	...		...
Louisiana	★	★	★	★(f)	...		...
Maine	...	★	...	...	...		...
Maryland	★	★	★	...	...		...
Massachusetts				------(a)------			
Michigan	★	...	...	(g)	...		...
Minnesota	...	★	...	★	★	End of regular session	...
Mississippi				------(a)------			
Missouri	...	★	...	★	...		...
Montana	...	★	...	...	★	None	★
Nebraska	...	★	...	★	★	Next regular session	...
Nevada	★	...	★	★	★	30 session days	...
New Hampshire	★	★	★	...	...		...
New Jersey				------(a)------			
New Mexico				------(a)------			
New York	★	★	★	...	...		...
North Carolina	★	...	★	★	...		...
North Dakota	★	★	★	...	...		...
Ohio	★	...	★	★	★	60 days	★
Oklahoma	...	★	...	...	★	30 days	...
Oregon	★	★	★	...	...		...
Pennsylvania	(h)	...	...	...	...		...
Rhode Island				------(a)------			
South Carolina	★	...	★	...	★	90 days after filed with legislature	...
South Dakota	★	★	★	★	★	30 days after convening of regular session	★
Tennessee	★	★	★	★	...		...
Texas	★	...	★	★	...		...
Utah				------(a)------			
Vermont	★	★	★	...	...		...
Virginia	★	...	★	★	★	End of regular session	★
Washington	★	★	★	...	...		...
West Virginia	★	★	...	...	★	End of session	★
Wisconsin	★	★	★	★	★	End of next regular session	...
Wyoming	...	★	...	...	...		...

Note: Even though a state legislature may not have a formal mechanism in place to take action on administrative rules and regulations, rules could be submitted and standing committees could review on an informal basis. In some states, the courts' determinations that statutes providing for formal legislative review of administrative rules were unconstitutional led the legislatures to reenact or revise those procedures. Consult annotated state statutes and court actions for more details.

Key:
★—Yes
...—No
(a) No formal mechanism for legislative review of administrative rules.
(b) It is not mandatory for legislature to approve or disapprove committee action. However, disapproval of a rule implementing a federally subsidized program must be sustained by legislature before end of the regular session or committee's action is reversed.
(c) Committee may disapprove a part of a rule.
(d) Reviews rules when adopted, amended or repealed.
(e) Until an interim committee or the next legislature can review the rule.
(f) If committee determines that rule is unacceptable, it submits a report to the governor. The governor has five days to accept or reject the report.
(g) Committee may suspend rules during interim only, if granted authorization to do so by legislature.
(h) Some rules may be submitted for "review and comment."

Table 24
LEGISLATIVE REVIEW OF ADMINISTRATIVE REGULATIONS:
STRUCTURES AND PROCEDURES

State	Type of reviewing committee	All rules reviewed	Time limits for submission of rules for review
Alabama	Joint	★	35 days before adoption
Alaska	Joint	★	45 days
Arizona	(a)	(b)	Immediately after adoption
Arkansas	Joint	★	10 days before agency hearing
California	--(c)--		
Colorado	Joint	★	20 days after approval by attorney general
Connecticut	Joint bipartisan	★	After approval by attorney general
Delaware	--(c)--		
Florida	Joint	★	21 days
Georgia	Standing cmtes.	★	30 days
Hawaii	(d)	(e)	None
Idaho	Standing cmtes. & germane jt. sub-cmtes.	★	Beginning of each session or upon adoption
Illinois	Joint bipartisan	★	45 days
Indiana	--(c)--		
Iowa	Joint	★	35 days(f)
Kansas	Joint	★	By Dec. 31 of each year
Kentucky	Joint subcmte.	★	None(g)
Louisiana	Standing cmtes.	★	15 days before adoption(h)
Maine	Joint standing cmtes.	. . .	None
Maryland	Joint	★	45 days before adoption
Massachusetts	--(c)--		
Michigan	Joint	★	None
Minnesota	Joint	★	None
Mississippi	--(c)--		
Missouri	Joint	★	None
Montana	Joint	★	None
Nebraska	Standing cmtes.	★	None
Nevada	Joint	★	After adoption
New Hampshire	Standing cmtes.	★	None
New Jersey	--(c)--		
New Mexico	--(c)--		
New York	Joint	★	21 days before effective date
North Carolina	Joint	★	Prior to filing with attorney general, usually 30 days before effective date
North Dakota	Joint interim	★	None
Ohio	Joint	(i)	60 days before adoption
Oklahoma	Standing cmtes.	★	10 days after adoption
Oregon	Joint	(j)	Within 10 days after filing with secretary of state
Pennsylvania	Standing cmtes.	. . .	None
Rhode Island	--(c)--		
South Carolina	Standing cmtes.	★	None(k)
South Dakota	Joint interim	★	20 days before agency hearing
Tennessee	Standing cmtes.(l)	★	45 days before effective date
Texas	Standing cmtes.	★	30 days before adoption
Utah	--(c)--		
Vermont	Joint	★	2 weeks before adoption
Virginia	Standing cmtes.	★	30 days before adoption
Washington	Joint	★	Immediately upon filing with code revisor
West Virginia	Joint	★	None
Wisconsin	Joint	★	None
Wyoming	Joint	★	20 days before adoption

Note: Even though a state legislature may not have a formal mechanism in place to take action on administrative rules and regulations, rules could be submitted and standing committees could review on an informal basis. In some states, the courts' determinations that statutes providing for formal legislative review of administrative rules were unconstitutional led the legislatures to reenact or revise those procedures. Consult annotated state statutes and court actions for more details.

Key:
★—Yes
. . .—No

(a) Not specified; presumably review done by appropriate committee.
(b) Provides only for legislative review of those rules promulgated by State Parks Board.
(c) No formal mechanism for legislative review of administrative rules.

(d) Review is by office of legislative auditor which submits reports to the legislature for appropriate action.
(e) Reviews rules when adopted, amended or repealed.
(f) Published in Iowa Administrative Code 35 days prior to adoption.
(g) But proposed rule cannot go into effect unless it is filed with the Legislative Research Commission and reviewed by subcommittee.
(h) Thirty days before the regular session, agencies must submit an annual report to the legislature on all rules adopted over the previous year.
(i) Certain rules exempt from review.
(j) Committee may review or may direct the legislative counsel to review a rule. Review is not automatic.
(k) But rule cannot go into effect until 90 days after submission. During interim, emergency regulations can be issued with an immediate effective date.
(l) House and Senate Government Operations committees.

Table 25

SUMMARY OF SUNSET LEGISLATION

State	Scope	Preliminary evaluation conducted by	Other legislative review	Other oversight mechanisms in bill	Phase-out period	Life of each agency (in years)	Other provisions
Alabama	C	Select Joint Committee	Dept. of Examiners of Public Accounts	Zero-base budg.	180/d	4	1-hour time limit on floor debate on each bill.
Alaska	R	Standing committees		Perf. audit	1/y	Varies	In addition to regulatory agencies, programs in other broad areas terminate in 1980-83; specific programs authorized for termination by Legislative Budget & Audit Cmte.
Arizona	C	Office of the Auditor General	Jt. Legislative Oversight Cmte.	Perf. audit	(a)	10	
Arkansas	(b)						
California	(c)						
Colorado	R	Until July 1, 1984, by the Dept. of Regulatory Agencies; after, by the Dept. of Admin. Reports to Legis. Council by July 1, preceding year of termination	Standing committees	Perf. audit	1/y	10	There is also legislation requiring a study of 20 principal depts. of state government on a schedule concluding in 1994.
Connecticut	R(d)	Legis. Prog. Review & Investigations Cmte.	Govt. Admnis. & Elections Cmte.	Perf. audit	1/y	5	
Delaware	C	Agencies under review submit report to Del. Sunset Comm. based on criteria for review and set forth in statute. Comm. staff conducts separate review		Perf. audit	Dec. 31 of next succeeding calendar year	4	Yearly Sunset Review schedules must include at least nine agencies. If the number automatically scheduled for review or added by the General Assembly is less than a full schedule, additional agencies shall be added in order of their appearance in the Del. Code to complete the review schedule.
Florida	R	Appropriate substantive cmte. shall begin review 15 months prior to repeal date			1/y	10	Provides for periodic review of limitations on the initial entry into a profession, occupation, business, industry or other endeavor.

State							
Georgia	R	Standing committees	Dept. of Audits	Perf. audit	1/y	6	The termination dates of the 10 agencies reviewed & scheduled for termination in 1978 were extended.
Hawaii	R	Legislative Auditor			None	6	
Idaho				—No program—			
Illinois	R	Select Jt. Cmte. on Regulatory Agency Reform	Standing cmtes. of each house	Performance evaluation; agency demonstrates need for continued existence	1/y	10	Upon receipt of report from Bur. of the Budget, the gov. may recommend continuation or abolition of agency. Gov. may also submit Select Jt. Cmte.'s recommendations as a reorganization plan.
Indiana	C	Legis. Serv. Agency, Off. of Fiscal & Mgt. Analysis	Jt. Interim Sunset Evaluation Cmte.	Gov. submits recommendations	None(e)		Each newly established agency subject to termination with 10-year life span. Agencies established by exec. order, terminate when a gov. leaves office. Agencies established by concurrent resolution by a General Assembly terminate after adjournment of the 2nd session.
Iowa	(c)						
Kansas	R(d)	Legis. Post Audit nine months prior to termination	Standing committees	Perf. audit	1/y	Subject to legislative discretion	Act terminates in July 1984 unless re-enacted.
Kentucky				—No program—			
Louisiana	C	Standing cmtes. of the two houses which have usual jurisdiction over the affairs of the entity. Process begins 2 years prior to the termination date	Bill authorizing re-creation referred to committee performing initial review	Zero-base budgeting	July 1 of year before end of legislative authority	9	Standing cmtes. may conduct a more extensive evaluation of selected statutory entities under their jurisdiction or of particular programs of such entities.
Maine	R	Legislative Finance Office		Perf. eval.	1/y	10	Performance reviews also scheduled for executive departments (no terminations).
Maryland	R	Dept. of Fiscal Serv.	Standing committees		None	6	
Massachusetts				—No program—			

SUMMARY OF SUNSET LEGISLATION—Continued

State	Scope	Preliminary evaluation conducted by	Other legislative review	Other oversight mechanisms in bill	Phase-out period	Life of each agency (in years)	Other provisions
Michigan	(c)						
Minnesota	(c)						
Mississippi	C	Standing committees	Jt. Cmte. on Performance Evaluation and Expenditure Review	Perf. audit; agency demonstrates need for continued existence	By Dec. 31 of year terminated	8	Act terminates in 1984 unless re-enacted. Newly created agencies subject to termination with 8-year life span. Governmental units established by exec. order shall terminate unless enacted into statutory law. (Those established after effective date of sunset legislation.)
Missouri				————No program————			
Montana	R(f)	Legis. Audit Cmte.	Standing committees		1/y	6	
Nebraska	(g)						
Nevada	(h)						
New Hampshire	D/C	Jt. Legis. Cmte. on Review of Agencies & Programs	Standing committees		9/m	6	
New Jersey	(c)						
New Mexico	R	Legis. Finance Cmte.			1/y	6	
New York				————No program————			
North Carolina	(i)						
North Dakota				————No program————			
Ohio	(c)						
Oklahoma	R	Standing or interim cmte.		Zero-base budgeting	1/y	6	Rules & regulations of terminated agencies continue in effect unless terminated by law; includes agencies established by exec. order.
Oregon	R	Interim cmte.	Standing committees		None	6	
Pennsylvania	S	Legislative Budget and Finance Cmte.		Perf. eval.	None	8	
Rhode Island	C	Oversight Commission	Auditor General	Zero-base budgeting	1/y	5	Oversight Commission established to conduct sunset reviews.
South Carolina	R	Legis. Audit Council	Reorganization Commission, standing committees	Perf. audit	1/y	6	

State		First body	Second body	Review type	Frequency	No.	Description
South Dakota	S	Special interim cmte.	Legislative Research Council	Perf. audit	180/d	10	The sunset review cycle pertains only to an agency's administrative rules. Only through legislation can an agency be terminated.
Tennessee	C	Special eval. cmte. in each house	State Auditor	Limited prog.	1/y	6	Establishment of new agencies subject to review by evaluation committee.
Texas	C	Sunset Advisory Commission		Perf. eval.	1/y	12	Initial review conducted by agencies themselves.
Utah	R	Interim study cmte.	Off. of Legislative Research	Interim cmte.'s discretion	1/y	6	
Vermont	R	Legis. Council staff	Standing committees		1/y	13	
Virginia	(j)						
Washington	C	Legis. Budget Cmte.	Standing committees	Prog. review	1/y	6	Select jt. cmte. prepares termination legislation.
West Virginia	S	Jt. Cmte. on Govt. Operations	Leg. Post Audit Div.	Perf. audit	1/y	6	Jt. Cmte. on Govt. Operations composed of 5 house members, 5 senate members & 5 citizens appointed by governor. Agencies may be reviewed more frequently.
Wisconsin	(c)						
Wyoming	S	Legis. Serv. Office	11-mbr. cmte. apptd. by Mgt. Council		1/y	Subject to legislative discretion	Every 2 years the legislature selects a group of agencies to undergo sunset review.

(d) Primarily.

(e) Through an executive order, the governor may provide a terminated agency with one year to wind up its affairs.

(f) Plus certain agencies within Departments of Social and Rehabilitative Services, Community Affairs and Institutions.

(g) Nebraska's Sunset Act terminated in 1983.

(h) Nevada law provided for a one-cycle pilot program under which three agencies were reviewed in 1980. No further expansion of the law has been enacted.

(i) North Carolina's sunset law terminated on June 30, 1983.

(j) By joint resolution, Senate and House of Delegates establish a schedule for review of "functional areas" of state government. Program evaluation is carried out by Joint Legislative Audit and Review Commission. Agencies are not scheduled for automatic termination. Commission reports are made to standing committees which conduct public hearings.

Key:
C—Comprehensive
R—Regulatory
S—Selective
D—Discretionary
d—day
y—year
m—month

(a) Agency termination is scheduled on July 1 of the year prior to the scheduled termination of statutory authority for that agency.

(b) Arkansas' sunset law terminated on June 30, 1983.

(c) While they have not enacted sunset legislation in the same sense as the other 33 states with detailed information in this table, the legislatures in California, Delaware, Iowa, Michigan, Minnesota, New Jersey, Ohio and Wisconsin have included sunset clauses in selected programs.

Table 26
LEGISLATIVE APPLICATIONS OF ELECTRONIC DATA PROCESSING

State	Statutory, bill systems, legal applications								Fiscal, budget, economic applications										Legislative management			
	Statutory retrieval	Bill drafting	Bill typing	Bill status report	Statutory revision	Case law retrieval	Redistricting	Other	Revenue forecasting	Revenue analysis	Budget comparison	Budget effects of legislation	Fiscal notes	Local fiscal notes	Economic impact note	Impact of salary and fringe changes	State aid formulas	Tracking federal dollars	Computer printing	Legislative accounting	Mailing lists	Other
Alabama	★	★	★	★	★		★		★	★	★	★	★	★	★	★	★	★	★	★	★	
Alaska	★			★	★	★			★	★			★			★	★		★	★ (c)		
Arizona																				★		
Arkansas	★	★	★	★	★		★		★	★	★	★	★	★		★	★	★	★	★	★	
California	★	★	★		★	★	★	(a,b)	★	★	★	★	★		★	★	★		★	★	★	
Colorado	★	★	★	★	★	★	★		★	★	★	★	★	★		★	★	★	★	★	★	
Connecticut	★	★	★	★	★		★		★	★	★	★	★	★	★	★	★		★	★	★	
Delaware	★	★	★		★	★							★							★	★	
Florida	★	★	★	★	★		★					★					★			★	★	
Georgia	★	★	★	★	★		★				★ (e)								★ (f)	★		(g)
Hawaii	★		★	★	★	★			★	★	★	★	★			★	★	★	★	★	★	
Idaho																						
Illinois	★	★	★	★	★	★	★				★ (d)	★	★	★		★	★		★	★	★	(g)
Indiana				★	★						★						★			★		
Iowa	★	★	★	★	★		★										★			★	★	
Kansas	★	★	★	★	★				(h)	(h)	(h)	(h)				(h)			(h)	(h)		(g,i,j)
Kentucky	★	★	★	★	★		★	(b,k)	★	★	★	★				★	★		★	★ (h)	★	(j)
Louisiana	★	★	★	★	★		★		★	★	★	★ (l)	★	★		★ (h)	★		★	★ (i)	★	
Maine		★	★	★	★	★			★	★	★	★	★	★		★	★	★	★	★	★	
Maryland	★		★	★	★		★		★	★	★	★	★				★ (m)			★	★	
Massachusetts	★	★	★	★	★	★	★					★					★		★	★	★	(n,o)
Michigan	★	★	★	★	★		★						★	★		★	★	★	★	★		
Minnesota	★	★	★	★	★		★						★				★		★	★	★	
Mississippi	★	★	★	★	★		★													★		
Missouri	★	★	★	★ (q)	★	★	★		★	★	★	★	★	★		★	★		★	★	★	
Montana	★	★	★	★	★		★										★			★	★	
Nebraska		★	★	★	★		★	(b)	★	★	★	★	★	★		★	★		★ (b)	★	★	(n,p)
Nevada						★														★		
New Hampshire(r)																						
New Jersey																						
New Mexico																						
New York	★		★	★	★		★		★	★	★	★	★			★	★	★	★	★	★	
North Carolina	★	★	★	★	★		★		★	★	★	★	★			★	★		★	★	★	
North Dakota		★ (s)	★	★	★				★											★		
Ohio	★	★	★	★	★	★		(b,t,u)	★	★	★		★			★	★		★	★	★	(v)

	(h)			(h)	(w)	(h)										(h)		(h)	(h)
Oklahoma	★	★	★	★		★										★		★	★
Oregon	★	★	★	★		★										★	★	★	★
Pennsylvania	★	★	★	★	★	★	★	★	★	★	★	★	★	★	★	★	★	★	★
Rhode Island	★	★	★	★ (b,x)															★
South Carolina																			
South Dakota	★	★	★	★	★	★	★		★	★	★	★	★	★	★	★	★	★	★
Tennessee																			
Texas	★	★	★	★	★	★	★	★	★	★	★	★	★	★	★	★	★	★	★
Utah	★	★	★	★		★	★	★	★		★		★	★	★	★	★	★	★
Vermont																			
Virginia	★	★	★	★		★						★	★	★	★	★	★	★	★
Washington	★	★	★ (z)	★													★	★	★
West Virginia	★	★	★	★														★	
Wisconsin	★	★	★	★	★	★	★	★	★	★	★	★	★	★	★	★	★	★	★
Wyoming	★	★	★	★		★													
														(h)	(g,i,y)

Key:

★—Existing application.

⋯—Not an existing application.

(a) Engrossing—House only.

(b) Preparation of journals and/or calendars. In Arkansas, journal for House only. In Nevada, also
preparation of supplements and annotations to *Nevada Revised Statutes.*

(c) Bureau of Legislative Research only.

(d) For internal comparison between executive and legislative budgets.

(e) General budget development and analysis.

(f) Computer photo composition.

(g) Inventory. In Louisiana, Senate only.

(h) Senate only.

(i) Payroll.

(j) Workload management.

(k) Committee reporting.

(l) In process.

(m) For education.

(n) Word processing.

(o) Electronic mail.

(p) Library services.

(q) Bill tracking.

(r) Electronic data processing used to varying degrees in performing activities.

(s) Bill registry for the tracking of bills being drafted.

(t) General bill analysis.

(u) Administrative Code and attorney general's opinions retrieval.

(v) Constituent letters.

(w) House only.

(x) Word searching of bills introduced and of state's statutes.

(y) Listing of registered lobbyists.

(z) Pilot project for 1984.

Table 27
LOBBYISTS: AS DEFINED IN STATE STATUTES

State	*"Lobbyist" includes:* Anyone receiving compensation to influence legislative action	Anyone spending money to influence legislation	Anyone representing someone else's interests	Anyone attempting to influence legislation(a)	*"Lobbyist" does not include:* Public officials acting in an official capacity	Anyone who speaks only before committees or boards	Anyone with professional knowledge acting as a professional witness	Members of the media	Representatives of religious organizations(b)	Anyone performing professional bill drafting services(c)	Others
Alabama	★	...	...	...	(d)	★	★	...	...	...	...
Alaska(e)	★	★	...	...	★	★	...	★	...	★	...
Arizona	★	...	★	★	★	★	...	...	...	★	(f,g)
Arkansas	★	...	★	...	(d)	...	...	...	...	...	...
California	★	...	...	...	★(h)	...	...	★	★	...	...
Colorado	★	...	...	...	★	★(i)	...	...	...	...	(f,j)
Connecticut	★(k)	★(k)	...	...	★	★	...	★	...	...	(l)
Delaware	★	★	★	...	★	★	★	...	★	★	...
Florida	...	...	...	★(m)	(d)	★	...	...	...	...	...
Georgia	★	...	...	★	★	★	...	...	...	★	...
Hawaii	★(k)	★(k)	★	...	★	★	★	★	...	★	...
Idaho	★	...	...	...	★	★	...	★	★	★	...
Illinois	★	...	★	...	(d)	★	★	★	★	★	(n)
Indiana	★(k)	★(k)	...	...	★	★	...	★	...	...	(o)
Iowa	★	★	★	...	★	★	...	★	...	...	(o)
Kansas	★	★(k)	★	...	★	...	...	...	...	...	(p)
Kentucky	★	★	...	★(q)	...	★	★	...	★	...	...
Louisiana	★	...	...	...	★	★	...	★	...	...	...
Maine	★(k)	★	★	...	★	★	...	...	...	...	(j)
Maryland	★(k)	★(k)	...	...	★	★	★	★	★	★	(r)
Massachusetts	★	...	...	...	...	...	...	...	...	...	...
Michigan	★(k)	★(k)	...	...	★(s)	...	★	★	...	...	...
Minnesota	★(k)	★(k)	...	...	★	...	★	★	...	...	(t)
Mississippi	★	...	...	...	...	★	...	★	...	★	...
Missouri	★	...	...	...	(d)	...	...	...	...	...	...
Montana	★	★(k)	...	...	★	...	...	...	...	...	...
Nebraska	...	...	★	...	★(u)	★	...	★	...	...	...
Nevada	...	...	★	★	★	★	★	★	...	...	(n,v)
New Hampshire	★	...	...	...	...	...	...	...	...	...	...
New Jersey	★(k)	...	...	...	★	...	...	★	★	...	(o,v)
New Mexico	★	...	...	...	★	★	...	...	...	...	(n)
New York	★	...	...	...	★(u)	★	★	★	...	★	(f,j)
North Carolina	★	...	...	...	★(d)	★	★	★	...	★	(j,v)
North Dakota	...	...	...	★	★(d)	★	...	...	...	...	(v)
Ohio	★	...	★	★	...	★	...	★	...	★	...
Oklahoma	★(k)	★(k)	★	...	★	★	★	...	...	...	(f,v)
Oregon	★(k)	★(k)	★	★(m)	(d,w)	★	...	★	...	...	...
Pennsylvania	★	★(k)	★	...	★	★	★	...	...	...	...
Rhode Island	★(k)	★(k)	★	...	★	...	...	...	...	...	...
South Carolina	★	...	★	★(q)	★	★	...	★	★	★	(v)
South Dakota	★	...	...	★(q,m)	...	★	★	★	...	...	(x)
Tennessee	...	★(k)	...	★(m)	★	★	...	★	★	...	(f,j)
Texas	★(k)	★(k)	...	...	★	★	...	★	...	...	(y)
Utah	★	★	...	...	★	★	...	★	★	★	(f,o)
Vermont	★	...	...	...	★	★	...	...	...	...	...
Virginia	...	...	★	...	★	★	...	...	...	...	...
Washington	...	★(k)	...	★	★	★	...	...	...	...	...
West Virginia	★	...	★	★	...	...	...	★	...	...	(o)
Wisconsin	★	★(k)	...	...	★	★	★	★	...	...	(j)
Wyoming	★	...	★	...	★	...	...	...	...	...	...

Note: Entries reflect a literal reading of statutes. Consult lobbyist regulation provisions in each state for more details.

Definitions used to determine who is required to register and, in most cases, report as lobbyist.

Key:

. . . .Not specifically included or excluded in statute wording.

(a) Does not link activity to compensation or expenditures.

(b) Persons representing a bona fide church or religious society for the purpose of protecting the public right to practice the doctrines of such church.

(c) Or advising clients as to the construction or effects of proposed legislation.

(d) Specifically excludes members of the state legislature. In Missouri, stipulates only elected officials.

(e) An individual who lobbies without compensation or who limits lobbying activities to appearances before the legislature, its committees or other public hearings may elect to register with and report to the secretary of state.

(f) Attorneys representing clients before any court or quasi-judicial body or proceedings.

(g) Anyone contacting an official for the sole purpose of acquiring information.

(h) Also does not apply to any state employee acting within the scope of employment, provided that an employee (other than a legislative official) who attempts to influence legislative action and who would otherwise be required to register as a lobbyist is not allowed to make gifts of more than $10/month to an elected state officer or legislative official.

(i) Unless person makes more than three such appearances in a calendar year.

(j) Communications by person in response to an inquiry or request for information. Lobbying as an activity in Colorado does not include communications made by a person in response to a statute, rule, regulation or order requiring such a communication.

(k) Compensation and/or expenditures or time spent lobbying must exceed a specific amount before individual is required to register as a lobbyist. Connecticut—compensation, reimbursement or expenditures (or combined total) of $500 or more/year. Hawaii—anyone who spends more than five hours/month or $275/six months for lobbying activities. Indiana—compensation or expenditures of $500 or more/year. Kansas—expenditures of $100 or more/year. Maine—anyone who spends more than eight hours/month on lobbying activities. Maryland—compensation of $500 or more/reporting period; expenditures of $2,000/reporting period. Michigan—"lobbyist agent" is an individual who receives at least $250/year in compensation; "lobbyist" is an individual who spends more than $1,000/year on activities (more than $250/year, if amount is spent on a single public official). Minnesota—anyone who spends more than five hours/month or more than $250/year. Montana—anyone who spends

more than $1,000/year. New Jersey—anyone who is reimbursed over $100/three months. Oklahoma—compensation or expenditures over $250/quarter. Oregon—anyone who spends over 16 hours/quarter or over $50/quarter. Pennsylvania—anyone who spends over $300/month. Rhode Island—compensation or expenditures over $100/year. Tennessee—anyone who spends more than $200/report period. Texas—compensation or expenditures over $200/quarter. Washington—anyone who spends more than four days/three months and over $25. Wisconsin—anyone who spends over $250/year.

(l) Lobbying as an activity does not include communications by or on behalf of a public service company in connection with public utilities control authority's rate hearings.

(m) Any public official who lobbies. In Florida, includes state executive and judicial or quasi-judicial department employees. In South Dakota, executive employees register as "public employee lobbyists."

(n) Legislative employees.

(o) Officers, employees or representatives of state political parties.

(p) Non-profit organizations which are interstate in their operations.

(q) Specifies legislation affecting private pecuniary interests.

(r) Appearances (as part of the official duties) by an officer, director, member or employee of an association engaged exclusively in lobbying for counties and municipalities.

(s) Although all elected and appointed officials of state or local government are excluded, the categorization itself does not refer to the employees of colleges and universities, townships and other local governments, the state executive departments, the judicial branch or appointed members of state-local boards and commissions.

(t) Individuals engaged in selling goods or services to be paid for by public funds; stockholders of family farm corporations not spending over $250/year in communication with public officials.

(u) College officials and employees are not excluded from lobbyist definition. In Nebraska, the University of Nebraska is specified.

(v) Persons who express a personal opinion to their legislators.

(w) Governor, secretary of state, treasurer, attorney general (and attendant deputies for the latter three officers), superintendent of public instruction and the commissioner of the Bureau of Labor and Industries.

(x) Public corporations.

(y) Persons whose only activity is to encourage or solicit members, employees or stockholders of an entity by whom individual is employed to communicate with legislative members to influence legislation; persons whose only activity is to compensate another to act on their behalf; persons whose only activity is to attend meetings or entertainment events attended by executive/legislative branch members.

Table 28
LOBBYISTS: REGISTRATION AND REPORTING

State	Lobbyist registers with	Frequency	Activity reports(a) Information required(b)						Penalties
			Total expenditures	Expenditures by category	Sources of income	Monies or gifts to individual officials	Legislation supported/ opposed by lobbyist	Other	
Alabama	Ethics Commn.	Monthly(c)	★	⋮	⋮	★	★	(d)	Fine of not more than $10,000 or imprisonment for not more than 10 years, or both.
Alaska	Public Offices Commn.	Monthly(e)	★	⋮	⋮	★	★	(d)	For failure to register or file report on time: $10/day until filed; for violation of provisions: fine of not more than $1,000 or imprisonment for not more than 1 year, or both.
Arizona	Secy. of State	Annually(f) + + +	★	⋮	⋮	★	⋮		Prosecuted as a Class 1 misdemeanor.
Arkansas	Clerk of House; Secy. of Sen.		⋮	⋮	⋮	★	★		None specified.
California	Secy. of State	Quarterly	⋮	⋮	★	★	★	(d)	Prosecuted as misdemeanor, subject to civil fines.
Colorado	Secy. of State	Monthly(g)	★	⋮	★	★	★	(h)	Fine of not more than $5,000 or imprisonment in county jail for 1 year, or both; revocation of registration at discretion of secretary of state.
Connecticut	Ethics Commn.	Quarterly(i)	★	★	★	★	⋮		Fine of not more than $1,000 or imprisonment for 1 year, or both.
Delaware	Legislative Council	Quarterly	★	⋮	★	★	⋮	(j)	For failure to register or for furnishing false information: prosecuted as a Class C misdemeanor; for failure to file report: deemed voluntary cancellation of registration.
Florida	Jt. Legislative Office(k)	Semi-annually	★	⋮	★	⋮	⋮		For violation of provisions: reprimand, censure, prohibition from lobbying for all or part of the legislative biennium during which violation occurred (l); for false swearing as to material fact: prosecuted as 2nd degree misdemeanor.
Georgia	Secy. of State	+ + +							For violation of provisions or non-compliance: prosecuted as a misdemeanor.
Hawaii	Ethics Commn.	Semi-annually	★	⋮	★	★	★		For failure to file statement or for falsifying statement: prosecuted as a misdemeanor.
Idaho	Secy. of State	Annually(i)	★	★	★	★	★		For registration and reporting violations: prosecuted as a misdemeanor and liable to max. civil fine of $250 or max. 6 months imprisonment, or both; for late filing of report: $10/day at discretion of secretary of state; for violation of statutory duties of lobbyists: possible revocation of registration.
Illinois	Secy. of State	Jan., Apr., July(m)	★	⋮	⋮	★	⋮		Prosecuted as a Class 3 felony(n).
Indiana	Secy. of State	Semi-annually	★	★	⋮	★	★	(o)	For failure to file report: $10/day (to max. of $100) until filed; for violation of provisions or false reporting: prosecuted as a Class D felony.
Iowa	Clerk of House; Secy. of Sen.	Monthly	★	⋮	⋮	★	⋮		For failure to file report: cancellation of registration.
Kansas	Secy. of State	Monthly(p)	★	★	★	★	⋮		Prosecuted as a Class B misdemeanor.
Kentucky	Attorney General	After session	★	★	⋮	⋮	★		Fine of not more than $5,000 or imprisonment for not more than 5 years, or both.
Louisiana	Clerk of House; Secy. of Sen.	+ + +							Prosecuted as a misdemeanor, punishable by fine of not more than $500 or imprisonment for not more than 6 months, or both.
Maine	Secy. of State	Monthly(c)	★	⋮	★	★	★		For failure to register or report: fine of $50.
Maryland	Ethics Commn.	Semi-annually	⋮	⋮	⋮	★	⋮	(o)	Prosecuted as a misdemeanor.

State	Administered by	Filing of Reports	Penalties
Massachusetts	Secy. of State	Semi-annually	For failure to register or report: fine of not less than $100 nor more than $5,000; additionally, for legislative agent, disqualification until end of 3rd regular session of legislature after conviction.
Michigan	Secy. of State	Annually(q)	For failure to register or file report: $10/day (to max. $300); for failure to register over 30 days: prosecuted as a misdemeanor, with fine of not more than $1,000.
Minnesota	Ethical Practices Bd.	Quarterly	For late registration or failure to report after first notice: $5/day (to max. $100); for failure to report after second notice: prosecuted as a misdemeanor.
Mississippi	Secy. of State	Annually	For first violation: fine of $1,000 or imprisonment for not more than 6 months, or both; for second offense: $5,000, imprisonment for not more than 3 years, or both.
Missouri	Clerk of House; Secy. of Sen.	3 times during session.	Prosecuted as a misdemeanor; may not register for 2 years.
Montana	Commr. of Political Practices	(r)	For violation of licensing provision: revocation. Prosecuted as a misdemeanor; subject to civil penalties of not less than $250 nor more than $7,500.
Nebraska	Clerk of Legislature	Monthly(c,s)	For violation of gifting provision: prosecuted as Class III misdemeanor.
Nevada	Dir., Legislative Counsel Bureau	After session(t)	For late reports: $5/day for first 30 days; $100 after period at discretion of Director. Prosecuted as a misdemeanor.
New Hampshire	Secy. of State	(u)	Prosecuted as a misdemeanor. For filing false statement: punished as perjury.
New Jersey	Attorney General	Quarterly(g)	Prosecuted as a misdemeanor.
New Mexico	Secy. of State	(v)	Prosecuted as a misdemeanor; fine of not more than $1,000.
New York	Temporary State Commn. on Lobbying	(w)	Prosecuted as a Class A misdemeanor.
North Carolina	Secy. of State	Annually	Prosecuted as a misdemeanor: fine of not less than $50 nor more than $1,000 or imprisonment for not more than 2 years, or both; upon conviction, may not lobby for 2 years.
North Dakota	Secy. of State	Annually	Prosecuted as a Class B misdemeanor.
Ohio	Jt. Cmte. on Agency Rule Review	Semi-annually	Prosecuted as a misdemeanor of the 4th degree.
Oklahoma	Jt. Legislative Ethics Cmte.	Semi-annually	For violation of provisions: prosecuted as a misdemeanor; for failure to register or report, liable for amt. equal to 3 times the expenditure; for third violation: prohibited from lobbying for 5 years.
Oregon	Govt. Ethics. Commn.	Quarterly	Either house of legislature may prescribe penalty.
Pennsylvania	Clerk of House; Secy. of Sen.	Semi-annually	Prosecuted as a 3rd degree misdemeanor.
Rhode Island	Secy. of State	3 times during session	For person, corporation or association engaging lobbyist: fine of not less than $200 nor more than $5,000; for legislative counsel or agent: fine of not less than $100 nor more than $1,000 and disqualification for 3 years.
South Carolina	Secy. of State	Annually	Prosecuted as a misdemeanor; upon conviction, disqualification for 2 years.
South Dakota	Secy. of State; State Librarian & Archivist	Annually; Annually	Disqualification from lobbying for 3 years.
Tennessee			For late filing: suspension of registration; for violation of registration or reporting provisions: prosecuted as a misdemeanor.
Texas	Secy. of State	Monthly(s)	For late filing: civil liability of $100; for failure to register or report: amt. equal to 3 times the compensation or expenditure; for violation of provisions: prosecuted as a Class A misdemeanor.
Utah	Lieutenant Governor	+++	For violation of provisions: prosecuted as a Class C misdemeanor.
Vermont	Secy. of State	Annually(y)	Fine of not more than $500.
Virginia	Secy. of Commonwealth	After session	For failure to report: $50/day until filed; for violation of provisions: prosecuted as a misdemeanor.
Washington	Public Disclosure Commn.	Monthly	Determined by Commn. No individual penalty may exceed $250; for multiple violations: max. aggregate penalty of $5,000.
West Virginia	Clerk of Senate(z)	After session	None specified.
Wisconsin	Secy. of State	Semi-annually(aa)	Fine of not more than $5,000 depending on offense.
Wyoming	Dir., Legislative Service Agy.	+++	For failure to register: prosecuted as a misdemeanor, subject to $200 fine.

Note: Entries reflect a literal reading of statutes. Consult lobbyist regulation provisions in each state for more details.

LOBBYISTS: REGISTRATION AND REPORTING—Notes

Key:
. . —Not required in report.
+ + —Report not required.

(a) When activity or financial reports are required, they are filed with the official or entity responsible for registering lobbyist.

(b) Reports must contain the stated information; however, additional information may be volunteered by the lobbyist or principal responsible for reporting.

(c) During legislative session.

(d) Statement of business association or partnership with any official; may include entities with which lobbyist has engaged in exchange.

(e) As long as individual continues to engage in lobbying activities.

(f) Supplemental reports filed monthly to show any single expenditure over $25 occurring during month.

(g) Also, annual cumulative disclosure statement.

(h) Media expenditures.

(i) Also, interim monthly reports of lobbying activities during legislative session.

(j) Terms of any contracts, agreements or promises.

(k) As defined by statute, a central office designated jointly by the president of the Senate and the speaker of the House and under the immediate responsibility of the secretary of the Senate and the clerk of the House.

(l) If a legislative committee finds there has been a violation of the lobbying provisions, it reports its findings to the presiding officer along with a recommended penalty. The presiding officer brings committee report and recommendations to entire chamber for determination by a majority of members.

(m) April and July of the year during which legislature is in regular session; within 20 days after adjournment of special session; and January each year for the preceding year during which the legislature was not in session.

(n) Corporations violating provisions are guilty of a business offense and receive a maximum fine of $10,000. Any individual convicted of violation is prohibited from lobbying (for compensation) for three years.

(o) Update of information required at registration.

(p) Only required for months during which expenditures are made, or gifts, payments or honoraria given.

(q) On Jan. 31, covering the calendar year ending Dec. 31, and on Aug. 31 covering immediately preceding Dec. 31 to July 31.

(r) Before Feb. 16 when legislature is in session; before the 16th day of the calendar month when principal spent $5,000 or more in the previous month; 60 days after adjournment.

(s) Also, during the interim. In Nebraska, once during interim. In Texas, quarterly during interim.

(t) Monthly during session if lobbyist is attempting to influence legislative action.

(u) If registered for regular session—file April and Aug. 15 of each odd year; if regular session days are held after Aug. 1 of odd year, must file 30 days after each calendar day in which legislative business is conducted. If registered for special session—15 days after conclusion.

(v) Upon filing registration statement, for all pre-session expenditures and 60th day after regular or special session.

(w) Any lobbyist who receives, spends or incurs over $2,000/year files by the 15th day following reporting period in which cumulative total equalled amount (reporting periods—Jan. 1-March 31; April 1-May 31; June 1-Aug. 31) and files an annual cumulative report.

(x) Monthly expenses incurred on behalf of each person in whose interest individual engaged in lobbying.

(y) Also after two months of legislative session.

(z) Copies of registration and report sent to clerk of House.

(aa) By principal.

Section IV THE JUDICIARY

STATE OF THE JUDICIARY

By Daina Farthing-Capowich

The phenomenal pace of change in our society has not left the state court systems untouched during the past two years. While the areas affected and adaptations required have been diverse, three key topics stand out, cutting across states and levels of courts. Due to their recent overriding significance, the following will be highlighted as fundamental developments in the state court systems: the continued move toward state funding of trial courts; application of technological advances to court operations; and the use of carefully formulated strategies to reduce delay in the disposition of court cases.

Continuation of a Trend: State Financing

Between 1980 and 1983, the number of states that assumed or committed themselves to assume total or substantial funding of their court systems increased from 22 to 29.[1] In addition, at least six other states are considering joining the ranks of the state-financed court systems.[2] The reasons recounted for this movement tend to center on the critical need for sufficient fiscal resources.

The shift from a limited local tax base assures courts an adequate, stable funding source. The centralized budgeting that accompanies state funding results in a more equitable distribution of money, thereby ensuring a more uniform delivery of court services. The extent of local control that remains varies, but integration of the budget usually saves money due to centralized purchasing, standardization of procedures, and additional support services that localities are otherwise unable to provide.

The scope and level of state funding vary considerably, however. The majority of states assume court funding gradually or incrementally.[3] Such an approach often eases the difficult transition to state funding by allowing for extensive planning, coordination and development of the necessary administrative structure. The establishment of clear lines of authority is also a part of the evolutionary process and leads ultimately to increased efficiency and accountability as the management system matures.

The initiation of state financing holds major implications for court personnel as well. The task of incorporating local court staff into the state personnel system is an arduous one that involves payroll transfers, personnel classification changes, modification of fringe benefit programs, and renegotiation of collective bargaining agreements. Yet commentators suggest that the outcome is a more effective, more qualified court staff who have broader professional opportunities available to them.[4]

The continued trend toward state funding of the courts, with its concomitant transformations of related administrative and fiscal processes, appears to be robust. A majority of the states have moved in this direction. To date, no evaluations of this trend have been conducted. Systematic evaluation will provide important insights concerning the impact of state funding on the effectiveness of court administration. However, reliable evaluation will be extremely difficult due to the wide variation among states.

The Promise of Technology

Experimentation with and use of technology by judges, administrators and court personnel are clearly on the rise. It is apparent that innovative application of a vast array of technological developments offers courts much in terms of time and fiscal savings as well as potential solutions to mounting dilemmas.[5] Pioneers in the courts are using scientific knowledge to improve performance and delivery of services. Transfer of these experiences, the successes and the pitfalls, is proceeding at a phenomenal pace as judges and administrators attempt to meet the challenges of ever increasing caseloads and limited resources. The impact of technology is now evident in many courts and others are anxious to learn from their varied experiences.

Use of computers is invariably the form of technology that comes to mind first. In fact, development of judicial information systems and other forms of automation represents the technological need most frequently discussed in state of the judiciary messages during 1982 and 1983.[6] Reported uses include word processing, computerized legal research, and automated jury selec-

---

Daina Farthing-Capowich is Staff Associate for the National Center for State Courts.

142

tion.[7] However, one of the most common computer uses in the courts involves case management. Delaware provides one example in this area. Its on-line information system encompasses the superior, family and common pleas courts as well as the state department of justice and the public defenders office. Subpoenas and calendars are computer-generated, and cases are transferred electronically from court to court as necessary.[8] New Jersey recently adopted a master plan to develop a statewide computer system that will ease the overwhelming manual workload, improve case management, and increase the collection of fines and fees.[9]

Innovative uses for videotape have also been employed by various courts. For example, experimentation with pre-recorded videotaped trials or segments of trials (particularly in Erie County, Ohio) has been instituted to save time, place absent witnesses in court, and improve jury utilization in California, Ohio and Wisconsin. The use of videotapes as demonstrative evidence and depositions is also being explored. Time savings and decreased security risks have been achieved using videotape, videophones and closed circuit television in preliminary hearings and arraignments in some states (such as Alaska, Idaho, Pennsylvania and Nevada).

The nature of court reporting has been shaped by changing technology during the last few years. The widespread increase in the volume and complexity of cases has caused court administrators to examine activities that can be modified to improve caseflow and efficiency. Court reporting is widely recognized as one such area, as exemplified by a recent study in an appellate court in Texas that pinpointed preparation of the record as the primary cause of delay in criminal appeals.[10] Stimulated by research in the federal courts, attempts to provide faster, accurate service in the state court systems have included experimentation and increased use of electronic sound recording, computer-aided transcription and videotape. Results of a 1983 survey of court reporting services conducted by the National Center for State Courts for the Conference of State Court Administrators confirms this trend. That study, as well as a second survey by the American Bar Association Appellate Judges' Conference, indicates that courts in at least 15 states and the District of Columbia use computer-aided transcription to some extent.[11] There is no doubt that the trend toward application of technological devices that eliminate the traditional manual court reporting method will continue throughout the 1980s.

Pressure for technological change has not entirely been the result of internal forces. Experimental television coverage in state courts has occurred in response to desires by the public and the media for increased involvement in judicial proceedings. The favorable experience of state courts that permit television coverage, accompanied by the adoption of guidelines that govern such coverage, appears to have put to rest the concerns about jury bias, unfairness and exploitation in favor of the educational benefits and promotion of public understanding of the judicial system. In 1981, 34 states permitted experimental or permanent television coverage of courtroom proceedings. By 1983, the number of state courts had increased to 40 and three more were considering experimental programs.[12] Cameras in the courtroom represent a practice whose time has come. Courts have risen to the challenge, exercised guidance and control, and adapted successfully to the effects and pressures of technology in this area.

These and other technological advances will continue to significantly affect the administration of justice.[13] The solutions to many of the problems courts now face will depend upon careful planning and innovative uses of the technology available.

Attacking Court Delay

Court caseloads have continued to rise, challenging the courts' capabilities to efficiently manage operations. The state courts have begun to study causes of delay in order to develop and implement programs designed to solve this problem. It is now generally accepted that there is no single cause of or remedy for delay in the disposition of court cases. Based on this understanding, the problem of delay is increasingly being addressed through development of comprehensive case management programs that encompass all actors involved in the judicial process.

Case management systems usually include changes in procedural rules that encourage or require pretrial settlement conferences and attempt to limit continuances, discovery and interrogatories. Rule changes are then enforced through strict scheduling, setting of firm trial dates, and occasionally the imposition of sanctions. Active monitoring of caseflow by trial judges or presiding judges in conjunction with such delay reduction methods is beginning to increase disposition rates and decrease processing time without necessarily increasing the number of judges or sacrificing the quality of justice or dignity of the judicial system. The adoption of time standards for case processing by the Conference of State Court Administrators and several states represents an important new element in initiating and successfully implementing a delay reduction program.[14] The American Bar Association has also recognized the importance of time standards and is developing guidelines for use at the trial and appellate level. Additional delay reduction methods employed at the trial court level include calendaring changes, use of part-time, temporary or retired judges, increased use of alternate dispute resolution mechanisms and jury streamlining.

Delay reduction efforts at the appellate level have taken several forms as well. Thirty-seven states have created and others are considering creation of an intermediate appellate court.[15] Other states have expanded the jurisdiction of the intermediate appellate court to ease demand on the court of last resort. In addition, appellate courts have instituted prehearing settlement conference programs, fast-tracking programs, and screening mechanisms as well as made more frequent use of *per curiam* opinions and court orders to dispose of appeals.

Increased awareness of court delay on the part of judges and court administrators has resulted in the judicial commitment necessary to induce change. Jurists and court managers will increasingly assume direct responsibility for the flow of criminal and civil cases from filing to conclusion rather than allowing control by lawyers and litigants.[16] Further research and the commitment of other actors in the process will be essential to successful experimentation and institutionalization of delay reduction programs in the state courts.

Conclusion

Each of the changes and innovations highlighted represents the continuing trend toward professional development of court administration and improvements in the delivery of judicial services. State courts have responded capably to many changes in their environment and have explored a variety of avenues to upgrade the quality of justice. It is clear that the resourcefulness of court officials in the recent past will continue as we rise to meet the challenges of the future.

Notes

1. Alabama, Alaska, Colorado, Connecticut, Delaware, Hawaii, Indiana, Iowa, Kansas, Kentucky, Maine, Maryland, Massachusetts, Michigan, Missouri,

Nebraska, New Hampshire, New Mexico, New York, North Carolina, North Dakota, Oklahoma, Oregon, Rhode Island, South Dakota, Vermont, Virginia, West Virginia and Wyoming. Michigan is included in this list although fiscal difficulties may hinder implementation of the 1980-81 legislative mandate.

2. Arkansas, Georgia, Louisiana, New Jersey, Washington and Wisconsin. Lawson, "State Court System Unification," *American University Law Review* 31 (1982): 273-78. Gold, *State and Local Fiscal Relations in the Early 1980s* (Washington, D.C.: Urban Institute Press, 1983) might include Montana and Nevada in this group if inclusion were defined on the basis of a state's assumption of additional or greater fiscal responsibilities.

3. For example, Iowa, Kansas and New York. See also Tobin, "Managing the Shift to State Court Financing," *Justice System Journal* 7 (1982): 70-102.

4. See Dosal, "Current Status of State Financing of Trial Courts," Institute for Court Management/National Center for State Courts Workshop on State Court Financing, Denver, Colorado, May 4-7, 1980; Lawson, footnote 2; and Tobin, footnote 3, for a more thorough discussion of the advantages of state funding.

5. A recent discussion is presented by Douglas, "How the New Technology Can Help You," *Judges' Journal* 22 (1983): 4-7; 58.

6. Chief justices in at least the following states referred to consideration of, experimentation with, and installation or expansion of computer systems for a multitude of purposes: Alaska, Delaware, Hawaii, Idaho, Kansas, Maine, Massachusetts, Michigan, Nevada, New Mexico, Oklahoma, Pennsylvania, South Dakota, Texas and Utah.

7. Examples of states in each category include Iowa, North Dakota, Pennsylvania and Washington; Idaho, New Mexico, South Dakota and Utah; Maine and Nevada, respectively.

8. State of the Judiciary Address, presented by Chief Justice Daniel L. Herrmann on June 2, 1982 to the Joint Bar and Bench Conference at the University of Delaware.

9. "New Jersey Adopts Statewide Computer Plan," National Center for State Courts *Report* 10 (1983): 1.

10. "The State of the Judiciary Message," presented by Chief Justice Jack Pope, *Texas Bar Journal* (March 1983): 362-67.

11. The states that reported such use were Arizona, California, Florida, Georgia, Hawaii, Illinois, Louisiana, Maryland, Minnesota, Missouri, Montana, Nevada, North Carolina, Texas and Vermont. "Court Reporting Practices Among the State Court Systems," study conducted by the National Center for State Courts under the auspices of the Conference of State Court Administrators, Committee to Examine Court Reporting Services, 1983; Appellate Judges' Conference Court Technology Committee, "A Survey on How Courts are Using (and Resisting) the New Technology," *Judges' Journal* 22 (1983): 8-9; 57.

12. Rockwell, "Television Coverage in the State Courts," *State Court Journal* 7 (1983): 14-15. Only two states terminated experimentation without extension.

13. Examples of innovations not discussed include teleconferencing for pretrial motions and conferences, juror phone-in systems, and use of updatable microfiche in court records management.

14. National Time Standards for Case Processing were adopted by the Conference of State Court Administrators at the 29th Annual Meeting, Savannah, Georgia on July 27, 1983. Trial time standards have been implemented or are being considered in courts in California, Kansas and Nebraska.

15. By 1981, 32 states had created intermediate appellate courts. Five more have followed suit since that time.

16. See Sipes, "The Journey Toward Delay Reduction in Trial Courts: A Traveler's Report," *State Court Journal* 6 (1982): 5-7; 32-37.

Table 1
STATE COURTS OF LAST RESORT

State or other jurisdiction	Name of court	Justices chosen(a) At large	Justices chosen(a) By district	No. of judges(b)	Term (in years)(c)	Chief justice Method of selection	Chief justice Term of service as chief justice
Alabama	S.C.	★		9	6	Popular election	6 years
Alaska	S.C.	★		5	10	By court	3 years(d)
Arizona	S.C.	★		5	6	By court	5 years
Arkansas	S.C.	★		7	8	Popular election	8 years
California	S.C.	★		7	12	Appointed by governor(e)	12 years
Colorado	S.C.	★		7	10	By court	At pleasure of court
Connecticut	S.C.	★		7 (f)	8	Nominated by governor, appointed by General Assembly	8 years
Delaware	S.C.	★		5	12	Appointed by governor, with consent of Senate	12 years
Florida	S.C.		★	7	6	By court	6 years
Georgia	S.C.	★		7	6	By court	6 years
Hawaii	S.C.	★		5	10	Appointed by governor, with consent of Senate	10 years
Idaho	S.C.	★		5	6	Justice with shortest remaining term(g)	Remainder of term
Illinois	S.C.		★	7	10	By court	3 years
Indiana	S.C.	★		5	10	Selected by judicial nominating commission from S.C. members	5 years
Iowa	S.C.	★		9	8	By court	Remainder of term
Kansas	S.C.	★		7	6	By seniority of service(h)	Remainder of term
Kentucky	S.C.	★	★	7	8	By court	4 years
Louisiana	S.C.	★	★	7	10	By seniority of service	Remainder of term
Maine	S.J.C.	★		7	7	Appointed by governor, with consent of Senate	7 years
Maryland	C.A.		★	7	10	Designated by governor	Remainder of term
Massachusetts	S.J.C.	★		7	To age 70	Appointed by governor	To age 70
Michigan	S.C.	★		9	8	By court	2 years
Minnesota	S.C.	★		9	6	Popular election	6 years
Mississippi	S.C.		★	9	8	By seniority of service	Remainder of term
Missouri	S.C.	★		7	12	By court	Fixed by court
Montana	S.C.	★		7	8	Popular election	8 years
Nebraska	S.C.	★	★	7	6	Appointed by governor	6 years
Nevada	S.C.	★		5	6	By seniority of service(i)	Remainder of term
New Hampshire	S.C.	★		5	To age 70	Appointed by governor and council	To age 70
New Jersey	S.C.	★		7	7(j)	Appointed by governor, with consent of Senate	7 years(j)

	Court					Selection of chief justice	Term
New Mexico	S.C.	★		5	8	By court	2 years
New York	C.A.	★		7	14	Appointed by governor, with consent of Senate	14 years
North Carolina	S.C.	★		7	8	Popular election	8 years
North Dakota	S.C.	★		5	10	By Supreme and district court judges	5 years(k)
Ohio	S.C.	★		7	6	Popular election	6 years
Oklahoma	S.C.		★	9	6	By court	2 years
	C.C.A.		★	3	6		
Oregon	S.C.	★		7	6	By seniority of service	6 years
Pennsylvania	S.C.	★		7	10	By seniority of service	Remainder of term
Rhode Island	S.C.			5	Life	By legislature	Life
South Carolina	S.C.	★		5	10	Joint public vote of General Assembly	10 years
South Dakota	S.C.	★		5	8	By court	4 years
Tennessee	S.C.	★		5	8	By court	18 months
Texas	S.C.	★		9	6	Popular election	6 years
	C.C.A.	★		9	6	Popular election(l)	6 years(l)
Utah	S.C.	★		5	10	Justice with shortest term(g)	Remainder of term
Vermont	S.C.	★		5	6	Appointed by governor, with consent of Senate	6 years
Virginia	S.C.	★		7	12	By seniority of service	Remainder of term
Washington	S.C.	★		9	6	Justice with shortest term(g)	Remainder of term
West Virginia	S.C.A.	★		5	12	By court	Pleasure of court
Wisconsin	S.C.	★		7	10	By seniority of service(m)	Remainder of term
Wyoming	S.C.	★		5	8	By court	Pleasure of court
Dist. of Col.	C.A.	★		9	15	Designated by President(n)	4 years
American Samoa	H.C.	★		8 (o)	(p)	Appointed by Secretary of the Interior	(p)
Puerto Rico	S.C.	★		8	To age 70	Appointed by President with consent of U.S. Senate	To age 70

Sources: State constitutions, statutes and court administration offices.

Key:
S.C.—Supreme Court
S.C.A.—Supreme Court of Last Resort
S.J.C.—Supreme Judicial Court
C.A.—Court of Appeals
C.C.A.—Court of Criminal Appeals
H.C.—High Court

(a) See table on Selection and Retention of Judges for details.
(b) Number includes chief justice.
(c) The initial term may be shorter. See table on Selection and Retention of Judges for details.
(d) A justice may serve more than one term as chief justice, but may not serve consecutive terms in that position.
(e) Subsequently, must run on record for retention.
(f) Includes chief court administrator who is also an associate justice on the Supreme Court.
(g) Not holding office by selection to fill a vacancy.
(h) If two or more qualify, then senior in age.
(i) If two or more qualify, then determined by lot.
(j) May be reappointed to age 70.
(k) Or expiration of term, whichever is first.
(l) Presiding judge of Court of Criminal Appeals.
(m) If two or more qualify, then justice with least number of years remaining in term.
(n) From list of nominees submitted by Judicial Nominating Commission.
(o) Chief justice and associate judges sit on appellate and trial divisions.
(p) For good behavior.

Table 2
NUMBER OF JUDGES AND TERMS FOR
INTERMEDIATE APPELLATE COURTS
AND MAJOR TRIAL COURTS

State or other jurisdiction	Intermediate appellate court			Major trial court		
	Name of court	No. of judges	Term (years)	Name of court	No. of judges	Term (years)
Alabama	Court of Criminal Appeals	5	6	Circuit courts	113	6
	Court of Civil Appeals	3	6			
Alaska	Court of Appeals	3	6	Superior courts	26	6
Arizona	Court of Appeals	15	6	Superior courts	91	4
Arkansas	Court of Appeals	6	8	Chancery courts	30	4
				Circuit courts	31	6
California	Courts of Appeal	77	12	Superior courts	637(a)	6
Colorado	Court of Appeals	10	8	District Court	102	6
Connecticut	Appellate Court	5	8	Superior courts	136(b)	8
Delaware				Superior courts	11(c)	12
Florida	District Court of Appeals	46	6	Circuit courts	339	6
Georgia	Court of Appeals	9	6	Superior courts	123	4(d)
Hawaii	Intermediate Appellate Court	3	10	Circuit courts	24	10
Idaho	Court of Appeals	3	6	District courts	33	4
Illinois	Appellate Court	34	10	Circuit courts	383(e)	6
Indiana	Court of Appeals	12	10	Circuit courts	89	6
Iowa	Court of Appeals	5	6	District courts	99(f)	6
Kansas	Court of Appeals	7	4	District courts	212(g)	4
Kentucky	Courts of Appeals	14	8	Circuit courts	91	8
Louisiana	Court of Appeals	48	10	District courts	150	6
Maine				Superior Court	14	7
Maryland	Court of Special Appeals	13	10	Circuit courts	81	15
				Circuit court for Baltimore City	23	15
Massachusetts	Appeals Court	10	To age 70	Trial Court	278	To age 70
Michigan	Court of Appeals	18	6	Circuit courts	170	6
Minnesota	Court of Appeals	12	6	District courts	99	6
Mississippi				Chancery courts	38	4
				Circuit courts	36	4
Missouri	Court of Appeals	24	12	Circuit courts	133(h)	6
Montana				District courts	36	6
Nebraska				District courts	48	6
Nevada				District courts	35	6
New Hampshire				Superior Court	18(i)	To age 70
New Jersey	Appellate Division of Superior Court	23	7	Superior Court	329	7

State	Intermediate appellate court	No. of judges	Term (yrs.)	Major trial court	No. of judges	Term (yrs.)
New Mexico	Court of Appeals	7	8	District courts	49	6
New York	Appellate Division of Supreme Court	24	5	Supreme Court	314	14
North Carolina	Court of Appeals	12	8	Superior Court	60	8
North Dakota	. . .			District courts	26	6
Ohio	Court of Appeals	53	6	Courts of common pleas	210	6
Oklahoma	Court of Appeals	12	6	District Court	71(j)	4
Oregon	Court of Appeals	10	6	Circuit courts	84	6
	Tax Court	1				
Pennsylvania	Superior Court	15	10	Courts of common pleas	309	10
	Commonwealth Court	9	10			
Rhode Island	. . .			Superior Court	19	Life
South Carolina	. . .			Circuit Court	31	6
South Dakota	. . .			Circuit courts	36	8
Tennessee	Court of Appeals	12	8	Chancery courts	27	8
	Court of Criminal Appeals	9	8	Circuit courts	84(k)	8
Texas	Court of Civil Appeals	80	6	District courts	29	4
Utah	. . .			District courts	10	6
Vermont	. . .			Superior courts	14	6
Virginia	(l)	(l)	(l)	Circuit courts	120	8
Washington	Court of Appeals	16	6	Superior courts	128	4
West Virginia	. . .			Circuit courts	60	8
Wisconsin	Court of Appeals	12	6	Circuit courts	190	6
Wyoming	. . .			District courts	17	6
Dist. of Col.	. . .			Superior Court	44	15
American Samoa	. . .			High Court: trial level	8(m)	(n)
Guam	. . .			Superior Court	5	7
Puerto Rico	. . .			Superior Court	92	12

Sources: State statutes and court administration offices.

Key:

. . . —Court does not exist in jurisdiction.

(a) Legislature has authorized 594 judgeships; however, an additional 43 have been authorized if sufficient funds are available and counties choose to add new positions.

(b) Includes the judges of the Supreme and appellate courts.

(c) Six associate judges, president judge and four associate justices required by the constitution.

(d) For judges of the Superior Court of the Atlanta Judicial Court, term of office is eight years.

(e) Plus 310 associate judges.

(f) Plus 39 district associate judges and 11 senior judges.

(g) Plus 69 district associate judges and 72 district magistrates.

(h) Plus 177 associate circuit judges.

(i) For 1984. In 1985, 21 judges; 1986, 25 judges.

(j) Plus 77 associate judges and 54 special judges.

(k) With civil jurisdiction, 58 judges; with criminal jurisdiction, 26.

(l) Effective January 1985, Court of Appeals with nine judges serving eight-year terms.

(m) Chief justice and associate judges sit on appellate and trial divisions.

(n) For good behavior.

Table 3

COMPENSATION OF JUDGES OF APPELLATE COURTS
AND MAJOR TRIAL COURTS

State or other jurisdiction	Appellate courts				Major trial courts	Salary
	Court of last resort	Salary	Intermediate appellate court	Salary		
Alabama	Supreme Court	$58,000(a)	Court of Criminal Appeals	$57,000(b)	Circuit courts	$48,000(c)
			Court of Civil Appeals	57,000(b)		
Alaska	Supreme Court	81,648(d)	Court of Appeals	76,188	Superior courts	73,620(d)
Arizona	Supreme Court	67,500	Court of Appeals	65,500	Superior courts	62,500
Arkansas	Supreme Court	54,410(a)	Court of Appeals	52,557(b)	Chancery court	50,703
					Circuit courts	50,703
California	Supreme Court	77,226(a)	Courts of Appeal	72,401	Superior courts	63,267
Colorado	Supreme Court	55,600(a)	Court of Appeals	51,152(b)	District Court	47,260
Connecticut	Supreme Court	65,500(a,b)	Appellate Court	62,500	Superior courts	59,600
Delaware	Supreme Court	56,600(a)	---	---	Superior courts	53,200(b)
Florida	Supreme Court	67,588	District Court of Appeals	60,994	Circuit courts	58,247
Georgia	Supreme Court	57,680	Court of Appeals	57,054	Superior courts	48,276(c)
Hawaii	Supreme Court	53,460(a)	Intermediate Appellate Court	51,975(b)	Circuit courts	50,490
Idaho	Supreme Court	47,300	Court of Appeals	46,300	District courts	45,300
Illinois	Supreme Court	75,000	Appellate Court	70,000	Circuit courts	60,500(b)
Indiana	Supreme Court	47,244(e)	Court of Appeals	47,244(e)	Circuit courts	39,932(f)
					Superior courts	39,932(f)
Iowa	Supreme Court	57,100(a)	Court of Appeals	54,200(b)	District courts	50,700(b)
Kansas	Supreme Court	52,864(a)	Court of Appeals	50,639(b)	District courts	(g)
Kentucky	Supreme Court	57,264(a)	Court of Appeals	54,927(b)	Circuit courts	52,589
Louisiana.........	Supreme Court	66,566	Court of Appeals	63,367	District courts	60,169(h)
Maine............	Supreme Judicial Court	44,431(a)	---	---	Superior Court	43,736
Maryland.........	Court of Appeals	62,500(a)	Court of Special Appeals	60,000(b)	Circuit courts	58,000
Massachusetts......	Supreme Judicial Court	62,500(a)	Appeals Court	62,500	Trial Court	60,000(b)
Michigan	Supreme Court	74,000	Court of Appeals	71,040	Circuit courts	40,700(c)
					Recorder's Court (Detroit)	63,480
Minnesota	Supreme Court	65,000(a)	Court of Appeals	60,000(b)	District courts	55,000
Mississippi........	Supreme Court	58,000(a)	---	---	Chancery courts	51,000
					Circuit courts	51,000
Missouri..........	Supreme Court	52,080(a)	Court of Appeals	49,530	Circuit courts	34,230(i)
Montana	Supreme Court	48,923(a)	---	---	District courts	47,693
Nebraska	Supreme Court	55,930	---	---	District courts	51,735
Nevada...........	Supreme Court	61,500	---	---	District courts	56,000
New Hampshire	Supreme Court	51,789(a)	---	---	Superior Court	50,434(b)
New Jersey	Supreme Court	78,000(a)	Appellate division of Superior Court	75,000	Superior Court	70,000(j)
New Mexico	Supreme Court	55,000(a)	Court of Appeals	52,000(b)	District courts	49,300
New York	Court of Appeals	80,892(a)	Appellate divisions of Supreme Court	69,657(b)	Supreme Court	65,163
North Carolina	Supreme Court	59,868 (a,k)	Court of Appeals	56,676(b,k)	Superior Court	50,328(b,k)
North Dakota......	Supreme Court	53,900(a)	---	---	District courts	50,600(b)
Ohio.............	Supreme Court	68,000(a)	Court of Appeals	64,000	Courts of common pleas	55,500(l)
Oklahoma	Supreme Court	59,136(a)	Court of Appeals	55,440	District Court	(m)
	Court of Criminal Appeals	59,136(a)				
Oregon...........	Supreme Court	53,308(a)	Court of Appeals	52,039(b)	Circuit courts	48,356
			Tax Court	49,967		
Pennsylvania.......	Supreme Court	76,500(a)	Superior Court	74,500(b)	Courts of common pleas	65,000(b)
			Commonwealth Court	74,500(b)		
Rhode Island.......	Supreme Court	(a,n)	---	---	Superior Court	(b,n)
South Carolina	Supreme Court	63,128(a)	---	---	Circuit Court	63,128
South Dakota	Supreme Court	48,755(a)	---	---	Circuit courts	45,500(b)
Tennessee	Supreme Court	65,650(a)	Court of Appeals	63,125(b)	Chancery courts	60,600
			Court of Criminal Appeals	63,125(b)	Circuit courts	60,600
					Criminal courts	60,600
Texas	Supreme Court	74,300(a)	Court of Civil Appeals	66,870(b,c)	District courts	52,900(c)
	Court of Criminal Appeals	74,300(a)				
Utah	Supreme Court	50,000(a)	---	---	District courts	45,000
Vermont	Supreme Court	47,350(a)	---	---	Superior courts	45,050(b)
					District courts	45,050(b)
Virginia	Supreme Court	61,400(a)	---	---	Circuit courts	57,000
Washington	Supreme Court	51,500	Court of Appeals	48,100	Superior courts	44,700
West Virginia	Supreme Court of Appeals	49,000	---	---	Circuit courts	45,000
Wisconsin	Supreme Court	57,687(a)	Court of Appeals	52,918	Circuit courts	50,659
Wyoming..........	Supreme Court	63,500	---	---	District courts	61,000
Dist. of Col.	Court of Appeals	69,570(a)	---	---	Superior Court	65,790(b)
American Samoa ...	High Court	70,026(a)	---	---	(o)	(o)
Puerto Rico........	Supreme Court	36,000(a)			Superior Court	30,000
					District Court	24,000
Virgin Islands	---	---	---	---	Territorial Court	57,200(b)

Source: National Center for State Courts, Survey of Judicial Salaries.

Note: Compensation is shown according to most recent legislation, even though laws may not yet have taken effect.

(a) These jurisdictions pay additional amounts to chief justices or presiding judges of court of last resort:

Alabama, Texas, District of Columbia—$500.
Arkansas—$4,830.
California—$4,828.
Colorado—$3,336.
Connecticut—$6,500.
Delaware, Puerto Rico—$600.
Hawaii—$2,970.
Iowa, Minnesota—$5,000.
Kansas—$2,782.
Kentucky—$1,168.
Maine—$2,083.
Maryland, North Dakota, Utah—$1,500.
Massachusetts, Missouri, Pennsylvania—$2,500.
Mississippi—chief justice, $2,000; presiding judges, $1,000.
Montana—$1,228.
New Hampshire—$2,008.
New Jersey, South Dakota—$2,000.
New Mexico—$1,000.
New York—$3,371.
North Carolina—$1,260.
Ohio—$4,000.
Oklahoma—$2,640.
Oregon—$1,329.
Rhode Island—see note (n).
South Carolina—$8,123.
Tennessee—$2,525.
Vermont—$2,300.
Virginia—$2,600 (plus $4,000 in lieu of travel expenses).
Wisconsin—$7,525.
American Samoa—$2,980.

(b) Additional amounts paid to various judges:

Alabama—presiding judge, $500.
Arkansas—chief judge, $927.
Colorado—chief judge, $1,112.
Connecticut—state court administrator who is also an associate judge of Supreme Court, $3,100.
Delaware—presiding judge, $500.
Hawaii—chief judge, $1,485.
Illinois—chief judge, $5,000.
Iowa—chief judge of court of appeals, $1,200; chief judge of district court, $2,300.
Kansas—chief judge, $1,113.
Kentucky—chief judge, $584.

Maryland—chief judge of court of special appeals, $1,500.
Massachusetts—chief judge of superior court, $2,500.
Minnesota—chief judge, $2,500.
Missouri—chief judge, see note (i).
New Hampshire—chief judge of superior court, $1,355.
New Mexico—chief judge, $1,000.
New York—presiding judge of appellate division of Supreme Court, $4,494.
North Carolina—chief judge of court of appeals, $1,272; senior judge of superior court, $1,566.
North Dakota—presiding judge, $1,200.
Oregon—chief judge, $1,269.
Pennsylvania—presiding judges of superior court and commonwealth court, $1,500; president judges of court of common pleas, amount varies depending on number of judges and population.
Rhode Island—presiding judge of superior court, see note (n).
South Dakota—presiding circuit judge, $1,000.
Tennessee—presiding judge of intermediate appeals court, $1,010.
Texas—chief judge, $450.
Vermont—administrative judges of superior and district courts, $2,300.
District of Columbia—chief judge of superior court, $500.
Virgin Islands—presiding judge of territorial court, $2,750.

(c) Plus local supplements, if any. In Texas, for court of appeals, supplements to salary $1,000 less than salary for Supreme Court justice; for district court, salary to $1,000 less than salary of court of appeals judge.

(d) Salaries range from $81,648 to $93,084 for Supreme Court justices and $73,620 to $86,508 for superior court judges, depending on location and cost-of-living differentials.

(e) Plus $3,000 subsistence allowance.

(f) Salaries range from $39,932 to $42,182.

(g) Salary varies according to designation: district judge designated administrative judge, $49,526; district judge, $48,969; associate district judge, $46,743; district magistrate judge, $21,146; associate district judge designated as administrative judge, $47,300.

(h) Base figure.

(i) Salaries range from $34,230 to $40,350; chief judges' salary, $46,980.

(j) Assignment judges receive $73,000.

(k) Plus 4.8 percent after five years and 9.6 percent after 10 years.

(l) Salaries range from $55,500 to $60,500.

(m) District judges, $49,280. Associate district judges paid on basis of population ranges: over 30,000—$44,352; 10,000 to 30,000—$39,424; under 10,000—$36,960.

(n) Salary varies depending on longevity: associate judges of Supreme Court—$50,070 to $60,084; chief judge of Supreme Court—$51,379 to $61,654; associate judges of superior court—$47,451 to $56,941; presiding judge of superior court—$48,760 to $58,512.

(o) General trial court responsibilities handled by the chief justice or associate judges of the High Court.

Table 4
QUALIFICATIONS OF JUDGES OF STATE APPELLATE COURTS AND TRIAL COURTS OF GENERAL JURISDICTION

State or other jurisdiction	U.S. citizenship (years) A	T	Years of minimum residence — In state A	T	In district A	T	Minimum age A	T	Member of state bar (years) A	T	Other A	T
Alabama	5	5	(a)	(a)	...	1	25	25	★	★	...	...
Alaska	★	★	5(a)	5(a)	...	...	...	...	★(b)	★(b)	...	...
Arizona	...	...	10(c)	5	3(d,e)	...	30(d)	30	10(c)	5	(f,g)	(f,g)
Arkansas	★	★	2	2	...	...	30	28	(h,i)	(h,i)	(f)	(f)
California	...	...	...	...	...	...	...	...	10(i)	10(i)	...	...
Colorado	...	...	(e)	...	...	(e)	...	...	5	5	(g)	(g)
Connecticut	...	...	...	...	...	...	...	...	★	★	...	...
Delaware	...	...	(a)	(a)	...	...	...	...	(h)	(h)	...	...
Florida	...	...	(e)	(e)	★	★	...	...	10	5	(g)	(g)
Georgia	3	3	(a)	(a)	...	...	30	30	7	7	...	...
Hawaii	★	★	★(a)	★(a)	...	...	...	...	10	10	...	...
Idaho	★	★	2	2	...	(e)	30	30	★	(h)	...	...
Illinois	★	★	...	...	★	★	...	...	★	★	...	...
Indiana	★	★	...	...	★	★	...	...	10(i)	★	...	...
Iowa	...	...	...	...	...	...	...	...	★	★	...	...
Kansas	...	...	...	...	...	★	30	30	★(i)	★(i)	...	...
Kentucky	★	★	2	2	2	2	...	...	8	8	...	...
Louisiana	...	...	...	...	2	2	...	...	5	5	...	...
Maine	...	...	...	...	...	...	...	...	(h)	(h)	(f)	(f)
Maryland	...	...	5(a,e)	5(a,e)	6 mo.	6 mo.	30	30	★	★	(f)	(f)
Massachusetts	...	...	...	...	...	...	...	...	...	...	...	...
Michigan	...	...	(e)	...	(e)	(e)	...	...	★	★	(g,j)	(g,j)
Minnesota	...	...	...	...	...	...	...	...	(h)	(h)	...	...
Mississippi	...	...	(a)	(a)	...	...	30	26	5	5	...	...
Missouri	15	10	(e)	(e)	★	1	30	30	★	★	...	...
Montana	★	★	2	2	...	...	...	...	5	5	...	...
Nebraska	★	★	3	...	★(e)	★	30	30	5(i)	5(i)	...	...
Nevada	...	...	2(e)	2(e)	...	...	25	25	★	★	(k)	(k)
New Hampshire	...	...	...	...	...	...	...	...	...	...	(l)	(l)
New Jersey	...	...	...	...	...	...	...	...	10	10	...	...
New Mexico	...	...	3	3	...	★	30	30	3(h,i)	3(h,i)	...	...
New York	...	...	...	...	...	...	...	...	10	10	...	...
North Carolina	...	...	...	...	...	...	...	...	★	★	...	...
North Dakota	★	★	★	★	...	...	...	...	★(h)	★(h)	...	...
Ohio	...	...	...	...	...	★	...	...	6(i)	6(i)	(g)	(g)
Oklahoma	...	...	(e)	...	(e)	(e)	30	...	5(i)	4(i)	...	...
Oregon	★	★	3	★	(e)	★	...	...	★	★	...	...
Pennsylvania	★	★	1(a)	(a)	...	1	...	...	★	★	...	...
Rhode Island	...	...	...	...	...	...	...	...	...	...	...	...
South Carolina	★	★	5(a)	5(a)	...	★(e)	26	26	5	5	...	...
South Dakota	★	★	★	★	★(e)	★(e)	...	...	★	★	...	...
Tennessee	...	...	5(a)	5	...	1	35(m)	30	★	★	...	...
Texas	★	★	(a)	(a)	(d)	2	35	25	★(i)	★(i)	...	...
Utah	...	...	5	3	...	★	30	25	★(h)	★	...	...
Vermont	...	...	★	★	...	...	...	...	★(i)	★(i)	...	...
Virginia	...	...	★	★	...	...	...	...	5	5	...	...
Washington	...	...	...	...	1	1	...	...	★(n)	★	...	...
West Virginia	...	...	5	5	...	...	30	30	★(i)	★(i)	...	...
Wisconsin	...	...	(e)	...	...	(e)	...	...	5	5	...	...
Wyoming	★	★	3	2	...	...	30	28	1(h,i)	1(h)	...	...
Dist. of Col.	★	★	...	...	...	...	...	...	5(i)	5(i)	...	...
American Samoa	★	★	...	...	...	...	...	...	★	★	...	...
Guam	...	★	...	...	...	...	...	...	...	(h)	...	...
No. Marianas Is.	...	★	...	...	...	...	...	30	...	(h)	...	...
Puerto Rico	★	★	...	...	...	...	...	25	★(i)	★(i)	...	...

Note: The information in this table is based on a literal reading of the state constitutions and statutes. Requirements that an individual be a member of the state bar or a qualified elector may imply additional requirements.

Key:

A—Judges of courts of last resort and intermediate appellate courts.

T—Judges of trial courts of general jurisdiction.

★—Provision; length of time not specified.

. . .—No specific provision.

(a) Citizen of the state. In Alabama, Mississippi and Tennessee (court of criminal appeals), five years; in Georgia, three years.

(b) Must have been engaged in active practice of law for specific number of years. Alaska: appellate—eight years; trial—five years.

(c) For court of appeals, five years.

(d) For court of appeals judges only.

(e) Qualified elector. For Arizona court of appeals, must be elector of county of residence. For Michigan Supreme Court, elector in state; court of appeals, elector of appellate circuit. For Missouri Supreme and appellate courts, electors for nine years; for circuit courts, electors for three years. For Oklahoma Supreme Court and Court of Criminal Appeals, elector for one year; court of appeals and district courts, elector for six months. For Oregon court of appeals, qualified elector in county.

(f) Specific personal characteristics. Arizona, Arkansas—good moral character. Maine—sobriety of manners. Maryland—integrity, wisdom and sound legal knowledge.

(g) Nominee must be under certain age to be eligible. Arizona—under 65. Colorado—under 72, except when name is submitted for vacancy. Florida—under 70, except upon temporary assignment or to complete a term. Michigan, Ohio—under 70.

(h) Learned in law.

(i) Years as a practicing lawyer and/or service on bench of court of record in state may satisfy requirement. Arkansas—appellate: eight years; trial: six years. Indiana—10 years admitted to practice or must have served as a circuit, superior or criminal court judge in the state for at least five years. Kansas—appellate: 10 years; trial: five years (must have served as an associate district judge in state for two years). Texas—appellate: 10 years; trial: four years. Vermont—five of 10 years preceding appointment. West Virginia—appellate: 10 years; trial: five years. Puerto Rico—appellate: 10; trial: five.

(j) A person convicted of a felony or breach of public trust is not eligible to the office for a period of 20 years after conviction.

(k) May not have been previously removed from judicial office.

(l) Except that record of birth is required.

(m) Thirty years for judges of court of appeals and court of criminal appeals.

(n) For court of appeals, admitted to practice for five years.

Table 5
SELECTION AND RETENTION OF JUDGES

Alabama .... Appellate, circuit, district and probate judges elected on partisan ballots. Municipal court judges appointed by the governing body of the municipality (majority vote of its members).

Alaska .... Supreme Court, court of appeals, superior court and district court judges appointed by governor from nominations submitted by Judicial Council. Supreme Court, court of appeals and superior court judges approved or rejected at first general election held more than three years after appointment. Reconfirmation every 10 and six years, respectively. District court judges approved or rejected at first general election held more than one year after appointment. Reconfirmation every four years. District court magistrates appointed by and serve at pleasure of presiding judge of superior court in each judicial district.

Arizona .... Supreme Court justices and court of appeals judges appointed by governor from a list of not less than three for each vacancy submitted by a nine-member Commission on Appellate Court Appointments. Superior court judges (in counties with population of at least 150,000) appointed by governor from a list of not less than three for each vacancy submitted by a nine-member commission on trial court appointments. Judges initially hold office for term ending 60 days following next regular general election after expiration of two year term. Judges who file declaration of intention to be retained in office run at next regular general election on non-partisan ballot. Superior court judges in counties having population less than 150,000 elected on non-partisan ballot; justices of the peace elected on partisan ballot; police judges and magistrates selected as provided by charter or ordinance; Tucson city magistrates appointed by mayor and council from nominees submitted by non-partisan Merit Selection Commission on magistrate appointments.

Arkansas .... All elected on partisan ballot.

California .... Supreme Court and courts of appeal judges appointed by governor, confirmed by Commission on Judicial Appointments. Judges run unopposed on non-partisan ballot at next general election after appointment. Superior court judges elected on non-partisan ballot or selected by method described above; judges elected to full term at next general election on non-partisan ballot. Municipal court and justice court judges initially appointed by governor and county board of supervisors, respectively, retain office by election on non-partisan ballot.

Colorado .... Supreme Court and court of appeals judges appointed by governor from nominees submitted by Supreme Court Nominating Commission. Other judges appointed by governor from nominees submitted by Judicial District Nominating Commission. After initial appointive term of two years, judges run on record for retention. Municipal judges appointed by municipal governing body. Denver County judges appointed by mayor from list submitted by nominating commission; judges run on record for retention.

Connecticut .... Supreme and superior court judges appointed by legislature from nominations submitted by governor. Judicial Review Council makes recommendations on nominations for reappointment. Probate judges elected on partisan ballots.

Delaware .... All appointed by governor with consent of majority of senate.

Florida .... Supreme Court and district court of appeals judges appointed by governor from nominees submitted by appropriate judicial nominating commission. Judges run for retention at next general election preceding expiration of term. Circuit and county court judges elected on non-partisan ballots.

Georgia .... Supreme Court, court of appeals and superior court judges elected on non-partisan ballots. Probate judges and justices of peace elected on partisan ballots. Other county and city court judges appointed.

Hawaii .... Supreme Court and intermediate appellate court justices and circuit court judges nominated by Judicial Selection Commission (on list of at least six names) and appointed by governor with consent of senate. District court judges nominated by Commission (on list of at least six names) and appointed by chief justice.

Idaho .... Supreme Court and court of appeals justices and district court judges elected on non-partisan ballot. Magistrates appointed on non-partisan merit basis by District Magistrates Commission and run for retention in first general election next succeeding the 18-month period following initial appointment; thereafter, run every four years.

Illinois .... Supreme Court, appellate court and circuit court judges nominated at primary elections or by petition and elected at general or judicial elections on partisan ballot. Circuit court associate judges appointed by circuit judges for four-year terms.

Indiana .... Supreme Court justices and court of appeals judges appointed by governor from list of three nominees submitted by seven-member Judicial Nominating Commission. Judges serve until next general election after two years from appointment date; thereafter, run for retention on record. Circuit, superior and county judges in most counties run on partisan ballot. Marion County municipal judges appointed by governor from nominees submitted by county nominating commission.

Iowa .... Supreme Court, court of appeals and district court judges appointed by governor from lists submitted by nominating commissions. Judges serve initial one-year term and until January 1 following next general election, then run on records for retention. Full-time judicial magistrates appointed by district judges in judicial election district from nominations submitted by county judicial magistrate appointing commission. Part-time magistrates appointed by county judicial magistrate appointing commission.

Kansas .... Supreme Court and court of appeals judges appointed by governor from nominations submitted by Supreme Court Nominating Commission. Judges serve until second Monday in January following first general election after one year in office; thereafter run on record for retention every six (Supreme Court) and four (court of appeals) years. District judges in most judicial districts selected by non-partisan commission plan.

Kentucky .... All judges elected on non-partisan ballot.

Louisiana .... All justices and judges (except Orleans Parish District and Family Court judges) elected on non-partisan ballot.

Maine .... All appointed by governor with confirmation of the senate, except probate judges who are elected on partisan ballot.

Maryland .... Court of appeals and special appeals judges nominated by Judicial Nominating Commission, and appointed by governor with advice and consent of senate. Judges run on record for retention after one year of service. Judges of circuit courts and Supreme Bench of Baltimore City nominated by Commission and appointed by governor. Judges run in first general election after year of service (may be challenged by other candidates). District court judges nominated by Commission and appointed by governor, subject to senate confirmation.

Massachusetts ...... All nominated and appointed by governor with advice and consent of Governor's Council. Judicial Nominating Commission, established by executive order, submits names on non-partisan basis to governor.

Michigan .... All elected on non-partisan ballot, except remaining municipal judges who are selected in accordance with local procedures for selecting public officials.

Minnesota .... All elected on non-partisan ballot.

Mississippi .... All elected on partisan ballot, except municipal court judges who are appointed by governing authority of each municipality.

Missouri .... Judges of Supreme Court, court of appeals and several circuit courts appointed initially by governor from nominations submitted by judicial selection commissions. Judges run for retention after one year in office. All other judges elected on partisan ballot.

Montana	All elected on non-partisan ballot. Judges unopposed in reelection effort, run for retention.
Nebraska	All judges appointed initially by governor from nominees submitted by judicial nominating commissions. Judges run for retention on non-partisan ballot in general election following initial three year term; subsequent terms are six years.
Nevada...........	All elected on non-partisan ballot.
New Hampshire	All appointed by governor and confirmed by majority vote of five-member Executive Council.
New Jersey	All appointed by governor with advice and consent of senate, except judges of municipal courts serving a single municipality who are appointed by governing body.
New Mexico	All elected on partisan ballot.
New York	All elected on partisan ballot, except judges of court of appeals who are appointed by governor with advice and consent of senate. Governor also appoints judges of court of claims and designates members of appellate division of Supreme Court. Mayor of New York City appoints judges of criminal and family courts in the city.
North Carolina	All elected on partisan ballot, except special judges of superior court who are appointed by governor.
North Dakota	All elected on non-partisan ballot.
Ohio	All elected on non-partisan ballot, except court of claims judges who may be appointed by chief justice of Supreme Court from ranks of Supreme Court, court of appeals, court of common pleas or retired judges.
Oklahoma	Supreme Court justices and court of criminal appeals judges appointed by governor from lists of three submitted by Judicial Nominating Commission. Judges run for retention on non-partisan ballot at first general election following completion of one year's service. Judges of court of appeals, and district and associate district judges elected on non-partisan ballot. Special judges appointed by district judges within judicial administrative districts. Municipal judges appointed by governing body of municipality.
Oregon	All judges elected on non-partisan ballot for six-year terms, except municipal judges who are generally appointed and serve as prescribed by city council.
Pennsylvania.......	All initially elected on partisan ballot and thereafter on non-partisan retention ballot, except judges of traffic court and magistrates (Pittsburgh) who are appointed by mayor.
Rhode Island.......	Supreme Court justices elected by legislature. Superior, district and family court judges appointed by governor with advice and consent of senate. By executive order, governor selects appointees from names submitted by a judicial nominating commission. Probate and municipal court judges appointed by city or town councils.
South Carolina	Supreme Court, circuit court and family court judges elected by legislature from names submitted on a non-partisan basis by judiciary committee of legislature. Probate judges elected on partisan ballot. Magistrates appointed by governor with advice and consent of senate. Municipal judges appointed by mayor and alderman of city.
South Dakota	Supreme Court justices appointed by governor from nominees submitted by Judicial Qualifications Commission. Justices run for retention at first general election after three years in office. Circuit court judges elected on non-partisan ballot. Magistrates appointed by presiding judge of judicial court.
Tennessee	Judges of intermediate appellate courts appointed initially by governor from list of three nominees submitted by Appellate Court Nominating Commission. Judges run for election to full term at biennial general election held more than 30 days after occurrence of vacancy. Supreme Court judges and all other judges elected on partisan ballot, except some municipal judges who are appointed by governing body of city.
Texas	All elected on partisan ballot (method of selection for municipal judges determined by city charter or local ordinance).
Utah	Supreme Court, district court and circuit court judges elected on non-partisan ballot. Judges may be challenged in reelection effort. Juvenile court judges appointed by governor from list of at least two nominees submitted by Juvenile Court Commission. County justices of the peace elected on non-partisan ballot. Selection method for municipal justices of the peace locally determined.
Vermont	Supreme Court justices, superior court and district court judges nominated by Judicial Nominating Board and appointed by governor with advice and consent of senate. Judges retained in office unless legislature votes for removal.
Virginia	All full-time judges elected by majority vote of legislature.
Washington........	All elected on non-partisan ballot (method of selection for some municipal judges locally determined).
West Virginia	Supreme Court of appeals judges, circuit court judges and magistrates elected on partisan ballot.
Wisconsin	Supreme Court, court of appeals and circuit court judges elected on non-partisan ballot. Method of selection for municipal judges determined locally.
Wyoming..........	Supreme Court justices, district and county court judges appointed by governor from list of three nominees submitted by judicial nominating commission. Judges run for retention on non-partisan ballot at first general election occurring more than one year after appointment. Justices of the peace elected on non-partisan ballot. Municipal (police) judges appointed by mayor with consent of council.
Dist. of Col.	Court of appeals and superior court judges nominated by president of the United States from a list of persons recommended by District of Columbia Judicial Nominating Commission; appointed upon advice and consent of U.S. Senate.
American Samoa ...	Chief justice and associate justice(s) appointed by the U.S. Secretary of the Interior pursuant to presidential delegation of authority. Associate judges appointed by governor of American Samoa on recommendation of the chief justice, and subsequently confirmed by the senate of American Samoa.
Guam	All appointed by governor with consent of legislature from list of nominees submitted by Judicial Council; thereafter, run on record for retention every seven years.
No. Mariana Is.	All appointed by governor with advice and consent of senate.
Puerto Rico........	All appointed by governor with advice and consent of senate.
Virgin Islands	All appointed by governor with advice and consent of legislature.

Sources: Larry Berkson, Scott Beller and Michele Grimaldi, *Judicial Selection in the United States: A Compendium of Provisions* (Chicago: American Judicature Society) and update; Donna Vandenberg, "Judicial Merit Selection: Current Status," American Judicature Society; and state constitutions and statutes.

Table 6
METHODS FOR REMOVAL OF JUDGES AND FILLING OF VACANCIES

State or other jurisdiction	How removed	Vacancies: how filled
Alabama	Judicial Inquiry Commission investigates, receives or initiates complaints concerning any judge. Complaints are filed with the Court of the Judiciary which is empowered to remove, suspend, censure or otherwise discipline judges in the state.	By gubernatorial appointment. At next general election held after appointee has been in office one year, office is filled for a full term. In some counties, vacancies in circuit and district courts are filled by gubernatorial appointment on nominations made by judicial commission.
Alaska	Justices and judges subject to impeachment for malfeasance or misfeasance in performance of official duties. On recommendation of Judicial Qualifications Commission or on its own motion, Supreme Court may suspend judge without salary when judge pleads guilty or no contest or is found guilty of a crime punishable as felony under state or federal law or of any other crime involving moral turpitude under that law. If conviction is reversed, suspension terminates and judge is paid salary for period of suspension. If conviction becomes final, judge is removed from office by Supreme Court. On recommendation of Judicial Qualifications Commission, Supreme Court may censure or remove a judge for action (occurring not more than six years before commencement of current term) which constitutes willful misconduct in office, willful and persistent failure to perform duties, habitual intemperance or conduct prejudicial to the administration of justice that brings the judicial office into disrepute. The Court may also retire a judge for a disability that seriously interferes with the performance of duties and is (or is likely to become) permanent.	By gubernatorial appointment, from nominations submitted by Judicial Council.
Arizona	Judges subject to recall election. Electors, equal in number to 25% of votes cast in last election for judge, may petition for judge's recall. All Supreme Court, court of appeals and superior court judges (judges of courts of record) are subject to impeachment. On recommendation of Commission on Judicial Qualifications or on its own motion, Supreme Court may suspend without salary, a judge who pleads guilty or no contest or is found guilty of a crime punishable as felony or involving moral turpitude under state or federal law. If If conviction is reversed, suspension terminates and judge is paid salary for period of suspension. If conviction becomes final, judge is removed from office by Supreme Court. Upon recommendation of Commission on Judicial Qualifications, Supreme Court may remove a judge for willful misconduct in office, willful and persistent failure to perform duties, habitual intemperance or conduct prejudicial to the administration of justice that brings the office into disrepute. The Court may also retire a judge for a disability that seriously interferes with performance of duties and is (or is likely to become) permanent.	Vacancies on Supreme Court, court of appeals and superior courts (in counties with population over 150,000) are filled as in initial selection. Vacancies on superior courts in counties of less than 150,000 may be filled by gubernatorial appointment until next general election when judge is elected to fill remainder of unexpired term. Vacancies on justice courts are filled by appointment by county board of supervisors.
Arkansas	Supreme, appellate, circuit and chancery court judges are subject to removal by impeachment or by the governor upon the joint address of 2/3 of the members elected to each house of General Assembly.	By gubernatorial appointment. Appointee serves remainder of unexpired term if it expires at next general election.
California	All judges subject to impeachment for misconduct. All judges subject to recall election. On recommendation of the Commission on Judicial Performance or on its own motion, the Supreme Court may suspend a judge without salary when the judge pleads guilty or no contest or is found guilty of a crime punishable as a felony or any other crime that involves moral turpitude under that law. If conviction is reversed, suspension terminates and judge is paid salary for period of suspension. If conviction becomes final, judge is removed from office by Supreme Court. Upon recommendation of Commission on Judicial Performance, Supreme Court may remove judge for willful misconduct in office, persistent failure or inability to perform duties, habitual intemperance or conduct prejudicial to the administration of justice that brings the office into disrepute. The Court may also retire a judge for disability that seriously interferes with performance of duties and is (or is likely to become) permanent.	Vacancies on appellate courts are filled by gubernatorial appointment with approval of Commission on Judicial Appointments until next general election at which appointee has the right to become a candidate. Vacancies on superior courts are filled by gubernatorial appointment until next election. Vacancies on municipal courts are filled by gubernatorial appointment for remainder of unexpired term; on justice courts by appointment of county board of supervisors or by nonpartisan special election.
Colorado	Supreme, appeals and district court judges are subject to impeachment for high crimes and misdemeanors or malfeasance in office by 2/3 vote of senate. Supreme Court, on its own motion or upon petition, may remove a judge from office upon final conviction for a crime punishable as felony under state or federal law or of any other crime involving moral turpitude under that law. Upon recommendation of Commission of Judicial Discipline, Supreme Court may remove or discipline a judge for willful misconduct in office, willful or persistent failure to perform the duties of office, intemperance or violation of judicial conduct, or for disability that seriously interferes with performance and is (or is likely to become) permanent. Denver county judges are removed in accordance with charter and ordinance provisions.	By gubernatorial appointment (or mayoral appointment in case of Denver county court) from names submitted by appropriate judicial nominating commission.
Connecticut	Supreme and superior court judges are subject to removal by impeachment or by the governor on the address of 2/3 of each house of the General Assembly. On recommendation of Judicial Review Council or on its own motion, the Supreme Court may remove or suspend a judge of the Supreme or superior court after an investigation and hearing. If the investigation involves a Supreme Court justice, such judge is disqualified from participating in the proceedings. If a judge becomes permanently incapacitated and cannot adequately fulfill the duties of office, the judge may be retired for disability by the Judicial Review Council on its own motion or on application of the judge.	If General Assembly is in session, vacancies are filled by gubernatorial nomination and legislative appointment. Otherwise vacancies are filled temporarily by gubernatorial appointment.

State or other jurisdiction	How removed	Vacancies: how filled
Delaware	Judges are subject to impeachment for treason, bribery or any high crime or misdemeanor. The Court on the Judiciary may (after investigation and hearing) censure or remove a judge for willful misconduct in office, willful and persistent failure to perform the duties of office or an offense involving moral turpitude or other persistent misconduct in violation of judicial ethics. The Court may also retire a judge for permanent mental or physical disability interfering with the performance of duties.	Vacancies are filled as in initial selection.
Florida	Supreme Court, district courts of appeal and circuit court judges are subject to impeachment for misdemeanors in office. On recommendation of Judicial Qualifications Commission, Supreme Court may discipline or remove a judge for willful or persistent failure to perform duties or for conduct unbecoming to member of the judiciary, or retire a judge for a disability that seriously interferes with the performance of duties and is (or is likely to become) permanent.	By gubernatorial appointment, from nominees recommended by appropriate judicial nominating commission.
Georgia	Judges are subject to impeachment for cause. Upon recommendation of the Judicial Qualification Commission (after investigation of alleged misconduct), the Supreme Court may retire, remove or censure any judge.	By gubernatorial appointment (by executive order) on nonpartisan basis from names submitted by Judicial Nominating Commission.
Hawaii	Upon recommendation of the Commission on Judicial Discipline (after investigation and hearings), the Supreme Court may reprimand, discipline, suspend (with or without salary), retire or remove any judge as a result of misconduct or disability.	Vacancies on Supreme, intermediate appellate and circuit courts are filled by gubernatorial appointment (subject to consent of senate) from names submitted by Judicial Selection Committee. Vacancies on district courts are filled by appointment by chief justice from names submitted by Committee.
Idaho	Judges are subject to impeachment for cause. Upon recommendation by Judicial Council, Supreme Court (after investigation) may remove judges of Supreme Court, court of appeals and district court judges. District court judges (or judicial district sitting en banc), by majority vote in accordance with Supreme Court rules, may remove magistrates for cause. District Magistrate's Commission may remove magistrates without cause during first 18 months of service.	Vacancies on Supreme Court, court of appeals and district courts are filled by gubernatorial appointment from names submitted by Judicial Council for unexpired term. Vacancies in magistrates' division of district court are filled by District Magistrate's Commission for remainder of unexpired term.
Illinois	Judges are subject to impeachment for cause. The Judicial Inquiry Board receives (or initiates) and investigates complaints, and files complaints with the Courts Commission which may remove, suspend without pay, censure or reprimand a judge for willful misconduct in office, persistent failure to perform duties or other conduct prejudicial to the administration of justice or that brings the judicial office into disrepute. The Commission may also suspend (with or without pay) or retire a judge for mental or physical disability.	Vacancies on Supreme, appellate and circuit courts are filled by appointment by Supreme Court until general election. Associate judge vacancies on circuit courts are filled as in initial selection.
Indiana	Upon the recommendation of the Judicial Qualifications Commission or on its own motion, the Supreme Court may suspend or remove an appellate judge for pleading guilty or no contest to a felony or crime involving moral turpitude. The Supreme Court may also retire, censure or remove a judge for other matters. The Supreme Court may also discipline or suspend without pay a non-appellate judge.	Appellate vacancies are filled as in initial selection. Vacancies on circuit courts are filled by gubernatorial appointment until general election. Vacancies on most superior courts are filled by gubernatorial appointment.
Iowa	Supreme and district court judges are subject to impeachment for misdemeanor or malfeasance in office. Upon recommendation of Commission of Judicial Qualifications, the Supreme Court may retire a Supreme, district or associate district judge for permanent disability, or remove such judge for failure to perform duties, habitual intemperance, willful misconduct, conduct which brings the office into disrepute or substantial violations of the canons of judicial ethics. Judicial magistrates may be removed by a tribunal in the judicial election district of the magistrate's residence.	Vacancies are filled as in initial selection.
Kansas	All judges are subject to impeachment for treason, bribery or other high crimes and misdemeanors. Supreme Court justices are subject to retirement upon certification to the governor (after a hearing by the Supreme Court nominating commission) that such justice is so incapacitated as to be unable to perform adequately the duties of office. Upon recommendation of the Judicial Qualifications Commission, the Supreme Court may retire for incapacity, discipline, suspend or remove for cause any judge below the Supreme Court level.	Vacancies on Supreme Court and court of appeals are filled as in initial selection. Vacancies on district courts (in areas where commission plan has not been adopted) are filled by gubernatorial appointment until next general election, when vacancy is filled for remainder of unexpired term; in areas where commission plan has been adopted, vacancies are filled by gubernatorial appointment from names submitted by judicial nominating commission.

Table 6—Continued

State or other jurisdiction	How removed	Vacancies: how filled
Kentucky	Judges are subject to impeachment for misdemeanors in office. Retirement and Removal Commission, subject to rules of procedure established by Supreme Court, may retire for disability, suspend without pay or remove for good cause any judge. The Commission's actions are subject to review by Supreme Court.	By gubernatorial appointment (from names submitted by appropriate judicial nominating comission) or by chief justice if governor fails to act within 60 days. Appointees serve until next general election after their appointment at which time vacancy is filled.
Louisiana	Judges are subject to impeachment for commission or conviction of felony or malfeasance or gross misconduct. Upon investigation and recommendation by Judiciary Commission, Supreme Court may censure, suspend (with or without salary), remove from office or retire involuntarily a judge for misconduct relating to official duties, willful and persistent failure to perform duties, persistent and public conduct prejudicial to the administration of justice that brings the office into disrepute, or conduct while in office which would constitute a felony or conviction of felony. The Court may also retire a judge for disability which is (or is likely to become) permanent.	Vacancies are filled by Supreme Court appointment if remainder of unexpired term is six months or less; if longer than six months, vacancies are filled in special election.
Maine	Judges are subject to removal by impeachment or by governor upon the joint address of the legislature. Upon recommendation of the Committee on Judicial Responsibility and Disability, the Supreme Judicial Court may remove, retire or discipline any judge.	Vacancies are filled as in initial selection.
Maryland	Judges are subject to impeachment. Judges of Court of Appeals, court of special appeals, trial courts of general jurisdiction and district courts are subject to removal by governor on judge's conviction in court of law, impeachment, or physical or mental disability. Judges are also subject to removal upon joint address of the legislature. Upon recommendation of the Commission on Judicial Disabilities (after hearing), the Court of Appeals may remove or retire a judge for misconduct in office, persistent failure to perform duties, conduct prejudicial to the proper administration of justice, or disability that seriously interferes with the performance of duties and is (or is likely to become) permanent. Elected judges convicted of felony or misdemeanor relating to public duties and involving moral turpitude may be removed from office by operation of law when conviction becomes final.	Vacancies are filled as in initial selection.
Massachusetts	Judges are subject to impeachment. The governor, with the consent of the Executive Council, may remove judges upon joint address of the legislature, and may also (after a hearing and with consent of the Council) retire a judge because of advanced age or mental or physical disability. The Commission on Judicial Conduct, using rules of procedure approved by the Supreme Judicial Court, may investigate the action of any judge that may, by consequence of willful misconduct in office, willful or persistent failure to perform his duties, habitual intemperance or other conduct prejudicial to the administration of justice, bring the office into disrepute.	Vacancies are filled as in initial selection.
Michigan	Judges are subject to impeachment. With the concurrence of 2/3 of the members of the legislature, the governor may remove a judge for reasonable cause insufficient for impeachment. Upon recommendation of Judicial Tenure Commission, Supreme Court may censure, suspend (with or without salary), retire or remove a judge for conviction of a felony, a physical or mental disability, or a persistent failure to perform duties, misconduct in office, habitual intemperance or conduct clearly prejudicial to the administration of justice.	Vacancies in all courts of record are filled by gubernatorial appointment from nominees recommended by a bar committee. Appointee serves until next general election at which successor is selected for remainder of unexpired term. Vacancies on municipal courts are filled by appointment by city councils.
Minnesota	Supreme and district court judges are subject to impeachment. Upon recommendation of Board of Judicial Standards, Supreme Court may censure, suspend (with or without salary), retire or remove a judge for conviction of a felony, physical or mental disability, or persistent failure to perform duties, misconduct in office, habitual intemperance or conduct prejudicial to the administration of justice.	As a result of executive order, by gubernatorial appointment from names submitted by appropriate committee on judicial nominations. Appointee serves until general election occurring more than one year after appointment at which time a successor is elected to serve a full term.
Mississippi	Judges are subject to impeachment. For reasonable cause which is not sufficient for impeachment, the governor may, on joint address of legislature, remove judges of Supreme and inferior courts. Upon recommendation of Commission on Judicial Performance, Supreme Court may remove, suspend, fine, publicly censure or reprimand a judge for conviction of a felony (in a court outside the state), willful misconduct, willful and persistent failure to perform duties, habitual intemperance or conduct prejudicial to the administration of justice which brings the office into disrepute. The Commission may also retire any judge for physical or mental disability that seriously interferes with performance of duties and is (or is likely to become) permanent.	By gubernatorial appointment, from names submitted by a nominating commission. The office is filled for remainder of unexpired term at next state or congressional election held more than seven months after vacancy.
Missouri	Upon recommendation of Commission on Retirement, Removal and Discipline, Supreme Court may retire, remove or discipline any judge.	Vacancies on Supreme Court, court of appeals and circuit courts which have adopted commission plan are filled as in initial selection. Vacancies on other circuit courts and municipal courts are filled, respectively, by special election and mayoral appointment.

State or other jurisdiction	How removed	Vacancies: how filled
Montana	All judges are subject to impeachment. Upon recommendation of Judicial Standards Commission, Supreme Court may suspend a judge and remove same upon conviction of a felony or other crime involving moral turpitude. The Supreme Court may also order censure, suspension, removal or retirement for cause.	Vacancies on Supreme and district courts are filled by gubernatorial appointment (with confirmation by senate) from names submitted by judicial nominating commission. Vacancies on municipal and city courts are filled by appointment by city councils for remainder of unexpired term.
Nebraska	Judges are subject to impeachment. In case of impeachment of Supreme Court justice, judges of district court sit as court of impeachment with 2/3 concurrence required for conviction. In case of other judicial impeachments, Supreme Court sits as court of impeachment. Upon recommendation of the Commission on Judicial Qualifications, the Supreme Court may reprimand, discipline, censure, suspend or remove a judge for willful misconduct in office, willful failure to perform duties, habitual intemperance, conviction of crime involving moral turpitude, disbarment or conduct prejudicial to the administration of justice that brings the office into disrepute. The Supreme Court also may retire a judge for physical or mental disability that seriously interferes with performance of duties and is (or is likely to become) permanent.	Vacancies are filled as in initial selection.
Nevada	All judges, except justices of peace, are subject to impeachment. Judges are also subject to removal by legislative resolution and by recall election. The Commission on Judicial Discipline may censure, retire or remove a Supreme Court justice or district judge for willful misconduct, willful or persistent failure to perform duties or habitual intemperance, or retire a judge for advanced age which interferes with performance of duties or for mental or physical disability that is (or is likely to become) permanent.	Vacancies on Supreme or district courts are filled by gubernatorial appointment from among three nominees submitted by Commission on Judicial Selection. Vacancies on justice courts are filled by appointment by board of county commissioners or by special election.
New Hampshire ..	Judges are subject to impeachment. Governor, with consent of Executive Council, may remove judges upon address of both houses of legislature.	Vacancies are filled as in initial selection.
New Jersey	Supreme and superior court judges are subject to impeachment by the legislature. Except for Supreme Court justices, judges are subject to a statutory removal proceeding that is initiated by the filing of a complaint by the Supreme Court on its own motion or the governor or either house of the legislature acting by a majority of its total membership. Prior to institution of the formal proceedings, complaints are usually referred to the Supreme Court's Advisory Committee on Judicial Conduct, which conducts a preliminary investigation, makes findings of fact and either dismisses the charges or recommends that formal proceedings be instituted. The Supreme Court's determination is based on a plenary hearing procedure, although the Court is supplied with a record created by the Committee. The formal statutory removal hearing may be either before the Supreme Court sitting en banc or before three justices or judges (or combination thereof) specifically designated by chief justice. If Supreme Court certifies to governor that it appears a Supreme Court or superior court judge is so incapacitated as to substantially prevent the judge from performing the duties of office, the governor appoints a commission of three persons to inquire into the circumstances. On their recommendation, the governor may retire the justice or judge from office, on pension, as may be provided by law.	Vacancies on Supreme, superior, appellate division of superior, county, district, tax and municipal courts are filled as in initial selection.
New Mexico	Judges are subject to impeachment. The Judicial Standards Commission may discipline or remove a judge for willful misconduct in office, willful and persistent failure to perform duties or habitual intemperance, or retire a judge for disability that seriously interferes with performance of duties and is (or is likely to become) permanent.	Vacancies on Supreme and district courts are filled by gubernatorial appointment (may use nominating commission). Appointee serves until next general election when a successor is elected for remainder of unexpired term. Vacancies on court of appeals are filled by gubernatorial appointment (may use nominating commission), with appointee serving until Dec. 31 following general election or the remainder of the unexpired term, whichever is longer.
New York	All judges are subject to impeachment. Court of Appeals and supreme court judges may be removed by 2/3 concurrence of both houses of legislature. Court of claims, county court, surrogate's court, family court, civil and criminal court (NYC) and district court judges may be removed by 2/3 vote of the senate on recommendation of governor. Commission on Judicial Conduct may determine that a judge be admonished, censured or removed from office for cause, or retired for disability, subject to appeal to the court of appeals.	Vacancies on Court of Appeals and appellate division of supreme court are filled as in initial selection. Vacancies in elective judgeships (outside NYC) are filled at the next general election for full term; until election, governor makes appointment (with consent of senate if in session).
North Carolina ...	Upon recommendation of Judicial Standards Commission, Supreme Court may censure or remove a court of appeals or trial court judge for willful misconduct in office, willful and persistent failure to perform duties, habitual intemperance, conviction of a crime involving moral turpitude, conduct prejudicial to the administration of justice that brings the office into disrepute, or mental or physical incapacity that interferes with the performance of duties and it (or is likely to become) permanent. Upon recommendation of Judicial Standards Commission, a seven-member panel of the court of appeals may censure or remove (for the above reasons) any Supreme Court judge.	Vacancies on Supreme, appeals and superior courts are filled by gubernatorial appointment until next general election. Superior court judges are selected from names submitted by judicial nominating commission.

State or other jurisdiction	How removed	Vacancies: how filled
North Dakota	Supreme and district court judges are subject to impeachment for habitual intemperance, crimes, corrupt conduct, malfeasance or misdemeanor in office. Governor may remove county judges after hearing. All judges are subject to recall election. On recommendation of Commission on Judicial Qualifications or on its own motion, Supreme Court may suspend a judge without salary when judge pleads guilty or no contest or is found guilty of a crime punishable as a felony under state or federal law or any other crime involving moral turpitude under that law. If conviction is reversed, suspension terminates and judge is paid salary for period of suspension. If conviction becomes final, judge is removed by Supreme Court. Upon recommendation of Commission on Judicial Qualifications, Supreme Court may censure or remove a judge for willful misconduct, willful failure to perform duties, willful violation of the code of judicial conduct or habitual intemperance. The court may also retire a judge for disability that seriously interferes with the performance of duties and is (or is likely to become) permanent.	Vacancies on Supreme and district courts are filled by gubernatorial appointment from nominees submitted by Judicial Nominating Committee until next general election, unless governor calls for a special election to fill vacancy for remainder of term. Vacancies on county courts are filled by appointment by board of county commissioners from names submitted by nominating commission.
Ohio	Judges are subject to impeachment. Judges may be removed by concurrent resolution of 2/3 members of both houses of legislature or removed for cause upon filing of a petition signed by 15% of electors in preceding gubernatorial election. The Board of Commissioners on Grievances and Discipline of the Judiciary may disqualify a judge from office when judge has been indicted for a crime punishable as felony under state or federal law. Board may also remove or suspend a judge for willful and persistent failure to perform duties, habitual intemperance, conduct prejudicial to the administration of justice or which would bring the office into disrepute, or suspension from practice of law, or retire a judge for physical or mental disability that prevents discharge of duties. Judge may appeal action to Supreme Court.	Vacancies are filled by gubernatorial appointment until next general election when successor is elected to fill unexpired term. If unexpired term ends within one year following such election, appointment is made for unexpired term.
Oklahoma	Judges are subject to impeachment for willful neglect of duty, corruption in office, habitual intemperance, incompetency or any offense involving moral turpitude. Upon recommendation of Council on Judicial Complaints, chief justice of Supreme Court may bring charges against any judge in the Court on the Judiciary. Court on the Judiciary may order removal of judge for gross neglect of duty, corruption in office, habitual intemperance, an offense involving moral turpitude, gross partiality in office, oppression in office, or any other ground specified by law. Judge may also be retired (with or without salary) for mental or physical disability that prevents performance of duties or for incompetence to perform duties.	Vacancies on Supreme Court and court of criminal appeals are filled as in initial selection. Vacancies on court of appeals and district courts are filled by gubernatorial appointment from nominees submitted by Judicial Nominating Commission. For court of appeals vacancies, judge is elected to fill unexpired term at next general election.
Oregon	On recommendation of Commission on Judicial Fitness, Supreme Court may remove a judge for conviction of a felony or crime involving moral turpitude, willful misconduct in office, willful or persistent failure to perform judicial duties, habitual intemperance, illegal use of narcotic drugs, willful violation of rules of conduct prescribed by Supreme Court or general incompetence. A judge may also be retired for mental or physical disability after certification by Commission. Judge may appeal action to Supreme Court.	Vacancies on Supreme Court, court of appeals and circuit courts are filled by gubernatorial appointment, until next general election when judge is selected to fill unexpired term.
Pennsylvania	All judges are subject to impeachment for misdemeanor in office. Upon recommendation of Judicial Inquiry and Review Board, a judge may be suspended, removed or otherwise disciplined by Supreme Court for specific forms of misconduct, neglect of duty or disability.	By gubernatorial appointment (with advice and consent of senate), from names submitted by appropriate nominating commission. Appointee serves until next election if the election is more than 10 months after vacancy occurred.
Rhode Island	All judges are subject to impeachment. The Supreme Court on its own motion may suspend a judge who pleaded guilty or no contest or was found guilty of a crime punishable as felony under state or federal law or any other crime involving moral turpitude. Upon recommendation of the Commission on Judicial Tenure and Discipline, the Supreme Court may censure, suspend, reprimand or remove from office a judge guilty of a serious violation of the canons of judicial ethics or for willful or persistent failure to perform duties, a disabling addiction to alcohol, drugs or narcotics, or conduct that brings the office into disrepute. The Supreme Court may also retire a judge for physical or mental disability that seriously interferes with performance of duties and is (or is likely to become) permanent. Whenever the Commission recommends removal of a Supreme Court justice, the Supreme Court transmits the findings to the speaker of the house of representatives recommending the initiation of proceedings for the removal of the justice by resolution of the legislature.	Vacancies on Supreme Court are filled by the two houses of the legislature in grand committee until the next election. In case of a judge's temporary inability, governor may appoint a person to fill vacancy. Vacancies on superior, family and district courts are filled by gubernatorial appointment (with advice and consent of senate) from names submitted by nominating commission.
South Carolina ...	Judges are subject to removal by impeachment or by governor on address of 2/3 of each house of legislature. Supreme Court may retire judges for mental and/or physical disability. Judicial Standards Commission enforces code of judicial conduct.	Vacancies are filled as in initial selection for remainder of unexpired term; if remainder is less than one year, vacancy is filled by gubernatorial appointment. Vacancies on probate courts are filled by gubernatorial appointment until next general election.
South Dakota	Supreme Court justices and circuit court judges are subject to removal by impeachment. Upon recommendation of Judicial Qualifications Commission, Supreme Court may remove a judge from office.	Vacancies on Supreme and circuit courts are filled by gubernatorial appointment from names submitted by Judicial Qualifications Commission for balance of unexpired term.

State or other jurisdiction	How removed	Vacancies: how filled
Tennessee	Judges are subject to impeachment for misfeasance or malfeasance in office. Upon recommendation of the Court of the Judiciary, the legislature (by concurrent resolution) may remove a judge for willful misconduct in office or physical or mental disability.	Vacancies on Supreme, circuit, criminal and chancery courts are filled by gubernatorial appointment until next biennial election held more than 30 days after vacancy occurred. At election, successor is chosen as in initial selection. Vacancies on court of appeals and court of criminal appeals are filled as in initial selection.
Texas	Supreme Court, court of appeals and district court judges are subject to removal by impeachment or by joint address of both houses. Supreme Court may remove district judges from office. District judges may remove county judges and justices of the peace. Upon charges filed by the Commission on Judicial Conduct, the Supreme Court may remove a judge for misconduct or retire a judge for disability.	Vacancies on appellate and district courts are filled by gubernatorial appointment until next general election, at which time a successor is chosen. Vacancies on county courts are filled by appointment by county commissioner's court until next election when successor is chosen. Vacancies on municipal courts are filled by governing body of municipality for remainder of unexpired term.
Utah	All judges, except justices of the peace, are subject to impeachment. Upon recommendation of Commission on Judicial Qualifications, Supreme Court may remove a judge for willful misconduct in office, final conviction of a crime punishable as a felony, persistent failure to perform duties, habitual use of alcohol or drugs which interferes with the performance of duties or conduct prejudicial to the administration of justice which brings the judicial office into disrepute. The court may also retire a judge for disability that seriously interferes with the performance of duties and is (or is likely to become) permanent. Lay justices of the peace may be removed for willful failure to participate in judicial education program.	Vacancies on Supreme, district and circuit courts are filled by gubernatorial appointment from candidates submitted by appropriate nominating commission.
Vermont	All judges are subject to impeachment. Supreme Court may discipline, impose sanctions on, or suspend from duties any judge in the state.	Vacancies on Supreme, superior and district courts are filled as in initial selection if senate is in session. Otherwise, by gubernatorial appointment from nominees submitted by judicial nominating board.
Virginia	All judges are subject to impeachment. Upon certification of charges against judge by Judicial Inquiry and Review Commission, Supreme Court may remove a judge.	Vacancies are filled as in initial selection if General Assembly is in session. Otherwise, by gubernatorial appointment, with appointee serving until 30 days after commencement of next legislative session.
Washington	A judge of any court of record is subject to impeachment. After notice, hearing and recommendation of Judicial Qualifications Commission, Supreme Court may censure, suspend or remove a judge for violating a rule of judicial conduct. The Supreme Court may also retire a judge for disability that seriously interferes with the performance of duties and is (or is likely to become) permanent.	Vacancies on appellate and general trial courts are filled by gubernatorial appointment until next general election when successor is elected to fill remainder of term.
West Virginia	Judges are subject to impeachment for maladministration, corruption, incompetency, gross immorality, neglect of duty or any crime or misdemeanor. The Supreme Court of Appeals may censure or suspend a judge for any violation of the judicial code of ethics or retire a judge who is incapable of performing duties because of advancing age, disease or physical or mental infirmity.	Vacancies on appellate and general trial courts are filled by gubernatorial appointment (from names submitted by nominating commission). If unexpired term is less than two years (or such additional period not exceeding three years), appointee serves for remainder of term. If unexpired term is more than three years, appointee serves until next general election, at which time successor is chosen to fill remainder of term.
Wisconsin	All judges are subject to impeachment. Supreme Court, court of appeals and circuit court judges are subject to removal by address of both houses of legislature with 2/3 of members concurring and by recall election. As judges of courts of record must be licensed to practice law in state, removal of judge may also be by disbarment. Upon petition of Judicial Commission or on its own motion, Supreme Court may declare a judgeship vacant for judge's misconduct or disability. In case of disability, judge receives salary and benefits for balance of term or until temporary vacancy terminates, whichever comes first.	Vacancies on Supreme Court, court of appeals and circuit courts are filled by gubernatorial appointment from nominees submitted by nominating commission.
Wyoming	All judges, except justices of peace, are subject to impeachment. Upon recommendation of Judicial Supervisory Commission, the Supreme Court may retire or remove a judge. After a hearing before a panel of three district judges, the Supreme Court may remove justices of the peace.	Vacancies are filled as in initial selection. Vacancies on justice of the peace courts are filled by appointment by county commissioners until next general election.

Table 6—Continued

State or other jurisdiction	How removed	Vacancies: how filled
Dist. of Col.	Commission on Judicial Disabilities and Tenure may remove a judge upon conviction of a felony (including a federal crime), for willful misconduct in office, willful and persistent failure to perform judicial duties or for other conduct prejudicial to the administration of justice which brings the office into disrepute.	Vacancies are filled as in initial selection, unless president of the United States fails to nominate candidate within 60 days of receipt of list of nominees from D.C. Judicial Nominating Commission; then Commission nominates and appoints, wth advice and consent of U.S. Senate.
American Samoa .	U.S. Secretary of the Interior may remove chief and associate justices for cause. Upon recommendation of governor, chief justice may remove associate judges for cause.	Vacancies are filled as in initial selection.
Guam	On recommendation of Judicial Qualification Commission, a special court of three judges may remove a judge for misconduct or incapacity.	By gubernatorial appointment.
No. Mariana Is. ..	Judges are subject to impeachment for treason, commission of a felony, corruption or neglect of duty. Upon recommendation of an advisory commission on the judiciary, the governor may remove, suspend or otherwise sanction a judge for illegal or improper conduct.	By gubernatorial appointment.
Puerto Rico	Supreme Court justices are subject to impeachment for treason, bribery, other felonies and misdemeanors involving moral turpitude. Supreme Court may remove other judges for cause (as provided by judiciary act) after a hearing on charges brought by order of chief justice, who disqualifies self from final proceedings.	Vacancies are filled as in initial selection.

Source: American Judicature Society, 1984 (used with permission).

Table 7
SELECTED DATA ON COURT ADMINISTRATIVE OFFICES

State or other jurisdiction	Title	Estab-lished	Appointed by(a)	Salary
Alabama	Administrative Director of Courts(b)	1971	CJ	$51,610
Alaska	Administrative Director	1959	CJ (c)	79,648
Arizona	Court Administrator	1960	SC	53,500
Arkansas	Executive Secretary, Judicial Department	1965	CJ (d)	38,462
California	Administrative Director of the Courts	1960	JC	70,665
Colorado	State Court Administrator	1959	SC	51,152
Connecticut	Chief Court Administrator(e)	1965	CJ	61,500 (f)
Delaware	Director, Delaware Court System	1971	CJ	43,600
Florida	State Courts Administrator	1972	SC	48,514
Georgia	Director, Administrative Office of the Courts	1973	JC	46,725
Hawaii	Administrative Director of the Courts	1959	CJ (c)	50,490
Idaho	Administrative Director of the Courts	1967	SC	46,620
Illinois	Administrative Director of the Courts	1959	SC	61,500
Indiana	Executive Director, Division of State Court Administration	1975	SC	46,500
Iowa	Court Administrator	1971	SC	46,700
Kansas	Judicial Administrator	1965	CJ	48,969
Kentucky	Administrative Director of the Courts	1976	CJ	44,993
Louisiana	Judicial Administrator	1954	SC	60,169
Maine	Court Administrator	1975	CJ	43,186
Maryland	State Court Administrator(b)	1955	CJ	57,300
Massachusetts	Administrator, Supreme Judicial Court(b)	1978	SC	62,500
Michigan	State Court Administrator	1952	SC	65,814
Minnesota	Director, State Court Administration	1963	SC	48,000-54,000
Mississippi	Executive Assistant to the Supreme Court	1974	SC	51,000
Missouri	Court Administrator	1970	SC	40,000
Montana	State Court Administrator	1975	SC	31,954
Nebraska	State Court Administrator	1972	CJ	40,750
Nevada	Director, Office of Court Administration	1971	SC	35,650
New Hampshire	Director of Administrative Services	1980	SC	46,406
New Jersey	Administrative Director of the Courts	1948	CJ	60,000
New Mexico	Director, Administrative Office of the Courts	1959	SC	48,000
New York	Chief Administrator of the Courts(g)	1978	CJ (h)	76,151
North Carolina	Director, Administrative Office of the Courts	1965	CJ	53,496
North Dakota	Court Administrator(i)	1971	CJ	48,508
Ohio	Administrative Director of the Courts	1955	SC	61,936
Oklahoma	Administrative Director of the Courts	1967	SC	55,440
Oregon	Court Administrator	1971	CJ	52,788
Pennsylvania	Court Administrator	1968	SC	60,000
Rhode Island	Court Administrator	1969	CJ	46,359-56,317 (j)
South Carolina	Director of Court Administration	1973	CJ	48,661
South Dakota	State Court Administrator	1974	SC	44,498
Tennessee	Executive Secretary of the Supreme Court	1963	SC	63,125
Texas	Administrative Director of the Courts(k)	1977	SC	47,600
Utah	Court Administrator	1973	SC	45,000
Vermont	Court Administrator(l)	1967	SC	42,900
Virginia	Executive Secretary to the Supreme Court	1952	SC	57,000
Washington	Administrator for the Courts	1957	SC (m)	40,200
West Virginia	Administrative Director of the Supreme Court of Appeals	1975	SC	46,000
Wisconsin	Director of State Courts	1978	SC	52,918
Wyoming	Court Coordinator	1974	SC	36,440
Dist. of Col.	Executive Officer of D.C. Courts	1971	(n)	65,790
American Samoa	Court Administrator	1977	CJ	20,177
Puerto Rico	Administrative Director of Court Administration	1952	CJ	30,600

Source: Salary information derived from "Survey of Judicial Salaries," National Center for State Courts.

Key:
SC—State court of last resort.
CJ—Chief justice or chief judge of court of last resort.
JC—Judicial council.
(a) Term of office for all court administrators is at pleasure of appointing authority.
(b) In addition, there is a court administrator to administer state trial courts.
(c) With approval of Supreme Court.
(d) With approval of Judicial Council.

(e) Administrator is an associate judge of the Supreme Court.
(f) Salary conditioned on administrator being a judge of the Supreme or superior court.
(g) If incumbent is a judge, the title is Chief Administrative Judge of the Courts.
(h) With advice and consent of Administrative Board of the Courts.
(i) Serves as secretary to Judicial Council.
(j) Longevity payments at 7, 11, 15, 20 and 25 years of state service.
(k) Serves as executive director of Judicial Council.
(l) Also clerk of the Supreme Court.
(m) Appointed from list of five submitted by governor.
(n) Joint Committee on Judicial Administration.

Section V
LEGISLATION, ELECTIONS AND CONSTITUTIONS
1. Legislation

TRENDS IN STATE LEGISLATION: 1982-83

By Elaine Stuart Knapp

The recession, high unemployment and federal budget cuts combined to cause budget problems for most states in the biennium. In addition to dealing with revenue problems, state legislatures cracked down on drunk driving and paid increased attention to education and economic development.

Taxes, Finance

Many states bit the bullet—raising taxes, slashing spending, freezing hiring or laying off workers, and making other changes to avoid deficits. Many which had cut taxes in response to the heralded tax revolt of the late 1970s found themselves without a cushion for continued hard times. In contrast to the previous biennium when states raised excise taxes to boost revenues, during 1982-83 many were forced to raise broad-based taxes. Sales taxes were raised in 21 states and personal income taxes in 20 states. Motor fuel taxes were increased in 27 states, with most acting in 1983 to take advantage of federal funds available under a nickel hike in the federal gasoline tax. Other excise taxes were increased as well: cigarette taxes were raised in 21 states and liquor taxes in at least 13 states. Vehicle and truck fees also went up. Despite their best efforts, 17 states closed with deficits during fiscal 1982 or 1983.

Economy, Labor

High unemployment depleted many state jobless compensation funds, and 28 were forced to borrow from the federal government during the biennium. Worse, the federal government began charging 10 percent interest on the previously interest-free loans as of April 1, 1982. Total loans and interest stood at $13.64 billion at the end of 1983. More than 40 states amended their unemployment compensation laws over the biennium. Many tightened benefits and increased revenues to return jobless funds to solvency.

The high technology or computer revolution became the object of state economic development efforts. Many states created high technology authorities, councils or facilities. Other economic development legislation included authorization of venture capital programs to provide financing for new businesses, passage of enterprise zone acts in at least 14 states, creation of new authorities and commissions, provision of tax credits and other incentives for creating new jobs, and encouragement of exports and tourism. State changes in banking laws included authority for interstate banking in several Northeast states, approval of branch banking and multibank holding companies, international banking, revision of interest rate ceilings and changes in credit laws. Jobs programs were launched by at least six states. Even more states provided job training and other aid programs for the unemployed.

Education

A number of national commission reports on education resulted in the examination of public education by many states in 1983. Mississippi set the stage with passage of a sales tax hike for education in late 1982, with at least seven other states raising taxes for education during the biennium. Education law changes included: tougher graduation requirements, more emphasis on math and science, evaluation and testing of teachers, merit raises for teachers, and steps toward a career ladder for teachers. Laws allowing silent prayer or moments of silence in school were struck down by courts in Alabama, New Jersey and Tennessee. Efforts to equalize school financing were made by Vermont, West Virginia and Wyoming.

Elaine Stuart Knapp is Editor of *State Government News*, the Council's monthly magazine.

Law Enforcement

Largely in response to citizen action groups, and with the boost of federal incentives in late 1982, legislatures in nearly every state toughened drunk driving laws during the biennium. Major changes included making a blood alcohol concentration (BAC) of .10 percent the legal definition of intoxication, mandating jail time, providing for treatment or alcohol education, increasing fines and providing for license suspensions. Drinking ages were raised in 11 states. Also in highway safety, child restraint laws requiring toddlers to be strapped in special car seats passed in at least 34 states. Truck size and weight limits were increased to conform to federal law in most states. Connecticut lost a court battle to ban twin-trailer trucks.

Overcrowded prisons continued to plague states, with most states under court order or in litigation over conditions. Funds for prison facilities were increased in at least 13 states. At least 11 states now provide for emergency release of inmates when prisons become overcrowded. States also expanded parole and probation provisions, authorized community service as an alternative to jail, provided more halfway houses, and required restitution to victims. Laws requiring consideration of victims in sentencing or otherwise assuring victims' rights passed in 10 states. At least four states assured criminals would not profit from writing about their crimes. Insanity defenses were revised by a dozen states, in continued response to the acquittal of John Hinckley Jr. by reason of insanity for shooting President Reagan. Some states abolished the insanity defense and others adopted guilty but mentally ill verdicts. States continued to crack down on child pornography and drug abuse. Imitation or "look-alike" drugs were banned in 13 states. Capital punishment was adopted in Massachusetts and New Jersey, while lethal injections were authorized for executions in Arkansas and Montana. Pari-mutuel betting was approved in Iowa, Minnesota and Oklahoma. Washington and Colorado joined the states with lotteries.

Environment, Energy

Toxic substances and hazardous waste continued to be major state concerns. Superfunds or other financing for cleanup of toxic waste passed in at least eight states. States also dealt with problems of locating or regulating waste facilities and regulating transporting of waste. Workers must be told of toxic substances in nine states under new laws and so-called "community right-to-know" laws passed in Connecticut and New Jersey as well. More than 30 states moved to join low-level nuclear waste compacts providing for regional disposal sites. Water legislation included protection for groundwater in Arizona, Florida, Kansas and Wisconsin; South Dakota's major water sale; a state water plan in Texas; and new water projects in Colorado, Oklahoma, South Dakota and Wyoming. Most energy legislation was aimed at holding down utility rate hikes. Metal beverage tabs were banned in Colorado and Louisiana and bottle deposits required in New York. Farmers were given some protection from grain buyers' bankruptcy in seven states.

Government

Legislative redistricting or reapportionment to meet new Census figures was completed in most states. Increased legislative review of rules or budgets was authorized in more states, although such an attempt was struck down by the court in Kentucky. Comparable pay for women state workers with male counterparts was the object of legislation in Iowa, Minnesota, Montana and Washington. Washington lost a major court suit on the issue as well. Presidential primaries were repealed in Kentucky, Louisiana, Michigan and Nevada. Alaska became the 31st state to call for a constitutional amendment for a balanced federal budget.

Health, Social Legislation

States continued to try to hold down health costs, with at least eight passing cost control legislation. Pre-paid health care as an alternative to Medicaid passed in Arizona. States stepped up enforcement of child support, with at least 13 enacting new legislation. States continued to extend protection from abuse to children and the elderly. Health legislation emphasized community and home care for the mentally ill, the handicapped and the elderly. Child custody laws continued to be revised and at least three states authorized shared custody agreements.

Table 1

INITIATIVE PROVISIONS FOR STATE LEGISLATION

State or other jurisdiction	Type(a)	Basis for number of signatures required on petition(b)
Alaska	D	10% of votes cast in last general election and resident in at least 2/3 of election districts
Arizona	D	10% of qualified electors based on votes cast in last general election for governor
Arkansas	D	8% of legal voters based on votes cast in last general election for governor
California	D	5% of votes cast in last general election for governor
Colorado	D	5% of votes cast in last general election for secretary of state
Idaho	D	10% of votes cast in last general election for governor
Maine	I	10% of votes cast in last general election for governor
Massachusetts	I	3% of votes cast in last general election for governor
Michigan	I	8% of votes cast in last general election for governor
Missouri..............	D	5% of voters in each of 2/3 of congressional districts
Montana	D	5% of qualified electors in each of at least 1/3 of legislative representative districts; total must be at least 5% of the total qualified electors in state
Nebraska	D	7% of votes cast in last general election for governor; petition must include 5% of electors of each of 2/5 of counties in state
Nevada...............	I	10% of votes cast in last general election in at least 75% of counties in state
North Dakota	D	2% of state's resident population at last federal decennial census
Ohio	B	3% of electors
Oklahoma	D	8% of legal voters based on total vote cast in last general election for state office receiving largest number of votes
Oregon	D	6% of total votes cast in last election for governor
South Dakota	I	5% of qualified voters based on votes cast in last general election for governor
Utah	B	10% (direct) or 5% (indirect) of total votes cast in last general election for governor with same percentage required from a majority of counties in state
Washington	B	8% of votes cast in last general election for governor
Wyoming.............	D	15% of qualified voters based on votes cast in last general election and resident in at least 2/3 of counties in state
Dist. of Col.	D	5% of registered qualified voters; total must include 5% of registered voters in each of five or more of the wards in the district
Guam	D	20% of voters in last general election for governor
No. Marianas	D	20% of qualified voters

Note: This table refers only to those jurisdictions that allow proposed state laws to be placed on a state ballot by citizen petition and enacted or rejected by the electorate.

(a) The initiative may be direct or indirect. The direct type, designated D in this column, allows proposed measures to be placed on the ballot by securing a specific number of signatures on a petition—no legislative action is required. The indirect type, designated I, requires that the petition for a proposed measure first be submitted to the legislature allowing the legislators an opportunity to enact or alter the measure before it is placed on the ballot for consideration by the electorate. In some states, both types, designated B, are used.

(b) A majority of the popular vote is required to enact a measure in every jurisdiction except the Northern Mariana Islands where enactment requires approval by 2/3 of the votes cast. In Massachusetts and Nebraska, apart from satisfying the requisite majority vote, the measure must receive, respectively, 30 and 35 percent of the total votes cast in favor.

Table 2

PROVISIONS FOR REFERENDUM ON STATE LEGISLATION

State or other jurisdiction	Basis of referendum(a)	Basis for number of signatures on citizen petition(b)
Alaska	Citizen petition	10% of votes cast in last general election for governor and resident in at least 2/3 of election districts
Arizona	Citizen petition Submission by legislature	5% of qualified voters
Arkansas	Citizen petition	6% of legal voters based on votes cast in last general election for governor
California	Citizen petition Constitutional requirement(c)	5% of votes cast in last general election for governor
Colorado	Citizen petition Submission by legislature	5% of votes cast in last general election for secretary of state
Connecticut	Submission by legislature	
Florida	Constitutional requirement(c)	
Georgia	Constitutional requirement(c)	
Idaho	Citizen petition	10% of votes cast in last general election for governor
Illinois	Submission by legislature(c)	
Iowa	Constitutional requirement(c)	
Kansas	Constitutional requirement(c)	
Kentucky	Citizen petition(d) Submission by legislature(d) Constitutional requirement(d)	5% of legal voters based on votes cast in last general election for governor
Maine	Citizen petition Submission by legislature Constitutional requirement(c)	10% of votes cast in last general election for governor
Maryland	Citizen petition	3% of qualified voters based on votes cast in last general election for governor; not more than 1/2 can be residents of Baltimore or any one county
Massachusetts	Citizen petition	2% of votes cast in last general election for governor
Michigan	Citizen petition Submission by legislature Constitutional requirement(c)	5% of votes cast in last general election for governor
Missouri	Citizen petition Submission by legislature	5% of legal voters in each of 2/3 of congressional districts
Montana	Citizen petition Submission by legislature	5% of total qualified electors and 5% in at least 1/3 of legislative districts
Nebraska	Citizen petition	5% of votes cast in last general election for governor
Nevada	Citizen petition	10% of votes cast in last general election
New Jersey	Submission by legislature Constitutional requirement(c)	
New Mexico	Citizen petition Constitutional requirement(c)	10% of qualified electors of each of 3/4 of counties; total must be at least 10% of qualified electors in state
New York	Constitutional requirement(c)	
North Carolina	Constitutional requirement	
North Dakota	Citizen petition	2% of state's resident population from last federal decennial census
Ohio	Citizen petition Constitutional requirement(c)	6% of electors
Oklahoma	Citizen petition Submission by legislature Constitutional requirement(c)	5% of votes cast for state office receiving largest number of votes in last general election
Oregon	Citizen petition	4% of votes cast in last election for governor
Pennsylvania	Constitutional requirement(c)	

State or other jurisdiction	Basis of referendum(a)	Basis for number of signatures on citizen petition(b)
Rhode Island	Constitutional requirement(c)	
South Dakota	Citizen petition	5% of votes cast in last general election for governor
Utah	Citizen petition	10% of votes cast in last general election for governor and same percentage required from a majority of the counties
Virginia	Submission by legislature Constitutional requirement(c)	
Washington	Citizen petition	4% of voters registered and voting in last general election for governor
	Submission by legislature Constitutional requirement(c)	
Wisconsin	Submission by legislature Constitutional requirement(c)	
Wyoming	Citizen petition	15% of voters in last general election and resident in at least 2/3 of counties
Dist. of Col.	Citizen petition	5% of registered qualified voters; total must include 5% of registered voters in each of five or more wards in district
Guam	Citizen petition	20% of persons voting in last general election for governor
	Submission by legislature	
No. Marianas	Citizen petition	20% of qualified voters
Puerto Rico	Citizen petition	20% of persons voting in last general election for governor
	Submission by legislature	

Note: This table refers only to those jurisdictions which provide for a process whereby a state law passed by the legislature may be referred to the voters before it goes into effect.

(a) Three forms of referendum exist: (1) Citizen petition—the people may petition for a referendum, usually with the intention of rejecting an act passed by the legislature (in many states, the right to petition for referendum may not extend to specific types of legislation); (2) Submission by legislature—the legislature may voluntarily submit laws to the voters for their approval; (3) Constitutional requirement—the state constitution may require that certain questions, such as debt authorization, be submitted to the voters.

(b) A majority of the popular vote is required to enact a referendum measure in every jurisdiction. In Massachusetts, the measure must also receive at least 30 percent of the total ballots cast in the election.

(c) Applies to laws regarding state debt authorization: California, Illinois (debt may be incurred by law passed by legislature or by submission of question to voters), Iowa, Kansas, New Jersey, New Mexico, New York, North Carolina, Oklahoma, Pennsylvania, Rhode Island, Virginia, Washington, Wisconsin; state bond issuance: Florida, Maine; taxation: Georgia (exemptions from ad valorem taxes), Michigan (taxing and spending over prescribed limits); and authorization of banking powers for associations: Iowa, Ohio.

(d) Applies only to referendum on legislation classifying property and providing for taxation on the same. The referendum, required by the state constitution, may be ordered by citizen petition or submitted by the legislature.

Table 3

PROVISIONS FOR RECALL OF STATE OFFICIALS

State or other jurisdiction	Officers to whom applicable	Basis for number of signatures on petition(a)
Alaska	All elective officials except judicial officers	25% of voters in last general election in jurisdiction of official sought to be recalled
Arizona	All elective officials	25% of votes cast in last election for office of official sought to be recalled
California	All elective officials	Statewide officers: 12% of votes cast in last election for officer sought to be recalled; signatures must be obtained from at least five different counties equal in number to 1% of last vote for office in each of the five counties. State legislators, members of Board of Equalization and courts of appeals justices: 20% of last vote for office
Colorado	All elective officials	25% of votes cast in last election for office of official sought to be recalled
Georgia	All elective officials	Statewide officers: 15% of electors registered and qualified to vote at the last general election for office of official sought to be recalled. At least 1/15 of electors must reside in each of the U.S. congressional districts in state. Others: 30% of electors registered and qualified to vote in last general election for office of official sought to be recalled
Idaho	All elective officials except judicial officers	Statewide officers: 20% of number of electors registered to vote in last general election for governor. Others: 20% of electors registered to vote in last general election in jurisdiction of official sought to be recalled
Kansas	All elective officials except judicial officers	40% of votes cast at last general election for office of official sought to be recalled
Louisiana	All elective officials except judicial officers	25% of electors in jurisdiction of official sought to be recalled
Michigan	All elective officials except judges of courts of records and courts of like jurisdiction	25% of voters in last election for governor in district of official sought to be recalled
Montana	All public officials elected or appointed(b)	Statewide officers: 10% of registered voters at last general election. Others: 15% of number registered to vote in last election in jurisdiction of official sought to be recalled
Nevada	All elective officials	25% of voters in last election in jurisdiction of official sought to be recalled
North Dakota	All elective officials	25% of electors voting in last general election for governor in jurisdiction of official sought to be recalled
Oregon	All elective officials	25% of electors voting in last election for Supreme Court justice
Washington	All elective officials except judges of courts of record	25% or 35% of qualified voters depending on office
Wisconsin	All elective officials	25% of votes cast in last general election for governor in jurisdiction of official sought to be recalled
Dist. of Col.	All elective officials except D.C. delegate to U.S. Congress	At-large officers: 10% of registered electors in each of five or more of the city's wards. Others: 10% of registered electors in ward of official sought to be recalled
Guam	Governor	50% of votes cast in last gubernatorial election(c)
No. Marianas	All elective officials	40% of persons qualified to vote for official sought to be recalled
Virgin Islands	Governor	50% of votes cast in last gubernatorial election(c)

Note: This table refers only to those jurisdictions that allow the voters to remove state elective officials from office in a recall election.

(a) A majority of the popular vote is required to recall an official in every jurisdiction except the Northern Mariana Islands where recall requires approval by 2/3 of votes cast. In Guam and the Virgin Islands, apart from satisfying the requisite majority vote, the "yes" votes must total 2/3 of the votes cast in the last gubernatorial election.

(b) An elective official may be recalled by qualified voters entitled to vote for individual's successor. An appointed official may be recalled by qualified voters entitled to vote for the successor(s) of the elective officer(s) authorized to appoint an individual to the position.

(c) Referendum on governor (recall) may be initiated by petition described above or by 2/3 vote of members of legislature.

Table 4
MINIMUM AGE FOR SPECIFIED ACTIVITIES

State or other jurisdiction	Age of majority (a)	Minimum age for marriage with consent(b)		Minimum age for making a will	Minimum age for buying		Minimum age for serving on a jury	Minimum age for leaving school(c)
		male	female		liquor	beer or wine		
Alabama	19	14(d)	14(d)	19	19	19	19	16
Alaska	18	16(e)	16(e)	18	21	21	18	16
Arizona	18	16(e)	16(e)	18	19	19	18	16
Arkansas	18	17(e)	16(e)	18	21	21	18	15
California	18	(f)	(f)	18	21	21	18	18
Colorado	18	16(e)	16(e)	18	21	18(g)	18	16
Connecticut	18	16(e)	16(e)	18	20	20	18	16(h,i)
Delaware	18	18(e,j)	16(e,j)	18	21	21	18	16
Florida	18	16(e)	16(e)	18	19	19	18	16
Georgia	18	16(e,j)	16(e,j)	18	19	19	18	16
Hawaii	18	16	16(e)	18	18	18	18	18(i)
Idaho	18	16(e)	16(e)	18(k)	19	19	18	16
Illinois	18	16(e)	16(e)	18	21	21	18	16
Indiana	18	17(e)	17(e)	18	21	21	18	16(h,i)
Iowa	18	16	16	18	19	19	18	16
Kansas	18	(f)	(f)	18	21	18(g)	18	16
Kentucky	18	(f)	(f)	18	21	21	18	16
Louisiana	18	18(e)	16(e)	16(k)	18	18	18	17(l)
Maine	18	16(e)	16(e)	18	20	20	18	16
Maryland	18	16(e)	16(e)	18	21	21	18	16
Massachusetts	18	(f)	(f)	18	20	20	18	16
Michigan	18	16	16	18	21	21	18	16
Minnesota	18	16(m)	16(m)	18	19	19	18	16
Mississippi	18	17(e)	15(e)	18	21	18(g)	21	14(n)
Missouri	18	15(e)	15(e)	18	21	21	21	16
Montana	18	18(e)	18(e)	18	19	19	18	16(o)
Nebraska	19	17	17	18	20	20	19	16
Nevada	18	16(e)	16(e)	18	21	21	18	17
New Hampshire	18	14(m)	13(m)	18	20	20	18	16
New Jersey	18	16(p)	16(p)	18	21	21	18	16
New Mexico	18	16(e)	16(e)	18	21	21	18	18(q)
New York	(r)	16	14(m)	18	19	19	18	17(s)
North Carolina	18	16	16(e)	18	21	19	18	16
North Dakota	18	16	16	18	21	21	18	18
Ohio	18	18(e)	16(e)	18	21	19	18	18
Oklahoma	18	16(e)	16(e)	18	21	21	18	16
Oregon	18	17	17	18	21	21	18	16(t)
Pennsylvania	21	16(e)	16(e)	18	21	21	18	16(t)
Rhode Island	18	18(e)	16(e)	18	20	20	18	16
South Carolina	18	18(e)	14(e)	18	21	18	18	16
South Dakota	18	16(e)	16(e)	18	21	19(g)	18	16
Tennessee	18	16(e)	16(e)	18	19	19	18	16
Texas	18	14(m)	14(m)	18(k)	19	19	18	17
Utah	18	(f)	(f)	18	21	21	18	18
Vermont	18	16(e)	16(e)	18	18	18	18	18
Virginia	18	16(e)	16(e)	18	21	19	18	17
Washington	18	17(e)	17(e)	18	21	21	18	18(t)
West Virginia	18	(u)	(u)	18	19	19	18	16
Wisconsin	18	16	16	18	18	18	18	16(t)
Wyoming	19	16(e)	16(e)	19	19	19	19	16
Dist. of Col.	18	16	16	18	21	18	18	16(i)

(a) Generally, the age at which an individual has legal control over own actions and business (e.g. ability to contract) except as otherwise provided by statute. In many states, age of majority is arrived at upon marriage if minimum legal marrying age is lower than prescribed age of majority.

(b) With parental consent. Minimum age for marrying without consent is 18 years in all states, except Mississippi (21 years) and Wyoming (19 years).

(c) Without graduating.

(d) Bond is required if under 18.

(e) Legal procedure for younger persons to obtain license.

(f) Statute provides that any unmarried male or female under 18 may marry with consent (usually with order of court granting permission).

(g) In Colorado, Kansas, Mississippi and South Dakota, 3.2 beer only.

(h) Unless parent or guardian is able to show child is receiving equivalent instruction.

(i) Younger, if lawfully employed. Connecticut, Iowa, District of Columbia, 14 years; Hawaii, 15 years.

(j) Parental consent not required when female is pregnant or applicants are parents of a living child.

(k) Age may be lower for a minor who is living apart from parents or legal guardians and managing own financial affairs, or who has con-

tracted a lawful marriage.

(l) Does not apply to those who have reached age 15 or completed ninth grade, or who otherwise have permission to leave.

(m) Parental consent and judicial consent required.

(n) Mississippi's compulsory attendance statute is being implemented in a staggered fashion (began with 1982-83 school year) until every child who is six years old and has not reached the age of 14 years is covered by the mandatory attendance provision.

(o) Or completion of eighth grade, whichever is earlier.

(p) Parental consent required for ages 16 to 18; judicial approval for individuals under 16.

(q) Does not apply to those who have completed 10th grade and have consent of parents and school officials.

(r) As defined in general obligations (for purposes of contracting) and civil rights codes, 18 years.

(s) In cities having over 4,500 population and union-free school districts.

(t) With certain exceptions.

(u) Under 16, must have parental consent and approval of circuit judge.

Table 5
LEGALIZED GAMING IN THE STATES
As of June 1983

State or other jurisdiction	Lotteries	Sports betting	Off-track betting	Horse racing	Dog racing	Jai alai	Casinos	Bingo
Alabama	...	...	...	...	★	...	...	★
Alaska	...	...	...	...	...	...	...	★
Arizona	★	...	•	...	...	...	...	★
Arkansas	...	...	...	★	★	...	...	...
California	...	...	...	★	...	...	...	★
Colorado	★	...	★(a)	★	★	...	...	★
Connecticut	★	...	★	•	★	★	...	★
Delaware	★	•	...	★	...	...	...	★
Florida	...	...	★	★	★	★	...	★
Georgia	...	...	...	...	...	...	...	★
Hawaii	...	...	...	...	...	...	...	...
Idaho	...	...	...	★	...	...	...	...
Illinois	★	...	★	★	...	...	...	★
Indiana	...	...	...	...	...	...	...	...
Iowa	...	...	...	•	•	...	...	★
Kansas	...	...	...	...	...	...	...	★
Kentucky	...	...	★	★	...	...	...	★
Louisiana	...	...	•	★	...	...	...	★
Maine	★	...	...	★	...	...	...	★
Maryland	★	...	...	★	...	...	...	★
Massachusetts	★	...	★	★	★	...	...	★
Michigan	★	...	...	★	...	...	...	★
Minnesota	...	...	...	...	...	...	...	★
Mississippi	...	...	...	...	...	...	...	...
Missouri	...	...	...	...	...	...	...	★
Montana	...	★(a)	...	★	...	...	...	★
Nebraska	...	...	...	★	...	...	...	★
Nevada	★	★(c)	★(c)	★	★	★	★	★(b)
New Hampshire	★	...	...	★	★	...	...	★
New Jersey	★	...	...	★	...	...	★	★
New Mexico	...	...	...	★	...	...	...	★
New York	★	...	★	★	...	...	...	★
North Carolina	...	...	...	...	...	...	...	★
North Dakota	...	...	...	...	...	...	...	★
Ohio	★	...	...	★	...	...	...	★
Oklahoma	...	...	•	•	...	...	...	★
Oregon	...	...	...	★	★	...	...	★
Pennsylvania	★	...	★	★	...	...	...	★
Rhode Island	★	...	...	★	★	★	...	★
South Carolina	...	...	...	...	...	...	...	★
South Dakota	...	...	...	★	★	...	...	★
Tennessee	...	...	...	...	...	...	...	★
Texas	...	...	...	...	...	...	...	★
Utah	...	...	...	...	...	...	...	...
Vermont	★	...	...	★	★	...	...	★
Virginia	...	...	...	...	...	...	...	★
Washington	★	★(a)	★	★	...	...	...	★
West Virginia	...	...	★	★	★	...	...	★
Wisconsin	...	...	...	...	...	...	...	★
Wyoming	...	...	...	★	...	...	...	★
Dist. of Col.	★	...	...	...	...	...	...	★

Source: Public Gaming Research Institute, Rockville, Md.
Key:
★—Legalized and operative.
•—Legalized but not now operative.
. . .—Not legalized.

(a) Includes betting at a track on races at other tracks in the same state (cross-track wagering), on races at tracks in other states (interstate wagering), telephone betting, branch office betting or satellite wagering and bookmaking on racing.
(b) Keno.
(c) Operated by bookmakers licensed by the state.

UNIFORM STATE LAWS

By John M. McCabe

In 1982 and 1983, the National Conference of Commissioners on Uniform State Laws (NCCUSL) completed 10 Uniform and Model Acts and two significant Amendments to the Uniform Probate Code:

1. Uniform Common Interest Ownership Act. This act deals with all common interest real estate forms, including condominiums, cooperatives and planned communities (planned unit developments). It provides for the creation, financing, management and termination of any common interest projects and places special emphasis on adequate management powers, regular transfer of control of the project from developer to unit owners, and self-government through the owners' association. Five basic protections are provided for buyers, including disclosure of all important facts concerning the project and warranties of sale.

2. Uniform Conflict of Laws—Limitations Act. This act treats statutes of limitations as substantive, rather than procedural. This means that a forum state, in choosing the law of another state through its choice-of-law rules, would also choose the applicable statute of limitations of that other state. There is one exception to the rule of this act: a state may choose its own statute of limitations if the borrowed statute is so unfair that it would deprive a litigant of a right to litigate. This act replaces and supersedes the Uniform Statute of Limitations on Foreign Claims Act.

3. Uniform Guardianship and Protective Proceedings Act. This act provides for the appointment and supervision of guardians and conservators for incapacitated adults and unemancipated minors. Guardians of the person and conservators of the estate are to be separate and distinct offices, and special care is taken to insure adequate due process to all persons subjected to a proceeding. This act requires courts to subject persons to the least restrictive alternative in qualifying guardians and conservators. Courts have substantial powers to order and validate transactions on behalf of the estate of a protected adult or minor.

4. Model Health-Care Consent Act. This act determines who may consent to the health care of any person. An adult and certain specially qualified minors have the power to consent to their own health care, or to delegate that power to another person in an appropriate, witnessed writing. For incapable adults and all other minors the act sets priority, by statute, for all those who have the power to consent.

5. Uniform Law on Notarial Acts. This law provides for notarization or signature verification for all forms of acknowledgment, oath taking, witnessing, and certifying, as required in the law of any state. It supersedes the Uniform Acknowledgment Act and the Uniform Recognition of Acknowledgments Act.

6. Uniform Marital Property Act. This act creates a new category of property known as marital property, composed of all property of spouses, with certain exceptions that remain as individual property. Each spouse has a present undivided one-half interest in the marital property. Although marital property exists, notwithstanding the title record, management and control generally follow title. The act provides, also, for creditors' rights, enforcement between marital partners, deferred employment benefits and life insurance ownership.

7. Uniform Premarital Agreements Act. This act authorizes prospective marital partners to enter into agreements concerning the marital relationship before the marriage takes place. Rights and obligations with respect to property, including the disposition of property at separation, divorce or death, may be settled in such agreements. Agreements must be entered voluntarily. Disclosure of information concerning property is required, unless waived.

8. Uniform Succession Without Administration Act. This act permits estates to be distributed without administration by a court of probate to heirs in intestate estates, and residuary devisees in testate estates, provided that all heirs or residuary devisees join in application for succession without administration. These "universal successors" agree to assume all liabilities of the decedent to the extent each shares the estate. They are also liable to any unfound or excluded

John M. McCabe is Legislative Director of the National Conference of Commissioners on Uniform State Laws.

distributees for their shares, as well. Universal succession is an alternative to administration of an estate.

9. Uniform Transboundary Pollution Reciprocal Access Act. This act allows out-of-state litigants injured by pollution originating in an enacting state or Canadian province the access to the courts of that state or province to sue for damages. It extends the privilege to litigants from those states and provinces that provide the same access, in a reciprocal fashion, to their courts. The act is meant for enactment in both Canada and the U.S. (and might possibly be used between states of the U.S. and of Mexico, as well), and was a joint project between the NCCUSLs of Canada and the U.S.

10. Uniform Transfers to Minors Act. This act supersedes the earlier Uniform Gifts to Minors Acts promulgated in 1956 and amended in 1965 and 1966. It permits transfers of property to a minor in care of a designated custodian. The custodian remains in control of the property, holding it, investing it, and expending it for the minor's benefit, until the minor reaches the age of 21. Any kind of property can be transferred under this act, and transfers can be made as gifts or in satisfaction of certain obligations.

11. Amendments to the Uniform Probate Code. Both the Uniform Guardianship and Protective Proceedings Act and the Uniform Succession Without Administration Act are available as amendments to the Uniform Probate Code.

The NCCUSL continues work on a large number of drafting projects. More details on the work of the NCCUSL can be obtained from the NCCUSL, 645 North Michigan Avenue, Suite 510, Chicago, Illinois 60611.

Table 1
RECORD OF PASSAGE OF UNIFORM AND MODEL ACTS
As of September 1, 1983

State or other jurisdiction	Acknowledgment (1939) (1960)	Adoption (1953) (1971)	Alcoholism and Intoxication Treatment (1971)	Anatomical Gift (1968)	Arbitration (1956)	Attendance of Out of State Witnesses (1931) (1936)	Audio-Visual Deposition (1978)	Certification of Questions of Law (1967)	Child Custody Jurisdiction (1968)	Civil Liability for Support (1954)	Class Actions (1976)	Commercial Code (1951) (1957) (1962) (1966)	Commercial Code—Article 8 (1977)	Commercial Code—Article 9 (1972)	Common Interest Ownership (1982)	Common Trust Fund (1938) (1952)	Comparative Fault (1977) (1979)	Condominium (1977) (1980)	Conflict of Laws-Limitations (1982)
Alabama	---	---	---	★	---	●	---	---	★	---	---	●	---	★	---	★	---	---	---
Alaska	---	---	★	★	★	●	---	---	★	---	---	●	---	★	---	★	---	★	---
Arizona	●	---	---	★	★	●	---	---	★	---	---	●	---	★	---	★	---	★	---
Arkansas	●	●	---	★	★	★	---	---	★	---	---	●	---	★	---	★	---	★	---
California	---	---	---	☆	---	●	---	---	★	★	---	●	---	★	---	★	---	---	---
Colorado	---	---	★	★	★	●	---	★	★	---	---	●	★	★	---	★	---	★	---
Connecticut	●	---	☆	★	☆	●	---	---	★	---	---	●	★	★	★	---	---	---	---
Delaware	●	---	★	★	★	●	---	---	★	---	---	●	★	---	---	★	---	---	---
Florida	★	---	☆	★	☆	●	---	☆	---	---	---	●	---	★	---	★	---	●	---
Georgia	---	---	★	★	☆	●	---	---	★	---	---	●	---	★	---	★	---	---	---
Hawaii	★	---	---	★	---	●	---	---	★	---	---	●	---	★	---	★	---	★	---
Idaho	★	---	★	★	★	★	---	---	★	---	---	●	---	★	---	★	---	★	---
Illinois	★	---	★	★	★	●	---	---	★	---	---	●	---	★	---	★	---	★	---
Indiana	---	---	★	★	☆	★	---	---	★	---	---	●	---	★	---	★	---	●	---
Iowa	★	●	★	★	★	☆	---	★	★	★	---	●	---	★	---	★	---	●	---
Kansas	●	---	★	★	★	●	---	★	★	---	---	●	---	★	---	★	---	★	---
Kentucky	---	---	---	★	---	●	---	---	★	---	---	●	---	★	---	★	---	---	---
Louisiana	---	---	---	☆	★	●	---	---	---	---	---	---	---	★	---	★	---	★	---
Maine	---	---	★	★	★	●	---	☆	★	★	---	●	---	★	---	★	---	●	---
Maryland	●	---	☆	★	★	●	---	★	★	---	---	●	---	★	---	★	---	---	---
Massachusetts	●	---	☆	★	★	●	---	★	---	---	---	●	---	★	---	★	---	●	---
Michigan	★	---	☆	★	★	★	☆	---	★	---	---	●	---	★	---	★	---	●	---
Minnesota	★	---	☆	★	★	●	---	★	★	---	---	●	★	★	---	★	---	●	---
Mississippi	---	---	---	★	---	●	---	---	★	---	---	●	---	★	---	★	---	●	---
Missouri	---	---	---	★	★	●	---	---	★	---	---	●	---	★	---	★	---	●	---
Montana	★	★	---	★	---	●	---	---	★	---	---	●	★	★	---	★	---	●	---
Nebraska	★	---	---	★	---	●	---	---	★	---	---	●	★	★	---	★	---	●	---
Nevada	★	---	★	★	★	●	---	---	★	---	---	●	---	★	---	★	---	---	---
New Hampshire	●	---	---	★	---	●	---	★	★	★	---	●	---	★	---	★	---	---	---
New Jersey	---	---	---	★	---	●	---	---	★	---	---	●	---	★	---	★	---	---	---
New Mexico	★	☆	---	★	★	●	---	---	★	---	---	●	---	★	---	★	---	●	---
New York	---	---	---	★	★	●	---	---	★	---	---	●	★	★	---	---	---	---	---
North Carolina	---	---	---	★	★	●	---	---	★	---	---	●	---	★	---	★	---	---	---
North Dakota	★	●	---	★	---	★	★	★	★	★	---	●	---	★	---	★	---	●	---
Ohio	---	---	---	★	☆	●	---	---	★	---	---	●	---	★	---	★	---	●	---
Oklahoma	---	★	★	★	★	●	---	★	★	---	---	●	---	★	---	★	---	●	---
Oregon	---	---	---	★	★	●	---	★	★	---	---	●	---	★	---	★	---	---	---
Pennsylvania	●	---	---	★	★	●	---	---	★	---	---	●	---	★	---	---	---	★	---
Rhode Island	---	---	☆	★	★	★	---	★	★	---	---	●	---	★	---	---	---	●	---
South Carolina	---	---	---	★	★	●	---	---	★	---	---	●	---	---	---	---	---	---	---
South Dakota	★	---	★	★	★	●	---	---	★	---	---	●	---	★	---	★	---	---	---
Tennessee	●	---	---	★	---	●	---	---	★	---	---	●	---	★	---	★	---	---	---
Texas	---	---	★	★	★	●	---	---	★	★	---	●	★	★	---	★	---	★	---
Utah	★	---	---	★	☆	●	---	---	★	★	---	●	---	★	---	★	---	---	---
Vermont	---	---	---	★	---	●	---	---	★	---	---	●	---	---	---	---	---	---	---
Virginia	---	---	---	★	---	●	★	---	★	---	---	●	---	★	---	★	---	---	☆	---
Washington	★	---	★	★	★	●	---	☆	★	---	---	●	---	★	---	★	---	★	☆	★
West Virginia	---	---	---	★	---	●	---	★	★	---	---	●	★	★	---	★	---	★	★	---
Wisconsin	●	---	★	★	☆	●	---	★	★	---	---	●	---	★	---	★	---	●	---
Wyoming	●	---	---	★	★	★	---	---	★	---	---	●	---	★	---	★	---	---	---
Dist. of Col.	---	---	☆	★	★	---	---	---	★	---	---	●	---	---	---	★	---	---	---
Puerto Rico	---	---	---	---	---	★	---	---	---	---	---	---	---	---	---	---	---	---	---
Virgin Islands	●	---	---	---	---	●	---	---	---	---	---	●	---	---	---	---	---	---	---

Key:
★—Enacted
. . .—Not enacted
●—Amended version
☆—Substantially similar version

RECORD OF PASSAGE OF UNIFORM AND MODEL ACTS—Continued
As of September 1, 1983

State or other jurisdiction	Conservation Easement (1981)	Consumer Credit Code (1968) (1974)	Consumer Sales Practices (1970) (1971)	Controlled Substances (1970) (1973)	Crime Victims Reparations (1973)	Criminal Extradition (1926) (1936)	Deceptive Trade Practices (1964) (1966)	Declaratory Judgments (1922)	Determination of Death (1978) (1980)	Disclaimer of Property Interests (1978) (1978)	Disclaimer of Transfers by Will, Intestacy or Appt. (1973) (1978)	Disclaimer of Transfers under Non-testamentary Instruments (1973) (1978)	Disposition of Community Property Rights at Death (1971)	Disposition of Unclaimed Property (1954) (1966)	Division of Income for Tax Purposes (1957)	Durable Power of Attorney (1979)	Duties to Disabled Persons (1972)	Enforcement of Foreign Judgments (1948) (1964)	Evidence, Rules of (1974)
Alabama	---	---	---	★	---	★	---	★	☆	●	---	---	---	★	---	★	---	---	---
Alaska	---	---	---	★	---	●	---	---	---	---	---	---	---	★	★	★	---	★	---
Arizona	---	---	---	★	---	★	---	★	---	---	---	---	---	★	★	★	---	★	---
Arkansas	★	---	---	☆	---	★	---	★	---	●	---	---	★	●	★	★	---	●	★
California	---	---	---	☆	---	●	---	---	---	---	---	---	---	---	---	★	---	---	---
Colorado	---	★	---	★	---	●	●	★	---	●	---	---	---	★	★	★	★	●	---
Connecticut	---	---	---	★	---	●	---	★	---	---	---	---	---	☆	☆	★	●	---	---
Delaware	---	---	---	★	---	●	★	★	---	---	---	---	---	---	---	★	---	●	---
Florida	---	---	---	☆	---	●	---	★	---	---	---	---	---	---	---	---	---	---	★
Georgia	---	---	---	☆	---	●	●	★	---	---	---	---	---	☆	☆	---	---	☆	---
Hawaii	---	---	---	☆	---	●	---	---	★	---	---	---	★	---	★	★	---	●	---
Idaho	---	★	---	★	---	★	---	★	●	●	---	---	---	★	★	★	---	●	---
Illinois	---	---	---	☆	---	●	★	★	---	---	★	---	---	★	★	---	---	★	---
Indiana	---	★	---	★	---	★	---	★	☆	---	---	---	---	●	★	★	---	●	---
Iowa	---	★	---	★	---	●	---	★	---	---	---	---	---	●	---	★	---	---	---
Kansas	---	★	★	★	☆	●	---	---	---	---	---	---	---	★	★	★	---	●	---
Kentucky	---	---	---	☆	★	●	---	---	---	---	★	---	---	★	---	★	☆	---	---
Louisiana	---	---	---	★	---	●	---	---	---	---	---	---	---	---	---	---	---	---	---
Maine	---	★	---	---	---	●	★	★	●	---	★	★	---	---	---	★	---	●	★
Maryland	---	---	---	★	---	●	---	★	☆	★	---	---	---	★	---	---	---	---	★
Massachusetts	---	---	---	★	---	●	---	★	---	---	---	---	---	★	★	★	---	●	---
Michigan	---	---	---	★	---	●	---	★	---	---	---	---	---	★	★	★	---	●	★
Minnesota	---	---	---	☆	☆	●	●	●	---	---	---	---	---	---	☆	★	★	●	★
Mississippi	---	---	---	★	---	---	---	★	●	---	---	---	---	---	---	---	---	---	---
Missouri	---	---	---	★	---	●	---	★	---	---	---	---	---	★	---	---	---	★	---
Montana	---	---	---	☆	★	●	---	★	●	---	---	---	---	●	★	★	---	---	★
Nebraska	---	---	---	★	---	●	---	★	---	---	---	---	---	●	★	★	---	★	☆
Nevada	★	---	---	★	---	●	★	★	★	---	---	---	---	●	★	★	---	●	---
New Hampshire	---	---	---	---	---	●	---	★	---	---	---	---	---	★	☆	★	---	---	---
New Jersey	---	---	---	★	---	●	---	★	---	---	★	★	---	---	---	---	---	---	---
New Mexico	---	---	---	★	---	●	☆	★	---	---	---	---	---	●	★	★	---	---	---
New York	---	---	---	★	---	●	---	★	---	---	---	---	---	★	---	☆	---	●	---
North Carolina	---	---	---	☆	---	●	---	★	---	---	---	---	★	---	★	☆	---	---	---
North Dakota	---	---	---	★	★	●	---	★	---	---	★	---	---	★	★	★	★	●	★
Ohio	---	---	☆	---	---	●	●	★	☆	---	---	---	---	☆	☆	★	---	●	---
Oklahoma	---	★	☆	★	---	●	★	★	---	---	---	---	---	●	---	---	---	★	★
Oregon	★	---	---	★	---	●	---	★	---	★	★	★	★	●	★	☆	★	●	---
Pennsylvania	---	---	---	★	---	●	---	★	●	●	---	---	---	★	---	☆	☆	●	---
Rhode Island	---	---	---	☆	---	●	---	★	●	☆	---	---	---	●	---	---	---	---	---
South Carolina	---	☆	---	★	---	---	---	★	---	---	---	---	---	☆	---	---	---	---	---
South Dakota	---	---	---	★	---	●	---	★	---	---	---	---	---	●	★	---	---	---	---
Tennessee	---	---	---	★	☆	●	---	★	●	---	---	---	---	●	☆	★	---	●	---
Texas	---	---	---	★	☆	●	---	★	●	---	---	---	---	●	---	★	---	●	---
Utah	---	★	●	★	---	●	---	★	---	---	---	---	---	☆	★	☆	---	---	---
Vermont	---	---	---	---	★	●	---	★	●	---	---	---	---	---	---	★	---	---	---
Virginia	---	---	---	☆	★	●	---	★	---	---	---	---	★	★	☆	☆	---	---	---
Washington	---	---	---	★	---	●	---	★	---	---	---	---	★	★	★	★	---	★	★
West Virginia	---	---	---	★	---	●	---	★	☆	●	---	---	---	★	---	---	---	---	---
Wisconsin	★	☆	---	★	---	●	---	★	☆	---	---	---	---	●	☆	★	---	---	---
Wyoming	---	★	---	★	---	★	---	★	☆	---	---	---	---	---	---	---	---	---	---
Dist. of Col.	---	---	---	☆	---	---	---	☆	●	---	---	---	---	☆	---	---	---	---	---
Puerto Rico	---	---	---	★	---	●	---	★	---	---	---	---	---	---	---	---	---	---	---
Virgin Islands	---	---	---	★	---	●	---	★	---	---	---	---	---	---	---	---	---	---	---

State or other jurisdiction	Facsimile Signatures of Public Officials (1958)	Federal Lien Registration (1978)	Federal Tax Lien Registration (1926) (1966)	Fiduciaries (1922)	Foreign Money Judgments Recognition (1962)	Fraudulent Conveyance (1918)	Gifts to Minors (1956) (1966)	International Wills (1977)	Interstate Arbitration of Death Taxes (1943)	Interstate Compromise of Death Taxes (1943)	Jury Selection and Service (1970) (1971)	Juvenile Court (1968)	Limited Partnership (1916) (1976)	Management of Institutional Funds (1972)	Mandatory Disposition of Detainers (1958)	Marriage and Divorce (1970) (1973)	Notarial Acts (1982)	Parentage (1973)	Partnership (1914)
Alabama	---	---	---	★	---	---	•	---	---	---	---	---	•	---	---	---	---	---	☆
Alaska	---	---	★	---	★	---	•	---	---	---	---	---	•	---	---	---	---	---	★
Arizona	---	---	•	★	---	★	★	---	---	---	---	---	•	---	★	★	---	---	★
Arkansas	★	---	★	---	---	---	•	---	---	---	---	---	•	☆	---	---	---	---	★
California	★	★	•	---	★	★	•	---	★	★	---	---	•	☆	---	---	---	★	★
Colorado	★	---	•	★	•	---	•	---	★	★	★	---	•	★	★	★	★	★	★
Connecticut	---	---	•	•	---	---	•	---	★	★	---	---	•	★	---	---	---	★	★
Delaware	★	---	★	---	---	•	•	---	---	---	---	---	•	★	---	---	---	★	★
Florida	★	---	•	•	---	---	★	---	---	---	---	---	★	---	---	---	---	★	★
Georgia	---	---	•	---	★	---	---	---	---	---	---	☆	★	---	---	☆	---	---	---
Hawaii	---	---	☆	★	---	---	•	---	---	---	---	---	★	---	---	---	---	★	★
Idaho	★	★	•	★	•	---	•	---	★	---	★	---	★	★	---	★	---	---	★
Illinois	★	---	☆	★	★	---	•	---	---	☆	---	---	★	★	★	---	---	---	★
Indiana	---	---	★	★	---	---	•	---	---	☆	---	---	•	---	---	---	---	---	★
Iowa	---	---	•	---	---	---	•	---	---	---	---	---	•	---	---	---	---	---	★
Kansas	★	---	•	---	---	---	•	---	---	---	---	---	•	☆	★	---	---	---	★
Kentucky	---	---	★	---	---	---	•	---	---	---	---	---	★	★	---	★	---	---	★
Louisiana	---	---	★	★	---	---	★	---	---	---	---	---	---	★	---	---	---	---	---
Maine	---	---	•	---	---	---	•	---	★	★	★	---	★	★	---	---	---	---	★
Maryland	★	★	•	★	★	★	•	---	★	★	---	---	★	★	---	---	---	---	★
Massachusetts	---	---	★	---	★	★	•	---	★	★	---	---	★	★	☆	---	---	---	★
Michigan	---	---	•	•	★	★	•	---	★	★	★	---	•	★	---	---	---	★	★
Minnesota	★	★	•	★	---	★	•	★	☆	★	•	---	★	★	★	☆	---	★	★
Mississippi	---	---	---	---	---	---	★	---	---	---	☆	---	★	---	---	---	---	---	★
Missouri	★	---	★	★	---	---	•	---	---	---	---	---	★	★	★	---	---	---	★
Montana	★	•	•	---	---	★	•	---	---	---	---	---	★	---	---	•	---	★	★
Nebraska	---	---	•	•	---	★	•	★	★	★	---	---	•	---	---	---	---	★	☆
Nevada	★	★	•	★	---	★	•	---	---	---	---	---	★	★	---	---	---	★	★
New Hampshire	★	---	•	---	---	★	•	---	---	★	---	---	★	★	---	---	---	★	★
New Jersey	---	---	•	★	---	★	•	---	---	---	---	---	★	★	---	---	---	★	★
New Mexico	★	---	•	---	★	★	•	---	---	---	---	---	★	---	---	---	---	---	★
New York	---	---	★	☆	★	★	•	---	---	★	---	---	★	☆	---	---	---	---	★
North Carolina	---	---	•	•	---	---	---	---	---	---	---	---	★	•	---	---	---	---	★
North Dakota	---	★	•	---	---	★	•	---	---	---	★	★	★	★	★	---	---	---	★
Ohio	---	---	---	★	---	★	★	---	---	---	---	---	★	☆	---	---	---	☆	★
Oklahoma	★	---	•	---	★	★	•	---	---	---	---	---	★	---	---	---	---	---	★
Oregon	---	---	•	•	★	---	---	---	---	---	---	---	☆	★	---	---	★	---	★
Pennsylvania	★	---	★	★	---	---	•	---	★	★	---	---	★	★	---	---	---	★	★
Rhode Island	★	---	★	☆	---	---	★	---	---	---	---	---	★	★	★	★	---	★	★
South Carolina	---	---	★	---	---	---	•	---	---	---	---	---	★	---	★	---	---	---	★
South Dakota	---	---	•	★	---	★	•	---	---	---	---	---	★	---	---	---	---	---	★
Tennessee	---	---	★	★	---	★	•	---	☆	☆	---	---	★	★	---	---	---	---	★
Texas	★	---	---	---	---	---	•	---	---	---	---	---	★	---	---	---	---	---	★
Utah	---	---	★	★	---	★	•	---	---	---	---	---	★	---	★	---	---	---	★
Vermont	---	---	•	---	---	---	★	---	★	★	---	---	★	---	---	---	---	---	★
Virginia	---	---	•	---	---	---	★	---	★	★	---	---	★	★	---	---	---	---	★
Washington	★	---	---	---	★	★	•	---	★	★	---	---	•	★	---	☆	---	★	★
West Virginia	★	---	•	---	---	•	•	---	★	★	---	---	•	★	★	---	---	★	★
Wisconsin	---	★	★	★	---	★	•	---	★	---	---	---	•	---	---	---	---	---	★
Wyoming	★	---	★	★	---	★	•	---	---	---	---	---	•	---	---	---	---	★	★
Dist. of Col.	---	---	---	★	---	---	•	---	---	---	---	---	★	★	---	---	---	---	★
Puerto Rico	---	---	---	---	---	---	---	---	---	---	---	---	---	---	---	---	---	---	---
Virgin Islands	---	---	★	---	★	★	---	---	---	---	---	---	★	---	---	---	---	---	★

RECORD OF PASSAGE OF UNIFORM AND MODEL ACTS—Continued
As of September 1, 1983

State or other jurisdiction	Photographic Copies as Evidence (1949)	Post-Conviction Procedure (1955) (1966) (1980)	Principal and Income (1931) (1962)	Probate Court (1969) (1975) (1977) (1979)	Public Assembly (1972)	Reciprocal Enforcement of Support (1950) (1958) (1968)	Recognition of Acknowledgments (1968)	Rendition of Accused Persons (1967)	Residential Landlord-Tenant (1972)	Securities (1956) (1958)	Simplification of Fiduciary Security Transfers (1958)	Simultaneous Death (1940) (1953)	State Antitrust (1973) (1979)	Status of Convicted Persons (1964)	Supervision of Trustees for Charitable Purposes (1954)	Testamentary Additions to Trusts (1960)	Trade Secrets (1979)	Transboundary Pollution Reciprocal Access (1982)	Trustees' Powers (1964)	Unclaimed Property (1981)
Alabama	★	---	★	---	---	•	---	☆	---	•	★	★	---	---	---	☆	---	---	---	---
Alaska	★	---	---	★	---	•	☆	---	★	•	★	★	---	---	---	★	---	---	---	---
Arizona	---	---	★	★	---	•	★	---	★	---	★	---	★	---	★	---	---	---	---	★
Arkansas	★	---	•	---	---	•	---	---	---	•	---	•	---	---	---	★	★	---	---	---
California	★	---	•	---	---	•	---	---	---	---	★	★	---	---	★	☆	---	---	---	---
Colorado	★	---	★	•	---	•	★	★	---	•	★	★	---	---	---	☆	---	---	---	---
Connecticut	★	---	•	---	---	•	★	---	★	•	★	★	---	---	---	★	★	---	---	---
Delaware	---	---	•	---	---	•	---	---	---	•	★	★	---	---	---	★	★	---	---	---
Florida	★	---	•	---	---	•	---	---	★	---	★	★	---	---	---	☆	---	---	★	---
Georgia	★	---	---	---	---	•	---	---	---	•	---	★	•	---	---	★	---	---	---	---
Hawaii	★	---	•	---	---	•	---	★	★	•	★	★	---	★	---	★	---	---	---	---
Idaho	★	•	•	★	---	•	---	★	★	•	★	★	★	---	---	★	★	★	---	★
Illinois	---	---	★	•	---	•	★	★	---	---	★	★	★	---	---	☆	★	---	---	---
Indiana	---	---	•	---	---	•	---	---	☆	★	★	★	★	---	---	☆	★	---	---	---
Iowa	★	•	---	---	---	•	---	---	★	☆	★	★	★	---	---	★	---	---	---	---
Kansas	★	---	•	---	---	•	★	---	☆	---	★	★	---	---	---	★	★	---	★	---
Kentucky	★	---	★	---	---	•	★	---	★	☆	---	•	---	---	---	★	---	---	★	---
Louisiana	---	---	★	---	---	•	---	---	---	★	---	---	---	---	---	---	---	---	---	---
Maine	★	---	•	•	---	•	★	---	---	•	★	★	---	---	---	★	---	---	---	---
Maryland	★	★	•	---	---	•	---	---	---	•	★	★	---	---	---	☆	---	---	---	---
Massachusetts	★	---	•	---	---	•	---	---	---	---	★	•	---	---	---	---	---	---	---	---
Michigan	---	---	•	☆	---	•	★	★	★	•	★	★	---	---	★	★	★	---	---	---
Minnesota	★	•	•	★	---	•	★	---	---	•	★	★	---	---	---	★	★	---	☆	---
Mississippi	---	---	•	---	---	•	---	---	---	•	★	★	---	---	---	☆	---	---	★	---
Missouri	---	---	•	---	---	•	---	---	---	•	★	★	---	---	---	---	---	---	---	---
Montana	★	★	•	★	---	•	---	---	★	•	★	★	---	☆	---	☆	---	---	★	☆
Nebraska	★	---	•	★	---	•	★	★	★	☆	★	★	---	---	---	★	---	---	---	★
Nevada	---	•	•	---	---	•	---	---	★	•	★	★	---	---	---	★	---	---	---	★
New Hampshire	★	---	•	---	---	•	★	---	---	•	---	★	---	★	---	★	---	---	★	---
New Jersey	★	---	•	☆	---	•	---	---	---	•	★	★	---	---	---	☆	---	---	---	---
New Mexico	★	---	•	★	---	•	---	---	★	•	★	---	---	---	---	★	---	---	---	---
New York	★	---	•	---	---	•	---	---	---	•	★	★	---	---	---	☆	---	---	---	---
North Carolina	★	---	•	---	---	•	---	---	---	•	★	★	---	---	---	☆	---	---	---	---
North Dakota	★	•	•	•	---	•	★	★	---	•	★	•	---	---	---	★	★	★	---	---
Ohio	---	---	---	---	---	•	---	---	---	---	---	---	---	---	---	☆	---	---	---	---
Oklahoma	★	•	★	---	★	•	★	---	★	•	★	★	---	---	---	★	---	---	---	---
Oregon	---	★	•	---	---	•	★	★	★	---	•	---	•	---	★	☆	---	---	★	★
Pennsylvania	★	---	★	☆	---	•	---	---	---	☆	---	★	---	---	★	☆	---	---	---	---
Rhode Island	★	•	---	---	---	•	---	---	---	•	★	★	---	---	---	---	---	---	---	---
South Carolina	---	•	•	---	---	•	★	---	---	•	★	★	---	---	---	★	---	---	---	---
South Dakota	★	•	---	---	---	•	★	---	---	•	★	★	---	---	---	★	---	---	---	---
Tennessee	★	---	★	---	---	•	---	---	★	•	★	★	---	---	---	★	---	---	---	---
Texas	---	---	★	---	---	•	---	---	---	•	★	★	---	---	---	☆	---	---	---	---
Utah	★	---	★	★	---	•	---	---	---	•	★	★	---	---	---	☆	---	---	★	★
Vermont	★	---	★	---	☆	•	---	---	---	•	★	★	---	---	---	★	---	---	---	---
Virginia	★	---	★	---	---	•	★	---	★	•	★	★	---	---	---	---	---	---	---	---
Washington	★	---	•	---	---	•	---	★	☆	•	★	★	---	---	---	☆	★	---	---	★
West Virginia	★	---	★	---	---	•	★	---	---	•	★	★	---	---	---	★	---	---	---	★
Wisconsin	★	---	★	---	---	•	★	---	---	•	★	★	---	---	---	---	---	---	---	---
Wyoming	★	---	•	---	---	•	---	---	---	•	★	★	---	---	---	☆	---	---	★	---
Dist. of Col.	---	---	---	---	---	•	---	---	---	•	★	•	---	---	---	☆	---	---	---	---
Puerto Rico	---	---	---	---	---	•	---	---	---	•	★	---	---	---	---	---	---	---	---	---
Virgin Islands	★	---	---	---	---	•	---	---	---	---	•	•	---	---	---	---	---	---	---	---

RECORD OF PASSAGE OF MODEL ACTS
As of September 1, 1983

State or other jurisdiction	Act to Provide for the Appointment of Commissioners (1944)	Anti-Discrimination (1966)	Anti-Gambling (1952)	Court Administrator (1948) (1960)	Foreign Bank Loan (1959)	Land Sales Practices (1966)	Minor Student Capacity to Borrow (1969)	Post-Mortem Examinations (1954)	Public Defender (1970) (1974)	Real Estate Cooperative (1981)	Real Estate Time-Share (1980) (1982)	State Administrative Procedure (1946) (1961) (1981)	State Witness Immunity (1952)	Statutory Construction (1965)	Water Use (1958)
Alabama	★	---	---	---	---	---	---	---	---	---	---	---	---	---	---
Alaska	---	---	---	---	★	★	---	---	---	---	---	---	---	---	---
Arizona	★	---	---	---	---	---	★	---	---	---	---	---	---	---	---
Arkansas	★	---	---	---	---	---	---	---	---	---	---	•	---	---	---
California	---	---	---	---	---	---	---	---	---	---	---	---	---	---	---
Colorado	---	---	---	---	---	---	---	---	---	---	---	---	---	★	---
Connecticut	---	---	★	---	---	★	★	---	---	---	---	•	---	---	---
Delaware	---	---	---	---	---	★	---	---	---	---	---	•	---	---	---
Florida	---	---	---	---	---	★	---	---	---	---	---	•	---	---	---
Georgia	---	---	---	---	---	☆	---	---	---	---	---	•	---	---	---
Hawaii	---	★	---	---	---	★	---	---	---	---	---	---	★	---	☆
Idaho	---	---	---	---	---	---	---	---	---	---	---	---	---	---	---
Illinois	---	---	---	★	---	---	---	---	---	---	---	---	★	---	---
Indiana	---	---	★	---	---	---	---	---	---	---	---	---	---	---	---
Iowa	★	---	---	---	---	---	---	☆	---	---	---	•	---	★	---
Kansas	★	---	---	---	---	★	---	---	---	---	---	---	---	---	---
Kentucky	★	---	---	---	---	---	---	---	---	---	---	---	---	---	---
Louisiana	---	---	---	---	---	---	---	---	---	---	☆	•	---	---	---
Maine	★	---	---	---	---	---	---	---	---	---	---	---	---	---	---
Maryland	---	---	---	---	---	---	---	☆	---	---	---	★	---	---	---
Massachusetts	---	---	---	---	---	---	---	---	---	---	---	---	---	---	---
Michigan	---	---	---	★	---	---	---	---	---	---	---	★	---	---	---
Minnesota	---	---	---	---	---	---	---	---	---	---	---	---	---	---	---
Mississippi	★	---	---	---	---	---	---	---	---	---	---	★	---	---	---
Missouri	---	---	---	---	---	---	---	---	---	---	---	★	---	---	---
Montana	★	---	---	☆	---	★	☆	---	---	---	---	•	---	---	---
Nebraska	★	---	---	---	---	---	---	---	---	---	---	---	---	---	---
Nevada	---	---	---	---	---	---	---	---	---	---	---	---	---	---	---
New Hampshire	★	---	---	---	---	---	---	---	---	---	---	---	---	---	---
New Jersey	---	---	---	---	---	---	---	---	---	---	---	---	---	---	---
New Mexico	---	---	---	---	---	---	---	---	---	---	---	---	---	---	---
New York	---	---	---	---	---	---	---	---	---	---	---	---	---	---	---
North Carolina	---	---	---	---	---	---	---	---	---	---	---	---	---	---	---
North Dakota	★	---	---	---	---	---	★	---	---	---	---	---	---	---	---
Ohio	---	---	---	---	---	---	---	---	---	---	---	---	---	---	---
Oklahoma	★	★	---	•	---	★	★	---	---	---	---	•	---	---	---
Oregon	★	---	---	---	---	---	★	---	---	---	---	★	---	---	---
Pennsylvania	---	---	---	---	---	---	---	---	---	---	---	•	---	---	---
Rhode Island	---	---	---	---	---	---	---	---	---	---	---	•	---	---	---
South Carolina	---	---	---	---	---	---	---	---	---	---	---	---	---	---	---
South Dakota	---	---	---	---	---	---	---	---	---	---	---	---	---	---	---
Tennessee	---	---	★	---	---	---	---	---	---	---	---	•	---	---	---
Texas	★	---	---	---	---	---	---	★	---	---	---	---	---	---	---
Utah	---	---	---	---	---	---	---	---	---	---	---	---	---	---	---
Vermont	---	---	---	---	---	---	---	---	---	---	---	---	---	---	---
Virginia	---	---	---	---	---	---	---	---	---	★	---	---	---	---	---
Washington	---	---	---	★	---	★	---	---	---	---	---	★	---	---	---
West Virginia	---	---	---	---	---	---	☆	---	---	---	---	☆	---	---	---
Wisconsin	★	---	---	---	---	---	---	---	---	---	---	★	---	★	---
Wyoming	---	---	---	---	---	---	---	---	---	---	---	•	---	---	---
Dist. of Col.	---	---	---	---	---	---	---	---	---	---	---	•	---	---	---
Puerto Rico	---	---	---	---	---	---	---	---	---	---	---	---	---	---	---
Virgin Islands	---	---	---	---	---	---	---	---	---	---	---	---	---	---	---

2.   Elections

ELECTION LEGISLATION

By Richard G. Smolka

For more than 10 years, the universal trend in state legislation has been to make voter registration easier and voting more convenient. The trend continued during the 1982-83 biennium, with newer laws easing the process for persons with physical handicaps, but examples of individuals and groups taking fraudulent advantage of easier registration and voting began to appear more frequently. Fraud indictments and convictions seemed to increase and even involved state legislators in at least three states. Numerous absentee ballot convictions were obtained, and many more voters than in recent years were identified as having fraudulently registered from addresses where they did not live. In general, states have responded by prosecution rather than by attempts to change existing laws.

Laws on campaign finance regulation changed very little, but new laws and procedures appeared in other areas as reactions to the external pressures of television and the courts. Following network projections of 1980 presidential election results while polls were still open from New York to California, several states amended laws on electioneering to make it more difficult for the media to conduct exit polls. Courts continued to upset laws on ballot access relating to third parties and independent candidates, making it easier for third parties to qualify for positions on the ballot and other benefits of party status.

The states have been compelled to react to the Federal Voting Rights Act Amendments of 1982, effective January 1, 1984, by allowing blind, illiterate or physically disabled voters to be assisted in voting by a person of their own choosing, other than the voter's employer or agent of that employer or officer or agent of the voter's union. Many states had a more restrictive definition of persons who could be assisted or who could provide assistance, and some also limited the number of voters any one person could assist.

Absentee Voting

Absentee voting procedures remain controversial and states have reacted to local situations, either easing or tightening the procedures as the situation warranted. After allegations of vote fraud and voter harassment, Missouri passed a law keeping secret until the Friday before the election the names of persons who requested absentee ballots. The law applied only to St. Louis City and Kansas City, but the legislature is considering making the provision statewide.

Candidates and political parties have solicited absentee ballot applications from voters favorable to them in states where any voter may apply for an absentee ballot without being required to state an acceptable reason such as absence, illness or physical disability. In some instances in California, the absentee ballots were mailed directly to a campaign headquarters for later delivery by campaign workers to the voter. The campaign workers also delivered the ballot to the county election official for the voter.

More than 36 percent of all votes cast in the April 1983 recall election of San Francisco Mayor Dianne Feinstein were by absentee ballot. Most of these had been solicited by the mayor's campaign organization from people favorable to her. A similar absentee ballot campaign took place in February 1984 during a special initiative on resort development in Kauai, Hawaii when one-third of the vote was absentee. Although a majority of those who voted at the polls were against development, 82 percent of the absentee voters favored development, providing the winning margin. In both states, legislation is being considered to control either the application or the role of third parties in handling absentee ballots or applications.

Overseas Absentee Voting. The Department of Justice, through its Federal Voting Assistance Program for military personnel, dependents and other Americans residing overseas, has begun vigorous efforts to ensure that state election calendars allow sufficient time for these persons to request and return absentee ballots. Three states, New York, Florida and Colorado, were sued and required to count absentee ballots received after the state deadline because there was insufficient time for overseas persons to obtain and return their ballots. The department has

Richard G. Smolka is Professor of Government at the American University and Editor of *Election Administration Reports.*

been working with the states to change election calendars to allow absentee ballots to be mailed 45 days before the election. Failing this, the agency is seeking to have absentee ballots counted up to 10 days after the election.

Elections by All-Mail Ballot

The idea of all-mail ballots as an option to in-person voting at the polls continued to spread. The all-mail option for special elections on issues, especially for smaller districts and non-controversial matters, has proven attractive because it costs less to administer and at the same time increase voter participation. The all-mail ballot was initiated in Monterey County, California in 1977 but the practice received great publicity when San Diego, in May 1981, mailed each of 430,000 registered voters a ballot on a city issue. Oregon based its 1981 all-mail experiment on the San Diego procedure but expanded it in 1983 to include, for the first time anywhere, elections in which candidates' names were on the ballot. The town of Gresham, Oregon filled vacancies in three council posts as well as adopted charter amendments in an all-mail ballot election November 8, 1983. Two of the council positions were closely contested, with margins of 90 and 140 votes respectively separating the winners and losers. A total of 6,552 city voters participated in the election. Kansas also passed a law allowing all-mail ballots, and the practice 1983 all-mail ballot elections for school district issues were favorably received. Many states are now considering authorizing optional all-mail ballot elections as substitutes for special elections on issues. However, there is still strong resistance to the idea of all-mail candidate elections. Although feared by opponents of all-mail elections, there is so far little evidence of fraud.

Voting Procedures for Handicapped Persons

Many states have passed or extended laws making it easier for physically handicapped persons to register and vote and all but 10 states allow most physically handicapped persons to register either by mail, at their own home, or at the polls on election day. In some states, a physically disabled person may be sent an absentee ballot automatically without making a separate request each election. All states permit the handicapped to vote by absentee ballot, but 14 retain some requirement for a physician's certificate under certain circumstances. Twenty-four states now require all polling places to be accessible for the handicapped in the same manner as other public buildings. Delaware, Georgia, Nebraska

and North Dakota laws exempt no polling places, but the other 20 states do allow some exemptions under specified conditions.

At least 18 states allow "curbside voting." Under these laws, polling place officials may take a ballot to the "curbside" to a voter who is physically unable to enter the polling place. Some states reassign handicapped persons who reside in a precinct with a nonaccessible polling place to a polling place which is accessible.

Voter Registration

For more than 10 years, new laws have made it easier for more people to register and remain on the rolls. A recent example is designating public officials or employees as deputy registrars. Among officials who may serve as deputy registrars are school principals or teachers and motor vehicle agency employees. Arizona law prevents a voter's name from being deleted from the rolls for nonvoting provided the voter retains a valid Arizona driver's license. Twenty-one states with more than half the population of the nation now provide for voter registration by mail.

Exit Polls

In an effort to eliminate or reduce the potentially adverse effects on voter turnout caused by media projections of election results while the polls are still open, several states have passed laws making it more difficult for the networks to conduct exit polls. In 1983, Washington, among other states, extended the distance from the polls in which various activities are prohibited. The Washington law prohibits electioneering and specifically exit polls within 300 feet of a polling place. This law became the target of a legal challenge by the three major networks which argued that it infringed upon freedom of the press. The state viewed its law as protecting voters from harassment, thereby protecting the right of the voter. It argued further that if freedom of the press allowed interviews close to the polls, freedom of speech would allow politicians or their supporters to approach voters in the same area. Among the factors at issue are the specific types of activity that can be prohibited. Georgia law, for example, has been interpreted to allow persons to conduct oral surveys but to prohibit interviewers from giving a respondent a sample ballot, questionnaire or other piece of paper within the restricted area. Unless the media or the states change positions, this is a controversy apparently headed for the U.S. Supreme Court.

Presidential Primaries

The number of presidential primary elections, which had been increasing, declined in 1984. The political parties or the state in Arkansas, Kansas, Kentucky, Louisiana, Michigan and South Carolina (states in which at least one party conducted a presidential primary in 1980) decided not to hold a presidential primary in 1984. Only one state without a 1980 primary, Alaska, introduced a 1984 primary election. Alaska then repealed the enacting legislation in January 1984 before the primary could be held because of costs of conducting an additional election, disagreements between state political parties and the national parties about how the primary should be conducted, and lack of interest in the process.

Federal Legislation

The Voting Rights Act Amendments of 1982 offer a very strong basis for challenge to state and local election laws throughout the nation. The law, broadly written to ensure that specific minorities are not denied the right to vote, includes language to ensure that the vote will have effect. Section 2 of the act, applicable nationally, prohibits jurisdictions from maintaining any practice that makes it difficult for protected minorities to achieve full participation and representation. At the time the law was debated, opponents argued that the provision would ultimately require proportional representation by race. The bill was amended to specify that this was not required but any jurisdiction that has a substantial minority population and a disproportionate representation of that minority in its elected governing units may be subject to a lawsuit and will have the burden of demonstrating that the result was not produced by the electoral practice. Lawyers for both sides agree that at-large elections and numbered post elections will be especially vulnerable to challenge. Any districting system that discriminates will also be subject to challenge under this section.

The same law provides that jurisdictions which are covered under the pre-clearance provisions of Section 5 of the act, and must now get federal approval for any change in any election procedure or practice, may bail-out from under this section if they meet certain tests. Briefly stated, these tests require a state or county to demonstrate full compliance with the act for a 10 year period prior to bail-out. All sub-units within the state or county must also be eligible for bail-out before the jurisdiction may bail-out. The state or county must also show evidence of a positive effort to eliminate election structures that inhibit minority participation.

Selected References

Alexander, Herbert E. and Jennifer W. Frutig. *Public Financing of State Elections.* Los Angeles: Citizens Research Foundation, 1983.

Berns, Walter, ed., *After the People Vote.* Washington, D.C.: American Enterprise Institute, 1983. An explanation of laws and procedures relating to the presidential election from the time the votes are cast until the president is sworn into office.

Malbin, Michael J., ed. *Money and Politics in the U.S.: Financing Elections in the 1980s.* Chatham, N.J.: American Enterprise Institute/Chatham House Publishers, 1984.

Palmer, James A. and Edward D. Feigenbaum. *Campaign Finance Law 1984.* Washington, D.C.: Federal Election Commission, 1984.

Smolka, Richard G. *Election Administration Reports.* A biweekly newsletter for election officials. Washington, D.C.

Table 1
CAMPAIGN FINANCE LAWS: FILING REQUIREMENTS
(As of January 1984)

State or other jurisdiction	Statements required from	Statements filed with	Time for filing
Alabama	Political committees.	Secy. of state for statewide and judicial offices. Probate judge in county of residence for legislative office.	15 days after primary or runoff and 30 days after any other election.
Alaska	Candidates; groups; individuals who contribute $250 or more per year to any group or candidate; a business entity, labor organization or municipality making a contribution or expenditure; suppliers receiving more than $250 from a candidate or group.	Alaska Public Offices Commission, central office.	30 days and 1 week before and 10 days after election; annually on Dec. 31 for contributions and expenditures received but not reported that year.(a)
Arizona	Candidates, committees and continuing political organizations.	Secy. of state.	10-15 days before and 20 days after primary; 10-15 days before and 30 days after general or special election; supplemental reports annually by Apr. 1 for contributions and expenditures subsequent to post-election report.
Arkansas	Candidates and persons acting on their behalf receiving contributions in excess of $250/election from any person.	Secy. of state and county clerk in county of residence.	Contributions: 25 and 7 days before and 30 days after election. Expenditures: 30 days after election. Supplemental reports for contributions and expenditures subsequent to post-election report.
California	Candidates receiving or spending more than $500 in an election; certain committees; elected officers.	Secy. of state, registrar of Los Angeles and San Francisco and clerk of county of residence; legislative candidates also file with clerk of county with largest number of registered voters in district.	Semiannual: July and Jan. 31; periodic: March and Sept. 22 and 12 days before 1st Tues. after 1st Mon. in June and Nov.; 40 and 12 days before and 65 days after any election not held on the 1st Tues. after the 1st Mon. of June or Nov.(b)
Colorado	Candidates; political committees; persons making independent expenditures of more than $100.	Secy. of state.	11 days before and 30 days after election. Supplemental reports annually on the anniversary of the election until no unexpended balance or deficit.(c)
Connecticut..........	Candidates, party committees and political committees receiving or spending over $500 in a single election.	Secy. of state.	2nd Thurs. of Jan., Apr., July, Oct.; 7 days before and 30 days after primary (45 days after general election or for political committees in any election). Supplemental reports for deficits: 90 days after election and within 30 days after any change and within 7 days after distribution of surplus funds.
Delaware	Candidates, committees.	State election commissioner.	20 days before election, Dec. 31 of election year, Dec. 31 of post election year and annually by Dec. 31 until fund closes.
Florida	Candidates; political committees; committees of continuous existence; party executive committees; persons making independent expenditures of $100 or more.	Qualifying officer and supervisor of elections in county of residence for the candidates. Division of elections and supervisor of elections in county where election is held for statewide committees.	Pre-election: 10th day of each calendar quarter from time treasurer is appointed through last day of qualifying for office; the Fri. preceding election for unopposed candidates, and the 4th, 18th and 32nd days preceding the election for all others. Post-election report 45 days after the election.
Georgia	Candidates, committees, certain other individuals or organizations.	Secy. of state and copy to probate judge in candidate's county of residence.	45 and 15 days before and 10 days after primary and 15 days before general or special election; Dec. 31 of election year; and annually on Dec. 31 for winning candidates with additional contributions or expenditures since filing post-election report.
Hawaii	Candidates, parties, committees.	Campaign Spending Commission.	10 working days before each election; 20 days after primary and 30 days after general or special election. Supplemental reports in event of surplus or deficit over $250 on 5th day after the last day of election year, and every 6 months thereafter.
Idaho	Candidates; political committees; organizations which contribute more than $500 to a political committee; persons making independent expenditures of more than $50.	Secy. of state.	Between 7 and 14 days before election, and 30 days after.(d) Supplemental reports on 10th day of Jan., Apr., July and Oct. annually in the event of an unexpended balance or expenditure deficit.

CAMPAIGN FINANCE LAWS: FILING REQUIREMENTS—Continued

State or other jurisdiction	Statements required from	Statements filed with	Time for filing
Illinois	Political committees.	State Board of Elections.	Contributions: 15 days before election and 90 days after each general election. Annual reports of contributions and expenditures: July 31.
Indiana	Political committees and any person making an independent expenditure.	State Election Board; legislative candidate committees file duplicate with elections board of candidate's county of residence.	10 days (if postmarked) or 8 days (if hand-delivered) before election or convention; 20 days after convention, if no pre-convention report is filed; annually by Jan. 15.
Iowa	Candidates and committees receiving contributions of or spending more than $250.	Finance Disclosure Commission.	The 20th day of Jan., May, July and Oct. annually. In years in which the candidate does not stand for election, the May and July reports are not required of a candidate committee.
Kansas	Candidates; political committees; party committees; persons making independent expenditures of more than $100.	Secy. of state.	6 days before election and Dec. 10 of election years.
Kentucky	Candidates, campaign committees, political party executive committee, permanent committees.	Kentucky Registry of Election Finance with duplicates to clerk of county where candidate resides. Campaign committees file with appropriate central campaign committees.	Candidates and campaign committees: 32 and 12 days before and 30 days after election. Political party executive committee: 30 days after election. Permanent committees: last day of each calendar quarter. Semiannual supplemental reports June 30 and Dec. 31 until no unexpended balance, continuing debts and obligations, expenditures or deficit.
Louisiana	Candidates spending more than $5,000 or receiving any single contribution in excess of $1,000; political committees spending or receiving $1,000 or more; any person (not a candidate) making independent expenditures or accepting contributions (other than to or from a candidate) of more than $500.	Supervisory Committee.	Candidates and committees: 180, 90, 30 and 10 days before primary; 10 days before and 40 days after general election; Jan. 15 annually until a deficit has been paid, or if the candidate or committee has received contributions or made expenditures during the year.(e)
Maine	Candidates; political committees; state party committees; political action committees; persons making independent expenditures of more than $50.	Commission on Governmental Ethics and Election Practices.	7 days before and 42 days after election; gubernatorial candidates also file Jan. 15 after non-election years if they received or spent more than $1,000 in that year, and 42 days before election. Disposition of surplus or deficit in excess of $50 on 1st day of each quarter of fiscal year until eliminated.(f)
Maryland	Candidates receiving contributions of or spending $300 or more; political committees; political clubs spending more than $51.	Board at which candidate filed certificate of candidacy. Central committees and political committees file with State Administrative Board of Election Laws.	4th Tues. before primary; 2nd Fri. before any election; the 3rd Tues. after general election or before taking office, whichever is earlier. Disposition of surplus or deficit 6 months after general election and annually on anniversary of election until eliminated.
Massachusetts	Candidates and political committees.	Director of campaign and political finance.	8 days before election and Jan. 10 of year after general election for General Assembly candidates; 3rd business day after designating depository and Jan. 10 of year after general election for others.
Michigan	Candidates; political committees; party committees; persons making independent expenditures of $100 or more.	Secy. of state.	11 days before and 30 days after election; committees other than independent committees by Jan. 31 of each year.(g)
Minnesota	Candidates; political committees; party committees; and individuals making independent expenditures over $100.	Ethical Practices Board. Legislative candidates file copies with auditor of each county in district.	10 days before election and Jan. 31 annually.(h)
Mississippi	Candidates and political committees.	Secy. of state for statewide candidates and committees; appropriate circuit clerk for legislative office.	Contributions: 5th day of each month of candidacy and Sat. before election. Expenditures: candidates report within 60 days after election; committees, within 30 days.

State or other jurisdiction	Statements required from	Statements filed with	Time for filing
Missouri	Candidates who spend or receive more than $500 or who receive a single contribution in excess of $50; committees; and persons making independent expenditures of $500 or more.	Secy. of state for statewide candidates and committees, and candidates for Supreme Court or Appellate Court; candidates for legislature file with secy. of state and election authority of candidate's place of residence.	40 and 7 days before and 30 days after election. Supplemental reports each Jan. 15 if contributions or expenditures of $500 or more were made or received since last report. Quarterly reports if post-election report shows outstanding debts of more than $500, until deficit is below $500.(i)
Montana	Candidates and political committees.	Commissioner of Political Practices and county clerk or recorder.	Statewide office: March 10 and Sept. 10 in election years. 15 and 5 days before and 20 days after election; supplemental reports March 10 and Sept. 10 until all debts and obligations are extinguished and no more contributions are accepted or expenditures made. Legislative office: 10 days before and 20 days after election.(j)
Nebraska	Candidates, political party committees, and other committees.	Nebraska Accountability and Disclosure Commission and election commissioner or clerk of candidate's county of residence.	30 and 15 days before and 40 days after election. June 1 annually for committees not supporting or opposing a candidate.(k)
Nevada	Candidates and persons advocating the election or defeat of a candidate.	Officer with whom candidate filed declaration of candidacy.	15 days before primary and 15 days before and 30 days after general election.
New Hampshire	Candidates; political committees spending over $500.	Secy. of state.	Wed. 3 weeks before and Wed. immediately before election; 2nd Fri. after election and every 6 months thereafter until outstanding debt or obligation is satisfied or surplus depleted.
New Jersey	Candidates; political committees; political parties and persons making independent expenditures over $100.	Election Law Enforcement Commission.	25 and 7 days before and 15 days after election; every 60 days after election until no balance remains. Political parties report March 1 annually.
New Mexico	Candidates spending more than $500; political committees.	Secy. of state.	10 days before and 30 days after election; 6 months after if any contributions are unspent or debt remains unpaid, and 12 months (and annually thereafter) if debt remains unpaid.
New York	Candidates and political parties spending or receiving more than $1,000 in a filing period.	State Board of Elections.	Primary election reports filed on the 32nd and 11th day before, and 10th day after; general election reports filed 32nd and 11th day before, and 27th day after. Additional statements on Jan. 15th and July 15th until satisfaction of all liabilities and disposition of all assets.(l)
North Carolina	Candidates; political committees; individuals making independent expenditures over $100.	State Board of Elections for statewide and multicounty district offices. County board of elections for others.	10 days before and after election (losing candidates in primary file 45 days after election). Supplemental reports due Jan. 7 after general election and annually following years in which contributions are received or expenditures made. Independent expenditure reports are filed within 10 days after expenditure is made.
North Dakota	Candidates receiving more than $100 in contributions, and political parties receiving contributions of more than $100 or contributing more than $100 to a candidate.	Secy. of state. Legislative candidates file with county auditor of candidate's county of residence.	Candidates: 10 days before election and 30 days after close of calendar year. Political parties: 30 days after close of calendar year.(m)
Ohio	Candidates, political committees, political parties.	Secy. of state. Legislative candidates file with Board of Elections for county with largest population.	12 days before and 45 days after election and last business day of Nov. annually.(n)
Oklahoma	Candidates, political parties and organizations.	State Election Board.	10 days before election and 40 days after general election. Political parties receiving checkoff funds must also report by Nov. 30 of each even-numbered year on expenditure of such funds. Supplemental reports within 6 months and 10 days after general election if any contributions are received or expenditures made within 6 months after general election.

CAMPAIGN FINANCE LAWS: FILING REQUIREMENTS—Continued

State or other jurisdiction	Statements required from	Statements filed with	Time for filing
Oregon	Candidates, political committees.	Secy. of state.	30-21 and 12-7 days before and 30 days after election. If post-election statement shows an unexpended balance of contributions or a deficit, supplemental reports are required annually on Sept. 10 until there is no balance or deficit.
Pennsylvania	Candidates and political committees receiving or spending over $250; political action committees.	Secy. of the commonwealth.	6th Tues. and 2nd Fri. before and 30 days after election. Annual reports required on Jan. 31 until there is no balance or debt in the report.(o)
Rhode Island	Candidates; political action committees; political party committees spending more than $5,000 or receiving any contribution in excess of $200; and those making independent expenditures of $200 or more.	Secy. of state; independent expenditures are to be reported to the appropriate candidate or party committee.	28 and 7 days before and 28 days after election. Party committees also file by March 1 annually. Supplemental reports are required at 90 day intervals commencing 120 days after election until dissolution.
South Carolina	Candidates and committees.	State Ethics Commission; Senate or House Ethics Committee for legislative office.	30 days after election and 10 days after end of each calendar quarter in which funds are received or spent.
South Dakota	Candidates and committees.	Secy. of state.	Last Tues. before election and Feb. 1 of each year (for statewide offices); July 1 and Dec. 31 of each year (for legislative office).(p) Supplemental report 1 year after election if statement shows an unexpended balance or a deficit.
Tennessee	Candidates and political campaign committees.	State librarian for state office. Clerk of the House or Senate for legislative office.	7 days before any election and 48 days after general election.
Texas	Candidates and committees.	Secy. of state.	30 and 7 days before and 30 days after election; annually on Jan. 15 if contributions are received or expenditures made.
Utah	Candidates for gov., lt. gov., state auditor, state treasurer, atty. gen., state senate or house of representatives; party committees.	State auditor.	10th day of July, Oct. and Dec. of election year and 5th day before election for state office candidates and for political parties; 30 days after election for legislative candidates.
Vermont	Candidates and political committees.	Secy. of state for state office and political committees. Senatorial or representative district clerk for legislative office.	State office and political committees: 40 and 10 days before any election and 10 days after general election. Legislative office: within 10 days after election. Supplemental reports for all candidates annually on July 15 until all expenditures are accounted for and all deficits are eliminated.
Virginia	Candidates, political action committees, political party committees meeting certain thresholds, and individuals making independent expenditures.	State Board of Elections and election board where candidate resides.	8 days before and 30 days after election. Statewide candidates and committees also report 30 days before election.(q)
Washington	Candidates and political committees.	Public Disclosure Commission and county auditor in county of candidate's residence. Continuing political committees: commission and auditor in county of treasurer's residence.	Initial report at time of appointment of treasurer; 21 and 7 days before election and 21 days after any election; reports of each contribution deposited after 1st day of the 4th month before a general election; 10th day of each month in which no other report is filed if total contributions or expenditures since last report exceed $200.(r)
West Virginia	Candidates and their financial agents; persons and treasurers of associations supporting or opposing any candidate.	Secy. of state for multicounty office. Clerk of county commission for single-county office.	Last Sat. in March or 15 days after that day before a primary; 5-10 days before and 30 days after any election.
Wisconsin	Candidates; political party committees; political committees; and others receiving or spending over $25.	State Elections Board. Legislative candidates also file duplicate with county clerk of counties in district.	8-14 days before election; continuing reports by committees and individuals, Jan. 1-31 and July 1-10 annually.(s)

State or other jurisdiction	Statements required from	Statements filed with	Time for filing
Wyoming............	Candidates, political party committees and political action committees.	Secy. of state. Legislative candidates also file with county clerk.	10 days after election. Committees: 7 days after election. Committees formed after election report July 1 and Dec. 31 of odd-numbered years until all debts are paid.
Dist. of Col.	Candidates; political committees; and individuals making independent expenditures of $50 or more.	Director of campaign finance.	Each year: Jan. 31. Election years: 10th day of March, June, Aug., Oct. and Dec. and 8 days before election. Nonelection years: July 31.(t)

Source: James A. Palmer and Edward D. Feigenbaum, *Campaign Finance Law 1984* (Washington, D.C.: National Clearinghouse on Election Administration, Federal Election Commission, 1984).

Note: This table deals with filing requirements for statewide and legislative offices in general terms. For detailed legal requirements or requirements for county and local offices, state statutes should be consulted.

(a) Contributions exceeding $250 made within one week before the election must be reported within 24 hours.

(b) Contributions or independent expenditures of $1,000 or more received after the final pre-election report must be reported within 48 hours.

(c) Contributions exceeding $500 received within 16 days before the election must be reported within 48 hours.

(d) Winning candidates in a primary do not file a post-primary report.

(e) Special report is required within 48 hours after receipt of a contribution of more than $2,000, or a candidate's expenditure of more than $200 to any candidate, committee, or other person required to file disclosure reports who makes endorsements during the period from 20 days before any election through election day.

(f) Contributions to or expenditures by candidates of $1,000 or more made after the 11th day and more than 48 hours before any election must be reported within 48 hours.

(g) Contributions of $200 or more received after the closing date of a pre-election statement, but before the second day prior to the election, must be reported within 48 hours after receipt.

(h) Contributions of $2,000 or more ($200 or more for a legislative candidate) received between the closing date of the last pre-election report and the election must be reported within 48 hours after receipt.

(i) Contributions of more than $1,000 ($500 for a legislative candidate) received after the closing date of the last pre-election report but before election day must be reported within 48 hours after receipt.

(j) Contributions of $500 or more received by a statewide candidate between the 10th day before the election and election day must be reported within 24 hours. Contributions of $100 or more received by a legislative candidate between the 15th day before the election and election day must be reported within 24 hours.

(k) Contributions of $500 or more received after last pre-election statement must be reported within 5 days after receipt.

(l) Contributions of more than $1,000 received after the final pre-election statement must be reported within 24 hours after receipt. A candidate who is unopposed in a primary and the candidate's authorized committee are not required to file the pre-election reports for the primary if the relevant information is furnished in the first pre-election report for the general election.

(m) Contributions of $500 or more received by a candidate in the 15-day period before any election must be reported within 48 hours of receipt.

(n) Initial report is not required of candidate committees which have received contributions or made expenditures of less than $1,000 at the close of business on the 20th day prior to the election.

(o) Contributions received or independent expenditures made of $500 or more after the final pre-election report must be reported within 24 hours.

(p) Contributions of $500 or more received within the nine days immediately prior to the election must be reported within 48 hours after receipt.

(q) Contributions of $1,000 or more received between the 11th day before any nomination or election and the day of nomination or election must be reported within 72 hours, but no later than the day prior to the day of nomination or election.

(r) Contributions of $500 or more made or received after the last pre-election report and before any election must be reported within 24 hours after the contribution is made or received.

(s) Contributions of more than $500 received after the last pre-election report must be reported within 24 hours after receipt.

(t) Contributions of $200 or more received after last pre-election report must be reported within 24 hours.

Table 2
CAMPAIGN FINANCE LAWS: LIMITATIONS ON CONTRIBUTIONS
BY ORGANIZATIONS
(As of January 1984)

State or other jurisdiction	*Corporate*	*Labor Union*	*Separate segregated fund— political action committee (PAC)*	*Regulated industry*	*Political party*
Alabama	Limited to $500 to any one candidate, political committee or political party per election.	Unlimited.	Unlimited.	Public utility regulated by public service commission may only contribute through a PAC.	Unlimited.
Alaska(a)...........	Limited to $1,000 per year for each elective office.	Same as corporate.	Same as corporate.	. . .	Unlimited.
Arizona	Prohibited.	Prohibited.	Unlimited.	Prohibited.	Unlimited.
Arkansas(a)..........	Limited to $1,500 per candidate, per election.	Same as corporate.	Same as corporate.	. . .	Limited to $2,500 per candidate, per election.
California(b).........	Unlimited.	Unlimited.	Unlimited.	. . .	Unlimited.
Colorado(b)	Unlimited.	Unlimited.	Unlimited.	. . .	Unlimited.
Connecticut(c)	Prohibited.	Prohibited.	Labor organization PAC limited to an aggregate of $50,000 per election, and same limits per candidate as individuals. Corporate PAC limited to an aggregate of $100,000 per election, and twice the limits per candidate as individuals.	Prohibited.	Unlimited.
Delaware(c)..........	Limited to $1,000 per statewide candidate per election, $500 per non-statewide candidate, per election.	Same as corporate.	Same as corporate.	. . .	. . .
Florida(a)	Limited to $3,000 for statewide office candidate per election; $2,000 for candidate for retention as district court of appeal judge; $1,000 for any other candidate or committee, per election.	Same as corporate.	Same as corporate.	. . .	Unlimited, except that party may not contribute to a candidate for judicial office.
Georgia	Unlimited.	Unlimited.	Unlimited.	Public utility corporation regulated by public service commission may not contribute, directly or indirectly.	Unlimited.
Hawaii(d)	Limited to $2,000 in any election period.	Same as corporate.	Same as corporate.	. . .	Sliding scale percentage limit based upon candidate expenditure limits.
Idaho	Unlimited.	Unlimited.	Unlimited.	. . .	Unlimited.
Illinois	Unlimited.	Unlimited.	Unlimited.	. . .	Unlimited.
Indiana.............	Limited to an aggregate of $5,000 for statewide candidates; an aggregate of $5,000 for state party central committees; an aggregate of $2,000 for other offices; and an aggregate of $2,000 for other party committees.	Same as corporate.	Unlimited.	. . .	Unlimited.

State or other jurisdiction	Corporate	Labor Union	Separate segregated fund—political action committee (PAC)	Regulated industry	Political party
Iowa	Prohibited.	Unlimited.	Unlimited.	Prohibited for insurance companies.	Unlimited.
Kansas	Limited to $3,000 per statewide candidate per election, and $750 per candidate, per election for other offices.	Same as corporate.	Same as corporate.	Prohibited.	Unlimited.
Kentucky(a)	Prohibited.	Unlimited.	Unlimited.	Prohibited.	Unlimited.
Louisiana(e)	Unlimited.	Unlimited.	Unlimited.	. . .	Unlimited.
Maine	Limited to $5,000 per candidate per election.	Same as corporate.	Same as corporate.	Same as corporate.	Same as corporate.
Maryland(a)	Limited to an aggregate of $2,500 per election and $1,000 per candidate, per election.	Same as corporate.	Unlimited.	. . .	Unlimited.
Massachusetts(c)	Prohibited.	Unlimited.	Unlimited.	Prohibited.	Unlimited.
Michigan(f)	Prohibited.	Limited to $1,700 for a statewide office, $450 for state senator, $250 for state representative candidates per election.	Same as labor union.	Prohibited.	State central committee is limited to $34,000 for a statewide office, $4,500 for state senator, $2,500 for state representative candidates, per election. Local party is limited to $17,000 for a statewide office, $4,500 for a state senator, $2,500 for state representative candidates, per election.
Minnesota	Prohibited.	Limited to $60,000 per election year for governor/lt. governor ($12,000 in non-election years); $10,000 per election year for attorney general ($2,000 in non-election years); $5,000 per election year for other statewide offices ($1,000 in non-election years); $1,500 per election year for state senate ($300 in non-election years); $750 per election year for state representative ($150 in non-election years).	Same as labor union.	Prohibited for insurance companies.	Limited to $300,000 per election year for governor/lt. governor ($60,000 in non-election years); $50,000 per election year for attorney general ($10,000 in non-election years); $25,000 per election year for other statewide offices ($5,000 in non-election years); $7,500 per election year for state senator ($1,500 in non-election years); $3,750 per election year for state representative ($750 in non-election years).
Mississippi	Limited to $1,000 per candidate per year and $250 for judicial office primary candidates.	Unlimited, except in contributions to judicial office primary candidates ($250 limit).	Same as labor union.	Generally prohibited.	Same as labor union.
Missouri(d)	Unlimited.	Unlimited.	Unlimited.	. . .	Unlimited.

Table 2—Continued

State or other jurisdiction	Corporate	Labor Union	Separate segregated fund—political action committee (PAC)	Regulated industry	Political party
Montana	Prohibited.	Limited for all elections in a campaign to $8,000 for governor/lt. governor; $2,000 for other statewide candidates; $1,000 for public service commissioner; $600 for state senator; $300 for other candidates.	Same as labor union.	Prohibited.	Contributions to judicial candidates are prohibited.
Nebraska(c)	Unlimited.	Unlimited.	Unlimited.	. . .	Unlimited.
Nevada	Unlimited.	Unlimited.	Unlimited.	. . .	Unlimited.
New Hampshire	Prohibited.	Prohibited.	. . .	Prohibited.	Unlimited.
New Jersey	Unlimited, except in contributions to governor in any primary or general election ($800 limit).	Same as corporate.	Same as corporate.	Prohibited for insurance corporations or associations and certain other corporations.	Unlimited, in state committee contribution to governor in general election ($800 limit).
New Mexico	Unlimited.	Unlimited.	Unlimited.	. . .	Prohibited in primary elections, otherwise unlimited.
New York(a)	Limited to an aggregate of $5,000 per calendar year.	Same as corporate.	Same as corporate.	Public utilities may not contribute from public service revenues unless cost is charged to shareholders.	Unlimited.
North Carolina(a)	Prohibited.	Prohibited.	Limited to $4,000 per committee or candidate, per election.	Prohibited for insurance companies.	Unlimited.
North Dakota	Prohibited.	Prohibited.	Unlimited.	Prohibited.	Unlimited.
Ohio(a)	Prohibited.	Unlimited.	Unlimited.	Prohibited for public utilities.	Unlimited.
Oklahoma	Prohibited.	Limited to $5,000 to a political party or organization or a state office, and $1,000 for a local office candidate.	Same as labor union.	Prohibited.	Same as labor union.
Oregon	Unlimited.	Unlimited.	Unlimited.	Generally prohibited.	Unlimited.
Pennsylvania(g)	Prohibited.	Prohibited.	Unlimited.	Prohibited.	Unlimited.
Rhode Island	Unlimited.	Unlimited.	Continued.	. . .	Unlimited.
South Carolina	Unlimited.	Unlimited.	Unlimited.	. . .	Unlimited.
South Dakota	Prohibited.	Prohibited.	Unlimited.	Prohibited.	Unlimited.
Tennessee	Prohibited.	Unlimited.	Unlimited.	Prohibited.	Unlimited.
Texas	Prohibited.	Prohibited.	Unlimited.	Prohibited.	Unlimited.
Utah	Unlimited.	Unlimited.	Unlimited.	. . .	Unlimited.
Vermont(c)	Limited to $5,000 per candidate or committee, per election.	Same as corporate.	Same as corporate.	. . .	Same as corporate.
Virginia	Unlimited.	Unlimited.	Unlimited.	. . .	Unlimited.
Washington	Unlimited.	Unlimited.	Unlimited.	. . .	Unlimited.

State or other jurisdiction	Corporate	Labor Union	Separate segregated fund—political action committee (PAC)	Regulated industry	Political party
West Virginia(c)	Prohibited.	Limited to $1,000 per candidate, per election.	Same as labor union.	Prohibited.	Same as labor union.
Wisconsin	Prohibited.	Limited according to formula for statewide candidates; and $1,000 for state senator; $500 for state representative; and $6,000 for political parties.	Same as labor union.	Public utilities may not offer special privileges to candidates.	Certain specified percentage limits per candidate.
Wyoming	Prohibited.	Prohibited.	Unlimited.	Prohibited.	Prohibited in primary elections.
Dist. of Col.(h)	Limited to an aggregate of $4,000 per election and $2,000 for mayor, $1,500 for council chairman, $1,000 for council member at-large, $400 for council member from a district and board of education member at-large, $200 for board of education member from a district or a party official, $25 for neighborhood advisory commission member.	Same as corporate.	Same as corporate.	. . .	. . .

Source: James A. Palmer and Edward D. Feigenbaum, *Campaign Finance Law 1984* (Washington, D.C.: National Clearinghouse on Election Administration, Federal Election Commission, 1984).
Note: Consult state statutes for more details.
Key:
. . .—No reference to contribution in the law.
(a) Cash contribution must be $100 or less.
(b) Cash contribution must be less than $100.
(c) Cash contribution must be $50 or less.
(d) Cash contribution of more than $100 requires a receipt to the donor and a record of the transaction.
(e) All cash contributions by corporations, labor organizations and associations must be by check.
(f) Cash contribution must be $20 or less.
(g) Cash contribution must be $100 or less per candidate.
(h) Cash contribution must be less than $50.

Table 3
CAMPAIGN FINANCE LAWS: LIMITATIONS ON CONTRIBUTIONS
BY INDIVIDUALS
(As of January 1984)

State or other jurisdiction	Individual	Candidate	Candidate's family member	Government employees	Anonymous or in name of another
Alabama	Unlimited.	Unlimited.	Unlimited.	No solicitation of state employees for state political activities. City employees may contribute to county/state political activities; county employees may contribute to city/state political activities.	. . .
Alaska(a)	Limited to $1,000 per year for each elective office.	Unlimited.	Same as individual.	Contribution may not be required of state employees.	Prohibited.
Arizona	Unlimited.	Unlimited.	Unlimited.	. . .	. . .
Arkansas(a)	Limited to $1,500 per candidate, per election.	Unlimited.	Same as individual.	Contribution may not be required of state employees. State division of social services/county board of public welfare employees may not solicit, nor may certain judges solicit for campaigns other than their own.	Anonymous contribution must be less than $50 per year. Contribution in the name of another prohibited.
California(b)	Unlimited.	Unlimited.	Unlimited.	Local agency employees may not solicit employees of their agency except incidentally through a large solicitation.	Anonymous contribution must be less than $100 per year. Contribution in the name of another prohibited.
Colorado(b)	Unlimited.	Unlimited.	Unlimited.	. . .	Contribution in the name of another prohibited.
Connecticut(c)	Limited to an aggregate of $15,000 per election and $2,500 for governor; $1,500 for other statewide office; $1,000 for sheriff; $500 for state senator or probate judge; $250 for state representative; $1,000 for town, city or borough office; $5,000 per year to state party.	Unlimited.	Unlimited.	May not be required.	Anonymous contribution must be less than $15. Contribution in the name of another prohibited.
Delaware(c)	Limited to $1,000 per statewide candidate, per election; $500 per non-statewide candidate per election.	Limited to $5,000 per election.	Same as candidate.	. . .	Prohibited.
Florida(a)	Limited to $3,000 for statewide office candidate per election; $2,000 for candidate for retention as district court of appeal judge; $1,000 for any other candidate or committee per election.	Unlimited.	Same as individual.	Judges not elected in public elections between competing candidates may not make contributions. Solicitation generally prohibited for state employees. Judges may not solicit contributions.	Contribution in the name of another prohibited.
Georgia	Unlimited.	Unlimited.	Unlimited.	Solicitation generally prohibited. State employee may not coerce another state employee.	Anonymous contribution prohibited.
Hawaii(d)	Limited to $2,000 in any election period.	Limited to an aggregate of $50,000 in any election year.	Same as candidate.	Solicitation of contributions prohibited. Contributions to other employees is prohibited.	Prohibited.

State or other jurisdiction	Individual	Candidate	Candidate's family member	Government employees	Anonymous or in name of another
Idaho	Unlimited.	Unlimited.	Unlimited.	Contributions permitted. Solicitation prohibited. State employee may not coerce another state employee.	Anonymous contribution must be $50 or less. Contribution in the name of another prohibited.
Illinois	Unlimited.	Unlimited.	Unlimited.	Generally prohibited.	Prohibited.
Indiana	Unlimited.	Unlimited.	Unlimited.	Contribution may not be required. Employees may not solicit or receive contributions.	Contribution in the name of another prohibited.
Iowa	Unlimited.	Unlimited.	Unlimited.	. . .	Prohibited.
Kansas	Limited to $3,000 per statewide candidate, per election; and $750 per candidate per election for other offices.	Unlimited.	Spouse is unlimited.	Contribution may not be required.	Anonymous contribution must be $10 or less. Contribution in the name of another prohibited.
Kentucky(a)	Limited to $3,000 per candidate per election.	Unlimited.	Same as individual.	Contribution may not be required. Contribution may be prohibited, depending on who is recipient.	Anonymous contribution must be $50 or less. Contribution in the name of another prohibited.
Louisiana(e)	Unlimited.	Unlimited.	Unlimited.	Contribution may not be solicited.	Anonymous contribution generally prohibited if more than $25. Contribution in the name of another prohibited.
Maine	Limited to an aggregate of $25,000 in a calendar year and $1,000 per candidate, per election.	Unlimited.	Spouse is unlimited.	State employee may not coerce another state employee.	Contribution in the name of another prohibited.
Maryland(a)	Limited to an aggregate of $2,500 per election and $1,000 per candidate per election.	Unlimited.	Spouse is unlimited.	Contribution may not be required.	Prohibited.
Massachusetts(c)	Limited to $1,000 per candidate, per year. Minors limited to $25 per year.	Unlimited.	Same as individual.	Contribution may not be required. Solicitation generally prohibited.	Contribution in the name of another prohibited.
Michigan(f)	Limited to $1,700 for statewide office, $450 for state senator, $250 for state representative candidates per election.	Limited to $25,000 per gubernatorial campaign.	Same as candidate.	Contribution may not be required.	Prohibited.
Minnesota	Limited to $60,000 per election year for governor/lt. governor ($12,000 in non-election years); $10,000 per election year for attorney general ($2,000 in non-election years); $5,000 per election year for other statewide offices ($1,000 in non-election years); $1,500 per election year for state senate ($300 in non-election years); $750 per election year for state representative ($150 in non-election years).	Unlimited.	Same as individual.	Contribution may not be required. Solicitation prohibited during hours of employment.	Anonymous contribution must be less than $20. Contribution in the name of another prohibited.

Table 3—Continued

State or other jurisdiction	Individual	Candidate	Candidate's family member	Government employees	Anonymous or in name of another
Mississippi	Unlimited, except in contributions to judicial office primary candidates ($250 limit).	Same as individual.	Same as individual.	Contribution may not be required. Highway patrol or correctional system employees may not contribute. Solicitation prohibited for state correctional system employees.	. . .
Missouri(d)	Unlimited.	Unlimited.	Unlimited.	. . .	Anonymous contribution must be $10 or less. Contribution in the name of another prohibited.
Montana	Limited for all elections in a campaign to $1,500 for governor/lt. governor; $750 for other statewide candidates; $400 for public service commissioner, district court judge, or state senator; $250 for other candidates.	Unlimited.	Same as individual.	Solicitation prohibited during hours of employment.	Contribution in name of another.
Nebraska(c)	Unlimited.	Unlimited.	Unlimited.	Solicitation prohibited during hours of employment.	Prohibited.
Nevada.............	Unlimited.	Unlimited.	Unlimited.	Employees may not solicit from other employees.	. . .
New Hampshire	Limited to $5,000.	Unlimited.	Same as individual.	Contribution may not be required.	Prohibited.
New Jersey	Unlimited, except in contribution to governor in any primary or general election ($800 limit). Contributor's spouse may contribute up to $800 for governor in general election.	Unlimited, but if receiving public funds for governor, limited to $25,000 per election from own funds.	Unlimited, except in contribution to governor in any primary or general election ($800 limit).	Contribution by certain public officeholders prohibited.	Prohibited.
New Mexico	Unlimited.	Unlimited.	Unlimited.	Solicitation prohibited while on duty.	Anonymous contribution in excess of $50 subject to special report.
New York(a)	Limited to an aggregate of $150,000 in a calendar year and $0.005 x number of registered voters in state or in party for statewide and state party elections, respectively; $0.05 x number of registered voters in district or in party in district for district office ($4,000 for state senator *or* amt. determined by above formula, and $2,500 for assembly member *or* amt. determined by above formula, whichever is greater in each case) with a min. of $1,000 and max. of $50,000.	Unlimited.	Family member contributions are aggregated and limited to $0.025 x number of registered voters in state or in party for statewide and state party elections; $0.25 x number of registered voters in district or in party in district for district office *or* $1,250, whichever is greater ($25,000 for state senator *or* amt. determined by above formula, and $12,500 for assembly member *or* amt. determined by above formula, whichever is greater in each case) with a max. of $100,000 per election.	Contributions permitted, but may not be required. Judicial candidates may not solicit government employees or receive contributions from them. Police force members may not solicit for contributions from government employees. State employees may not coerce other state employees.	Prohibited.

State or other jurisdiction	Individual	Candidate	Candidate's family member	Government employees	Anonymous or in name of another
North Carolina(a)	Limited to $4,000 per committee or candidate, per election.	Unlimited.	Unlimited.	State employee may not coerce another state employee.	Prohibited.
North Dakota	Unlimited.	Unlimited.	Unlimited.	. . .	. . .
Ohio(a)	Unlimited.	Unlimited.	Unlimited.	Contribution by certain employees with taxation duties is prohibited. Employees may not solicit or be solicited.	Anonymous contribution generally prohibited. Contribution in the name of another prohibited.
Oklahoma	Limited to $5,000 to a political party or organization or a state office, and $1,000 for a local office candidate, per person or family.	Unlimited.	Same as individual.	State employee may not solicit. Certain state employees may not receive contributions.	Anonymous contribution generally prohibited. Contribution in the name of another prohibited.
Oregon	Unlimited.	Unlimited.	Unlimited.	Contribution may not be required. Solicitation prohibited during hours of employment.	Contribution in the name of another prohibited.
Pennsylvania(g)	Unlimited.	Unlimited.	Unlimited.	State employees may not be solicited, and may not solicit from other state employees.	Prohibited.
Rhode Island	Unlimited.	Unlimited.	Unlimited.	State employees may not be solicited, and may not solicit other state employees.	Prohibited.
South Carolina	Unlimited.	Unlimited.	Unlimited.	. . .	. . .
South Dakota	Limited to $1,000 for any statewide candidate; $250 for any other candidate; or $3,000 to a political party in any calendar year.	Unlimited.	Unlimited.	. . .	. . .
Tennessee	Unlimited.	Unlimited.	Unlimited.	Employees may not solicit during hours of employment. Superiors may not solicit their employees. Certain government contractors may not be solicited.	. . .
Texas	Unlimited.	Unlimited.	Unlimited.	. . .	. . .
Utah	Unlimited.	Unlimited.	Unlimited.	Contribution may not be required. Solicitation prohibited during hours of employment.	. . .
Vermont(c)	Limited to $1,000 per candidate or committee, per election.	Unlimited.	Unlimited.	Solicitation by employees prohibited.	. . .
Virginia	Unlimited.	Unlimited.	Unlimited.	. . .	. . .
Washington	Unlimited.	Unlimited.	Unlimited.	Contribution may not be required.	Prohibited.
West Virginia(c)	Limited to $1,000 per candidate, per election.	Same as individual.	Same as individual.	Contribution may not be solicited.	. . .

Table 3—Concluded

State or other jurisdiction	Individual	Candidate	Candidate's family member	Government employees	Anonymous or in name of another
Wisconsin	Limited to $10,000 for statewide candidates; $1,000 for state senator; $500 for state representative; other offices by formula, with an aggregate limit of $10,000.	Unlimited.	Unlimited as to funds or property owned jointly by candidate and spouse.	Contribution and solicitation prohibited during hours of employment.	Anonymous contribution must be less than $10. Contribution in the name of another prohibited.
Wyoming	Limited to an aggregate of $25,000 and $1,000 per candidate in any general election and the year preceding.	Unlimited.	Unlimited.	. . .	. . .
Dist. of Col.(h)	Limited to an aggregate of $4,000 per election and $2,000 for mayor, $1,500 for council chairman, $1,000 for council member at-large, $400 for council member from a district or board of education member at-large, $200 for board of education member from a district or a party official, $25 for neighborhood advisory commission member.	Same as individual.	Same as individual.	Contributions permitted, but district employees may not solicit or collect political contributions.	Contribution in the name of another prohibited.

Source: James A. Palmer and Edward D. Feigenbaum, *Campaign Finance Law 1984* (Washington, D.C.: National Clearinghouse on Election Administration, Federal Election Commission, 1984).
Note: Consult state statutes for more details.
Key:
. . .—No reference to contribution in the law.
(a) Cash contribution must be $100 or less.
(b) Cash contribution must be less than $100.
(c) Cash contribution must be $50 or less.
(d) Cash contribution of more than $100 requires a receipt to the donor and a record of the transaction.
(e) All cash contributions of more than $300 must be by written instrument.
(f) Cash contribution must be $20 or less.
(g) Cash contribution must be $100 or less per candidate.
(h) Cash contribution must be less than $50.

Table 4
FUNDING OF STATE ELECTIONS: TAX PROVISIONS AND PUBLIC FINANCING
(As of January 1984)

State or other jurisdiction	Tax provisions relating to individuals				Public financing	
	Credit	Deduction	Checkoff	Surcharge	Source of funds	Distribution of funds
Alabama	...	...	...	$1(a)	Surcharge	To political party designated by taxpayer
Alaska	$50	...	...	...	...	
Arizona	...	$100(a)	...	...		
Arkansas	...	$25	...	...		
California	...	$100	...	$1, $5, $10 or $25(b)	Surcharge and an equal amount matched by state	To political parties for party activities and distribution to state-wide general election candidates
Hawaii	...	$100 for contributions to central or county party committees or $500 for contributions to candidates who abide by expenditure limits, with max. of $100 of a total contribution to a single candidate deductible	$2(a)	...	Checkoff, appropriated funds, other moneys	To candidates for all non-federal elective offices
Idaho	50% of contribution to max. $5(a)	...	$1	...	Checkoff	To political party designated by taxpayer
Iowa	...	...	$1(a)	$2(a)	Checkoff/surcharge	To political party designated by taxpayer; if not specified, amount divided among qualifying parties for party activities and distribution to general election candidates
Kentucky	...	...	$2(a)	...	Checkoff	To political party designated by taxpayer for party activities and distribution to general election candidates
Maine	...	...	...	$1	Surcharge	To political party designated by taxpayer
Massachusetts	...	...	...	$1(a)	Surcharge	To candidates in statewide primary and general elections
Michigan	...	...	$2(a)	...	Checkoff and an equal amount matched by state	To candidates in gubernatorial primaries and candidates for governor and lt. governor in general election
Minnesota	50% of contribution to max. $50(a)	...	$2(a)	...	Checkoff and excess anonymous contribution	To candidates for governor, lt. governor, attorney general, secretary of state, state auditor, state treasurer, state senator and representative in primary and general elections
Montana	...	...	$1(a)	$1(a) for those with no tax liability	Checkoff/surcharge	To candidates opposed in elections for governor, lt. governor, Supreme Court chief justice and justices

FUNDING OF STATE ELECTIONS: TAX PROVISIONS AND PUBLIC FINANCING
(As of January 1984)—Continued

| State or other jurisdiction | Tax provisions relating to individuals | | | | Public financing | |
	Credit	Deduction	Checkoff	Surcharge	Source of funds	Distribution of funds
New Jersey	...	...	$1(a)	...	Direct appropriations; Gubernatorial Gen. Elec. Fund from checkoff	To gubernatorial candidates
North Carolina	...	$25	$1(a)	...	Checkoff	Divided among political parties according to registration; of amount—50% goes to party, 50% for other purposes
Oklahoma	...	$100	$1(a)	...	Checkoff	50% to political parties(c) and 50% to eligible general election candidates(d)
Oregon	50% of contribution to max. $25(a) unless taxpayer has claimed a federal tax credit for political contributions	...	...	...		
Rhode Island	$1(a)	...	(e)	...	Credit/checkoff	To political party designated by taxpayer; other funds allocated to parties based on number of elected state officials and of votes in most recent election
Utah	...	...	$1	...	Checkoff	50% to state central committee of each party, 50% to county central committees of party designated by taxpayer
Wisconsin	...	...	$1(a)	...	Checkoff	According to formula, to general election candidates for state-wide and legislative offices(f)
Dist. of Col.	50% of contribution to max. $50(a)	...	...	...		

Source: James A. Palmer and Edward D. Feigenbaum, *Campaign Finance Law 1984* (Washington, D.C.: National Clearinghouse on Election Administration, Federal Election Commission, 1984).

Note: This table shows only those states that have a tax provision relating to individuals or a provision for public financing of state elections. Credits and deductions may be allowed only for certain types of candidates and/or political parties. Consult state laws for further details.

Key:
. . .—No provision.
(a) For joint returns, amount indicated above may be doubled.

(b) And a separate designation of $1, $5, $10 or $25.
(c) 10 percent to each party and remainder divided according to registration figures.
(d) 20 percent for governor, 15 percent for lieutenant governor, 15 percent for attorney general and 10 percent each for state treasurer, state auditor and inspector, commissioner of insurance, superintendent of public instruction and corporation commissioner.
(e) See credit. Designated to specified party or to non-partisan general account.
(f) Candidates must meet certain qualifications.

Table 5
VOTER REGISTRATION INFORMATION

State or other jurisdiction	Mail registration allowed for all voters	Minimum state residence requirement (days)	Closing date for registration before general election (days)	Persons eligible for absentee registration(a)	Automatic cancellation of registration for failure to vote after _____ years
Alabama		1	10	D,S,T	
Alaska	★	30	30	(b)	2
Arizona		50	50	S,T	2
Arkansas		. . .	20	D	4
California	★	29	29	(b)	4
Colorado		32	32	D,S,T	2
Connecticut		. . .	21(c)	D	
Delaware	★	. . .	3rd Sat. in Oct. (c)	(b)	4
Florida		. . .	30	(d)	2
Georgia		. . .	30	B,D,R, S,T	3
Hawaii		. . .	30	B,D,E, R,S,T	2
Idaho		30	17/10(e)	B,D,S,T	4
Illinois		30	28	(f)	4
Indiana		30	29(g)	B,D,S,T	2
Iowa	★	. . .	10	(b)	4
Kansas	★	20	20	(b)	4
Kentucky	★	30	30	(b)	4
Louisiana		. . .	24(c)	D,T	4
Maine	★	. . .	Election day	(b)	
Maryland	★	29	29	(b)	5
Massachusetts		. . .	28	D,T	
Michigan		30	30	D,S,T	10
Minnesota	★	20	Election day	(b)	4
Mississippi		30	10	(f)	4
Missouri	★	. . .	28	(b)	
Montana	★	30	30	(b)	4
Nebraska		. . .	10	D,S,T	
Nevada		30	30	S,T	2
New Hampshire		10	10	B,D,R,S	
New Jersey	★	30	29	(b)	4
New Mexico		. . .	42	T	2
New York	★	30	30	(b)	4
North Carolina		30	21(h)	D	8
North Dakota(i)		30			
Ohio	★	30	30	(b)	4
Oklahoma		. . .	10	D	4
Oregon	★	20	Election day	(b)	2
Pennsylvania	★	30	30	(b)	2
Rhode Island		30	30	D	5
South Carolina		. . .	30	D,S,T	
South Dakota		. . .	15	S,T	4
Tennessee	★	50	30	(b)	4
Texas	★	. . .	30	(b)	
Utah	★	30	5	(b)	4
Vermont		. . .	17	(d)	4
Virginia		. . .	31	(f)	4
Washington		30	30	(f)	2
West Virginia	★	30	30	(b)	4
Wisconsin	★	10	Election day	(b)	2
Wyoming		. . .	30	B,D,E, S,T	2
Dist. of Col.	★	30	30	(b)	4
Puerto Rico		. . .	50	(f)	2
Virgin Islands		45	45	S	4

Source: Adapted from *Easy Does It.* League of Women Voters Education Fund, 1730 M St., N.W., Washington, D.C. (Copyright 1984).

Key:

. . .—No residence requirement.

(a) In this column: B—Absent on business; D—Disabled persons; E—Not absent, but prevented by employment from registering; R—Absent for religious reasons; S—Students; T—Temporarily out of jurisdiction.

(b) All voters. See column on mail registration.

(c) Closing date differs for primary election. In Connecticut, 14 days; Delaware, 21 days; Louisiana, 30 days.

(d) Anyone unable to register in person.

(e) With precinct registrar, 17 days before; with county clerk, 10 days.

(f) No one is eligible to register absentee.

(g) Before deputy registrar, 45 days.

(h) Business days.

(i) No voter registration.

Table 6
POLLING HOURS: GENERAL ELECTIONS

State or other jurisdiction	Polls open	Polls close	Notes on hours(a)
Alabama	No later than 8 a.m.	Between 6 and 8 p.m.	Polls must be open at least 10 consecutive hours; hours set by county commissioner.
Alaska	8 a.m.	8 p.m.	
Arizona	6 a.m.	7 p.m.	
Arkansas	Between 7 and 8 a.m.	7:30 p.m.	
California	7 a.m.	8 p.m.	
Colorado	7 a.m.	7 p.m.	
Connecticut	6 a.m.	8 p.m.	
Delaware	7 a.m.	8 p.m.	
Florida	7 a.m.	7 p.m.	
Georgia	7 a.m.	7 p.m.	
Hawaii	7 a.m.	6 p.m.	
Idaho	Between 7 and 8 a.m.	8 p.m.	Polls may close earlier if all registered electors in a precinct have voted.
Illinois	6 a.m.	7 p.m.	
Indiana	6 a.m.	6 p.m.	
Iowa	7 a.m.	9 p.m.	
Kansas	Between 6 and 7 a.m.	Between 7 and 8 p.m.	Hours may be changed by county election officer, but polls must be open at least 12 consecutive hours between 6 a.m. and 8 p.m.
Kentucky	6 a.m.	6 p.m.	Persons in line may vote only until 7 p.m.
Louisiana	6 a.m.	8 p.m.	
Maine	Between 6 and 10 a.m.	8 p.m.	Opening hour is determined by municipal election officer. Municipalities using voting machines may close at 9 p.m.
Maryland	7 a.m.	8 p.m.	
Massachusetts	Between 5:45 and 10 a.m.	8 p.m.	In cities and towns, the polls must be open at least 10 hours.
Michigan	7 a.m.	8 p.m.	
Minnesota	7 a.m.	8 p.m.	Municipalities of less than 1,000 may establish hours of no later than 9 a.m. to 8 p.m.
Mississippi	7 a.m.	6 p.m.	
Missouri	6 a.m.	7 p.m.	
Montana	7 a.m. noon	8 p.m. 8 p.m.	In precincts of over 200 registered voters. In precincts of less than 200 registered voters, polls may close when all registered electors have voted.
Nebraska	7 a.m. 8 a.m.	7 p.m. 8 p.m.	Mountain Time Zone. Central Time Zone.
Nevada	7 a.m.	7 p.m.	
New Hampshire	Varies	Varies	Cities: Polls open not less than 4 hours and may be opened not earlier than 6 a.m. nor later than 8 p.m. Small towns: In towns of less than 700 population the polls must be open at least five consecutive hours. On written request of seven registered voters the polls shall be kept open until 6 p.m. In towns of less than 100 population, the polls close if all registered voters have appeared. Other towns: Polls may not open later than 10 a.m. and may not close earlier than 6 p.m. On written request of 10 registered voters the polls may close at 7 p.m.
New Jersey	7 a.m.	8 p.m.	
New Mexico	8 a.m.	7 p.m.	
New York	6 a.m.	9 p.m.	
North Carolina	6:30 a.m.	7:30 p.m.	In precincts where voting machines are used, county board of elections may permit closing at 8:30 p.m.
North Dakota	Between 7 and 9 a.m.	Between 7 p.m. & 9 p.m.	In precincts where less than 75 votes were cast in previous election, polls may open at noon.
Ohio	6:30 a.m.	7:30 p.m.	
Oklahoma	7 a.m.	7 p.m.	
Oregon	8 a.m.	8 p.m.	
Pennsylvania	7 a.m.	8 p.m.	
Rhode Island	Between 7 a.m. & noon	9 p.m.	Opening hours vary across cities and towns.

State or other jurisdiction	Polls open	Polls close	Notes on hours(a)
South Carolina	8 a.m.	7 p.m.	
South Dakota	7 a.m. 8 a.m.	7 p.m. 8 p.m.	Mountain Time Zone. Central Time Zone.
Tennessee	Varies.	7 p.m. (CST); 8 p.m. (EST)	Counties with population over 120,000 may not open later than 8 a.m.
Texas	7 a.m.	7 p.m.	Counties with population over one million may open polls at 6 a.m.
Utah	7 a.m.	8 p.m.	
Vermont	Between 6 and 10 a.m.	No later than 7 p.m.	
Virginia	6 a.m.	7 p.m.	
Washington..........	7 a.m.	8 p.m.	
West Virginia	6:30 a.m.	7:30 p.m.	
Wisconsin	7 a.m. Between 7 and 9 a.m.	8 p.m. 8 p.m.	1st, 2nd and 3rd class cities. 4th class cities, towns and villages.
Wyoming............	8 a.m.	7 p.m.	
Dist. of Col.	7 a.m.	8 p.m.	
American Samoa	6 a.m.	6 p.m.	
Guam	8 a.m.	8 p.m.	
Puerto Rico..........	9 a.m.	3 p.m.	
Virgin Islands	8 a.m.	6 p.m.	

Note: Hours for primary, municipal and special elections may differ from those noted.

Sources: State statutes and state election administration offices.
(a) In all states, voters standing in line when the polls close are allowed to vote; however, provisions for handling those voters vary across jurisdictions.

Table 7
STATE OFFICERS TO BE ELECTED: 1984 AND 1985

State or other jurisdiction	Date of general elections in 1984(a)	Governor	Lieutenant governor	Secretary of state	Attorney general	Treasurer	Auditor	Judges of court of last resort(b)	Judges of intermediate appellate court(b)	Board of education members	Public utilities commissioners	Superintendent of public instruction	Other	State legislatures: members to be elected — Senate	State legislatures: members to be elected — House
Alabama	Nov. 6							2	(c)	4	(d)			1/2	All
Alaska	Nov. 6							1						All	All
Arizona	Nov. 6							2	8		2		State mine inspector	1/2(e)	All
Arkansas	Nov. 6	★	★	★	★	★	★	2	2				Land commr.	1/2	All
California	Nov. 6							(c)	(c)					1/2	All
Colorado	Nov. 6							1	5	2			3 Univ. of Colorado regents	1/2	All
Connecticut	Nov. 6													All	All
Delaware	Nov. 6	★	★										insurance commr.	1/2(e)	All
Florida	Nov. 6							2	9					1/2	All
Georgia	Nov. 6							2	3		2			All	All
Hawaii	Nov. 6									13				1/2(e)	All
Idaho	Nov. 6							2	1					All	All
Illinois	Nov. 6							1	4				3 Univ. of Illinois trustees	1/3(e)	All
Indiana	Nov. 6	★	★						2			★		1/2	All
Iowa	Nov. 6							2	4					1/2	All
Kansas	Nov. 6							3	4	5				All	All
Kentucky	Nov. 6							1	1	2	2				All
Louisiana	(f)							1	9	2	2				All
Maine	Nov. 6							1						All	All
Maryland	Nov. 6							1	6						All
Massachusetts	Nov. 6							3	6				8 executive councillors	All	All
Michigan	Nov. 6							5	6	2			6 trustees of state universities		All
Minnesota	Nov. 6							4							All
Mississippi	Nov. 6							4							All
Missouri	Nov. 6	★	★	★	★	★	★	3	4					1/2	All
Montana	Nov. 6	★	★	★	★		★	2	7		3	★		1/2(e)	All
Nebraska	Nov. 6							1		4	1		2 Univ. of Nebraska regents	1/2(e)	U
Nevada	Nov. 6							2		4			3 university regents	1/2(e)	All
New Hampshire	Nov. 6	★											5 executive councillors	All	All
New Jersey(1985)	Nov. 5	★													All
New Mexico	Nov. 6							2	2	10			1 corporation commr.	All	All
New York	Nov. 6							2	6					All	All
North Carolina	Nov. 6	★	★	★	★	★	★					★	Commr. of agriculture; commr. of insurance; commr. of labor	All	All
North Dakota	Nov. 6	★	★	★	★	★	★	2		7	1	★	Commr. of agriculture; commr. of insurance; tax commr.	1/2	All
Ohio	Nov. 6							2	12	7				1/2	All

State or other jurisdiction	Date of election	Governor	Lt. Governor	Secretary of state	Attorney general	Treasurer	Other executive	Supreme court	Appellate court	Other court	State senate	State house	Other offices up for election
Oklahoma	Nov. 6	...	...	...	★	...	...	(g)2	4	1	1/2	All	...
Oregon	Nov. 6	...	...	★	★	★	...	...	3	...	1/2	All	...
Pennsylvania	Nov. 6	...	...	...	...	★	★	...	...	...	1/2	All	...
Rhode Island	Nov. 6	...	...	★	★	★	...	...	...	...	All	All	...
South Carolina	Nov. 6	...	...	...	...	...	...	...	...	...	All	All	...
South Dakota	Nov. 6	...	...	★	★	★	...	2	1	1	All	All	Commr. of school and public lands
Tennessee	Aug. 9	...	...	...	...	...	...	...	...	...	1/2(e)	...	...
Texas	Nov. 6	...	...	...	...	...	...	(h)1	7	...	1/2(e)	...	Railroad commr.
Utah	Nov. 6	★	★	...	★	★	...	...	9	1	All	...	...
Vermont	Nov. 6	★	★	★	★	★	...	...	4	...	...	All	...
Virginia (1985)	Nov. 5	★	★	...	★	...	...	3	6	...	1/2(e)	All	insurance commr.; commr. of public lands
Washington	Nov. 6	...	...	★	★	★	...	2	...	★	1/2	All	Commr. of agriculture
West Virginia	Nov. 6	★	★	★	★	★	...	1	3	...	...	All	...
Wisconsin	Apr. 3	...	...	...	...	...	...	1	...	...	1/2(e)	...	...
	Nov. 6	...	...	...	...	...	...	2	...	★	1/2(e)	All	...
Wyoming (1985)	Apr. 2 / Nov. 6	...	...	...	...	...	...	...	...	...	...	All	...
Dist. of Col.	Nov. 6	...	...	...	★	...	...	...	...	...	(i)	U	...
American Samoa	Nov. 6	★	...	...	...	...	...	...	...	...	All	All	...
Guam	Nov. 6	★	★	...	...	...	★	...	...	...	All	U	19 village commrs.; 4 asst. village commrs.
No. Marianas (1985)	Nov. 5	★	★	...	...	...	...	...	...	...	All	All	...
Puerto Rico	Nov. 6	...	...	...	...	...	...	...	...	...	All	All	...
Virgin Islands	Nov. 6	...	...	...	...	...	...	...	...	...	(j)	U	...

Source: State election administration offices.

Note: In several states, elections for some state offices do not occur in 1984 or 1985. When a number appears in a column instead of a star, the figure indicates the number of individuals on the state court or other governmental entity up for election in 1984 or 1985. The information in this table is current as of February 1984.

Key:
★—Office up for election.
...—Office not up for election.
U—Unicameral legislative body.
(a) Elections for 1985 are indicated by (1985) before date for general election.
(b) For some states, information on number of judges facing election in 1984 or 1985 is tentative given the nature of the initial selection and retention processes.

(c) Court of civil appeals (3); court of criminal appeals (4).
(d) President of Public Service Commission.
(e) Approximately 1/2 of the membership. Actual number of seats up for election: Arkansas (18); Delaware (10); Hawaii (13); Illinois (20); Montana (25); Nebraska (25); Nevada (10); Tennessee (16); Texas (15); Utah (14); Washington (25); Wisconsin (17); Wyoming (16).
(f) Under Louisiana's election law, candidates of all parties run together on a single ballot in September; if no candidate for an office wins a majority of the vote, the top two finishers oppose each other in a November runoff. In 1984, the elections will be held on September 29 and November 6.
(g) Supreme Court (3); Court of Criminal Appeals (1).
(h) Supreme Court (3); Court of Criminal Appeals (3).
(i) Six members of the Council of the District of Columbia.
(j) Thirteen members.

Table 8
METHODS OF NOMINATION FOR STATE OFFICIALS

State or other jurisdiction	Method(s) of nominating candidates
Alabama	Primary election; however, the state executive committee or other governing body of any political party may choose instead to hold a state convention for the purpose of nominating candidates (meetings must be held at least 60 days prior to the date on which primaries are conducted).
Alaska	Primary election.
Arizona	Primary election.
Arkansas	Primary election.
California	Primary election.
Colorado	Primary election; however, a political party may hold a pre-primary convention (at least 55 days before the primary) for the designation of candidates. Each candidate who receives at least 20 percent of the convention delegates' votes is listed on the primary ballot, with the candidate receiving the most votes listed first.
Connecticut	Convention/primary election. Political parties hold state conventions (convening not earlier than the 61st day and closing not later than the 43rd day before the date of the primary) for the purpose of endorsing candidates. If no one challenges the endorsed nominee (who received at least 20 percent of the delegate vote), no primary election is held. However, if anyone challenges the nominee by filing a candidacy of nomination (having also received at least 20 percent of the delegate vote), a primary election is held to determine the party candidate for the general election.
Delaware	Primary election.
Florida	Primary election.
Georgia	Primary election; however, the state executive committee or other governing body of any political party may choose instead to hold a state convention for the purpose of nominating candidates (meetings must be held at least 90 days before the date on which primaries are held).
Hawaii	Primary election.
Idaho	Primary election.
Illinois	Primary election; however, state conventions are held for the nomination of candidates for trustees of the University of Illinois.
Indiana	Primary election held for the nomination of candidates for governor and U.S. senator; state party conventions held for the nomination of candidates for other state offices.
Iowa	Primary election; however, if there are more than two candidates for any nomination and none receives at least 35 percent of the primary vote, the primary is deemed inconclusive and the nomination is made by party convention.
Kansas	Primary election; however, candidates of any political party whose secretary of state did not poll at least 5 percent of the total vote cast for all candidates for that office in the preceding general election are restricted to nomination by delegate or mass convention.
Kentucky	Primary election.
Louisiana	Primary election.
Maine	Primary election.
Maryland	Primary election.
Massachusetts	Primary election.
Michigan	Primary election held for the nomination of candidates for governor, U.S. congressional seats and state senators and representatives; state conventions held for the nomination of candidates for lieutenant governor, secretary of state and attorney general.
Minnesota	Primary election.
Mississippi	Primary election.
Missouri	Primary election.
Montana	Primary election.

State or other jurisdiction	Method(s) of nominating candidates
Nebraska	Primary election.
Nevada	Primary election.
New Hampshire	Primary election.
New Jersey	Primary election.
New Mexico	Primary election; however minor parties (those receiving less than 15 percent of the total number of votes cast at the last general election for governor or U.S. president) may nominate candidates by political convention.
New York	Convention/primary election. The person who receives the majority vote at the state party committee meeting becomes the designated candidate for nomination; however, all other persons who received at least 25 percent of the convention vote may demand that their names appear on the primary ballot as candidates for nomination.
North Carolina	Primary election.
North Dakota	Primary election.
Ohio	Primary election.
Oklahoma	Primary election.
Oregon	Primary election.
Pennsylvania	Primary election.
Rhode Island	Primary election.
South Carolina	Primary election; however, the state executive committee or other governing body of any political party may choose instead to hold a state convention for the purpose of nominating candidates (nominations must be announced no later than poll closing time on the date of the primary election).
South Dakota	Primary election. Any candidate who receives a plurality of the primary vote becomes the nominee; however, if no individual receives at least 35 percent of the vote for the candidacy for the offices of governor or U.S. congressman, the nominee is selected by party convention.
Tennessee	Primary election.
Texas	Primary election.
Utah	Convention/primary election. Delegates from the county primary conventions are elected to the state primary convention for the purpose of selecting the political party nominees to run at the regular primary election.
Vermont	Primary election.
Virginia	Primary election; however, the state executive committee or other governing body of any political party may choose instead to hold a state convention for the purpose of nominating candidates (party opting for convention can only do so within 32 days prior to date on which primary elections are normally held).
Washington	Primary election.
West Virginia	Primary election.
Wisconsin	Primary election.
Wyoming	Primary election.
Dist. of Col.	Primary election.

Note: The nominating methods described here are for state offices; procedures may vary for local candidates. Also, independent candidates may have to petition for nomination. For more information on primaries, see table on Primary Elections for State Officers.

Table 9
PRIMARY ELECTIONS FOR STATE OFFICERS

State or other jurisdiction	Dates of 1984 primaries for state officers(a) Primary	Runoff primary(b)	Party affiliation for primary voting — Voters must declare/change affiliation prior to election day	Voters select party on election day	Voters receive ballot of: One party (c)	All parties participating(d)
Alabama	Sept. 4	Sept. 25		★	★	
Alaska	Aug. 28			(e)		★(e)
Arizona	Sept. 11		At least 50 days before		★	
Arkansas	May 29	June 12		★	★	
California	June 5		At least 29 days before		★	
Colorado	Sept. 11		At least 32 days before		★	
Connecticut	Sept. 11		At least 6 months before(f)		★	
Delaware	Sept. 8		At least 21 days before		★	
Florida	Sept. 4	Oct. 2	At least 30 days before		★	
Georgia	Aug. 14	Sept. 4		★	★	
Hawaii	Sept. 22			★		★
Idaho	May 22			★		★
Illinois	March 20			★	★	
Indiana	May 8			★	★	
Iowa	June 5			★	★	
Kansas	Aug. 7		(g)	(g)	★	
Kentucky	May 29		At least 30 days before		★	
Louisiana	Sept. 29(h)	Nov. 6(h)		(h)		(h)
Maine	June 12		(g)	(g)	★	
Maryland	May 8		At least 4 months before(f)		★	
Massachusetts	Sept. 18		(g)	(g)	★	
Michigan	Aug. 7			★		★
Minnesota	Sept. 11			★		★
Mississippi	June 5	June 26		★	★	
Missouri	Aug. 7			★	★	
Montana	June 5			★		★
Nebraska	May 15		At least 10 days before		★	
Nevada	Sept. 4		At least 30 days before		★	
New Hampshire	Sept. 11		At least 10 days before		★	
New Jersey (1985)	June 5 June 4		(g)	(g)	★	
New Mexico	June 5		At least 42 days before(i)		★	
New York	Sept. 11		At least 1 year before(f)		★	
North Carolina	May 8	June 5	At least 21 days before(j)		★	
North Dakota	June 12			★	★	★
Ohio	May 8			★	★	
Oklahoma	Aug. 28	Sept. 18	(g)	(g)	★	
Oregon	May 15		At least 20 days before(f)		★	
Pennsylvania	April 10		At least 30 days before		★	
Rhode Island	Sept. 11		(g)	(g)	★	
South Carolina	June 12	June 26		★	★	
South Dakota	June 5		At least 15 days before		★	
Tennessee	Aug. 2			★	★	
Texas	May 5	June 2		★	★	
Utah	Aug. 21			★		★
Vermont	Sept. 11			★		★
Virginia (1985)	June 12 June 11			★	★	
Washington	Sept. 18			(e)		★(e)
West Virginia	June 5		At least 30 days before		★	
Wisconsin	Sept. 11			★		★
Wyoming	Sept. 11			★	★	
Dist. of Col.	May 1		At least 30 days before		★	
Puerto Rico	June 10		At least 14 days before		★	
Virgin Islands	Sept. 11		At least 30 days before		★	

Sources: Federal Election Commission; League of Women Voters, *Easy Does It*; state election administration offices.

(a) Primaries for state offices in 1985 have (1985) before the date.

(b) A runoff election between the top two candidates is held if the leading candidate does not get a majority of the votes cast in the first primary.

(c) The type of primary in which voters receive only the ballot of their party choice in a primary (voters must declare their affiliation on, or prior to, election day) is generally referred to as a *closed* primary.

(d) The type of primary in which voters receive a ballot for all parties and select the party of their choice in the privacy of the voting booth is generally referred to as an *open* primary.

(e) Voters are not restricted to one party. In Alaska and Washington, voters participate in a *blanket* primary. As in regular open primaries, voters receive a ballot that contains the primary ballot for all parties. However, a voter in the blanket primary may pick and choose among the parties in moving through the lists of candidates for various offices. The only restriction is that the voter can indicate only one preference for each office.

(f) Applies to previously affiliated registered voters. In Connecticut, unaffiliated voters must declare at least 14 days before. In Maryland and Oregon, new registrants declare at time of registration. In New York, new voters declare affiliation at least 30 days before, while previously eligible voters declare at least 60 days before.

(g) Procedures vary for affiliated and previously unaffiliated or new voters. Kansas: unaffiliated voters may declare on election day; others must change affiliation at least 20 days before. Maine: unaffiliated voters may declare on election day; others must withdraw previous affiliation 90 days before. Massachusetts: unaffilated voters select party on election day; others must change affiliation at least 28 days before. New Jersey: new voters declare party on election day; others must change affiliation at least 50 days before. Oklahoma: new registrants declare at time of registration; however, no changes in affiliation are allowed between July 1 and September 30 in an even-numbered year. Rhode Island: unaffiliated voters declare on election day; affiliated voters must change at least 90 days before.

(h) Louisiana has an open primary which requires all candidates, regardless of party affiliation, to appear on a single ballot. If a candidate receives over 50 percent of the vote in the primary, he is elected to the office. If no candidate receives a majority vote, then a single election is held between the two candidates receiving the most votes.

(i) Previously affiliated voters may not change party affiliation after proclamation of primary.

(j) Business days.

Table 10
VOTER TURNOUT FOR PRESIDENTIAL ELECTIONS: 1972, 1976 AND 1980
(In thousands)

State or or other jurisdiction	1980 Voting age population (a)	1980 Number registered	1980 Number voting (b)	1976 Voting age population (a)	1976 Number registered	1976 Number voting (b)	1972 Voting age population (a)	1972 Number registered	1972 Number voting (b)
United States	164,383	112,946	86,519	152,309	105,838	82,645	140,776	92,702	78,902
Alabama	2,748	2,142	1,342	2,554	1,865	1,183	2,325	1,764	1,051
Alaska	274	259	158	257	207	128	203	149	99
Arizona	1,956	1,121	874	1,611	980	765	1,315	862	648
Arkansas	1,629	1,189	838	1,502	1,021	768	1,354	1,010	651
California	17,513	11,361	8,587	15,598	9,982	8,137	14,062	10,466	8,596
Colorado	2,114	1,434	1,184	1,838	1,349	1,082	1,604	1,220	954
Connecticut	2,307	1,706	1,406	2,201	1,669	1,408	2,091	1,648	1,409
Delaware	432	301	236	412	301	236	379	293	236
Florida	7,585	4,810	3,687	6,408	4,094	3,151	5,313	3,487	2,583
Georgia	3,868	2,467	1,597	3,494	2,302	1,467	3,153	2,043	1,179
Hawaii	696	403	303	624	363	309	547	338	287
Idaho	643	581	437	567	520	355	490	397	310
Illinois	8,224	6,212	4,750	7,939	6,252	4,839	7,576	6,215	4,883
Indiana	3,883	2,944	2,242	3,692	3,010	2,279	3,498	3,019	2,126
Iowa	2,091	1,747	1,318	2,026	1,407	1,279	1,917	(c)	1,226
Kansas	1,726	1,291	980	1,628	1,113	958	1,539	(c)	922
Kentucky	2,590	1,803	1,295	2,434	1,713	1,167	2,223	1,455	1,067
Louisiana	2,915	2,015	1,549	2,623	1,866	1,278	2,389	1,785	1,122
Maine	810	760	523	759	696	486	692	616	421
Maryland	3,082	2,065	1,540	2,920	1,950	1,440	2,721	1,816	1,354
Massachusetts	4,281	3,143	2,524	4,132	2,912	2,594	3,963	3,096	2,508
Michigan	6,526	5,726	3,910	6,214	5,202	3,722	5,876	4,763	3,490
Minnesota	2,927	2,787	2,052	2,726	2,566	1,979	2,537	(c)	1,774
Mississippi	1,716	1,486	893	1,603	(c)	769	1,462	N.A.	646
Missouri	3,577	2,841	2,100	3,408	2,553	1,954	3,240	(c)	1,866
Montana	559	496	364	519	455	339	470	387	327
Nebraska	1,128	856	641	1,081	841	624	1,021	712	592
Nevada...........	601	298	248	457	251	206	367	231	185
New Hampshire	671	551	384	593	478	359	525	450	345
New Jersey	5,417	3,761	2,976	5,220	3,770	3,037	5,010	3,673	3,030
New Mexico	896	653	457	783	527	426	669	505	396
New York	12,945	7,870	6,202	12,892	8,199	6,668	12,717	9,207	7,323
North Carolina	4,265	2,775	1,856	3,907	2,554	1,679	3,548	2,358	1,519
North Dakota	465	(c)	302	442	(c)	309	411	(c)	289
Ohio	7,731	5,887	4,284	7,461	4,693	4,195	7,149	4,628	4,220
Oklahoma	2,199	1,469	1,150	1,990	1,401	1,108	1,818	1,247	1,057
Oregon...........	1,921	1,569	1,182	1,679	1,420	1,049	1,495	1,198	953
Pennsylvania	8,785	5,754	4,562	8,531	5,750	4,621	8,207	5,872	4,592
Rhode Island......	710	547	416	689	545	411	682	532	416
South Carolina	2,204	1,236	894	1,993	1,113	803	1,762	1,034	674
South Dakota	485	448	328	469	426	301	443	392	308
Tennessee	3,313	2,359	1,618	3,033	1,912	1,476	2,763	1,990	1,201
Texas	10,117	6,640	4,542	8,789	6,319	4,072	7,719	5,500 (d)	3,471
Utah	936	782	604	791	705	548	689	621	480
Vermont	369	312	213	337	284	194	308	273	194
Virginia	3,920	2,309	1,866	3,613	2,124	1,716	3,257	2,107	1,457
Washington........	3,030	2,237	1,742	2,601	2,065	1,585	2,330	1,975	1,520
West Virginia	1,395	1,035	738	1,314	1,084	751	1,219	1,063	774
Wisconsin	3,383	(c)	2,273	3,163	2,566	2,104	2,965	(c)	1,853
Wyoming..........	332	219	177	267	195	160	226	N.A.	152
Dist. of Col.	493	289	175	525	268	171	537	305	166

Sources: U.S. Department of Commerce, Bureau of the Census, *Statistical Abstract of the United States, 1982-83.* (Compiled from U.S. Bureau of the Census, *Current Population Reports* and unpublished data from the National Republican Congressional Committee.)
   N.A.—Not available.

   (a) Estimated population as of November of year indicated. Includes armed forces in each state, aliens and institutional population.
   (b) For 1980, total persons voting are total votes cast for president. For 1972 and 1976, total persons voting restricted to number of ballots recorded by secretaries of state as having been cast for any electoral office or referendum; or in those states which do not count total number of ballots, the largest number of votes cast for a particular office.
   (c) No statewide registration required. Excluded from totals for persons registered.
   (d) Estimated.

Table 11
VOTER TURNOUT IN NON-PRESIDENTIAL ELECTION YEARS:
1974, 1978 AND 1982
(In thousands)

State or other jurisdiction	1982 Voting age population (a)	1982 Number registered	1982 Number voting (b)	1978 Voting age population (a)	1978 Number registered	1978 Number voting (b)	1974 Voting age population (a)	1974 Number registered	1974 Number voting (b)
United States	169,339	110,477	67,592	158,373	104,829	61,038	145,031	97,303	57,357
Alabama	2,812	2,136	1,128(c)	2,669	1,938	730(d)	2,404	1,793	598(c)
Alaska	287	266	195(c)	269	238	130	213	169	99
Arizona	2,061	1,141	726(c)	1,766	969	551	1,444	891	564
Arkansas	1,650	1,116	789(c)	1,575	1,047	524(c)	1,420	997	546(c)
California	18,277	11,559	7,876(c)	16,546	10,130	7,132	14,595	9,928	6,635
Colorado	2,225	1,456	956(c)	1,974	1,345	848	1,710	1,227	829(c)
Connecticut	2,378	1,647	1,084(c)	2,254	1,626	1,061	2,149	1,562	1,125
Delaware	443	286	191(d)	426	278	166	390	279	160(e)
Florida	8,169	4,866	2,689(c)	6,862	4,217	2,530	5,856	3,621	1,828(c)
Georgia	4,040	2,316	1,169(c)	3,667	2,183	663(c)	3,251	2,090	936(c)
Hawaii	716	405	312(c)	657	395	293	574	343	273
Idaho	661	541	327(c)	612	526	297	528	440	264
Illinois	8,346	5,965	3,691(f)	8,132	5,809	3,343	7,612	5,906	3,085
Indiana	3,904	2,937	1,817(d)	3,812	2,851	1,405	3,577	2,937	1,753(d)
Iowa	2,094	1,586	1,038(c)	2,075	1,588	843(c)	1,958	1,013	920(c)
Kansas	1,759	1,186	763(c)	1,681	1,182	749(d)	1,581	1,143	794(d)
Kentucky	2,620	1,827	700(e)	2,528	1,666	477(d)	2,284	1,473	746(d)
Louisiana.........	3,055	1,965	(g)	2,760	1,821	840	2,443	1,727	546(e)
Maine............	831	766	460(c)	791	692	375(d)	714	632	364(c)
Maryland	3,190	1,968	1,139(c)	3,014	1,888	1,012(c)	2,783	1,738	949(c)
Massachusetts......	4,394	3,027	2,051(d)	4,213	2,920	2,044	4,054	2,928	1,896
Michigan	6,554	5,625	3,040(c)	6,406	5,230	2,985	6,077	4,786	2,657(c)
Minnesota	2,988	2,668	1,805(d)	2,823	2,511	1,625	2,631	1,922	1,296
Mississippi	1,745	1,508	645(d)	1,672	1,150(h)	584(d)	1,505	1,152	306(e)
Missouri	3,640	2,749	1,544(d)	3,499	2,579	1,546(i)	3,306	2,165	1,224(d)
Montana	569	446	321(d)	548	410	297	494	374	260
Nebraska	1,144	832	548(c)	1,108	833	511	1,056	788	467
Nevada...........	661	322	240(d)	520	268	195	390	237	172
New Hampshire	697	462	285(c)	638	489	279	551	421	236
New Jersey	5,544	3,681	2,194(c)	5,326	3,602	2,060	5,070	3,502	2,184
New Mexico	936	583	407(c)	841	598	357	717	504	339
New York	13,153	7,635	5,222(c)	12,912	7,801	4,929	12,701	8,341	5,544
North Carolina	4,417	2,675	1,321(e)	4,088	2,430	1,136(d)	3,677	2,280	1,020(d)
North Dakota......	473	(j)	262(d)	455	(j)	235	425	(j)	242
Ohio..............	7,793	5,674	3,395(d)	7,638	5,222	3,018	7,296	4,442	3,151
Oklahoma	2,299	1,614	883(c)	2,081	1,366	801	1,872	1,341	822
Oregon............	1,954	1,517	1,042(c)	1,808	1,473	911(c)	1,581	1,143	793
Pennsylvania......	8,883	5,703	3,684(c)	8,673	5,590	3,742(c)	8,312	5,529	3,500(c)
Rhode Island.......	726	534	343(d)	707	534	332	654	514	322(c)
South Carolina	2,291	1,229	672(c)	2,104	1,098	633(d)	1,842	998	523(c)
South Dakota......	482	426	279(c)	480	421	260(c)	459	402	279(d)
Tennessee	3,375	2,273	1,260(d)	3,179	2,138	1,190(c)	2,859	1,960	1,064
Texas	10,793	6,415	3,191(c)	9,350	5,682	2,370(c)	8,075	5,348	1,655(c)
Utah..............	986	749	531(d)	858	667	385	741	620	423
Vermont	379	316	169(c)	353	286	125	316	267	145
Virginia	4,078	2,234	1,415(d)	3,794	2,027	1,251	3,375	2,051	924(e)
Washington	3,154	2,106	1,368(d)	2,792	1,961	1,029	2,419	1,896	1,044
West Virginia	1,408	948	565(d)	1,363	1,021	493	1,240	1,025	416(e)
Wisconsin	3,464	(j)	1,580(c)	3,263	1,682	1,501(c)	3,090	(j)	1,199
Wyoming..........	354	230	169(c)	296	201	142	245	185	132
Dist. of Col.	487	361	111(e)	515	250	103	515	273	108(k)

Sources: U.S. Department of Commerce, Bureau of the Census, *Statistical Abstract of the United States* and unpublished data from the Republican National Committee.

(a) Estimated as of November 1 of the year indicated. Includes armed forces stationed in each state, aliens and institutional population.

(b) Number represents total voting in general election for all races for the year indicated, except where noted. Total persons voting restricted to number of ballots recorded by secretaries of state as having been cast.

(c) Total vote for largest race—governor.

(d) Total vote for largest race—senator.

(e) Total vote for largest race—congressional.

(f) Total vote for largest race—secretary of state.

(g) Under Louisiana's election law, candidates of all parties run together on a single non-partisan ballot in September. If no candidate wins a majority of the vote, the top two finishers, regardless of party, oppose each other in a November runoff. In 1982, the congressional incumbents were reelected in the September race.

(h) Estimated.

(i) Total vote for largest race—state auditor.

(j) No required statewide registration.

(k) Total vote for largest race—mayor.

Table 12
VOTING STATISTICS FOR GUBERNATORIAL ELECTIONS

State	Primary			General election						
	Republican	Democrat	Total	Republican	Per-cent	Democrat	Per-cent	Other	Per-cent	Total
Alabama	unopposed	1,000,295 (a)	1,000,295	440,815	39.1	650,538	57.6	37,372	3.3	1,128,725
Alaska	81,732	55,315	137,047	72,291	37.1	89,918	46.1	32,676	16.7	194,885
Arizona	176,245	166,051	342,296	235,877	32.5	453,795	62.5	36,692	5.0	726,364
Arkansas	13,347	567,125 (a)	580,472	357,496	45.3	431,855	54.7	0	0.0	789,351
California	2,281,115	2,827,348	5,108,463	3,881,014	49.3	3,787,669	48.1	208,015	2.6	7,876,698
Colorado	unopposed	unopposed	0	302,740	31.7	627,960	65.7	25,321	2.6	956,021
Connecticut	(b)	(b)	(b)	497,773	45.9	578,264	53.4	8,119	0.7	1,084,156
Delaware †	unopposed	unopposed	0	159,004	70.6	64,217	28.5	1,860	0.8	225,081
Florida	376,448	993,534	1,369,982	949,013	35.3	1,739,553	64.7	0	0.0	2,688,566
Georgia	61,410	899,990 (a)	961,400	434,496	37.2	734,090	62.8	455	0.0	1,169,041
Hawaii	12,395	239,452	251,847	81,507	26.2	141,043	45.2	89,303	28.6	311,853
Idaho	99,554	unopposed	99,554	161,157	49.4	165,365	50.6	0	0.0	326,522
Illinois	606,446	unopposed	606,446	1,816,101	49.4	1,811,027	49.3	46,553	1.3	3,673,681
Indiana †	unopposed	541,961	541,961	1,257,383	57.7	913,116	41.9	7,904	0.4	2,178,403
Iowa	unopposed	196,071	196,071	548,313	52.8	483,291	46.5	6,625	0.6	1,038,229
Kansas	235,828	131,565	367,393	339,356	44.4	405,772	53.2	18,135	2.4	763,263
Kentucky §	97,836	658,454	756,290	454,650	44.1	561,674	54.5	14,347	1.4	1,030,671
Louisiana §	(c)	(c)	1,615,905	(c)	(c)	(c)	(c)	(c)	(c)	(c)
Maine	84,794	74,209	159,003	172,949	37.6	281,066	61.1	6,280	1.3	460,295
Maryland	134,590	590,648	725,238	432,826	38.0	705,910	62.0	413	0.0	1,139,149
Massachusetts	178,683	1,181,421	1,360,104	749,679	36.6	1,219,109	59.4	81,466	4.0	2,050,254
Michigan	641,377	810,184	1,451,561	1,369,582	45.1	1,561,291	51.4	109,135	3.5	3,040,008
Minnesota	309,292	538,603	847,895	715,796	40.0	1,049,104	58.6	24,639	1.4	1,789,539
Mississippi §	unopposed	828,211 (a)	828,211	288,764	38.9	409,209	55.1	44,764	6.0	742,737
Missouri †	352,079	665,557	1,017,636	1,098,950	52.6	981,884	47.0	7,194	0.3	2,088,028
Montana †	71,566	136,364	207,930	160,892	44.6	199,574	55.4	0	0.0	360,466
Nebraska	184,819	123,853	308,672	270,203	49.3	277,436	50.7	263	0.0	547,902
Nevada...........	68,986	108,236	177,222	100,104	41.8	128,132	53.4	11,515	4.8	239,751
New Hampshire	83,434	unopposed	83,434	145,389	51.9	132,287	46.4	4,882	1.7	282,588
New Jersey ‡	398,359	633,322	1,031,681	1,145,999	49.5	1,144,202	49.4	27,038	1.1	2,317,239
New Mexico	65,599	177,490	243,089	191,626	47.0	215,840	53.0	0	0.0	407,466
New York	576,045	1,297,256	1,873,301	2,494,827	47.5	2,675,213	50.9	84,851	1.6	5,254,891
North Carolina †	147,609	753,684	901,293	691,449	37.4	1,143,145	61.9	12,838	0.7	1,847,432
North Dakota †	79,322	unopposed	79,322	162,230	53.6	140,391	46.4	0	0.0	302,621
Ohio	673,564	1,030,418	1,703,982	1,303,962	38.9	1,981,882	59.0	70,877	2.1	3,356,721
Oklahoma	113,846	459,036	572,882	332,207	37.6	548,159	62.1	2,764	0.3	883,130
Oregon	252,798	313,376	566,174	639,841	61.4	374,316	35.9	27,852	2.7	1,042,009
Pennsylvania	unopposed	756,818	756,818	1,872,784	50.8	1,772,353	48.1	38,848	1.1	3,683,985
Rhode Island......	unopposed	unopposed	0	79,602	23.6	247,208	73.3	10,449	3.1	337,259
South Carolina	20,944	unopposed	20,944	202,806	30.2	468,819	69.8	0	0.0	671,625
South Dakota	unopposed	41,017	41,017	197,426	70.9	81,136	29.1	0	0.0	278,562
Tennessee	unopposed	635,830	635,830	737,963	59.6	500,937	40.4	27	0.0	1,238,927
Texas	265,851	1,317,814	1,583,665	1,465,937	45.9	1,697,870	53.2	27,284	0.9	3,191,091
Utah †	(b)	(b)	(b)	266,578	44.4	330,974	55.2	2,467	0.4	600,019
Vermont	unopposed	17,645	17,645	93,111	55.0	74,394	44.0	1,746	1.0	169,251
Virginia ‡	(b)	(b)	(b)	659,398	46.4	760,357	53.5	856	0.1	1,420,611
Washington †	399,577	569,950	969,527	981,083	56.7	749,813	43.3	0	0.0	1,730,896
West Virginia †	unopposed	321,002	321,002	337,240	45.4	401,863	54.1	3,047	0.4	742,150
Wisconsin	334,347	586,127	920,474	662,838	41.9	896,812	56.8	20,694	1.3	1,580,344
Wyoming..........	70,667	52,116	122,783	62,128	36.9	106,427	63.1	0	0.0	168,555

Source: *America Votes* and state election administration offices.
Note: Figures are for 1982 except where indicated: †1980; ‡1981; §1983.
(a) Total shown is for first Democratic primary. Total votes for runoff election: Alabama, 1,000,647; Arkansas, 445,567; Georgia, 911,024; Mississippi, 773,301.
(b) Candidates nominated by convention.
(c) Louisiana has an open primary which requires all candidates, regardless of party affiliation, to appear on a single ballot. If a candidate receives over 50 percent of the vote in the primary, he is elected to the office. If no candidate receives a majority vote, then a single election is held between the two candidates receiving the most votes. In 1983, 62.3 percent of the votes in the open primary were cast for one candidate, who was therefore considered elected.

3. Constitutions

STATE CONSTITUTIONS: 1982-1983

By Albert L. Sturm and Janice C. May

The pace of state constitutional change, both comprehensive and piecemeal, was somewhat slower in 1982-83 than during the preceding biennium, and far slower than in the 1970s. During 1982-83, a total of 345 proposed changes were submitted to the voters in 45 states; 258, including six amendments adopted in Delaware by legislative action only, were approved. As Table A indicates, the percentage of voter adoptions during 1982-83 was higher than during the previous biennium and very substantially higher than adoptions in 1970-71. Highlight of the past biennium was the ratification in November 1982 of Georgia's 10th constitution, which became effective July 1, 1983. Although no state constitutional convention was active during the period, the voters of New Hampshire approved a convention call in 1982. Also in 1982, a constitutional convention elected by the voters of the District of Columbia drafted a new constitution in preparation for hoped-for statehood. The relative decline of constitutional activity during the period probably resulted from state constitutional revision successes in the previous two decades, reducing the pressure for major changes. Other contributing factors were the diversion of state attention to pressing fiscal and policy issues in a time of recession, taxpayers' revolts and diminished federal aid.

Four methods of initiating proposals for constitutional amendment and revision have been authorized by the states: proposal by the state legislature, available in all states; the constitutional initiative, authorized by 17 state constitutions; the constitutional convention, which is expressly authorized in 41 organic laws but is available in all states; and the constitutional commission, which is specifically authorized only in the Florida constitution. Only the Florida document expressly provides for all four methods. In all states except Delaware, where action by the General Assembly only is required for proposal and adoption, all proposals must be submitted to the voters. Tables 2, 3 and 4 summarize the procedures for use of the three methods available in more than one state. During 1982-83, only legislative proposal and the constitutional initiative were used to propose constitutional change.

Legislative proposal, by far the most commonly used method of originating proposed alterations in state constitutions, accounted for 330 or 95.7 percent of the 345 proposals in 1982-83. The rate of adoptions is far higher than that of the other methods historically, and in 1982-83 reached 75.5 percent. In addition to proposing constitutional amendments, legislatures play other major roles in constitutional revision; in fact, they are the key actors in the process and have even proposed entire state constitutions. The constitutions of Florida, Georgia and Oregon expressly authorize the legislature to do so. The Georgia General Assembly exercised this power in initiating the revision process in 1977 and in finally approving a new constitution for submission to the voters at the November 1982 general election. In some states, exemplified by Virginia, the entire responsibility for initiating constitutional change rests with the legislature.

In contrast with legislative proposal, which may be used to originate all forms of constitutional alteration, the constitutional initiative is appropriate only for limited change. The constitutional initiative enables proponents of reform to have their proposals submitted to the electorate by petition when lawmaking bodies fail to act. Table 3 summarizes the salient requirements in the 17 states that authorize use of the constitutional initiative. The results of referendums over the years, which vary greatly in the degree of voter approval, reflect the ephemeral nature of popular support for initiative proposals. During 1982-83, only three of 15 constitutional initiatives submitted to the electorates in nine states were adopted, or only 20 percent. As Table A indicates, this was somewhat lower than the adoption rate in the preceding biennium and the same as that for 1970-71. The numbers of constitutional initiatives proposed and adopted in the nine states during the biennium were as follows:

Albert L. Sturm is Professor Emeritus, Center for Public Administration and Policy, Virginia Polytechnic Institute and State University, Blacksburg, Virginia, and Janice C. May is Associate Professor in the Department of Government, The University of Texas at Austin. They are co-authors of this and the following two articles.

California (2-0), Colorado (1-0), Michigan (2-0), Nebraska (1-1), Nevada (2-1), North Dakota (1-0), Ohio (4-0), Oregon (1-0) and South Dakota (1-1).

Probably no governmental institution is more American than the constitutional convention, which is the oldest, best known and most traditional method for extensive revision of an old constitution or writing a new one. Through 1983, at least 230 such bodies had been convened in American states. An increasing number of state constitutions require periodic submission to the voters of the question of calling a convention to consider constitutional revision. The number of such provisions has increased from eight in 1939 to 14 in 1983. As Table 4 indicates, eight states provide for submission of the convention question to the voters every 20 years, one state every 16 years, four states every 10 years, and one every nine years.

No state constitutional convention convened during 1982-83. In the November 1982 general election, however, the voters in three states—Alaska, Missouri and New Hampshire—voted on convention calls, in each case in compliance with the automatic submission requirement in their respective state constitutions. Results of the referendums were as follows: rejection by the electorates of Alaska (63,544 for, 107,855 against) and Missouri (402,742 for, 914,216 against); approval by the voters of New Hampshire (115,351 for, 105,027 against). Although the vote in New Hampshire was relatively close, the result was not unexpected. Until 1964, all constitutional amendments were proposed by conventions in that state, which has held 16 such constituent assemblies to lead all states in the use of this method of initiating proposed constitutional alterations.

As Table 6 indicates, New Hampshire's 16th constitutional convention, which adjourned June 26, 1974, is a continuing body officially for 10 years or until its successor is authorized and selected. The state's 17th constituent assembly is scheduled to convene on May 9, 1984. The 400 delegates (the same number as the membership of the lower house of the General Court) will be elected on February 28, 1984 from lower house districts on a nonpartisan basis. Funded by an appropriation not to exceed $400,000, the convention will have unlimited powers to propose alterations in the organic law. Proposed changes must be approved by a three-fifths vote of the convention delegates before submission to the voters.

Our summary in the last volume of *The Book of the States* indicated that on November 4, 1980 District of Columbia voters approved calling a constitutional convention to draft a constitution for submission to Congress as a basis for statehood (Vol. 24, p. 130). The 45 convention delegates, who were elected on a nonpartisan basis on November 3, 1981, convened on January 30, 1982 and approved a proposed "Constitution of the State of New Columbia" on May 29. Following voter ratification of the document on November 2, 1982 by a close vote of 61,405 to 54,964, the Mayor of the District transmitted it to Congress on September 9, 1983. On September 12, D.C. Delegate Fauntroy introduced H.R. 3861, the New Columbia Admissions Act, on which hearings are expected to be held in 1984.

Adoption of the New Columbia Admissions Act requires only a majority vote in each house of Congress. Any modification of the document will require resubmission to the voters of the District of Columbia. Otherwise, the document, if approved by Congress, would become effective and the state of New Columbia a member of the Union after a further approval by D.C. voters and a presidential proclamation.

Constitutional commissions serve two princi-

Table A

State Constitutional Changes by Method of Initiation
1970-71, 1980-81 and 1982-83

Method of Initiation	Number of states involved			Total proposals			Total adopted			Percentage adopted		
	1970 -71	1980 -81	1982 -83	1970 -71	1980 -81	1982 -83	1970 -71	1980 -81	1982 -83	1970 -71	1980 -81	1982 -83
All methods	48	46	45	403	388	345	224	272	258	55.6	70.1	73.0 (a)
Legislative proposal	47	46	45	392	362	330	222	265	255	55.6	73.2	75.5 (a)
Constitutional initiative	4	11	9	5	18	15	1	5	3	20.0	27.8	20.0
Constitutional convention	2	2	-	6	8	-	1	2	-	16.7	25.0	-
Constitutional commission	-	-	-	-	-	-	-	-	-	-	-	-

(a) In calculating these percentages, the six amendments adopted in Delaware (where proposals are not submitted to the voters) are excluded.

pal purposes: to study the state constitution and recommend appropriate changes, and to prepare for a constitutional convention. As shown in Table 5, during 1982-83 constitutional commissions operated officially in three states—Georgia, Utah and New Hampshire. The Georgia and Utah commissions are study commissions, which comprise by far the larger number and usually serve as auxiliary staff arms or legislative assemblies, which normally have full discretion to accept, modify, or reject their recommendations. The New Hampshire body was established primarily to make preparations for the constitutional convention scheduled to convene in May 1984.

In Georgia, the Select Committee on Constitutional Revision provided overall policy direction and coordination for revision and drafting of the state's 10th constitution. Created initially in 1977, the life of this body has been extended officially to June 30, 1986. The Select Committee's activities diminished greatly after adoption of the constitution in November 1982, but it continued to operate officially through 1983. Besides legislative implementation of the new constitution's provisions, much attention in the immediate future will be directed to the disposition of approximately 1,200 local amendments ratified by Georgia voters over the years. In addressing the problem of local amendments, the Office of Legislative Counsel has played, and will continue to play, a major role.

The Utah Constitutional Revision Commission, which has been a permanent body since 1977, is mandated to report recommendations for constitutional revision to the legislature at least 60 days before each legislature convenes. Through 1983, voter action on the commission's recommendations has included approval of revised articles on the executive branch and revenue and taxation, after having previously rejected proposed revisions of these articles, and actions on more limited changes. The commission will submit proposed revisions of the legislative, judicial and education articles for legislative review in 1984.

To prepare for the 1984 constitutional convention, the New Hampshire General Court created a 10-member Constitutional Convention Task Force. Members of this preparatory body were appointed by the speaker of the house (3), the president of the senate (3), the governor (2) and the state Supreme Court (2). In addition to studying the constitution and recommending needed changes to the convention, the task force was directed to prepare a report containing any proposed changes with supporting factual and explanatory data for wide general distribution by January 1984. Organized during the fall, the task force held a series of public hearings throughout the state in late 1983. Recommendations of this body will provide a major basis for the deliberations of the state's 17th convention scheduled to convene May 9, 1984.

STATE CONSTITUTIONAL CHANGES

By Albert L. Sturm and Janice C. May

Adoption of Georgia's 10th constitution in November 1982 was the only comprehensive constitutional revision that occurred in 1982-83. Salient substantive features of the new Georgia document were summarized in the last volume of *The Book of the States* (Vol. 24, p. 119). A proposed new constitution for Alabama, submitted by the legislature, was scheduled for voter action at the November 8, 1983 election only to be removed from the ballot less than a week before the election by the Alabama Supreme Court. The Court ruled that only a constitutional convention, the call for which must be approved by the voters, was authorized by the Alabama constitution to propose a new constitution (*Seigelman v. Manley*, 18 A.B.R.90, decided November 2, 1983). Generally, piecemeal changes characterized constitutional revision during the biennium, although a few states approved revisions of entire articles in their organic laws and some achieved limited editorial revision.

Table B provides a rough index of the general subject matter of constitutional changes during the last two bienniums and in 1970-71. All proposals are grouped into two major categories: those of statewide application, which are by far the most numerous and involved 45 states during 1982-83; and proposed local amendments, submitted by the legislatures in six states. Of the 226 statewide proposals in 1982-83, 149 or 65.9 percent were adopted, an adoption percentage slightly higher than during the preceding biennium and substantially greater than in 1970-71. The rate of adoption of local amendments, 107 of 123 or 87 percent, was substantially greater than that for the statewide proposals and the highest of the bienniums cited in Table B. Statewide amendments are further classified under the principal areas of state constitutional systems, which are identified for convenience by the titles of articles found in practically all state constitutions.

By far the largest number of proposals during the current and other bienniums cited in Table B related to taxation and finance, encompassing taxation, debt and fiscal administration. Excepting the new constitution approved by the Georgia voters (tabulated under general revision pro-

posals), the highest rate of adoption of statewide proposals was achieved by proposed changes in state bills of rights, followed by adoption percentages of 80 percent or better for proposals relating to suffrage and elections, the judiciary, and miscellaneous proposals.

Most changes affecting individual rights concerned criminal justice, with approximately half relating to limitations on the right to bail. California voters approved a "Victims' Bill of Rights," which repealed the existing guarantee of the right of bail and added new provisions altering criminal justice procedures, punishments and constitutional rights, including provisions for restitution to victims, right to safe schools, admission of relevant evidence, public safety bail and use of prior convictions. Massachusetts restored the death penalty. A few states, including Nevada and New Hampshire, specified a right to keep and bear arms under stated conditions. The right to be free from unreasonable searches and seizures was the subject of an approved Florida amendment.

Alterations concerning suffrage and elections included removal by Idaho voters of obsolete and gender-biased language and provisions nullified by the U.S. Constitution or U.S. Supreme Court decisions, such as lowering the voting age to 18. Virginia made changes in the voter registration certificate but rejected a provision authorizing the restoration of the rights of felons, which would apply to voting. The Delaware General Assembly approved the use of absentee ballots by persons unable to vote on a particular day because of religious belief.

Ranking next to taxation and finance in the number of proposed constitutional changes during the biennium were the three branches of government, with those concerning the legislature outnumbering the others. The judicial proposals, however, enjoyed the higher adoption rate, which occurred in two of the three bienniums cited in Table B.

Proposed changes concerning the legislative branch related mainly to members and their compensation, reapportionment, legislative organization and procedure, and legislative powers. Washington voters approved establishment of a bipartisan reapportionment commission, but a similar commission was rejected in California. Missouri rejected a commission to redraw congressional districts, but approved revision of procedures for state legislative redistricting. Of several legislative compensation proposals, a salary commission was approved in Utah but rejected in Arizona (where the proposal included other elective state officers). Montana voters authorized the legislature to override a post-session veto through a poll of its members by the secretary of state. Legislative review of administrative regulations was approved in Connecticut, but rejected in Missouri. Texas voters approved a provision for alternate legislators and other legislative changes in times of enemy attack. Legislative reforms rejected included four-year legislative terms in North Carolina and Rhode Island, annual sessions in Montana, and removal of the lieutenant governor as president of the senate in California.

State electorates approved only nine of 19 proposals concerning the executive branch. In Texas, the governor lost authority over paroles but gained the power to appoint all members of the Board of Pardons and Paroles. In South Carolina, the secretary of agriculture was added to the state elective offices, and the Georgia electorate rejected the prohibition against governors succeeding themselves. New Hampshire voters turned down the four-year term for governor; Michigan voters disapproved a department of state police; North Dakota voters defeated election of the governor and lieutenant governor in off-year, nonpresidential elections; and Ohio voters rejected election of the public utilities commission.

Proposed changes in state judiciaries, dealing mainly with selection, tenure and assignment of judges, court organization and structure, and jurisdiction, met with a large measure of success. New appellate courts were approved in Connecticut and Minnesota. Mississippi voters adopted a comprehensive judicial redistricting proposal. Alaska and Colorado approved alterations in their commissions on judicial conduct, and Alabama voters authorized establishment of a judicial compensation commission. An Idaho amendment provided for the Chief Justice of the Supreme Court to serve as administrative head of the courts, as well as his election by a majority of Supreme Court justices for a four-year term. In North Carolina, recall of judges in the appellate division for temporary service was adopted, New Mexico voters rejected a proposal for merit selection of judges, and Texas voters authorized temporary transfers of probate judges and a re-

duction in the number of justices of the peace. Various jurisdictional changes were approved in Missouri, Nevada and North Carolina; others were rejected in Arkansas and Nevada.

Local government proposals covered many subjects, including some dealing with local finance. The new article governing political subdivisions adopted in North Dakota included provisions for county home rule and authorization for extensive intergovernmental cooperation. Voters in at least four states took action on proposals concerning the office of sheriff, with approvals in Delaware and Wisconsin, rejections in New Mexico and West Virginia. In Alabama, the voters validated a law establishing eight classes of municipalities and adopted an authorization for compensation of county officers. Idaho approved a four-year term for prosecuting attorneys in counties. In Ohio, a proposal for a high-speed intercity passenger transportation system was rejected. Oklahoma voters turned down a regional transportation authority.

Substantive changes in finance and taxation articles (including state and local debt) are almost too numerous to classify, comprising one-third of the 226 statewide proposals. Excepting Utah where a revised article on taxation was adopted and Colorado's approval of a general revision of the property tax provisions, piecemeal revision was the general rule during 1982-83. The property tax continued to draw numerous amendments, including exemptions (some approved, some rejected), property tax classification to permit different tax rates and assessment ratios, and abolition of the state property tax (Texas). Housing financed by state bonds was approved in at least three states; in two, this applied only to veterans. Several new trust funds were established, although Oklahoma voters rejected such a proposal. In Louisiana, the Louisiana Investment Fund for Enhancement (LIFE) was created to capture windfall revenues from deregulation of oil and gas. These are illustrative of the wide variety of proposed changes dealing with tax levies, assessments, exemptions, financial administration and policy and other financial matters on which voters acted during the biennium.

In comparison with 1978-79, when California voters by approving Proposition 13 initiated a series of taxpayers' revolts in numerous states, no major fiscal limitation was adopted in the past biennium. In fact, Ohio voters in 1983 rejected a much publicized rollback, an initiative proposal that would have nullified, as of June 30, 1984, changes in the tax laws enacted between January 1, 1983 and the effective date of the proposed amendment, including recent increases in the state income tax. Also, the Ohio electorate rejected an initiative that raised from a simple majority to a three-fifths majority the vote required in both legislative chambers for approval of new taxes. The proposal closest to a general fiscal limitation was adopted in Alaska, where a spending limitation was imposed; however, the voters will be able to reconsider it at the 1986 general election.

Alterations were made in various policy areas of state constitutional systems during 1982-83. Most prominent of these was public education, including both primary and secondary and higher education; other principal areas with changes during the biennium included corporations, natural resources and the environment, state institutions, public works and welfare.

Only two proposals submitted to the voters in the biennium concerned amendment and revision of state constitutions. In Alabama, a new procedure for approving proposed constitutional amendments affecting only one county was adopted. Missouri voters rejected proposed changes in the method of selecting delegates to a constitutional convention.

Of the 10 proposals in the miscellaneous category, eight or 80 percent were adopted. The two rejections related to gambling: North Dakota voters rejected an initiative proposal for limitation of authorized gambling to raffles and bingo, and the South Dakota electorate refused authorization for the legislature to provide for games of chance, subject to local option. Minnesota voters authorized on-track parimutuel betting on horse racing in a manner provided by law. Other approved changes concerned sovereign immunity (Georgia), boundaries (Nevada), and editorial revision (Wisconsin).

Local amendments, which apply to only one or a few political subdivisions, comprised more than a third of the total proposals submitted to the voters. Six states, located mainly in the South, accounted for these proposals. They were: Alabama (42 proposed, 36 adopted), Georgia (76 proposed, 68 adopted), Louisiana (1 proposed and rejected), Maryland (2 proposed and adopted), Missouri (1 proposed and rejected), and Texas (1 proposed and adopted). Although the percentage of adoptions for local amendments is substantially greater than for statewide proposals, they have long been acknowledged to be a problem by constitution makers. One of the most significant features of the new Georgia constitution is elimination of the need for local amendments.

Finally, it is appropriate to note the major substantive contents of the proposed constitution for New Columbia, which was approved by D.C. voters and has been submitted to Congress. Containing 18 articles, 250 sections, and approximately 18,000 words, the document is highly unusual in proposing numerous reforms, both traditional and novel. Salient features include: a bill of rights containing guarantees for various new "freedoms," "rights," and "privileges," some of controversial nature; a 40-member unicameral legislature to be elected from single-member districts for four-year terms; requirement of a code of ethics governing members of the three branches of government; joint election of the governor and lieutenant governor for four-year terms with ineligibility for re-election after two

Table B

Substantive Changes in State Constitutions:
Proposed and Adopted, 1970-71, 1980-81, 1982-83

Subject Matter	Total Proposed			Total Adopted			Percentage Adopted		
	1970-71	1980-81	1982-83	1970-71	1980-81	1982-83	1970-71	1980-81	1982-83
Proposals of statewide applicability	300	254	226	176	160	149	58.2	63.0	65.9
Bill of rights	13	13	13	11	10	13	84.6	76.9	100.0
Suffrage and elections	39	5	5	23	5	4	59.0	100.0	80.0
Legislative branch	42	43	32	19	21	18	45.2	48.8	56.3
Executive branch	27	21	19	22	10	9	81.5	47.6	47.4
Judicial branch	17	23	26	11	17	21	64.7	73.9	80.8
Local government	21	11	13	15	4	9	71.4	36.4	69.2
Finance and taxation	50	77	48	29	52	28	58.0	67.5	58.3
State and local debt	25	20	26	10	13	19	40.0	65.0	73.1
State functions	46	23	31	26	16	18	56.5	69.6	58.1
Amendment and revision	13	9	2	7	7	1	53.8	77.8	50.0
General revision proposals	7	1	1	3	0	1	42.9	0	100.0
Miscellaneous proposals	(a)	8	10	(a)	5	8	(a)	62.5	80.0
Local amendments	103	134	123	48	112	107	46.6	83.6	87.0

(a) Not compiled for 1970-71.

terms; appointment of department heads by the governor subject to advice and consent of the legislature; limitation of principal executive departments to 20, with specified exceptions; a two-tiered, unified judicial system; selection of judges/justices by gubernatorial appointment from nominations by a judicial nomination commission; life tenure for judges/justices subject to retention elections at specified intervals; inclusion of articles on education, land and the environment, banking and corporations, public services, labor, apportionment, the initiative, referendum and recall, and intergovernmental relations. Principal criticisms of the document have focused on provisions that permit public employees to strike, guarantee a right to employment, abolish sovereign immunity, and make various change in the criminal justice system.

SOURCES ON STATE CONSTITUTIONS

By Albert L. Sturm and Janice C. May

The biennium saw a few additions to the large body of materials on state constitutions and constitutional revision accumulated over the years, much of it during the productive 1960s and 1970s. One development of particular significance was the publication in 1982 of the second series of *Sources and Documents of United States Constitutions*, a valuable reference collection edited and annotated by William F. Swindler. The original series of 10 volumes included annotations of the significant sections of state constitutions, historical background notes, analytical tables tracing the development of specific provisions in successive constitutions, a selected bibliography and a separate index for each state. Composed of three volumes, the new series is designed to integrate national and state constitutional documents into a "complete reference collection on American constitutional development as a whole," including chronologies and indices. A comparative analysis of state constitutional subjects in Volume 2 complements the *Model State Constitution* and the *Index Digest of State Constitutions*. The *Model State Constitution*, first published in 1921 by the National Municipal League (recently renamed the Citizens Forum on Self-Government) and since revised six times, most recently in 1968, has been widely recognized and used as a valuable resource on constitutional revision. The *Index Digest of State Constitutions*, which was first prepared for the New York Constitutional Convention of 1915 by the Legislative Drafting Research Fund of Columbia University, was revised in 1959. In 1980, the fund introduced the first of a series of subject matter indices that will replace the *Index Digest*. The second in the series was released in October 1982.

Another source of documents for state constitutions from 1776 to 1978 is the Congressional Information Service (CIS). One collection consists of major publications of state constitutional conventions and commissions active between 1776 and 1959; the second collection covering the years 1959 to 1978 includes official publications of revision bodies as well as those relating to amendment by legislative proposal and constitutional initiative and even unofficial items. All of these are on microfiches. The two-volume bibliographical guide issued by CIS to accompany the 1959 to 1978 file is a helpful reference in its own right.

Illustrative of innovations in citizen education on state constitutions and general constitutional principles is *A Citizen's Guide to the Alaska Constitution* by George S. Harrison, published in 1982 by the University of Alaska. Modeled after the *Citizens' Guide to the Texas Constitution* (1972) and the *Citizens' Guide to the Proposed New Texas Constitution* (1975) by George Braden, the Alaska *Guide* was prepared in time for citizens to evaluate the need for a constitutional convention to revise the Alaska constitution. As noted earlier, the call for a convention was on the November 1982 general election ballot.

Also during the biennium, the literature on state constitutional law continued to grow in what has been called a rediscovery of state constitutions by the legal profession. Illustrative of recent legal articles are a special 100-page section on the Connecticut Constitution in the *Connecticut Law Review*, 15 (Fall 1982): 1-107 and a 178-page interpretive study in the *Harvard Law Review* entitled, "The Interpretation of State Constitutional Rights" 95 (April 1982): 1326-1502.

The selected list of references at the end of the summary analysis necessarily excludes many specific items on constitutional reform efforts in particular states and numerous special studies. Students, planners and participants in constitutional revision should consult official proceedings, debates and reports of state constitutional conventions and state constitutional commissions and special studies prepared for constitution making in given states, as well as publications of The Council of State Governments, the U.S. Advisory Commission on Intergovernmental Relations, the Citizens Forum on Self-Government and the League of Women Voters. Particularly useful are complete, annotated and comparative analyses of the Illinois and Texas constitutions prepared for the delegates to the constitutional conventions in those states in the 1970s. In addition, a vast quantity of ephemeral materials is stored in the archives and libraries of states where major constitutional reform efforts have occurred. Excepting the holdings in the Library of Congress, probably the most extensive collections of fugitive and published materials on state constitutions are those of the Citizens Forum on Self-Government and The Council of State Governments.

Two sources of periodic reviews and updates of state constitutional developments are the biennial summaries of official actions in *The Book of the States* and the annual surveys in the *National Civic Review,* which have appeared in the January or February issue each year since 1970. Written by one of the authors, the latter contains state-by-state accounts of substantive changes during the year. A 50-year review of state constitutional materials is included in the biennial survey of state constitutional developments in *The Book of the States, 1982-83.*

Selected Bibliography

Browne, Cynthia E., comp. *State Constitutional Conventions: From Independence to the Completion of the Present Union. A Bibliography.* Westport, Conn.: Greenwood Press, 1973.

Clem, Alan L., ed. *Contemporary Approaches to State Constitutional Revision.* Vermillion, S.D.: Governmental Research Bureau, University of South Dakota, 1970.

Constitutions of the United States: National and State. 2nd ed. 2 vols. Dobbs Ferry, N.Y.: Oceana Publications, 1974. Loose leaf. Updated periodically.

Cornwell, Elmer E., Jr., et al. *Constitutional Conventions: The Politics of Revision.* New York, N.Y.: National Municipal League, 1974. (In second series of the National Municipal League's *State Constitution Studies.*)

Dishman, Robert B. *State Constitutions: The Shape of the Document.* Rev. ed. New York, N.Y.: National Municipal League, 1968. (In first series of the National Municipal League's *State Constitution Studies.*)

Edwards, William A., ed. *Index Digest of State Constitutions.* 2nd ed. Dobbs Ferry, N.Y.: Oceana Publications, 1959. Prepared by the Legislative Drafting Research Fund, Columbia University.

Elazar, Daniel J., ed. Series of articles on American state constitutions and the constitutions of selected foreign states. *Publius: The Journal of Federalism* 12, 2 (Winter 1982): entire issue.

Grad, Frank P. *The State Constitution: Its Function and Form for Our Time.* New York, N.Y.: National Municipal League, 1968. Reprinted from *Virginia Law Review* 54, 5 (June 1968). (In first series of the National Municipal League's *State Constitution Studies.*)

Graves, W. Brooke. "State Constitutional Law: A Twenty-five Year Summary." *William and Mary Law Review* 8, 1 (Fall 1966): 1-48.

_____, ed. *Major Problems in State Constitutional Revision.* Chicago: Public Administration Service, 1960.

Leach, Richard H., ed. *Compacts of Antiquity: State Constitutions.* Atlanta, Ga.: Southern Newspaper Publishers Association Foundation, 1969.

May, Janice C. "Texas Constitutional Revision: Lessons and Laments." *National Civic Review* 66, 2 (February 1977): 64-69.

_____. *The Texas Constitutional Revision Experience in the Seventies.* Austin, Tx.: Sterling Swift Publishing Company, 1975.

Model State Constitution. 6th ed. New York, N.Y.: National Municipal League, 1963. Revised 1968.

Pisciotte, Joseph P., ed. *Studies in Illinois Constitution Making.* 10 vols. Urbana, Ill.: University of Illinois Press, 1972-1980.

Sachs, Barbara Faith, ed. *Index to Constitutions of the United States: National and State.* London, Rome and New York: Oceana Publications, 1980. Prepared by the Legislative Drafting Research Fund, Columbia University. The first two in the series are: *Fundamental Liberties and Rights: A Fifty-State Index* (1980), and *Laws, Legislatures and Legislative Procedures: A Fifty-State Index* (1982).

State Constitutional Convention Studies. 11 vols. New York, N.Y.: National Municipal League, 1969-1978.

State Constitution Studies. 10 vols. in two series. New York, N.Y.: National Municipal League, 1960-1965.

State Constitutional Conventions, Commissions, and Amendments, 1959-1978: An Annotated Bibliography. 2 vols. Washington, D.C.: Congressional Information Service, 1981. This bibliography incorporates the contents of the following two supplements to the Browne bibliography:

> Yarger, Susan Rice, comp. *State Constitutional Conventions, 1959-1975: A Bibliography.* Westport, Conn.: Greenwood Press, 1976.

> Canning, Bonnie, comp. *State Constitutional Conventions, Revisions, and Amendments, 1959-1976: A Bibliography.* Westport, Conn.: Greenwood Press, 1977.

State Constitutional Conventions, Commissions, and Amendments on Microfiche. 4 pts. [Microform]. Westport, Conn.: Greenwood Press, 1972-76; Washington, D.C.: Congressional Information Service, 1977-1981.

Sturm, Albert L. *A Bibliography on State Constitutions and Constitutional Revision, 1945-1975.* Englewood, Colo.: The Citizens Conference on State Legislatures, August 1975.

_____. Annual summary analyses of state constitutional developments. Published in the January or February issues of the *National Civic Review* since 1970.

_____. *Thirty Years of State Constitution Making, 1938-1968.* New York, N.Y.: National Municipal League, 1970.

Swindler, William F., ed. *Sources and Documents of United States Constitutions.* 10 vols. Dobbs Ferry, N.Y.: Oceana Publications, Inc., 1973-1979.

_____. ed. *Sources and Documents of United States Constitutions.* Second Series. 3 vols. Dobbs Ferry, N.Y.: Oceana Publications, Inc., 1982-1983.

Wheeler, John P., Jr. *The Constitutional Convention: A Manual on Its Planning, Organization and Operation.* New York, N.Y.: National Municipal League, 1961.

_____. ed. *Salient Issues of Constitutional Revision.* New York, N.Y.: National Municipal League, 1961.

Table 1
GENERAL INFORMATION ON STATE CONSTITUTIONS
(As of December 31, 1983)

State or other jurisdiction	Number of consti-tutions*	Dates of adoption	Effective date of present constitution	Estimated length (number of words)	Number of amendments Submitted to voters	Adopted
Alabama	6	1819, 1861, 1865, 1868, 1875, 1901	Nov. 28, 1901	172,000	640	443
Alaska	1	1956	Jan. 3, 1959	13,000	26	19
Arizona	1	1911	Feb. 14, 1912	28,876(a)	176	104
Arkansas	5	1836, 1861, 1864, 1868, 1874	Oct. 30, 1874	40,720(a)	151	69(b)
California	2	1849, 1879	July 4, 1879	33,350	745	442
Colorado	1	1876	Aug. 1, 1876	43,215	223	105
Connecticut	4	1818(c), 1965	Dec. 30, 1965	8,575	21	20
Delaware	4	1776, 1792, 1831, 1897	June 10, 1897	19,000	(d)	113
Florida	6	1839, 1861, 1865, 1868, 1886, 1968	Jan. 7, 1969	25,100	55	34
Georgia	10	1777, 1789, 1798, 1861, 1865, 1868, 1877, 1945, 1976, 1982	July 1, 1983	25,000	0	0
Hawaii	1(f)	1950	Aug. 21, 1959	17,466(a)	81	75
Idaho	1	1889	July 3, 1890	21,500	181	102
Illinois	4	1818, 1848, 1870, 1970	July 1, 1971	13,200	6	3
Indiana	2	1816, 1851	Nov. 1, 1851	10,225(a)	63	34
Iowa	2	1846, 1857	Sept. 3, 1857	12,500	46	43(g)
Kansas	1	1859	Jan. 29, 1861	11,865	107	80(g)
Kentucky	4	1792, 1799, 1850, 1891	Sept. 28, 1891	23,500	53	25
Louisiana	11	1812, 1845, 1852, 1861, 1864, 1868, 1879, 1898, 1913, 1921, 1974	Jan. 1, 1975	36,146(a)	19	15
Maine	1	1819	March 15, 1820	13,500	175	150(h)
Maryland	4	1776, 1851, 1864, 1867	Oct. 5, 1867	41,055	226	194
Massachusetts	1	1780	Oct. 25, 1780	36,675(a,i)	141	116
Michigan	4	1835, 1850, 1908, 1963	Jan. 1, 1964	20,000	38	14
Minnesota	1	1857	May 11, 1858	9,500	201	107
Mississippi	4	1817, 1832, 1869, 1890	Nov. 1, 1890	23,500	123	54
Missouri	4	1820, 1865, 1875, 1945	March 30, 1945	42,000	93	56
Montana	2	1889, 1972	July 1, 1973	11,866(a)	15	8
Nebraska	2	1866, 1875	Oct. 12, 1875	20,048(a)	272	179
Nevada	1	1864	Oct. 31, 1864	20,770	157	99(g)
New Hampshire	2	1776, 1784(k)	June 2, 1784	9,200	176(j)	77(j)
New Jersey	3	1776, 1844, 1947	Jan. 1, 1948	17,086	42	32
New Mexico	1	1911	Jan. 6, 1912	27,100	212	103
New York	4	1777, 1822, 1846, 1894	Jan. 1, 1895	80,000	263	197
North Carolina	3	1776, 1868, 1970	July 1, 1971	11,000	28	22
North Dakota	1	1889	Nov. 2, 1889	31,000	203(k)	115(k)
Ohio	2	1802, 1851	Sept. 1, 1851	36,900	240	141
Oklahoma	1	1907	Nov. 16, 1907	68,500	237(l)	107(l)
Oregon	1	1857	Feb. 14, 1859	25,100	341	171
Pennsylvania	5	1776, 1790, 1838, 1873, 1968(m)	1968	21,675	20(m)	15(m)
Rhode Island	2	1842(c)	May 2, 1843	19,026(a,i)	82	43
South Carolina	7	1776, 1778, 1790, 1861, 1865, 1868, 1895	Jan. 1, 1896	22,500(n)	628(o)	444(o)
South Dakota	1	1889	Nov. 2, 1889	23,300	177	92
Tennessee	3	1796, 1835, 1870	Feb. 23, 1870	15,300	55	32
Texas	5	1845, 1861, 1866, 1869, 1876	Feb. 15, 1876	62,000	408	263
Utah	1	1895	Jan. 4, 1896	17,500	116	68
Vermont	3	1777, 1786, 1793	July 9, 1793	6,600	206	49
Virginia	6	1776, 1830, 1851, 1869, 1902, 1970	July 1, 1971	18,500	17	14
Washington	1	1889	Nov. 11, 1889	29,400	135	74
West Virginia	2	1863, 1872	April 9, 1872	25,600	91	55
Wisconsin	1	1848	May 29, 1848	13,500	161	118(g)
Wyoming	1	1889	July 10, 1890	31,800	87	49
American Samoa	2	1960, 1967	July 1, 1967	6,000	13	7
No. Mariana Islands	1	1977	Oct. 24, 1977	---	---	---
Puerto Rico	1	1952	July 25, 1952	9,281(a)	6	6

GENERAL INFORMATION ON STATE CONSTITUTIONS—Notes

*The constitutions referred to in this table include those Civil War documents customarily listed by the individual states.

(a) Actual word count.

(b) Eight of the approved amendments have been superseded and are not printed in the current edition of the constitution. The total adopted does not include five amendments that were invalidated.

(c) Colonial charters with some alterations served as the first constitutions in Connecticut (1638, 1662) and in Rhode Island (1663).

(d) Proposed amendments are not submitted to the voters in Delaware.

(e) The new Georgia constitution eliminates the need for local amendments, which have been a long-term problem for state constitution makers.

(f) As a kingdom and a republic, Hawaii had five constitutions.

(g) The figure given includes amendments approved by the voters and later nullified by the state supreme court in Iowa (three), Kansas (one), Nevada (six) and Wisconsin (two).

(h) The figure does not include one amendment approved by the voters in 1967 that is inoperative until implemented by legislation.

(i) The printed constitution includes many provisions that have been annulled. The length of effective provisions is an estimated 24,122 words (12,490 annulled) in Massachusetts and 11,399 words (7,627 annulled) in Rhode Island.

(j) The constitution of 1784 was extensively revised in 1792. Figures show proposals and adoptions since 1793, when the revised constitution became effective.

(k) The figures do not include submission and approval of the constitution of 1889 itself and of Article XX; these are constitutional questions included in some counts of constitutional amendments and would add two to the figure in each column.

(l) The figures include five amendments submitted to, and approved by,the voters which were, by decisions of the Oklahoma or U.S. Supreme Courts, rendered inoperative or ruled invalid, unconstitutional, or illegally submitted.

(m) Certain sections of the constitution were revised by the limited constitutional convention of 1967-68. Amendments proposed and adopted are since 1968.

(n) Of the estimated length, approximately two-thirds is of general statewide effect; the remainder is local amendments.

(o) Of the 626 proposed amendments submitted to the voters, 130 were of general statewide effect and 496 were local; the voters rejected 83 (12 statewide, 71 local). Of the remaining 543, the General Assembly refused to approve 100 (22 statewide, 78 local), and 443 (96 statewide, 347 local) were finally added to the constitution.

Table 2
CONSTITUTIONAL AMENDMENT PROCEDURE: BY THE LEGISLATURE
Constitutional Provisions

State or other jurisdiction	Legislative vote required for proposal(a)	Consideration by two sessions required	Vote required for ratification	Limitation on the number of amendments submitted at one election
Alabama	3/5	No	Majority vote on amendment	None
Alaska	2/3	No	Majority vote on amendment	None
Arizona	Majority	No	Majority vote on amendment	None
Arkansas	Majority	No	Majority vote on amendment	3
California	2/3	No	Majority vote on amendment	None
Colorado	2/3	No	Majority vote on amendment	None(b)
Connecticut	(c)	(c)	Majority vote on amendment	None
Delaware	2/3	Yes	Not required	No referendum
Florida	3/5	No	Majority vote on amendment	None
Georgia	2/3	No	Majority vote on amendment	None
Hawaii	(d)	(d)	Majority vote on amendment(e)	None
Idaho	2/3	No	Majority vote on amendment	None
Illinois	3/5	No	(f)	3 articles
Indiana	Majority	Yes	Majority vote on amendment	None
Iowa	Majority	Yes	Majority vote on amendment	None
Kansas	2/3	No	Majority vote on amendment	5
Kentucky	3/5	No	Majority vote on amendment	4
Louisiana	2/3	No	Majority vote on amendment(g)	None
Maine	2/3(h)	No	Majority vote on amendment	None
Maryland	3/5	No	Majority vote on amendment	None
Massachusetts	Majority(i)	Yes	Majority vote on amendment	None
Michigan	2/3	No	Majority vote on amendment	None
Minnesota	Majority	No	Majority vote in election	None
Mississippi	2/3(j)	No	Majority vote on amendment	None
Missouri	Majority	No	Majority vote on amendment	None
Montana	2/3(h)	No	Majority vote on amendment	None
Nebraska	3/5	No	Majority vote on amendment(e)	None
Nevada	Majority	Yes	Majority vote on amendment	None
New Hampshire	3/5	No	2/3 vote on amendment	None
New Jersey	(k)	(k)	Majority vote on amendment	None(l)
New Mexico	Majority(m)	No	Majority vote on amendment(m)	None
New York	Majority	Yes	Majority vote on amendment	None
North Carolina	3/5	No	Majority vote on amendment	None
North Dakota	Majority	No	Majority vote on amendment	None
Ohio	3/5	No	Majority vote on amendment	None
Oklahoma	Majority	No	Majority vote on amendment	None
Oregon	(n)	No	Majority vote on amendment	None
Pennsylvania	Majority(o)	Yes(o)	Majority vote on amendment	None
Rhode Island	Majority	No	Majority vote on amendment	None
South Carolina	2/3(p)	Yes(p)	Majority vote on amendment	None
South Dakota	Majority	No	Majority vote on amendment	None
Tennessee	(q)	Yes(q)	Majority vote in election(r)	None
Texas	2/3	No	Majority vote on amendment	None
Utah	2/3	No	Majority vote on amendment	None
Vermont	(s)	Yes	Majority vote on amendment	None
Virginia	Majority	Yes	Majority vote on amendment	None
Washington	2/3	No	Majority vote on amendment	None
West Virginia	2/3	No	Majority vote on amendment	None
Wisconsin	Majority	Yes	Majority vote on amendment	None
Wyoming	2/3	No	Majority vote in election	None
American Samoa	3/5	No	Majority vote on amendment(t)	None
Puerto Rico	2/3(u)	No	Majority vote on amendment	3

Table 2—Notes

(a) In all states not otherwise noted, the figure shown in the column refers to the proportion of elected members in each house required for approval of proposed constitutional amendments.

(b) Legislature may not propose amendments at the same session to more than six articles in Colorado.

(c) Three-fourths vote in each house at one session, or majority vote in each house in two sessions between which an election has intervened.

(d) Two-thirds vote in each house at one session, or majority vote in each house in two sessions.

(e) Majority on amendment must be at least 50 percent of the total votes cast at the election; or, at a special election, a majority of the votes tallied which must be at least 30 percent of the total number of registered voters.

(f) Majority voting in election or three-fifths voting on amendment.

(g) If five or fewer political subdivisions of state affected, majority in state as a whole and also in affected subdivision(s) is required.

(h) Two-thirds of both houses.

(i) Majority of members elected sitting in joint session.

(j) The two-thirds must include not less than a majority elected to each house.

(k) Three-fifths of all members of each house at one session, or majority of all members of each house for two successive sessions.

(l) If a proposed amendment is not approved at the election when submitted, neither the same amendment nor one which would make substantially the same change for the constitution may be again submitted to the people before the third general election thereafter.

(m) Amendments concerning certain elective franchise and education matters require three-fourths vote of members elected and approval by three-fourths of electors voting in state and two-thirds of those voting in each county.

(n) Majority to amend constitution, two-thirds to revise (revise includes all or a part of the constitution).

(o) Emergency amendments may be passed by two-thirds vote of each house, followed by ratification by majority vote of electors in election held at least one month after legislative approval.

(p) Two-thirds of members of each house, first passage; majority of members of each house after popular ratification.

(q) Majority of members elected to both houses, first passage; two-thirds of members elected to both houses, second passage.

(r) Majority of all citizens voting for governor.

(s) Two-thirds vote senate, majority vote house, first passage; majority both houses, second passage. As of 1974, amendments may be submitted only every four years.

(t) Within 30 days after voter approval, governor must submit amendment(s) to Secretary of the Interior for approval.

(u) If approved by two-thirds of members of each house, amendment(s) submitted to voters at special referendum; if approved by not less than three-fourths of total members of each house, referendum may be held at next general election.

Table 3
CONSTITUTIONAL AMENDMENT PROCEDURE: BY INITIATIVE
Constitutional Provisions

State	Number of signatures required on initiative petition	Distribution of signatures	Referendum vote
Arizona	15% of total votes cast for all candidates for governor at last election.	None specified.	Majority vote on amendment.
Arkansas	10% of voters for governor at last election.	Must include 5% of voters for governor in each of 15 counties.	Majority vote on amendment.
California	8% of total voters for all candidates for governor at last election.	None specified.	Majority vote on amendment.
Colorado	5% of total legal votes for secretary of state at last election.	None specified.	Majority vote on amendment.
Florida	8% of total votes cast in the state in the last election for presidential electors.	8% of total votes cast in each of 1/2 of the congressional districts.	Majority vote on amendment.
Illinois(a)	8% of total votes cast for candidates for governor at last election.	None specified.	Majority voting in election or 3/5 voting on amendment.
Massachusetts(b)	3% of total votes cast for governor at preceding biennial state election (not less than 25,000 qualified voters).	No more than 1/4 from any one county.	Majority vote on amendment which must be 30% of total ballots cast at election.
Michigan	10% of total voters for governor at last election.	None specified.	Majority vote on amendment.
Missouri	8% of legal voters for all candidates for governor at last election.	The 8% must be in each of 2/3 of the congressional districts in the state.	Majority vote on amendment.
Montana	10% of qualified electors, the number of qualified electors to be determined by number of votes cast for governor in preceding general election.	The 10% to include at least 10% of qualified electors in each of 2/5 of the legislative districts.	Majority vote on amendment.
Nebraska	10% of total votes for governor at last election.	The 10% must include 5% in each of 2/5 of the counties.	Majority vote on amendment which must be at least 35% of total vote at the election.
Nevada	10% of voters who voted in entire state in last general election.	10% of total voters who voted in each of 75% of the counties.	Majority vote on amendment in two consecutive general elections.
North Dakota	4% of population of the state.	None specified.	Majority vote on amendment.
Ohio	10% of total number of electors who voted for governor in last election.	At least 5% of qualified electors in each of 1/2 of counties in the state.	Majority vote on amendment.
Oklahoma	15% of legal voters for state office receiving highest number of voters at last general state election.	None specified.	Majority vote on amendment.
Oregon	8% of total votes for all candidates for governor elected for 4-year term at last election.	None specified.	Majority vote on amendment.
South Dakota	10% of total votes for governor in last election.	None specified.	Majority vote on amendment.

(a) Only Article IV, The Legislature, may be amended by initiative petition.

(b) Before being submitted to the electorate for ratification, initiative measures must be approved at two sessions of a successively elected legislature by not less than one-fourth of all members elected, sitting in joint session.

Table 4
PROCEDURES FOR CALLING CONSTITUTIONAL CONVENTIONS
Constitutional Provisions

State or other jurisdiction	Provision for convention	Legislative vote for submission of convention question(a)	Popular vote to authorize convention	Periodic submission of convention question required(b)	Popular vote required for ratification of convention proposals
Alabama	Yes	Majority	ME	No	Not specified
Alaska	Yes	No provision(c,d)	(c)	10 yrs.(c)	Not specified(c)
Arizona	Yes	Majority	(e)	No	MP
Arkansas	No		No		
California	Yes	2/3	MP	No	MP
Colorado	Yes	2/3	MP	No	ME
Connecticut	Yes	2/3	MP	20 yrs.(f)	MP
Delaware	Yes	2/3	MP	No	No provision
Florida	Yes	(g)	MP	No	Not specified
Georgia	Yes	(d)	None	No	MP
Hawaii	Yes	Not specified	MP	9 years	MP(h)
Idaho	Yes	2/3	MP	No	Not specified
Illinois	Yes	3/5	(i)	20 years	MP
Indiana	No		No		
Iowa	Yes	Majority	MP	10 yrs.; 1970	MP
Kansas	Yes	2/3	MP	No	MP
Kentucky	Yes	Majority(j)	MP(k)	No	No provision
Louisiana	Yes	(d)	None	No	MP
Maine	Yes	(d)	None	No	No provision
Maryland	Yes	Majority	ME	20 yrs.; 1970	MP
Massachusetts	No			No	Not specified
Michigan	Yes	Majority	MP	16 yrs.; 1978	MP
Minnesota	Yes	2/3	ME	No	3/5 on P
Mississippi	No		No		
Missouri	Yes	Majority	MP	20 yrs.; 1962	Not specified(l)
Montana	Yes(m)	2/3(n)	MP	20 years	MP
Nebraska	Yes	3/5	MP(o)	No	MP
Nevada	Yes	2/3	ME	No	No provision
New Hampshire	Yes	Majority	MP	10 years	2/3 on P
New Jersey	No		No		
New Mexico	Yes	2/3	MP	No	Not specified
New York	Yes	Majority	MP	20 yrs.; 1957	MP
North Carolina	Yes	2/3	MP	No	MP
North Dakota	No		No		
Ohio	Yes	2/3	MP	20 yrs.; 1932	MP
Oklahoma	Yes	Majority	(e)	20 years	MP
Oregon	Yes	Majority	(e)	No	No provision
Pennsylvania	No		No		
Rhode Island	Yes	Majority	MP	10 years	MP
South Carolina	Yes	(d)	ME	No	No provision
South Dakota	Yes	(d)	(d)	No	M(p)
Tennessee	Yes(q)	Majority	MP	No	MP
Texas	No		No		
Utah	Yes	2/3	ME	No	MP
Vermont	No		No		
Virginia	Yes	(d)	None	No	MP
Washington	Yes	2/3	ME	No	Not specified
West Virginia	Yes	Majority	MP	No	Not specified
Wisconsin	Yes	Majority	MP	No	No provision
Wyoming	Yes	2/3	ME	No	Not specified
American Samoa	Yes	(r)	None	No	ME(s)
Puerto Rico	Yes	2/3	MP	No	MP

Key:
MP—Majority voting on the proposal.
ME—Majority voting in the election.

(a) In all states not otherwise noted, the entries in this column refer to the proportion of members elected to each house required to submit to the electorate the question of calling a constitutional convention.

(b) The number listed is the interval between required submissions on the question of calling a constitutional convention; where given, the date is that of the first required submission of the convention question.

(c) Unless provided otherwise by law, convention calls are to conform as nearly as possible to the act calling the 1955 convention, which provided for a legislative vote of a majority of members elected to each house and ratification by a majority vote on the proposals. The legislature may call a constitutional convention at any time.

(d) In these states, the legislature may call a convention without submitting the question to the people. The legislative vote required is two-thirds of the members elected to each house in Georgia, Louisiana, South Carolina and Virginia; two-thirds concurrent vote of both branches in Maine; three-fourths of all members of each house in South Dakota; and not specified in Alaska, but bills require majority vote of membership of each house. In South Dakota, the question of calling a convention may be initiated by the people in the same manner as an amendment to the constitution (see Table 3) and requires a majority vote on the question for approval.

(e) The law calling a convention must be approved by the people.

(f) The legislature shall submit the question 20 years after the last convention, or 20 years after the last vote on the question of calling a conven-tion, whichever date is last.

(g) The power to call a convention is reserved to the people by petition.

(h) The majority must be 50 percent of the total votes cast at a general election or at a special election, a majority of the votes tallied which must be at least 30 percent of the total number of registered voters.

(i) Majority voting in the election, or three-fifths voting on the question.

(j) Must be approved during two legislative sessions.

(k) Majority must equal one-fourth of qualified voters at last general election.

(l) Majority of those voting on the proposal is assumed.

(m) The question of calling a constitutional convention may be submitted either by the legislature or by initiative petition to the secretary of state in the same manner as provided for initiated amendments (see Table 3).

(n) Two-thirds of all members of the legislature.

(o) Majority must be 35 percent of total votes cast at the election.

(p) Convention proposals are submitted to the electorate at a special election in a manner to be determined by the convention.

(q) Conventions may not be held more often than once in six years.

(r) Five years after effective date of constitutions, governor shall call a constitutional convention to consider changes proposed by a constitutional committee appointed by the governor. Delegates to the convention are to be elected by their county councils.

(s) If proposed amendments are approved by the voters, they must be submitted to the Secretary of the Interior for approval.

Table 5
STATE CONSTITUTIONAL COMMISSIONS
(Operative during January 1, 1982-December 31, 1983)

State	Name of commission	Method and date of creation and period of operation	Membership: number and type	Funding	Purpose of commission	Proposals and action
Georgia	Select Committee on Constitutional Revision	Statutory: HR 135-588, Res. Act No. 26, March 30, 1977; May 9, 1977-June 30, 1986	11 members (most ex officio): gov., lt. gov., speaker of house, chf. justice of Sup. Ct., chf. judge of ct. of appeals, atty. gen., chmn. of sen. jud. cmte., chmn. of house jud. cmte., trial judge apptd. by jud. council, pres. pro tem of sen., pres. pro tem of house	No specified amount; funded from General Assembly appropriation	Provide overall policy direction and coordination for a continuing study and revision of the constitution	Under the auspices of the select committee, nine article revision committees prepared proposed revisions which were reviewed in 1981 by a 62-member Legislative Overview Committee and submitted to the General Assembly. The General Assembly approved a proposed new constitution on Sept. 18, 1981 for submission to the voters and further refined it during the 1982 regular session. The Georgia electorate approved the state's 10th constitution on Nov. 2, 1982 (567,663 to 211,342), which became effective July 1, 1983.
New Hampshire	Constitutional Convention Task Force	Statutory; N.H. Laws, 1983, Ch. 469: 125-129. Appointed in the fall, 1983, the task force will fulfill its mission when its recommendations are submitted to the convention, which convenes May 9, 1984	10 members: appointed by the speaker of the house (3), the pres. of the sen. (3), the gov. (2), and the Sup. Ct. (2)	$15,000 appropriation for the fiscal year 1984	Study the constitution and if amendments are needed, recommend such amendments to the next constitutional convention	Mandated to hold public hearings, prepare report containing proposed changes and explanatory material before Jan. 1, 1984, give report wide public dissemination, and submit report to the 17th constitutional convention in 1984
Utah	Utah Constitutional Revision Commission	Statutory; Ch. 89, Laws of Utah, 1969; amended by Ch. 107, Laws, 1975; amended by Ch. 159, Laws, 1977, which made the commission permanent as of July 1, 1977	16; 1 ex officio, 9 apptd.: by speaker of house (3), pres. of sen. (3) and gov. (3)—no more than 2 of each group to be from same party; and 6 additional members apptd. by the 9 previously appt. members	Appropriations through 1983 totaled $373,000. (The 1983 appropriation was $54,000, the same as for 1982)	Study constitution and recommend desirable changes, including proposed drafts	Mandated to report recommendations at least 60 days before legislature convenes. Voter action on the commission's recommendations through 1983 included: approval of revised articles on the executive branch and revenue and taxation, previous rejection of proposed revisions of the executive branch and revenue and taxation articles, and action on other more limited proposals. Proposed revisions of the judicial, legislative, and education articles will be submitted to the legislature in 1984.

Table 6

CONSTITUTIONAL CONVENTIONS
1982-83

State	Convention dates	Type of convention	Referendum on convention question	Preparatory bodies	Appropriations	Convention delegates	Convention proposals	Referendum on convention proposals
New Hampshire ..	May 8-June 26, 1974 (met 12 days). The 16th constitutional convention is a continuing body for 10 years or until successor is authorized and selected.	Unlimited	Nov. 7, 1972 Vote: 96,793 73,365	Commission to Study the State Constitution	$180,000	400 (elected March 5, 1974 from house districts; non-partisan)	27 proposed amendments were voted on during the period 1974-80	Nov. 5, 1974: 5 proposed amendments, 2 adopted; Feb. 24, 1976: 5 proposed, 5 rejected; Nov. 2, 1976: 7 proposed, 4 adopted; Nov. 7, 1978: 4 proposed, 2 adopted; Feb. 26, 1980: 3 proposed, 3 rejected; Nov. 4, 1980: 3 proposals, 2 adopted. (Total convention proposed: 27; 10 adopted).

Note: On November 2, 1982, the voters of New Hampshire approved a convention call by a vote of 115,351 to 105,027. The 400 delegates to New Hampshire's 17th constitutional convention will be elected on February 28, 1984 from lower house districts on a non-partisan basis, and the convention will convene on May 9, 1984.

A Note on Use

Symbols: Unless otherwise noted, all tables in *The Book of the States* use the following scheme:

. . .—no data
blank cell—not applicable
0—zero quantity.

Sources: Unless otherwise noted, the sources of data for tables are surveys and research by The Council of State Governments.

Section VI   ADMINISTRATION
1.   Financial Administration

STATE FINANCIAL ADMINISTRATION

By Kay T. Pohlmann

Effective financial management is very important to state government. Resources must be used efficiently in the face of inflation, increased demands for government services, and new problems such as revenue shortfalls and reduced federal aid. With this pressure on state government, managers must have reliable financial information at the proper time in order to make sound fiscal policy decisions. Financial management tools include the budget process, the accounting system, the cash management system, the financial reporting system and audits.

Cash Management

Cash management is the collection, processing, disbursement and investment of cash funds. Actions in each of these areas have an effect on available cash resources. Improved cash management can partially compensate for inflation and increase revenue by streamlining the collection procedures, taking advantage of the highest interest rates and reducing "float" time.

The importance of effective cash management practices is emphasized by the significant number of states that have recently reviewed their cash management practices. Eighteen states reviewed or updated all or some segment of their cash management practices in 1982, and 20 additional states continuously review or update all or some segment of their cash management practices.

States use various cash management techniques including: lockbox services, wire transfers, zero balance accounts, account reconcilement services and service bureaus. Twenty-eight states use some type of collection service, 41 states use the Federal Reserve wire transfer system, 37 states use the bank wire transfer system, and 28 states use depository transfer checks for funds mobilization. Disbursement techniques used include: zero balance accounts (20 states), bank drafts (11 states), and a controlled disbursement program (17 states). Cash management information services are used by 35 states; account reconcilement services are used by 33 states; and data transmission services are used by 16 states. Eighteen states use a business service or service bureau and 20 states use the automated clearinghouse facilities.

Float within the states' collection and disbursement processes is analyzed (either internally or by consultants) by 36 states, and 15 states have an automated system for forecasting cash flow.

Accounting and Reporting

Accounting and reporting systems are the basic components of financial management. The National Council on Governmental Accounting in *Governmental Accounting and Financial Reporting Principles* indicated that: "A governmental accounting system must make it possible both: (a) to present fairly and with full disclosure the financial position and results of financial operations of the funds and account groups of the governmental unit in conformity with generally accepted accounting principles; and (b) to determine and demonstrate compliance with finance-related legal and contractual provisions."

Several states have converted or are in the process of converting to generally accepted accounting principles (GAAP). Several states, including Illinois, New York, Tennessee and Maryland, have GAAP financial statements, and approximately 15 other states are in varying stages of implementing GAAP.

In addition to providing a more accurate measure of fiscal condition, GAAP financial statements also affect the states' bond ratings. Standard & Poor's now takes into account the quality of reporting and accounting standards being used by the issuers under review. Standard & Poor's said in a 1980 policy statement that financial statements should be prepared in accordance with GAAP and that these statements should be independently audited either by a certified public

Kay T. Pohlmann is the Staff Director of the National Association of State Auditors, Comptrollers and Treasurers, The Council of State Governments.

accounting firm or by a qualified independent state or local agency, on a timely basis; i.e., no later than six months after the fiscal year end. Maryland, one of the first states to adopt GAAP, has maintained a Triple A rating on general obligation bonds. According to Comptroller Louis V. Goldstein, the savings in interest have paid for the cost of the new accounting system, plus independent audits.

Auditing

Auditing is an important management tool. The increase in government programs, both federal and state, brought with it an increased demand for full accountability by those administering the programs, and auditing is an integral part of that accountability.

Several years ago the major concern was financial audits; however, today auditors are also interested in the economy, efficiency and effectiveness of government operations. Legislators, investors, public officials and citizens want to know not only whether government funds are handled properly and in accordance with laws and regulations, but also whether the programs are achieving the purposes intended and whether they are doing so economically and efficiently. This type of audit is often called "post audit" to distinguish it from the activities of some auditors who approve expenditures before payment is made—the pre-audit.

Over the past several years, there has been an effort by state post auditors to improve the operations of their offices and the quality of their audits. Most state auditors are independent and are responsible for auditing all state agencies. Several state auditors are also responsible for auditing local government units and prescribing the scope and nature of audits of local governments by others.

Table 1
STATE CASH MANAGEMENT

State	Investment policy governed by	Determines investment policy	Responsible for investing funds	Restrictions on investing funds	Investment counseling	Bank selection policy	Responsible for selecting banks for demand deposits	Bank selection method for demand deposits
Alabama	S	State Treas.—E	State Treas.	Yes	SE	S,A	State Treas.—E	All banks used
Alaska	—	State Treas.—E	Investment Officer—Treas. Office	Yes	SE,IC,IF	—	Bd. of Deposit/ St. Treas.—G,E	Competitive bid
Arizona	C,S		State Treas.	Yes	SE	—	State Treas.—E	Size/location
Arkansas	S	State Bd. of Fin.—E,G	State Treas.	Yes	SE	C,S	State Treas.—E	Geographic coverage of the state with requirement of a Sacramento branch
California	S	Money Investment Bd.—E,G	Chief of Investments—Treas. Office	Yes	SE	A	Cash Mgt. Chief	
Colorado	S	State Treas.—E(a)	Chief Investment Officer—Treas. Dept.	Yes	SE	T(b)	State Treas.—E	Competitive bid
Connecticut	S,A	State Treas.—E	Dep. State Treas.	Yes	SE,IC	A	State Treas.—E	Combination(c)
Delaware	S	Cash Mgt. Policy Bd.—G	State Treas.	Yes	SE,IC,IF	S	Cash Mgt. Policy Bd.—G	Competitive bid
Florida	S	Statute	State Treas.	Yes	SE	(d)	State Treas.—E	Competitive bid
Georgia	S	State Depository Bd.—E,G	Dir., Fiscal Div., Dept. of Administrative Services	Yes	SE	(e)	State Depository Bd.—E,G	Location/size
Hawaii	S,A	Dir. of Finance—G	Chief, Fin. Div., Dept. of Budget & Finance	Yes	SE	S,A	State Dir. of Finance—G	Competitiveness of int. rates; depository's size; ability to fully collateralize state deposits (f)(g)
Idaho	S,A	State Treas.—E	State Treas. & Senior Deputy Treas. Investments	Yes	SE	(f)	(f)	Size
Illinois	C,S,A	State Treas.—E	Chief Fiscal Officer, Treas. Office	Yes	(h)	A	State Treas.—E	Discretion of State Treas.
Indiana	S	State Treas.—E	State Treas. & Investment Mgr., Treas. Office	Yes	SE	T	State Treas.—E	All Federal Reserve Banks in Des Moines
Iowa	S	State Treas.—E(a)	State Treas., Dept. of Investment	Yes	IC	S,A	State Treas.—E	
Kansas	S(i)	State Treas. & Money Invest. Bd.—E,G	State Treas. & Money Invest. Bd.	Yes	—	(j)	Money Investment Bd.—G,E	Competitive bid
Kentucky	S	State Invest. Comm.—E,G	State Treas.	Yes	SE	S	State Treas.—E	Negotiated agreement
Louisiana	S	State Treas.—E	Asst. State Treas. & Office of Depository & Investment, Dept. of Treas.	Yes	—	A	State Treas.—E	Interim Emergency Bd.(k)
Maine	S	Deputy State Treas.—CS	State Treas.	Yes	SE	S,A	State Treas.—L	Competitive bid
Maryland	S	State Treas.—L	State Treas.	Yes	SE	S	State Treas.—L	Competitive bid/negotiation
Massachusetts	S	State Treas.—E	First Deputy, Treas. Dept., Investment Div.	Yes	IC	A	State Treas.—E	Competitive bid/lowest responsible bidder
Michigan	S,A	State Treas.—G	State Treas./Dir. of Investments	Yes	SE	A	State Treas.—G	Location/convenience
Minnesota	A	State Bd. of Investment—E	State Bd. of Investment	Yes	(l)	A	Commr., Dept. of Fin.—G	Competitive bid
Mississippi	S,A	State Depository Commission & State Treas.—E	State Depository Commission & State Treas.	Yes	—	S	State Auditor—E	State Auditor(n)
Missouri	C,S,A	State Treas.—E	State Treas.	Yes	SE	C,S,A	State Treas.—E	Competitive bid/convenience & rotation on collection accts.
Montana	S	Bd. of Investments	Bd. of Investments, Dir., Investment Council	Yes	SE,IC,IF	S,A	Admin., Treas. Div.—CS	All banks used
Nebraska	S	Investment Council—G		Yes	SE,IC,IF	A	State Treas.—E	The five major correspondent banks utilized (clearing accts.)
Nevada	C,S,A	State Treas.—E	State Treas. & Treas. Deputy	Yes	SE	S	State Treas.—E	Competitive bid/level of services available
New Hampshire	S	State Treas.—E	State Treas.	Yes	SE	A	State Treas.—E	Size/geographic location
New Jersey	S,A	State Investment Council—G,S	Dir., Div. of Investment	Yes	SE	A	State Treas.—G	Competitive bid & convenience

STATE CASH MANAGEMENT—Continued

State	Investment policy governed by	Determines investment policy	Responsible for investing funds	Restrictions on investing funds	Investment counseling	Bank selection policy	Responsible for selecting banks for demand deposits	Bank selection method for demand deposits
New Mexico	C,S,A	State Legislature—E	State Treas./Deputy Comptroller	Yes	IC	S	Secy. Dept. of Fin. & Admin.—G	Competitive bid/convenience/quality & price of services
New York	S	Comptroller—E	Comptroller Office of State Comptroller,	Yes	SE	S	Comptroller—E	
North Carolina	S	State Treas.—E	Invest. & Cash Mgmt. Div. State Treas., Investment & Banking Div.	Yes	IC	S,A	State Treas.—E	Convenience & safety in receiving & disbursing state monies/all banks eligible
North Dakota	S	State Investment Bd.—E,G	State Treas., Invest. Dept.	Yes	(n)	S	(o)	(o)
Ohio	S	State Bd. of Deposit—E	Dir. of Investment, Treas. Office	Yes	IF	A	State Treas.—E	All banks used
Oklahoma	---	---	---	---	---	(p)	---	---
Oregon	S	Investment Council—E,G	Treas. Dept.—Invest. Div.	Yes	SE	S	State Treas.—E	All banks used
Pennsylvania	S	State Treas.—E	Dir., Treas. Dept., Bureau of Cash Mgmt.	Yes	SE		Bd. of Fin. & Rev.—E,G	Size/geography
Rhode Island	S,A	Investment Commission—E,G,L,CS	Gen. Treas./Deputy Gen. Treas., Treas. Dept.	No	(q)	A	Gen. Treas.—E	All banks used
South Carolina	S	State Treas.—E	State Treas.	Yes	IF	A	State Treas.—E	All banks used
South Dakota	S	Investment Office—L	State Investment Office, Treas. Dept., Investment Div.	No	IC	A	State Treas.—E	Competitive bid
Tennessee	C,S,A	State Treas.—L	State Treas.	Yes	SE	S	Treas./Commr. of Fin. & Admin./Governor—E,G,L(s)	State requirement(r)
Texas	---	---	---	---	---	---	---	---
Utah	S	State Treas.—E	State Investment Officer, Treas. Office	Yes	---	A	State Treas.—E	Competitive bid
Vermont	S	State Treas.—E	State Treas.	Yes	SE,IC,IF	T	State Treas.—E	Divided among largest state banks with Montpelier offices
Virginia	S	State Treas.—G	Investment Officer, Dept. of Treas.	Yes	SE	A	State Treas.—G	Service capability(b)
Washington	C,S	State Treas.—E	Investment Officer, Treas. Office	Yes	SE	A	State Treas.—E	Competitive bid
West Virginia	C,S,A	State Bd. of Investment—E	Dir. of Invest., Treas. Office	Yes	SE,IF	S	Bd. of Investment—E	All banks used
Wisconsin	S	Investment Bd.—G	State Investment Bd. staff	Yes	IC	S	Depository Selection Bd.—E,G	Competitive bid
Wyoming	S,A,C	State Treas.—E	Dep. State Treas., Treas. Office	Yes	SE	A	State Treas.—E	Banks are invited to make proposals for the state account

Source:

Key:
S—Statute
C—Constitution
A—Administrative practice
E—Elected
G—Appointed by governor
L—Appointed by legislature
CS—Civil service
SE—State employee
IC—Investment council
IF—Investment firm

(a) Treasurer of state for all but retirement funds.
(b) Established and in operation for three or more years/competitive bidding.
(c) Competitive bid for disbursing accounts (3); Convenience for deposit and various economic and service criteria for others (32).
(d) Not limited.
(e) State Depository Board.
(f) Negotiated bids not limited.
(g) Law requires that all banks requesting deposits receive them in proportion to their capital and surplus, with amount covered by federal insurance excluded from apportionment by this formula.

(h) Chief fiscal officer.
(i) Statute, State Investment Board.
(j) Statute, Money Investment Board.
(k) Banks must be approved fiscal agents of state in order to have state funds. Approval is secured from the Interim Emergency Board.
(l) Representation from the local financial community.
(m) Selection by state auditor's approval of agency request. State treasurer rotates clearing account among capital city banks.
(n) Bank of North Dakota.
(o) All held in Bank of North Dakota.
(p) Agencies have choice of bank deposit location based on convenience.
(q) Advised by major banking firm.
(r) Request by bank, meeting statute requirements, authorized by governor, treasurer and commissioner of finance and administration.
(s) The state does not maintain demand deposit accounts as operating accounts. Rather, taxpayers are permitted to deposit tax payments to local banks. These depository accounts are drawn down on a daily basis to concentrate state cash for subsequent investment. State warrants are redeemed through Federal Reserve Bank in Nashville, Tennessee.
(t) Some restrictions will likely be established.

Table 2

STATE ACCOUNTING AND REPORTING

State	Who establishes state accounting principles	Responsible for statewide general purpose financial statements	Accounting function centralized	If centralized, who is responsible	Pre-audit function	Method of payment for goods & services	Who issues check or warrant	If checks are used, are warrants used in internal processing	If yes, who is responsible for issuing warrants
Alabama	Legislature	Comptroller—CS	Yes	Comptroller	Comptroller—CS	Warrant	Comptroller—CS	---	---
Alaska	Legislature	Commr. of Admin.	Yes	Commr. of Admin.	Commr. of Admin.	Warrant	Commr. of Admin.	---	---
Arizona	Asst. Dir. for Fin.—G	Asst. Dir. for Fin.—G	Yes	Asst. Dir. for Fin.	Agency	Warrant	Asst. Dir. for Fin.—G	---	---
Arkansas	Chief fiscal officer—G	Adm. Office of Acctg. (chief fiscal officer)	Yes	Adm. Office of Acctg.	Dept. of Fin. & Admin. (chief fiscal officer)	Warrant	State auditor—E	---	---
California	Dir. of Fin.—G	State Controller—E	Yes	State Controller	State Controller—E	Warrant	State Controller—E	---	---
Colorado	State Controller—CS	State Controller—CS	Yes	State Controller	State Controller—CS	Warrant	State Controller—CS	Yes	---
Connecticut	State Comptroller—E	State Comptroller—E	Yes	State Comptroller	State Comptroller—E	Check	State Comptroller—E	No	State Comptroller
Delaware	Budget Director—G	Budget Director—G	Yes	Dir., Div of Acctg.	Dir., Div of Acctg.	Check	Dir., Div of Acctg. (Appt., Secy. of Fin.)	---	---
Florida	State Comptroller—E	State Comptroller—E	Yes	State Comptroller	State Comptroller—E	Warrant	State Comptroller—E	Yes	---
Georgia	State Auditor—L	State Auditor—L	---	---	Dir., Office of Planning & Bud.	Check	Fiscal Officer (various depts.)—CS	Yes	Dir., Office of Planning & Budget
Hawaii	Comptroller—G	Comptroller—G	Yes	Comptroller	Comptroller—G	Warrant	Comptroller—G	---	---
Idaho	State Auditor—E	Financial Mgt.—G	Yes	State Auditor	State Auditor—E	Warrant	State Auditor—E	---	---
Illinois	State Comptroller—E	State Comptroller—E	Yes(a)	State Comptroller	State Comptroller—E	Warrant	State Comptroller—E	---	---
Indiana	State Auditor—E	State Auditor—E	Yes	State Auditor	State Auditor—E	Warrant	State Auditor—E	---	---
Iowa	State Comptroller—G	State Comptroller—G	Yes	State Comptroller	State Comptroller—G	Warrant	State Auditor—G	---	---
Kansas	Dir., Div. of Accts. & Reports—CS	Dir., Div. of Accts. & Reports—CS	Yes	Dir., Div. of Accts. & Reports	Dir., Div. of Accts. & Reports—CS	Warrant	Dir., Div. of Accts. & Reports—CS	Yes	Dir., Div. of Accts.
Kentucky	Dir., Div. of Accts.—G	Dir., Div. of Accts.—G	Yes	Dir., Div. of Accts.	Dir., Div. of Accts., Pre-Aud. Section—G	Check	State Treasurer—E	Yes	State Treasurer
Louisiana	Commr. of Admin.—G	Commr. of Admin.—G	Yes(b)	Commr. of Admin.	Legislative Auditor—L	Check	State Treasurer—L	Yes	State Controller
Maine	State Controller (Fin. Commission)	State Controller (Fin. Commission)	Yes	State Controller	State Controller (Fin. Commission)	Check	State Treasurer—L	Yes	State Controller
Maryland	Comptroller—E	Comptroller—E	Yes(c)	Comptroller	Comptroller—E	Check	State Treasurer—L	Yes	Comptroller
Massachusetts	State Comptroller—G	State Comptroller—G	Yes	State Comptroller	State Comptroller—G	Check	State Treasurer—E	Yes	State Comptroller
Michigan	Dir. of Acctg.—CS	Dir. of Acctg.—CS	Yes	Dir. of Acctg.	Delegated to agencies—CS	Warrant	State Treasurer—G	---	---
Minnesota	Commr. of Fin.—G	Commr. of Fin.	Yes	Commr. of Fin.	Commr. of Fin.—G	Warrant	Commr. of Fin.—G	---	---
Mississippi	State Aud. of Pub. Accts.—E	State Aud. of Pub. Accts.—E	Yes(d)	Aud. of Pub. Accts.	Dept. of Pub. Accts.—E	Warrant	State Aud. of Pub. Accts.—E	---	---
Missouri	Commr. of Admin.—G	Commr. of Admin.—G	Yes	Dir. of Acctg.	Dir. of Acctg.—G	Check	State Treas.—E	Yes	Dir. of Acctg.
Montana	Dir., Dept. of Admin.—G	Dir., Dept. of Admin.—G	Yes	Dir., Dept. of Admin.	Dir., Dept. of Admin.—G	Warrant	State Auditor—E	---	---
Nebraska	Dir. of Adm. Serv.—G	Dir. of Adm. Serv.—G	Yes	State Acctg. Admin.	State Acctg. Adm. (Dir. of Adm. Serv.)	Warrant	Dir. of Adm. Serv.—G	---	---
Nevada	State Controller—E	State Controller—E	Yes(e)	State Controller	State Budget Offr.—G	Warrant	State Controller—E	Yes	State Controller
New Hampshire	Dir. of Accts.—G	Dir. of Accts.—G	Yes	Dir. of Accts.	Dir. of Accts.—G	Check	State Treasurer—L	Yes	Gov. & Council
New Jersey	State Comptroller—G	Asst. State Comptroller—CS	Yes	State Comptroller	Agency Approval Officers & Accountants in Treas. Bureau—CS	Check	Dir., Div. of Budget & Acctg. & State Treasurer—G	No	---
New Mexico	Dir., Fin. Control Div.—G	Dir., Fin. Control	Yes	Dir., Fin. Control Div.	Dir., Fin. Control Div.—G	Warrant	Dir., Fin. Control Div.—G	---	---
New York	Comptroller—E	Comptroller—E	Yes	Comptroller	State Comptroller—E	Check	State Comptroller & State Treas., jointly—E,G	Yes	State Comptroller

State	Who establishes state accounting principles	Responsible for statewide general purpose financial statements	Accounting function centralized	If centralized, who is responsible	Pre-audit function	Method of payment for goods & services	Who issues check or warrant	If checks are used, warrants used in internal processing	If yes, who is responsible for issuing warrants
North Carolina	State Auditor—E	State Auditor—E	---	---	Each Departmental Controller—CS	Check	Departmental Controllers—CS	Yes	Off. of State Bud.
North Dakota	Dir., Off. of Mgt. & Budget—G	Dir., Off. of Mgt. & Budget—G	Yes	Dir., Off. of Mgt. & Budget	Dir., Off. of Mgt. & Budget—G	Check	State Treasurer—E	No	---
Ohio	---	---	---	---	---	Warrant	State Treasurer—E	---	---
Oklahoma	Dir. of State Fin.—G	Chief Analyst, Budget Div.—CS	Yes	State Comptroller	State Comptroller—CS	Check	State Treasurer—E	---	---
Oregon	Admin., Acctg. Div. (Appt., Dir. of Exec. Dept.)	Admin., Acctg. Div. (Appt., Dir. of Exec. Dept.)	---	---	Agency level	Check	Agency level	Yes	Admin. Acctg. Div.
Pennsylvania	Secy. of Budget & Admin.—G	Dep. Secy. for Comptroller Operations—G	Yes(f)	Dir., Bureau of Fin. Mgmt.	Comptroller—G / State Treasurer—E	Check	State Treasurer—E	Yes	State Treasurer
Rhode Island	Dir. of Admin.—G	State Controller—CS	Yes	State Controller	State Controller—CS	Check	State Controller—CS	Yes	State Controller
South Carolina	Comptroller General—E	Comptroller General—E	Yes	Comptroller General	Comptroller General—E	Check	State Treasurer—E	Yes	Comptroller General
South Dakota	Commr., Bureau of Fin. & Mgt.—CS	Chief Accountant, Bureau of Fin. & Mgt.—CS	Yes	Commr., Bureau of Fin. & Mgt.	State Auditor—E	Warrant	State Auditor—E	---	---
Tennessee	Commr. of Fin. & Admin.—G / Comptroller of the Treas.—L	Commr. of Fin. & Admin.—G	Yes	Asst. Commr. for Acctg.	Dir. of Accts.—CS	Warrant	Commr. of Fin. & Admin.—G	---	---
Texas	Comptroller of Pub. Accts.—E / State Auditor—L	Comptroller of Pub. Accts.—E	Yes	Comptroller of Pub. Accts.	Comptroller of Pub. Accts.—E	Warrant	Comptroller of Pub. Accts.—E	---	---
Utah	Dir. of Fin. (Appt. by Dir. of Adm. Serv.)	Dir. of Fin. (Appt. by Dir. of Adm. Serv.)	Yes	Dir. of Fin.	Dir. of Fin. (Appt. by Dir. of Adm. Serv.)	Warrant	Dir. of Fin. (Appt., Dir. of Adm. Serv.)	---	---
Vermont	Dept. of Fin. & Info. Support—G	Dept. of Fin. & Info. Support	Yes	Dept. of Fin. & Info. Support	Dept. of Fin. & Info. Support—G	Check	State Treasurer—E	Yes	Dept. of Fin. & Info. Support
Virginia	Comptroller—G	Comptroller—E	Yes	Comptroller	Comptroller	Check	State Treasurer—G	Yes	Comptroller
Washington	Dir. Office of Fin. Mgt.—G	Dir., Office of Fin. Mgt.—G	---	---	Each Agency	Warrant	State Treasurur—E	---	---
West Virginia	Comm. Dept. of Fin. & Admin.—G	State Auditor—E	Yes	State Auditor	State Auditor—E	Warrant	State Auditor—E	---	---
Wisconsin	State Fin. Dir. (Appt. by Secy. of Admin.)	State Fin. Dir. (Appt. by Secy. of Admin.)	Yes	State Fin. Dir.	State Fin. Dir. (Appt. by Secy. of Admin.)	Check	State Fin. Dir. (Appt. by Secy. of Admin.)	(f)	(f)
Wyoming	State Auditor—E	State Auditor—E	Yes	State Auditor	State Auditor—E	Warrant	State Auditor—E	---	---

and certain Trust Funds. These reports are folded in with data from the centralized systems and year-end closing packages to produce the Statewide GPFS.

(d) Large departments maintain detailed accounts. Statements are obtained from colleges and universities and from Employment Security Commission (for FY 1981, for the first time) and combined with amounts handled through State Treasury which are recorded by Department of Public Accounts.

(e) Centralized—however, individual agencies prepare all input to the accounting system run by the controller. Certain enterprise and trust funds and all pension funds are maintained as separate accounting systems by the agencies administering them; however, those funds are then consolidated into Controller's CAFR.

(f) General Fund is centralized. Special Funds decentralized but consolidated centrally. For financial statement preparation, agency comptrollers submit individual fund trial balances to the Bureau of Financial Management. These are then compiled and summarized by the Bureau. For management reports computer tape output is interfaced with Central Accounting System for Major Funds.

Key:
E—Elected
G—Appointed by governor.
L—Appointed by legislature.
CS—Civil service.

(a) Treasury held funds are centralized. Non-Treasury held funds are decentralized. Certain information is obtained from an annual form prepared by agencies and sent to the comptroller for inclusion in statewide general purpose financial statements.

(b) Approximately 65 percent centralized, 35 percent decentralized. Annual financial statements prepared by agencies.

(c) Centralized—however, basic financial data is obtained from decentralized agency accounting offices. Centralized accounting and reporting systems and year-end closing packages. Separate financial reports are prepared by proprietary organizations (higher education funds and other enterprise funds)

Table 3
STATE AUDITING

State/Agency	Audit all state agencies	State agencies permitted to arrange for own audits	Regulation of local govt. acctg., auditing & reporting practices	Audit local governments	Types of local government audits	Prescribe scope & nature for other auditors	Types of audits performed State	Local
Alabama								
State Auditor..............	Yes	No	Yes	Yes	CI	No	---	F,C
Chief Examiner...........	Yes(a)	No	Yes	Yes	CO,SD,OT	Yes	F,C,E,P	F,C
Alaska								
Legislative Auditor........	Yes	Yes	Yes	Yes	OT	No	F,C,E,P	---
Internal Auditor..........	Yes	Yes	No	No		---	---	---
Arizona								
Auditor General..........	No	Yes	Yes	Yes	CO,SD	Yes	F,C,E,P	F,C
Arkansas								
Legislative Auditor........	No	Yes	Yes	Yes	CI,CO,SD	No	F,E	F
State Auditor..............	Yes(b)	No	Yes	No		---	---	---
California								
Auditor General..........	Yes	Yes	Yes	Yes	CI,CO,SD	No	F,C,E	E
Dept. of Finance...........	Yes	No	No	Yes	CO,SD	Yes	F,C(c),E	C(i)
State Controller...........	Yes	Yes	Yes	Yes	CO,OT,(e)(u),SD	Yes	F,C,P	F,C,P
Colorado								
State Auditor..............	Yes	No	Yes	No		No	F,C(c)	E,P
Connecticut								
Auditors of Accounts......	Yes	No	Yes	No		---	F,C(d)	---
Delaware								
Auditor of Accounts.......	Yes	No	No	No		No	F,C,E	---
Florida								
Auditor General..........	Yes	No	Yes	Yes	SD,OT	Yes	F,C,E,P	F,C
Georgia								
State Auditor..............	No	No	Yes	Yes	SD	No	F,C,E,P	F,C
Hawaii								
Legislative Auditor........ (Post Audits)	Yes	Yes	No	Yes(v)	CO	No	F,C,E,P(e)	F,C
Idaho								
Legislative Auditor........	Yes(f)	Yes(g)	Yes(h)	No(i)		No(h)	F,C,E,P(c)(j)	---
Illinois								
Auditor General..........	Yes	No	No	Yes	OT	No	F,C,E,P	---
State Comptroller..........	No		No	No		No	---	---
Indiana								
State Examiner............	Yes	No	Yes	Yes	CI,CO,SD,OT		F,C	F,C
Iowa								
Auditor of State...........	Yes	No	Yes	Yes	CI,CO,SD	Yes	F,C(c)	F,C
Kansas								
Legislative Auditor........	Yes	No	No	No		No	F,C(c),E,P	---
Kentucky								
Aud. of Public Accts........	No	Yes	Yes	Yes	CO	Yes	F,C	F,C
Louisiana								
Legislative Auditor........	Yes	Yes	Yes	Yes	(k)	Yes	F,C	F,C
Maine								
State Auditor..............	Yes	Yes(l)	Yes	Yes	CI,CO,SD,OT	Yes	F,C	F,C
Maryland								
Legislative Auditor........	Yes	No	Yes	No		Yes	F,C,E,P	---
Massachusetts								
State Auditor..............	Yes	Yes	Yes	Yes	OT	No	F,C(c)	---
Legislative Auditor........	No	Yes	Yes	No		No	E,P	---
Michigan								
Legislative Auditor General..	Yes	No	No	No		No	F,C(c),E,P(p)	---
Local Govt. Audit Div......			Yes	Yes	CI,CO,SD,OT	Yes	---	F,C(m)
Minnesota								
Legislative Auditor........	Yes(a)	No(n)	No	No		No	F,C(c)(o),E,P	---
State Auditor..............	No		Yes	Yes	CI,CO,SD,OT (o)	Yes	---	F,C(c)
Mississippi								
Department of Audit.......	Yes	No	Yes	Yes	CI,CO,SD	Yes	F,C(c)	F,C(e)
Jt. Leg. Comt. Perf. & Expend. Review...........	Yes			Yes	CI,CO,SD,OT	No	E,P(e)	E,P
Missouri								
State Auditor..............	Yes	Yes	No	Yes	CO	No	F,C(c),E	F,C(c),E
Montana								
Legislative Auditor........	Yes	No	No	No		No	F,C(c),E,P(p)	---
Nebraska								
Aud. of Public Accts........	Yes	No	Yes	Yes	CO	Yes	F,C,E	F,C,E

State/Agency	Audit all state agencies	State agencies permitted to arrange for own audits	Regulation of local govt. acctg., auditing & reporting practices	Audit local governments	Types of local government audits	Prescribe scope & nature for other auditors	Types of audits performed State	Local
Nevada								
Legislative Auditor.........	Yes	No	No	No		No	F,C(c)	---
New Hampshire								
Legislative Budget Asst...... Post-Audit Div.	Yes	No	No	No		No	F,C,E,P	---
New Jersey								
State Auditing............	Yes	Yes(q)	Yes	No		No	F,C	---
New Mexico								
State Auditor..............	Yes	Yes	Yes	Yes	CI,CO,SD,OT	Yes	F,C	F,C
New York								
State Comptroller..........	Yes	No	Yes	Yes	CI,CO,SD,OT	Yes(r)	F,C,E,P	F,C,-P(cc)
Leg. Comm. on Exp. Review	Yes		No	Yes	CI,CO,SD	No	E,P	E,P
North Carolina								
State Auditor..............	Yes	No	No	No		Yes	F,C(c),E	
North Dakota								
State Auditor..............	Yes	No	Yes	Yes	CI,CO,SD	Yes	F,C	F,C
Leg. Bud. Anal. & Aud......	No	No	No	No		Yes	C,E,P	---
Ohio								
State Auditor..............	Yes	Yes	Yes	Yes	CI,CO,SD	Yes	F,C(c)	F,C
Oklahoma								
Leg. Fiscal Office..........	Yes	Yes	No	No		No	C,E,P	
State Aud. & Inspector......	Yes	No	Yes	Yes	CO	Yes	F,C	F,C
Oregon								
Div. of Audits.............	Yes	No	Yes(s)	Yes	CI,CO,SD,OT	Yes	F,C,P	F,C
Pennsylvania								
Auditor General..........	No	Yes	No	Yes	CI,CO,SD,OT	No	F,C,E,P	F,C,E,P
Leg. Bud./Fin. Cmte.......	No	No	No	No		No	E,P	----
Rhode Island								
Bureau of Audits..........	Yes	No	Yes	Yes	CI,SD,OT	No	F,C	F,C
Auditor General..........	No	Yes	Yes	No		Yes	F,C(c),E(t),P	---
South Carolina								
State Auditor..............	Yes	Yes	No	Yes		No	F,C(m)	---
Leg. Audit Council.........	No	No	No	No (dd)	SD,OT	---	F,C,E,P	---
South Dakota								
State Auditor..............	No	No	No	No	---	---	(bb)	---
Auditor General..........	Yes	Yes	Yes	Yes	CI,CO,SD,OT	Yes	F,C(c)	F,C
Tennessee								
Comptroller of Treasury....	Yes	No	Yes	Yes	CI(u),CO, SD(u),OT(u)	Yes	F,C(c),E,P(p)	F,C
Texas								
State Auditor..............	Yes	No	Yes	No		No	F,C,E	---
Leg. Budget Office.........	Yes	No	No	No		No	P,E(p)	---
Utah								
Legis. Aud. General.......	Yes	No	No(v)	No(v)		No	E,P(p)	---
State Auditor..............	Yes	No	Yes	No(v)		Yes	F,C(c)	---
Vermont								
Auditor of Accts..........	Yes	No	No	No		No	F,C(c)	---
Virginia								
Aud. of Public Accts........	Yes	Yes(w)	Yes	Yes	CI,CO,OT	Yes	F,C	F,C
Jt. Legis. Aud. & Review....	Yes		Yes	Yes(x)	CI,CO,OT	No	E,P	E,P
Washington								
State Auditor..............	Yes	No	Yes	Yes	CI,CO,SD,OT	No	F,C	F,C
Legislative Auditor.........	Yes	No	Yes	Yes	CI,CO,SD	No	P	---
West Virginia								
Legislative Auditor.........	Yes	No	Yes	No		No	F,C,E,P	---
State Tax Dept.............	No		Yes	Yes	CI,CO,SD,OT	Yes		F,C,E,P
Wisconsin								
State Auditor..............	Yes	Yes	No	No		---	F,C,E,P	---
Dept. of Revenue..........			No	Yes(aa)	CI,CO,SD,OT	No	C(d),E	F,C
Dept. of Public Instruction..			Yes(r)	No		Yes(n)		
Wyoming								
State Auditor..............	No	Yes	No	No	---	No	C	---
Leg. Services Office........	(y)		No	Yes	CI,CO,OT(z)	No	P(p),C(d),E	---
State Exam. Office.........	No	Yes	Yes	Yes	CI,OT	Yes	F,C	F,C

Key:
CI—City
CO—County
SD—School districts
OT—Other
F—Financial audits
C—Compliance audits
E—Efficiency/economy audits
P—Program results audits

(a) Except other legislative agencies.
(b) All Treasury funds of state agencies.
(c) Financial and compliance audits combined.
(d) Have elements of all types.
(e) Includes sunset audits.
(f) Authorized to audit all state agencies including universities.
(g) Legislative auditor must approve contract provisions and may review private auditor papers.
(h) Authorized to issue regulation on all aspects of governmental auditing for government units subordinate to state.
(i) Authorized to audit local units upon direction of Joint Finance Appropriation Committee.
(j) Authorized to perform comprehensive audits, F,C,EE,P. Present audits are complying with OMB Circ. A-102, Att. P as applicable.
(k) All units except municipalities.
(l) Federal grants only.
(m) Also fraud investigations.
(n) Exceptions are certain activities financed by review bonds.
(o) State auditor does not actually audit all local governments. CPA firms perform a good share of certain local government types.
(p) Efficiency and economy and program results combined.
(q) With the express approval of auditor.
(r) For school districts only.
(s) Budgeting, auditing and reporting only.
(t) Financial, compliance, and economy and efficiency combined.
(u) Monitor.
(v) Has the authority.
(w) Grant audits.
(x) To the extent state funds are involved.
(y) At present, sunset audits only.
(z) If they have state funding.
(aa) At the request of local governing bodies.
(bb) Pre-audit state agencies.
(cc) New York City only.
(dd) Fraud investigations as requested by the attorney general of the State Law Enforcement Division.

2. Budgeting

BUDGETING IN THE 1980s

By Robert P. Kerker

Sometime in the early 1970s, subtle changes began to take place in state budgeting, changes that are gathering momentum and bringing about major revisions in the way executive budget agencies are organized, the way budget officers spend their time, and the relationships of executive and legislative branches.

The purpose of this essay is to identify some principal sources of change that are only beginning to receive widespread attention, and to speculate briefly on their potential impact on the framework of state budgeting in the current decade. Nothing could be more hazardous or arbitrary, of course, than such an attempt at generalization. The situation undoubtedly looks different from the Northeastern states than it does from states with severance taxes. And, the diverse patterns of historical development among 50 states will always make the deviation in one state seem a "return to normalcy" in another.

However, change is upon us, as conference after conference in budgeting and public administration affirms, and it does not seem out of order in a work devoted to the synthesis of experience to attempt to look at some of its roots.

Change is often well along before it is realized that anything is happening, and even major change is initially treated as aberration, attributable to isolated events, personalities or caprice, a departure from the norm that will be corrected when those who have real experience in the field and a real love for the institutions regain control.

In all probability, the changes discussed below would have come about anyway. But, they were hurried forward by the growth in government in the 1960s, almost as dramatic in the state capitals as in Washington, and by the fiscal crisis of the 1970s, in which some cities and states often seemed to teeter on the edge of bankruptcy.

Consider the new power relationships that are emerging in budgeting. First and foremost, we see everywhere revitalized and far more aggressive legislatures. From the end of World War II to roughly 1960, the executive was dominant in the budgetary process to a degree scarcely achieved before or since. Revenue growth was steady if not spectacular. Budget agencies, stimulated by the new sense of professionalism symbolized by the establishment at the beginning of the period of the National Association of State Budget Officers (NASBO), increased staff resources in both quality and quantity, expanded their capacity for both fiscal research and management analysis, became far more interventionist in the lives of program agencies, and established the agenda and provided the background for debate on nearly every critical financial question. Even battles lost on the floors of legislative bodies could be won later through uncontested executive control of the execution process.

All this began to change rapidly in the late 1960s—even in states like New York which had been widely viewed as the prototypes of strong executive systems. Reapportionments following "one-man one-vote" decisions unhinged state party structures and produced new brands of leadership in legislative bodies. A legislative perspective increasingly independent of both executive control and state party structure began to demand independent staff resources and research capability and was less and less willing to accept at face value the assumptions of the executive. This growth, well along by the 1960s, accelerated in the following decade as the states groped with constricting resources and sometimes fiscal crisis. The legislatures rethought institutional relationships, took extraordinary steps to cap expenditures and redirect and control the flow of revenues, tried to influence if not control municipal budgets and the decisions and policies of once independent public authorities, and bent the rules in extraordinary ways in a patchwork of efforts to deal with impending disasters.

For the executive charged with crisis management, the price of legislative cooperation was often a sharing of power in areas that had theretofore been the preserve of the governor and his budget staff. Prolonged deadlocks over the budget stretched beyond the beginning of the fiscal year in state after state; if it embarrassed legislative bodies, the embarrassment was at least collective. For governors it was all too personal,

Robert P. Kerker is a Deputy Chief Budget Examiner, New York State Division of the Budget.

and new mechanisms aimed at reconciling economic assumptions and revenue estimates seemed increasingly attractive even to strong chief executives. Legislative overrides of executive vetoes, or credible threats of such overrides, were commonplace, even where at least one house of the legislature formally shared a governor's political persuasion.

If the rise of the legislative branch is changing the framework of budgeting, the third branch of government has been almost as effective in reshaping the structure. Despite ebb and flow from decision to decision, the judiciary will continue to play a critical role in defining the equity of budgetary decisions and in influencing budget procedures. The courts have set standards for an increasing array of dependent populations, with striking budgetary as well as political and managerial effects in such diverse locales as Alabama, New York and Texas. The comparable pay issue in the state of Washington is being watched everywhere with interest and with apprehension. Advocacy groups, pushing for long overdue reforms in their areas of special concern, are not likely to be impressed by the competitive demands of other groups and even less by those seeking tax reductions.

How the courts will react to class action in the 1980s is not clear at this point, but litigation is likely to continue to seem a viable option for any group that fails to carry the day in the legislative and political process. And, regardless of the validity of the claim, judicial intervention continues to raise significant questions about the ability of the budget process to perform its classic role: balancing through political decisions the public's perception of need with its readiness to commit its resources.

A third major catalyst for change in the 1980s is the growing impact of the financial markets on government budgets and budgetary processes. The reasons for this are not hard to find. Nothing demonstrated so vividly the depth of the New York City crisis in 1975 as the loss of its ability to borrow. Looming over the state of New York was the potential loss of its own credit standing. Nothing symbolized recovery so much as the return to the market.

Overall, the effects of the new relationship with rating services and banks have probably been salutary. The increasingly voluminous prospectuses that accompany the notes and bonds offered for sale discuss—with a candor rarely sought and never achieved by standard budget presentations—the vulnerability of revenue and expenditure estimates, the potentially damaging effects of adverse court or administrative rulings, and the magnitude of unfunded liabilities. And, the focus of the rating services on overall financial health and the soundness of the financial structure have done as much as anything else to focus attention on budget aggregates. The question of whether the budget is in fact "in balance" has given a powerful thrust toward "macrobudgeting." It has also produced, probably inevitably, curious institutional alignments within state governments. Regardless of party, officials, such as governors and comptrollers, who are charged with defending a financial plan in its entirety before the markets, frequently find themselves at odds with those in the legislative branch who must be responsive to specific constituencies.

State budgeting as it moves through the 1980s is an institution in flux. Some of the forces are potentially centrifugal: the impacts of changing relationships among the three branches of government. One of them, however, the emergent relationship with the money market, with its unavoidable focus on the aggregates of macrobudgeting, is definitely centripetal. And it serves to remind state budgeters of latent strengths, strengths viewed wistfully by some at the federal level who see the national budget process disintegrating in the wake of the reform legislation of the mid-1970s. The states, let us not forget, must already operate within a balanced budget, generally have a line-item veto (admittedly more effective some places than others), and for the most part continue to make the executive presentation the centerpiece of attention—even if the result is often far removed from what the executive had in mind. Those are important advantages, and will be important ingredients in assuring coherence as the decade progresses.

Table 1
STATE BUDGETARY PRACTICES

State or other jurisdiction	Budget-making authority	Date estimates must be submitted by dept. or agencies	Power of legislature to change budget(a)	Fiscal year begins	Frequency of budget
Alabama	Governor	Oct. 15 for Jan. session; Nov. 15 for Feb. session	Unlimited	Oct. 1	Annual
Alaska	Governor	Oct. 1	Unlimited	July 1	Annual
Arizona	Governor	Sept. 1 each year	Unlimited	July 1	Annual
Arkansas	Governor	Sept. 1 in even years	Unlimited	July 1	Biennial, odd yr.(b)
California	Governor	Specific date for each agency set by Dept. of Finance	Unlimited	July 1	Annual
Colorado	Governor	Aug. 1-15	Unlimited	July 1	Annual
Connecticut	Governor	Sept. 1	Unlimited	July 1	Annual
Delaware	Governor	Sept. 15; schools, Oct. 15	Unlimited	July 1	Annual
Florida	Governor	Nov. 1 each year	Unlimited	July 1	Biennial
Georgia	Governor	Sept. 1	Unlimited	July 1	Annual
Hawaii	Governor(c)	Aug. 31	Unlimited	July 1	Biennial, odd yr.(b,d)
Idaho	Governor	Sept. 1 before Jan. session	Unlimited	July 1	Annual
Illinois	Governor	Specific date for each agency set by Bureau of the Budget	Unlimited	July 1	Annual
Indiana	Governor	Sept. 1 in even years, flexible policy	Unlimited	July 1	Biennial, odd yr.(b)
Iowa	Governor	Sept. 1	Unlimited	July 1	Biennial, odd yr.(b)
Kansas	Governor	Not later than Oct. 1	Unlimited	July 1	Annual
Kentucky	Governor	Specific date set by administrative action but may not be later than Nov. 15 of each odd year	Unlimited	July 1	Biennial, even yr.(b)
Louisiana	Governor	Dec. 15	Unlimited	July 1	Annual
Maine	Governor	Sept. 1 in even years	Unlimited	July 1	Biennial, odd yr.(b)
Maryland	Governor	Sept. 1	Limited: legislature may decrease but not increase, except appropriations for legislature and judiciary	July 1	Annual
Massachusetts	Governor	Set by administrative action	Unlimited	July 1	Annual
Michigan	Governor	Set by administrative action	Unlimited	Oct. 1	Annual
Minnesota	Governor	Oct. 1 preceding convening of legislature	Unlimited	July 1	Biennial, odd yr.(b)
Mississippi	Commission of Budget & Accounting (e)	Aug. 1 preceding convening of legislature	Unlimited	July 1	Annual
Missouri	Governor	Oct. 1	Unlimited	July 1	Annual
Montana	Governor	Sept. 1 of year before each session	Unlimited	July 1	Biennial, odd yr.
Nebraska	Governor	Not later than Sept. 15	Limited: 3/5 vote required to increase governor's recommendations; majority vote required to reject or decrease such items	July 1	Annual
Nevada	Governor	Sept. 1	Unlimited	July 1	Biennial, odd yr.(b)
New Hampshire	Governor	Oct. 1 in even years	Unlimited	July 1	Biennial, odd yr.(b)
New Jersey	Governor	Oct. 1	Unlimited	July 1	Annual
New Mexico	Governor	Sept. 1	Unlimited	July 1	Annual
New York	Governor	Early in Sept.	Limited: may strike out items, reduce items, or add separate items of expenditure	April 1	Annual

State or other jurisdiction	Budget-making authority	Date estimates must be submitted by dept. or agencies	Power of legislature to change budget(a)	Fiscal year begins	Frequency of budget
North Carolina	Governor	Sept. 1 preceding session	Unlimited	July 1	Biennial, odd yr.(b)
North Dakota	Governor	July 15 in even years; may extend 45 days	Unlimited	July 1	Biennial, odd yr.
Ohio	Governor	Nov. 1; Dec. 1 when new governor is elected	Unlimited	July 1	Biennial, odd yr.(b)
Oklahoma	Governor	Sept. 1	Unlimited	July 1	Annual
Oregon	Governor	Sept. 1 in even year preceding legislative year	Unlimited	July 1	Biennial, odd yr.
Pennsylvania	Governor	Nov. 1 each year	Unlimited	July 1	Annual
Rhode Island	Governor	Oct. 1	Unlimited	July 1	Annual
South Carolina	State Budget & Control Board(f)	Sept. 15 or discretion of board	Unlimited	July 1	Annual
South Dakota	Governor	Sept. 1	Unlimited	July 1	Annual
Tennessee	Governor	Oct. 1	Unlimited	July 1	Annual
Texas	Governor, Legislative Budget Board	Date set by budget director and Legislative Budget Board	Unlimited	Sept. 1	Biennial, odd yr.(b)
Utah	Governor	Sept. 1-30(g)	Unlimited	July 1	Annual
Vermont	Governor	Sept. 1	Unlimited	July 1	(h)
Virginia	Governor	Feb.-Sept. in odd years	Unlimited	July 1	Biennial, even yr.(b)
Washington	Governor	Date set by governor	Unlimited	July 1	Biennial, odd yr.(b)
West Virginia	Governor	Aug. 15	Limited: may not increase items of budget bill except appropriations for legislature and judiciary	July 1	Annual
Wisconsin	Governor	Dates are set by secretary, Department of Administration	Unlimited	July 1	Biennial, odd yr.(b)
Wyoming	Governor	Sept. 15 preceding session in Feb.	Unlimited	July 1	Biennial, even yr.(b)
Guam	Governor	Date set by director, Bureau of Budget & Management Resource	Unlimited	Oct. 1	Annual
Puerto Rico	Governor	Oct. 15	Unlimited	July 1	Annual
Virgin Islands	Governor	Dec. 30	Unlimited	Oct. 1	Annual

Note: For further information on the budget processes in the states, see the following tables—Budget: Officials or Agencies Responsible for Preparation, Review and Controls; Legislative Appropriations Process: Budget Documents and Bills; and Enacting Legislation: Veto, Veto Override and Effective Date.

(a) Limitations listed in this column relate to legislative power to increase or decrease budget items generally. Specific limitations, such as constitutionally earmarked funds or requirement to enact revenue measures to cover new expenditure items, are not included.

(b) Budget is adopted biennially, but appropriations are made for each year of the biennium separately. Maine—budget is reviewed annually. Minnesota and Wisconsin—a few appropriations are made for the biennium. Virginia—amendments to current budget can be made in any year, but there is no formal provision for annual review of the entire biennial appropriation. North Carolina, Washington and Wyoming—biennial appropriations with annual review. Wisconsin—statutes authorize an annual budget review, and the governor may in even years recommend changes.

(c) Governor has budget-making authority for executive branch only. Judiciary and legislative branch budgets are the responsibility of the respective branches, and the governor may only veto the budget bills as a whole, not by item.

(d) Increases or decreases may be made in even-year sessions.

(e) Composition of commission: governor (ex-officio chairman), lieutenant governor, president pro tempore of Senate, chairman of Senate Finance Committee, chairman of Senate Appropriations Committee, one senator appointed by lieutenant governor, speaker of the House, chairman of House Ways and Means Committee, chairman of House Appropriations Committee and two representatives appointed by speaker.

(f) Composition of board: governor (chairman), treasurer, comptroller general, chairman Senate Finance Committee, chairman House Ways and Means Committee.

(g) Thirty days prior to each department or agency hearing before the governor.

(h) 1981 legislature authorized annual or biennial budget at governor's discretion. Submission of annual budget began with fiscal 1982.

Table 2
BUDGET AGENCY FUNCTIONS

State or other jurisdiction	Revenue estimating primary	Revenue estimating secondary	Fiscal research	Fiscal notes	Organization and management analysis	Accounting primary	Accounting secondary	Data processing primary	Data processing secondary	Legislative review	Planning	Program policy issue analysis	Program evaluation	Federal/state relations	Debt management	Economic analysis
Alabama	★		★		★		★					★	★		★	
Alaska	★		★	★	★					★		★	★			★
Arizona	★		★	★					★	★		★		Y,Z		★
Arkansas	★		★							★	C	★	★			
California			★	★						★		★	★	V		★
Colorado			★		(a)			★		★	C,P	★	★	V,W		★
Connecticut	★(b)		★		★		★(c)			★	C,P (a)	★	★	(a)		★
Delaware		(b)	★	(d)	★					★		★	★	W,Y,Z		★
Florida	★(b)		★	(e)	★			★		★	C,P	★	★	V,W,Y,Z		★
Georgia			★		★	★		★		★	P	★	★	V,W		
Hawaii	(f)		★		★					★		★	★	Y		★
Idaho			★	★	★					★	C,F,P	★	★	V,W		★
Illinois		(f)	★		★		★			★	P	★	★	W,Y,Z	★	
Indiana			★		★					★		★	★	V	★	★
Iowa	★		★	★	★					★		★		V,W,Y	★	★
Kansas			★	★	★					★	P	★	★	V(g)		★
Kentucky		(f)	★		★			★		★	P	★	★	(h)		
Louisiana		(f)	★(a)		★					★		★	★	V		(a)
Maine	★		★	★	★					★		★	★	V,Y	★	★
Maryland	★		★		★			★		★	P	★	★	V		★
Massachusetts	(e)		★		★					★	C,P	★	★	V		
Michigan	(a)	(g)	★	★	(i)	(a)		(i)		★	P	★	(j)	V,W(a)	(a)	★
Minnesota	★	(h)	★	★						★	C,L,P	★	★			
Mississippi	(k)		★	★	★					★		★	★	Y,Z		
Missouri	★		★		★					★		★	★			
Montana	(l)		★		★					★	C,L,P	★		V		
Nebraska	★	(g)	★	★	★					★	F,P	★	★	(h)		★
Nevada	★	(h)	★	★	★	★		★		★		★	★			
New Hampshire	★	(f)	★		★	★				★	P	★	★	Y		
New Jersey			★		★					★	P	★				★
New Mexico	★		★	★	★					★	P	★	★			★
New York	★		★		★	★				★	P	★	★	V,W,Y,Z	★	★
North Carolina			★		★	★				★	P	★	★			
North Dakota			★							★		★				
Ohio	(m)		★		★	(a)		(a)		★		★	★	V,Y,Z		
Oklahoma	★		★							★		★				
Oregon	★		★		★					★		★			★	★
Pennsylvania			★	★						★		★		V		★
Rhode Island	★	★	★	★	★	★	★	★	★	★		★	★	V	★(n)	★
South Carolina	★		★	★	★				★	★	C,P	★	★	V		★

State														
South Dakota	★	★	(d)	★	★	★	⋯	⋯	★	★	★	★	★
Tennessee	★	★ (o)	⋯	★	★	⋯	⋯	⋯	★	★	★	⋯	⋯
Texas	★	⋯	⋯	★	★	C,L,P	⋯	★	★	★	v	★	★
Utah	★	⋯	⋯	⋯	★	⋯	⋯	★	★	★	v,w	⋯	★
Vermont	★	★	★	★	★	⋯	★	★	★	★	⋯	⋯	★
Virginia	⋯	⋯	★	⋯	⋯	(p)	⋯	⋯	⋯	⋯	⋯	⋯	⋯
Washington	★ (f)	★	★	★	★	C,P	★	★	★	★	w,z	⋯	★
West Virginia	★ (e)	⋯	⋯	⋯	⋯	C,P	⋯	⋯	⋯	⋯	⋯	★	★
Wisconsin	★	(a)	(a)	(a)	(a) ★	L	(a) ★	⋯	⋯	★	v	⋯	★
Wyoming	★	(a)	⋯	⋯	⋯	C,F,P	★	⋯	★	★	v,w,z	★	★
Guam	★ (e)	★	★	★	★	P	★	⋯	★	★	w	⋯	⋯
Puerto Rico	★	★	★	★	⋯	P	★	⋯	★	★	⋯	⋯	★
Virgin Islands	⋯ (q)	★	★	★	⋯	C,P	★	★	⋯	★	⋯	★	★

Source: National Association of State Budget Officers; updated by The Council of State Governments.

Note: In addition to the functions listed, the following states indicated additional duties. Alabama—keep all allotment records; Colorado—approval of fund transfers; Delaware—coordinate state policies and federal programs and resources by providing staff support to State Clearinghouse Committee and operating Washington, D.C. office; New Hampshire—management supervision of all state agencies; New Jersey—monitor programs and their objectives to determine progress in reaching objectives; New Mexico—review contracts for professional services and out-of-state travel requests, propose and administer salary plans for exempt employees (political appointments), serve as revenue sharing liaison, draft general appropriations act, prepare capital budgets and plans, budget adjustments; New York—participates in management assistance and coordination, state-local relations, employee relations and compensation; Rhode Island—negotiations of hospital rates; Virginia—development, storage, retrieval and dissemination of data on social, economic, physical and governmental aspects of the state to provide information for use by state and other governmental bodies; Guam—local auditing of territorial programs within the executive branch; Virgin Islands—coordination of state energy policy.

Key:
★—Yes
⋯—No
C—Comprehensive state
F—Functional
L—Local
P—Policy
V—Approval of agency grant applications.
W—Planning assistance for and monitoring of grant applications.

Y—Information on grant awards.
Z—Assistance to agencies and local governments on obtaining grants or information on grants.

(a) Performed by another division in same office or department.
(b) Performed or executed by another budgetary-related department or body.
(c) Budget director establishes and maintains accounting system and procedures; secretary of Department of Finance processes documents, conducts pre-audits and maintains central accounting records.
(d) Upon request.
(e) Joint responsibility with another office or department.
(f) Responsibility of revenue-collection agency. Hawaii—constitutional requirement for Council on Revenues. Washington—Revenue Department responsible for primary revenue estimating for most major taxes; however, budget agency has responsibility for all estimates used for budget.
(g) Recommendations on applications.
(h) Review only.
(i) Department of Administration.
(j) Legislative auditor.
(k) Approval of estimates made by State Tax Commission.
(l) General fund only.
(m) Provides input and data to State Board of Equalization which makes the official estimates.
(n) Recommend bond sales, including amount by project and term.
(o) Comptroller of Public Accounts.
(p) By statute, budget agency responsible for revenue estimating; however, Department of Revenue provides assistance.
(q) Approval of personnel action and fund transfers.

Table 3
BUDGET: OFFICIALS OR AGENCIES RESPONSIBLE FOR
PREPARATION, REVIEW AND CONTROLS

State or other jurisdiction	*Official/agency responsible for preparing budget document*	*Special budget review agency in legislative branch*	*Agency(ies) responsible for budgetary and related accounting controls*
Alabama	Budget Officer, Dept. of Finance	Leg. Fiscal Off.; Joint Fiscal Cmte.	Div. of Control & Accounts, Dept. of Finance
Alaska	Dir., Off. of Budget & Mgmt.	Leg. Budget & Audit Cmte.	Div. of Treasury, Dept. of Revenue
Arizona	Executive Budget Officer, Finance Div., Dept. of Admin.	Joint Leg. Budget Cmte.	Div. of Finance, Dept. of Admin.
Arkansas	Administrator, Off. of Budget, Dept. of Finance & Admin.	Budget & Fiscal Review Section, Bur. of Leg. Research	Dept. of Finance & Admin.
California	Dir., Dept. of Finance	Joint Leg. Budget Cmte.	Dept. of Finance; Off. of the Controller
Colorado	Executive Dir., Off. of State Planning & Budgeting	Joint Budget Cmte.	Div. of Accounts & Control, Dept. of Admin.
Connecticut	Undersecy. for Budget, Off. of Policy & Mgmt.	Off. of Fiscal Analysis, Joint Cmte. on Leg. Mgmt.	Off. of Policy & Mgmt.; Off. of the Comptroller
Delaware	Dir. Off. of the Budget	Controller General	Dept. of Finance
Florida	Dir., Off. of Planning & Budgeting	Senate, House Appropriations; Senate, House Finance & Taxation cmtes.	Comptroller; Finance Div., Dept. of Banking & Finance
Georgia	Dir., Off. of Planning & Budget	Off. of Leg. Budget Analyst, Leg. Services Cmte.	Fiscal Div., Dept. of Administrative Services.
Hawaii	Dir., Dept. of Budget & Finance	Off. of the Leg. Auditor	Dept. of Budget & Finance; Comptroller, Dept. of Accounting & General Services
Idaho	Administrator, Div. of Financial Mgmt., Off. of the Governor	Leg. Budget Off., Joint Finance & Appropriations Cmte.	Div. of Financial Mgmt., Off. of the Governor, Off. of State Auditor
Illinois	Bur. of the Budget	Economic & Fiscal Comm.; Senate, House Appropriations cmtes.	Off. of the Comptroller
Indiana	Dir., Budget Agency	Off. of Fiscal & Mgmt. Analysis, Leg. Services Agency	Budget Agency; Off. of State Auditor
Iowa	State Comptroller	Leg. Fiscal Bur.	Off. of the Comptroller
Kansas	Dir., Div. of the Budget, Dept. of Admin.	Off. of Leg. Fiscal Analyst, Leg. Research Dept.	Div. of Accounts & Reports, Dept. of Admin.
Kentucky	Secy., Finance & Admin. Cabinet	Budget Review, Leg. Research Comm.	Off. of Policy & Mgmt., Finance & Admin. Cabinet
Louisiana	Budget Dir., Div. of Admin., Off. of the Governor	Leg. Fiscal Off.	Div. of Admin., Off. of the Governor
Maine	State Budget Officer, Bur. of the Budget, Dept. of Finance & Admin.	Joint Cmte. on Appropriations & Financial Aff.; Leg. Finance Off.	Bur. of Accounts & Control Dept. of Finance & Admin.
Maryland	Secy., Budget & Fiscal Planning Dept.	Joint Cmte. Budget & Audit; Div. of Budget Review, Dept. of Fiscal Services	Comptroller of the Treasury
Massachusetts	Budget Dir., Div. of Fiscal Aff., Off. for Admin. & Finance	Senate, House Ways & Means cmtes.	Off. for Admin. & Finance; Comptroller's Div.
Michigan	Dir., Dept. of Mgmt. & Budget	Senate, House Fiscal agencies	Dept. of Mgmt. & Budget
Minnesota	Commr., Dept. of Finance	Senate Fiscal Analysts; House Appropriations Cmte.	Dept. of Finance
Mississippi	Commission of Budget & Accounting(a)	(a)	Commission of Budget & Accounting(a); Off. of State Audit
Missouri	Dir., Div. of Budget & Planning, Off. of Admin.	Cmte. on State Fiscal Aff.; Senate Appropriations Cmte.; House Budget Cmte.	Off. of Admin.
Montana	Dir., Off. of Budget & Program Planning	Leg. Audit Cmte.; Leg. Finance Cmte.	Dept. of Admin.
Nebraska	Administrator, Budget Div., Dept. of Administrative Services	Leg. Fiscal Off.	Dept. of Administrative Services
Nevada	Dir., Dept. of Admin.	Fiscal Analysis Div., Leg. Counsel Bur.	Off. of the Comptroller
New Hampshire	Comptroller, Dept. of Admin. & Control	Fiscal Cmte. of the General Court	Comptroller, Dept. of Admin. & Control
New Jersey	Comptroller, Div. of Budget & Accounting, Dept. of Treasury	Div. of Budget & Program Review, Off. of Leg. Services	Div. of Budget & Accounting, Dept. of Treasury
New Mexico	Dir., Budget Div., Dept. of Finance & Admin.	Leg. Finance Cmte.	Dept. of Finance & Admin.
New York	Dir., Div. of Budget	Senate Finance Cmte.; Assembly Ways & Means Cmte.	Comptroller, Dept. of Audit & Control
North Carolina	Budget Officer, Off. of Budget & Mgmt.	Fiscal Research Div., Leg. Ser. Comm.	Off. of Budget & Mgmt.
North Dakota	Exec. Budget Analyst; Dir., Off of Mgmt. & Budget	Off. of Leg. Budget Analyst & Auditor, Leg. Council	Off. of Mgmt. & Budget
Ohio	Dir., Off. of Budget & Mgmt.	Leg. Budget Off.	Dept. of Administrative Services

State or other jurisdiction	Official/agency responsible for preparing budget document	Special budget review agency in legislative branch	Agency(ies) responsible for budgetary and related accounting controls
Oklahoma	Dir., Off. of State Finance	Leg. Fiscal Off.	Off. of State Finance
Oregon	Administrator, Budget & Mgmt. Div.	Leg. Fiscal Off.	Accounting Div., Exec. Dept.
Pennsylvania	Secy., Off. of Budget	Senate, House Appropriations Cmtes.; Leg. Budget & Finance Cmte.	Comptroller Operations, Off. of the Governor
Rhode Island	Finance & Planning, Dept. of Admin.	Senate, House Finance cmtes.	Accounts & Control, Dept. of Admin.
South Carolina	Exec. Dir., State Budget & Control Bd.	State Budget & Control Bd.; State Auditor	Off. of Comptroller General; State Budget & Control Bd.
South Dakota	Commissioner, Bureau of Finance & Mgmt.	Chief Fiscal Analyst, Leg. Research Council	Bur. of Finance & Mgmt.; Off. of State Auditor
Tennessee	Commissioner, Budget Div., Dept. of Finance & Admin.	Fiscal Review Cmte.	Dept. of Finance & Admin.; Off. of Comptroller
Texas	Dir., Governor's Off. of Mgmt. & Budget	Leg. Budget Bd.	Comptroller, Public Accounts
Utah	Dir., Off. of the State Budget	Leg. Fiscal Analyst, Leg. Mgmt. Cmte.	Div. of Finance, Dept. of Admin. Ser.
Vermont	Commissioner, Dept. of Budget & Mgmt.	Joint Fiscal Cmte.	Dept. of Finance, Agency of Admin.
Virginia	Dir., Dept. of Planning & Budget	Senate Finance Cmte.; House Appropriations Cmte.	Comptroller, Dept. of Accounts
Washington	Dir., Off. of Financial Mgmt.	Leg. Budget Cmte.	Off. of Financial Mgmt.
West Virginia	Dir., Budget Div.; Commissioner, Dept. of Finance & Admin.	Leg. Auditor; Joint Cmte. on Government & Finance	Dept. of Finance & Admin.
Wisconsin	Administrator, State Exec. Budget & Planning, Dept. of Admin.	Joint Cmte. on Finance; Leg. Fiscal Bur.	Bureau of State Finance, State Finance & Program Mgmt., Dept. of Admin.
Wyoming	Administrator, Budget Div., Dept. of Admin. & Fiscal Control	Leg. Ser. Off.	Off. of State Auditor
American Samoa	Dir., Program Planning & Budget Development, Off. of the Governor	Leg. Fiscal Officer, Leg. Reference Bur.	Administrative Ser.
Guam	Dir., Bur. of Budget & Mgmt. Resource	Leg. Cmte. on Ways & Means	Div. of Accounts, Dept. of Admin.
No. Mariana Is.	Planning & Budgeting, Off. of the Governor	Senate Consultant on Fiscal Aff.; House Appropriations Cmte. Consultant	Dept. of Finance
Puerto Rico	Dir., Off. of Budget Mgmt.	Economic Div., Off. of Leg. Ser.	Off. of Budget Mgmt.
Virgin Islands	Dir., Off. of the Budget	Leg. Finance Cmte.; Leg. Post Auditor	Dept. of Finance

(a) Commission of Budget and Accounting members: governor (ex-officio chairman), lieutenant governor, president pro tempore of Senate, chairman of Senate Finance Committee, chairman of Senate Appropriations Committee, one senator appointed by lieutenant governor, speaker of the House, chairman of House Ways and Means Committee, chairman of House Appropriations Committee, two representatives appointed by speaker.

3.   Purchasing

PROCUREMENT CHALLENGES

By Glenn R. Cummings

Thus far in the 1980s, state purchasing faces challenges that affect not only the way states do business but the very fabric of society and even individual safety. Many of the challenges are remnants from the previous decade, others have sprung from new technology and legal decisions that require changes in procurement thinking and methodology.

1. The Model Procurement Code. Since the Model Procurement Code was approved and drafts were distributed, there has been much discussion and activity concerning its adoption or adaptation by the states. Both the National Association of State Purchasing Officials and the National Institute of Governmental Purchasing have endorsed the concept of the code. Since it is a model, not a uniform code, the state procurement community is of the opinion that the Model Procurement Code, or parts of it, can be adapted to the needs of most state purchasing functions. However, since 1979, only nine states have adopted code-based legislation. Another six states have either introduced legislation or are actively considering such activity. Many other states are studying various aspects of the code, and may be interested in changing sections of their legislation. However, not all states endorse the code or are actively pursuing its eventual adoption. A great number have not initiated any activity whatsoever. The adoption of the code by all states appears to be a remote possibility that will, at best, take years.

2. Attachment "O". OMB Circular A-102, Revised, *Uniform Administrative Requirements for Grants in Aid—to State and Local Governments* effective October 1, 1979, was designed to reduce paperwork by relying on state and local purchasing under federal grants, after the state systems have been certified by the federal government. Everyone applauds the idea of reducing bureaucratic interference and the idea of relying on local procedures for procurement under federal grants. However, most states remain uncertified. Several hypotheses may be promulgated for this phenomenon. Attachment "O" relies heavily on the adoption of the Model Procurement Code or similar legislation. As noted above, many states have not seriously considered the Model Procurement Code nor do they apparently feel a need for changing their present procurement statutes. Without the codification of the Model Procurement Code, it is difficult for some states to acquire certification even under the self-certification program (which most states that are certified have used). Further, certification by one federal agency does not necessarily mean other agencies will accept the state procurement system without going through the process of certification once again.

Attachment "O", as well as the Model Procurement Code, tends toward standardization of state procurement functions. With this standardization, the creativity and innovation of independent states may well be lost.

3. Socioeconomic Issues. Owing, to a great degree, to the recent poor economic conditions, many states have been reevaluating the viability of remedying socioeconomic ills through the procurement process, a practice that has taken many forms including buy-America acts, small business and minority set-aside legislation, and in-state preference. This interest has been fostered in spite of the procurement officials' uniquely unqualified position to adjudicate socioeconomic issues. Indeed, preferences of any type are antithetical to the principles of competitive bidding.

The result of socioeconomic procurement legislation, almost without exception, is to increase the cost of acquisition. The National Association of State Purchasing Officials, National Institute of Governmental Purchasing, and the National Governors' Association have passed resolutions against resident vendor preferences, which are considered particularly onerous to free competition. These laws delegate to the purchasing practitioner the duty of making social decisions in lieu of his normal role of making the most prudent investment of public funds.

4. Acquisition of Professional Services. The manner in which professional services are obtained, whether they are engineering, architectural, legal or medical, etc., is slowly being changed in state government. Increasingly, the

---

Glenn R. Cummings is Director of Purchasing for West Virginia.

responsibility for this contracting is being given to the purchasing officials of the states. With this transfer of responsibility, a debate has ensued over whether professional service can or should be competitively bid. Many of the practitioners of professional services feel it is degrading to have their services placed on a figurative auction block as if they were fungible commodities. Many state purchasing officials view these services as the most complex procured by the state. Most state purchasing organizations have attempted to devise methods to evaluate the qualifications of each proposed professional and make rational decisions based on qualifications and benefits to be derived by the state government. Almost all state purchasing officials believe that both price and qualifications, as well as need, should be considered. In the future, some understanding must be reached between the buyer and the seller of professional services to devise a universally acceptable method that will obtain the services needed by the states at a reasonable cost.

5. *Telecommunications.* Because of the recent break-up of the Bell System, state purchasing professionals have been catapulted into acquisition of high technology communications equipment previously leased on a non-competitive basis. State governments can no longer rely on the local telephone company to provide these services, but must competitively bid new switching gear, telephone systems and possibly even telephone instruments. In order to deal with this new challenge, many states have formed separate divisions to plan acquisition of systems in this revolutionary market, while other states are attempting to devise methods of assuring continued communications within state government, almost on a crisis basis.

To deal with this new industry, the most sophisticated purchasing procedures are used, namely requests for proposals and other complex procurement methods. The combative nature of the vendors in this field along with new ideas, technology and terminology assure that this area of purchasing must be mastered by purchasing officials within a very short time.

6. *Hazardous Waste Removal.* Almost every state has problems with hazardous waste or low level nuclear waste disposal. State governments also must deal with liability when waste is removed, containerized and stored, either within or outside the state's boundaries. Purchasing will be brought into these controversial areas more and more in the future. Because most state governments do not have the ability to ascertain

the proper methods of disposal, outside services must be contracted to prevent contamination of soil, water and atmosphere. While the courts decree and regulatory agencies mandate clean up of the environment, in many instances purchasing will have to find a vendor and issue a contract, assuring the safe disposal of hazardous materials.

7. *The Robinson-Patman Act.* The recent court decision, in *Jefferson County Pharmaceutical v. Abbott Laboratories*, in which the U.S. Supreme Court declared that manufacturers cannot give special prices to state governments if the commodities are for resale, has raised many questions for state purchasers. The exemption of states from application of the Robinson-Patman Act has been questioned under the *Jefferson County Pharmaceutical* case. While this ruling appears to be of no great concern to most state governments, the questions raised are far-reaching. If manufacturers or distributors cannot competitively bid prices to state governments, the entire competitive process, as known in the states, is in jeopardy. The set commercial price may become a "take it or leave it" offer and state governments may be denied the opportunity to obtain the best possible pricing for goods or services.

The next few years in state purchasing will present challenges never before imagined. Some of these challenges have been briefly discussed here while others are addressed in more detail in the recent publication by the National Association of State Purchasing Officials and The Council of State Governments, *State and Local Government Purchasing, 2nd Edition.* The state purchasing official must not only be resourceful and innovative to meet these challenges but must receive aid from others in state governments. Too often, the value of state public purchasing has been ignored, resulting in inadequate funding and staffing of this vital function. Only with adequate resources and a determined effort will state purchasing personnel be able to meet the new procurement challenges.

4.   Information Systems

STATE INFORMATION MANAGEMENT

By Lorraine Amico

Over the past 10 years, the number and complexity of state data systems have grown significantly. This growth has focused on technology (hardware and software) in particular and data production in general. While this aspect of information delivery remains basic in state data activities, the federal budget cuts of 1981 and 1982 brought attention to the nation's statistical system. Public hearings examined how budget cuts would affect the information derived from approximately 97 federally funded statistical programs. Witnesses, including public policymakers, program managers and private sector decision-makers, spoke of their need for and uses of particular data sets. They testified on how the loss of available data and the reduced data reliability, timeliness and geographic detail of specific data series might affect their ability to make informed decisions.

Courtenay Slater, former Chief Economist with the U.S. Department of Commerce, stated at a statistical meeting in March 1983 that the budget cuts are not the primary problem with our nation's statistical system even though the decreased funding served as a catalyst to focus attention on information issues. She indicated that the single most serious problem is the continuing lack of information management or a systematic approach to the collection, analysis, dissemination and use of voluminous amounts of data in our largely decentralized statistical system. The Federal Paperwork Reduction Act of 1980 was intended to establish in the Office of Management and Budget (OMB) central policy-making and coordination for statistical programs at the federal level; however, the authority exercised to date has been minimal.

Because of the weakened federal role in coordinating statistical programs and the increasing need of state government staff to use information to manage programs such as block grants, the issue of state-level comprehensive information management has been heightened in a number of states within the past two years. For example, 10 states are participating in a State Statistical Task Force, and in addition, Alaska, New York, Maine, Georgia and Massachusetts have conducted a variety of projects. The issue is not new. Several states have existing legal mandates dating back to 1966 to manage information.

Statewide information management and statistical coordination is defined here to mean activities comparable to the coordination and oversight envisioned in the Federal Paperwork Reduction Act—activities that deal with statewide information policy and management practices which crosscut individual agency statistical work. Information policy is concerned with the development, implementation and oversight of uniform and consistent information management principles, standards and guidelines; initiation and review of proposed changes in legislation, regulations and agency procedures; and coordination of agency information practices. Information management to improve the production, dissemination and use of data includes the inter-agency capability to:

• Plan strategically and operationally for comprehensive information activities and systems implementation.

• Manage staff and fiscal resources related to information production and use.

• Manage automated technology and apply it cost efficiently to data systems implementation.

• Provide training to state and substate staffs.

In December 1983 the State Statistical Task Force surveyed information management practices in the states. Forty-nine states responded to the telephone survey. As can be seen in Table 1, 15 of the 49 respondents reported their state coordinates inter-program statistical activities. In nine of the 15 states these activities were authorized by law or executive order; six states conduct these activities on a more informal basis using such mechanisms as an inter-agency task force. Five of the 15 receive targeted money for these activities. Hawaii, South Carolina, Utah and Washington receive state general revenue funds, and West Virginia receives funds on a cost reimbursable basis. Six states have staff assigned to this activity. Nine states have a user committee to provide input.

Lorraine Amico is Project Director in the National Governors' Association Center for Policy Research. Data were collected by the State Statistical Task Force.

The finding that only 30 percent of the states have a mechanism for overall statistical coordination is not surprising if the primary state role in many of the statistical programs is considered. In each program area states are required to respond to federal standards, definitions and methodologies regarding the various data sets that are funded in whole or part with federal funds. These programs, which comprise a large portion of the statistical activities conducted in the states, include both administrative records and statistical surveys that are federal programs or federal-state cooperative efforts. Because of this states to a large extent have not built and depended upon their own capabilities to manage statistical programs but rather have supported a strong federal role.

States, however, have taken responsibility for statistical coordination in specific issue areas. For example, in the 1960s several natural resources information systems were funded with state monies to centralize information capabilities and to maintain common data bases to assist data users. Information management practices in the human resources area began later in the 1970s, with the State Data Center program, a non-financial federal-state cooperative program intended primarily to disseminate decennial census information, and also with the State Occupational Information Coordinating Committees, which are federally funded to coordinate occupational data producers and users and to develop an integrated system containing multiple data sources.

The states that did enact overall statistical coordination laws presumably considered the management of information resources to be an issue of efficiency and good government management. The state laws range in comprehensiveness from minimal to extensive. For example, the Georgia law enacted in 1970 assigns responsibility for statistical coordination and standardization to the Office of Planning and Budget but does not enumerate specific activities. At the other extreme, the Hawaii administrative directive dated 1966 establishes the position of state statistician and authorizes the Department of Planning and Economic Development to coordinate state statistical programs and serve as a liaison with various public and private sector entities. The directive very specifically defines the objectives and responsibilities of the department and state statistician to coordinate, not centralize, various activities in developing a statewide statistical reporting system. Somewhere between these extremes, the Virginia law authorizes

the Department of Planning and Budget to coordinate existing sources of data and to approve new data programs. In Wyoming, the law specifies the overall supervisory and coordinating authority of the Division of Research and Statistics in the Department of Administration and Fiscal Control to perform a variety of activities including establishing uniform criteria, maintaining a central depository of state government operational data, developing data management programs and preparing an annual catalog of available information.

The authority that is exercised based on these legal mandates varies from state to state. Hawaii indicated that the authority has been used, as is also the case in Virginia where a statistical coordination procedure defining specific responsibilities and review processes was established. In Wyoming, however, the law has not been exercised to the fullest extent possible. The level of interest of key state decision-makers in the information management issue varies over time. For example, in Massachusetts Governor Dukakis made statistical coordination mandatory during his first term. His successor abolished the law. Now, during the second Dukakis term, interest has peaked again and will probably result in action in the state.

There are selected activities in the majority of the states with no overall statistical coordination. Fifteen separate statistical coordination activities are displayed in Table 2. In one state, although there is no overall coordination, 12 of the 15 activities are conducted. At the other extreme, several states have only one of the 15 activities. On the average, states conducted five activities. The 15 functions are ranked in Table 3. As can be seen, the most common (43 of 49 states) is coordinating the approval of equipment procurement. This can be attributed to the emphasis on technology and computer acquisition of the past decade. A statistical compendium was prepared in 28 states. Household surveys are conducted and information release procedures set in the fewest states.

A major concern in information management is the reduction of paperwork reporting burden. Eliminating duplication of effort to improve the efficiency of the system is extremely important in times of budgetary constraint. States generally indicated that duplication did exist and that the human resource development area was perhaps the worst. Duplication is possible when an economically disadvantaged, physically handicapped vocational education student who is also a veteran could potentially provide input to four different data reporting systems.

A key to reducing the data reporting burden is the use of a common identifier to allow multi-agency access to data in order to meet specific record-keeping requirements and user needs. A conflict exists when a privacy act discourages use of a common identifier such as a social security number. At the federal level, this conflict will have to be resolved before a consolidated federal statistical policy can be established. Eleven states indicated that they had made efforts to reduce the data reporting burden (see Table 2). Seven states conduct activities to secure the confidentiality of information. Only one state, Utah, is working in both areas simultaneously. Most states have separate freedom of information and confidentiality laws, and almost half of the states (23 out of 49) have specific program confidentiality laws rather than a single omnibus law. If states are to seriously consider reduction of the reporting burden then they will also have to address the issue of how to eliminate duplicative data collection efforts, while protecting confidential information.

The cost-effective use of data is as important as the cost-effective production of data, and the mechanisms to achieve this are key to the information management issue. Twenty-one states try to maximize use by coordinating and facilitating access to information. Often multiple data sets, particularly projections data, are available to the user. The debate for users in the decision-making process becomes which data set is used rather than the substantive implications of the data. The production and use of official projections by all user groups is a cost-effective use of limited resources. The states surveyed indicated (see Table 4) that population projections are the most, revenue forecasts the next and economic forecasts the third most commonly available official projections. In most cases there was a formal or informal input mechanism used in the development of these data sets. In fewer cases there is user training provided.

As states face the implications of a decreased federal presence in many programs and tighter budgets to carry out greater responsibilities, the effective use of information will continue to grow. The state capacity to effectively manage information should be an increasingly important concern for the key decision-makers who need and use data as a basis for the administration of state responsibilities.

Table 1
STATE STATISTICAL ACTIVITIES

State	Overall statistical coordination performed	Legal basis exists for activities	State funds support activities	State staff perform activities	User committee provides input	State has freedom of information law	State has confidentiality law	
							Agency specific	Omnibus/general
Alabama						★	★	
Alaska								
Arizona							★	
Arkansas						★	★	
California	★				★	★	★	
Colorado						★	★	
Connecticut	★					★	★	
Delaware						★	★	
Florida	★	★			★	★	★	
Georgia	★	★		★	★	★	★	
Hawaii	★	★	★	★	★	★	★	
Idaho						★	★	
Illinois						★	★	★
Indiana						★		
Iowa								★
Kansas						★		
Kentucky								
Louisiana								
Maine	★	★		★				
Maryland								
Massachusetts						★		
Michigan						★	★	★
Minnesota								★
Mississippi						★	★	
Missouri						★	★	
Montana						★		
Nebraska						★		
Nevada						★		
New Hampshire						★	★	
New Jersey						★	★	

State	1	2	3	4	5	6	7	8
New Mexico	★	.	★	.	.	.	.	.
New York	★	.	★	.	.	.	★	.
North Carolina	.	★	★	.	★	.	.	★
North Dakota	★	.	★	.	.	.	.	.
Ohio	★	.	★	.	.	.	★	.
Oklahoma	★	.	★	.	★	.	★	★
Oregon	.	★	★	.	.	.	.	.
Pennsylvania	.	★	★	.	.	.	.	.
Rhode Island	.	★	★	.	.	.	★	.
South Carolina	.	★	★	★	.	.	.	★
South Dakota	★	.	.	.	.	.	.	.
Tennessee	.	.	.	.	.	.	.	.
Texas	★	.	★	.	★	★	.	★
Utah	★	.	★	★	★	.	★	★
Vermont	.	★	.	★	.	★	★	★
Virginia	★	.	★	★	.	.	★	★
Washington	★	.	★	★	.	★	★	★
West Virginia	★	.	★	.	.	★	.	★
Wisconsin	.	.	★	.	.	.	.	.
Wyoming	.	★	.	.	.	.	.	★

Key:
★ —Yes
. —No

257

Table 2

STATE INTERAGENCY STATISTICAL COORDINATION

State	Information policy-making	Budget review of information activities	Serve as federal liaison for data activities	Serve as local liaison for data activities	Information standards setting	Reduce data reporting burden	Assure quality control	Set information release procedures	Approve equipment procurement	Protect privacy/maintain security of information	Conduct household survey on ongoing basis	Facilitate access of information	Make personnel policy	Publish compendium of state data	Coordinate training
Alabama	★	★	★	★	★	★			★					★	★
Alaska									★					★	
Arizona						★			★					★	
Arkansas	★	★	★	★								★		★	
California									★			★			
Colorado				★					★			★			★
Connecticut				★					★						
Delaware	★	★	★	★					★				★		
Florida			★	★					★					★	
Georgia									★					★	★
Hawaii				★		★	★	★	★			★			★
Idaho		★	★						★						★
Illinois									★		★				★
Indiana	★								★						
Iowa									★						
Kansas									★			★		★	★
Kentucky								★	★		★	★		★	
Louisiana		★		★					★						★
Maine				★					★						★
Maryland	★														
Massachusetts	★								★			★	★	★	★
Michigan			★	★		★			★			★	★	★	★
Minnesota				★					★				★		★
Mississippi									★						
Missouri									★					★	
Montana						★			★	★				★	
Nebraska		★	★	★					★	★		★			★
Nevada		★		★											★
New Hampshire					★				★				★	★	
New Jersey									★			★	★	★	

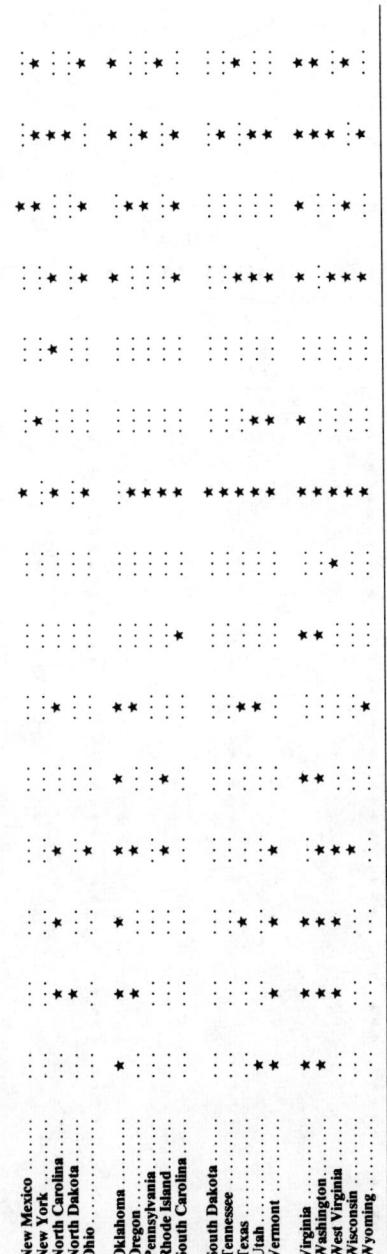

Key:
★—Yes
...—No

Table 3
RANK ORDER OF STATISTICAL FUNCTIONS PERFORMED

Function	Rank	Number of states
Approve equipment procurement	1	43
Publish compendium of state data	2	28
Serve as local liaison	3	22
Facilitate access of data	4	21
Coordinate training	5	19
Serve as federal liaison	6	18
Make personnel policy concerning information	7	17
Review information related budgets	8	16
Make information policy	9.5	11
Reduce data reporting burden	9.5	11
Set standards	11	9
Protect privacy/maintain security	12	7
Assure quality control	13	5
Conduct household survey	14.5	4
Set information release procedures	14.5	4

Table 4
AVAILABILITY OF OFFICIAL STATE PROJECTIONS

State	Economic forecast	Revenue forecast	Program need projections	Population projections	Intercensal estimates	Availability of user input mechanism	Training provided in use
Alabama	★	★	...	★	★	...	...
Alaska	...	...	...	...	...	...	...
Arizona	★	★	★	★	★	★	...
Arkansas	...	...	...	...	...	...	...
California	★	★	★	★	★	★	...
Colorado	...	★	...	★	...	...	...
Connecticut	★	★	...	★	★	...	...
Delaware	...	★	★	★	★	★	...
Florida	★	★	★	★	★	★	...
Georgia	...	...	...	★	★	★	...
Hawaii	★	★	...	★	★	★	★
Idaho	★	★	...	★	...	...	...
Illinois	...	...	...	★	★	★	...
Indiana	★	★	★	★	...	...	...
Iowa	...	...	...	★	★	...	...
Kansas	★	★	...	★	★	★	...
Kentucky	...	...	...	...	...	...	...
Louisiana	★	★	...	★	★	...	★
Maine	★	★	★	★	★	★	...
Maryland	★	★	★	★	★	...	...
Massachusetts	★	★	★	★	★	★	★
Michigan	...	★	...	★	★	...	★
Minnesota	★	★	★	★	★	★	...
Mississippi	...	★	...	★	...	...	...
Missouri	...	...	...	...	...	...	...
Montana	★	★	★	★	★	★	★
Nebraska	★	★	...	★	★	★	★
Nevada	★	★	★	★	...	★	...
New Hampshire	★	...	...	★	★	★	★
New Jersey	...	...	...	★	★	★	★
New Mexico	★	★	★	★	...	★	★
New York	...	...	...	★	★	...	...
North Carolina	★	★	...	★	★	...	...
North Dakota	★	★	...	★	★	★	★
Ohio	...	★	...	★	★	★	★
Oklahoma	★	★	...	★	★	★	...
Oregon	★	★	★	★	★	★	...
Pennsylvania	★	★	★	...	★	...	...
Rhode Island	★	★	...	★	★	★	...
South Carolina	★	★	...	★	★	★	...
South Dakota	★	...	...	★	★	★	★
Tennessee	★	★	...	...	★	...	...
Texas	...	★	...	...	...	★	★
Utah	★	★	...	★	★	★	...
Vermont	★	★	...	★	★	★	...
Virginia	★	★	...	★	★	★	...
Washington	★	★	★	★	★	★	...
West Virginia	...	★	★	★	★	...	...
Wisconsin	★	★	...	★	★	★	★
Wyoming	★	★	...	★	★	...	...

Key:
★—Yes
...—No

STATE INFORMATION SYSTEMS

By Carl W. Vorlander

In a recent survey, state information system administrators were asked to identify problems that are external to the organization and over which they have very little control. Table 1 depicts those concerns for the five years from 1979 to 1983. The data gathered this year indicates that management commitment has moved from fourth to first place among problems causing concern for these managers. Several states raised new issues in the survey: a lack of communications planning and policies, a lack of microcomputer policies, and a lack of concern for cost controls. Added to these responses were those directed to internal problems for which managers are held responsible. Again new problem areas arose: the need for effective disaster recovery and security programs and plans.

These new responses point out the challenges which face the information resources of state governments at a time when those governments are becoming evermore reliant on the use of those resources.

Communications are rapidly becoming an integral part of the information system. The interoffice, intracity and intercity networks are the arteries carrying the life blood of information between governmental agencies. The technology of communications is, if anything, changing faster than that of the computer itself. Organizations of state government officials are implementing interstate networks for the sharing of information and ideas. Data is being made available to all governors and legislators. Information concerning actions of the federal government can be made instantly available to all state capitols. At the same time that these rapid technological changes are occurring, the very framework of the communications industry is undergoing an upheaval of great dimension. The breakup of AT&T has created a number of separate new companies all operating in their own best interests. New service offerings are waiting in the wings. New companies spring up weekly. All of these events have placed a new challenge before the state information manager of a magnitude which cannot yet be fully measured. To meet this challenge the National Association for State Information Systems (NASIS) has created a new standing committee to review the impacts

of divestiture, to look at new management structures to meet these changes, and to develop new cost containment methods.

The second new concern that NASIS feels must be resolved is the establishment of a rationale for coordinating the explosive proliferation of the inexpensive micro and personal computer. These devices are capable of performing many of the computations that would have required a large central processing unit only a few years ago and at a far lower cost. However, they do have certain disadvantages if their use is not coordinated. The redundant collection of data will increase and new program activities will be undertaken without effective review by administrators and policy-makers. Staff may well be hired to service a not-so-necessary installation. That these devices have an important place in the provision of information services is not the question, but how to best use them is.

The issues raised in the foregoing paragraphs lead into the third and possibly most serious problem confronting the state information director. How do you protect the dual assets of the system itself and the data which it contains? Every time a communication link is used, the information is vulnerable to interception. Every time a terminal is installed, the systems may become open to misuse. Each minicomputer put in place requires a greater effort to insure its proper use. Everyone has heard of the multi-million dollar rip-offs through the felonious entry into the Electronic Funds Transfer (EFT) system. In the same way, welfare checks have been improperly issued, driver records have been fraudulently issued or improperly altered, and criminal records have been looked at by unauthorized persons. While some of this may be the work of the so-called computer "hacker" the bright high school student with an advanced knowledge of computers, it cannot be considered mischief. It is an important crime and needs to have proper statutory deterrence. In 1981, NASIS drafted a model computer crime act which was published in that year's volume of *Suggested State Legislation.* A recent Council of

---

Carl W. Vorlander is Executive Director of the National Association for State Information Systems.

State Governments *Backgrounder* paper said: "Enacting legislation to combat computer crime is one way to deter information systems pilfering . . . ." As of this writing less than 50 percent of the states have enacted this legislation, and it has yet to emerge from a congressional committee.

The second concern in the security area is the illegal use of this expensive equipment for personal gains. There have been cases of equine bloodstock recordkeeping and privately operated service bureaus using state-owned equipment. Programs developed at state expense have been sold to the private sector for private profit. These are not the unauthorized printing of Merry Christmas signs or new calendars. These are premeditated crimes of some magnitude, undertaken with the intent of making money for the perpetrator. Such a situation can have dire consequences.

Table 1
STATE INFORMATION SYSTEMS: EXTERNAL PROBLEMS 1979-1983

Problem category	Aggregate rank					Number of states reporting problems 1983	
	1979	*1980*	*1981*	*1982*	*1983*	*More serious*	*Less serious*
Management understanding	2	2	2	3	3	11	13
Lack of definitive plan	3	4	3	2	4	14	10
Management commitment	4	3	4	4	1	12	11
Management interest	8	7	8	9	6	7	18
Resistance to consolidation	7	8	6	10	9	5	17
User unfamiliarity with information system	5	6	9	6	7	5	19
User agency cooperation	9	8	7	7	8	5	18
Recruitment of qualified personnel	1	1	1	1	2	19	6
Inadequate financing	10	5	5	5	5	17	8
Lack of standards	6	10	10	8	10	5	8
Need for documentation	11	12	11	12	11	4	19
Need for common data base	12	11	12	11	12	12	13

Table 2
STATE INFORMATION SYSTEMS: INTERNAL PROBLEMS 1979-1983

Problem category	Aggregate rank					Number of states reporting problems 1983	
	1979	*1980*	*1981*	*1982*	*1983*	*More serious*	*Less serious*
Missed programming schedules	1	2	1	1	3	11	9
Costs too high	2	1	2	3	1	17	6
Cost overruns	6	4	4	4	4	10	11
Inflexibility of programs	4	5	5	5	5	9	13
Programming backlog	3	2	3	2	2	16	6
Missed production schedules	5	6	6	6	8	5	16
Poor input control	7	7	7	8	8	4	17
Poor systems/program documentation	8	9	8	7	6	5	18
Inaccurate output	10	10	12	9	10	1	19
Systems design too primitive	9	8	10	11	7	5	16
Systems design too sophisticated	12	11	9	10	12	7	13
Poor operations documentation	11	12	11	10	11	5	18

Table 3

STATE INFORMATION SYSTEMS: SECURITY

(45 states reporting)

	Physical security					
	Total physical security plan				*I.D. badges required*	*Entrance guards required*
States reporting	*Issued*	*Implemented*	*Enforced*	*Audited*		
Yes	31	30	29	19	31	19
No	14	13	15	18	10	20

	Data security					
	Total data security plan				*Off-site back-up storage used*	*S & P documentation included*
	Issued	*Implemented*	*Enforced*	*Audited*		
Yes	24	21	20	15	38	22
No	20	19	22	23	5	18

STATE LIBRARY AGENCIES

By Lester L. Stoffel

Provision of library services to state governments, leadership in promotion of library development (including the administration of both federal and state grants), and coordinating the planning for library services are functions generally held in common by state library agencies.

All but one state library agency provide public services, principally to departments of state governments. This research assists public policy decision-making. Most agencies coordinate documents depository collections, and a large number administer audio-visual collections. Legislative reference service is provided by 22 agencies, while twice that number are responsible for services to the blind and physically handicapped readers.

All of the agencies consider statewide development of library services an important responsibility. This responsibility usually is carried out through the administration of state and federal funds, the provision of consultant services, the publication of library statistics and long-range planning. Library services to state-supported institutions, especially correctional institutions and increasingly for state institutions for mental health, are the responsibility of many state library agencies, either directly or through assignment to libraries.

Significant progress in library development has been made through the creation of library systems. The first state-supported public library system was formed in New York in 1958 and brought together autonomous local libraries in a region for the purpose of sharing materials and services. Since then, library systems have become the common method for states to carry out their obligations of moving toward equalized library services. In several states, public library systems have been the mechanism through which residents of one jurisdiction can borrow from public libraries located elsewhere.

In more recent years, state library agencies have carried the library system idea further by promoting resource sharing among libraries of every type. The federal Library Services and Construction Act (LSCA), which had supplied funds to states to strengthen public library services throughout the nation, was broadened in 1966 by the addition of Title III. Under the new title, funds were appropriated to "establish and maintain local, regional, state or interstate networks for the systematic and effective coordination of the resources of school, public, academic, and special libraries or special information centers." Eligibility for funding depended on all types of libraries collaborating in the development of comprehensive statewide plans for access to all of the state's resources. This legislation furthered the evolution to multitype library systems.

Meanwhile, the library profession has adopted networking as a useful means of sharing materials to satisfy the needs of library clientele. The 1983 *American Library Directory* lists 325 "Networks, Consortia & Other Cooperative Library Organizations," and separately lists 348 public library and 90 multitype library systems.

A number of library networks cross state boundaries, such as the New England Library Network (NELINET), while others are computer-based and are open to libraries anywhere in the nation. For example, the not-for-profit On Line Computer Library Center (OCLC) has 3,300 member libraries, over 10 million bibliographic records, and over 147 million location listings in all 50 states and in seven foreign countries.

OCLC is just one example of how networking and automation together have advanced the ability of libraries to locate and share needed materials. To facilitate the delivery of shared materials, a few states support statewide delivery systems.

The planning role of state library agencies has been reinforced by increased cooperation and the spread of the automation of library functions. Joint planning with all libraries has become a necessity to provide efficient and effective ways to share resources.

To carry out their rapidly growing responsibilities, state library agencies must attract compe-

Lester L. Stoffel is Executive Director of the Suburban Library System in Burr Ridge, Illinois. Sandra M. Cooper, Executive Director of the Association of Specialized and Cooperative Library Agencies, supplied materials and suggestions.

tent professional personnel capable of providing leadership in each state's library community. By working with libraries of all types, library organizations, government agencies and citizen groups, strong state library networks can be created as links in the rapidly developing national information network.

Selected References

American Library Association. Association of Specialized and Cooperative Library Agencies. *The State Library Agencies*. A Survey Project Report. Chicago, 1983.

Eberhart, W. Lyle. "State Library Agencies in the United States." *World Encyclopedia of Library and Information Services*. Chicago, 1980.

American Association of State and Cooperative Libraries. *Standards for Library Functions at the State Level*. Draft revision of the 1970 edition, n.d.

McCrossan, John A., ed. "State Library Development Agencies." *Library Trends* 27, 2, (Fall 1978).

American Library Directory. 36th edition. New York: R.R. Bowker Co., 1983.

Table 1
STATE LIBRARY AGENCIES
Structure and Appropriations
Fiscal 1984

			Appropriations					
			State		Federal			
State	Organization structure(a)	Agency reports to:(b)	Agency appropriation	Direct assistance to public libraries & networks	Library Services and Construction Act(c)	Other(d)	Other sources of income	Total
All states			$115,023,969	$217,790,040	$69,940,838	$40,749,160	$10,173,796	$453,677,803
Alabama	I	B	1,536,644	1,957,846	1,233,493	1,165,334		5,893,317
Alaska	U	E	3,345,500	485,000	364,300		72,500	4,267,300
Arizona	U	B		300,000				300,000
Arkansas	U	E	1,324,985	1,994,871	902,104			4,221,960
California	U	E	7,233,000	11,685,000	7,153,796	5,590,000		31,661,796
Colorado	U	E	726,401	1,585,651	1,099,320		85,142	3,496,514
Connecticut.........	U	B	4,429,989	1,426,000	1,033,774			6,889,763
Delaware	U	D	428,800	75,000	392,095	182,499		1,078,394
Florida	U	S	1,488,309	5,523,934	2,741,184	1,617,633		11,371,060
Georgia	U	E	746,123	14,011,475	1,635,592	918,387		17,311,577
Hawaii	U	E	12,176,866	(e)	486,447	216,857		12,880,170
Idaho	U	B,E	862,200	251,000	480,900	255,100	25,000	1,874,200
Illinois	U	S	3,057,795	23,753,515	3,156,549	2,881,157	2,250,000	35,099,016
Indiana	I	G	1,574,992	1,778,095	1,642,142	1,421,662		6,416,891
Iowa	I	C	936,607	1,130,808	984,049	547,612		3,599,076
Kansas	I	G	750,795	744,545	945,432	421,071	91,396	2,953,239
Kentucky	I	G	5,967,696	2,074,304	1,175,076		224,000	9,441,076
Louisiana...........	U	R	894,361	1,472,080	1,205,767	953,298	155,000	4,680,506
Maine	U	E	1,665,435	363,000	527,221	260,966		2,816,622
Maryland	U	E	920,415	14,156,311	1,316,897	909,245		17,302,868
Massachusetts........	I	A	1,165,052(f)	10,207,601	1,706,055	929,960		14,008,668
Michigan	U	L	2,371,000	15,390,000	2,607,500	3,017,100	60,000	23,445,600
Minnesota	U	E	706,100	4,569,000	1,281,328			6,556,428
Mississippi	I	C	1,598,352	1,740,179	982,956	616,645		4,938,132
Missouri............	U	E	511,595	1,500,000	1,495,878	831,861		4,339,334
Montana	U	C	600,497	389,000	364,560	220,523	3,000	1,577,580
Nebraska	I	G	1,183,348	304,690	536,603	315,107		2,339,748
Nevada.............	I	G	999,428	142,968	444,194	315,793		1,902,383
New Hampshire	I	G	1,200,000		475,000	234,000		1,909,000
New Jersey	U	E	2,749,062	7,715,000	2,271,614	1,153,361		13,889,037
New Mexico	U	R	1,737,900	340,100	572,049	363,431	50,000	3,063,480
New York	U	E	5,999,900	38,305,162	4,726,627	2,718,381		51,750,070
North Carolina	U	R	2,476,224	7,789,462	1,740,258	985,616	4,000	12,995,560
North Dakota	U	I	386,500	550,000	406,000			1,342,500
Ohio	I	B	3,377,553	1,059,310	2,999,196	2,784,004	437,458	10,657,521
Oklahoma	A	B	2,455,312	1,467,128	1,284,856	524,490	101,960	5,833,746
Oregon	I	G	1,606,894	200,000	728,810	800,000	10,225	3,345,929
Pennsylvania........	U	G	2,262,000	17,664,000	3,270,841	3,720,788	13,000	26,930,629
Rhode Island........	I	G	655,501	1,782,332	477,598	322,072		3,237,503
South Carolina	I	B	1,264,511	2,339,406	1,036,600			4,640,517
South Dakota	U	R	1,115,955		403,080	190,560	175,889	1,885,484
Tennessee	U	S	1,461,900	3,681,100	1,200,600		110,500	6,454,100
Texas	I	C	5,402,856	4,652,964	3,874,080		197,746	14,127,646
Utah	U	D	1,839,100		613,148	313,746	659,500	3,425,494
Vermont	I	G	1,149,797		386,456		8,000	1,544,253
Virginia	I	G	10,295,630		2,000,000			12,295,630
Washington..........	I	C	3,642,548		1,138,858	1,107,220	4,575,580	10,464,206
West Virginia	I	G	1,529,679	5,314,703(g)	737,911	642,477		8,224,770
Wisconsin	U	E	2,224,900	5,917,500	1,441,893	1,301,204	63,900	10,949,397
Wyoming............	I	B	987,962		260,151		800,000	2,048,113

Source: Chief Officers of State Library Agencies and Ann Carlson and Noreen Kaminski, Association of Specialized and Cooperative Library Agencies.

Note: Appropriations vary depending on the state library's functions; therefore, the reader is advised to view appropriation figures in Table 1 in tandem with information provided in Table 2: Functions and Responsibilities. For further information, consult: *The State Library Agencies: A Survey Project Report, 1983* (Chicago: American Library Association/ASCLA, 1983).

(a) Abbreviations: I—Independent; U—Unit within larger unit.

(b) Abbreviations: A—Department of Administration; B—Board; C—Commission; D—Department of Community Affairs and Economic Development; E—Department of Education; G—Governor or Gover-

nor's Board; I—Director of Institutions; L—Legislature; R—Department of Cultural Resources; S—Secretary of State.

(c) Congress had not completed action on LSCA fiscal 1984 appropriations at the time of this survey; therefore, data reported herein reflect budgeted estimates.

(d) "Other" includes LSCA II appropriations which were one-time supplemental emergency job funds.

(e) Hawaii: A totally integrated system exists; all public and state library support is included in previous column.

(f) Massachusetts: Reflects agency appropriations for the state library and the Board of Library Commissioners (state library development agency).

(g) West Virginia: Includes $400,000 for construction.

Table 2
FUNCTIONS AND RESPONSIBILITIES
OF STATE LIBRARY AGENCIES

State	Library services to state governments							Statewide library services development															
	Documents	Information and reference service	Legislative reference	Law library	Genealogy and state history	Archives	Liaison with institutional libraries	Coordination of academic libraries	Coordination of public libraries	Coordination of school libraries	Coordination of institutional libraries	Research	Coordination of library systems	Consulting services	Interlibrary loan, reference and bibliographic service	Statistical gathering and analysis	Library legislation review	Interstate library compacts and other cooperative efforts	Specialized resource centers	Direct service to the public	Annual reports	Public relations	Continuing education
Alabama		★					★		★		★	★	★	★	★	★	★	★	★	†	★	★	★
Alaska	★	★	†	†	★		★	†	★	†	★	★	★	★	★	★	†	★	★	†	★	†	★
Arizona	★	★	★	★	★	★	★	★	★	★	★	★	★	★	★	★	★	★	★	†	★	†	★
Arkansas	★	★					★	†	★	†	★	★	★	★	★	★	★	★	★		★	†	★
California	★	★	★	★	★		★	†	★		†	★	★	★	★	★	†	★	†	★	†	★	†
Colorado	★	★		★			★	†	★	†	†	★	★	★	★	★	†	†		★	†	†	†
Connecticut	★	★	★	★	★	★	★		★	†	†	★	★	★	★	★	★	★		★	†	★	†
Delaware	†	★	†	†		†	★		★		★	†	†	★	★	★	†	★	★	★	★	★	★
Florida	★	★	†			★	★	†	★		†	★	★	★	★	★	★	★	★	★	★	★	†
Georgia	†	★					★		★	†	★	★	★	★	★	★	★		★	★	★	★	†
Hawaii	★	★					★		★		★	†	†	★	†	†				★	★	†	†
Idaho	†	★	†	†	†	†	★		★		★	†	★	★	†	†			★	★	★	★	★
Illinois	★	★	†		★		†	†	★	†	†	★	†	★	★	†	†	†	†	★		★	†
Indiana	★	★	†		★	★	★		★	†	★	†	†	★	†	†	†	★	★		★	★	†
Iowa	★	★	†	★	†		★		†	†	★	★	★	★	★	★	★	★		★	★	†
Kansas	★	★		★			★	†	★	†	†	★	★	★	★	★	★	†	★	†	★	†	†
Kentucky	†	★	†	†	★	★	★	†	★	†	†	★	★	★	★	★	†	★	†	★	†	★	†
Louisiana	†	★	†		★		★	†	★	†	†	★	★	★	★	★	★	†	★	†	†	★	†
Maine	★	★	†		★		★	†	★	★	†	★	★	★	★	★	★		★	†	★	★	★
Maryland	†	†					★	†	★	★	★	★	★	★	★	★	†		★	†	★	★	★
Massachusetts		†					★		★		★	★	★	†	†	†	★	★		★	†	†	†
Michigan	★	★	†	★	★	★	★		†	†	★	†	†	★	†	†	★	†	†	†	†	†	†
Minnesota		†					†	†	★	†	†	★	★	★	★	★	★	†	★	†	★	★	★
Mississippi	★	†	†				★	†	★	†	★	†	★	★	★	★	†	★	†	★	★	†	†
Missouri	†	†	†				★	†	★	†	★		★	★	★	†		★	★	★	★	★	★
Montana	†	★	†			†		★	†	★	†	★	†	★	★	★	†	†	†	★	★	★	★
Nebraska	★	★	†				★	†	★	†	†	★	†	★	★	†	★	★	★	★	★	★	†
Nevada	★	★	†	†	†	★	★	†	★	†	★	★	★	★	★	★	†	★	★	★	★	★	★
New Hampshire	★	★	★	★	★	★			★	†	†	★	★	★	★	★	†	★		★	★	★	★
New Jersey	★	★	†	★	★		†	†	★	★	†	†	★	★	★	†	★	†		★	†	†
New Mexico	★	★	†		★	†	★	†	★	†	★	★	★	★	★	★	★	†	†	★	★	★
New York	★	★	†	★	★	†	★	★	★	†	★	★	★	★	★	★	★	★	★	†	★	†	†
North Carolina	★	★	†	†	†	†	★	†	†	†	†	†	★	★	★	★	†	†	★	★	★	★	★
North Dakota	★	★	†		†	†	★	★	★	★	†	★	★	★	★	★	†	†	†	★	★	★	★
Ohio	★	★	†		†		★	†	★	†	†	★	★	★	★	★	★	†	†	★	★	★	†
Oklahoma	★	★	★	★	†	★	★	†	★	†	★	★	★	★	★	★	★	★	†		★	†	★
Oregon	★	★	†				★		★		†	★	★	★	★	†	†		★	★	★	★	★
Pennsylvania	★	★	★	†	★	†	★	★	★	†	★	★	★	★	★	★	†		★	★	★	★	★
Rhode Island		†					★	★	★	★	†	★	★	★	★	★	†	★	★	★	†	★	†
South Carolina	†	★	★			★	★	†	★	†	★	★	★	★	★	★	★	†			★	†	★
South Dakota	★	★	★			★	★	†	†	★	†	★	★	★	★	★	★	†	★	★	★	★	★
Tennessee	★	†	†	†		★	†	†	★	†	†	★	★	★	★	★	†	★	†	★	★	★	†
Texas	★	★			★	★	★	†	★	†	†	†	†	★	★	★	†	†	†		★	†	★
Utah	★	★	†				★			★	†	★	★	★	★	†	†	†	★	†	★	★	★
Vermont	★	★	†	★	†		★			★	†	★	★	★	★	★	†	†	★	†	★	★	†
Virginia	★	†	†		★	★	★		★		★	†	★	★	★	★	†	†	†	†	†	†	†
Washington	★	★	★		†	★	★	†		★	†	★	★	★	★	★	★	†	†	†	★	★	★
West Virginia	†	†	†				★	†	★	†	†	★	★	★	★	★	†	†	†	★	★	★	★
Wisconsin	†	†	†				★	†	★	★	★	★	★	★	★	†	†	†	★	★	★	★	★
Wyoming	★	★			†	†	★	★	★	★	†		★	★	★	★			★	†	★	★	†

Source: Modified by Ann Carlson and Noreen Kaminski, Association of Specialized and Cooperative Library Agencies, from the Association for State Library Agencies.
Key: ★—Primary. †—Shared. . . .—None.

State	Long-range planning	Determination of size and scope of collections in the state	Mobilization of resources	Subject and reference centers	Resources—books	Resources—other printed materials	Resources—multimedia	Resources—materials for the blind and handicapped	Coordination of resources	Little-used materials	Planning of information networks	Provision of centralized facilities	Exchange of information and materials	Interstate cooperation	Administration of federal aid	Administration of state aid	Financing of library systems and networks
Alabama	★	★	★	★	★	★	★	★	★	…	★	†	★	★	★	★	★
Alaska	★	†	†	†	†	†	★	★	★	…	†	★	†	★	★	★	†
Arizona	★	★	★	★	★	★	★	★	★	…	★	★	★	★	★	★	★
Arkansas	★	★	★	★	★	★	★	★	★	★	†	†	★	★	★	★	★
California	★	†	†	†	†	†	†	†	★	†	†	†	★	★	★	★	★
Colorado	★	†	†	†	†	†	†	†	★	†	†	†	★	†	★	★	★
Connecticut	★	★	†	★	★	†	★	★	★	†	★	★	★	★	★	★	★
Delaware	★	†	★	†	★	†	★	★	★	†	★	★	★	★	★	★	★
Florida	★	†	†	★	†	†	†	†	★	★	★	★	★	★	★	★	★
Georgia	★	★	★	★	★	★	★	★	★	…	★	★	★	★	★	★	★
Hawaii	†	†	†	†	†	†	†	★	†	★	†	†	†	†	†	†	†
Idaho	★	†	★	†	†	★	★	★	†	★	★	†	★	★	★	★	★
Illinois	†	†	†	†	†	†	†	†	†	…	†	†	†	†	★	★	★
Indiana	★	…	†	†	†	†	†	†	†	…	†	†	†	†	★	★	★
Iowa	★	★	★	★	★	★	★	†	★	★	★	★	★	★	★	★	★
Kansas	★	†	†	†	†	†	†	†	★	†	★	†	★	★	★	★	★
Kentucky	★	†	†	†	†	†	†	★	★	†	†	★	★	★	★	★	★
Louisiana	†	†	†	†	†	†	†	★	†	…	†	★	★	★	★	★	★
Maine	★	★	★	★	★	★	★	★	★	†	★	★	★	★	★	★	★
Maryland	★	…	…	★	…	…	…	★	…	…	★	…	★	★	★	★	★
Massachusetts	†	…	†	…	†	†	†	†	†	†	★	†	†	★	★	★	★
Michigan	★	†	†	†	†	†	†	†	†	†	★	…	†	★	★	★	★
Minnesota	★	†	★	†	†	†	†	★	★	★	★	†	★	★	★	★	★
Mississippi	★	†	★	★	★	★	†	†	★	★	★	†	★	†	★	★	†
Missouri	★	†	★	★	★	★	†	†	★	★	★	★	★	★	★	★	★
Montana	★	★	★	★	★	★	★	†	†		†	†	★	★	★	…	★
Nebraska	★	…	★	★	★	★	★	★	★	…	★	…	†	★	★	★	★
Nevada	★	†	†	†	†	†	†	†	★	†	★	★	★	★	★	★	★
New Hampshire	★	★	★	★	★	★	★	★	★	★	★	★	★	★	★	★	★
New Jersey	★	…	★	†	†	†	†	★	†	†	★	★	★	★	★	★	★
New Mexico	★	†	★	…	†	†	†	★	★	…	★	★	★	†	†	★	★
New York	★	†	★	†	★	★	†	★	★	…	★	★	★	★	★	★	★
North Carolina	★	†	†	†	★	★	†	★	★	†	★	★	★	★	★	★	★
North Dakota	★	…	★	★	★	★	★	★	★	★	★	★	★	★	★	★	★
Ohio	★	†	†	†	†	†	★	★	†		★	…	★	★	★	★	★
Oklahoma	★	†	★	★	★	★	★	★	★	★	★	★	★	★	★	★	★
Oregon	★	★	★	…	†	★	†	★	†	†	★	…	★	★	★	★	†
Pennsylvania	★	†	★	†	†	†	★	★	★	…	★	★	★	…	★	★	★
Rhode Island	★	†	★	†	†	†	†	★	★	…	★	★	★	★	★	★	★
South Carolina	★	†	…	★	†	†	†	★	★	…	★	★	★	★	★	★	…
South Dakota	★	†	†	†	★	†	†	★	★	★	†	★	★	★	★	…	★
Tennessee	★	†	†	†	†	†	†	★	★	†	★	†	★	★	★	★	★
Texas	★	†	†	†	★	★	†	★	★	†	★	†	★	★	★	★	★
Utah	★	†	†	†	†	…	†	★	★	…	†	†	★	★	†	★	†
Vermont	★	†	†	†	†	†	†	★	★	†	†	†	★	★	★	★	†
Virginia	★	†	†	†	†	†	†	†	†	†	★	★	★	★	★	★	†
Washington	★	…	★	†	…	…	…	…	…	…	★	★	★	★	★	…	★
West Virginia	★	…	…	†	★	†	†	★	★	★	†	★	†	★	★	★	†
Wisconsin	★	†	†	†	†	†	†	★	†	†	†	★	★	★	★	★	★
Wyoming	★	†	†	†	†	†	†	†	★	★	†	†	★	★	★	…	…

Statewide development of library resources — Statewide development of information networks — Financing library programs

A Note on Use

Symbols: Unless otherwise noted, all tables in *The Book of the States* use the following scheme:

　. . .—no data
　blank cell—not applicable
　0—zero quantity.

Sources: Unless otherwise noted, the sources of data for tables are surveys and research by The Council of State Governments.

5. Employment

STATE GOVERNMENT EMPLOYMENT

By Alan V. Stevens

State governments employed 3,747,000 workers as of October 1982, slightly less than the peak employment level of 3,753,000 recorded in October 1980. Gross salaries and wages for state government workers were $5 billion for the month of October 1982, up an average of 8.3 percent per year from $4.3 billion in October 1980. On a full-time equivalent basis, state government employment in October 1982 was 3,083,000.[1]

The changes in state government employment and payrolls since 1980 reflect major adjustments to the trends of the 1970s, when state employment increased an average of 3.1 percent per year and payrolls increased an average of 10.3 percent per year.

Changing Trends in Government Employment

Federal, state and local governments employed a total of 15.9 million civilian workers in October 1982; local governments accounted for 58.5 percent of these employees, state governments accounted for 23.5 percent, and the federal government accounted for 18 percent.

The number of civilian government workers has declined 1.8 percent since reaching its highest level of 16.2 million in October 1980. A decrease of 1.5 percent, or 245,000 employees, occurred between October 1980 and October 1981; much

of this decline was attributed to the elimination of the public service employment portions of the Comprehensive Employment and Training Act. A further decrease of 0.2 percent, or 35,000 employees, occurred between October 1981 and October 1982; this decrease was primarily attributed to declining general economic conditions that resulted in reduced or stagnant revenue levels in many governments. Table A summarizes government employment and payroll levels and rates of change for the period 1970-1982.

The data in Table A illustrate that while state government employment followed the growth trend of the 1970s and cutback trend of the early 1980s, its rate of growth was greater in the 1970s and its rate of decline has been less severe in the early 1980s than employment at the federal and local government levels.

These general trends in state employment have not been consistent across all state government activities nor have they mirrored the trend within certain broad activity or functional groups. The most notable exceptions to the major trends have been the fairly consistent employment decline in state highway activities since 1970 and a continued strong growth of employment in state correctional activities during the 1980-1982 period. Employment trends in the major state functional areas for the periods 1970-1980 and 1980-1982 are shown in Table B.

Ratio of Employment to Population

States employed an average of 133 full-time equivalent employees per 10,000 population in 1982, down slightly from the 1980 ratio of 137 per 10,000 population. Local governments employed 335 full-time equivalent employees per 10,000 population in 1982, also down from their 1980 level of 351 per 10,000 population.

The ratio of full-time equivalent state employment to population for major state functions is summarized in Table C. States with high ratios of full-time equivalent employment to population tend to have smaller populations than those

Table A
Government Employment and Payrolls
1970-1982

Employment and payrolls	All governments	Federal government	State governments	Local governments
Employment (thousands):				
October 1982	15,933	2,862	3,747	9,324
October 1980	16,222	2,907	3,753	9,562
October 1970	13,028	2,881	2,755	7,392
Payrolls (millions of dollars):				
October 1982	22,558.6	5,393.7	5,027.7	12,137.1
October 1980	19,945.8	5,215.7	4,284.7	10,445.4
October 1970	8,334.2	2,427.9	1,612.2	4,294.2
Average annual rate of change (percent):				
Employment, Oct. 1980- Oct. 1982	-0.9	-0.8	-0.1	-1.3
Employment, Oct. 1970- Oct. 1980	2.2	0.1	3.1	2.6
Payroll, Oct. 1980- Oct. 1982	6.2	1.7	8.3	7.8
Payroll, Oct. 1970- Oct. 1980	9.1	7.9	10.3	9.3

Alan V. Stevens is Chief of the Employment Branch, Governments Division, U.S. Bureau of the Census.

271

Table B
State Employment by Major Functions
1970-1982

Function	Total employment			Average annual rate of change (percent)	
	1970	1980	1982	1970-1980	1980-1982
Higher education	1,093,637	1,474,326	1,496,349	3.0	0.7
Hospitals	450,382	577,721	570,173	2.5	-0.7
Highways	301,896	258,377	244,339	-1.6	-2.8
Natural resources*	150,817	191,948	186,618	2.4	-1.4
Correction	91,505	153,086	185,477	5.3	3.9
Public welfare	99,489	173,909	174,456	5.7	0.1
Financial and general government administration**	145,429	237,225	163,321	5.0	17.0
All other functions	370,416	573,871	609,296	4.5	1.2

* Includes state parks and recreation.
** Includes courts and legislatures.

with low ratios. The states with the highest and lowest ratios of full-time equivalent employment per 10,000 population as of October 1982 were:

Highest Ratios	Lowest Ratios
Alaska — 442	California — 100
Hawaii — 380	Illinois — 102
Delaware — 277	Ohio — 102
New Mexico — 241	Pennsylvania — 104
Rhode Island — 211	Florida — 107

While small population size tends to be a major factor contributing to a high employment/population ratio, other factors are also significant. Some of these other factors include: (1) more extensive state higher education systems in certain states that have few private institutions of higher education, or where community colleges are operated by the state government rather than by local governments; and (2) instances where the state government has major responsibility for a function that is primarily performed by local governments in other states, such as administration of public welfare programs.

Employee Average Earnings

Full-time state government employees were paid an average of $1,625 for the month of October 1982 (equivalent to an annualized rate of

Table C
State Full-time Equivalent Employment Per
10,000 Population
October 1980

Function	Full-time equivalent employment per 10,000 population
Total, all functions	133
Higher education	41
Hospitals	24
Highways	10
Correction	8
Public welfare	7
Natural resources*	7
Financial administration	5
Health	5
General control**	5
Police protection	3
All other activities	18

* Includes parks and recreation.
** Includes legislatures and state courts.

$19,500), up an average of 8.8 percent a year from $1,373 paid in October 1980. In comparison, local governments increased full-time employee pay by an average annual rate of 9 percent during this period, from an average of $1,323 in October 1980 to $1,572 in October 1982.

The average October 1982 pay for full-time state employees ranged from a high of $2,407 in Alaska to less than half that amount in Mississippi, $1,191. Table D shows a ranking of state governments by average October 1982 pay for full-time employees.

Table D
State Government Average Full-time Pay
October 1982

State	Pay	State	Pay
Alaska	$2,407	Connecticut	$1,521
California	2,063	Alabama	1,520
Minnesota	1,912	Virginia	1,520
Michigan	1,903	Oklahoma	1,505
Wyoming	1,875	Vermont	1,503
Nevada	1,867	Massachusetts	1,499
Arizona	1,780	Maryland	1,488
New York	1,745	Kansas	1,478
Washington	1,738	Tennessee	1,476
Illinois	1,734	New Mexico	1,473
Colorado	1,730	Maine	1,470
Indiana	1,722	Florida	1,469
Wisconsin	1,716	Georgia	1,436
New Jersey	1,714	South Dakota	1,432
Montana	1,699	Delaware	1,431
Ohio	1,670	Kentucky	1,417
Iowa	1,655	South Carolina	1,412
Oregon	1,647	North Carolina	1,400
Hawaii	1,645	Louisiana	1,394
Texas	1,644	Arkansas	1,361
AVERAGE	1,625	Missouri	1,301
North Dakota	1,616	New Hampshire	1,295
Rhode Island	1,595	Nebraska	1,293
Idaho	1,595	West Virginia	1,272
Utah	1,578	Mississippi	1,191
Pennsylvania	1,570		

Many things affect the rankings of state governments by average pay for full-time employees. Some of the principal factors are general cost of living in areas where workers are employed, the proportions of higher paying jobs or occupations with those of lower pay levels, general economic conditions in each state and executive and legislative decisions concerning employee compensation.

Note

1. Full-time equivalent is a computed statistic representing the number of full-time workers that could be employed with no increase in total salary and wage costs if all personnel were engaged on a full-time basis at the average October pay prevailing for full-time employees.

Table 1
SUMMARY OF STATE GOVERNMENT EMPLOYMENT: 1952-1982

| | Employment (in thousands) | | | | | | Monthly payrolls (in millions of dollars) | | | Average monthly earnings of full-time employees | | |
| | Total, full-time and part-time | | | Full-time equivalent | | | | | | | | |
Year	All	Educa-tion	Other	All	Educa-tion	Other	All	Educa-tion	Other	All	Educa-tion	Other
October:												
1982	3,747	1,616	2,131	3,083	1,051	2,032	$5,027.7	$1,874.0	$3,153.7	$1,625	$1,789	$1,551
1981	3,726	1,603	2,123	3,087	1,063	2,024	4,667.5	1,768.0	2,899.5	1,507	1,671	1,432
1980	3,753	1,599	2,154	3,106	1,063	2,044	4,284.7	1,608.0	2,676.6	1,373	1,523	1,305
1979	3,699	1,577	2,122	3,072	1,046	2,026	3,869.3	1,451.4	2,417.9	1,257	1,399	1,193
1978	3,539	1,508	2,032	2,966	1,016	1,950	3,483.0	1,332.9	2,150.2	1,167	1,311	1,102
1977	3,491	1,484	2,007	2,903	1,005	1,898	3,194.6	1,234.4	1,960.1	1,096	1,237	1,031
1976	3,343	1,434	1,910	2,799	973	1,827	2,893.7	1,111.5	1,782.1	1,031	1,163	975
1975	3,271	1,400	1,870	2,744	952	1,792	2,652.7	1,021.7	1,631.1	964	1,080	909
1974	3,155	1,357	1,798	2,653	929	1,725	2,409.5	932.7	1,476.9	906	1,023	855
1973	3,013	1,280	1,733	2,547	887	1,660	2,158.2	822.2	1,336.0	843	952	805
1972	2,957	1,267	1,690	2,487	867	1,619	1,936.6	746.9	1,189.7	778	871	734
1971	2,832	1,223	1,609	2,384	841	1,544	1,741.7	681.5	1,060.2	731	826	686
1970	2,755	1,182	1,573	2,302	803	1,499	1,612.2	630.3	981.9	700	797	605
1969	2,614	1,112	1,501	2,179	746	1,433	1,430.5	554.5	876.1	655	743	597
1968	2,495	1,037	1,458	2,085	694	1,391	1,256.7	477.1	779.6	602	687	544
1967	2,335	940	1,395	1,946	620	1,326	1,105.5	406.3	699.3	567	666	526
1966	2,211	866	1,344	1,864	575	1,289	975.2	353.0	622.2	522	614	483
1965	2,028	739	1,289	1,751	508	1,243	849.2	290.1	559.1	484	571	450
1964	1,873	656	1,217	1,639	460	1,179	761.1	257.5	503.6	464	560	427
1963	1,775	602	1,173	1,558	422	1,136	696.4	230.1	466.3	447	545	410
1962	1,680	555	1,126	1,478	389	1,088	634.6	201.8	432.8	429	518	397
1961	1,625	518	1,107	1,435	367	1,068	586.2	192.4	393.8	409	482	383
1960	1,527	474	1,053	1,353	332	1,021	524.1	167.7	356.4	386	439	365
1959	1,454	443	1,011	1,302	318	984	485.4	136.0	349.4	373	427	352
1958	1,408	406	1,002	1,259	284	975	446.5	123.4	323.1	355	416	333
April 1957	1,300	375	925	1,153	257	896	372.5	106.1	266.4	320	355	309
1956	1,268	353	915	1,136	250	886	366.5	108.8	257.7	321	358	309
1955	1,199	333	866	1,081	244	837	325.9	88.5	237.4	302	334	290
1954	1,149	310	839	1,024	222	802	300.7	78.9	221.8	294	325	283
1953	1,082	294	788	966	211	755	278.6	73.5	205.1	289	320	278
1952	1,060	293	767	958	213	745	260.3	65.1	195.2	271	298	262

Source: U.S. Bureau of the Census, annual *Public Employment* reports.

Note: Because of rounding, detail may not add to totals.

Table 2
EMPLOYMENT AND PAYROLLS OF STATE AND LOCAL GOVERNMENTS, BY FUNCTION: OCTOBER 1982

| Function | All employees, full-time and part-time (in thousands) | | | October payrolls (in millions of dollars) | | | Average October earnings of full-time employees |
	Total	State govern-ments	Local govern-ments	Total	State govern-ments	Local govern-ments	
All functions	13,071	3,747	9,324	$17,165	$5,028	$12,137	$1,587
Education	6,733	1,616	5,117	8,526	1,874	6,652	1,640
Local schools	4,756	23	4,732	6,276	33	6,243	1,594
Instructional personnel only	3,090	15	3,076	4,899	25	4,874	1,775
Institutions of higher education	1,881	1,496	385	2,107	1,697	410	1,827
Instructional personnel only	650	455	195	1,069	823	246	2,502
Other education	96	96	. . .	143	143	. . .	1,605
Functions other than education	6,338	2,131	4,207	8,639	3,154	5,485	1,540
Highways	527	244	283	729	370	360	1,438
Public welfare	393	174	219	495	245	250	1,335
Hospitals	1,157	570	587	1,432	737	694	1,339
Health	250	117	133	348	176	172	1,520
Police protection	665	76	589	1,063	139	925	1,786
Police officers only	493	50	444	895	102	793	1,908
Local fire protection	310	. . .	310	446	. . .	446	1,949
Fire fighters only	285	. . .	285	423	. . .	423	1,968
Natural resources	195	158	36	264	224	41	1,583
Correction	285	185	100	438	290	148	1,579
Social insurance administration	103	103	. . .	158	158	. . .	1,658
Financial administration	312	121	191	405	182	224	1,436
General control	550	119	431	669	211	457	1,598
Utilities	396	18	378	696	42	654	1,859
Other	1,194	245	950	1,494	381	1,114	1,493

Source: U.S. Bureau of the Census, *Public Employment in 1982*.

Note: Statistics for local governments are subject to sampling variation. Because of rounding, detail may not add to totals.

Table 3
STATE AND LOCAL GOVERNMENT EMPLOYMENT, BY STATE:
OCTOBER 1982

State or other jurisdiction	All employees (full-time and part-time)		Full-time equivalent employment					
			Number			Number per 10,000 population		
	State	Local	Total	State	Local	Total	State	Local
United States............	3,746,967	9,323,726	10,828,915	3,083,233	7,745,682	468	133	335
Alabama.................	73,310	150,442	189,780	61,244	128,536	481	155	326
Alaska	20,697	19,117	35,918	19,338	16,580	820	442	379
Arizona	47,823	119,196	134,868	35,726	99,142	472	125	347
Arkansas	43,016	80,541	103,683	35,637	68,046	453	156	297
California................	305,116	1,089,454	1,097,501	247,539	849,962	444	100	344
Colorado	58,984	131,703	149,330	42,521	106,809	490	140	351
Connecticut..............	56,019	105,525	137,835	48,435	89,400	437	154	284
Delaware	19,211	16,496	31,357	16,664	14,693	521	277	244
Florida	128,525	401,667	467,396	111,787	355,609	449	107	341
Georgia.................	93,686	248,683	301,682	82,880	218,802	535	147	388
Hawaii	46,574	12,590	49,457	37,742	11,715	498	380	118
Idaho	17,962	39,215	45,194	13,586	31,608	468	141	328
Illinois..................	146,466	457,841	486,572	116,913	369,659	425	102	323
Indiana	88,803	207,356	237,357	62,474	174,883	434	114	320
Iowa	51,179	130,286	142,182	41,487	100,695	489	143	347
Kansas	50,992	111,035	127,560	38,631	88,929	530	160	369
Kentucky	67,091	106,299	149,038	56,652	92,386	406	154	252
Louisiana................	96,272	155,407	224,451	81,919	142,532	515	188	327
Maine	23,172	42,385	50,602	18,144	32,458	447	160	286
Maryland	87,616	166,688	218,560	80,234	138,326	512	188	324
Massachusetts	85,938	216,874	256,758	74,649	182,109	444	129	315
Michigan	148,262	359,145	392,485	113,591	278,894	431	125	306
Minnesota	72,084	181,793	189,345	52,693	136,652	458	127	331
Mississippi	44,506	100,680	126,397	39,276	87,121	495	154	342
Missouri	73,926	186,544	220,696	64,194	156,502	446	130	316
Montana	19,848	36,104	42,439	14,390	28,049	530	180	350
Nebraska	32,964	80,564	89,617	27,388	62,229	565	173	392
Nevada..................	14,902	34,630	42,252	12,318	29,934	480	140	340
New Hampshire	17,784	32,521	39,776	13,573	26,203	418	143	276
New Jersey...............	99,899	322,239	358,825	85,826	272,999	482	115	367
New Mexico..............	41,699	48,834	76,661	32,812	43,849	564	241	323
New York................	254,181	866,702	963,387	235,801	727,586	546	134	412
North Carolina	101,328	244,613	288,310	86,861	201,449	479	144	335
North Dakota	17,248	34,238	33,583	12,637	20,946	501	189	313
Ohio	149,853	430,012	457,955	110,531	347,424	424	102	322
Oklahoma	75,254	120,254	168,398	62,338	106,060	530	196	334
Oregon	51,634	111,556	128,802	39,803	88,999	486	150	336
Pennsylvania	145,484	399,731	458,259	123,196	335,063	386	104	282
Rhode Island	26,688	26,313	43,666	20,214	23,452	456	211	245
South Carolina	63,814	113,222	156,181	58,046	98,135	488	181	306
South Dakota	15,814	30,704	34,101	11,915	22,186	494	172	321
Tennessee................	77,031	167,879	213,794	64,946	148,848	460	140	320
Texas	208,457	614,240	727,233	175,926	551,307	476	115	361
Utah	32,710	54,496	68,919	27,528	41,391	443	177	266
Vermont.................	11,994	17,507	24,167	10,668	13,499	468	207	262
Virginia.................	116,174	197,282	266,713	94,178	172,535	486	172	314
Washington	92,139	145,710	192,491	67,251	125,240	453	158	295
West Virginia.............	40,480	65,768	94,415	34,181	60,234	485	175	309
Wisconsin	80,578	212,934	213,842	57,317	156,525	449	120	328
Wyoming	11,780	29,427	33,058	9,633	23,425	659	192	467
Dist. of Col..............		49,284	46,067		46,067	730		730

Source: U.S. Bureau of the Census, *Public Employment in 1982.*
Note: Statistics for local governments are estimates subject to sampling variation. Because of rounding, detail may not add to totals.

Table 4
STATE AND LOCAL GOVERNMENT PAYROLLS AND
AVERAGE EARNINGS OF FULL-TIME EMPLOYEES,
BY STATE: OCTOBER 1982

State or other jurisdiction	Amount of payroll (in thousands of dollars)			Percentage of October payroll		Average earnings of full-time state and local government employees (dollars)		
	Total	State government	Local governments	State government	Local governments	All	Education employees	Other
United States	$17,164,868	$5,027,727	$12,137,140	29.3	70.7	$1,587	$1,641	$1,540
Alabama	244,741	93,342	151,400	38.1	61.9	1,284	1,361	1,217
Alaska	93,221	46,237	46,984	49.6	50.4	2,606	2,585	2,620
Arizona	233,359	63,684	169,675	27.3	72.7	1,736	1,729	1,744
Arkansas	121,013	48,663	72,350	40.2	59.8	1,165	1,197	1,129
California	2,192,363	511,049	1,681,314	23.3	76.7	2,003	2,029	1,984
Colorado	239,647	74,158	165,489	30.9	69.1	1,601	1,637	1,566
Connecticut.........	212,762	73,984	138,778	34.8	65.2	1,549	1,633	1,467
Delaware	47,873	24,621	23,251	51.4	48.6	1,508	1,585	1,436
Florida	664,269	164,434	499,835	24.8	75.2	1,424	1,436	1,415
Georgia	378,487	118,954	259,533	31.4	68.6	1,260	1,270	1,251
Hawaii	82,544	62,490	20,054	75.7	24.3	1,662	1,751	1,596
Idaho	61,765	21,603	40,162	35.0	65.0	1,373	1,372	1,373
Illinois	862,235	203,375	658,860	23.6	76.4	1,781	1,874	1,699
Indiana.............	341,765	109,321	232,444	32.0	68.0	1,430	1,567	1,275
Iowa	213,986	69,464	144,523	32.5	67.5	1,498	1,561	1,426
Kansas	172,465	56,749	115,716	32.9	67.1	1,354	1,399	1,305
Kentucky	197,429	80,192	117,237	40.6	59.4	1,335	1,396	1,264
Louisiana...........	297,433	114,445	182,987	38.5	61.5	1,327	1,410	1,248
Maine	65,958	26,599	39,360	40.3	59.7	1,306	1,280	1,337
Maryland	362,278	117,679	244,598	32.5	67.5	1,669	1,838	1,528
Massachusetts.......	408,299	112,142	296,157	27.5	72.5	1,598	1,691	1,526
Michigan	742,365	214,078	528,287	28.8	71.2	1,900	1,987	1,810
Minnesota	333,303	100,236	233,067	30.1	69.9	1,775	1,864	1,691
Mississippi	136,036	47,127	88,909	34.6	65.4	1,077	1,134	1,021
Missouri............	294,585	84,740	209,845	28.8	71.2	1,331	1,391	1,279
Montana	66,715	24,552	42,163	36.8	63.2	1,576	1,737	1,417
Nebraska	123,269	35,526	87,743	28.8	71.2	1,384	1,368	1,398
Nevada.............	76,221	23,018	53,203	30.2	69.8	1,807	1,784	1,821
New Hampshire	50,738	17,415	33,323	34.3	65.7	1,279	1,289	1,270
New Jersey	589,101	147,663	441,438	25.1	74.9	1,648	1,842	1,469
New Mexico	110,598	48,697	61,901	44.0	56.0	1,436	1,518	1,351
New York	1,723,973	411,330	1,312,642	23.9	76.1	1,797	1,972	1,706
North Carolina	374,674	121,860	252,814	32.5	67.5	1,302	1,349	1,252
North Dakota	54,817	20,484	34,333	37.4	62.6	1,638	1,853	1,392
Ohio	707,240	187,208	520,032	26.5	73.5	1,542	1,649	1,444
Oklahoma	226,055	94,212	131,843	41.7	58.3	1,337	1,390	1,286
Oregon	211,676	66,381	145,294	31.4	68.6	1,644	1,633	1,654
Pennsylvania.........	714,863	193,051	521,812	27.0	73.0	1,568	1,647	1,499
Rhode Island	71,052	32,358	38,694	45.5	54.5	1,630	1,799	1,496
South Carolina	194,219	82,123	112,096	42.3	57.7	1,248	1,301	1,191
South Dakota	42,712	16,885	25,827	39.5	60.5	1,249	1,252	1,245
Tennessee	289,409	96,321	193,087	33.3	66.7	1,361	1,505	1,238
Texas	1,053,898	289,131	764,767	27.4	72.6	1,452	1,451	1,452
Utah	104,383	43,461	60,922	41.6	58.4	1,526	1,458	1,617
Vermont	32,750	16,027	16,723	48.9	51.1	1,351	1,333	1,374
Virginia	382,837	144,146	238,691	37.7	62.3	1,441	1,509	1,372
Washington..........	344,411	117,696	226,716	34.2	65.8	1,798	1,779	1,814
West Virginia	119,198	43,716	75,481	36.7	63.3	1,265	1,353	1,159
Wisconsin	349,859	97,256	252,603	27.8	72.2	1,649	1,691	1,608
Wyoming............	54,203	17,845	36,358	32.9	67.1	1,655	1,731	1,582
Dist. of Col.	95,819		95,819		100.0	2,088	2,143	2,072

Source: U.S. Bureau of the Census, *Public Employment in 1982.*

Note: Statistics for local governments are estimates subject to sampling variation. Because of rounding, detail may not add to totals.

Table 5
STATE GOVERNMENT EMPLOYMENT (FULL-TIME EQUIVALENT), TOTAL AND FOR SELECTED FUNCTIONS, BY STATE: OCTOBER 1982

| State | All functions | Education | | | Selected functions other than education | | | | | | | |
		Institutions of higher education	Other education	Highways	Public welfare	Hospitals	Correction	Police protection	Natural resources	Financial administration	General control
All states	3,083,233	942,338	108,452	241,499	171,147	544,526	182,426	75,086	138,175	117,870	109,613
Alabama	61,244	20,739	3,820	3,691	3,906	11,200	2,294	981	2,718	2,185	2,563
Alaska	19,338	2,990	2,891	3,333	886	405	737	417	2,555	1,099	1,436
Arizona	35,726	14,354	2,435	2,904	1,992	2,131	2,748	1,723	1,135	1,445	801
Arkansas	35,637	11,198	2,317	3,524	2,046	5,037	1,359	768	2,089	1,407	461
California	247,539	79,245	4,711	15,284	2,860	32,098	13,554	9,053	15,302	11,553	6,126
Colorado	42,521	18,497	826	3,028	1,192	6,816	2,102	740	1,897	2,001	1,976
Connecticut	48,435	10,072	2,361	4,085	1,885	9,547	3,297	1,286	371	1,504	3,547
Delaware	16,664	5,269	245	1,312	603	2,733	1,215	590	420	738	1,001
Florida	111,787	24,427	2,369	7,827	5,636	19,861	12,677	2,720	5,896	4,065	7,204
Georgia	82,880	24,053	2,768	6,102	5,758	13,733	6,700	1,663	4,455	1,868	1,660
Hawaii	37,742	5,599	16,556	857	869	2,854	860	. . .	1,272	716	1,618
Idaho	13,586	4,480	406	1,565	1,176	1,155	508	222	1,327	624	355
Illinois	116,913	39,051	2,696	6,970	10,942	18,034	7,580	3,372	3,308	6,448	3,810
Indiana	62,474	29,357	3,523	4,983	1,288	8,703	3,251	1,700	2,466	1,800	980
Iowa	41,487	13,599	1,254	3,255	3,444	8,967	1,679	801	2,324	1,650	999
Kansas	38,631	14,740	811	3,540	2,356	5,473	1,642	687	2,264	2,107	1,868
Kentucky	56,652	17,280	3,911	5,335	4,207	6,393	2,505	1,636	3,061	1,425	2,776
Louisiana	81,919	21,499	3,897	7,702	4,370	19,583	5,084	1,347	4,489	3,071	1,297
Maine	18,144	4,668	1,104	2,640	1,551	1,854	799	540	1,474	768	646
Maryland	80,234	22,413	2,125	4,822	6,214	13,185	6,004	2,164	3,448	3,537	2,491
Massachusetts	74,649	14,550	1,602	5,337	8,237	18,510	5,150	1,616	1,517	3,508	5,489
Michigan	113,591	45,568	2,205	4,041	13,458	16,339	6,331	2,999	4,118	2,051	3,529
Minnesota	52,693	22,624	1,499	4,525	1,216	8,558	1,601	840	3,234	2,111	944
Mississippi	39,276	12,433	1,354	2,956	2,694	6,204	1,736	925	3,622	1,271	470
Missouri	64,194	18,172	1,953	5,671	5,059	13,486	3,020	1,697	2,638	1,951	3,050
Montana	14,390	3,780	394	1,711	1,010	1,270	618	303	2,146	981	327
Nebraska	27,388	11,890	717	2,149	1,083	3,894	1,312	504	2,142	595	776
Nevada	12,318	3,602	225	1,288	667	638	1,141	291	629	645	421
New Hampshire . .	13,573	4,500	292	1,727	1,115	2,075	423	278	511	186	349
New Jersey	85,826	19,934	2,337	8,336	4,439	16,449	4,940	4,352	1,986	3,762	4,045
New Mexico	32,812	11,421	428	2,453	1,733	3,714	1,497	639	1,422	1,615	1,367
New York	235,801	29,933	5,276	14,161	6,912	73,254	19,046	5,080	3,127	11,055	18,114
North Carolina . . .	86,861	26,307	2,974	10,342	987	15,445	7,570	2,442	5,266	2,322	4,163
North Dakota	12,637	4,963	341	810	450	2,250	266	180	1,058	338	245
Ohio	110,531	43,477	2,372	8,359	1,424	21,597	6,412	1,904	3,984	3,709	2,072
Oklahoma	62,338	20,481	2,505	3,610	7,812	10,601	3,565	1,398	2,715	1,478	1,530
Oregon	39,803	11,113	883	3,402	3,172	5,760	1,926	982	2,953	1,869	1,099
Pennsylvania	123,196	21,389	2,371	15,393	11,323	30,119	4,318	4,703	4,952	5,985	3,364
Rhode Island	20,214	4,941	862	874	1,681	2,636	966	238	483	912	1,024
South Carolina . . .	58,046	17,513	2,781	4,395	3,891	10,359	3,349	1,277	1,947	1,848	1,399
South Dakota	11,915	4,047	387	1,154	903	1,430	331	276	786	325	535
Tennessee	64,946	23,512	2,625	5,067	4,732	9,735	4,401	925	2,174	2,367	1,377
Texas	175,926	67,299	3,428	14,158	11,692	35,866	8,420	2,879	8,115	6,232	2,405
Utah	27,528	13,294	762	1,639	1,471	3,503	935	479	1,086	683	617
Vermont	10,668	3,218	327	1,057	727	945	469	430	637	521	518
Virginia	94,178	31,328	2,459	10,263	870	18,612	7,750	2,010	3,621	3,136	2,420
Washington	67,251	26,791	1,394	4,966	5,019	8,415	3,969	1,262	3,841	1,893	1,418
West Virginia	34,181	9,398	1,051	5,720	2,746	5,319	733	837	1,754	1,259	953
Wisconsin	57,317	28,790	1,422	1,597	948	6,718	3,215	674	2,636	2,552	1,691
Wyoming	9,633	2,540	200	1,579	495	1,063	421	256	804	699	287

Source: U.S. Bureau of the Census, *Public Employment in 1982.*

Table 6
STATE GOVERNMENT PAYROLLS,
TOTAL AND FOR SELECTED FUNCTIONS, BY STATE: OCTOBER 1982
(In thousands of dollars)

State	All functions	Education		Selected functions other than education							
		Institution of higher education	Other education	Highways	Public welfare	Hospitals	Correction	Police protection	Natural resources	Financial administration	General control
All states	$5,027,727	$1,697,298	$176,741	$369,624	$244,952	$737,357	$290,051	$138,688	$223,519	$181,796	$211,475
Alabama	93,342	35,280	6,261	5,370	5,459	14,589	3,331	1,648	3,397	3,268	4,460
Alaska	46,237	5,912	7,228	7,505	1,738	828	1,915	1,498	6,367	2,819	4,035
Arizona	63,684	28,666	3,609	4,915	3,168	3,915	4,365	3,407	1,944	2,105	1,583
Arkansas	48,663	17,317	3,108	4,935	2,377	5,903	1,534	1,098	2,707	1,668	1,022
California	511,049	171,956	9,091	30,223	5,764	56,245	27,645	18,161	32,043	19,522	11,760
Colorado	74,158	37,102	1,471	626	2,077	11,717	3,998	1,376	3,634	3,510	3,764
Connecticut	73,984	18,058	4,106	6,433	2,621	12,683	5,006	2,116	687	2,324	6,099
Delaware	24,621	8,938	432	1,901	779	2,995	1,784	1,123	520	920	1,596
Florida	164,434	43,463	3,375	10,400	6,244	23,486	19,089	4,364	7,979	5,950	14,110
Georgia	118,954	39,101	4,201	8,060	7,605	18,227	8,307	2,222	6,051	2,765	2,928
Hawaii	62,490	11,602	27,365	1,417	1,215	3,925	1,143	. . .	2,222	1,128	2,736
Idaho	21,603	7,155	630	2,580	1,528	1,472	752	306	2,428	949	873
Illinois	203,375	75,245	4,357	12,699	16,415	27,758	12,567	6,543	5,177	9,062	8,481
Indiana	109,321	58,569	4,263	6,418	1,501	12,343	9,802	2,788	3,199	2,433	1,992
Iowa	69,464	27,235	2,050	4,695	4,912	12,261	2,503	1,692	3,305	3,199	1,986
Kansas	56,749	22,425	1,229	5,384	3,484	6,842	2,282	1,140	3,494	2,829	2,788
Kentucky	80,192	27,732	5,758	6,996	5,370	7,532	3,206	2,812	4,065	1,978	4,188
Louisiana	114,445	33,649	6,619	11,574	5,335	20,163	7,163	2,152	6,290	4,936	2,675
Maine	26,599	7,171	1,642	3,850	2,151	2,449	1,202	894	2,353	1,026	992
Maryland	117,679	32,960	3,614	6,820	6,317	18,226	9,262	4,486	4,175	5,407	4,081
Massachusetts	112,142	25,236	2,403	7,998	11,938	22,731	8,077	2,919	2,140	5,372	9,432
Michigan	214,078	83,331	4,591	8,501	24,806	28,960	12,748	6,715	7,663	4,044	7,904
Minnesota	100,236	47,139	2,838	8,896	1,993	13,268	2,996	1,672	5,470	3,445	2,637
Mississippi	47,127	17,048	1,752	3,218	2,760	5,529	1,775	1,302	4,304	1,661	1,109
Missouri	84,740	28,916	2,034	7,689	5,724	13,898	3,512	2,618	4,095	2,098	4,535
Montana	24,552	8,018	648	3,161	1,474	1,850	957	516	2,683	1,411	752
Nebraska	35,526	15,479	964	3,061	1,367	4,406	1,658	779	2,605	795	1,254
Nevada	23,018	6,640	451	2,547	1,223	1,184	2,108	557	1,194	1,060	839
New Hampshire	17,415	5,741	407	2,144	1,337	2,264	609	392	710	274	602
New Jersey	147,663	40,568	4,372	15,136	6,935	21,784	7,815	7,433	3,083	5,819	9,216
New Mexico	48,697	19,473	632	3,297	2,375	4,668	2,166	1,071	2,488	2,196	2,089
New York	411,330	53,360	9,270	22,710	12,485	108,852	31,869	11,085	5,965	17,454	39,413
North Carolina	121,860	39,634	4,363	12,828	1,478	18,721	9,969	4,182	7,583	3,434	5,774
North Dakota	20,484	8,917	549	1,336	704	2,590	398	326	1,951	478	499
Ohio	187,208	84,729	3,944	13,447	2,252	28,043	10,359	3,468	7,125	5,877	4,536
Oklahoma	94,212	34,372	4,047	5,276	10,920	12,663	4,983	2,364	4,101	2,294	2,998
Oregon	66,381	21,085	1,436	5,436	4,661	7,851	3,068	2,087	4,826	2,822	2,361
Pennsylvania	193,051	41,331	4,066	21,680	15,751	39,577	7,392	9,342	8,506	8,852	5,195
Rhode Island	32,358	8,271	1,465	1,484	2,448	4,168	1,664	647	726	1,389	1,769
South Carolina	82,123	29,633	4,087	4,851	4,791	11,357	4,241	1,963	2,529	2,382	2,469
South Dakota	16,885	6,002	573	1,718	1,117	1,478	455	418	1,200	492	882
Tennessee	96,321	40,921	3,407	6,067	5,598	14,028	5,039	1,328	3,768	3,088	2,801
Texas	289,131	121,279	5,592	23,350	17,590	46,595	13,150	5,133	13,689	10,845	5,546
Utah	43,461	19,455	1,370	3,140	2,311	4,843	1,619	910	1,923	1,085	1,325
Vermont	16,027	5,316	482	1,494	985	1,180	647	825	985	701	825
Virginia	144,146	57,884	3,655	13,198	1,263	23,003	10,412	3,238	5,509	4,345	3,890
Washington	117,696	51,524	2,407	9,223	7,135	11,967	6,388	2,652	6,384	3,096	2,621
West Virginia	43,716	14,535	1,420	7,010	2,987	5,003	768	1,192	2,400	1,493	1,495
Wisconsin	97,256	46,938	2,724	3,662	1,667	9,874	5,711	1,145	4,286	4,546	3,929
Wyoming	17,845	4,983	383	3,268	818	1,463	643	586	1,593	1,152	632

Source: U.S. Bureau of the Census, *Public Employment in 1982.*
Note: Because of rounding, detail may not add to totals.

FINANCES OF STATE-ADMINISTERED
PUBLIC EMPLOYEE RETIREMENT SYSTEMS

By Maurice Criz

The 190 public employee retirement systems administered by state governments in 1982, although slightly less in number than in 1977, served a membership that is 8 percent larger. The increase can be attributed to growth in the number of employees and to extension of state systems to more groups of local government employees. These state systems accounted for 9 percent of all state revenue in fiscal 1982, 4 percent of all state government expenditure, and 57 percent of all state government cash and security holdings. The systems have been of increasing fiscal importance in recent years, not only in absolute terms but also in their impact on state government operations generally, on the size of future liabilities created, and on effective operation of personnel systems.

Coverage

The 190 state-administered public employee retirement systems provided coverage to 10,141,062 members in 1982, or 185,000 less than in 1980, but an increase of 734,000 over 1977. These figures demonstrate the increases in state and local government employment in the 1970s and retrenchment in the early 1980s. It should be noted that the Census Bureau defines retirement systems for public employees as only those systems sponsored by a recognized unit of government and whose members are public employees compensated with public funds. There must be an identifiable employee retirement fund, financed in whole or in part with public contributions. Excluded from this census count are public employee pension plans in which direct payments to retired or disabled individuals are made by appropriation of general funds or payments are made to a private trustee or insurance carrier who administers the investments and benefit payments.

The 62 general coverage systems are open to all employees with little or no exception. All states except Nebraska have general, state-administered systems that cover the bulk of state employees, either by themselves or in some combination with local employees. Nebraska maintains a privately administered pension plan for its state employees, which is not included here in the count of government-operated retirement systems.

Limited coverage systems are restricted by occupational area and therefore tend to be smaller in size. There were 128 limited coverage state systems in 1982.

As is indicated in Table 1, 4 million active members of state-administered systems were also covered by Social Security as reported in the 1982 Census of Governments. This figure, however, is considerably short of the actual total since all of the state systems in nine states and some of the systems in six states reported that the data were not available.

Benefit Operations

The number of beneficiaries under state-administered systems totalled 2,262,175 in 1982, an increase of 12.6 percent over 1980 and 36.2 percent over 1977. Not only is the absolute amount surging upward, but the ratio of beneficiaries receiving periodic benefit payments to total membership has been constantly increasing. This ratio reached 22.3 percent in the last month of fiscal 1982 as compared to 19.4 percent in 1980, 17.7 percent in 1977, and 11.7 percent in 1967. This trend reflects the increasing proportion of elderly in the population nationwide, as well as the recent cutbacks in government employment.

Average benefit payments were $410 nationally in 1982, with considerable variation among the states (Table 5). The average monthly payments for all persons receiving periodic benefits ranged from $142 in Nebraska, $153 in Wyoming and $154 in Kansas, to $823 in Alaska, $659 in Louisiana and $649 in Maryland.

Several factors affect the computation of average benefit payments: differences in salary levels among professions, varying length-of-service requirements, regional economic differences, and the degree of employee unionization.

Maurice Criz is Senior Advisor, Governments Division, U.S. Bureau of the Census. Data are from the Bureau of the Census report, *Employee-Retirement Systems of State and Local Governments,* 1982 Census of Governments, Volume 6, No. 1, and annual and census reports from prior years.

Also affecting the computations are particular nuances in the survey data. For example, the low average benefit in Nebraska reflects the absence of any general coverage, statewide system.

Financial Operations

During fiscal 1982, inflation subsided and corporate and federal bond yields remained at all-time high yields while the economy was in deep recession. Returns on recently purchased fixed investments produced income at very good levels, but investment portfolios that contained older bonds did not perform well in 1982. Common stocks yielded dividend-price ratios about equal to the inflation rate for the year.

Income and expenditures of the state systems have increased constantly over the years. Receipts amounted to $37.9 billion in 1982, an increase of 97 percent over 1977 and 309 percent over 1972 (Table 2). Benefits and withdrawal payments amounted to $13.1 billion in 1982, an increase of 90 percent over 1977 and 312 percent over 1972.

The sources of income for state-administered systems have changed interestingly in the past two decades (Table A). Government contributions (state and local) provided 44.3 percent of total receipts in 1962, reached a high of 45.5 percent in 1980, and then dropped off to 41.6 percent in 1982. Employee contributions amounted to 35 percent in 1962 and have dropped steadily to 17.6 percent in 1982. Earnings on investments have increased steadily from 20.7 percent of receipts in 1962 to 40.8 percent in 1982.

Local government contributions ranged as high as 49.7 percent in Florida and 35 percent in New York.

An upward trend in the relationship between benefit payments and total receipts halted, at least temporarily. From 1957 to 1978, the ratio of such payments to receipts increased steadily from 23.7 percent to 31.7 percent. Since then, the ratio declined to 29.9 percent in 1981 and increased slightly to 30.1 percent in 1982. Individual state ratios ranged from 11.3 percent in Wyoming and 11.5 percent in Utah, to more than 50 percent in Louisiana, Maine and Massachusetts.

Asset holdings of the retirement systems are an important segment of the national economy, amounting to $193.3 billion at the close of fiscal 1982 (Table 2). Since these funds currently increase by $20-30 billion annually, they constitute an important source of funds for the nation's credit markets. The largest portion of these holdings is in corporate bonds (35.7 percent), next is corporate stocks (22.8 percent), and federal securities are third (22.4 percent).

In the past decade, there has been a significant change in the composition of cash and security holdings of these systems. Holdings of federal government securities doubled to 22.4 percent of the total in 1982. Correspondingly, the level of corporate bond holdings dropped from 57.8 percent of total assets to 35.7 percent. The percentage of holdings invested in corporate stocks remained steady at one-fifth, while investment in mortgages decreased slightly from 12 to 9.2 percent.

Table A
PERCENTAGE DISTRIBUTION OF TOTAL RECEIPTS, SELECTED YEARS: 1962 TO 1982

Item	1981-82	1980-81	1979-80	1971-72	1962
Employee contributions	17.6	17.9	18.5	28.4	35.0
Government contributions	41.6	44.2	45.5	43.3	44.3
Earnings on investments	40.8	37.8	36.0	28.2	20.7

As one might expect, the relative importance of specific sources of revenue varies considerably among the states (Table 5). Employee contributions amounted to about one-third of receipts in 1982 in Arizona, Louisiana, North Dakota, South Dakota and Utah, but comprised less than 5 percent in Florida, Michigan and New York. State government contributions amounted to 57.2 percent of receipts in Oklahoma, 51.2 percent in Nevada, and 47.9 percent in Connecticut.

Table 1
NUMBER, MEMBERSHIP AND BENEFITS OF STATE-ADMINISTERED EMPLOYEE RETIREMENT SYSTEMS, BY SYSTEM CHARACTERISTICS: 1981-82

Systems	Number of systems	Membership, last month of fiscal year		Recurrent benefit operations, last month of fiscal year			Lump-sum survivors benefit payments during the month (in thousands)
		Number(a)	Covered by Social Security(b,c)	Number of beneficiaries	Amount (in thousands)(c)	Average per beneficiary (c)	
All systems	190	10,141,062	4,065,944	2,262,175	$927,217	$410	$43,443
General coverage	62	6,445,853	2,890,729	1,431,636	483,601	338	15,550
State employees only	12	844,236	428,977	218,200	81,984	376	3,629
State employees and all local employees	18	2,403,679	1,051,201	463,155	155,964	337	1,712
State employees and local nonschool employees	16	2,412,224	848,462	609,677	204,798	336	8,394
State employees and local school employees	2	70,341	36,654	13,646	5,040	369	99
State employees and teachers	1	230,213	230,213	43,031	18,239	424	398
Local employees other than teachers	13	485,160	295,222	83,927	17,576	209	1,319
Limited coverage	128	3,695,209	1,175,215	830,539	444,652	535	27,893
Teachers only	18	1,550,951	366,169	384,983	232,334	603	3,076
All school employees	18	1,784,480	456,193	343,678	142,617	415	4,748
All other	92	359,778	352,853	101,878	69,701		20,069

Source: Compiled from unpublished data received in the U.S. Bureau of the Census 1982 survey on finances of public employee retirement systems.

(a) Includes both active and inactive membership.
(b) Includes only active members also covered under Social Security.
(c) Data not available for all systems.

Table 2
NATIONAL SUMMARY OF FINANCES OF STATE-ADMINISTERED EMPLOYEE RETIREMENT SYSTEMS, SELECTED YEARS: 1972-1982

Item	Amount (in millions of dollars)							Percentage distribution			
	1981-82	1980-81	1979-80	1978-79	1977-78	1976-77	1971-72	1981-82	1979-80	1976-77	1971-72
Receipts	$37,944	$33,340	$28,603	$24,659	$21,488	$19,287	$9,285	100.0	100.0	100.0	100.0
Employee contributions	6,674	5,982	5,285	4,968	4,619	4,223	2,637	17.6	18.5	21.9	28.4
Government contributions	15,777	14,749	13,010	11,490	10,000	8,898	4,026	41.6	45.5	46.1	43.3
From states	8,898	8,353	7,399	6,318	5,736	4,847	2,428	23.5	25.9	25.1	26.1
From local governments	6,879	6,395	5,611	5,173	4,264	4,051	1,598	18.1	19.6	21.0	17.2
Earnings on investments	15,492	12,609	10,308	8,200	6,868	6,167	2,621	40.8	36.0	32.0	28.2
Benefits and withdrawal payments	13,134	11,393	10,257	8,937	7,811	6,930	3,187	100.0	100.0	100.0	100.0
Benefits	11,430	9,964	8,809	7,704	6,821	6,048	2,694	87.0	85.9	87.3	84.5
Withdrawals	1,704	1,429	1,448	1,233	990	882	493	13.0	14.1	12.7	15.5
Cash and security holdings at end of fiscal year, total	193,295	164,624	144,682	125,803	110,357	94,913	51,158	100.0	100.0	100.0	100.0
Cash and deposits	2,427	2,611	2,647	1,883	1,304	818	419	1.3	1.8	0.9	0.8
Governmental securities	44,216	34,292	26,724	20,872	14,743	10,096	2,925	22.9	18.5	10.6	5.7
Federal	43,368	33,716	26,213	20,510	14,425	9,500	2,241	22.4	18.1	10.0	4.4
U.S. Treasury	24,494	19,503	13,814	10,375	6,680	4,729		12.7	9.5	5.0	
Federal agency	18,874	14,212	12,399	10,136	7,745	4,770		9.8	8.6	5.0	
State and local	848	577	511	362	318	596	684	0.4	0.4	0.6	1.3
Nongovernmental securities	146,652	127,721	115,311	103,048	94,309	83,998	47,814	75.9	79.7	88.5	93.5
Corporate bonds	68,948	65,246	60,871	55,108	51,266	45,364	29,570	35.7	42.1	47.8	57.8
Corporate stocks	44,025	36,438	31,146	26,987	24,404	21,733	9,209	22.8	21.5	22.9	18.0
Mortgages	17,742	14,174	11,966	10,711	9,794	10,228	6,138	9.2	8.3	10.8	12.0
Other securities	12,525	9,684	10,677	8,944	7,637	6,361	2,897	6.5	7.4	6.7	5.7
Other investments	3,412	2,179	651	1,298	1,208	312		1.8	0.4	0.3	

Source: U.S. Bureau of the Census, Census of Governments reports for 1972, 1977, and 1982: *Employee Retirement Systems of State and Local Governments* (Volume 6, No. 1), and annual reports for other years: *Finances of Employee Retirement Systems of State and Local Governments.*

Table 3
MEMBERSHIP AND BENEFIT OPERATIONS OF STATE-ADMINISTERED EMPLOYEE RETIREMENT SYSTEMS: LAST MONTH OF FISCAL 1982

| State | Membership, last month of the fiscal year | Beneficiaries receiving periodic benefit payments | | | | Benefit Operations, last month of fiscal year | | | | |
| | | | | | | Periodic benefit payment for the month (dollars) | | | | Lump-sum survivors benefit payments during the month (dollars) |
		Total(a)	Persons retired on account of age or length of service	Persons retired on account of disability	Survivors of deceased former members (no. of payees)	Total(a)	Persons retired on account of age or length of service	Persons retired on account of disability	To survivors of deceased former members	
All states	10,141,062	2,262,175	1,958,960	149,092	154,123	$927,217,000	$825,219,000	$ 60,527	$41,472,000	$43,443,000
Alabama	148,771	29,137	25,760	1,755	1,622	10,662,000	9,933,000	493,000	236,000	186,000
Alaska	37,713	4,430	4,186	125	119	3,644,000	3,400,000	151,000	93,000	40,000
Arizona	136,783	21,028	20,543	210	275	6,265,000	5,956,000	164,000	145,000	375,000
Arkansas	94,223	16,781	14,501	1,369	911	4,627,000	4,112,000	340,000	174,000	3,000
California	897,765	277,492	233,565	27,428	16,499	139,951,000	124,732,000	12,737,000	2,482,000	23,244,000
Colorado	103,928	21,758	17,667	3,134	957	10,637,000	8,886,000	1,396,000	355,000	0
Connecticut	98,360	28,720	25,757	1,976	987	16,835,000	15,605,000	919,000	311,000	130,000
Delaware	25,302	6,091	4,612	592	887	2,106,000	1,798,000	144,000	164,000	0
Florida	392,344	64,372	51,815	5,428	7,129	25,711,000	22,302,000	1,464,000	1,945,000	0
Georgia	232,196	35,954	30,031	2,504	3,419	16,143,000	14,000,000	1,189,000	954,000	86,000
Hawaii	50,317	13,656	12,615	985	56	7,418,000	6,977,000	416,000	25,000	139,000
Idaho	48,620	12,055	10,708	371	976	3,334,000	2,973,000	178,000	183,000	29,000
Illinois	430,269	106,039	84,965	4,919	16,155	39,532,000	34,285,000	2,319,000	2,928,000	4,675,000
Indiana	197,456	46,221	42,653	2,530	1,038	17,348,000	16,563,000	464,000	320,000	8,000
Iowa	183,544	35,943	35,846	28	69	6,713,000	6,665,000	23,000	25,000	775,000
Kansas	113,193	29,349	27,761	117	1,471	4,511,000	4,240,000	62,000	210,000	52,000
Kentucky	148,149	31,726	31,684	2	40	11,483,000	11,460,000	1,000	21,000	0
Louisiana	231,966	42,440	37,752	2,738	1,950	27,968,000	25,606,000	1,341,000	1,021,000	62,000
Maine	65,247	17,812	14,244	617	2,951	7,839,000	6,689,000	413,000	737,000	27,000
Maryland	92,812	31,796	31,796	0	0	20,635,000	20,635,000	0	0	222,000
Massachusetts	160,928	49,417	49,291	37	89	27,615,000	27,572,000	20,000	23,000	147,000
Michigan	365,706	80,154	76,807	1,989	1,358	30,033,000	29,145,000	510,000	378,000	116,000
Minnesota	226,693	41,180	34,888	1,603	4,689	12,073,000	10,625,000	523,000	925,000	83,000
Mississippi	192,044	21,541	18,429	1,310	1,802	6,172,000	5,446,000	312,000	414,000	106,000
Missouri	131,260	30,002	25,883	2,083	2,036	9,565,000	8,666,000	479,000	420,000	
Montana	54,820	12,158	10,747	894	517	4,284,000	3,806,000	311,000	168,000	42,000
Nebraska	33,471	5,687	5,561	82	44	810,000	785,000	11,000	14,000	0
Nevada	56,018	7,000	5,938	421	641	2,863,000	2,587,000	171,000	104,000	0
New Hampshire	28,950	6,017	6,017	0	0	1,666,000	1,666,000	0	0	87,000
New Jersey	359,088	81,602	77,385	412	3,805	42,676,000	40,094,000	307,000	2,276,000	850,000

New Mexico	78,701	12,288	11,119	779	390	4,424,000	4,214,000	113,000	97,000	0
New York	888,165	225,484	202,030	10,293	13,161	88,914,000	81,868,000	4,486,000	2,561,000	5,412,000
North Carolina	318,265	55,330	43,805	7,051	4,474	21,397,000	17,444,000	2,762,000	1,191,000	564,000
North Dakota	23,454	4,197	3,800	79	318	788,000	731,000	15,000	43,000	0
Ohio	753,483	176,763	143,138	13,118	20,507	70,689,000	58,560,000	6,745,000	5,385,000	548,000
Oklahoma	112,823	30,318	27,142	1,249	1,927	12,473,000	11,387,000	547,000	539,000	26,000
Oregon	124,280	35,436	32,783	2,630	23	9,043,000	8,320,000	711,000	12,000	64,000
Pennsylvania	424,365	128,749	114,857	6,454	7,438	56,417,000	52,241,000	2,300,000	1,877,000	3,270,000
Rhode Island	34,243	9,608	9,488	0	120	4,646,000	4,600,000	0	46,000	91,000
South Carolina	239,795	27,776	22,494	3,679	1,603	9,866,000	8,266,000	1,185,000	415,000	0
South Dakota	28,881	6,367	5,658	104	605	1,074,000	952,000	24,000	98,000	0
Tennessee	162,802	40,181	37,869	2,312	0	12,907,000	12,557,000	350,000	0	133,000
Texas	659,031	96,422	85,229	5,781	5,412	43,020,000	39,105,000	1,868,000	2,047,000	1,007,000
Utah	69,901	12,606	11,952	654	0	2,725,000	2,568,000	157,000	0	42,000
Vermont	17,969	4,269	4,054	62	153	1,384,000	1,339,000	22,000	23,000	0
Virginia	238,005	39,384	32,840	5,038	1,506	15,018,000	12,700,000	1,900,000	418,000	0
Washington	217,911	59,240	20,317	19,476	19,447	26,918,000	9,041,000	8,942,000	8,935,000	0
West Virginia	119,028	28,521	24,662	1,568	2,291	9,109,000	8,225,000	439,000	445,000	27,000
Wisconsin	249,982	56,062	50,934	3,028	2,100	14,419,000	13,100,000	1,067,000	252,000	773,000
Wyoming	42,042	5,616	5,382	78	156	862,000	791,000	33,000	38,000	0

Source: U.S. Bureau of the Census, *Employee Retirement Systems of State and Local Governments,* 1982 Census of Governments, Volume 6, No. 1.

(a) Detail may not add to totals because detail was not always available.

Table 4

FINANCES OF STATE-ADMINISTERED EMPLOYEE RETIREMENT SYSTEMS, BY STATE: 1981-82

(In thousands of dollars)

State	Total	Employee contributions	Government contributions From state	Government contributions From local governments	Earnings on investments	Benefits and withdrawal payments Total	Benefits	Withdrawals
All states.................	$37,943,651	$6,673,867	$8,897,943	$6,879,352	$15,492,489	$13,133,714	$11,429,730	$1,703,984
Alabama...................	564,960	98,819	200,705	27,379	238,057	162,227	139,962	22,265
Alaska....................	272,552	50,653	77,890	61,699	82,310	60,499	50,320	10,179
Arizona	456,246	141,001	81,295	68,680	165,270	113,629	73,931	39,698
Arkansas	254,034	37,584	96,152	13,697	106,602	68,387	54,907	13,480
California................	5,870,963	1,084,615	1,095,204	1,249,142	2,442,002	1,950,894	1,725,567	225,327
Colorado	488,138	130,592	91,030	136,641	129,874	158,416	123,858	34,558
Connecticut..............	486,323	79,817	233,860	7,317	167,329	219,492	200,414	19,078
Delaware	119,097	8,198	55,641	0	55,267	23,836	22,739	1,097
Florida	905,552	10,699	178,359	449,938	266,555	295,855	286,204	9,651
Georgia..................	787,056	167,066	231,473	73,037	315,480	222,810	191,473	31,337
Hawaii	366,096	78,479	129,342	22,672	135,603	98,352	89,564	8,788
Idaho	121,790	30,040	20,272	36,636	34,843	49,604	40,799	8,805
Illinois..................	1,343,017	382,735	297,356	102,384	560,541	559,267	489,603	69,664
Indiana	449,980	80,773	166,540	53,231	149,436	189,026	169,365	19,661
Iowa	340,326	66,434	49,680	62,020	162,192	100,803	79,188	21,615
Kansas	254,285	58,977	59,587	27,991	107,730	79,847	59,440	20,407
Kentucky	457,413	101,899	137,910	29,714	187,888	170,819	151,222	19,597
Louisiana	638,545	205,479	194,275	75,489	163,303	367,975	333,232	34,743
Maine	177,502	35,974	76,310	19,805	45,413	102,329	92,156	10,173
Maryland	595,881	89,548	241,350	14,615	250,369	286,643	251,421	35,222
Massachusetts	627,958	150,951	297,020	0	179,986	384,910	331,681	53,229
Michigan	1,364,918	16,383	370,620	265,356	712,559	371,276	359,584	11,692
Minnesota	746,136	147,941	146,726	88,495	362,976	170,470	139,907	30,563
Mississippi	310,217	85,886	50,959	76,016	97,356	101,259	78,418	22,841
Missouri	517,826	98,036	87,481	104,790	227,519	142,873	112,390	30,483
Montana..................	139,441	41,015	29,635	15,095	53,694	66,041	51,462	14,579
Nebraska	53,664	13,389	7,460	5,946	26,868	13,220	9,091	4,129
Nevada	375,378	21,730	192,301	63,178	98,168	42,887	35,909	6,978
New Hampshire	85,480	23,255	8,606	10,842	42,777	25,686	19,036	6,650
New Jersey	1,435,745	277,354	408,392	104,091	645,909	528,300	492,625	35,675
New Mexico..............	251,935	72,028	63,258	14,710	101,938	70,417	53,249	17,168
New York................	4,280,550	93,809	637,636	1,499,085	2,050,019	1,243,685	1,182,961	60,724
North Carolina	1,000,797	223,106	277,421	42,448	457,821	290,326	239,514	50,812
North Dakota	56,711	19,277	6,413	14,472	16,550	13,013	9,116	3,897
Ohio	2,859,913	636,790	268,661	797,926	1,156,535	1,103,200	985,130	118,070
Oklahoma	511,919	62,214	292,931	27,907	128,867	155,387	142,421	12,966
Oregon	452,391	113,222	74,560	137,398	127,211	137,538	108,348	29,190
Pennsylvania	1,879,855	298,879	597,739	248,566	734,672	882,552	794,051	88,501
Rhode Island	151,828	32,266	40,599	22,842	56,121	61,700	55,252	6,448
South Carolina	479,368	107,407	70,134	80,289	221,537	137,588	111,422	26,166
South Dakota	69,189	20,724	8,631	12,616	27,218	18,159	12,519	5,640
Tennessee................	551,292	90,241	210,826	30,147	220,079	163,571	139,377	24,194
Texas....................	2,005,207	512,479	596,063	41,254	855,410	662,664	516,391	146,273
Utah	268,287	81,995	4,229	84,735	97,329	54,941	30,905	24,036
Vermont..................	51,326	9,658	18,009	555	23,103	101,172	16,188	84,984
Virginia..................	541,741	124,861	136,514	98,623	181,743	196,186	161,385	34,801
Washington	787,495	195,543	77,305	177,577	337,070	367,515	323,202	44,313
West Virginia.............	215,891	62,072	73,214	14,056	66,549	121,592	108,169	13,423
Wisconsin................	819,496	73,986	117,196	246,551	381,764	208,091	173,341	34,750
Wyoming	99,943	27,997	13,171	21,699	37,076	16,783	11,320	5,463

Source: U.S. Bureau of the Census, *Employee Retirement Systems of State and Local Governments,* 1982 Census of Governments, Volume 6, No. 1.

Note: Because of rounding, detail may not add to totals.

Table 4—Part 2

FINANCES OF STATE-ADMINISTERED EMPLOYEE RETIREMENT SYSTEMS, BY STATE: 1981-82

(In thousands of dollars)

			Cash and security holdings at end of fiscal year				
			Governmental securities				
			Federal securities				
State	Total	Cash and deposits	Total	U.S. Treasury	Federal agency	State and local	Non-governmental securities
All states	$193,294,855	$2,426,923	$43,367,530	$24,493,911	$18,873,619	$848,145	$146,652,256
Alabama.................	2,537,373	49,528	6,410	0	6,410	0	2,481,435
Alaska	1,042,543	163,907	282,600	282,600	0	0	596,037
Arizona	2,700,537	139	994,496	992,134	2,362	0	1,705,903
Arkansas	1,277,763	22,098	443,148	290,335	152,814	0	812,517
California...............	31,010,650	286,731	4,862,383	1,252,838	3,609,545	11,541	25,849,994
Colorado	2,876,553	42,794	362,059	211,006	151,052	102	2,471,596
Connecticut.............	2,067,857	27,603	58,954	58,954	0	0	1,981,300
Delaware	368,461	682	21,092	20,542	550	0	346,687
Florida	4,879,429	11,822	1,522,380	801,754	720,626	0	3,345,227
Georgia.................	3,455,876	117,895	990,913	693,842	297,071	0	2,347,068
Hawaii(a)	1,634,520	29,430	439,500	43,340	387,160	137	1,174,453
Idaho	480,049	50,351	49,684	26,840	22,844	0	380,014
Illinois.................	7,203,624	187,812	927,040	436,627	490,412	0	6,088,772
Indiana	1,896,021	61,746	741,473	340,010	401,464	0	1,092,802
Iowa	1,742,109	2,045	535,323	335,574	199,749	0	1,204,741
Kansas	1,294,160	143,881	321,758	206,285	115,472	15,270	813,251
Kentucky	2,166,651	135,449	437,372	189,163	248,209	1,160	1,592,670
Louisiana	3,000,687	181,674	1,289,903	717,704	572,199	1,694	1,527,416
Maine	434,280	87,512	74,621	63,267	11,355	0	272,146
Maryland	2,782,795	31,622	0	0	0	0	2,751,173
Massachusetts	2,026,595	38,720	802,586	39,573	763,013	0	1,185,290
Michigan	7,433,541	2,669	1,555,459	216,218	1,339,241	2,918	5,872,494
Minnesota	3,733,641	12,080	760,885	456,476	304,409	1,385	2,959,290
Mississippi	1,418,482	7,436	818,389	358,834	459,555	0	592,657
Missouri	2,775,740	34,360	656,844	185,570	471,273	0	2,084,536
Montana	586,590	3,350	21,221	20,371	850	1,473	560,546
Nebraska	287,825	57	109,446	69,748	39,698	3,392	174,930
Nevada.................	1,024,558	168	281,658	185,228	96,431	0	742,731
New Hampshire	409,904	42,340	77,583	59,556	18,027	0	289,981
New Jersey..............	7,952,484	37	1,242,527	61,328	1,181,199	625	6,709,295
New Mexico.............	1,137,543	18,085	497,300	229,406	267,895	0	622,158
New York...............	25,408,075	9,000	7,512,280	6,054,099	1,458,181	776,166	17,110,629
North Carolina	5,395,379	77,240	1,216,523	665,340	551,183	0	4,101,616
North Dakota	229,749	22,666	77,425	47,783	29,642	0	129,658
Ohio	15,408,615	115,976	2,810,572	1,768,669	1,041,904	2,214	12,479,853
Oklahoma	1,512,295	184,436	482,008	272,728	209,280	0	845,851
Oregon	2,182,731	45	96,891	1,000	95,891	0	2,085,796
Pennsylvania............	9,224,251	23.631	1,569,725	1,569,725	0	69	7,630,827
Rhode Island	625,696	43,370	225,253	223,653	1,600	26,444	330,539
South Carolina	2,448,122	9,917	1,492,592	555,687	936,905	3,089	942,525
South Dakota	334,204	3,364	148,625	148,625	0	0	182,215
Tennessee...............	2,532,891	18,552	799,580	702,912	96,668	0	1,714,758
Texas	9,685,487	85,614	3,353,057	1,498,957	1,854,100	0	6,246,816
Utah	1,180,267	0	242,681	176,000	66,681	0	937,586
Vermont................	222,020	1,385	26,742	24,784	1,957	0	193,894
Virginia.................	2,319,383	4,551	899,014	899,014	0	112	1,415,706
Washington	3,820,699	12,316	712,033	711,765	268	351	3,095,999
West Virginia............	789,389	10,428	291,144	135,211	155,933	0	487,816
Wisconsin	5,866,775	2	52,801	52,801	0	0	5,813,972
Wyoming	470,078	10,411	182,577	140,035	42,542	0	277,090

Table 5
COMPARATIVE STATISTICS FOR STATE-ADMINISTERED PUBLIC EMPLOYEE RETIREMENT SYSTEMS: 1981-82

State	Percent of receipts paid by			Annual benefit payments as a percentage of		Average benefit payments(a)	Investment earnings as a percentage of cash and asset holdings	Percentage distribution of cash and security holdings				
	Employee contribution	State government	Local government	Annual receipts	Cash and security holdings			Total	Cash and deposits	Governmental securities		Nongovernmental securities
										Federal	State and local	
All states	17.6	23.5	18.1	30.1	5.9	$410	8.0	100.0	1.3	22.4	0.4	75.9
Alabama	17.5	35.5	4.8	24.8	5.5	366	9.4	100.0	2.0	0.3	0	97.8
Alaska	18.6	28.6	22.6	18.5	4.8	823	7.9	100.0	15.7	27.1	0	57.2
Arizona	30.9	17.8	15.1	16.2	2.7	298	6.1	100.0	0	36.8	0	63.2
Arkansas	14.8	37.9	5.4	21.6	4.3	276	8.3	100.0	1.7	34.7	0	63.6
California	18.5	18.7	22.0	29.4	5.6	504	7.9	100.0	0.9	15.7	0	83.4
Colorado	26.8	18.6	28.0	25.4	4.3	489	4.5	100.0	1.5	12.6	0	85.9
Connecticut	16.3	47.9	1.5	41.0	9.7	586	8.1	100.0	1.3	2.9	0	95.8
Delaware	6.9	46.7	0	19.1	6.2	346	15.0	100.0	0.2	5.7	0	94.1
Florida	1.2	19.7	49.7	31.6	5.9	399	5.5	100.0	0.2	31.2	0	68.6
Georgia	21.2	29.4	9.3	24.3	5.5	462	9.1	100.0	3.4	28.7	0	67.9
Hawaii	21.4	35.3	6.2	24.5	5.5	543	8.3	100.0	1.8	26.3	0	71.9
Idaho	24.7	16.6	30.1	33.5	8.5	247	7.3	100.0	10.5	10.3	0	79.2
Illinois	28.5	22.1	7.6	36.5	6.8	373	7.8	100.0	2.6	12.9	0	84.5
Indiana	18.0	37.0	11.8	37.6	8.9	375	7.9	100.0	3.3	39.1	0	57.6
Iowa	19.5	14.6	18.2	23.3	4.5	187	9.3	100.0	0.1	30.7	0	69.2
Kansas	23.2	23.4	11.0	23.4	4.6	154	8.3	100.0	11.1	24.9	1.2	62.8
Kentucky	22.3	30.1	6.5	33.1	7.0	362	8.7	100.0	6.3	20.2	0.1	73.5
Louisiana	32.2	30.4	11.8	52.2	11.1	659	5.4	100.0	6.1	43.0	0.1	50.9
Maine	20.3	43.0	11.2	51.9	21.2	440	10.5	100.0	20.2	17.2	0	62.7
Maryland	15.0	40.5	2.5	42.2	9.0	649	9.0	100.0	1.1	0	0	98.9
Massachusetts	24.0	47.3	0	52.8	16.4	559	8.9	100.0	1.9	39.6	0	58.5
Michigan	1.2	27.2	19.4	26.3	4.8	364	9.6	100.0	0	20.9	0	79.0
Minnesota	19.8	19.7	11.9	18.8	3.7	258	9.7	100.0	0.3	20.8	0	78.9
Mississippi	27.7	16.4	24.5	25.3	5.5	287	6.9	100.0	0.5	57.7	0	41.8
Missouri	18.9	16.9	20.2	21.7	4.0	319	8.2	100.0	1.2	23.7	0	75.1
Montana	29.4	21.3	10.8	36.9	10.5	352	11.0	100.0	0.6	3.6	0.3	95.6
Nebraska	25.0	13.9	11.1	16.9	3.2	142	9.3	100.0	0	38.0	1.2	60.8
Nevada	5.8	51.2	16.8	12.5	3.5	409	9.6	100.0	0	27.5	0	72.5
New Hampshire	27.2	10.1	12.7	22.2	4.6	277	10.4	100.0	10.3	18.9	0	70.7
New Jersey	19.3	28.4	7.3	34.3	6.2	523	8.1	100.0	0	15.6	0	84.4

New Mexico	28.6	25.1	5.8	21.1	4.7	360	9.0	100.0	1.6	43.7	0	54.7
New York	2.2	14.9	35.0	27.6	4.7	394	8.1	100.0	0	29.6	3.1	67.3
North Carolina	22.3	27.7	4.2	23.9	4.4	387	8.5	100.0	1.4	22.5	0	76.0
North Dakota	34.0	11.3	25.5	16.1	4.0	188	7.2	100.0	9.9	33.7	0	56.4
Ohio	22.3	9.4	27.9	34.4	6.4	400	7.5	100.0	0.8	18.2	0	81.0
Oklahoma	12.2	57.2	5.5	27.8	9.4	411	8.5	100.0	12.2	31.9	0	55.9
Oregon	25.0	16.5	30.4	24.0	5.0	255	5.8	100.0	0	4.4	0	95.6
Pennsylvania	15.9	31.8	13.2	42.2	8.6	438	8.0	100.0	0.3	17.0	0	82.7
Rhode Island	21.3	26.7	15.0	36.4	8.8	484	9.0	100.0	6.9	36.0	4.2	52.8
South Carolina	22.4	14.6	16.7	23.2	4.5	355	9.0	100.0	0.4	61.0	0.1	38.5
South Dakota	30.0	12.5	18.2	18.1	3.7	169	8.1	100.0	1.0	44.5	0	54.5
Tennessee	16.4	38.2	5.5	25.3	5.5	321	8.7	100.0	0.7	31.6	0	67.7
Texas	25.6	29.7	2.1	25.8	5.3	446	8.8	100.0	0.9	34.6	0	64.5
Utah	30.6	1.6	31.6	11.5	2.6	216	8.2	100.0	0	20.6	0	79.4
Vermont	18.8	35.1	1.1	31.5	7.3	324	10.4	100.0	0.6	12.0	0	87.3
Virginia	23.0	25.2	18.2	29.8	7.0	381	7.8	100.0	0.2	38.8	0	61.0
Washington	24.8	9.8	22.5	41.0	8.5	454	8.8	100.0	0.3	18.6	0	81.0
West Virginia	28.8	33.9	6.5	50.1	13.7	319	8.4	100.0	1.3	36.9	0	61.8
Wisconsin	9.0	14.3	30.1	21.2	3.0	257	6.5	100.0	0	0.9	0	99.1
Wyoming	28.0	13.2	21.7	11.3	2.4	153	7.9	100.0	2.2	38.8	0	58.9

Source: U.S. Bureau of the Census, *Employee Retirement Systems of State and Local Governments,* Volume 6, No. 1.

(a) Average benefit payment for last month of fiscal year.

DEVELOPMENTS IN STATE PERSONNEL SYSTEMS

By Keon S. Chi

There were few structural changes in state personnel systems during the 1982-1983 biennium. As in the past, states maintain a centralized personnel office along with between 25 and 50 agency personnel offices. State government employees are under two or more jurisdictions for classification and compensation purposes. Separate personnel systems are used in most states for legislative staff, judicial personnel, executive managers, and those in the law enforcement and education fields. Although a majority (34) of the states use classification systems revised in the past two decades, it is interesting to note that seven states still use personnel systems adopted before 1945.

Major developments in state personnel administration in the past two years are related to affirmative action, cutback management, productivity, executive manager training, unionization, performance evaluation and employee compensation. And, state personnel executives were confronted with other issues arising from federal fund cuts and state revenue shortfalls. Due to limited space, three topics—collective bargaining, evaluation and compensation—are described here with particular focus on the pay equity question.

Collective Bargaining

In 1983, Illinois and Ohio joined 23 other states to allow collective bargaining for state government employees. Under the new laws of the two states, both effective in 1984, collective bargaining rights are guaranteed for all public employees except police and firefighters. Currently, collective bargaining is legally allowed in nearly all the Eastern and Midwestern states while government unionization movements led by AFSCME and others have been less successful in Western states. In 1983, Florida was the only state in the South with a collective bargaining law. Of the states with collective bargaining laws, 10 have "right to work" provisions under which state government employees can choose to remain non-union.

Performance Appraisal

State governments continue to use employee appraisal. The main purposes of performance

evaluation cited by state personnel executives, in order of frequency of mention in a 50-state survey, are communication between supervisors and employees (44 states), productivity improvement (38), and salary adjustment (37). Other objectives include promotion, layoff and dismissal, and employee training. All but two states have either statutory or administrative requirements for employee evaluation, and 32 states use a statewide, uniform appraisal system.

Most (45) states evaluate employees annually, but it is difficult to characterize the effects of evaluation. For instance, compensation specialists in one-third of the states reported in 1983 that employee evaluations did not have much weight in their compensation adjustments. The most popular evaluation method used by state governments is management by objective (MBO), followed by numerical rating scales and behaviorally anchored rating scales (BARS). Factors that are considered most heavily in employee evaluation are productivity, knowledge of work, planning and organization, work habits and dependability.

Compensation Practices

The past two years have not been generous to many state government employees in at least 16 states where salaries were frozen. One state had a 6 percent across-the-board reduction for its general fund agencies. Yet the pay situation nationwide in 1982-83 was not as bad as it appeared; 32 states gave a cost of living increase of between 6 and 10 percent to their government employees. As economic conditions began to improve, most states projected an increase in employee compensation in the next two years.

A majority of the states have recently adopted the concept of total compensation comparability (TCC), incorporating fringe benefits into overall pay policy, and only 15 states' pay plans are not based on the TCC concept. Fringe benefits that most state governments give to their employees are social security, retirement, health insurance, holidays, sick leave and vacation leave, while

Keon S. Chi is Research Associate for The Council of State Governments and teaches at Georgetown College, Kentucky.

many states still do not give disability, unemployment compensation, or life insurance benefits. A slight majority (29) of the states allocate between 30 percent and 40 percent of the base salary for fringe benefits, with 13 states under 30 percent and five states slightly over 40 percent, but no state over 50 percent.

A great deal of variation exists in decision-making involving employee compensation. Some states have constitutional provisions on compensation while other states have statutory provisions only. Seven states have neither. Legislative action is needed to adjust compensation plans, either annually or biannually, in 35 states, although the nature of legislative control over pay plans differs from state to state. One thing common to almost all states, however, is the fact that compensation plans may or may not be adjusted depending on availability of funds.

Pay Equity

The establishment or maintenance of internal equity and external equity is essential to a sound compensation plan. Thirty-nine states (or 78 percent) reported in 1983 that their pay plans were based on the "equal pay for equal work" principle, and all but five states have recently adopted the external equity principle, comparing their pay plans with compensation in the labor market.

It must be noted that the adoption of the external equity principle may not necessarily mean actual comparability of salaries and fringe benefits for employees in state governments and their counterparts in the private labor market. In fact, most compensation specialists in state governments reported that their salary plans are generally behind the private sector. The question is: how much behind are state government compensations as compared to the labor market? This question may be answered differently depending upon measurement method. State governments may be grouped into three categories: (1) states in which employee salaries are lower across-the-board compared to the labor market; (2) states in which salaries are higher compared to the labor market in small cities and rural areas, but lower compared to the labor market in certain metropolitan areas in the states; and (3) states in which salaries for lower-level positions are higher compared to the same or similar jobs in the private sector, while salaries for professional and executive positions in state governments are behind the labor market. In these three categories, states vary greatly in percentage differences.

Comparable Worth

One of the most controversial developments in the personnel management field relates to another aspect of the pay equity question: comparable worth. Much of the attention to comparable worth has been due to the recent ruling of a federal judge in the state of Washington that the state government had "historically engaged in employment discrimination on the basis of sex." Judge Jack Tanner, U.S. District Court for the Western District of Washington, ruled in September 1983 in *AFSCME et. al. vs. the State of Washington et. al.* that the state had committed sex discrimination in violation of Title VII of the 1964 Civil Rights Act and ordered immediate pay increases and four years' back pay for more than 15,000 female employees. Currently, four states (California, Iowa, Minnesota and Washington) have laws requiring equal pay for comparable worth in their state personnel systems, and a growing number of the states, faced with pressure mostly from women's groups, have begun compensation studies to define comparable worth, measure pay gender gaps, and determine methods of adjustment.

The concept of comparable worth is different from the equal pay for equal work principle. A common definition of comparable worth concerns the value of work or equal pay for work of comparable value. California law (S.B. 459) defines the term "comparability of the value of the work" as meaning "the value of the work performed by an employee, or group of employees within a class or salary range, in relation to the value of the work of another employee, or group of employees, to any class or salary range within state service." Minnesota law (H.R. No. 2005) defines comparable worth as "the value of the work measured by the composite of the skill, effort, responsibility and working conditions normally required in the performance of the work." And, according to Washington law (SSB 3248), comparable worth means the provision of "similar salaries for positions that require or impose similar responsibilities, judgments, knowledge, skills and working conditions."

It is not difficult to document the gender pay gap that exists in state governments. In 1982, female employees in state and local governments on average earned 71 cents for each dollar paid to male employees. (The wage gap between female and male workers in the labor market was wider: 63 cents for each dollar.) Gender pay gaps exist because of several factors, including childhood socialization, lack of education and training, marketplace economic conditions, male-dominated union movements, job segregation or occupational concentration. As in the private sector, a considerable number of large occupational classes in state governments are dominated over 80 percent by either males or females.

One way of measuring comparable worth involves assigning a numerical rating to every job in order to set appropriate salaries. For example, predominantly male-dominated state government jobs such as carpenter, security officer and mechanic are ranked with predominantly female-dominated jobs such as social worker, telephone operator and medical record analyst. Comparable worth studies require a systematic comparison of jobs and salaries in a "sex-neutral manner," according to proponents. Yet there seem to be no easy answers to the controversial question as reflected in policy issues raised by the Comparable Worth Task Force in Michigan: What should be the role of labor market rates in the determination of pay for classified employees? Can effects of social values and societal sex bias be separated from economic labor market factors? How long would be an appropriate time period to eliminate completely wage discrimination based on sex? Should elimination of wage discrimination based on sex in collective bargaining units be adjusted exclusively through employee-employer negotiations? How should any cost-incurring wage adjustments be financed? And, what impact, if any, on the business climate and labor relations in the private sector in the state can be anticipated from comparable worth implemented in the state government?

Legal and financial implications of comparable worth appear to be significant. While the state of Washington decided to appeal the case, the pay equity issue might have to be decided ultimately by the U.S. Supreme Court. In 1981, the Supreme Court ruled in *County of Washington v. Gunther* that plaintiffs can prevail by providing that their wages were "depressed" because of intentional sex discrimination even though their jobs were not equal to jobs held by men with higher wages. The Court, however, avoided endorsing the theory of comparable worth.

The pay equity issue will continue to remain controversial at all levels of government. Comparative worth bills (S. Con. Res. 83, and H.R. 4237) have been introduced in U.S. Congress to correct inequities in pay practices in the federal government; local officials highlighted the comparable worth issue at a national conference in January 1984 co-sponsored by the American Ar-bitration Association and the U.S. Conference of Mayors; and the National Association of State Personnel Executives met in February 1984 to discuss strategies to deal with comparable worth in state governments.

Note

This article is based on data collected by The Council of State Governments. Additional information was taken from other sources including 1982 and 1983 issues of *State Personnel View* (National Association of State Personnel Executives), *Hotline AGE* (Assembly of Government Employees), *IPMA News* (International Personnel Management Association) and *Governors' Bulletin*.

Table 1
STATE EMPLOYEES: PERSONNEL SYSTEM ORGANIZATION AND COLLECTIVE BARGAINING

| State | Board/commission members(a) | | | More than one personnel system in state(b) | Collective bargaining | |
	Number	Method of selection	Term(years)		Allowed in state	Employees may choose to remain nonmembers of bargaining unit
Alabama	5	(c)	6	...	(d)	
Alaska	3	G(e)	6	...	★	...
Arizona	5	G(e)	3	★	...	
Arkansas	5	G	5	...	...	
California	5	G(e)	10	★	★	★
Colorado	5	(f)	5	★	...	
Connecticut				★	★	...
Delaware	5	G	3	★	★	...
Florida	7	G(g)	4	★	★	★
Georgia	5	G(e)	5	...	...	
Hawaii	7	G(e)	4	★	★	..
Idaho	5	G	6	...	...	
Illinois				★	★(h)	(h)
Indiana	7	G	4	...	...	
Iowa	5	G(e)	6	★	★	...
Kansas	5	G(e)	4	★	(i)	★
Kentucky	7	(j)	4	★	...	
Louisiana	7	G(k)	6	...	...	
Maine	5	G(e)	4	...	★	(l)
Maryland				★	...	
Massachusetts	5	G	5	...	★	...
Michigan	4	G	8	★	★	...
Minnesota	3	G(e)	3	...	★	...
Mississippi	8	(m)	4	★	...	
Missouri	3	G(e)	6	★	...	
Montana	3	G	6	...	★	...
Nebraska	5	G(e)	5	★	★	★
Nevada	5	G	4	★	...	
New Hampshire	3	G(n)	3	...	★	
New Jersey	5	G(e)	5	...	★	(o)
New Mexico	5	G(e)	5	...	★	...
New York	3	G(e)	6	★	★	(p)
North Carolina	7	G(e)	6	...	...	
North Dakota	5	(q)	6	...	...	
Ohio				...	★(r)	...
Oklahoma	7	G	7	...	...	
Oregon				★	★	(s)
Pennsylvania	3	G	6	...	★	★
Rhode Island				★	★	(t)
South Carolina	5	(u)	4	...	...	
South Dakota	5	G(e)	4	★	★	★
Tennessee	5	G	6	★	...	
Texas	6	G(e)	6	★	...	
Utah	5	G	4	...	...	
Vermont				...	★	★
Virginia	7	G(e)	4	★	...	
Washington	3	G(e)	6	★	...	
West Virginia	3	G(e)	6	...	...	
Wisconsin	5	(v)	5	...	★	(w)
Wyoming	3	G	3	★	...	

Source: Information on number of personnel systems and collective bargaining derived from The Council of State Governments' survey of state personnel agencies on government employee compensation plans and practices (May 1983).

Table 1—Notes

(a) Members of entity generally referred to as the state personnel board or commission. Exceptions: Arkansas, Louisiana, Minnesota, Montana and Texas—Merit system boards or councils; Florida, Wyoming—Career service commissions; Hawaii, Kansas, Massachusetts, Michigan, New Jersey, New York, Pennsylvania, Tennessee and West Virginia—Civil service commissions; Iowa—Merit Employment Commission.

(b) May include separate systems for university-related, legislative, judicial and/or non-merit personnel, among other categories of employees.

(c) Two appointed by governor; one appointed by speaker of the House; one appointed by lieutenant governor (as president of Senate); one elected by majority vote of full-time state employees.

(d) Employee organization exists only for one department.

(e) Confirmed by legislature.

(f) Three appointed by governor with consent of Senate; two elected by persons certified to classes in system.

(g) With approval of three cabinet members and confirmation by Senate.

(h) Collective bargaining authorized by executive order (effective 1984); employees may opt for non-representation.

(i) Employee groups/unions represent employees in "meet and confer" discussions and agreements.

(j) Five appointed by governor (with consent of Senate); two elected by classified employees.

(k) Six appointed by governor; one elected by employees.

(l) Employees who are assigned to bargaining unit, but who choose to remain non-members may pay an 80 percent (of membership cost) service fee or no fee if union services are not desired.

(m) Two House members appointed by speaker; two Senate members appointed by lieutenant governor; four members appointed by governor.

(n) With the advice of the Executive Council.

(o) Agency shop act permits employees to remain non-union, but pay up to 85 percent of the equivalent dues to union representing their respective classifications.

(p) Employees are in negotiating units which can vote to certify or decertify a labor organization. Once the organization is certified, an employee can elect not to join, but must pay an agency fee.

(q) One constitutionally elected official; one member appointed by Board of Education; one appointed by governor; two elected by employees.

(r) Effective 1984.

(s) Employees in bargaining units vote on "fair-share" payments for non-member employees.

(t) Must be exempted by State Labor Relations Board by job, or employees may choose non-membership by paying a service fee equal to union dues.

(u) Three constitutionally elected; two appointed by legislature.

(v) All nominated by governor: one of governor's personal choice, one from list submitted by Senate president; one from list submitted by speaker of Assembly; one from list submitted by minority leader of Senate; and another from list submitted by minority leader of Assembly.

(w) Employees are required to pay union dues only if 2/3 of the eligible employees approve in a fair share referendum.

Table 2
STATE EMPLOYEES: COMPENSATION PROVISIONS AND SELECTED BENEFITS

State	General provisions for compensation plans		Selected employee benefits			
	Statutory provision on compensation	Legislative action necessary to adjust compensation plan	Health insurance (monthly cost to state)(a)	Retirement plans (state contribution rate)(b)	Annual leave (days)	Sick leave (annual accrual rate) (days)
Alabama	...	...	$75	7.83%	13(c)	13
Alaska	★(d)	★	195	12.71	15(c)	15
Arizona	★(e)	★	55.56	7	12(c)	12
Arkansas	★	★	34.76	12	12(c)	12
California	★	★	71	18.34	10.5(c)	12
Colorado	★	...	42.12	12.2	12(c)	15
Connecticut	★	...	113.33	6.91	12(c,f)	15
Delaware	★	★	55.78	14.2	15(c)	15
Florida	★	...	39.83	10.93	13(c)	13
Georgia	...	★	varies	15.25	15(c)	15
Hawaii	★	★	15.98	23.92	21	21
Idaho	★	★	73.10	8.75	12(c)	12
Illinois	★	...	67.10	6.5	10(c)	12
Indiana	★	★	41.40	varies	12(c)	12
Iowa	★	★	66	5.75	10(c)	18
Kansas	...	★	84.78	4.8	12(c)	12
Kentucky	★	...	46.10	7.25	12(c)	12
Louisiana	★	...	47.33	9	12(c)	12
Maine	★	★	47.22	16.15	12(c)	12
Maryland	★	★	55	11.3	10(c)	15
Massachusetts	★	★	47.39	(g)	10(c)	15
Michigan	★	★	82.15	18.5	13(c)	13
Minnesota	★	★	61.20	5.6	13(c)	13
Mississippi	★	★	48.80	8.75	15(c,h)	15
Missouri	★	...	54	13.1	15(c)	15
Montana	★	★	77.80	6.3	15(c)	12
Nebraska	...	★	29.80	5.62(i)	12(c)	12
Nevada	★	★	86	8	15(c)	15
New Hampshire	★	★	(j)	2.7	15(c)	15
New Jersey	★	★	45	varies	12(c)	15
New Mexico	★	★	29.73	7.85	15	12
New York	★	★	52.49	15.64	14(c)	13
North Carolina	★	(k)	47.75	9.93	10(c)	10
North Dakota	...	...	50	5.12	12(c)	12
Ohio	★	...	59	13.75	10(c)	7
Oklahoma	...	★	57	14	15(c)	15
Oregon	★	★	48	17.01	12(c)	12
Pennsylvania	...	...	110	17.85	15(c)	15
Rhode Island	...	...	36.25	5.5	10(c)	15
South Carolina	★	★	48.02	7.3	15(c)	15
South Dakota	★	★	46.58	5	15(c)	14
Tennessee	★	...	21	11.07	12(c)	12
Texas	★	★	68	8	10.5(c)	12
Utah	★	★	48.74	13	13(c)	13
Vermont	★	★	29	9	12(c)	12
Virginia	★	...	96	12.33	12(c)	15
Washington	★	★	111.30	6.5	12(c)	12
West Virginia	★	...	46.40	9.5	15(c)	18
Wisconsin	★	...	90.58	10.8	10(c)	13
Wyoming	★	★	55	7.5	12(c)	12

Note: For information on paid holidays granted state employees, see table on State Employees: Paid Holidays.

Source: Information derived from The Council of State Governments' survey of state personnel agencies on government employee compensation plans and practices (May 1983).

Key:
★—Yes
. . .—No
(a) For individual employee coverage. Monthly cost to state for family coverage may vary.
(b) As percentage of employee salary.
(c) Additional days after a specified number of years.
(d) Covers those employees not covered by collective bargaining.
(e) Department of Administration required to make annual recommendations to legislature of a salary plan and adjustments for over half of the state employees, and advisory recommendations for statutorily-estab-

lished agency heads, statutorily-approved agency heads and members of boards of commissions, statutorily-exempt division heads within state services and other exempted positions.
(f) Individuals hired before July 1977 receive 15 days. Individuals hired after July 1977 receive additional days after specified number of years.
(g) State contribution funded via annual appropriation.
(h) Individuals employed from six months to one year receive six days. Individuals with one to five years of service receive 15 days.
(i) At rate of 5.62 percent of salary on first $24,000 and 7.49 percent on amount over $24,000.
(j) Amount for employee coverage not available. Family coverage at cost of $152/m.
(k) Action necessary for across-the-board increases resulting in adjustment of entire salary schedule; however, not necessary for adjustments of salary grade assignments for individual classifications or groups of classifications.

Table 3
STATE EMPLOYEES: PAID HOLIDAYS

State or other jurisdiction	Major holidays(a)	Martin Luther King's Birthday(b)	Lincoln's Birthday	Washington's Birthday(c)	Good Friday	Memorial Day(d)	Columbus Day(e)	Veterans Day	Day after Thanksgiving	Day before or after Christmas	Day before or after New Year's	Election Day(f)	Other(g)
Alabama	★			★		★	★	★					★★
Alaska	★		★	★		★		★		Before			★★
Arizona	★	(h)		★		★		★					
Arkansas	★		★	★		★		★					★★
California	★	★	★	★		★	★	★					★
Colorado	★			★		★	★	★				★	
Connecticut	★	★	★	★	★★	★	★	★					
Delaware	★			★		★		★	★				★
Florida	★				★	★		★					★
Georgia	★			★(i)		★	★	★	(i)	(i)			
Hawaii	★		★	★		★	★(j)	★	★				★
Idaho	★	★	★	★	★	★	★	★(l)					
Illinois	★			★		★	★	★				★	
Indiana	★		★	★(l)	★	★	★	★	★			★(k)	★★
Iowa	★					★		★(l)					
Kansas	★	★			(m)★	★		★	★(n)	Before (n)	Before (n)		
Kentucky	★	★		★	★	★	★					★(o)	
Louisiana	★		★	★		★	★	★	(i)				★
Maine	★			★		★	★	★	★			★	
Maryland	★			★		★	★	★					★
Massachusetts	★	★	★	★		★	★	★	★★	Before	Before		★
Michigan	★			★		★		★	★				(p)
Minnesota	★			★		★		★				★	★★
Mississippi	★	★	★	★		★		★					★
Missouri	★			★		★	★	★	★	Before		★(k)	★(p)
Montana	★		★	★		★	★	★	★			★(o)	★★
Nebraska	★			★	★	★	★	★				★★	★★
Nevada	★	★		★		★	★	★	★			★	
New Hampshire	★			★		★		★		Before		★★	★
New Jersey	★	★	★	★	★	★	★	★				★	★
New Mexico	★		★(i)	★(i)		★		★	(i)	(i)			
New York	★	★	★	★		★	★	★		★(q)		★(o)	★★
North Carolina	★			★		★		★	★			★	
North Dakota	★	★		★★	★	★	★★	★				★★	
Ohio	★					★		★				★	
Oklahoma	★			★		★		★	(i)	Before		★	
Oregon	★	★			★	★		★					
Pennsylvania	★	★		★	★	★	★	★				★(k)	★
Rhode Island	★			★		★	★	★				★★	
South Carolina	★			★		★		★	★	After		★★	★

Note: In some states, the governor may proclaim additional holidays or select from a number of holidays for observance by state employees. In some states, the list of paid holidays is determined by the personnel department at the beginning of each year; as a result, the number of holidays may change from year to year. Number of paid holidays may also vary across some employee classifications.

Holidays in addition to any other authorized paid personal leave granted state employees.

Key:

. —Paid holiday not granted.

★ —Paid holiday not granted.

(a) New Year's Day, Independence Day, Labor Day, Thanksgiving Day and Christmas Day.

(b) With the adoption of Martin Luther King's birthday as a federal holiday, other states may be in the process of adding the day to their list of paid holidays.

(c) Third Monday in February. In some states, the holiday is called President's Day or Washington-Lincoln Day.

(d) Last Monday in May in all states indicated, except Delaware, Maryland, New Hampshire, New Mexico, Ohio, South Dakota and Vermont, where holiday is observed on May 30.

(e) Second Monday in October on all states indicated, except Maryland, where holiday is observed on October 12.

(f) General election day only unless otherwise indicated.

(g) Additional holidays:

Alabama—Robert E. Lee's Birthday (Jan. 16), Mardi Gras Day (varies), Thomas Jefferson's Birthday (April 13), Jefferson Davis' Birthday (June 4).

Alaska—Seward's Day (last Mon. in March), Alaska Day (Oct. 18).

Arkansas—Robert E. Lee's Birthday (or Martin Luther King's) (Jan. 16), employee's birthday.

California—Admission Day (Sept. 9).

Colorado—Colorado Day (Aug. 6).

Georgia—Robert E. Lee's Birthday (Jan. 16), Confederate Memorial Day (April 26), Jefferson Davis' Birthday (June 4).

Hawaii—Prince Jonah Kuhio Kalanianaole Day (March 26), King Kamehameha Day (June 11), Admission Day (3rd Friday in Aug.).

Louisiana—Mardi Gras Day (varies), Inauguration Day (every four years, in Baton Rouge only).

Maine—Patriot's Day (April 16).

Maryland—Maryland Day (March 26), Defender's Day (Sept. 12).

Massachusetts—Evacuation Day (March 17) and Bunker Hill Day (June 17) in Boston and Suffolk County; state offices outside the county remain open on those days; however, employees outside county may choose two other days as paid holidays.

Mississippi—Robert E. Lee's Birthday (Jan. 16), Confederate Memorial Day (April 26), Jefferson Davis' Birthday (June 4).

Missouri—Harry Truman's Birthday (May 8).

Nebraska—Arbor Day (April 23).

Nevada—Admissions Day (Oct. 31).

New Hampshire—Fast Day (April 23).

North Carolina—Easter Monday.

Rhode Island—Victory Day (2nd Mon. in Aug.).

South Dakota—Pioneer Day (2nd Mon. in Oct.).

Texas—Confederate Heroes' Day (Jan. 19), Texas Independence Day (March 2-not observed on another day if falls on weekend), Lyndon Johnson's Birthday (Aug. 27), San Jacinto Day (April 21-not observed on another day if falls on weekend), Emancipation Day (June 19).

Utah—Pioneer Day (June 25).

Vermont—Town Meeting Day (1st Tues. in March), Battle of Bennington Day (Aug. 16).

Virginia—Lee/Jackson Day (3rd Mon. in Jan., same as Martin Luther King's Birthday).

West Virginia—West Virginia Day (June 20).

District of Columbia—Inauguration Day (every four years).

American Samoa—Flag Day (April 17).

Guam—Guam Discovery Day (1st Mon. in March), Liberation Day (July 21), Lady of Camarin Day (Dec. 8).

Northern Mariana Islands—Commonwealth Day (Jan. 9), Covenant Day (March 24), Constitution Day (Dec. 8).

Puerto Rico—Three Kings Day (Jan. 6), DeHostos' Birthday (Jan. 11), Jose de Diego's Birthday (April 16), Luis Munoz Rivera's Birthday (July 17), Commonwealth Constitution Day (July 25), Jose C. Barbosa's Birthday (July 27), Discovery of Puerto Rico Day (Nov. 19).

Virgin Islands—Three Kings Day (Jan. 6), Transfer Day (March 31), Holy Thursday (varies), Easter Monday, Traditional Market Fair (3rd Tues. after Easter), Carnival Children's Parade (3rd Fri. after Easter), Organic Act Day (3rd Mon. in June), Emancipation Day (July 3), Hurricane Supplication Day (4th Mon. in July), Local Thanksgiving (3rd Mon. in Oct.).

(h) On Robert E. Lee's Birthday.

(i) Because legislature was in session during their normal occurrences, the paid holidays of Robert E. Lee's and Washington's Birthdays in Georgia and Lincoln's and Washington's Birthdays in New Mexico will be observed instead on Nov. 23 (day after Thanksgiving) and Dec. 24 (Christmas Eve).

(j) Discoverer's Day.

(k) Also, primary election day.

(l) Floating holidays.

(m) Half days. In Wisconsin, half day before Christmas and New Year's Day.

(n) One extra day designated for each holiday.

(o) Presidential election day only.

(p) One floating holiday.

(q) One or two days depending on whether days preceding or following Christmas are normally workdays.

(r) Martin Luther King's Birthday *and* Lee/Jackson Day.

(s) Before Thanksgiving.

(t) Half day before and full day after.

Table 4
STATE EMPLOYEE EVALUATION SYSTEMS
(As of May 1983)

State	Requirements for employee performance evaluation — Statutory	Requirements for employee performance evaluation — Administrative	Formal statewide evaluation system(a)	Evaluation method(s)(b)	Salary adjustment	Promotion/demotion	Dismissal/layoff	Employee training	Communication between supervisor & employees	Manpower planning	Productivity improvement
Alabama	★		★	N	★	★	★		★		★
Alaska	★	★	★	E,G	★	★	★	★	★		★
Arizona	★		★	MBO		★			★		
Arkansas	★		★	BARS	★	★	★	★	★		★
California			(c)	E,G	★	★	★		★		★
Colorado	★	★	★	BARS,E,N	★	★	★		★		★
Connecticut	★	★	(d)	BARS,MBO(e)	★	★	★		★		★
Delaware		★	★	MBO	★	★	★		★		★
Florida	★	★	(c)	C(f)	★	★			★		★
Georgia			★(g)	MBO,N					★		★
Hawaii	★	★	★	PS		★		★	★		★
Idaho	★		•	MBO	★	★	★	★	★		★
Illinois	★		•	MBO	★	★		★	★		★
Indiana	★	★	★	BARS	★	★	★	★	★		★
Iowa	★	★	★	MBO,N	★	★			★		
Kansas	★	★	★	(h)	★	★	★		★	★	★
Kentucky	★	★	★	MBO	★	★	★	★	★		★
Louisiana	★	★	★(i)	P	★	★	★	★	★		★
Maine	★	★		BARS,N(j)	★	★	★	★	★		
Maryland	★	★	(c)	E							
Massachusetts	★	★	•	MBO,N	★	★			★		★
Michigan		★	•	(k)	★	★	★	★	★	★	★
Minnesota	★		•	MBO							
Mississippi	★	★	★	BARS,E,MBO,N	★	★	★	★	★	★	★
Missouri	★		(l)	G,MBO(l)	★	★	★	★	★	★	★

State	Method
Montana	MBO,PS
Nebraska	C,N
Nevada	PS
New Hampshire	C,N
New Jersey	BARS,MBO
New Mexico	E,N
New York	MBO
North Carolina	C,E,MBO,N
North Dakota	N
Ohio	N
Oklahoma	BARS,MBO,N
Oregon	N
Pennsylvania	G,MBO
Rhode Island	BARS
South Carolina	MBO
South Dakota	N
Tennessee	C,E,G,MBO
Texas	MBO
Utah	MBO
Vermont	C,E(e),MBO,N
Virginia	N
Washington	C
West Virginia	MBO
Wisconsin	N
Wyoming	C,E,MBO

Source: The Council of State Governments' survey of state personnel agencies on government employee compensation plans and practices (May 1983).

Note: With few exceptions, respondents indicated non-probationary employees face evaluation on an annual basis. In New York, however, employees are subject to semi-annual evalutions, and in Rhode Island, performance evaluations are required only for the six-month probation-ary period.

(a) In this column only: ★—one formal statewide system; •—two or more systems.

(b) In this column: BARS—Behaviorally anchored rating scales; C—Checklist; E—Essay method; G—Graphical rating scales; MBO—Management by objectives; N—Numerical rating scales; PS—Performance standards.

(c) Separate evaluation systems for state agencies.

(d) Different evaluation systems for different bargaining units.

(e) For managers only. In Vermont, essay method is employed only for certain managerial-type positions.

(f) At time of survey, a combination MBO and task anchored rating scale had been developed, but not implemented.

(g) State agencies may develop separate systems with approval of Merit System of Personnel Administration.

(h) System approximates BARS and MBO types.

(i) At time of survey, system was being implemented.

(j) Ratings based on evaluation of performance standards using BARS.

(k) Each department may have its own evaluation method.

(l) At time of survey, a formal statewide system existed in merit agencies and more than two systems in other agencies. A new system, employing MBO evaluation method and applicable to all agencies, had been developed and was being implemented (estimated completion, 1985).

(m) For promotion only.

(n) For layoff only.

(o) Statewide evaluation system applies only to agencies covered by civil service. Individual agencies may also develop an evaluation system in compliance with the civil service system rules and regulations.

A Note on Use

Symbols: Unless otherwise noted, all tables in *The Book of the States* use the following scheme:

. . .—no data

blank cell—not applicable

0—zero quantity.

Sources: Unless otherwise noted, the sources of data for tables are surveys and research by The Council of State Governments.

Section VII   FINANCES
1.   Revenue, Expenditure and Debt

STATE AND LOCAL GOVERNMENT FINANCES IN 1981-82

By Maurice Criz

The national economy in 1981-82 contained many road blocks for financial operations of state and local governments. While the pace of high inflation that had prevailed for a decade was broken, the price was two recessions beginning in January 1980 and mid-1981 and lasting through most of 1982. Real gross national product (GNP) was stagnant, at the same level in 1982 as in 1979. However, the 4.6 percent increase in the GNP implicit price deflator between the fourth quarters of 1981 and 1982 was less than half the 10.2 percent rate of increase between the 1979 and 1980 fourth quarters. The slowdown in the economy increased the unemployment rate to 10.8 percent by December 1982, adding 4 million more unemployed than in January 1981 when the unemployment rate was 7.5 percent.

On the plus side, interest rates fell sharply in 1981 and 1982. Rates for three-month Treasury bills, for example, went from a high of 16.295 percent in May 1981 to 8.013 percent in December 1982, while the prime rate charged by banks fell from 21.50 in January 1981 to 11.50 in December 1982. This decline stimulated residential investment and consumer purchases of durable goods in 1982. Lower financing costs resulted in an upturn of automobile sales, and housing starts showed the first increase in five years.

Business fixed investment increased by 4.7 percent between the 1980 and 1981 fourth quarters, but decreased by 8.4 percent between the 1981 and 1982 fourth quarters.

Increasingly, federal government deficits became a central issue in their effect on economic recovery and interest rates. The deficit amounted to $57.9 billion in fiscal 1981 and increased to $110.7 billion in fiscal 1982; it subsequently grew to $195.4 billion in fiscal 1983 with prospects for continuing at that level for several more years. In order to raise the funds to finance these deficits, the government must compete with private, state and local borrowers, thereby increasing the cost of money. It is a difficult juggling act for policy-makers to finance huge deficits without bringing back double-digit inflation, or to reduce deficits by cutting expenditures or

increasing taxes without jeopardizing a strong economic recovery. And this must be done while providing an investment climate which reduces unemployment.

Effects of the foregoing economic relationships were felt throughout state and local government finances. The annual growth of tax revenue slowed in fiscal 1982, and income generally fell short of budget estimates. About one-half the states enacted tax rate increases or broadened taxes, and many local governments increased property tax valuations and rates and user charges. Even so, many states had to draw on previous fund balances in order to meet financial obligations, and they had to cut expenses where possible. Hiring of new employees was limited, payrolls were trimmed, and some employees were put on unpaid furloughs. There were program cuts both selectively and across the board. Travel was restricted, and some expenditure was postponed into the next fiscal year. In total, general revenue of state and local governments (that is, excluding utility, liquor stores and insurance trust revenue) increased by 7.7 percent in fiscal 1982 over 1981, as compared with annual increases of 10.7 and 11.4 percent in fiscal 1981 and 1980, respectively. Similarly, general expenditure went up 6.8 percent in 1982, less than the increases of 10.4 percent in 1981 and 12.7 percent in 1980.

Revenue

Fiscal 1982 saw the first decrease in the dollar amount of intergovernmental revenue from the federal government since World War II. This revenue source increased steadily from 7 to 11 percent of state and local general revenue in the 1940s to 17 to 22 percent in the 1970s and early 1980s. In fiscal 1982, revenue from the federal government fell off by $3.3 billion to $86.9 billion, a drop of 3.9 percent from fiscal 1981, and amounted to 19.1 percent of state and local general revenue. The largest decreases in federal

Maurice Criz is Senior Advisor, Governments Division, U.S. Bureau of the Census.

expenditures were $2.3 billion in unemployment compensation for federal employees, ex-servicemen and temporary extended benefits; $2.5 billion for labor and manpower (largely due to termination of the Comprehensive Employment and Training Act program); $1.7 billion in education grants-in-aid; and $.5 billion for health and hospitals. There were significant increases in several categories: $.5 billion for public welfare medical assistance; $.3 billion for refugee assistance; and $.3 billion for housing and urban renewal.

State and local general revenue from own sources achieved a sizable increase of 10.8 percent in fiscal 1982 compared to 11.3 percent in 1981, and amounted to $369.2 billion in 1982. This growth came despite the depressed state of the economy and high unemployment rates, through extensive increases in tax rates and broadened coverage of taxes, increases in fees and user charges, and higher collections from interest earnings.

Tax revenue increased by 8.9 percent in fiscal 1982, slightly less than in 1981. However, individual income taxes went up by 9.4 percent in 1982, better than the 7.8 percent increase in 1981 but substantially less than the 16.6 percent rise in 1980. Corporation net income taxes increased by 6.3 percent in 1982, about the same as in 1981, but less than the 1980 figure of 9.8 percent. One of the factors in the lower rate of growth the past two years was federal changes in tax treatment of depreciation, which were incorporated in many state tax laws. Several states have since deviated from the federal depreciation rules or have raised tax rates to avoid the revenue losses.

Sales and gross receipts taxes were the primary sources of tax revenue for state and local governments, yielding 35.2 percent of their taxes and 20.5 percent of total general revenue in fiscal 1982. Even with the lagging economy, these taxes produced 8.9 percent more revenue in 1982 as compared to a 7.6 percent increase in 1981. This feat was accomplished through widespread tax increases in one-half the states and the District of Columbia. Four states increased the general sales tax rate, while Oklahoma extended the coverage of its tax to include services. Fifteen states increased tax rates on motor fuel, 12 on alcoholic beverages, and six on cigarettes and tobacco products.

Property taxes, the second largest revenue source, produced 30.8 percent of state and local tax revenue and 18.0 percent of their total general revenue. Property taxes increased by 9.3 percent in fiscal 1982 over 1981, about the same

rate of growth as in 1981 but considerably larger than the 5.5 percent rate in 1980. The tax revolt of the 1970s that restricted property taxes and other revenue sources, highlighted by California's Proposition 13 and Massachusetts' Proposition 2½, was apparently outweighed by state and local revenue needs created in part by reduced federal aid to state governments. States in turn limited grants to local governments. The recent growth in property tax collections also resulted from sharply higher assessed valuations that were catching up with inflationary market prices in combination with higher tax rates in many jurisdictions.

Current charges or user fees have been increasing at a faster rate than taxes. Total charges went up by 11.6 percent in fiscal 1982, somewhat lower than the 1981 increase of 13.2 percent. Charges for education services grew by 12.1 percent and 11.4 percent in the same periods, and hospital charges increased by 12.2 and 15.9 percent.

Expenditure

The fiscal stresses on state and local governments in 1982 resulted in self-imposed limits on spending. General fund balances were depleted throughout the country in order to provide financial support for services. Budget-balancing measures included limits on hiring, program cuts, restrictions on travel, postponement of repair of infrastructure, conversion of capital spending from current to bond funds, unpaid furloughs and postponement of expenditures and payments into the next fiscal year.

Application of these and other restraints helped keep the annual increase in state and local general expenditure down to 6.8 percent in fiscal 1982, as compared with an increase of 10.4 percent in 1981. Such a low growth rate has been seen in only three years since World War II (1977, 1962 and 1959). General government expenditure for current operations increased in fiscal 1982 by 8.4 percent, slightly more than the total, while assistance and subsidies went up by only 3 percent, reflecting stricter eligibility requirements for Aid to Families with Dependent Children called for by federal legislation and state limitations on cost-of-living adjustments. Capital outlay expenditure decreased by 3.8 percent, resulting from sizable cutbacks in education, road and sewer construction. Interest on general debt increased by 16.6 percent as interest rates for state and local borrowing rose throughout 1981 to an all-time high in January 1982 and remained near that level through the first half of the year. Subsequently, in fiscal 1983, interest rates on municipals dropped sharply.

Analysis of general expenditure by function shows that corrections increased in 1982 by 14.7 percent, housing and urban renewal by 14.3 percent, hospitals by 12.2 percent, fire protection by 10.9 percent, police protection by 10.1 percent and health by 9.6 percent. Public welfare increased by 7.3 percent, half the growth of 14.4 percent in 1981. Education expenditure increased by 6 percent in 1982 compared with 9.4 and 11.5 percent in fiscal 1981 and 1980, respectively. Highway expenditure decreased by .2 percent and sewerage by 3 percent.

Indebtedness

State and local debt outstanding at the end of fiscal 1982 continued an upward trend that was stronger than revenue or expenditure. The amount outstanding at the end of the year was $399.3 billion, 9.7 percent greater than 1981. As has been typical in recent years, there was a continuation of the swing from long-term, full faith and credit debt (general obligations) to nonguaranteed (revenue) debt. The former decreased by .4 percent in 1982 over 1981, while the latter increased by 16.5 percent. Tax supported, long-term debt has been holding at about an even level while revenue bond issues have been expanding rapidly for such purposes as industrial development, pollution control, residential mortgage financing, civic centers, hospitals, public housing and various types of utilities. Short-term debt outstanding at the end of fiscal 1982 soared to $19.1 billion, an increase of 22.7 percent over 1981 which in turn exceeded the prior year by 18.4 percent. This was a direct result of the financial straits of governments, which forced both state and local officials to borrow short-term money at relatively high interest rates in order to maintain services.

Cash and Security Holdings

State and local governments, at the end of fiscal 1982, had cash and security holdings amounting to $504.7 billion—an increase of 11.1 percent over 1981. Of this total, almost one-half is held by state or locally administered employee retirement systems. These trust funds, and another 4 percent in other insurance trust systems, are not available for other government purposes and therefore cannot be used for general expenditure.

Securities represented 78.4 percent of total asset holdings, and consisted of federal securities 22 percent, state and local government securities 2.3 percent, and corporate stocks and bonds, mortgages and other securities 54.1 percent. Cash and deposits amounted to 21.6 percent.

Table 1
INDEBTEDNESS OF STATE AND LOCAL GOVERNMENTS
AT END OF FISCAL 1982, BY STATE
(In millions of dollars, except per capita amounts)

State or other jurisdiction	Total	Long-term debt		Short-term debt	Per capita debt	
		Total	Full faith and credit		Total	Long-term only
United States	$399,349.5	$380,252.1	$151,199.7	$19,097.4	$1,762.77	$1,678.47
Alabama	5,279.5	5,086.8	1,760.4	192.8	1,355.81	1,306.31
Alaska	6,765.8	6,765.7	2,057.3	0.1	16,830.25	16,830.13
Arizona	6,612.2	6,310.1	1,918.8	302.1	2,432.75	2,321.60
Arkansas	2,454.5	2,416.6	467.4	37.9	1,073.69	1,057.13
California	28,801.3	28,317.8	11,215.3	483.5	1,216.89	1,196.46
Colorado	5,158.0	5,141.5	1,918.6	16.5	1,784.79	1,779.06
Connecticut	6,605.1	5,969.1	3,231.0	636.0	2,125.20	1,920.55
Delaware	2,013.1	1,948.5	755.4	64.6	3,389.06	3,280.33
Florida	13,134.1	12,683.5	3,959.8	450.6	1,347.64	1,301.41
Georgia	7,550.3	7,213.1	1,986.2	337.2	1,382.08	1,320.36
Hawaii	2,447.2	2,392.3	1,779.7	54.9	2,535.93	2,479.08
Idaho	932.2	873.9	205.2	58.4	987.55	925.71
Illinois	16,875.2	15,478.0	7,509.7	1,397.2	1,476.78	1,354.51
Indiana	4,105.1	3,888.2	938.5	216.9	747.73	708.23
Iowa	4,113.4	4,047.8	867.0	65.6	1,411.60	1,389.10
Kansas	5,100.5	4,923.9	1,100.2	176.6	2,157.57	2,082.86
Kentucky	8,322.3	8,307.6	1,023.7	14.7	2,273.86	2,269.84
Louisiana	9,720.0	9,603.3	3,967.7	116.6	2,310.98	2,283.25
Maine	1,493.7	1,459.1	754.9	34.6	1,327.77	1,297.02
Maryland	9,358.8	8,904.9	5,550.5	453.9	2,219.30	2,111.67
Massachusetts	11,069.4	10,151.3	5,534.8	918.0	1,929.47	1,769.45
Michigan	12,308.2	11,922.9	6,247.5	385.2	1,328.89	1,287.30
Minnesota	10,414.6	10,214.2	4,140.1	200.4	2,555.10	2,505.93
Mississippi	2,321.2	2,273.1	1,456.0	48.1	920.75	901.67
Missouri	5,017.9	4,824.7	1,348.7	193.2	1,020.52	981.23
Montana	1,311.0	1,305.0	255.1	6.0	1,665.79	1,658.22
Nebraska	5,208.9	4,938.9	740.2	270.0	3,317.77	3,145.78
Nevada	1,593.1	1,591.1	768.2	2.0	1,991.37	1,988.84
New Hampshire	1,705.7	1,588.8	656.4	116.9	1,852.00	1,725.05
New Jersey	15,841.7	13,708.5	5,150.7	2,133.1	2,150.94	1,861.31
New Mexico	3,025.3	3,011.3	360.6	14.0	2,321.78	2,311.03
New York	49,450.2	45,635.8	17,266.7	3,814.4	2,816.39	2,599.15
North Carolina	5,838.6	5,419.3	2,657.5	419.3	992.62	921.33
North Dakota	949.1	938.8	345.6	10.4	1,453.50	1,437.65
Ohio	12,143.5	10,634.2	5,089.4	1,509.4	1,124.61	984.83
Oklahoma	3,783.1	3,723.2	1,129.3	59.8	1,250.60	1,230.82
Oregon	8,817.4	8,636.0	6,976.8	181.4	3,348.79	3,279.91
Pennsylvania	20,234.2	19,387.1	7,786.8	847.1	1,705.52	1,634.11
Rhode Island	2,554.2	2,432.7	621.8	121.5	2,697.16	2,568.90
South Carolina	4,791.3	4,452.8	1,450.4	338.5	1,534.68	1,426.25
South Dakota	1,168.9	1,166.5	98.9	2.5	1,691.66	1,688.09
Tennessee	6,664.9	5,841.4	2,626.7	823.6	1,451.74	1,272.35
Texas	24,343.0	24,118.4	10,772.8	224.6	1,710.80	1,695.02
Utah	3,547.7	3,534.5	690.6	13.2	2,428.26	2,419.20
Vermont	914.2	871.4	379.4	42.8	1,789.00	1,705.20
Virginia	6,978.2	6,459.0	2,714.3	519.3	1,305.08	1,207.96
Washington	16,183.8	15,712.2	3,812.2	471.6	3,916.71	3,802.57
West Virginia	3,780.7	3,747.8	1,095.6	32.9	1,938.82	1,921.93
Wisconsin	6,027.2	5,820.6	4,165.5	206.6	1,280.75	1,236.85
Wyoming	1,687.2	1,685.3	390.8	1.9	3,589.75	3,585.73
Dist. of Col.	2,833.0	2,773.7	1,502.8	59.3	4,440.44	4,347.49

Source: U.S. Bureau of the Census, *Governmental Finances in 1981-82.*

Note: Because of rounding, detail may not add to total.

Table 2
SUMMARY OF GOVERNMENTAL FINANCES, BY LEVEL OF GOVERNMENT: 1981-82
(In millions of dollars, except per capita amounts)

Sources	All governments	Federal government	State and local governments			Per capita		
			Total	State	Local	Total	Federal government	State and local governments
Total revenue	$1,144,787	$687,647	$545,897 (a)	$330,949	$313,131 (a)	$5,053.20 (a)	$3,035.34	$2,409.64 (a)
Total general revenue	865,257 (a)	497,833	456,182 (a)	275,162	279,203 (a)	3,819.33 (a)	2,197.48	2,013.63 (a)
Intergovernmental revenue	(a)	1,812	86,945 (a)	69,166	115,963	(a)	8.00	383.79
From federal government	(a)	0	86,945	66,026	20,919	(a)	0	383.79
From state government	(a)	1,812	(a)	0	95,044	(a)	8.00	(a)
From local governments	(a)	0	(a)	3,139	(a)	(a)	0	(a)
Revenue from own sources	1,144,787	685,835	458,952	261,784	197,168	5,053.20	3,027.34	2,025.86
General revenue from own sources	865,257	496,021	369,236	205,996	163,240	3,819.33	2,189.48	1,629.84
Taxes	671,424	405,125	266,299	162,658	103,641	2,963.73	1,788.26	1,175.47
Property	81,918	0	81,918	3,113	78,805	361.59	0	361.59
Individual income	348,896	298,111	50,785	45,708	5,078	1,540.06	1,315.89	224.17
Corporation income	64,240	49,207	15,033	14,006	1,027	283.56	217.20	66.36
Sales and gross receipts	139,311	45,675	93,636	78,800	14,836	614.93	201.61	413.32
Customs duties	8,917	8,917	0	0	0	39.36	39.36	0
General sales and gross receipts	60,583	0	60,583	50,343	10,240	267.42	0	267.42
Selective sales and gross receipts	69,811	36,758	33,053	28,458	4,596	308.15	162.25	145.90
Motor fuel	15,534	4,950	10,584	10,437	146	68.57	21.85	46.72
Alcoholic beverages	8,388	5,439	2,949	2,723	226	37.03	24.01	13.02
Tobacco products	6,674	2,559	4,135	3,958	177	29.46	11.21	18.25
Public utilities	9,845	2,075	7,770	4,957	2,813	43.46	9.16	34.30
Other	29,371	21,755	7,616	6,382	1,234	129.64	96.03	33.62
Motor vehicle and operators licenses	6,460	0	6,460	6,051	409	28.52	0	28.52
Death and gift tax	10,341	7,991	2,350	2,350	0	45.65	35.27	10.37
All other	20,258	4,141	16,117	12,630	3,487	89.42	18.28	71.14
Charges and miscellaneous general revenue	193,833	90,896	102,937	43,338	59,599	855.60	401.22	454.37
Current charges	102,324	46,283	56,041	21,043	34,998	451.67	204.30	247.37
Miscellaneous general revenue	91,509	44,613	46,896	22,295	24,601	403.93	196.93	207.00
Utility revenue	30,267	0	30,267	2,085	28,182	133.60	0	133.60
Liquor stores revenue	3,344	0	3,344	2,854	490	14.76	0	14.76
Insurance trust revenue	245,919	189,814	56,105	50,848	5,257	1,085.51	837.86	247.65
Total expenditure	1,231,436 (a)	796,483	522,760 (a)	310,292	311,375 (a)	5,435.68 (a)	3,515.75	2,307.51 (a)
Intergovernmental expenditure	(a)	86,014	1,793 (a)	98,743	1,957 (a)	(a)	379.67	7.91 (a)
To federal government	(a)	0	1,793	1,793	0	(a)	0	7.91
To state governments	(a)	63,768	(a)	0	1,957	(a)	281.48	(a)
To local governments	(a)	22,246	(a)	96,950	(a)	(a)	98.20	(a)
Direct expenditure	1,231,436	710,469	520,967	211,549	309,418	5,435.68	3,136.08	2,299.60
By type:								
General expenditure	915,889	482,359	433,530	170,747	262,783	4,042.82	2,129.18	1,913.64
Utility expenditure	45,135	0	45,135	3,730	41,405	199.23	0	199.23
Liquor stores expenditure	2,836	0	2,836	2,408	428	12.52	0	12.52
Insurance trust expenditure	267,576	228,110	39,466	34,664	4,802	1,181.11	1,006.90	174.21
By character and object:								
Current operation	639,524	265,891	373,633	133,152	240,481	2,822.92	1,173.67	1,649.25
Capital outlay	129,249	62,835	66,414	23,466	42,948	570.52	277.36	293.16
Construction	61,457	8,177	53,280	19,560	33,720	271.28	36.09	235.18
Equipment, land and existing structures	67,792	54,658	13,134	3,906	9,228	299.24	241.27	57.97

Assistance and subsidies	69,182	51,817	17,365	10,867	6,498	305.38	228.73	76.65
Interest on debt	125,904	101,816	24,088	9,400	14,688	555.75	449.43	106.33
Insurance benefits and repayments	267,576	228,110	39,466	34,664	4,802	1,181.11	1,006.90	174.21
Exhibit: expenditure for salaries and wages	294,439	104,285 (b)	190,154	56,627	133,527	1,299.68	460.32	839.36
Direct general expenditure, by function	915,889	482,359	433,530	170,747	262,783	4,042.82	2,129.18	1,913.64
Selected federal programs:								
National defense and international relations	204,275	204,275	0	0	0	901.69	901.69	0
Postal service	21,761	21,761	0	0	0	96.06	96.06	0
Space research and technology	6,181	6,181	0	0	0	27.28	27.28	0
Education services:								
Education	166,057	11,484	154,573	42,301	112,272	732.99	50.69	682.30
Local schools	106,101	0	106,101	1,054	105,047	468.34	0	468.34
Institutions of higher education	41,521	0	41,521	34,296	7,225	183.28	0	183.28
Other	18,435	11,484	6,951	6,951	0	81.37	50.69	30.68
Libraries	2,180	185	1,995	147	1,848	9.62	.82	8.81
Social services and income maintenance:								
Public welfare	78,821	22,564	56,257	41,513	14,744	347.92	99.60	248.32
Categorical cash assistance	22,081	9,047	13,034	7,337	5,697	97.47	39.93	57.54
Other cash assistance	1,675	0	1,675	875	801	7.40	0	7.40
Other public welfare	55,064	13,517	41,547	33,301	8,246	243.06	59.67	183.39
Hospitals	35,551	5,998	29,553	13,874	15,678	156.92	26.48	130.45
Health	17,215	6,509	10,706	5,524	5,182	75.99	28.73	47.26
Social insurance administration	5,409	3,123	2,286	2,278	8	23.88	13.79	10.09
Veterans' services	15,023	14,959	64	64	0	66.31	66.03	.28
Transportation:								
Highways	35,121	576	34,545	20,103	14,441	155.03	2.54	152.48
Air transportation	5,396	2,578	2,818	346	2,472	23.82	11.38	12.44
Water transport and terminals	3,544	2,122	1,422	513	909	15.64	9.37	6.28
Parking facilities	390	0	390	0	390	1.72	0	1.72
Public safety:								
Police protection	18,461	2,000	16,461	2,396	14,064	81.49	8.83	72.66
Fire protection	6,926	0	6,926	0	6,926	30.57	0	30.57
Correction	8,905	422	8,483	5,524	2,959	39.31	1.86	37.44
Protective inspection and regulation	2,802	0	2,802	1,905	897	12.37	0	12.37
Environment and housing:								
Natural resources	45,486	38,974	6,512	5,165	1,348	200.78	172.03	28.75
Sewerage	10,797	0	10,797	359	10,438	47.66	0	47.66
Housing and urban renewal	16,008	7,910	8,098	488	7,610	70.66	34.92	35.74
Parks and recreation	8,783	1,375	7,408	1,362	6,046	38.77	6.07	32.70
Sanitation other than sewerage	4,137	0	4,137	0	4,137	18.26	0	18.26
Governmental administration:								
Financial administration	11,895	3,875	8,020	3,669	4,352	52.51	17.10	35.40
General control	13,057	2,165	10,892	3,772	7,120	57.63	9.56	48.08
General public buildings (state-local)	3,312	0	3,312	867	2,445	14.62	0	14.62
Interest on general debt	21,786	101,816	19,970	9,015	10,955	537.57	449.43	88.15
Other and unallocable	46,614	21,507	25,107	9,564	15,543	205.76	94.93	110.83
Indebtedness								
Gross debt outstanding at end of fiscal year	1,546,336	1,146,986	399,350	147,470	251,870	6,825.67	5,062.90	1,762.77

Source: U.S. Bureau of the Census, *Governmental Finances in 1981-82.*
Note: Because of rounding, detail may not add to totals. Local government amounts are estimates subject to sampling variations.

(a) Duplicative transactions between levels of government are excluded.
(b) Includes pay and allowance for military personnel, amounting to $57,991 million.

Table 3
SUMMARY OF STATE AND LOCAL GOVERNMENT FINANCES: 1977-78 TO 1981-82
(In millions of dollars, except per capita amounts)

Sources	1981-82			1980-81	1979-80	1978-79	1977-78	Per capita				
	Total	State	Local					1981-82	1980-81	1979-80	1978-79	1977-78
Revenue, total	$545,897	$327,810	$218,087	$506,728	$451,537	$404,934	$371,607	$2,409.63	$2,236.75	$1,993.50	$1,839.78	$1,704.11
From federal government	86,945	66,026	20,919	90,294	83,029	75,164	69,592	383.78	398.57	366.56	341.50	319.14
Revenue from own sources	458,952	261,784	197,168	416,433	368,509	329,770	302,014	2,025.86	1,838.17	1,626.93	1,498.28	1,384.97
General revenue from own sources	369,236	205,996	163,240	333,109	299,293	268,115	246,368	1,629.84	1,470.38	1,321.35	1,218.15	1,129.75
Taxes	266,299	162,658	103,641	244,514	223,463	205,514	193,642	1,175.47	1,079.31	986.57	933.74	888.00
Property	81,918	3,113	78,805	74,969	68,499	64,944	66,422	361.59	330.92	302.42	295.07	304.60
Sales and gross receipts	93,636	78,800	14,836	85,971	79,927	74,247	67,596	413.32	379.49	352.87	337.34	309.98
General	60,583	50,343	10,240	55,641	51,328	46,559	41,473	267.42	245.61	226.61	211.53	190.19
Selective	33,053	28,458	4,596	30,330	28,599	27,689	26,123	145.90	133.88	126.26	125.80	119.80
Individual income	50,785	45,708	5,078	46,426	42,080	36,932	33,176	224.17	204.93	185.78	167.80	152.14
Corporation net income	15,033	14,006	1,027(a)	14,143	13,321	12,128	10,738	66.36	62.43	58.81	55.10	49.24
Other taxes	24,927	21,031	3,896	23,004	19,636	17,264	15,710	110.03	101.54	86.69	78.44	72.04
Charges and miscellaneous	102,937	43,338	59,599	88,595	75,830	62,600	52,726	454.37	391.07	334.78	284.42	241.79
Insurance trust revenue	56,105	50,848	5,257	53,429	43,656	39,027	35,635	247.65	235.84	192.74	177.31	163.42
Utility revenue	30,267	2,085	28,182	26,617	22,359	19,730	17,252	133.60	117.49	98.71	89.64	79.12
Liquor stores revenue	3,344	2,854	490	3,278	3,201	2,898	2,759	14.76	14.47	14.13	13.17	12.65
Expenditure, total	522,760	213,342	309,418	487,048	434,073	381,867	346,786	2,307.51	2,149.88	1,916.39	1,734.98	1,590.29
To federal government	1,793	1,793	—	1,873	1,746	1,493	1,472	7.91	8.27	7.71	6.78	6.75
Direct expenditure by character and object	520,967	211,549	309,418	485,175	432,327	380,374	345,313	2,299.60	2,141.61	1,908.69	1,729.86	1,583.54
Current operation	373,633	133,152	240,481	343,623	307,811	274,167	249,222	1,649.25	1,516.78	1,358.96	1,245.65	1,142.88
Capital outlay	66,414	23,466	42,948	67,596	62,894	53,196	44,769	293.16	298.38	277.67	241.69	205.30
Construction	53,280	19,560	33,720	54,950	51,492	43,326	36,199	235.18	242.55	227.33	196.85	166.00
Equipment, land and existing structures	13,134	3,906	9,228	12,646	11,402	9,870	8,570	57.97	55.82	50.34	44.84	39.30
Assistance and subsidies	17,365	10,867	6,498	16,861	15,222	14,044	13,753	76.65	74.43	67.20	63.81	63.07
Insurance benefits and repayments	39,466	34,664	4,802	36,583	28,797	23,504	23,525	174.21	161.48	127.14	106.79	107.89
Interest on debt	24,088	9,400	14,688	20,511	17,604	15,463	14,044	106.33	90.54	77.72	70.25	64.40
Exhibit: Expenditure for salaries and wages	190,154	56,627	133,527	180,261	163,896	149,104	137,703	839.36	795.69	723.59	677.44	631.48
Direct expenditure, by function	520,967	211,549	309,418	485,174	432,327	380,374	345,313	2,299.60	2,141.60	1,908.69	1,729.86	1,583.54
Direct general expenditure	433,530	170,747	262,783	405,576	367,340	326,024	295,510	1,913.64	1,790.25	1,621.77	1,481.26	1,355.15
Education	154,573	42,301	112,272	145,784	133,211	119,448	110,758	682.30	643.51	588.11	542.70	507.91
Local schools	106,101	1,054	105,047	100,534	92,930	83,385	76,703	468.34	443.77	410.28	378.85	351.74
Institutions of higher education	41,521	34,296	7,225	38,114	33,919	30,059	28,391	183.28	168.24	149.75	136.57	130.19
Other education	6,951	6,951		7,136	6,362	6,004	5,664	30.68	31.50	28.09	27.28	25.98
Public welfare	56,257	41,513	14,744	52,248	45,552	40,418	37,679	248.32	230.63	201.11	190.36	172.79
Highways	34,545	20,103	14,442	34,603	33,311	28,440	24,609	152.48	152.74	147.07	129.22	112.85
Hospitals	29,553	13,874	15,678	26,330	23,787	21,039	18,648	130.45	116.22	105.02	95.59	85.51
Police protection	16,461	2,396	14,064	14,947	13,494	12,207	11,306	72.66	65.98	59.57	55.46	51.85
Sewerage	10,797	359	10,438	11,121	9,892	8,795	7,142	48.08	49.09	43.67	39.96	32.75
General control	10,892	3,772	7,120	9,541	8,697	7,742	7,001	48.08	42.11	38.40	35.17	32.11
Health	10,706	5,524	5,182	9,771	8,387	7,179	6,303	47.26	43.13	37.03	32.62	28.90
Natural resources	6,512	5,165	1,348	6,175	5,509	4,706	4,225	28.75	27.26	24.32	21.38	19.38
Financial administration	8,020	3,669	4,352	7,230	6,719	6,071	5,292	35.40	31.91	29.66	27.58	24.27
Fire protection	6,926	—	6,926	6,336	5,718	5,147	4,802	30.57	27.97	25.25	23.38	22.02
Parks and recreation	7,408	1,362	6,046	7,064	6,520	5,896	5,270	32.70	31.18	28.79	26.79	24.17

Correction	8,483	5,524	2,959	7,393	6,448	5,534	4,981	37.44	32.63	28.47	25.15	22.84
Housing and urban renewal	8,098	488	7,610	7,086	6,062	4,724	3,699	35.74	31.28	26.76	21.46	16.96
General public buildings	3,312	867	2,445	3,230	3,018	2,829	2,561	14.62	14.26	13.32	12.85	11.74
Sanitation other than sewerage	4,137	—	4,137	3,777	3,322	2,992	2,727	18.26	16.67	14.67	13.59	12.51
Employment security administration	2,286	2,278	8	2,276	2,009	1,806	1,764	10.09	10.05	8.87	8.21	8.09
Airports	2,818	346	2,473	2,743	2,501	1,906	1,617	12.44	12.11	11.04	8.66	7.42
Interest on general debt	19,970	9,015	10,955	17,131	14,747	12,987	11,983	88.15	75.62	65.11	59.01	54.95
Other and unallocable	31,780	12,193	19,586	30,790	28,436	26,157	23,143	140.29	135.92	125.54	118.84	106.13
Insurance trust expenditure	39,466	34,664	4,802	36,583	28,797	23,504	23,525	174.21	161.48	127.14	106.79	107.89
Utility expenditure	45,135	3,730	41,405	40,290	33,599	28,429	23,960	199.23	177.84	148.34	129.17	109.88
Liquor stores expenditure	2,836	2,408	428	2,726	2,591	2,416	2,317	12.52	12.03	11.44	10.98	10.63
Debt outstanding at end of fiscal year	399,350	147,470	251,870	363,892	335,603	304,103	280,433	1,762.77	1,606.25	1,481.66	1,381.66	1,286.01
Long-term	380,252	143,702	236,550	348,329	322,456	292,302	269,003	1,678.47	1,537.56	1,423.62	1,328.05	1,233.59
Full faith and credit	151,200	51,507	99,692	151,750	149,802	145,385	142,523	667.41	669.84	661.36	660.54	653.58
Nonguaranteed	229,053	92,195	136,858	196,579	172,654	146,917	126,481	1,011.06	867.72	762.25	667.50	580.01
Short-term	19,097	3,768	15,329	15,562	13,147	11,801	11,430	84.30	68.69	58.04	53.62	52.41
Long-term debt issued	48,379	19,436	28,943	43,819	42,364	42,085	39,980	213.55	193.42	187.03	191.21	183.34
Long-term debt retired	21,012	7,982	13,030	18,929	17,404	27,056	16,715	92.75	83.55	76.84	122.93	76.65
Cash and security holdings, by type	504,693	338,273	166,419	454,393	407,815	362,359	318,676	2,227.76	2,005.73	1,800.47	1,646.35	1,461.38
Unemp. Comp. Fund balance in U.S. Treasury	6,967	6,967	—	11,736	11,994	11,341	7,431	30.75	51.80	52.95	51.53	34.08
Other deposits and cash	102,136	35,222	66,913	93,438	89,743	85,138	73,296	450.83	412.44	396.20	386.82	336.12
Securities	395,589	296,084	99,505	349,220	306,077	265,881	237,950	1,746.17	1,541.49	1,351.30	1,208.01	1,091.19
Federal	111,228	71,742	39,486	95,135	81,669	72,284	63,449	490.97	419.94	360.56	328.41	290.96
State and local government	11,449	7,597	3,852	10,707	11,379	10,248	12,078	50.54	47.26	50.24	46.56	55.38
Other	272,912	216,745	56,167	243,378	213,031	183,350	162,422	1,204.66	1,074.29	940.51	833.03	744.83

Source: U.S. Bureau of the Census, *Governmental Finances in 1981-82,* and prior annual reports.
(a) Minor amount included in individual income tax figure.

Table 4
GENERAL REVENUE OF STATE AND LOCAL GOVERNMENTS
BY SOURCE AND BY STATE: 1981-82
(In millions of dollars)

State or other jurisdiction	Total general revenue	From federal government	All general revenue from own sources	Taxes Total	Taxes Property	Taxes Other	Charges and miscellaneous general revenue
United States..........	$456,182	$86,945	$369,236	$266,299	$81,918	$184,381	$102,937
Alabama	6,069	1,380	4,690	2,973	347	2,627	1,717
Alaska	6,333	424	5,909	2,813	361	2,452	3,096
Arizona	4,995	756	4,239	2,880	897	1,983	1,358
Arkansas	3,262	827	2,435	1,666	357	1,309	769
California.............	55,179	10,745	44,433	32,481	8,324	24,157	11,952
Colorado	6,126	1,065	5,061	3,434	1,202	2,232	1,628
Connecticut............	6,153	1,027	5,126	4,115	1,756	2,359	1,011
Delaware	1,366	285	1,081	722	110	613	359
Florida	16,213	2,865	13,348	9,221	3,156	6,065	4,127
Georgia	9,850	2,183	7,667	5,167	1,390	3,777	2,500
Hawaii	2,329	465	1,863	1,381	254	1,127	482
Idaho	1,515	325	1,190	811	223	588	379
Illinois	21,889	4,300	17,588	13,678	4,866	8,813	3,910
Indiana................	8,352	1,505	6,847	4,810	1,702	3,108	2,037
Iowa	5,517	918	4,598	3,293	1,273	2,020	1,306
Kansas	4,554	735	3,819	2,530	1,013	1,517	1,290
Kentucky	5,496	1,327	4,169	3,130	550	2,580	1,039
Louisiana	8,863	1,549	7,313	4,633	566	4,067	2,680
Maine	1,937	475	1,463	1,151	431	719	312
Maryland	9,075	1,672	7,404	5,368	1,431	3,937	2,036
Massachusetts	12,320	2,729	9,590	7,762	2,926	4,837	1,828
Michigan	20,250	3,962	16,288	11,397	4,843	6,554	4,891
Minnesota	9,677	1,765	7,912	5,257	1,392	3,865	2,655
Mississippi	3,965	1,038	2,927	1,893	410	1,483	1,034
Missouri...............	7,231	1,546	5,684	4,144	1,127	3,017	1,540
Montana	1,772	349	1,423	965	458	508	458
Nebraska	2,974	497	2,476	1,645	705	940	831
Nevada................	1,820	287	1,533	1,014	185	829	519
New Hampshire	1,442	285	1,157	852	527	325	305
New Jersey	15,233	2,486	12,747	9,965	4,354	5,611	2,782
New Mexico............	3,374	558	2,816	1,488	199	1,289	1,328
New York	48,285	9,001	39,284	31,427	10,079	21,348	7,857
North Carolina	8,974	1,876	7,098	5,205	1,211	3,994	1,893
North Dakota	1,545	299	1,247	738	200	539	508
Ohio	17,983	3,411	14,572	10,504	3,545	6,960	4,068
Oklahoma	5,995	936	5,060	3,659	525	3,134	1,401
Oregon	5,785	1,187	4,598	2,954	1,271	1,683	1,644
Pennsylvania	21,549	4,324	17,225	13,239	3,458	9,781	3,986
Rhode Island	2,032	460	1,572	1,158	486	672	414
South Carolina	4,802	992	3,810	2,628	626	2,003	1,182
South Dakota	1,268	302	966	633	266	367	333
Tennessee..............	6,668	1,562	5,106	3,545	895	2,650	1,561
Texas	26,049	3,702	22,347	15,359	5,212	10,147	6,988
Utah	2,975	647	2,328	1,478	404	1,074	851
Vermont................	1,042	285	757	565	232	334	191
Virginia	9,154	1,682	7,472	5,510	1,606	3,903	1,963
Washington	8,621	1,571	7,050	4,841	1,432	3,410	2,209
West Virginia...........	3,380	811	2,569	1,862	312	1,550	708
Wisconsin	9,988	1,845	8,143	5,928	2,068	3,860	2,215
Wyoming...............	2,170	379	1,792	1,197	418	779	595
Dist. of Col.	2,782	1,342	1,440	1,227	339	888	213

Source: U.S. Bureau of the Census, *Governmental Finances in 1981-82.*
Note: Because of rounding, detail may not add to total.

Table 5
PER CAPITA GENERAL REVENUE OF STATE AND LOCAL GOVERNMENTS BY SOURCE AND BY STATE: 1981-82

State or other jurisdiction	Total	From federal government	All general revenue from own sources	Taxes Total	Taxes Property	Taxes Other	Charges and miscellaneous general revenue
U.S. Average..........	$2,013.62	$ 383.78	$1,629.84	$1,175.47	$ 361.59	$ 813.87	$ 454.37
Alabama	1,558.67	354.30	1,204.37	763.56	89.06	674.50	440.81
Alaska	15,754.31	1,055.61	14,698.70	6,997.50	898.46	6,099.04	7,701.20
Arizona	1,837.77	278.32	1,559.45	1,059.70	330.11	729.59	499.75
Arkansas	1,426.76	361.63	1,065.12	728.88	156.30	572.58	336.24
California.............	2,331.36	454.01	1,877.35	1,372.38	351.70	1,020.68	504.98
Colorado	2,119.82	368.50	1,751.32	1,188.12	415.86	772.26	563.20
Connecticut...........	1,979.86	330.60	1,649.26	1,324.01	564.90	759.10	325.25
Delaware	2,299.98	480.23	1,819.74	1,215.72	184.37	1,031.35	604.02
Florida...............	1,663.56	293.97	1,369.59	946.17	323.82	622.35	423.42
Georgia	1,803.01	399.53	1,403.48	945.80	254.44	691.36	457.68
Hawaii	2,412.96	482.30	1,930.66	1,431.28	263.62	1,167.66	499.38
Idaho	1,604.99	344.38	1,260.61	858.87	235.88	622.99	401.74
Illinois	1,915.53	376.33	1,539.20	1,197.02	425.81	771.21	342.18
Indiana	1,521.31	274.05	1,247.26	876.14	309.98	566.16	371.11
Iowa	1,893.13	315.12	1,578.01	1,129.94	436.70	693.24	448.07
Kansas	1,926.43	310.79	1,615.65	1,070.03	428.50	641.53	545.62
Kentucky	1,501.77	362.69	1,139.07	855.17	150.23	704.94	283.91
Louisiana	2,107.13	368.40	1,738.73	1,101.46	134.57	966.89	637.27
Maine	1,722.18	421.88	1,300.30	1,022.73	383.47	639.26	277.57
Maryland	2,152.05	396.40	1,755.65	1,272.95	339.35	933.60	482.70
Massachusetts..........	2,147.39	475.71	1,671.68	1,353.04	509.98	843.06	318.64
Michigan	2,186.40	427.81	1,758.59	1,230.49	522.90	707.59	528.10
Minnesota	2,374.15	432.97	1,941.18	1,289.70	341.50	948.19	651.48
Mississippi	1,572.96	411.82	1,161.14	751.02	162.59	588.43	410.12
Missouri	1,470.54	314.50	1,156.05	842.80	229.16	613.64	313.25
Montana	2,251.72	443.47	1,808.25	1,226.70	581.72	644.98	581.55
Nebraska	1,893.96	316.72	1,577.24	1,047.90	448.94	598.96	529.35
Nevada	2,275.32	359.17	1,916.15	1,267.24	230.99	1,036.25	648.91
New Hampshire	1,565.94	309.33	1,256.60	925.55	572.15	353.40	331.06
New Jersey............	2,068.27	337.56	1,730.71	1,353.00	591.14	761.87	377.71
New Mexico...........	2,589.71	428.59	2,161.12	1,141.97	152.83	989.13	1,019.15
New York	2,750.03	512.64	2,237.39	1,789.92	574.07	1,215.85	447.47
North Carolina	1,525.62	318.92	1,206.70	884.87	205.86	679.00	321.83
North Dakota	2,366.60	457.18	1,909.42	1,130.71	305.72	825.00	778.71
Ohio	1,665.44	315.92	1,349.52	972.81	328.28	644.53	376.72
Oklahoma	1,981.95	309.26	1,672.69	1,209.58	173.57	1,036.01	463.11
Oregon	2,197.25	450.88	1,746.37	1,122.03	482.73	639.29	624.35
Pennsylvania...........	1,816.32	364.44	1,451.88	1,115.91	291.51	824.40	335.97
Rhode Island	2,145.73	485.30	1,660.42	1,222.74	513.21	709.53	437.68
South Carolina	1,538.00	317.59	1,220.41	841.90	200.43	641.47	378.51
South Dakota	1,835.45	437.29	1,398.16	916.11	385.53	530.59	482.05
Tennessee.............	1,452.38	340.17	1,112.21	772.14	194.96	577.18	340.07
Texas	1,830.70	260.18	1,570.53	1,079.43	366.32	713.12	491.09
Utah	2,036.28	442.59	1,593.70	1,011.49	276.67	734.82	582.21
Vermont...............	2,039.23	558.61	1,480.61	1,106.42	453.68	652.74	374.19
Virginia	1,712.04	314.56	1,397.49	1,030.41	300.37	730.03	367.08
Washington	2,086.49	380.20	1,706.29	1,171.71	346.48	825.23	534.58
West Virginia..........	1,733.36	415.85	1,317.51	954.68	159.87	794.81	362.83
Wisconsin	2,122.45	392.13	1,730.32	1,259.66	439.42	820.25	470.66
Wyoming	4,618.02	805.89	3,812.13	2,546.39	888.83	1,657.55	1,265.74
Dist. of Col.	4,360.82	2,103.40	2,257.42	1,923.88	531.56	1,392.32	333.53

Source: U.S. Bureau of the Census, *Governmental Finances in 1981-82.*

Table 6
ORIGIN AND ALLOCATION, BY LEVEL OF GOVERNMENT,
OF GENERAL REVENUE OF STATE AND LOCAL GOVERNMENTS: 1981-82
(Dollar amounts in millions)

| State or other jurisdiction | Total general revenue | By originating level of government (before transfers among governments) | | | | | | By final recipient level of government (after intergovernmental transfers) | | | |
| | | Amount | | | Percent | | | Amount | | Percent | |
		Federal	State	Local	Federal	State	Local	State(a)	Local	State	Local
United States	$456,181.5	$86,945.4	$205,996.1	$163,240.0	19.1	45.2	35.8	$180,117.7	$276,063.9	39.5	60.5
Alabama	6,069.5	1,379.6	2,980.2	1,709.6	22.7	49.1	28.2	3,068.3	3,001.2	50.6	49.4
Alaska	6,333.2	424.4	5,215.8	693.1	6.7	82.4	10.9	4,910.0	1,423.2	77.5	22.5
Arizona	4,995.1	756.5	2,364.4	1,874.2	15.1	47.3	37.5	1,624.3	3,370.8	32.5	67.5
Arkansas	3,261.6	826.7	1,537.6	897.3	25.3	47.1	27.5	1,600.8	1,660.8	49.1	50.9
California	55,178.7	10,745.4	25,615.7	18,817.5	19.5	46.4	34.1	17,492.4	37,686.2	31.7	68.3
Colorado	6,126.3	1,065.0	2,338.9	2,722.4	17.4	38.2	44.4	2,091.1	4,035.2	34.1	65.9
Connecticut	6,153.4	1,027.5	2,997.9	2,128.0	16.7	48.7	34.6	3,181.3	2,972.0	51.7	48.3
Delaware	1,366.2	285.3	846.3	234.7	20.9	61.9	17.2	864.9	501.3	63.3	36.7
Florida	16,213.0	2,865.0	6,412.2	6,935.8	17.7	39.5	42.8	4,873.3	11,339.8	30.1	69.9
Georgia	9,849.8	2,182.6	3,813.4	3,853.8	22.2	38.7	39.1	3,861.1	5,988.8	39.2	60.8
Hawaii	2,328.5	465.4	1,457.5	405.6	20.0	62.6	17.4	1,805.8	522.7	77.6	22.4
Idaho	1,515.1	325.1	735.8	454.2	21.5	48.6	30.0	693.7	821.4	45.8	54.2
Illinois	21,888.8	4,300.4	8,896.8	8,691.6	19.6	40.6	39.7	8,310.3	13,578.5	38.0	62.0
Indiana	8,352.0	1,504.5	3,953.4	2,894.0	18.0	47.3	34.7	3,088.3	5,263.7	37.0	63.0
Iowa	5,516.6	918.2	2,491.9	2,106.5	16.6	45.2	38.2	2,085.4	3,431.2	37.8	62.2
Kansas	4,554.1	734.7	1,835.4	1,984.0	16.1	40.3	43.6	1,779.3	2,774.8	39.1	60.9
Kentucky	5,496.5	1,327.5	3,147.3	1,021.7	24.2	57.3	18.6	3,143.3	2,353.2	57.2	42.8
Louisiana.........	8,862.6	1,549.5	4,584.8	2,728.3	17.5	51.7	30.8	4,071.4	4,791.2	45.9	54.1
Maine.............	1,937.5	474.6	938.7	524.2	24.5	48.4	27.1	1,097.8	839.6	56.7	43.3
Maryland.........	9,075.2	1,671.6	4,289.9	3,113.6	18.4	47.3	34.3	3,916.3	5,158.9	43.2	56.8
Massachusetts.....	12,319.6	2,729.2	5,789.6	3,800.8	22.2	47.0	30.9	5,797.9	6,521.7	47.1	52.9
Michigan.........	20,250.4	3,962.4	8,213.1	8,074.9	19.6	40.6	39.9	8,371.6	11,878.9	41.3	58.7
Minnesota........	9,677.0	1,764.8	4,650.5	3,261.7	18.2	48.1	33.7	3,290.7	6,386.4	34.0	66.0
Mississippi........	3,965.4	1,038.2	1,848.7	1,078.5	26.2	46.6	27.2	1,765.8	2,199.6	44.5	55.5
Missouri..........	7,230.7	1,546.4	2,851.0	2,833.3	21.4	39.4	39.2	2,882.6	4,348.1	39.9	60.1
Montana	1,772.1	349.0	796.3	626.8	19.7	44.9	35.4	864.1	908.0	48.8	51.2
Nebraska	2,973.5	497.3	1,153.5	1,322.7	16.7	38.8	44.5	1,186.7	1,786.8	39.9	60.1
Nevada...........	1,820.3	287.3	871.6	661.3	15.8	47.9	36.3	621.5	1,198.8	34.1	65.9
New Hampshire ...	1,442.2	284.9	537.4	619.9	19.8	37.3	43.0	665.7	776.6	46.2	53.8
New Jersey	15,232.8	2,486.1	7,115.3	5,631.4	16.3	46.7	37.0	5,839.0	9,393.9	38.3	61.7
New Mexico	3,374.4	558.4	2,296.4	519.5	16.5	68.1	15.4	1,947.1	1,427.3	57.7	42.3
New York	48,285.0	9,000.8	18,121.8	21,162.4	18.6	37.5	43.8	13,852.3	34,432.7	28.7	71.3
North Carolina....	8,973.7	1,875.9	4,587.1	2,510.8	20.9	51.1	28.0	3,867.9	5,105.8	43.1	56.9
North Dakota.....	1,545.4	298.5	873.1	373.8	19.3	56.5	24.2	835.4	710.0	54.1	45.9
Ohio	17,983.5	3,411.3	7,629.2	6,942.9	19.0	42.4	38.6	6,507.4	11,476.1	36.2	63.8
Oklahoma	5,995.4	935.5	3,442.6	1,617.3	15.6	57.4	27.0	3,116.5	2,878.8	52.0	48.0
Oregon...........	5,785.4	1,187.2	2,428.9	2,169.3	20.5	42.0	37.5	2,354.1	3,431.2	40.7	59.3
Pennsylvania......	21,548.8	4,323.7	9,634.3	7,590.8	20.1	44.7	35.2	9,040.9	12,507.9	42.0	58.0
Rhode Island......	2,032.0	459.6	1,028.3	544.1	22.6	50.6	26.8	1,211.3	820.7	59.6	40.4
South Carolina.....	4,801.6	991.5	2,519.4	1,290.8	20.6	52.5	26.9	2,433.0	2,368.7	50.7	49.3
South Dakota	1,268.3	302.2	541.1	425.0	23.8	42.7	33.5	644.0	624.3	50.8	49.2
Tennessee	6,667.9	1,561.2	2,687.9	2,418.2	23.4	40.3	36.3	2,950.1	3,717.8	44.2	55.8
Texas	26,049.1	3,702.0	11,914.7	10,432.4	14.2	45.7	40.0	10,358.7	15,690.4	39.8	60.2
Utah	2,975.0	646.6	1,298.2	1,030.2	21.7	43.6	34.6	1,349.5	1,625.5	45.4	54.6
Vermont	1,042.0	285.5	481.7	274.9	27.4	46.2	26.4	660.7	381.4	63.4	36.6
Virginia	9,154.3	1,681.9	4,400.4	3,072.0	18.4	48.1	33.6	4,170.3	4,984.0	45.6	54.4
Washington........	8,621.4	1,571.0	4,265.4	2,785.0	18.2	49.5	32.3	3,485.1	5,136.3	40.4	59.6
West Virginia	3,380.0	810.9	1,787.6	781.5	24.0	52.9	23.1	1,788.5	1,591.6	52.9	47.1
Wisconsin	9,988.2	1,845.3	4,743.5	3,399.4	18.5	47.5	34.0	3,663.1	6,325.1	36.7	63.3
Wyoming..........	2,170.5	378.8	1,033.7	758.0	17.5	47.6	34.9	1,037.4	1,133.1	47.8	52.2
Dist. of Col.	2,782.2	1,342.0		1,440.2	48.2		51.8		2,782.2		100.0

Source: U.S. Bureau of the Census, *Governmental Finances in 1981-82.*
Note: Because of rounding, detail may not add to totals. Local government amounts are estimates subject to sampling variation.

(a) Data not adjusted for federal receipts of $1,812 million from state governments (mainly for Supplemental Security Income program).

Table 7
DIRECT GENERAL EXPENDITURE OF STATE AND LOCAL GOVERNMENTS, FOR SELECTED ITEMS, BY STATE: 1981-82
(In millions of dollars)

State or other jurisdiction	Total	Education Other than capital outlay	Total	Local schools only	Public welfare	Health and hospitals	Highways Total	Other than capital outlay	Interest on general debt
United States	$433,530	$379,546	$154,573	$112,272	$56,257	$40,258	$34,545	$16,841	$19,970
Alabama	5,987	5,173	2,386	1,277	542	768	567	311	242
Alaska	3,487	2,609	880	470	171	111	304	110	416
Arizona	5,146	4,194	2,161	1,495	243	380	455	165	210
Arkansas	3,081	2,732	1,242	806	363	345	321	185	131
California	53,088	48,515	17,901	13,302	8,968	4,722	2,350	1,319	1,330
Colorado	5,737	4,979	2,373	1,634	570	495	507	285	224
Connecticut	5,735	5,230	1,958	1,497	803	373	413	229	396
Delaware	1,295	1,093	470	252	98	66	117	60	101
Florida	16,224	13,336	5,619	4,515	1,223	1,909	1,344	519	542
Georgia	9,450	8,028	3,094	2,218	929	1,782	1,012	319	257
Hawaii	2,254	1,909	644	0	290	156	143	60	147
Idaho	1,459	1,244	579	390	120	132	162	64	49
Illinois	20,517	18,082	7,108	5,423	3,198	1,389	1,626	828	1,032
Indiana	7,986	7,023	3,523	2,285	817	857	647	366	210
Iowa	5,470	4,682	2,197	1,549	633	567	694	356	128
Kansas	4,352	3,780	1,684	1,205	446	395	509	236	278
Kentucky	5,341	4,574	1,903	1,162	738	364	656	266	409
Louisiana	8,597	7,214	2,943	1,983	873	995	755	175	523
Maine	1,869	1,671	649	453	325	81	215	129	91
Maryland	8,632	7,246	3,059	2,232	904	635	845	252	451
Massachusetts	11,297	10,407	3,296	2,625	2,078	1,048	625	369	610
Michigan	19,072	17,466	7,153	5,167	3,043	1,954	1,079	571	646
Minnesota	9,671	8,357	3,306	2,335	1,431	852	895	427	608
Mississippi	3,976	3,409	1,436	984	451	568	534	232	108
Missouri	6,954	6,102	2,611	1,969	794	771	617	309	235
Montana	1,539	1,331	620	466	154	86	203	91	58
Nebraska	2,822	2,393	1,145	818	250	278	378	162	81
Nevada...........	1,801	1,477	553	391	115	191	173	75	69
New Hampshire	1,488	1,318	523	376	197	73	180	120	115
New Jersey	14,506	12,938	5,083	4,151	1,870	890	958	512	890
New Mexico	2,843	2,361	1,162	772	220	250	356	132	149
New York	46,355	41,609	13,436	10,919	7,907	4,653	2,547	1,416	3,130
North Carolina	8,707	7,844	3,769	2,618	831	921	624	390	244
North Dakota	1,431	1,181	551	359	109	76	182	83	47
Ohio	18,068	15,857	6,587	4,895	2,634	1,759	1,246	699	716
Oklahoma	5,229	4,483	2,202	1,388	690	505	495	264	160
Oregon...........	5,872	5,175	2,196	1,709	483	350	511	234	531
Pennsylvania	19,912	17,835	6,717	5,268	3,415	1,372	1,607	1,069	1,189
Rhode Island	1,969	1,814	646	414	351	154	93	55	161
South Carolina	4,601	4,133	2,029	1,299	473	641	221	171	137
South Dakota	1,201	1,017	430	294	113	61	192	104	59
Tennessee	6,284	5,395	2,181	1,410	691	763	588	256	314
Texas	24,066	19,730	10,001	7,349	1,679	2,267	2,789	1,028	967
Utah	2,663	2,234	1,265	792	214	161	245	94	98
Vermont	998	897	389	235	129	50	112	66	55
Virginia	8,874	7,803	3,443	2,360	951	807	789	430	352
Washington........	8,526	7,091	3,320	2,130	852	605	863	426	303
West Virginia	3,218	2,724	1,189	890	273	299	465	176	222
Wisconsin	10,132	8,727	3,957	2,872	1,185	1,005	1,009	522	333
Wyoming..........	1,585	1,169	610	477	65	128	237	79	108
Dist. of Col.	2,164	1,953	392	392	353	202	88	43	107

Source: U.S. Bureau of the Census, *Governmental Finances in 1981-82.*
Note: Because of rounding, detail may not add to totals.

Table 8
PER CAPITA DIRECT GENERAL EXPENDITURE OF STATE AND LOCAL GOVERNMENTS, FOR SELECTED ITEMS, BY STATE: 1981-82

State or other jurisdiction	Total	Other than capital outlay	Education Total	Education Local schools only	Public welfare	Health and hospitals	Highways	Interest on general debt
United States	$1,913.63	$1,675.34	$ 682.30	$ 468.34	$248.32	$177.70	$152.48	$ 88.15
Alabama	1,537.43	1,328.35	612.77	354.02	139.24	197.13	145.69	62.21
Alaska	8,673.17	6,490.98	2,189.32	1,577.94	424.40	276.60	756.87	1,035.73
Arizona	1,893.43	1,543.04	795.04	483.13	89.41	139.87	167.32	77.27
Arkansas	1,347.71	1,194.90	543.35	354.54	158.70	150.74	140.53	57.39
California	2,243.02	2,049.80	756.34	484.74	378.93	199.51	99.28	56.17
Colorado	1,984.98	1,722.97	821.22	555.77	197.14	171.21	175.49	77.48
Connecticut	1,845.13	1,682.62	630.11	481.74	258.43	120.11	132.81	127.39
Delaware	2,180.09	1,840.72	791.30	424.93	165.63	110.52	197.63	170.37
Florida	1,664.65	1,368.31	576.58	412.44	125.50	195.85	137.94	55.64
Georgia	1,729.85	1,469.56	566.32	402.74	170.05	326.17	185.21	46.95
Hawaii	2,335.94	1,978.04	667.72	397.84	300.99	161.65	148.45	151.82
Idaho	1,545.74	1,317.67	613.25	393.63	127.11	139.53	172.03	52.09
Illinois	1,795.53	1,582.42	622.03	430.68	279.87	121.53	142.30	90.28
Indiana	1,454.72	1,279.25	641.77	416.15	148.84	156.15	117.83	38.32
Iowa	1,877.19	1,606.78	753.91	478.68	217.39	194.68	238.15	44.04
Kansas	1,840.74	1,598.82	712.38	472.96	188.57	166.90	215.16	117.77
Kentucky	1,459.18	1,249.85	519.95	318.05	201.58	99.44	179.30	111.76
Louisiana	2,044.01	1,715.07	699.61	475.60	207.52	236.57	179.44	124.34
Maine	1,661.02	1,485.77	577.33	404.83	289.30	72.12	190.82	80.89
Maryland	2,046.97	1,718.23	725.49	483.44	214.25	150.59	200.46	107.03
Massachusetts	1,969.13	1,814.04	574.55	456.12	362.19	182.64	108.95	106.30
Michigan	2,059.15	1,885.81	772.28	517.22	328.58	210.93	116.54	69.71
Minnesota	2,372.74	2,050.39	811.02	572.77	351.15	209.08	219.69	149.15
Mississippi	1,577.23	1,352.25	569.56	340.78	178.95	225.30	211.94	42.83
Missouri	1,414.37	1,241.02	530.92	379.77	161.51	156.85	125.48	47.89
Montana	1,955.40	1,691.18	788.18	583.99	195.13	109.09	257.41	73.62
Nebraska	1,797.72	1,524.26	729.51	486.33	159.09	177.28	241.02	51.59
Nevada..........	2,250.85	1,845.92	691.00	488.98	143.55	238.37	216.56	85.83
New Hampshire	1,615.15	1,431.30	568.16	408.09	214.39	78.93	194.92	124.86
New Jersey	1,969.59	1,756.63	690.17	535.21	253.92	120.82	130.09	120.89
New Mexico	2,182.09	1,812.11	891.69	604.89	169.21	192.16	272.84	114.19
New York	2,640.13	2,369.81	765.21	559.42	450.33	265.00	145.08	178.26
North Carolina	1,480.30	1,333.63	640.74	403.83	141.35	156.61	106.15	41.49
North Dakota	2,191.10	1,808.74	844.47	537.70	166.80	115.97	278.76	71.54
Ohio	1,673.28	1,468.51	609.99	444.46	243.90	162.91	115.41	66.33
Oklahoma	1,728.56	1,482.12	727.96	461.66	228.05	167.07	163.70	52.98
Oregon	2,230.10	1,965.47	834.07	584.49	183.32	132.80	194.06	201.85
Pennsylvania.......	1,678.35	1,503.27	566.14	431.54	287.86	115.65	135.44	100.19
Rhode Island	2,078.77	1,915.98	682.39	437.04	371.03	162.33	98.38	170.27
South Carolina	1,473.64	1,323.83	649.80	428.36	151.49	205.47	70.69	43.76
South Dakota	1,737.54	1,471.79	622.12	426.12	163.95	87.97	277.46	84.99
Tennessee	1,368.71	1,175.16	475.05	307.17	150.57	166.10	128.00	68.31
Texas	1,691.31	1,386.60	702.87	481.75	117.99	159.33	196.00	67.96
Utah	1,822.84	1,529.25	865.64	541.97	146.57	110.00	167.80	67.24
Vermont	1,953.61	1,755.08	761.92	460.53	252.39	97.58	218.89	108.31
Virginia	1,659.64	1,459.33	643.95	441.33	177.91	150.86	147.49	65.88
Washington.......	2,063.37	1,716.09	803.38	541.15	206.11	146.45	208.98	73.37
West Virginia	1,650.17	1,396.97	609.95	456.66	140.23	153.16	238.24	113.70
Wisconsin	2,153.06	1,854.46	840.91	554.34	251.74	213.45	214.51	70.74
Wyoming.........	3,373.09	2,486.27	1,297.96	923.51	138.26	272.27	503.85	229.85
Dist. of Col.	3,391.94	3,061.48	614.87	508.73	553.08	316.18	137.76	168.03

Source: U.S. Bureau of the Census, *Governmental Finances in 1981-82.*

Table 9
RELATION OF SELECTED ITEMS OF STATE AND LOCAL GOVERNMENT
FINANCES TO PERSONAL INCOME: 1981-82

| State or other jurisdiction | General revenue per $1,000 of personal income | | | | | Direct general expenditure per $1,000 of personal income | | | | |
	Total	From federal government	All state and local general revenue sources	Taxes	Charges and miscellaneous general revenue	All general expenditures	Education	Highways	Public welfare	Health and hospitals
U.S. Average..........	$189.63	$ 36.14	$153.49	$110.70	$ 42.79	$180.22	$ 64.26	$14.36	$23.39	$16.74
Alabama	188.50	42.85	145.66	92.34	53.31	185.94	74.11	17.62	16.84	23.84
Alaska	1,117.56	74.88	1,042.68	496.38	546.30	615.25	155.30	53.69	30.11	19.62
Arizona	183.27	27.76	155.51	105.67	49.84	188.82	79.28	16.69	8.92	13.95
Arkansas	176.62	44.77	131.85	90.23	41.62	166.83	67.26	17.40	19.65	18.66
California..............	191.27	37.25	154.03	112.59	41.43	184.03	62.05	8.15	31.09	16.37
Colorado	184.22	32.02	152.19	103.25	48.94	172.50	71.37	15.25	17.13	14.88
Connecticut	153.21	25.58	127.62	102.46	25.17	142.78	48.76	10.28	20.00	9.30
Delaware	205.75	42.96	162.79	108.76	54.04	195.03	70.79	17.68	14.82	9.89
Florida	156.65	27.68	128.96	89.09	39.87	156.75	54.29	12.99	11.82	18.44
Georgia	197.80	43.83	153.97	103.76	50.21	189.77	62.13	20.32	18.66	35.78
Hawaii	215.14	43.00	172.14	127.62	44.53	208.28	59.54	13.24	26.84	14.41
Idaho	176.71	37.92	138.79	94.56	44.23	170.19	67.52	18.94	13.99	15.36
Illinois	164.98	32.41	132.57	103.10	29.47	154.65	53.57	12.26	24.11	10.47
Indiana	157.15	28.31	128.84	90.50	38.34	150.27	66.29	12.17	15.37	16.13
Iowa	181.69	30.24	151.45	108.45	43.00	180.16	72.36	22.86	20.86	18.68
Kansas	176.78	28.52	148.26	98.19	50.07	168.91	65.37	19.74	17.30	15.32
Kentucky	178.25	43.05	135.20	101.50	33.70	173.19	61.71	21.28	23.93	11.80
Louisiana	216.16	37.79	178.36	112.99	65.37	209.68	71.77	18.41	21.29	24.27
Maine	200.38	49.09	151.29	119.00	32.30	193.26	67.17	22.20	33.66	8.39
Maryland	185.48	34.16	151.31	109.71	41.60	176.42	62.53	17.28	18.47	12.98
Massachusetts	191.75	42.48	149.27	120.82	28.45	175.83	51.30	9.73	32.34	16.31
Michigan	203.90	39.90	164.01	114.76	49.25	192.04	72.02	10.87	30.64	19.67
Minnesota	219.50	40.03	179.47	119.24	60.23	219.37	74.98	20.31	32.47	19.33
Mississippi	211.50	55.37	156.13	100.98	55.15	212.08	76.58	28.50	24.06	30.29
Missouri	151.64	32.43	119.21	86.91	32.30	145.85	54.75	12.94	16.66	16.17
Montana	237.61	46.80	190.81	129.45	61.37	206.34	83.17	27.16	20.59	11.51
Nebraska	181.91	30.42	151.49	100.65	50.84	172.67	70.07	23.15	15.28	17.03
Nevada	186.08	29.37	156.71	103.64	53.07	184.08	56.51	17.71	11.74	19.49
New Hampshire	154.25	30.47	123.78	91.17	32.61	159.10	55.97	19.20	21.12	7.78
New Jersey.............	169.65	27.69	141.96	110.98	30.98	161.56	56.61	10.67	20.83	9.91
New Mexico............	297.99	49.32	248.67	131.40	117.27	251.08	102.60	31.39	19.47	22.11
New York	239.24	44.60	194.65	155.72	38.93	229.68	66.57	12.62	39.18	23.05
North Carolina	174.27	36.43	137.84	101.08	36.76	169.09	73.19	12.13	16.15	17.89
North Dakota	229.80	44.39	185.41	109.79	75.61	212.76	82.00	27.07	16.20	11.26
Ohio	161.75	30.68	131.07	94.48	36.59	162.51	59.24	11.21	23.69	15.82
Oklahoma	188.71	29.45	159.26	115.17	44.09	164.58	69.31	15.59	21.71	15.91
Oregon	218.10	44.76	173.35	111.37	61.97	221.36	82.79	19.26	18.20	13.18
Pennsylvania	175.06	35.13	139.93	107.55	32.38	161.76	54.57	13.05	27.74	11.15
Rhode Island	210.00	47.50	162.51	119.67	42.84	203.45	66.79	9.63	36.31	15.89
South Carolina	188.62	38.95	149.67	103.25	46.42	180.72	79.69	8.67	18.58	25.20
South Dakota	209.43	49.90	159.53	104.53	55.00	198.26	70.99	31.66	18.71	10.04
Tennessee.............	171.16	40.09	131.07	91.00	40.08	161.30	55.98	15.09	17.75	19.57
Texas	164.42	23.37	141.05	96.95	44.11	151.90	63.13	17.60	10.60	14.31
Utah	235.76	51.24	184.52	117.11	67.41	211.04	100.22	19.43	16.97	12.74
Vermont...............	231.72	63.48	168.24	125.72	42.52	221.99	86.58	24.87	28.68	11.09
Virginia	162.91	29.93	132.98	98.05	34.93	157.93	61.28	14.04	16.93	14.36
Washington	181.29	33.03	148.25	101.80	46.45	179.28	69.80	18.16	17.91	12.72
West Virginia...........	206.71	49.59	157.12	113.85	43.27	196.79	72.74	28.41	16.72	18.27
Wisconsin	209.93	38.79	171.15	124.59	46.55	212.96	83.17	21.22	24.90	21.11
Wyoming	378.26	66.01	312.25	208.58	103.68	276.29	106.32	41.27	11.33	22.30
Dist. of Col.	325.71	157.10	168.61	143.69	24.91	253.34	45.92	10.29	41.31	23.62

Source: U.S. Bureau of the Census, *Governmental Finances in 1981-82.*

STATE FINANCES IN 1982

By Maurice Criz

The fiscal condition of state governments changed dramatically in fiscal 1982. Revenue from the federal government decreased for the first time since the 1940s. The deep economic recession affected all tax bases to such an extent that state tax revenue growth slowed to 8.6 percent in 1982 over 1981, compared to an average increase of 11.6 percent annually in the 1970s. The decline would have been sharper if 26 states had not enacted rate increases or broadened coverage in general and selective sales taxes, individual and corporate income taxes, and motor vehicle and operators license taxes. However, even with the rate increases, practically all states received less revenue than estimated, and they had to draw on fund balances and apply the axe to spending programs.

Part of the drop in tax revenue resulted from the widespread tax revolt in the late 1970s, enactment of tax and spending limits in about 30 states, and income tax indexing in 10 states.

A survey conducted by the Federation of Tax Administrators to determine the effect of the economy on state tax revenues showed that in fiscal 1982 general fund revenues were below the amounts anticipated when the budgets were adopted in nearly two-thirds of the states.[1] The sales tax had the greatest number of shortfalls, about four-fifths of the reporting states.

State fiscal condition is usually analyzed in terms of the general fund. The balance of all state general funds totalled $6.5 billion at the start of fiscal 1982, as compared with $11.8 and $11.2 billion in the two preceding years.[2] By the end of the year, balances dropped by $2 billion and amounted to only 3 percent of 1982 expenditures, a figure that is lower than a desirable minimum by a couple of percentage points. It has been estimated that fiscal 1983 statistics will show a further drop of $4.2 billion to almost a zero balance ($0.3 billion), or only 0.2 percent of expenditure. What makes matters even worse than these figures show is that one state (Texas) had a balance of $1.5 billion in 1982 and $0.6 billion in 1983, which indicates the pressures on the other states. In fact, if Texas is excluded, the 49 state total would show a deficit in 1983.

The annual fiscal survey of the states by the National Governors' Association and National Association of State Budget Officers also shows that the majority of states applied a variety of cost-cutting measures as well as tax increases aimed at balancing their budgets. Programs most frequently used in fiscal 1982 were hiring limits (37 states), selective program cuts (25), restricted out-of-state travel (24), and temporary or permanent revenue increases (26). Other austerity measures adopted were: converting capital spending from current to bond funds (5 states); moving general funds to special funds (8 states); postponing expenditure or payment into the next fiscal year (13 states); and forcing unpaid furloughs (5 states). These budget-balancing measures were intensified in fiscal 1983: hiring limits increased in number to 42 states, and personnel were laid off in 22 states; selective program cuts went up to 37 and across-the-board cuts to 27; 27 states enacted permanent revenue increases and 24 enacted or proposed temporary tax increases; 32 states restricted out-of-state travel, and 24 restricted in-state travel.

Revenue

Total revenue of the 50 states continued the annual upward trend in fiscal 1982, reaching a peak of $330.9 billion or 6.5 percent more than 1981. The highest rates of increase were in Wyoming (34.6 percent), Nevada (17.2 percent), Alaska (14.7 percent) and Oklahoma (14.6 percent). Three states experienced decreases in revenue: Michigan (3.0 percent), Arkansas (0.9 percent) and Oregon (0.9 percent).

In Census Bureau reporting, state government financial statistics include four sectors of activity: general government, state-operated utilities, state alcoholic beverage monopolies and insurance trust operations. In 1982, general revenue contributed $275.2 billion of the total, insurance trusts $50.8 billion, liquor stores $2.9 billion, and utilities $2.1 billion.

Maurice Criz is Senior Advisor, Governments Division, U.S. Bureau of the Census. Fiscal 1982 data are for fiscal years which ended on June 30, 1982, except for four states with other closing dates: Alabama, September 30; Michigan, September 30; New York, March 31; and Texas, August 31.

General revenue increased by 6.6 percent in 1982 over 1981. Taxes comprised 59.1 percent of general revenue and increased by 8.6 percent in 1982 compared to 1981. Sales and gross receipts taxes accounted for 28.6 percent of general revenue, and continued to show strength, increasing by 8.3 percent in 1982. Public utilities taxes were the largest gainer in this group with an annual increase of 15.3 percent. Individual income taxes comprised 16.6 percent of general revenue and had an annual increase of 11.8 percent as employment levels generally remained high and personal income continued an upward trend. Severance taxes continued to enlarge their role in state finances with an increase of 22.7 percent in 1982 to a 2.9 percentage of general revenue, this rise coming on top of a 53.1 percent increase in 1981 versus 1980. This growth is particularly interesting because there are nine leading energy producing states that in 1982 had the following percentages of severance taxes to general revenue: Wyoming 28.5; Alaska, 28.1; Oklahoma, 17.5; Louisiana, 17.0; North Dakota, 16.3; Texas, 16.2; Montana, 13.7; New Mexico, 13.6; and Kentucky, 6.0.

Current charges and miscellaneous revenue were significant contributors to the 1982 increase in general revenue. Current charges were 7.7 percent of general revenue and increased by 13.5 percent compared to 1981, as states resorted to higher fees for tuition at universities and colleges and at hospitals and parks. Interest earnings were one of the biggest gainers of the year, increasing by 23.4 percent in 1982 to 4.4 percent of general revenue as the result of sustained high interest rate levels.

State revenue from the federal government, including grants-in-aid and reimbursements for performance of general government functions and specific services, decreased in fiscal 1982 in dollar amounts for the first time in a third of a century. The drop amounted to 2.7 percent compared to 1981, and resulted in revenue from the federal government sinking to 24.0 percent of state general revenue from 26.3 percent in 1981. While this was a not unexpected event since it had been announced by the administration and had been discussed in detail with state officials, it nevertheless created difficulties for state finances especially in light of the then existing recession. In terms of major state functions, the 1982 decreases amounted to 6.7 percent for education, 11.4 percent for highways, 3.5 percent for health and hospitals, and 3.0 percent for natural resources. In addition, states no longer received General Revenue Sharing funds. The only increase in this area was revenue for public welfare, which grew by 9.0 percent in 1982.

Insurance trust revenue totalled $50.8 billion in 1982, an increase of 5.8 percent over 1981. Every state operates a system of unemployment insurance and one or more public employee retirement systems. Most of the states also administer workers' compensation systems, and a few have other insurance systems involving the payment of cash benefits from accumulated fund reserves. Transactions of these various systems, exclusive of administrative costs (treated as general expenditure) and of state contributions (classified as intergovernmental transactions), are reported as insurance trust revenue and insurance trust expenditure. Employee retirement revenue increased by 15.5 percent in 1982, and workers' compensation revenue went up by 11.5 percent, while unemployment compensation revenue decreased by 8.7 percent.

Liquor stores revenue in the 17 states that maintain such systems increased by 1.8 percent in 1982. Utility revenue in the 14 states that had some form of utility operation during 1982 increased by 14.2 percent. These systems were for water supply, electric power and transit operations.

Expenditure

General expenditure of all state governments reflected the fiscal stresses created by the national recession, revenue shortfalls from smaller growth in taxes and diminished federal aid, the need to draw down fund balances, and high rates of unemployment. Consequently, general expenditure increased by only 6.2 percent in fiscal 1982 compared to 1981, while the increase in 1981 amounted to 11.1 percent. The slowdown affected both intergovernmental expenditure to local governments (6.2 percent growth in 1982 versus 10.3 percent in 1981) and direct expenditure to employees, suppliers, beneficiaries, etc. (6.4 percent increase in 1982 as against 11.7 percent in 1981). The slowdown was evident in practically all major functional areas, which showed 1982 annual rates of increase as follows with 1981 in parenthesis: education, 6.3 (10.2); public welfare, 7.4 (16.4); hospitals, 9.2 (12.2); health, 6.5 (20.7); highways, -1.2 (1.6); police protection, 6.7 (13.0); corrections, 15.6 (14.5); natural resources, 9.5 (15.2); financial administration, 12.1 (9.9); general control, 14.3 (5.8); and interest on general debt, 14.9 (16.0).

Education is the largest state general expenditure, amounting to $103.0 billion in fiscal 1982 or 38.2 percent of the total. Of this amount,

$60.7 billion (59 percent) went to school districts and other local governments as grants-in-aid and compensation for services performed. Public welfare is the second largest at $55.3 billion or 20.5 percent of general expenditure. Highways rank third at $25.1 billion (9.3 percent), followed by hospitals with $14.0 billion and health with $8.3 billion. Interest on general debt, due to considerable growth in debt outstanding and to high interest rates, amounted in 1982 to $9.0 billion or 3.4 percent of general expenditure.

In state finance sectors other than general expenditure, insurance trust expenditure totalled $34.7 billion in 1982, an increase of 7.6 percent over 1981. Employee retirement expenditure increased by 15.0 percent to $13.1 billion, unemployment compensation increased slightly to $18.0 billion, and workmen's compensation increased 23.5 percent to $2.5 billion. Liquor stores expenditure grew by 4.4 percent to $2.4 billion, and utility expenditure went up by 11.4 percent to $3.7 billion.

Indebtedness

Total indebtedness of all state governments reached $147.5 billion at the end of fiscal 1982, or $653 per capita. Long-term debt increased by 8.4 percent to $143.7 billion, while short-term debt went up by 62 percent to $3.8 billion. The large increase in short-term debt was the result of revenue shortfalls.

The shift from full faith and credit debt (backed by state government powers of taxation) to revenue bonds and other forms of non-guaranteed debt continues at a strong pace. Full faith and credit debt, which comprised 49.8 percent of long-term state debt at the end of fiscal 1972, declined to 35.8 percent in 1982, while non-guaranteed debt increased from 50.2 percent to 64.2 percent in the same period. In fact, full faith and credit debt decreased by 2.0 percent in 1982, while non-guaranteed debt increased by 15.3 percent. The increased use of non-guaranteed debt reflects greater state involvement in financing enterprise-type operations (sewage facilities, hospitals, utilities, public housing, etc.) as well as an increased level of state financing of facilities for private enterprise. These include activities for pollution control, industrial development and housing construction for private ownership.

Cash and Security Holdings

Financial assets of state governments represent a significant factor in the nation's banking and investment sectors. Not only are states' cash and security holdings very large, but there is constant turnover of sizable amounts of funds. In fiscal 1982, these holdings totalled $338.3 billion, an increase of 10.8 percent compared to 1981.

Securities represented 87.5 percent of these asset holdings and consisted of federal securities 21.2 percent, state and local government securities 2.3 percent, and corporate stocks and bonds, mortgages, and other securities 64.1 percent. Cash and deposits amounted to 12.5 percent of total holdings.

Notes

1. *The Impact of the Economy on State Tax Revenues Fiscal Year 1982 and Current Fiscal Year*, Research Memorandum 553 (March 1983), p. 1.

2. National Governors' Association and National Association of State Budget Officers, *Fiscal Survey of the States 1983*, p. 6.

Table 1
SUMMARY FINANCIAL AGGREGATES, BY STATE: 1982
(In millions of dollars)

	Revenue						Expenditure					Debt redemption
State	Total	General	Insurance trust	Liquor stores	Utilities	Borrowing	Total	General	Insurance trust	Liquor stores	Utilities	
All states	$330,949	$275,162	$50,848	$2,854	$2,085	$20,273	$310,292	$269,490	$34,664	$2,408	$3,730	$7,197
Alabama	4,823	4,159	544	120	0	742	4,667	4,181	367	119	0	104
Alaska	5,889	5,583	306	0	0	1,397	3,281	3,034	139	0	107	95
Arizona	3,501	2,888	605	0	8	102	3,245	2,966	271	0	8	4
Arkansas	2,506	2,238	268	0	0	94	2,362	2,159	203	0	0	11
California	42,247	34,421	7,798	0	29	1,829	40,444	35,492	4,948	0	4	476
Colorado	3,805	3,174	631	0	0	57	3,635	3,216	420	0	0	31
Connecticut	4,300	3,846	438	0	16	645	3,994	3,498	445	0	50	436
Delaware	1,190	1,066	121	0	4	365	1,084	1,005	70	0	9	69
Florida	9,364	8,338	1,019	0	7	17	9,322	8,757	544	0	21	105
Georgia	6,144	5,376	768	0	0	379	6,007	5,523	484	0	0	112
Hawaii	2,146	1,843	303	0	0	360	1,994	1,826	168	0	0	104
Idaho	1,237	1,009	187	41	0	74	1,209	1,021	157	31	0	20
Illinois	14,441	11,879	2,562	0	0	870	14,138	12,031	2,107	0	0	313
Indiana	5,657	5,099	558	0	0	42	5,694	5,146	546	0	0	46
Iowa	3,885	3,271	477	136	0	30	3,903	3,449	358	96	0	14
Kansas	2,751	2,428	323	0	0	0	2,634	2,403	231	0	0	23
Kentucky	4,885	4,252	634	0	0	222	4,726	4,225	501	0	0	134
Louisiana	6,453	5,785	668	0	0	752	6,463	5,773	690	0	0	121
Maine	1,572	1,361	167	44	0	87	1,527	1,307	176	44	0	59
Maryland	6,281	5,591	647	0	42	442	6,260	5,416	656	0	188	218
Massachusetts	8,752	7,883	867	0	2	752	8,631	7,771	837	0	23	627
Michigan	14,587	11,441	2,723	423	0	592	13,997	11,506	2,137	353	0	204
Minnesota	7,060	6,095	965	0	0	462	6,925	6,385	539	0	0	190
Mississippi	3,230	2,724	396	110	0	3	3,039	2,725	220	94	0	50
Missouri	4,745	4,003	742	0	0	423	4,410	3,966	444	0	0	148
Montana	1,331	1,088	199	44	0	93	1,135	944	154	38	0	19
Nebraska	1,658	1,561	98	0	0	54	1,646	1,576	70	0	0	5
Nevada	1,552	1,102	414	0	35	111	1,413	1,110	242	0	61	17
New Hampshire	1,051	789	112	150	0	234	1,005	822	62	121	0	51
New Jersey	11,341	9,254	1,960	0	127	1,429	11,152	9,215	1,510	0	427	264
New Mexico	3,020	2,773	247	0	0	137	2,392	2,272	119	0	0	80
New York	33,396	26,513	5,484	0	1,399	2,143	30,160	25,533	2,523	0	2,104	1,014
North Carolina	7,128	6,123	1,005	0	0	351	6,851	6,180	670	0	0	109
North Dakota	1,286	1,142	143	0	0	126	1,191	1,119	72	0	0	16
Ohio	15,308	10,170	4,793	345	0	480	13,742	10,416	3,026	300	0	207
Oklahoma	4,692	4,237	352	0	102	32	4,162	3,697	298	0	168	37
Oregon	4,382	3,356	871	155	0	397	4,210	3,445	673	91	0	184
Pennsylvania	16,290	12,973	2,726	591	0	314	15,328	12,353	2,434	541	0	341
Rhode Island	1,686	1,421	257	0	8	389	1,628	1,402	203	0	23	121
South Carolina	4,209	3,344	559	0	307	727	4,110	3,216	356	0	538	125
South Dakota	873	793	79	0	0	39	829	794	34	0	0	24
Tennessee	4,521	3,953	569	0	0	244	4,298	3,813	485	0	0	130
Texas	16,365	14,691	1,674	0	0	100	14,152	13,189	963	0	0	95
Utah	2,324	1,862	395	67	0	153	1,994	1,756	190	48	0	17
Vermont	832	738	64	30	0	46	888	720	139	29	0	46
Virginia	6,614	5,772	595	247	0	606	6,298	5,683	402	213	0	166
Washington	7,446	5,621	1,588	237	0	876	7,256	5,893	1,165	197	0	64
West Virginia	3,100	2,468	555	78	0	68	2,842	2,351	430	61	0	106
Wisconsin	7,533	6,296	1,237	0	0	293	6,895	6,202	693	0	0	236
Wyoming	1,559	1,366	156	36	0	93	1,123	1,002	90	31	0	11

Source: U.S. Bureau of the Census, *State Government Finances in 1982.*

Note: Details do not add up to totals due to rounding.

Table 2
NATIONAL TOTALS OF STATE GOVERNMENT FINANCES, SELECTED YEARS: 1960-82

Item	Amounts in millions									Percentage change 1981 to 1982	Per capita 1982
	1982	1981	1980	1978	1976	1974	1972	1970	1960		
Revenue and borrowing	$351,222	$329,213	$293,696	$238,475	$199,626	$148,775	$120,931	$93,463	$35,149	6.7	$1,555
Borrowing	20,273	18,385	16,734	13,464	15,805	7,959	8,622	4,523	2,312	10.3	90
Revenue total	330,949	310,828	276,962	225,011	183,821	140,816	112,309	88,939	32,838	6.5	1,465
General revenue	275,162	258,159	233,592	189,099	152,118	122,327	98,632	77,755	27,363	6.6	1,218
Taxes total	162,658	149,738	137,075	113,261	89,256	74,207	59,870	47,961	18,036	8.6	720
Intergovernmental revenue	69,166	70,786	64,326	53,461	44,717	33,170	27,981	20,248	6,745	-2.3	306
From federal government	66,026	67,868	61,892	50,200	42,013	31,632	26,791	19,252	6,382	-2.7	292
Public welfare	31,510	28,892	24,680	20,007	16,867	13,320	12,289	7,818	2,048	9.0	139
Education	13,149	14,100	12,765	9,819	8,661	6,720	5,984	4,554	727	-6.7	58
Highways	8,304	9,369	8,860	6,301	6,262	4,503	4,871	4,431	2,883	-11.4	37
General revenue sharing	(b)	1,118	2,278	1,887	1,658	1,295	1,148	0	0	—	
Employment security administration	2,352	2,362	2,050	2,255	2,102	2,045	1,191	769	319	-0.4	10
Other	10,711	12,027	11,258	9,931	6,463	3,749	1,308	1,681	406	-10.9	47
From local governments	3,139	2,918	2,434	3,261	2,704	1,538	1,190	995	363	7.7	14
Charges and miscellaneous revenue	43,338	37,636	32,190	22,377	18,145	14,950	10,780	9,545	2,583	15.2	192
Utility revenue(a)	2,085	1,823	1,304	962	0	0	0	0	0	14.2	9
Liquor stores revenue	2,854	2,805	2,765	2,388	2,196	2,049	1,904	1,748	1,128	1.8	13
Insurance trust revenue	50,848	48,041	39,301	32,562	29,508	16,439	11,773	9,437	4,347	5.8	225
Unemployment compensation	16,854	18,443	13,468	13,083	15,068	5,711	3,588	3,090	2,316	-8.7	75
Employee retirement	29,035	25,122	21,146	16,026	12,171	8,919	6,827	5,205	1,558	15.5	129
Other	4,959	4,476	4,686	3,452	2,269	1,809	1,359	1,143	472	10.8	22
Debt outstanding at end of fiscal year, total	147,470	134,847	121,958	102,569	84,825	65,296	53,833	42,008	18,543	9.4	653
Long-term	143,702	132,521	119,821	99,671	78,814	61,697	50,379	38,903	18,128	8.4	636
Non-guaranteed	92,195	79,940	70,457	53,356	39,972	30,842	25,314	21,167	9,216	15.3	408
Full faith and credit	51,507	52,582	49,364	46,316	38,842	30,855	25,065	17,736	8,912	-2.0	228
Short-term	3,768	2,325	2,137	2,897	6,011	3,599	3,454	3,104	415	62.0	17
Net long-term	87,047	81,538	79,810	72,089	62,488	53,847	45,082	34,479	15,595	6.8	385
Full faith and credit only	39,766	41,429	39,357	39,147	33,708	26,967	21,932	14,832	6,711	-4.0	176
Expenditure and debt redemption	317,482	297,466	263,494	208,533	184,511	134,948	111,933	87,152	32,496	6.7	1,406
Debt redemption	7,190	5,938	5,682	4,701	3,585	2,814	2,690	2,096	900	21.1	32
Expenditure total	310,292	291,527	257,812	203,832	180,926	132,134	109,243	85,055	31,596	6.6	1,374
General expenditure	269,490	253,654	228,223	179,802	153,690	119,891	98,810	77,642	27,228	6.2	1,193
Education	102,984	96,921	87,939	69,702	59,630	46,860	38,348	30,865	5,461	6.3	456
Intergovernmental expenditure	60,684	57,257	52,688	40,125	34,084	27,107	21,195	17,085	2,856	6.0	269
State institutions of higher education	34,296	31,488	27,927	23,259	19,707	15,395	13,381	11,011	540	8.9	152
Other	8,005	8,175	7,324	6,318	5,839	4,358	3,773	2,769	2,065	-2.1	35
Public welfare	55,257	51,463	44,219	35,776	29,633	22,538	19,191	13,206	3,704	7.4	245
Intergovernmental expenditure	13,744	12,882	10,977	10,047	9,476	7,369	6,944	5,003	1,483	6.6	61
Cash assistance, categorical programs	7,337	7,579	6,831	5,712	5,203	4,984	5,089	3,534	1,728	-3.2	32
Cash assistance, other	875	799	623	623	353	212	192	145	76	9.5	4
Other public welfare	33,301	30,201	25,725	19,393	14,601	9,974	6,967	4,523	417	10.3	147
Highways	25,131	25,439	25,044	18,479	18,100	15,847	15,380	13,483	7,317	-1.6	111
Regular state highway facilities	19,078	19,659	19,652	13,970	14,223	11,887	12,089	10,482	5,812	-3.0	84
State toll highway facilities	1,025	1,028	1,009	687	636	749	658	562	259	-0.3	5
Intergovernmental expenditure	5,028	4,751	4,383	3,821	3,241	3,211	2,633	2,439	1,247	5.8	22

Item											
Health and hospitals	22,284	20,593	17,855	13,883	11,110	8,443	6,963	5,355	2,072	8.2	99
State hospitals and institutions for handicapped	13,681	12,360	11,015	8,979	7,572	5,957	4,825	3,941	1,618	10.6	61
Other	8,603	8,233	6,840	4,905	3,538	2,486	2,138	1,414	454	4.5	38
Natural resources	5,485	5,008	4,346	3,411	3,863	3,053	2,595	2,223	862	9.5	24
Corrections	5,889	5,093	4,449	3,275	2,480	1,812	1,389	1,104	433	15.6	26
Financial administration	3,735	3,331	3,031	2,482	1,955	1,594	1,235	1,032	447	12.1	17
General control	3,909	3,419	3,232	2,331	1,688	1,273	944	717	216	14.3	17
Employment security administration	2,278	2,269	2,001	1,757	1,570	1,304	1,133	767	313	0.3	10
Police	2,730	2,558	2,263	1,826	1,569	1,262	983	741	251	6.7	12
Miscellaneous and unallocable	39,808	37,560	33,843	26,879	22,091	15,906	10,647	8,149	2,755	6.0	176
State aid for unspecified purposes	10,044	9,570	8,501	6,819	5,674	4,804	3,752	2,958	806	5.0	44
Interest	9,015	7,844	6,763	5,268	4,140	2,863	2,135	1,499	536	14.9	40
Veterans' services	64	57	61	54	64	156	51	67	112	12.2	0
Other (includes intergovernmental aid for specified purposes not elsewhere classified)(a)	20,685	20,089	18,518	14,738	12,213	8,083	4,709	3,626	1,300	3.0	92
Utility expenditure	3,730	3,347	2,401	1,544		0	0	0	0	11.4	17
Liquor store expenditure	2,408	2,305	2,206	1,991	1,781	1,653	1,495	1,404	907	4.4	11
Insurance trust expenditure	34,664	32,221	24,981	20,495	25,455	10,590	8,938	6,010	3,461	7.6	153
Unemployment compensation	18,027	17,846	12,006	10,672	17,780	4,673	4,722	2,713	2,359	1.0	80
Employee retirement	13,133	11,419	10,257	7,811	6,045	4,591	3,175	2,376	700	15.0	58
Other	3,503	2,955	2,718	2,011	1,629	1,326	1,041	921	402	18.5	16
Total expenditure by character and object	310,292	291,527	257,812	203,832	180,926	132,134	109,243	85,055	31,596	6.6	1,374
Direct expenditure	211,549	198,348	173,307	136,545	123,069	86,193	72,483	56,163	22,152	6.7	936
Current operation	133,152	122,794	108,131	86,153	68,175	50,803	39,790	30,971	9,534	8.4	589
Capital outlay	23,466	24,286	23,325	16,064	18,009	15,417	15,283	13,295	6,607	-3.4	104
Construction	19,560	20,632	19,736	13,260	15,285	12,655	13,022	11,185	5,509	-5.2	87
Purchase of land and existing structures	1,316	1,152	1,345	1,171	1,274	1,540	1,369	1,240	296	14.2	6
Equipment	2,590	2,502	2,243	1,633	1,450	1,222	892	870	2,015	3.5	11
Assistance and subsidies	10,867	10,889	9,818	8,341	7,290	6,521	6,337	4,387	536	-0.2	48
Interest on debt	9,400	8,157	7,052	5,493	4,140	2,863	2,135	1,499		15.2	42
Insurance benefits and repayments	34,664	32,221	24,981	20,495	25,455	10,590	8,938	6,010	3,461	7.6	153
Intergovernmental expenditure	98,743	93,180	84,504	67,287	57,858	45,941	36,759	28,892	9,443	6.0	1,497
Cash and security holdings at end of fiscal year	338,274	305,237	273,047	212,107	157,210	134,493	99,791	84,810	33,940	10.8	30
Unemployment fund balance in U.S. Treasury	6,789	11,634	11,945	7,450	4,425	10,773	8,964	12,236	6,597	-41.7	157
Cash and deposits	35,400	32,797	30,782	25,345	18,477	18,387	12,372	8,463	4,175	7.9	1,311
Securities	296,084	260,806	230,320	179,312	134,308	105,332	78,456	64,110	23,168	13.5	
Total by purpose:											
Insurance trust	211,493	187,158	166,656	124,371	94,679	80,840	62,991	54,995	20,264	13.0	936
Debt offsets	56,655	50,983	40,011	27,582	15,880	7,849	5,309	4,424	2,533	11.1	251
Other	70,126	67,096	66,381	60,154	46,651	45,804	31,514	25,404	11,144	4.5	310

Source: U.S. Bureau of the Census, annual reports on *State Government Finances* and *Historical Statistics on Governmental Finances and Employment* (vol. 6, no. 4, of the 1977 Census of Governments).

(a) Reported separately only since 1977; previously included with general revenue or general expenditure.
(b) State participation ended September 1980.

Table 3
STATE GENERAL REVENUE, BY SOURCE AND BY STATE: 1982
(In thousands of dollars)

State	Total general revenue(a)	Taxes — Total	Sales and gross receipts — Total	General	Motor fuels	Licenses — Total	Motor vehicle	Individual income	Corporation net income	Intergovernmental revenue	Charges and miscellaneous general revenue
All states	$275,161,865	$162,657,820	$78,800,227	$50,342,651	$10,437,350	$10,099,095	$6,051,063	$45,707,515	$14,006,175	$69,165,793	$43,338,252
Alabama	4,158,745	2,195,831	1,341,497	629,453	237,698	125,905	40,443	480,969	123,218	1,178,508	784,406
Alaska	5,582,926	2,539,193	65,216		31,096	54,217	13,691	1,488	703,663	367,144	2,676,589
Arizona	2,888,380	1,856,009	1,036,711	800,921	122,343	123,698	93,837	438,985	114,759	524,000	508,371
Arkansas	2,238,436	1,263,746	680,330	419,378	133,384	96,098	69,256	353,733	91,706	700,848	273,842
California	34,420,723	21,818,694	9,672,042	7,720,805	835,281	837,026	611,272	7,467,709	2,643,946	8,804,999	3,797,030
Colorado	3,174,292	1,690,034	873,367	612,900	138,802	105,900	59,342	548,944	91,400	835,420	648,838
Connecticut	3,846,307	2,339,524	1,647,425	1,004,164	149,176	125,348	91,159	137,726	349,283	848,432	658,351
Delaware	1,065,586	594,816	86,910	0	34,554	166,882	24,688	286,069	36,138	219,324	251,446
Florida	8,337,735	5,555,936	4,189,571	2,783,889	431,686	399,933	268,047	0	383,827	1,925,500	856,299
Georgia	5,376,281	3,281,065	1,697,558	1,088,279	350,803	100,220	58,626	1,182,783	267,683	1,562,884	532,332
Hawaii	1,843,279	1,066,225	716,535	576,927	33,196	16,929	8,456	283,000	43,202	385,826	391,228
Idaho	1,009,106	578,613	239,573	146,206	56,805	67,160	41,409	220,073	45,602	273,298	157,195
Illinois	11,878,859	7,429,268	3,728,482	2,333,153	364,705	469,299	375,757	2,222,143	714,196	2,982,031	1,467,560
Indiana	5,099,096	3,063,657	1,972,883	1,510,453	286,066	147,250	110,192	748,769	125,845	1,145,675	889,764
Iowa	3,270,832	1,996,971	853,848	523,397	180,037	193,276	151,369	720,883	147,115	778,956	494,905
Kansas	2,428,389	1,442,737	695,803	470,762	116,416	107,825	74,341	459,822	122,549	593,005	392,647
Kentucky	4,251,541	2,491,052	1,134,335	682,432	202,444	105,628	59,098	600,823	166,815	1,104,216	656,273
Louisiana	5,784,891	3,127,229	1,421,829	926,912	190,761	184,010	57,898	220,134	291,953	1,200,100	1,457,562
Maine	1,361,185	730,979	394,640	248,943	49,579	58,118	36,149	209,585	36,090	422,505	207,701
Maryland	5,591,135	3,193,087	1,403,046	797,397	192,032	119,532	90,848	1,354,613	148,857	1,301,191	1,096,857
Massachusetts	7,882,932	4,803,664	1,606,587	917,362	269,297	162,476	119,096	2,324,052	598,283	2,093,341	985,927
Michigan	11,440,971	6,307,161	2,616,857	1,843,651	421,922	316,622	244,743	2,126,630	952,280	3,227,867	1,905,943
Minnesota	6,094,728	3,799,371	1,528,231	875,008	258,868	231,721	169,701	1,549,121	325,295	1,444,213	851,144
Mississippi	2,723,626	1,462,293	980,569	767,072	101,656	113,501	48,981	168,471	70,987	874,946	386,387
Missouri	4,002,908	2,313,057	1,189,282	839,003	193,579	197,627	116,407	760,711	123,072	1,151,889	537,962
Montana	1,088,341	529,144	102,803	0	49,416	46,155	24,909	143,804	44,630	292,061	267,136
Nebraska	1,560,764	860,527	491,082	288,517	125,715	73,623	46,134	226,560	48,498	407,237	293,000
Nevada	1,102,274	745,460	637,592	375,973	55,704	84,173	32,783	0	0	230,684	126,130
New Hampshire	789,273	325,515	152,676	0	59,855	55,852	32,833	15,076	79,808	251,853	211,905
New Jersey	9,253,811	5,577,236	2,864,703	1,379,206	287,756	479,955	274,470	1,305,567	724,869	2,138,528	1,538,047

New Mexico	2,773,047	1,226,543	698,678	533,809	86,791	60,804	40,779	14,263	60,265	476,633	1,069,871
New York	26,512,744	15,438,003	5,232,121	3,196,779	443,825	533,706	334,280	8,034,066	1,342,051	8,390,965	2,683,776
North Carolina	6,123,494	3,790,035	1,673,132	779,512	372,159	286,649	160,141	1,449,370	277,460	1,536,436	797,023
North Dakota	1,142,455	532,631	219,232	146,935	34,711	48,452	29,647	35,342	37,734	269,401	340,423
Ohio	10,170,249	5,819,461	3,308,846	1,819,381	527,012	506,838	304,025	1,243,618	548,091	2,541,012	1,809,776
Oklahoma	4,237,497	2,712,960	906,874	481,996	137,724	230,882	175,643	641,428	139,022	794,874	729,663
Oregon	3,356,364	1,552,313	190,943	0	91,303	175,237	111,865	968,264	124,171	927,496	876,555
Pennsylvania	12,973,482	8,185,625	4,063,385	2,229,436	573,298	870,115	405,580	1,985,270	869,714	3,339,170	1,448,687
Rhode Island	1,421,454	674,792	365,753	199,809	48,659	23,825	17,868	215,156	52,524	393,168	353,494
South Carolina	3,343,611	1,959,205	1,073,137	646,544	213,882	81,413	44,763	641,838	131,546	824,236	560,170
South Dakota	793,458	328,785	282,915	178,687	55,609	27,395	15,919	0	1,041	252,321	212,352
Tennessee	3,952,564	2,146,242	1,629,914	1,117,859	280,145	205,169	118,283	44,469	206,835	1,264,630	541,692
Texas	14,691,385	9,099,849	5,696,833	3,480,790	496,415	914,070	340,972	0	0	2,776,697	2,814,839
Utah	1,862,191	950,869	513,248	387,624	83,615	38,531	23,018	331,145	40,894	564,007	347,315
Vermont	738,119	332,308	150,973	48,440	25,385	38,601	29,484	112,520	24,954	256,437	149,374
Virginia	5,771,565	3,235,829	1,356,653	670,512	325,384	164,762	113,197	1,446,187	176,965	1,371,167	1,164,569
Washington	5,620,729	3,528,362	2,546,054	1,892,066	261,403	198,870	114,336	0	0	1,355,331	737,036
West Virginia	2,467,841	1,468,886	1,028,556	781,223	95,287	80,123	55,553	305,964	34,400	680,247	318,708
Wisconsin	6,296,324	3,934,495	1,560,687	961,068	285,706	193,192	131,730	1,680,372	322,939	1,552,840	808,989
Wyoming	1,365,940	762,533	280,310	228,018	38,405	54,502	38,045	0	0	332,244	271,163

Source: U.S. Bureau of the Census, *State Government Finances in 1982.*

(a) Total general revenue equals total taxes plus intergovernmental revenue plus charges and miscellaneous revenue. Columns do not add to totals due to rounding.

Table 4

STATE GOVERNMENT EXPENDITURE, BY CHARACTRISTIC AND OBJECT AND BY STATE: 1982
(In thousands of dollars)

State	Intergovernmental expenditure	Direct expenditure Total	Current operation	Capital outlay Total	Construction	Land and existing structures	Equipment	Assistance and subsidies	Interest on debt	Insurance benefits and repayments	Exhibit: Total salaries and wages
All states	$98,742,976	$211,549,151	$133,152,143	$23,465,895	$19,560,179	$1,315,635	$2,590,081	$10,866,929	$9,400,451	$34,663,733	$56,626,523
Alabama	1,136,158	3,530,664	2,403,952	501,784	440,996	13,728	47,060	153,874	103,883	367,171	1,023,228
Alaska	992,519	2,288,366	1,301,947	552,330	422,079	76,620	53,631	44,605	250,017	139,467	643,396
Arizona	1,192,237	2,052,866	1,390,882	303,994	237,602	12,692	53,700	77,129	9,447	271,414	737,822
Arkansas	667,184	1,695,197	1,201,534	191,695	156,883	10,278	24,534	64,370	34,354	203,244	541,396
California	17,625,121	22,818,722	15,752,744	1,349,680	1,044,219	157,628	147,833	214,993	553,550	4,947,755	6,126,797
Colorado	1,200,839	2,434,526	1,719,850	210,975	149,580	25,445	35,950	37,133	47,009	419,559	894,216
Connecticut	760,415	3,233,326	2,013,715	243,488	214,435	10,352	18,701	239,845	291,076	445,202	879,276
Delaware	214,619	869,373	548,679	144,750	122,465	3,766	18,519	39,408	66,462	70,074	274,854
Florida	3,512,218	5,810,137	3,811,328	965,228	799,707	68,716	96,805	312,589	176,767	544,225	2,020,939
Georgia	1,781,763	4,225,312	2,737,945	741,852	687,117	3,841	50,894	193,688	68,017	483,810	1,184,181
Hawaii	27,875	1,966,484	1,287,272	264,299	216,437	11,531	36,331	118,352	128,139	168,422	698,531
Idaho	353,787	854,937	518,216	121,606	102,049	3,430	16,127	28,932	29,133	157,050	222,422
Illinois	3,725,170	10,413,067	5,695,034	921,933	807,514	29,452	84,967	1,217,734	471,080	2,107,286	2,005,986
Indiana	2,045,228	3,648,788	2,488,295	488,303	348,990	70,406	68,907	62,069	64,265	545,856	1,110,710
Iowa	1,262,391	2,640,792	1,771,205	315,421	246,306	14,525	54,590	167,108	28,878	358,180	850,587
Kansas	711,548	1,922,895	1,313,762	221,497	174,770	14,426	32,301	134,728	21,902	231,006	668,288
Kentucky	1,107,357	3,618,435	2,155,448	583,300	506,000	26,723	50,577	171,671	207,002	501,014	1,110,882
Louisiana	1,599,993	4,862,595	2,960,188	800,707	653,262	82,803	64,642	184,772	227,303	689,625	1,343,753
Maine	297,274	1,229,802	811,983	106,032	84,624	8,730	12,678	81,301	54,312	176,174	298,328
Maryland	1,708,142	4,552,163	2,742,940	656,624	583,756	14,519	58,349	289,917	207,116	655,566	1,094,976
Massachusetts	2,315,564	6,315,926	4,007,399	459,471	381,862	43,176	34,433	573,676	438,002	837,378	1,532,935
Michigan	3,824,824	10,172,005	6,143,349	540,792	449,187	33,859	57,746	1,105,955	244,614	2,137,295	2,432,073
Minnesota	3,016,693	3,907,995	2,764,308	384,896	310,840	31,214	42,842	58,327	161,021	539,443	1,252,430
Mississippi	948,128	2,090,718	1,472,868	256,559	205,317	15,596	35,646	99,291	42,331	219,669	543,022
Missouri	1,167,399	3,242,565	2,105,411	366,505	285,110	40,893	40,502	217,715	109,376	443,558	963,829
Montana	243,384	891,456	559,474	123,230	103,810	6,668	12,752	27,726	27,441	153,585	264,142
Nebraska	456,728	1,163,550	811,091	196,847	161,266	7,916	17,665	63,361	22,307	69,944	428,280
Nevada	139,824	956,419	511,777	160,192	140,767	9,003	10,422	26,580	26,580	242,142	250,418
New Hampshire	139,824	865,268	619,290	67,823	54,321	3,610	9,892	35,555	80,848	61,752	222,430
New Jersey	4,030,065	7,121,514	4,129,886	848,179	642,268	38,554	167,357	117,309	516,068	1,510,072	1,682,932

New Mexico	829,899	1,561,862	1,054,090	271,179	224,380	8,661	38,138	64,101	53,170	119,322	531,818
New York	11,849,950	18,309,809	11,227,434	2,048,891	1,883,165	61,320	104,406	531,163	1,979,238	2,523,083	4,554,980
North Carolina	2,440,069	4,410,634	2,951,352	451,477	359,968	4,508	87,001	213,074	124,329	670,402	1,491,274
North Dakota	355,610	835,312	589,905	133,486	114,738	5,459	13,289	21,264	18,502	72,155	246,611
Ohio	3,561,699	10,180,623	5,151,701	1,013,941	882,442	27,853	103,646	660,550	328,385	3,026,046	1,974,936
Oklahoma	1,160,761	3,001,587	2,093,800	386,219	308,313	23,672	54,234	156,123	67,636	297,809	867,871
Oregon	1,014,603	3,195,083	1,721,506	255,350	196,286	23,790	35,274	129,257	415,817	673,153	711,576
Pennsylvania	4,014,697	11,313,689	6,312,719	646,269	548,918	10,487	86,864	1,498,802	421,631	2,434,268	2,125,889
Rhode Island	235,816	1,392,226	882,912	89,387	60,415	13,916	15,056	89,974	126,822	203,131	347,940
South Carolina	1,024,500	3,085,692	2,084,758	355,125	291,566	12,882	50,677	107,993	181,648	356,168	1,015,102
South Dakota	160,201	668,761	464,750	96,479	75,135	6,395	14,949	24,634	48,411	34,487	196,391
Tennessee	1,067,709	3,230,672	2,126,706	421,208	343,842	34,178	43,188	95,986	101,440	485,332	930,910
Texas	4,252,176	9,899,633	6,629,706	1,807,734	1,533,548	69,901	204,285	349,407	150,222	962,564	2,838,467
Utah	525,165	1,469,011	974,752	206,607	162,300	11,722	32,585	61,942	36,127	189,583	446,192
Vermont	110,722	777,608	477,856	63,288	53,098	1,938	8,252	52,003	45,198	139,263	181,255
Virginia	1,658,077	4,640,257	3,346,338	510,633	413,596	35,221	61,816	219,939	160,958	402,389	1,665,776
Washington	2,128,066	5,127,471	2,829,684	696,509	588,462	36,029	72,018	291,587	144,447	1,165,244	1,295,399
West Virginia	674,956	2,166,723	1,258,180	315,859	281,037	13,164	21,658	62,524	100,518	429,642	548,570
Wisconsin	2,761,315	4,133,209	2,809,455	412,899	332,791	18,412	61,696	71,236	147,008	692,611	1,138,302
Wyoming	369,903	753,426	412,767	193,363	172,640	6,027	14,696	16,509	40,644	90,143	214,205

Source: U.S. Bureau of the Census, State Government Finances in 1982.

Table 5
STATE GENERAL EXPENDITURE IN TOTAL AND FOR SELECTED FUNCTIONS, BY STATE: 1982
(In thousands of dollars)

	Total general expenditure(a)	Education	Public welfare	Highways	Hospitals	Natural resources	Health	Corrections	Financial administration	General control	Employment security administration	Police
All states	$269,490,133	$102,984,441	$55,257,202	$25,131,092	$13,938,144	$5,485,297	$8,346,011	$5,889,202	$3,691,801	$2,721,564	$2,249,626	$2,730,261
Alabama	4,180,657	1,990,096	535,510	448,287	293,527	85,798	110,079	90,192	56,480	49,170	26,710	35,413
Alaska	3,034,203	812,820	174,964	259,070	16,765	205,407	81,690	61,498	42,900	60,248	18,579	40,834
Arizona	2,966,027	1,430,439	178,661	340,936	108,010	50,727	106,895	110,416	57,152	14,564	25,711	65,178
Arkansas	2,159,137	934,440	358,628	289,186	110,362	70,007	62,447	36,314	38,927	11,751	24,411	19,691
California	35,492,261	13,645,871	10,112,067	1,537,374	1,080,382	928,383	1,151,376	670,040	493,731	175,347	192,740	320,557
Colorado	3,215,806	1,453,517	552,968	337,405	180,433	106,382	81,371	67,562	53,545	45,717	18,431	35,602
Connecticut	3,498,262	982,480	763,521	281,164	260,111	27,322	86,560	85,445	48,602	63,488	41,886	37,707
Delaware	1,005,187	398,387	98,578	98,064	39,762	21,661	25,451	35,629	19,558	16,629	6,696	16,752
Florida	8,757,490	3,932,992	1,135,095	993,621	369,101	271,134	423,156	241,361	86,613	91,876	51,284	127,114
Georgia	5,523,265	2,370,270	914,303	840,843	271,958	131,307	226,824	160,374	70,427	27,879	46,215	46,579
Hawaii	1,825,937	644,041	290,303	94,446	82,471	46,299	68,318	24,974	21,244	60,232	14,039	1,453
Idaho	1,020,638	470,039	115,125	131,414	23,741	51,777	35,651	14,883	15,763	8,198	16,109	9,131
Illinois	12,030,951	4,412,716	3,142,803	1,168,806	473,148	132,092	301,721	268,871	177,201	104,235	112,388	105,539
Indiana	5,148,160	2,390,074	706,860	566,925	214,085	91,914	136,472	103,356	52,603	20,722	45,137	48,195
Iowa	3,448,835	1,525,793	586,329	471,451	242,404	85,610	35,051	62,369	38,309	18,861	31,624	23,702
Kansas	2,403,437	1,070,430	435,522	285,303	173,035	72,419	40,619	45,567	42,655	38,074	16,869	16,354
Kentucky	4,224,778	1,665,439	726,570	619,899	166,711	118,266	118,196	75,473	37,200	64,998	13,655	77,984
Louisiana	5,772,963	2,138,001	851,757	535,086	430,797	173,215	144,952	138,070	67,702	56,184	19,629	86,758
Maine	1,307,256	440,061	326,489	144,103	34,713	52,156	35,393	19,942	32,258	14,639	13,797	15,443
Maryland	5,416,462	1,735,656	911,444	756,396	348,377	84,476	174,916	186,690	80,924	53,133	28,767	139,121
Massachusetts	7,770,784	1,836,659	2,153,368	421,046	358,414	56,836	411,510	155,218	89,668	141,479	62,265	38,930
Michigan	11,506,487	3,864,659	3,254,048	894,366	690,902	140,663	552,998	242,133	97,702	118,763	149,814	115,239
Minnesota	6,385,245	2,784,446	1,175,282	553,520	295,925	155,837	88,150	70,557	63,685	39,783	51,484	44,309
Mississippi	2,724,684	1,147,964	440,642	354,509	142,039	87,987	68,295	40,858	24,343	11,061	38,173	29,858
Missouri	3,966,406	1,614,328	790,710	424,510	257,475	111,235	111,416	68,055	43,158	51,414	52,264	41,716
Montana	943,647	337,512	137,836	140,692	27,495	59,175	35,214	17,192	30,377	8,076	6,379	12,232
Nebraska	1,576,241	526,158	238,725	264,624	97,683	67,516	46,308	34,495	13,106	15,065	16,609	15,379
Nevada	1,109,878	431,320	106,798	122,700	23,781	23,589	27,228	51,943	31,147	7,474	17,423	10,318
New Hampshire	821,874	216,673	153,852	123,593	38,246	15,494	30,565	12,221	12,154	7,480	8,234	10,806
New Jersey	9,214,556	2,714,199	1,862,637	619,554	467,315	132,550	160,842	177,374	102,218	76,319	50,403	89,921

New Mexico	2,272,439	1,009,935	215,130	287,873	100,703	50,756	91,196	56,006	42,464	28,448	14,804	23,185
New York	25,532,765	7,752,257	6,736,380	1,214,221	1,910,267	131,885	752,809	635,475	389,641	561,525	216,972	155,485
North Carolina	6,180,301	3,030,321	790,161	555,696	353,433	150,316	189,565	217,702	52,968	80,069	31,908	64,098
North Dakota	1,118,767	448,593	104,494	147,760	53,540	43,017	20,853	10,388	14,263	9,278	4,911	4,987
Ohio	10,416,409	3,813,417	2,432,316	1,012,258	671,547	133,709	454,684	184,212	169,864	41,303	115,174	63,207
Oklahoma	3,696,802	1,744,930	695,616	426,541	226,678	68,052	82,348	78,897	54,269	25,661	28,626	35,656
Oregon	3,445,047	1,107,521	465,867	394,179	162,130	116,604	76,213	64,145	102,940	23,815	27,444	39,721
Pennsylvania	12,353,481	4,031,629	3,374,247	1,332,078	732,772	190,165	408,112	156,596	181,047	133,031	156,884	156,840
Rhode Island	1,402,142	398,184	357,077	56,645	102,814	11,227	49,344	25,319	23,652	25,320	16,108	13,502
South Carolina	3,216,183	1,541,587	470,366	247,822	201,444	77,713	120,637	78,062	43,338	22,089	33,459	30,042
South Dakota	794,475	233,587	109,090	129,822	24,562	41,509	22,387	8,194	18,714	12,100	10,883	6,912
Tennessee	3,813,049	1,541,746	662,529	510,449	215,056	68,665	126,960	103,700	42,571	20,228	44,101	27,684
Texas	13,189,245	6,749,901	1,622,657	1,963,494	812,489	227,367	256,237	311,808	154,470	64,594	114,883	102,493
Utah	1,756,141	926,614	213,426	178,629	80,293	47,564	47,381	36,425	26,804	13,022	23,589	17,843
Vermont	720,099	239,790	134,046	80,997	22,141	28,062	26,082	12,980	13,946	9,359	11,001	11,918
Virginia	5,682,647	2,240,740	888,732	677,121	470,384	73,947	186,116	226,760	106,761	68,298	39,901	177,008
Washington	5,893,401	2,966,916	863,114	626,319	170,997	167,210	155,217	165,331	76,264	40,109	56,184	49,435
West Virginia	2,351,487	935,591	271,400	436,707	90,380	57,265	68,260	16,526	37,835	25,295	22,592	20,848
Wisconsin	6,201,913	2,044,895	1,555,146	546,393	191,258	110,087	209,413	117,461	80,253	40,540	53,066	39,808
Wyoming	1,001,826	309,417	64,013	187,195	26,088	32,943	22,533	14,143	18,385	4,621	9,411	11,774

Source: U.S. Bureau of the Census, *State Government Finances in 1982*.

Note: Totals do not add, due to rounding.

(a) Does not represent sum of state figures because total includes miscellaneous expenditure not shown separately.

Table 6
STATE DEBT OUTSTANDING AT END OF FISCAL YEAR, BY STATE: 1982
(In thousands of dollars, except per capita amounts)

State	Total	Per capita	Long-term Total	Full faith and credit	Non-guaranteed	Short-term	Net long-term(a) Total	Full faith and credit
All states	$147,341,980	$ 650.38	$143,573,917	$51,529,485	$92,044,432	$3,768,063	$86,918,955	$39,788,000
Alabama	1,958,569	502.97	1,916,819	626,085	1,290,734	41,750	1,590,231	614,346
Alaska	3,700,774	9,205.91	3,700,774	842,413	2,858,361	0	2,561,476	842,000
Arizona	240,258	88.40	232,300	0	232,300	7,958	217,250	0
Arkansas	554,540	242.58	538,300	0	538,300	16,240	127,573	0
California	10,330,999	436.50	10,228,649	4,123,473	6,105,176	102,350	6,554,712	1,310,141
Colorado	741,305	256.51	736,048	0	736,048	5,257	261,356	0
Connecticut.........	4,620,575	1,486.67	4,492,006	2,035,546	2,456,460	128,569	2,295,143	1,859,213
Delaware	1,359,539	2,288.79	1,328,706	539,049	789,657	30,833	1,118,604	539,049
Florida	2,993,388	307.14	2,993,388	1,141,317	1,852,071	0	2,036,388	526,306
Georgia	1,645,941	301.29	1,645,941	866,886	779,055	0	1,230,579	829,198
Hawaii	2,109,692	2,186.21	2,056,240	1,464,487	591,753	53,452	1,785,827	1,461,102
Idaho	427,178	452.52	427,178	580	426,598	0	83,067	572
Illinois	7,470,299	653.74	7,229,616	3,054,200	4,175,416	240,683	4,204,641	2,891,127
Indiana............	1,024,784	186.66	894,327	0	894,327	130,457	637,442	0
Iowa	458,042	157.19	458,042	0	458,042	0	179,802	0
Kansas	397,481	168.14	397,481	27,800	369,681	0	342,333	27,800
Kentucky...........	2,659,592	726.66	2,655,262	245,525	2,409,737	4,330	1,713,525	239,561
Louisiana...........	4,146,609	985.88	4,098,781	2,082,414	2,016,367	47,828	2,875,867	2,079,156
Maine	860,782	765.14	858,635	252,537	606,098	2,147	345,387	252,537
Maryland	4,212,457	998.92	4,042,253	2,219,010	1,823,243	170,204	2,744,667	2,164,806
Massachusetts.......	6,420,794	1,119.19	6,150,152	3,059,100	3,091,052	270,642	3,729,963	3,040,898
Michigan	3,859,420	416.69	3,816,800	594,610	3,222,190	42,620	2,200,671	578,581
Minnesota	2,659,518	652.48	2,621,107	969,049	1,652,058	38,411	1,046,428	823,392
Mississippi	748,192	296.78	745,868	696,703	49,165	2,324	704,886	663,123
Missouri...........	1,836,490	373.50	1,786,490	78,135	1,708,355	50,000	1,154,886	68,534
Montana	399,215	507.26	399,215	42,220	356,995	0	178,054	41,620
Nebraska	295,479	188.20	295,479	0	295,479	0	22,203	0
Nevada.............	648,313	810.39	648,313	188,006	460,307	0	354,166	155,996
New Hampshire	1,270,612	1,379.60	1,205,612	318,600	887,012	65,000	691,054	308,787
New Jersey	8,795,893	1,194.28	8,756,578	2,165,796	6,590,782	39,315	5,954,857	2,128,730
New Mexico	823,500	632.00	820,842	22,021	798,821	2,658	277,655	15,802
New York	25,813,504	1,470.18	25,301,009	3,895,573	21,405,436	512,495	15,421,802	3,197,708
North Carolina	1,591,067	270.50	1,586,502	905,848	680,654	4,565	1,205,043	875,871
North Dakota	324,836	497.45	316,745	8,490	308,255	8,091	44,605	0
Ohio	4,999,271	462.98	4,686,353	2,303,730	2,382,623	312,918	4,313,209	2,298,540
Oklahoma	1,171,937	387.42	1,171,884	157,794	1,014,090	53	967,257	65,076
Oregon	6,220,641	2,362.57	6,130,680	5,583,406	547,274	89,961	298,924	182,520
Pennsylvania.........	6,244,149	526.31	6,081,550	3,820,515	2,261,035	162,599	5,155,536	3,769,171
Rhode Island	1,987,036	2,098.24	1,985,344	256,225	1,729,119	1,692	573,178	255,725
South Carolina	3,077,471	985.74	2,817,021	557,823	2,259,198	260,450	1,790,295	312,786
South Dakota	708,707	1,025.63	706,810	0	706,810	1,897	48,424	0
Tennessee	1,587,121	345.70	1,350,106	617,340	732,766	237,015	673,588	519,718
Texas	2,458,997	172.82	2,458,997	836,705	1,622,292	0	1,354,875	145,808
Utah	722,510	494.53	722,510	81,490	641,020	0	324,258	69,329
Vermont	673,362	1,317.73	668,377	268,493	399,884	4,985	333,928	268,493
Virginia	2,614,239	488.92	2,389,145	229,139	2,160,006	225,094	392,931	200,057
Washington..........	2,492,091	603.12	2,084,032	1,739,506	344,526	408,059	1,811,234	1,739,506
West Virginia	1,804,135	925.20	1,794,974	874,256	920,718	9,161	992,488	719,181
Wisconsin	2,647,931	562.67	2,611,931	1,737,590	874,341	36,000	1,925,227	1,706,134
Wyoming	532,745	1,133.50	532,745	0	532,745	0	71,460	0

Source: U.S Bureau of the Census, *State Government Finances in 1982.*

(a) Long-term debt outstanding minus long-term debt offsets.

Note: Debt figures include revenue bonds and other special obligations of state agencies as well as state general obligations.

2. Taxation

RECENT TRENDS IN STATE TAXATION

By John Gambill

More state tax increases were enacted during 1982 and 1983 than during any biennium in the past decade. Nineteen states increased sales tax rates, 17 states increased personal income tax rates, 16 increased corporation income tax rates, 26 raised motor fuel tax rates, 21 increased cigarette tax rates and 15 increased taxes on alcoholic beverages.

General Sales Taxes

In 1982, sales tax rates were increased in Florida (4 to 5 percent), Indiana (4 to 5 percent), Minnesota (5 to 6 percent), Missouri (3.125 to 4.125 percent), Mississippi (5 to 5.5 percent, effective January 1984), Nebraska (3 to 3.5 percent), New Jersey (5 to 6 percent), Vermont (3 to 4 percent) and Wisconsin (4 to 5 percent). Washington reduced its rate from 5.5 to 5.4 percent, but suspended its exemption for food.

In 1983, sales tax rates were increased in Arizona (4 to 5 percent), Arkansas (3 to 4 percent), Colorado (3 to 3.5 percent), Idaho (from 3 to 4 percent, and then by separate action to 4.5 percent), Illinois (from 4 to 5 percent), Iowa (from 3 to 4 percent), Mississippi (from 5 to 6 percent), Nebraska (from 3.5 to 4 percent), New Mexico (3.5 to 3.75 percent), North Dakota (from 3 to 4 percent), Utah (from 4 to 4.125 and then to 4.625 percent) and Washington (from 5.4 to 6.5 percent).

Illinois and Nebraska exempted food from their sales taxes in 1983.

Personal Income Taxes

1982 Rate Increases. Alabama increased its income tax rates and Indiana raised its rate from 1.9 to 3 percent. Michigan raised its rate from 4.6 to 5.6 percent for six months. Minnesota imposed a 7 percent surtax for 1982 and 5 percent for 1983. Mississippi imposed a 5 percent rate on incomes over $10,000. Nebraska increased its tax from 15 to 18 percent of federal tax liability. New Jersey imposed a 3.5 percent rate on income over $50,000. Ohio raised the tax rate on incomes over $80,000 and imposed a 25 percent surtax. Oregon increased its tax rates and Rhode Island increased its tax from 19.24 to 21.9 percent of federal tax liability. Vermont increased its tax from 23 to 24 percent of federal tax liability.

1983 Rate Increases. Illinois increased its tax from 2.5 to 3 percent. Michigan increased its tax from 4.6 to 6.35 percent. Minnesota increased its surtax from 5 to 10 percent. Nebraska increased its rate from 18 to 20 percent of federal tax liability. New Mexico increased its tax by 30 percent. North Dakota increased its tax from 7.5 to 10.5 percent of federal tax liability. Ohio revised its brackets from a range of .5-5 percent to .95-9.5 percent. Pennsylvania raised its tax from 2.2 to 2.45 percent. Rhode Island raised its rate from 21.9 to 27.5 percent of federal tax liability for the first half of 1983 and to 26 percent thereafter. Vermont raised its tax from 24 to 26 percent of federal tax liability. West Virginia imposed a 12 percent surtax for incomes over $10,000 and also raised its rates for the higher brackets. Wisconsin imposed a 10 percent surtax.

In 1982, Connecticut repealed its unincorporated business tax. In 1983, it increased the rate of its tax on dividends and capital gains, extended the tax to include interest, and increased the exemption from $20,000 to $50,000.

Corporation Income Taxes

1982 Rate Increases. Indiana increased its rate from 6 to 7 percent. Iowa increased the tax on incomes over $250,000 from 10 to 12 percent. Mississippi imposed a 5 percent rate on incomes over $10,000. Nebraska increased its rates from 3.75 percent on the first $25,000 and 4.125 percent on additional amounts to 4.5 percent on the first $50,000 and 6.3 percent on additional amounts. Ohio extended its 5.75 percent surtax for another year. Wisconsin imposed a 10 percent surtax.

1983 Rate Increases. Connecticut increased its rate from 10 to 11.5 percent. Idaho raised its rate from 6.7 percent (6.5 for income over $250,000) to 7.7 percent. Illinois increased its rate from 4 to 4.8 percent. Maine increased its rates for larger incomes and reduced them for smaller incomes. Nebraska increased its rates from 4.5 and 6.3 percent to 5 and 7 percent. New Hampshire imposed a 19.5 percent surtax for the fiscal year

John Gambill is Senior Research Associate and Director of Publications, Federation of Tax Administrators.

ending June 30, 1984, and 13.5 percent for the following year. New Mexico enacted a 20 percent increase in its corporate tax. North Dakota raised its rate range from 2-7 percent to 3-10.5 percent. Ohio increased its rates from 4.6 and 8.7 percent to 5.1 and 9.2 percent. Rhode Island raised its rate from 8 to 9 percent. Utah increased its rate from 4 to 4.65 percent. West Virginia increased the rate on income over $50,000 from 6 to 7 percent and imposed a 15 percent surtax. Wisconsin extended its 10 percent surtax. Colorado delayed a scheduled tax reduction for two years.

Motor Fuel Taxes

In 1982, motor fuel tax rates were increased in Arizona (8 to 10 cents per gallon, with subsequent increases to 12 and 13 cents), Idaho (11.5 to 12.5 cents), Kentucky (9.5 to 10 cents, via a new minimum for its variable-rate tax), Maryland (9 to 11 cents, and then to 13.5 cents) and Michigan (11 to 13 cents). Vermont imposed a 14 cents per gallon tax on diesel fuel, which had previously not been taxed.

In 1983, motor fuel taxes were increased by 18 states: Colorado (9 to 12 cents for gasoline, 9 to 13 cents for diesel fuel), Connecticut (11 to 14 cents), Idaho (12.5 to 14.5 cents), Illinois (7.5 to 11 cents, with subsequent increases to 13 cents and with increases to 15.5 cents for diesel fuel), Kansas (8 to 10 cents, with a subsequent increase to 11 cents for gasoline and with an increase from 10 to 12 to 13 cents for diesel fuel), Maine (9 to 14 cents), Massachusetts (9.9 to 11 cents, via a new minimum for its variable-rate tax), Minnesota (13 to 16 to 17 cents), Montana (9 to 15 cents for gasoline, 11 to 17 cents for diesel fuel), North Dakota (8 to 13 cents), Oregon (8 to 9 to 10 cents), Pennsylvania (11 to 12 cents), Rhode Island (11 to 13 cents, via a new minimum for its variable-rate tax), Vermont (from 11 to 13 cents for gasoline but no increase in the 14 cent diesel fuel tax), Washington (from 12 to 16 to 18 cents, repealing its variable-rate law) and Wisconsin (13 to 15 to 16 cents).

Variable-rate Laws. Provisions for automatic increases in motor fuel tax rates were enacted in Florida, Kansas, Maryland, Michigan, West Virginia and Wisconsin. In Florida and West Virginia, these provisions took the form of sales taxes based on the average price of the fuel. Michigan and Wisconsin followed Ohio in basing their variable-rate provisions on the cost of highway maintenance and the amount of fuel sold in the state. The Florida, Michigan and West Virginia enactments resulted in immediate

rate increases. The variable-rate laws resulted in rate increases in Nebraska, New Mexico, Ohio and the District of Columbia.

Gross Receipts Taxes. Rhode Island and Virginia imposed taxes on the gross receipts of petroleum companies. New York revised its gross receipts franchise tax. Pennsylvania raised the rate of its tax.

Cigarette and Tobacco Taxes

In 1982, cigarette tax rates were increased in nine states: Michigan (11 to 21 cents per pack), Missouri (9 to 13 cents), Nebraska (14 to 18 cents), New Jersey (from 19 to 24 cents), Oregon (from 16 to 19 cents), Rhode Island (from 18 to 23 cents), Utah (10 to 12 cents), Washington (20 to 23 cents) and Wisconsin (from 20 to 25 cents). New Jersey also provided that beginning January 1, 1983, the cigarette tax will be redetermined semiannually based on the wholesale price of cigarettes. Washington also increased its tax on other tobacco products.

In 1983, cigarette tax rates were increased in 13 states: Arkansas (from 17.75 to 21 cents), Colorado (from 10 to 15 cents), Connecticut (from 21 to 26 cents), Kansas (from 11 to 16 cents), Maine (from 16 to 20 cents), Massachusetts (from 21 to 26 cents), Montana (12 to 16 cents), Nevada (10 to 15 cents), New Hampshire (12 to 17 cents), New Jersey (from 24 to 25 cents, by operation of the variable-rate provision described above), New York (15 to 21 cents), North Dakota (12 to 18 cents) and Vermont (12 to 17 cents). Nevada imposed a 30 percent tax on the wholesale price of tobacco products other than cigarettes.

Alcoholic Beverage Taxes

In 1982, taxes on one or more categories of alcoholic beverages were increased in Alabama (beer), Kentucky (beer, wine and spirits), Utah (wine and spirits), Virginia (spirits) and Washington (beer and wine).

In 1983, 11 states increased their taxes on one or more categories of alcoholic beverages. Of these, seven increased the rates on beer, wine and spirits: Alaska, Connecticut, Florida, Kansas, New Mexico, New York and South Carolina. States that confined their increases to one or two categories of alcohol were: Arkansas (beer and spirits), Nevada (beer and wine), New Hampshire (beer) and Utah (beer).

Table 1
AGENCIES ADMINISTERING MAJOR STATE TAXES
(As of January 1, 1984)

State or other jurisdiction	Income	Sales	Gasoline	Motor vehicle
Alabama	Dept. of Rev.	Dept. of Rev.	Dept. of Rev.	Dept. of Rev.
Alaska	Dept. of Rev.	---	Dept. of Rev.	Dept. of Pub. Sfty.
Arizona	Dept. of Rev.	Dept. of Rev.	Dept. of Trans.	Dept. of Trans.
Arkansas	Dept. of Fin. & Admin.	Dept. of Fin. & Admin.	Dept. of Fin. & Admin.	Dept. of Fin. & Admin.
California	Fran. Tax Bd.	Bd. of Equal.	Bd. of Equal.	Dept. of Mot. Veh.
Colorado	Dept. of Rev.	Dept. of Rev.	Dept. of Rev.	Dept. of Rev.
Connecticut	Dept. of Rev. Serv.	Dept. of Rev. Serv.	Dept. of Rev. Serv.	Dept. of Mot. Veh.
Delaware	Div. of Rev.	---	Dept. of Pub. Sfty.	Dept. of Pub. Sfty.
Florida	Dept. of Rev.	Dept. of Rev.	Dept. of Rev.	Div. of Mot. Veh.
Georgia	Dept. of Rev.	Dept. of Rev.	Dept. of Rev.	Dept. of Rev.
Hawaii	Dept. of Tax.	Dept. of Tax.	Dept. of Tax.	County Treasr.
Idaho	Dept. of Rev./Tax.	Dept. of Rev./Tax.	Dept. of Rev./Tax.	Trans. Dept.
Illinois	Dept. of Rev.	Dept. of Rev.	Dept. of Rev.	Secy. of State
Indiana	Dept. of Rev.	Dept. of Rev.	Dept. of Rev.	Bur. of Mot. Veh.
Iowa	Dept. of Rev.	Dept. of Rev.	Dept. of Rev.	Dept. of Trans.
Kansas	Dept. of Rev.	Dept. of Rev.	Dept. of Rev.	Dept. of Rev.
Kentucky	Rev. Cabinet	Rev. Cabinet	Rev. Cabinet	Trans. Cabinet
Louisiana	Dept. of Rev./Tax.	Dept. of Rev./Tax.	Dept. of Rev./Tax.	Dept. of Pub. Sfty.
Maine	Bur. of Tax.	Bur. of Tax.	Bur. of Tax.	Secy. of State
Maryland	Comptroller	Comptroller	Comptroller	Dept. of Trans.
Massachusetts	Dept. of Rev.	Dept. of Rev.	Dept. of Rev.	Reg. of Mot. Veh.
Michigan	Dept. of Treas.	Dept. of Treas.	Dept. of Treas.	Secy. of State
Minnesota	Dept. of Rev.	Dept. of Rev.	Dept. of Rev.	Dept. of Pub. Sfty.
Mississippi	Tax Com.	Tax Com.	Tax Com.	Tax Com.
Missouri	Dept. of Rev.	Dept. of Rev.	Dept. of Rev.	Dept. of Rev.
Montana	Dept. of Rev.	---	Dept. of Rev.	Div. of Mot. Veh.
Nebraska	Dept. of Rev.	Dept. of Rev.	Dept. of Rev.	Dept. of Mot. Veh.
Nevada	---	Dept. of Tax.	Dept. of Rev.	Dept. of Mot. Veh.
New Hampshire	Dept. of Rev. Admin.	---	Dept. of Sfty.	Dept. of Sfty.
New Jersey	Dept. of Treas.	Dept. of Treas.	Dept. of Treas.	Dept. of Law & Pub. Sfty.
New Mexico	Tax & Rev. Dept.	Tax & Rev. Dept.	Tax & Rev. Dept.	Trans. Dept.
New York	Dept. of Tax. & Fin.	Dept. of Tax. & Fin.	Dept. of Tax. & Fin.	Dept. of Mot. Veh.
North Carolina	Dept. of Rev.	Dept. of Rev.	Dept. of Rev.	Dept. of Trans.
North Dakota	Tax Commr.	Tax Commr.	Tax Commr.	Dept. of Mot. Veh.
Ohio	Dept. of Tax.	Dept. of Tax.	Dept. of Tax.	Bur. of Mot. Veh.
Oklahoma	Tax Com.	Tax Com.	Tax Com.	Tax Com.
Oregon	Dept. of Rev.	---	Dept. of Trans.	Dept. of Trans.
Pennsylvania	Dept. of Rev.	Dept. of Rev.	Dept. of Rev.	Dept. of Trans.
Rhode Island	Dept. of Admin.	Dept. of Admin.	Dept. of Admin.	Dept. of Trans.
South Carolina	Tax Com.	Tax Com.	Tax Com.	Dept. of Hwy./Pub. Trans.
South Dakota	---	Dept. of Rev.	Dept. of Rev.	Dept. of Pub. Sfty.
Tennessee	Dept. of Rev.	Dept. of Rev.	Dept. of Rev.	Dept. of Rev.
Texas	---	Comptroller	Comptroller	Dept. Hwy./Pub. Trans.
Utah	Tax. Com.	Tax Com.	Tax Com.	Tax Com.
Vermont	Commr. of Taxes	Commr. of Taxes	Commr. of Taxes	Mot. Veh. Dept.
Virginia	Dept. of Tax.	Dept. of Tax.	Div. of Mot. Veh.	Div. of Mot. Veh.
Washington	---	Dept. of Rev.	Dept. of Licensing	Dept. of Licensing
West Virginia	Tax Dept.	Tax Dept.	Tax Dept.	Dept. of Mot. Veh.
Wisconsin	Dept. of Rev.	Dept. of Rev.	Dept. of Rev.	Dept. of Trans.
Wyoming	---	Dept. of Rev. & Tax.	Dept. of Rev. & Tax.	Dept. of Rev. & Tax.
Dist. of Col.	Dept. of Fin. & Rev.	Dept. of Fin. & Rev.	Dept. of Fin. & Rev.	Dept. of Trans.

Source: The Federation of Tax Administrators

AGENCIES ADMINISTERING MAJOR STATE TAXES—Continued
(As of January 1, 1984)

State or other jurisdiction	Tobacco	Death	Alcoholic beverage	Number of agencies
Alabama	Dept. of Rev.	Dept. of Rev.	Al. Bev. Cont. Bd.	2
Alaska	Dept. of Rev.	Dept. of Rev.	Dept. of Rev.	2
Arizona	Dept. of Rev.	Dept. of Rev.	Dept. of Rev.	2
Arkansas	Dept. of Fin. & Admin.	Dept. of Fin. & Admin.	Dept. of Fin. & Admin.	1
California	Bd. of Equal.	Controller	Bd. of Equal.	4
Colorado	Dept. of Rev.	Dept. of Rev.	Dept. of Rev.	1
Connecticut	Dept. of Rev. Serv.	Dept. of Rev. Serv.	Dept. of Rev. Serv.	2
Delaware	Div. of Rev.	Div. of Rev.	Div. of Rev.	2
Florida	Dept. of Bus. Reg.	Dept. of Rev.	Dept. of Bus. Reg.	3
Georgia	Dept. of Rev.	Dept. of Rev.	Dept. of Rev.	1
Hawaii	Dept. of Tax.	Dept. of Tax.	Dept. of Tax.	2
Idaho	Dept. of Rev./Tax.	Dept. of Rev./Tax.	Dept. of Rev./Tax.	2
Illinois	Dept. of Rev.	Atty. Gen.	Dept. of Rev.	3
Indiana	Dept. of Rev.	Dept. of Rev.	Dept. of Rev.	2
Iowa	Dept. of Rev.	Dept. of Rev.	Dept. of Rev.	2
Kansas	Dept. of Rev.	Dept. of Rev.	Dept. of Rev.	1
Kentucky	Rev. Cabinet	Rev. Cabinet	Rev. Cabinet	2
Louisiana	Dept. of Rev./Tax.	Dept. of Rev./Tax.	Dept. of Rev./Tax.	2
Maine	Bur. of Tax.	Bur. of Tax.	Liquor Com.	3
Maryland	Comptroller	Local	Comptroller	3
Massachusetts	Dept. of Rev.	Dept. of Rev.	Dept. of Rev.	2
Michigan	Dept. of Treas.	Dept. of Treas.	Liquor Contr. Com.	3
Minnesota	Dept. of Rev.	Dept. of Rev.	Dept. of Rev.	2
Mississippi	Tax Com.	Tax Com.	Tax Com.	1
Missouri	Dept. of Rev.	Dept. of Rev.	Dept. of Rev.	1
Montana	Dept. of Rev.	Dept. of Rev.	Dept. of Rev.	2
Nebraska	Dept. of Rev.	Dept. of Rev.	Liquor Cont. Com.	3
Nevada	Dept. of Tax.	. . .	Dept. of Tax	2
New Hampshire	Dept. of Rev. Admin.	Dept. of Rev. Admin.	Liquor Com.	3
New Jersey	Dept. of Treas.	Dept. of Treas.	Dept. of Treas.	2
New Mexico	Tax & Rev. Dept.	Tax & Rev. Dept.	Tax & Rev. Dept.	2
New York	Dept. of Tax. & Fin.	Dept. of Tax. & Fin.	Dept. of Tax. & Fin.	2
North Carolina	Dept. of Rev.	Dept. of Rev.	Dept. of Rev.	2
North Dakota	Tax Commr.	Tax Commr.	Treasurer	3
Ohio	Dept. of Tax.	Dept. of Tax.	Dept. of Tax.	2
Oklahoma	Tax Com.	Tax Com.	Tax Com.	1
Oregon	Dept. of Rev.	Dept. of Rev.	Liquor Cont. Com.	3
Pennsylvania	Dept. of Rev.	Dept. of Rev.	Dept. of Rev.	2
Rhode Island	Dept. of Admin.	Dept. of Admin.	Dept. of Admin.	2
South Carolina	Tax Com.	Tax Com.	Tax Com.	2
South Dakota	Dept. of Rev.	Dept. of Rev.	Dept. of Rev.	2
Tennessee	Dept. of Rev.	Dept. of Rev.	Dept. of Rev.	1
Texas	Comptroller	Comptroller	Al. Bev. Com.	3
Utah	Tax Com.	Tax Com.	Tax Com.	1
Vermont	Commr. of Taxes	Commr. of Taxes	Commr. of Taxes	2
Virginia	Dept. of Tax.	Dept. of Tax.	Dept. of Tax.	2
Washington	Dept. of Rev.	Dept. of Rev.	Liquor Cont. Bd.	3
West Virginia	Tax Dept.	Tax Dept.	Al. Bev. Cont. Commr.	3
Wisconsin	Dept. of Rev.	Dept. of Rev.	Dept. of Rev.	2
Wyoming	Dept. of Rev. & Tax.	Dept. of Rev. & Tax.	Liquor Com.	2
Dist. of Col.	Dept. of Fin. & Rev.	Dept. of Fin. & Rev.	Dept. of Fin. & Rev.	2

Table 2
FOOD AND DRUG SALES TAX EXEMPTIONS
(As of January 1, 1984)

State or other jurisdiction	Tax rate	Exemptions Food	Exemptions Pre-scription drugs	Related income tax credit	State or other jurisdiction	Tax rate	Exemptions Food	Exemptions Pre-scription drugs	Related income tax credit
Alabama	4		★		New Jersey	6	★	★	
Arizona	5	★	★		New Mexico	3.75			★
Arkansas	4		★		New York	4	★	★	
California	4.75	★	★		North Carolina	3		★	
Colorado	3.5	★	★		North Dakota	4	★	★	
Connecticut	7.5	★	★		Ohio	5	★	★	
Florida	5	★	★		Oklahoma	2		★	
Georgia	3				Pennsylvania	6	★	★	
Hawaii	4			★	Rhode Island	6	★	★	
Idaho	4.5		★	★	South Carolina	4		★	
Illinois	5	★	★		South Dakota	4		★	
Indiana	5	★	★		Tennessee	4.5		★	
Iowa	4	★	★		Texas	4	★	★	
Kansas	3		★		Utah	4.625		★	
Kentucky	5	★	★		Vermont	4	★	★	★
Louisiana	3	★	★		Virginia	3		★	
Maine	5	★	★		Washington	6.5	★	★	
Maryland	5	★	★		West Virginia	5	★	★	
Massachusetts	5	★	★		Wisconsin	5	★	★	
Michigan	4	★	★		Wyoming	3		★	
Minnesota	6	★	★		Dist. of Col.	6	★	★	
Mississippi	6		★						
Missouri	4.125		★						
Nebraska	4	★	★						
Nevada	5.75	★	★						

Source: The Federation of Tax Administrators (based on legislation enacted at 1983 session).

Table 3
STATE EXCISE RATES
(As of January 1, 1984)

State or other jurisdiction	Sales and gross receipts (percent)	Cigarettes (cents per pack)	Distilled spirits(b) (dollars per gallon)	Motor fuel(a) (cents per gallon)			
				Gasoline	Diesel	Liquefied petroleum gas	Gasohol
Alabama	4	16	---	11	12	No tax	8
Alaska	---	8	5.60	8	---	No tax	No tax
Arizona	5(c)	13	2.50	12	---	---	---
Arkansas	4	21	2.50	9.5	10.5	7.5	No tax
California	4.75	10	2.00(d)	9	---	6	---
Colorado	3.5	15	2.28(e)	12	13	No tax	7
Connecticut	7.5	26	3.00	14	---	---	13
Delaware	---	14	2.25	11	---	---	---
Florida	5(g)	21	6.50(h)	9.7(f)	---	---	4
Georgia	3	12	3.79(e)	7.5	---	---	---
Hawaii	4(i)	40% of wholesale price	20% of wholesale price	8.5	---	6	---
Idaho	4.5	9.1	---	14.5	---	---	10.5
Illinois	5	12	2.00	11	13.5	---	---
Indiana	5(j)	10.5	2.68	11.1	---	---	---
Iowa	4	18	---	13	15.5	---	10
Kansas	3	16	2.50	11	13	10	6
Kentucky	5	3.1	1.92	10(k)	---	---	6.5
Louisiana	3	11	2.50(e)	8	---	---	No tax
Maine	5	20	---	14	---	---	---
Maryland	5	13	1.50(e)	13.5	---	---	10.5
Massachusetts	5	26	4.05	11	---	6.7	---
Michigan	4	21	---	15	---	---	11
Minnesota	6(l)	18	4.39(e)	17	---	---	9
Mississippi	6(m)	11	---	9	10	8	---
Missouri	4.125	13	2.00	7	---	---	---
Montana	---	16	---	15	17	No tax	8
Nebraska	4	18	2.75	15.4	---	---	10.4
Nevada	5.75(n)	15	2.05	12(o)	---	---	11
New Hampshire	---	17	---	14	---	---	9
New Jersey	6	25	2.80	8	---	4	---
New Mexico	3.75	12	3.94(e)	11	---	---	No tax
New York	4	21	4.09(e)	8	10	---	---
North Carolina	3(p)	2	---	12	---	---	11
North Dakota	4(q)	18	4.05	13	---	---	8
Ohio	5	14	---	12	---	---	8.5
Oklahoma	2	18	4.00	6.58	---	---	---
Oregon	---	19	---	9	---	---	---
Pennsylvania	6	18	---	12	---	---	---
Rhode Island	6	23	2.50	13	---	---	---
South Carolina	4	7	2.96(e,r)	13	---	---	---
South Dakota	4	15	3.80	13	---	11	9
Tennessee	4.5(s)	13	4.00	9(t)	---	---	5
Texas	4	18.5	2.00	5	6.5	---	No tax
Utah	4.625	12	---	11	---	---	6
Vermont	4	17	---	13	14	No tax	---
Virginia	3	2.5	---	11(u)	---	---	3
Washington	6.5(v)	23	---	16	---	No tax	13.44
West Virginia	5(w)	17	---	15.35(f)	---	---	---
Wisconsin	5	25	3.25(e)	15	---	---	---
Wyoming	3	8	---	8	No tax	No tax	4
Dist. of Col.	6(x)	13	1.50	14.8	No tax	No tax	---

Source: The Federation of Tax Administrators (based on legislation enacted at the 1983 sessions).

Key:

. . .—Not applicable

(a) Under motor fuel, a dash indicates the tax is the same as on gasoline. Thirteen states and the District of Columbia have variable rate motor fuel taxes, under which the motor fuel tax rate is periodically changed by administrative action according to a statutory formula. The states that have these provisions, the variable on which the formula is based, and the dates that the rate changes become effective are: Indiana, retail price of motor fuel, January 1 and July 1. Kansas, retail price of motor fuel, July 1, beginning 1985. Kentucky, wholesale price of motor fuel, January 1, April 1, July 1 and October 1. Maryland, wholesale price of motor fuel, January 1 and July 1, beginning July 1, 1984. Massachusetts, wholesale price of motor fuel, January 1, April 1, July 1 and October 1. Michigan, highway maintenance costs and fuel consumption, January 1. Nebraska, price of fuel purchased by state government, January 1, April 1, July 1 and October 1. New Mexico, wholesale price of motor fuel, July 1. Ohio, highway maintenance costs and fuel consumption, March 1. Rhode Island, wholesale price of motor fuel, January 1, April 1, July 1 and October 1. Wisconsin, highway maintenance costs and fuel consumption, April 1, beginning in 1985. District of Columbia, consumer price index for Washington, D.C., June 1. See also Florida and West Virginia.

Connecticut, New York, Pennsylvania, Rhode Island and Virginia have gross receipts or franchise taxes on oil companies, which are not covered in this table.

(b) Seventeen states have liquor monopoly systems (Alabama, Idaho, Iowa, Maine, Michigan, Mississippi, Montana, New Hampshire, Ohio, Oregon, Pennsylvania, Utah, Vermont, Virginia, Washington, West Virginia and Wyoming). (North Carolina has county-operated stores on a local option basis.) Some of the monopoly states impose taxes, generally expressed in terms of percentage of retail price. Only gallonage taxes imposed by states with license systems are reported in the table. Excise tax rates shown are general rates; some states tax distilled spirits manufactured in the state from state-grown products at lower rates.

(c) Arizona: This rate is for retailers. Selected businesses are taxed at rates ranging from 0.46875 to 5 percent.

(d) California: If not over 50 percent alcohol by weight. If over 50 percent, $4.00 per gallon.

(e) In several states, the tax rate is expressed in metric units: Colorado—$0.6026 per liter; Georgia—$1.00 per liter; Louisiana—$0.66 per liter; Maryland—$0.3963 per liter; Minnesota—$1.16 per liter; New Mexico—$1.04 per liter; New York—$1.08 per liter; South Carolina—$0.7828925 per liter (includes 9 percent surcharge); and Wisconsin—$0.8586 per liter. On gallon equals 3,7854 liters.

(f) The rates shown for Florida and West Virginia include motor fuel sales tax imposed on a cents-per-gallon basis. Eight other states impose a sales tax based on the actual selling price.

(g) Florida: Self-propelled or power-driven farm equipment is taxed at 3 percent.

(h) Florida: On beverages containing 14 to 48 percent alcohol. The tax rate on beverages containing more than 48 percent alcohol is $9.53 per gallon.

(i) Hawaii: Wholesalers and manufacturers, 0.5 percent; retailers, 4 percent.

(j) Indiana: In addition to the 4 percent sales tax, a gross income tax is imposed, under which wholesale and retail sales are taxed at 0.325 percent in 1984. Thereafter, the gross income tax will be reduced annually until 2010, when it goes out of existence.

(k) Kentucky: Heavy equipment motor carriers pay a 12.2 cents per gallon tax on a use basis.

(l) Minnesota: Farm machinery is taxed at 4 percent.

(m) Mississippi: Among other rates imposed under the tax: aircraft, automobiles, trucks and truck tractors, 3 percent; manufacturing or processing machinery and farm tractors, 1.0 percent; contractors (on compensation exceeding $10,000), 2.5 percent.

(n) Nevada: Includes mandatory, statewide, state-collected 3.75 percent county and school sales tax.

(o) Nevada: Includes uniform local tax.

(p) North Carolina: Motor vehicles, boats, railway cars and locomotives, and airplanes, 2 percent with a maximum tax of $300. A tax of 1 percent is imposed on various items used in agriculture and industry. On some items subject to the 1 percent rate, the maximum tax is $80 per article.

(q) North Dakota: The tax on farm machinery, agricultural irrigation equipment and mobile homes is 2 percent. A 5 percent tax is imposed on alcoholic beverages.

(r) South Carolina: Includes 9 percent surtax. In addition, there is a tax of $5.84 ($5.36 plus 9 percent surtax) per case on wholesale sales.

(s) Tennessee: The tax on water sold to or used by manufacturers is 1 percent. The tax on various fuels is 1.5 percent.

(t) Tennessee: Also subject to special privilege tax of 1.0 cents per gallon.

(u) Virginia: A 13 cents per gallon tax is imposed on motor carriers of property on a use basis.

(v) Washington: Also has a gross income tax with rates varying from 0.01 percent to 1 percent according to type of business. Retailers are subject to a 0.4708 percent tax under the business and occupation tax.

(w) West Virginia: Sales of mobile homes to be used by purchasers as their principal year-round residence and dwelling are taxed at 3 percent. West Virginia also has a gross income tax at rates ranging from 0.27 to 8.63 percent, according to type of business. Retailers are subject to a 0.55 percent rate under this tax.

(x) District of Columbia: Parking charges are taxed at 12 percent; hotel lodging and accommodations at 10 percent; food or drink for immediate consumption at 8 percent; rental vehicles at 8 percent; and food or drink sold from vending machines at 2 percent.

Table 4
STATE INDIVIDUAL INCOME TAXES
(As of January 1, 1984)

State	Rate range(a) (percent)	Income brackets		Personal exemptions			Federal income tax deductible
		Lowest (ends)	Highest (over)	Single	Married	Dependents	
Alabama	2.0-5.0(3)	$500	$3,000	$1,500	$3,000	$300	
Arizona(b).............	2.0-8.0(7)	1,017	6,102(c)	1,759	3,518	1,056	★
Arkansas	1.0-7.0(6)(d)	3,000	25,000	17.50(e)	35(e)	6(e)	★
California(b)...........	1.0-11.0(11)	4,600(f)	25,430(f)	38(e)	76(e)	12(e)	. . .
Colorado(b)	3.0-8.0(11)(g)	1,415	14,153	1,203	2,406	1,203	. . .
Delaware	1.4-13.5(15)	1,000	50,000	600	1,200	600	★
Georgia	1.0-6.0(6)	750(i)	7,000(i)	1,500(j)	3,000(j)	700	★(h)
Hawaii	2.25-11.0(11)(k)	1,300	30,800	1,000	2,000	1,000	. . .
Idaho	2.0-7.5(6)(l)	1,000	5,000	1,000(l,m)	2,000(l,m)	1,000(l,m)	. . .
Illinois	3.0	—— Flat rate ——		1,000	2,000	1,000	. . .
Indiana	3.0	—— Flat rate ——		1,000	2,000(n)	500	. . .
Iowa(b)	0.5-13.0(13)(o)	1,023	76,725	20(e)	40(e)	15(e)	★
Kansas	2.0-9.0(8)	2,000(c)	25,000(c)	1,000	2,000	1,000	★
Kentucky	2.0-6.0(5)	3,000	8,000	20(e)	40(e)	20(e)	★
Louisiana	2.0-6.0(3)	10,000	50,000	4,500(q)	9,000(q)	1,000	★
Maine(b)	1.0-10.0(8)	2,000(c)	25,000(c)	1,000	2,000	1,000	. . .
Maryland	2.0-5.0(4)	1,000	3,000	800	1,600	800	. . .
Massachusetts	5.375(r)	—— Flat rate ——		2,200	4,400(s)	700	. . .
Michigan	6.1(t)	—— Flat rate ——		1,500	3,000	1,500	. . .
Minnesota(b)	1.6-16.0(13)(d)	672	36,925	68(e)	136(e)	68(e)	★
Mississippi	3.0-5.0(3)	5,000	10,000	6,000	9,500	1,500	. . .
Missouri	1.5-6.0(10)	1,000	9,000	1,200	2,400	400	★
Montana(b)............	2.0-11.0(10)	1,200	42,000	960	1,920	960	★
Nebraska	20% U.S. tax	. . .	. . .	. . .	. . .	. . .	. . .
New Jersey.............	2.0-3.5(3)	20,000	50,000	1,000	2,000	1,000	. . .
New Mexico	0.7-7.8(19)(u)	1,000	100,000	1,000(m)	2,000(m)	1,000(m)	. . .
New York	2.0-14.0(13)(v)	1,000	23,000	800	1,600	800	. . .
North Carolina	3.0-7.0(5)	2,000	10,000	1,100	3,300	800	. . .
North Dakota	2.0-9.0(8)(w)	3,000	50,000	1,000(m)	2,000(m)	1,000(m)	★
Ohio	0.95-9.5(8)	5,000	100,000	1,000(aa)	2,000(aa)	1,000(aa)	. . .
Oklahoma	0.5-6.0(7)(x)	1,000	7,500	1,000	2,000	1,000	(x)
Oregon(b)	4.2-10.7(7)	500	5,000	85(e)	170(e)	85(e)	★(h)
Pennsylvania	2.45	—— Flat rate ——		0	0	0	. . .
Rhode Island	26% of U.S. tax	. . .	. . .	. . .	. . .	. . .	. . .
South Carolina(b)	2.0-7.0(6)	2,000	10,000	800	1,600	800	★(h)
Utah	2.75-7.75(6)	750(c)	3,750(c)	750(m)	1,500(m)	750(m)	★
Vermont...............	26% of U.S. tax(y)	. . .	. . .	. . .	. . .	. . .	. . .
Virginia	2.0-5.75(4)	3,000	12,000	600	1,200	600	. . .
West Virginia	2.1-13.0(24)	2,000(z)	60,000(z)	800	1,600	800	. . .
Wisconsin(b)...........	3.4-10.0(8)	3,900	51,600	20(e)	40(e)	20(e)	. . .
Dist. of Col.	2.0-11.0(10)	1,000	25,000	750	1,500	750	. . .

Source: The Federation of Tax Administrators (based on legislation enacted at 1983 sessions).

Note: The table excludes the following state taxes: Connecticut taxes interest and dividends at 6 to 13 percent and capital gains at 7 percent. New Hampshire taxes interest and dividends at 5 percent. Tennessee taxes dividends and interest at 6 percent; it imposes a 4 percent tax on dividends from corporations with property at least 75 percent of which is assessable for property tax in Tennessee.

(a) Figure in parentheses is the number of steps in range. For California and Hawaii amount shown for lowest bracket includes zero bracket amount and lowest positive bracket.

(b) Ten states have statutory provisions for automatic adjustment of tax brackets or personal exemptions, as well as other features, to reflect changes in the price level. Adjustments to be made for 1984 tax years will generally not be made until the latter part of 1984. The 1983 adjustment is shown when available.

(c) For joint returns, the tax is twice the tax imposed on half the income.

(d) Provides for the exemption of or the imposition of lower rates on taxpayers with incomes below certain levels.

(e) Tax credits.

(f) The range reported is for single persons. For married persons, the tax is twice the tax imposed on half the income. For heads of households, different rates apply.

(g) Imposes a surtax of 2 percent on gross income from intangibles which exceed $15,000. A credit is allowed on taxable income up to $9,000, computed by dividing taxable income by 200.

(h) The federal tax deduction is limited: in Delaware to $300 for single persons and $600 for joint returns; in Oregon to $7,000; and in South Carolina to $500.

(i) The range reported is for single persons. For joint returns and heads of households the same rates are applied to income brackets ranging from $1,000 to $10,000. For married persons filing separately, the income brackets range from $500 to $5,000.

(j) In addition, low-income taxpayers are allowed a tax credit up to $15 for single persons and $30 for heads of households or married persons filing jointly.

(k) The range reported is for single persons. For joint returns, the tax is twice the tax imposed on half the income. Different rates and brackets apply to heads of households.

(l) In the case of joint returns, the tax is twice the tax imposed on half the income. A filing fee of $10 is imposed on each return. A credit of $15 is allowed for each personal exemption.

(m) These states by definition allow personal exemptions provided in the Internal Revenue Code. Under existing law, Idaho follows the federal code as of January 1, 1983; North Dakota as of March 11, 1983, Utah (for purposes of personal exemptions) as of December 31, 1974, and the District of Columbia (for personal exemptions) as of July 1, 1975. New Mexico automatically accepts amendments to the federal code.

(n) Allows $1,000 for individual taxpayers and $500 for dependents. On joint returns, each spouse may subtract the lesser of $1,000 or adjusted gross income; the minimum exemption is $500 for each spouse.

(o) No tax is imposed on persons whose net income does not exceed $5,000.

(q) Combined personal exemption and standard deduction.

(r) A 10.75 percent rate is applied to interest and dividends (other than from savings deposits) and on net capital gains. The 5.375 percent rate applies to all other income, including earned income and interest and dividends from savings deposits. These rates include a 7.5 percent surtax.

(s) Maximum allowance; spouse's exemption is $1,000 plus the amount of earnings, but the total exemption for taxpayer and spouse may not exceed $4,400.

(t) The rate may be reduced depending on the state unemployment rate and other factors.

(u) The rate range reported is for single persons. For joint returns and heads of households, tax rates range from 0.7 percent on income not over $2,000 to 7.8 percent on income over $200,000. For married persons filing separately, a separate set of rates and brackets applies.

(v) Maximum rate of 10 percent on personal service income.

(w) Taxpayers have the option of paying 10.5 percent of adjusted federal income tax liability.

(x) The rate range is for single persons not deducting federal income tax. Married persons filing jointly, surviving spouses, and heads of households have the same rates and brackets that are twice as wide. Separate schedules, with rates ranging from 0.5 percent to 17 percent, apply to taxpayers deducting federal income taxes.

(y) If Vermont tax liability for any taxable year exceeds Vermont tax liability determinable under federal law in effect January 1, 1980, the taxpayer will be entitled to a credit equal to the excess plus 6 percent of that amount. A credit is allowed to taxpayers with an adjusted gross income of under $7,000.

(z) The range reported is for single persons and heads of households. For joint returns, the same rates are applied to brackets ranging from $4,000 to $400,000. A 12 percent surtax is imposed through June 30, 1985.

(aa) Or $650 deduction, plus $20 credit per exemption, at taxpayer's option.

Table 5
STATE SEVERANCE TAXES: 1983

State	Title and application of tax(a)	Rate
Alabama	Iron Ore Mining Tax	3ᶜ/ton
	Forest Products Severance Tax	Varies by species and ultimate use
	Oil and Gas Severance Tax	8% of gross value at point of production; 4% for wells producing less than 10 bbls./day
	Oil and Gas Production Tax	2% of gross value at point of production
	Coal Severance Tax(b)	13.5ᶜ/ton
	Coal and Lignite Severance Tax	20ᶜ/ton in addition to Coal Severance Tax
Alaska	Fisheries Business Tax	3% to 5% of fish value based on type of fish
	Oil and Gas Production Tax	The greater of 60ᶜ/bbl. for old crude oil (80ᶜ for all other) or 15% of gross value at production point (multiplied by economic limit factor); the greater of $.064/1,000 cu. ft. of gas or 10% of gross value at production point (multiplied by economic limit factor). Additional $.125/bbl. of oil as oil and gas regulation and conservation tax
Arizona	Severance Tax(c)	2.5% of net severance base for mining; 1.5% of value for timbering
Arkansas	Natural Resources Severance Tax	Separate rate for each substance
	Oil and Gas Conservation Tax	Maximum 25 mills/bbl. of oil and 5 mills/1,000 cu. ft. of gas
California	Oil and Gas Production Tax	Rate determined annually by Department of Conservation
Colorado	Severance Tax(d)	Separate rate for each substance
	Oil and Gas Conservation Tax	Maximum 1 mill/$1 of market value at wellhead
Florida	Oil and Gas Production Tax	8% (oil) and 5% (gas) of gross value at point of production; additional 12.5% for escaped oil. Wells producing less than 100 bbls./day or oil produced by tertiary methods are taxed at 5% of gross value at point of severance
	Solid Minerals Tax(e)	5% of market value at point of production
Georgia	Tax on Phosphates	$1/ton
Idaho	Ore Severance Tax	2% of net value
	Oil and Gas Production Tax	Maximum of 5 mills/bbl. of oil and 5 mills/50,000 cu. ft. of gas(f)
	Additional Oil and Gas Production Tax	2% of market value at site of production
Illinois	Timber Fee	4% of purchase price(g)
Indiana	Petroleum Production Tax(h)	1% of value
Kansas	Severance Tax(i)	8% of gross value of oil and gas; $1/ton of coal; 4ᶜ/ton of salt
	Oil and Gas Production Tax	$.002/bbl. of oil and $.00006/1,000 cu. ft. of gas, in addition to $.003/bbl. of oil or petroleum and $.0008/1,000 cu. ft. of gas produced, sold, marketed or used(j)
Kentucky	Oil Production Tax	4.5% of market value
	Coal Severance Tax	4.5% of gross value
	Natural Resource Severance Tax(k)	4.5% of gross value
Louisiana	Natural Resources Severance Tax	Rate varies according to substance
Maine	Mining Excise Tax	The greater of a tax on facilities and equipment or a tax on gross proceeds
Maryland	Coal and Gas Severance Taxes(l)	40¢/ton; 7% of wholesale market value of gas
Michigan	Gas and Oil Severance Tax	5%, 6.6%, and 4% of gross cash market value of the total production of gas, oil, and oil from stripper wells and marginal properties. Maximum additional fee of 1% of gross cash market value on all oil and gas produced in state in previous year
Minnesota	Iron Severance Tax(m)	15% to 15.5% of value (depending on ore) minus credits
	Ore Royalty Tax	15% to 15.5% of royalty (depending on ore) minus credits
	Taconite, Iron Sulphides and Agglomerate Taxes	$1.25/ton (5ᶜ /ton for agglomerates), plus 1.6% of total tax/ton based on percentage of iron content
	Semi-Taconite Tax	10ᶜ/ton (5ᶜ/ton if agglomerated in state), plus $.1/ton depending on percentage of iron content
	Copper-Nickel Taxes	1% of value of ores mined or produced (occupation tax); 2.5ᶜ/ gross ton, plus 10% of base tax/ton depending on copper-nickel content(n)
Mississippi	Oil and Gas Severance Tax	The greater of 6% of value at point of production or 6ᶜ/bbl. of oil; the greater of 6% of value at point of production or 3 mills/1,000 cu. ft. of gas
	Timber Severance Tax	Varies depending on type of wood and ultimate use
	Salt Severance Tax	3% of value of entire production in state

336

State	Title and application of tax(a)	Rate
Montana	Coal Severance Tax	Varies by quality of coal and type of mine
	Metalliferous Mines License Tax(o)	Progressive gross value tax from 0.5% to 1.5%(p)
	Oil or Gas Producers' Severance Tax	License Tax: 6% of gross value of oil (until March 31, 1985, 5% thereafter); 2.65% of gross value of gas. Conservation tax: maximum 0.2% of market value/bbl. of oil and of each 10,000 cu. ft. of gas(f)
	Micaceous Minerals License Tax	5ᶜ/ton
	Cement License Tax(q)	22ᶜ/ton of cement, 5ᶜ/ton of cement, plaster, gypsum or gypsum products
	Mineral Mining Tax	$25 plus 0.5% of gross value over $5,000
Nebraska	Oil and Gas Severance Tax	3% of value of nonstripper oil and natural gas; 2% of value of stripper oil
	Oil and Gas Conservation Tax	Maximum 4 mills/$1 of value at wellhead(f)
	Uranium Tax	2% of gross value over $5 million
Nevada	Net Proceeds of Mine Tax	Total property tax rate of place where mine is located
	Oil and Gas Conservation Tax	50 mills/bbl. of oil and 50 mills/50,000 cu. ft. of gas
New Hampshire	Refined Petroleum Products Tax	0.1% of fair market value
New Mexico	Resources Excise Tax(r)	0.75% for most substances
	Severance Tax(r)	Varies according to substance
	Oil and Gas Severance Tax	3.75% of value (less credits) of oil, other liquid hydrocarbons and carbon dioxide; 14.7ᶜ/1,000 cu. ft. of gas
	Oil and Gas Privilege Tax	3.15% of value
	Natural Gas Processor's Tax	0.45% of value
	Oil and Gas Ad Valorem Production Tax	Varies
	Oil and Gas Conservation Tax(s)	Variable percentage
North Carolina	Oil and Gas Conservation Tax	Maximum 5 mills/bbl. of oil and 0.5 mill/1,000 cu. ft. of gas(f)
	Primary Forest Product Assessment Tax	40ᶜ or 50ᶜ/1,000 board ft. and 12ᶜ or 20ᶜ/cord depending on type of wood and use
North Dakota	Oil and Gas Gross Production Tax	5% of gross value at well
	Coal Severance Tax	85ᶜ/ton and 1ᶜ/ton for every four-point increase in wholesale price index
	Oil Extraction Tax	6.5% of gross value at well
Ohio	Resource Severance Tax(t)	10ᶜ/bbl. of oil; 2.5ᶜ/1,000 cu. ft. of gas; 4ᶜ/ton of coal and salt; 1ᶜ/ton of sand, gravel, limestone and dolomite
Oklahoma	Oil, Gas, and Mineral Gross Production Tax(u)	Separate rate for each substance
	Natural Gas and Casinghead Gas Conservation Excise Tax	7ᶜ/1,000 cu. ft., less 7% of gross value of each 1,000 cu. ft. of gas
Oregon	Forest Products Harvest Tax	23ᶜ/1,000 board ft. and additional 12ᶜ/1,000 board ft. until July 1, 1985(v)
	Oil and Gas Gross Production Tax	6% of gross value at well
	Severance Tax on Eastern Oregon Timber	5% of immediate harvest value, plus additional severance tax
	Severance Tax on Western Oregon Timber	6.5% of value, plus additional severance tax
South Dakota	Precious Metals Severance Tax(w)	6% of gross yield from sale of metals
	Energy Minerals Severance Tax	4.5% of taxable value of any energy minerals
	Conservation Tax	2.4 mills of taxable value of any energy minerals
Tennessee	Oil and Gas Severance Tax	3% of sales price
	Coal Severance Tax	35ᶜ/ton
Texas	Natural Gas Production Tax	7.5% of market value
	Oil Production Tax	The greater of 4.6% of market value or 4.6ᶜ/bbl.
	Sulphur Production Tax	$1.03/long ton
	Cement Production Tax	2.75ᶜ/100 lbs.
Utah	Mining Occupation Tax(x)	1% of gross value for metals; 2% of value for oil and gas and other hydrocarbons at wellhead
	Oil and Gas Conservation Tax	2 mills/$1 of market value at wellhead
Virginia	Forest Products Tax	Varies by species and ultimate use
	Coal Surface Mining Reclamation Tax	Varies depending on balance of Coal Surface Mining Reclamation Fund
Washington	Uranium and Thorium Milling Tax	5ᶜ/lb.
	Food Fish and Shellfish Tax	0.07% to 5% of the selling price depending on species and additional 7% of basic tax rate

STATE SEVERANCE TAX—Continued

State	Title and application of tax(a)	Rate
Wisconsin	Metalliferous Minerals Occupation Tax	Progressive net proceeds tax from 3% to 15%
Wyoming	Oil and Gas Production Tax	Maximum 0.8 mill/$1 of value at wellhead(f)
	Mining Excise and Severance Taxes	Varies by substance from 1.5% to 7.25% of value

Source: Commerce Clearing House, *State Tax Guide.*

(a) Application of tax is same as that of title unless otherwise indicated by a footnote.

(b) Tax scheduled to terminate upon the redemption of all bonds issued by the Alabama State Docks Department.

(c) Timber, metalliferous minerals.

(d) Metallic minerals, coal, oil shale, and oil and gas.

(e) Clay, gravel, phosphate rock, lime, shells, stone, sand, heavy minerals and rare earths.

(f) Actual rate set by administrative actions.

(g) Buyer deducts amount from payment to grower; amount forwarded to Department of Conservation.

(h) Petroleum, oil, gas and other hydrocarbons.

(i) Coal, salt, oil and gas.

(j) Figures are total parts of tax designed for pollution and conservation.

(k) Coal and oil excepted.

(l) Limited to certain counties. Coal tax expires June 30, 1987.

(m) All ores.

(n) Additional ore royalty tax of 1% of royalties plus 1% of amount of royalty paid on precious metals.

(o) Metals, precious and semi-precious stones and gems.

(p) Over $250,000 gross value to over $1 million.

(q) Cement and gypsum or allied products.

(r) Natural resources except oil, natural gas, liquid hydrocarbons or carbon dioxide.

(s) Oil, coal, gas, liquid hydrocarbons, geothermal energy, carbon dioxide and uranium.

(t) Oil, gas, coal, salt, limestone, dolomite, sand and gravel.

(u) Asphalt, oil, gas, uranium and metals.

(v) Plus additional tax of 15¢/1,000 board ft. for harvesting on protected west and east side forest lands.

(w) Does not apply if less than 1,000 ozs. of gold or silver severed annually.

(x) Metals, oil, gas, other hydrocarbons and uranium.

Table 6
RANGE OF STATE CORPORATE INCOME TAX RATES
(As of January 1, 1984)

State or other jurisdiction	Tax rate* (percent)	Federal income tax deductible	State or other jurisdiction	Tax rate* (percent)	Federal income tax deductible
Alabama		★	**Minnesota**		---
Business corporations	5		$0 to $25,000	6	
Banks & financial corps.	6		Over $25,000	12	
Alaska		---	**Mississippi**		---
Business corporations:			$0 to $5,000	3	
$0 to $10,000	1		Over $10,000	5(3)	
Over $90,000	9.4(10)		**Missouri**		★
Banks & finan. institutions	7(a)		Business corporations	5	
Arizona		★	Banks & trust companies	7	
$0 to $1,000	2.5		**Montana**	6.75(m)	---
Over $6,000	10.5(7)		**Nebraska**		---
Arkansas		---	$0 to $50,000	5	
$0 to $3,000	1		Over $50,000	7(2)(n)	
Over $25,000	6(5)		**New Hampshire**	9.56(o)	---
California		---	**New Jersey**	9(p)	---
Business corporations	9.6(b)		**New Mexico**		---
Banks & financial corps.	11.6(b)		$0 to $1 million	4.8	
Colorado	5(c)	---	Over $2 million	7.2(3)	
Connecticut	11.5(d)	---	**New York**		---
Delaware	8.7	---	Business corporations	10(q)	
Florida	5(e)	---	Banks & financial corps.	12(r)	
Georgia	6	---	**North Carolina**	6	---
Hawaii		---	**North Dakota**		★
Business corporations			Business corporations		
$0 to $25,000	5.85(f)		$0 to $3,000	3	
Over $25,000	6.435(2)		Over $50,000	10.5(6)	
Banks & financial corps.	11.7		Banks & financial corps.	5(s)	
Idaho	7.7(g)	---	**Ohio**		---
Illinois	7.3(h)	---	$0 to $25,000	5.1(t)	
Indiana	7(i)	---	Over $25,000	9.2(2)(t)	
Iowa		(j)	**Oklahoma**	4	---
Business corporations			**Oregon**	7.5(u)	---
$0 to $25,000	6		**Pennsylvania**	10.5	---
Over $250,000	12(4)		**Rhode Island**	8(v)	---
Financial institutions	5		**South Carolina**		---
Kansas		---	Business corporations	6	
Business corporations	4.5(k)		Banks	4.5	
Banks	4.25(k)		Financial associations	8	
Trust companies & savings			**South Dakota**		★
& loan associations	4.5(k)		Banks & financial corps.	6(w)	
Kentucky		---	**Tennessee**	6	---
$0 to $25,000	3		**Utah**	4(x)	---
Over $100,000	6(4)		**Vermont**		---
Louisiana		★	$0 to $10,000	5	
$0 to $25,000	4		Over $250,000	7.5(4)(y)	
Over $200,000	8(5)		**Virginia**	6	---
Maine		---	**West Virginia**		---
$0 to $25,000	3.5		$0 to $50,000	6.9	
Over $250,000	8.93(4)		Over $50,000	8.05	
Maryland	7	---	**Wisconsin**	7.9	---
Massachusetts		---			
Business corporations	9.4962(l)		**Dist. of Col.**	9.9(z)	---
Banks & trust companies	12.54				
Utility corporations	6.5				

Source: The Federation of Tax Administrators (based on legislation enacted at 1983 sessions.)

*Figure in parentheses is number of steps in range.

(a) Banks and other financial institutions are subject to a license tax.

(b) Minimum tax is $200.

(c) A credit was suspended for 1983 and 1984 but is scheduled to resume in 1985.

(d) Or 3.1 mills per dollar of capital stock and surplus (maximum tax $100,000), or $250, or 5 percent of 50 percent of net income of corporation plus salaries and other compensation paid to officers and certain shareholders, whichever is greater.

(e) An exemption of $5,000 is allowed.

(f) Taxes capital gains at 3.08 percent.

(g) Minimum tax is $20. An additional tax of $10 is imposed on each return.

(h) Includes 2.5 percent personal property tax replacement tax.

(i) Consists of 3 percent basic rate plus a 4 percent supplemental tax.

(j) 50 percent of federal income tax deductible.

(k) Plus a surtax of 2.25 percent of taxable income in excess of $25,000 (2.125 percent for banks).

(l) Rate includes a 14 percent surtax, as does the following: Plus a tax of $2.60 per $1,000 on taxable tangible property (or net worth allocable to state, for intangible property corporations). Minimum tax of $228 including surtax. Corporations engaged exclusively in interstate or foreign commerce are taxed at 5 percent of net income, and are not subject to surtax.

(m) Minimum tax is $50; for small business corporations, $10.

(n) 25 and 35 percent of individual income tax rate, determined annually, imposed on net taxable income.

(o) Business profits tax imposed on both corporations and unincorporated business. Includes a 13.5 percent surtax.

(p) This is the corporation business franchise tax rate, plus a net worth tax at millage rates ranging from 2 mills to 0.2 mill; minimum tax is $250. Corporations not subject to the franchise tax are subject to a 7.25 percent

income tax. Savings institutions are subject to a 3 percent tax.

(q) Or $250; 1.78 mills per dollar of capital; or 10 percent of 30 percent of net income plus salaries and other compensation to officers and stockholders owning more than 5 percent of the issued capital stock less $30,000 and any net loss, if any of these is greater than the tax computed on net income.

(r) Minimum tax is $250 or 1.6 mills per dollar of capital stock; for savings institutions, the minimum tax is $250 or 2 percent of interest credited to depositors in preceding year.

(s) Minimum tax is $50; plus an additional 2 percent tax.

(t) Or 5.82 mills times the value of the taxpayer's issued and outstanding shares of stock as determined according to the total value of capital surplus, undivided profits, and reserves; minimum tax $50. An additional litter tax is imposed equal to 0.11 percent on the first $25,000 of income, 0.22 percent on income over $25,000, or 0.14 mills on net worth. Corporations manufacturing or selling litter stream products are subject to an additional 0.22 percent tax on income over $25,000 or 0.14 mills on net worth.

(u) Minimum tax is $10.

(v) Or, for business corporations, the tax is 40 cents per $100 of net worth, if greater than the tax computed on net income. For banks, if a greater tax results, the alternative tax is $2.50 per $10,000 of capital stock; minimum tax is $100.

(w) Minimum tax is $200 per authorized location.

(x) Minimum tax is $25. There is a graduated gross receipts tax on corporations not otherwise required to pay income or franchise taxes, ranging up to 1 percent on receipts in excess of $1 billion.

(y) Minimum tax is $50.

(z) Includes 10 percent surtax. Minimum tax is $100.

Note: Michigan imposes a single business tax (sometimes described as a business activities or value added tax) of 2.35 percent on the sum of federal taxable income of the business, compensation paid to employees, dividends, interest and royalties paid, and other items.

STATE TAX COLLECTIONS IN 1983

By Maurice Criz

State tax collections increased a little more than 5 percent in fiscal 1983, but it took many rate increases and postponement of scheduled rate decreases to offset the sluggish national economy, relatively high interest rates and decreasing federal assistance. Gross national product increased by 6.6 percent, personal income went up by 5.9 percent, and personal consumption expenditures advanced by 8.8 percent. The rate of inflation dropped from 6 to 4 percent. Employment ended the year at about the same level it started, with some sag in the middle, while unemployment increased during the first half of the fiscal year and fell steadily the last half. The fact that the trough in the economic recession came in the fourth quarter of 1982 was not of great help to fiscal 1983 state tax revenue, since it is several months after the economy starts moving before tax collections are affected. This time lag is reflected in the 7.5 percent increase in state tax collections in the second quarter of calendar 1983 over the same quarter a year earlier, which was somewhat higher than the 4.7 percent increase in the 1982 second quarter over 1981, but less than the increases of 11.7 and 9.9 percent in 1981 and 1980, respectively.[1]

State tax collections totaled $171.4 billion in fiscal 1983, an increase of $8.8 billion over 1982 and $21.6 billion more than 1981. In per capita terms, there was an increase from $720.01 in 1982 to $739.72 in 1983.

Individual income taxes were the star performers of the year. They grew by 9 percent over 1982. Contributing factors were growth in personal income, bracket creep, enactment of tax rate increases in 12 states, postponement of indexing provisions in several states, and smaller federal income tax deductions (where permissible) in view of lower federal tax rates.

Corporation net income tax collections, in contrast, fell by 6.1 percent—this was the second successive yearly decrease. In 1982, the drop was 1 percent, following a 6.2 percent increase in 1981. The 1983 decrease was significant ($849 million) and very damaging to state budgets. The downtrend was found in 27 of the 46 states with corporation net income taxes. This drop resulted not only from depressed earnings due to the recession but also from the federal Economic Re-

covery Tax Act of 1981 (ERTA) which, in part, established a more rapid system of depreciation (ACRS) and safe-harbor leasing. Those states following federal depreciation schedules saw sharp drops in their income taxes, although there was some correction subsequently when the Tax Equity and Fiscal Responsibility Act of 1982 (TEFRA) restricted buying and selling tax benefits through safe-harbor leasing. Tennessee denied ACRS safe-harbor leasing provisions for state tax purposes, and Virginia required that corporations add back to federal taxable income the estimated benefits derived from ACRS over the previous depreciation system. Other states also uncoupled from the federal rapid depreciation allowance.

General sales and gross receipts taxes increased by 6.5 percent in 1983, a poorer showing than the increases of 8.5 and 7.5 percent in 1982 and 1981. That there was any growth at all can be attributed to better than expected personal consumption expenditure and tax rate increases in 14 states, several of which were enacted toward the end of the fiscal year.

Major Tax Sources

Sales and gross receipts taxes have produced from 50 to 60 percent of all state taxes since general sales taxes were first enacted in the 1930s until 1980 when they fell below the one-half mark. The sales tax percentage decline started in fiscal 1967 and has continued at a steady pace downward to 48.4 percent in 1982 and 48.9 percent in 1983.

Sales taxes include both general sales and gross receipts taxes, currently imposed by 45 states, and a variety of selective sales taxes on specific goods or services. General sales and gross receipts taxes totaled $53.6 billion during fiscal 1983, amounting to $231 per capita nationwide. The annual rate of increase dropped to 6.5 percent as compared to 8.5 percent in fiscal 1982— the lowest rate of growth in more than two decades.

Maurice Criz is Senior Advisor, Governments Division, U.S. Bureau of the Census.

Table A

**Percentage Distribution of State Tax Collections,
by Major Tax Category, Selected Years 1957-1983**

Year	Sales and gross receipts taxes	Income taxes	License taxes	Other
1957	58.1	17.6	15.1	9.2
1967	58.2	22.4	11.4	8.0
1977	51.8	34.3	7.1	6.8
1982	48.4	36.7	6.2	8.6
1983	48.9	36.7	6.2	8.1

Income taxes accounted for 36.7 percent of total state tax revenue, the same ratio as in fiscal 1982. Individual income taxes were up 9 percent to $49.8 billion, less than the 11.7 percent increase in 1982. Taxes on corporation net income, however, decreased by 6.1 percent following a 1 percent drop in fiscal 1982, both resulting not only from the economic recession but also from accelerated depreciation and safe-harbor leasing under ERTA.

Motor fuel sales tax collections were up slightly by 3.1 percent in 1983 as compared to an increase of 7.5 percent in 1982. These taxes accounted for 6.3 percent of all state tax revenue in 1983. The states have been attempting to offset falling tax revenue, resulting from fuel-efficient vehicles and considerably lower fuel consumption, by increasing motor fuel sales tax rates.

Individual State Comparisons

As one might expect, there was considerable variation among the states in both the direction and rate of change in 1983 tax collections. While the U.S. total state tax increase in fiscal 1983 was 5.4 percent, there was a wide range from +19 to -19 percent among the states. Eleven states had increases exceeding 10 percent: Arizona, Florida, Kansas, Michigan, Minnesota, Missouri, Nebraska, New Jersey, Ohio, Oregon and Washington. Eight states had tax collection decreases ranging from .9 percent to 5.2 percent, while Alaska showed a decrease of 19.4 percent that was primarily due to a drop of $437.3 million in corporation net income taxes. The other eight states were Louisiana, Montana, New Mexico, North Dakota, Oklahoma, South Dakota, Texas and Wyoming.

Five states had annual percentage increases in general sales and gross receipts taxes considerably above the U.S. total of 6.5 percent: Vermont (37.7), Washington (29.7), Wisconsin (25.8), Nebraska (23.6) and New Jersey (20.4). These were followed by eight states with increases ranging from 10 to 20 percent: Connecticut, Florida, Idaho, Massachusetts, Minnesota, Missouri, New York and Ohio. At the other ex-

treme, three states had decreases of 10 percent or more in general sales and gross receipts taxes: Wyoming (16.7 percent), Oklahoma (15.1 percent) and New Mexico (10.7 percent). An additional seven states had decreases of up to 10 percent.

Individual income tax collections exhibited the strongest uptrend among major taxes in 1983, a total increase of 9 percent, and more states were in the higher part of the plus column. Two states headed the list—Ohio with 58.6 percent (surtax was increased) and Connecticut with 29.6 percent (a change in collection cycle). In six other states this tax source grew by 20 to 30 percent: Minnesota (27.7), Nebraska (23.9), Hawaii (22.6), Oregon (22), Rhode Island (21.4) and Michigan (20.7). In another 12 states increases ranged between 10 and 20 percent. There were only two states that experienced a drop in individual income taxes in 1983: Illinois (1 percent) and North Dakota (.6).

The picture for corporation net income taxes was much bleaker than for individual income. The total for all states was -6.1 percent, a decrease in tax collections noted above as resulting not only from the recession but also from federal legislation accelerating depreciation and providing for safe-harbor leasing subsequently restricted. States that allowed for depreciation deduction under federal procedures found much of the tax base dissipated, and receipts suffered. Three states had very large percentage decreases of corporation net income taxes in 1983: Alaska (62.2), primarily due to legislation applying to oil and gas companies; Hawaii (49), which allowed credits for 1982 tax liability; and Colorado (38.5), due to reduced rates. Five states had decreases of 20 to 32 percent: Idaho, Minnesota, Ohio, Oklahoma and Utah. In addition, seven states had decreases of 10 to 20 percent, and in 14 states collections fell off by up to 10 percent. There were two states that had increases of 30 percent or more, excluding South Dakota which has nominal revenue from corporate net income taxes: Arizona (40) and West Virginia (31.2). Five states had increased revenue of 10 to 20 percent, and 10 states increased by up to 10 percent.

Revenue from various selective sales and gross receipts taxes increased by 6.3 percent overall in 1983 over 1982. A large number of states increased tax rates and imposed surtaxes or new taxes on the commodities and services in this group in attempts to maintain balanced budgets. These were the actions taken on motor fuel sales in 10 states, on tobacco products in 10 states, and on alcoholic beverage sales in seven states. Even with the tax increases, however, these three sales taxes showed very small annual revenue increases compared to sales and gross receipts taxes on public utilities and insurance. The 1983 percentage increases were as follows: public utilities, 15.4; insurance, 11.4; motor fuels, 3.1; tobacco products, 1.2; and alcoholic beverages, .8 percent. The number of states with revenue decreases in 1983 was notable—18 states in motor fuel sales taxes, 30 states in tobacco product sales taxes, and 21 states in alcoholic beverage sales taxes.

Among the states with significant amounts of revenue from sales and gross receipts taxes on public utilities, the following had large increases in 1983: Minnesota, 59.9 percent; New Jersey, 24.8 percent; New York, 21.1 percent; Ohio, 27 percent; and Texas, 15.5 percent.

States with larger amounts of revenue from insurance sales and gross receipts taxes and with notable percentage increases in 1983 were California (36.1), Illinois (40.3), Louisiana (21.3) and Missouri (51). In California and Missouri changes in tax collection cycles affect the annual comparison.

Notes

1. U.S. Bureau of the Census, *Quarterly Summary of Federal, State and Local Tax Revenue*, April-June 1983.

Table 1
NATIONAL SUMMARY OF STATE GOVERNMENT TAX REVENUE, BY TYPE OF TAX: 1981 TO 1983

Tax source	Amount (in thousands)			Percent change year-to-year		Percent distribu-tion, 1983	Per capita, 1983
	1983 (prelim.)	1982	1981	1982 to 1983	1981 to 1982		
Total collections	$171,370,096	$162,607,136	$149,751,851	5.4	8.6	100.0	$739.72
Sales and gross receipts	83,840,134	78,788,928	72,759,573	6.4	8.3	48.9	361.90
General.....................	53,626,783	50,356,889	46,412,126	6.5	8.5	31.3	231.48
Selective	30,213,351	28,432,039	26,347,447	6.3	7.9	17.6	130.42
Motor fuels	10,793,333	10,473,023	9,741,863	3.1	7.5	6.3	46.59
Public utilities	5,650,815	4,894,702	4,295,626	15.4	13.9	3.3	24.39
Tobacco products...........	4,001,392	3,955,155	3,893,171	1.2	1.6	2.3	17.27
Insurance	3,857,437	3,462,603	3,321,350	11.4	4.3	2.3	16.65
Alcoholic beverages	2,743,092	2,722,195	2,613,426	0.8	4.2	1.6	11.84
Other	3,167,283	2,924,361	2,482,011	8.3	17.8	1.8	13.67
Licenses	10,651,435	10,105,709	9,487,892	5.4	6.5	6.2	45.98
Motor vehicles...............	5,777,676	5,548,666	5,266,082	4.1	5.4	3.4	24.94
Corporations in general	1,848,127	1,760,577	1,611,720	5.0	9.2	1.1	7.98
Hunting and fishing	534,569	491,928	464,003	8.7	6.0	0.3	2.31
Motor vehicle operators........	503,157	487,254	428,988	3.3	13.6	0.3	2.17
Alcoholic beverages	223,470	213,789	212,407	4.5	0.7	0.1	0.96
Other	1,764,436	1,603,495	1,504,692	10.0	6.6	1.0	7.62
Individual income	49,788,567	45,667,517	40,895,235	9.0	11.7	29.1	214.91
Corporation net income..........	13,152,503	14,001,709	14,143,497	-6.1	-1.0	7.7	56.77
Severance	7,396,743	7,829,520	6,379,191	-5.5	22.7	4.3	31.93
Property	3,280,844	3,115,511	2,948,883	5.3	5.7	1.9	14.16
Death and gift	2,544,640	2,350,092	2,228,968	8.3	5.4	1.5	10.98
Other.........................	715,230	748,150	908,612	-4.4	-17.7	0.4	3.09

Source: U.S. Bureau of the Census, *State Government Tax Collections in 1983.*
Note: Because of rounding, detail may not add to totals. Population figures as of July 1, 1983 were used to calculate per capita amounts.

Table 2
SUMMARY OF STATE GOVERNMENT TAX REVENUE, BY STATE:
1981 TO 1983

State	Amount (in thousands)			Percent change year-to-year		
	1983 (prelim.)	1982	1981	1982 to 1983	1981 to 1982	Per capita, 1983
United States............	$171,370,096	$162,607,136	$149,751,851	5.4	8.6	$ 739.72
Alabama.................	2,341,229	2,192,251	2,148,415	6.8	2.0	595.43
Alaska	2,046,086	2,539,193	2,316,823	-19.4	9.6	4,487.03
Arizona	2,060,817	1,857,887	1,785,775	10.9	4.0	702.15
Arkansas	1,337,881	1,264,614	1,188,851	5.8	6.4	577.17
California...............	22,259,976	21,818,694	20,504,787	2.0	6.4	894.44
Colorado	1,743,225	1,690,034	1,445,777	3.1	16.9	562.88
Connecticut.............	2,537,725	2,342,572	2,071,885	8.3	13.1	812.59
Delaware	639,261	594,817	550,943	7.5	8.0	1,063.66
Florida.................	6,224,717	5,555,936	5,314,376	12.0	4.5	588.24
Georgia.................	3,504,220	3,281,065	3,019,847	6.8	8.7	619.01
Hawaii	1,150,503	1,066,225	1,088,330	7.9	-2.0	1,188.54
Idaho	620,035	583,822	536,757	6.2	8.8	630.76
Illinois.................	7,420,382	7,405,578	7,322,572	0.2	1.1	648.07
Indiana.................	3,194,741	3,063,657	2,808,811	4.3	9.1	583.73
Iowa	2,014,289	1,996,971	1,835,807	0.9	8.8	693.86
Kansas	1,565,625	1,402,736	1,392,277	11.6	0.8	653.16
Kentucky	2,601,949	2,491,052	2,276,170	4.5	9.4	707.24
Louisiana...............	3,011,347	3,138,278	2,804,570	-4.0	11.9	683.31
Maine	780,052	730,979	674,316	6.7	8.4	686.67
Maryland	3,468,193	3,193,087	2,956,088	8.6	8.0	815.28
Massachusetts	5,155,631	4,803,664	4,335,648	7.3	10.8	896.32
Michigan	7,022,658	6,318,984	6,171,246	11.1	2.4	775.30
Minnesota	4,319,483	3,799,371	3,373,726	13.7	12.6	1,042.60
Mississippi	1,537,705	1,498,812	1,396,745	2.6	7.3	599.50
Missouri................	2,640,325	2,313,057	2,142,965	14.1	7.9	533.08
Montana	513,658	529,247	466,575	-2.9	13.4	632.58
Nebraska	987,454	860,527	803,960	14.8	7.0	623.00
Nevada.................	779,338	745,460	515,303	4.5	44.7	886.62
New Hampshire	329,458	325,515	268,752	1.2	21.1	345.34
New Jersey..............	6,128,035	5,526,136	5,029,336	10.9	9.9	823.22
New Mexico.............	1,163,021	1,226,543	1,179,280	-5.2	4.0	841.55
New York...............	16,207,994	15,438,003	13,928,143	5.0	10.8	918.87
North Carolina	4,028,477	3,790,035	3,430,723	6.3	10.5	674.11
North Dakota	526,006	532,631	450,755	-1.2	18.2	786.26
Ohio	6,734,008	5,819,461	5,240,844	15.7	11.0	627.41
Oklahoma	2,627,487	2,713,324	2,232,278	-3.2	21.6	804.99
Oregon	1,783,670	1,552,313	1,608,423	14.9	-3.5	670.55
Pennsylvania............	8,430,271	8,185,625	7,597,010	3.0	7.7	709.44
Rhode Island	726,421	674,792	607,951	7.7	11.0	764.65
South Carolina	2,112,640	1,959,205	1,825,935	7.8	7.3	660.41
South Dakota	324,587	328,785	297,813	-1.3	10.4	468.38
Tennessee................	2,246,288	2,146,242	1,958,427	4.7	9.6	481.73
Texas	9,019,075	9,099,849	8,173,759	-0.9	11.3	579.00
Utah	974,098	950,869	849,148	2.4	12.0	604.28
Vermont.................	358,097	332,592	294,243	7.7	13.0	682.09
Virginia.................	3,477,988	3,235,829	3,035,683	7.5	6.6	645.63
Washington	4,191,161	3,524,903	3,125,815	18.9	12.8	988.02
West Virginia............	1,470,331	1,468,886	1,269,671	0.1	15.7	748.64
Wisconsin	4,296,576	3,934,495	3,629,459	9.2	8.4	904.54
Wyoming	735,902	762,533	469,058	-3.5	62.6	1,442.95

Source: U.S. Bureau of the Census, *State Government Tax Collections*
in 1983.
Note: Because of rounding, detail may not add to totals. Population
figures as of July 1, 1983 were used to calculate per capita amounts; see
Table 6.

Table 3
STATE GOVERNMENT TAX REVENUE, BY TYPE OF TAX: 1983
(In thousands of dollars)

State	Total	Sales and gross receipts	Licenses	Individual income	Corporation net income	Property	Death and gift	Severance	Documentary and stock transfer	Other
Number of states using tax	50	50	50	44	46	43	49	32	28	14
United States	$171,370,096	$83,840,134	$10,651,435	$49,788,567	$13,152,503	$3,280,844	$2,544,640	$7,396,743	$677,003	$38,227
Alabama	2,341,229	1,385,536	119,384	556,390	133,717	53,285	9,179	77,144	6,594	
Alaska	2,046,086	74,614	56,316	1,540	266,302	152,580	700	1,494,034		
Arizona	2,060,817	1,145,486	140,594	480,716	160,429	121,358	12,234	28,393		
Arkansas	1,337,881	706,742	112,428	388,341	86,921	4,558	7,229	28,684	2,608	
California	22,259,976	9,952,672	846,144	7,649,231	2,553,948	740,021	489,276			661
Colorado	1,743,225	885,909	99,359	655,491	56,184	5,272	9,118	27,056		4,836
Connecticut	2,537,725	1,798,600	128,045	178,535	357,364	11	75,169			1
Delaware	639,261	90,052	176,263	313,986	29,790		16,619		12,550	1
Florida	6,224,717	4,795,751	444,038		371,453	131,327	79,335	137,933	264,880	
Georgia	3,504,220	1,784,280	107,037	1,342,092	238,834	14,290	11,865		5,070	752
Hawaii	1,150,503	755,861	17,687	347,016	22,026	242	6,416		1,497	
Idaho	620,035	288,608	71,919	223,774	31,114		3,572	806		
Illinois	7,420,382	3,869,061	438,628	2,200,670	603,900	165,025	138,544		4,554	
Indiana	3,194,741	2,009,813	153,309	819,220	139,968	28,575	42,240	1,616		
Iowa	2,014,289	889,277	195,156	724,127	138,483		65,148		2,098	
Kansas	1,565,625	728,372	111,243	530,657	141,347	24,232	27,435	2,339		
Kentucky	2,601,949	1,187,337	131,423	647,170	172,120	203,340	38,317	221,445	797	
Louisiana	3,011,347	1,356,288	196,701	229,261	321,372	2,750	35,510	869,465		
Maine	780,052	421,911	63,883	235,933	33,043	12,541	11,699		1,042	
Maryland	3,468,193	1,546,318	134,438	1,458,654	148,423	112,213	29,396		29,847	8,904
Massachusetts	5,155,631	1,735,723	159,308	2,472,278	660,654	2,110	111,850		13,708	
Michigan	7,022,658	2,773,197	366,545	2,567,038	1,004,269	166,344	63,894	81,371		
Minnesota	4,319,483	1,698,291	262,331	1,977,991	253,970	4,131	18,497	84,693	19,579	
Mississippi	1,537,705	1,023,288	120,915	201,114	68,794	923	8,043	114,628		
Missouri	2,640,325	1,387,915	210,009	885,272	118,625	6,210	31,826	25		443

State										
Montana	513,658	107,323	47,989	151,784	35,825	26,027	6,398	137,599		713
Nebraska	987,454	560,707	81,100	280,662	51,635	3,570	3,131	5,217	1,432	
Nevada	779,338	669,071	86,152			24,115	10,580		7,020	
New Hampshire	329,458	158,975	56,568	16,727	73,960	5,545	147,861	83	20,081	
New Jersey	6,128,035	3,309,264	478,007	1,440,183	664,415	68,224				
New Mexico	1,163,021	656,835	62,548	16,626	61,742	9,056	4,871	351,343	26,728	
New York	16,207,994	5,727,816	554,437	8,275,754	1,339,005		283,854			
North Carolina	4,028,477	1,763,988	296,402	1,550,107	306,594	62,003	48,246	1,197		
North Dakota	526,006	219,338	51,938	35,136	30,594	1,746	2,727	184,527		
Ohio	6,734,008	3,685,835	469,132	1,972,089	415,017	109,342	78,625	3,968		
Oklahoma	2,627,487	800,614	254,891	651,202	103,325	159	32,740	777,687	5,441	1,587
Oregon	1,783,670	211,859	182,136	1,181,731	125,110	117,783	31,841	49,662	1,172	
Pennsylvania	8,430,271	4,175,875	927,887	2,044,544	830,108	7,725	250,618		83,456	
Rhode Island	726,421	374,083	29,735	261,139	42,446	8,671	9,987		1,306	
South Carolina	2,112,640	1,140,747	89,311	718,861	128,180		15,658		11,212	
South Dakota	324,587	279,173	28,352		2,565		8,821	5,676	21,985	
Tennessee	2,246,288	1,704,157	214,928	52,151	203,858	1,109	37,072	3,419		8,718
Texas	9,019,075	5,671,153	999,948			369	92,137	2,254,728		
Utah	974,098	527,377	47,282	345,813	31,592	477	1,977	19,688	3,259	
Vermont	358,097	175,176	38,134	113,775	25,400		1,376			500
Virginia	3,477,988	1,440,702	208,536	1,549,147	183,215	35,865	17,819	1,347	37,202	4,155
Washington	4,191,161	3,116,201	234,267			691,394	27,975	41,122	80,202	
West Virginia	1,470,331	1,005,196	87,234	310,583	45,146	1,041	16,765		2,662	1,704
Wisconsin	4,296,576	1,825,864	205,079	1,734,056	339,781	109,314	67,257	952	9,021	5,252
Wyoming	735,902	241,903	55,939			45,971	3,193	388,896		

Source: U.S. Bureau of the Census, *State Government Tax Collections in 1983.*

Table 4
STATE GOVERNMENT SALES AND GROSS RECEIPTS TAX REVENUE: 1983
(In thousands of dollars)

State	Total	General sales or gross receipts	Selective sales and gross receipts								
			Total	Motor fuels	Alcoholic beverages	Tobacco products	Insurance	Public utilities	Parimutuels	Amusements	Other
Number of states using tax	50	45	50	50	50	50	50	41	31	28	35
United States	$83,840,134	$53,626,783	$30,213,351	$10,793,333	$2,743,092	$4,001,392	$3,857,437	$5,650,815	$729,269	$366,044	$2,071,969
Alabama	1,385,536	659,663	725,873	240,850	88,368	68,226	76,710	214,603		69	37,047
Alaska	74,614		74,614	36,675	10,413	5,290	13,842	1,445			6,949
Arizona	1,145,486	845,306	300,180	151,780	23,712	42,205	39,485	32,861	10,137		
Arkansas	706,742	437,474	269,268	132,781	23,888	55,236	38,226		19,137		
California	9,952,672	7,766,551	2,186,121	925,560	136,172	262,351	658,704	30,453	118,473		54,408
Colorado	885,909	622,548	263,361	143,016	24,543	36,630	47,871	2,178	8,735	388	
Connecticut	1,798,600	1,104,136	694,464	159,014	26,237	73,669	77,705	235,945	61,233	12,444	48,217
Delaware	90,052		90,052	37,707	5,111	12,336	13,619	18,810	520	2	1,947
Florida	4,795,751	3,334,207	1,461,544	451,940	316,644	275,294	125,715	136,653	111,789	2,348	41,161
Georgia	1,784,280	1,173,027	611,253	353,429	101,871	85,597	70,356				
Hawaii	755,861	601,127	154,734	33,761	9,299	17,609	27,670	66,395			
Idaho	288,608	165,403	123,205	77,327	8,092	10,382	23,517	2,177	339		1,371
Illinois	3,869,061	2,394,075	1,474,986	361,416	73,394	173,287	110,091	646,207	69,023	7,882	33,686
Indiana	2,009,813	1,521,846	487,967	316,935	33,945	79,054	57,977			56	
Iowa	889,277	571,087	318,190	188,271	16,728	60,384	49,432	3,106			269
Kansas	728,372	498,495	229,877	115,180	34,599	33,481	44,901	905		811	
Kentucky	1,187,337	700,407	486,930	197,100	49,408	20,771	99,334		10,097	275	109,945
Louisiana	1,356,288	838,511	517,777	186,105	55,950	60,987	121,780	39,738	25,869	196	27,152
Maine	421,911	270,309	151,602	55,440	30,716	23,988	15,842	24,381	1,235		
Maryland	1,546,318	865,087	681,231	233,407	28,984	68,640	66,040	83,397	16,891	910	182,962
Massachusetts	1,735,723	1,051,712	684,011	250,425	82,709	142,912	134,890		35,457	10,108	27,510
Michigan	2,773,197	1,969,377	803,820	456,490	96,751	126,889	102,345		21,303	42	
Minnesota	1,698,291	992,259	706,032	262,101	53,093	85,008	68,776	113,237		5	123,812
Mississippi	1,023,288	761,391	261,897	135,226	34,650	35,067	56,650			304	
Missouri	1,387,915	984,874	403,041	194,290	24,243	77,929	105,532	1,047			
Montana	107,323		107,323	48,890	15,071	11,162	24,799	5,864	125		1,412
Nebraska	560,707	356,608	204,099	119,752	13,774	29,935	25,599	789	8,964	962	4,324
Nevada	669,071	368,332	300,739	66,871	11,564	13,399	15,440	3,253	202	189,716	294
New Hampshire	158,975		158,975	60,994	5,991	25,515	15,143	519	7,217		43,596
New Jersey	3,309,264	1,660,284	1,648,980	288,981	59,716	214,543	103,599	828,816	11,750	130,985	10,590

State											
New Mexico	656,835	476,664	180,171	93,509	17,146	15,033	25,191	5,465	2,134	95	21,598
New York	5,727,816	3,531,930	2,195,886	436,796	142,292	330,976	222,619	885,373	100,891	968	75,971
North Carolina	1,763,988	825,703	938,285	379,480	116,465	17,512	98,722	304,277			21,829
North Dakota	219,338	146,377	72,961	35,539	6,427	10,492	10,153	4,025			6,325
Ohio	3,685,835	2,004,589	1,681,246	588,531	70,359	188,393	152,556	639,406	24,596		17,405
Oklahoma	800,614	409,125	391,489	128,102	38,476	80,533	67,490	12,569			64,319
Oregon	211,859		211,859	97,118	10,587	61,941	34,154	2,785	5,274	164	
Pennsylvania	4,175,875	2,365,061	1,810,814	558,402	135,401	250,733	177,102	503,648	21,864		163,500
Rhode Island	374,083	212,446	161,637	44,493	7,609	29,292	14,487	50,913	8,101	104	6,638
South Carolina	1,140,747	691,575	449,172	213,909	101,393	29,671	52,906	25,051		6,000	20,242
South Dakota	279,173	173,539	105,634	55,155	9,190	10,634	14,853	460	2,279		13,063
Tennessee	1,704,157	1,177,234	526,923	282,937	59,113	79,211	72,663	25,042		476	7,481
Texas	5,671,153	3,319,992	2,351,161	490,375	272,345	354,965	223,693	309,722		223	699,838
Utah	527,377	391,346	136,031	85,895	11,176	13,261	22,984	2,715	878		34,974
Vermont	175,176	66,711	108,465	28,134	14,070	9,568	7,236	13,605			34,974
Virginia	1,440,702	721,580	719,122	321,394	78,487	17,532	87,071	116,041		77	98,520
Washington	3,116,201	2,453,969	662,232	241,353	105,460	104,151	53,619	144,895	12,395	359	
West Virginia	1,005,196	745,360	259,836	106,290	6,723	36,486	34,938		12,335		63,064
Wisconsin	1,825,864	1,209,440	616,424	287,576	42,557	127,931	45,691	112,044		75	
Wyoming	241,903	190,046	51,857	36,631	2,180	5,301	7,719	26			550

Source: U.S. Bureau of the Census, *State Government Tax Collections in 1983.*

Table 5

STATE GOVERNMENT LICENSE TAX REVENUE: 1983

(In thousands of dollars)

State	Total	Motor vehicles	Motor vehicle operators	Corporations in general	Public utilities	Alcoholic beverages	Amusements	Occupations and businesses, n.e.c.	Hunting and fishing	Other
Number of states using tax	50	50	49	49	31	49	34	50	50	48
United States	$10,651,435	$5,777,676	$504,157	$1,848,127	$158,432	$223,470	$103,799	$1,405,542	$534,569	$96,663
Alabama	119,384	32,756	8,377	54,595	1,172	1,702	176	11,659	9,123	
Alaska	56,316	15,820	366	934		1,593	388	28,041	9,297	89
Arizona	140,594	101,402	4,169	1,508		2,870	475	11,783	7,690	10,784
Arkansas	112,428	67,341	6,756	3,465	7,202	1,046	423	12,375	13,614	154
California	846,144	537,725	58,073	6,273	13,277	33,455		150,105	41,982	4,831
Colorado	99,359	54,354	3,431	2,342		2,228	124	15,485	18,645	2,750
Connecticut	128,045	75,290	13,604	5,331		6,257	55	22,055	2,196	3,257
Delaware	176,263	26,544	1,099	80,031	3,205	516	52	63,787	517	512
Florida	444,038	274,468	25,466	11,760	9,113	16,695	550	91,175	9,366	5,445
Georgia	107,037	55,792	7,411	11,711		1,759		19,414	10,298	652
Hawaii	17,687	8,777	1,636	841	2,558	718		5,291	141	79
Idaho	71,919	35,472	38,933	315	2,263	1,999	935	19,886	11,543	86
Illinois	438,628	308,329	(a)	43,026		7,709	65	31,029	12,939	1,438
Indiana	153,309	118,414		3,555	186	5,097		15,193	7,705	482
Iowa	195,156	146,728	6,091	17,454	95			12,763	5,002	1,926
Kansas	111,243	69,376	4,093	8,976	1,010	1,145	20	18,578	7,536	509
Kentucky	131,423	71,625	6,134	20,291	3,069	2,157	472	17,220	9,942	513
Louisiana	196,701	51,928	9,067	110,772	1,021	2,199	107	16,095	5,130	382
Maine	63,883	32,993	5,102	923		1,522	194	14,953	7,088	1,108
Maryland	134,438	85,194	7,228	3,349		279	346	33,246	4,233	563
Massachusetts	159,308	93,018	24,363	9,313	11,118	841	26,252	3,744	1,107	
Michigan	366,545	258,794	12,035	3,457		20,004	65	34,634	23,705	2,733
Minnesota	262,331	183,823	9,016	1,754		507		41,465	20,734	5,032
Mississippi	120,915	47,328	8,462	38,240	1,337	2,571	502	16,021	6,856	100
Missouri	210,009	117,529	5,531	37,819	5,190	2,207		28,243	11,773	1,215

Montana	47,989	24,339	1,428	542	973	1,344		7,225	12,062	76
Nebraska	81,100	44,932	2,634	6,007		175		13,670	7,061	6,621
Nevada	86,152	30,789	1,810	2,529		24	39,696	6,936	3,235	1,133
New Hampshire	56,568	28,894	2,500	3,247	1,129	1,903	64	13,023	3,322	2,486
New Jersey	478,007	259,230	21,118	127,025	84	3,434	34,865	25,162	6,018	1,071
New Mexico	62,548	38,994	1,632	5,911	163	943	87	7,812	7,006	1,449
New York	554,837	318,642	18,356	15,847	44,074	34,257	7,251	92,051	22,910	856
North Carolina	296,402	151,585	22,466	71,435		1,797	2,598	37,861	7,804	7
North Dakota	51,938	29,107	1,032	524	8	234	1,260	16,084	3,682	
Ohio	469,132	293,080	13,786	70,789	3,845	16,167		55,098	13,996	2,371
Oklahoma	254,891	180,890	6,955	26,981	3	1,038	1,504	17,555	9,812	10,153
Oregon	182,136	111,638	8,570	3,159	4,568	1,570	961	33,412	16,699	1,559
Pennsylvania	927,887	362,293	40,367	371,046	21,441	11,460	27	88,440	28,619	4,194
Rhode Island	29,735	21,784	(a)	1,954		152	91	5,076	450	228
South Carolina	89,311	42,782	2,888	6,486		4,186	8,373	15,843	6,546	2,207
South Dakota	28,352	14,486	1,390	524		120		5,342	6,169	321
Tennessee	214,928	106,939	11,783	58,659	1,363	1,378		23,948	9,965	893
Texas	999,948	308,612	25,724	572,022	3,889	13,242	142	53,776	18,621	3,920
Utah	47,282	26,990	3,638			210		7,434	8,756	254
Vermont	38,134	26,962	2,318	420		504	266	4,256	3,036	372
Virginia	208,536	144,330	14,083	7,670	6,860	3,151	16	26,856	10,292	2,138
Washington	234,267	119,460	16,907	8,093	6,761	6,921	808	54,123	20,982	113
West Virginia	87,234	59,010	(a)	3,896	15	2,231		6,158	6,885	2,293
Wisconsin	205,079	124,935	16,041	3,090	1,440	110		30,530	25,369	4,989
Wyoming	55,939	36,153	288	2,236		14		1,123	14,473	212

Source: U.S. Bureau of the Census, *State Government Tax Collections in 1983.*
(a) Included with motor vehicle licenses.

Table 6
FISCAL YEAR, POPULATION AND PERSONAL INCOME, BY STATE

State	Date of close of fiscal year in 1983	Total population (excluding armed forces overseas) (in thousands)(a)		Personal income, calendar year 1982(b)		State government portion of state-local tax revenue in fiscal 1981-82(c) (percent)
		July 1, 1983 (provisional)	July 1, 1982	Amount (in millions)	Per capita	
United States...............		231,669	229,498	$2,562,406	$ 11,097	61.4
Alabama.....................	September 30	3,932	3,917	34,101	8,649	73.9
Alaska......................	June 30	456	421	7,118	16,257	90.3
Arizona	June 30	2,935	2,866	29,100	10,173	64.4
Arkansas	June 30	2,318	2,297	19,430	8,479	75.9
California...................	June 30	24,887	24,408	310,704	12,567	67.2
Colorado	June 30	3,097	3,027	37,453	12,302	49.2
Connecticut	June 30	3,123	3,111	43,351	13,748	56.9
Delaware	June 30	601	595	7,065	11,731	82.4
Florida	June 30	10,582	10,378	114,327	10,978	60.3
Georgia.....................	June 30	5,661	5,578	54,035	9,583	63.5
Hawaii	June 30	968	942	11,579	11,652	77.2
Idaho	June 30	983	972	8,716	9,029	71.4
Illinois......................	June 30	11,450	11,427	138,519	12,100	54.3
Indiana	June 30	5,473	5,476	54,819	10,021	63.7
Iowa	June 30	2,903	2,905	31,347	10,791	60.6
Kansas	June 30	2,397	2,380	28,325	11,765	57.0
Kentucky	June 30	3,679	3,658	32,762	8,934	79.6
Louisiana	June 30	4,407	4,346	44,633	10,231	67.5
Maine	June 30	1,136	1,127	10,249	9,042	63.5
Maryland	June 30	4,254	4,228	52,195	12,238	59.5
Massachusetts	June 30	5,752	5,737	69,882	12,088	61.9
Michigan	September 30	9,058	9,105	99,802	10,956	55.3
Minnesota	June 30	4,143	4,131	46,184	11,175	72.3
Mississippi	June 30	2,565	2,547	19,840	7,778	77.2
Missouri	June 30	4,953	4,919	50,346	10,170	55.8
Montana....................	June 30	812	800	7,673	9,580	54.8
Nebraska	June 30	1,585	1,577	16,939	10,683	52.3
Nevada	June 30	879	865	10,552	11,981	73.5
New Hampshire	June 30	954	944	10,202	10,729	38.3
New Jersey..................	June 30	7,444	7,401	97,361	13,089	56.0
New Mexico.................	June 30	1,382	1,351	12,492	9,190	82.5
New York....................	March 31	17,639	17,541	217,457	12,314	49.1
North Carolina	June 30	5,976	5,921	54,431	9,044	72.8
North Dakota	June 30	669	661	7,287	10,876	72.2
Ohio	June 30	10,733	10,761	115,217	10,677	55.4
Oklahoma	June 30	3,264	3,193	36,119	11,370	74.1
Oregon	June 30	2,660	2,666	27,373	10,335	52.5
Pennsylvania	June 30	11,883	11,866	129,985	10,955	61.8
Rhode Island	June 30	950	947	10,278	10,723	58.3
South Carolina	June 30	3,199	3,158	27,231	8,502	74.5
South Dakota	June 30	693	688	6,675	9,666	52.0
Tennessee...................	June 30	4,663	4,633	41,420	8,906	60.5
Texas.......................	August 31	15,577	15,186	174,493	11,419	59.2
Utah	June 30	1,612	1,565	13,788	8,875	64.3
Vermont....................	June 30	525	520	4,907	9,507	58.8
Virginia.....................	June 30	5,387	5,327	60,923	11,095	58.7
Washington	June 30	4,242	4,222	49,074	11,560	72.9
West Virginia................	June 30	1,964	1,960	17,078	8,769	78.9
Wisconsin...................	June 30	4,750	4,744	51,341	10,774	66.4
Wyoming	June 30	510	506	6,207	12,372	63.7

Source: U.S. Bureau of the Census, *State Government Tax Collections in 1983.*

Note: Because of rounding, detail may not add to totals.

(a) Bureau of the Census, *Current Population Reports.* Series P-25, January 1984.

(b) U.S. Department of Commerce, *Survey of Current Business,* August 1983.

(c) Bureau of the Census, *Governmental Finances in 1981-82,* October 1983.

SECTION VIII MAJOR STATE SERVICES
1. Education

EDUCATION, 1982-1983

By Nancy M. Berve and John Augenblick, with Christian Pipho

The economic recession that began early in 1980 rapidly worsened in 1982 and 1983, severely affecting state budgets and financing for education. In 1982, about 40 percent of the states experienced zero or deficit budget balances. By the end of fiscal 1983, almost 90 percent of the states faced year-end balances of less than 5 percent, considered the safe level, and 20 percent suffered budget deficits. Although public school systems suffered from the recession, they were affected less than public colleges and universities, which were faced with immediate problems caused by mid-year budget cuts mandated in state after state. In fiscal 1981, 20 percent of the states made mid-year budget adjustments. In 1982, this figure increased to more than 40 percent and in 1983 to almost 70 percent. Even the oil-rich states such as Oklahoma, Louisiana, Texas, North Dakota and Alaska were forced to retrench on education expenditures as the price of oil dropped and severance tax revenue eroded.

As the midpoint of the decade approaches, a more optimistic picture for education is beginning to emerge. According to the U.S. Secretary of Education, nearly one-third of all Americans are currently involved in education, and fiscal 1984 expenditures for the nation's schools and colleges are expected to total $230 billion. National polls conducted in 1982 and 1983 noted that American taxpayers will support increased funding for education in the states, but only if improvements in quality can be assured.

1983 was the year of the report on American education. More than 20 reports were published, 10 of which received considerable national visibility. Each report recommended ways to improve education (see addendum). Although these reports focused primarily on elementary-secondary education, the impact of their recommendations will be significant for colleges and universities. One report, issued by the Carnegie Foundation for the Advancement of Teaching, called upon colleges and universities to establish a comprehensive partnership with one or more high schools to help improve the quality of American secondary education.[1] In another move to create ties between universities and public schools, the presidents of six leading re-search universities agreed that their institutions should play a more active role if excellence in a full-access system of primary and secondary schools is to be assured.

It is clear that education will continue to receive much attention in the 1980s, both nationally and at the state level. The issue will almost certainly be one of the primary agenda items in the 1984 state legislative sessions as well as an important topic during the 1984 presidential and congressional campaigns.

State Support for Education

State support for education continued to grow between 1980-81 and 1982-83; in 1982-83, the 50 states provided $82.7 billion in state aid to education—$58.4 billion for elementary-secondary schools and $24.3 billion for colleges and universities.[2] On the average, states increased their support for elementary-secondary education by 13.4 percent over the two-year period 1981-83, while they increased their support for higher education by 16.3 percent. For fiscal 1984, the state appropriations for colleges and universities showed a more modest increase—5 percent over 1982-83 and an 11 percent two-year increase over fiscal 1982. There were, however, large variations among the states, reflecting differences in rates of enrollment growth or decline and differences in economic conditions. In all but seven states, average daily attendance in elementary-secondary schools decreased, with an overall decline of 3.8 percent across all states. On the other hand, full-time equivalent enrollments in public colleges grew by 3.6 percent with enrollments decreasing in only seven states.

After reducing expenditures dramatically in 1982, many states chose to increase revenues in 1983. Between November 1982 and May 1983, 20 states raised their sales or income taxes.[3] Actions designed to reduce expenditures and increase

Nancy M. Berve is former coordinator of Postsecondary Education for the Education Commission of the States and now a consultant in education. John Augenblick is a partner in Augenblick, Van de Water & Associates, Educational Policy/Planning Services in Denver, Colorado. Christian Pipho is Senior Policy Analyst for the Education Commission of the States.

revenues kept most 1983 state budgets in balance, preparing the way for a rosier fiscal picture in 1984. Education did not suffer as much as other state functions in the cutbacks and the combination of increased national attention to education and better economic conditions is likely to lead to improved funding for schools and colleges in the future.

Due to declining enrollments and specific actions taken to protect elementary-secondary education, per pupil state support for public schools increased more rapidly than per student state support of colleges and universities between 1980-81 and 1982-83. States increased their public school aid from $1,367 per student to $1,611, by 17.9 percent, over the two-year period. At the same time, state aid per higher education student increased by 13 percent—from $3,171 in 1980-81 to $3,582 in 1982-83. There is enormous variation among the states in their support of education. New Hampshire provided only $189 per pupil in 1982-83 and six other states provided less than $1,200 per pupil in school aid. At the same time, Alaska provided $5,920 per pupil in school aid, with another six states providing over $2,000 per pupil. In 1982-83, 11 states allocated less than $3,000 per student for public higher education while 14 states allocated more than $4,000 per student. This variation reflects differences in the traditional role of the states in supporting education and in reliance on local revenue for support of public elementary-secondary schools and tuition as a source of revenue for higher education.

The state share of all revenue for elementary-secondary schools has steadily increased over the past decade, in part reflecting the influence of the school finance reform movement. Even between 1980-81 and 1982-83, when most states were not involved in court-mandated or voluntary reform, the state share increased from 48.8 percent to 50.3 percent of all revenue. In 14 states, state aid now provides in excess of 60 percent of all school revenues. In part, this increasing reliance on state support also reflects the diminishing role of the federal government in supporting schools. In the last two years, federal aid decreased as a proportion of all school revenues in 43 states.[4]

State support for higher education has not increased so uniformly across the states. In 21 states, per student state support increased by less than 10 percent between 1980-81 and 1982-83. Tuition and fees charged by public institutions of higher education have continued to rise rapidly, a trend begun in fall 1980. Between 1981-82 and 1982-83, tuition increased by 19.5 percent at public four-year institutions and by 26.9 percent at public two-year institutions. With an increase of over 8 percent in tuition reported for public four-year institutions for 1983-84 and an estimated 16 plus percent over the two-year period from fall 1983 to 1985, this trend is predicted to continue. This pattern reflects an increasing reliance on user fees by the states.

A number of issues will face state policymakers as they determine how much support should be provided for education in the future. Expectations about the quality of the system have risen, and many states are trying new ways to fund education improvement. In the public schools, most attention has focused on the quality of teachers, and numerous suggestions have been made to improve the attractiveness of the profession. Merit pay plans and career ladders are two ideas that have been at the center of discussion accompanied by a perception that salary levels, on average, should be increased. In the last two years, teacher salaries have risen by 16.6 percent across the states. Statewide average annual salary levels range from $14,285 in Mississippi to nearly $34,000 in Alaska. The number of teachers declined by 2.8 percent across the country between 1980-81 and 1982-83, slightly less than the decline in enrollments.[5]

Other suggestions to improve the schools include increasing the length of the school day or the school year, strengthening graduation requirements and integrating new technological advances into the curriculum. While some of these suggestions might not cost a great deal to implement and could save money in the long run, most will require an influx of new funds. Because federal support for education continues to decrease and since local property taxes remain unpopular, it is likely that states will be asked to bear the burden. At the postsecondary education level, increasing attention is being paid by state policy leaders to new state aid distribution mechanisms designed to promote improvements in education quality by providing direct incentives to institutions or by increasing the flexibility of institutions to spend state funds.

Notes

1. Carnegie Foundation for the Advancement of Teaching, *High School: A Report on American Secondary Education*, October 1983.

2. John Augenblick and Gordon Van de Water, *State Support for Education, 1982-83*, Augenblick, Van de Water & Associates, December 1983.

3. Steven D. Gold and Karen Benker, "State Budget Actions in 1983," National Conference of State Legislatures, September 1983.

4. National Education Association, *Estimates of School Statistics, 1982-83*, January 1983.

5. Ibid.

Addendum

In 1983, over 20 reports were issued that focused primarily on the improvement of American education, 10 of which received national attention and major discussion throughout the country. Twelve of the 20 reports are summarized below, in alphabetical order.

1. Business-Higher Education Forum, *America's Competitive Challenge: The Need for a National Response*, April 1983. Stating that the nation must give top priority to improving America's competitiveness in global markets, this report includes several recommendations for presidential and private sector action. Available from: Business-Higher Education Forum, (202) 833-4716.

2. Carnegie Foundation for the Advancement of Teaching, *The Condition of Teaching: A State-by-State Analysis*, September 1983. Analyzes data from each state on teacher salaries, enrollment trends and teacher certification requirements to determine the current condition of the teaching profession. Concludes that teaching is in crisis, primarily due to low pay, poor professional preparation, chaotic credentialling, and low morale. Available from: Princeton University Press, (609) 896-1344.

3. Carnegie Foundation for the Advancement of Teaching, *High School: A Report on American Secondary Education*, October 1983. Based on extensive field studies, this report focuses on all aspects of the American high school, including goals, curriculum, teaching and learning, the role of technology, and the transition from high school to college and the workplace. Available from: Harper and Row, (212) 593-7065.

4. The College Board, *Academic Preparation for College: What Students Need to Know and Be Able to Do*, 1983. Through dialogues with teachers, deans, curriculum specialists and education policy leaders, consensus was reached on the knowledge and skills needed by high school students to perform successfully in college. Available from: The College Board (New York City Office), (212) 582-6210.

5. Congressional Research Service, "Comparison of Recommendations from Selected Education Reform Reports," June 1983. This paper compares the reports of the National Commission on Excellence in Education, the Twentieth Century Fund Task Force and the Education Commission of the States' Task Force on Education for Economic Growth. Available from: Each state's congressional offices.

6. Education Commission of the States, Task Force on Education for Economic Growth, *Action for Excellence*, June 1983. This report focuses on kindergarten through high school education; links educational improvement to each state's future economic growth and stresses public-private sector partnerships. Contains many recommendations including that state plans for improving education in the public schools be developed and implemented as promptly as possible. Available from: Education Commission of the States, (303) 830-3600, $5.00 per copy.

7. John I. Goodlad, *A Place Called School: Prospects for the Future*, 1983. With a focus on elementary-secondary education, the report analyzes findings from an eight-year research project that included visits to more than 1,000 classrooms in seven states; advocates a complete overhaul of all American education. Available from: McGraw-Hill Book Company, 1221 Avenue of the Americas, New York, NY 10020, $17.95 per copy.

8. National Association of Secondary School Principals, National Association of Independent Schools, *A Study of High Schools*, 1984. This report will eventually include three publications: (1) A Celebration of Teaching, by Theodore Sizer, focusing upon the student-teacher-content triangle in classrooms (January 1984); (2) a historical survey by Robert Hampel describing the changes taking place in American society and in American high schools since 1940 (Spring 1984); and (3) an analysis by Arthur Powell, David Cohen and Eleanor Farrar of 15 public and private high schools in five states (Fall 1984). Available from: National Association of Secondary School Principals, (703) 860-0200.

9. National Commission on Excellence in Education, *A Nation at Risk*, April 1983. With a focus on the high school, this report contains recommendations under five general headings—content, standards and expectations, time, teaching and leadership and fiscal support; the report was the first of the so-called excellence reports to raise educational mediocrity as a national issue and has both fueled and shaped the current debate on how to improve learning and teaching. Available from: Superintendent of Documents, U.S. Government Printing Office, Washington, D.C. 20402; stock No. 065-000-00177-2, $4.50 per copy.

10. National Science Foundation's National Science Board Commission on Precollege Education in Mathematics, Science and Technology, *Educating Americans for the 21st Century*, September 1983. Contains a plan of action to insure that academic achievement of American students is the "best in the world" by 1995. Available from: National Science

Foundation, (202) 357-7700.

11. Diane Ravitch, *The Troubled Crusade: American Education, 1945-1980*, 1983. A report on the nation's "crusade against ignorance" since World War II. Particularly critical of single-issue approaches to school reform and the progressive education movement. Available from: Basic Books, 10 East 53rd Street, New York, NY 10022, $19.95 per copy.

12. Twentieth Century Fund Task Force on Federal Elementary and Secondary Education Policy, *Making the Grade*, 1983. The only major report to focus exclusively on the federal role in elementary-secondary education; contains seven major recommendations for the federal government. Available from: Twentieth Century Fund, 41 East 17th Street, New York, NY 10021, $6.00 per copy.

Source: National Conference of State Legislatures.

ELEMENTARY-SECONDARY EDUCATION ISSUES

By Christian Pipho

An awakening public interest in education brought on by more than 20 national reports released in 1983 set the stage for reform in public school programs. Excellence became the watchword as states moved to strengthen curricular standards and teacher qualifications. In part the various reports focusing on excellence were stimulated by the assumption that the nation's economy could be improved by first improving the education system. Critics felt the country's technology lag could be attributed to a decline in the number of students enrolled in mathematics and science courses and the quality of instruction in these areas. The inability to compete in the international arena and the sluggish economy also were identified as problems that could be improved by upgrading the quality of education programs at the K-12 and postsecondary education levels.

Instructional Standards

Between 1980 and 1983, more than half the states increased high school graduation standards. For the most part, the number of units of mathematics and science required of all high school students has been increased. Several states also increased the total number of academic or basic skills units required for graduation while decreasing the number of electives students are permitted to earn. Many colleges and universities are raising admission requirements as well, and in some cases, state or local education boards have responded by establishing two kinds of high school diplomas—one with higher standards for college-bound students and one with lower standards for other students.

While *A Nation at Risk*, the first of the excellence reports, calls for students to be prepared in new technological basics, only Rhode Island, by early 1984, had added computer literacy as a state high school graduation requirement, and then only for the college-bound student. Several other states, however, encourage computer education in their schools. In Delaware, computer literacy must be considered an instruction objective, rather than a graduation requirement, but all high schools are encouraged to offer computer literacy electives. In Georgia, students must take either fine arts, vocational education

or computer technology. In Idaho, Illinois and West Virginia, one year of mathematics may be in the area of computer technology, and in Indiana, every school district must have a plan for computer literacy by August 1984. The Nevada Department of Education encourages school districts to offer coursework in computers and calculators, and in Virginia, each student must receive educational experience as outlined in a state publication on computer literacy.

While states have been studying the issue of computers and the educational and public media have given lots of space to computers and their use in schools, it is not likely that many more states will immediately add this requirement for all students. At stake will be the large outlays of money for computer hardware, software and teacher training. In addition, some critics are wary of the proliferation of the use of computers in the schools and warn that not only could computer buying become a fad among schools, but that available educational software leaves much to be desired. The U.S. Secretary of Education chastised the schools in early January 1984 on their use of computer software and noted that most of the computer software now is "electronic page-turning" and not designed to do a good job of interacting with students' minds. He reported that the U.S. Department of Education will finance research on new ways to use computers to teach children algebra and composition.

Minimum Competency

Student minimum competency testing continues to be a popular means to assure a minimum level of student achievement. By the end of 1983, 40 states had either used or were still using some form of the test. Nineteen states were using the test for high school graduation and four states were using the tests for grade-to-grade promotion at the elementary level. Only Louisiana had embarked on a program to make grade promotion at all grade levels contingent upon passing the state test. The concept will still be attracting interest in the 1984 legislative sessions when no less than five states will be considering

Christian Pipho is Senior Policy Analyst for the Education Commission of the States.

bills to extend or create a minimum competency testing program.

Teacher Quality

States have regulated the certification of teachers for many years. Every state requires prospective teachers to complete an approved program with required courses, and approximately 35 states impose at least some of the requirements themselves (in the remaining states, institutions of higher education approve programs). Twenty-three states currently have or are seriously considering imposing statewide teacher tests. Seven states require that prospective teachers have minimum college grade-point averages before they can be certified. A few states require teaching practicums or internships that often involve extensive evaluation. Several states are attempting to lure better-qualified students into schools of education. Two of the most popular methods are offering scholarships in exchange for five-year teaching commitments and offering low-interest loans to qualified education majors, as in programs established in Kentucky and Louisiana. Revamping the education school curriculum to make it more attractive to students has received some attention at the state level, but most of the interest in curriculum revision thus far has come from schools of education.

In the 1984 legislative sessions, several states will consider legislation creating alternative certification plans to allow individuals to become certified without taking education courses. These states hope this plan will help attract people from business and industry into teacher shortage areas, such as mathematics and science.

One of the more interesting trends to grow out of the excellence movement is the use of new approaches to paying teachers, including merit pay and career ladders. These approaches are gaining attention and will likely be implemented in some states in order to attract better qualified people into the teaching profession and retain them in the future. The merit pay plan rewards outstanding teachers with extra money in order to provide an incentive for better performance and encouragement to remain in the profession. The career ladder in some ways replaces the single salary schedule approach, differentiating salary among teachers who provide leadership in addition to being good teachers. In 1983, Tennessee considered legislation, which will be reintroduced in 1984, creating a four-step career ladder—apprentice, professional, senior and distinguished senior teacher. In some plans the top level of teacher also has responsibility to assist with the evaluation of other teachers. One of the key elements of a merit pay or career ladder program is the evaluation of teachers. Organized teacher groups have opposed many of the legislative proposals because they considered current or proposed evaluation plans too weak. Some experts were predicting that as many as 20 states would consider merit pay or career ladder programs in 1984.

POSTSECONDARY EDUCATION

By Nancy M. Berve and Gordon Van de Water

Although many of the states faced financial difficulties during 1983, the majority continued to provide at least a modest increase in their support for higher education. State tax appropriations for the 50 states to support operating costs of colleges and universities total $25.4 billion for 1983-84, an 11 percent increase over 1981-82. Although this is the smallest gain since 1960, it still is an increase in an era when less money, rather than more, is the norm. However, when the 1983-84 appropriations are adjusted for the inflation rate in the two-year period from 1981 to 1982, there is an actual decline in real support for higher education in 16 of the 50 states. Overall, inflation turned a two-year increase of 11 percent into a gain of about 2 percent.[1] On the optimistic side, there is a general consensus that, with the current administration continuing to reduce federal funds and returning financial responsibilities to the states, the state legislatures will step into the breach and continue to maintain at least the current support of education, and perhaps even increase support.

Disappointing revenue collections in the states during the last three years have produced a new phenomenon in postsecondary education—the mid-year budget adjustment. Although all state agencies suffered from this problem, it has been particularly troublesome in postsecondary education because a large percentage of the budget is devoted to personnel costs—a difficult area in which to make short-term budget adjustments. A 1983 survey by the Education Commission of the States identified mid-year adjustments in fiscal year 1982 ranging from 0.7 percent to 10 percent in 14 of the 33 states reporting. In fiscal 1983, the number jumped to 23 states out of the 33 reporting states. In general, the percentage reduction required of the higher education budgets was the same as those required of other state agencies. Compared to elementary-secondary education, however, the higher education segment typically was mandated to cut a greater percentage of its budget.

Postsecondary institutions adopted a variety of tactics to meet mid-year budget adjustment requirements. These tactics included some combination of leaving positions vacant, delaying capital construction, delaying facility renovation or maintenance, restricting travel and reducing equipment purchases. While none of these, if viewed separately during a single year, would be cause for undue alarm, it is the cumulative effects of actions over several years that threaten the health and vitality of public colleges and universities.[2]

Student Assistance

Two recent studies of student assistance report that not only has federal support of student aid programs decreased radically, but the federal programs have been seriously eroded. According to the National Commission on Student Financial Assistance, established by the Congress in 1981, federal financial aid for the country's most needy college students has been eroded by a "quiet, unintended shift of attention and funding" toward programs helping those from middle-income families. The commission notes that unless that trend is checked, "we will drift into becoming a country where only the wealthy can be healthy and wise."[3] A study by the College Board, released in January 1984, reported the amount of financial aid available for college students dropped by $2 billion from 1981-82 to 1983-84, with most of the reduction in federal funds. The effect of this decline, from a total of $18 billion in fiscal 1982, is even greater if inflation is taken into account. The real value of student aid, according to the College Board's study, has dropped 21 percent in the 1980s. The study traces the major reasons for the decline to the decision of the Reagan administration and the 1981 Congress to phase out Social Security benefits for college students, to eligibility restrictions for the guaranteed student loans, and to a drop in the use of veterans benefits.[4]

In contrast to the erosion of federal funds for needy students, the states continue to provide a greater portion of funds for these students. The rate of increase of state funds has remained fairly consistent since 1980, increasing at an average

---

Nancy M. Berve is a consultant in education. Gordon Van de Water is a partner in Augenblick, Van de Water & Associates, Educational Policy/Planning Services, Denver, Colorado.

annual rate of 10 percent. In 1983-84, state grants to needy undergraduates will top $1 billion, according to the annual survey conducted by the National Association of State Scholarship and Grant Programs (NASSGP). In 1983-84, states will provide aid to about 1,281,193 students, an increase of 2.5 percent over the previous year.

The NASSGP survey found that many states are reevaluating their student aid programs, and recently 20 states have created special commissions to study tuition and aid policies, 14 states are considering the establishment of new aid programs, and of these, eight may develop their own work-study programs, modeled after the federal College Work-Study Program. Since 1981, seven states have established work-study programs. In addition, in the last few years, 10 states have initiated financial incentive programs to encourage students to choose teaching careers in mathematics and science for elementary-secondary schools.[5]

The Search for Quality

State-level policy-makers traditionally have left judgments of quality in higher education to the institutions and their accrediting agencies. Policy-makers have focused on equitable funding patterns, access and opportunity. These interests are reflected in budget processes tied to enrollment levels and program costs, and are not overtly concerned about quality. Indeed, when closely examined, such processes often include disincentives to improving quality. For example, enrollment-driven funding formulas create pressure to continually expand enrollment levels, thus providing an incentive for lower admission and retention standards. Similarly, state-imposed salary schedules may work against an institution trying to upgrade its faculty or retain its best teachers.

With an era of fiscal constraint coming on the heels of 15 years of expansion and emphasis on access, state-level policy-makers are now focusing on issues of accountability and quality. Even though quality is difficult to define and relate to budget processes, several states are attempting to move in this direction. Three strategies have emerged. Under one strategy, institutions are provided with greater latitude to determine how state funds are to be spent, what programs will be offered and how much tuition will be charged. Success is measured by the marketplace, that is, how many students choose to attend given the quality, diversity and cost of the programs offered. Colorado has recently adopted such an approach.

Under a second strategy, specific areas are singled out for improvement using several approaches. Some states encourage private fund raising by setting up matching grants from state funds, as in Texas, Virginia and Florida. Other states use competitive grants to stimulate new ideas at the campus level, as is done in Louisiana and Virginia. Where there is a specific problem, such as inadequate teacher preparation or failure to recruit good students to teaching, then the use of categorical funding mechanisms, the third strategy, can be effective. The clearer the definition of the improvement goal, the more useful this process can be. If the goal is one that can be accomplished in a relatively short period of time, this strategy is more likely to succeed. Since 1974, Florida has been using this strategy to develop "centers of excellence" at its state universities. Consistency over time is the major determinant of the success of such approaches.[6]

Strengthening Admission Standards and Policies

As noted in the earlier section on elementary-secondary education, admission policies for public colleges and universities are becoming stricter at the same time the state school systems are tightening graduation requirements from high school. A 1982 survey by the Connecticut Board of Higher Education revealed that 25 states had made changes in their admission requirements and 15 others have current policies under review. The trend is toward increasing the number of academic courses required, usually in the areas of mathematics, science and social science. The new norm includes four years of English, two or three years of mathematics, science and social science, and strong recommendations for two or more years of a foreign language. In addition, the desired minimum high school grade-point average has been increased and, in a few cases, the minimum acceptable test score—either American College Testing (ACT) or Scholastic Aptitude Test (SAT)—has been raised.[7]

Campus Developments

The following summarizes the major highlights of campus developments during the two-year period 1981-1983:

Enrollments. Enrollments have inched up steadily the past three years. Total enrollment increased about 1.9 percent in fall 1981, 1.57 percent in fall 1982 and, based on preliminary surveys, 1.1 percent during fall 1983. Although the

18-year-old population took its first big drop in 1983-84 (down 4 percent from 1982-83), the predicted overall decline thus far has not occurred. Full-time enrollments on the campuses have remained essentially the same, but part-time enrollments continue to account for the major portion of the increases. In fall 1983, part-time enrollments rose by 4.6 percent at public community colleges and by 9.8 percent at private junior colleges, the latter having lost enrollment in fall 1982. Graduate enrollments increased in fall 1983 for the first time in three years, gaining 1.4 percent as compared to a decline of 1.1 percent in 1982-83.

Faculty. More than 4,000 faculty members, 1,200 of them with tenure, have been dismissed over the last five years because of fiscal problems at four-year colleges and universities. Virtually all of the layoffs were at relatively small public institutions that had recently expanded programs or in less well-known private colleges. Tenure has become much more difficult to obtain over the past five years as more institutions have toughened standards for awarding tenure. There are an estimated 490,000 faculty members teaching either full or part-time at four-year institutions, and of the total, 43 percent have tenure and an additional 23 percent are in positions that could lead to tenure.

According to the U.S. Bureau of Labor Statistics, the demand for college and university faculty will decline by 15 percent from 1982 through 1995. The bureau projects that the total faculty of 744,000 will drop to 632,000 and the number of graduate assistants will drop from 140,000 to 124,000 in the same period. The demand for vocational-education teachers at the postsecondary education level will increase rapidly because of growth that is projected in job training and retraining programs.

Average faculty salaries rose by 6.4 percent in 1982-83. Women in the top three professorial ranks earned an average of 19 percent less than men during fiscal 1983. Although in the past few years, starting salaries for women in higher education have come closer to those of men, the higher the rank, the greater the difference between salaries of male and female faculty members, according to the National Center for Education Statistics.

Teacher Education Programs. In a survey conducted by the National Center for Education Statistics for the National Commission on Excellence in Education, about 75 percent of the nation's colleges and universities have raised their admission standards for teacher education programs. Over 85 percent of the institutions surveyed have revised their programs and made their curricula more rigorous in an effort to improve the quality of teachers. About 5 percent of the institutions have extended their teacher education programs from four to five years.

Voluntary Support. Gifts to education in 1982 totaled nearly $8.6 billion, an increase of 13 percent over 1981, according to the American Association of Fund-Raising Council. Individuals accounted for 80 percent of all charitable giving in the United States and for nearly half of all gifts to colleges and universities. Preliminary figures for 1983 indicate that major fund-raising programs of American universities are receiving substantially more support than given during the same period in 1982.[8]

Notes

1. M.M. Chambers, *State Tax Funds for Operating Expenses of Higher Education, 1983-84*, National Association of State Universities and Land-Grant Colleges, October 1983.

2. Gordon Van de Water and Van Dougherty, "The Effect of State Budget Reductions on Higher Education in Fiscal Year 1983-84," Education Commission of the States, October 1983.

3. *The Chronicle of Higher Education*, November 16, 1973, p. 1.

4. The College Board, *Trends in Student Aid: 1963-1983*, January 1984.

5. *The Chronicle of Higher Education*, January 4, 1984, p. 13.

6. John K. Folger, "Financing Quality Improvements in Higher Education," Vanderbilt University, October 1983.

7. Connecticut Board of Higher Education, *Admission Standards: National Trends in Public Higher Education*, May 1983.

8. *The Chronicle of Higher Education*, October 26, November 2, 9, 23, 30, December 7, 1983; January 11, 18, 1984.

Table 1
CHANGES IN TOTAL STATE SUPPORT FOR EDUCATION,
1980-81 TO 1982-83
(Dollar amounts in millions)

State	Elementary/Secondary Education			Higher Education		
	1982-83	1980-81	Percent change	1982-83	1980-81	Percent change
All States	$58,444.4	$51,544.2	13.4%	$24,249.3	$20,857.2	16.3%
Alabama	735.9	705.4	4.3	407.1	385.3	5.6
Alaska	469.1	339.8	38.0	146.8	81.9	79.3
Arizona	640.0	634.1	0.9	322.5	280.4	15.0
Arkansas	505.6	426.5	18.5	198.1	187.6	5.6
California	8,189.6	7,840.3	4.5	3,274.9	3,158.9	3.7
Colorado	668.4	609.0	9.8	350.0	264.0	32.6
Connecticut........	660.3	525.3	25.7	252.6	209.8	20.4
Delaware	244.2	216.2	13.0	76.9	63.8	20.5
Florida	2,600.0	2,097.4	24.0	905.8	718.5	26.1
Georgia	1,358.2	1,179.6	15.1	534.2	432.0	23.7
Hawaii	458.4	396.8	15.5	185.1	135.4	36.7
Idaho	288.5	231.7	24.5	104.0	94.1	10.5
Illinois	2,327.3	2,271.7	2.4	1,029.3	989.9	4.0
Indiana............	1,562.8	1,376.6	13.5	485.3	459.6	5.6
Iowa	635.0	564.1	12.6	381.1	318.9	19.5
Kansas	606.1	498.9	21.5	312.0	259.9	20.1
Kentucky	1,054.0	915.2	15.2	363.6	307.6	18.2
Louisiana..........	1,072.5	959.0	11.8	501.8	398.3	26.0
Maine	274.5	233.0	17.8	71.9	62.6	14.8
Maryland..........	956.2	843.8	13.3	432.7	367.7	17.7
Massachusetts......	1,141.4	1,262.7	-9.6	412.4	322.5	27.9
Michigan	2,066.8	1,750.0	18.1	865.0	757.8	14.2
Minnesota	1,181.8	1,375.7	-14.1	520.9	478.0	9.0
Mississippi	527.8	452.1	16.7	296.4	261.3	13.4
Missouri...........	857.7	745.8	15.0	358.1	353.3	1.4
Montana	230.6	196.0	17.7	95.3	67.3	41.6
Nebraska	190.0	198.2	-4.1	189.6	166.2	14.1
Nevada............	217.1	168.4	28.9	71.9	62.1	15.8
New Hampshire	28.0	29.9	-6.4	35.2	32.9	6.9
New Jersey	1,947.8	1,612.0	20.8	498.1	434.2	14.7
New Mexico	646.1	441.0	46.5	184.1	143.3	28.5
New York	4,492.0	3,957.8	13.5	2,010.0	1,644.4	22.2
North Carolina	1,622.8	1,441.1	12.6	793.4	660.6	20.1
North Dakota	175.0	138.7	26.2	108.5	75.7	43.4
Ohio	2,136.0	1,749.7	22.1	846.3	719.9	17.6
Oklahoma	1,037.5	821.3	26.3	399.9	271.2	47.5
Oregon............	601.7	467.1	28.8	240.5	250.4	-4.0
Pennsylvania........	2,850.0	2,521.2	13.0	871.0	780.2	11.6
Rhode Island.......	174.5	143.8	21.3	91.1	78.3	16.3
South Carolina	785.8	673.8	16.6	373.8	344.5	8.5
South Dakota	95.0	83.7	13.5	53.5	53.7	-0.4
Tennessee	882.7	755.8	16.8	374.3	338.2	10.7
Texas	4,159.0	3,254.0	27.8	2,035.5	1,464.9	39.0
Utah..............	480.0	380.3	26.2	196.4	160.9	22.1
Vermont	98.0	69.1	41.7	37.7	30.5	23.8
Virginia	1,115.6	969.3	15.1	616.5	509.7	20.9
Washington.........	1,682.1	1,569.8	7.2	497.8	467.7	6.4
West Virginia	606.0	497.2	21.9	193.1	169.8	13.7
Wisconsin	979.0	846.0	15.7	550.1	511.1	7.6
Wyoming...........	130.0	108.2	20.1	97.2	70.5	37.9

Sources: Augenblick, Van de Water & Associates (Denver, Co.), National Education Association and National Association of State Universities and Land-Grant Colleges.

Table 2
CHANGES IN ENROLLMENTS IN PUBLIC EDUCATION,
1980-81 TO 1982-83

State	Elementary/Secondary Education (ADA)			Higher Education (FTE)		
	1982-83	1980-81	Percent change	1982-83	1980-81	Percent change
All States	36,273,884	37,712,077	-3.8%	6,690,542	6,505,732	3.6%
Alabama	698,696	701,925	-0.5	116,843	113,821	2.7
Alaska	79,238	78,211	1.3	12,542	10,399	20.6
Arizona	513,278	518,211	-1.0	124,473	116,916	6.5
Arkansas	408,859	417,080	-2.0	52,972	53,711	-1,4
California	3,766,736	4,014,917	-6.2	967,113	938,132	3.1
Colorado	507,125	527,720	-3.9	112,577	107,076	5.1
Connecticut.	464,900	504,976	-7.9	66,463	65,449	1.5
Delaware	79,252	89,609	-11.6	22,095	21,160	4.4
Florida	1,262,866	1,387,475	-9.0	228,210	223,392	2.2
Georgia	975,267	988,600	-1.3	115,837	106,229	9.0
Hawaii	147,976	151,713	-2.5	34,391	32,534	5.7
Idaho	192,402	190,007	1.3	26,808	26,303	1.9
Illinois	1,630,800	1,726,079	-5.5	333,841	318,124	4.9
Indiana.	892,370	944,424	-5.5	146,955	138,297	6.3
Iowa	480,000	501,403	-4.3	88,000	80,518	9.3
Kansas	365,290	374,451	-2.4	90,083	88,490	1.8
Kentucky	601,910	614,676	-2.1	88,452	75,897	16.5
Louisiana.	702,000	715,900	-1.9	119,070	110,604	7.7
Maine	196,000	207,554	-5.6	24,641	24,055	2.4
Maryland	635,600	683,533	-7.0	130,042	126,868	2.5
Massachusetts	877,001	897,060	-2.2	125,582	128,402	-2.2
Michigan	1,620,954	1,721,239	-5.8	301,888	311,393	-3.1
Minnesota	676,220	710,089	-4.8	127,771	121,829	4.9
Mississippi	438,500	446,515	-1.8	79,820	71,316	11.9
Missouri	722,938	754,179	-4.1	127,373	122,582	3.9
Montana	135,100	139,810	-3.4	27,553	26,208	5.1
Nebraska	248,640	263,883	-5.8	56,389	53,182	6.0
Nevada	141,420	138,400	2.2	23,038	19,763	16.6
New Hampshire	148,522	151,016	-1.7	20,972	20,102	4.3
New Jersey	1,083,814	1,143,700	-5.2	169,338	164,659	2.8
New Mexico	255,655	257,804	-0.8	44,465	41,020	8.4
New York	2,397,010	2,547,134	-5.9	422,214	417,987	1.0
North Carolina	1,024,237	1,055,651	-3.0	179,831	171,289	5.0
North Dakota	112,213	113,091	-0.8	28,999	28,116	3.1
Ohio	1,710,120	1,801,900	-5.1	283,452	271,998	4.2
Oklahoma	545,000	542,800	0.4	102,016	100,658	1.3
Oregon.	401,190	417,002	-3.8	91,129	98,309	-7.3
Pennsylvania	1,633,700	1,740,300	-6.1	227,678	221,601	2.7
Rhode Island	124,978	135,096	-7.5	28,154	24,451	15.1
South Carolina	571,200	581,103	-1.7	85,799	84,688	1.3
South Dakota	118,000	121,663	-3.0	21,851	20,331	7.5
Tennessee	774,814	797,237	-2.8	115,273	115,805	-0.5
Texas	2,733,000	2,656,523	2.9	459,190	434,806	5.6
Utah	341,246	323,048	5.6	48,538	47,057	3.1
Vermont	85,300	88,351	-3.5	14,089	14,203	-0.8
Virginia	903,026	938,794	-3.8	172,438	170,033	1.4
Washington	685,973	704,655	-2.7	150,008	183,722	-18.4
West Virginia	345,116	351,823	-1.9	53,016	51,462	3.0
Wisconsin	723,248	742,366	-2.6	184,569	175,651	5.1
Wyoming	95,184	91,381	4.2	16,701	15,132	10.4

Sources: National Education Association and National Center for Education Statistics.
Note: ADA is average daily attendance; FTE is full-time-equivalent based on full-time plus one-third of part-time students.

Table 3
CHANGES IN PER STUDENT STATE SUPPORT FOR EDUCATION, 1980-81 TO 1982-83

State	Elementary/Secondary Education			Higher Education		
	1982-83	1980-81	Percent change	1982-83	1980-81	Percent change
All States	$1,611	$1,367	17.9%	$3,582	$3,171	13.0%
Alabama	1,053	1,005	4.8	3,463	3,364	3.0
Alaska	5,920	4,345	36.2	11,705	7,874	48.7
Arizona	1,247	1,224	1.9	2,591	2,399	8.0
Arkansas	1,237	1,023	21.0	3,740	3,492	7.1
California	2,174	1,953	11.3	3,386	3,367	0.6
Colorado	1,318	1,154	14.2	3,109	2,465	26.1
Connecticut	1,420	1,040	36.5	3,801	3,206	18.6
Delaware	3,081	2,412	27.7	3,480	3,016	15.4
Florida	2,059	1,512	36.2	3,969	3,216	23.4
Georgia	1,419	1,193	18.9	4,612	4,066	13.4
Hawaii	3,098	2,616	18.4	5,383	4,161	29.4
Idaho	1,499	1,219	22.9	3,879	3,579	8.4
Illinois	1,427	1,316	8.4	3,050	3,078	-0.9
Indiana	1,751	1,458	20.1	3,302	3,324	-0.6
Iowa	1,323	1,125	17.6	4,331	3,960	9.4
Kansas	1,659	1,332	24.5	3,463	2,937	17.9
Kentucky	1,751	1,489	17.6	4,111	4,052	1.4
Louisiana	1,528	1,340	14.1	4,184	3,578	16.9
Maine	1,401	1,123	24.8	2,918	2,604	12.1
Maryland	1,504	1,234	21.8	3,238	2,820	14.8
Massachusetts	1,301	1,408	-7.6	3,284	2,512	30.8
Michigan	1,275	1,017	25.4	2,865	2,433	17.7
Minnesota	1,748	1,937	-9.8	4,053	3,885	4.3
Mississippi	1,204	1,013	18.9	3,713	3,664	1.3
Missouri	1,186	989	19.9	2,811	2,882	-2.5
Montana	1,707	1,402	21.8	3,459	2,570	34.6
Nebraska	764	751	1.7	3,362	3,124	7.6
Nevada	1,535	1,216	26.2	3,121	3,143	-0.7
New Hampshire	189	198	-4.6	1,678	1,638	2.5
New Jersey	1,797	1,409	27.5	2,853	2,553	11.8
New Mexico	2,527	1,711	47.7	4,140	3,494	18.5
New York	1,824	1,554	17.4	4,462	3,702	20.5
North Carolina	1,584	1,365	16.0	4,412	3,857	14.4
North Dakota	1,564	1,226	27.5	3,742	2,691	39.1
Ohio	1,249	971	28.6	2,961	2,622	12.9
Oklahoma	1,904	1,513	25.8	3,921	2,694	45.5
Oregon	1,500	1,120	33.9	2,639	2,547	3.6
Pennsylvania	1,745	1,449	20.5	3,625	3,348	8.3
Rhode Island	1,396	1,064	31.2	3,236	3,203	1.0
South Carolina	1,376	1,160	18.7	4,357	4,068	7.1
South Dakota	805	688	17.0	2,448	2,643	-7.4
Tennessee	1,139	948	20.1	3,247	2,920	11.2
Texas	1,522	1,225	24.3	4,307	3,269	31.8
Utah	1,407	1,177	19.5	4,046	3,418	18.4
Vermont	1,149	783	46.8	2,676	2,144	24.8
Virginia	1,235	1,033	19.6	3,564	2,998	18.9
Washington	2,452	2,228	10.1	3,318	2,546	30.3
West Virginia	1,756	1,413	24.3	3,642	3,300	10.4
Wisconsin	1,354	1,140	18.8	2,980	2,910	2.4
Wyoming	1,366	1,184	15.4	5,820	4,659	24.9

Source: Augenblick, Van de Water & Associates (Denver, Co.).

Table 4

TOTAL REVENUES FOR ELEMENTARY/SECONDARY EDUCATION AND PERCENTAGE SHARE OF TOTAL REVENUES BY SOURCE, 1980-81 and 1982-83
(Dollar amounts in millions)

State	1982-83				1980-81			
	Total Revenue	Percent State	Percent Local	Percent Federal	Total Revenue	Percent State	Percent Local	Percent Federal
All States	$115,954	50.3	42.3	7.4	$102,445	48.8	42.7	8.5
Alabama	1,145	64.3	21.0	14.8	1,083	65.6	19.5	15.0
Alaska	599	78.3	16.0	5.7	467	69.6	17.3	13.1
Arizona	1,400	45.7	42.9	11.4	1,312	44.9	44.0	11.2
Arkansas	930	54.3	32.4	13.3	781	53.7	31.6	14.7
California	9,545	85.8	8.9	5.3	9,260	73.4	19.4	7.1
Colorado	1,813	36.9	57.7	5.4	1,498	40.6	52.9	6.5
Connecticut.........	1,815	36.4	58.7	4.9	1,526	34.4	59.8	5.8
Delaware	361	67.6	21.2	11.2	324	66.8	21.6	11.6
Florida	4,200	61.9	31.0	7.1	3,803	55.0	34.7	10.3
Georgia	2,441	55.6	34.2	10.2	2,117	55.7	33.2	11.1
Hawaii	511	89.8	0.3	9.9	448	86.3	2.3	11.4
Idaho	461	62.6	30.4	6.9	382	61.5	30.1	8.4
Illinois	6,118	38.0	53.4	8.5	5,663	40.1	50.5	9.4
Indiana............	2,665	58.6	35.1	6.3	2,216	59.7	34.8	5.5
Iowa	1,508	42.1	50.6	7.3	1,345	41.9	52.0	6.0
Kansas	1,365	44.4	50.8	4.8	1,111	44.9	48.8	6.3
Kentucky	1,494	70.5	18.7	10.7	1,312	69.8	17.8	12.5
Louisiana..........	1,918	55.9	34.7	9.4	1,630	55.2	32.5	12.3
Maine	553	49.7	40.2	10.1	477	48.8	42.1	9.1
Maryland	2,381	40.2	53.9	5.9	2,125	39.7	52.7	7.6
Massachusetts........	2,900	39.4	55.8	4.8	3,265	38.7	54.3	7.0
Michigan	5,725	36.1	55.8	8.1	4,886	35.8	56.2	8.0
Minnesota	2,417	48.9	46.3	4.7	2,382	57.7	36.5	5.7
Mississippi	991	53.3	23.7	23.0	859	53.1	22.8	24.1
Missouri............	2,166	39.6	52.3	8.1	1,921	38.8	52.1	9.1
Montana	487	47.4	44.2	8.5	418	46.9	44.3	8.9
Nebraska...........	681	27.9	65.0	7.1	692	16.7	75.7	7.6
Nevada............	358	60.6	31.8	7.6	297	51.7	40.5	7.8
New Hampshire	406	6.9	89.2	3.9	389	7.3	88.4	4.3
New Jersey	4,865	40.0	56.4	3.5	4,117	39.2	57.2	3.6
New Mexico	830	77.8	12.0	10.2	676	65.2	19.2	15.6
New York	10,709	41.9	54.1	4.0	9,693	40.8	54.2	4.9
North Carolina	2,641	61.5	22.4	16.1	2,240	65.4	21.2	13.4
North Dakota	341	51.5	41.1	7.3	253	45.4	46.6	7.9
Ohio	5,251	40.7	54.3	5.0	4,448	41.6	50.7	7.7
Oklahoma	1,722	60.2	29.5	10.3	1,392	59.3	29.2	11.5
Oregon............	1,633	36.8	54.4	8.8	1,380	33.8	57.2	9.0
Pennsylvania	6,312	45.2	47.4	7.5	5,520	45.3	47.1	7.6
Rhode Island........	471	37.0	58.3	4.7	399	36.0	58.4	5.6
South Carolina	1,377	57.1	29.3	13.6	1,195	56.4	29.2	14.4
South Dakota	344	27.6	63.7	8.7	263	27.4	59.4	13.1
Tennessee	1,868	47.2	39.8	13.0	1,575	48.5	37.8	13.7
Texas	8,223	50.6	39.5	10.0	6,761	49.4	40.0	10.6
Utah..............	853	56.3	38.5	5.2	708	53.9	38.4	7.6
Vermont	278	35.2	57.8	7.0	218	27.0	66.8	6.1
Virginia	2,683	41.6	51.8	6.6	2,341	41.4	49.6	9.0
Washington..........	2,237	75.2	19.4	5.4	1,879	74.9	16.6	8.6
West Virginia	970	62.4	28.5	9.0	827	60.2	28.7	11.2
Wisconsin	2,617	37.4	57.2	5.4	2,294	36.8	57.0	6.3
Wyoming...........	375	34.7	61.3	4.0	277	28.6	64.7	6.7

Source: National Education Association, *Estimates of School Statistics, 1982-83* (and 1981-82).

Table 5
CHANGES IN NUMBER OF TEACHERS AND AVERAGE TEACHER SALARY, 1980-81 TO 1982-83

State	Number of Teachers			Teacher Salary		
	1982-83	1980-81	Percent change	1982-83	1980-81	Percent change
All States	2,133,663	2,194,869	-2.8%	$20,531	$17,602	16.6%
Alabama	39,400	39,714	-0.8	17,850	15,205	17.4
Alaska	5,630	5,224	7.8	33,953	29,048	16.9
Arizona	28,856	26,200	10.1	18,849	17,201	9.6
Arkansas	23,505	24,111	-2.5	15,156	13,273	14.2
California	170,397	179,938	-5.3	23,555	20,729	13.6
Colorado	29,000	29,840	-2.8	21,500	17,917	20.0
Connecticut	31,698	33,850	-6.4	20,300	17,419	16.5
Delaware	5,344	5,589	-4.4	20,665	18,025	14.6
Florida	82,041	80,285	2.2	18,538	15,406	20.3
Georgia	57,016	56,970	0.1	17,412	15,445	12.7
Hawaii	8,124	8,082	0.5	24,796	21,147	17.3
Idaho	10,125	9,938	1.9	17,549	15,109	16.1
Illinois	104,249	107,404	-2.9	22,618	19,425	16.4
Indiana............	50,692	53,111	-4.6	20,067	17,255	16.3
Iowa	31,013	32,433	-4.4	18,709	16,131	16.0
Kansas	26,280	26,371	-0.3	18,299	15,250	20.0
Kentucky	32,200	33,301	-3.3	18,400	15,750	16.8
Louisiana...........	42,499	42,700	-0.5	19,265	16,557	16.4
Maine	12,277	12,381	-0.8	15,722	13,994	12.3
Maryland	37,746	40,780	-7.4	22,786	18,998	19.9
Massachusetts	52,000	65,817	-21.0	19,000	18,703	1.6
Michigan	77,206	80,526	-4.1	23,965	21,213	13.0
Minnesota	40,643	44,103	-7.8	22,296	17,777	25.4
Mississippi	24,842	25,631	-3.1	14,285	13,017	9.7
Missouri	48,257	49,004	-1.5	17,726	15,421	14.9
Montana	8,906	9,139	-2.5	19,463	15,954	22.0
Nebraska	16,249	16,802	-3.3	17,412	14,882	17.0
Nevada.............	7,442	6,972	6.7	20,944	17,700	18.3
New Hampshire	10,105	9,846	2.6	15,353	13,412	14.5
New Jersey	73,291	76,550	-4.3	21,642	18,245	18.6
New Mexico	14,250	14,156	0.7	20,600	16,812	22.5
New York	163,100	167,510	-2.6	25,100	21,326	17.7
North Carolina	56,459	55,343	2.0	17,836	15,858	12.5
North Dakota	7,499	7,119	5.3	18,390	13,865	32.6
Ohio	95,010	100,530	-5.5	20,360	16,904	20.4
Oklahoma	33,900	33,985	-0.3	18,110	15,182	19.3
Oregon.............	24,500	25,730	-4.8	22,334	18,047	23.8
Pennsylvania	102,700	109,930	-6.6	21,000	17,890	17.4
Rhode Island	8,758	9,218	-5.0	23,175	20,088	15.4
South Carolina	32,080	31,935	0.5	16,380	14,353	14.1
South Dakota	7,974	8,109	-1.7	15,595	13,674	14.0
Tennessee	39,233	40,940	-4.2	17,425	15,118	15.3
Texas	166,800	161,560	3.2	19,500	15,728	24.0
Utah	14,889	14,397	3.4	19,677	16,864	16.7
Vermont	6,591	6,650	-0.9	15,338	13,006	17.9
Virginia	56,892	58,082	-2.0	18,707	15,535	20.4
Washington.........	34,497	35,612	-3.1	23,413	21,268	10.1
West Virginia	22,001	21,988	0.1	17,370	14,948	16.2
Wisconsin	52,200	53,113	-1.7	20,940	17,607	18.9
Wyoming...........	7,297	6,350	14.9	24,000	18,718	28.2

Source: National Education Association, *Estimates of School Statistics, 1982-83* (and 1981-82).

Table 6
STATE COURSE REQUIREMENTS FOR HIGH SCHOOL GRADUATION

State	Total	Language Arts	Social Studies	Mathematics	Science	PE/ Health	Electives	Other
Alabama	20	4	3	2	1	3½	6½	
Alaska	19	1	1	1	1	1		
Arizona	20	4	2	2	2		9½	½—essentials of the free enterprise system
Arkansas	16	4	1			1	10	
California	13	3	3	2	2	2		1—fine arts or foreign language
Connecticut	18							
Delaware	19	4	3	2	2	1½	6½	
Florida	24	4	3	3	3	1	9	½—practical arts; ½—fine arts
Georgia	21	4	3	2	2	1	8	1—fine arts, vocational education or computer technology
Hawaii	20	4	4	2	2	1½	6	½—guidance
Idaho	20	4	2	2	2½	1½	6	1—reading/speech; 1—humanities
Illinois	16	3	2	2	1	4	1	¼—consumer education
Indiana	19½	4	2	2	2	1½	8	
Iowa		1½				1		
Kansas	20	4	3	2	2	1	8	
Kentucky	20	3	2	3	3	1	8	
Louisiana	22	4	2	3	2	2	8½	½—free enterprise system
Maine		4	1					
Maryland	20	4	3	2	2	1	8	
Massachusetts			1			4		
Michigan			½					
Minnesota	15	3	2			1		
Mississippi	16	3	2½	1	1	1	8½	
Missouri	20	1	1	1	1	1	11	2—English, social studies, math or science; 1—practical arts; 1—fine arts
Montana	16	4	2	2	2	1	2	1—fine arts; 2—practical arts
Nevada	20	3	2	2	1	2½		
New Hampshire	16	4	2	1	1		8	
New Jersey	14½	4	2	2	1	4		1—fine, practical or performing arts; ½—career exploration
New Mexico	21	4	2	2	2	1	9	1—practical or fine arts
New York								
Local diploma	16	4	3	1	1	½	6½	
Regents diploma	18	4	3	1	1	½	8½	
North Carolina	20	4	2	2	2	1	9	
North Dakota	19	4	3	2	2	1	7	
Ohio	18	3	2	2	1	1	9	
Oklahoma	20	4	2	2	2		10	
Oregon	21	3	3½	1	1	2	9	½—career development; 1—fine arts or foreign language
Pennsylvania	13	3	2	1	1			
Rhode Island								
General	16	4	1	1	1		9	
College-bound	18	4	2	3	2		4	2—foreign language; ½—arts; ½—computer literacy
South Carolina	20	4	3	3	2	1	7	
South Dakota	18	4	2	2	2		8	
Tennessee	20	4	1½	2	2	1½	9	
Texas	18	3	2½	2	2	2	6½	
Utah	15	3	2	1	1	1½	6½	
Virginia	20	4	3	2	2	2	6	1—additional science or math
Washington	48	9	7½	6	6		16½	3—occupational education
West Virginia	20	4	3	2	1	2	8	
Wyoming	18		1					
Dist. of Col.								
Comprehensive	20½	4	2	2	2	1½	8	1—foreign language
Career/vocational	23	4	2	2	2	1½	1½	1—foreign language; 9—specialized preparation

Source: Education Commission of the States.   *Note:* Numbers refer to years of instruction.

Table 7
STATE MINIMUM COMPETENCY TESTING FOR PUPILS

States Using Minimum Competency Testing	Government Level Setting Standards	Grade Levels Assessed	Expected Uses					First Graduating Class Assessed
			Grade Promotion	High School Graduation	Early Exit	Remediation	Other	
Alabama	State	3, 6, 9+		X		X		1985
Arizona	State/local	8, 12	(a)	X			X	1976
Arkansas	State	3, 4, 6, 8		X				
California	State/local	4-11, 16 yr. old +	X	X	X	X		1979
Colorado	Local	9, 12		Local option				
Connecticut	State/local	3, 5, 7, 8				X	X	
Delaware	State	11		X				1981
Florida	State/local	3, 5, 8, 11	X	X	X			1983
Georgia	State	4, 8, 10		X		X	X	1985
Hawaii(b)	State	9-12		X		X		1983
Idaho	State	9-12		Local option				1982
Illinois	Local	Local option					Local option	
Indiana	Local	3, 6, 8, 10				X	X	
Kansas(c)	State	2-4, 6, 8, 9, 11, 12					Local option	
Kentucky	State/local	3, 5, 7, 8, 10, 11					X	
Louisiana	State	4, 8, 11	X	X			X	1992
Maine(d)	State	8, 11					X	
Maryland	State	3, 7, 9, 11	X	X		X		1982
Massachusetts	Local	Local option					X	
Michigan	State	4, 7, 10					Local option	
Missouri	State	8					X	
Nebraska	Local	5+					X	
Nevada	State	3, 6, 9, 12		X		X		1982
New Hampshire	State	4, 8, 12					Local option	
New Jersey	State	9-12		X		X	X	1989
New Mexico	State	Local option, 10					X	1981
New York	State	3, 6, 8-12		X		X		1979
North Carolina	State	1-3, 6, 9, 11		X				1980
Ohio	Local	Local option					Local option	
Oklahoma	None	3, 6, 9, 12					X	
Oregon	Local	Local option		X				1978
Rhode Island	State	4, 8, 10					X	
South Carolina	State	1-3, 6, 8, 11				X	X	1989
Tennessee	State/local	4-6, 8, 11, 12		X		X	X	1983
Texas	Not reported	3, 5, 9+				X		
Utah	Local	Local option		X				1980
Vermont	State	K-12		X			X	1981
Virginia	State/local	K-6, 9-12		X				1981
Washington(e)	Local	4, 8					Local option	
Wisconsin	Local	1-4, 5-8, 9-10		Local option		X		

Source: Education Commission of the States.

(a) 1983 legislation calls for Arizona to develop a minimum course of study and criteria for high school graduation standards and for grade to grade promotion criteria. Local school districts are to implement standards.

(b) In Hawaii, students have three options: paper-pencil test, performance test or course.

(c) Kansas test expired in 1983—the state legislature is expected to renew for a five-year period in 1984.

(d) The Maine legislature discontinued use of the test after one year.

(e) The Washington Department of Education discontinued use of this test in the late 1970s.

Table 8
TOTAL ENROLLMENTS IN HIGHER EDUCATION: 1982
(Including degree credit and non-degree credit students)

State or other jurisdiction	Total enrollment		Public institutions		Private institutions	
	Number of students, 1982	Percentage change, 1980-82	Number of students, 1982	Percentage change, 1980-82	Number of students, 1982	Percentage change, 1980-82
Total	12,588,520	2.9	9,762,245	2.6	2,826,275	4.0
Alabama	167,753	2.1	147,032	2.3	20,721	0.4
Alaska	24,556	15.3	23,479	14.2	1,077	46.5
Arizona	210,683	3.9	200,599	3.4	10,084	16.2
Arkansas	76,972	-0.8	65,895	-0.3	11,077	-4.2
California	1,842,963	2.9	1,646,116	2.9	196,847	3.0
Colorado	171,821	5.5	151,666	4.2	20,155	16.4
Connecticut	162,194	1.6	101,268	3.6	60,926	-1.5
Delaware	32,454	-1.5	28,314	-0.04	4,140	-11.5
Florida	436,606	6.0	353,639	5.8	82,967	7.0
Georgia	198,367	7.7	152,333	8.7	46,034	4.6
Hawaii	51,788	9.8	47,210	9.1	4,578	17.0
Idaho	42,975	-0.1	34,519	0.08	8,456	-0.8
Illinois	683,969	6.2	528,675	7.6	155,294	1.5
Indiana	253,529	2.5	194,977	3.0	58,552	0.9
Iowa	147,862	5.3	104,757	7.5	43,105	0.3
Kansas	141,661	3.7	126,573	3.8	15,088	3.2
Kentucky	144,159	0.8	114,963	0.07	29,196	3.6
Louisiana	176,505	10.3	152,599	11.6	23,906	2.4
Maine	47,719	10.3	32,654	2.4	15,065	32.3
Maryland	234,585	4.0	202,445	3.8	32,140	5.5
Massachusetts	407,557	-2.7	177,969	-3.3	229,588	-2.2
Michigan	508,240	-2.3	439,961	-3.2	68,279	3.5
Minnesota	214,133	3.6	168,532	3.8	45,601	2.9
Mississippi	105,932	3.5	94,701	4.5	11,231	-4.2
Missouri	244,238	4.2	173,990	5.3	70,248	1.5
Montana	36,811	4.7	32,860	5.4	3,951	-1.2
Nebraska	94,390	5.5	77,526	5.5	16,864	5.5
Nevada	42,212	4.4	41,849	3.9	363	107.4
New Hampshire	52,208	11.6	26,018	7.9	26,190	15.5
New Jersey	322,284	0.2	256,099	3.7	66,185	-12.7
New Mexico	63,483	8.9	60,493	9.8	2,990	-7.2
New York	1,012,421	2.0	573,113	1.8	439,308	2.4
North Carolina	300,910	4.7	241,736	6.0	59,174	-0.4
North Dakota	36,224	6.3	33,551	5.8	2,673	13.3
Ohio	532,361	8.8	389,432	2.0	142,929	33.11
Oklahoma	168,186	4.9	145,047	5.7	23,139	0.1
Oregon	141,312	-11.4	124,052	-12.9	17,260	-0.6
Pennsylvania	529,341	4.3	299,838	2.5	229,503	6.6
Rhode Island	68,351	2.2	34,707	-1.0	33,644	5.8
South Carolina	136,727	3.2	108,802	1.0	27,925	12.6
South Dakota	35,074	7.1	26,284	8.0	8,790	4.2
Tennessee	201,806	-1.4	154,796	-1.3	47,010	-1.6
Texas	758,839	8.2	667,306	8.8	91,533	4.2
Utah	99,431	5.9	65,231	9.5	34,200	-0.6
Vermont	30,648	0.07	18,266	1.6	12,382	-2.1
Virginia	281,026	0.2	245,179	-0.5	35,847	5.4
Washington	227,812	-33.3	198,071	-39.4	29,741	7.9
West Virginia	82,891	1.1	71,612	0.5	11,279	5.0
Wisconsin	276,176	2.6	241,950	2.9	34,226	0.9
Wyoming	22,713	7.4	22,713	7.4	0	-100.0
Dist. of Col.	82,793	-4.7	14,561	4.8	68,232	-6.7
U.S. Service Schools	60,129	20.7	60,129	20.7	0	0
Territories(a)	162,740	18.15	66,158	9.0	96,582	25.34

Source: Fall Enrollment in Higher Education, 1980 (Washington, D.C.: U.S. Department of Education, National Center for Education Statistics), 1982 figures National Center for Education Statistics, unpublished data.

(a) Includes American Samoa, Guam, Puerto Rico, Trust Territory of the Pacific Islands and Virgin Islands.

Table 9
APPROPRIATIONS OF STATE TAX FUNDS
FOR OPERATING EXPENSES OF HIGHER EDUCATION
(In thousands)

State	Fiscal year			1982-84		1974-84	
	1973-74	1981-82	1983-84	2-year change	Percentage	10-year gain	Percentage
All states	$9,797,005	$22,954,495	$25,476,649	$2,522,154	11.0	$15,679,644	160.1
Alabama..................	165,996	376,591	410,038	33,447	8.9	244,042	147.0
Alaska	23,399	122,439	150,752	28,313	23.1	127,353	544.3
Arizona	135,998	306,801	336,080	29,279	9.6	200,082	147.1
Arkansas	73,411	183,980	197,321	13,341	7.3	123,910	168.8
California................	1,156,254	3,328,706	3,150,376	-178,330	-5.7	1,994,122	172.5
Colorado	140,315	305,791	366,747	60,956	19.9	226,432	161.4
Connecticut..............	119,918	229,406	273,706	44,300	19.3	153,788	128.3
Delaware	33,573	72,125	77,792	5,667	7.9	44,219	131.7
Florida	346,056	802,316	956,258	153,942	19.2	610,202	176.3
Georgia.................	218,660	498,919	570,170	71,251	14.3	351,510	160.8
Hawaii	57,295	154,755	181,560	26,805	17.3	124,265	216.9
Idaho	40,737	95,100	101,107	6,007	6.3	60,370	148.2
Illinois.................	550,904	1,025,211	1,106,007	80,796	7.9	555,103	100.8
Indiana	233,379	482,494	503,484	20,990	4.4	270,105	115.7
Iowa	144,476	321,494	372,128	50,634	15.8	227,652	157.6
Kansas	108,927	278,662	306,473	27,811	10.0	197,546	181.4
Kentucky	131,118	339,632	400,529	60,897	17.9	269,411	205.5
Louisiana	158,855	453,422	503,086	49,664	11.0	344,231	216.7
Maine	39,828	66,940	76,653	9,713	14.5	36,825	92.5
Maryland	172,826	385,949	437,028	51,079	13.2	264,202	152.9
Massachusetts	176,707	417,938	537,263	119,325	28.6	360,556	204.1
Michigan	464,029	848,532	887,471	38,939	4.6	423,442	91.3
Minnesota	230,604	545,503	612,209	66,706	12.2	381,605	165.5
Mississippi	112,868	300,524	345,370	44,846	14.9	232,502	206.0
Missouri	180,719	323,860	363,689	39,829	12.3	182,970	101.3
Montana	36,792	83,693	103,617	19,924	23.8	66,825	181.6
Nebraska	68,000	181,645	193,925	12,280	6.8	125,925	185.2
Nevada.................	26,632	65,851	75,360	9,509	14.4	48,728	183.0
New Hampshire	17,403	39,323	41,141	1,818	4.6	23,738	136.4
New Jersey	257,708	464,787	531,891	67,104	14.4	274,183	106.4
New Mexico..............	54,902	171,576	187,600	16,024	9.3	132,698	241.7
New York................	983,941	1,855,429	2,166,908	311,479	16.8	1,182,967	120.2
North Carolina	287,115	758,466	864,658	106,192	14.0	577,543	201.2
North Dakota	31,730	108,539	108,725	186	0.2	76,995	242.7
Ohio	345,759	739,309	883,761	144,452	19.5	538,002	155.6
Oklahoma	96,038	325,553	389,167	63,614	19.5	293,129	305.2
Oregon	123,476	252,602	272,969	20,367	8.1	149,493	121.1
Pennsylvania.............	429,366	820,477	902,253	81,776	10.0	472,887	110.1
Rhode Island	42,439	83,588	97,651	14,063	16.8	55,212	130.1
South Carolina	147,612	360,902	392,471	31,569	8.8	244,859	165.9
South Dakota	26,964	57,106	53,070	-4,036	-7.6	26,106	96.8
Tennessee...............	150,799	357,016	387,738	30,722	8.6	236,939	157.1
Texas	500,095	1,905,007	2,282,342	377,335	19.8	1,782,247	356.4
Utah	66,373	174,139	198,060	23,921	13.7	131,687	198.4
Vermont.................	18,453	33,876	40,343	6,467	19.1	21,890	118.6
Virginia.................	206,458	543,961	617,283	73,322	13.5	410,825	199.0
Washington	252,224	497,822	566,477	68,655	13.8	314,253	124.6
West Virginia............	81,796	192,092	199,319	7,227	3.8	117,523	143.7
Wisconsin	304,546	532,002	595,843	63,841	12.0	291,297	95.7
Wyoming	23,532	82,644	100,780	18,136	22.0	77,248	328.3

Source: M. M. Chambers, *Appropriations of State Tax Funds for Operating Expenses of Higher Education, 1983-1984* (Washington, D.C.: National Association of State Universities and Land-Grant Colleges, October 1983).

Table 10
PROGRAMS OF STUDENT FINANCIAL AID, BASED UPON NEED, FOR STATE RESIDENTS TO ATTEND EITHER PUBLIC OR NON-PUBLIC COLLEGES OR UNIVERSITIES: 1981-82 TO 1983-84

State or other jurisdiction	Number of monetary awards		2-year percentage change, 1981-82 to 1983-84	Payout of dollars (thousands)		2-year percentage change 1981-82 to 1983-84	Average award amount	
	1981-82	1983-84	1983-84	1981-82	1983-84	1983-84	1981-82	1983-84
United States..........	1,210,126	1,281,193	5.9	$890,141	$1,051,978	18.2	$ 736	$ 821
Alabama	1,068	2,167	102.9	505	1,751	246.7	473	808
Alaska	247	127	-94.5	329	191	-72.3	1,332	1,504
Arizona	3,153	2,950	-6.9	2,283	2,042	-11.8	724	692
Arkansas	9,922	10,801	8.7	1,603	2,183	36.2	162	202
California	62,577	62,763	0.3	86,363	89,025	3.1	1,380	1,418
Colorado	10,635	10,000	-6.4	7,278	7,354	1.1	684	735
Connecticut...........	11,640	11,950	2.7	8,792	9,412	7.1	755	788
Delaware	859	858	-0.1	544	573	5.3	633	668
Florida	14,112	20,033	42.0	12,322	14,028	13.9	873	700
Georgia	12,668	12,800	1.0	3,493	3,741	7.1	276	292
Hawaii	1,900 (a)	1,400	-35.7	736 (a)	493	-49.3	387 (a)	352
Idaho	887	746	-18.9	496	379	-30.9	559	508
Illinois	95,450	119,350	25.0	89,634	104,589	16.7	939	876
Indiana...............	36,037	41,202	14.3	20,576	22,629	10.0	571	549
Iowa	13,190	13,811	4.71	15,629	20,268	29.7	1,185	1,468
Kansas	6,400	5,800	-10.4	5,004	4,664	-7.3	782	804
Kentucky	16,311	20,500	25.7	6,322	8,228	30.2	388	401
Louisiana.............	4,135	3,500	-18.2	2,220	1,707	-30.1	537	488
Maine	1,550	2,900	87.1	537	490	-9.6	346	169
Maryland	12,341	12,453	0.9	5,921	5,525	-7.2	478 (a)	444
Massachusetts	26,298	32,710	24.4	17,071	27,101	58.8	649	829
Michigan	39,036	31,748	-23.0	28,626	30,632	7.0	733	965
Minnesota	50,131	45,283 (b)	-10.7	28,019	43,534	55.4	559	961
Mississippi	2,260	2,000	-13.0	1,321	1,015	-30.2	585	508
Missouri..............	10,412	13,425	28.9	8,941	8,796	-1.7	859	655
Montana	900	650	-38.5	390	331	-17.8	433	509
Nebraska	1,998	1,800	-11.0	1,119	860	-26.6	560	478
Nevada	450 (a)	654	45.3	150 (a)	327	118.0	333 (a)	500
New Hampshire	1,652	1,443	-14.5	592	529	-11.9	358	367
New Jersey............	71,093	72,480	2.0	39,774	49,679	24.9	559	685
New Mexico...........	1,500 (a)	1,500 (b)	0	720 (a)	1,000 (b)	38.9	480 (a)	667 (b)
New York	332,500	332,500	0	280,280	327,320	16.8	843	984
North Carolina	5,410	6,003	11.0	3,299	4,172	26.5	610	695
North Dakota	1,668	1,550	-7.6	672	665	-1.1	403	429
Ohio	61,000	63,000	3.3	31,864	40,000	25.5	522	635
Oklahoma	9,214 (c)	18,800	104.0	2,265	7,168	216.5	246	381
Oregon	15,114	15,132	0.1	7,669	8,836	15.2	507	584
Pennsylvania..........	123,345	120,140	-2.7	77,592	86,039	10.9	629	716
Rhode Island	8,687	11,842	36.3	5,936	7,393	24.6	683	624
South Carolina	8,011	7,000	-14.5	12,631	12,578	-0.4	1,577	1,796
South Dakota	470 (a)	1,273	170.9	431 (a)	270	-59.6	917 (a)	212
Tennessee.............	8,995	14,600	62.3	6,439	7,081	10.0	716	485
Texas	24,330	24,100	-1.0	18,697	25,530	36.6	768	1,059
Utah	1,599	1,689	5.6	1,171	1,199	2.4	732	710
Vermont	7,703	9,115	18.3	5,531	7,114	28.6	718	780
Virginia	18,027	7,000	-157.5	3,733	4,079	9.3	207	583
Washington	11,783	10,604	-11.1	5,304	7,398	39.5	450	698
West Virginia..........	6,425	5,870	-9.5	4,300	4,389	2.1	669	748
Wisconsin	40,874	34,341	-19.0	20,829	23,523	12.9	510	685
Wyoming..............	81	279 (b)	244.4	49	204 (b)	316.3	605	731 (b)
Dist. of Col.	850 (a)	760 (c)	-11.9	1,118 (a)	876	-27.6	1,315 (a)	1,153
American Samoa	162 (a)	162 (a)	0	719 (a)	719 (a)	0	4,438 (a)	4,438 (a)
Guam	60 (a)	60 (a)	0	235 (a)	235 (a)	0	3,917 (a)	3,917 (a)
Puerto Rico	1,940 (a)	34,503	1,678.5	1,458 (a)	11,505	689.1	752 (a)	333
Trust Territory	1,000 (a)	1,000 (a)	0	505 (a)	505 (a)	0	505 (a)	505 (a)
Virgin Islands	66 (a)	66 (a)	0	104 (a)	104 (a)	0	1,576 (a)	1,576 (a)

Note: Comprehensive undergraduate competitive and non-competitive state grant and scholarship programs. All figures include both state and federal State Student Incentive Grant Program funds; 1983-84 figures are estimates of the states in November 1983.

Source: 14th Annual Survey, 1982-83 Academic Year and 15th Annual Survey, 1983-84 Academic Year, National Association of State Scholar-

ship and Grant Programs (Harrisburg, Pa., Pennsylvania Higher Education Assistance Agency, 1982, 1983).
(a) 1981-82 preliminary data; final figures for 1981-82 data not available.
(b) 1982-83 data; 1983-84 data not available.
(c) All data listed as undergraduate as data could not be broken down into undergraduate versus graduate.

Table 11
NUMBER OF INSTITUTIONS OF HIGHER EDUCATION AND BRANCHES:
1980-81 and 1982-83

State or other jurisdiction	All institutions			Publicly controlled institutions			Privately controlled institutions		
	1980-81	1982-83	Change	1980-81	1982-83	Change	1980-81	1982-83	Change
United States	3,221	3,269	48	1,487	1,482	-5	1,734	1,787	53
Alabama	57	60	3	37	37	0	20	23	3
Alaska	15	15	0	12	12	0	3	3	0
Arizona	28	29	1	19	19	0	9	10	1
Arkansas	35	35	0	19	19	0	16	16	0
California	268	273	5	135	137	2	133	136	3
Colorado	44	47	3	27	27	0	17	20	3
Connecticut	47	47	0	24	24	0	23	23	0
Delaware	10	8	-2	6	5	-1	4	3	-1
Florida	79	85	6	37	37	0	42	48	6
Georgia	76	80	4	34	34	0	42	46	4
Hawaii	12	12	0	9	9	0	3	3	0
Idaho	9	9	0	6	6	0	3	3	0
Illinois	157	160	3	63	63	0	94	97	3
Indiana	74	74	0	28	28	0	46	46	0
Iowa	61	60	-1	21	21	0	40	39	-1
Kansas	52	53	1	29	29	0	23	24	1
Kentucky	57	57	0	21	21	0	36	36	0
Louisiana	32	32	0	20	20	0	12	12	0
Maine	28	29	1	12	12	0	16	17	1
Maryland	57	57	0	32	32	0	25	25	0
Massachusetts	116	117	1	33	31	-2	83	86	3
Michigan	93	92	-1	45	44	-1	48	48	0
Minnesota	70	67	-3	30	28	-2	40	39	-1
Mississippi	42	42	0	25	25	0	17	17	0
Missouri..........	86	92	6	28	28	0	58	64	6
Montana	16	16	0	9	9	0	7	7	0
Nebraska	30	28	-2	16	13	-3	14	15	1
Nevada...........	7	8	1	6	6	0	1	2	1
New Hampshire	25	27	2	10	11	1	15	16	1
New Jersey	62	60	-2	31	30	-1	31	30	-1
New Mexico	19	20	1	16	16	0	3	4	1
New York	293	296	3	86	86	0	207	210	3
North Carolina	126	128	2	73	74	1	53	54	1
North Dakota	16	18	2	11	11	0	5	7	0
Ohio	135	139	4	60	59	-1	75	80	5
Oklahoma	45	45	0	29	29	0	16	16	0
Oregon	45	45	0	21	21	0	24	24	0
Pennsylvania.......	200	202	2	61	61	0	139	141	2
Rhode Island......	13	13	0	3	3	0	10	10	0
South Carolina	61	62	1	33	33	0	28	29	1
South Dakota	20	20	0	8	8	0	12	12	0
Tennessee	77	80	3	23	24	1	54	56	2
Texas	153	157	4	96	98	2	57	59	2
Utah	14	14	0	9	9	0	5	5	0
Vermont	21	22	1	6	6	0	15	16	1
Virginia	69	69	0	39	39	0	30	30	0
Washington........	49	50	1	33	33	0	16	17	1
West Virginia	28	29	1	16	16	0	12	13	1
Wisconsin	65	63	-2	31	30	-1	34	33	-1
Wyoming..........	9	8	-1	8	8	0	1	0	-1
Dist. of Col.	18	18	0	1	1	0	17	17	0

Source: National Center for Education Statistics, *1980-81 and 1982-83*
Supplement to the Education Directory, Colleges and Universities
(Washington, D.C.: U.S. Department of Education, 1981, 1983).

Table 12
NUMBER OF POSTSECONDARY SCHOOLS WITH OCCUPATIONAL PROGRAMS, BY STATE AND BY TYPE OF SCHOOL: 1982

State or other jurisdiction	Total	College/ University	Junior/ Community College	Vocational/ Technical	Specialized/ Trade Schools	Hospital/ Allied Health Schools	Art/ Design Schools	Other
United States	9,208	597	1,017	891	5,010	1,169	248	298
Alabama	132	13	24	27	58	9	0	1
Alaska	30	1	6	2	18	0	0	3
Arizona	175	4	11	4	126	16	5	9
Arkansas	94	12	10	24	43	5	0	0
California	1,043	18	100	48	692	115	48	44
Colorado	152	10	16	13	94	7	6	6
Connecticut	187	10	18	28	99	19	8	5
Delaware	30	2	5	0	16	5	1	1
Florida	339	12	21	54	192	34	6	20
Georgia	231	17	22	31	123	24	10	4
Hawaii	38	4	6	3	18	3	1	3
Idaho	50	4	3	3	35	3	0	2
Illinois	408	14	59	15	231	71	11	7
Indiana	217	29	16	11	137	16	3	5
Iowa	136	9	21	4	70	31	0	1
Kansas	119	15	21	16	52	12	1	2
Kentucky	179	16	11	55	73	16	2	6
Louisiana	209	17	7	55	117	8	2	3
Maine	61	9	8	5	21	17	1	0
Maryland	167	4	21	7	88	25	11	11
Massachusetts	259	13	35	27	124	33	14	13
Michigan	320	30	37	8	190	36	8	11
Minnesota	160	7	22	39	68	23	1	0
Mississippi	72	6	20	1	43	0	2	0
Missouri	289	24	16	44	153	43	4	5
Montana	56	4	3	6	33	4	2	4
Nebraska	89	12	9	4	50	11	1	2
Nevada	54	2	3	5	32	1	1	10
New Hampshire	38	9	8	1	15	5	0	0
New Jersey	252	9	19	41	109	53	9	12
New Mexico	54	7	6	9	31	1	0	0
New York	535	42	81	13	268	94	22	15
North Carolina	158	12	70	2	57	14	1	2
North Dakota	44	8	5	2	17	12	0	0
Ohio	422	28	32	36	201	78	17	30
Oklahoma	122	2	6	29	72	7	3	3
Oregon	143	6	14	3	104	6	5	5
Pennsylvania	459	38	28	69	206	102	10	6
Rhode Island	52	8	2	1	29	7	3	2
South Carolina	117	8	24	15	57	9	0	4
South Dakota	46	13	3	5	17	8	0	0
Tennessee	180	21	21	37	80	17	4	0
Texas	522	20	55	14	313	92	8	20
Utah	65	4	7	5	40	5	2	2
Vermont	21	7	1	1	7	4	1	0
Virginia	233	7	25	21	143	24	2	11
Washington	173	4	26	9	122	4	6	2
West Virginia	97	14	8	22	34	16	1	2
Wisconsin	115	5	18	8	58	22	1	3
Wyoming	27	0	7	4	16	0	0	0
Dist. of Col.	37	7	0	5	18	2	4	1

Source: U.S. Department of Education, National Center for Education Statistics.

Table 13
AVERAGE SALARIES OF FULL TIME INSTRUCTIONAL FACULTY ON 9-MONTH CONTRACTS, IN INSTITUTIONAL UNITS OF HIGHER EDUCATION: 1982-83

State or other jurisdiction	All institutional units				All public institutional units				All private institutional units			
	Pro-fessors	Associ-ate pro-fessors	Assist-ant pro-fessors	Instruc-tors	Pro-fessors	Associ-ate pro-fessors	Assist-ant pro-fessors	Instruc-tors	Pro-fessors	Associ-ate pro-fessors	Assist-ant pro-fessors	Instruc-tors
United States	$35,540	$26,921	$22,056	$17,601	$35,473	$27,346	$22,538	$18,003	$35,701	$25,876	$21,054	$16,675
Alabama	31,289	24,836	20,648	16,524	32,300	25,382	21,016	16,915	24,605	19,850	17,823	15,460
Alaska	54,671	43,477	35,837	29,810	54,671	43,644	35,945	29,810	---	24,300	21,834	---
Arizona	39,681	29,426	23,779	18,429	39,997	29,731	23,920	18,941	28,761	23,881	20,438	14,433
Arkansas	30,027	23,997	20,529	16,726	30,956	24,469	20,842	16,943	25,063	21,398	18,562	15,625
California	37,949	28,107	23,182	20,386	37,337	27,926	22,976	22,053	40,923	28,651	23,574	18,395
Colorado	33,001	25,750	21,656	17,729	32,753	25,577	21,714	17,502	35,040	26,710	21,429	18,403
Connecticut	38,699	27,454	22,802	19,170	36,737	27,641	23,479	19,594	40,997	27,211	22,043	18,558
Delaware	39,048	27,661	21,889	17,648	40,430	28,193	22,518	18,430	20,672	19,677	17,122	12,063
Florida	34,657	25,666	21,191	16,903	35,417	26,049	21,880	17,672	32,162	24,423	19,566	15,649
Georgia	33,565	25,807	21,187	16,301	35,666	27,066	22,010	16,967	25,694	20,554	17,543	14,239
Hawaii	37,167	27,706	22,703	17,774	37,783	28,440	23,199	19,940	22,918	20,461	17,171	13,098
Idaho	28,640	23,755	20,343	18,377	29,299	24,067	20,519	18,857	23,628	19,907	17,322	15,530
Illinois	35,079	26,357	22,186	18,268	33,904	26,414	22,478	18,442	37,098	26,256	21,683	17,853
Indiana	33,187	25,713	20,845	16,027	34,034	26,125	21,084	15,652	31,226	24,828	20,375	16,789
Iowa	32,689	25,601	21,051	17,569	36,554	27,688	22,619	17,908	27,043	22,421	18,977	17,031
Kansas	32,248	24,424	20,591	16,506	33,772	25,672	21,776	17,481	21,687	18,487	16,417	14,307
Kentucky	30,656	24,215	20,236	16,513	32,036	24,968	20,925	17,260	24,774	20,599	17,199	14,462
Louisiana	32,481	26,507	22,021	17,415	32,564	26,780	22,455	17,554	32,141	25,447	19,958	16,446
Maine	32,359	24,742	19,539	15,935	30,861	24,602	19,483	15,280	35,597	25,204	19,613	17,448
Maryland	36,595	28,107	22,699	17,328	35,994	28,508	23,171	17,525	38,731	25,771	20,685	15,486
Massachusetts	39,380	28,517	23,369	18,301	34,466	28,098	23,209	18,362	42,308	28,800	23,452	18,238
Michigan	35,127	26,742	22,373	18,100	36,107	27,372	23,158	18,936	28,990	23,603	19,417	15,734
Minnesota	35,155	26,760	21,832	17,451	36,236	27,786	22,517	17,676	32,115	25,160	20,782	17,208
Mississippi	29,221	24,018	19,460	15,721	29,791	24,395	19,979	15,913	23,639	19,832	15,256	13,628
Missouri..........	32,097	25,269	20,568	16,629	31,987	26,077	21,227	16,896	32,320	23,491	19,131	15,713
Montana	31,040	25,576	21,357	18,170	31,498	26,100	21,884	18,776	23,956	19,535	17,482	15,289
Nebraska	30,820	24,409	20,025	16,479	31,592	24,935	20,419	16,497	27,524	23,154	19,285	16,440
Nevada	37,780	29,366	24,106	21,151	37,780	29,366	24,106	21,151	---	---	---	---
New Hampshire	32,145	24,222	20,029	16,216	28,905	24,075	19,511	16,189	36,094	24,424	20,613	16,245
New Jersey	40,019	29,940	23,682	18,317	40,478	30,624	24,167	18,781	39,232	27,573	22,037	16,719
New Mexico	35,801	27,234	22,546	18,693	35,838	27,510	22,725	18,833	18,900	18,722	16,247	15,574
New York	38,518	29,477	23,346	18,389	38,371	30,381	24,249	18,824	38,692	28,221	22,399	17,797
North Carolina	32,205	25,044	20,628	17,073	34,383	26,363	21,763	18,941	26,050	21,539	17,728	14,530
North Dakota	31,785	26,758	22,314	18,877	31,886	26,881	22,483	19,311	27,300	23,732	19,653	15,405
Ohio	34,672	26,861	21,676	17,721	36,561	27,834	22,595	18,225	30,802	24,164	19,700	16,315
Oklahoma	34,056	27,992	24,121	20,118	35,048	28,918	25,048	20,684	29,827	25,022	20,053	16,599
Oregon	30,942	24,423	20,481	16,751	31,039	24,748	21,018	17,274	30,602	23,527	19,292	13,818
Pennsylvania......	36,130	27,335	22,242	17,088	35,498	27,847	22,706	17,155	36,861	26,613	21,766	17,003
Rhode Island	35,641	26,674	21,997	17,713	32,562	25,861	22,269	15,585	39,459	28,151	21,630	18,960
South Carolina ...	31,872	23,879	20,894	15,454	34,856	25,074	22,179	16,146	24,245	19,662	16,496	13,924
South Dakota	26,981	22,210	19,097	15,742	27,813	22,876	19,728	16,418	23,538	19,951	17,352	14,087
Tennessee	31,241	24,174	19,925	16,279	31,322	24,403	20,310	16,473	31,056	23,474	18,925	15,740
Texas	35,937	27,931	23,102	18,746	36,740	28,698	23,674	19,291	33,468	25,064	20,947	16,311
Utah	35,195	26,461	21,869	17,571	35,293	26,486	21,933	17,615	21,937	20,387	17,268	12,020
Vermont	32,031	24,379	20,243	17,539	32,790	25,264	21,053	18,264	30,851	23,210	19,411	16,899
Virginia	33,510	25,681	21,039	16,748	34,724	26,291	21,571	17,125	29,149	22,757	18,736	15,086
Washington........	32,470	25,403	20,966	17,828	33,073	25,718	21,393	17,932	29,679	24,659	20,382	17,802
West Virginia	27,518	22,790	19,114	15,640	28,202	23,228	19,642	15,839	23,316	20,401	17,096	14,799
Wisconsin	34,645	26,243	22,205	18,874	35,228	26,667	22,872	20,163	31,046	24,683	20,450	16,135
Wyoming..........	38,772	31,396	25,365	21,311	38,772	31,396	25,365	21,311	---	---	---	---
Dist. of Col.	37,481	28,389	22,773	18,908	36,373	28,831	23,466	20,237	37,737	28,266	22,555	18,581

Source: National Center for Education Statistics, U.S. Dept. of Education. Data collected by the 17th Annual Higher Education General Information Survey (HEGIS XVII) on the Salaries, Tenure and Fringe Benefits of Full-Time Instructional Faculty in Institutions of Higher Education for Academic Year 1982-83.

Table 14

AVERAGE SALARIES OF FULL TIME INSTRUCTIONAL FACULTY ON 12-MONTH CONTRACTS, IN INSTITUTIONAL UNITS OF HIGHER EDUCATION: 1982-83

State or other jurisdiction	All institutional units				All public institutional units				All private institutional units			
	Professors	Associate professors	Assistant professors	Instructors	Professors	Associate professors	Assistant professors	Instructors	Professors	Associate professors	Assistant professors	Instructors
United States	$43,897	$34,273	$27,944	$21,987	$45,109	$35,227	$28,963	$22,787	$38,852	$30,956	$24,972	$19,874
Alabama	39,942	32,417	25,746	19,824	41,098	33,200	27,117	20,309	21,597	19,268	18,052	17,101
Alaska	67,264	40,478	37,847	38,470	72,317	66,310	50,953	38,470	42,000	34,020	27,362	---
Arizona	45,816	35,949	29,356	23,089	46,492	35,961	29,356	23,089	20,604	34,500	---	---
Arkansas	37,190	31,219	25,208	20,636	38,686	32,210	25,717	20,706	29,423	26,557	23,084	19,095
California	45,628	32,797	28,270	21,903	48,731	35,142	30,787	32,198	43,373	31,696	26,845	21,143
Colorado	43,872	35,160	29,904	24,059	43,840	37,081	31,413	23,346	43,990	30,117	20,096	27,390
Connecticut	51,855	39,176	32,107	21,927	65,200	49,240	40,248	---	39,464	34,665	27,019	21,927
Delaware	43,681	34,317	26,834	21,273	44,092	35,058	26,943	21,273	25,170	20,614	22,260	---
Florida	40,857	31,243	26,638	19,949	41,467	31,981	27,855	20,815	37,259	25,676	19,844	17,459
Georgia	48,677	37,014	28,958	21,797	49,199	37,526	29,492	22,019	33,450	27,225	23,648	18,693
Hawaii	44,287	33,287	27,773	21,899	44,878	34,017	29,219	21,899	19,788	27,078	20,544	---
Idaho	38,033	31,898	24,664	23,654	38,548	32,120	24,664	23,654	28,496	24,787	---	---
Illinois	43,125	34,460	28,668	20,417	43,541	34,713	28,520	21,149	41,768	33,908	29,101	19,635
Indiana	45,432	33,902	26,935	18,638	47,225	35,312	27,717	19,133	28,285	23,752	21,732	17,029
Iowa	46,669	35,408	28,534	21,035	47,327	37,535	30,539	24,691	35,246	27,236	23,787	17,660
Kansas	40,007	31,997	25,202	21,002	40,874	33,725	26,291	21,623	22,999	19,231	18,994	15,916
Kentucky	40,981	32,916	28,143	18,563	41,987	34,220	28,973	20,072	25,774	21,354	18,706	15,797
Louisiana	43,348	35,550	28,323	23,061	44,294	36,214	28,700	23,144	30,848	27,068	22,252	21,182
Maine	33,141	27,323	22,877	14,332	37,660	29,719	23,685	19,504	24,425	24,356	22,496	11,100
Maryland	48,653	36,116	29,256	22,139	46,672	36,235	29,663	22,213	52,464	35,776	28,428	21,555
Massachusetts	39,459	30,653	26,124	23,992	35,388	28,030	23,132	18,465	43,013	33,736	28,645	24,288
Michigan	46,252	35,433	27,615	20,420	47,204	35,363	28,558	22,065	40,819	35,605	24,833	17,300
Minnesota	39,899	34,577	28,836	23,785	46,466	36,394	30,865	26,050	22,039	26,064	22,568	18,954
Mississippi	39,389	33,270	26,648	21,418	39,627	33,519	26,723	21,534	29,801	25,558	23,346	18,000
Missouri	39,771	32,291	25,669	21,068	41,694	34,738	27,529	22,246	36,785	29,243	23,694	20,082
Montana	40,986	31,620	27,677	26,375	40,986	31,792	27,995	26,375	---	29,293	24,172	---
Nebraska	41,463	33,060	25,086	19,042	41,943	32,723	26,997	18,496	36,031	34,153	23,746	20,278
Nevada...........	43,861	35,640	29,240	18,129	43,861	35,640	29,240	18,129	---	---	---	---
New Hampshire	32,384	23,086	20,045	16,284	34,416	23,557	22,350	16,714	17,655	19,708	15,978	15,807
New Jersey	53,166	38,784	29,172	21,597	53,401	39,674	29,323	21,620	50,449	33,338	27,846	21,005
New Mexico	43,936	32,311	26,729	22,778	43,936	32,423	26,729	22,778	---	23,383	---	---
New York	45,770	35,976	27,585	24,731	49,148	40,583	31,821	26,341	40,548	30,417	23,268	18,982
North Carolina	44,454	33,720	28,872	20,405	46,248	34,774	29,184	20,572	28,670	22,223	17,899	18,567
North Dakota......	40,686	33,373	28,466	22,793	40,686	33,373	28,696	22,793	---	---	17,012	---
Ohio	44,036	34,460	28,801	21,820	47,160	35,906	30,114	23,057	35,824	31,297	25,020	20,111
Oklahoma	44,628	35,350	28,015	23,409	45,142	35,490	28,066	23,437	24,652	23,208	25,501	21,000
Oregon...........	41,681	32,582	24,892	20,687	42,983	33,423	28,640	21,205	35,335	29,680	20,446	18,774
Pennsylvania	46,448	34,810	27,110	20,107	48,774	36,371	28,179	20,636	35,902	29,134	24,277	18,862
Rhode Island......	43,717	31,719	24,641	20,121	40,495	31,472	25,299	18,531	51,199	34,555	23,934	20,783
South Carolina	42,450	32,528	28,071	20,010	44,317	33,387	28,445	20,616	24,856	21,456	20,603	15,335
South Dakota	34,842	27,816	23,656	19,360	35,085	27,987	24,350	19,577	28,609	22,001	20,049	17,518
Tennessee	35,078	29,736	25,395	19,380	35,506	29,473	24,283	18,755	34,461	30,275	27,250	21,931
Texas	49,427	39,799	32,746	24,099	51,520	41,202	34,097	25,221	37,915	31,594	24,507	19,280
Utah	41,312	30,254	24,484	20,666	43,169	33,032	26,840	21,922	22,742	17,372	16,946	15,013
Vermont	39,696	32,466	26,013	20,500	39,696	32,466	26,013	20,500	---	---	---	---
Virginia	45,222	36,111	29,093	23,183	46,809	36,947	29,509	23,901	30,938	23,477	22,051	17,946
Washington........	46,896	35,081	29,487	20,753	47,222	35,173	29,776	22,182	37,904	33,766	23,359	18,611
West Virginia	36,230	29,196	24,039	20,887	37,067	30,017	24,507	21,723	22,462	18,241	19,044	18,379
Wisconsin	41,094	34,904	28,797	20,384	44,445	34,441	29,999	25,122	31,999	35,178	28,057	18,661
Wyoming..........	43,483	39,958	31,258	27,059	43,483	39,958	31,258	27,059	---	---	---	---
Dist. of Col.	49,794	38,604	30,719	23,423	---	---	---	---	49,794	38,604	30,719	23,423

Source: National Center for Education Statistics, U.S. Dept. of Education. Data collected by the 17th Annual Higher Education General Information Survey (HEGIS XVII) on the Salaries, Tenure and Fringe Benefits of Full-Time Instructional Faculty in Institutions of Higher Education for Academic Year 1982-83.

2. Transportation

TRANSPORTATION IN THE 1980s

The United States faces a dilemma of rising costs and declining revenues in the decade of the 1980s. While varying in substance and degree from state to state, this will be true for both highway and mass transit systems, and urban and rural systems.

The close of the 1970s found many of our nation's roads, bridges and mass transit systems in decay. Rapidly rising costs of operations and day-to-day maintenance meant that major repairs and rehabilitation generally had been deferred. The road systems—local, state and federal—will need repair during the 1980s. Studies show that the federally-aided urban and secondary system roads are in the poorest condition of all, requiring resurfacing or reconstruction within the decade. Of the more than 500,000 bridges in the U.S., nearly half are considered unsafe or obsolete. Mass transit systems, particularly the older systems of the Northeast and Midwest, need immediate infusions of money for structural repairs and to replace antiquated equipment. The rehabilitation of our highway and transit systems can be deferred no longer.

From the state perspective, the situation appears bleak, as states are increasingly expected to shoulder a greater share of the transportation burden. The 1983 Maryland *State Report on Transportation* said: "During the past decade, major changes in program responsibilities have taken place, particularly the substantial increase in state-funded transit operating subsidies." The 1982 state of New York annual report on public transportation found the state doubly hit by decreases in both federal and local transit assistance. Local and state aid for transit operations in New York had been an equal match through 1979. By the end of 1982, the state match had increased from 6.5 percent to 17 percent, while the local match had decreased from 6.5 percent to 4 percent. This situation is not unique to Maryland and New York. The goal of the current administration in Washington is to completely phase out federal mass transit operating assistance, and localities everywhere are looking to the states to fill the revenue gap caused by the declining federal dollars and increasing transit deficits.

Financing the nation's roads has historically

been a federal, state and local partnership. While the landmark Surface Transportation Assistance Act of 1982 (STAA) increased money flowing into the Highway Trust Fund and enacted other reforms in the area of highway and mass transit finance, it likewise increased the state burden in matching fund requirements. Under the STAA, states will be required to raise about $8 billion in matching funds during the four years of the act. Some of the STAA's other reforms, such as the Buy America provisions and the 10 percent minority business requirement, further increase costs to the states. Additionally, new regulations under the act stipulate that states will lose all federal highway funds if they do not permit 80,000 pound trucks on their highways. Studies show that even with the higher federal and state taxes on trucks, these heavy trucks still pay considerably less than the cost of the damage they do to the roads.

While the transportation picture is not rosy, it is not entirely desperate. States are in a position to take the lead in reversing the decline of the 1970s, and many states have already begun. Efforts are being made on a number of fronts, with the primary emphasis on raising revenue. States are increasing revenues from traditional sources, such as dedicated taxes, vehicle registration and license fees, bond issues, highway user taxes and tolls. And, states are exploring new, innovative funding sources such as local option taxes, special assessment districts, taxes on private entities such as oil companies, public-private ventures, earmarking lottery funds, and new bonding mechanisms.

The state of Washington has local option retail sales and motor vehicle excise taxes dedicated to transit. Oregon has a local-option self employment tax, whereby a tax is levied on the net earnings from self-employment of individuals working within special transit districts. Several states, such as Virginia and Florida, have contracted out to private operators to provide commuter van-pool services. New York has implemented Service Contract Bonds as special issues of the New York Metropolitan Transit Au-

Prepared by the Finance and Taxation staff of The Council of State Governments.

thority, which are being used to finance a portion of New York's transit capital programs and are backed by state appropriations. Both Arizona and Pennsylvania have earmarked a percentage of their state lottery proceeds for transit and road repairs.

Several factors, in addition to decreases in federal and local assistance, have contributed to the present crisis facing the transit industry. Transportation planning has generally been short-range and piecemeal. Many reduced fare plans were implemented during the 1970s, and fare structures in general were not kept in line with the increased costs of operations. Labor costs have risen astronomically, due to increasing wages and benefits, decreasing labor productivity, and restrictive labor agreement provisions. And, changes in patterns of transit ridership, due to suburban migration and rush-hour ridership, were not reflected in transit routes and service.

States are looking beyond revenue-raising mechanisms to resolve these other transit problems. Several states are in the midst of or already have renegotiated labor contracts. Fare structures are being revised to more accurately reflect system costs. Comprehensive transportation planning is being undertaken at the state level. Most importantly, states are making state transit subsidies contingent upon system financial and operating performance standards. Illinois is currently implementing a major plan to financially and organizationally restructure the Chicago Regional Transportation Authority.

Transportation is but another of the major areas of state activity that will face both struggle and opportunity in the 1980s. The major tasks will be to find sufficient revenue and to plan well the use of available resources.

References

Much of the information and data on highways and the Surface Transportation Assistance Act came from Craft, Ralph. "Highways: Financing for the Future," *State Legislative Report*. National Conference of State Legislatures, July 1983.

1982 Annual Report on Policy and Finance, Public Transportation Operating Assistance Programs in New York State. Transit Division, New York Department of Transportation, November 1982.

Draft *State Report on Transportation, Overview/ Maryland Transportation Plan,* Maryland Department of Transportation, September 1983.

Pickrell, Don H. *The Causes of Rising Transit Operating Deficits*. Prepared for the U.S. Department of Transportation, July 1983.

Table 1
TOTAL ROAD AND STREET MILEAGE: 1982
(Classified by jurisdiction)

State or other jurisdiction	Rural mileage				Urban mileage			Total rural and urban mileage
	Under state control	Under local control(a)	Under federal control(b)	Total rural roads	Under state control	Under local control(a)	Total urban mileage(c)	
United States	825,385	2,139,790	260,565	3,225,740	102,671	536,192	640,556	3,866,296
Alabama	10,285	63,163	307	73,755	1,326	12,402	13,728	87,483
Alaska	8,713	0	0	8,713	974	198	1,172	9,885
Arizona	6,152	26,016	35,232	67,400	466	8,424	8,890	76,290
Arkansas(d)	15,034	52,805	1,457	69,296	1,095	6,258	7,353	76,649
California	14,762	63,531	33,081	111,374	3,052	59,451	62,514	173,888
Colorado	8,539	57,699	0	66,238	638	8,557	9,195	75,433
Connecticut(d)	2,314	7,109	0	9,423	1,590	8,466	10,056	19,479
Delaware	3,679	228	3	3,910	994	365	1,359	5,269
Florida	8,086	57,215	0	65,301	3,498	24,998	28,496	93,797
Georgia(d)	16,350	72,295	0	88,645	1,921	13,687	15,608	104,253
Hawaii	854	1,926	72	2,852	194	1,104	1,320	4,172
Idaho	4,945	25,898	35,307	66,150	260	1,985	2,245	68,395
Illinois	13,383	90,394	281	104,058	4,336	25,996	30,347	134,405
Indiana	9,499	64,533	0	74,032	1,569	16,053	17,622	91,654
Iowa	9,236	94,733	115	104,084	883	7,217	8,104	112,188
Kansas	10,091	113,758	0	123,849	593	7,765	8,358	132,207
Kentucky	23,412	38,033	301	61,746	1,683	5,059	6,928	68,674
Louisiana	15,210	31,105	538	46,853	1,193	8,886	10,079	56,932
Maine	7,852	11,691	170	19,713	261	1,969	2,240	21,953
Maryland(d)	4,335	12,619	355	17,309	1,150	8,603	9,824	27,133
Massachusetts	1,741	11,387	87	13,215	1,865	18,691	20,585	33,800
Michigan	7,697	84,583	0	92,280	1,773	23,372	25,145	117,425
Minnesota	12,385	104,201	1,636	118,222	1,163	11,829	12,992	131,214
Mississippi	9,831	54,351	295	64,477	737	5,559	6,312	70,789
Missouri	104,742	3	0	104,745	6,414	7,451	13,865	118,610
Montana	7,263	53,375	8,497	69,135	154	2,140	2,297	71,432
Nebraska	10,000	77,501	100	87,601	322	3,978	4,300	91,901
Nevada	4,914	23,346	13,215	41,475	269	2,105	2,375	43,850
New Hampshire	3,847	8,103	141	12,091	620	1,756	2,376	14,467
New Jersey	1,586	9,850	21	11,457	1,576	20,461	22,235	33,692
New Mexico	11,549	31,493	6,283	49,325	901	3,526	4,427	53,752
New York	12,451	60,980	0	73,431	3,902	32,492	36,394	109,825
North Carolina	69,413	3,266	3,156	75,835	7,282	9,562	17,086	92,921
North Dakota	7,058	76,760	662	84,480	190	1,371	1,561	86,041
Ohio	16,569	65,337	29	81,935	3,625	25,590	29,215	111,150
Oklahoma	12,230	86,243	0	98,473	792	10,610	11,402	109,875
Oregon	10,085	33,490	81,743	125,318	763	7,615	8,416	133,734
Pennsylvania	87,801	304	0	88,105	19,525	8,334	27,859	115,964
Rhode Island	254	2,393	0	2,647	1,701	1,927	3,628	6,275
South Carolina	35,480	19,874	598	55,952	4,450	2,613	7,063	63,015
South Dakota	8,885	61,172	1,622	71,679	167	1,403	1,570	73,249
Tennessee	9,657	60,862	1,302	71,821	1,468	10,468	11,936	83,757
Texas	65,689	145,912	961	212,562	5,462	54,403	59,865	272,427
Utah	4,979	21,990	12,165	39,134	634	4,379	5,013	44,147
Vermont(d)	2,699	10,479	69	13,247	54	632	695	13,942
Virginia	50,200	796	1,519	52,515	4,326	7,859	12,390	64,905
Washington	16,331	37,590	14,596	68,517	1,013	13,161	14,807	83,324
West Virginia	29,995	641	998	31,634	1,165	1,769	2,934	34,568
Wisconsin	11,202	82,892	186	94,280	1,321	12,458	13,779	108,059
Wyoming	6,121	25,865	3,465	35,451	259	1,235	1,494	36,945
Dist. of Col.	0	0	0	0	1,102	0	1,102	1,102

Source: Federal Highway Administration, U.S. Department of Transportation. Compiled for calendar year ending Dec. 31, 1982, from reports of state authorities.

Note: This table does not include mileage of non-public roads.

(a) Includes mileage not identified by administrative authority.

(b) Mileage in federal parks, forests and reservations that are not a part of the state and local highway systems.

(c) Total includes additional urban mileage (1,513) under federal control in 17 states: California, 11; Hawaii, 22; Illinois, 15; Iowa, 4; Kentucky, 186; Maine, 10; Maryland, 71; Massachusetts, 29; Mississippi, 16; Montana, 3; Nevada, 1; New Jersey, 18; North Carolina, 242; Oregon, 38; Vermont, 9; Virginia, 205; Washington, 633.

(d) Incomplete 1982 data submitted for these states. Totals include additional areawide data and available data from previous submittals included and factored to 1982 level. For Georgia and Vermont, 1981 areawide data are used for totals.

Table 2

STATE RECEIPTS FOR HIGHWAYS: 1982
(In thousands of dollars)

State or other jurisdiction	State highway user tax revenues	Roads and crossing tolls(a)	Other state imposts, general fund revenues	Miscellaneous income	Federal funds Federal Highway Administration	Other agencies	Transfers from local governments	Bond proceeds (b)	Total receipts
United States	$15,540,375	$1,555,149	$1,607,103	$1,366,718	$8,325,658	$330,725	$311,678	$1,541,538	$30,578,948
Alabama	289,840		61,353	16,250	186,205	3,867	342	54,253	612,109
Alaska	26,611	13,492	54,592	16,030	131,043	3,473		45,600	290,841
Arizona	211,150			18,311	101,356	5,738	7,138	168,824	512,516
Arkansas	198,479		8,828	12,530	93,857	27,641	3,039		344,376
California	1,245,608	53,381		145,225	514,485	23,061	50,597	24,072	2,056,430
Colorado	190,638		49,525	11,924	146,055	2,197	5,534		405,874
Connecticut.........	171,314	67,066		11,223	96,824	1,497		32,134	380,058
Delaware	56,467	28,917	11,015	12,579	41,214	568		57,606	208,366
Florida	608,149	101,123		165,108	301,807	5,447	3,083	7,144	1,191,861
Georgia	287,237		161,841	76,259	193,606	3,741	6,053		728,738
Hawaii	46,262		17,066	1,290	49,883	866		19,000	134,367
Idaho	94,364			3,385	56,223	3,279	1,486		158,738
Illinois.............	627,168	99,385	127,214	38,572	429,565	6,003	24,415	115,023	1,467,347
Indiana.............	402,303	35,027	2,377	37,283	162,176	4,264	5,756		649,189
Iowa...............	306,893	2,313	63,743	24,548	117,411	2,528	3,641		521,077
Kansas	176,153	24,868		41,521	125,128	2,474	12,435		382,578
Kentucky	359,032	19,836		42,161	173,241	3,324	2,127	378	640,031
Louisiana...........	252,993		102,158	3,663	180,252	5,405		265,840	810,311
Maine	81,393	18,509	1,389	3,490	47,410	778	4,865	42,255	200,091
Maryland	384,660	62,016		52,993	369,130	2,868	463	34,620	906,751
Massachusetts	297,924	79,650	34,595	12,291	139,375	2,499		75,000	641,334
Michigan	570,725	7,396	102,110	41,779	219,317	6,839	12,482		960,648
Minnesota	401,364		27,755	33,120	200,694	4,083	15,322	32,100	714,435
Mississippi	169,786		102,445	48,674	102,172	15,396	4,476	8,547	451,495
Missouri.............	286,480		40,684	11,434	192,830	3,405	6,135		540,968
Montana	75,683			4,738	100,822	10,001			191,244
Nebraska	151,660		40,707	8,664	74,047	1,111	7,722		283,910
Nevada.............	81,670			5,625	66,324	592	5,782	25,041	185,034
New Hampshire	89,641	15,420		6,337	48,485	911	6,040	13,000	179,835
New Jersey	170,405	230,386		64,359	150,103	6,478		95,000	716,731
New Mexico	142,278		28,576	6,183	76,447	2,225	924	29,695	286,328
New York	719,796	308,809	125,938	85,637	417,984	8,429			1,666,593
North Carolina	507,320	919		37,210	165,847	4,241	3,421	75,394	794,352
North Dakota	66,040		22,495	558	45,972	1,011	6,672		142,748
Ohio	873,925	59,640		52,483	249,996	7,573	22,014		1,265,632
Oklahoma	299,417	39,500	132,561	16,936	61,701	1,732	8,832		560,679
Oregon.............	193,107	1,380	14,832	1,547	185,088	25,220	11,994		433,170
Pennsylvania........	1,089,971	154,544		61,841	485,166	11,000	7,998		1,810,519
Rhode Island	50,288	5,617		469	32,247	304			88,925
South Carolina	254,609			1,640	91,049	3,373	509	710	351,890
South Dakota	77,421		16,729	4,122	51,543	1,078	2,308		153,202
Tennessee	345,724		30,883	9,361	175,283	4,313	1,893		567,456
Texas	912,364	11,429	22,615	74,593	436,440	7,748	24,846	145,817	1,635,851
Utah	101,762		3,756	1,202	92,797	1,297	3,365		204,179
Vermont	70,472		3,191	853	48,813	998			124,327
Virginia	493,710	49,869	30,495	3,568	190,235	5,805	7,417	57,000	838,099
Washington	348,258	46,166		21,586	303,991	28,056	3,780	75,431	827,269
West Virginia	199,568	18,491	56,556	8,416	183,287	3,545			469,862
Wisconsin	383,958			919	134,909	3,556	15,014	15,590	553,946
Wyoming............	65,569		61,689	6,228	53,836	48,106	1,762		237,191
Dist. of Col.	32,766		6,700		31,987	781		27,220	99,453

Source: Federal Highway Administration, U.S. Department of Transportation. Compiled for calendar year ending Dec. 31, 1982 from reports of state authorities.

(a) Toll receipts allocated for non-highway purposes are excluded.
(b) Par value of bonds issued and redeemed by refunding is excluded.

Table 3
STATE DISBURSEMENTS FOR HIGHWAYS: 1982
(In thousands of dollars)

State or other jurisdiction	Capital outlay				Mainten-ance and traffic services	Adminis-tration and highway police	Bond interest	Grants-in-aid to lo-cal govern-ments	Bond retirement	Total disburse-ments
	State adminis-tered high-ways(a)	County and township roads	Local munici-pal streets	Total						
United States......	$12,398,957	$624,970	$537,803	$13,561,730	$5,330,136	$3,931,793	$1,137,058	$4,740,964	$1,227,319	$29,929,000
Alabama	242,425	33,389	917	276,731	64,622	51,009	17,872	119,380	74,930	604,544
Alaska	144,347		5,103	149,450	91,411	39,308	6,294	10,412	5,144	302,019
Arizona	150,159	9,462	13,628	173,249	37,349	44,521	1,454	88,609	2,050	347,232
Arkansas	154,412	8,014	579	163,005	63,797	45,497		79,106		351,405
California	602,272	9,833	26,587	638,692	319,472	456,995	7,875	580,720	8,778	2,012,532
Colorado	155,682	1,944	17,493	175,119	89,485	45,769		100,415		410,788
Connecticut........	140,889	4,646		145,535	54,371	55,790	39,334	20,241	81,213	396,484
Delaware	71,837			71,837	20,873	30,016	18,108	2,000	25,294	168,128
Florida	607,014	1,064		608,078	135,747	92,226	45,142	205,466	46,562	1,133,221
Georgia	371,903	87,581	29,700	489,184	82,242	71,968	40,108	9,671	34,504	727,677
Hawaii	77,505	1,271		78,776	11,076	8,138	7,750	18,228	9,216	133,184
Idaho	54,116	7,217		61,333	28,572	38,095		32,133		160,133
Illinois.............	633,285	59,880	1,643	694,808	209,944	182,708	82,246	260,658	51,889	1,482,253
Indiana.............	235,944	18,791	28,241	282,976	112,454	53,090	24,147	179,014	20,302	671,983
Iowa	151,923			151,923	65,499	67,365	334	213,226	620	498,967
Kansas	147,375	24,030	8,457	179,862	70,608	44,130	17,391	37,831	16,439	366,261
Kentucky	332,712	10,964	4,264	347,940	122,030	68,385	73,868	53,984	25,416	691,623
Louisiana...........	570,463		2,359	572,812	68,378	89,056	45,128	1,106	35,200	811,680
Maine	76,845	374		77,219	63,162	19,812	4,698	8,904	11,841	185,636
Maryland	256,633	4,877		261,510	87,909	104,908	44,893	346,480	28,370	874,070
Massachusetts.......	190,268			190,268	88,623	74,307	73,266	38,027	62,975	527,466
Michigan	249,746	13,240	63,661	326,647	128,638	177,624	4,870	346,565	31,858	1,016,202
Minnesota	262,329	40,606	7,166	310,101	107,544	72,752	9,410	158,242	13,184	671,233
Mississippi	207,676	57,331	6,890	271,897	36,279	43,979	52,527	51,233	28,609	484,524
Missouri............	207,397	2,395	1,578	211,370	135,700	92,067		68,109		507,246
Montana	86,255	11,656	3,364	101,275	31,751	17,936		22,553		173,515
Nebraska	102,166	16,783	7,365	126,314	39,376	26,476	465	76,931	1,000	270,562
Nevada.............	102,172	172	2	102,346	18,059	30,097	77	13,043		163,622
New Hampshire	80,349	1,179	4,359	85,887	53,510	34,627	5,953	8,801	8,500	197,278
New Jersey	228,575	20,955	95,784	345,314	164,236	117,020	93,118	1,618	130,521	851,827
New Mexico	163,610			163,610	46,591	58,609	8,530	12,578	10,810	300,728
New York	689,180	49,807	47,150	786,137	290,037	259,530	64,457	125,363	127,709	1,653,233
North Carolina	251,392			251,392	236,176	126,610	18,858	43,102	17,000	693,138
North Dakota	51,718	9,257	3,215	64,190	24,578	13,140		34,277		136,185
Ohio	388,329	9,728	46,056	444,113	178,817	187,086	26,562	304,618	57,886	1,199,082
Oklahoma	223,848	4,365		228,213	70,034	79,468	13,510	138,631	9,529	539,385
Oregon.............	180,364	10,812	35,716	226,892	48,740	53,935	3,628	80,339	3,300	416,834
Pennsylvania	681,561			681,561	517,378	185,443	131,406	207,784	93,722	1,817,294
Rhode Island	41,995			41,995	18,533	10,437	6,163	387	10,506	88,021
South Carolina	136,333	2,839		139,172	83,588	47,906	3,118	15,865	10,132	299,781
South Dakota	60,505	8,817	5,881	75,203	28,513	22,488		17,713		143,917
Tennessee	241,139	35,977	1,505	278,621	90,688	46,155	5,742	116,702	16,720	554,628
Texas	1,018,383		1,456	1,019,839	397,225	176,969	15,595	64,858	10,417	1,684,903
Utah	110,000	5,200	3,800	119,000	33,254	23,444		23,854		199,552
Vermont	57,816			57,816	26,631	15,260	4,065	12,055	8,872	124,699
Virginia	336,421			336,421	236,862	106,806	17,670	71,449	14,105	783,313
Washington.........	343,653	8,587	5,190	357,430	131,429	91,146	31,287	169,542	18,070	798,904
West Virginia	235,773			235,773	115,331	47,000	47,997		47,086	493,257
Wisconsin	170,853	27,380	13,477	211,710	85,184	50,575	8,173	140,005	12,872	508,519
Wyoming...........	121,420	4,547		125,967	38,393	27,382		9,136		200,878
Dist. of Col.			45,217	45,217	29,437	6,663	13,969		4,168	99,454

Source: Federal Highway Administration, U.S. Department of Transportation. Compiled for calendar year ending Dec. 31, 1982 from reports of state authorities.

(a) Expenditures for county roads under state control in Alabama (10 counties), Delaware, North Carolina, Virginia (all but 2 counties) and West Virginia are included with expenditures for state-administered highways.

Table 4
APPORTIONMENT OF FEDERAL-AID HIGHWAY FUNDS: FISCAL 1983
(In thousands of dollars)

State or other jurisdiction	Highway system funds				Interstate resurfacing funds(b)	Forest highway funds(c)	Highway safety funds(a,d,e)	Other program funds(c,d,f)	Total (g)
	Consolidated primary(a)	Rural secondary (a)	Urban system (a)	Interstate (b)					
United States	$1,803,179(h)	$633,815	$780,080	$3,162,527	$780,080	$6,840	$487,969	$1,423,796	$9,078,286
Alabama	33,185	13,540	10,097	81,223	14,071	20	9,024	28,811	189,971
Alaska	59,686	34,895	3,900	15,114	6,617	596	4,405	4,224	129,437
Arizona	24,005	10,024	10,076	42,773	17,062	385	5,835	4,177	114,337
Arkansas	22,932	11,599	4,762	15,114	9,365	93	6,493	28,080	98,438
California	129,623	24,320	98,778	334,474	73,540	980	37,461	40,936	740,112
Colorado	25,923	11,003	10,455	51,992	15,384	491	6,659	15,725	137,632
Connecticut	19,281	4,229	11,193	94,886	9,560		4,535	21,943	165,627
Delaware	8,886	3,169	3,900	15,114	3,900		2,092	3,699	40,760
Florida	58,385	14,019	37,213	160,330	24,238	40	16,844	29,408	340,477
Georgia	43,384	17,018	14,842	134,999	28,606	24	12,320	27,944	279,137
Hawaii	8,886	3,169	3,900	60,366	3,900		1,980	3,699	85,900
Idaho	14,861	7,957	3,900	15,114	7,713	696	3,914	5,221	59,376
Illinois	70,005	18,601	42,806	40,113	30,471	8	23,108	51,559	276,671
Indiana	41,011	14,969	15,503	15,114	20,468	5	13,371	39,486	159,927
Iowa	29,212	14,347	7,096	15,114	11,286		10,145	38,457	125,657
Kansas	26,902	13,172	6,633	23,487	9,708		10,266	43,775	133,943
Kentucky..........	31,103	13,327	7,934	80,739	14,714	14	7,823	27,960	183,614
Louisiana..........	30,375	10,825	12,650	143,553	12,826	16	8,731	34,465	253,441
Maine.............	11,482	5,682	3,900	15,114	3,900	3	2,639	7,276	49,996
Maryland..........	26,051	5,935	15,347	202,441	11,305		6,323	24,749	292,151
Massachusetts......	33,940	6,268	21,750	90,442	10,441		8,385	26,299	197,525
Michigan	63,947	19,734	29,413	49,272	25,953	73	17,823	18,008	224,223
Minnesota	35,963	16,391	11,795	53,473	14,976	95	11,259	25,155	169,107
Mississippi	25,088	11,795	4,974	15,114	9,900	32	6,455	38,669	112,027
Missouri..........	41,049	17,277	14,600	27,326	22,711	35	11,868	68,867	203,733
Montana	21,327	11,921	3,900	15,114	12,311	545	4,154	10,567	79,839
Nebraska..........	20,757	10,506	4,294	15,114	7,196	6	6,635	24,422	88,930
Nevada...........	14,847	7,532	3,900	15,114	6,550	123	2,524	3,772	54,362
New Hampshire	8,886	3,169	3,900	15,114	3,900	37	2,264	8,542	45,812
New Jersey	40,574	5,530	29,961	90,382	8,896		10,803	55,811	241,957
New Mexico	19,953	10,110	4,103	15,114	13,364	274	3,609	3,823	70,350
New York	102,959	19,569	67,505	150,657	19,016		26,190	141,352	527,248
North Carolina	50,063	19,900	12,086	45,644	15,786	42	11,925	59,654	215,100
North Dakota	14,680	8,106	3,900	15,114	6,829		5,564	7,567	61,760
Ohio	72,131	19,846	35,625	49,635	32,862	4	20,309	41,540	271,952
Oklahoma	27,723	12,807	8,680	25,754	11,641	5	8,893	29,222	124,725
Oregon	23,982	10,975	7,757	32,888	12,168	942	7,317	16,179	112,208
Pennsylvania.......	82,719	24,065	36,607	151,685	22,795	18	20,362	84,089	422,340
Rhode Island.......	8,886	3,169	3,900	57,615	3,900		2,039	4,833	84,342
South Carolina	25,599	10,070	7,165	45,010	12,012	22	7,242	13,140	120,260
South Dakota	15,715	8,779	3,900	15,114	7,977	54	4,293	5,849	61,681
Tennessee	36,970	14,691	12,194	35,548	21,494	23	9,570	50,167	180,657
Texas	105,377	39,391	50,383	156,944	63,723	22	30,855	65,488	512,183
Utah	15,200	6,720	5,484	40,929	11,339	227	3,636	3,855	87,390
Vermont	8,886	3,169	3,900	15,114	4,026	12	2,236	6,722	44,065
Virginia	39,050	14,199	15,804	98,574	20,654	44	9,537	19,136	216,998
Washington........	30,854	10,873	13,513	131,129	16,665	475	8,990	28,292	240,811
West Virginia	18,458	8,365	3,900	70,039	6,061	27	4,417	30,507	141,774
Wisconsin	38,679	15,213	13,135	17,714	11,733	38	11,374	28,550	136,436
Wyoming..........	13,738	7,608	3,900	15,114	10,647	292	2,576	3,776	57,651
Dist. of Col.	7,836		3,900	33,553	3,900		1,769	14,333	65,291
American Samoa ...							1,259		1,259
Guam.............							1,259		1,259
No. Mariana Is.							1,259		1,259
Puerto Rico........	22,165	4,267	9,367			2	4,092	4,016	43,909
Virgin Islands							1,259		1,259

Source: Federal Highway Administration, U.S. Department of Transportation.

Note: This table does not include funds from the mass transit account of the Highway Trust Fund.

(a) Total of funds apportioned Oct. 18, 1982 and Jan. 6, 1983.

(b) Apportionment of funds provided by the Federal-Aid Highway Act of 1978 as amended by the Federal-Aid Highway Act of 1981. Interstate funds are made available one year earlier than other federal-aid funds.

(c) Apportionment of funds provided by the Federal-Aid Highway Act of 1982 at a ratio of 78/365. The Surface Transportation Assistance Act of 1982 eliminated the apportionment of forest highway funds by legislative formula.

(d) Apportioned Jan. 6, 1983.

(e) Apportionment of funds provided by the Highway Safety Act of 1978 as amended by the Omnibus Budget Reconciliation Act of 1981. Includes $96 million administered by the National Highway Traffic Safety Administration and $9.8 million administered by the Federal Highway Administration.

(f) Does not include funds from the following programs: discretionary priority primary, emergency relief, discretionary bridges, federal lands, great river road and other special programs authorized for fiscal year 1983. These funds are allocated from the Highway Trust Fund.

(g) Amounts in this column are paid from the Highway Trust Fund. The totals are of the funds shown in this table. They do not include the Eighty-Five Percent Minimum Allocation Funds authorized by the Highway Improvement Act of 1982.

(h) Total does not include $7,456,843 apportioned to the territories.

Table 5
MOTOR VEHICLE LAWS
(As of September 1982)

State or other jurisdiction	Age for driver's license Regular	Age for driver's license Learner's	Age for driver's license Restrictive	Drivers license renewal (in years)	Liability laws(a)	Vehicle inspection (b)	Transfer of plates to new owner	Child restraint laws(c)
Alabama	16	15(d)	14(e)	4	S	(f)	★	★
Alaska	18		16(g)	5	S	spot	★	...
Arizona	18	15 + 7mo.(d,g)	16(g)	3	C	(h)	★	...
Arkansas	18	(d)	14(g,i)	2 or 4	S,NF	★	...	...
California	18	15(i,j)	16(j)	4	(k)	...	★	★
Colorado	21	15 + 6mo.(d)	16(g)	4	S,NF	(l)	...	...
Connecticut	18		16(j)	2 or 4	S,NF	★	...	★
Delaware	18	(d,i)	16(j)	4	S,NF	★	★	★
Florida	16	(d)	15(g)	4	(m)	...	...	★
Georgia	18	15	16(g)	4	C,NF	...	★	...
Hawaii	18	(d)	15(g)	2 or 4(n)	S,NF	★	★	...
Idaho	16	(d)	14(j)	3	S,C	...	...	...
Illinois	18	(d)	16(g,j)	3	S	(o)	...	★
Indiana	18	15(p)	16 + 1mo.(g,j)	4	S	★	...	...
Iowa	18	14	16(j)	2 or 4(n)	S	spot(q)	...	...
Kansas	16		14(i)	4	NF	(q)	...	★
Kentucky	18	(d)	16(g)	4	C,NF	...	★	★
Louisiana	17		15(r)	4	C	★	★	...
Maine	17	(d)	15(j)	2 or 4(n)	S	★	...	★
Maryland	18	(d)	16(g,j)	4	NF	(q)	...	...
Massachusetts	18	(d)	16 + 6mo.(g,j)	4	C,NF	★	...	★
Michigan	18		16(g,j)	2 or 4	C,NF	spot	...	★
Minnesota	18	(d)	16(j)	4	NF	spot(f)	★	★
Mississippi	15	(d)		4	S,F	★	★	...
Missouri	16		15(p)	3	S	★	...	...
Montana	18	(d)	15(g,j)	4	C	...	...	...
Nebraska	16	15(d,i)	14	4	F	...	...	★
Nevada	18	15 + 6mo.	16(g)	4	F,C	(q)	...	...
New Hampshire	18	(s)	16(j)	4	S,F	★	...	...
New Jersey	17	(i)	16	3	S,NF,UJ	★	...	...
New Mexico	16	15(i)	14(p)	4	S,UM	...	...	★
New York	17(j)	(i)	16(g)	4	S,C,NF,UM	★	...	★
North Carolina	18	15(i,j)		4	S,C	★	...	...
North Dakota	16	(d)	14(g,j)	4	S,C,NF, UM,UJ	spot	★	...
Ohio	18(t)	(i)	14(u)	4	F	spot		...
Oklahoma	16	(p)	15 + 6mo.(j)	2	S,C	★	★	...
Oregon	16	15(d)	14	4	F,C,NF	spot	★	...
Pennsylvania	17(j)	(d)	16(g,r)	4	NF	★	...	...
Rhode Island	18	(d)	16(j)	2	S	★	...	★
South Carolina	16	15(i)	15	4	C,NF,UM	★	★	...
South Dakota	16	14(d)	14(r)	4	F,NF	...	★	...
Tennessee	16	15(d)		2	S,F	(f)	...	★
Texas	16(j)	15(i)	15(u)	4	S,F,UM,C	★	★	...
Utah	16(j)	(d)		4	S,NF	★	...	...
Vermont	18	15(i)	16(i)	2 or 4	S	★	...	...
Virginia	18	15 + 8mo.(d,g)	16(g,j)	4	S,NF	★	...	★
Washington	18	15(d,p)	16(j)	4	S,F	spot	★	...
West Virginia	18	(d)	16(g)	4	S,C	★	...	★
Wisconsin	18	(d)	16(j)	4	S	spot	...	★
Wyoming	18	15(g,i)	16(g)	4	S,C	...	...	...
Dist. of Col.	18	(d)	16(g)	4	S	★	...	...
American Samoa	18	(d)	16(g,j)	2 or 3	C	★	★	...
Guam	18	15(g,i)	16(g)	3	S	★	★	...
Puerto Rico	18	(d)	16(g)	4	(v)	★	★	...
Virgin Islands	18		16(g)	3	C	★	★	...

Source: American Automobile Association, *Digest of Motor Laws,* (1983).

*Note:*All jurisdictions except Guam have chemical test laws for intoxication. All except the District of Columbia have an implied consent provision.

Key:
★—Provision.
. . .—No provision.

(a) All jurisdictions except Colorado, Hawaii, American Samoa, Guam, Puerto Rico and the Virgin Islands have a non-resident service of process law. In this column only: S—"Security-type" financial responsibility law (following accident report, each driver/owner of the vehicles involved must show ability to pay damages which may be charged in subsequent legal actions arising from accident); F—"Future-proof type" financial responsibility law (persons who have been convicted of certain serious traffic offenses or who have failed to pay a judgment against them for damages arising from an accident must make a similar showing of financial responsibility); C—"Compulsory insurance" law (motorists must show proof of financial responsibility—liability insurance—usually as a condition of vehicle registration; NF—"No-fault insurance" law (vehicle owner looks to own insurance company for reimbursement for accident damages, rather than having to prove in court that the other party was responsible); UJ—"Unsatisfied judgment funds" law (financed with fees from motorists unable to provide evidence of insurance or from assessments levied on auto insurance companies to cover pedestrians and others who do not have no-fault insurance); UM—"Uninsured motorist" law (insurance companies must offer coverage against potential damage by uninsured motorists).

(b) "Spot" indicates spot check, usually for reasonable cause, or random roadside inspection for defective equipment.

(c) Use of child restraints is mandatory in all states so designated by a star in this column, with the exception of Maine where use is recommended for ages four and under. In Alabama and Rhode Island—for ages three and under. In California, Connecticut, Delaware, Michigan, Minnesota, Tennessee, Virginia and Wisconsin—for ages four and under. In Florida, Illinois, Massachusetts, New York and West Virginia—for ages five and under. In Kansas and North Carolina—for ages two and under. In Kentucky—for children under 40 inches tall. In Nebraska—for child care centers.

(d) Permit required. In Arizona, under certain circumstances. In Arkansas, for 30 days prior to taking driving test. In Delaware, for up to two months prior to 16th birthday.

(e) Restricted to mopeds.

(f) Cities have authority to maintain inspection stations. In Alabama, state troopers also authorized to inspect at their discretion.

(g) Guardian or parental consent required.

(h) Emission inspection required in Maricopa and Pima counties.

(i) Driver must be accompanied by licensed operator. In California, New York, Texas, Vermont (restrictive license) and Wyoming—a licensed operator 18 years or older. In Nebraska—a licensed operator 19 years or older. In South Carolina and Vermont (learner's permit)—a licensed operator 21 years or older. In Guam, must be accompanied by parent or guardian.

(j) Must have completed approved driver education course.

(k) Financial responsibility required of every driver/owner of motor vehicle at all times.

(l) Mandatory annual emissions test in many counties.

(m) State requires proof of personal injury protection and has a judgment-type financial responsibility law applicable in event of accident causing injury, death or property damage wherein a court judgement has been rendered.

(n) Depending upon age of driver. In Hawaii, two years for drivers 15-24 or 65 and over. In Iowa, two years for drivers under 18 and over 70. In Maine, two years for drivers over 65.

(o) Trucks and buses only.

(p) Must be enrolled in driver education course. In New Mexico, permit valid only when accompanied by instructor.

(q) Mandatory inspection only under certain circumstances. In Iowa, complete inspection required prior to first registration and on all transfers. In Kansas, prior to first registration and on all resales. In Maryland, all used cars upon resale or transfer. In Nevada, used cars registered to new owner and emissions test for first-time registration in Clark and Washoe counties.

(r) Driving hours restricted. In Louisiana, drivers under 17 not permitted to operate vehicles between hours of 11 p.m. and 5 a.m. Monday through Thursday; between midnight and 5 a.m. Friday through Sunday. In Pennsylvania, driver not permitted to operate vehicle between midnight and 5 a.m., unless accompanied by parent or spouse 18 years or older or in possession of employer's affidavit. In South Dakota, driver not permitted to operate vehicle between 8 p.m. and 6 a.m. unless accompanied by licensed driver.

(s) Required for motorcyclists only. Otherwise, unlicensed persons who are being taught to drive must be accompanied by licensed operator 21 years or older.

(t) Probationary license issued to persons 16-18 upon completion of approved driver education course.

(u) Upon proof of hardship.

(v) Has financial responsibility law; details not available.

Table 6
STATE NO-FAULT MOTOR VEHICLE INSURANCE LAWS

State or other jurisdiction	Purchase of first-party benefits	Minimum tort liability threshold(a)	Maximum first-party (no-fault) benefits			
			Medical	Income loss	Replacement services	Survivors/funeral benefits
Arkansas	O	None	$5,000 if incurred within 2 yrs. of accident	70% of lost income up to $140/wk. beginning 8 days after accident, for up to 52 wks.	Up to $70/wk. beginning 8 days after accident, for up to 52 wks.	$5,000
Colorado	M	$500	$25,000 if incurred within 3 yrs. (additional $25,000 for rehabilitation expenses incurred within 5 yrs. of accident)	Up to $125/wk. for up to 52 wks.	Up to $15/day for up to 52 wks.	$1,000
Connecticut	M	$400	—————————————$5,000 overall max. on first-party benefits————————————			
			Limited only by total benefits limit	85% of lost income up to $200/wk.	85% of replacement services up to $200/wk.	85% of actual loss for income and replacement services up to $200/wk. Funeral benefit: $2,000
Delaware	M	None, but amt. of no-fault benefits received cannot be used as evidence in suits for general damage	————$10,000 per person, $20,000 per accident overall max. on first-party benefits————			
			Limited only by total benefits limit, but must be incurred within 2 yrs. of accident	Limited only by total benefits limit, but must be incurred within 2 yrs. of accident	Limited only by total benefits limit, but must be incurred within 2 yrs. of accident	Funeral benefit: $2,000 (must be incurred within 2 yrs of accident)
Florida	M	No dollar threshold(b)	—————————————$10,000 overall max. on first-party benefits————————————			
			80% of all costs	60% of lost income	Limited only by total benefits limit	Funeral benefit: $1,750
Georgia	M	$500	—————————————$5,000 overall max. on first-party benefits————————————			
			$2,500	85% of lost income up to $200/wk.	$20/day	Max. wage loss and replacement services amounts. Funeral benefit: $1,500
Hawaii	M	Floating threshold set annually by insurance commissioner	—————————————$15,000 overall max. on first-party benefits————————————			
			Limited only by total benefits limit	Up to $800/mo. for income loss and replacement services		Up to $800/mo. Funeral benefit: $1,500
Kansas	M	$500	$2,000 (additional $2,000 for rehabilitation)	85% of lost income up to $650/mo. for 1 yr.	$12/day for 365 days	Up to $650/mo. for lost income and $12/day for replacement services for up to 1 yr., less disability payments received before death. Funeral benefit: $1,000
Kentucky	(c)	$1,000	—————————————$10,000 overall max. on first-party benefits————————————			
			Limited only by total benefits limit	85% of lost income (more if tax advantage is less than 15%) up to $200/wk.	Up to $200/wk.	Up to $200/wk. each for survivors' economic loss and survivors' replacement services loss. Funeral benefit: $1,000
Maryland	M	None	—————————————$2,500 overall max. on first-party benefits————————————			
			—————————————for expenses incurred within 3 yrs. of accident————————————			
			Limited only by total benefits limit	Limited only by total benefits limit	Limited only by total benefits limit; payable only to non-wage earners	Funeral benefit: limited only by total benefits limit
Massachusetts....	M	$500	—————————————$2,000 overall max. on first-party benefits————————————			
			Limited only by total benefits limit, if incurred within 2 yrs.	Up to 75% of lost income	Limited only by total benefits limit; payments made to nonfamily members for services that would have been performed by victim	Funeral benefit: limited only by total benefits limit

State or other jurisdiction	Pur-chase of first-party benefits	Minimum tort liability threshold(a)	Maximum first-party (no-fault) benefits			
			Medical	Income loss	Replacement services	Survivors/funeral benefits
Michigan(d)	M	No dollar thres-hold(e)	Unlimited	85% of lost in-come up to $1,475/30-day pe-riod for up to 3 yrs.; max. amt. ad-justed annually for cost of living	$20/day for up to 3 yrs.	Up to $1,475/30-day period for lost income for up to 3 yrs. and $20/day for replacement services. Funeral benefits: $1,000
Minnesota	M	$4,000	$20,000	—$10,000 max. for first-party benefits other than medical— 85% of lost in-come up to $200/ wk.	$15/day, beginning 8 days after acci-dent	Up to $200/wk. ea. for income loss and replacement services. Funeral benefit: $1,250
New Jersey	M	$200	Unlimited	Up to $100/wk. to max. of $5,200/ person	Up to $12/day to a max. of $4,380/ person	Max. amount of benefits victim would have re-ceived. Funeral benefit: $1,000
New York	M	No dollar thres-hold(f)	Limited only by total benefits limit	—$50,000 overall max. on first-party benefits— 80% of lost in-come up to $1,000/mo. for 3 yrs.	$25/day for 1 yr.	$2,000 in addition to other benefits
North Dakota	M	$1,000	Limited only by total benefits limit	—$15,000 overall max. on first-party benefits— 85% of lost in-come up to $150/ wk.	$15/day	Up to $150/wk. for survivors income loss and $15/day for replacement services. Funeral benefit: $1,000
Oregon	M	None	$5,000 if incurred within 1 yr. of accident	If victim is dis-abled at least 14 days, 70% of lost income up to $750/mo. for up to 52 wks.	If victim is dis-abled at least 14 days, up to $18/ day for up to 52 wks.	Funeral benefit: $1,000
Pennsylvania	M	$750	Unlimited	Up to $15,000(g)	Up to $25/day for 1 yr.	Up to $5,000 for survivors loss and income loss benefits victim would have received. Funeral benefit: $1,500
South Carolina ...	O	None	Limited only by total benefits limit if incurred within 3 yrs. of accident	—$1,000 overall max. on first-party benefits— Limited only by total benefits limit	Limited only by total benefits limit	Funeral benefit: limited only by total benefits limit
South Dakota	O	None	$2,000 if incurred within 2 yrs. of accident	$60/wk. for up to 52 wks. for dis-ability extending beyond 14 days of date of accident	None	$10,000 if death oc-curs within 90 days of accident
Texas	O	None	Limited only by total benefits limit if incurred within 3 yrs. of accident	—$2,500 overall max. on first-party benefits— Limited only by total benefits limit if incurred within 3 yrs. of accident	Limited only by total benefits limit if incurred within 3 yrs. of accident. Payable only to non-wage earners	Limited only by total benefits limit if incurred within 3 yrs. of accident
Utah	M	$500	$2,000	85% of lost in-come up to $150/ wk. for up to 52 wks. subject to 3-day waiting period which does not ap-ply if disability lasts longer than 2 wks.	$12/day for up to 365 days subject to 3-day waiting period which does not apply if dis-ability lasts longer than 2 wks.	$2,000 survivors benefit. Funeral benefit: $1,000

NO-FAULT INSURANCE LAWS—Continued

State or other jurisdiction	Pur- chase of first- party benefits	Minimum tort liability threshold(a)	Maximum first-party (no-fault) benefits			
			Medical	Income loss	Replacement services	Survivors/funeral benefits
Virginia	O	None	$2,000 if incurred within 1 yr. of accident	100% of lost income up to $100/ wk. for up to 52 wks.	None	Funeral benefit: included in medical benefit
Dist. of Col.	M	$5,000 (to be adjusted annually to reflect cost-of-living changes)	$100,000 (medical and rehabilitation)	80% of lost income up to $2,000/mo. (max. of $24,000)	Up to $50/day up to 3 yrs. (max. of $24,000)	Funeral benefit: $2,000

Source: No Fault Press Reference Manual, State Farm Insurance Companies.

Key: O—Optional; M—Mandatory.

(a) Refers to minimum amount of medical expenses necessary before victim can sue for general damages ("pain and suffering"). Lawsuits allowed in all states for injuries resulting in death and permanent disability. Some states allow lawsuits for one or more of the following: serious and permanent disfigurement, certain temporary disabilities, loss of body member, loss of certain bodily functions, certain fractures or economic losses (other than medical) which exceed stated limits.

(b) Victim cannot sue for general damages unless injury results in significant and permanent loss of important body function, permanent injury, significant and permanent scarring or disfigurement, or death.

(c) Accident victim is not bound by tort restriction if (1) he has rejected the tort limitation in writing or (2) he is injured by a driver who has rejected the tort limitation in writing. Rejection bars recovery of first-party benefits.

(d) Liability for property damage for all states with no-fault insurance is under the state tort system. Michigan has no tort liability for vehicle damage.

(e) Victim cannot sue for general damages unless injuries result in death, serious impairment of bodily function or serious permanent disfigurement.

(f) Victim cannot recover general damages unless injury results in inability to perform usual daily activities for at least 90 days during the 180 days following the accident; dismemberment; significant disfigurement; fracture; permanent loss of use of a body organ, member, function, or system; permanent consequential limitation of use of a body organ or member; significant limitation of use of a body function or system; or death.

(g) Maximum monthly income loss benefit is $1,000 multiplied by the percentage that the state's per capita income bears to the nation's per capita income. Up to 20 percent can be subtracted to offset income tax savings.

Table 7
STATE MOTOR VEHICLE REGISTRATIONS: 1982

State or other jurisdiction	Automobiles(a)	Motorcycles(a)	Buses(a,b)	Trucks(a)	Comparison of total motor vehicle registrations		Percentage change
					1981	1982	
United States	123,697,863	5,743,463	559,197	35,252,765	164,287,143	165,253,288	0.6
Alabama....................	2,194,794	70,895	8,300	836,366	3,084,613	3,110,355	0.8
Alaska.....................	199,956	10,462	1,580	117,014	297,572	329,012	10.6
Arizona	1,582,896	102,639	4,540	628,113	2,199,834	2,318,188	5.4
Arkansas	965,330	25,976	5,863	510,173	1,691,226	1,507,342	-10.9
California.................	13,420,945	687,110	34,111	3,675,347	17,530,169	17,817,513	1.6
Colorado	1,843,399	118,895	5,197	653,131	2,601,448	2,620,622	0.7
Connecticut	2,099,377	75,975	9,214	149,384(c)	2,180,330	2,333,950	7.0
Delaware	333,803	11,812	1,634	79,327	416,314	426,576	2.5
Florida	6,753,616	226,403	32,178	1,548,800	8,194,081	8,560,997	4.5
Georgia...................	2,995,234	115,395	13,819	906,766	3,965,497	4,031,214	1.6
Hawaii	528,125	7,462	3,378	54,803	587,952	593,768	1.0
Idaho	529,194	53,495	2,862	340,580	912,839	926,131	1.5
Illinois...................	5,855,187	295,115	23,304	1,363,491	7,902,639	7,537,097	-4.6
Indiana	2,874,145	161,494	18,417	991,055	4,063,904	4,045,111	-0.4
Iowa	1,667,984	235,900	7,907	669,914	2,590,203	2,581,705	-0.3
Kansas	1,392,762	124,694	4,030	664,382	2,139,599	2,185,868	2.1
Kentucky	1,809,711	62,551	8,562	797,068	2,658,164	2,677,892	0.7
Louisiana	2,010,151	70,994	18,237	772,039	2,902,905	2,871,421	-1.1
Maine	541,222	48,166	2,448	199,187	778,773	791,023	1.6
Maryland	2,421,184	76,295	10,243	461,998	2,932,983	2,969,720	1.3
Massachusetts	3,296,631	98,711	11,142	441,795	3,875,665	3,848,279	-0.7
Michigan	5,005,544	238,542	20,210	1,224,535	6,410,298	6,488,831	1.2
Minnesota	2,338,304	172,856	17,166	922,955	3,335,736	3,451,281	3.5
Mississippi	1,214,950	29,472	7,910	370,161	1,605,286	1,622,493	1.1
Missouri..................	2,540,190	99,523	9,766	861,549	3,438,728	3,511,028	2.1
Montana..................	451,097	43,675	2,267	304,560	774,237	801,599	3.5
Nebraska	804,626	47,334	4,017	406,348	1,261,338	1,262,325	0.1
Nevada	513,450	22,361	1,641	194,875	718,019	732,327	2.0
New Hampshire	660,588	56,543	1,540	111,436(c)	815,478	830,107	1.8
New Jersey	4,389,581	104,726	14,423	513,375(c)	4,802,621	5,022,105	4.6
New Mexico	779,944	60,367	3,483	409,734	1,099,848	1,253,528	14.0
New York.................	7,201,767	191,432	32,503	1,000,587(c)	8,310,324	8,426,289	1.4
North Carolina	3,445,754	115,860	30,520	1,107,031	4,660,904	4,699,165	0.8
North Dakota	380,683	31,359	1,887	270,456	672,539	684,385	1.8
Ohio	6,324,670	279,523	24,906	1,286,284	8,008,527	7,915,383	-1.2
Oklahoma	1,787,616	135,461	11,229	980,955	2,745,820	2,915,261	6.2
Oregon	1,467,482	83,919	8,898	598,316	2,171,780	2,158,615	-0.6
Pennsylvania	5,617,934	228,541	28,332	1,078,473(c)	7,235,249	6,953,280	-3.9
Rhode Island	507,284	27,101	1,562	77,214(c)	619,893	613,161	-1.1
South Carolina	1,518,689	35,168	11,677	444,376	2,012,753	2,009,910	-0.1
South Dakota	376,735	38,500	2,164	236,487	650,751	653,886	0.5
Tennessee.................	2,765,974	83,419	11,624	603,618	3,616,612	3,464,635	-4.2
Texas.....................	7,992,738	337,756	38,549	3,356,546	11,461,291	11,725,589	2.3
Utah	712,027	66,067	1,136	325,248	1,099,672	1,104,478	0.4
Vermont..................	269,966	22,237	1,319	79,596	366,316	373,118	1.9
Virginia...................	3,153,409	80,973	12,886	539,052	3,928,718	3,786,320	-3.6
Washington	2,296,429	141,181	9,996	930,429	3,477,089	3,378,035	-2.8
West Virginia.............	792,707	54,001	3,430	345,799	1,389,808	1,195,937	-13.9
Wisconsin.................	2,560,470	206,886	11,929	589,938	3,302,367	3,369,223	2.0
Wyoming	298,847	22,274	2,453	206,301	509,736	529,875	4.0
Dist. of Col.................	212,762(d)	5,967	2,808	15,798	278,695	237,335	-14.8

Source: Federal Highway Administration, U.S. Department of Transportation. Compiled for the calendar year ending Dec. 31, 1982, from reports of state authorities.

Note: Where the registration year is not more than one month removed from the calendar year, registration-year data are given. Where the registration year is more than one month removed, registrations are given for the calendar year.

(a) Includes federal, state, county and municipal vehicles. Vehicles owned by the military services are not included.

(b) The numbers of private and commercial buses included in the figures are estimates by the Federal Highway Administration of the numbers in operation, rather than the registration counts of the states.

(c) The following farm trucks, registered at a nominal fee and restricted to use in the vicinity of the owner's farm, are not included in this table: Connecticut, 5,681; New Hampshire, 4,673; New Jersey, 6,530; New York, 19,406; Pennsylvania, 19,948; and Rhode Island, 1,318.

(d) Includes 3,476 automobiles of the diplomatic corps.

Table 8
MOTOR VEHICLE OPERATORS AND CHAUFFEURS LICENSES: 1982

State or other jurisdiction	Operators licenses			Chauffeurs licenses			Estimated total licenses in force during 1982 (in thousands(a))
	Years for which issued	Renewal date	Amount of fees	Years for which issued	Renewal date	Amount of fees	
Alabama	4	Birthday	$15.00(b)				2,316
Alaska	5	Birthday	5.00				321
Arizona	3	Birthday	5.00	3	Birthday	$ 7.50	2,086
Arkansas	2 or 4	Birth month	7.00 or 13.00	2 or 4	Birth month	11.00 or 21.00	1,591
California*	4	Birthday	10.00				16,299
Colorado*	4(c)	Birthday	5.50				2,182
Connecticut*	4	Birthday	21.00(b)	1	June 30	5.00(b)	2,235
Delaware*	4(d)	Birthday	10.00(d)				433
Florida	4	Birthday	6.50(b)	4	Birthday	10.50(b)	7,979
Georgia*	4	Birthday	4.50				3,605
Hawaii*	2 or 4(e)	Birthday	5.50 or 8.50(e)				561
Idaho	3	Birthday	7.00	3	Birthday	9.00	663
Illinois*	3	Birthday	8.00(f)				6,965
Indiana	4	Birth month	6.00(f)	2	Birth month	4.00	3,345
Iowa*	2 or 4(g)	Birthday	5.00 or 10.00(g)	2 or 4(g)	Birthday	10.00 or 20.00(g)	1,927
Kansas*	4(h)	Birthday	6.50(b)				1,694
Kentucky	4	Birth month	8.00	4	Birth month	8.00	2,141
Louisiana*	4(i)	Birthday	7.00(i)	4(i)	Birthday	18.00(i,j)	2,540
Maine*	2 or 4(k)	Birthday	8.00 or 18.00(k)				757
Maryland*	4	Birthday	6.00(l)				2,741
Massachusetts*	4	Birthday	20.00(b)				3,641
Michigan*	4(m)	Birthday	6.00(l)	4(l)	Birthday	14.50(l)	6,390
Minnesota*	4	Birthday	9.00(n)				2,397
Mississippi	4	Birth month	13.00(n)	4	Birth month	21.00(n)	1,734
Missouri	3	Issuance	3.00	3	Issuance	10.00	3,297
Montana	4	Birthday	8.00	4	Birthday	8.00	492
Nebraska*	4(o)	Birthday	10.00(o)				1,084
Nevada*	4	Birthday	7.00(f,l)				655
New Hampshire* ...	4	Birthday	20.00				677
New Jersey*	2(p)	Issuance	8.00(p)				5,338
New Mexico*	4(c)	30 days after Birthday	8.00				943
New York*	4	Birthday	4.00				8,992
North Carolina*	4	Birthday	10.00				3,903
North Dakota*	4	Birthday	8.00				428
Ohio	4	Birthday	5.00(n)	4	Birthday	5.00(n)	7,669
Oklahoma	2	Birth month	7.00(l)	2	Birth month	11.00	2,039
Oregon	4	Birthday	11.00(l)	4	Birthday	5.00(l)	1,894
Pennsylvania*	4(c)	Birth month	21.50(c)				7,351
Rhode Island*	2	Birthday	8.00(b)				600
South Carolina*	4	Birthday	4.00				1,959
South Dakota	4	Birthday	6.00				486
Tennessee	2	Birthday	6.00	2	Birthday	8.00	2,902
Texas	4	Birthday	7.00	2	Birthday	13.00	10,154
Utah*	4	Birthday	10.00	4	Birthday	10.00	914
Vermont	4	Birthday	16.00				355
Virginia*	4	Birth month	9.00	2	Birth month	12.00	3,625
Washington*	4	Birthday	14.00(b)				2,774
West Virginia	4	Issuance	10.00(q)	4	Issuance	15.00(q)	1,411
Wisconsin*	2	Birthday	4.00(b,l)	1	Birthday	4.00(b,l)	3,036
Wyoming	4	Birthday	2.50(r)				398
Dist. of Col.	4	Issuance	15.00				385

Sources: Federal Highway Administration, U.S. Department of Transportation. Compiled for the calendar year ending Dec. 31, 1982, from reports of state authorities and other sources.

Key:

*—Classified drivers licenses are issued; permit qualified persons to operate specified vehicles on the public highways.

(a) Includes all classes and types of licenses except "motorcycle only." Allowance has been made for deaths, emigration and revocations in the states that were able to do so. In Kentucky and Wisconsin, chauffeurs licenses have not been added to operators licenses since they require an operators license in addition to the chauffeurs.

(b) The following examination fees are in addition to the fee shown for original license: Alabama, Massachusetts, Rhode Island and Wisconsin—$5; Connecticut—$6.50 for operators and $2.50 for public service (chauffeurs) license; Florida and Washington—$3; Kansas—$6.

(c) Colorado—term is two years for persons 16-17 years and three years for persons 18-20 years; New Mexico—persons 75 years and over renew annually at no charge; Pennsylvania—drivers over 65 renew for two years at $11.50.

(d) A driver who has had a Delaware drivers license for three consecutive years and has a motor-vehicle operation record that shows no previous arrest or conviction may apply for a permanent license for an initial fee of $25 plus every four years the driver must be reexamined and pay a $1 photo fee.

(e) Licenses issued for two years to persons 15-24 years and 65 years and over. Cost varies depending on place of issuance; fees shown are for Honolulu.

(f) Illinois—$4 for persons 69 years and over; Indiana—$3 for two-year renewal license for persons 75 years and over; Nevada—$3 for original or renewal license for persons over 70 years.

(g) Two-year operators and chauffeurs licenses at $5 and $10, respectively, issued to persons under 18 and over 70 years old.

(h) Original licenses are issued for six to 59 months and expire on licensee's birthday in second even- or odd-numbered calendar year after issuance, depending on licensee's birth year.

(i) Two-year licenses for persons over 60 years. Fees are: operators—$3.50; chauffeurs—$9, except in New Orleans Parish where fee is $11.

(j) $22 in New Orleans Parish and municipalities over 300,000 population.

(k) Two-year license for persons 65 years and over at $8 (without photo) or $10 (with optional photo).

(l) Maryland—$20 for original operators license; Michigan—$7.50 for original operators, $16 for original chauffeurs (expires first birthday after issue date), $4 annual renewal for persons 60 years and over; Nevada—$10 for original operators; Oklahoma—additional $2 for license application before obtaining original operators; Oregon—$16 for original operators and $10 for original chauffeurs; Wisconsin—$6.50 for original operators and $6 for original chauffeurs.

(m) Persons with unsatisfactory driving records renew for two-year term.

(n) The following fees are in addition to the license fee shown: Minnesota—$1 service charge if issued by local clerk of district court or agent; Mississippi—$.25 mailing fee; Ohio—$1 deputy issuance fee.

(o) Original license expires on licensee's birthday in the first year after issuance that licensee's age is divisible by four. Fees are: $3.50 for one year; $5.50 for two years; $8 for three years.

(p) Persons under 21 years are issued three-year basic driver permits for $12 (plus $1.50 photo fee).

(q) Driver license can be obtained without examination by a new resident who has a valid out-of-state license, by payment of the regular fee plus $1.

(r) $5 renewed by mail.

3. Health and Human Services

PUBLIC WELFARE

Growing concern about fairness to the poor and the rising tide of unemployment in 1983 put an end to the spate of changes that sharply reduced federal spending on public welfare during 1981-82. Congress blocked the Reagan administration's further attempts to restrict eligibility for welfare assistance and shift social program responsibilities to states and localities. And to ameliorate the adverse effects of the recession on the poor and jobless, the lawmakers—with administration support—even added more money for social and health services, food assistance and shelter. The drive to contain domestic spending focused instead on the large federal entitlement programs—Social Security and Medicare.

Income Assistance

Aid to Families with Dependent Children (AFDC)—Financial assistance is provided to poor families with children by the AFDC program, Title IV-A of the Social Security Act. A family is eligible if it is both needy and one of the parents has died, is continuously absent from the home, or is permanently incapacitated. States also have the option to cover poor, two-parent families on the basis of one parent's unemployment; currently, only 21 states, the District of Columbia and Guam do so, as many states have been forced by budgetary pressures to drop the option.

AFDC is financed and administered jointly by the federal, state and—in 18 states—local governments. The states receive reimbursement from the federal government for the costs of paying benefits and running the program. Reimbursement for benefit expenditures varies according to a state's per capita income and, in fiscal 1983, ranged from a low of 50 percent to a high of 77.63 percent. Administrative costs are matched at the rate of 50 percent. Within general guidelines established and enforced by the federal Office of Family Assistance, states and their political subdivisions are responsible for the day-to-day operation of AFDC. States determine AFDC benefit levels and many of the eligibility requirements, with the result that access to the program and payment amounts differ from one state to the next. Also, states that make erroneous payments are subject to the loss of federal reimbursement.

In fiscal 1982, AFDC served an average monthly caseload of 3.6 million families, representing 10.4 million individuals. The total cost of the program—to all levels of government—was $13.8 billion, of which $12 billion (roughly 54 percent of it federal money) went toward benefits and $1.8 billion for administration. By comparison, in fiscal 1981—prior to enactment of legislation narrowing eligibility for the program—AFDC served an average of 11.1 million persons a month, at a total cost of around $14.2 billion.

A number of changes have been made in the AFDC program as a result of the Omnibus Budget Reconciliation Act of 1981. To assure that benefits only go to eligible people in the correct amount, states must use systems for retrospective budgeting (basing a family's benefit on income in the prior month) and monthly reporting (requiring recipients to file monthly reports on their circumstances with the welfare office). Limits have been placed on the amount of a working recipient's earnings that may be deducted for employment and child care expenses in determining eligibility and benefits, and the deduction of a portion of earned income as a work incentive is now subject to a time limit, too. In addition, the law bars families from owning more than $1,000 in resources, restricts AFDC payments to families in which the principal earner is the one unemployed, and requires that part of the income of a child's step-parent or an alien's sponsor be deemed available to that child or alien when calculating AFDC eligibility and benefits.

The Reconciliation Act also toughened the program's work requirements. All applicants and recipients of AFDC must register for work, except: children under age 16 and full-time students under age 18; ill, elderly and incapacitated persons; people who live too far from work training sites to participate; and persons needed at home to care for others. States may offer a variety of work programs for recipients. All states operate a work incentive (WIN) program

---

These two articles were prepared by the Department of Government Affairs and Social Policy, American Public Welfare Association.

or WIN demonstration, both of which provide a range of employment, training and social services to help AFDC recipients become self-supporting wage earners. States may also choose to conduct community work experience programs (CWEP), known as workfare, in which recipients are required to work off their AFDC benefits in a community service job or work supplementation programs in which the AFDC grant is used to subsidize a private sector job for the recipient.

Child Support Enforcement (CSE)—The child support enforcement program, Title IV-D of the Social Security Act, is used by the states to help establish paternity for and secure parental support of both AFDC children and those not receiving AFDC. AFDC applicants and recipients are required, as a condition of eligibility, to cooperate with the states in determining paternity and obtaining support from absent parents. The Office of Child Support Enforcement located in the Social Security Administration oversees the program. The federal government pays 70 percent of the states' administrative cost—as a result of a law adopted in 1982 lowering the reimbursement rate from 75 percent. The same law, beginning in fiscal 1984, reduces the federal incentive payments that are made to states and localities based on the amount of child support they collect. Further legislative changes to strengthen the child support enforcement program are likely in the near future, owing to the large proportion of absent fathers who do not meet their support obligations.

Total federal expenditures for administration of the program in fiscal 1982 were $592 million. Child support collections equalled $1.771 billion—$787 million obtained on behalf of AFDC recipients and $984 million on behalf of persons not on the welfare rolls. Approximately $2.99 was collected for each dollar spent on administration.

Supplemental Security Income (SSI)—For indigent persons who are 65 or older, legally blind, or permanently or totally disabled, cash assistance is available from the SSI program. Unlike AFDC, in which the states determine payment levels, basic SSI benefits are set and administered by the federal government. As of July 1983, a qualified individual could receive a basic monthly grant of $304 and an eligible couple $456. Supplements to the basic benefits are provided by the states, half of which contract with the Social Security Administration to administer all or part of these additional payments.

In fiscal 1982, an average of 4 million people drew SSI benefits each month, at a total federal cost for the year of $7.65 billion. State supplements accounted for an additional expenditure of $2.09 billion.

Low Income Home Energy Assistance—The federal low income home energy assistance program, administered by the Office of Family Assistance, allows states to help needy people with their heating and cooling bills. Eligibility is limited to households in which at least one person receives AFDC, SSI, food stamps, or certain veterans' benefits, or households with income that does not exceed 150 percent of the state poverty level or 60 percent of the state median income, whichever is higher. Federal energy assistance funds are distributed to the states in the form of a need-based block grant. Each year, a state may reserve a reasonable amount of the grant for energy crisis assistance and use up to 15 percent for economical weatherization and 10 percent for program administration. In addition, as much as 25 percent of a state's annual allocation may be held for use in the following year, and 10 percent may be transferred by the state to other federal block grants for health, social services and community services. In fiscal 1982, states received low-income energy assistance funds totalling $1.875 billion.

General Assistance—Most states and many localities operate programs of general assistance which are financed and operated without federal support. Eligibility standards, benefit levels and types, and administrative arrangements vary widely from one jurisdiction to the next. For the most part, general assistance is used to aid persons who do not qualify for AFDC and SSI. In September 1981, an estimated one million people were receiving general assistance in 40 states.

FOOD STAMPS, MEDICAID, SOCIAL SERVICES AND AGING

The primary means of helping poor people obtain adequate nutrition in the United States is the food stamp program, which provides needy households with a monthly allotment of coupons for their use in buying food. The amount of the allotment varies with the size and net income (after certain deductions have been taken) of the household. The food stamp program is unique, since it is the only federally funded welfare program that extends benefits to virtually all poor people—not just the categories served by AFDC and SSI.

The federal government bears the entire cost of the benefits and splits administrative expenses evenly with the states. Although the states run the program, eligibility and most other program rules are set by the U.S. Department of Agriculture. In fiscal 1982, the food stamp program served an average of 21 million persons a month, at an annual cost of $11.1 billion.

Frequent changes have been made in the program to control its growth. Eligibility has been tightened by: (1) limiting a household's gross income to 130 percent and net income to 100 percent of the poverty level; (2) barring boarders, children living with parents who are under age 60, and adult siblings from qualifying as separate households; and (3) excluding strikers and most students from participation. Benefit levels have been made less sensitive to inflation and reduced to cover only that part of the month during which a household participates in the program. As in AFDC, retrospective budgeting and monthly reporting have been mandated, the authority to establish work programs and requirements in the states has been expanded, and financial penalties have been created for states that issue benefits erroneously.

Medicaid

Medicaid, Title XIX of the Social Security Act, is the chief source of health care coverage for the nation's poor. All AFDC and SSI recipients qualify for Medicaid, and in 30 states, coverage is also extended to the medically needy, those whose income exceeds AFDC or SSI limits but is insufficient to meet their medical needs. Under federal policy administered by the Health Care Financing Administration, a state's Medicaid program must offer inpatient and outpatient care, laboratory and x-ray services, skilled nursing and home health care, physician services, family planning, rural health clinics, and health screening for children. States may also cover other services, such as intermediate care facilities, eyeglasses and dental care. For the cost of benefits (paying health care providers for the services they furnish) and program administration, states are reimbursed at the same rates as in AFDC.

Currently, approximately 22 million people receive Medicaid benefits. The total expenditure for services in the program reached $33.5 billion in fiscal 1982, with the state share of these costs equal to around $15.1 billion. In fiscal 1982, the last year for which data are available, total administrative costs were $1.567 billion.

Changes made by the 1981 reconciliation legislation gave states more flexibility and stronger financial incentives to control Medicaid costs. States may receive federal waivers to set up home and community-based alternatives to institutionalization for long-term care patients and to establish more efficient health care delivery systems such as primary care networks (in which a recipient is assigned to a single physician who determines what care is needed and who will provide it). States also have more discretion in setting reimbursement rates for hospitals that participate in the program, in limiting coverage of the medically needy, and in restricting recipient freedom in choosing providers. To encourage use of these and other cost-saving options, states faced the loss of some federal reimbursement during fiscal 1982-84 unless they met certain cost containment standards. As a result of the increased flexibility and incentives, states were able to keep Medicaid expenditure growth to under 10 percent in fiscal 1982, a large drop from the 15 percent annual rate of growth of the five previous years.

As in AFDC and food stamps, fiscal sanctions are levied against states that make erroneous Medicaid payments.

Social Services

Social Services Block Grant—The main source of federal funding for social services is the social service block grant, Title XX of the Social Security Act. The block grant was enacted in 1981 as part of President Reagan's plan to increase state and local control of human services and replaced a somewhat more restrictive version of Title XX that had operated since 1975. Under the new program, states are essentially free to determine what services will be provided to whom and through what mechanisms (public or private deliverers). An annual report on how it plans to spend the grant is required of each state, and every two years, the state must both report on what it has done to carry out its plans and arrange for an independent expenditure audit. Title XX received $2.4 billion in fiscal 1982, $2.675 billion in fiscal 1983, and $2.7 billion in fiscal 1984—compared to $2.991 billion in fiscal 1981, the year before the block grant took effect. Federal administration of Title XX is lodged in the Office of Human Development Services.

Community Services Block Grant—In 1981, Congress also, at the administration's request, established the community services block grant to states, consolidating the remnants of the federal antipoverty effort of the 1960s and 1970s. State discretion in using the block grant is limited, since 90 percent of the funds they get must be passed on to local agencies that were federal grantees immediately prior to the enactment of the new program. Governors have sought unsuccessfully to have this restriction removed by Congress. Although annual funding of the block grant is authorized at $389 million from fiscal year 1982 through 1986, the yearly appropriation for the program has not yet exceeded $350 million. Like Title XX, the federal Office of Human Development Services is responsible for administration.

Child Welfare Services—States provide foster care, adoption assistance, and a variety of other child welfare services under Titles IV-E and IV-B of the Social Security Act. The Adoption Assistance and Child Welfare Act of 1980 (P.L. 96-272) established Title IV-E—which finances foster care and, for the first time, adoption assistance payments—and made several changes in Title IV-B, which is a general source of funds for child welfare services, to help states find permanent homes for the children in their care. Title IV-E operates as an entitlement, meaning that federal funds are available to help cover the cost of care for any child who qualifies for the program within the state. The law requires states to implement a number of "good practices" to receive extra money under the flexible Title IV-B program, including: completion of an inventory

of all children in foster care longer than six months; implementation of a foster care case review system; establishment of an information system to track children in a state's foster care system; and development of services to help children return to or remain in their own homes. For fiscal 1984, federal funding of Title IV-B is set at $165 million and Title IV-E is estimated to cost the federal government $442.2 million. The Office of Human Development Services administers both programs.

Programs for the Aging

The economic needs of older people are met through various sources. The bulk of their income is derived from earnings, private pensions and Social Security payments. The largest public income support program, Social Security, in 1982 paid out $134.7 billion in benefits to 32.2 million retirees, disabled persons, and their dependents and survivors. Legislation enacted in 1983 to shore up the financing of the program makes a number of revisions in the benefit and revenue provisions of the program including: a delay in the annual cost-of-living adjustment in benefits; taxation of the benefits of higher income retirees; acceleration of scheduled payroll tax increases; higher payroll taxes for the self-employed; and required participation by employees of nonprofit organizations and new federal employees. The poor elderly may also obtain income assistance from the SSI and food stamp programs.

Health care is available to the elderly under Medicare and Medicaid. Medicare provides acute-care health insurance for nearly all people 65 years of age or older. Part A of Medicare covers hospitals and Part B pays for a substantial portion of physicians' services. To contain rising Part A costs, Congress, in 1983, adopted a new hospital reimbursement system which pays hospitals a fixed amount based on a patient's diagnosis. The Medicare program is financed largely by Social Security taxes, with additional revenue obtained through coinsurance, premiums and deductibles paid by the elderly themselves. In fiscal 1982, Medicare expenditures equalled $49.1 billion. Indigent older people who cannot pay the out-of-pocket expenses of Medicare may also qualify for Medicaid, which will cover these expenses as well as services not available under Medicare, particularly nursing home care.

The primary source of federal funding for social services for the elderly is the Older Americans Act. The law's main purpose is to stimulate the availability of services and support needed specifically by the elderly. The long-term aim of the act is to develop a comprehensive, coordinated social service system for older people in all parts of the country. Leadership for this resides in the Administration on Aging of the Office of Human Development Services, with program implementation the responsibility of state and area agencies on aging. The Older Americans Act provided funding to 57 state agencies and 670 area agencies in 1983; total expenditures for the act were $671.7 million.

Table 1
AID TO FAMILIES WITH DEPENDENT CHILDREN:
RECIPIENTS OF CASH PAYMENTS AND AMOUNT BY STATE
(As of January 1983)

State or other jurisdictions	Number of families (in thousands)	Number of recipients (in thousands)	Payments to recipients		
			Total (in thousands)	Average per	
				Family	Recipient
United States	3,632.0	10,620.7	$1,131,001.0	$311.40	$106.49
Alabama	54.7	152.4	6,042.3	110.52	39.63
Alaska	4.4	10.0	2,511.2	566.61	244.31
Arizona	23.8	66.5	4,896.7	205.66	73.63
Arkansas	22.3	63.6	2,951.1	132.18	46.39
California	537.5	1,580.4	249,171.6	463.57	157.66
Colorado	29.0	84.3	8,283.5	286.12	98.29
Connecticut	43.5	126.9	18,685.9	429.57	147.31
Delaware	9.4	25.9	2,178.8	232.93	84.06
Florida	102.2	278.2	19,431.4	190.20	69.84
Georgia	89.3	240.5	15,507.8	173.62	64.47
Hawaii	17.8	54.9	7,357.6	412.31	134.02
Idaho	7.0	18.9	1,869.1	268.90	98.97
Illinois	234.8	732.8	68,820.5	293.07	93.92
Indiana	57.2	165.5	12,068.5	211.04	72.94
Iowa	36.5	100.7	11,848.2	324.94	117.64
Kansas	24.8	71.8	7,512.6	303.25	104.61
Kentucky	56.6	150.2	10,364.0	183.12	69.01
Louisiana.........	65.8	199.7	11,105.2	168.78	55.61
Maine.............	16.7	47.9	4,951.2	296.71	103.33
Maryland.........	70.1	192.4	18,785.2	268.02	97.62
Massachusetts.....	90.8	255.5	33,745.9	371.63	132.09
Michigan	237.9	746.6	99,141.7	416.66	132.78
Minnesota	46.8	135.9	18,590.8	397.62	136.83
Mississippi	50.8	147.9	4,664.2	91.90	31.54
Missouri..........	64.2	179.5	15,601.1	243.10	86.91
Montana	6.1	16.7	1,786.1	292.13	106.89
Nebraska	13.8	39.9	4,370.4	315.76	109.49
Nevada...........	4.8	13.3	928.7	192.23	69.67
New Hampshire	7.2	19.5	1,984.1	276.68	101.68
New Jersey	133.1	399.1	43,719.6	328.47	109.55
New Mexico	17.7	48.4	3,533.2	199.44	73.00
New York	359.6	1,089.2	141,846.6	394.43	130.24
North Carolina....	69.3	173.9	12,273.6	177.22	70.58
North Dakota......	3.9	10.7	1,235.3	313.85	114.99
Ohio	208.6	626.2	54,928.4	263.38	87.71
Oklahoma	24.3	70.3	6,235.3	257.01	88.67
Oregon...........	27.7	74.2	7,982.6	288.21	107.62
Pennsylvania......	197.0	587.7	62,554.2	317.46	106.44
Rhode Island......	16.1	45.8	6,528.0	405.54	142.60
South Carolina	49.9	135.4	6,416.9	128.47	47.41
South Dakota	6.0	16.9	1,463.0	241.89	86.45
Tennessee	58.2	152.4	6,849.0	117.75	44.95
Texas	101.3	304.4	10,516.4	103.86	34.55
Utah.............	12.1	35.9	4,347.8	358.02	121.13
Vermont	7.1	21.0	2,739.5	383.63	130.30
Virginia	60.8	162.1	13,855.6	227.72	85.48
Washington.......	54.7	145.1	21,446.8	392.19	147.76
West Virginia	28.1	78.7	5,037.4	178.99	64.01
Wisconsin	85.6	260.0	38,426.2	448.83	147.80
Wyoming..........	2.8	7.1	855.7	310.83	119.96
Dist. of Col.	24.5	64.0	7,168.6	292.85	112.01
Guam.............	1.4	4.9	315.8	232.41	64.14
Puerto Rico.......	55.2	184.9	5,316.4	96.36	28.75
Virgin Islands	1.3	3.7	254.0	196.11	67.87

Source: *Monthly Benefit Statistics*, U.S. Department of Health and
Human Services, Social Security Administration, Office of Policy, Office
of Research, Statistics and International Policy, No. 6.

Table 2
FOOD STAMP PROGRAM
(As of October 1982)

State or other jurisdiction	Monthly household recipients	Monthly individual recipients	Monthly total value issued	Monthly average value per person	Monthly average value per household
United States........	7,503,980	20,655,829	$890,793,487	$43.13	$118.70
Alabama	207,456	622,048	27,274,378	43.84	131.47
Alaska	5,723	17,652	1,234,246	69.92	215.66
Arizona	72,388	218,724	11,981,920	54.78	165.52
Arkansas	105,058	306,989	12,312,877	40.10	117.20
California	605,025	1,711,455	58,795,358	34.35	97.17
Colorado	65,683	176,218	7,788,849	44.20	118.58
Connecticut..........	63,155	165,982	5,714,456	34.42	90.48
Delaware	18,326	49,108	2,374,834	48.39	129.58
Florida	320,350	845,788	40,208,715	47.54	125.51
Georgia	208,198	614,357	25,739,003	41.89	123.62
Hawaii	38,036	100,370	6,701,556	66.76	176.19
Idaho	22,790	65,688	3,222,676	49.06	141.40
Illinois	407,021	1,068,725	50,484,760	47.23	124.03
Indiana.............	148,168	450,301	20,868,348	46.23	140.84
Iowa	72,398	190,531	8,146,846	42.75	112.52
Kansas	50,015	129,464	5,492,760	42.42	109.82
Kentucky............	175,954	544,400	24,772,267	45.50	140.79
Louisiana............	180,284	542,313	22,940,413	42.30	127.24
Maine	49,183	124,851	5,727,651	45.87	116.45
Maryland	126,965	315,643	15,014,309	47.56	118.25
Massachusetts.........	165,386	399,228	16,589,505	41.55	100.30
Michigan(a)	401,540	1,012,958	44,184,367	43.61	110.03
Minnesota	78,883	216,995	8,186,410	37.72	103.77
Mississippi	160,069	507,473	21,694,452	42.75	135.53
Missouri.............	138,069	394,104	17,417,013	44.19	126.14
Montana	18,121	49,276	2,095,773	42.53	115.65
Nebraska.............	30,172	83,020	3,125,509	37.64	103.59
Nevada..............	13,834	32,956	1,655,020	50.21	119.63
New Hampshire	18,302	44,946	2,064,851	45.94	112.82
New Jersey...........	197,102	534,733	24,638,830	46.07	125.00
New Mexico	53,875	171,032	7,700,740	45.02	142.93
New York(a)..........	728,685	1,796,525	74,435,420	41.43	102.15
North Carolina	187,634	536,924	21,918,217	40.82	116.81
North Dakota	10,013	29,336	1,152,362	39.28	115.08
Ohio(a)	394,210	1,061,398	51,727,377	48.73	131.21
Oklahoma	81,831	211,191	7,860,335	37.21	96.05
Oregon(a)............	96,753	249,592	12,704,784	50.90	131.31
Pennsylvania	428,640	1,052,080	44,860,994	42.64	104.65
Rhode Island	33,328	81,670	3,054,808	37.40	91.65
South Carolina(a)	140,457	431,837	18,380,822	42.56	130.86
South Dakota	16,172	49,507	2,075,034	41.91	128.31
Tennessee	223,045	621,225	26,987,231	43.44	120.99
Texas	378,970	1,237,546	55,341,027	44.71	146.03
Utah(a)	23,483	76,654	3,227,583	42.10	137.44
Vermont(a)	14,816	44,506	1,788,058	40.17	120.68
Virginia(a)...........	153,372	420,338	17,737,703	42.19	115.65
Washington	118,468	294,111	12,133,584	41.25	102.42
West Virginia	82,785	256,842	10,865,183	42.30	131.24
Wisconsin	118,474	337,200	10,449,935	30.99	88.20
Wyoming.............	6,482	18,135	739,785	40.79	114.12
Dist. of Col.	35,800	85,920	3,930,189	45.74	109.78
Guam	5,189	24,298	1,488,062	61.24	286.77
Virgin Islands	7,844	31,666	1,786,302	56.41	227.72

Source: Food Stamp Program Statistical Summary of Operations, U.S. Department of Agriculture, Food and Nutrition Service, October 1982.
  (a) State totals exclude SSI/Elderly Cash-Out Demonstration Project.

Table 3
SUPPLEMENTAL SECURITY INCOME, BY STATE: 1982
(In thousands)

State or other jurisdiction	Total	Federal SSI	State supplementation
United States	$8,669,504	$6,832,380(a)	$1,837,124(b)
Alabama	224,643	224,643	
Alaska	6,514	6,514	
Arizona	62,206	62,206	
Arkansas	119,064	119,013	51
California	2,113,232	879,805	1,233,427
Colorado	53,242	53,242	
Connecticut.........	47,414	47,414	
Delaware	12,936	12,477	459
Florida	354,617	354,617	
Georgia	268,509	268,466	43
Hawaii	23,411	19,033	4,378
Idaho	13,394	13,394	
Illinois	244,232	244,232	
Indiana............	71,906	71,906	
Iowa	40,279	39,239	1,040
Kansas	32,713	32,659	54
Kentucky	177,634	177,634	
Louisiana...........	246,040	245,939	101
Maine	33,075	28,188	4,887
Maryland	96,516	96,364	152
Massachusetts.......	258,551	138,307	120,244
Michigan	257,753	199,214	58,539
Minnesota	47,672	47,672	
Mississippi	198,818	198,753	65
Missouri...........	145,222	145,222	
Montana	12,517	11,782	735
Nebraska	22,424	22,424	
Nevada.............	14,274	11,649	2,625
New Hampshire	9,503	9,503	
New Jersey	197,202	156,914	40,288
New Mexico	48,005	48,005	
New York	872,630	650,949	221,681
North Carolina	243,233	243,233	
North Dakota	9,688	9,688	
Ohio	233,350	233,270	80
Oklahoma	108,017	108,017	
Oregon.............	42,001	42,001	
Pennsylvania........	344,591	288,366	56,225
Rhode Island	29,012	21,896	7,116
South Carolina	145,137	145,137	
South Dakota	12,216	12,183	33
Tennessee	230,457	230,457	
Texas	419,164	419,164	
Utah...............	13,943	13,943	
Vermont	17,749	12,631	5,118
Virginia	143,311	143,311	
Washington..........	94,213	78,175	16,038
West Virginia	83,983	83,983	
Wisconsin	133,418	73,359	60,059
Wyoming...........	2,929	2,929	
Dist. of Col.	35,528	31,626	3,902
Northern Mariana Is...	1,542	1,542	

Source: Office of Research and Statistics, Social Security Administration.

(a) Federal payments of $92,000 not reported by state.

(b) The total amount of state payments was reduced by $85,000 to reflect returned checks and overpayment refunds in some states where amount is not shown. In addition, a reduction of $131,000 was made to reflect adjustments not applicable to specific states.

Table 4
SUPPLEMENTAL SECURITY INCOME FOR AGED, BLIND AND DISABLED
May 1983

State or other jurisdiction	Number of persons receiving federally administered payments				Payment (in thousands)					
	Total	Aged	Blind	Disabled	Total federal payments	Federal SSI	Federally administered state supplementation	Aged	Blind	Disabled
United States(a) ..	3,855,896	1,522,908	78,065	2,254,923	$758,909	$609,104	$149,805	$221,225	$18,875	$518,809
Alabama(b)	125,765	65,035	1,895	58,835	19,821	19,821	...	7,775	373	11,672
Alaska(b)	3,010	1,108	57	1,845	584	584	...	173	13	398
Arizona(b)	28,769	10,017	604	18,148	5,579	5,579	...	1,439	138	4,002
Arkansas	70,407	35,531	1,387	33,489	10,224	10,217	7	3,937	262	6,024
California	654,682	271,836	17,885	364,961	178,541	80,045	98,496	57,647	5,867	115,027
Colorado(b)	27,969	10,377	392	17,200	4,702	4,702	...	1,272	74	3,356
Connecticut(b)	23,286	6,442	450	16,394	4,408	4,408	...	842	100	3,466
Delaware	6,686	2,037	154	4,495	1,179	1,143	36	219	29	931
Florida	168,430	77,095	2,838	88,497	31,340	31,339	1	12,521	596	18,223
Georgia	144,694	60,994	2,855	80,845	23,273	23,269	4	7,262	576	15,435
Hawaii	9,880	4,454	168	5,258	2,145	1,759	386	824	40	1,282
Idaho(b)	7,253	2,120	122	5,011	1,223	1,223	...	224	24	975
Illinois(c)	117,880	29,479	2,017	86,384	22,180	22,180	...	3,949	432	17,799
Indiana(c)	40,070	11,731	1,195	27,144	6,680	6,680	...	1,236	237	5,206
Iowa	24,491	8,784	1,030	14,677	3,738	3,633	105	839	192	2,707
Kansas	19,052	6,094	323	12,635	2,984	2,979	5	666	62	2,256
Kentucky(b)	90,835	35,441	2,024	53,370	15,947	15,947	...	4,314	459	11,174
Louisiana	122,245	52,683	2,049	67,513	20,939	20,927	12	6,904	428	13,607
Maine	20,220	8,044	304	11,872	2,892	2,499	393	651	53	2,188
Maryland	46,297	13,718	704	31,875	8,778	8,765	13	1,675	153	6,949
Massachusetts	107,652	53,522	4,932	49,198	22,332	12,677	9,655	8,064	1,276	12,992
Michigan	108,301	30,265	1,943	76,093	23,269	18,311	4,959	4,187	467	18,615
Minnesota(b)	29,369	10,181	620	18,568	4,347	4,347	...	1,087	105	3,156
Mississippi(b)	107,741	53,703	1,789	52,249	17,245	17,240	5	6,450	358	10,437
Missouri(b)	76,199	31,028	1,245	43,926	12,623	12,623	...	3,642	232	8,748
Montana(b)	6,473	1,785	131	4,557	1,138	1,066	72	183	25	931
Nebraska(b)	12,713	4,140	231	8,342	1,996	1,996	...	399	43	1,554
Nevada	6,755	3,271	437	3,047	1,251	1,023	228	485	109	658
New Hampshire(b) .	5,153	1,636	106	3,411	892	892	...	170	18	704
New Jersey	82,976	28,596	1,136	53,244	17,709	14,463	3,247	4,682	262	12,765

New Mexico(b)	24,010	9,059	470	14,481	4,255	4,255	18,650	1,136	97	3,021
New York	334,389	113,988	4,037	216,364	76,400	57,750	···	19,785	982	55,634
North Carolina(b)	131,491	54,725	2,894	73,872	21,451	21,451	···	6,337	592	14,523
North Dakota(b)	5,790	2,552	80	3,158	835	835	···	260	15	560
Ohio	113,606	27,785	2,325	83,496	20,958	20,946	12	3,251	473	17,234
Oklahoma(b)	58,710	26,875	946	30,889	9,205	9,205	···	3,309	198	5,698
Oregon(b)	21,912	6,246	508	15,158	3,809	3,809	···	714	95	3,000
Pennsylvania	152,351	46,704	3,057	102,590	31,527	26,123	5,404	6,436	728	24,363
Rhode Island	14,264	5,038	212	9,014	2,612	1,978	634	629	51	1,933
South Carolina(b)	79,389	33,023	1,873	44,493	12,756	12,756	···	3,790	391	8,575
South Dakota	7,654	3,110	148	4,396	1,109	1,106	3	314	30	766
Tennessee	122,893	51,276	1,983	69,634	20,163	20,162	1	5,853	423	13,887
Texas(c)	239,700	123,964	4,233	111,503	36,332	36,332	···	14,748	853	20,730
Utah(c)	7,609	1,999	177	5,433	1,274	1,274	···	263	36	974
Vermont	8,508	3,017	116	5,375	1,628	1,151	478	380	28	1,221
Virginia(c)	77,953	30,110	1,453	46,390	12,853	12,853	1,399	3,455	290	9,109
Washington	42,677	12,320	634	29,723	8,521	7,123	···	1,665	140	6,717
West Virginia(c)	38,926	11,028	650	27,248	7,538	7,538	5,257	1,407	145	5,985
Wisconsin	61,787	24,078	982	36,727	12,040	6,783	···	3,084	244	8,712
Wyoming(b)	1,701	607	41	1,053	274	274	···	62	9	203
Dist. of Col.	14,695	3,915	206	10,574	3,267	2,924	344	554	47	2,667
No. Mariana Is.(c)	617	339	17	261	138	74	···	74	4	60
Unknown	11	3	···	8	6	6	···	2	···	4

Source: *Monthly Benefit Statistics*, U.S. Department of Health and Human Services, Social Security Administration, Office of Policy, Office of Research, Statistics and International Policy, No. 6.

(a) Includes persons with federal SSI payments and/or federally administered state supplementation, unless otherwise indicated.

(b) Data for federal SSI payments only. State has state-administered supplementation.

(c) Data for federal SSI payments only; state supplementary payments not made.

Table 5
MEDICAID EXPENDITURES: FISCAL 1981
(In thousands)

State or other jurisdiction	Total expenditure for Medicaid assistance payments	Total expenditure for state administration	Total expenditure computable for federal funding	Federal share of total expenditure
United States	$28,431,817	$1,327,657	$29,759,474	$16,681,025
Alabama	291,655	10,129	301,784	223,964
Alaska	44,333	2,114	46,447	23,538
Arizona	State did not operate a Medicaid program in fiscal 1981			
Arkansas	281,206	8,965	290,171	213,001
California	3,733,516	190,501	3,924,017	1,997,620
Colorado	217,807	8,474	226,281	127,917
Connecticut	379,777	16,891	396,668	199,712
Delaware	55,188	2,374	57,562	29,736
Florida	512,476	27,779	540,255	314,767
Georgia	553,847	23,457	577,304	381,055
Hawaii	111,116	6,155	117,271	59,854
Idaho	60,246	3,479	63,725	43,756
Illinois	1,481,947	55,021	1,536,968	762,146
Indiana	448,936	18,292	467,228	264,511
Iowa	278,003	9,662	287,665	159,935
Kansas	222,828	8,159	230,987	123,247
Kentucky	371,293	17,385	388,678	264,189
Louisiana	420,534	18,103	438,637	331,880
Maine	162,280	6,988	169,268	120,771
Maryland	480,728	19,973	500,701	241,859
Massachusetts	1,159,932	28,520	1,188,452	597,876
Michigan	1,375,480	59,778	1,435,258	720,672
Minnesota	679,653	25,085	704,738	393,622
Mississippi	253,534	11,283	264,817	206,955
Missouri	383,779	14,101	397,880	267,840
Montana	87,741	4,443	92,184	57,888
Nebraska	126,502	7,954	134,456	81,335
Nevada	62,187	4,261	66,448	34,091
New Hampshire	84,494	4,463	88,957	53,828
New Jersey	846,861	32,641	879,502	462,194
New Mexico	91,905	5,959	97,864	69,024
New York	5,072,503	257,762	5,330,265	2,824,565
North Carolina	486,523	27,794	514,317	348,193
North Dakota	60,551	4,411	64,962	40,190
Ohio	1,054,083	42,826	1,096,909	611,678
Oklahoma	361,737	27,551	389,288	245,020
Oregon	198,602	19,838	218,440	123,997
Pennsylvania	1,492,896	67,980	1,560,876	847,957
Rhode Island	183,441	6,354	189,795	112,323
South Carolina	300,889	10,863	311,752	215,187
South Dakota	72,212	2,798	75,010	50,906
Tennessee	434,718	16,317	451,035	316,593
Texas	1,200,298	88,129	1,288,427	743,504
Utah	92,607	6,103	98,710	73,267
Vermont	71,610	4,728	76,338	57,057
Virginia	440,988	17,503	458,491	274,928
Washington	415,809	22,495	438,304	232,853
West Virginia	129,036	8,860	137,896	91,341
Wisconsin	848,625	28,866	877,491	516,035
Wyoming	16,936	860	17,796	8,844
Dist. of Col.	160,684	9,136	169,820	85,806
Guam	2,866	45	2,911	900
Northern Mariana Is ..	49	59	108	96
Puerto Rico	72,570	4,332	76,902	30,000
Virgin Islands	1,905	500	2,405	1,000

Source: *Medicaid Financial Management Report for FY 1981*, Health Care Financing Administration.

Table 6
CHILD SUPPORT ENFORCEMENT: FISCAL 1982
(In thousands)

State or other jurisdiction	AFDC collections	Non-AFDC collections	AFDC expenditures	Non-AFDC expenditures	AFDC child support caseload	Non-AFDC child support caseload
Alabama	$ 8,060	$ 160	$ 7,020	$ 128	82,444	895
Alaska	1,048	6,340	2,062	745	10,497	3,534
Arizona	1,250	9,171	2,306	354	9,178	14,664
Arkansas	3,032	2,521	3,501	1,254	46,691	4,675
California	136,394	110,630	83,996	24,971	657,207	320,924
Colorado	5,990	10,948	5,787	842	93,976	28,819
Connecticut	21,308	15,770	8,263	1,206	40,687	13,218
Delaware	1,958	5,426	1,275	851	10,287	8,747
Florida	14,286	5,988	12,308	1,758	256,789	10,742
Georgia	8,107	1,393	6,877	207	119,448	64,165
Hawaii	3,345	4,879	1,649	83	20,972	6,086
Idaho	3,433	765	1,595	90	20,092	3,310
Illinois	17,015	4,585	15,135	1,593	278,792	24,187
Indiana	11,650	2,939	7,342	84	138,978	10,401
Iowa	18,114	8,696	5,255	846	55,826	9,486
Kansas	7,787	1,835	4,642	23	97,228	3,273
Kentucky	3,752	10,895	5,880	1,198	136,818	11,032
Louisiana	9,301	13,018	9,832	1,016	104,448	20,846
Maine	5,991	1,474	2,128	504	31,020	593
Maryland	16,317	39,513	11,284	2,857	136,115	43,235
Massachusetts	40,368	23,244	12,923	2,406	92,600	11,000
Michigan	101,339	139,099	29,640	· 6,571	399,520	92,893
Minnesota	23,125	14,709	11,667	2,943	67,136	16,774
Mississippi	2,396	295	2,280	152	14,960	1,310
Missouri	12,437	6,152	5,436	2,136	111,764	10,344
Montana	1,237	513	1,015	33	24,971	856
Nebraska	3,176	13,949	3,295	282	16,678	9,829
Nevada	1,510	3,202	2,136	518	16,620	6,199
New Hampshire	2,303	2,927	1,420	94	6,121	1,090
New Jersey	33,606	96,887	23,098	9,320	247,169	75,207
New Mexico	2,218	1,252	2,084	586	66,850	3,037
New York	54,632	97,171	56,223	14,249	586,925	115,862
North Carolina	12,795	9,472	9,752	1,465	113,308	15,673
North Dakota	1,763	549	1,064	146	14,831	603
Ohio	30,082	872	18,379	195	308,620	22,124
Oklahoma	2,607	1,289	5,284	867	50,331	7,171
Oregon	16,599	30,725	7,737	3,579	39,443	41,346
Pennsylvania	40,586	214,895	17,651	17,559	236,589	240,288
Rhode Island	3,869	1,512	1,897	76	16,723	5,466
South Carolina	4,712	1,441	2,260	181	71,435	1,055
South Dakota	1,432	690	993	162	14,894	748
Tennessee	5,901	11,591	4,330	1,260	91,036	37,506
Texas	6,869	6,973	15,184	1,461	90,597	91,654
Utah	10,065	1,883	5,186	309	29,224	1,519
Vermont	3,039	219	722	87	7,774	922
Virginia	10,398	1,832	7,299	385	1,830	1,255
Washington	22,160	14,467	8,726	4,278	48,594	21,175
West Virginia	2,488	149	2,880	81	35,114	5,937
Wisconsin	32,020	11,132	13,945	1,145	128,428	12,027
Wyoming	619	258	343	43	7,761	471
Dist. of Col.	1,813	761	3,708	160	46,444	2,092
Guam	165	95	216	18	1,660	1,460
Puerto Rico	675	16,697	1,200	620	57,208	18,105
Virgin Islands	179	479	175	109	134,467	3,230

Source: *Child Support Enforcement,* 7th Annual Report to Congress for the period ending September 30, 1982.

Table 7
FEDERAL ALLOTMENTS TO STATES FOR TITLE XX SOCIAL SERVICES: FISCAL 1981-1984
(In thousands)

State or other jurisdiction	1981	1982	1983	1984
United States	$2,991,100	$2,400,000	$2,450,000	$2,675,000
Alabama	50,729	40,989	41,843	45,440
Alaska	5,469	4,215	4,302	4,779
Arizona	32,382	28,640	29,237	32,412
Arkansas	30,472	24,088	24,590	26,635
California	302,631	249,403	254,599	280,689
Colorado	35,576	30,442	31,076	34,396
Connecticut.........	47,169	32,749	33,432	36,356
Delaware	7,905	6,270	6,400	6,937
Florida	116,497	102,631	104,770	118,129
Georgia	69,055	57,575	58,774	64,662
Hawaii	12,163	10,168	10,380	11,380
Idaho	11,900	9,947	10,154	11,125
Illinois	152,455	120,313	122,819	132,966
Indiana.............	73,161	57,849	59,054	63,432
Iowa	39,265	30,695	31,334	33,630
Kansas	31,834	24,899	25,418	27,644
Kentucky	48,003	38,576	39,380	42,481
Louisiana...........	54,073	44,298	45,221	49,975
Maine	15,139	11,854	12,101	13,143
Maryland	56,178	44,424	45,350	49,453
Massachusetts.......	78,936	60,451	61,711	66,970
Michigan	124,587	97,553	99,585	106,772
Minnesota	54,340	42,960	43,855	47,493
Mississippi	32,676	26,564	27,117	29,361
Missouri............	65,886	51,811	52,890	57,319
Montana	72,077	8,293	8,465	9,199
Nebraska	21,221	16,543	16,888	18,294
Nevada.............	8,947	8,419	8,594	9,803
New Hampshire	11,805	9,705	9,907	10,858
New Jersey	99,354	77,595	79,212	85,891
New Mexico	16,712	13,698	13,984	15,406
New York	243,943	185,000	188,854	204,194
North Carolina	76,325	61,895	63,184	69,058
North Dakota	8,951	6,881	7,024	7,633
Ohio	145,743	113,769	116,139	125,066
Oklahoma	39,056	31,875	32,539	35,962
Oregon	32,123	27,744	28,322	30,753
Pennsylvania........	160,251	124,044	127,649	137,711
Rhode Island	12,874	9,979	10,187	11,055
South Carolina	39,557	32,865	33,550	36,739
South Dakota	9,356	7,271	7,422	7,958
Tennessee	59,066	48,376	49,384	53,502
Texas	177,795	149,922	153,045	171,295
Utah	18,017	15,395	15,715	17,610
Vermont	6,880	5,384	5,497	5,986
Virginia	70,092	56,331	57,505	62,991
Washington	51,425	43,518	44,425	48,920
West Virginia	25,980	20,547	20,975	22,644
Wisconsin	63,640	49,577	50,610	55,010
Wyoming	5,924	4,953	5,066	5,708
Dist. of Col.	9,198	6,723	6,863	7,320
Guam	500	414	422	461
Northern Mariana Is ..	106	1,283	84	
Puerto Rico	16,000	12,414	12,672	13,836
Virgin Islands	500	414	422	461

Source: U.S. Department of Human Services.

STATE HEALTH AGENCY PROGRAMS

By Jeffrey L. Lake and James T. Dimas

The American public health system is a partnership of federal, state and local agencies, which together provide a wide range of preventive and curative health services aimed at protecting and improving the health and well-being of the entire United States population. Within each state, the District of Columbia and the six U.S. territories, primary responsibility for ensuring the public health has been vested in a single, state-level agency. Generally, these state health agencies (SHAs) are responsible for setting statewide priorities, carrying out national and state mandates, responding to disease outbreaks and other health hazards, controlling the spread of infectious diseases, and assuring access to health care for underserved residents. As advocates and providers of preventive health services, and as providers of care to the medically indigent, SHAs play a unique and important role in the American health care system.

This chapter presents an overview of the organization, responsibilities, services, expenditures and funding sources of 51 of the nation's SHAs during fiscal 1982.[1] The data used were voluntarily submitted to the Association of State and Territorial Health Officials (ASTHO) Foundation by the nation's SHAs.[2]

SHA Organization and Responsibilities

Each SHA is headed by a health commissioner or director, appointed by the governor, state legislature or a board of health. The organization of public health services in a state affects how services are delivered and, to an extent, which services are provided. While some generalizations about public health organizations are possible, there is considerable variation from state to state.

The organizational structure of SHAs may be characterized by two models: (1) a freestanding, independent agency responsible directly to the governor or a board of health; or (2) one component of a superagency structure. Thirty-one of the 51 reporting SHAs follow the first model, while 20 SHAs are characterized by the second.

Variations in the SHAs' organizational structure are reflected in the range of their designated responsibilities. For example, of the SHAs reporting for fiscal 1982:

- 40 SHAs were the designated State Crippled Children's Agency (Title V, SSA).
- 12 SHAs were the designated State Mental Health Authority (PL 94-63).
- Nine SHAs were the designated Medicaid Single State Agency (Title XIX, SSA).
- 29 SHAs were the designated State Health Planning and Development Agency (PL 93-641).
- 18 SHAs acted as the lead environmental agency in their states.
- 21 SHAs operated hospitals or other health care institutions.

SHA Services

Despite differences in their structures and responsibilities, many SHAs share common features. Nearly all SHAs offer services related to maternal and child health, communicable disease control (including sexually transmitted diseases, tuberculosis and vaccine-preventable diseases), chronic diseases (such as cancer and hypertension), dental health, public health nursing (including home visits), nutrition, health education, consumer protection and sanitation, water quality, health statistics, and diagnostic laboratory tests.

In fiscal 1982, the 51 reporting SHAs provided direct public health services to 63 million people—nearly three in every 10 in the U.S. Table 2 displays the number of persons receiving direct services from SHAs. The SHAs demonstrated their strong commitment to health promotion and disease prevention during fiscal 1982 by:

- Preventing communicable diseases among preschool and school age children and influenza among the elderly and other high risk populations by immunizing nearly 11 million people.
- Using quick, effective and low-cost screening techniques to detect and prevent disease among nearly 44 million people, including screening 14 million for sexually transmitted diseases, 10

Jeffrey L. Lake is Analyst and James T. Dimas is Assistant Director for Planning and Analysis, Association of State and Territorial Health Officials (ASTHO) Foundation.

million for visual acuity, nine million for hearing acuity, seven million for nutritional status, three million for dental disease and three million for tuberculosis.

• Making 1.1 million inspections of restaurants and other food-related facilities to ensure the availability of wholesome, unadulterated food and milk products.

• Reviewing 112,000 design specifications for water supply facilities and issuing nearly 151,000 licenses, registrations and permits for treatment facilities, water supply sources, storage tanks and line extensions.

• Preventing human exposure to toxic chemicals by making 232,000 field inspections of solid and hazardous waste disposal sites.

• Collecting vital records and health statistics to provide essential population-based information on the health and demographic characteristics of communities and states.

• Fluoridating community water supplies to prevent tooth decay.

• Preventing and responding to disease outbreaks using epidemiologic methods, including disease surveillance.

• Training nearly 2,000 persons to respond to environmental emergencies caused by hazardous chemicals, radiation exposure and contaminated air, water and food.

• Analyzing 26 million laboratory samples and specimens to prevent and detect disease and identify environmental contaminants.

• Detecting and promoting control of hypertension by screening nearly seven million people for high blood pressure and diagnosing over 131,000 as hypertensive. Public health agencies often provided follow-up services to those requiring treatment, including nutritional counseling.

Expenditures

The nation's state health agencies spent $5.04 billion for their public health programs in fiscal 1982 (including direct SHA expenditures and intergovernmental transfers to local health departments, but excluding SHA Medicaid expenditures). SHA expenditures ranged from $11.2 million in Wyoming to $482.6 million in California. Several factors account for the tremendous range in SHA public health expenditures, including variation in state populations and differences in the responsibilities of these agencies. Some SHAs have responsibility only for such traditional public health services as communicable disease control, general sanitation, maternal and child health and vital statistics. In contrast,

others have such additional responsibilities as the provision of mental health services and the operation of hospitals. Furthermore, the balance of responsibility for public health services between state and local governments varies greatly among the states.

Of the $5.04 billion in SHA expenditures, 73 percent ($3.68 billion) was spent for personal health programs, including $937 million for the SHA-operated institutions in 21 states. Expenditures for health resources programs were $350 million (7 percent of the total), expenditures for environmental health programs were $344 million (7 percent), and expenditures for laboratory programs were $176 million (3 percent). Expenditures for general administration were reported to be $285 million (6 percent of the total). The remaining $204 million was reported as "funds to local health departments not allocated to program areas."

The ASTHO Foundation estimates that SHAs spent $1.1 billion for hospital and other institutional inpatient services. This amount included $888 million spent for inpatient care in SHA-operated institutions, as well as $199 million for inpatient care services purchased from institutions other than those operated by the SHA. The $1.1 billion in purchased and SHA-provided inpatient care accounted for 30 percent of all personal health expenditures.

Sources of Funds

State Health Agencies are funded primarily by state, federal and local governments. Additional funding is collected from fees and reimbursements for services, and other sources such as grants from foundations. State funds provide the core of support for public health programs and typically include both the required match for federal grants and general revenue support of state programs. Of the $5.04 billion spent by the 51 reporting SHAs in fiscal 1982, $2.89 billion (57 percent of the total) came from state funds. Federal grants and contracts, excluding direct federal assistance provided in lieu of cash, accounted for $1.72 billion (34 percent) of the total. Funds from local sources, fees, reimbursements and other sources made up the remaining 9 percent.

Of the $1.72 billion in federal grant and contract funds spent by the SHAs, $867 million (51 percent) came from the U.S. Department of Agriculture's Special Supplemental Food Program for Women, Infants and Children (WIC). Although administered by the SHAs, WIC is primarily a food distribution program. Grants and contracts from the Department of Health and Human Services (DHHS) accounted for $740 million (43 percent) of the federal funds spent by SHAs, and the remaining 6 percent was from the Environmental Protection Agency, the Departments of Labor and Transportation, and other federal agencies.

Among the federal grants for public health administered by DHHS, the Maternal and Child Health Services (MCH) and Preventive Health and Health Services (PHHS) block grants (created by the Omnibus Budget Reconciliation Act of 1981) are of special interest. These two newly-created block grants encompassed 15 previously categorical grant programs. The 51 reporting SHAs spent a total of $172 million from block grant funds in 1982—$144 million (86 percent) from the MCH Block Grant and $27 million (14 percent) from the PHHS Block Grant.[3]

Nearly all (96 percent) of the MCH Block Grant funds was spent for personal health programs. The remaining 4 percent was distributed among health resources, environmental health, and laboratory programs and general administration. Over two-thirds ($19 million) of the PHHS Block Grant expenditures by SHAs went for personal health programs; 8 percent ($2 million) was spent for health resources programs, 7 percent for environmental health programs, 5 percent for laboratory programs and 3 percent for general administration. The remaining 8 percent was reported as "funds provided to local health departments but not allocable to program areas."

Local Health Departments

In 46 states and Puerto Rico, there are more than 3,000 local health departments (LHDs) providing direct community health services. In the 10 states and territories with no LHDs, the SHA usually is the primary provider of community health services.[4] The nation's LHDs provide preventive health services such as childhood immunizations, restaurant inspections, food-borne and water-borne disease investigation, lead-based paint poisoning prevention and urban rat control.

The structure of LHDs varies considerably— some serve rural populations of a few thousand people, while others are located in urban areas, serving millions of people. Some have only a few employees, such as a public health nurse, a sanitarian and a clerical worker. On the other end of the scale, some LHDs have multi-million dollar budgets and hundreds of employees. Most LHDs, however, lie somewhere between these extremes.

In fiscal 1982, 37 SHAs granted $1.02 billion to LHDs in their states. About two-thirds (65 percent) of the funds were reported as personal health expenditures, 8 percent as environmental health, 2 percent as health resources, 4 percent as general administration and 1 percent as laboratory program expenditures. The remaining 20 percent was unallocable to program areas. Nearly two-thirds (62 percent) came from state revenues, while federal grants and contracts accounted for 26 percent. The other 12 percent came from local sources, fees and reimbursements and other sources.

Of the $259 million in federal funds provided to local health departments by SHAs, 17 percent was from the MCH and PHHS block grants. Under the block grants, certain programs that traditionally were implemented at the local level (e.g., rat control and lead-based paint poisoning prevention) are still operated by local governments with funding "pass throughs" at the discretion of the SHAs.

In addition to receiving funds from SHAs, LHDs received funds directly from local governments, federal grants and contracts, and other sources. An additional $1.32 billion was spent by LHDs from sources other than the SHA, with 70 percent of this amount from local governments. Altogether, LHDs spent an estimated $2.34 billion in fiscal 1982, including funds from the SHAs and other sources.

Medicaid

Title XIX of the Social Security Act requires the designation of a single agency in each state to administer the state plan for the medical assistance program—Medicaid. Nine reporting SHAs were the designated Medicaid Single State Agencies (MSSAs) for their states in fiscal 1982; their MSSA expenditures are entirely separate from the public health expenditures discussed in this chapter. Together these nine SHAs spent $5.6 billion for their Medicaid programs alone, an amount that is greater than the total spent by all SHAs for all public health programs. This $5.6 billion represents nearly 20 percent of the $29.9 billion spent by all MSSAs in fiscal 1982.[5]

Notes

1. There are 57 state health agencies. The public health agencies in three states (Maine, Montana and Wisconsin) and three territories (American Samoa, Guam and the Northern Mariana Islands) did not provide complete data for fiscal 1982.

2. More complete information on specific programs, including state-by-state detail on services, ex-

penditures and sources of funds appears in: *Public Health Agencies 1982, Volumes 1-4* (Kensington, Maryland: Association of State and Territorial Health Officials Foundation, 1984).

3. For several reasons the amount of block grant funds spent by the SHAs during their 1982 fiscal year was substantially smaller than the amount appropriated by Congress. First, the 1982 fiscal year in most states began July 1, 1981, but block grant funds were not available until October 1, 1981. This resulted in block grant funds being available to most SHAs for a maximum of nine months during their 1982 fiscal periods. Second, some states (e.g. California and New York) did not assume control of the block grants during their 1982 fiscal years. These states continued to receive a *pro rata* share of categorical funding. Finally, overlap existed between the budget periods of many of the categorical programs that were included in the block grants, and the budget periods of many of the programs not included. As a result, significant sums of (federal) fiscal 1981 categorical funds were spent by the SHAs during their 1982 fiscal periods. This enabled them to conserve a portion of their 1982 block grant allotments for expenditure the following year.

4. The nine states and territories without LHDs were: Arkansas, Delaware, the District of Columbia, Rhode Island, Vermont, American Samoa, the Northern Mariana Islands, the Trust Territory and the Virgin Islands.

5. Health Care Financing Administration, Personal Communication, 1984.

Table 1
SELECTED PUBLIC HEALTH RESPONSIBILITIES DELEGATED TO STATE HEALTH AGENCIES: FISCAL 1982

State or other jurisdiction	SHA Organizational Structure		SHA designated as:					
	Freestanding independent agency	Component of superagency	State crippled children's agency (Title V, SSA)	Mental health authority (PL 94-63)	Medicaid single state agency (Title XIX, SSA)	State Health planning & development agency (PL 93-641)	Lead environmental agency	SHA operates institutions
United States	31	20	40	12	9	29	18	21
Alabama	★	...	...	...	...	...	★	...
Alaska	...	★	★	...	...	...	...	...
Arizona	★	...	★	★	★	★	★	★
Arkansas	★	...	...	...	...	...	...	...
California	...	★	★	...	★	...	...	...
Colorado	★	...	★	...	...	★	★	...
Connecticut	★	...	★	...	...	★	...	★
Delaware	...	★	★	...	...	...	...	★
Florida	...	★	...	...	...	...	...	★
Georgia	...	★	★	...	...	...	...	...
Hawaii	★	...	★	★	...	★	★	★
Idaho	...	★	★	...	...	...	...	...
Illinois	★	...	...	...	...	★	...	...
Indiana	★	...	...	...	...	★	★	...
Iowa	★	...	...	...	...	★	...	...
Kansas	★	...	★	...	...	★	★	...
Kentucky	...	★	★	★	...	★	...	★
Louisiana	...	★	★	...	...	...	...	...
Maine	...	...	...	...	...	...	...	...
Maryland	★	...	★	★	...	★	★	★
Massachusetts	...	★	★	...	...	...	★	★
Michigan	★	...	★	...	...	...	...	★
Minnesota	★	...	★	...	...	...	...	...
Mississippi	★	...	★	...	...	...	★	...
Missouri	...	★	★	...	...	...	...	★
Montana	...	...	...	...	...	...	...	...
Nebraska	★	...	...	★	...	★	...	...
Nevada	...	★	★	...	...	...	...	...
New Hampshire	...	★	★	...	...	...	...	...
New Jersey	★	...	★	...	...	★	...	...
New Mexico	★	...	★	★	...	★	★	★
New York	★	...	★	...	...	★	...	★
North Carolina	...	★	★	...	...	...	...	★
North Dakota	★	...	...	★	...	★	...	...
Ohio	★	...	★	...	...	★	...	...
Oklahoma	★	...	...	...	...	...	★	...
Oregon	...	★	...	...	...	...	...	...
Pennsylvania	★	...	★	...	...	★	...	★
Rhode Island	★	...	★	...	...	★	...	...
South Carolina	★	...	★	...	...	★	★	★
South Dakota	★	...	★	...	...	★	...	...
Tennessee	★	...	★	...	★	...	★	...
Texas	★	...	★	...	...	...	...	★
Utah	★	...	★	...	★	...	★	...
Vermont	...	★	★	...	...	...	...	...
Virginia	★	...	★	...	★	★	...	...
Washington	...	★	★	...	...	...	...	...
West Virginia	★	...	...	★	...	...	★	★
Wisconsin	...	★	...	...	...	...	★	...
Wyoming	...	★	★	...	★	★	...	...
Dist. of Col.	...	★	★	★	★	...	...	★
American Samoa ...	...	...	...	...	...	...	...	...
Guam	...	...	...	...	...	...	...	...
No. Marianas Is. ...	...	...	...	...	...	...	...	...
Puerto Rico	★	...	★	★	...	★	...	★
Trust Territory	...	★	★	★	...	★	★	★
Virgin Islands	...	★	★	★	★	★	★	★

Source: Association of State and Territorial Health Officials (ASHTO) Foundation, Kensington, Maryland.

Key:
★ —Yes
. . .—No

Table 2
PERSONS RECEIVING SELECTED PERSONAL HEALTH SERVICES
FROM STATE HEALTH AGENCIES: FISCAL 1982
(In thousands)

State or other jurisdiction	Receiving any services	Health screening	Immuniza-tion	Maternity services	Infant and child child health ambulatory services	WIC nutrition services	Family planning services	Genetic counseling	Dental services	Handicap-ped children's ambulatory services
United States	62,632	43,817	10,524	650	2,952	3,984	3,219	111	2,296	461
Alabama	1,164C	896C	237C	18C	54C	110C	86C	U	9	...
Alaska	387E	286E	93E	5	15	33E	6	1	5	4
Arizona	1,274E	999	150E	21	25	46	33	★	5E	15
Arkansas	472E	440E	79E	7	41C	32	42	...	2	...
California	3,678E	2,085E	1,183E	16	17E	329	498E	U	33E	1
Colorado	402E	174E	170E	3	57	31C	30	2	1	U
Connecticut	650E	377E	220	2	8	52	2	1	2	3
Delaware	285E	223E	36	2	14	10	20	★	9C	6
Florida	1,758E	1,111E	430	31	275	135	148	1	40	...
Georgia	1,416E	1,260E	1	7	2	75	154	★	41	17E
Hawaii	507E	397E	2	1	161E	21	12E	★	76E	4
Idaho	315E	179E	100	1	U	23	19	★	★	3
Illinois	4,224	3,923E	201	35	59	145	4	U	U	...
Indiana	592E	355E	91E	U	★	55	U	U	160	U
Iowa	336E	258E	46	5	11	45E	30	2	4	...
Kansas	1,291E	946E	349E	8	55E	97E	42E	5E	1E	4
Kentucky	1,323E	976C	143	14	11E	97	92E	1E	3E	13E
Louisiana	1,507E	1,167E	292E	24	100	114E	79	2	6	17E
Maine	...	...	...	...	...	...	...	...	...	...
Maryland	687E	368E	92C	38E	56E	84E	130E	3	33C	23
Massachusetts	2,359E	1,505	680	2	39	39	6	1C	3E	8
Michigan	1,490E	780	579	U	U	82	92	1E	3	8
Minnesota	1,700E	782E	252	33	236	80E	49E	1	★	11
Mississippi	1,099E	756E	177E	23	95	73	93	...	150	6
Missouri	906E	626E	195	14	19	72	8	1	21	7
Montana	...	...	...	...	...	...	...	...	...	...
Nebraska	259E	248E	9	3	6	17	22	2	14C	...
Nevada...........	266E	195E	45	1E	4E	24E	9E	U	4	2
New Hampshire	127E	125E	54	1E	7E	10	16	1	21	2
New Jersey	963E	662E	102	12	67	79	70	4	5	14E
New Mexico	273E	123E	54	3	21	25	18	1	16	4
New York	1,610E	961E	438	24E	51C	180E	271	★	1C	5E
North Carolina	2,483E	1,158	180	27	155E	139	39	7	355E	26
North Dakota	254E	191E	32	★	17	10	22E	★	...	...
Ohio	2,918E	2,565E	313	11	51	172	85	3	23	25
Oklahoma	925E	683E	188E	3E	51E	49E	60E	★E	3	...
Oregon...........	375E	295E	53	1	24	41	39	...	29	...
Pennsylvania	4,078E	2,992E	442	30	204E	274E	20E	18	564	125E
Rhode Island......	297E	163E	109E	1	6	21	10	1	13	3
South Carolina	727E	497E	248	★	69	109	95	...	4E	7
South Dakota	308	312E	81	1	12	23	26	...	...	2
Tennessee	1,407E	862E	263E	18E	18E	50E	159E	37E	184E	8E
Texas	8,967E	7,567	600C	62	167	431	133	13	71	21
Utah	476E	276E	145E	4	21E	15	4	3	1	5
Vermont	191E	121E	54E	1	1E	23	15	U	24	4C
Virginia	1,293	724	126	1	5	126	93	...	52	18
Washington.......	1,307C	609C	537	29	128C	68	86	1	7E	6
West Virginia	692E	294E	184E	4	74E	50	97E	2	103E	...
Wisconsin	...	...	...	...	...	...	...	...	...	...
Wyoming..........	462E	271E	79	3	7	10	1	★	2	2
Dist. of Col.	553E	349	31E	5	42E	11	11	U	21	10E
American Samoa ...	...	...	...	...	...	...	...	...	...	...
Guam	...	...	...	...	...	...	...	...	...	...
No. Mariana Is.	...	...	...	...	...	...	...	...	...	...
Puerto Rico........	1,571E	702E	326E	95E	393E	141E	138E	U	172E	23E
TTPI	U	U	U	U	U	...	U	U	U	U
Virgin Islands	30	5E	30	2	3	9	6	...	U	U

Source: Association of State and Territorial Health Officials (ASHTO)
Foundation, Kensington, Maryland.
Key:
★—Small number, unspecified.
E—Estimated.
C—Data combined with reporting of another service or program.
U—Data unobtainable.

State or other jurisdiction	Communicable disease ambulatory services			Chronic disease ambulatory services						
	Veneral disease	Tuberculosis	Other	Cancer	Diabetes	Hypertension	Cardiovascular diseases	Mental retardation	Renal dialysis	Other
United States	2,757	544	172	56	43	297	140	51	20	79
Alabama	65C	11C	...	★C	U	3C	...	1	...	...
Alaska	16	7E	U	...	...	U	...	1	...	...
Arizona	25	7	...	U	1	4	3	...	★	U
Arkansas	18E	U	4E	1	...	3E	...	...	...	...
California	852E	★	U	U	U	U	U	...	U	U
Colorado	13	U	...	...	...	U	U	1	...	...
Connecticut	26E	1	...	1	...	★	...	1	...	...
Delaware	6	1	7	★	U	U	U	...	★	1
Florida	125	120	...	★	7	3	★	U	★	1
Georgia	86	12	...	1	U	50	U	★	★	7
Hawaii	6	20	1	★	★	6	1	5	★	1
Idaho	7	1	25	...	...	...	...	...	...	...
Illinois	52	U	...	...	★	...	...	1	3E	1
Indiana	U	U	...	U	...	10E	U	...	★	★
Iowa	8E	2	1	...	...	5E	...	...	★	...
Kansas	3	5	2	...	U	★C	★	★E	★	3
Kentucky	17	20E	38E	24E	2E	27E	3E	8	...	3E
Louisiana	100	5	U	...	U	U	U	...	...	★
Maine	...	...	...	...	...	...	...	...	...	...
Maryland	20E	12E	U	2E	...	★	...	16E	2	U
Massachusetts	50	18E	...	1E	...	★	1E	...	★E	1E
Michigan	100	7	...	U	2E	50	...	U	...	...
Minnesota	26	13	77	6	6	0C	86C	2	U	23
Mississippi	27	9	...	1	4	15	2	...	...	...
Missouri	50	5	...	1	...	12E	1	U	...	★
Montana	...	...	...	...	...	...	...	...	...	...
Nebraska	3	★	...	...	...	...	...	★	★	...
Nevada	21E	10E	...	★	★	★	★	...	...	...
New Hampshire	11	★E	...	U	...	U	★	★	...	...
New Jersey	49	2	...	...	...	...	...	...	2	...
New Mexico	11	12	5	2	★	7	1	2	...	★
New York	40	63	...	U	U	U	U	...	U	...
North Carolina	66	1	U	2	U	20	U	2	★	U
North Dakota	2	8	1	★	...	...	1	★	...	1
Ohio	76	4	...	★	★	24	1	U	U	U
Oklahoma	47	8E	1	1	U	4	U	★	...	★
Oregon	130	3	2	...	...	...	...	...	...	...
Pennsylvania	97	43	...	1E	4E	9E	7E	...	4	1E
Rhode Island	7	1	...	1	★	18	★	1	★	...
South Carolina	22	7	...	5	1	★	1	...	★	...
South Dakota	4	6	...	...	...	...	...	...	1	3
Tennessee	94	2	...	U	U	U	U	★	1	3
Texas	221	59E	★	1E	2	...	11E	1	5	26E
Utah	10	3	...	U	...	U	★	1	U	★
Vermont	1	2	U	...	...	...	★	U	...	U
Virginia	49	11	1	...	★	7	2	★	...	★
Washington	57E	4	...	★	...	U	...	...	★	2
West Virginia	5E	3	★	★	★	1	2	7E	U	3
Wisconsin	...	...	...	...	...	...	...	...	...	...
Wyoming..........	6	2	1	★	...	...	★	★	★	...
Dist. of Col.	28	6E	...	...	U	U	★E	★	...	...
American Samoa ...	...	...	...	...	...	...	...	...	...	...
Guam	...	...	...	...	...	...	...	...	...	...
No. Mariana Is.	...	...	...	...	...	...	...	...	...	...
Puerto Rico	★E	5E	★	3E	13E	12E	15E	1	U	U
TTPI	U	U	...	U	...	U	U	...	U	...
Virgin Islands	4	★	4	★	1	5	★	U	...	...

Table 2—Continued
PERSONS RECEIVING SELECTED PERSONAL HEALTH SERVICES
FROM STATE HEALTH AGENCIES: FISCAL 1982
(In thousands)

State or other jurisdiction	Mental health, alcohol and drug abuse services			General ambulatory care	Home health care	Inpatient care
	Mental health	Alcohol abuse	Drug abuse			
United States	300	183	73	2,033	247	475
Alabama	U	U	. . .	U	9C	★
Alaska	1E	★	U	50	1	1E
Arizona	32	12	5	6	. . .	16
Arkansas	★	. . .	. . .	★	5	★
California	1	. . .	U	13	U	15
Colorado	U	U	U	23	U	1
Connecticut	. . .	. . .	. . .	5E	★	1
Delaware	★	. . .	. . .	2	3E	1
Florida	. . .	. . .	. . .	37	4	★
Georgia......................	. . .	. . .	. . .	33	U	17E
Hawaii	20E	★	★	106E	1E	26
Idaho	. . .	3	★	★	1	3
Illinois.......................	. . .	. . .	. . .	1	. . .	8
Indiana	U	. . .	. . .	U	21	U
Iowa	. . .	. . .	. . .	. . .	16	★
Kansas	★	★	★	69	5E	★
Kentucky	49	19	6	2E	7	22E
Louisiana	. . .	. . .	. . .	4	1	3
Maine	. . .	. . .	. . .	. . .	. . .	. . .
Maryland	44	13E	16	391E	10E	29E
Massachusetts	1E	40E	1E	17E	1E	53E
Michigan	U	18	15	32	★	18
Minnesota	7	1	1	249	25	1
Mississippi	. . .	. . .	. . .	2E	5	2E
Missouri	U	. . .	. . .	U	8	8
Montana.....................	. . .	. . .	. . .	. . .	. . .	. . .
Nebraska	. . .	. . .	. . .	10	★	★
Nevada......................	U	. . .	. . .	2E	. . .	2
New Hampshire	2	U	. . .	★	★E	★
New Jersey	U	7	16	2	23	10E
New Mexico..................	26	7	3	. . .	★	10
New York....................	U	. . .	. . .	U	U	1
North Carolina	. . .	10	. . .	49E	26	4
North Dakota	★	★	★	4	. . .	. . .
Ohio	★	8	1	2	. . .	6
Oklahoma	14	★	★	★	2	★
Oregon	. . .	. . .	. . .	. . .	. . .	. . .
Pennsylvania	9	36C	★C	21E	1E	28C
Rhode Island	U	. . .	. . .	1E	U	★
South Carolina	. . .	. . .	. . .	★	16	13
South Dakota	★	2	1	57	3	3E
Tennessee....................	2E	. . .	. . .	71E	7	2
Texas........................	. . .	. . .	. . .	2	9	7
Utah	1	U	U	46E	. . .	1
Vermont	. . .	. . .	. . .	5	1	★
Virginia......................	. . .	. . .	. . .	317	10	1
Washington	. . .	. . .	. . .	. . .	U	1
West Virginia.................	★E	5	1	16E	13	7E
Wisconsin....................	. . .	. . .	. . .	. . .	. . .	. . .
Wyoming	. . .	. . .	. . .	22	2	★
Dist. of Col..................	18	2	6	79C	10	8
American Samoa..............	. . .	. . .	. . .	. . .	. . .	. . .
Guam	. . .	. . .	. . .	. . .	. . .	. . .
No. Mariana Is................	. . .	. . .	. . .	. . .	. . .	. . .
Puerto Rico	69	U	U	247E	1E	143E
TTPI........................	. . .	U	. . .	U	. . .	U
Virgin Islands................	2	★	★	37	★	★

Table 3
PUBLIC HEALTH PROGRAM EXPENDITURES
OF STATE HEALTH AGENCIES, BY PROGRAM: FISCAL 1982
(In thousands)

State or other jurisdiction	Total	Personal health	Environmental health	Health resources	Laboratory	General administration	Funds to LHDs not allocated to program areas
United States	$5,041,195	$3,682,062	$344,384	$349,888	$175,976	$284,516	$204,370
Alabama...................	58,526	35,627	5,299	3,296	4,319	3,256	6,729
Alaska	21,944	17,155	139	1,874	1,749	1,028	. . .
Arizona	107,771	85,035	12,672	2,627	1,962	5,475	. . .
Arkansas	42,160	28,850	5,347	1,637	1,857	4,468	. . .
California.................	482,578	232,991	27,214	28,146	17,222	44,495	132,510
Colorado	61,898	36,664	8,580	3,115	2,036	7,949	3,554
Connecticut...............	47,241	32,178	1,342	6,554	4,320	1,843	1,004
Delaware	25,869	23,065	1,133	434	600	636	. . .
Florida	165,554	109,767	25,685	10,450	6,905	12,745	. . .
Georgia	110,828	77,587	299	3,600	3,056	1,016	25,271
Hawaii	148,308	123,626	6,184	13,849	1,359	3,290	. . .
Idaho	20,099	12,183	3,534	1,988	1,705	688	. . .
Illinois...................	83,381	53,058	4,857	9,139	3,163	7,956	5,208
Indiana	45,832	23,867	16,136	2,655	3,175	. . .	. . .
Iowa	25,371	20,397	378	3,365	. . .	1,231	. . .
Kansas	29,632	15,339	6,485	3,377	1,787	2,642	. . .
Kentucky	163,475	140,808	3,341	5,061	1,844	3,703	8,717
Louisiana.................	92,446	73,497	10,933	2,369	4,012	1,635	. . .
Maine	. . .	. . .					. . .
Maryland	390,150	329,922	24,082	10,955	5,404	19,787	. . .
Massachusetts	126,810	111,784	3,106	3,994	4,345	3,581	. . .
Michigan	188,453	143,551	15,350	11,219	11,280	7,054	. . .
Minnesota	56,274	26,910	2,763	7,322	2,643	4,927	11,709
Mississippi	66,079	56,794	3,098	2,100	1,250	2,837	. . .
Missouri	67,421	57,252	1,705	5,642	1,512	1,105	205
Montana	. . .	. . .					. . .
Nebraska	16,760	10,647	1,243	3,714	651	504	. . .
Nevada...................	15,253	10,930	1,157	1,171	796	513	686
New Hampshire	12,063	8,461	839	1,509	523	731	. . .
New Jersey................	104,530	74,120	4,713	12,854	5,065	7,778	. . .
New Mexico...............	82,422	62,173	8,684	4,587	3,012	3,967	. . .
New York.................	397,703	259,294	11,988	64,563	32,642	29,215	. . .
North Carolina	122,693	106,943	6,213	1,791	5,149	2,597	. . .
North Dakota	13,365	6,827	2,642	1,540	1,208	652	496
Ohio	102,372	76,288	3,381	11,433	3,896	7,374	. . .
Oklahoma	61,986	38,785	13,601	3,886	1,238	4,476	. . .
Oregon	27,548	17,111	1,536	4,885	2,496	767	753
Pennsylvania	187,863	155,635	6,064	20,189	2,829	3,146	. . .
Rhode Island	26,969	14,088	3,671	4,333	3,349	1,529	. . .
South Carolina	120,321	81,862	23,384	3,948	3,202	7,924	. . .
South Dakota	12,930	9,837	365	1,419	937	372	. . .
Tennessee.................	103,636	79,605	10,419	6,184	3,526	3,902	. . .
Texas	211,045	153,218	18,602	20,652	5,214	13,359	. . .
Utah	26,304	14,784	5,152	2,085	2,568	1,715	. . .
Vermont..................	15,195	11,931	969	1,127	876	292	. . .
Virginia...................	141,644	90,159	20,795	5,573	1,418	19,579	4,120
Washington	45,082	35,259	3,115	3,755	2,267	686	. . .
West Virginia	111,729	96,280	1,487	4,603	2,037	3,913	3,410
Wisconsin	. . .	. . .					. . .
Wyoming.................	11,191	8,878	435	1,249	462	166	. . .
Dist. of Col...............	80,529	73,300	. . .	1,887	1,002	4,341	. . .
American Samoa	. . .	. . .	. . .	. . .	. . .	. . .	. . .
Guam	. . .	. . .	. . .	. . .	. . .	. . .	. . .
No. Mariana Is.............	. . .	. . .	. . .	. . .	. . .	. . .	. . .
Puerto Rico	300,355	270,488	2,888	14,066	503	12,410	. . .
TTPI.....................	13,191	11,512	626	648	. . .	405	. . .
Virgin Islands	48,416	35,738	754	1,466	1,604	8,855	. . .

Source: The Association of State and Territorial Health Officials
(ASTHO) Foundation, Kensington, Maryland.

Table 4

PUBLIC HEALTH EXPENDITURES OF STATE HEALTH AGENCIES, BY SOURCE OF FUNDS: FISCAL 1982

(In millions of dollars)

Source of funds	Total	Personal health		Environmental health	Health resources	Laboratory	General administration	Funds to LHDs not allocated to program areas
		Noninstitutional	SHA-operated institutions					
Total	$5,041.2	$2,745.5	$936.6	$344.4	$349.9	$176.0	$284.5	$204.4
Subtotal, excluding federal grant and contract funds	3,325.7	1,288.5	908.4	258.8	255.0	161.6	254.9	198.5
State funds	2,894.1	1,111.2	779.7	210.8	219.9	149.6	226.4	196.4
Local funds	122.9	76.0		27.2	1.7	1.7	14.8	1.6
Fees	238.0	72.4	118.5	16.1	19.6	6.9	3.9	0.6
Patient fees & reimbursements from Medicaid	89.3	24.2	64.3		0.3	0.1	0.2	
Patient fees & reimbursements from other sources	96.6	35.1	54.1	2.1	0.9	1.4	2.4	0.6
Other fees	52.0	13.1		14.0	18.4	5.3	1.3	
Other	70.7	28.9	10.1	4.7	13.9	3.3	9.8	
Subtotal, federal grant and contract funds(a)	1,715.5	1,457.0	28.2	85.5	94.9	14.4	29.6	5.8
Department of Health and Human Services	739.7	585.9	23.6	12.5	88.7	9.2	13.8	5.8
Public Health Service	618.9	517.4	14.3	12.4	49.4	8.8	10.7	5.8
Alcohol, Drug Abuse & Mental Health Administration	70.5	66.3		0.1	3.8		0.4	
ADAMHA Block Grant (P.L. 97-35)	21.2	19.7			1.2		0.2	
Other ADAMHA	49.3	46.6		0.1	2.6		0.1	
Centers for Disease Control	130.4	89.1		9.7	22.3	3.1	2.4	4.0
Preventive Health & Health Services Block Grant (P.L. 97-35)	27.2	18.7		1.9	2.1	1.4	0.7	2.3
Immunization (PHSA Sec. 317)	11.8	11.6				0.1	0.1	
Refugee Assistance Act of 1980 (Sec. 412C3)	6.0	4.6			0.1		0.1	1.1
Venereal Disease (PHSA Sec. 318)	20.5	19.6				0.8	0.1	
Diabetes Control (PHSA Sec. 301)	9.1	8.8			0.2		0.1	
Fluoridation (PHSA Sec. 317)	3.1	2.7		0.4				
Health Education/Risk Reduction (PHSA Sec. 1703(a) & P.L. 95-626)	14.2	12.9			0.3		0.9	
Emergency Medical Services (PHSA Title XII)	18.4	0.2			17.9			
Hypertension (PHSA Sec. 317)	8.5	8.5				0.3		
Rat Control (PHSA Sec. 317)	8.2			6.6	1.5		0.2	
Health Incentive Grant (PHSA Sec. 314(d))	1.4	0.5		0.1		0.2	0.1	0.6
Other CDC	1.9	0.8		0.6	0.1	0.2	0.2	
Food & Drug Administration	1.5			1.4				

Health Resources and Services Administration	386.6	354.4	1.7	1.1	19.5	2.1	5.8	1.8
Maternal and Child Health Services Block Grant (P.L. 97-35)	144.4	138.6		0.5	0.5	0.8	2.8	1.2
Community Health Centers (PHSA Sec. 330)	5.3	5.1					0.1	
Family Planning (PHSA Title X)	76.5	76.1					0.3	
Migrant Health (PHSA Sec. 319)	2.9	2.7		0.2				
Crippled Children (SSA Title V)	33.2	30.5	1.4		0.3	0.4	0.7	
Genetic Disease (PHSA Sec. 1101)	6.2	6.2						
SIDS (PHSA Sec. 1121)	1.3	1.3						
Maternal and Child Health (SSA Title V)	83.2	80.1		0.2	0.3	0.9	1.0	0.6
Services for Blind/Disabled Children (SSI, Sec. 1615 SSA)	5.9	5.6	0.3					
Lead-Based Paint Poisoning Prevention (PHSA Sec. 316)	1.0	0.9		0.1			0.1	
National Health Planning & Resources Development Act (P.L. 93-641)	17.6	0.1		0.2	17.0		0.4	
Other HRSA	9.1	7.3		0.1	1.4		0.3	
National Institutes of Health	27.3	7.6	12.6		1.7	3.6	1.7	
National Center for Health Statistics	2.5				2.1		0.4	
Health Care Financing Administration	77.6	29.4	7.6		37.4	0.3	2.9	
Medicaid grants and contracts (SSA Title XIX)	64.9	25.7	7.1		29.3		2.8	
Medicare grants and contracts (SSA Title XVIII)	10.7	2.9	0.5		7.0	0.3	0.1	
Other HCFA	2.1	0.9	0.1		1.2			
Social Security Administration	4.2	3.1	0.9	0.1	0.9		0.1	
Office of Human Development Services	37.3	35.5	0.1	0.1	0.7			
Developmental Disabilities (P.L. 91-517, P.L. 94-103)	3.2	2.5	0.4		0.5			
Grants for Services (SSA Title XX)	33.3	32.6	0.4		0.2			
Other OHDS	0.8	0.4						
Other DHHS	1.7	0.4	0.7		0.3		0.2	
Other Federal Agencies	964.1	870.5	4.5	72.9	5.7	5.1	5.4	
Department of Agriculture	872.5	863.3	0.6	4.8	0.8	0.1	3.0	
WIC	866.8	862.5		0.5	0.8		3.0	
Other	5.8	0.8	0.6	4.3		0.1		
Department of Labor	5.2	0.9		3.7	0.5	0.1	0.1	
Department of Transportation	5.0	0.6			3.6	0.7		
Environmental Protection Agency	65.9	0.1		62.1	0.1	2.9	0.7	
Regional Commissions	1.3	0.3	0.4		0.5			
Other	14.2	5.3	3.5	2.2	0.2	1.3	1.7	
Unidentified federal	11.7	0.6		0.1	0.4	0.1	10.3	

Key:
—Dollar amounts less than $50,000.

(a) Four of the predecessor categorical grants were transferred from one federal agency to another when the block grants were created. In the table above, these four grants are reported under the agency that administered them as part of the block grants. Thus expenditures from Emergency Medical Services, Hypertension and Home Health Services grant funds are included in the Centers for Disease Control for both fiscal years 1981 and 1982. Expenditures from lead-based paint poisoning prevention grant funds are included in Health Resources and Services Administration for both years.

A Note on Use

Symbols: Unless otherwise noted, all tables in *The Book of the States* use the following scheme:

  . . .—no data
  blank cell—not applicable
  0—zero quantity.

Sources: Unless otherwise noted, the sources of data for tables are surveys and research by The Council of State Governments.

4. Safety and Public Protection

CORRECTIONS, COURTS AND CRIMINAL JUSTICE

By Edward D. Feigenbaum

Prison overcrowding led the list of state criminal justice concerns in 1983. When the U.S. Department of Justice reported yet another increase in the growth of the prison population during the first six months of 1983, few were surprised. The total number of incarcerated individuals rose to a record high of more than 431,000 by June 30, 1983, following yearly increases of 12 percent in 1981 and 1982,[1] and an overall growth rate of 42 percent since 1979.[2] Probation and parole cutbacks were not responsible; the number of offenders released under supervision increased proportionally during the period.[3]

Several factors contribute to the burgeoning prison population. Criminals among the "baby boom" generation of the 1940s and 1950s are now entering their peak years of activity.[4] Arrest rates since the late 1970s have increased.[5] New, harsher state sentencing policies have also exacerbated the problem. Nine states have determinate sentencing, which reduces the parole board's discretionary power over early release.[6] Almost all of the states have mandatory prison terms for one or more of the broad offense categories of violent crime, habitual crime, narcotics violation, and use or possession of a firearm in a crime, leaving a judge no option but to impose a prison sentence.[7] Nine states have some form of sentencing guidelines, which limit the judge's discretion in imposing a sentence.[8] Policies in 14 states and the District of Columbia also severely restrict parole board alternatives.[9]

While a recent survey of the states showed that all but four jurisdictions—the District of Columbia, Rhode Island, South Dakota and Vermont—were either constructing new prisons, renovating or expanding prisons, or seeking legislative approval for capital improvements, new accommodations for an expected 50,000 additional inmates will fall far short of coping with the current condition in the states.[10] The dilemma that the states face is immediate. Prison overcrowding has led to court orders or litigation to improve prison conditions in 38 states and the District of Columbia,[11] with 23 state correctional systems under direct court order to correct overcrowding, according to an early 1983 study. The cost for implementing these court orders can run as high as $1 billion or more for some state governments.[12]

To ease overcrowding and attempt to comply with court requirements, at least 16 states have adopted emergency early release provisions, resulting in the commutation of sentences for approximately 15,000 offenders since 1980.[13] The states have used a variety of release options. Michigan's law requires the governor to declare an emergency if the capacity of the state prisons (13,047) is exceeded for 30 consecutive days. In such a situation the governor must order the release of enough offenders so as to bring the prison population down to 95 percent of capacity. The sentences of virtually all inmates (except violent offenders) are reduced by 30 days, with the reductions being cumulative.

In Illinois, officials had liberally interpreted provisions for cutting sentences on the basis of "good behavior time," often allowing such time in blocks of three to nine months instead of a day at a time, but this system was recently ruled unconstitutional by the Illinois Supreme Court. Wisconsin screens out violent offenders from early release candidates and imposes strict supervision by parole officers of those released. South Carolina has an automatic release provision, but allows the governor to intercede in the process and overrule any early release decision. Minnesota, interestingly, uses available prison capacity as a consideration in setting the length of terms. Many other states, such as Alabama, Arizona, Connecticut, Missouri, New Jersey, North Carolina, Ohio, Oklahoma, Texas, Utah and Washington have similar systems that range from bestowing considerable discretion upon officials in granting early parole (as in Mississippi) to the use of a scientific risk assessment scoring system that assists officials in evaluating candidate offenders for early release (as developed by Iowa).[14]

As the prison population continues to increase and states adopt early emergency release provisions, offender risk characteristic assessment systems will gain greater popularity across the nation.

Edward D. Feigenbaum is an attorney and Legal Affairs Program Manager, The Council of State Governments.

Considerable attention has also been focused on sentencing that provides alternatives to prison for non-violent offenders and that offers benefits to society. Restitution programs allow offenders to avoid incarceration and require that they compensate the victim or society for the crime. Community service work may be imposed as a sentence where there has been no direct monetary loss, such as in a first-time conviction for driving under the influence, or trespassing. Aid to senior citizens, community service organizations or youth groups have been increasingly popular alternatives, along with the traditional "road crew" or community cleanup sentence. Judges have also become less reluctant to impose fines upon offenders, with revenues often used to help defray costs of offender processing. Finally, specialized probation, or the referral of individuals to programs specifically designed to meet their needs, has grown significantly in recent years. Drug and alcohol programs, psychological treatment plans and individually-oriented programs have come into special favor in the states.

Other Significant Activities

Drunk Driving. The attention generated by several highly-publicized, multiple fatality vehicle crashes and an intense grass-roots lobbying effort by concerned citizens have sparked more than 40 states since 1982 to enact improved legislation governing driving under the influence of alcohol or drugs. Even more states have established executive and leadership commissions or task forces to examine the problem, identify deficiencies in the system and recommend potential solutions. As of late 1983, 19 states had laws requiring a minimum legal purchase age of 21 for all alcoholic beverages; nine other states restricted liquor sales to those at least 21 years of age.[15] In 36 states, it is illegal to operate a motor vehicle if the driver's blood alcohol content is 0.10 percent or higher.[16] Fifteen states now require a mandatory jail sentence upon the initial conviction, while 39 states make a jail sentence mandatory upon a second or subsequent conviction.[17] Recommendations issued by the Presidential Commission on Drunk Driving in late 1983 are expected to encourage additional states to increase their minimum legal purchasing age for alcoholic beverages, restrict alcoholic beverage consumption in motor vehicles, and increase enforcement through selective enforcement and police road blocks. Increased chemical testing of suspect drunk drivers, lowering the presumptive under-the-influence BAC level to 0.08 percent

and making 0.10 percent illegal per se are also likely trends.[18]

Hazardous Waste. Another recent development in the criminal justice field is the move toward criminal enforcement of state laws governing hazardous waste handling and disposal. This phenomenon has its genesis in the Northeastern states, but has also been successfully employed in other areas of the country. Many states have established or are in the process of setting up hazardous waste "strike forces," comprised of attorneys, state police investigators and highly trained technical support personnel. Maryland's strike force has successfully prosecuted approximately 20 criminal cases since its organization in 1981.[19] The New England and mid-Atlantic states have joined to create an 11-state regional strike force, the Northeast Hazardous Waste Coordination Committee, which serves as a centralized repository for criminal enforcement data, conducts training sessions, and brings officials and investigators together to work closely on matters that transcend state boundaries, such as the involvement of organized crime in hazardous waste disposal operations in the region.[20]

Notes

1. News release, Bureau of Justice Statistics, October 23, 1983.
2. News release, Bureau of Justice Statistics, September 18, 1983.
3. Ibid.
4. Dave Ahearn, "States Spending $8 Billion on Prisons to Cope With Rise in Inmate Population," *The Bond Buyer*, September 6, 1983, p. 7.
5. Bureau of Justice Statistics, October 23, 1983.
6. Bureau of Justice Statistics, *Setting Prison Terms* (Washington, D.C., 1983), p. 2.
7. Ibid., p. 3.
8. Ibid., pp. 3-4.
9. Ibid., p. 4.
10. *Corrections Compendium* 7, 12 (July 1983): 1.
11. *Corrections Compendium* 7, 11 (June 1983): 1.
12. Linda Harriman and Jeffrey D. Strausman, "Do Judges Determine Budget Decisions? Federal Court Decisions in Prison Reform and State Spending For Corrections," *Public Administration Review* 43, 4 (July/August 1983): 1-4.
13. Howard Kurtz, "Michigan Will Release 500 From Overcrowded Prisons," *The Washington Post*, September 17, 1983, p. A-2.
14. Keon Chi, *Offender Risk Assessment: The Iowa Model* (Lexington, Kentucky: The Council of State Governments, 1983); *Prison Overcrowding Emergency Powers Act: The Michigan Experience* (Lexington, Kentucky: The Council of State Governments, 1984).

15. National Highway Traffic Safety Administration, *A Digest of State Alcohol-Highway Safety-Related Legislation* (2nd Edition) (Washington, D.C., 1983), p. 2-2.

16. Ibid.

17. Ibid., p. 2-4.

18. Presidential Commission on Drunk Driving, *Final Report*, 1983.

19. James Lyko, "EPA Must Establish Enforcement Legitimacy," *Hazardous Waste Report*, December 26, 1983, p. 2.

20. Steven J. Madonna, "Organized Crime in the Hazardous Waste Industry," *National Association of Attorneys General Environmental Protection Report* (November 1983): 1.

Table 1
STATE DEATH PENALTY
(As of December 1983)

State or other jurisdiction	Method of execution	No. of women on death row	Persons on death row	State or other jurisdiction	Method of execution	No. of women on death row	Persons on death row
Alabama	Electrocution	2	67	Nebraska	Electrocution	0	11
Alaska	. . .			Nevada	Lethal injection	1	20
Arizona	Gas chamber	0	52	New Hampshire	+ + +	0	0
Arkansas	Lethal injection (or choice of electrocution for those sentenced before March 24, 1983)	0	23	New Jersey	Lethal injection	0	2
				New Mexico	Lethal injection	0	6
				New York(a)	Electrocution	0	1
				North Carolina	Gas chamber or lethal injection	1	35
California	Gas chamber	0	150	North Dakota	. . .		
				Ohio	Electrocution	2	19
Colorado	Gas chamber	0	2				
Connecticut	+ + +	0	0	Oklahoma	Lethal injection	2	37
Delaware	Lethal injection	0	6	Oregon	. . .		
Florida	Electrocution	0	207	Pennsylvania	Electrocution	0	55
Georgia	Electrocution	3	112	Rhode Island	. . .		
				South Carolina	Electrocution	0	29
Hawaii	. . .						
Idaho	Lethal injection or firing squad	0	7	South Dakota	+ + +	0	0
				Tennessee	Electrocution	0	35
Illinois	Lethal injection	0	59	Texas	Lethal injection	0	166
Indiana	Electrocution	0	21	Utah	Firing squad	0	4
Iowa	. . .			Vermont(b)	+ + +	0	0
Kansas	. . .			Virginia	Electrocution	0	21
Kentucky	Electrocution	0	19	Washington	Lethal injection or hanging	0	4
Louisiana	Electrocution	0	38				
Maine	. . .			West Virginia	. . .		
Maryland	Gas chamber	1	11	Wisconsin	. . .		
				Wyoming	Gas chamber	0	3
Massachusetts	+ + +	0	0				
Michigan	. . .			Dist. of Col.	. . .		
Minnesota	. . .						
Mississippi	Gas chamber	1	38				
Missouri	Gas chamber	0	23				
Montana	Lethal injection or hanging	0	4				

Source: NAACP Legal Defense and Educational Fund, Inc.
Key:
. . .—State has no capital punishment statute.
+ + +—State has capital punishment statute, but no sentences imposed.

(a) In *People v. Davis*, 43 N.Y.2d 17 (1977), the New York Court of Appeals invalidated most of the death penalty statute but left open the question of the death sentence for inmates convicted of murder while serving a life sentence.
(b) The Vermont statute predates *Furman vs. Georgia*, 408 U.S. 238 (1972), but there has been no state action since 1971 to revalidate it.

Table 2
TRENDS IN STATE PRISON POPULATION

State or other jurisdiction	Total population			Population by maximum length of sentence					
				More than a year			Year or less and unsentenced		
	1981	1980	Percentage change	1981	1980	Percentage change	1981	1980	Percentage change
United States	340,639	305,458	11.5	330,998	295,363	12.1	9,641	10,095	-4.5
Alabama....................	7,657	6,543	17.0	7,199	6,368	13.0	458	175	161.7
Alaska(a)	1,019	822	24.0	708	571	24.0	311	251	23.9
Arizona	5,223	4,372	19.5	5,199	4,360	19.2	24	12	100.0
Arkansas	3,328	2,911	14.3	3,297	2,911	13.3	31	0	ND
California..................	29,202	24,569	18.9	27,913	23,264	20.0	1,289	1,305	-1.2
Colorado	2,772	2,629	5.4	2,770	2,609	6.2	2	20	-90.0
Connecticut(a)	4,647	4,308	7.9	2,995	2,750	8.9	1,652	1,558	6.0
Delaware(a)	1,712	1,474	16.1	1,248	1,087	14.8	464	387	19.9
Florida....................	23,589	20,735	13.8	23,200	20,211	14.8	389	524	-25.8
Georgia....................	12,444	12,178	2.2	12,377	11,922	3.8	67	256	-73.8
Hawaii(a)	1,207	985	22.5	757	624	21.3	450	361	24.7
Idaho	957	817	17.1	957	817	17.1	0	0	ND
Illinois....................	13,206	11,899	11.0	12,996	10,724	21.2	210	1,175	-82.1
Indiana	8,022	6,683	20.0	7,559	6,281	20.3	463	402	15.2
Iowa	2,670	2,481	7.6	2,554	2,479	3.0	116	2	5,700
Kansas	2,770	2,494	11.1	2,770	2,494	11.1	0	0	ND
Kentucky	4,167	3,588	16.1	4,167	3,588	16.1	0	0	ND
Louisiana	9,415	8,889	5.9	9,415	8,889	5.9	0	0	ND
Maine	992	814	21.9	806	671	20.1	186	143	30.1
Maryland	9,335	7,731	20.7	9,335	7,731	20.7	0	0	ND
Massachusetts	3,889	3,185	22.1	3,791	3,150	20.3	98	35	180.0
Michigan	15,157	15,124	0.2	15,157	15,124	0.2	0	0	ND
Minnesota	2,024	2,001	1.1	2,024	2,001	1.1	0	0	ND
Mississippi	4,624	3,902	18.5	4,494	3,793	18.5	130	109	19.3
Missouri...................	6,489	5,726	13.3	6,489	5,726	13.3	0	0	ND
Montana...................	831	739	12.4	828	738	12.2	3	1	200.0
Nebraska	1,653	1,446	14.3	1,640	1,402	17.0	13	44	-70.5
Nevada	2,116	1,839	15.1	2,116	1,839	15.1	0	0	ND
New Hampshire	398	326	22.1	398	326	22.1	0	0	ND
New Jersey(b)	7,011	5,884	19.2	6,861	5,564	23.3	150	320	-53.1
New Mexico................	1,497	1,279	17.0	1,345	1,199	12.2	152	80	90.0
New York..................	25,599	21,815	17.3	25,599	21,639	18.3	0	176	-100.0
North Carolina	15,791	15,513	1.8	14,854	14,456	2.8	937	1,057	-11.4
North Dakota	280	253	10.7	218	185	17.8	62	68	-8.8
Ohio	14,968	13,489	11.0	14,968	13,489	11.0	0	0	ND
Oklahoma	5,281	4,796	10.1	5,281	4,796	10.1	0	0	ND
Oregon	3,295	3,177	3.7	3,292	3,172	3.8	3	5	-40.0
Pennsylvania	9,365	8,171	14.6	9,291	8,112	14.5	74	59	25.4
Rhode Island(a)	962	813	18.3	689	611	12.8	273	202	35.1
South Carolina	8,538	7,862	8.6	8,010	7,427	7.8	528	435	21.4
South Dakota	693	635	9.1	662	609	8.9	31	26	19.2
Tennessee..................	7,897	7,022	12.5	7,897	7,022	12.5	0	0	ND
Texas(c)	31,502	29,892	5.4	31,502	29,892	5.4	0	0	ND
Utah	1,140	932	22.3	1,126	928	21.3	14	4	250.0
Vermont(a)	534	480	11.2	395	342	15.5	139	138	0.7
Virginia....................	9,388	8,920	5.2	9,013	8,581	5.0	375	339	10.6
Washington	5,336	4,399	21.3	5,336	4,399	21.3	0	0	ND
West Virginia...............	1,565	1,257	24.5	1,565	1,257	24.5	0	0	ND
Wisconsin..................	4,416	3,980	11.0	4,416	3,980	11.0	0	0	ND
Wyoming	587	534	9.9	587	534	9.9	0	0	ND
Dist. of Col.(a)	3,479	3,145	10.6	2,932	2,719	7.8	547	426	28.4

Sources: Bureau of Justice Statistics, U.S. Department of Justice; data collected by U.S. Bureau of the Census, Department of Commerce.

Note: This table reports all prisoners subject to confinement under the jurisdiction of a given correctional system, whether or not they are in its physical custody.

Key:

ND—Not definable

(a) Figures include both jail and prison inmates; jails and prisons form an integrated system.

(b) Official prison population count excludes state prisoners held in local jails to ease overcrowding.

(c) All data are custody figures; jurisdiction counts are not available.

STATE REGULATION OF OCCUPATIONS AND PROFESSIONS

By Frances Stokes Berry and R. Douglas Roederer

Occupational licensing is a common form of state regulation that affects most businesses and professions. It is an exercise of the state's inherent police power to protect the health, safety and welfare of its citizens. Generally accepted criteria for the appropriate exercise of licensure authority are: (1) unqualified practice poses a serious risk to a consumer's life, health, safety or economic well-being; (2) such risks are likely to occur; (3) the public cannot accurately judge a practitioner's qualifications; (4) benefits to the public clearly outweigh potential harmful effects of licensure (such as a decrease in the supply of practitioners). Failure to meet these criteria, in general, indicates that licensure is not justified, or that some alternative form of regulation such as registration or certification, may be appropriate.[1]

State officials and others concerned with occupational and professional licensing currently face at least five major issues: (1) setting appropriate criteria for determining which groups to license; (2) questions about the organization, structure and composition of licensure boards; (3) evaluating the performance of licensure boards through sunset; (4) assuring the continuing competency of licensed practitioners; and (5) creating mechanisms for exchanging information.

Criteria for Licensure

Occupational and professional groups seek licensure for many reasons. It offers an opportunity for increased status for the practitioners; it is sometimes a prerequisite for third-party reimbursement; and it offers mechanisms for keeping unqualified or unscrupulous practitioners from engaging in the occupations or professions. Professional groups usually draft legislation providing for regulation of the profession and then attempt to convince legislators of the utility of that regulation.

The benefits of protecting the public from incompetent practitioners are not without negative side effects, however. Several pitfalls of occupational regulation are now recognized. Licensure laws frequently place restrictions on advertising and on various business structures and practices. By restricting the number of people entering a profession and the ability of new professions to work independently, licensure may increase the cost to consumers of some professional services.[2] The mobility of practitioners has been hampered,[3] and in many fields auxiliaries have been underused. Licensure often focuses on testing applicants for the initial license and is less concerned about the competence and performance of practitioners after the license is granted.

Several states have instituted formal "sunrise" processes for evaluating requests for regulation in an attempt to restrict licensure only to those occupations that meet established criteria. Washington, Virginia,[4] Kansas and New York are among the states using a sunrise process. The evaluation generally asks: (1) will regulation benefit the public? (2) will obvious harm result from unregulated practice? and (3) is there any cost-beneficial means to protect the public short of regulation?

Organization of Licensure Boards

Historically, most licensure boards have been autonomous.[5] Over 35 states have now established a central agency for some or all licensure boards. Frequently, the health boards are organized in an agency separate from the non-health boards.

However, central agencies differ widely in their statutorily-mandated responsibilities and the extent of the authority exercised over board decision.[6] In a majority of states, the central agency is responsible for administrative functions such as processing applications, issuing licenses, record keeping, fee collection and routine correspondence, while the boards continue to exercise primary policy-making powers such as conducting examinations, exercising disciplinary authority and drafting administrative regulations. In other states, such as Illinois, New York, Florida and Connecticut, the central agency's powers extend to authority over board personnel, budgets, investigations and examinations.

Frances Stokes Berry is Program Manager for Licensure and Regulation and R. Douglas Roederer is Director of Research and State Services at The Council of State Governments.

The trend since the late 1970s to centralize administrative services for licensing boards continues. In the last two years, Indiana and New Mexico have established central agencies and other states, such as Maine, are bringing additional boards into already-established agencies.

The composition of licensure boards is changing as well. Traditionally, boards have been comprised exclusively of members of the regulated profession. Most states now tend to place one or more public or lay members on licensure boards. The California Public Member Act requires that boards be made up of a majority of lay members except for health and accountancy boards which are to have one-third lay members. A related trend adds to board membership practitioners who are specialists or auxiliaries to the profession regulated by the board, such as adding a dental hygienist to a board of dentistry.

While states continue to add public members to licensing boards, the debate continues about whether public members are effective. A Michigan study found public members had limited impact on licensing policies and procedures.[7]

Opponents of the trend toward centralization of licensure contend that it adds to bureaucracy and red tape and reduces the responsiveness of the licensure authority to both licensee needs and citizen complaints. Further, they argue that individual licensure boards with professional members best understand the issues of examinations, professional practice and discipline.

Evaluation of Licensing Boards

Until the late 1970s, there was little evaluation of the performance of boards or of the need for state regulation of each profession. State sunset laws, beginning with Colorado in 1976, changed that neglect. Indeed, nearly all of the 37 states that have enacted sunset laws have applied them to occupational and professional licensing boards.[8] While licensing boards continue to be reviewed on a regular cycle, usually every five to seven years, more states now include the major line agencies under sunset performance evaluations.[9] Some states have eliminated repeat reviews of licensing boards.

Specific changes in health regulatory laws resulting from sunset reviews include the following: (1) the composition of boards was altered to include lay members and auxiliary health practitioners; (2) board meetings were opened to the public; (3) scopes of practice were expanded or changed to accommodate emerging health care practitioners; (4) specialists and auxiliary health care practitioners were granted broader scopes of practice to perform functions independently or with less supervision; (5) licensing examination guidelines were strengthened or clarified; (6) reciprocal licensure arrangements with other states were encouraged; (7) grounds for disciplinary action were expanded with new definitions of negligence, incompetence, malpractice and others; (8) mechanisms were created and strengthened for receiving and processing complaints; and (9) enforcement staff has been increased, reflecting emphasis on strengthened enforcement policies.

Another type of evaluation in which licensing boards participate is the administrative rules review process. Most rules review bodies are joint legislative commissions, although California houses its Office of Administrative Law in the executive branch. Under rules review processes, regulations are checked for appropriateness, clarity and statutory authority.

Continuing Competence

There is a growing recognition that the state government regulatory system that attempts to insure beginning practitioners' competence should also attempt to insure that practitioners continue to practice above minimum levels. Since 1971 when the New Mexico Board of Medical Examiners first adopted mandatory continuing education (MCE) requirements for license renewal, professions have passed MCE to promote continuing competence.

Over a decade later, however, there are serious questions as to whether MCE achieves its desired goal. Concerns include the high cost of MCE to practitioners, the unproven relationship between course work taken and practitioner performance, and the uneven substance of course work offered to MCE.[10] A 1983 study of continuing education requirements by the California Department of Consumer Affairs reported that: (1) most licensing board staff found little or no benefit to the public or the licensees from MCE; and (2) licensees in the department spend approximately $240,000 annually (excluding lost income), to meet the MCE requirements.[11] Other options to assess competency in addition to MCE include practical examinations, simulations, peer review, self assessment tests and audits.[12]

Strengthened disciplinary and enforcement procedures may be more effective than continuing education in protecting the public from incompetent or fraudulent practitioners. Under this approach, state governments' efforts are directed at the small percentage of practitioners who practice below minimum levels rather than toward the large majority of competent practitioners. For example, a 1983 review of Michigan's law to develop continuing competency programs for all licensed professionals found the state had not progressed far toward this goal. Instead, the report recommended that the limited funds available for continuing competency assessment be directed toward improving the enforcement program.

Table 1 shows the status of MCE requirements from 16 professions. Optometrists, CPAs and Nursing Home Administrators must meet MCE requirements in more states than any of the other professions. The trend since 1977 has been to adopt MCE requirements across the professions, although since 1982 few states have passed new MCE requirements. Several, including Colorado, have revoked MCE for selected health professions. In a 50 state comparison since 1982, only physicians and LPNs have fewer states mandating continuing education in 1984 of the professions listed in Table 1.[13]

Exchanging Information

Responding to the expressed need for a forum to share information and discuss common problems, state licensing officials formed the National Clearinghouse on Licensure, Enforcement and Regulation (C.L.E.A.R.) in 1980.

C.L.E.A.R., with staff support from The Council of State Governments, maintains an information library on state licensing practices and procedures. Twelve publications provide comparative state information on model investigative practices, licensing structures, sunset audits, public membership and financing patterns. An annual national conference, regional meetings and a newsletter provide forums for information exchange on mutual problems and innovative solutions.

In response to the states' needs for enforcement information, C.L.E.A.R. has established the National Disciplinary Information System, which provides information to states on disciplinary actions taken by states against licensed practitioners.

Notes

1. See *Occupational Licensing: Questions A Legislator Should Ask* (Lexington, Ky.: The Council of State Governments, 1978) for further clarification on the forms of regulation and the questions to answer in deciding among forms of regulation.

2. For an extensive review of the empirical research which generally supports the position that licensure is an anti-competitive barrier to entry see *Law and Human Behavior* (September 1983).

3. For example, see N. Kleiner, et. al., "Licensing, Migration: Some Empirical Insights," a paper presented at symposium on regulatory policy, University of Houston, Texas, November 19, 1979.

4. For a full report on Virginia's criteria, see *The Regulation of the Health Professions* (Bethesda, Maryland: Alpha Center, 1983).

5. For a brief description of the regulatory system and a cogent discussion of key occupational licensing issues, see Benjamin Shimberg, *Occupational Licensing, A Public Perspective* (Princeton, New Jersey: Educational Testing Service, 1982).

6. See *Centralizing State Licensing Functions* (Lexington, Ky.: The Council of State Governments, 1980).

7. See "A Report on the Role and Effectiveness of Public Members on Licensing Boards," Michigan Department of Licensing and Regulation, 1980.

8. See *The Status of Sunset in the States: A Common Cause Report* (Washington, D.C.: Common Cause, 1982).

9. For a schedule of sunset reviews in states through 1992, see *Sunset: A Schedule of State Sunset Reviews* (Lexington, Ky.: The Council of State Governments, 1983).

10. For excellent consideration of issues and current activities in continuing education, see Milton R. Stern, ed. *Power and Conflict in Continuing Professional Education* (Belmont, California: Wadsworth Publishing, 1983).

11. See Benjamin Shimberg, "What's Competence? How Can It Be Assessed?" in *Power and Conflict in Continuing Education.*

12. *Evaluation of the Effectiveness, Costs and Benefits of Continuing Education Requirements*, California Department of Consumer Affairs, December 1982.

13. Analysis is from "Trends in MCE Requirements," unpublished data compiled by Louis Phillips, University of Georgia, 1984.

Table 1
STATUS OF MANDATORY CONTINUING EDUCATION
FOR SELECTED PROFESSIONS
(As of February 1984)

State or other jurisdiction	Architects	Certified public accountants	Dentists	Engineers (Prof.)	Lawyers	Nurses	Nursing home administrators	Optometrists	Psychologists	Pharmacists	Physical therapists	Physicians	Real estate agents	Social workers	Licensed practical nurses	Veterinarians
Alabama	...	★	...	...	★	...	★	★	...	★	...	★	...	★	...	★
Alaska	...	★	...	...	...	S	...	★	★	★	...	★	...	...	...	...
Arizona	•	★	...	...	S	...	★	★	★	★	...	★	★	...	...	★
Arkansas	...	★	...	...	S	...	★	★	•	★	...	•	...	★	...	★
California	...	★	★	...	S	★	★	...	...	★	...	★	★	★	★	...
Colorado	...	★	...	...	★	★	...	...	...	...	...	...	...	★	★	★
Connecticut	...	★	...	...	...	...	...	★	...	...	...	...	...	...	...	...
Delaware	•	...	...	...	...	...	★	★	★	★	...	...	...	★	★	★
Florida	•	★	...	...	S	★	★	★	★	★	...	★	★	★	★	★
Georgia	...	★	...	...	S	...	★	★	...	★	...	...	...	...	...	...
Hawaii	...	...	...	...	...	...	★	★	...	...	...	★	...	...	...	...
Idaho	...	★	...	...	★	S	★	★	...	★	...	...	...	...	...	...
Illinois	...	★	...	...	...	...	★	★	...	★	...	...	...	...	...	...
Indiana	...	★	...	...	...	...	•	★	...	★	...	...	...	...	...	•
Iowa	★	★	★	★	★S	★	★	★	★	★	★	★	★	...	★	★
Kansas	...	★	★	...	...	★	★	★	•	★	★	★	★	★	★	★
Kentucky	...	★	★	...	...	★	★	★	•	★	...	•	★	★	★	★
Louisiana	...	★	...	...	...	...	★	★	•	★	...	...	★	★	★	...
Maine	...	★	...	...	...	...	★	★	...	★	...	...	★	★	★	★
Maryland	...	★	...	...	...	...	★	★	★	...	...	...	★	★	★	...
Massachusetts	...	★	★	...	...	★	★	★	★	★	...	...	★	...	★	★
Michigan	•	★	...	...	...	★	★	★	•	★	...	...	★	★	...	★
Minnesota	•	★	★	•	★	★	★	★	•	★	...	...	★	★	...	★
Mississippi	...	★	...	...	...	S	★	★	...	★	...	...	★	...	S	★
Missouri	...	...	...	...	...	...	★	★	...	...	...	...	...	...	...	...
Montana	...	★	...	★	★	...	★	★	...	★	•	...	...	★	...	★
Nebraska	...	★	...	...	...	★	★	★	...	★	...	•	...	...	...	★
Nevada	...	★	...	...	★	★	★	★	★	★	...	•	★	...	★	★
New Hampshire	•	★	...	...	...	S	★	★	...	★	...	...	S	...	...	★
New Jersey	•	...	S	...	...	...	★	★	...	★	...	...	...	...	...	...
New Mexico	•	★	★	...	S	★	★	★	★	★	★	...	...	...	★	★
New York	...	...	...	...	...	...	★	★	•	•	...	...	★	...	...	...
North Carolina	...	★	...	•	...	...	★	★	•	•	...	...	★	★	...	...
North Dakota	...	★	★	...	★	...	★	★	...	...	...	...	★	★	...	★
Ohio	...	★	...	...	...	...	★	★	•	★	...	...	★	...	...	★
Oklahoma	...	★	...	...	...	...	★	★	★	...	...	...	★	★	...	★
Oregon	...	★	★	...	...	S	★	★	★	★	...	...	...	★	...	★
Pennsylvania	...	★	...	...	...	...	★	★	...	★	...	S	...	...	...	★
Rhode Island	...	★	...	...	...	...	★	★	...	★	...	...	★	...	...	...
South Carolina	...	★	...	...	★S	...	★	★	...	...	...	...	...	...	...	...
South Dakota	...	★	★	...	...	...	★	★	...	★	...	...	★	★	★	★
Tennessee	...	★	...	...	...	...	★	★	★	...	...	...	S	★	...	★
Texas	...	•	...	...	S	...	★	★	•	★	...	...	S	★	...	★
Utah	★	...	...	...	...	...	★	★	★	★	•	•	★	S	★	...
Vermont	...	★	...	...	...	...	★	★	•	•	...	...	...	...	...	...
Virginia	...	...	...	...	...	...	★	★	...	...	...	...	...	★	...	...
Washington	...	★	...	...	★	•	★	★	★	★	...	...	...	...	...	★
West Virginia	...	...	...	...	...	...	★	★	★	...	...	...	...	...	...	...
Wisconsin	...	...	...	...	★	...	★	★	...	...	...	...	★	★	...	...
Wyoming	...	★	...	...	★	...	★	★	•	★	...	...	★	...	...	...
Dist. of Col.	...	★	...	...	...	...	...	...	...	•	...	...	...	...	...	...

Source: Copyright, Louis E. Phillips, University of Georgia, Athens, Georgia. Information obtained from national professional associations.

Key: ★—Required by statute or regulation.
    •—Enabling legislation passed.
    S—Required under certain circumstances.
    ...—Profession not licensed.

STATE POLICE AND HIGHWAY PATROLS

By R. H. Sostkowski

Law enforcement at the state level is generally perceived as a police force that provides services on the nation's highways and in the unincorporated areas of the states. This description, however, is only partially accurate. There are a number of state-level law enforcement agencies with differing responsibilities, and most states, in fact, have more than one state-level law enforcement agency. The International Association of Chiefs of Police (IACP) divides state-level law enforcement agencies into the following broad categories: state police, highway patrols, state departments of law enforcement and state law enforcement units.[1] The factor that distinguishes state police or highway patrols from all other state-level enforcement agencies is the operation of a *uniformed* patrol force that acts *throughout* the state, as opposed to within narrowly defined areas of jurisdiction.

Even narrowing the scope to state police and highway patrols, there are still differences between the agencies in the several states, and the 49 state law enforcement agencies cannot be compared solely by grouping them according to title.[2] The mission and jurisdictional boundaries vary between states. In some—California, for example—a highway patrol is responsible for all traffic matters, and county agencies, such as sheriff's departments, are responsible for all criminal matters and providing police service to incorporated areas. In other states, there may not be a clear-cut line of authority, and the state police and county sheriff respond to the same calls for service, with the agency first responding having primary jurisdiction. Such is the case in Michigan. In yet other cases—for example, Texas—an umbrella "department of public safety" houses both a highway patrol and state police, with the different divisions within the parent organization having differing jurisdictions or responsibilities.

The major distinguishing factor between a state police and a highway patrol is that the former's responsibility is to provide a full range of police service, while the latter directs its primary efforts to the enforcement of highway safety, motor vehicle regulations and traffic safety programs. Current federal priorities, however, have resulted in a shift in the responsibilities of

the state police to become more closely aligned to a highway patrol. The following programs exemplify this.

Ten years ago, the federal government established the 55 National Maximum Speed Limit (NMSL) and provided funding to law enforcement agencies to assist in their enforcement of this law. Initially, a national public information campaign was launched, enforcement was greatly increased, and the motoring public generally slowed their speed to the 55 limit. In recent years, however, emphasis on the 55 NMSL has decreased, and speeds have increased. Sanctions against the states in the form of a loss in highway construction monies are in effect, and several states currently are close to being affected by the increasing speeds on their highways. Even with the possibility of losing federal funds, states cannot control speeds due to lack of public support and insufficient resources to increase patrols. Because of the many issues surrounding the 55 NMSL, the U.S. Congress has mandated a study of this issue, to be conducted by the National Academy of Sciences.

State police and highway patrols have greatly increased emphasis on the drinking driver problem. While this issue has been dealt with by law enforcement for years, it has not been until recently that such a great expenditure in manpower and resources has been devoted to this effort. With the advent of groups such as Mothers Against Drunk Drivers (MADD), Students Against Drunk Driving (SADD) and Remove the Intoxicated Driver (RID), federal officials have increased national attention to the problem of drunk drivers. The Congress developed an incentive grant program which provides funding to those states meeting established criteria relating to drunk driving programs. Currently, 13 states have met the criteria and are eligible to receive funding for expanded DWI programs. Additionally, the U.S. Department of Transportation has designated the drinking driver problem as a national priority and assists states in developing and enhancing their DWI programs. The federal

R.H. Sostkowski is the Director of the Division of State and Provincial Police of the International Association of Chiefs of Police.

attention on DWI, combined with the support received by public interest groups such as MADD and RID, results in greatly increased efforts at enforcing the DWI statutes within the states.

A third federal initiative which has been responsible for state police agencies leaning more heavily toward the highway safety aspect of their responsibilities is the occupant protection program currently underway. The Department of Transportation identified occupant restraints as a national priority due to their proven effectiveness and has attempted to educate the motoring public on their value and promote their voluntary use. The emphasis on this issue resulted in legislation in more than 40 states requiring the use of child restraints, with the enforcement of these laws falling primarily on the state-level law enforcement agencies.

The current trend, as an outgrowth of the child restraint legislation, is the mandatory use of occupant restraints by adults as well. In an effort to provide viable alternatives, vehicle manufacturers have developed passive restraints such as the air bag, making it more convenient for motorists. To assist in the testing of such equipment, several state police agencies have installed air bags in their vehicles for "real world" testing.

As evidenced above, the federal priorities and programs heavily affect the state law enforcement mission at any given time. Today's national programs have resulted in a heavy emphasis on highway safety and traffic services. In the near future, the trends will remain the same in large measure. It is anticipated that highway safety will continue to be a high priority, expanding to take into consideration the deteriorating condition of our highways and shifts in traffic patterns as larger and heavier trucks are produced, while automobiles are smaller and lighter.

Notes

1. For definitions and responsibilities of these agencies, see R.H. Sostkowski, "State Police and Highway Patrols," *The Book of the States, 1982-83* (Lexington, Ky.: The Council of State Governments, 1982), pp. 556-60.

2. Hawaii has neither a state police agency nor a highway patrol.

NUMBER OF STATE LAW ENFORCEMENT PERSONNEL: 1982

State	Number of law enforcement employees					State	Number of law enforcement employees				
		Officers		Civilians				Officers		Civilians	
	Total(a)	Male	Female	Male	Female		Total(a)	Male	Female	Male	Female
Total	66,927	45,221	863	9,364	11,096	Nebraska	503	379	4	60	60
						Nevada	258	181	2	15	60
Alabama	1,175	688	6	185	296	New Hampshire	278	215	2	32	29
Alaska	825	424	13	103	285	New Jersey	3,224	1,918	43	760	503
Arizona	1,504	906	28	304	266	New Mexico	652	378	8	104	162
Arkansas	628	468	13	63	84						
California	7,306	4,917	127	1,025	1,237	New York	3,830	3,257	66	153	354
						North Carolina	1,419	1,110	3	195	111
Colorado	681	472	9	82	118	North Dakota	123	101	1	2	19
Connecticut	1,242	813	21	202	206	Ohio	1,916	1,128	18	373	397
Delaware	565	417	8	67	73	Oklahoma	1,319	812	12	231	264
Florida	1,830	1,265	39	202	324						
Georgia	1,489	801	9	348	331	Oregon	958	816	19	19	104
						Pennsylvania	4,799	3,721	56	481	541
Idaho	170	137	1	18	14	Rhode Island	200	163	1	28	8
Illinois	2,054	1,503	42	243	266	South Carolina	884	740	9	50	85
Indiana	1,665	1,077	13	288	287	South Dakota	184	131		35	18
Iowa	776	539	11	105	121						
Kansas	565	415	3	81	66	Tennessee(c)	947	560	4		
						Texas	4,706	2,644	37	607	1,418
Kentucky	1,612	901	8	396	307	Utah	444	363	3	20	58
Louisiana	1,176	869	9	100	198	Vermont	382	252	5	50	75
Maine	463	326	3	64	70	Virginia	1,862	1,304	19	156	383
Maryland	2,114	1,462	51	216	385						
Massachusetts	1,123	924	33	113	53	Washington	1,257	741	8	309	199
						West Virginia	823	528	7	85	203
Michigan	3,072	2,041	53	542	436	Wisconsin	609	443	24	87	55
Minnesota	615	464	6	101	44	Wyoming	205	161		9	35
Mississippi	882	552	3	97	230						
Missouri	1,613	794	3	558	258						
Montana(b)	.....										

Source: U.S. Department of Justice, *Crime in the United States* (Washington, D.C.: U.S. Government Printing Office, 1983), p. 251.
   (a) Due to rounding, details do not add up to totals.
   (b) Law enforcement employee data were not furnished to the National Uniform Crime Reporting Program by the Montana Board of Crime Control.
   (c) Male and female breakdowns not available for civilians.

DEVELOPMENTS IN PUBLIC UTILITIES REGULATION

By James E. Suelflow

The decade of the 1980s is undoubtedly one of the most unsettled times in the history of public utilities and their regulation.

Energy conservation, cost-based pricing, protection of the environment, competitive forms of communications, consumerism, and promotion of competition are all demanding stricter regulations. Governor Snelling of Vermont stated this very well a few years ago. To paraphrase the governor, it will no longer be possible for regulators to regard themselves merely as umpires or as protectors of those they regulate. Regulators must be more accountable to both the public and the utilities. If we are to have efficient public utilities, we must have regulators who are willing to reward good management with rate increases and increased stability and to penalize poorly-run utilities by denying requests for rate increases and letting them fail. Well-managed utilities should thrive; poorly-managed utilities should wither and eventually be taken over by their stronger, more efficient rivals. Whether one agrees or not with this evaluation, the increased demands on regulators are evident.

The term "public utility" generally refers to suppliers of electricity, natural gas firms (including production, transmission and distribution), telephone and telegraph companies, water and sewage operations, and in some instances cable television (CATV) companies. Regulation takes place at one or more governmental levels. In the case of water and sewage utilities and CATV companies, most regulation is local. Ultimate regulation for the more traditional energy and communication utilities' service is usually overseen by state regulatory bodies. Any activities involving interstate commerce must be controlled by federal regulators. In some instances, various aspects of a utility's operations simultaneously come under all three forms of control, and often jurisdictional boundaries are unclear.

The magnitude of state regulatory activities is illustrated by the number of utilities agencies are required to oversee: approximately 1,510 telephone companies, 33 telegraph companies, 245 CATV systems, 353 investor-owned (private) electric companies, 656 rural electricity cooperatives, 711 municipal, regional and other publically (governmentally)-owned electric sys-

tems, 950 investor and 227 publically-owned gas distribution utilities. In addition, these agencies regulate a significant portion of more than 6,635 private and publically-owned water utilities, 1,856 sewer systems and 760 combination water-sewage utilities.

Regulation, while at times no more than advisory oversight, generally includes the determination of revenue requirements, approval of individual rates, sanctioning of entry, exit and expansion, safety and territorial market limits. In order to accomplish these tasks, commissions, among other things, prescribe uniform accounting systems and procedures, perform accounting and management audits, oversee financial practices, provide safety regulations, and oversee both the quantity and quality of services rendered. While a number of these tasks may be carried out informally, the more important regulation of revenue requirements and rates is generally accomplished through formal rate hearings and procedures that are similar to traditional legal methods.

The Industries—Regulatory Update

In the following discussion, states named in parentheses have instituted regulatory action concerning the issue. Further information may be obtained by contacting the respective commissions.

Water. In a May 1983 study, the National Regulatory Research Institute found that 45 commissions have responsibility for the regulation of small water utilities. Regulation of these utilities by traditional methods is becoming of concern because of the increased workload placed upon both the utility and the regulator. Part of the concern is due to the relatively large number of such companies, weak management and the fact that many are not economically viable. To help overcome the dilemma, a number of commissions (for example, Illinois and Maryland) have issued orders on the simplification of rate case procedures for both small water and sewage utilities.

James E. Suelflow is Professor of Business Administration in the Graduate School of Business at Indiana University, Bloomington.

Electricity. Among the specific regulatory issues related to electric utilities are those concerning treatment of the costs of abandoned nuclear power plants (Oregon, Connecticut, South Dakota), excess capacity (Kansas, New Jersey), construction work in progress (California, Kentucky, Oklahoma), cogeneration (Idaho, Mississippi, New Hampshire) and hydro-relicensing (Wyoming). Major questions arise with virtually every one of these issues due to the magnitude of the costs and who pays, consumer or investors. Most state regulatory statutes emphasize that plants can only be charged back to customers through rates if the facility is used and useful and, in many states if the initial investment was prudent. Consumers continue to demand increased service at reasonable rates and at the same time continue to balk at higher costs to produce such service. Over the coming years commissions will have to cope with these issues while keeping investors content.

To elaborate on the hydro-licensing controversy, in 1920 legislation was passed (and amended in 1935) authorizing the Federal Power Commission (now FERC) to issue 50-year licenses to construct all hydroelectric dams on navigable waterways. After the original license expired, renewal preference was to be given to public authorities. In Vermont, the commission ruled that it could independently review applications for renewal in the interest of the state. The decision was later overruled on the basis of the dominance of federal authority. However, the Merwin Dam decision by the FERC appears to give preference for license renewal to the existing licensee unless doing so does not meet certain public interest standards.

Another issue is paying the costs of decommissioning nuclear plants when their useful life is at an end. Commissions are constructing methods for developing these costs, as well as ways to account for and recover them from present or future rate payers (California, Michigan, Florida).

Natural Gas. The important question for state regulators is how the various legislative proposals affecting wellhead prices based on the NEGPA and involving deregulation, price increases, contract clauses and market distortions are likely to affect retail gas rates. Among those states making recent decisions on these issues are Wisconsin, Michigan, Missouri and Georgia.

Energy. Regulatory concerns which encompass all energy utilities (electricity and gas) center around separate but related issues. Assistance to the needy, particularly with respect to service cutoffs, continues to be a problem. The utilities as well as the regulators come under considerable moral and political pressure to assist the disadvantaged. Such assistance, particularly if it is provided through delayed billing, budget billing, lifeline rates, etc., might have an adverse effect on other rate payers.

Additional assistance involves energy conservation and the implications of low-cost loans by utilities or their subsidiaries for insulation and weather-stripping and the subsequent effects on the utilities' cost of service.

Communications. State regulatory interest continues to center around the restructuring of domestic telecommunications, prompted by the so-called "Modified Final Judgment" found as an appendix to the antitrust suit decision *United States vs. American Telephone and Telegraph Co.* (552 F. Supp. 121, 225 D.D.C. 1982) and the *Computer II* decision (35 PUR 4th 143; 39 PUR 4th 319; 88 FCC 2d 512; and 697 F2d 198).

Decisions to be made involve regulation of consumer premises equipment, toll calls within and among local access and transport areas (LATAs), the role of competing carriers, intrastate access charges to the toll network, and rules and regulations which might be applied to bypass technology, which may allow inter-LATA carriers to connect with ultimate consumers without use of local phone company networks.

State Regulation—General. With continued pressures from specific interest groups, at least 13 states have recently discussed the possibilities of electing public utility regulatory commissioners rather than having them appointed. The purpose is to provide better representation; yet studies have been inconclusive as to the grater effectiveness of elected over appointed officials. Additionally, there have been suggestions and legislative enactments (Indiana) to increase the number of commissioners for the purposes of better representation.

Commissioners will continue to cope with diversification by utilities—particularly diversification through the purchase of unregulated subsidiaries such as coal mines and real estate. These transactions are often attempts to better the financial position of the utilities, yet they present some very sticky regulatory problems with respect to rate base, cost of capital and, eventually, consumer rates.

Similarly, deregulation has put additional burdens on state regulators. For example, in a few instances, cooperatives were removed from commission jurisdiction, and the commission now finds it difficult to meet certain requirements of the Public Utility Regulatory Policies Act of 1978 (Colorado).

State vs. Federal Regulation. Jurisdictional issues have long plagued public utility regulators. The basis for this responsibility rests in the U.S. Constitution. The Commerce Clause authorizes federal control of interstate commerce while the 10th Amendment provides for state regulation. Several of the regulatory areas mentioned above also include jurisdictional issues. In addition, cellular mobile telephone service currently produces similar regulating problems (Arizona, North Carolina and Pennsylvania).

Electric utilities also face the problems of jurisdictional authority. At one time the distinction between retail and wholesale rates was the guideline; however, subsequent cases have changed the earlier Attleboro decision (Mississippi, Illinois, Indiana). State commissions must be alert to a possible jurisdictional conflict in the energy field.

Finally, CATV is not exempt from the controversy. While most regulation is at the local level, eight states have regulatory authority with five of these states adapting federal guidelines. Authority to control pole attachments as well as cross-ownership with other utilities share state and federal scrutiny.

Aid for State Commissions. A number of organizations continued to provide assistance to state regulatory bodies. These include the National Association of Regulatory Utility Commissioners, Electric Power Research Institute (EPRI) and the Edison Electric Institute (EEI), which have jointly engaged in massive rate design projects. EEI members have available to them a computerized data bank known as "URAP" to help utility companies become acquainted with useful rate-case information. Finally, in order to meet the research needs of state regulators as well as to provide on-site technical assistance and conduct workshops, the National Regulatory Research Institute (NRRI) was organized. NRRI studies have produced information to aid commissions on water utility rate procedures, electric rate reforms, conservation, operating efficiencies, fuel clause adjustments and regulatory problems associated with the reorganization of the telecommunications industry. A series of publications on regulatory information exchange is issued quarterly.

Table 1
STATE PUBLIC UTILITY COMMISSIONS

State or other jurisdiction	Regulatory authority	Members		Selection of chair	Length of commissioners' terms (in years)	Number of full-time employees
		Number	Selection			
Alabama	Public Service Commission	3	E	E	4	112
Alaska	Public Utilities Commission	5	GL	G	6	40
Arizona	Corporation Commission	3	E	C	6	139
Arkansas	Public Service Commission	3	GS	G	6	89
California	Public Utilities Commission	5	GS	G	6	866
Colorado	Public Utilities Commission	3	GS	G	6	95
Connecticut	Public Utilities Control Authority	5	GL	G	4	107
Delaware	Public Service Commission	5	GS	G	5	17
Florida	Public Service Commission	5	GS	C	4	322
Georgia	Public Service Commission	5	E	C	6	108
Hawaii	Public Utilities Commission	3	GS	G	6	17
Idaho	Public Utilities Commission	3	GS	G	6	55
Illinois	Commerce Commission	5	G	G	5	279
Indiana	Public Service Commission	3	G	G	4	96
Iowa	State Commerce Commission	3	GS	G	6	156
Kansas	State Corporation Commission	3	GS	C	4	194
Kentucky	Public Service Commission	3	G	G(d)	3	80
Louisiana	Public Service Commission	5	E	C	6	91
Maine	Public Utilities Commission	3	GS	G	7	75
Maryland	Public Service Commission	5	GS	G	6	117
Massachusetts	Dept. of Public Utilities	3	G	G	4	115
Michigan	Public Service Commission	3	GS	G	6	313
Minnesota	Public Utilities Commission	5	GS	G	6	24
Mississippi	Public Service Commission	3	E	C	4	73
Missouri	Public Service Commission	5	GS	G	6	244
Montana	Public Service Commission	5	E	C	4	44
Nebraska	Public Service Commission	5	E	C	6	54
Nevada	Public Service Commission	3	G	G	4	72
New Hampshire	Public Utilities Commission	3	G	G	6	51
New Jersey	Board of Public Utilities	3	GS	G	6	164
New Mexico	Public Service Commission	3	GS	G	6	40
New York	Public Service Commission	6	GS	G(a)	6	731
North Carolina	Utilities Commission	7	GL	G	8	168
North Dakota	Public Service Commission	3	E	C	6	56
Ohio	Public Utilities Commission	3	GS	G	6	333
Oklahoma	Corporation Commission	3	E	C	6	413
Oregon	Public Utility Commissioner	1	G	. . .	4	343
Pennsylvania	Public Utility Commission	5	GS	G	10	561
Rhode Island	Public Utilities Commission	3	GS	G	6	41
South Carolina	Public Service Commission	7	GS	(b)	4	145
South Dakota	Public Utilities Commission	3	E	C	6	30
Tennessee	Public Service Commission	3	E	C	6	142
Texas	Public Utility Commission	3	GS	C	6	110
	Railroad Commission	3	E	C	6	700
Utah	Public Service Commission	3	GS	G	6	35
Vermont	Public Service Board	3	GS	G	6(c)	26
Virginia	State Corporation Commission	3	L	C	6	460
Washington	Utilities and Transportation Commission	3	GS	G	6	205
West Virginia	Public Service Commission	3	G	G(d)	6	193
Wisconsin	Public Service Commission	3	GS	G	6	152
Wyoming	Public Service Commission	3	GS	C	6	41
Dist. of Col.	Public Service Commission	3	M	C	3	31
Puerto Rico	Public Service Commission	5	GS	GS	4	256

Source: National Association of Regulatory Utility Commissioners, *Annual Report on Utility and Carrier Regulation*, 1981. (Washington, D.C.: 1982).

Key:
G— Appointed by governor.
GS— Appointed by governor, with confirmation by senate.
GE— Appointed by governor, confirmation by executive council.
GL— Appointed by governor, approved by joint session of legislature.
E— Elected.
C— Elected by commission.
L— Appointed by legislature.
M— Appointed by mayor.

(a) Chairman designated by and serves at pleasure of governor.
(b) Rotates annually.
(c) Chairman appointed by governor for two years.
(d) Chairman appointed by governor for one year.

Table 2
CERTAIN REGULATORY FUNCTIONS OF
STATE PUBLIC UTILITIES COMMISSIONS

State or other jurisdiction(a)	Controls rates of privately owned utilities on sales to ultimate consumers of				Agency has authority to											
					Prescribe temporary rates, pending investigation			Require prior authorization of rate changes			Suspend proposed rate changes			Initiate rate investigations on its own motion		
	Electric	Gas	Telephone	CATV	Electric	Gas	Telephone	Electric	Gas	Telephone	Electric	Gas	Telephone	Electric	Gas	Telephone
Alabama PSC	★	★	★		★	★	...	★	★	★	★	★	★	★	★	★
Alaska PUC	★	★	★	★(b)	★	★	★	★	★	★	★	★	★	★	★	★
Arizona CC	★	★	★	...	★	★	★	★	★	★	...	...	...	★	★	★
Arkansas PSC	★	★	★	...	★	★	★	★	★	★	★	★	★	★	★	★
California PUC	★	★	★	...	★	★(c)	★(c)	★	★	★	★	★	★	★	★	★
Colorado PUC	★	★	★	...	★(d)	★(d)	★(d)	★	★	★	★	★	★	★	★	★
Connecticut PUCA	★	★	★	★	★	★	★	★	★	★	★	★	★	★	★	★
Delaware PSC	★	★	★	★	★	★	★	★	★	★	★	★	★	★	★	★
Florida PSC	★	★	★	...	★	★	★	★	★	★	★	★	★	★	★	★
Georgia PSC	★	★	★	...	★	★	★	★	★	★	★	★	★	★	★	★
Hawaii PUC	★	★	★	(e)	★	★	★	★	★	★	...	...	...	★	★	★
Idaho PUC	★	★	★	...	★	★	★	★(f)	★(f)	★(f)	★	★	★	★	★	★
Illinois CC	★	★	★	...	★	★	★	★	★	★	★	★	★	★	★	★
Indiana PSC	★	★	★	...				★	★	★	★	★	★	★	★	★
Iowa SCC	★	★	★(g)	...	★(h)	★(h)	★(h)	★	★	★	★	★	★(g)	★	★	★(g)
Kansas SCC	★	★	★	...	★	★	★	★	★	★	★	★	★	★	★	★
Kentucky PSC	★	★	★	...	★	★	★	★	★	★	★	★	★	★	★	★
Louisiana PSC	★	★(i)	★	...	★	★	★	★	★	★	★	★	★	★	★	★
Maine PUC	★	★	★	...	★	★	...	★	★	★	★	★	★	★	★	★
Maryland PSC	★	★	★	...	★	★	★	★	★	★	★	★	★	★	★	★
Massachusetts DPU	★	★	★	...	★	★	★	★	★	★	★	★	★	★	★	★
Michigan PSC	★	★	★	...	★(j)	★(j)	★(j)	★	★	★	(k)	(k)	(k)	★	★	★
Minnesota PUC	★	★	★(l)	...	★	★	★(l)	★	★	★(l)	★	★	★(l)	★	★	★(l)
Mississippi PSC	★	★	★	...	★	★	★	★	★	★	★	★	★	★	★	★
Missouri PSC	★	★	★	...	★	★	★	★	★	★	★	★	★	★	★	★
Montana PSC	★	★	★	...	★	★	★	★	★	★	★	★	★	★	★	★
Nebraska PSC(m)	...	...	★	...	...	...	★	...	...	★	...	...	★	...	...	★
Nevada PSC	★	★	★	...	★	★	★	★	★	★	★	★	★	★	★	★
New Hampshire PUC	★	★	★	...	★	★	★	★	★	★	★	★	★	★	★	★
New Jersey BPU	★	★	★	★	★	★	★	★	★	★	★	★	★	★	★	★
New Mexico PSC	★	★	★	...	★	★	★	★	★	★	★	★	★	★	★	...
New York PSC	★	★	★	...	★	★	★	★	★	★	★	★	★	★	★	★
North Carolina UC	★	★	★	...	★	★	★	★	★	★	★	★	★	★	★	★
North Dakota PSC	★	★	★	...	★	★	★	★	★	★	★	★	★	★	★	★
Ohio PUC	★	★	★	...	★	★	★	★	★	★	...	...	...	★	★	★
Oklahoma CC	★	★	★	...	★	★	★	★	★	★	★	★	★	★	★	★
Oregon PUC	★	★	★	...	(n)	(n)	(n)	★	★	★	★	★	★	★	★	★
Pennsylvania PUC	★	★	★	...	★	★	★	★	★	★	★	★	★	★	★	★
Rhode Island PUC	★	★	★	★	★	★	★	★	★	★	★	★	★	★	★	★
South Carolina PSC	★	★	★	...	★	★	★	★	★	★	★	★	★	★	★	★
South Dakota PUC	★	★	★(o)	...	★	★	★	★	★	★	★	★	★	★	★	★
Tennessee PSC	★	★	★	...	★	★	★	★	★	★	★	★	★	★	★	★
Texas PUC	★	★	★	...	★	★	★	★	★	★	★	★	★	★	★	★
RC	...	★	...	...	...	★	...	...	★	...	...	★	...	...	★	...
Utah PSC	★	★	★	...	★	★	★	★	★	★	★	★	★	★	★	★
Vermont PSB	★	★	★	★	★	★	★	★	★	★	★	★	★	★	★	★
Virginia SCC	★	★	★	...	★	★	★	★	★	★	★	★	★	★	★	★
Washington UTC	★	★	★	...	★	★	★	★	★	★	★	★	★	★	★	★
West Virginia PSC	★	★	★	...	★	★	★	★	★	★	★	★	★	★	★	★
Wisconsin PSC	★	★	★	...	★	★	★	★	★	★	(k)	(k)	(k)	★	(k)	★
Wyoming PSC	★	★	★	...	★	★	★	★	★	★	★	★	★	★	★	★
Dist. of Col. PSC	★	★	★	...	...	...	...	★	★	★	★	★	★	★	★	★
Puerto Rico PSC	...	★	(p)	★	...	...	(p)	...	...	(p)	...	...	(p)	...	★	(p)

Source: National Association of Regulatory Utility Commissioners, *1981 Annual Report on Utility and Carrier Regulation* (Washington, D.C.: 1982).

Key:
★—Yes
...—No

(a) Full names of commissions on Table 1.
(b) Regulation is limited, until July 1, 1983, to communities with populations of less than 3,500 and not located on a state road or marine highway.
(c) May fix temporary rates, but practice is not followed.
(d) No specific statutory authority.
(e) Regulated by the Cable Television Division of the Department of Regulatory Services.
(f) Rates become effective after seven months if commission does not take action.

(g) Not for companies with less than 13,000 stations.
(h) Interim rates must be approved and are collected under bond, subject to refund.
(i) Except no authority over rates charged to industrial customers by any gas company.
(j) Commission has authority to grant partial and immediate rate relief during pendency of final order, after statutory requirements are met.
(k) Specific authority required to change rates. Rates do not become effective after a specified period; consequently, no suspension is required.
(l) The commission no longer sets rates for telephone cooperatives—effective June 6, 1979.
(m) Telephone is the only regulated utility.
(n) Grant emergency increases only.
(o) PUC does not require rates of rural telephone companies.
(p) The Puerto Rico Telephone Authority, a state public corporation, purchased the Puerto Rico Telephone Company.

Table 3
AVERAGE MONTHLY BILLS, BY CUSTOMER CLASS,
FOR ELECTRICITY AND GAS: 1981

State or other jurisdiction	Electricity			Gas(a)		
	Residential(b)	Commercial(c)	Industrial(d)	Residential	Commercial	Industrial
U.S. average	$66.84	$509.34	$4,685	$36.35	$216.42	$12,083.65
Alabama	53.92	392.42	3,940	32.43	166.41	19,053.75
Alaska	53.26	376.76	3,506	32.44	94.74	2,792.86
Arizona	65.49	498.56	4,438	18.82	132.82	9,838.11
Arkansas	48.06	292.78	2,677	20.57	94.83	12,199.30
California	74.20	505.03	4,888	21.82	228.29	10,165.70
Colorado	58.53	425.79	3,583	33.23	197.82	10,306.03
Connecticut	86.93	666.08	5,389	50.49	313.92	3,647.85
Delaware	86.54	593.77	5,045	40.44	319.41	19,942.50
Florida	69.21	418.62	4,368	16.76	253.29	58,578.65
Georgia	50.10	540.20	4,269	36.85	215.70	18,436.09
Hawaii	119.19	777.95	7,237	33.08	474.09	1,254.41
Idaho	27.46	215.81	2,203	32.93	213.33	43,274.17
Illinois	61.88	542.57	4,660	49.81	272.60	5,396.83
Indiana	54.35	357.59	2,962	40.81	185.28	14,100.13
Iowa	60.05	460.60	4,045	37.32	172.91	15,913.99
Kansas	57.92	432.46	3,801	27.66	142.55	9,586.90
Kentucky	46.80	336.97	2,964	35.87	156.24	12,677.76
Louisiana	51.08	391.33	3,246	23.11	114.27	44,609.03
Maine	65.80	419.37	3,824	27.79	218.30	3,148.33
Maryland	58.82	395.11	3,497	41.04	237.05	4,428.99
Massachusetts	75.88	578.82	4,753	48.03	342.61	3,010.98
Michigan	56.18	436.21	4,230	50.15	337.37	7,463.26
Minnesota	55.78	352.65	3,193	42.83	204.02	5,679.92
Mississippi	51.99	439.01	3,750	26.37	114.40	27,430.69
Missouri	51.89	405.33	3,473	36.99	259.69	21,868.44
Montana	33.78	250.34	1,548	42.83	201.01	5,679.42
Nebraska	44.01	259.73	2,445	32.69	134.17	7,042.50
Nevada	55.00	385.97	3,678	31.60	535.64	147,883.33
New Hampshire	74.90	506.57	4,513	43.53	239.28	3,949.17
New Jersey	83.20	602.69	5,417	43.63	200.63	6,087.11
New Mexico	74.25	495.11	5,260	26.61	130.72	5,226.52
New York	102.77	845.54	7,670	41.14	190.59	4,533.98
North Carolina	56.61	342.32	3,062	40.50	220.77	16,146.08
North Dakota	53.04	363.88	3,215	41.87	294.71	5,387.50
Ohio	63.21	484.58	4,288	48.29	245.99	13,416.09
Oklahoma	45.64	305.64	2,590	21.52	119.63	17,880.79
Oregon	30.86	266.06	2,478	34.91	194.85	25,601.39
Pennsylvania	70.16	542.17	4,763	48.40	281.27	15,675.94
Rhode Island	73.40	486.73	4,263	47.67	219.87	2,630.54
South Carolina	57.49	346.86	3,162	30.00	198.84	19,481.74
South Dakota	58.60	377.55	3,477	33.97	168.21	2,351.39
Tennessee	44.77	318.75	3,741	27.31	170.00	14,226.81
Texas	58.46	413.01	3,857	24.20	157.86	30,957.34
Utah	60.94	503.10	3,380	32.84	128.41	16,185.56
Vermont	67.51	486.25	4,428	60.41	351.96	24,195.00 (e)
Virginia	62.26	408.46	4,060	40.46	293.00	7,033.70
Washington	22.99	154.96	1,558	38.84	279.16	12,111.35
West Virginia	50.62	338.19	2,900	43.97	228.80	43,595.83
Wisconsin	50.30	370.42	3,386	45.71	239.00	5,961.92
Wyoming	35.26	210.92	1,870	32.11	157.20	31,413.33
Dist. of Col.	50.42	484.07	4,501	47.37	415.69	-0-

(a) *Gas Facts, 1981 Data* (Arlington, Va.: American Gas Association, 1981), pp. 78 and 108.
(b) 1,000 kwhs. *Typical Electric Bills—January 1, 1981* (Washington, D.C.: U.S. Department of Energy, Energy Information Administration, November 12, 1981).
(c) 30 KW-6,000 KWH.
(d) 300 KW-60,000 KWH.
(e) Estimate as number of customers not exact.

5. Development and Housing

STATE ECONOMIC DEVELOPMENT

By Robert J. Reinshuttle

In recent years, we have witnessed an increasing desire and willingness of state and local governments to become involved in economic development. Enormous amounts of resources—both human and financial—have been spent in order to promote economic growth and jobs. But perhaps of even greater significance are the new and creative approaches state governments are taking. In no fewer than 27 states, special advisory bodies appointed by the governors have recommended programs to promote research and development, improve education and training, and facilitate industrial growth. In addition, some development programs feature assistance to small businesses with financial problems and reform of regulatory policies that business and industry have found to be particularly repugnant.

These new policies are distinctly different from the traditional industrial development policies that states pursued over the years with varying degrees of intensity. Smokestack chasing, or "chip chasing" as it has come to be called, continues to be prevalent, as do various tax incentives states have devised in order to lure businesses. However, the new strategies and approaches seem to be taking hold. The objectives are twofold: to concentrate on industries that offer long-term potential for growth and employment, such as high-tech companies, and to assist new and small businesses to flourish by providing loans and venture capital, if necessary. But, assistance is not taking a form which will be beneficial to all businesses. Incentives such as special grants are offered very selectively to businesses with the greatest potential.

Since the dawn of the Industrial Revolution in America, many of the Northeast and Midwestern states have experienced a rollercoaster economy. When times were good, they were very, very good, but when times were bad, many experienced hardship and unemployment. In the early 1970s, a few of the New England states, such as Connecticut and Massachusetts, decided to jump off the rollercoaster and attempt to devise an economy which was broadly based, stable, and comprised of industries which would remain viable through the coming decades. In 1972, Connecticut took the first step through the creation of a Product Development Corporation to finance new products in exchange for royalties. This approach has been put in place in several states. Michigan, New Mexico and New York provide direct venture capital to infant technology-based enterprises.

The states are also forging new links between universities and the private sector. Last year a significant number of states appointed commissions or task forces to examine the role of government in attracting new, particularly high-tech, industries. Several of these reports have recommended ideas such as advanced technology centers at private and public universities which would receive state funding for equipment and research. Such programs would likely be similar to the Ben Franklin Partnership Program in Pennsylvania, which also includes foundation grants and private sector funding. Other states are developing independent "hothouses" and incubation facilities to attract new industries. One of the foremost examples is the Industrial Technology Institution in Michigan, which was designed to work on robotics and factories of the future. This project is also funded through a joint effort by the state, private sector concerns and foundations. In many instances partnerships such as these have proven effective and may, in fact, be essential to the development of a successful project.

This same base of support was also used in another innovative program in the state of Michigan—the Michigan Investment Fund. In light of rapid changes in the automobile industry and high rates of unemployment, the Mott Foundation, a longtime supporter of community economic development programs, commissioned the National Development Council (NDC) to investigate setting up a financial mechanism that could provide equity investments in small businesses. The report recommended a profit-making partnership arrangement which is unique for a number of reasons. Its major partners include the Mott Foundation, Kellogg Foundation, Dow Foundation, the State of Michigan Employee Pension Fund and the University of

Robert J. Reinshuttle is Program Manager for Finance and Taxation for The Council of State Governments.

Michigan Endowment Fund. The involvement of foundations in a venture capital arrangement is unusual, but it does represent a new investment vehicle for philanthropy. Secondly, the fund is primarily a Michigan fund, although it is national as an investor. And finally, the motivation of the investors is to profit but also to strengthen the state's industry and economy.

Rhode Island devised the most ambitious plan—"The Greenhouse Compact." This comprehensive and lengthy economic development plan was the work of a gubernatorially appointed commission comprised of leaders from business, finance, organized labor, higher education, public service and environmental advocacy groups. The commission analyzed the Rhode Island economy and then proposed a strategic plan for the state's economic future. If the plan is adopted by voters in spring 1984, the entire state may become a laboratory of economic development initiatives and new ideas that may be emulated throughout the country. The objectives of the compact are to reduce levels of unemployment to 25-30 percent below the national average, to create 60,000 new jobs and to raise the standard of living for Rhode Island citizens.

Achieving these goals involves raising $250 million in order to stimulate a $750 million investment program to revitalize the economy over the next seven years. This includes a current bond issue ($90 million) and another issue in three years ($30 million). Other important sections of the plan include a product-market development incentive plan to encourage Rhode Island firms to pioneer new products by sharing the risk of associated investments; creation of a series of venture capital-limited partnerships licensed by the commission to offer tax incentives by investors and specialized tax incentives to entrepreneurs; and the formation of four research greenhouses in areas to be designated by the commission.

New ideas are contributing to very interesting and exciting times for economic development efforts at the state level, but concepts which have been around for a few years are also taking hold and proving their effectiveness. For example, with the recent addition of Nevada, Texas, Oklahoma and New Jersey, 19 states now have their own free-standing enterprise zone programs. Customized industrial training has proven very effective in several states, particularly the Bay State Skills Corporation in Massachusetts and the California Worksite Education and Training Act Program (CWETA).

On another front, joint research and development ventures are producing some of the nation's most useful technological innovations. Such cooperative efforts are particularly helpful to the development of small businesses because they spread the costs and risks of expensive, uncertain endeavors. These arrangements also offer other advantages such as facilitating capital formation and easing entry into higher tech fields. Successful joint ventures of this type are being undertaken by the private sector in many states, and they are without question a valuable component of state efforts to reduce unemployment through the creation of new jobs and to stimulate their economic climate.

However, no single innovation will generate a sudden increase in business births or the rapid growth of small businesses throughout a particular state. A comprehensive, thoughtful and ambitious strategy is required. Ingredients such as equitable tax policies, regulatory reform, programs to expand the availability of equity capital and policies to assist entrepreneurs and distressed communities are important elements and will continue to receive a great deal of attention by state officials.

HOUSING AND COMMUNITY DEVELOPMENT

By Carol H. Hartwell

The state role in housing and community development has grown in importance over recent years. State programs for housing continue to develop and expand, despite the withdrawal of federal support and unrelenting attacks on tax-exempt financing, the centerpiece of state housing activities. In community development, a change in federal law has shifted part of the responsibility for the major funding program to states, which have responded ably to the new challenge.

Housing

Government involvement in housing generally falls into three broad categories: regulation, not only of construction and building conditions but also to protect against discrimination in the housing market; support for mortgage lending through measures that maintain and increase the availability of housing credit; and assistance for those unable to afford or obtain suitable housing through the private market.

Historically, states have functioned largely as regulators, leaving the problems of capital availability and housing assistance to the federal government. Early in the 1970s, however, states began to expand their involvement in housing through mortgage lending programs designed to serve residents whose needs were not being met through the private market. They created state housing finance agencies (HFAs) to undertake these new housing activities.

By 1983, state HFAs existed in 49 states (all but Kansas), plus the District of Columbia, Puerto Rico and the Virgin Islands. Established by state law, these agencies raise funds for housing by issuing tax-exempt bonds. In turn, they lend the proceeds from these bond issues for residential mortgages. The bonds are supported by revenues earned from mortgage investments and generally are not backed by the general obligation of the state.

Because interest earned on HFA bonds is exempt from federal taxation, the agency pays a below market interest rate to investors and passes this savings on to borrowers. While tax-exempt financing programs clearly depend on this interest rate advantage, they were neither created nor originally authorized by the federal government. Rather, they developed out of the exemption for state obligations that has existed as long as the federal income tax itself.

Collectively, state HFAs have over $35 billion in debt outstanding. They have financed about one million housing units, roughly half for homeowners and half for renters. In 1983, state HFAs issued $9.4 billion in tax-exempt revenue bonds, $8.1 billion for owner-occupied housing and $1.3 billion for rental housing. Along with housing bonds issued by their local government counterparts, these tax-exempt housing bonds represented about 18.6 percent of the municipal bond market in 1983.

Proceeds from state HFA bond issues are used for three kinds of programs: home mortgage loans, rental housing development and home improvement loans.

Home Mortgage Loans. Almost every state operates a mortgage program to assist families who otherwise might not be able to buy a home. The HFA makes loans available through participating financial institutions for borrowers who meet state and federal eligibility requirements. Some programs are targeted to geographic areas and some to new construction; most limit eligibility by income. In the year ending June 30, 1983, state HFAs made about 65,000 mortgage loans.

While not created by Congress, these programs have nevertheless been regulated by federal law since 1980. In that year, Congress enacted legislation to control the use of these bonds by limiting the amount each state could issue, by restricting eligibility almost entirely to first-time buyers, and by establishing sales price limits. The 1980 act also contained a "sunset" provision, requiring Congress to act before December 31, 1983 to continue the federal tax exemption on these bonds.

At the start of the 1983 session, bills were introduced in both houses of Congress to eliminate the sunset date on mortgage revenue bonds. Three quarters of the members of both the House and the Senate co-sponsored these bills,

---

Carol H. Hartwell is Director of Research and Policy for the Council of State Housing Agencies.

which also had the support of the nation's governors, state legislatures, mayors, home builders, realtors and many other groups. Despite overwhelming support for continuation of the program, Congress was unable to pass a tax bill before the end of 1983, and the sunset date was allowed to go into effect.

As of January 1, 1984, bonds issued for homeownership programs were no longer eligible for federal tax exemption (except for general obligation bonds issued for veterans' programs). It is generally expected that the tax exemption will be restored in 1984, though the fate of the program will again be tied to the politics of larger tax issues.

Rental Housing Development. Many states also operate mortgage loan programs to support the development of rental housing. Again, the HFA raises funds in the tax-exempt bond market, lending them to private—either for-profit or non-profit—developers of rental housing. In the year ending June 30, 1983, state HFAs provided permanent financing for more than 45,000 rental housing units, representing about $1.9 million in mortgages.

Historically, most state HFAs have combined tax-exempt financing with federal subsidies for rental housing. The federal assistance has allowed state housing programs to reach a very low income market, both through "Section 236" interest subsidies during the early 1970s and "Section 8" rent assistance provided from the mid-1970s until recently. State HFAs have financed about 250,000 newly constructed and substantially rehabilitated rental units under the Section 8 program and deserve a great deal of credit for the high level of production achieved under that program.

Federal support for rental housing development has all but disappeared, leaving states without the resources they depended on in the past. State HFAs are working to develop programs to finance affordable rental housing without the backing of deep federal subsidies. From July 1982 through June 1983, about one-third of the rental units financed by state HFAs were "unassisted." State financing may also become an important part of the new federal development grant program for rental housing, authorized by Congress at the end of 1983 and modeled after the urban development action grant program.

Another new direction for state HFAs is to finance the rehabilitation of rental housing, where the need is for improvements rather than rebuilding. State HFAs have begun to develop these programs, known as "moderate rehabilitation," with and without federal support. A new federal program will begin in 1984, relying on states to administer rental rehab grants outside of entitlement communities (but excluding rural areas).

As with homeownership programs, the federal government restricts the tax exemption on bonds for rental housing development. The tax code classifies these as "industrial development bonds" (IDBs). Congress is expected to enact new limits on the use of IDBs during 1984, and while rental housing is likely to be exempted from the worst of these, any new restrictions will make it even more difficult for states to operate rental programs.

Home Improvement Loans. Along with financing home purchases and the development of rental housing, some states also offer small loans to eligible homeowners to finance needed improvements. For the year ending June 30, 1983, 12 state HFAs operated home improvement or energy conservation loan programs, originating a total of about 6,500 loans. Over time, states have made more than 56,000 home improvement loans, many with additional subsidies provided by state contributions or coordination with community development block grants.

The Internal Revenue Code treats tax-exempt financing for home improvement and energy loan programs under the same section as home purchase programs. Thus, these programs also fell victim to Congressional inaction on the December 31, 1983 sunset date and will not operate again until the tax exemption is reauthorized.

Community Development

Since the mid-1970s, the major program for community development across the country has been the Department of Housing and Urban Development's community development block grant program. Until recently, states had no role in this program. Block grants went straight from the federal government to local communities, on an entitlement basis for large cities and urban counties and on a competitive basis for small cities. States were completely bypassed in the process.

In 1981, Congress enacted legislation creating a fundamental change in the CDBG program. It authorized states to receive and distribute block grants for small cities, representing 30 percent of the total funds appropriated for the program annually.

In fiscal year 1983, 46 states (all but Hawaii, Kansas, Maryland and New York) administered the small cities CDBG program. They allocated grants totaling about $1.1 billion for housing, economic development, public works and other eligible uses. Each state develops its own program guidelines and selection process.

So far, states have received positive reviews for the job they have done. The General Accounting Office has issued a report titled "States are Making Good Progress in Implementing the Small Cities Community Development Block Grant Program." Based on a study of seven state programs, the GAO report observes that "the majority of grantees and unsuccessful applicants perceived their state's program as being equivalent to or better than HUD's program."

STATE HOUSING FINANCE AGENCIES

State or other jurisdiction	Enabling legislation adopted	1983 Bond Issues		Cumulative Loans (through 6/83)		
		Owner-occupied (in millions)	Rental housing (in millions)	Home mortgage loans	Rental housing development	Home improvement loans
Alabama	1980	$200.0	$80.3	7,567	3,942	0
Alaska(a)	1971	200.0	31.4	4,155		0
Arizona	1981	113.5	0		0	0
Arkansas	1977	200.0	0	8,667	1,232	1,382
California	1975	312.0	54.6	12,334		903
Colorado	1973	149.2	12.9			
Connecticut.........	1969	200.0	0	31,400	10,194	104
Delaware	1968	32.8	9.3	4,160	2,710	0
Florida	1980	215.5	184.1	1,098	4,626	0
Georgia	1974	56.2	0	6,082	0	0
Hawaii	1979	141.0	0	2,237		0
Idaho	1972	90.0	3.7	5,792	2,020	727
Illinois	1967	198.5	54.7	981	15,054	0
Indiana.............	1978	200.0	2.4	5,478	369	0
Iowa	1979	24.6	0	4,947	1,928	0
Kansas(b)						
Kentucky	1972	69.9	0	19,964	4,170	0
Louisiana...........	1980	100.0	100.6	2,600	282	0
Maine	1969	124.2	0	7,800	4,455	1,808
Maryland	1970	142.0	40.4	6,809	9,840	1,424
Massachusetts	1968	200.0	26.0	5,118	38,516	0
Michigan	1966	200.0	37.1	10,979	32,980	10,477
Minnesota	1971	147.8	0	12,092	16,201	35,832
Mississippi	1980	127.2	0	3,734	0	0
Missouri............	1969	143.5	50.0	12,304	13,693	
Montana	1975	200.0	0	5,989	568	0
Nebraska	1978	199.9	4.4	6,207	557	750
Nevada	1975	100.0	16.6	4,934	2,619	0
New Hampshire	1975	60.0	0	8,555	2,142	0
New Jersey	1967	274.3	80.4	10,084	31,084	
New Mexico	1975	79.7	0	11,432	296	0
New York	1960	376.0	237.2	32,000	91,523	0
North Carolina	1973	189.0	28.6	4,111	2,268	
North Dakota	1980	120.0	0	144	498	0
Ohio	1983	410.0	0	5		0
Oklahoma	1975	199.6	63.5	4,300	2,910	400
Oregon.............	1973	0	0	8,174	4,616	0
Pennsylvania........	1972	176.6	19.4	9,850	17,500	0
Rhode Island........	1973	199.9	0	25,944	8,770	0
South Carolina	1971	99.8	0	7,600	704	0
South Dakota	1973	175.8	13.3	14,124	2,274	
Tennessee	1973	138.5	31.5	17,000	3,412	0
Texas	1979	238.8	764.0	3,196	3,265	0
Utah	1975	198.3	9.6	9,119	1,530	0
Vermont	1974	57.8	7.6	6,036	1,880	867
Virginia	1972	237.6	66.4	22,778	16,652	621
Washington	1983	193.5	0	0	0	0
West Virginia	1968	38.8	0	6,753	8,453	0
Wisconsin	1972	195.0	3.1	6,185	14,546	5,266
Wyoming...........	1975	200.0	0	8,126	0	0
Dist. of Col.	1980	30.0	0	0	257	0

Source: Council of State Housing Agencies.

(a) Represents tax-exempt financing programs only; Alaska also operates large financing program with taxable bonds.
(b) Kansas does not have a state housing finance agency.

BUSINESS AND INDUSTRIAL DEVELOPMENT

Economic recovery is here. All the indicators are up: personal income, the GNP, employment and corporate profits. And all are expected to continue to rise through 1984. But a new era of tight budgets and sly taxes may also be here. Recovery or no, the Reagan administration cuts in aid to the states are not likely to be restored in the near future, and we may have entered an era of *de facto* New Federalism.

Indeed, the present situation may have been in the making for some while. The states have already moved ahead in areas once regarded as purely federal domains: enterprise zone legislation and job training and retraining programs. In 1983, the Job Training Partnership Act and the Small Cities Community Development Block Grant further decentralized the process of economic development, making it more flexible and adaptable to the needs of both localities and business.

In 1983, as in 1982, budgets and taxes were the primary concern of state legislatures still adjusting to the effects of the Reagan funding cuts and the lingering damage of the recession. The states managed to avoid deficits by a combination of budget cuts and tax increases. In 1983, the states increased taxes by $10 billion. Twenty-six states increased taxes on personal income or sales or both, while 15 raised corporate income tax rates. Additional increases hit motor fuel, cigarettes and alcohol. In all, 35 states and the District of Columbia had increased taxes in at least one category by September of the year. Still, at year's end, a majority of the states had a balance in their treasuries of less than one percent of their annual expenditures.

States hard hit by unemployment and therefore hard pressed to fund their compensation programs scrambled to restructure them and pay back federal loans. The top borrower, Pennsylvania, set the pattern for other states when it cut benefits and raised unemployment taxes. Other states taking such actions included Louisiana, Michigan, Minnesota and Oklahoma.

The search for revenue led some states to a form of taxation far more onerous to corporate America than any ordinary increase in corporate income tax: the unitary tax. This method of assessment allows a state to tax a corporation not only on the basis of its assets and activities within state borders but also on total worldwide profits. California, which led the way with the unitary method, assesses a company's property, sales and payroll, in California and worldwide. The tax is then levied on the California fraction of worldwide income.

Some had hoped for relief from the unitary tax when Container Corp. of America challenged California in the U.S. Supreme Court in the summer of 1983, but the justices, by a five-to-three decision, ruled in favor of the state. The decision was a strong stance in support of states' rights, and business leaders who petitioned President Reagan met with a lukewarm response.

The president did, however, establish the Worldwide Unitary Taxation Working Group, headed by Secretary of the Treasury Donald Regan and consisting of representatives from federal and state governments, as well as members of multinational corporations, to review the issues at stake and make policy recommendations.

Besides California, 14 states employ some form of the unitary method of taxation: Alaska, Colorado, Florida, Idaho, Illinois, Indiana, Maine, Massachusetts, Minnesota, Montana, New Hampshire, North Dakota, Oklahoma, Oregon and Utah. New York repealed its unitary tax on June 26, the day before the Supreme Court ruled on *Container v. California*.

The federal government was also concerned with sources of revenue in 1983, and its efforts to raise taxes bore down hard on industrial revenue bonds, already under heavy attack for several years. The Tax Reform Act (H.R. 4170) was the major federal legislation affecting IRB financing. In its original form, H.R. 4170 would have ended the tax exemption for bond issues guaranteed by the federal government, modified the use of accelerated depreciation on IRB-financed projects, and disallowed IRB use for the purchase of land or existing facilities except in

This article was prepared by Conway Data, Inc., Atlanta, Georgia, based on data from *Industrial Development*, January/February 1984, copyright Conway Data, Inc., 1984.

cases of farmland or of the substantial rehabilitation and renovation of facilities.

But the heart of H.R. 4170 is a proposed $150 per capita state volume cap on tax-exempt, private purpose bond issues. Such a limit could have a detrimental effect on the growth of large and small businesses in most states. U.S. Treasury Department estimates of state IRB issues per capita in 1983 show that 12 states—24 percent of the country—met or exceeded the proposed cap, while an additional four came within a few dollars of it.

In a marathon session just before adjournment, the House Ways and Means and Rules committees achieved a compromise on H.R. 4170 that will remove multi-family housing IRBs from the state bond volume cap; continue to allow IRB use for buying land, but limit to 25 percent the amount of an issue's proceeds that may be used for this purpose; continue to allow IRB use for buying existing buildings, so long as proceeds equal to 15 percent of the structure's cost are used for rehabilitation; and continue to allow direct and indirect federal guarantees for multi-family IRBs and public housing bonds.

In other action, the Internal Revenue Service issued temporary regulations implementing the IRB restrictions included in the Tax Equity and Fiscal Responsibility Act (TEFRA) of 1982. The regulations concern TEFRA's public approval and information reporting requirements and call for a public hearing before bonds are issued and for their approval by voters or elected representatives.

Late in 1983, South Carolina challenged the reporting requirements of TEFRA in court, arguing that the registration requirements erode the states' power to borrow money and that they impose a tremendous financial burden on the states. Texas took the lead among the states supporting South Carolina and filed a brief on behalf of 26 other states.

Bills seeking to protect communities and states from the effects of business shutdowns by requiring prenotification of closing were few in number in 1983 and fared poorly before the state legislatures. Those that passed, such as Connecticut's nine-point job protection plan, sought to avoid restrictive or punitive regulation and to foster, instead, cooperation among the affected parties—business, labor and government.

Though federal enterprise zone legislation remains stalled, states and cities continue to move ahead in this experiment in urban restoration. In 1983, Alabama, Arkansas, Georgia, Minnesota, Mississippi, New Jersey, Ohio, Oklahoma and Texas joined the list of 14 states that had already enacted enterprise zone legislation.

The emerging industries of high technology also captured the attention of state governments in 1983. Fifteen states have established agencies to work solely toward attracting high technology industrial investment. Louisiana and New Jersey established venture capital programs and tax credits designed to appeal to high tech entrepreneurs. Minnesota, on the other hand, allocated $5.7 million for public school computer learning from kindergarten through the 12th grade.

On the darker side of high tech, both state and federal legislators confronted the question of how to safeguard electronically stored, processed and transmitted data. Among the states that have legislation to protect against data theft are Alabama, California, Maryland, Massachusetts, Pennsylvania, Tennessee and Virginia.

On balance, state government actions in 1983 favored business and may mark the beginning of a new era of healthy competition for industrial investment among the states. Placed in a fiscal vise by the worst economy in postwar history and cut loose from dependence on federal largess, the states have been forced to reexamine and redefine their own roles in the process of economic development. The result has been a more innovative and flexible attitude toward business generally and toward the actions government can take to create and sustain an environment conducive to growth.

Table 1
FINANCIAL ASSISTANCE FOR INDUSTRY

State or other jurisdiction	State-sponsored industrial development authority	Privately sponsored Development Credit Corporation	State authority or agency revenue bond financing	State authority or agency general obligation bond financing	City and/or county revenue bond financing	City and/or county general obligation bond financing	State loans for building construction	State loans for equipment/machinery	City and/or county loans for building construction	City and/or county loans for equipment/machinery	State loan guarantees for building construction	State loan guarantees for equipment/machinery	City and/or county loan guarantees for building construction	City and/or county loan guarantees for equipment/machinery	State financing aid for existing plant expansion	State matching funds for city and/or county industrial financing programs	State incentive for establishing industrial plants in areas of high unemployment	City and/or county incentive for establishing industrial plants in areas of high unemployment
Alabama	★(q)	★★			★★	★★(a)									★(b,j)	★		
Alaska	★★				★★	★★									★★			
Arizona	★	★★(e)	★(i)	★	★★	★★	★	★							★★★★(u)		★★	★★
Arkansas		★(d)			★★★★				★(a)	★(a)	★★(k)	★(k)			★★★(d)		★★(d)	★★(a)
California	★(d)	★★(d)			★★★★	★★(c)		★(u)	★★★(a)	★★★(a)	★★	★★			★★★(d)		★★★(r)	★★★
Colorado	★★	★	★★		★★★★	★★	★								★			★
Connecticut	★★	★★			★★★★				★	★					★			★★
Delaware			★★		★★★★	★★									★			
Florida	★★	★★★★	★★	★	★★★★	★★	★	★	★	★	★	★			★	★	★	★★★
Georgia	★★	★★★	★★		★★★★	★★★			★	★					★★		★★	★★★
Hawaii	★	★★★★	★		★★★★★										★			
Idaho		★★			★★★★★		★(u)	★(u)										
Illinois	★★	★★★	★★		★★★★★	★★	★	★	★	★	★	★			★★★		★★	★★★
Indiana	★★	★★	★		★★★★★										★			
Iowa		★			★★★★★										★		★	★★★
Kansas	★	★★★★	★	★	★★★★★	★★			★	★					★★		★	★★★
Kentucky	★	★★(d)	★★★		★★★★★	★★	★	★	★	★	★	★			★		★	★
Louisiana		★★★★★	★★★★		★★★★★	★★	★★★★(d)											
Maine	★★	★★★	★★★	★★	★★★★★	★★★	★★★		★★(t)		★★★(m)	★★★(m)			★★★★(b)	★(g)	★★★★	★★★★
Maryland	★	★★★	★★★(b)		★★★★★	★★★									★★★		★	★
Massachusetts	★★★	★★★★	★★★		★★★★★	★★									★★		★	★
Michigan	★★★	★★★★	★★★		★★★★★	★★									★★		★	★
Minnesota	★★★	★★★★	★★★	★★	★★★★★	★★★	★★★★(m)	★★★(m)	★★★(h)	★★★(h)	★★★(m)	★★★(m)			★★★★(b)	★★	★★★	★★★
Mississippi	★★★★	★★★★★	★	★★	★★★★★	★★	★★★(m)	★★(m)	★★(h)	★★	★★(m)	★★(m)			★★	★★	★	★★★
Missouri		★★★★	★★★★		★★★★★				★(o)									
Montana		★★★★	★★★★	★★	★★★★★										★★			★★★★
Nebraska	★	★★★★★	★★★★		★★★★★										★★★★		★★★★	★★★★
Nevada	★★	★★★★			★★★★★(v)				★★(v)	★(v)			★(v)	★(v)	★★(b)			★★(a)
New Hampshire	★★		★	★	★★★★★(i)	★★(i)			★★(i)	★(i)			★(v)	★(v)		★★		★
New Jersey	★★	★★★★	★★★★★		★★★★★		★	★	★★	★★	★★	★★			★★		★	★

New Mexico
New York
North Carolina
North Dakota
Ohio
Oklahoma
Oregon
Pennsylvania
Rhode Island
South Carolina
South Dakota
Tennessee
Texas
Utah
Vermont
Virginia
Washington
West Virginia
Wisconsin
Wyoming
Puerto Rico

Source: Adapted from copyrighted data supplied by Conway Data, Inc., Atlanta, Ga. 30341, U.S.A.

Key:
★—Yes
—No
(a) Permitted only in specified municipalities.
(b) State allows cities or counties to offer financial aid for existing plant expansions. In Louisiana, state financing aid is directly involved only in the case of those port authorities whose obligations are backed by the full faith and credit of the state.
(c) For public projects only (water, sewer treatment, etc.).
(d) Authorized but none is active.
(e) State-sponsored but privately operated non-profit Regional Job Development Corporations may be established in low-income areas to provide loans to small businesses.
(f) Available through the Minority Business Development Agency.
(g) Limited to EDA-designated areas.
(h) Permitted for processing products of agriculture, including forestry and timber production.
(i) Applies only to pollution control equipment.
(j) Alabama offers site grants of up to $150,000 to industries needing grading of land and roads; grants may also be applied toward drainage needs.
(k) Guarantee applies to Act 9 industrial revenue bonds up to $1 million.
(l) State and local program of participation in building construction.
(m) Small business program.
(n) For acquiring and developing sites.
(o) Authorized if a one-mill, multi-purpose tax levy is approved by local voters.
(p) State funds are available to local governments to help industry in the 16 poorest counties.
(q) State grants to assist in industrial site preparation.
(r) Corporate income tax credits of 50 percent of contributions to eligible community development projects, 25 percent of wages of employees hired from designated areas and an economic revitalization tax incentive credit to new or expanding business located in designated areas.
(s) In city of Portland and in Coos, Curry and Douglas counties from EDA revolving loan fund.
(t) Has been used in city of Baltimore.
(u) State manages federal SBA 503 program.
(v) By special statute in specified communities.

Table 2

TAX INCENTIVES FOR INDUSTRY AND OTHER PERTINENT LAWS

State or other jurisdiction	Corporate income tax exemption	Personal income tax exemption	Excise tax exemption	Tax exemption or moratorium on land capital improvements	Tax exemption or moratorium on equipment/machinery	Inventory tax exemption on goods in transit (free port)	Tax exemption on manufacturers' inventories	Sales/use tax exemption on new equipment	Tax exemption on raw materials used in manufacturing	Tax incentive for creation of jobs	Tax incentive for industrial investment	Tax credits for use of specified state products	Tax stabilization agreements for specified industries	Tax exemption to encourage research and development	Accelerated depreciation of industrial equipment	State right to work law	State minimum wage law	State fair employment practice code	Statewide uniform property tax evaluation law	Statewide industrial noise abatement law
Alabama	★	★	★★	★★	★	★	★	★★	★★★★★					★	★ (am)	★	★		★★★★★	
Alaska	★	★		★ (b)	★ (b)	★★★	★★★		★★★★★	★ (ay)		(c)			★★	★	★	★★	★	★
Arizona	★ (be)		(e)																★	★★
Arkansas	★ (a)	(f)	(e)	(b)	(b)	(w)	(w)	(bi)	(av)	(az)	(az)	★		(az)	(a)	★		★★★	★	
California	★	(p)	(e)		(d)			(v)			(g)			★	(aq)		★	★	★	★★
Colorado																				
Connecticut	★ (a)	★★	★★		★ (d)	★★★	★★★	★★★★★	★★★★★	(az) ★★★	(az) ★★★			★	★★★		★★★	★★★★★	★★★	★★
Delaware	★★					★★★	★★★			(g) ★★★	(g) ★★★				(a) ★★★			★	★★★	
Florida	★			(l)	(l)		(w)					(ak)			(bf)	★★		★★★★★	★★★	★
Georgia														(r)			★		★	★
Hawaii															★		★	★★	★★★★★	★
Idaho	★			(q) ★★	(t) ★★	(aw) ★★	(aw) ★★★	(ai) ★★	(av) ★★★	(z)	(q)				(am)	★	★	★	★★★	★
Illinois				(ax) ★★	(at)	(l)	(i)		(j) ★★						(am)		★	★★★	★★★★★	★
Indiana		★		★	★		(au)	(bg)	★★★★		(q)			★	(am)		★★★★	★★	★★★★	★
Iowa	★★ (h)			(n) ★★	(l) ★★	(l) ★★	(l) ★★	(m) ★★	(o) ★★						(am)		★★★	★★★★★	★
Kansas	★ (ar)			(k) ★★	(k) ★★	(l)	(au)	(bg)	(l) ★★	(z) (ba)	(z)				(am)		★★	★★★	★★★	★
Kentucky				(z) ★★	(t) ★★		(l)	★★★★★	(l) ★★		(z)				(a)	★	★★	★★★★★	★★★	★
Louisiana	★ (m)	★	★	(n) ★★	(at)				(av) ★★		(z)		★		(am)		★★		★★★	★★
Maine	★★	★				★★	★★	★★★							(am)		★★★	★★★	★★★	★
Maryland	★		★													★	★★	★★	★★★★★	★
Massachusetts	★★				★	★★★★★	★★★★	★★	★★★★★						(am)		★★	★★★	★★★	★
Michigan	★★	★★★	★		★	★★★★★	★★★★	★★	★★★★★		★★			★	(am)		★★★	★★★	★★★	★
Minnesota		★★★		(s) ★★	(t) ★★			(u)							(am)		★★★	★★★	★★★	★
Mississippi				(a)												★		★	★★★	
Missouri	★	★	★	★	★	★★★★★	★★★★★		★★★★★		★★★★			★		★		★★★	★★★★	
Montana	★ (p)	★	★★					★★ (v)		★ (p)					(am)		★★★★	★★★	★★★	★
Nebraska	★ (f)	★ (f)			★			★★ (v)			★		★	★	(am)	★★	★★★★★	★★★	★★★	★
Nevada	★	★ (f)	(e)													★★		★	★	
New Hampshire		★ (f)															★★★	★★★	★★★	
New Jersey				★	★ (at)	★★ (x)	★★★★★	★★	★★★	★	★				★ (at)		★★★★★	★★★★★	★★★★★	★★

New Mexico			★(aa,ab) ★(aa)	★(e)	★	★	★(ac)	★(ac)	★(ac)	★(ac)	★	★(aa)			★(ab)	★(am)	★ ★
New York					★	★	★(ac)	★(x)	★(bh)						★(r)	★(a)	★ ★
North Carolina					★(af)	★(ag)	★(ac)	★(ac)	★(ac)	★(ad)							★ ★
Ohio		★								★(ae)							★
Oklahoma					★	★(ag)	★(ah)	★(ai)	★(ai)			★(bb)				★(am)	★ ★
Oregon				★(ag)												★(a)	
Pennsylvania	★(bd)	★			★(ag)	★(ah)	★(ai)	★(ai)	★(ai)	★(ah)							★ ★
Rhode Island																	★
South Carolina																	
South Dakota	★(f)	★(f)			★	★(l)	★(l)	★(l)	★(y)	★(as)	★(bc)						★
Tennessee	★(f)	★(f)			★	★(al)	★(al)	★(al)			★(ak)						★ ★
Utah																	★
Vermont	★(e)																
Virginia	★(f)	★(f)			★	★(l)	★(l)	★(y)	★(y)	★(an)	★(bi)	★(bi)			★(ao)	★(am)	★
Washington	★(f)	★(f)			★												★
West Virginia	★(ap)																
Wisconsin	★(f)	★(f)			★												★
Wyoming																	★
Puerto Rico																	

Source: Adapted from copyrighted data supplied by Conway Data, Inc., Atlanta, Ga. 30341, U.S.A.

Key:

★—Yes

⋮—No

(a) Applies only to pollution control equipment.

(b) Exempt using Act 9 in some cities.

(c) Seven year ad valorem tax exemption on textile plants.

(d) Equipment and machinery acquired after the 1973 assessment date is exempt from local property tax.

(e) Delaware, Florida and New York do not collect an excise tax.

(f) Nevada, South Dakota, Texas, Washington and Wyoming do not tax corporate or personal income. Connecticut, Florida and New Hampshire do not tax personal income.

(g) Corporate income tax credit equal to 25 percent of wages paid by business employing residents from designated areas and a corporate income tax credit for investment in new or expanded business in designated areas.

(h) Fifty percent of federal tax paid is exempt from corporate income tax on profits from sales outside Iowa. Corporate income tax is figured only on profits from sales in Iowa. Iowa has adopted the Federal Accelerated Cost Recovery System.

(i) Personal property taxes are being phased out. First $175,000 of assessed taxable value of personal property is exempt. An additional exemption is added by the county, and the amount varies by county.

(j) Inventory, goods in process and finished goods are taxed only the value of raw materials.

(k) Applicable to Industrial Revenue Bond financed property only. A 10-year exemption is allowed.

(l) In Kentucky, the exemption is applicable at the local level only. In Maryland, the exemption may be applicable at the county or local level. In Tennessee, the exemption is applicable to plants financed with industrial revenue bonds. In Virginia localities have the option of totally or partially exempting certified pollution control, facilities and equipment, certified solar energy equipment and facilities and energy conversion equipment of manufacturers from taxation. In Florida, the exemption is a local option, and school and special district taxes are excluded from the exemption.

(m) Applicable under the tax equalization law, Enterprise Zone Act and Flood, Fire and Famine Act.

(n) Exemption applicable to capital improvements only.

(o) Allowed except for sales/use tax when purchased for use as an ingredient in tangible personal property for sale.

(p) A 1 percent tax credit, based on wages paid, is allowed for the first three years to new and expanding industry engaged in the mechanical or chemical transformation of materials or substances into new products. "Expanding" means to expand a present operation so as to increase total permanent jobs by 30 percent.

(q) Ten year partial property tax abatement in designated areas of all cities and towns for renovation or new construction of facilities.

(r) R&D equipment is classified as manufacturer's machinery and equipment and, as such, is eligible for tax exemptions.

(s) Local option, in designated redevelopment areas.

(t) For industrial access roads only.

(u) Exemption is allowed on separate, detachable accessory tools and equipment which have a useful life of less than 12 months.

(v) State does not collect sales/use tax.

(w) State has no inventory tax.

(x) Applicable to goods stored in bonded warehouses.

(y) Applies to imported goods if they have not lost their status as imports and to inventory which is imported or scheduled for export and is located in a foreign trade zone.

(z) Limited to state designated enterprise zones.

(aa) A tax credit equal to 6 percent of qualified capital invested in new production facilities may be applied against the business corporate franchise tax or personal income tax liability. The tax credit is restricted to investment in buildings, equipment and facilities which have a useful life of at least four years and are used in manufacturing, processing, assembling, refining, mining, agricultural, commercial, fishing or specified retail activities. Experimental research and development facilities may elect this option in place of the write-off described in footnote (ab). A particular investment is not eligible for both the investment credit and other state tax incentives, except that eligible firms maintaining or increasing employment in the state may deduct an additional credit of one-half of the original credit in each of the three years succeeding the investment. This results in a potential credit of 15 percent over four years. Corporate franchise taxpayers must pay the minimum tax of $250 but may carry unused credits forward until exhausted. New firms may elect to receive as a refund any unused part of the earned tax credit.

(ab) Costs paid or incurred in a taxable year by incorporated business for experimental R&D facilities, for industrial waste treatment facilities and/or for air pollution control facilities may be deducted

TAX INCENTIVES FOR INDUSTRY AND OTHER PERTINENT LAWS—Continued

from net income for tax purposes. The credit described in footnote (aa) may be taken in lieu of this credit. In lieu of all other credits, a firm may take a credit against the corporate franchise/income tax of 10 percent of the cost of tangible personal property purchased for R&D use.

(ac) Tangible and intangible personal property is not subject to ad valorem taxes.

(ad) Manufacturing machinery is allowed a preferential rate of 1 percent, with a maximum tax of $80 per article.

(ae) Leaf tobacco is allowed an exemption of 40 percent of property tax rate, and peanuts an 80 percent exemption. No property tax exemption is allowed for other raw materials. All raw materials used in manufacturing are exempt from sales and use tax.

(af) In North Dakota, exemption extends only to new construction. In Oregon, exemption is allowed while facility is under construction only.

(ag) Tax credits allowed to manufacturers and processors for property taxes paid on goods in process.

(ah) Exclusion from sales and use tax on industrial purchases used directly in industrial production and research.

(ai) Exclusion of tangible personal property from taxation at local level. State has no inventory tax.

(aj) Phased exemption; fully exempt by 1984.

(ak) In Tennessee, tax credits are allowed for products of state soil. In Florida, tax credit applies only to alcoholic beverages produced from specified Florida-grown agricultural products.

(al) Seven-year annexation or de-annexation exemption.

(am) Allowable depreciation is similar to that which is permitted under federal laws.

(an) Exempt from sales/use tax, but not from intangible personal property tax.

(ao) Local governments may classify separately the tangible personal property of research and development firms from that of other taxpayers and tax it at different rates. Sales and use tax exemptions are allowed for research and development.

(ap) A credit is allowed for sales tax paid on energy.

(aq) Carried out through local development corporations.

(ar) An income tax credit is allowed for a period of 10 years against the income taxes generated by the operation of a new business activity. The credit is based on the number of new jobs created as well as the capital investment involved.

(as) Raw materials for processing are exempt from sales and use taxes. However, a personal property inventory tax is levied at the local level on raw materials a manufacturer has on hand on January 1. Finished goods are exempt from taxation.

(at) Seventy percent reduction on property tax on newly acquired computers and manufacturing equipment/machinery.

(au) Applicable to goods stored in licensed and bonded warehouse, provided that 35 percent or more of the previous year's sales or shipments from the storage area were shipped in interstate commerce to a point outside the state.

(av) Sales/use tax exemption.

(aw) Finished goods stored in public or private warehouses destined for out-of-state shipment are exempt.

(ax) Five-year local option tax exemption on new industrial building construction and expansions.

(ay) Targeted jobs tax credit program.

(az) Connecticut Urban Jobs Program, available in 18 "distressed" and 29 "high unemployment" communities.

(ba) $100 per job created by any business enterprise. However, in high unemployment areas $225 per job can be credited. The Rural Enterprise Zone Act allows a tax credit of $2,500 per job.

(bb) A gross production tax on textile mills in lieu of property tax.

(bc) One percent of investment in industrial machinery against corporate excise tax. Fully effective July 1, 1984.

(bd) Pennsylvania has adopted ACRS.

(be) A $100 credit for each employee hired because of new plant location or a plant expansion. Total yearly credit may be up to 50 percent of corporate tax and may be carried over three years.

(bf) State corporate tax code is "piggy-backed" to the federal internal revenue code.

(bg) Applicable to permanent or fixed property financed with industrial revenue bonds.

(bh) No exemption, but limited income tax credit allowed where qualifying inventories are excessive.

(bi) Applies in urban enterprise zones.

Table 3
SPECIAL SERVICES FOR INDUSTRIAL DEVELOPMENT

State or other jurisdiction	State financed speculative building	City and/or county financed speculative building	State provides free land for industry	Cities and/or counties provide freeland for industry(a)	State-owned industrial park sites	City and/or county-owned industrial park sites	State funds for city and/or county development-related public works projects	State funds for city and/or county master plans	State funds for city and/or county recreational projects	State funds for private recreational projects	State program to promote research and development	State program to increase export of products	University R&D facilities available to industry	State and/or universities conduct feasibility studies to attract or assist new industry	State recruiting, screening of industrial employees	State supported training of industrial employees	State re-training of industrial employees	State supported training of "hard-core" unemployed	State incentive to industry to train "hard-core" unemployed	State help in bidding on federal procurement contracts	State science and/or technology advisory council
Alabama	★	★		(c)★	★	★	★	★	★		★	★	★	★	★	★	★	★			★
Alaska	★			(c)★		★			★		★	★	★	★	★	★	★		★		★
Arizona	★			(c)★		★	★	★	★		★	★	★	★	★	★	★				★
Arkansas		(c)★		(c)★		★	★	★	★		★	★	★	★	★	★	★	★	★		★
California		(c)★		★		★			★	★	★	★	★	★	★	★	★	★	★	★	
Colorado		(c)★		(c)★		★					★	★	★	★	★	★	★		★	★	★
Connecticut		★			★	★		(d)★	★	★	★	★	★	★	★	★	★	★	★	★	★
Delaware	★			★		★	(q)★	★		(r)★	★	★	(e)★	★	★	★	★	(f)★		★	★
Florida						★					★	★	★	★	★	★	★	★	★	★	
Georgia				(c)★		★			★		★	★	★	★	★	★	★	★	★	★	★
Hawaii						★					★	★	★	★	★	★	★			★	★
Idaho				(c)★		★			★	(j)★	★	★	(h)★	★	★	★	★		★	★	
Illinois	(a)★			(i)★		★				(k)★	★	★		★	★	★	★		★	★	★
Indiana	★			(i)★		★					★	★	(e)★	★	★	★	★	★	★	★	★
Iowa	(s)★			(c)★		★					★	★	★	★	★	★	★			★	
Kansas		(g)★		(c)★		★			★		★	★	★	★	★	★	★		★	★	★
Kentucky	(a)★			(l)★		★			★		★	★	★	★	★	★	★	★	★	★	★
Louisiana	★			(i)★		★					★	★	★	★	★	★	★		★	★	★
Maine						★					★	★	★	★	★	★	★		★	★	★
Maryland						★					★	★	★	★	★	★	★		★	★	★
Massachusetts						★			★		★	★	★	★	★	★	★		★	★	★
Michigan				(l)★		★					★	★	★	★	★	★	★			★	★
Minnesota						★		★			★	★	★	★	★	★	★	★	★	★	★
Mississippi						★			★		★	★	★	★	★	★	★			★	★
Missouri						★						★	★	★	★	★	★			★	★
Montana				(c)★		★	(m)★	★(m)				★	★	★	★	★	★		★	★	★
Nebraska		(g)★				★	★	★	★		★	★	★	★	★	★	★				★
Nevada						★					★	★	★	★	★	★	★		★	★	★
New Hampshire	★				★	★		★		★	★	★	★	★	★	★	★	★	★	★	★
New Jersey	★				★	★	★	★	★		★	★	★	★	★	★	★	★	★	★	★

SPECIAL SERVICES FOR INDUSTRIAL DEVELOPMENT—Continued

State or other jurisdiction	State financed speculative building	City and/or county financed speculative building	State provides free land for industry	Cities and/or counties provide freeland for industry(a)	State-owned industrial park sites	City and/or county-owned industrial park sites	State funds for city and/or county development-related public works projects	State funds for city and/or county master plans	State funds for city and/or county recreational projects	State funds for private recreational projects	State program to promote research and development	State program to increase export of products	University R&D facilities available to industry	State and/or universities conduct feasibility studies to attract or assist new industry	State recruiting, screening of industrial employees	State supported training of industrial employees	State re-training of industrial employees	State supported training of "hard-core" unemployed	State incentive to industry to train "hard-core" unemployed	State help in bidding on federal procurement contracts	State science and/or technology advisory council
New Mexico	·	★	·	·	★	★	·	·	·	·	★	★	★	★	★	★	★	★	★	★	★
New York	·	★	·	·	·	★	★	★	★	·	★	★	★	★	★	★	★	★	·	★	★
North Carolina	★	★	·	·	·	★	★	·	★	·	★	★	★	★	★	★	★	★	★	★	★
North Dakota	★	★	·	★	·	★	★	★	★	·	★	★	★	★	★	★	★	★	·	★	★
Ohio	·	·	·	·	·	·	★	·	★	·	★	★	★	★	★	★	★	★	·	★	·
Oklahoma	·	★	·	★	★	★	★(b)	★	★	·	★	★	★	★	★	★	★	★	★	★	★
Oregon	·	·	·	★	·	★	★(b)	·	★	·	★	★	★	★	★	★	★	·	·	★	★
Pennsylvania	★(t)	·	·	★(u)	★	★	★	★	★	·	★	★	★	★	★	★	★	★	★	★	★
Rhode Island	·	·	·	·	·	★	★	★	★	·	★	★	★	★	★	★	★	★	★	★	★
South Carolina	·	★	·	★(c)	★	★	★	★	★	·	★	★	★	★	★	★	★	★	★	·	★
South Dakota	★	★	·	·	★	★	·	·	★	·	★	·	★	★	★	★	★	★	★	★	★
Tennessee	·	·	·	·	·	★	·	★	★	·	★	★	★	★	★	★	★	★	★	★	★
Texas	★	★	·	·	·	★	·	★	★	·	★	★	★	★	★	★	★	★	★	★	★
Utah	·	·	·	·	★	★	·	★	★	·	★	★	★	★	★	★	★	·	·	★	★
Vermont	★	·	·	·	·	★	★(o)	★(p)	★	·	★	★	★	★	★	★	★	★	·	★	·
Virginia	·	★(g)	·	·	·	★(g)	★	·	★	·	★	★	★	★	★	★	★	★	·	·	★
Washington	·	·	·	·	·	★(n)	★	★	★	★	★	★	★	★	★	★	★	★	★	★	★
West Virginia	·	·	·	·	·	★	★	·	★	·	★	·	★	★	★	★	★	★	·	★	★
Wisconsin	·	·	·	·	·	★	★	·	★	★	★	★	★	★	★	★	★	★	·	·	★
Wyoming	·	·	·	·	·	·	·	·	·	·	·	·	★	★	★	★	★	·	·	★	·
Puerto Rico	★	·	★	·	·	·	★	·	★	·	★	★	★	★	★	★	★	★	★	★	★

Source: Adapted from copyrighted data supplied by Conway Data, Inc., Atlanta, Ga. 30341, U.S.A.

Key:
★—Yes
·—No

(a) Authorized but none is active.
(b) For industrial access roads only.
(c) Provided only in rare instances. In California, a few cities and counties will lease land they own at nominal rates.
(d) Limited to technical assistance.
(e) Facilities available on contract basis.
(f) State vocational education program keyed to federally funded program.
(g) Carried out through local development corporations.
(h) Available to industry on a contract and/or consulting basis.
(i) City-owned land only. Cities may not purchase land for purpose of providing free land to industry.
(j) Highway Commission will build first two miles of road into new ski areas.
(k) Maryland Industrial Development Financing Authority will guarantee up to 80 percent of the mortgages for land and 70 percent for equipment for recreational projects.
(l) Activity limited to certain units.
(m) A coal tax fund is available to areas directly impacted by coal development.
(n) Port districts only.
(o) Funds are from Public Health for solid wastes disposal projects.
(p) State matches funds from U.S. Department of Housing and Urban Development.
(q) Specially appropriated funds for economic development road projects and other targeted projects.
(r) State matching funds for private non-profit organizations for recreational projects.
(s) State pays interest on spec buildings until they have been sold or leased.
(t) Pennsylvania provides loans for small business incubators on a limited basis.
(u) Selectively, in Pittsburgh and Philadelphia.

6. NATURAL RESOURCES

ENVIRONMENTAL MANAGEMENT: EMERGING ISSUES

By Jon Grand

The 1970s were characterized by expanding fiscal, legislative and program commitments to the protection and enhancement of the nation's land, air and water resources. Backed by strong legislation and grant dollars, the states expanded their programs in a variety of environmental areas. The state role, as envisioned in the legislation and as it actually evolved, was to take the lead in program implementation and enforcement with the federal government providing technical assistance, program oversight and enforcement backup. Within the context of a nationally defined set of goals and standards, the states were free to develop programs to solve their individual environmental problems.

However, at the beginning of the 1980s, the intense interest in and support of environmental programs at the national level began to wane. Under the guise of a New Federalism both the federal role and the available federal dollars to support state programs diminished with no concurrent decrease in mandated state activities. The result was the gradual overburdening of state resources and capabilities in environmental management.

Recently, however, environmental management has again been thrust into the forefront of national concern. Alleged improprieties related to the cleanup of hazardous waste sites focused attention on both the threat posed by the improper disposal of hazardous materials and on the manner in which the U.S. Environmental Protection Agency was carrying out its responsibilities. Concerns about acid rain, groundwater contamination and a host of other issues further attracted the attention of Congress just as the major pieces of environmental legislation were scheduled for reauthorization.

The result has been a close scrutiny of the existing legislation and an aggressive attempt to tighten existing loopholes during the reauthorization process. Coupled with a better knowledge of environmental management, this will mean new and increased responsibilities at both the state and federal levels. It will be the challenge of the 1980s to maintain the quality of current programs while advancing into new areas.

Water Quality[1]

The federal Clean Water Act faces an uncertain reauthorization course through Congress in 1984. The Federal Water Pollution Control Act of 1972 amended by the Clean Water Act of 1977 and the Safe Drinking Water Act of 1974 are the keystones of the nation's water quality program.

The Clean Water Act provided a comprehensive approach to water quality management through the establishment of water quality standards, the development of stream classification systems, the implementation of a pollution discharge permit system, the provision of grants for the construction of wastewater treatment facilities, and the encouragement of water quality management and planning activities.

The Clean Water Act is the oldest and most ambitious of the major pieces of environmental legislation. The current reauthorization process allows both the states and the Congress an opportunity to fine tune the nation's water quality management program. In particular, the reauthorization process has focused on: nonpoint sources of pollution; pretreatment; dredge and fill activities; delegation of the National Pollution Discharge Elimination System (the discharge permits); and elimination of toxic discharges. Before reauthorization proceeds, these issues must be resolved.

Water Problems

Nonpoint Sources of Pollution. Nonpoint sources contribute pollutants from diffuse rather than specific origins. In spite of the progress made in controlling point source discharges, nonpoint sources continue to significantly affect water quality in many areas of the country. One fifth of the states reported in 1982 that eliminating nonpoint sources of pollution would mean identifying particular kinds of problem activities (for example, farming practices that cause polluting run-off) as well as specific site controls.[2]

Financing. The funding of construction and rehabilitation of water and wastewater treatment facilities continues to concern both the states

---

Jon Grand is Program Manager for Environment and Natural Resources for The Council of State Governments.

and the federal government. According to the U.S. EPA needs survey,[3] the capital investment required to meet water quality goals through construction or rehabilitation of wastewater treatment plants will be $19 billion between 1980 and the year 2000. The costs of financing the repair and replacement of urban water supply and treatment facilities are equally staggering: ranging from $80 to $115 billion by the year 2000.

Groundwater. With 50 percent of the nation's population currently dependent on groundwater as the primary source of fresh water, widespread and repeated reports of groundwater contamination have caused increasing alarm. The federal groundwater programs are now fragmented between a number of different program areas including water quality, drinking water and hazardous waste. The inconsistencies are repeated as state programs attempt to mirror the requirements of the various federal program areas. In January 1984, the U.S. EPA released a draft of its groundwater strategy paper. This strategy represents a necessary first step toward a comprehensive groundwater policy but stops short of supplying the detail necessary to help the states develop realistic, compatible groundwater management strategies.

Air Quality

The Clean Air Act of 1970, as amended in 1977, was due for reauthorization in 1981, but remains stalled while Congress considers the State Implementation Process (SIP), mobile sources, Prevention of Significant Deterioration (PSD) requirements, long-range transport of pollutants, and state-federal roles.

However, the reauthorization process has not been stymied by any of these issues. The sticking point has been, and continues to be, acid rain.

Acid Rain. The long-range transport of air pollutants, particularly those contributing to the formation of acid precipitation, has become a major interstate, interregional and international concern. Approximately one-half of the sulfur emissions deposited in Eastern Canada are said to originate in the United States. Emissions from the urban areas of Los Angeles and San Francisco are blamed for acid depositions in the Sierra Nevada. In the Colorado Rockies, damage resulting from acid precipitation on the western slope is said to originate at coal-fired electrical generating plants in the Four Corners region.[4]

Research into the causes and effects of acid rain continues, as do demands for legislation to deal with the problem. The Reagan administration, despite the recommendations of its own Office of Science and Technology and the National Academy of Sciences, continues to advocate further research and study before defining steps to reduce sulfur emissions.

A wide range of legislative proposals have been introduced in the Congress, running the gamut from urging additional research to requiring specific reductions of sulfur emissions. Supporters of the alternatives reflect the regional interests of their constituencies. Thus, while the scientific complexity of the issue hampers the development of an easily defined response, the political and economic issues create a climate unfavorable to the necessary political compromise.

It now appears that no major acid rain legislation will be forthcoming until late 1984 or 1985. In the meantime, the reauthorization of the Clean Air Act will continue to be stymied.

Solid and Hazardous Waste[5]

Solid and hazardous wastes are dealt with through two major pieces of legislation: the Resource Conservation and Recovery Act of 1976 (RCRA) and the Comprehensive Environmental Response Compensation and Liability Act of 1980 (CERCLA also called Superfund). Both are currently before Congress for reauthorization. Hazardous wastes tend to resist decomposition and can persist in the environment in a highly toxic state for years.

The Resource Conservation and Recovery Act of 1976. RCRA established the regulatory framework for the proper disposal of waste materials. Under Subtitle C of the act, hazardous wastes were regulated from "cradle to grave" through the control of the generation, transportation and disposal of hazardous materials. Both houses of Congress currently are considering reauthorization bills that seek to plug existing loopholes and spur the promulgation of necessary regulations.

One major concern is to bring the small quantity generators (defined as those producing less than 1,000 kilograms per month) under the control of the legislation. With at least 130,000 small businesses generating wastes from painting solvents to dry cleaning agents, the problem is too large to ignore any longer.

Other concerns being addressed through the reauthorization process include banning the disposal of EPA-listed hazardous wastes in landfills, prohibiting the use of surface impoundments for disposal, and restricting the disposal of wastes through incineration. Congress is also considering legislatively mandated regulations if EPA fails to promulgate regulations within specified time limits.

The chances for passage of a reauthorization RCRA bill during 1984 appear good. However, the impact of the proposed changes on the states remains in question. As envisioned by the bills currently pending, a greater workload would fall to the state agencies without significantly increased funding. Recently offered amendments seek to incorporate the state funding concerns, but the final resolution is still in doubt.

The Comprehensive Environmental Response Compensation and Liability Act. CERCLA or, more commonly, Superfund, created a five-year, $1.6 billion fund for use in event of spills of hazardous substances or to clean up leaking disposal facilities. The fund will be used to clean up approximately 400 sites nationwide, although it is estimated that the total number of sites requiring Superfund dollars could range from 1,000 to 2,000. The fund is paid for by a tax on generators (87.5 percent) and federal appropriations (12.5 percent). Reimbursements by responsible parties to the federal government also will go into the fund, along with any damage awards. The Superfund law envisions that the costs of clean up will be borne by the responsible parties. These parties may pay for the clean up themselves or reimburse the government for the costs.

In order to ensure that the most serious threats were dealt with first, EPA developed the National Priority List. However, the 546 currently listed sites represent only a fraction of the potential sites which may contain hazardous materials. The priority sites were identified using a ranking system which evaluated the immediacy and magnitude of the threat posed by the site. The list is updated on a regular basis.

In order to trigger remedial action, a state must assure that: (1) the site will be maintained in the future; (2) there is off-site disposal capability; and (3) that it will pay 10 percent of the costs (50 percent if the site was state or locally owned).

A major concern to some states is whether the federal Superfund preempts states' collection of fees and taxes to support state funds. New Jersey's spill compensation and control fund surcharge collection is currently being challenged by five petrochemical companies. The outcome of the New Jersey case leaves the legal status of many state funds in question. Florida has reacted by adding language to its state fund indicating that it will not be used in a manner inconsistent with CERCLA. State laws authorizing the establishment of trust funds often spell out the funding source. California recently enacted Superfund legislation in response to a 1980 state survey which identified 67 hazardous waste sites in need of clean-up. The $100 million California fund, to be collected over the next 10 years, will be supported entirely by industry-paid fees on hazardous waste disposal. Several states can activate their funds to provide for emergency response and clean up. Other funds, as in Kentucky and Massachusetts, have been set up to also encourage volume reduction and alternatives to land disposal of hazardous wastes.

A number of issues are being examined during the reauthorization of CERCLA. Of these, the most critical to the states include state matching fund requirements and victim compensation.

The requirements for state matching funds have meant no activity at many sites simply because states lack the necessary match dollars. In 1983, EPA waived its requirements that the states match 10 percent of the initial investigation costs, although they still must contribute to costs of clean up. Proposed changes would allow those costs to be offset by crediting of costs incurred by the states at hazardous waste sites in the three years before enactment of CERCLA.

Originally, CERCLA provided a mechanism to help compensate victims of hazardous materials contamination or exposure. However, those provisions were deleted, forcing victims to the courts for protracted hearings and subject to current statutes of limitations. However, the Congress did mandate a study on the adequacy of existing remedies. That report, along with a report from the Environmental Law Institute, urged a plan that would ease the problems of compensating victims.

Summary

States, chafing under federal requirements on standards and administration, have long argued for a greater state voice and flexibility in design and implementation of environmental programs. The expanded responsibilities thrust upon the states provide a test of their capability to plan, manage and finance environmental programs. States have the potential to assume an expanded role in environmental policy development and problem-solving, and they have demonstrated a capacity to deal with environmental and natural resource problems with realism and moderation. Many pioneered innovations later adopted for national use. With immediate knowledge of particular environmental problems, states can implement programs and target investments far more effectively than federal programs and agencies.

Less optimism can be voiced over states' capability to support environmental management activities at levels commensurate with federal programs. Even with savings through more efficient program administration, individual states are unlikely to have the financial resources to substitute for federal funds. Federal money has supported technical staff, planning and research activities, and basic environmental management programs. States have depended upon federal agencies and federally sponsored research for data gathering, issue analyses and technical assistance. Reductions in federal direct and indirect assistance, combined with revenue and spending limitations in the states, cast uncertainty on the ease with which states can assume expanded responsibilities to manage and enforce environmental programs.

As the states take on expanded responsibilities for environmental programs, several issues continue to cloud the state-federal partnership. States remain concerned over the terms and speed with which federal programs incorporating national objectives are being transferred. The prospective size and timing of reduced federal support create problems for an orderly transfer and stable management of programs. The degree of administrative flexibility and the access to new funding sources remain unknown. Redefining the federal-state partnership in environmental management will be a major task confronting the states in the upcoming years.

Notes

1. This section is based on Linda Eichmiller and Jon Grand, "Congress Considers the Clean Water Act," *State Government News* (March 1984): 12-13, 18.

2. Testimony of William Ruckelshaus, Administrator, U.S. EPA, before the Subcommittee on Water Resources, U.S. House of Representatives Committee on Public Works and Transportation, November 15, 1983.

3. George Peterson, "Clean Water: The Financing Gap," in *Funding Clean Water*, H. Clyde Reeves, ed. (Lexington, Mass.: Lexington Books, 1984).

4. Anne Stubbs and Leslie Cole, "Environmental Management," *The Book of the States, 1982-83* (Lexington, Ky.: The Council of State Governments, 1982), p. 596.

5. Parts of this section appeared in John Cromwell and Jon Grand, "Hazardous Waste Controls Up for a Change in Congress," *State Government News* (April 1984): 14-16.

Table 1
STATE ENVIRONMENTAL ORGANIZATIONS

State	Date of reorganization	Health department(a)	Little EPA(b)	Environmental superagency(c)	Partially consolidated or unconsolidated agency	Citizen environmental council/ commission
Alabama	1982	...	...	★	...	...
Alaska	1971	...	...	★	...	...
Arizona	...	★	...	...	...	★
Arkansas	1971	...	★	...	...	...
California	1975	...	...	...	★	...
Colorado	...	★	...	...	...	...
Connecticut	1971	...	...	★	...	...
Delaware	1970	...	...	★	...	...
Florida	1969	...	★	...	...	...
Georgia	1972	...	...	★	...	...
Hawaii	...	★	...	...	...	★
Idaho	1972	★	...	...	...	...
Illinois	1970	★	★	...	...	...
Indiana	...	★	★	...	...	...
Iowa	1972	...	★	...	...	...
Kansas	1974	★	...	...	...	★
Kentucky	1973	...	...	★	...	★
Louisiana	1982	...	...	★	...	★
Maine	1971	...	★	...	...	...
Maryland	1969	★	...	...	...	...
Massachusetts	1969	...	...	★	...	...
Michigan	1973	...	...	★	...	...
Minnesota	1967	...	★	...	...	...
Mississippi	1979	...	...	★	...	...
Missouri	1974	...	...	★	...	★
Montana	1971	★	...	...	...	★
Nebraska	1971	...	★	...	...	★
Nevada	1975	...	★	...	...	★
New Hampshire	1980	...	★	...	...	★
New Jersey	1970	...	...	★	...	...
New Mexico	1971	★	...	...	...	...
New York	1970	...	...	★	...	...
North Carolina	1977	...	...	★	...	★
North Dakota	...	★	...	...	...	...
Ohio	1972	...	★	...	...	...
Oklahoma	...	★	...	...	...	...
Oregon	1969	...	★	...	...	...
Pennsylvania	1970	...	...	★	...	...
Rhode Island	1977	...	...	★	...	...
South Carolina	1973	★	...	...	...	★
South Dakota	1981	...	...	★	...	...
Tennessee	...	★	...	...	...	★
Texas	...	...	...	...	★	★
Utah	...	★	...	...	...	...
Vermont	1970	...	...	★	...	...
Virginia	...	...	...	...	★	...
Washington	1971	...	...	★	...	...
West Virginia	...	...	...	...	★	...
Wisconsin	1967	...	...	★	...	...
Wyoming	1973	...	★	...	...	★

Key:
★—Yes
...—No

(a) Health Department Model: 15 states currently include their pollution control programs within their state health or health and human resources department. While a few states have chosen explicitly to consolidate their previously fragmented pollution control programs within a reorganized health department, in most states this model represents the historical relationship between environmental protection programs and public health considerations.

(b) Little EPA Model: 12 states currently have what might be called little EPAs because they mirror the U.S. Environmental Protection Agency in their program responsibilities.

(c) Environmental Superagency Model: 19 states consolidate their pollution control functions into an environmental superagency, defined as the inclusion of the three major pollution control programs with at least one other state conservation or development program.

Table 2
HAZARDOUS WASTE FACILITY SITING

| State | Agency responsible | Date of siting legislation | Under law, siting must consider: | | | |
			Surface water	Ground-water	Geology	Physical/chemical studies
Alabama	Dept. of Environ. Mgmt., Land Div.	1981	...	...	...	...
Alaska	Dept. of Environ. Conservation					
Arizona	Dept. of Health Serv., Div. of Environ. Health	1980, amended '81, '82	★	★	★	★
Arkansas	Dept. of Pollution Control & Ecology	1979	...	...	...	...
California	Dept. of Health Serv., Toxic Substance Control Div.	1982	★	★	...	...
Colorado	Dept. of Health, Waste Mgmt. Div.	1981, amended '83	★	★	★	★
Connecticut	Dept. of Environ. Protection (administers RCRA); Siting Council (approves new sites or modifications); Hazardous Waste Mgmt. Serv. (inventories generators and identifies sites)	1981	★	★	★	★
Delaware	Dept. of Natural Res. & Environ. Control	1980	...	...	...	...
Florida	Dept. of Environ. Reg.	1983	...	...	...	...
Georgia	Dept. of Natural Res., Environ. Protection Div.	1972, 1981	...	★	...	...
Hawaii	Dept. of Health, Environ. Protection & Health Serv. Div.	None	...	...	...	...
Idaho	Dept. of Health, Welfare, Div. of Environ.	None	...	...	...	...
Illinois	Environ. Protection Agency	1982	...	...	...	...
Indiana	State Bd. of Health; Solid Waste Site Approval Authority	1981	...	★	...	...
Iowa	Dept. of Water, Air & Waste Mgmt.	1981	...	...	★	...
Kansas	Dept. of Health & Environ.	1983	...	...	...	...
Kentucky	Dept. of Natural Res. & Environ. Protection	None	...	...	...	...
Louisiana	Dept. of Environ. Affairs	1979	★	★	★	★
Maine	Dept. of Environ. Protection	1983	★	★	★	★
Maryland	Hazardous Waste Siting Bd.	1980	★	★	★	★
Massachusetts	Dept. of Environ. Mgmt.; Dept. of Environ. Quality Engineering; Hazardous Waste Facility Site Safety Council	1980	★	★	★	★
Michigan	Dept. of Natural Res.	1979	★	★	★	★
Minnesota	Waste Mgmt. Bd.	1980	...	...	...	...
Mississippi	Dept. of Natural Res.	1981	...	...	★	★
Missouri	Dept. of Natural Res.	1982	...	...	...	...

Key:
★—Yes
...—No

HAZARDOUS WASTE FACILITY SITING—Continued

State	Agency responsible	Date of siting legislation	Under law, siting must consider:			
			Surface water	Ground-water	Geology	Physical/chemical studies
Montana	Dept. of Health & Environ. Sciences, Div. of Environ. Sciences		...	...	...	...
Nebraska	Dept. of Environ. Control	1971	★	★	★	★
Nevada	Dept. of Conservation & Natural Res., Div of Environ. Protection	1981	...	...	...	★
New Hampshire	Dept. of Health & Welfare	1983				
New Jersey	Dept. of Environ. Protection; Hazardous Waste Facilities Siting Comm.	1981	★	★		
New Mexico	Dept. of Health & Environ.	None	...	...	...	...
New York	Dept. of Environ. Conservation	1979	...	...	...	...
North Carolina	Dept. of Human Res.	1982	★	★	★	★
North Dakota	Dept. of Health	1981	...	...	...	...
Ohio	Hazardous Waste Facility Approval Bd.	1980	...	...	...	...
Oklahoma	Dept. of Health	1981	...	...	...	...
Oregon	Dept. of Environ. Quality, Solid Waste Div.	1971	...	...	...	...
Pennsylvania	Dept. of Environ. Res.	1980	...	...	...	...
Rhode Island	Dept. of Environ. Mgmt.	1979	...	...	...	...
South Carolina	Dept. of Health & Environ. Control	None	...	...	...	...
South Dakota	Dept. of Water & Natural Res.	None	...	...	...	...
Tennessee	Dept. of Health & Environ., Div. of Solid Waste	1977	...	...	...	...
Texas	Dept. of Health, Dept. of Water Res.	None	...	...	...	...
Utah	Dept. of Health, Div. of Environ. Health	1981	★	★	★	★
Vermont	Agency of Environ. Conser.	1983	...	...	...	...
Virginia	Dept. of Health	Siting bill passed Gen. Asmby. is due to take effect July 1, 1984 if Gov. signs	...	...	...	...
Washington	Dept. of Ecology, Off. of Hazardous Substances/Air Qual. Control	1976	...	...	...	★
West Virginia	Dept. of Natural Res.	None	...	...	...	...
Wisconsin	Dept. of Natural Res.	Revision due June 1984	★	★	★	★
Wyoming	Dept. of Environ. Qual.	None	...	...	...	...

Table 3
WASTE DISPOSAL SITES

State or other jurisdiction	Number of disposal impoundments(a)	Number of hazardous waste sites EPA National Priority List(b)	State or other jurisdiction	Number of disposal impoundments(a)	Number of hazardous waste sites EPA National Priority List(b)
Total	132,709	546 (c)			
Alabama	1,590	7	New Mexico	16,176	4
Alaska	130	0	New York	960	29
Arizona	332	6 (d)	North Carolina	1,038	3
Arkansas	953	6	North Dakota	2,784	1
California	3,721	19	Ohio	13,196	22
Colorado	5,237	9	Oklahoma	2,006	4
Connecticut..........	96	6	Oregon	757	3
Delaware	63	9	Pennsylvania.........	15,341	39
Florida	2,035	29	Rhode Island........	30	6
Georgia	1,438	4	South Carolina	911	10
Hawaii	78	0	South Dakota	650	1
Idaho	584	4	Tennessee	776	6
Illinois	3,667	11	Texas	8,436	11
Indiana..............	2,538	17	Utah	669	1
Iowa	1,466	3	Vermont	329	2
Kansas	6,086	4	Virginia	2,116	4
Kentucky............	2,141	7 (d)	Washington..........	1,045	14
Louisiana............	9,997	5 (d)	West Virginia	2,803	4
Maine	237	5	Wisconsin	985	20
Maryland	523	3	Wyoming............	5,179	1
Massachusetts........	73	16	American Samoa		1
Michigan	3,229	48 (d)	Guam		1
Minnesota	1,540	23	Pacific Trust		1
Mississippi	1,676	1	Puerto Rico..........		8
Missouri.............	2,757	7	Virgin Islands		0
Montana	1,363	5	No. Mariana Isl.......		1
Nebraska	2,329	0			
Nevada..............	261	0			
New Hampshire	105	10			
New Jersey	277	85			

(a) Source: Veronica N. Pye, Ruth Patrick, John Quarles.
(b) Source: *Groundwater Contamination in the United States* (University of Pennsylvania Press: 1983), p. 62-63.
(c) Total includes sites pending rulemaking.
(d) Rulemaking pending.

STATE PARKS AND OUTDOOR RECREATION

By John Karel

Webster's New International Dictionary defines "recreation" as: "Act of recreating, or state of being recreated; refreshment of the strength and spirits after toil . . . ."

To be reminded of the essential meaning of recreation, and by deduction of outdoor recreation, is to be reminded that such a function is essential in any society. Our own is no exception. Americans traditionally place a very high value on outdoor recreation and a high quality natural environment. The opportunity to camp, hike, picnic, swim or just loaf in the great outdoors continues to be extremely important to millions of Americans. Even at a time of basic reassessment of almost all governmental services, the enduring popularity of state parks is proven by continued growth in the number of Americans who visit and use them.

Though very diverse in features, facilities, size and operating philosophy, the state parks are by any measure a primary cornerstone of outdoor recreation in America. It is thus of major importance that the 1980s are proving to be a watershed for state parks and a time of facing fundamental issues.

Trends

Attendance at state parks has grown steadily, with a total of approximately 644,844,000 visitors in the most recent statistical year, 1983. This was almost 14 million more visitors than for the previous year. At the same time, the general nationwide cutback in governmental funding has held state park acreage virtually at a standstill. There is increasing pressure on the existing state parks across the country. New construction starts for facilities to serve these visitors were down in 1983 by 21 percent from the previous year: here again, more people, more pressure per facility.

Given population growth, continued restrictions on state funding and federal support, and an obviously finite land base, it is almost certain that state parks will be accommodating more and more people in a static or nearly static land area. The era of a decade ago, of continued expansion of park systems as a response to increasing needs, is at an end, at least for the time being. The emphasis now is on making the best use of existing park lands, without compromising the quality of the resource or the experience: in other words, taking care of what we have. Obviously, great challenges lie ahead.

Funding: Crisis and Response

Any discussion of the nation's state park system in 1984 must focus on the issue of funding. In a recent address, Don Davison, Director of Parks and Recreation for Minnesota and immediate past president of the National Association of State Park Directors, summed it up: "There is not a state park system in the United States that has escaped budget reductions in the 1980s. Dollar-stress is not the exception . . . it is the rule in park management."

Budget shortage has recently been a big theme for most public services, but park systems have probably suffered disproportionately because of a combination of high vulnerability to reduced federal support and moderate to low priority ranking by most state legislatures.

1983 was the Golden Anniversary year for the Civilian Conservative Corps, or CCC. Many states participated in ceremonies and activities which acknowledged the incredible job done by the CCC in the 1930s. Besides other work, hundreds of state parks around the country were initially developed or improved by the CCC. It was ironic that this CCC anniversary fell at a time of all-time low federal support for state parks.

One bright spot was the revival of the Land and Water Conservation Fund after a one-year hiatus. Despite its lower than normal level of funding, many state parks benefitted last year from this assistance. Another federal appropriation that helped many state park systems around the country during the summer of 1983 was the "Job's Bill" funded program that was earmarked for outdoor landscaping through the Small Business Administration. In many states, long overdue outdoor landscaping projects were carried out with these funds. In general, though, traditional sources of federally supported labor assistance programs, such as Young Adult Conservation Corps (YACC) and Comprehensive

John Karel is Director of the Division of Parks and Historic Preservation for Missouri.

Employment and Training Assistance (CETA), were eliminated or drastically reduced.

The principal funding source for most state park systems is the appropriation of state revenues, and in this arena also most state park systems have suffered. As a result, numerous services have been curtailed, and some parks actually closed.

In response, earnest brainstorming on the part of park agencies has produced a host of innovations aimed at maintaining, or even enhancing, state park public services. Almost universally, fees of all kinds have gone up; 33 states now have entrance fees. Many services have been dropped, and some facilities have even been culled permanently from the park systems. Volunteer assistance has been sought more vigorously. Various schemes for earmarking special taxes have been promoted, specific developments have been pursued through lease-agreements with private industry, fund raising special events have been offered, and studies have been commissioned to demonstrate the economic importance of state parks. Revenue generation has been emphasized almost everywhere more than in the past. In a general strategic sense, many park systems have drawn tighter alliances with tourism agencies and also with citizen constituency groups.

At least one major initiative on the federal level is the proposal for creation of an American Conservation Corps, or ACC, modelled to some extent in the spirit of the old CCC. There is widespread support for this revival of public service. There is a general if not universal consensus, however, that the era of tighter funding is likely to endure.

Technology

State park systems are rapidly converting to the computer world, using the most cost effective software technologies available. In the increasingly demanding job of serving the public, stewarding fragile resources, and managing technically complex facilities, the requirements for education, background and training of park personnel continue to stiffen.

Maintaining Identity

One of the hallmark characteristics of America's state parks is their rich diversity, individually and as systems. This diversity is not limited to the types of scenery and resources, but also includes the philosophies that underlie parks. All share a common goal of providing a wide variety of high quality outdoor recreation experiences.

Virtually all states also place a high priority on the preservation of outstanding natural and scenic resources. But, there are widely varying degrees of emphasis on amounts and types of facility development, ranging from resort parks to wilderness parks. Most states have a mix of offerings.

Nevertheless, current fiscal stress is causing many if not most state park systems to reassess their mission. The most fundamental issue raised by the funding crisis is the identity of the state parks. Just what is a state park supposed to be and do?

Traditional park purposes of preservation, interpretation and passive forms of recreation are being supplemented or even challenged by new purposes of revenue generation, more active recreation programming, and in a few cases resource development. Park administrators are wrestling with questions of competing uses and values. Many states are working to clarify the specific mission of their particular park systems. They hope to better guide major decisions about revenue-related development, compatible uses and resource exploitation.

There is a proposal pending in Congress to reconstitute an Outdoor Recreation Resources Review Commission. The first ORRRC, which submitted its final report in 1962, was a major watershed in national direction for outdoor recreation at federal, state and local levels, strongly influencing developments for two decades. A new commission could likewise chart a fresh course for all aspects of outdoor recreation. It is a landmark opportunity and should not be missed.

Conclusion

Whatever may be said about fiscal difficulties and shrinking public expectations for services, it remains clear that Americans love their state parks, and that state parks and outdoor recreation remain integral parts of American life. Use figures alone show that.

The soul-searching exercises being conducted, even though in the face of adverse budgets, could prove a tonic to the state parks in the long run. This will be especially true where states use the opportunity to clearly identify what it is that they want their park systems to be and then secure the resources to accomplish those missions.

STATE PARK STATISTICS

State	Administrative agency	Total attendance	Total areas	Total acres	Income generated	Operating budget	Capital outlay budget
Alabama	Dept. of Conservation & Natural Resources, Div. of State Parks	5,171,845	22	48,027	$ 7,985,404	$11,852,906	$ 230,000
Alaska	Dept. of Natural Resources, Div. of Parks	3,600,000	98	3,029,949	...	5,365,000	2,367,799
Arizona	State Parks Board	2,089,344	20	33,891	...	3,324,345	685,730
Arkansas	Dept. of Parks & Tourism, State Parks Div.	6,604,357	43	44,235	6,338,920	12,533,156	
California	Dept. of Parks & Recreation	61,258,748	274	1,116,301	...	80,859,255	60,499,218
Colorado	Dept. of Natural Resources, Div. of Parks & Outdoor Recreation	6,410,392	27	159,693	4,270,968	5,798,334	2,045,099
Connecticut	Dept. of Environmental Protection, Parks & Recreation Unit	9,149,272	193	167,119	...	8,000,000	1,550,000
Delaware	Dept. of Natural Resources & Environmental Control, Div. of Parks & Recreation	2,890,077	12	10,129	1,698,834	2,634,700	977,400
Florida	Dept. of Natural Resources, Div. of Recreation & Parks	14,819,917	126	252,696			
Georgia	Dept. of Natural Resources, Div. of Parks, Recreation & Historic Sites	10,199,363	65	60,233	6,179,862	16,158,713	1,311,749
Hawaii	Dept. of Land & Natural Res., Div. of State Parks, Outdoor Recreation & Historic Sites	11,924,584	71	20,534	...	3,899,569	4,627,714
Idaho	Dept. of Parks & Recreation	1,922,654	44	41,713	390,700	1,895,000	1,446,200
Illinois	Dept. of Conservation, Bureau of Lands & Historic Sites	30,544,225	168	273,358	...	21,596,776	14,191,863
Indiana	Dept. of Natural Resources, Div. of State Parks	8,602,585	20	54,143	6,575,706		...
Iowa	State Conservation Commission, Park Section	14,829,000	173	161,195	1,156,840	4,828,691	...
Kansas	Park & Resources Authority	4,396,000	24	31,316	1,642,622	4,605,545	1,150,407
Kentucky	Dept. of Parks	22,890,440	43	42,813	27,246,847	42,043,847	1,500,000
Louisiana	Dept. of Culture, Recreation & Tourism, Office of State Parks	1,162,896	53	36,624	42,919	5,868,072	12,652,917
Maine	Dept. of Conservation, Bureau of Parks & Recreation	2,614,633	155	66,451	...	2,977,910	8,779
Maryland	Dept. of Natural Resources, Forest/Park Service	5,582,436	58	217,327	3,664,655	9,089,818	3,591,000
Massachusetts	Dept. of Environmental Management, Div. of Forests & Parks	11,462,167	175	261,354	401,510	13,728,510	17,702,175
Michigan	Dept. of Natural Resources, Parks Div.	20,676,603	89	247,737	12,050,000	14,658,000	5,300,000
Minnesota	Dept. of Natural Resources, Div. of Parks & Recreation	6,070,138	75	182,143	2,069,386	9,485,052	2,029,000
Mississippi	Dept. of Natural Resources, Bureau of Recreation & Parks	4,452,724	28	20,542	3,386,250	10,899,330	756,452
Missouri	Dept. of Natural Resources, Div. of Parks & Historic Preservation	9,709,386	71	97,670	2,320,748	7,535,710	8,292,462
Montana	Dept. of Fish, Wildlife & Parks, State Parks Div.	3,608,000	316	49,275	123,740	2,093,047	2,152,780
Nebraska	Game & Parks Commission	7,869,787	92	136,935	1,415,496	4,813,813	984,579
Nevada	Dept. of Conservation & Natural Resources, Div. of State Parks	4,219,914	21	152,964	473,188	2,413,138	1,336,667
New Hampshire	Dept. of Resources & Economic Development, Div. of Parks & Recreation	4,209,888	50	70,979	340,703	4,316,215	3,846,227
New Jersey	Dept. of Environmental Protection, Div. of Parks & Forestry	8,949,991	116	290,353	...	13,225,397	500,000

New Mexico	Dept. of Natural Resources, State Park & Recreation Div.	4,960,028	42	108,938	791,200	4,599,000	1,843,000
New York	Office of Parks & Recreation	49,400,000	181	255,911	...	73,825,000	15,549,576
North Carolina	Dept. of Natural Resources & Community Development, Div. of Parks & Recreation	5,211,328	40	120,335	708,866	4,770,813	1,883,089
North Dakota	Parks & Recreation Dept.	930,836	31	15,259	449,347	2,097,104	904,522
Ohio	Dept. of Natural Resources, Div. of Parks & Recreation	62,124,783	71	111,797	8,965,297	28,103,312	5,807,391
Oklahoma	Tourism & Recreation Dept., Div. of State Parks	17,831,314	115	99,830	4,019,756	17,384,856	3,112,890
Oregon	Dept. of Transportation, State Parks & Recreation Div.	32,249,000	226	88,494	5,328,000	13,215,000	1,262,000
Pennsylvania	Dept. of Environmental Resources, Bureau of State Parks	33,071,467	112	278,909	3,861,861	29,250,861	...
Rhode Island	Dept. of Environmental Management, Div. of Parks & Recreation	7,700,000	79	10,596	...	877,530	...
South Carolina	Dept. of Parks, Recreation & Tourism, Div. of State Parks	11,335,334	60	81,206	6,219,485	8,949,330	1,403,076
South Dakota	Dept. of Game, Fish & Parks, Div. of Parks & Recreation	4,897,479	63	90,485	1,303,919	3,656,564	1,778,805
Tennessee	Dept. of Conservation, Div. of Parks & Recreation	20,033,129	109	166,548	11,756,908	20,463,858	8,511,746
Texas	Dept. of Parks & Wildlife, Parks Div.	18,071,609	116	194,296	10,660,398	22,579,477	9,837,961
Utah	Dept. of Natural Resources, Div. of Parks & Recreation	5,713,956	44	96,176	1,545,830	6,124,029	3,344,951
Vermont	Dept. of Forests, Parks & Recreation, Div. of Parks	919,360	80	177,320	1,640,400	2,523,200	382,735
Virginia	Dept. of Conservation & Economic Development, Div. of Parks	3,255,618	36	49,998	3,190,857	4,339,755	3,002,080
Washington	State Parks & Recreation Commission	39,593,798	195	220,000	8,680,007	15,952,682	4,767,142
West Virginia	Dept. of Natural Resources, Div. of Parks & Recreation	8,228,013	51	149,951	...	14,127,606	1,355,366
Wisconsin	Dept. of Natural Resources, Bureau of State Parks & Recreation	10,797,804	66	120,792	4,825,967	8,174,721	2,848,971
Wyoming	Recreation Commission	627,657	54	123,486	...	2,058,791	1,878,020

Source: 1984 Annual Information Exchange compiled by the National Association of State Park Directors for period July 1, 1982 to June 30, 1983.

A Note on Use

Symbols: Unless otherwise noted, all tables in *The Book of the States* use the following scheme:

   . . .—no data
   blank cell—not applicable
   0—zero quantity.

Sources: Unless otherwise noted, the sources of data for tables are surveys and research by The Council of State Governments.

STATE AGRICULTURE

By Edward H. Glade Jr. and Mae Dean Johnson

The United States farm economy during the decade of the 1980s has been, and will continue to be, significantly affected by conditions and events beyond control. Worldwide economic recession, foreign currency devaluations, high interest rates and weather-related problems have consequences in agricultural communities in every state. State departments of agriculture are called on to work closely with farm groups, suppliers and local financial organizations in adjusting to the effects of ever-changing economic conditions and commodity supplies.

Agricultural Transportation

The transportation of agricultural products from the nation's 2.3 million farms to ultimate domestic and foreign customers is undergoing important adjustments which require cooperative efforts between the carrier industries and departments of agriculture in each state.

With wide year-to-year swings in crop output and carryover stocks, the nation's transportation and storage system must constantly react to sharp changes in the demand for services. Moreover, recent railroad deregulations are likely to increase competition in many areas between rail and motor carriers, but will permit abandonment of some lines in other areas causing problems at peak shipping periods. Transportation rates will vary more throughout the year and make forward contracting for services increasingly necessary.

State departments of agriculture must monitor these developments, with particular attention to rapidly changing rate structures, to insure that local farming communities are provided the transportation services so necessary in moving agricultural products from farms to final markets. Since most states depend heavily on fuel taxes as a major source of state highway funds, a viable agricultural transportation system also benefits those beyond the farm gate as well.

Agricultural Finance

During the early 1980s, excessive U.S. crop production in combination with weak global demand for agricultural commodities caused financial distress in farm states. Sharp declines in farm income in the face of rising production costs re-

duced producers' ability to pay current debts. Some producers were forced to leave farming altogether, while others had to liquidate assets or borrow heavily to remain in business.

Low farm income also affected farmland values. Producers' expectations about future real growth in earnings (inflation-adjusted) reduced the demand for farmland by both farm and nonfarm investors. Farmland values fell an average of 6 percent during the year ending April 1, 1983, after falling 1 percent the previous year. This drop was a sharp contrast to the annual average increase of 13 percent in the 1970s. A principal effect of the decline in real farm equity was the decline in farmers' borrowing capacity. This came at a time when income was low and farmers wanted to borrow against equity accumulated during the 1970s. Further, many farmers who tried to cover production expenses by selling some of their land had difficulty doing so in the weak land market, or else realized a lower price than expected. Lower farmland values reduced community tax bases, with local governments feeling the effects on their operating revenues.

State departments of agriculture continue to provide assistance to financially troubled farm areas. Through interaction with USDA's Farmers Home Administration (FmHA), local production credit associations, and other lending agencies throughout the states, efforts have been made to establish additional lines of credit, stop farm foreclosures, and extend repayment periods. Prospects now point to gradually improving farm financial conditions with only modest growth in farm debt. But, if crop production continues to vary widely with no corresponding movement in market demands, sharp changes in farm income will likely result.

Farm Policy

State departments of agriculture are concerned about U.S. agricultural policies and pro-

Edward H. Glade Jr. is Economist and Mae Dean Johnson is Economic Assistant, U.S. Department of Agriculture, Economic Research Service, National Economics Division.

grams and how these affect their respective states. Federal farm policy requires state and local agricultural agencies to provide educational services, technical assistance, and carry a wide range of financial and record-keeping responsibilities.

As the direction of farm policy has changed over the years, the extent of state involvement has changed also. From the 1950s to the early 1970s, U.S. farm policy relied on strict control of production through acreage allotments, marketing quotas and high loan rates. Large quantities of farm commodities were taken over under the government loan program and enormous price-depressing stocks accumulated. Producers were essentially isolated from market conditions. However, with the passage of the Agriculture and Consumer Protection Act of 1973, a more flexible program was established whereby producers were free to determine production levels and practices and make marketing decisions. Price and income support were provided through a target price and loan rate system. The price support loan rate is set at, or below, market-clearing levels and provides a price floor and interim financing for producers. A direct payment is made (outside of the market) if the market price falls below the target price. The Food and Agriculture Act of 1977 established the farmer-owned grain reserve to protect farmers from lower prices while ensuring adequate stocks to meet world and domestic needs.

As a result of these market-oriented programs, however, producers are now more vulnerable to wide swings in prices and farm income. Also, because of the rigid formulas used to adjust target prices and loan rates, federal government expenditures under current programs can be excessive. Future agricultural programs will likely maintain many of the flexible features of current legislation, but give Congress and the USDA more freedom to adjust support levels to changing market conditions. In the years ahead, state departments of agriculture will play increasingly important roles in the implementation and operation of farm programs and will be called on to supply vital information and services to the farm sector in each state.

State-USDA Programs

The long-standing close cooperation between the states and the U.S. Department of Agriculture in agricultural production, marketing and processing is the primary link between federal actions and farm decisions. State departments of agriculture and various USDA agencies also cooperate on programs that insure the conservation of natural resources and environmental quality. Cooperative market news programs are conducted in 43 states under 62 individual agreements, covering fruits and vegetables, dairy and poultry, livestock, grain, cotton and tobacco. In addition, the USDA and departments of agriculture in 45 states assist each other to enforce livestock and poultry licensing registration and bonding laws by providing ownership, volume and operational information to each other. Agencies remain exclusively responsible for enforcement of their own statutes and do not exchange funds.

The collection and dissemination of agricultural statistics provide the basic data necessary for appraising the current and future conditions of state agriculture. In 47 states there are joint state-USDA offices gathering data under the supervision of a state statistician who is a federal employee. The cooperative state agency in most cases is a state department of agriculture or, in a few states, a branch of the state university. Regulatory programs are conducted in animal health and plant pest control, including cooperative programs with all states, Puerto Rico, and the Virgin Islands to control and eradicate diseases and plant pests. There are also cooperative programs to prevent the introduction of as yet unknown plant pests or pests not widely distributed in the United States. In addition, there are 3,000 state conservation districts organized by local people under state law. The USDA's Soil Conservation Service receives appropriations from Congress earmarked for assistance to these local conservation districts. Each district is legally responsible for soil and water conservation work within its boundaries. These state-USDA programs, along with others, are a foundation for continued progress in state agriculture and help the farmer to adjust to the changing agricultural environment.

Table 1
FARM INCOME: 1982
(In thousands of dollars)

State	Cash receipts from farming				Farm income			
	Total	Livestock & products	Crops	Government payments	Total net income	Realized gross farm income	Farm production expense	Net change in farm inventories
All states.................	$148,043,274	$70,198,559	$74,352,750	$3,491,965	$22,051,212	$164,006,733	$148,043,278	$-1,852,243
Alabama...................	2,303,044	1,217,415	1,054,192	31,437	495,965	2,641,333	2,059,250	-86,118
Alaska....................	16,900	6,408	10,081	411	502	20,298	20,061	265
Arizona	1,716,829	682,421	974,961	59,447	140,831	11,872,191	1,619,996	-111,364
Arkansas	3,535,880	1,625,772	1,790,763	119,345	552,372	3,904,516	3,042,036	-310,108
California................	14,455,276	4,380,722	9,940,053	134,501	3,009,632	15,363,649	11,979,394	-374,623
Colorado	3,072,388	2,010,969	992,655	68,764	265,109	3,316,101	3,010,526	-40,466
Connecticut...............	309,595	192,172	116,920	503	55,847	364,138	305,401	-2,890
Delaware	405,287	287,204	117,371	712	100,681	428,543	334,411	6,549
Florida	4,257,740	942,336	3,307,911	7,493	1,392,267	4,517,840	3,173,197	47,624
Georgia...................	3,239,045	1,659,905	1,549,798	29,342	559,544	3,526,239	3,032,360	65,665
Hawaii	484,791	77,859	406,277	655	58,171	507,254	448,984	-99
Idaho	2,153,717	813,818	1,288,332	51,567	286,291	2,388,506	2,134,056	31,184
Illinois..................	7,552,565	2,372,494	5,061,913	118,158	1,012,765	8,288,743	7,557,125	281,147
Indiana	4,643,923	1,763,137	2,823,242	57,544	307,887	5,291,333	4,574,393	-409,053
Iowa	10,559,214	6,013,068	4,330,277	215,869	1,168,334	11,456,608	10,057,058	-231,216
Kansas	6,089,587	3,323,940	2,485,383	280,264	886,691	6,567,876	5,706,567	25,382
Kentucky	2,916,342	1,273,495	1,629,930	12,917	894,056	3,375,773	2,602,672	120,955
Louisiana	1,926,847	506,357	1,337,371	83,119	246,033	2,204,928	1,818,842	-140,053
Maine	410,719	248,991	159,441	2,287	-17,849	453,799	486,272	14,624
Maryland	1,057,171	714,602	339,989	2,580	221,451	1,260,903	1,038,225	-1,227
Massachusetts	341,716	134,926	206,150	640	67,607	401,784	327,404	-6,773
Michigan	2,903,037	1,175,038	1,687,582	40,417	448,527	3,374,448	2,953,530	27,609
Minnesota	6,855,057	3,540,614	3,131,586	182,857	1,087,067	7,524,979	6,339,323	-98,589
Mississippi	2,535,224	943,162	1,488,133	103,929	316,386	2,839,855	2,380,346	-143,123
Missouri	3,753,300	2,055,493	1,617,982	79,825	241,160	4,359,037	4,265,345	147,468
Montana...................	1,749,858	652,614	980,328	116,916	40,307	1,929,822	1,863,674	-25,841
Nebraska	7,364,328	4,231,406	2,855,444	277,478	647,037	7,749,057	6,735,320	-366,700
Nevada	240,768	166,140	70,198	4,430	19,390	279,266	248,772	-11,104
New Hampshire	104,697	75,046	29,001	650	2,783	127,663	123,866	-1,014
New Jersey................	517,063	126,440	389,547	1,076	108,098	653,208	547,085	1,975
New Mexico................	692,229	627,148	33,142	31,939	74,965	1,147,829	1,041,458	-31,406
New York..................	2,601,519	1,867,295	720,457	13,767	187,133	2,876,035	2,728,346	39,444
North Carolina	4,128,767	1,592,649	2,519,654	16,464	970,387	4,601,182	3,607,172	-23,623
North Dakota	2,910,567	604,524	2,105,867	200,176	414,310	3,142,228	2,777,489	49,571
Ohio	3,716,204	1,551,303	2,122,503	42,398	391,352	4,274,173	3,901,050	18,229
Oklahoma	3,258,753	2,091,014	1,040,012	127,727	502,302	3,712,555	3,130,886	-79,367
Oregon	1,805,935	651,843	1,123,470	30,622	323,815	2,125,370	1,752,722	-48,833
Pennsylvania	2,998,392	2,165,564	825,390	7,438	451,255	3,410,598	2,863,841	-95,502
Rhode Island	32,793	14,010	18,678	105	1,122	41,604	40,423	-59
South Carolina	1,173,097	394,939	761,005	17,153	128,326	1,314,156	1,206,626	20,796
South Dakota	2,680,121	1,635,733	951,667	92,721	604,935	2,896,286	2,639,510	348,159
Tennessee.................	2,140,585	885,251	1,227,256	28,078	406,069	2,609,815	2,201,083	-2,663
Texas.....................	10,323,263	5,430,712	4,248,953	643,598	829,035	11,361,882	10,191,283	-341,564
Utah	550,816	411,499	130,138	9,179	42,244	678,983	645,293	8,554
Vermont...................	409,137	373,821	33,696	1,620	91,923	454,438	377,928	15,413
Virginia..................	1,687,072	1,005,429	674,186	7,457	113,450	2,019,745	1,835,001	-71,294
Washington	3,099,832	993,101	2,029,758	76,973	863,788	3,457,696	2,568,759	-15,149
West Virginia	227,877	170,457	54,952	2,468	-39,797	348,878	378,178	-10,497
Wisconsin.................	5,293,626	4,103,752	1,143,411	46,463	1,135,754	5,921,056	4,716,661	-68,641
Wyoming	540,772	414,551	115,744	10,477	-56,098	622,534	704,078	25,446

Source: Economic Research Service, U.S. Department of Agriculture.

Table 2

FARM ACREAGE AND INCOME PER FARM: 1982

State	Farms		Realized gross income per farm	Realized net income per farm (a)	Total net income per farm (b)	Value of farm real estate (in millions) (c)
	Number of farms	Total acreage (in thousands)				
All states.................	2,400,370	1,038,530	$ 74,458	$ 9,929	$ 9,233	$818,926
Alabama....................	56,000	12,300	47,167	10,394	8,857	11,341
Alaska.....................	420	1,530	48,329	564	1,195	108
Arizona	7,200	39,000	260,027	35,027	19,560	11,466
Arkansas	57,000	16,400	68,500	15,131	9,691	18,106
California..................	80,000	33,700	192,046	42,303	37,620	64,199
Colorado	25,800	35,800	128,531	11,844	10,276	15,000
Connecticut	4,300	490	84,683	13,660	12,988	1,291
Delaware	3,400	660	126,042	27,686	29,612	1,095
Florida	41,000	13,000	110,191	32,796	33,958	18,616
Georgia...................	58,000	15,200	60,797	8,515	9,647	12,798
Hawaii	4,400	1,960	115,285	13,243	13,221	2,258
Idaho	24,200	15,100	98,699	10,514	11,830	11,370
Illinois....................	104,000	28,700	79,699	7,035	9,738	55,678
Indiana...................	88,000	16,900	60,129	8,147	3,499	29,155
Iowa	117,000	33,800	97,920	11,962	9,986	60,908
Kansas	76,000	48,500	86,419	11,333	11,667	28,373
Kentucky	102,000	14,500	33,096	7,579	8,765	14,442
Louisiana	37,500	10,200	58,798	10,296	6,561	15,412
Maine	7,900	1,560	57,443	-4,110	-2,258	992
Maryland	18,000	2,750	70,050	12,371	12,303	6,644
Massachusetts	5,300	630	75,808	14,034	12,756	1,075
Michigan	65,000	11,500	51,915	6,476	6,900	13,708
Minnesota	103,000	30,400	73,058	11,511	10,554	36,389
Mississippi	53,000	14,500	53,582	8,670	5,970	14,500
Missouri	118,000	31,400	36,941	794	2,044	27,381
Montana..................	24,000	62,100	80,409	2,756	1,679	15,773
Nebraska	63,000	47,600	123,001	16,091	10,279	29,798
Nevada	2,900	8,900	96,299	10,515	6,686	2,510
New Hampshire	3,200	540	39,895	1,187	870	587
New Jersey.................	9,500	1,030	68,759	11,171	11,379	3,212
New Mexico...............	13,500	47,400	85,024	7,879	5,553	10,001
New York..................	50,000	9,500	57,521	2,954	3,743	7,467
North Carolina	88,000	11,100	52,286	11,296	11,027	14,252
North Dakota	38,000	41,700	82,690	9,598	10,903	18,181
Ohio	93,000	16,200	45,959	4,012	4,208	23,879
Oklahoma	71,000	34,300	52,290	8,193	7,075	23,873
Oregon	36,000	18,200	59,038	10,351	8,995	11,181
Pennsylvania	60,000	8,800	56,843	9,113	7,521	11,722
Rhode Island	750	80	55,472	1,575	1,496	224
South Carolina	33,000	6,100	39,823	3,258	3,889	5,600
South Dakota	37,000	44,500	78,278	6,940	16,350	12,950
Tennessee.................	95,000	13,400	27,472	4,302	4,274	13,025
Texas.....................	185,000	138,400	61,416	6,328	4,481	79,718
Utah	12,900	12,300	52,634	2,612	3,275	7,257
Vermont..................	7,500	1,700	60,592	10,201	12,256	1,328
Virginia...................	60,000	9,800	33,662	3,079	1,891	10,192
Washington	39,000	16,300	88,659	22,537	22,148	14,474
West Virginia..............	20,600	4,300	16,936	-1,421	-1,931	3,565
Wisconsin.................	92,000	18,500	64,359	13,091	12,345	19,851
Wyoming	9,100	35,300	68,410	-8,960	-6,164	6,001

Source: Economic Research Service and Statistical Reporting Service,
U.S. Department of Agriculture.

(a) Excludes net inventory changes.
(b) Includes net inventory changes.
(c) This value includes farm households.

Table 3
PRODUCTION OF MAJOR GRAINS, BY STATE: 1982*

State	Feed grains				Food grains			
	Corn	Oats	Barley	Sorghum	Wheat	Rye	Rice	Soybean
All states..................	8,443,334	616,981	522,387	841,079	2,808,737	20,817	154,216	2,276,976
Alabama.....................	29,700	2,080	...	2,600	26,400	...	...	53,300
Alaska........................	...	...	...	...	...	...	...	...
Arizona	3,375	...	6,615	1,092	12,407	...	...	...
Arkansas	2,460	2,046	...	15,780	68,640	...	57,037	109,200
California....................	42,900	2,480	38,440	10,010	81,625	...	36,651	...
Colorado	110,390	2,800	17,020	12,920	87,504	228	...	...
Connecticut(a)	...	...	...	...	...	...	...	...
Delaware	18,564	...	2,166	...	2,058	136	...	6,480
Florida	15,190	...	...	...	...	...	...	15,606
Georgia......................	69,275	5,490	...	5,670	48,840	1,470	...	68,850
Hawaii	...	...	...	...	...	...	...	...
Idaho	7,800	3,174	74,520	...	94,200	...	...	...
Illinois(b)....................	1,524,920	11,800	...	6,560	67,500	299	...	366,990
Indiana......................	815,280	6,080	...	949	46,440	260	...	183,200
Iowa	1,591,150	56,000	...	650	3,000	112	...	320,625
Kansas	140,220	7,520	2,337	207,700	462,000	240	...	47,060
Kentucky	157,940	308	1,350	2,812	26,325	56	...	53,120
Louisiana....................	3,120	...	...	7,875	19,000	...	24,862	76,700
Maine(a).....................	...	2,400	...	...	...	...	...	...
Maryland	70,620	1,102	5,723	...	6,120	290	...	11,745
Massachusetts(a)..............	...	...	...	...	...	...	...	...
Michigan	307,380	28,350	2,016	...	24,600	638	...	32,240
Minnesota	734,500	107,580	51,040	...	126,809	3,300	...	174,600
Mississippi	51,580	...	...	6,900	39,900	...	9,870	93,600
Missouri.....................	204,880	3,198	...	70,470	75,820	72	3,582	184,275
Montana......................	1,400	7,650	76,440	...	183,560	...	...	...
Nebraska	770,340	24,650	1,175	121,910	101,500	1,107	...	82,800
Nevada	...	...	2,560	...	1,890	...	...	...
New Hampshire(a)	...	...	...	...	...	...	...	...
New Jersey	11,424	336	1,260	...	1,968	319	...	4,250
New Mexico..................	9,900	...	2,442	14,570	13,250	...	...	...
New York(b)	67,160	18,200	...	...	5,438	341	...	...
North Carolina	164,630	4,845	3,276	3,710	21,600	550	...	52,500
North Dakota	35,360	62,100	108,120	...	330,785	3,400	...	7,245
Ohio(b)......................	475,020	23,800	...	...	55,000	155	...	138,010
Oklahoma	6,000	3,420	1,344	19,890	227,700	874	...	5,320
Oregon	4,760	6,750	14,080	...	64,500	145	...	...
Pennsylvania	126,100	19,765	3,744	...	8,208	408	...	3,200
Rhode Island(a)..............	...	...	...	...	...	...	...	...
South Carolina	30,600	2,900	1,650	1,610	19,800	621	...	40,700
South Dakota	192,720	133,800	23,435	17,250	99,630	4,680	...	25,730
Tennessee(b)	61,100	405	...	4,424	33,660	...	...	63,450
Texas........................	119,700	10,730	1,610	305,250	144,000	504	22,214	23,920
Utah	2,006	960	13,202	...	9,572	...	...	...
Vermont(a)	...	...	...	...	...	...	...	...
Virginia	62,475	816	5,700	477	14,060	364	...	18,620
Washington	27,550	1,500	49,410	...	138,880	...	...	...
West Virginia................	6,900	561	392	...	324	...	...	...
Wisconsin....................	361,800	48,360	1,960	...	5,596	248	...	13,640
Wyoming	5,145	3,025	9,360	...	8,628	...	...	...

Source: Economic Research Service, U.S. Department of Agriculture.
*Amounts in 1,000 bushels, except rice which is in 1,000 cwt.
(a) All acreage harvested is for silage.
(b) Estimates discontinued after 1980 crop.

Table 4
LIVESTOCK ON U.S. FARMS, BY STATE: 1982
(In thousands)

	Cattle and calves		Other livestock		Poultry	
	Total	Milk cows	Hogs and pigs	Sheep and lambs	Chicken	Turkeys
All states..................	115,604	11,012	58,688	12,966	378,509	165,453
Alabama.....................	1,950	60	540	...	17,350	...
Alaska......................	9	1	3	4	81	...
Arizona	1,000	80	170	377	500	...
Arkansas	2,100	84	585	...	25,030	13,000
California..................	5,000	940	160	1,210	41,600	20,000
Colorado	3,025	75	330	710	3,450	4,065
Connecticut	107	49	10	6	5,946	25
Delaware	35	10	40	...	923	238
Florida	2,350	190	257	...	16,600	...
Georgia.....................	1,950	131	1,520	...	28,564	2,680
Hawaii	228	13	55	...	1,148	...
Idaho	1,850	168	150	498	1,405	...
Illinois....................	2,800	234	6,450	195	6,050	291
Indiana	1,750	207	4,100	138	23,450	6,807
Iowa	6,850	389	16,300	485	10,300	7,650
Kansas	6,000	124	1,770	200	2,230	202
Kentucky	2,600	240	1,040	25	2,940	...
Louisiana	1,450	102	130	10	2,800	...
Maine	146	59	10	15	7,710	...
Maryland	405	122	250	19	4,368	69
Massachusetts	98	47	49	8	1,540	145
Michigan	1,450	396	690	130	7,800	1,400
Minnesota	3,880	905	4,300	335	13,300	26,000
Mississippi	1,950	97	370	...	8,619	...
Missouri	5,400	245	3,400	133	7,700	12,000
Montana.....................	2,900	29	200	616	970	...
Nebraska	7,250	122	4,100	225	4,050	715
Nevada	700	16	13	129	15	...
New Hampshire	74	30	9	8	842	22
New Jersey..................	100	41	45	10	1,218	75
New Mexico..................	1,500	55	62	615	1,548	...
New York....................	1,959	921	165	70	9,500	267
North Carolina	1,160	134	1,980	8	19,200	27,000
North Dakota	2,000	92	280	280	510	950
Ohio	1,900	382	2,050	313	15,600	2,700
Oklahoma	5,800	110	245	105	4,700	2,055
Oregon	1,800	97	90	540	3,400	1,050
Pennsylvania	2,100	730	750	125	22,500	5,300
Rhode Island	8	4	6	...	340	...
South Carolina	700	48	490	...	8,550	2,616
South Dakota	3,900	160	1,710	750	2,050	1,600
Tennessee...................	2,500	215	900	10	4,700	...
Texas.......................	13,700	325	700	2,400	17,200	5,200
Utah	920	86	40	636	2,326	2,404
Vermont.....................	360	190	9	10	440	...
Virginia....................	1,850	172	640	170	5,576	10,081
Washington	1,580	207	60	83	6,213	...
West Virginia...............	620	36	52	110	800	2,115
Wisconsin	4,450	1,830	1,380	125	4,800	6,731
Wyoming	1,390	12	33	1,130	57	...

Source: Economic Research Service, U.S. Department of Agriculture.

Table 5
AGRICULTURAL PRODUCTION, BY COMMODITY, FOR SELECTED ITEMS, BY STATE: 1982
(In thousands)

State	Vegetables Fresh (tons)	Vegetables Processed (tons)	Fruits Citrus (tons)	Fruits Non-citrus (tons)	Other crops Potatoes (cwt.)	Other crops Cotton (bales)	Other crops Tobacco (lbs.)	Other crops Hay (tons)
All states	204,974	11,212,470	12,113	15,742	347,702	12,019	1,961,941	152,424
Alabama	541	2,630	...	8	2,004	460	...	1,235
Alaska	...	...	...	...	...	...	...	...
Arizona	12,572	...	458	14	1,434	1,226	...	1,241
Arkansas	200	10,040	...	31	...	530	...	1,584
California	105,838	6,172,160	2,597	7,763	21,145	3,050	...	7,656
Colorado	4,419	15,750	...	28	14,264	...	...	3,661
Connecticut	202	...	...	30	423	...	3,840	202
Delaware	...	61,670	...	1,566	...	...	...	48
Florida	22,804	24,600	8,250	51	6,744	19	20,135	569
Georgia	200	2,200	...	65	...	230	105,500	1,200
Hawaii	172	...	...	634	...	...	...	...
Idaho	2,475	200,360	...	80	89,890	...	...	4,446
Illinois	304	261,200	...	44	583	...	...	3,615
Indiana	175	151,960	...	38	1,342	...	22,050	2,495
Iowa	...	32,300	...	5	308	...	...	8,260
Kansas	...	...	...	6	...	...	...	6,013
Kentucky	...	...	...	6	...	...	573,730	3,397
Louisiana	43	...	...	5	88	870	...	772
Maine	...	10,950	...	45	26,500	...	...	428
Maryland	231	115,920	...	49	328	...	37,530	633
Massachusetts	823	...	...	116	770	...	838	293
Michigan	7,249	246,470	...	716	9,645	...	...	4,379
Minnesota	723	796,100	...	12	13,401	...	...	8,264
Mississippi	...	...	...	2	...	1,760	...	1,575
Missouri	...	1,750	...	27	...	210	6,235	6,530
Montana	...	...	...	3	1,924	...	...	5,105
Nebraska	...	...	...	...	2,307	...	...	7,810
Nevada	...	...	...	...	4,095	1	...	1,131
New Hampshire	...	...	...	28	...	...	...	203
New Jersey	2,490	131,530	...	120	2,054	...	...	311
New Mexico	2,905	2,160	...	8	1,260	90	...	1,384
New York	8,702	275,580	...	767	12,015	...	...	5,283
North Carolina	619	17,730	...	76	2,657	100	693,314	664
North Dakota	...	...	...	...	17,250	...	...	5,588
Ohio	2,138	368,480	...	98	2,628	...	30,135	3,580
Oklahoma	...	4,500	...	5	...	250	...	3,176
Oregon	6,809	580,070	...	354	21,105	...	...	2,967
Pennsylvania	1,498	116,000	...	394	5,758	...	25,350	4,840
Rhode Island	...	...	...	3	720	...	...	21
South Carolina	1,277	430	...	103	...	155	124,195	484
South Dakota	...	...	...	...	1,550	...	...	8,635
Tennessee	538	17,870	...	3	257	346	172,475	2,190
Texas	10,617	31,230	808	7	3,228	2,722	...	6,708
Utah	730	9,500	...	38	1,305	...	...	2,118
Vermont	...	...	...	25	129	...	...	962
Virginia	843	32,650	...	229	2,228	...	123,851	1,677
Washington	4,333	618,030	...	1,901	52,800	...	...	2,889
West Virginia	2,504	330	...	137	...	...	3,060	882
Wisconsin	...	900,320	...	102	22,575	...	19,703	13,158
Wyoming	...	...	...	...	988	...	...	2,162

Source: Economic Research Service, U.S. Department of Agriculture.

Table 6
U.S. AGRICULTURAL LANDHOLDINGS OF FOREIGN OWNERS,
BY STATE, DECEMBER 1982

State or other jurisdiction	1,000 acres		Foreign-owned agricultural land (acres)	Percent of foreign-owned, private agricultural land
	Total area of state(a)	Privately owned agricultural land(b)		
Total................	2,265,238	1,290,302	13,461,028	1.0
Alabama	32,491	29,467	590,145	2.0
Alaska	365,333	400	753	0.2
Arizona	72,645	10,983	225,755	2.1
Arkansas	33,330	28,834	116,401	0.4
California...............	100,031	47,353	898,711	1.9
Colorado	66,301	37,527	461,796	1.2
Connecticut..............	3,118	2,267	801	NEG.
Delaware	1,236	1,064	8,051	0.8
Florida	34,658	26,529	491,723	1.9
Georgia	37,156	33,253	944,154	2.8
Hawaii	4,112	1,992	56,374	2.8
Idaho	52,744	15,166	165,594	1.1
Illinois	35,613	32,326	148,774	0.5
Indiana	22,996	20,909	95,581	0.5
Iowa	35,818	33,912	35,529	0.1
Kansas	52,338	49,911	68,003	0.1
Kentucky	25,388	22,915	40,403	0.2
Louisiana...............	28,494	26,463	147,807	0.6
Maine	19,837	18,829	2,658,669	14.1
Maryland	6,295	5,146	44,492	0.9
Massachusetts	5,007	3,322	442	NEG.
Michigan	36,450	26,117	192,012	0.7
Minnesota	50,911	36,204	103,218	0.3
Mississippi	30,229	26,629	336,661	1.3
Missouri................	44,125	40,025	61,721	0.2
Montana	93,048	54,189	347,810	0.6
Nebraska	49,052	45,397	85,348	0.2
Nevada.................	70,332	7,586	70,147	0.9
New Hampshire	5,756	4,682	103,166	2.2
New Jersey..............	4,780	2,894	23,988	0.8
New Mexico.............	77,654	34,451	661,744	1.9
New York	30,321	24,257	358,384	1.5
North Carolina	31,259	27,321	268,728	1.0
North Dakota	44,351	39,617	19,205	NEG.
Ohio	26,243	22,979	43,902	0.2
Oklahoma	43,939	38,875	28,435	0.1
Oregon	61,558	25,685	527,400	2.1
Pennsylvania	28,728	22,380	158,785	0.7
Rhode Island	675	439	0	0
South Carolina	19,330	15,932	507,140	3.2
South Dakota	48,609	38,241	41,379	0.1
Tennessee...............	26,339	22,901	347,395	1.5
Texas	167,691	156,768	912,784	0.6
Utah	52,527	10,779	239,445	2.2
Vermont................	5,935	5,251	94,318	1.8
Virginia	25,411	21,499	127,353	0.6
Washington	42,567	23,028	398,411	1.7
West Virginia............	15,436	13,744	58,240	0.4
Wisconsin	34,833	27,637	18,664	NEG.
Wyoming	62,073	26,142	123,563	0.5
Guam	135	85	336	NEG.
Puerto Rico	---	---	1,388	NEG.

Source: Economic Research Service, U.S. Department of Agriculture.
Key:
NEG.—Negligible

(a) 1980 land area from geography division, Census Bureau.
(b) Privately held land based on unpublished data; T. Frey, Economic Research Service, U.S. Department of Agriculture, 1979. Estimate of total land less public, Indian, transportation and urban lands. Includes forest, pasture, crop, range and miscellaneous lands.

Table 7
FARM REAL ESTATE VALUES: 1982

State	Average value per acre	State rank	Total value (millions)	State rank
All states..................	$789		$816,556	
Alabama.....................	922	25	11,341	30
Alaska......................	...	...	...	...
Arizona	294	43	11,466	28
Arkansas	1,104	18	18,106	15
California..................	1,905	6	64,198	2
Colorado	419	42	15,000	18
Connecticut.................	2,634	3	1,291	43
Delaware	1,659	10	1,095	44
Florida	1,432	13	18,616	13
Georgia.....................	842	29	12,798	26
Hawaii				
Idaho	753	33	11,370	29
Illinois....................	1,940	5	55,678	4
Indiana	1,715	8	29,155	7
Iowa	1,802	7	60,908	3
Kansas	585	39	28,372	8
Kentucky	996	23	14,442	21
Louisiana	1,511	11	15,412	17
Maine	636	35	992	46
Maryland	2,416	4	6,644	36
Massachusetts	1,707	9	1,075	45
Michigan	1,192	17	13,708	23
Minnesota	1,197	16	36,389	5
Mississippi	1,000	22	14,500	19
Missouri	872	28	27,381	9
Montana.....................	254	46	15,773	16
Nebraska	626	36	29,798	6
Nevada	282	45	2,510	41
New Hampshire	1,087	19	587	47
New Jersey..................	3,118	1	3,212	40
New Mexico..................	211	47	10,001	33
New York....................	786	31	7,467	34
North Carolina	1,284	15	14,252	22
North Dakota	436	41	18,181	14
Ohio	1,474	12	23,879	10
Oklahoma	696	34	23,873	11
Oregon	611	37	11,181	31
Pennsylvania	1,332	14	11,722	27
Rhode Island	2,804	2	224	48
South Carolina	918	26	5,600	38
South Dakota	291	44	12,949	25
Tennessee	972	24	13,025	24
Texas.......................	576	40	79,718	1
Utah	590	38	7,257	35
Vermont.....................	781	32	1,328	42
Virginia....................	1,040	21	10,192	32
Washington	888	27	14,474	20
West Virginia...............	829	30	3,565	39
Wisconsin...................	1,073	20	19,850	12
Wyoming.....................	170	48	6,001	37

Source: Economic Research Service, U.S. Department of Agriculture.

STATE FORESTRY ADMINISTRATION
AND MANAGEMENT

By Leslie Cole

For decades, forests have contributed significantly to the nation's socioeconomic well-being through exports, energy and tax revenues. In recent years, however, several factors combined to give forests a new or increased role in many states' economic development and recovery strategies. For example, the growth of timber industries in the South has led to the need for maintaining economic growth and fiscal stability. Long-range economic growth and stabilization is a prime concern in the Pacific Coastal states in light of the predicted shortages of the region's domestic supplies of timber. The role of forest resources in state economic diversification is increasingly recognized in the highly industrialized Northern states suffering from economic dislocation. In addition, the high prices of non-renewable energy sources in many parts of the country, particularly the Northeast, add new economic dimensions to wood as a fuel. And last, technological development, such as waferboard, will continue to open new markets for forest products.

With the recent emphasis on economic development, states have begun to refocus their efforts in forestry to meet current and future social and economic needs. Many states are refining timber taxation policies and increasing financial incentives to forest landowners in addition to maintaining traditional programs of fire protection and insect and disease control. The recent development of forest resource plans in 48 states, Guam and Puerto Rico has also upgraded the balanced development of the forest resources.

State Activities

In the past, federal programs such as the Cooperative Forestry Assistance Act have enabled many states to assist landowners to protect and manage their forests. Subsequently, state forest policy objectives mirror broad federal objectives. Three major objectives stand out:
- To correct imperfections in the market place.
- To ensure adequate supplies of public goods.
- To ensure environmental quality.

In addition to administering federal programs of fire protection, insect and disease control, and cost-sharing, states have adopted many of their own policies and programs. For the most part, state programs include a combination of the following:
- Indirect financial assistance—primarily through tax revisions, loans and insurance.
- Technical assistance and education—service to owners from a variety of sources to assist, encourage and educate.
- Regulation of land use, forest practices and industry.
- Direct financial assistance—cost-sharing or payments to carry out projects or manage lands according to a state plan.

Taxation. State indirect assistance in the form of various state tax laws is recognized in many states as a major policy tool bearing directly on the management of forest resources. Special forest property tax laws can be grouped into three classes: exemption taxes, yield taxes and modified property taxes.

Exemption laws provide for the removal of forest land or timber from tax rolls, either permanently or for a specified number of years. Ten states currently provide tax exemptions. Under a yield tax structure, land and timber values are separated. Land values remain subject to annual property taxation, although sometimes in modified form. Timber values go untaxed until harvest time. When harvested, a tax equal to some percentage of stumpage value is imposed. Sixteen states are using some form of yield taxation.

The most popular timber tax law provides for a modified form of property taxation. Five states have modified rate statutes. Modified rate laws assess forest land and timber like other forms of property but at a lower tax rate. The most widely used tax structure involves modified assessment. Thirty-eight states currently employ modified assessment statutes. Modified assessment laws provide that forest properties are valued differently from other forms of property. Thirty-four states assess woodland at its value for timber production rather than on its market value for speculative use.

Leslie Cole is Staff Professional for The Council of State Governments' Environment and Natural Resources Program.

Several questions have been raised concerning the use of the modified assessment state property tax. Charges of tax inequality and market interference indicate the controversial nature of these tax laws. Their impact on a locality's ability to raise tax revenues has also been criticized.

States offer various death tax options for forest estates. Special use valuation in lieu of fair market value is authorized in 25 states upon meeting certain prerequisites, such as a continuation of a forest management program.

Most state income tax incentive programs are found in the Western and Southern states where forestry plays an important role in the economy. However, states that use federal adjusted gross income as the basis for computing taxable income automatically offer federal incentives to timber investors for state tax purposes. State income tax laws in the South may be divided into three broad categories in terms of their effect on timber revenues: six states use federal adjusted gross income for computing taxable income; five compute their own adjusted gross income; three have no income tax.

Education. State resource managers recognize that programs to educate and motivate landowners are necessary to assure that the benefits of forest management and protection are known. Almost every state has some type of outreach and education service that assumes people will change their behavior if they are given adequate information. Education is viewed favorably because it is relatively low-cost, not as an approach that can guarantee success. However, public education has never been carried out intensively except in the areas of fire control and prevention. Maryland is developing an extensive educational program promoting the economic benefits of forest management employing television, radio and printing, and will be aimed at certain areas in the state. Other states and forestry interests are exploring landowner associations to enlist cost-efficiency into educational programs.

Regulation. State regulation of forest resources has been more effective in stopping undesirable activity than promoting desirable activity. Fifteen states regulate harvesting practices, environmental protection or reforestation.[1] Regulation of forest lands, while measurably helpful in some states for establishing prompt regeneration and conserving soil, is not universally popular within the forest community. The effectiveness of the regulatory approach, its cost efficiency and political acceptability have been questioned. A majority of states approach

forest regulation through indirect means—approved management plans and tax penalties for land conversion, improper harvesting or regeneration practices.

Cost-Sharing. Seven states offer direct financial assistance to supplement the federal cost-share programs offering small landowner assistance in tree planting and timber stand improvement. The cost-share approach has become popular because participation is not mandatory, although administrative costs can be high.

Cost-sharing for forestry practices similar to the federal Forest Incentive Practices (FIP) program is offered in six states: Minnesota, Mississippi, North Carolina, South Carolina, Virginia and California. Most programs are financed by a severance tax on forest products. The Texas Reforestation Foundation, which is funded by industry, recently initiated a 65 percent cost-sharing program. Oregon and Washington offered state cost-sharing incentives programs that only lasted two years (1977 and 1978).

Forest Resource Planning

Encouraged by the federal Forest Resource Planning Act, 48 states have begun to develop comprehensive management programs for forest resources.[2] Some states are incorporating these plans into their statewide economic development and recovery strategies.

Michigan Governor James J. Blanchard has unveiled a wide-ranging program for expanding existing activity in Michigan's forest product industry that will strengthen the state's economy and create employment opportunities. The governor's support for the planning process came when the completed plan was used to sponsor a governor's conference on expanding the state's forest products industry. Blanchard's administration notes that the industry currently employs 63,000 people and contributes $4 billion in direct value to the state. Michigan's plan calls for increasing employment to 110,000 full-time workers, more than doubling value added to the state's economy.

Michigan's planning program targets a rise of annual roundwood harvests from 200 million cubic feet to 500 million cubic feet. Michigan's timber growth has far exceeded removals. The recent estimate of 19.2 billion cubic feet is nearly double 1952s inventory; similar statistics occur for other North Central and Northeastern states. Michigan today grows more than it consumes, but is harvesting only one third of consumption. By reducing imports and using their own resources, Michigan aims to diversify and substantially improve its economy.

Mississippi used its forest resource planning process to explore its potential contribution to state economic and social development. Leading the effort was Governor William F. Winter, who was interested in establishing a state policy to increase the wealth of the Mississippi forest industry. Mississippi's forest industry provides one of every five manufacturing jobs. But, even though the state ranks sixth in timber harvesting, it is only 24th in value added from wood processing. Narrowing this gap could provide many employment opportunities.

California's resource planning comes when the state is undergoing economic and demographic changes. Rural areas are growing faster in population and industrial expansion than the rest of the state, providing the opportunity for getting more multiple outputs from the land. Through the planning process, California is: identifying income generating ideas for landowners willing to lease hunting rights; improving compatibility between range and forest management practices; studying new uses for the state's hardwoods; increasing use of exports; emphasizing better water management for more output; and investing in the Lake Tahoe Basin, where 60 percent of construction is second homes for absentee owners.

Notes

1. Forest practices are regulated in Alaska, California, Idaho, Indiana, Maine, Maryland, Massachusetts, Mississippi, Nebraska, Nevada, New Hampshire, New Mexico, Oregon, Virginia and Washington.

2. Forest resource planning is not active in Connecticut and Idaho.

Table 1
FOREST RESOURCES
1982
(In thousands of acres)

State or other jurisdiction	Total land area	Total forest area	Private forest area	State forest area	Federal forest area
All states(a)	2,257,127	737,408	347,485	23,495	99,461
Alabama	32,231	21,361	20,324	156	800
Alaska	362,485	119,145	289	2,328	8,317
Arizona	72,580	18,494	166	32	2,480
Arkansas	33,091	18,282	15,233	237	2,718
California	99,847	40,152	7,628	79	8,434
Colorado	66,283	22,271	3,118	189	7,932
Connecticut...........	3,082	1,861	1,659	120	2
Delaware	1,232	392	370	13	1
Florida	33,994	17,040	13,214	466	1,616
Georgia	36,796	25,256	23,268	94	1,417
Hawaii	4,109	1,986	494	442	12
Idaho	52,676	21,727	3,021	861	9,570
Illinois	35,442	3,810	3,413	11	268
Indiana..............	22,951	3,943	3,405	170	239
Iowa	35,634	1,561	1,348	51	55
Kansas	52,127	1,344	1,150	8	27
Kentucky	25,282	12,161	11,007	76	819
Louisiana............	28,409	14,558	13,524	299	694
Maine	19,729	17,718	16,323	354	73
Maryland	6,289	2,653	2,280	185	25
Massachusetts	5,007	2,952	2,432	240	10
Michigan	36,172	19,270	12,359	3,838	2,454
Minnesota	50,382	16,709	6,367	2,650	1,870
Mississippi	29,930	16,716	14,828	95	1,202
Missouri.............	43,868	12,876	10,757	187	1,313
Montana	92,896	22,559	4,565	530	8,635
Nebraska	48,828	1,029	710	11	58
Nevada	70,295	7,683	69	3	61
New Hampshire	5,731	5,014	4,112	79	472
New Jersey...........	4,775	1,928	1,538	246	28
New Mexico	77,669	18,060	1,927	171	2,867
New York	30,357	17,218	13,351	711	58
North Carolina	30,956	20,043	17,799	320	1,318
North Dakota	43,939	422	281	10	52
Ohio	26,121	6,147	5,642	195	150
Oklahoma	43,728	8,513	3,755	91	348
Oregon...............	61,356	29,810	9,084	820	13,817
Pennsylvania	28,592	16,826	12,453	2,796	502
Rhode Island..........	664	404	363	20	0
South Carolina	19,143	12,249	11,081	206	862
South Dakota	48,381	1,702	361	70	965
Tennessee	26,290	13,161	11,555	324	919
Texas	167,283	23,279	11,717	48	737
Utah	52,505	15,557	661	239	2,431
Vermont..............	5,907	4,512	4,008	168	213
Virginia	25,286	16,417	14,017	183	1,669
Washington...........	42,456	23,181	8,728	2,084	5,382
West Virginia	15,335	11,669	10,363	229	892
Wisconsin	34,616	14,908	9,792	568	1,383
Wyoming..............	62,055	10,028	855	111	3,245
Guam	135	51	19	11	21
Puerto Rico	2,200	800	702	70	28

Source: An Analysis of the Timber Situation in the United States 1952-2030, USDA, Forest Service, Forest Resource Report, no. 23, December 1982.
Note: Commercial timberland only—excludes unproductive, reserved and deferred lands.
(a) Totals may not add because of rounding.

Table 2
RURAL FIRE PREVENTION AND CONTROL PROGRAM

State	1982		1978-82	
	State & private lands protected (thousands of acres)(a)	Federal & state fire control expenditures (thousands of dollars)	Average number of fires per year	Average acreage burned per year
All states..................	877,309	$299,612	126,880	1,860,975
Alabama.....................	25,029	5,672	7,211	190,574
Alaska......................	58,645	3,820	212	25,181
Arizona.....................	18,328	403	183	38,274
Arkansas	20,698	6,174	3,495	78,189
California..................	32,843	124,766	10,427	220,943
Colorado	25,958	3,536	1,124	11,014
Connecticut.................	2,390	404	1,684	2,467
Delaware	557	135	33	2,141
Florida	27,102	16,346	7,961	204,879
Georgia.....................	27,279	16,362	12,162	55,319
Hawaii	3,306	600	349	8,021
Idaho	7,127	3,727	434	28,178
Illinois....................	8,453	272	122	3,102
Indiana.....................	7,328	533	215	2,665
Iowa	7,612	460	2,047	8,114
Kansas	19,793	1,715	2,834	66,748
Kentucky	16,865	*	2,760	154,339
Louisiana	20,939	9,117	6,937	75,939
Maine	17,743	3,926	990	2,956
Maryland	3,700	951	960	12,916
Massachusetts	3,581	1,779	8,801	9,521
Michigan	19,675	5,650	671	5,180
Minnesota	22,830	1,557	1,385	43,859
Mississippi	19,858	5,930	8,542	120,837
Missouri....................	16,587	2,400	3,772	42,765
Montana.....................	34,839	3,775	371	4,178
Nebraska	27,154	477	1,861	27,796
Nevada	8,777	2,500	201	8,577
New Hampshire	4,631	523	938	486
New Jersey..................	2,705	2,900	1,845	8,986
New Mexico..................	40,199	1,132	302	12,411
New York....................	16,957	1,399	675	4,815
North Carolina	20,817	11,995	4,972	62,926
North Dakota	31,483	344	293	5,904
Ohio	5,823	1,264	1,032	4,022
Oklahoma	5,087	3,397	1,640	41,816
Oregon	13,099	11,175	853	7,753
Pennsylvania	19,541	3,297	1,580	8,997
Rhode Island	512	*	565	614
South Carolina	13,289	6,902	8,102	40,349
South Dakota	25,816	500	854	27,201
Tennessee...................	12,766	5,971	4,087	44,784
Texas.......................	22,123	5,107	2,439	30,349
Utah	14,724	1,496	370	22,248
Vermont.....................	4,638	188	211	620
Virginia....................	18,519	3,948	3,311	10,629
Washington..................	13,177	8,076	900	5,814
West Virginia...............	12,833	1,108	2,073	46,488
Wisconsin...................	18,898	3,589	1,535	7,697
Wyoming.....................	21,341	3,114	559	11,394

Sources: U.S. Forest Service, National Association of State Foresters.
(a) Acres protected do not equal total forest lands (Table 1) because areas with other classifications are also included.

Table 3
SUMMARY OF FORESTRY INCENTIVE PROGRAMS
AND RURAL FORESTRY ASSISTANCE EXPENDITURES

State	FP-1, Planting trees (fiscal 1983)		FP-2, Improving a stand of trees (fiscal 1983)		Rural forestry assistance expenditures (fiscal 1983) (thousands of dollars)(a)		
	Acres planted	Total cost share	Acres improved	Total cost share	Federal	State	Total
All states	143,273	$8,465,502	58,353	$1,692,628	$7,315	$44,888	$52,203
Alabama	15,584	1,064,921	2,089	21,120	363	2,200	2,563
Alaska					120	200	320
Arizona			51	2,486	69	80	149
Arkansas	11,057	489,558	4,710	117,798	231	1,881	2,112
California	430	59,211	704	83,209	134	5,274	5,408
Colorado	12	991	148	7,473	82	440	522
Connecticut	149	5,133	20	720	37	37	74
Delaware	250	27,804	92	2,101	31	85	116
Florida	13,185	652,543	358	5,514	364	1,902	2,266
Georgia	13,510	1,139,766	406	11,264	350	3,282	3,632
Hawaii					51	86	137
Idaho	120	13,968	203	17,841	78	261	339
Illinois	83	5,375	1,747	51,534	73	73	146
Indiana	191	12,481	4,593	74,631	94	803	897
Iowa	99	6,393	426	8,201	44	446	490
Kansas	24	1,814	172	6,818	72	834	906
Kentucky	157	17,485	2,489	71,308	289	1,447	1,736
Louisiana	8,478	514,705	2,089	62,842	219	928	1,147
Maine	260	28,365	707	37,589	103	261	364
Maryland	1,746	106,083	352	11,753	125	889	1,014
Massachusetts	5	687	1,163	40,009	51	342	393
Michigan	1,516	69,004	2,106	53,120	135	390	525
Minnesota	1,067	94,978	527	23,046	161	275	436
Mississippi	14,989	564,214	1,209	29,027	270	1,124	1,394
Missouri	363	23,566	4,111	68,395	195	389	584
Montana			109	7,671	85	450	535
Nebraska	20	543	16	341	53	1,116	1,169
Nevada	138	6,171			46	135	181
New Hampshire			1,236	49,178	84	220	304
New Jersey			614	11,252	78	90	168
New Mexico			250	10,912	58	291	349
New York	77	6,102	4,225	113,436	185	2,350	2,535
North Carolina	12,918	631,931	900	22,343	403	2,014	2,417
North Dakota					50	292	342
Ohio	516	24,053	4,243	137,981	103	869	972
Oklahoma	1,585	93,542	748	18,716	98	355	453
Oregon	2,418	294,155	1,766	89,158	146	155	301
Pennsylvania	78	3,816	2,229	110,298	177	1,666	1,843
Rhode Island			121	6,537	30	30	60
South Carolina	11,034	819,807	290	13,327	246	246	492
South Dakota			212	11,712	48	339	387
Tennessee	1,898	102,378	391	9,299	176	775	951
Texas	10,826	558,823	2,841	63,095	246	3,027	3,273
Utah					79	230	309
Vermont	13	1,351	598	18,599	97	441	538
Virginia	14,585	600,357	1,309	31,676	391	3,432	3,823
Washington	1,575	264,451	238	18,585	180	180	360
West Virginia	299	20,702	2,914	38,420	112	545	657
Wisconsin	2,018	138,275	2,065	70,146	177	1,229	1,406
Wyoming			566	32,147	43	205	248
Guam					35	55	90
Puerto Rico					135	183	318
Virgin Islands					13	39	52

Source: U.S. Forest Service.

(a) Includes forest management, wood utilization, seedlings, nurseries and tree improvement activities.

Table 4
INSECT AND DISEASE MANAGEMENT EXPENDITURES, URBAN AND COMMUNITY EXPENDITURES, PROFESSIONAL FORESTRY PERSONNEL, AND STATE NURSERY PROGRAMS

State or other jurisdiction	Insect and disease management expenditures FY 1983 (in thousands)	Urban and community expenditures (in thousands)	Professional state forestry personnel	State nursery programs FY 1983, state only (in thousands)	
				Number of tree seedlings produced by state nurseries	Acres of seed orchard
All states	$19,944	$4,622	3,146	742,412	4,779
Alabama	444	198	57	72,000	362
Alaska	0	37	44	308	0
Arizona	58	11	9	0	0
Arkansas	150	50	52	15,836	78
California	2,106	0	178	4,246	34
Colorado	1,728	822	49	1,404	0
Connecticut	0	0	23	1,758	9
Delaware	18	10	6	736	6
Florida	141	357	90	73,300	796
Georgia	453	230	72	97,921	682
Hawaii	70	30	29	341	0
Idaho	121	33	44	440	31
Illinois	10	47	42	3,902	73
Indiana	96	31	44	4,816	44
Iowa	67	42	23	5,520	14
Kansas	24	88	18	202	37
Kentucky	. . .	. . .	. . .	10,618	41
Louisiana	120	79	72	76,500	335
Maine	4,345	31	94	2,231	3
Maryland	0	359	33	3,252	25
Massachusetts	403	22	25	0	0
Michigan	178	29	80	6,052	0
Minnesota	703	51	281	20,864	21
Mississippi	137	75	107	62,146	209
Missouri	150	500	64	10,352	29
Montana	104	12	51	754	13
Nebraska	37	98	13	0	20
Nevada	32	0	11	205	0
New Hampshire	61	142	31	485	15
New Jersey	40	15	53	176	15
New Mexico	0	51	29	0	0
New York	153	176	111	5,907	175
North Carolina	77	45	117	51,660	134
North Dakota	19	24	9	1,096	6
Ohio	61	194	. . .	6,688	97
Oklahoma	63	72	24	2,037	41
Oregon	182	11	72	19,000	113
Pennsylvania	6,144	109	166	4,017	99
Rhode Island	. . .	. . .	. . .	0	0
South Carolina	145	110	76	45,632	191
South Dakota	52	28	46	1,064	0
Tennessee	64	32	71	6,753	291
Texas	478	78	63	19,414	210
Utah	1	104	10	337	0
Vermont	89	12	30	300	20
Virginia	150	80	89	62,765	406
Washington	199	20	250	15,977	20
West Virginia	0	1	70	5,028	14
Wisconsin	233	32	206	18,372	70
Wyoming	163	0	12	0	0
Guam	5	26	. . .	. . .	. . .
Puerto Rico	0	18	. . .	. . .	. . .

Source: National Association of State Foresters, State Forestry Statistics, 1983. *1981 Directory of Forest Tree Seed Orchards in the United States,* page vi.

Table 5
ADMINISTRATION OF STATE FOREST AGENCIES

State	Within natural resource or conservation unit	Within environmental protection unit	Independent board or commission	Executive level forestry unit	Other
Alabama	...	...	★	...	
Alaska	★	...	...	...	
Arizona	...	...	...	...	State Land Department
Arkansas	...	...	★	...	
California	...	...	...	★	
Colorado	...	...	...	...	State Forest Service-Colorado State Univ.
Connecticut	...	★	...	...	
Delaware	...	...	...	...	Dept. Natural Resources & Environ. Control
Florida	...	...	...	...	Dept. of Agriculture
Georgia	...	...	★	...	
Hawaii	★	...	...	...	
Idaho	★	...	...	...	
Illinois	★	...	...	...	
Indiana	★	...	...	...	
Iowa	...	...	★	...	
Kansas	...	...	...	...	Forestry Dept.-Kansas State Univ.
Kentucky	...	...	...	...	Dept. Natural Resources & Environ. Protection
Louisiana	★	...	...	...	
Maine	★	...	...	...	
Maryland	★	...	...	...	
Massachusetts	...	★	...	...	
Michigan	★	...	...	...	
Minnesota	★	...	...	...	
Mississippi	...	...	★	...	
Missouri	★	...	...	...	
Montana	...	...	...	...	Dept. of Lands
Nebraska	...	...	...	...	State Forest Service-Univ. of Nebraska
Nevada	★	...	...	...	
New Hampshire	...	...	...	...	Dept. Resources & Economic Development
New Jersey	...	★	...	...	
New Mexico	★	...	...	...	
New York	...	★	...	...	
North Carolina	★	...	...	...	
North Dakota	...	...	...	...	State Forest Service-Univ. North Dakota
Ohio	★	...	...	...	
Oklahoma	...	...	...	...	Dept. of Agriculture
Oregon	...	...	...	★	
Pennsylvania	...	★	...	...	
Rhode Island	...	★	...	...	
South Carolina	...	...	★	...	
South Dakota	...	...	...	...	Dept. Game, Fish, Parks
Tennessee	★	...	...	...	
Texas	...	...	...	...	State Forest Service-Texas A&M Univ.
Utah	★	...	...	...	
Vermont	...	...	...	...	Dept. Forests, Parks & Recreation
Virginia	...	...	...	...	Dept. Conservation & Economic Develop.
Washington	★	...	...	...	
West Virginia	★	...	...	...	
Wisconsin	★	...	...	...	
Wyoming	...	...	...	...	Office of Public Lands

Source: McCann, Ellefson. *Organizational Patterns and Administrative Procedures for Forest Resources Planning*, August 1982, Staff paper series.
Key:
★—Yes.
...—No.

Table 6
TYPES OF DEATH TAX INCENTIVES
APPLIED TO FORESTLAND: 1982

State	State statute	Federal incentive statutes incorporated into state law	State statute applying to agriculture land (with forest land considered)
Alabama	...	★	...
Alaska	...	★	...
Arizona	...	★	...
Arkansas	...	★	...
California	★	...	...
Colorado	...	★	...
Connecticut	...	★	★
Delaware	★	...	...
Florida	...	★	...
Georgia	...	★	...
Hawaii	...	...	...
Idaho	...	...	...
Illinois	★	...	...
Indiana	...	...	...
Iowa	...	...	...
Kansas	★	...	...
Kentucky	...	...	★
Louisiana	...	...	...
Maine	...	...	...
Maryland	★	...	...
Massachusetts	...	...	★
Michigan	...	...	...
Minnesota	★	...	...
Mississippi	★	...	...
Missouri	...	...	...
Montana	★	...	...
Nebraska	...	...	...
Nevada	...	...	...
New Hampshire	...	...	...
New Jersey	...	...	(a)
New Mexico	...	★	...
New York	★	...	...
North Carolina	...	...	...
North Dakota	...	★	...
Ohio	...	...	...
Oklahoma	...	...	...
Oregon	...	...	(a)
Pennsylvania	★	...	...
Rhode Island	...	...	...
South Carolina	...	...	...
South Dakota	...	...	...
Tennessee	★	...	...
Texas	...	...	...
Utah	...	★	...
Vermont	...	★	...
Virginia	...	★	...
Washington	★	...	...
West Virginia	...	...	...
Wisconsin	...	...	...
Wyoming	...	...	...

Source: William Siegel, USFS National Research Program in Forest Resource Law and Taxation, Southern Forest Experiment Station, New Orleans, La.
Key:
★—Yes.
...—No.
(a) Under ad valorem property tax structure—Administration decision on whether forest land qualifies.

Table 7
TYPES OF PROPERTY TAXES APPLIED
TO STANDING OR SEVERED TIMBER: 1982

State	Exemption	Yield	Modified property
Alabama	★	★	★
Alaska	...	...	...
Arizona	...	...	★
Arkansas	...	...	★
California	...	★	★
Colorado	★	...	...
Connecticut	...	★	★
Delaware	★	...	★
Florida	...	...	★
Georgia	...	...	...
Hawaii	★	★	★
Idaho	★	★	★
Illinois	...	...	★
Indiana	...	...	★
Iowa	★	...	★
Kansas	...	...	...
Kentucky	...	...	★
Louisiana	...	★ (b,c)	★
Maine	...	...	★
Maryland	...	...	★
Massachusetts	...	★	★
Michigan	...	★	...
Minnesota	...	★ (c)	★
Mississippi	...	★	★
Missouri	...	...	★
Montana	...	★	...
Nebraska	...	...	...
Nevada	...	...	★
New Hampshire	★ (a)	★	★
New Jersey	★	...	★
New Mexico	...	...	★
New York	...	★ (c)	★
North Carolina	★	...	★
North Dakota	...	...	★
Ohio	...	...	★
Oklahoma	...	...	★
Oregon	...	★ (b)	★
Pennsylvania	...	...	★
Rhode Island	★	...	★
South Carolina	...	...	★
South Dakota	...	...	...
Tennessee	★	...	★
Texas	...	...	★
Utah	...	...	...
Vermont	...	...	★
Virginia	...	...	★
Washington	...	★ (c)	★
West Virginia	...	...	★
Wisconsin	...	★	★
Wyoming	...	...	...

Source: Clifford Hickman, "Emerging Patterns of Forest Property and Yield Taxes," USFS Southern Exp. Station, February 1982.
Key:
★—Yes.
...—No.
(a) Rebate law.
(b) Yield tax known as severance tax.
(c) Remains in effect for only properties already enrolled.

SOIL AND WATER CONSERVATION

By Neil Sampson and Eugene Lamb

Since colonial days, Americans have been concerned for the condition of America's soil and water resources. The federal government became involved in 1928, when Hugh Hammond Bennett, a scientist with the federal Bureau of Chemistry and Soils, published a circular entitled "Soil Erosion: A National Menace." This led, in 1929, to the first federal appropriations for soil conservation. The money—$160,000—was used to set up 10 soil erosion measurement stations, which provided information that Bennett and his co-workers widely publicized.

In 1933, President Franklin D. Roosevelt named Bennett director of the newly established Soil Erosion Service in the Department of the Interior and gave him $5 million to employ people on erosion control projects. The Civilian Conservation Corps (CCC) eventually put 3 million idle young men to work on America's farms, forests and streambanks.

That early work largely resulted in demonstration projects, although "demonstration" is a misnomer, since it implies some knowledge about what will be demonstrated. Often, the first workers did not know what to do or what would result; however, through their projects came confidence that soil erosion could be controlled and the beginnings of the science of how to do it.

USDA Takes Over, Turns to States

Bennett's call for a coordinated program resulted in the 1935 Soil Conservation Act, which created the Soil Conservation Service as a permanent agency within the Department of Agriculture (USDA) to develop and execute a continuing program of soil and water conservation. In order to carry out the new program, the USDA decided that soil conservation districts should be established as independent, special purpose governments at the local level to take major responsibility for planning and operating the program. These districts would handle soil and water conservation as their only mission, much like school districts operate only schools. USDA lawyers drafted a suggested state law, and after much review within the administration, President Roosevelt sent a letter in February 1937 to all state governors, enclosing the "standard" enabling act and suggesting that each state adopt such a law as part of an effective national effort to conserve the soil.

Arkansas and Oklahoma were the first, and by the end of 1937 a total of 22 states had enacted the soil district law. Within the following decade, every state, Puerto Rico and the Virgin Islands established the legal framework for landowners to create soil conservation districts. The final state laws varied, but generally included provisions for establishing a state soil conservation agency (called a committee, commission or board in the various states) to oversee the operation of districts, a petition and referendum procedure for creating local districts, and a statement of the authorities that would be granted to the new units of special purpose governments.

At the local level, districts entered into a memorandum of understanding with the secretary of Agriculture and the Soil Conservation Service (SCS), by which SCS agreed to provide technical assistance to the districts and their cooperating landowners. Assistance was in the form of federal technicians who would live in the districts and help farmers solve soil and water problems.

Evolution of Conservation Districts

In the early 1960s, rapid shifts in land use away from agriculture, excessive erosion and sedimentation from construction, and the growing public concern for environmental quality presented new challenges for conservation districts. In many cases, this meant activities not originally authorized by state enabling laws, and over 200 amendments to state soil and water conservation laws were adopted between the late 1960s and 1975.

Some of the changes included broadening the scope of the law in 30 states to encompass such issues as flood prevention, drainage, irrigation, water quality and stormwater runoff; inclusion

Neil Sampson is Executive Vice President and Eugene Lamb is State Programs Specialist for the National Association of Conservation Districts, Washington, D.C.

of urban areas within districts; authorization for levying taxes or assessments; the exercise of eminent domain; and allowing districts to receive funds from counties.

New urgency was added to the conservation effort by Section 208 of the Federal Water Pollution Control Act Amendments of 1972. This brought the threat of federal regulation over farm activities if, as the law proposed, the Environmental Protection Agency exercised its authority to stop pollution wherever it originated. Farmers and their organizations adamantly opposed such federal regulation.

In a cooperative effort with The Council of State Governments (CSG), USDA and EPA, the National Association of Conservation Districts (NACD) worked out a model state erosion and sediment control act. CSG included the model act in its *Suggested State Legislation* for 1973, and NACD held 42 state sediment control conferences to increase awareness of erosion and sediment control, to explain provisions of the model act and to encourage state action to meet the challenges that water pollution posed. As a result, 20 states, the District of Columbia and the Virgin Islands established erosion and sediment control programs. Most laws prohibit local governments from issuing subdivision approvals or building permits that lack erosion and sediment control plans approved by conservation districts.

State Agencies Expand Roles

For most of the 1940-1960 period, the role of state agencies was limited to helping form local districts and providing guidance in their operations. As district programs became more independent and active, state appropriations to support them became more common. State funds were used to hire district employees and to pay for other district programs. Thus, the state soil conservation agency became more active in monitoring district programs, understanding district needs and telling state legislators what funds bought and why new appropriations were needed.

Long-range programs to guide state investments and coordinate them with other conservation activities were unnecessary for many years. However, as states took a more active role in funding district efforts, the need for states to develop their own soil and water conservation programs increased. When the Soil and Water Resources Conservation Act of 1977 (RCA) required SCS to develop a national report on conservation program needs, SCS in turn en-

couraged each state to inventory and appraise its soil and water resources. From that base, most state soil conservation agencies have developed long-range plans for solving resource problems.

State Programs

State long-range plans follow several different formats, according to the particular authorities and responsibilities delegated to the state soil conservation agency. Common features include an assessment of the overall condition of the state's soil and water resources and a program to guide the state agency in coordinating conservation district activities. Data used to develop state plans come from district long-range plans, state water quality plans and other sources, such as the National Resources Inventories conducted by SCS.

An important outcome of state long-range plans has been more widespread recognition of soil conservation issues by state government, as well as wider recognition of the constructive role the state must play in a truly intergovernmental effort. Many states, for example, have used their plans as a basis for new state legislation and to develop budget priorities, including state-funded technical and financial assistance for landowners, data collection, watershed management and public education.

The expansion in state and local activity has resulted in a major increase in financial contributions to conservation work. Initially, almost all soil and water conservation funds came from the federal government. Today, substantial contributions come from state and local governments and private interests. Table A shows the rapid growth in state and local funds for soil and water conservation programs—a trend that is expected to continue. (For comparison, the federal soil and water conservation effort in 1983 was about $1 billion.)

The number of state and locally funded employees working in conservation districts has risen dramatically in recent years. Of the approximately 5,500 employees working in the nation's 2,932 conservation districts in 1983, over 4,400

Table A
GROWTH OF STATE AND LOCAL GOVERNMENT FUNDS IN SOIL CONSERVATION DISTRICT PROGRAMS, 1957-1983, IN ACTUAL DOLLARS
(In millions)

Source of funds	1983	1979	1973	1968	1963	1957
State............	$ 96	$ 65	$ 42	$ 30	$ 14	$ 4
County and local.	90	87	44	33	17	9
Total...........	$186	$152	$ 86	$ 63	$ 31	$ 13

Source: NACD RCA Note Number 7, July 25, 1980; USDA Soil Conservation Service, 1983. Figures are rounded.

were employed with state and local funds. From 1979 to 1983, the total number of district employees hired with state and local funds increased by slightly over 7 percent a year. This indicates the tremendous movement on the part of districts in the past few years to strengthen their contribution to the on-the-land assistance available to farmers—a service formerly provided almost entirely by federally paid technicians.

Early state funding efforts were aimed almost exclusively at helping districts provide assistance or develop resource information. Recently, however, a number of new programs have been developed that provide funds to help farmers implement conservation practices. Sixteen states now have state funded cost-sharing programs for either conservation application or private land reforestation. Montana and Utah have low-interest revolving loan programs for range and grassland improvement and other conservation purposes. The state soil and water conservation agency and conservation districts administer the programs, with the exception of four reforestation projects. In addition, some of the new state laws allow cost-sharing in urban areas, a feature not available in USDA programs.

Most observers of the conservation scene forecast a continuation of the trend toward greater state and local involvement in soil and water conservation efforts. States and localities are realizing that investments to protect the resource base are essential to environmental and economic health, as well as the nation's future.

Table 1
MAJOR STATE SOIL AND WATER CONSERVATION PROGRAMS

State or other jurisdiction	Status of long-range plan	Major resource concerns								Major program needs				
		Soil erosion	Food/fiber production	Water Quality	Loss of ag. lands	Forestry	Water quantity	Flooding	Prime farmland	Water management	Technical assistance	Cost-share	Clerical assistance	Information/education
Alabama	...										★		★	
Alaska	Complete	★	★	★		★		★	★	★	★			
Arizona	Complete	★	★	★	★	★	★	★		★	★			★
Arkansas	Draft	★	★	★	★	★	★	★		★				
California	January 1984													
Colorado	Complete	★		★	★	★		★		★	★		★	★
Connecticut	Complete	★		★	★	★	★		★		★			
Delaware	Complete	★	★	★	★	★	★		★		★		★	★
Florida	Complete	★		★	★		★		★	★		★	★	★
Georgia	Complete	★	★			★		★	★		★			
Hawaii	Complete	★	★	★	★	★	★	★	★	★	★			
Idaho	Complete	★	★		★	★	★	★		★	★			
Illinois	Complete			★						★	★			
Indiana	Complete	★	★	★	★	★				★		★	★	★
Iowa	Complete	★	★	★	★	★	★	★	★	★	★	★		
Kansas	Complete	★	★				★			★		★		
Kentucky	Complete	★		★		★	★	★		★	★		★	
Louisiana	Complete	★	★	★	★	★	★	★	★		★			
Maine	Complete	★	★	★		★		★		★	★		★	
Maryland	Complete	★		★	★		★			★	★		★	
Massachusetts	Complete	★			★	★	★	★	★					★
Michigan	Complete	★			★	★				★		★		
Minnesota	Complete	★		★		★	★	★		★		★	★	
Mississippi	Complete	★						★						
Missouri	Complete	★	★		★	★								
Montana	Complete	★					★							
Nebraska	Complete	★		★	★	★	★	★						
Nevada(a)	January 1984													
New Hampshire	Complete	★		★		★	★	★					★	★
New Jersey(a)	March 1984										★		★	
New Mexico	Complete	★	★	★	★	★	★	★	★	★	★			
New York	Complete			★	★		★			★	★	★		
North Carolina	Complete	★		★	★	★		★		★	★			
North Dakota	Complete	★	★	★	★	★	★			★	★			
Ohio	Complete	★	★	★	★	★	★	★	★		★			
Oklahoma	Complete	★	★	★		★	★	★		★	★		★	
Oregon	Complete	★	★	★		★	★	★	★		★			★
Pennsylvania	Complete	★	★	★	★	★	★	★	★		★	★		
Rhode Island	January 1982												★	
South Carolina(a)	April 1984										★		★	
South Dakota	Complete										★			
Tennessee	Complete	★	★	★	★	★	★	★		★	★			★
Texas	Complete	★	★	★		★		★		★	★			★
Utah	Complete	★	★	★			★		★	★	★		★	
Vermont(a)	October 1984										★		★	
Virginia	Complete	★		★	★		★	★	★	★	★			★
Washington	Complete	★				★				★	★			★
West Virginia	Complete	★		★		★	★		★	★			★	★
Wisconsin	Complete	★		★		★	★	★	★	★				
Wyoming	Complete	★	★	★		★	★			★				
Puerto Rico	Complete	★	★								★			
Virgin Islands	...										★			★

Key:
★—Yes
...—No
(a) Estimated completion date.

Table 2
CONSERVATION DISTRICTS

State or other jurisdiction	Date district law became effective	Districts organized(a) (number)	Approximate area and farms within organized districts		Land in farms (1,000 acres)	Districts having memoranda of understanding with USDA(b) (number)
			Total area (1,000 acres)	Farms (thousands)		
Total.................		2,921	2,200,808	2,348	1,048,049	2,906
Alabama	March 18, 1939	64	33,030	54	13,100	64
Alaska	March 25, 1947	1	375,304	1	1,700	1
Arizona	June 16, 1941	31	60,378	6	40,400	30
Arkansas	July 1, 1937	76	33,826	57	16,800	76
California...............	June 26, 1938	127	75,201	60	32,300	126
Colorado	May 6, 1937	83	61,432	26	37,700	83
Connecticut............	July 18, 1945	8	3,132	4	450	8
Delaware	April 2, 1943	3	1,266	3	620	3
Florida	June 10, 1937	61	34,866	35	13,800	60
Georgia	March 23, 1937	34	37,959	54	16,000	26
Hawaii	May 19, 1947	15	4,089	4	2,290	15
Idaho	March 9, 1939	51	52,285	24	15,500	51
Illinois	July 9, 1937	98	29,095	105	28,600	98
Indiana................	March 11, 1937	92	23,102	88	16,900	92
Iowa	July 4, 1939	100	36,012	119	34,000	100
Kansas	April 10, 1937	105	52,649	72	48,200	105
Kentucky	June 11, 1940	121	25,377	94	14,300	121
Louisiana..............	July 27, 1938	38	28,214	35	10,200	38
Maine	March 25, 1941	16	17,539	8	1,640	16
Maryland	June 1, 1937	24	6,282	16	2,780	24
Massachusetts...........	June 28, 1945	16	4,973	5	650	15
Michigan	July 23, 1937	84	37,241	63	10,500	84
Minnesota	April 26, 1937	92	50,659	104	30,300	92
Mississippi	April 4, 1938	82	30,269	48	14,500	82
Missouri...............	July 23, 1943	110	42,154	117	32,300	110
Montana	February 28, 1939	59	89,724	22	62,000	59
Nebraska	May 18, 1937	24	48,982	63	47,800	24
Nevada................	March 30, 1937	30	70,605	2	8,990	30
New Hampshire	May 10, 1945	10	5,955	8	580	10
New Jersey.............	July 1, 1937	16	4,813	8	990	16
New Mexico.............	March 11, 1937	47	62,415	11	46,700	47
New York	July 20, 1940	57	30,489	44	9,800	57
North Carolina	March 22, 1937	93	31,229	98	12,300	93
North Dakota	March 16, 1937	62	45,148	40	41,690	62
Ohio	June 5, 1941	88	26,383	96	16,200	88
Oklahoma	April 15, 1937	88	43,726	71	34,500	88
Oregon	April 7, 1939	47	60,603	31	18,600	47
Pennsylvania............	July 2, 1937	66	29,352	61	9,000	66
Rhode Island	April 26, 1943	3	677	1	63	3
South Carolina	April 17, 1937	46	19,345	35	6,500	46
South Dakota	July 1, 1937	69	49,309	41	45,450	69
Tennessee...............	March 10, 1939	95	26,450	92	13,600	95
Texas	April 24, 1939	201	169,890	159	138,400	198
Utah	March 23, 1937	40	49,229	12	12,600	40
Vermont................	April 18, 1939	14	5,935	6	1,740	14
Virginia	April 1, 1938	42	25,630	60	9,700	42
Washington	March 17, 1939	52	37,073	34	16,100	50
West Virginia...........	June 12, 1939	14	15,411	20	4,180	14
Wisconsin	July 1, 1937	72	34,858	94	18,600	72
Wyoming	May 22, 1941	38	59,944	7	35,100	38
Dist. of Col.	July 13, 1982	1	42	0	0	. . .
Puerto Rico	July 1, 1946	17	2,189	30	1,336	17
Virgin Islands	June 1946	1	110	. . .	. . .	1

Source: Soil Conservation Service, U.S. Department of Agriculture. The term conservation district may be prefixed by resource, soil, water, natural resource, or other descriptive names due to variance in individual state laws.

(a) For specific procedure on organization of soil conservation districts, reference should be made to each of the respective state soil conservation districts' laws.

(b) Upon request, the U.S. Department of Agriculture enters into memoranda of understanding with districts for such assistance from the departmental agencies as may be available.

Table 3
CONSERVATION DISTRICT EMPLOYEES
(As of January 1983)

State	*Total*	State/locally funded employees	CETA & green thumb funded employees	Seasonal/ temporary employees
All States	5,566	4,419	625	522
Alabama....................	77	77	0	0
Alaska....................	1	1	0	0
Arizona(a)..................	30	30	0	0
Arkansas	77	76	1	0
California..................	31	30	1	0
Colorado	67	59	1	7
Connecticut................	20	15	1	4
Delaware	33	27	0	6
Florida	51	51	0	0
Georgia....................	33	25	8	0
Hawaii	4	4	0	0
Idaho	64	54	8	2
Illinois....................	191	155	22	14
Indiana....................	131	119	3	9
Iowa	187	177	10	0
Kansas	133	133	0	0
Kentucky	130	130	0	0
Louisiana..................	135	143	2	0
Maine	23	18	0	5
Maryland	101	97	4	0
Massachusetts	13	13	0	0
Michigan	104	99	0	5
Minnesota	236	217	3	16
Mississippi	69	69	0	0
Missouri...................	130	125	3	2
Montana...................	77	66	0	11
Nebraska	228	228	0	0
Nevada....................	19	17	2	0
New Hampshire	11	10	0	1
New Jersey.................	60	57	3	0
New Mexico................	34	34	0	0
New York..................	723	258	465	0
North Carolina	148	148	0	0
North Dakota	340	207	0	133
Ohio	280	253	13	14
Oklahoma	243	205	1	37
Oregon	35	28	6	1
Pennsylvania...............	156	145	10	1
Rhode Island...............	6	6	0	0
South Carolina	79	70	9	0
South Dakota	218	76	6	136
Tennessee..................	108	94	14	0
Texas......................	237	205	8	24
Utah	25	11	2	12
Vermont...................	17	17	0	0
Virginia....................	102	89	1	12
Washington	62	44	18	0
West Virginia..............	97	37	0	60
Wisconsin..................	148	138	0	10
Wyoming	32	32	0	0

(a) Includes five Indian districts.

7. Labor Relations

LABOR LEGISLATION: 1982-1983

By Richard R. Nelson

State labor legislation enacted during the 1982-83 biennium covered a wide variety of subjects. Among these were emerging issues of equal pay for jobs of comparable worth, the impact of plant closings on workers and communities, and the right of employees to receive information on their workplace exposure to toxic substances. Significant laws also were adopted in more conventional labor standards fields, including minimum wage, employment discrimination, public employee collective bargaining, workers' compensation and job training.

Wages and Hours

Minimum Wages. While the number of state minimum wage rate increases was less in 1982 and 1983 than during the prior four years when the federal rate was increasing annually and many states were adopting corresponding changes, wage rates for some or all workers were increased in 14 states and the District of Columbia.[1] Some increases resulted from escalation schedules adopted in previous years, but most were the result of new legislation.[2] New Mexico and New York increased the rate for farmworkers to $3.35 per hour, eliminating previous wage differentials for this group.

Twenty-two jurisdictions now have a minimum rate for some or all occupations equal to or exceeding the $3.35 per hour federal standard (Table 5), and Illinois is scheduled to reach $3.35 in 1985. Alaska, Connecticut and the District of Columbia have rates higher than the federal.

The minimum cash wage for tipped employees was increased in Delaware, Illinois and New Mexico.

Wage Garnishment and Assignment. Many legislatures addressed the problem of non-payment of court-ordered support payments. In doing so, 21 states adopted measures concerning the use of wage garnishment or assignment as a means of assuring that payment is made. Most of these laws dealt with child-support payments and set limits on the amount of earnings subject to these actions.

Employees in nine states were protected from employer disciplinary action because of the garnishment or assignment,[3] while the Louisiana law was amended to permit discharge of persons whose wages have been subjected to three garnishments or more for unrelated debts in a two-year period. Among other actions, Alaska increased the amount exempt from garnishment and provided for future biennial changes linked to changes in the Consumer Price Index for Anchorage, and a constitutional amendment permitting garnishment of wages for enforcement of child support payments was passed by Texas voters in the November 1983 general election.

Prevailing Wage. There are currently 37 states with prevailing wage laws.[4] These laws, which specify that wage rates paid on publicly funded construction contracts be not less than those prevailing in the locality, continued to be of interest as well as controversial at both the state and federal levels.

One or more amendments were introduced in most of the states with these laws. Some bills were to strengthen or extend existing laws, but most sought reduced coverage or repeal. Repeal measures passed the Idaho Legislature in both 1982 and 1983 but were vetoed. Amendments to the Kentucky law reduced coverage, eliminated the "30 percent rule," and increased the threshold dollar amount.

Other noteworthy measures included amendments to the Maryland law extending coverage to local and school construction contracts receiving less than the total state funding previously required, and amendments to the New York law requiring use of the collectively bargained rate as the prevailing rate where at least 30 percent of the workers in a locality receive that rate.

At the federal level, the U.S. Supreme Court in January 1984 declined to review an appeals court ruling largely upholding revised regulations under the Davis-Bacon Act, issued by the secretary of labor in May 1982, thus clearing the way for their implementation, which had been stayed.

Richard R. Nelson is a State Standards Adviser in the Division of State Employment Standards Programs, Office of State Liaison and Legislative Analysis, Employment Standards Administration, U.S. Department of Labor.

Equal Employment Opportunity

Legislation addressing one or more of the various forms of job discrimination was enacted in 36 jurisdictions during the biennium. These enactments included comprehensive laws applicable to both the public and private sectors in Louisiana and North Dakota, and a similar law in Texas applicable to just the private sector. Delaware prohibited differentials in pay for equal work based on sex under a new equal pay law. Kansas adopted an age discrimination in employment act for both the public and private sectors, Louisiana extended coverage of its age discrimination act to public sector employees, and California abolished mandatory retirement ages for most public employees. Several states enacted new protections for handicapped workers.

Increased attention was focused on the concept of "comparable worth" in setting state government salaries in male or female-dominated occupations on the basis of value of the work performed. Among the enactments, comparable worth is to be implemented for executive branch employees in Minnesota, and is to be achieved by June 30, 1993 for Washington state employees. Iowa adopted a policy to begin in 1984 of payment to state employees based on comparable worth, and the Montana Department of Administration is to work toward the goal of establishing a standard of equal pay for state jobs of comparable worth.

In September 1983, U.S. District Court Judge Tanner ruled that the state of Washington was guilty of discrimination against its female employees. In December 1983 he ruled that the state must pay wage adjustments within 18 months, depending on whether retroactive pension payments must be included.

Industrial Relations

Collective bargaining laws were enacted for state and local public sector employees in Ohio, and in Illinois for teachers and most other public employees except police and firefighters. A limited right to strike is permitted under both new Illinois laws following exhaustion of impasse procedures. Delaware repealed provisions regulating professional negotiations and enacted a comprehensive Public School Employment Relations Act, and California state employers and employee organizations were authorized to enter into union security agreements in the form of fair share fee deductions as a condition of employment.

Occupational Safety and Health

"Right-to-know" laws requiring employees to be informed of and given training on toxic substances found in the workplace received considerable attention. Laws of this type have been enacted in 14 states,[5] with eight adopted in 1983 and one in 1982. New federal regulations on "Chemical Hazard Communication" were published November 25, 1983. These regulations, which are being challenged in court, cover chemical manufacturers and importers and raise the issue of federal preemption. Prior to issuance of the new federal regulations, the West Virginia law survived a constitutional challenge in 1983.

Other legislation was adopted in several jurisdictions covering a wide variety of subjects, including mine safety and inspection of boilers and elevators.

Of the 24 state plans approved under the federal Occupational Safety and Health Act (Table 3), 21 were certified as of December 1983[6]—Oregon, Puerto Rico and Washington within the last two years.

Workers' Compensation*

Workers' compensation was the subject of significant legislative activity during this biennium. Over 2,200 proposals were introduced and 432 were enacted into law. Basic changes focused on coverage, benefit levels, occupational disease, medical and rehabilitative services, insurance rates and funding mechanisms.

Major changes occurred in Minnesota and Louisiana. Minnesota became the first state in 50 years to establish a competitive state fund. Minnesota also created a competitive system for setting workers' compensation insurance rates, in addition to establishing a two-tier benefit system for workers suffering permanent impairments. Louisiana increased its maximum weekly benefits for injured workers from two-thirds to three-fourths of the state's average weekly wage, established a supplemental earnings benefit system, and now provides benefits for disfigurement of any part of the body.

Twenty-three states enacted laws expanding coverage. Most changes provided coverage to groups who previously had none, such as volunteer firefighters and rescue personnel. Coverage was extended to teachers and other workers who

---

*This section was prepared by Mark L. Grobman, State Standards Adviser, Division of State Workers' Compensation Programs, Office of State Liaison and Legislative Analysis, Employment Standards Administration, U.S. Department of Labor.

are subjected to physical or sexual assault. Benefit levels for temporary total disability were increased in 47 jurisdictions (Table 1). Fifteen states enacted provisions on occupational disease. Sixteen states expanded medical and rehabilitative services. To meet increasing costs (Table 2), 10 states established additional funds. Insurance rate reductions were mandated in 14 states.

Private Employment Agencies

Private employment agency regulatory laws were repealed in Idaho in 1982 and Colorado in 1983 (similar actions took place in New Mexico in 1979, Florida in 1980, and South Dakota in 1981). Forty-two states, the District of Columbia and Puerto Rico currently have private employment agency laws.

Among other developments, Iowa passed a measure prohibiting employers from requiring job applicants to pay a fee as a condition of application or hire, including reimbursement for fees paid to employment agencies. California required licensing of job listing services, and in Georgia, career consultants, who do not guarantee actual job placement but who perform such activities as counseling, were specifically made subject to the Fair Business Practices Act.

Child Labor/School Attendance

While only a little activity related to child labor law or regulation, there were a few major developments. Comprehensive new regulations in South Carolina are the same as their federal counterparts in most respects, including limitations on hours of work, and prohibitions on work in hazardous occupations. In Louisiana, 60 day blanket work permits may now be issued to employers under certain circumstances, and changes were made in nightwork and maximum weekly hour requirements for minors under age 16. Changes were also made in the Virginia nightwork hours (Table 4).

Mississippi enacted a new Compulsory School Attendance Law. Implementation is scheduled on a staggered basis with one year added to the compulsory age bracket each year until by the 1989-1990 school year, attendance will be required of children six to 14.

Other Laws

Plant Closings. Aid to workers and communities facing mass layoffs or plant closings remained an area of concern. Among actions taken, California, Illinois and New York initiated programs to assist employees of plants that are about to be closed or relocated to acquire such plants and operate them as employee-owned corporations. The problem of health insurance was addressed by a new law in Connecticut and an amendment in Minnesota which provided for continuation of group insurance for terminated workers.

Civil Money Penalties. The last two years saw increased use of civil money penalties as an enforcement tool. They may now be assessed in minimum wage actions in California and Illinois, in child labor violation cases in Virginia, and in New Jersey for violation of the employment agency law. The labor commissioner in New Hampshire was authorized to impose a civil penalty for any labor law violation.

Agricultural Workers. A federal Migrant and Seasonal Agricultural Worker Protection Act was passed replacing the Farm Labor Contractor Registration Act. Among provisions of the new law, state agencies must submit written state plans in order to be considered for delegated authority by the U.S. Secretary of Labor.

Job Training. Several states enacted legislation to implement participation under the new federal Job Training Partnership Act. Also, additional states passed laws designed to create new jobs in economically depressed areas designated as enterprise zones.

Other. Iowa and West Virginia prohibited employers from requiring employees or applicants to take a polygraph examination as a condition of employment. Workers were protected from discharge because of required jury service in additional states; new laws were enacted giving preference to state contractors or residents on public works projects; and the Labor Department in Kentucky was elevated to cabinet level status headed by a secretary of labor.

Notes

1. Arkansas, Colorado, Delaware, District of Columbia, Illinois, Kentucky, Minnesota, Montana, New Mexico, New York, North Carolina, Oklahoma, Rhode Island, South Dakota and West Virginia.

2. Arkansas, Colorado, Delaware, District of Columbia, Illinois, Kentucky, New Mexico, New York, Oklahoma and South Dakota.

3. Michigan, Minnesota, New Hampshire, New Jersey, North Dakota, South Dakota, Texas, Utah and Virginia.

4. Alaska, Arkansas, California, Colorado, Connecticut, Delaware, Hawaii, Idaho, Illinois, Indiana, Kansas, Kentucky, Louisiana, Maine, Maryland, Massachusetts, Michigan, Minnesota, Missouri, Montana, Nebraska, Nevada, New Hampshire, New Jersey, New Mexico, New York, Ohio, Oklahoma, Oregon, Penn-

sylvania, Rhode Island, Tennessee, Texas, Washington, West Virginia, Wisconsin and Wyoming.

5. Alaska, California, Connecticut, Illinois, Maine, Massachusetts, Michigan, Minnesota, New Hampshire, New Jersey, New York, Rhode Island, West Virginia and Wisconsin.

6. Certification indicates that a state has successfully completed its developmental commitments and meets federal requirements. State performance continues to be monitored for at least one year following certification before final approval is given and federal jurisdiction removed. No state has yet received this final approval, but final approval proceedings have been initiated for Hawaii and the Virgin Islands.

Table 1
MAXIMUM BENEFITS FOR TEMPORARY TOTAL DISABILITY
PROVIDED BY WORKERS' COMPENSATION STATUTES
(As of November 1983)

State or other jurisdiction	Maximum percentage of wages	Maximum payment per week		Maximum period		Total maximum stated in law
		Amount	Based on*	Duration of disability	Number of weeks	
Federal (FECA)(a)..	66-2/3-75(b)	$910.31	(b) 66-2/3% or 75% of the pay of specific grade level in federal civil service	★	...	...
(LHWCA)(a)	66-2/3	524.70	200% of NAWW	★	...	...
Alabama	66-2/3	$184.00	66-2/3% of SAWW	...	300	...
Alaska	66-2/3	996.00(c)	200% of SAWW	★	...	...
Arizona	66-2/3	203.86(d)	...	★	...	...
Arkansas	66-2/3	154.00	...	...	450	$69,300
California	66-2/3	196.00(e)	...	★	...	...
Colorado	66-2/3	296.80(f)	80% of SAWW	★	...	...
Connecticut........	66-2/3	345.00(g)	100% of SAWW	★	...	...
Delaware	66-2/3	223.78	66-2/3% of SAWW	★	...	...
Florida	66-2/3	271.00(c)	100% of SAWW	...	350	...
Georgia	66-2/3	135.00	...	★	...	...
Hawaii	66-2/3	266.00	100% of SAWW	★	...	...
Idaho	60-90	238.50 - 331.25(i)	90% of SAWW		52(j)	...
Illinois	66-2/3	456.33	133-1/3% of SAWW	★	...	...
Indiana............	66-2/3	156.00(k)	...	...	500	78,000(l)
Iowa	80 of worker's spendable earnings	563.00	200% of SAWW	★	...	...
Kansas	66-2/3	218.00	75% of SAWW	★	...	75,000
Kentucky..........	66-2/3	277.66	100% of SAWW	★	...	...
Louisiana..........	66-2/3	245.00(m)	75% of SAWW	★	...	...
Maine	66-2/3	426.43(m)	166-2/3% of SAWW	★	...	...
Maryland	66-2/3	292.00	100% of SAWW	★	...	...
Massachusetts.......	66-2/3	320.29(n)	100% of SAWW	★	...	(o)
Michigan	80 of worker's spendable earnings	330.00(p)	90% of SAWW	★	...	...
Minnesota	66-2/3	313.00	100% of SAWW	★	...	...
Mississippi	66-2/3	112.00		...	450	50,400
Missouri............	66-2/3	202.09	66-2/3% of SAWW	...	400	...
Montana	66-2/3	277.00(f)	100% of SAWW	★	...	...
Nebraska	66-2/3	200.00	...	★	...	...
Nevada.............	66-2/3	314.18	100% of SAWW	★	...	...
New Hampshire	(q)	418.00	100% of SAWW	★	...	...
New Jersey	70	236.00	75% of SAWW	...	400	...
New Mexico	66-2/3	271.76	100% of SAWW	...	600	(r)
New York	66-2/3	255.00	...	★	...	...
North Carolina	66-2/3	248.00	100% of SAWW	★	...	...
North Dakota	66-2/3	278.00(s)(t)	100% of SAWW	★	...	...
Ohio	72 for first 12 weeks; thereafter 66-2/3	321.00(u)	100% of SAWW	★	...	...
Oklahoma	66-2/3	212.00	66-2/3% of SAWW	...	300	...
Oregon.............	66-2/3	316.23	100% of SAWW	★	...	...
Pennsylvania........	66-2/3	306.00	100% of SAWW	★	...	...
Rhode Island........	66-2/3	257.00(v)	100% of SAWW	★	...	...
South Carolina	66-2/3	254.38	100% of SAWW	...	500	...
South Dakota	66-2/3	238.00	100% of SAWW	★	...	...
Tennessee	66-2/3	136.00	...	★	...	54,400
Texas	66-2/3	189.00(w)	...	...	401	...
Utah	66-2/3	300.00(x)	100% of SAWW	...	312	...
Vermont	66-2/3	262.00(y)	100% of SAWW	★	...	...
Virginia	66-2/3	277.00	100% of SAWW	...	500	...
Washington.........	60 - 75	249.33(f)	75% of SAMW	★	...	...
West Virginia	70	318.87	100% of SAWW	...	208	...
Wisconsin	66-2/3	294.00(f)	100% of SAWW	★	...	...
Wyoming............	66-2/3	346.17	100% of SAMW	★	...	...
Dist. of Col.	66-2/3 or 80 of spendable earnings	396.78	100% of SAWW(h)	★	...	...
Puerto Rico..........	66-2/3	45.00	...	...	312	...
Virgin Islands	66-2/3	165.00	66-2/3% of SAWW	★	...	...

Source: Division of State Workers' Compensation Programs, Office of State Liaison and Legislative Analysis, Employment Standards Administration, U.S. Department of Labor.

*SAWW—State's average weekly wage; SAMW—State's average monthly wage; NAWW—National average weekly wage; AWW—Average weekly wage.

(a) Federal Employees' Compensation Act and the Longshoremen's and Harbor Workers' Compensation Act. LHWCA benefits are for private-sector maritime employees (not seamen) who work on navigable waters of the U.S., including dry docks.

(b) Benefits under (FECA) are computed at 66-2/3 percent of the pay of specific grade level in the federal Civil Service for a claimant with no dependents; at 75 percent of pay for a claimant with one or more dependents.

(c) Payments subject to Social Security and Unemployment Insurance benefits offsets.

(d) Additional $10 monthly added to benefits of dependents residing in the U.S.

(e) Effective January 1, 1984 maximum weekly benefit will be $224.

(f) Payments subject to Social Security benefit offsets.

(g) Additional $10 weekly for each dependent child under 18 years of age, up to 50 percent of basic benefit, not to exceed 75 percent of worker's wage.

(h) D.C. AWW or $396.78, whichever is greater.

(i) Additional 7 percent ($18.55) of SAWW is payable for each dependent child up to five children.

(j) After 52 weeks, payments are 60 percent of SAWW for duration of disability.

(k) Effective July 1, 1984 maximum weekly benefit will be $166.

(l) Effective July 1, 1984 maximum total amount payable will be $83,000.

(m) Payments subject to Unemployment Insurance benefit offsets.

(n) Additional $6 will be added per dependent if weekly benefits are below $150.

(o) Total maximum payable not to exceed 250 times the SAWW in effect at time of injury.

(p) Payments subject to reduction by Unemployment Insurance and Social Security benefits, in addition to benefits paid by an employer disability, retirement or pension plan.

(q) Benefits set by a "wage and compensation schedule" up to AWW of $138 (maximum benefit $92). If over $138, compensation will be 66-2/3 percent of worker's AWW not to exceed 100 percent of SAWW.

(r) Total maximum equals the sum of 600 multiplied by the maximum weekly benefit payable at time of injury.

(s) Additional $5 per week for each dependent child, not to exceed worker's net wage.

(t) Payments are reduced by 50 percent of Social Security benefits.

(u) Payments are subject to offset if concurrent and/or duplicate with those under employer non-occupational benefits plan.

(v) Additional $9 for each dependent; including a non-working wife; aggregate not to exceed 80 percent of worker's AWW.

(w) Each cumulative $10 increase in the AWW for manufacturing production workers will increase the maximum weekly benefit by $7 per week.

(x) Additional $5 for dependent spouse and each dependent child up to four, but not to exceed 100 percent of SAWW.

(y) Additional $10 will be paid for each dependent under age 21.

(z) Payments reduced by the amount of benefits received for same disability under another state workers' compensation law.

Table 2
PRELIMINARY ESTIMATES FOR WORKERS' COMPENSATION PAYMENTS: 1980 AND 1981
(In thousands)

State or other jurisdiction	1981				1980				Percentage change in total payment from 1980 to 1981
	Total	Insurance losses paid by private insurance(b)	State and federal fund disbursement(c)	Self insurance payments(d)	Total	Insurance losses paid by private insurance(b)	State and Federal fund disbursement(c)	Self insurance payments(d)	
United States(a)	$14,955,161	$7,868,106	$4,586,624	$2,500,431	$13,562,034	$7,022,707	$4,333,190	$2,206,137	10.3
Alabama	122,362	87,362		35,000	112,440	80,440	…	32,000	8.8
Alaska	62,179	51,779		10,400	59,721	51,921		7,800	4.1
Arizona	133,051	68,101	52,850	12,100	119,777	60,608	48,796	10,373	11.1
Arkansas	102,169	77,969		24,200	82,511	63,961		18,550	23.8
California	1,809,323	1,068,512	242,811	498,000	1,627,715	950,288	233,427	444,000	11.2
Colorado	139,522	47,696	73,426	18,400	114,496	39,970	60,826	13,700	21.9
Connecticut	160,596	138,696		21,900	132,396	117,196		15,200	21.3
Delaware	21,714	16,914		4,800	20,618	16,218		4,400	5.3
Florida	400,165	322,715		77,450	362,000	299,000		63,000	10.5
Georgia	215,867	182,467		33,400	184,828	156,328		28,500	16.8
Hawaii	74,849	54,399		20,450	59,695	44,295		15,400	25.4
Idaho	41,469	29,465		4,300	37,606	26,266		3,700	10.3
Illinois	658,527	553,527	7,704	105,000	665,212	559,212	7,640	106,000	-1.0
Indiana	119,433	98,533		20,900	109,715	91,015		18,700	8.9
Iowa	108,500	88,600		19,900	98,962	82,462		16,500	9.6
Kansas	95,219	80,489		14,730	84,478	72,138		12,340	12.7
Kentucky	164,243	123,075		41,168	160,576	109,508		51,068	2.3
Louisiana	350,923	292,423		58,500	300,629	254,729		45,900	16.7
Maine	108,801	85,201		23,600	81,263	64,463		16,800	33.9
Maryland	212,943	143,690	24,503	44,750	186,841	129,534	19,007	38,300	14.0
Massachusetts	341,505	312,780		28,725	295,770	272,409		23,361	15.5
Michigan	670,392	379,424	22,968	268,000	626,266	343,057	33,209	250,000	7.0
Minnesota	296,558	253,558		43,000	257,484	219,984		37,500	15.2
Mississippi	66,607	60,507		6,100	60,285	54,183		6,100	
Missouri	137,537	113,737		23,800	123,710	104,910		18,800	11.2
Montana	45,253	15,659	24,162(e)	5,432	40,872	14,441	21,724(e)	4,707	10.7
Nebraska	48,768	43,168		5,600	42,457	37,557		4,900	14.9
Nevada	80,899	930	77,620	2,349	69,136	456	66,680	2,000	17.0
New Hampshire	54,911	49,287		5,624	47,965	42,585		5,380	14.5
New Jersey	329,223	298,223		31,000	316,426	284,576		31,850	4.0

New Mexico	68,751	64,851		3,900	54,104	50,104		4,000	27.1
New York	688,815	373,791	193,524	121,500	637,108	346,766	178,025	112,317	8.1
North Carolina	146,806	118,806		28,000	130,817	106,917		23,900	12.2
North Dakota	18,564	137	18,427		16,976	95	16,881		9.4
Ohio	904,918	2,840	587,078	315,000	776,323	1,684	507,639	267,000	16.6
Oklahoma	161,316	110,485	24,831	26,000	133,545	89,084	22,961	21,500	20.8
Oregon	298,349	90,669	144,243	63,437	274,915	81,985	139,565	53,365	8.5
Pennsylvania	656,681	447,204	62,386(e)	147,091	571,908	386,320	56,514	129,074	14.8
Rhode Island	64,805	58,405		6,400	55,319	49,819		5,500	17.1
South Carolina	90,135	75,535		14,600	79,284	66,453		12,831	13.7
South Dakota	15,226	13,226		2,000	13,133	11,433		1,700	15.9
Tennessee	149,738	133,738		16,000	129,112	115,312		13,800	16.0
Texas	808,617	808,617			700,775	700,775			15.4
Utah	45,722	12,880	25,592	7,250	39,280	10,414	22,866	6,000	16.4
Vermont	18,600	17,100		1,500	15,334	14,084		1,250	21.3
Virginia	199,485	157,085		42,400	173,490	136,590		36,900	15.0
Washington	370,461	16,636	272,667	81,158	324,201	12,427	240,960	70,814	14.3
West Virginia	201,764	1,813	132,694	67,257	176,161	145	119,319	56,697	14.5
Wisconsin	191,464	157,164		34,300	171,544	140,844		30,700	11.6
Wyoming	19,436	3,459	15,977		14,072	250	13,822		38.1
Dist. of Col.	78,839	64,779	14,060		69,454	57,494	11,960		13.5
Federal: Civilian Employee Program(f)	842,053		842,053		776,403		776,403		8.5
Black Lung Benefits Program(g)	1,734,592		1,734,592		1,738,548		1,738,548		-0.2
Other(h)	6,516		6,516		8,378		8,378		-22.2

Note: The above figures are the most recent ones available for worker's compensation payment estimates.

Source: Daniel N. Price, Division of Retirement and Survivors Studies, Office of Retirement and Survivors Insurance, Social Security Administration.

(a) Data for 1981 preliminary. Calendar-year figures, except for Montana and West Virginia, for federal civilian employees and "other" federal worker's compensation, and for state fund disbursements in Maryland, Nevada, North Dakota, Utah and Wyoming represent fiscal years ended in 1979 and 1980. Includes benefit payments under Longshoremen's and Harbor Worker's Compensation Act and Defense Bases Compensation Act for the states in which such payments are made.

(b) Net cash and medical benefits paid during the calendar year by private insurance carriers under standard worker's compensation policies. Data primarily from A.M. Best Company, a national data-collecting agency for private insurance.

(c) Net cash and medical benefits paid by state funds compiled from state reports (published and unpublished); estimated for some states.

(d) Cash and medical benefits paid by self-insurers, plus the value of medical benefits paid by employers carrying worker's compensation policies that do not include the medical coverage. Estimated from available state data.

(e) Includes payment of supplemental pensions from general funds.

(f) Payments to civilian federal employees (including emergency relief workers) and their dependents under the Federal Employees' Compensation Act.

(g) Includes $706,538,000 in 1980 and $653,332,000 in 1981 paid by the Department of Labor.

(h) Primarily payments made to dependents of reservists who died while on duty in the Armed Forces, to individuals under the War Hazards Act, War Claims Acts, and Civilian Benefits Act, and to Civil Air Patrol and Reserve Officers Training Corp personnel, persons involved in maritime war risks and law-enforcement officers under Public Law 90-921.

Table 3
STATUS OF STATE PLANS DEVELOPED IN ACCORDANCE WITH THE FEDERAL OCCUPATIONAL SAFETY AND HEALTH ACT
(As of December 19, 1983)

State	States with approved plan(a)	Plan withdrawn by state		Plan submitted: Additional requirements necessary for approval	No plan ever submitted
		After approval	Before approval		
Alabama	...	...	...	★	...
Alaska	★	...	...	...	...
Arizona	★	...	...	...	...
Arkansas	...	...	...	★	...
California	★	...	...	...	...
Colorado	...	★		...	...
Connecticut	★(b,c)	★	...	...	...
Delaware	...	...	...	★	...
Florida	...	...	...	★	...
Georgia	...	...	★	...	...
Hawaii	★	...	...	...	...
Idaho	...	...	...	★	...
Illinois	...	★	...	...	...
Indiana	★	...	...	...	...
Iowa	★	...	...	...	...
Kansas	...	...	...	...	★
Kentucky	★	...	...	...	...
Louisiana	...	...	...	...	★
Maine	...	...	★	...	...
Maryland	★	...	...	...	...
Massachusetts	...	...	...	★	...
Michigan	★	...	...	...	...
Minnesota	★	...	...	...	...
Mississippi	...	...	★	...	...
Missouri	...	...	...	★	...
Montana	...	★	...	...	...
Nebraska	...	...	...	...	★
Nevada	★	...	...	...	...
New Hampshire	...	...	★	...	...
New Jersey	...	★(d)	...	...	...
New Mexico	★(c)	...	...	...	...
New York	...	★(e)	...	...	...
North Carolina	★	...	...	...	...
North Dakota	...	★	...	...	...
Ohio	...	...	...	...	★(d)
Oklahoma	...	...	...	★	...
Oregon	★	...	...	...	...
Pennsylvania	...	...	★	...	...
Rhode Island	...	...	★	...	...
South Carolina	★	...	...	...	...
South Dakota	...	...	...	...	★
Tennessee	★	...	...	...	...
Texas	...	...	...	★	...
Utah	★	...	...	...	...
Vermont	★	...	...	...	...
Virginia	★(c)	...	...	...	...
Washington	★	...	...	...	...
West Virginia	...	...	...	★	...
Wisconsin	...	★(d)	...	...	...
Wyoming	★	...	...	...	...
Dist. of Col.	...	...	...	★	...
American Samoa	...	...	...	★	...
Guam	...	...	...	★(d)	...
Puerto Rico	★	...	...	...	...
Trust Territories	...	...	...	★	...
Virgin Islands	★	...	...	...	...

Source: Based on information prepared by the Directorate of Federal Compliance and State Programs, Occupational Safety and Health Administration, U.S. Department of Labor.

Key:

★—Yes.

. . .—No.

(a) Section 18(b) of the federal Occupational Safety and Health Act provides that any state desiring to assume responsibility for development and enforcement of standards relating to any occupational safety or health issue with respect to which a federal standard has been promulgated under the law shall submit a state plan for the development of such standards and their enforcement. Specific criteria for approval of state plans, including a requirement that they be at least as effective as the federal program, are specified in Section 18(c). The federal funding share may not exceed 50 percent of the total cost to the state of such a program. Federal certification of successful completion of developmental commitments has been achieved in all jurisdictions except as noted in footnote (c).

(b) Enforcement in public sector (state and local government) only as of October 1, 1978. The plan applicable to the private sector was withdrawn after approval.

(c) Federal certification of successful completion of developmental commitments pending in Connecticut, New Mexico and Virginia. All other states have been certified.

(d) Although the jurisdictions do not have approved state plans, the federal Occupational Safety and Health Administration has enforcement agreements with three states (New Jersey, Ohio and Wisconsin) under which state agencies conduct safety and health inspections of migrant labor camps. An enforcement agreement with Guam authorizes that jurisdiction to conduct inspections of all private industry.

(e) New York subsequently submitted a second plan proposing coverage of state and local government employers only which has not yet been approved.

Notes:

1. Concurrent federal enforcement jurisdiction has been suspended in all state plan states (in areas covered by the states) through the vehicle of an Operational Status Agreement.

2. All jurisdictions except Louisiana provide onsite consultation services to employers, either through agreements under Section 7(c)(1) of the federal Occupational Safety and Health Act (47 jurisdictions) or as part of their approved state plan (eight jurisdictions). Up to 90 percent federal funding is provided to state agencies which, at the request of employers, provide onsite and offsite services to assist in recognizing and correcting safety and health hazards. Priority is accorded to smaller businesses in high-hazard industries.

Table 4
SELECTED STATE CHILD LABOR STANDARDS AFFECTING MINORS UNDER 18
(As of December 1983)
(Occupational coverage, exemptions and deviations usually omitted)

State or other jurisdiction	Documentary proof of age required up to age indicated(a)	Maximum daily and weekly hours and days per week for minors under 16 unless other age indicated(b)	Nightwork prohibited for minors under 16 unless other age indicated(b)
Federal (FLSA)	(c)	8-40, non-school period. Schoolday/week: 3-18(d).	7 p.m. (9 p.m. June 1 through Labor Day) to 7 a.m.
Alabama	17; 19 in mines and quarries.	8-40-6. Schoolday/week: 4-28.	8 p.m. to 7 a.m.
Alaska	18	6-day week, under 18. Schoolday/week: 9(f)-23.	9 p.m. to 5 a.m.
Arizona	(e)	8-40. Schoolday/week: 3-18.	9:30 p.m. to 6 a.m.
Arkansas	16	8-48-6. 10-54-6, 16 and 17.	7 p.m. (9 p.m. before non-schoolday) to 6 a.m. 11 p.m. before schoolday to 6 a.m., 16 and 17.
California	18	8-48-6, under 18. Schoolday/week: 4-28(g) under 18, except 8 before non-schoolday, 16 and 17.	10 p.m. (12:30 a.m. before non-schoolday) to 5 a.m., under 18.
Colorado	16	8-40, under 18. Schoolday: 6.	9:30 p.m. to 5 a.m., before schoolday.
Connecticut	18	9-48, under 18. 8-48-6, under 18 in stores, and under 16 in agriculture. (Overtime permitted in certain industries.)	10 p.m. to 6 a.m., under 18. 11 p.m. (midnight before non-schoolday or if not attending school) to 6 a.m., 16 and 17 in restaurants or as usher in non-profit theater.
Delaware	18	8-48-6.	7 p.m. (9 p.m. in stores on Friday, Saturday and vacation) to 6 a.m.
Florida	18	10-40-6. Schoolday: 4 when followed by schoolday, except if enrolled in vocational program.	9 p.m. (11 p.m. before non-schoolday) to 6:30 a.m. 1 a.m. to 5 a.m., 16 and 17.
Georgia	18	8-40. Schoolday: 4.	9 p.m. to 6 a.m.
Hawaii	18	8-40-6. Schoolday: 10(f).	7 p.m. to 7 a.m. (9 p.m. to 6 a.m. June 1 through day before Labor Day).
Idaho	(e)	9-54.	9 p.m. to 6 a.m.

Illinois	16	8-48-6. Schoolday/week: 3 [8(f)]-23(g).	7 p.m. (9 p.m. June 1-Labor Day) to 7 a.m.
Indiana	17	8-40-6, under 17, except minors of 16 not enrolled in school. 9-48 during summer vacation, minors of 16 enrolled in school. Schoolday/week: 3-23.	7 p.m. (9 p.m. before non-schoolday) to 6 a.m. 10 p.m. (midnight before non-schoolday) to 6 a.m., minors of 16 enrolled in school.
Iowa	18	8-40. Schoolday/week: 4-28.	7 p.m. (9 p.m. June 1 through Labor Day) to 7 a.m.
Kansas	16(e)	8-40.	10 p.m. before schoolday to 7 a.m.
Kentucky	18	8-40 Schoolday/week: 3-18, under 16. 6 (8 Saturday and Sunday) - 40, 16 and 17 if attending school.	7 p.m. (9 p.m. June 1 through Labor Day) to 7 a.m. 11:30 p.m. (1 a.m. Friday and Saturday) to 6 a.m. when school in session, 16 and 17.
Louisiana	18	8-40-6. Schoolday: 3.	10 p.m. to 7 a.m.
Maine	16	8-48-6. Schoolday/week: 4-28.	9 p.m. to 7 a.m., under 15. 10 p.m. to 7 a.m., 15.
Maryland	18	8-40. Schoolday/week:4-23(g), under 16. 12(f), under 18	8 p.m. (9 p.m. Memorial Day-Labor Day) to 7 a.m. 8 hours of non-work, non-school time required in each 24-hour day, 16 and 17.
Massachusetts	18	8-48-6. 4-24 in farmwork, under 14. 9-48-6, 16 and 17.	6 p.m. to 6:30 a.m. 10 p.m. (midnight in restaurants on Friday, Saturday and vacation) to 6 a.m., 16 and 17.
Michigan	18	10-48-6, under 18. Schoolweek: 48(f), under 18.	9 p.m. to 7 a.m. 10:30 p.m. to 6 a.m., 16 and 17 if attending school. 11:30 p.m. to 6 a.m., 16 and 17 if not attending school.
Minnesota	18	8-40.	9:30 p.m. to 7 a.m.
Mississippi	(e)	8-44 in factory, mill, cannery or workshop.	7 p.m. to 6 a.m. in factory, mill, cannery or workshop.
Missouri	16	8-40-6.	7 p.m. (10 p.m. before non-schoolday and for minors not enrolled in school) to 7 a.m.
Montana	18	...	...
Nebraska	16	8-48.	8 p.m. to 6 a.m. under 14. 10 p.m. (beyond 10 p.m. before non-schoolday with special permit) to 6 a.m., 14 and 15.
Nevada	17(e)	8-48.	
New Hampshire	18	8 on non-schoolday, 48-hour week during vacation, if enrolled in school. 10-48 at manual or mechanical labor in manufacturing. 10¼-54 at such labor in other employment, under 16 if not enrolled in school, and 16 and 17. Schoolday/week: 3-23 if enrolled in school.	9 p.m. to 7 a.m. if enrolled in school.

Table 4—Continued

SELECTED STATE CHILD LABOR STANDARDS AFFECTING MINORS UNDER 18

State or other jurisdiction	Documentary proof of age required up to age indicated(a)	Maximum daily and weekly hours and days per week for minors under 16 unless other age indicated(b)	Nightwork prohibited for minors under 16 unless other age indicated(b)
New Jersey	18	8-40-6, under 18. 10-hour day, 6-day week in agriculture. Schoolday: 8(f).	6 p.m. to 7 a.m. 11 p.m. to 6 a.m., 16 and 17 during school term, with specified variations.
New Mexico	16	8-44 (48 in special cases), under 14.	9 p.m. to 7 a.m., under 14.
New York	18	8-40-6. 8-48-6, 16 and 17. Schoolday/week: 3-23, under 16. 4-28, 16 if attending school.	7 p.m. to 7 a.m. Midnight to 6 a.m., 16 and 17.
North Carolina	18	8-40. Schoolday/week: 3-18(g).	7 p.m. (9 p.m. before non-schoolday) to 7 a.m.
North Dakota	16	8-48-6, under 18. Schoolday/week: 3-24 if not exempted from school attendance.	7 p.m. (9 p.m. June 1 through Labor Day) to 7 a.m.
Ohio	18	8-40. Schoolday/week: 3-18.	7 p.m. (9 p.m. June 1 through September 1 or during school holidays of 5 days or more) to 7 a.m.
Oklahoma	16	8-48.	6 p.m. to 7 a.m. in factories, factory workshops, pool halls or steam laundries.
Oregon	18	10-44 (emergency overtime with permit)-6. 44-hour week (emergency overtime with permit), 16 and 17.	6 p.m. to 7 a.m., except with special permit.
Pennsylvania	18	8-44-6, under 18. Schoolday/week: 4-26(g), under 16. 28 in schoolweek, 16 and 17 if enrolled in regular day school.	7 p.m. (10 p.m. during vacation from June to Labor Day) to 7 a.m. 11 p.m. (midnight before non-schoolday) to 6 a.m., 16 and 17 if enrolled in regular day school.
Rhode Island	18	8-40. 9-48, 16 and 17.	7 p.m. to 6 a.m. 11:30 p.m. (1:30 a.m. before non-schoolday) to 6 a.m., 16 and 17 if regularly attending school.
South Carolina	(e)	8-40. Schoolday/week: 3-18.	7 p.m. (9 p.m. June 1 through Labor Day) to 7 a.m.
South Dakota	16	8-40.	After 7 p.m. in mercantile establishments, under 14.
Tennessee	18	8-40. Schoolday/week: 3-18.	7 p.m. to 7 a.m. (9 p.m. to 6 a.m. before non-schooldays).
Texas	18(e)	8-48.	10 p.m. (midnight before non-school day or in summer if not enrolled in summer school) to 5 a.m.
Utah	(e)	8-40. Schoolday: 4.	9:30 p.m. to 5 a.m. before schoolday.

Vermont	16(e)	8-48-6. 9-50, 16 and 17.	7 p.m. to 6 a.m.
Virginia	16	8-40-6.	7 p.m. (9 p.m. before non-schoolday and June 1 to Labor Day or with special permit) to 7 a.m.
Washington.........	18	8-hour day, 5-day week, under 18. Schoolday/week: 3-18.	7 p.m. (9 p.m. during summer vacation) to 7 a.m. After 9 p.m. on consecutive nights preceding school-day, 16 and 17.
West Virginia	18	8-40-6	8 p.m. to 5 a.m.
Wisconsin	18	8-24-6 when school in session and 8-40-6 in non-schoolweek. 8-40-6 when school in session and 8-48-6 in non-schoolweek (voluntary overtime per day and week permitted in non-schoolweek up to 50-hour week), 16 and 17 if required to attend school.	8 p.m. (9:30 p.m. before non-schoolday) to 7 a.m. 12:30 a.m. to 6 a.m., except where under direct adult supervision, and with 8 hours rest between end of work and schoolday, 16 and 17 if required to attend school.
Wyoming..........	16	8-56.	10 p.m. (midnight before non-schoolday and for minors not enrolled in school) to 5 a.m. Midnight to 5 a.m., girls 16 and 17.
Dist. of Col.	18	8-48-6, under 18.	7 p.m. (9 p.m. June 1 through Labor Day) to 7 a.m. 10 p.m. to 6 a.m., 16 and 17.
Guam	16	8-40-6, under 18. Schoolday: 9(f), under 18.	After 10 p.m. on schoolday, under 18.
Puerto Rico........	18	8-40-6, under 18. Schoolday: 8(f)	6 p.m. to 8 a.m. 10 p.m. to 6 a.m., 16 and 17.

Source: Division of State Employment Standards Programs, Office of State Liaison and Legislative Analysis, Employment Standards Administration, U.S. Department of Labor.

(a) Many states require an employment certificate for minors under 16 and an age certificate for 16 and 17 year olds; in a few states other types of evidence are acceptable as proof of age. In most states the law provides that age certificates may be issued upon request for persons above the age indicated, or although not specified in the law, such certificates are issued in practice.

(b) State hours limitations on a schoolday and in a schoolweek usually apply only to those enrolled in school. Several states exempt high school graduates from the hours and/or nightwork or other provisions, or have less restrictive provisions for minors participating in various school-work programs. Separate nightwork standards in messenger service and street trades are common, but are not displayed in table.

(c) Not required. State age or employment certificates which show that the minor has attained the minimum age for the job are accepted under the Fair Labor Standards Act.

(d) Students of 14 and 15 enrolled in approved Work Experience and Career Exploration programs may work during school hours up to three hours on a schoolday and 23 hours in a schoolweek.

(e) Proof of age is not mandatory under state law in Arizona, Idaho, Mississippi, South Carolina, Texas and Utah; or in Kansas for minors enrolled in secondary schools, and in Nevada and Vermont for employment outside school hours. For purposes of the Fair Labor Standards Act, federal age certificates are issued upon request by the State Department of Labor in South Carolina and by Wage and Hour Offices in Mississippi and Texas. In Utah, state law directs schools to issue age certificates upon request.

(f) Combined hours of work and school.

(g) More hours are permitted when school is in session less than five days.

Table 5
CHANGES IN BASIC MINIMUM WAGES IN NON-FARM EMPLOYMENT UNDER STATE LAW: SELECTED YEARS 1965 TO 1984

State or other jurisdiction	1965(a)	1968(a)	1970(a)	1972	1976(a)	1979	1980	1981	1982	1983	1984
Federal (FLSA)	$1.15 & $1.25	$1.15 & $1.60	$1.30 & $1.60	$1.60	$2.20 & $2.30	$2.90	$3.10	$3.35	$3.35	$3.35	$3.35
Alabama	..	..	..	..	..	..	..	..	..	..	..
Alaska	1.75	2.10	2.10	2.10	2.80	3.40	3.60	3.85	3.85	3.85	3.85
Arizona	18.72-26.40/wk.(b)	18.72-26.40/wk.(b)	18.72-26.40/wk.(b)	18.72-26.40/wk.(b)	..	..	..	..	..	..	..
Arkansas	1.25/day(b)	1.25/day(b)	1.10	1.20	1.90	2.30	2.55	2.70	2.80	2.95	3.05
California	1.30(b)	1.65(b)	1.65(b)	1.65(b)	2.00	2.90	2.90	3.35	3.35	3.35	3.35
Colorado	.60-1.00(b)	1.00-1.25(b)	1.00-1.25(b)	1.00-1.25(b)	1.00-1.25(b)	1.90	1.90	1.90	1.90	1.90	2.50
Connecticut	1.25	1.40	1.60	1.85	2.21 & 2.31	2.91	3.12	3.37	3.37	3.37	3.37
Delaware	..	1.25	1.25	1.60	2.00	2.00	2.00	2.00	2.00	2.00	3.00
Florida	..	..	..	..	..	..	..	..	..	..	..
Georgia	..	..	..	1.25	1.25	1.25	1.25	1.25	1.25	1.25	1.25
Hawaii	1.25	1.25	1.60	1.60	2.40	2.65	2.90	3.10	3.35	3.35	3.35
Idaho	1.00	1.15	1.25	1.40	1.60	2.30	2.30	2.30	2.30	2.30	2.30
Illinois	..	..	..	1.40	2.10	2.30	2.30	2.30	2.30	2.30	2.65
Indiana	..	1.15	1.25	1.25	1.25	2.00	2.00	2.00	2.00	2.00	2.00
Iowa	..	..	..	..	..	..	..	..	..	..	..
Kansas	.65-.75(b)	.65-.75(b)	.65-.75(b)	.65-.75(b)	1.60	1.60	1.60	1.60	1.60	1.60	1.60
Kentucky	..	..	..	..	..	2.00	2.15	2.15	2.15	2.60	2.60
Louisiana	..	..	..	..	..	..	..	..	..	..	..
Maine	1.00	1.40	1.60	1.40-1.80	2.30	2.90	3.10	3.35	3.35	3.35	3.35
Maryland	..	1.00 & 1.15	1.30	1.60	2.20 & 2.30	2.90	3.10	3.35	3.35	3.35	3.35
Massachusetts	1.25	1.60	1.60	1.75	2.10	2.90	3.10	3.35	3.35	3.35	3.35
Michigan	1.00	1.25	1.25	1.60	2.20	2.90	3.10	3.35	3.35	3.35	3.35
Minnesota	.70-1.15(b)	.70-1.15(b)	.70-1.15(b)	.75-1.60	1.80	2.30	2.90	3.10	3.35	3.35	3.35
Mississippi	..	..	..	..	..	..	..	..	..	..	..
Missouri	..	..	..	..	..	..	..	..	..	..	..
Montana	..	1.00	1.00	1.60	1.80	2.00	2.00	2.00	2.50	2.75	2.75
Nebraska	1.15(b)	1.25	1.30	1.00	1.60	1.60	1.60	1.60	1.60	1.60	1.60
Nevada	1.25	..	..	1.60	2.20 & 2.30	2.75	2.75	2.75	2.75	2.75	2.75
New Hampshire	..	1.40	1.45-1.60	1.60	2.20-2.30	2.90	3.10	3.35	3.35	3.35	3.35
New Jersey	1.00-1.50(b)	..	1.50	1.50	2.20	2.50	3.10	3.35	3.35	3.35	3.35

State											
New Mexico	.70–.80	1.15–1.40	1.30–1.60	1.30–1.60	2.00	2.30	2.65	2.90	3.35	3.35	3.35
New York	1.25	1.60	1.60	1.85	2.30	2.90	3.10	3.35	3.35	3.35	3.35
North Carolina	.85	1.00	1.25	1.45	2.00	2.50	2.75	2.90	3.10	3.35	3.35
North Dakota	.75–.85(b)	1.00–1.25	1.00–1.45	1.00–1.45	2.00–2.20	2.10–2.30	2.60–3.10	2.80–3.10	2.80–3.10	2.80–3.10	2.80–3.10
Ohio	.70–1.00(b)	.75–1.25(b)	.75–1.25(b)	.75–1.25(b)	1.60	2.30	2.30	2.30	2.30	2.30	2.30
Oklahoma	.75–1.00	1.00	1.40	1.40	1.80	2.00	2.00	3.10	3.10	3.10	3.35
Oregon	.75–1.00	1.25	1.25	1.25	2.30	2.30	2.90	3.10	3.10	3.10	3.10
Pennsylvania	1.00	1.15	1.30	1.60	2.20	2.30	3.00	3.35	3.35	3.35	3.35
Rhode Island	1.25	1.40	1.60	1.60	2.30	2.30	2.65	2.90	3.10	3.35	3.35
South Carolina	…	…	…	…	…	…	…	…	…	…	…
South Dakota	17.00–20.00/wk.(b)	17.00–20.00/wk.	1.00	2.00	2.30	2.30	2.30	2.80	2.80	2.80	2.80
Tennessee	…	…	…	…	1.40	1.40	1.40	1.40	1.40	1.40	1.40
Texas	.95–1.10(b)	1.00–1.15(b)	1.20–1.35(b)	1.55–1.70(b)	2.20–2.45(b)	2.35–2.60(b)	2.50–2.75(b)	2.50–2.75(b)	2.50–2.75(b)	2.50–2.75(b)	2.50–2.75(b)
Utah	1.00	1.40	1.60	1.60	2.30	2.90	3.10	3.35	3.35	3.35	3.35
Vermont	1.40	1.60	1.60	2.30	2.90	3.10	3.35	3.35	3.35	3.35	3.35
Virginia	1.25	1.60	1.60	2.00	2.35	2.35	2.65	2.65	2.65	2.65	2.65
Washington	1.00	1.00	1.20	1.20	2.30	2.30	2.30	2.30	2.30	2.30	2.30
West Virginia	1.00–1.10(b)	1.30(b)	1.45(b)	2.00	2.20	2.20	2.75	3.05	3.05	3.05	3.05
Wisconsin	1.25(b)	1.30(b)	1.45(b)	2.10	2.80	3.00	3.25	3.25	3.25	3.25	3.25
Wyoming	.75	1.20	1.30	1.50	1.60	1.60	1.60	1.60	1.60	1.60	1.60
Dist. of Col.	40.00–46.00/wk.(b)	1.25–1.40	1.60–2.00	1.60–2.25	2.25–2.75	2.46–3.00	2.50–3.50	2.50–3.75	2.50–3.90	2.90–3.90	3.50–3.90
Puerto Rico	.35–1.25	.43–1.60	.65–1.60	.76–2.50	1.20–2.50	1.20–3.10	1.20–3.35	1.20–3.35	1.20–3.35	1.20–3.35	1.20–3.35

Source: Prepared by the Division of State Employment Standards Programs, Employment Standards Administration, U.S. Department of Labor.

Note: Rates are for January 1 of each year, except in 1968 and 1972 which show rates as of February. The rates are per hour unless otherwise indicated. A range of rates, as in North Dakota and a few other states, reflects rates which differ by industry, occupation, geographic zone or other factors, as established under wage-board type laws or by statute.

(a) Under the federal Fair Labor Standards Act (FLSA), the two rates shown in 1965, 1968, 1970 and 1976 reflect the former multiple-track minimum wage system in effect from 1961 to 1978. The lower rate applied to newly covered persons brought under the act by amendments, whose rates were gradually phased in. A similar dual-track system was also in effect in certain years under the laws in Connecticut, Maryland and Nevada.

(b) The law applies only to women and minors.

Table 6
SELECTED DATA ON STATE UNEMPLOYMENT INSURANCE OPERATIONS, BY STATE: CALENDAR 1982

State or other jurisdiction	Employers subject to state law	Initial claims	Beneficiaries	Avg. weekly benefit amount paid for total unemployment	Average duration of benefits (weeks)	Total benefit payments	Actual avg. employer contribution rate during year	Funds available for benefits at end of year (in thousands)
Total	4,833,702	30,291,774	11,648,448	$119.34	15.92	$21,529,740,547	2.53	$-2,644,584
Alabama	65,882	631,506	239,884	80.24	12.53	233,960,595	2.33	9,252
Alaska	13,227	74,580	39,720	130.25	14.87	74,884,982	4.02	133,984
Arizona	56,414	246,893	107,506	100.10	15.61	166,276,136	1.19	215,257
Arkansas	44,037	335,638	120,896	96.06	13.34	146,647,998	2.48	-77,042
California	600,524	3,572,604	1,326,992	99.87	18.10	2,353,965,883	2.80	2,707,650
Colorado	77,818	231,479	114,863	140.83	12.30	195,257,912	1.02	-3,853
Connecticut	76,890	385,816	174,608	122.47	13.22	271,492,603	2.24	-252,415
Delaware	13,627	77,832	31,686	98.04	14.36	43,214,410	3.42	-34,795
Florida	225,234	556,972	277,294	95.28	13.21	344,414,910	0.96	865,621
Georgia	103,561	839,519	318,280	96.39	10.77	316,557,299	1.37	397,109
Hawaii	22,441	92,880	41,392	129.82	14.74	75,369,264	1.85	108,019
Idaho	22,431	145,543	58,937	116.45	15.33	99,599,168	2.07	28,916
Illinois	264,074	1,391,134	613,544	146.01	18.81	1,675,946,167	3.79	-2,069,018
Indiana	93,219	775,648	307,305	94.24	13.88	396,511,314	2.73	62,717
Iowa	64,087	315,257	151,520	137.26	14.64	292,906,783	2.27	-63,332
Kansas	55,269	219,019	113,728	128.05	15.19	217,803,266	2.37	142,188
Kentucky	62,095	506,700	192,431	116.01	15.86	339,137,190	3.55	-121,396
Louisiana	82,735	422,392	203,967	144.75	17.17	495,076,418	1.99	-102,343
Maine	30,819	172,856	51,097	101.40	15.36	74,516,779	3.08	-3,819
Maryland	80,284	413,188	177,484	116.14	16.30	330,053,669	1.38	219,984
Massachusetts	120,862	705,299	285,051	115.36	16.29	518,600,351	3.22	436,344
Michigan	159,927	1,784,526	603,996	154.38	17.32	1,594,276,494	3.91	-2,185,816
Minnesota	86,982	379,860	194,261	137.08	16.55	432,105,550	2.15	-287,953
Mississippi	42,749	353,176	130,435	79.72	13.82	141,548,060	2.94	257,154
Missouri	113,971	677,530	237,824	93.72	13.71	292,152,974	2.65	-64,307
Montana	23,346	83,409	40,788	122.11	13.85	64,671,544	2.09	9,216
Nebraska	38,463	102,864	53,947	96.73	13.40	67,923,237	1.23	71,531
Nevada	20,962	119,802	58,538	116.00	15.35	102,595,735	1.78	122,431
New Hampshire	23,645	95,920	53,992	95.37	9.31	46,267,437	1.37	74,817
New Jersey	166,580	827,021	417,986	120.09	16.66	813,221,220	3.20	-423,357
New Mexico	29,208	92,385	41,805	105.49	16.50	72,139,308	1.68	101,427
New York	391,760	1,708,270	634,294	98.88	19.65	1,187,938,102	3.11	819,262
North Carolina	103,506	1,700,853	431,599	104.02	10.95	461,508,871	1.66	400,345
North Dakota	18,467	59,350	27,539	127.61	13.63	47,500,379	2.65	11,304
Ohio	196,231	1,641,069	616,139	143.59	17.77	1,547,753,790	2.83	-1,658,127
Oklahoma	66,850	241,376	120,498	137.22	11.77	181,980,378	0.85	108,387
Oregon	65,885	468,626	170,731	117.48	17.89	352,658,267	2.85	160,561
Pennsylvania	201,996	2,154,475	764,904	146.38	18.47	1,949,535,203	4.58	-2,145,252
Rhode Island	23,079	181,841	68,730	107.67	15.39	111,018,382	4.10	-76,261
South Carolina	54,264	884,816	227,118	93.83	11.78	245,447,127	1.90	50,447
South Dakota	17,528	39,459	15,028	109.53	12.51	20,319,075	1.32	8,554
Tennessee	77,417	859,155	262,214	87.02	15.17	343,015,332	2.45	14,954
Texas	287,807	904,347	421,905	126.91	12.35	648,909,311	0.61	-142,462
Utah	29,973	132,997	65,425	129.68	15.54	129,969,643	1.76	10,108
Vermont	14,273	70,095	29,901	107.42	14.94	45,964,034	3.06	-26,879
Virginia	95,744	577,177	209,952	108.17	10.95	240,279,435	1.83	13,585
Washington	95,478	613,801	250,001	130.68	18.20	569,969,247	2.99	150,264
West Virginia	32,734	180,417	122,607	129.58	15.80	243,604,064	4.56	-144,197
Wisconsin	87,317	761,525	311,125	136.62	15.59	654,791,624	2.59	-412,947
Wyoming	16,595	47,526	29,154	136.56	13.40	52,440,575	2.25	46,006
Dist. of Col.	18,598	44,116	30,994	141.15	22.86	98,864,999	2.19	-56,662
Puerto Rico	54,525	375,350	52,685	65.92	29.84	100,730,753	2.95	-46,857
Virgin Islands	2,332	7,885	4,148	87.01	20.32	7,255,300	3.18	-2,890

Source: Unemployment Insurance Service, Employment and Training Administration, U.S. Department of Labor.

Table 7
TOTAL UNEMPLOYMENT AND UNEMPLOYMENT RATES, BY STATE
ANNUAL AVERAGES: 1976-1981

State or other jurisdiction	Unemployment (in thousands)						Unemployment rates					
	1976	1977	1978	1979	1980	1981	1976	1977	1978	1979	1980	1981
Alabama	102	117	104	119	147	178	6.8	7.4	6.3	7.1	8.8	10.7
Alaska	14	16	20	17	18	18	8.0	9.4	11.2	9.2	9.7	9.3
Arizona	97	85	66	58	83	78	9.8	8.2	6.1	5.1	6.7	6.1
Arkansas	63	62	60	61	76	94	7.1	6.6	6.3	6.2	7.6	9.1
California	906	852	775	702	790	872	9.2	8.2	7.1	6.2	6.8	7.4
Colorado	73	81	74	68	88	84	5.9	6.2	5.5	4.8	5.9	5.5
Connecticut	136	105	78	80	94	98	9.5	7.0	5.2	5.1	5.9	6.2
Delaware	23	24	22	23	22	23	8.9	8.4	7.6	8.0	7.7	7.9
Florida	326	305	262	248	251	308	9.0	8.2	6.6	6.0	5.9	6.8
Georgia	184	161	137	25	163	165	8.1	6.9	5.7	5.1	6.4	6.4
Hawaii	40	31	32	26	21	24	9.8	7.3	7.7	6.3	4.9	5.4
Idaho	21	24	24	25	34	32	5.7	5.9	5.7	5.7	7.9	7.6
Illinois	336	325	329	98	458	474	6.5	6.2	6.1	5.5	8.3	8.5
Indiana	149	142	147	169	252	263	6.1	5.7	5.7	6.4	9.6	10.1
Iowa	53	56	57	59	82	98	4.0	4.0	4.0	4.1	5.8	6.9
Kansas	46	44	34	39	53	50	4.2	4.1	3.1	3.4	4.5	4.2
Kentucky	83	72	84	89	133	140	5.6	4.7	5.2	5.6	8.0	8.4
Louisiana	104	111	116	115	121	156	6.8	7.0	7.0	6.7	6.7	8.4
Maine	43	40	30	36	39	37	8.9	8.4	6.1	7.2	7.8	7.2
Maryland	128	119	115	125	141	157	6.8	6.1	5.6	5.9	6.5	7.3
Massachusetts	260	224	172	159	162	188	9.5	8.1	6.1	5.5	5.6	6.4
Michigan	373	336	289	335	534	528	9.4	8.2	6.9	7.8	12.4	12.3
Minnesota	109	97	75	85	125	118	5.9	5.1	3.8	4.2	5.9	5.5
Mississippi	64	73	71	59	80	88	6.6	7.4	7.1	5.8	7.5	8.3
Missouri	133	131	114	104	167	178	6.2	5.9	5.0	4.5	7.2	7.7
Montana	20	22	22	19	22	26	6.1	6.4	6.0	5.1	6.1	6.9
Nebraska	24	28	23	25	31	32	3.3	3.7	2.9	3.2	4.1	4.1
Nevada	29	25	17	20	27	33	9.0	7.0	4.4	5.1	6.2	7.1
New Hampshire	26	25	16	14	22	24	6.4	5.9	3.8	3.1	4.7	5.0
New Jersey	345	317	247	246	259	262	10.4	9.4	7.2	6.9	7.2	7.3
New Mexico	44	40	31	36	42	42	9.1	7.8	5.8	6.6	7.5	7.3
New York	788	703	602	570	597	612	10.3	9.1	7.7	7.1	7.5	7.6
North Carolina	163	159	120	134	187	188	6.2	5.9	4.3	4.8	6.6	6.4
North Dakota	10	14	14	11	15	16	3.6	4.8	4.6	3.7	5.0	5.0
Ohio	370	312	268	298	426	490	7.8	6.5	5.4	5.9	8.4	9.6
Oklahoma	66	62	49	45	66	52	5.6	5.0	3.9	3.4	4.8	3.6
Oregon	104	85	74	85	107	131	9.5	7.4	6.0	6.8	8.3	9.9
Pennsylvania	407	401	367	370	425	458	7.9	7.7	6.9	6.9	7.8	8.4
Rhode Island	36	39	30	31	34	36	8.1	8.6	6.6	6.6	7.2	7.6
South Carolina	91	96	78	69	96	119	6.9	7.2	5.7	5.0	6.9	8.4
South Dakota	11	10	10	12	16	17	3.4	3.3	3.1	3.5	4.9	5.1
Tennessee	112	123	113	119	152	192	6.0	6.3	5.8	5.8	7.3	9.1
Texas	327	318	299	273	352	373	5.7	5.3	4.8	4.2	5.2	5.3
Utah	30	29	22	26	40	43	5.7	5.3	3.8	4.3	6.3	6.7
Vermont	19	16	14	12	16	15	8.7	7.0	5.7	5.1	6.4	5.7
Virginia	138	128	133	119	128	158	5.9	5.3	5.4	4.7	5.0	6.1
Washington	140	148	124	131	156	189	8.7	8.8	6.8	6.8	7.9	9.5
West Virginia	52	50	47	53	74	84	7.5	7.1	6.3	6.7	9.4	10.7
Wisconsin	120	107	116	106	167	185	5.6	4.9	5.1	4.5	7.2	7.8
Wyoming	7	7	7	6	9	10	4.1	3.6	3.3	2.8	4.0	4.1
Dist. of Col.	31	33	29	25	24	28	9.1	9.7	8.5	7.5	7.3	9.0
Puerto Rico	176	186	175	167	171	202	19.5	19.9	18.1	17.0	17.1	19.9

Source: Unemployment Insurance Service, Employment and Training Administration, U.S. Department of Labor.

Section IX   THE STATE PAGES

The following section presents information on all the states of the United States and the District of Columbia; the commonwealths of Puerto Rico and the Northern Mariana Islands; the territories of American Samoa, Guam and the Virgin Islands; and the United Nations trusteeships of the Federated States of Micronesia, the Marshall Islands and the Republic of Belau.*

Included are listings of executive officials, the justices of the courts of last resort and officers of the legislatures. Lists of all officials are as of early 1984. Comprehensive listings of state legislators and other state officials appear in other publications of The Council of State Governments. Concluding each state listing are population figures and other statistics provided by the U.S. Bureau of the Census, based on the 1980 enumeration.

Preceding the state pages are three tables. The first lists the official names of states, the state capitols with zip codes and the telephone numbers of state central switchboards. The second table presents historical data on all the states, commonwealths and territories. The third presents a compilation of selected state statistics from the state pages.

---

*The Northern Mariana Islands, the Federated States of Micronesia, the Marshall Islands and the Republic of Belau (formerly Palau) have been administered by the United States since July 18, 1947, as part of the Trust Territory of the Pacific Islands (TTPI), a trusteeship of the United Nations. The Northern Mariana Islands separated themselves from TTPI in March 1976 and now operate under a constitutional government instituted January 9, 1978. The Federated States of Micronesia approved a constitution on July 12, 1978, which became effective May 10, 1979. The Marshall Islands approved a constitution on March 1, 1979, which became effective May 1, 1979. The Republic of Belau adopted a constitution on July 9, 1980, which became effective January 1, 1981, and changed the name from Palau to Belau.

Table 1

OFFICIAL NAMES OF STATES AND JURISDICTIONS, CAPITOLS, ZIP CODES AND CENTRAL SWITCHBOARDS

State or other jurisdiction	Name of state capitol(a)	Capital	Zip code	Area code	Central switchboard
Alabama, State of	State Capitol	Montgomery	36130	205	832-6011
Alaska, State of	State Capitol	Juneau	99811	907	465-2111
Arizona, State of	State Capitol	Phoenix	85007	602	255-4900
Arkansas, State of	State Capitol	Little Rock	72201	501	371-3000
California, State of	State Capitol	Sacramento	95814	916	322-9900
Colorado, State of	State Capitol	Denver	80203	303	866-5000
Connecticut, State of	State Capitol	Hartford	06115	203	566-2211
Delaware, State of	Legislative Hall	Dover	19901	302	736-4000
Florida, State of	State Capitol	Tallahassee	32301	904	488-1234
Georgia, State of	State Capitol	Atlanta	30334	404	656-2000
Hawaii, State of	State Capitol	Honolulu	96813	808	548-2211
Idaho, State of	State Capitol	Boise	83720	208	334-2411
Illinois, State of	State House	Springfield	62706	217	782-2000
Indiana, State of	State House	Indianapolis	46204	317	232-3140
Iowa, State of	State Capitol	Des Moines	50319	515	281-5011
Kansas, State of	State House	Topeka	66612	913	296-0111
Kentucky, Commonwealth of	State Capitol	Frankfort	40601	502	564-2500
Louisiana, State of	State Capitol	Baton Rouge	70804	504	342-6600
Maine, State of	State House	Augusta	04333	207	289-1110
Maryland, State of	State House	Annapolis	21401	301	269-6200
Massachusetts, Commonwealth of	State House	Boston	02133	617	727-2121
Michigan, State of	State Capitol	Lansing	48909	517	373-1837
Minnesota, State of	State Capitol	St. Paul	55515	612	296-6013
Mississippi, State of	New Capitol	Jackson	39201	601	359-1000
Missouri, State of	State Capitol	Jefferson City	65101	314	751-2151
Montana, State of	State Capitol	Helena	59620	406	449-2511
Nebraska, State of	State Capitol	Lincoln	68509	402	471-2311
Nevada, State of	State Capitol	Carson City	89710	702	885-5000
New Hampshire, State of	State House	Concord	03301	603	271-1110
New Jersey, State of	State House	Trenton	08625	609	292-2121
New Mexico, State of	State Capitol	Santa Fe	87503	505	827-4011
New York, State of	State Capitol	Albany	12224	518	474-2121
North Carolina, State of	State Capitol	Raleigh	27611	919	733-1110
North Dakota, State of	State Capitol	Bismarck	58505	701	224-2000
Ohio, State of	State House	Columbus	43215	614	466-2000
Oklahoma, State of	State Capitol	Oklahoma City	73105	405	521-2011
Oregon, State of	State Capitol	Salem	97310	503	378-3131
Pennsylvania, Commonwealth of	The Capitol	Harrisburg	17120	717	787-2121
Rhode Island and Providence Plantations, State of	State House	Providence	02903	401	277-2000
South Carolina, State of	State House	Columbia	29211	803	758-0221
South Dakota, State of	State Capitol	Pierre	57501	605	773-3011
Tennessee, State of	State Capitol	Nashville	37219	615	741-3011
Texas, State of	State Capitol	Austin	78701	512	475-2323
Utah, State of	State Capitol	Salt Lake City	84114	801	533-4000
Vermont, State of	State House	Montpelier	05602	802	828-1110
Virginia, Commonwealth of	State Capitol	Richmond	23219	804	786-0000
Washington, State of	Legislative Building	Olympia	98504	206	753-5000
West Virginia, State of	State Capitol	Charleston	25305	304	348-3456
Wisconsin, State of	State Capitol	Madison	53702	608	266-2211
Wyoming, State of	State Capitol	Cheyenne	82002	307	777-7011
District of Columbia	District Building	Washington	20004	202	727-1000
American Samoa, Territory of	Maota Fono	Pago Pago	96799	. . .	633-4116
Federated States of Micronesia	. . .	Kolonia	96941	. . .	NCS
Guam, Territory of	Congress Building	Agana	96910	. . .	477-7821
Marshall Islands	. . .	Majuro	96960	. . .	NCS
Northern Mariana Is., Commonwealth of	Civic Center	Saipan	96950	. . .	NCS
Puerto Rico, Commonwealth of	The Capitol	San Juan	00904	809	721-7000
Republic of Belau	. . .	Koror	96940	. . .	NCS
Virgin Islands, Territory of	Government House	Charlotte Amalie	00801	809	774-0880

NCS—No central switchboard.
(a) In some instances the name is not official.

Table 2
THE STATES OF THE UNION—HISTORICAL DATA

State or other jurisdiction	Capitol	Source of state lands	Date organized as territory	Date admitted to Union	Chrono-logical order of admission to Union
Alabama	Montgomery	Mississippi Territory, 1798(a)	March 3, 1817	Dec. 14, 1819	22
Alaska	Juneau	Purchased from Russia, 1867	Aug. 24, 1912	Jan. 3, 1959	49
Arizona	Phoenix	Ceded by Mexico, 1848(b)	Feb. 24, 1863	Feb. 14, 1912	48
Arkansas..........	Little Rock	Louisiana Purchase, 1803	March 2, 1819	June 15, 1836	25
California	Sacramento	Ceded by Mexico, 1848	(c)	Sept. 9, 1850	31
Colorado	Denver	Louisiana Purchase, 1803(d)	Feb. 28, 1861	Aug. 1, 1876	38
Connecticut	Hartford	Fundamental Orders, Jan. 14, 1638; Royal charter, April 23, 1662(e)	. . .	Jan. 9, 1788(f)	5
Delaware..........	Dover	Swedish charter, 1638; English charter, 1683(e)	. . .	Dec. 7, 1787(f)	1
Florida	Tallahassee	Ceded by Spain, 1819	March 30, 1822	March 3, 1845	27
Georgia	Atlanta	Charter, 1732, from George II to Trustees for Establishing the Colony of Georgia(e)	. . .	Jan. 2, 1788(f)	4
Hawaii	Honolulu	Annexed, 1898	June 14, 1900	Aug. 21, 1959	50
Idaho.............	Boise	Treaty with Britain, 1846	March 4, 1863	July 3, 1890	43
Illinois	Springfield	Northwest Territory, 1787	Feb. 3, 1809	Dec. 3, 1818	21
Indiana	Indianapolis	Northwest Territory, 1787	May 7, 1800	Dec. 11, 1816	19
Iowa	Des Moines	Louisiana Purchase, 1803	June 12, 1838	Dec. 28, 1846	29
Kansas............	Topeka	Louisiana Purchase, 1803(d)	May 30, 1854	Jan. 29, 1861	34
Kentucky	Frankfort	Part of Virginia until admitted as state	(c)	June 1, 1792	15
Louisiana	Baton Rouge	Louisiana Purchase, 1803(g)	March 26, 1804	April 30, 1812	18
Maine	Augusta	Part of Massachusetts until admitted as state	(c)	March 15, 1820	23
Maryland	Annapolis	Charter, 1632, from Charles I to Calvert(e)	. . .	April 28, 1788(f)	7
Massachusetts	Boston	Charter to Massachusetts Bay Company, 1629(e)	. . .	Feb. 6, 1788(f)	6
Michigan	Lansing	Northwest Territory, 1787	Jan. 11, 1805	Jan. 26, 1837	26
Minnesota.........	St. Paul	Northwest Territory, 1787(h)	March 3, 1849	May 11, 1858	32
Mississippi	Jackson	Mississippi Territory(i)	April 7, 1798	Dec. 10, 1817	20
Missouri	Jefferson City	Louisiana Purchase, 1803	June 4, 1812	Aug. 10, 1821	24
Montana..........	Helena	Louisiana Purchase, 1803(j)	May 26, 1864	Nov. 8, 1889	41
Nebraska	Lincoln	Louisiana Purchase, 1803	May 30, 1854	March 1, 1867	37
Nevada	Carson City	Ceded by Mexico, 1848	March 2, 1861	Oct. 31, 1864	36
New Hampshire....	Concord	Grants from Council for New England, 1622 and 1629. Made royal province, 1679(e)	. . .	June 21, 1788(f)	9
New Jersey	Trenton	Dutch settlement, 1618; English charter, 1664(e)	. . .	Dec. 18, 1787(f)	3
New Mexico	Santa Fe	Ceded by Mexico, 1848(b)	Sept. 9, 1850	Jan. 6, 1912	47
New York	Albany	Dutch settlement, 1623; English control, 1664(e)	. . .	July 26, 1788(f)	11
North Carolina	Raleigh	Charter, 1663, from Charles II(e)	. . .	Nov. 21, 1789(f)	12
North Dakota	Bismarck	Louisiana Purchase, 1803(k)	March 2, 1861	Nov. 2, 1889	39
Ohio	Columbus	Northwest Territory, 1787	May 7, 1800	March 1, 1803	17
Oklahoma.........	Oklahoma City	Louisiana Purchase, 1803	May 2, 1890	Nov. 16, 1907	46
Oregon	Salem	Settlement and treaty with Britain, 1846	Aug. 14, 1848	Feb. 14, 1859	33
Pennsylvania	Harrisburg	Grant from Charles II to William Penn, 1681(e)	. . .	Dec. 12, 1787(f)	2
Rhode Island	Providence	Charter, 1663, from Charles II(e)	. . .	May 29, 1790(f)	13
South Carolina	Columbia	Charter, 1663, from Charles II(e)	. . .	May 23, 1788(f)	8
South Dakota	Pierre	Louisiana Purchase, 1803	March 2, 1861	Nov. 2, 1889	40
Tennessee	Nashville	Part of North Carolina until land ceded to U.S. in 1789	June 8, 1790(l)	June 1, 1796	16
Texas.............	Austin	Republic of Texas, 1845	(c)	Dec. 29, 1845	28
Utah	Salt Lake City	Ceded by Mexico, 1848	Sept. 9, 1850	Jan. 4, 1896	45
Vermont	Montpelier	From lands of New Hampshire and New York	(c)	March 4, 1791	14
Virginia	Richmond	Charter, 1609, from James I to London Company(e)	. . .	June 25, 1788(f)	10
Washington	Olympia	Oregon Territory, 1848	March 2, 1853	Nov. 11, 1889	42
West Virginia	Charleston	Part of Virginia until admitted as state	(c)	June 20, 1863	35
Wisconsin	Madison	Northwest Territory, 1787	April 20, 1836	May 29, 1848	30
Wyoming	Cheyenne	Louisiana Purchase, 1803(d,j)	July 25, 1868	July 10, 1890	44
Dist. of Col.	. . .	Maryland(m)		. . .	. . .
American Samoa ...	Pago Pago	————————Became a territory, 1900————————			
Federated States of Micronesia	Kolonia	. . .	May 10, 1979	. . .	. . .
Guam	Agana	Ceded by Spain, 1898	Aug. 1, 1950	. . .	. . .
Marshall Islands....	Majuro	. . .	May 1, 1979	. . .	. . .
No. Mariana Is.	Saipan	. . .	March 24, 1976	. . .	. . .
Puerto Rico	San Juan	Ceded by Spain, 1898	. . .	July 25, 1952(n)	. . .
Republic of Belau ..	Koror	. . .	Jan. 1, 1981		. . .
Virgin Islands	Charlotte Amalie	——————————Purchased from Denmark, March 31, 1917——————————			

(a) By the Treaty of Paris, 1783, England gave up claim to the 13 original Colonies, and to all land within an area extending along the present Canadian border to the Lake of the Woods, down the Mississippi River to the 31st parallel, east to the Chattahoochie, down that river to the mouth of the Flint, east to the source of the St. Mary's, down that river to the ocean. The major part of Alabama was acquired by the Treaty of Paris, and the lower portion from Spain in 1813.

(b) Portion of land obtained by Gadsden Purchase, 1853.

(c) No territorial status before admission to Union.

(d) Portion of land ceded by Mexico, 1848.

(e) One of the original 13 Colonies.

(f) Date of ratification of U.S. Constitution.

(g) West Feliciana District (Baton Rouge) acquired from Spain, 1810; added to Louisiana, 1812.

(h) Portion of land obtained by Louisiana Purchase, 1803.

(i) See footnote (a). The lower portion of Mississippi was also acquired from Spain in 1813.

(j) Portion of land obtained from Oregon Territory, 1848.

(k) The northern portion of the Red River Valley were acquired by treaty with Great Britain in 1818.

(l) Date Southwest Territory (identical boundary as Tennessee's) was created.

(m) Area was originally 100 square miles, taken from Virginia and Maryland. Virginia's portion south of the Potomac was given back to that state in 1846. Site chosen in 1790, city incorporated 1802.

(n) On this date, Puerto Rico became a self-governing commonwealth by compact approved by the U.S. Congress and the voters of Puerto Rico as provided in U.S. Public Law 600 of 1950.

Table 3
STATE STATISTICS

State or other jurisdiction	Land area in square miles	Rank in nation	Population	Rank in nation	Percentage change 1970 to 1980	Density per square mile	No. of representatives in Congress	Capital	Population	Rank in state	Largest city	Population
Alabama	50,767	28	3,893,888	22	13.1	76.7	7	Montgomery	177,857	3	Birmingham	284,413
Alaska	570,833	1	401,851	50	32.8	0.7	1	Juneau	19,528	3	Anchorage	174,431
Arizona	113,508	6	2,718,215	29	53.1	23.9	5	Phoenix	789,704	1	Phoenix	789,704
Arkansas	52,078	27	2,286,435	33	18.9	43.9	4	Little Rock	158,461	1	Little Rock	158,461
California	156,299	3	23,667,902	1	18.5	151.4	45	Sacramento	275,741	7	Los Angeles	2,966,850
Colorado	103,595	8	2,889,964	28	30.8	27.9	6	Denver	492,365	1	Denver	492,365
Connecticut	4,872	48	3,107,576	25	2.5	637.8	6	Hartford	136,392	2	Bridgeport	142,546
Delaware	1,932	49	594,338	47	8.4	30.76	1	Dover	23,512	3	Wilmington	70,195
Florida	54,153	26	9,746,324	7	43.5	180.0	19	Tallahassee	81,548	11	Jacksonville	540,920
Georgia	58,056	21	5,463,105	13	19.1	94.1	10	Atlanta	425,022	1	Atlanta	425,022
Hawaii	6,425	47	964,691	39	25.3	150.1	2	Honolulu(a)	762,874	1	Honolulu(a)	762,874
Idaho	82,412	11	943,935	41	32.4	11.5	2	Boise	102,451	1	Boise	102,451
Illinois	55,645	24	11,426,518	5	2.8	205.3	22	Springfield	99,637	4	Chicago	3,005,072
Indiana	35,932	38	5,490,224	12	5.7	152.8	10	Indianapolis	700,807	1	Indianapolis	700,807
Iowa	55,965	23	2,913,808	27	3.1	52.1	6	Des Moines	191,003	1	Des Moines	191,003
Kansas	81,778	13	2,363,679	32	5.1	28.9	5	Topeka	115,266	3	Wichita	275,282
Kentucky	39,669	37	3,660,777	23	13.7	92.3	7	Frankfort	25,973	9	Louisville	298,451
Louisiana	44,521	33	4,205,900	19	15.4	94.5	8	Baton Rouge	219,419	2	New Orleans	557,515
Maine	30,995	39	1,124,660	38	13.2	36.3	2	Augusta	21,819	6	Portland	61,572
Maryland	9,837	42	4,216,975	18	7.5	428.7	8	Annapolis	31,740	5	Baltimore	786,775
Massachusetts	7,824	45	5,737,037	11	0.8	733.3	11	Boston	562,994	1	Boston	562,994
Michigan	56,954	22	9,262,078	8	4.3	162.6	18	Lansing	130,414	5	Detroit	1,203,339
Minnesota	79,548	14	4,075,970	21	7.1	51.2	8	St. Paul	270,230	2	Minneapolis	370,951
Mississippi	47,233	31	2,520,638	31	13.7	53.4	5	Jackson	202,895	1	Jackson	202,895
Missouri	68,945	18	4,916,686	15	5.1	71.3	9	Jefferson City	33,619	12	St. Louis	453,085
Montana	145,388	4	786,690	44	13.3	5.4	2	Helena	23,938	5	Billings	66,798
Nebraska	76,644	15	1,569,825	35	5.7	20.5	3	Lincoln	171,932	1	Omaha	314,255
Nevada	109,894	7	800,493	43	63.8	7.3	2	Carson City	32,022	5	Las Vegas	164,674
New Hampshire	8,993	44	920,610	42	24.8	102.4	2	Concord	30,400	3	Manchester	90,936
New Jersey	7,468	46	7,364,823	9	2.7	986.2	14	Trenton	92,124	5	Newark	329,248
New Mexico	121,335	5	1,302,894	37	28.1	10.7	3	Santa Fe	48,953	2	Albuquerque	331,767
New York	47,377	30	17,558,072	2	-3.7	370.6	34	Albany	101,727	6	New York	7,071,639
North Carolina	48,843	29	5,881,766	10	15.7	120.4	11	Raleigh	150,255	2	Charlotte	314,447
North Dakota	69,300	17	652,717	46	5.7	9.4	1	Bismarck	44,485	3	Fargo	61,383
Ohio	41,004	35	10,797,630	6	1.3	263.3	21	Columbus	564,871	2	Cleveland	573,822

State or other jurisdiction	Land area in square miles	Rank in nation	Population	Rank in nation	Percentage change 1970 to 1980	Density per square mile	No. of representatives in Congress	Capital	Population	Rank in state	Largest city	Population
Oklahoma	68,655	19	3,025,290	26	18.2	44.1	6	Oklahoma City	403,213	1	Oklahoma City	403,213
Oregon	96,184	10	2,633,105	30	25.9	27.4	5	Salem	89,233	3	Portland	366,383
Pennsylvania	44,888	32	11,863,895	4	0.5	264.3	23	Harrisburg	53,264	10	Philadelphia	1,688,210
Rhode Island	1,055	50	947,154	40	−0.3	897.8	2	Providence	156,804	1	Providence	156,804
South Carolina	30,203	40	3,121,820	24	20.5	103.4	6	Columbia	101,208	1	Columbia	101,208
South Dakota	75,952	16	690,768	45	3.7	9.1	1	Pierre	11,973	9	Sioux Falls	81,343
Tennessee	41,155	34	4,591,120	17	16.9	111.6	9	Nashville	455,651	2	Memphis	646,356
Texas	262,017	2	14,229,191	3	27.1	54.3	27	Austin	345,496	6	Houston	1,595,138
Utah	82,073	12	1,461,037	36	37.9	17.8	3	Salt Lake City	163,033	1	Salt Lake City	163,033
Vermont	9,273	43	511,456	48	15.0	55.2	1	Montpelier	8,241	5	Burlington	37,712
Virginia	39,704	36	5,346,818	14	14.9	134.7	10	Richmond	219,214	3	Norfolk	266,979
Washington	66,511	20	4,132,156	20	21.1	62.1	8	Olympia	27,447	15	Seattle	493,846
West Virginia	24,119	41	1,949,644	34	11.8	80.8	4	Charleston	63,968	1	Charleston	63,968
Wisconsin	54,426	25	4,705,767	16	6.5	86.5	9	Madison	170,616	2	Milwaukee	636,212
Wyoming	96,989	9	469,557	49	41.3	4.8	1	Cheyenne	47,283	2	Casper	51,016
Dist. of Col.	63		638,333		−15.6	10,132.3	1(b)		638,333			
American Samoa	77		32,297		18.9	419.0	...	Pago Pago	3,075		Pago Pago	3,075
Federated States of Micronesia	271		73,160		24.7	507.1	1(b)	Kolonia, Ponape	5,549		Moen, Truk	10,351
Guam	209		105,979		34.9	441	...	Agana	896		Tamuning	8,862
Marshall Islands	70		30,873				1(b)	Majuro	11,791		Majuro	11,791
Northern Mariana Islands	184		16,780		74.1	91.2		Saipan	14,549		Saipan	14,549
Puerto Rico	3,421		3,196,520		17.9	924.1	1(b)	San Juan	424,600		San Juan	424,600
Republic of Belau	192		12,116		8.1	63.1		Koror	7,585		Koror	7,585
Virgin Islands	132		96,569		54.6	731.6	1(b)	Charlotte Amalie, St. Thomas	11,842		Charlotte Amalie	11,842

Source: 1980 Bureau of the Census PC 80-1A final reports.

(a) Honolulu County.
(b) Delegate with committee voting privileges only.

Alabama

Nickname .... The Heart of Dixie
Motto................ *We Dare Defend Our Rights*
Flower .... Camellia
Bird .... Yellowhammer
Tree .... Southern (Longleaf) Pine
Song .... *Alabama*
Stone .... Marble
Mineral .... Hematite
Fish .... Tarpon
Entered the Union .... December 14, 1819
Capital .... Montgomery

SELECTED OFFICIALS

Governor .... George C. Wallace
Lieutenant Governor .... Bill Baxley
Secretary of State .... Don Siegelman
Attorney General .... Charlie Graddick
Treasurer .... Annie Laurie Gunter
Auditor .... Jan Cook
Commr. of Agri. & Ind. .... Albert McDonald

SUPREME COURT

C. C. Torbert Jr., Chief Justice
Oscar W. Adams
Reneau P. Almon
Samuel A. Beatty
T. Eric Embry
James H. Faulkner
Richard L. Jones
Alva Hugh Maddox
Janie L. Shores

LEGISLATURE

President of the Senate .... Bill Baxley
President Pro Tem of the Senate
.... John A. Teague
Secretary of the Senate .... McDowell Lee
Speaker of the House .... Tom Drake
Speaker Pro Tem of the House .... Roy Johnson
Clerk of the House .... John W. Pemberton

STATISTICS

Land Area (square miles) 50,767
　Rank in Nation 28th
Population 3,893,888
　Rank in Nation 22nd
　Density per square mile 76.7
Number of Representatives in Congress.......... 7
Capital City .... Montgomery
　Population 177,857
　Rank in State 3rd
Largest City .... Birmingham
　Population 284,413
Number of Places over 10,000 Population 40

Alaska

Motto .... *North to the Future*
Flower .... Forget-me-not
Bird .... Willow Ptarmigan
Tree .... Sitka Spruce
Song .... *Alaska's Flag*
Gem .... Jade
Fish .... King Salmon
Purchased from Russia by the
　United States .... March 30, 1867
Entered the Union .... January 3, 1959
Capital .... Juneau

SELECTED OFFICIALS

Governor .... Bill Sheffield
Lieutenant Governor .... Stephen McAlpine
Attorney General .... Norman C. Gorsuch

SUPREME COURT

Edmond W. Burke, Chief Justice
Allen Compton
Warren Matthews
Daniel Moore
Jay A. Rabinowitz

LEGISLATURE

President of the Senate .... Jalmar M. Kerttula
Majority Leader .... Bill Ray
Secretary of the Senate .... Peggy Mulligan
Speaker of the House .... Joe L. Hayes
Majority Leader .... Ramona L. Barnes
Chief Clerk of the House .... Irene Cashen

STATISTICS

Land Area (square miles) 570,833
　Rank in Nation 1st
Population 401,851
　Rank in Nation 50th
　Density per square mile 0.7
Number of Representatives in Congress.......... 1
Capital City .... Juneau
　Population 19,528
　Rank in State 3rd
Largest City .... Anchorage
　Population 174,431
Number of Places over 10,000 Population 3

Arizona

Nickname .... The Grand Canyon State
Motto .... *Ditat Deus* (God Enriches)
Flower .... Blossom of the Saguaro Cactus
Bird .... Cactus Wren
Tree .... Palo Verde
Song .... *Arizona March Song*
Gemstone .... Turquoise
Entered the Union .... February 14, 1912
Capital .... Phoenix

SELECTED OFFICIALS

Governor .... Bruce Babbitt
Secretary of State .... Rose Mofford
Attorney General .... Bob K. Corbin
Treasurer .... Ray Rottas
Supt. of Public Instruction .... Carolyn Warner
Mine Inspector .... James H. McCutchan

SUPREME COURT

Frank A. Holohan, Chief Justice
Frank X. Gordon Jr., Vice Chief Justice
James Duke Cameron
Stanley G. Feldman
Jack D. H. Hays

LEGISLATURE

President of the Senate .... Stan Turley
President Pro Tem of the Senate .... Jack Taylor
Secretary of the Senate .... Shirley Wheaton

Speaker of the House .... Frank Kelley
Speaker Pro Tem of the House
.... Sam A. McConnell Jr.
Chief Clerk of the House .... Jane Richards

STATISTICS

Land Area (square miles) 113,508
 Rank in Nation 6th
Population 2,718,215
 Rank in Nation 29th
 Density per square mile 23.9
Number of Representatives in Congress 5
Capital City .... Phoenix
 Population 789,704
 Rank in State 1st
Largest City .... Phoenix
Number of Places over 10,000 Population 17

Arkansas

Nickname .... The Land of Opportunity
Motto .... *Regnat Populus* (The People Rule)
Flower .... Apple Blossom
Bird .... Mockingbird
Tree .... Pine
Song .... *Arkansas*
Stone .... Diamond
Entered the Union .... June 15, 1836
Capital .... Little Rock

SELECTED OFFICIALS

Governor .... Bill Clinton
Lieutenant Governor .... Winston Bryant
Secretary of State .... Paul Riviere
Attorney General .... Steve Clark
Treasurer .... Jimmie Lou Fisher
Auditor .... Julia Hughs Jones
Land Commissioner .... Bill McCuen

SUPREME COURT

Richard B. Adkisson, Chief Justice
Robert H. Dudley
Steele Hays
Darrell Hickman
Les Hollingsworth
John I. Purtle
George Rose Smith

GENERAL ASSEMBLY

President of the Senate .... Winston Bryant
Pres. Pro Tem of the Senate .. William D. Moore Jr.
Secretary of the Senate .... Hal Moody

Speaker of the House .... John Paul Capps
Speaker Pro Tem of the House .... B.G. Hendrix
Chief Clerk of the House .... Mrs. Jim Childers

STATISTICS

Land Area (square miles) 52,078
 Rank in Nation 27th
Population 2,286,435
 Rank in Nation 33rd
 Density per square mile 43.9
Number of Representatives in Congress 4
Capital City .... Little Rock
 Population 158,461
 Rank in State 1st
Largest City .... Little Rock
Number of Places over 10,000 Population 29

California

Nickname......................The Golden State
Motto.................. *Eureka* (I Have Found It)
Flower..........................Golden Poppy
Bird......................California Valley Quail
Tree......................California Redwood
Reptile................California Desert Tortoise
Song..................... *I Love You, California*
Stone.............................Serpentine
Mineral........................Native Gold
Animal...................California Grizzly Bear
Fish.....................California Golden Trout
Insect.............California Dog-Face Butterfly
Marine Mammal..........California Gray Whale
Fossil........................Saber-Toothed Cat
Entered the Union..............September 9, 1850
Capital............................Sacramento

SELECTED OFFICIALS

Governor....................George Deukmejian
Lieutenant Governor..............Leo McCarthy
Secretary of State................March Fong Eu
Attorney General.............John Van de Kamp
Treasurer......................Jesse M. Unruh
Controller ....Kenneth Cory
Supt. of Public Instruction ....Louis Honig

SUPREME COURT

Rose Elizabeth Bird, Chief Justice
Allen E. Broussard
Otto M. Kaus
Anthony Kline
Stanley Mosk
Cruz Reynoso
(Vacancy)

LEGISLATURE

President of the Senate .... Leo T. McCarthy
President Pro Tem of the Senate .. David A. Roberti
Secretary of the Senate...........Darryl R. White
Speaker of the Assembly .... Willie L. Brown Jr.
Speaker Pro Tem of the Assembly ... Frank Vicencia
Chief Clerk of the Assembly......James D. Driscoll

STATISTICS

Land Area (square miles)................156,299
   Rank in Nation......................3rd
Population..........................23,667,902
   Rank in Nation........................1st
   Density per square mile..............151.4
Number of Representatives in Congress....45
Capital City.....................Sacramento
   Population.......................275,741
   Rank in State.........................7th
Largest City......................Los Angeles
   Population.......................2,966,850
Number of Places over 10,000 Population......256

Colorado

Nickname..................The Centennial State
Motto........................ *Nil Sine Numine*
(Nothing Without Providence)
Flower..............Rocky Mountain Columbine
Bird.............................Lark Bunting
Tree....................Colorado Blue Spruce
Song.............. *Where the Columbines Grow*
Stone...........................Aquamarine
Animal.......... Rocky Mountain Bighorn Sheep
Entered the Union................August 1, 1876
Capital............................Denver

SELECTED OFFICIALS

Governor....................Richard D. Lamm
Lieutenant Governor.................Nancy Dick
Secretary of State................Natalie Meyer
Attorney General................Duane Woodard
Treasurer.......................Roy R. Romer

SUPREME COURT

William H. Erickson, Chief Justice
Jean Dubofsky
Howard M. Kirshbaum
George E. Lohr
William D. Neighbors
Joseph R. Quinn
Luis D. Rovira

GENERAL ASSEMBLY

President of the Senate ....Ted L. Strickland
President Pro Tem of the Senate
.........................Robert J. Allshouse
Secretary of the Senate .... Marjorie L. Nielson

Speaker of the House..........Carl "Bev" Bledsoe
Chief Clerk of the House.....Lorraine F. Lombardi

STATISTICS

Land Area (square miles)................103,595
   Rank in Nation.........................8th
Population..........................2,889,964
   Rank in Nation.......................28th
   Density per square mile...................27.9
Number of Representatives in Congress...........6
Capital City...........................Denver
   Population..........................492,365
   Rank in State..........................1st
Largest City...........................Denver
Number of Places over 10,000 Population 25

Connecticut

Nickname .... The Constitution State
Motto .... *Qui Transtulit Sustinet*
(He Who Transplanted Still Sustains)
Animal ....Sperm Whale
Flower .... Mountain Laurel
Bird ....American Robin
Tree .... White Oak
Song .... *Yankee Doodle*
Mineral .... Garnet
Insect .... Praying Mantis
Entered the Union .... January 9, 1788
Capital .... Hartford

SELECTED OFFICIALS

Governor .... William A. O'Neill
Lieutenant Governor .... Joseph J. Fauliso
Secretary of State .... Julia H. Tashjian
Attorney General .... Joseph Lieberman
Treasurer .... Henry E. Parker
Comptroller .... J. Edward Caldwell

SUPREME COURT

John A. Speziale, Chief Justice
Maurice J. Sponzo, Chief Court Administrator
Anthony E. Grillo
Arthur H. Healey
Leo Parskey
Ellen A. Peters
David M. Shea

GENERAL ASSEMBLY

President of the Senate .... Joseph J. Fauliso
President Pro Tem of the Senate
.... James J. Murphy Jr.
Clerk of the Senate .... Mark C. Hauslaib

Speaker of the House .... Irving J. Stolberg
Deputy Speaker of the House .... Robert F. Frankel
Clerk of the House .... Thomas P. Sheridan

STATISTICS

Land Area (square miles) 4,872
 Rank in Nation 48th
Population 3,107,576
 Rank in Nation 25th
 Density per square mile 637.8
Number of Representatives in Congress 6
Capital City .... Hartford
 Population 136,392
 Rank in State 2nd
Largest City .... Bridgeport
 Population 142,546
Number of Places over 10,000 Population 22

Delaware

Nickname .... The First State
Motto .... *Liberty and Independence*
Flower .... Peach Blossom
Bird .... Blue Hen Chicken
Tree .... American Holly
Song .... *Our Delaware*
Entered the Union .... December 7, 1787
Capital .... Dover

SELECTED OFFICIALS

Governor .... Pierre S. du Pont IV
Lieutenant Governor .... Michael N. Castle
Attorney General .... Charles M. Oberly III
Treasurer .... Janet C. Rzewnicki
Auditor .... Dennis E. Greenhouse
Insurance Commissioner .... David H. Elliott

SUPREME COURT

Daniel L. Herrmann, Chief Justice
Andrew D. Christie
Henry R. Horsey
John J. McNeilly
Andrew G.T. Moore II

GENERAL ASSEMBLY

President of the Senate .... Michael N. Castle
President Pro Tem of the Senate
.... Richard S. Cordrey
Secretary of the Senate .... Betty Jean Caniford

Speaker of the House .... Orlando J. George Jr.
Chief Clerk of the House .... Doris Dayton

STATISTICS

Land Area (square miles) 1,932
 Rank in Nation 49th
Population 594,338
 Rank in Nation 47th
 Density per square mile 307.6
Number of Representatives in Congress 1
Capital City .... Dover
 Population 23,512
 Rank in State 3rd
Largest City .... Wilmington
 Population 70,195
Number of Places over 10,000 Population 3

Florida

Nickname . . . . The Sunshine State
Motto . . . . *In God We Trust*
Flower . . . . Orange Blossom
Bird. . . . . .Mockingbird
Tree . . . . Sabal Palmetto Palm
Song. . . . . *Old Folks at Home*
Stone. . . . . .Agatized Coral
Gem. . . . . .Moonstone
Saltwater Mammal . . . . Dolphin
Marine Mammal . . . . .Manatee
Saltwater Fish . . . . Atlantic Sailfish
Freshwater Fish . . . . .Florida Large Mouth Bass
Shell . . . . Horse Conch
Animal . . . . .Florida Panther
Beverage. . . . . .Orange Juice
Entered the Union . . . . March 3, 1845
Capital . . . . Tallahassee

SELECTED OFFICIALS

Governor . . . . Bob Graham
Lieutenant Governor . . . . Wayne Mixson
Secretary of State. . . . . .George Firestone
Attorney General. . . . . .Jim Smith
Treasurer/Comm. of Insurance . . . . .Bill Gunter
Comptroller .Gerald A. Lewis
Commissioner of Education . . .Ralph D. Turlington
Commissioner of Agriculture . . . . .Doyle Conner

SUPREME COURT

James E. Alderman, Chief Justice
James C. Adkins
Joseph A. Boyd Jr.
Raymond Ehrlich
Parker Lee McDonald
Ben F. Overton
Leander J. Shaw, Jr.

LEGISLATURE

President of the Senate . . . . Curtis Peterson
President Pro Tem of the Senate . . . Jack D. Gordon
Secretary of the Senate . . . . Joe Brown

Speaker of the House . . . . H. Lee Moffitt
Speaker Pro Tem of the House . . . . Steve Pajcic
Clerk of the House . . . . Allen Morris

STATISTICS

Land Area (square miles) 54,153
   Rank in Nation 26th
Population. 9,746,324
   Rank in Nation 7th
   Density per square mile 180
Number of Representatives in Congress. 19
Capital City . . . . Tallahassee
   Population 81,548
   Rank in State 11th
Largest City . . . . Jacksonville
   Population 540,920
Number of Places over 10,000 Population 96

Georgia

Nickname . . . . The Empire State of the South*
Motto . . . . *Wisdom, Justice and Moderation*
Flower. . . . . .Cherokee Rose
Bird . . . . Brown Thrasher
Tree . . . . .Live Oak
Song . . . . *Georgia on My Mind*
Fish . . . . Largemouth Bass
Entered the Union . . . . January 2, 1788
Capital . . . . .Atlanta

*Unofficial

SELECTED OFFICIALS

Governor. .Joe Frank Harris
Lieutenant Governor . . . . Zell Miller
Secretary of State . . . . Max Cleland
Attorney General. . . . . .Michael J. Bowers
Comptroller General . . . . .Johnnie L. Caldwell
Superintendent of Schools . . . . . . .Charles McDaniel
Commissioner of Agriculture . . . . . .Thomas T. Irvin
Commissioner of Labor . . . . .Sam Caldwell

SUPREME COURT

Harold N. Hill Jr., Chief Justice
Thomas O. Marshall, Presiding Justice
Richard Bell
Harold G. Clarke
Hardy Gregory Jr.
George T. Smith
Charles L. Weltner

GENERAL ASSEMBLY

President of the Senate . . . . Zell B. Miller
President Pro Tem of the Senate . . . . . . Joe Kennedy
Secretary of the Senate . . . . Hamilton McWhorter Jr.

Speaker of the House . . . . Thomas B. Murphy
Speaker Pro Tem of the House. . . . . . . .Jack Connell
Clerk of the House . . . . Glenn W. Ellard

STATISTICS

Land Area (square miles) 58,056
   Rank in Nation 21st
Population. 5,463,105
   Rank in Nation 13th
   Density per square mile 94.1
Number of Representatives in Congress. 10
Capital City . . . . .Atlanta
   Population 425,022
   Rank in State. 1st
Largest City . . . . Atlanta
Number of Places over 10,000 Population 39

Hawaii

Nickname......................The Aloha State
Motto .... *Ua Mau Ke Ea O Ka Aina I Ka Pono*
(The Life of the Land Is Perpetuated
in Righteousness)
Flower ....Hibiscus
Bird............................Hawaiian Goose
Tree..................................Candlenut
Song ....*Hawaii Ponoi*
Entered the Union................August 21, 1959
Capital..............................Honolulu

SELECTED OFFICIALS

Governor .... George R. Ariyoshi
Lieutenant Governor................John Waihee

SUPREME COURT

Herman T.F. Lum, Chief Justice
Yoshimi Hayashi
Edward Nakamura
Frank Padgett
James H. Wakatsuki

LEGISLATURE

President of the Senate .... Richard S. H. Wong
Vice President of the Senate ..... Duke T. Kawasaki
Clerk of the Senate.............T. David Woo Jr.

Speaker of the House .... Henry Haalilio Peters
Vice Speaker of the House .... Daniel J. Kihano
Clerk of the House .... George M. Takane

STATISTICS

Land Area (square miles) 6,425
    Rank in Nation 47th
Population 964,691
    Rank in Nation 39th
    Density per square mile 150.1
Number of Representatives in Congress...........2
Capital City .... Honolulu
    Population (county & city) 762,874
    Rank in State............................1st
Largest City........................Honolulu
Number of Places over 10,000 Population 12

Idaho

Nickname......................The Gem State
Motto .... *Esto Perpetua* (Let It Be Perpetual)
Flower ....Syringa
Bird .... Mountain Bluebird
Tree .... Western White Pine
Song .... *Here We Have Idaho*
Gemstone .... Idaho Star Garnet
Horse .... Appaloosa
Entered the Union .... July 3, 1890
Capital.................................Boise

SELECTED OFFICIALS

Governor........................John V. Evans
Lieutenant Governor.............David H. Leroy
Secretary of State...............Pete T. Cenarrusa
Attorney General.....................Jim Jones
Treasurer ....Marjorie Ruth Moon
Auditor ....Joe R. Williams
Supt. of Public Instruction.........Jerry L. Evans

SUPREME COURT

Charles R. Donaldson, Chief Justice
Robert E. Bakes
Stephen Bistline
Robert G. Huntley Jr.
Allan G. Shepard

LEGISLATURE

President of the Senate .... David H. Leroy
President Pro Tem of the Senate .... James Risch
Secretary of the Senate .... Dorthea Baxter

Speaker of the House .... Tom W. Stivers
Chief Clerk of the House .... Phyllis Watson

STATISTICS

Land Area (square miles) 82,412
    Rank in Nation 11th
Population 943,935
    Rank in Nation 41st
    Density per square mile 11.5
Number of Representatives in Congress...........2
Capital City..............................Boise
    Population 102,451
    Rank in State............................1st
Largest City .... Boise
Number of Places over 10,000 Population 11

Illinois

Nickname . . . . The Prairie State
Motto . . . . *State Sovereignty-National Union*
Flower . . . . Native Violet
Bird . . . . Cardinal
Tree . . . . White Oak
Song . . . . *Illinois*
Mineral . . . . Fluorite
Animal . . . . White-tailed deer
Insect . . . . Monarch Butterfly
Entered the Union . . . . December 3, 1818
Capital . . . . Springfield

SELECTED OFFICIALS

Governor . . . . James R. Thompson
Lieutenant Governor . . . . George H. Ryan
Secretary of State . . . . Jim Edgar
Attorney General . . . . Neil F. Hartigan
Treasurer . . . . James H. Donnewald
Comptroller . . . . Roland W. Burris

SUPREME COURT

Howard C. Ryan, Chief Justice
William G. Clark
Joseph H. Goldenhersh
Thomas J. Moran
Seymour Simon
Robert C. Underwood
Daniel P. Ward

GENERAL ASSEMBLY

President of the Senate . . . . Philip J. Rock
Secretary of the Senate . . . . Kenneth A. Wright

Speaker of the House . . . . Michael J. Madigan
Chief Clerk of the House . . . . John F. O'Brien

STATISTICS

Land Area (square miles) 55,645
   Rank in Nation 24th
Population 11,426,518
   Rank in Nation 5th
   Density per square mile 205.3
Number of Representatives in Congress 22
Capital City . . . . Springfield
   Population 99,637
   Rank in State 4th
Largest City . . . . Chicago
   Population 3,005,072
Number of Places over 10,000 Population 177

Indiana

Nickname . . . . The Hoosier State
Motto . . . . *Crossroads of America*
Flower . . . . Peony
Bird . . . . Cardinal
Tree . . . . Tulip Poplar
Song . . . . *On the Banks of the Wabash, Far Away*
Stone . . . . Limestone
Entered the Union . . . . December 11, 1816
Capital . . . . Indianapolis

SELECTED OFFICIALS

Governor . . . . Robert D. Orr
Lieutenant Governor . . . . John M. Mutz
Secretary of State . . . . Edwin J. Simcox
Attorney General . . . . Linley E. Pearson
Treasurer . . . . Julian L. Ridlen
Auditor . . . . Otis E. Cox
Supt. of Public Instruction . . . . . . Harold H. Negley
Clerk of Supreme Ct. and Ct. of Appeals
. . . . Marjorie H. O'Laughlin

SUPREME COURT

Richard M. Givan, Chief Justice
Roger O. DeBruler
Donald H. Hunter
Alfred J. Pivarnik
Dixon W. Prentice

GENERAL ASSEMBLY

President of the Senate . . . . John M. Mutz
President Pro Tem of the Senate
. . . . Robert Garton
Secretary of the Senate . . . . Sandra B. Culp

Speaker of the House . . . . J. Roberts Dailey
Speaker Pro Tem of the House . . . . Nelson J. Becker
Principal Clerk of the House
. . . . Sharon Cummins Thuma

STATISTICS

Land Area (square miles) 35,932
   Rank in Nation 38th
Population 5,490,224
   Rank in Nation 12th
   Density per square mile 152.8
Number of Representatives in Congress 10
Capital City . . . . Indianapolis
   Population 700,807
   Rank in State 1st
Largest City . . . . Indianapolis
Number of Places over 10,000 Population 61

Iowa

Nickname . . . . The Hawkeye State
Motto . . . . *Our Liberties We Prize and
Our Rights We Will Maintain*
Flower . . . . Wild Rose
Bird . . . . Eastern Goldfinch
Tree . . . . Oak
Song . . . . *The Song of Iowa*
Stone . . . . Geode
Entered the Union . . . . December 28, 1846
Capital . . . . Des Moines

SELECTED OFFICIALS

Governor . . . . Terry E. Branstad
Lieutenant Governor . . . . Robert T. Anderson
Secretary of State . . . . Mary Jane Odell
Attorney General . . . . Tom Miller
Treasurer . . . . Michael L. Fitzgerald
Auditor . . . . Richard D. Johnson
Secretary of Agriculture . . . . . Robert H. Lounsberry

SUPREME COURT

W. Ward Reynoldson, Chief Justice
James H. Carter
K. David Harris
Jerry L. Larson
Mark McCormick
A. A. McGiverin
Louis W. Schultz
Harvey Uhlenhopp
Charles R. Wolle

GENERAL ASSEMBLY

President of the Senate . . . . Robert T. Anderson
President Pro Tem of the Senate
. . . . Charles Miller
Secretary of the Senate . . . . K. Marie Thayer

Speaker of the House . . . . Don Avenson
Speaker Pro Tem of the House . . . . . . John Connors
Chief Clerk of the House . . . . Joseph O'Hern

STATISTICS

Land Area (square miles) 55,965
  Rank in Nation 23rd
Population 2,913,808
  Rank in Nation 27th
  Density per square mile 52.1
Number of Representatives in Congress 6
Capital City . . . . Des Moines
  Population 191,003
  Rank in State 1st
Largest City . . . . Des Moines
Number of Places over 10,000 Population 29

Kansas

Nickname . . . . The Sunflower State
Motto . . . . *Ad Astra per Aspera*
(To the Stars through Difficulties)
Flower . . . . Native Sunflower
Bird . . . . Western Meadowlark
Tree . . . . Cottonwood
Song . . . . *Home on the Range*
Animal . . . . American Buffalo
Insect . . . . Honeybee
Entered the Union . . . . January 29, 1861
Capital . . . . Topeka

SELECTED OFFICIALS

Governor . . . . John Carlin
Lieutenant Governor . . . . Tom Docking
Secretary of State . . . . Jack H. Brier
Attorney General . . . . Robert T. Stephan
Treasurer . . . . Joan Finney
Commissioner of Insurance . . . . Fletcher Bell

SUPREME COURT

Alfred G. Schroeder, Chief Justice
Harold S. Herd
Richard W. Holmes
Tyler C. Lockett
Kay McFarland
Robert H. Miller
David Prager

LEGISLATURE

President of the Senate . . . . Ross O. Doyen
Vice President of the Senate . . . . . . Charlie L. Angell
Secretary of the Senate . . . . Lu Kenney

Speaker of the House . . . . Mike Hayden
Speaker Pro Tem of the House . . . . Ben Foster
Chief Clerk of the House . . . . Geneva Seward

STATISTICS

Land Area (square miles) 81,778
  Rank in Nation 13th
Population 2,363,679
  Rank in Nation 32nd
  Density per square mile 28.9
Number of Representatives in Congress 5
Capital City . . . . Topeka
  Population 115,266
  Rank in State 3rd
Largest City . . . . Wichita
  Population 279,272
Number of Places over 10,000 Population 34

Kentucky

Nickname................... The Bluegrass State
Motto.......... *United We Stand, Divided We Fall*
Flower............................ Goldenrod
Bird................................. Cardinal
Tree.............................. Coffee Tree
Song.................... *My Old Kentucky Home*
Entered the Union.................. June 1, 1792
Capital............................ Frankfort

SELECTED OFFICIALS

Governor.................. Martha Layne Collins
Lieutenant Governor........... Steven L. Beshear
Secretary of State................... Drexell Davis
Attorney General............... David Armstrong
Treasurer.................... Frances Jones Mills
Auditor of Public Accounts...... Mary Ann Tobin
Supt. of Public Instruction....... Alice McDonald
Commissioner of Agriculture....... David Boswell

SUPREME COURT

Robert F. Stephens, Chief Justice
J. Calvin Aker
William Gant
Charles Leibson
James B. Stephenson
Roy Vance
Donald Wintersheimer

GENERAL ASSEMBLY

President of the Senate......... Steven L. Beshear
President Pro Tem of the Senate . Joseph W. Prather
Chief Clerk of the Senate....... Marjorie Wagoner

Speaker of the House........ Bobby H. Richardson
Speaker Pro Tem of the House ... Donald Blandford
Chief Clerk of the House.......... Evelyn Marston

STATISTICS

Land Area (square miles).................. 39,669
   Rank in Nation.......................... 37th
Population..........................3,660,777
   Rank in Nation.......................... 23rd
   Density per square mile.................... 92.3
Number of Representatives in Congress........... 7
Capital City........................ Frankfort
   Population.......................... 25,973
   Rank in State........................... 9th
Largest City......................... Louisville
   Population......................... 298,451
Number of Places over 10,000 Population 30

Louisiana

Nickname..................... The Pelican State
Motto............. *Union, Justice and Confidence*
Flower............................ Magnolia
Bird.................... Eastern Brown Pelican
Tree.............................. Bald Cypress
Songs.................... *Give Me Louisiana* and
                            You Are My Sunshine
Entered the Union .... April 30, 1812
Capital.......................... Baton Rouge

SELECTED OFFICIALS

Governor.................... Edwin W. Edwards
Lieutenant Governor.......... Robert L. Freeman
Secretary of State............... James H. Brown
Attorney General............. William J. Guste Jr.
Treasurer.................... Mary Evelyn Parker
Supt. of Education........... Thomas G. Clausen
Commissioner of Agriculture........... Bob Odom
Commissioner of Insurance.... Sherman A. Bernard
Commissioner of Elections .... Jerry M. Fowler

SUPREME COURT

John A. Dixon Jr., Chief Justice
Fred A. Blanche Jr.
Pascal F. Calogero Jr.
James L. Dennis
Harry T. Lemmon
Walter F. Marcus Jr.
Jack Crozier Watson

LEGISLATURE

President of the Senate........ Samuel B. Nunez Jr.
President Pro Tem of the Senate
                           ....Thomas Hudson
Secretary of the Senate .... Michael S. Baer III

Speaker of the House................. John Alario
Speaker Pro Tem of the House
                           ....Joe Delpit
Clerk of the House .... Alfred Speer

STATISTICS

Land Area (square miles).................. 44,521
   Rank in Nation.......................... 33rd
Population..........................4,205,900
   Rank in Nation.......................... 19th
   Density per square mile.................... 94.5
Number of Representatives in Congress........... 8
Capital City....................... Baton Rouge
   Population......................... 219,419
   Rank in State........................... 2nd
Largest City .... New Orleans
   Population......................... 557,515
Number of Places over 10,000 Population 34

Maine

Nickname................... The Pine Tree State
Motto........................ *Dirigo* (I Direct)
Flower.............. White Pine Cone and Tassel
Bird............................... Chickadee
Tree....................... Eastern White Pine
Song..................... *State of Maine Song*
Mineral......................... Tourmaline
Fish...................... Landlocked Salmon
Insect............................. Honeybee
Animal............................... Moose
Entered the Union............... March 15, 1820
Capital.............................. Augusta

SELECTED OFFICIALS

Governor.................... Joseph E. Brennan
Secretary of State.............. Rodney S. Quinn
Attorney General............... James E. Tierney

SUPREME JUDICIAL COURT

Vincent L. McKusick, Chief Justice
Gene Carter
Edward S. Godfrey
David A. Nichols
David G. Roberts
Elmer H. Violette
Daniel E. Wathen

LEGISLATURE

President of the Senate......... Gerard P. Conley
Secretary of the Senate............ Joy J. O'Brien

Speaker of the House............. John L. Martin
Clerk of the House............... Edwin H. Pert

STATISTICS

Land Area (square miles)................. 30,995
    Rank in Nation......................... 39th
Population.......................... 1,124,660
    Rank in Nation......................... 38th
    Density per square mile.................. 36.3
Number of Representatives in Congress........... 2
Capital City....................... Augusta
    Population........................... 21,819
    Rank in State........................... 6th
Largest City....................... Portland
    Population........................... 61,572
Number of Places over 10,000 Population....... 12

Maryland

Nickname................... The Old Line State
Motto.............. *Fatti Maschii, Parole Femine*
    (Manly Deeds, Womanly Words)
Flower...................... Black-eyed Susan
Bird......................... Baltimore Oriole
Tree............................. White Oak
Song.................... *Maryland, My Maryland*
Animal................. Chesapeake Bay Retriever
Fish........................... Striped Bass
Entered the Union................ April 28, 1788
Capital............................ Annapolis

SELECTED OFFICIALS

Governor..................... Harry R. Hughes
Lieutenant Governor........ J. Joseph Curran Jr.
Secretary of State........... Lorraine M. Sheehan
Attorney General............... Stephen H. Sachs
Comptroller of Treasury........ Louis L. Golstein

COURT OF APPEALS

Robert C. Murphy, Chief Judge
Harry A. Cole
James F. Couch Jr.
Rita C. Davidson
John C. Eldridge
Lawrence F. Rodowsky
Marvin H. Smith

GENERAL ASSEMBLY

President of the Senate....... Melvin A. Steinberg
President Pro Tem of the Senate
    .... Frederick C. Malkus Jr.
Secretary of the Senate.............. Oden Bowie

Speaker of the House......... Benjamin L. Cardin
Speaker Pro Tem of the House
    .... Thomas B. Kernan
Chief Clerk of the House....... Jacqueline M. Spell

STATISTICS

Land Area (square miles).................. 9,837
    Rank in Nation......................... 42nd
Population.......................... 4,216,975
    Rank in Nation......................... 18th
    Density per square mile................. 428.7
Number of Representatives in Congress........... 8
Capital City....................... Annapolis
    Population........................... 31,740
    Rank in State........................... 5th
Largest City....................... Baltimore
    Population.......................... 786,775
Number of Places over 10,000 Population....... 17

Massachusetts

Nickname . . . . The Bay State
Motto . . *Ense Petit Placidam Sub Libertate Quietem*
(By the Sword We Seek Peace,
but Peace Only under Liberty)
Flower . . . . Mayflower
Bird . . . . Chickadee
Tree . . . . American Elm
Song . . . . *All Hail to Massachusetts*
Fish . . . . Cod
Insect . . . . Ladybug
Horse . . . . Morgan
Dog . . . . Boston Terrier
Beverage . . . . Cranberry Juice
Mineral . . . . Babingtonite
Entered the Union . . . . February 6, 1788
Capital City . . . . Boston

SELECTED OFFICIALS

Governor . . . . Michael S. Dukakis
Lieutenant Governor . . . . John F. Kerry
Secretary of the Commonwealth
. . . . Michael J. Connolly
Attorney General . . . . Francis X. Bellotti
Treasurer . . . . Robert Q. Crane
Auditor of the Commonwealth . . . . John J. Finnegan

SUPREME JUDICIAL COURT

Edward F. Hennessey, Chief Justice
Ruth I. Abrams
Paul J. Liacos
Neil L. Lynch
Joseph R. Nolan
Francis P. O'Connor
Herbert P. Wilkins

GENERAL COURT

President of the Senate . . . . William M. Bulger
Clerk of the Senate . . . . Edward B. O'Neill

Speaker of the House . . . . Thomas W. McGee
Clerk of the House . . . . Robert MacQueen

STATISTICS

Land Area (square miles) 7,824
  Rank in Nation 45th
Population 5,737,037
  Rank in Nation 11th
  Density per square mile 733.1
Number of Representatives in Congress 11
Capital City . . . . Boston
  Population 562,994
  Rank in State 1st
Largest City . . . . Boston
Number of Places over 10,000 Population 149

Michigan

Nickname . . . . The Wolverine State
Motto . . . . *Si Quaeris Peninsulam Amoenam
Circumspice* (If You Seek a Pleasant Peninsula,
Look About You)
Flower . . . . Apple Blossom
Bird . . . . Robin
Tree . . . . White Pine
Song . . . . *Michigan, My Michigan*
Stone . . . . Petoskey Stone
Gem . . . . Chlorastrolite
Fish . . . . Trout
Entered the Union . . . . January 26, 1837
Capital . . . . Lansing

SELECTED OFFICIALS

Governor . . . . James Blanchard
Lieutenant Governor . . . . Martha Griffiths
Secretary of State . . . . Richard H. Austin
Attorney General . . . . Frank J. Kelley

SUPREME COURT

G. Mennen Williams, Chief Justice
Patricia J. Boyle
James H. Brickley
Michael F. Cavanagh
Thomas G. Kavanagh
Charles L. Levin
James L. Ryan

LEGISLATURE

President of the Senate . . . . Martha Griffiths
President Pro Tem of the Senate
. . . . Harry A. DeMaso
Secretary of the Senate . . . . William C. Kandler

Speaker of the House . . . . Gary M. Owen
Speaker Pro Tem of the House . . . Matthew McNeely
Clerk of the House . . . . William A. Ryan

STATISTICS

Land Area (square miles) 56,954
  Rank in Nation 22nd
Population 9,262,078
  Rank in Nation 8th
  Density per square mile 162.6
Number of Representatives in Congress 18
Capital City . . . . Lansing
  Population 130,414
  Rank in State 5th
Largest City . . . . Detroit
  Population 1,203,339
Number of Places over 10,000 Population 88

Minnesota

Nickname.................The North Star State
Motto.....*L'Etoile du Nord* (The Star of the North)
Flower.............Pink and White Lady's-Slipper
Bird............................Common Loon
Tree................................Red Pine
Song.......................*Hail! Minnesota*
Gemstone..................Lake Superior Agate
Fish..................................Walleye
Grain...............................Wild Rice
Entered the Union..................May 11, 1858
Capital..............................St. Paul

SELECTED OFFICIALS

Governor........................Rudy Perpich
Lieutenant Governor............Marlene Johnson
Secretary of State..........Joan Anderson Growe
Attorney General........Hubert H. Humphrey III
Treasurer....................Robert W. Mattson
Auditor.........................Arne Carlson

SUPREME COURT

Douglas K. Amdahl, Chief Justice
M. Jeanne Coyne
Glenn E. Kelley
C. Donald Peterson
George M. Scott
John E. Simonett
John J. Todd
Rosalie E. Wahl
Lawrence R. Yetka

LEGISLATURE

President of the Senate........Jerome M. Hughes
Secretary of the Senate.......Patrick E. Flahaven

Speaker of the House.........Harry A. Sieben Jr.
Chief Clerk of the House......Edward A. Burdick

STATISTICS

Land Area (square miles)..................79,548
    Rank in Nation.........................14th
Population...........................4,075,970
    Rank in Nation.........................21st
    Density per square mile....................51.2
Number of Representatives in Congress...........8
Capital City..........................St. Paul
    Population........................270,230
    Rank in State............................2nd
Largest City.....................Minneapolis
    Population........................370,951
Number of Places over 10,000 Population.......65

Mississippi

Nickname...................The Magnolia State
Motto.......*Virtute et Armis* (By Valor and Arms)
Flower................................Magnolia
Bird...............................Mockingbird
Tree................................Magnolia
Song.........................*Go, Mississippi*
Entered the Union.............December 10, 1817
Capital...............................Jackson

SELECTED OFFICIALS

Governor......................William A. Allain
Lieutenant Governor...................Brad Dye
Secretary of State..................Dick Molpus
Attorney General...........Edwin Lloyd Pittman
Treasurer.....................William J. Cole III
Auditor of Public Accounts............Ray Mabus
Supt. of Public Education.....Charles E. Holladay
Commissioner of Agric. and Comm...Jim Buck Ross
Commissioner of Insurance..........George Dale

SUPREME COURT

Neville Patterson, Chief Justice
Vernon H. Broom, Presiding Justice
Harry Walker, Presiding Justice
Francis S. Bowling
Armis E. Hawkins
Dan M. Lee
Roy Noble Lee
Lenore L. Prather
James Robertson

LEGISLATURE

President of the Senate.................Brad Dye
President Pro Tem of the Senate
.........................Tommy N. Brooks
Secretary of the Senate.........Charles H. Griffin

Speaker of the House..............C. B. Newman
Clerk of the House..........Charles J. Jackson Jr.

STATISTICS

Land Area (square miles)..................47,233
    Rank in Nation.........................31st
Population...........................2,520,638
    Rank in Nation.........................31st
    Density per square mile....................53.4
Number of Representatives in Congress...........5
Capital City...........................Jackson
    Population........................202,895
    Rank in State............................1st
Largest City...........................Jackson
Number of Places over 10,000 Population.......27

Missouri

Nickname . . . . The Show Me State
Motto . . . . *Salus Populi Suprema Lex Esto*
(The Welfare of the People Shall Be
the Supreme Law)
Flower . . . . Hawthorn
Bird . . . . Bluebird
Tree . . . . Dogwood
Song . . . . *Missouri Waltz*
Stone . . . . Mozarkite
Entered the Union . . . . August 10, 1821
Capital . . . . Jefferson City

SELECTED OFFICIALS

Governor . . . . Christopher S. Bond
Lieutenant Governor . . . . Kenneth J. Rothman
Secretary of State . . . . James C. Kirkpatrick
Attorney General . . . . John Ashcroft
Treasurer . . . . Mel Carnahan
Auditor . . . . James F. Antonio

SUPREME COURT

Albert Rendlen, Chief Justice
William H. Billings
Charles Blackmer
Robert T. Donnelly
Andrew J. Higgins
Warren D. Welliver

GENERAL ASSEMBLY

President of the Senate . . . . . . Kenneth J. Rothman
President Pro Tem of the Senate
. . . . John E. Scott
Secretary of the Senate . . . . Terry Spieler

Speaker of the House . . . . Robert F. Griffin
Speaker Pro Tem of the House . . . . Patrick J. Hickey
Chief Clerk of the House . . . . . . Douglas W. Burnett

STATISTICS

Land Area (square miles) 68,945
  Rank in Nation 18th
Population 4,916,686
  Rank in Nation 15th
  Density per square mile 71.3
Number of Representatives in Congress 9
Capital City . . . . Jefferson City
  Population 33,619
  Rank in State 12th
Largest City . . . . St. Louis
  Population 453,085
Number of Places over 10,000 Population 51

Montana

Nickname . . . . The Treasure State
Motto . . . . *Oro y Plata* (Gold and Silver)
Flower . . . . Bitterroot
Animal . . . . Grizzley Bear
Bird . . . . Western Meadowlark
Tree . . . . Ponderosa Pine
Song . . . . *Montana*
Stones . . . . Sapphire and Agate
Fish . . . . Blackspotted Cutthroat Trout
Grass . . . . Bluebunch Wheatgrass
Entered the Union . . . . November 8, 1889
Capital . . . . Helena

SELECTED OFFICIALS

Governor . . . . Ted Schwinden
Lieutenant Governor . . . . George Turman
Secretary of State . . . . Jim Waltermire
Attorney General . . . . Mike Greely
Auditor . . . . E.V. "Sonny" Omholt
Supt. of Public Instruction . . . . Ed Argenbright

SUPREME COURT

Frank I. Haswell, Chief Justice
L.C. Gulbrandson
John C. Harrison
Frank B. Morrison
Daniel J. Shea
John C. Sheehy
Fred J. Weber

LEGISLATURE

President of the Senate . . . . Stan Stephens
President Pro Tem of the Senate . . . Allen C. Kolstad
Secretary of the Senate . . . . John W. Larson

Speaker of the House . . . . Daniel Kemmis
Speaker Pro Tem of the House . . . . Joe Brand
Chief Clerk of the House . . . . Jo Ann Owens

STATISTICS

Land Area (square miles) 145,388
  Rank in Nation 4th
Population 786,690
  Rank in Nation 44th
  Density per square mile 5.4
Number of Representatives in Congress 2
Capital City . . . . Helena
  Population 23,938
  Rank in State 5th
Largest City . . . . Billings
  Population 66,798
Number of Places over 10,000 Population 9

Nebraska

Nickname.................The Cornhusker State
Motto..................*Equality Before the Law*
Flower.............................Goldenrod
Bird......................Western Meadowlark
Tree.....................Western Cottonwood
Song......................*Beautiful Nebraska*
Gemstone.........................Blue Agate
Fossil..............................Mammoth
Grass.....................Little Blue Stem
Insect..............................Honeybee
Rock............................Prairie Agate
Entered the Union.................March 1, 1867
Capital...............................Lincoln

SELECTED OFFICIALS

Governor.......................Robert Kerrey
Lieutenant Governor...........Donald McGinley
Secretary of State..............Allen J. Beermann
Attorney General...............Paul L. Douglas
Treasurer............................Kay Orr
Auditor of Public Accounts.....Ray A.C. Johnson

SUPREME COURT

Norman M. Krivosha, Chief Justice
Leslie Boslaugh
D. Nick Caporale
William C. Hastings
Hale McCown
Thomas M. Shanahan
C. Thomas White

LEGISLATURE

President of the Legislature......Donald McGinley
Speaker of the Legislature.......William E. Nichol
Chairman of Executive Board,
    Legislative Council..............Vard Johnson
Vice Chairman of Executive Board,
    Legislative Council..............Shirley Marsh
Clerk of the Legislature.......Patrick J. O'Donnell

STATISTICS

Land Area (square miles).................76,644
    Rank in Nation.........................15th
Population.........................1,569,825
    Rank in Nation.........................35th
    Density per square mile...................20.5
Number of Representatives in Congress...........3
Capital City..........................Lincoln
    Population.......................171,932
    Rank in State...........................2nd
Largest City............................Omaha
    Population.......................314,255
Number of Places over 10,000 Population.......12

Nevada

Nickname......................The Silver State
Motto......................*All for Our Country*
Flower.............................Sagebrush
Bird......................Mountain Bluebird
Tree.........................Single-leaf Pinon
Song.....................*Home Means Nevada*
Animal....................Desert Bighorn Sheep
Metal..................................Silver
Grass....................Indian Rice Grass
Fossil...........................Ichthyosaur
Entered the Union...............October 31, 1864
Capital...........................Carson City

SELECTED OFFICIALS

Governor........................Richard Bryan
Lieutenant Governor...........Robert A. Cashell
Secretary of State.........William D. Swackhamer
Attorney General...................Brian McKay
Treasurer.....................Patricia Cafferata
Controller.....................Darrel R. Daines

SUPREME COURT

Noel E. Manoukian, Chief Justice
E.M. Gunderson
John C. Mowbray
Charles E. Springer
Thomas L. Steffen

LEGISLATURE

President of the Senate..........Robert A. Cashell
President Pro Tem of the Senate
    ....Keith Ashworth
Secretary of the Senate..........Janice L. Thomas

Speaker of the Assembly.........John M. Vergiels
Speaker Pro Tem of the Assembly
    ....James W. Schofield
Chief Clerk of the Assembly...Mouryne B. Landing

STATISTICS

Land Area (square miles).................109,894
    Rank in Nation..........................7th
Population...........................800,493
    Rank in Nation.........................43rd
    Density per square mile....................7.3
Number of Representatives in Congress...........2
Capital City.........................Carson City
    Population.........................32,022
    Rank in State............................5th
Largest City.........................Las Vegas
    Population.......................164,674
Number of Places over 10,000 Population........6

New Hampshire

Nickname . . . . The Granite State
Motto . . . . *Live Free or Die*
Flower . . . . Purple Lilac
Bird . . . . Purple Finch
Tree . . . . White Birch
Song . . . . *Old New Hampshire*
Insect . . . . Ladybug
Entered the Union . . . . June 21, 1788
Capital . . . . Concord

SELECTED OFFICIALS

Governor . . . . John H. Sununu
Secretary of State . . . . William M. Gardner
Attorney General . . . . Gregory H. Smith

SUPREME COURT

John W. King, Chief Justice
William F. Batchelder
Maurice P. Bois
David A. Brock
Charles G. Douglas III

GENERAL COURT

President of the Senate . . . . Vesta M. Roy
Vice President of the Senate
. . . . George E. Freese Jr.
Clerk of the Senate . . . . Wilmont S. White

Speaker of the House . . . . John B. Tucker
Clerk of the House . . . . Carl A. Peterson

STATISTICS

Land Area (square miles) 8,993
    Rank in Nation 44th
Population 920,610
    Rank in Nation 42nd
    Density per square mile 102.4
Number of Representatives in Congress 2
Capital City . . . . Concord
    Population 30,400
    Rank in State 3rd
Largest City . . . . Manchester
    Population 90,936
Number of Places over 10,000 Population 12

New Jersey

Nickname . . . . The Garden State
Motto . . . . *Liberty and Prosperity*
Flower . . . . Purple Violet
Bird . . . . Eastern Goldfinch
Tree . . . . Red Oak
Insect . . . . Honeybee
Animal . . . . Horse
Entered the Union . . . . December 18, 1787
Capital . . . . Trenton

SELECTED OFFICIALS

Governor . . . . Thomas H. Kean
Secretary of State . . . . Jane Burgio
Attorney General . . . . Irwin I. Kimmelman

SUPREME COURT

Robert N. Wilentz, Chief Justice
Robert L. Clifford
Marie L. Garibaldi
Alan B. Handler
Daniel J. O'Hern
Stewart G. Pollock
Sidney M. Schreiber

LEGISLATURE

President of the Senate . . . . Carmen A. Orechio
President Pro Tem of the Senate
. . . . Joseph Hirkala
Secretary of the Senate . . . . Robert E. Gladden

Speaker of the Assembly . . . . Alan J. Karcher
Speaker Pro Tem of the Assembly
. . . . Thomas J. Deverin
Clerk of the Assembly . . . . John J. Miller Jr.

STATISTICS

Land Area (square miles) 7,468
    Rank in Nation 46th
Population 7,364,823
    Rank in Nation 9th
    Density per square mile 986.2
Number of Representatives in Congress 14
Capital City . . . . Trenton
    Population 92,124
    Rank in State 5th
Largest City . . . . Newark
    Population 329,248
Number of Places over 10,000 Population 110

New Mexico

Nickname............The Land of Enchantment
Motto........*Crescit Eundo* (It Grows As It Goes)
Flower................................Yucca
Bird.............................Roadrunner
Tree...............................Pinon
Songs..................*Asi es Nuevo Mexico* and
O, Fair New Mexico
Gem...............................Turquoise
Animal...........................Black Bear
Fish............................Cutthroat Trout
Entered the Union................January 6, 1912
Capital............................Santa Fe

SELECTED OFFICIALS

Governor........................Toney Anaya
Lieutenant Governor...............Mike Runnels
Secretary of State..................Clara P. Jones
Attorney General..............Paul G. Bardacke
Treasurer.......................Earl E. Hartley
Auditor..........................Albert Romero
Commissioner of Public Lands..........Jim Baca

SUPREME COURT

William R. Federici, Chief Justice
William F. Riordan
Dan Sosa Jr.
Harry E. Stowers Jr.
Mary Walters

LEGISLATURE

President of the Senate.............Mike Runnels
President Pro Tem of the Senate......I. M. Smalley
Chief Clerk of the Senate.........Juanita M. Pino

Speaker of the House........Raymond G. Sanchez
Chief Clerk of the House..............Steve Arias

STATISTICS

Land Area (square miles).................121,335
  Rank in Nation..........................5th
Population..........................1,302,894
  Rank in Nation.........................37th
  Density per square mile...................10.7
Number of Representatives in Congress...........3
Capital City..........................Santa Fe
  Population..........................48,953
  Rank in State..........................2nd
Largest City......................Albuquerque
  Population..........................331,767
Number of Places over 10,000 Population.......13

New York

Nickname.....................The Empire State
Motto...................*Excelsior* (Ever Upward)
Flower................................Rose
Bird.............................Bluebird
Tree...........................Sugar Maple
Fruit...............................Apple
Gem................................Garnet
Animal..............................Beaver
Fish................................Trout
Beverage..............................Milk
Entered the Union..................July 26, 1788
Capital...............................Albany

SELECTED OFFICIALS

Governor.....................Mario M. Cuomo
Lieutenant Governor..........Alfred B. DelBello
Attorney General.................Robert Abrams
Comptroller....................Edward V. Regan

COURT OF APPEALS

Lawrence H. Cooke, Chief Judge
Matthew J. Jasen
Hugh R. Jones
Judith S. Kaye
Bernard S. Meyer
Richard D. Simons
Sol Wachtler

LEGISLATURE

President of the Senate........Alfred B. Del Bello
President Pro Tem of the Senate
......................Warren M. Anderson
Secretary of the Senate............Stephen Sloan

Speaker of the Assembly............Stanley Fink
Speaker Pro Tem of the Assembly
......................William F. Passannante
Clerk of the Assembly.........Catherine A. Carey

STATISTICS

Land Area (square miles).................47,377
  Rank in Nation..........................30th
Population........................17,558,072
  Rank in Nation..........................2nd
  Density per square mile................370.6
Number of Representatives in Congress.........34
Capital City...........................Albany
  Population..........................101,727
  Rank in State..........................6th
Largest City.....................New York
  Population.......................7,071,639
Number of Places over 10,000 Population.......86

North Carolina

Nickname	The Tar Heel State
Motto	*Esse Quam Videri*
	(To Be Rather Than to Seem)
Flower	Dogwood
Bird	Cardinal
Tree	Long Leaf Pine
Song	*The Old North State*
Mammal	Gray Squirrel
Gem	Emerald
Fish	Channel Bass
Insect	Honey Bee
Reptile	Turtle
Rock	Granite
Entered the Union	November 21, 1789
Capital	Raleigh

SELECTED OFFICIALS

Governor	James B. Hunt Jr.
Lieutenant Governor	James C. Green
Secretary of State	Thad Eure
Attorney General	Rufus L. Edmisten
Treasurer	Harlan E. Boyles
Auditor	Edward Renfrow
Supt. of Public Instruction	A. Craig Phillips
Commissioner of Agriculture	James A. Graham
Commissioner of Labor	John C. Brooks
Commissioner of Insurance	John R. Ingram

SUPREME COURT

Joseph Branch, Chief Justice
J. William Copeland
James G. Exum Jr.
Henry E. Frye
Harry C. Martin
Louis B. Meyer
Burley B. Mitchell Jr.

GENERAL ASSEMBLY

President of the Senate	James C. Green
President Pro Tem of the Senate	W. Craig Lawing
Principal Clerk of the Senate	Sylvia Fink
Speaker of the House	Liston B. Ramsey
Speaker Pro Tem of the House	Allan C. Barbee
Principal Clerk of the House	Grace Collins

STATISTICS

Land Area (square miles)	48,843
Rank in Nation	29th
Population	5,881,766
Rank in Nation	10th
Density per square mile	120.4
Number of Representatives in Congress	11
Capital City	Raleigh
Population	150,255
Rank in State	3rd
Largest City	Charlotte
Population	314,447
Number of Places over 10,000 Population	43

North Dakota

Nicknames	The Flickertail State and
	The Sioux State
Motto	*Liberty and Union, Now and*
	Forever, One and Inseparable
Flower	Wild Prairie Rose
Bird	Western Meadowlark
Tree	American Elm
Song	*North Dakota Hymn*
March	*Spirit of the Land*
Stone	Teredo Petrified Wood
Fish	Northern Pike
Grass	Western Wheatgrass
Entered the Union	November 2, 1889
Capital	Bismarck

SELECTED OFFICIALS

Governor	Allen I. Olson
Lieutenant Governor	Ernest Sands
Secretary of State	Ben Meier
Attorney General	Robert Wefald
Treasurer	John Lesmeister
Auditor	Robert Peterson
Supt. of Public Instruction	Joe Crawford
Commissioner of Agriculture	Kent Jones
Commissioner of Labor	Orville Hagen
Commissioner of Insurance	J.O. Wigen
Tax Commissioner	Kent Conrad

SUPREME COURT

Ralph J. Erickstad, Chief Justice
H.F. Gierke
Vernon R. Pederson
Paul Sand
Gerald W. VandeWalle

LEGISLATIVE ASSEMBLY

President of the Senate	Ernest Sands
President Pro Tem of the Senate	Russell Thane
Secretary of the Senate	Leo Leidholm
Speaker of the House	Tish Kelly
Chief Clerk of the House	Charles Fleming

STATISTICS

Land Area (square miles)	69,300
Rank in Nation	17th
Population	652,717
Rank in Nation	46th
Density per square mile	9.4
Number of Representatives in Congress	1
Capital City	Bismarck
Population	44,485
Rank in State	2nd
Largest City	Fargo
Population	61,383
Number of Places over 10,000 Population	9

Ohio

Nickname . . . . The Buckeye State
Motto . . . . *With God, All Things Are Possible*
Flower . . . . Scarlet Carnation
Bird . . . . Cardinal
Tree . . . . Buckeye
Song . . . . *Beautiful Ohio*
Stone . . . . Ohio Flint
Insect . . . . Ladybug
Beverage . . . . Tomato Juice
Entered the Union . . . . March 1, 1803
Capital . . . . Columbus

SELECTED OFFICIALS

Governor . . . . Richard F. Celeste
Lieutenant Governor . . . . Myrl H. Shoemaker
Secretary of State . . . . Sherrod Brown
Attorney General . . . . Anthony J. Celebrezze Jr.
Treasurer . . . . Mary Ellen Withrow
Auditor . . . . Thomas E. Ferguson

SUPREME COURT

Frank D. Celebrezze, Chief Justice
Clifford F. Brown
William B. Brown
James Celebreeze
Robert E. Holmes
Ralph S. Locher
A. William Sweeney

GENERAL ASSEMBLY

President of the Senate . . . . Harry Meshel
President Pro Tem of the Senate
. . . . Neal F. Zimmers Jr.
Clerk of the Senate . . . . Thomas A. Smith

Speaker of the House . . . . Vernal G. Riffe Jr.
Speaker Pro Tem of the House . . . . . . Barney Quilter
Legislative Clerk of the House . . . . Ty Marsh
Executive Secretary of the House
. . . . Thomas R. Winters

STATISTICS

Land Area (square miles) 41,004
   Rank in Nation 35th
Population 10,797,630
   Rank in Nation 6th
   Density per square mile 263.5
Number of Representatives in Congress 21
Capital City . . . . Columbus
   Population 564,871
   Rank in State 2nd
Largest City . . . . Cleveland
   Population 573,822
Number of Places over 10,000 Population 150

Oklahoma

Nickname . . . . The Sooner State
Motto . . . . *Labor Omnia Vincit*
             (Labor Conquers All Things)
Flower . . . . Mistletoe
Bird . . . . Scissor-tailed Flycatcher
Tree . . . . Redbud
Grass . . . . Indian Grass
Song . . . . *Oklahoma*
Poem . . . . "Howdy Folks"
Stone . . . . Barite Rose (Rose Rock)
Animal . . . . American Buffalo
Reptile . . . . Mountain Boomer Lizard
Fish . . . . White Bass
Entered the Union . . . . November 16, 1907
Capital . . . . Oklahoma City

SELECTED OFFICIALS

Governor . . . . George Nigh
Lieutenant Governor . . . . Spencer Bernard
Attorney General . . . . Mike Turpin
Treasurer . . . . Leo Winters
Auditor and Inspector . . . . Clifton Scott
Supt. of Public Instruction . . . . Leslie R. Fisher
Insurance Commissioner . . . . Gerald Grimes

SUPREME COURT

Don Barnes, Chief Justice
Robert D. Simms, Vice Chief Justice
John B. Doolin   Marian P. Opala
Rudolph Hargrave   Alma Wilson
Ralph B. Hodges   (Vacancy)
Robert E. Lavender

COURT OF CRIMINAL APPEALS

Hez J. Bussey, Presiding Judge
Tom Brett
Tom R. Cornish

LEGISLATURE

President of the Senate . . . . Spencer Bernard
President Pro Tem of the Senate . . . . . . Marvin York
Secretary of the Senate . . . . Lee Slater

Speaker of the House . . . . Jim L. Barker
Speaker Pro Tem of the House . . . . Mike Murphy
Chief Clerk of the House/Administrator
. . . . Irene McConathy

STATISTICS

Land Area (square miles) 68,655
   Rank in Nation 19th
Population 3,025,290
   Rank in Nation 26th
   Density per square mile 44.1
Number of Representatives in Congress 6
Capital City . . . . Oklahoma City
   Population 403,213
   Rank in State 1st
Largest City . . . . Oklahoma City
Number of Places over 10,000 Population 33

Oregon

Nickname . . . . The Beaver State
Motto . . . . *The Union*
Flower . . . . Oregon Grape
Bird . . . . Western Meadowlark
Tree . . . . Douglas Fir
Song . . . . *Oregon, My Oregon*
Stone . . . . Thunderegg
Animal . . . . Beaver
Fish . . . . Chinook Salmon
Insect . . . . Swallowtail Butterfly
Entered the Union . . . . February 14, 1859
Capital . . . . Salem

SELECTED OFFICIALS

Governor . . . . Victor Atiyeh
Secretary of State . . . . Norma Paulus
Attorney General . . . . Dave Frohnmayer
Treasurer . . . . Bill Rutherford
Supt. of Public Instruction . . . . Verne A. Duncan
Labor Commissioner . . . . Mary Roberts

SUPREME COURT

Edwin J. Peterson, Chief Justice
J.R. Campbell
Wallace P. Carson Jr.
Robert E. Jones
Berkeley Lent
Hans A. Linde
Betty Roberts

LEGISLATIVE ASSEMBLY

President of the Senate . . . . Edward N. Fadeley
President Pro Tem of the Senate
. . . . William McCoy
Secretary of the Senate . . . . Maribel Cadmus

Speaker of the House . . . . Grattan Kerans
Speaker Pro Tem of the House . . . . Rick Bauman
Chief Clerk of the House . . . . (Vacancy)

STATISTICS

Land Area (square miles) 96,184
  Rank in Nation 10th
Population 2,632,105
  Rank in Nation 30th
  Density per square mile 27.4
Number of Representatives in Congress 5
Capital City . . . . Salem
  Population 89,233
  Rank in State 3rd
Largest City . . . . Portland
  Population 366,383
Number of Places over 10,000 Population 29

Pennsylvania

Nickname . . . . The Keystone State
Motto . . . . *Virtue, Liberty and Independence*
Flower . . . . Mountain Laurel
Game Bird . . . . Ruffed Grouse
Tree . . . . Hemlock
Dog . . . . Great Dane
Animal . . . . Whitetail Deer
Insect . . . . Firefly
Fish . . . . Brook Trout
Entered the Union . . . . December 12, 1787
Capital . . . . Harrisburg

SELECTED OFFICIALS

Governor . . . . Richard L. Thornburgh
Lieutenant Governor . . . . . . William W. Scranton III
Attorney General . . . . Leroy S. Zimmerman
Treasurer . . . . R. Budd Dwyer
Auditor General . . . . Al Benedict

SUPREME COURT

Robert N.C. Nix Jr., Chief Justice
John P. Flaherty
William D. Hutchinson
Rolf Larsen
James T. McDermott
Nicholas P. Papadakos
Stephen A. Zappala

GENERAL ASSEMBLY

President of the Senate . . . . William W. Scranton III
President Pro Tem of the Senate
. . . . Henry G. Hager
Secretary of the Senate . . . . Mark R. Corrigan

Speaker of the House . . . . K. Leroy Irvis
Chief Clerk of the House . . . . John J. Zubeck

STATISTICS

Land Area (square miles) 44,888
  Rank in Nation 32nd
Population 11,863,895
  Rank in Nation 4th
  Density per square mile 264.3
Number of Representatives in Congress 23
Capital City . . . . Harrisburg
  Population 53,264
  Rank in State 10th
Largest City . . . . Philadelphia
  Population 1,688,210
Number of Places over 10,000 Population 83

Rhode Island

Nickname .... Little Rhody
Motto .... *Hope*
Flower .... Violet
Bird .... Rhode Island Red
Tree .... Red Maple
Song .... *Rhode Island*
Rock .... Cumberlandite
Mineral .... Bowenite
Entered the Union .... May 29, 1790
Capital .... Providence

SELECTED OFFICIALS

Governor .... J. Joseph Garrahy
Lieutenant Governor .... Thomas R. DiLuglio
Secretary of State .... Susan L. Farmer
Attorney General .... Dennis J. Roberts II
General Treasurer .... Anthony J. Solomon

SUPREME COURT

Joseph A. Bevilacqua, Chief Justice
Thomas F. Kelleher
Florence K. Murray
Donald F. Shay
Joseph R. Weisberger

GENERAL ASSEMBLY

President of the Senate .... Thomas R. DiLuglio
President Pro Tem of the Senate
.... William O'Neill
Secretary of the Senate .... Susan L. Farmer

Speaker of the House .... Matthew J. Smith
First Deputy Speaker of the House
.... Maureen E. Maigret
Reading Clerk of the House
.... Eugene J. McMahon

STATISTICS

Land Area (square miles) 1,055
   Rank in Nation 50th
Population 947,154
   Rank in Nation 40th
   Density per square mile 897.8
Number of Representatives in Congress 2
Capital City .... Providence
   Population 156,804
   Rank in State 1st
Largest City .... Providence
Number of Places over 10,000 Population 27

South Carolina

Nickname .... The Palmetto State
Mottos .... *Animis Opibusque Parati*
   (Prepared in Mind and Resources) and
  Dum Spiro Spero (While I Breathe, I Hope)
Flower .... Carolina Jessamine
Bird .... Carolina Wren
Tree .... Palmetto
Song .... *Carolina*
Stone .... Blue Granite
Entered the Union .... May 23, 1788
Capital .... Columbia

SELECTED OFFICIALS

Governor .... Richard W. Riley
Lieutenant Governor .... Mike Daniel
Secretary of State .... John T. Campbell
Attorney General .... Travis Medlock
Treasurer .... Grady L. Patterson Jr.
Comptroller General .... Earle E. Morris Jr.
Supt. of Education .... Charlie G. Williams
Commissioner of Agriculture .... Les Tindal
Adjutant General .... Eston Marchant

SUPREME COURT

James Woodrow Lewis, Chief Justice
George Tillman Gregory Jr.
David W. Harwell
Bruce Littlejohn
Julius B. Ness

GENERAL ASSEMBLY

President of the Senate .... Mike Daniel
President Pro Tem of the Senate
.... Rembert Dennis
Clerk of the Senate .... James P. Fields Jr.

Speaker of the House .... Ramon Schwartz Jr.
Speaker Pro Tem of the House
.... W. Sterling Anderson
Clerk of the House .... Lois T. Shealy

STATISTICS

Land Area (square miles) 30,203
   Rank in Nation 40th
Population 3,121,820
   Rank in Nation 24th
   Density per square mile 103.4
Number of Representatives in Congress 6
Capital City .... Columbia
   Population 101,208
   Rank in State 1st
Largest City .... Columbia
Number of Places over 10,000 Population 26

South Dakota

Nickname . . . . The Coyote State
Motto . . . . *Under God the People Rule*
Flower . . . . Pasque Flower
Bird . . . . Ringnecked Pheasant
Tree . . . . Black Hills Spruce
Song . . . . *Hail, South Dakota*
Mineral . . . . Rose Quartz
Gem . . . . Fairburn Agate
Animal . . . . Coyote
Insect . . . . Honey Bee
Grass . . . . Western Wheat Grass
Entered the Union . . . . November 2, 1889
Capital City . . . . Pierre

SELECTED OFFICIALS

Governor . . . . William J. Janklow
Lieutenant Governor . . . . Lowell C. Hansen II
Secretary of State . . . . Alice Kundert
Attorney General . . . . Mark Meierhenry
Treasurer . . . . David L. Volk
Auditor . . . . Vern Larson
Commissioner of School and Public Lands
. . . . David L. Volk

SUPREME COURT

Jon Fosheim, Chief Justice
Francis G. Dunn
Frank E. Henderson
Robert E. Morgan
Roger Wollman

LEGISLATURE

President of the Senate . . . . Lowell C. Hansen II
President Pro Tem of the Senate . . Mary A. McClure
Secretary of the Senate . . . . Joyce Hazeltine

Speaker of the House . . . . Jerome B. Lammers
Speaker Pro Tem of the House . . . . . Donald J. Ham
Chief Clerk of the House . . . . Paul Inman

STATISTICS

Land Area (square miles) 75,952
   Rank in Nation 16th
Population 690,768
   Rank in Nation 45th
   Density per square mile 9.1
Number of Representatives in Congress 1
Capital City . . . . Pierre
   Population 11,973
   Rank in State 9th
Largest City . . . . Sioux Falls
   Population 81,343
Number of Places over 10,000 Population 10

Tennessee

Nickname . . . . The Volunteer State
Motto . . . . *Agriculture and Commerce*
Flower . . . . Iris
Bird . . . . Mockingbird
Tree . . . . Tulip Poplar
Wildflower . . . . Passion Flower
Songs . . . . *When It's Iris Time in Tennessee;*
   The Tennessee Waltz; My Homeland, Tennessee;
                 and *My Tennessee*
Stone . . . . Agate
Animal . . . . Raccoon
Insects . . . . Ladybug and Firefly
Gem . . . . Tennessee Pearl
Rock . . . . Limestone
Slogan . . . . Tennessee—America at Its Best
Entered the Union . . . . June 1, 1796
Capital City . . . . Nashville

SELECTED OFFICIALS

Governor . . . . Lamar Alexander
Lieutenant Governor . . . . John S. Wilder
Secretary of State . . . . Gentry Crowell
Attorney General . . . . William M. Leech Jr.

SUPREME COURT

William H.D. Fones, Chief Justice
Ray L. Brock Jr.
Robert E. Cooper
Frank F. Drowota III
William J. Harbison

GENERAL ASSEMBLY

Speaker of the Senate . . . . John S. Wilder
Chief Clerk of the Senate
. . . . Clyde W. McCullough Jr.

Speaker of the House . . . . Ned R. McWherter
Speaker Pro Tem of the House
. . . . Harper Brewer Jr.
Chief Clerk of the House . . . . Bryant Millsaps

STATISTICS

Land Area (square miles) 41,155
   Rank in Nation 34th
Population 4,591,120
   Rank in Nation 17th
   Density per square mile 111.6
Number of Representatives in Congress 9
Capital City . . . . Nashville
   Population 455,651
   Rank in State 2nd
Largest City . . . . Memphis
   Population 646,356
Number of Places over 10,000 Population 37

Texas

Nickname .... The Lone Star State
Motto .... *Friendship*
Flower .... Bluebonnet
Bird .... Mockingbird
Tree .... Pecan
Song .... *Texas, Our Texas*
Stone .... Palmwood
Gem .... Topaz
Grass .... Sideoats Grama
Dish .... Chili
Entered the Union .... December 29, 1845
Capital .... Austin

SELECTED OFFICIALS

Governor .... Mark White
Lieutenant Governor .... William P. Hobby
Attorney General .... Jim Mattox
Treasurer .... Ann Richards
Comptroller of Public Accounts ...... Bob Bullock
Commissioner of Agriculture ...... Jim Hightower
Commissioner of General Land Office
.... Garry Mauro

SUPREME COURT

Jack Pope, Chief Justice

Charles W. Barrow	C.L. Ray
Robert M. Campbell	Ted Robertson
Bill Kilgarlin	Franklin Spears
Sears McGee	James P. Wallace

COURT OF CRIMINAL APPEALS

John F. Onion Jr., Presiding Judge

Charles F. Campbell Jr.	Michael J.
Sam Houston Clinton	McCormick
Thomas G. Davis	Charles Miller
Wilbur C. Davis	Wendell Odom
	Marvin O. Teague

LEGISLATURE

President of the Senate .... William P. Hobby
President Pro Tem of the Senate
.... Lloyd Doggett
Secretary of the Senate .... Betty King

Speaker of the House .... Gibson D. Lewis
Speaker Pro Tem of the House ...... Hugo Berlanga
Chief Clerk of the House .... Betty Murray

STATISTICS

Land Area (square miles) 262,017
  Rank in Nation 2nd
Population 14,229,191
  Rank in Nation 3rd
  Density per square mile 54.3
Number of Representatives in Congress 27
Capital City .... Austin
  Population 345,496
  Rank in State 6th
Largest City .... Houston
  Population 1,595,138
Number of Places over 10,000 Population 151

Utah

Nickname .... The Beehive State
Motto .... *Industry*
Flower .... Sego Lily
Bird .... Seagull
Tree .... Blue Spruce
Song .... *Utah, We Love Thee*
Gem .... Topaz
Entered the Union .... January 4, 1896
Capital .... Salt Lake City

SELECTED OFFICIALS

Governor .... Scott M. Matheson
Lieutenant Governor .... David S. Monson
Attorney General .... David L. Wilkinson
Treasurer .... Edward T. Alter
Auditor .... W. Val Oveson

SUPREME COURT

Gordon R. Hall, Chief Justice
Christine M. Durham
Richard C. Howe
Dallin H. Oaks
I. Daniel Stewart

LEGISLATURE

President of the Senate .... Miles Ferry
Secretary of the Senate .... Sophia C. Buckmiller

Speaker of the House .... Norman H. Bangerter
Chief Clerk of the House .... Allan M. Acomb

STATISTICS

Land Area (square miles) 82,073
  Rank in Nation 12th
Population 1,461,037
  Rank in Nation 36th
  Density per square mile 17.8
Number of Representatives in Congress 3
Capital City .... Salt Lake City
  Population 163,033
  Rank in State 1st
Largest City .... Salt Lake City
Number of Places over 10,000 Population 22

Vermont

Nickname . . . . The Green Mountain State
Motto . . . . *Freedom and Unity*
Flower . . . . Red Clover
Bird . . . . Hermit Thrush
Tree . . . . Sugar Maple
Song . . . . *Hail, Vermont!*
Animal . . . . Morgan Horse
Insect . . . . Honeybee
Entered the Union . . . . March 4, 1791
Capital . . . . Montpelier

SELECTED OFFICIALS

Governor . . . . Richard A. Snelling
Lieutenant Governor . . . . Peter Smith
Secretary of State . . . . James H. Douglas
Attorney General . . . . John J. Easton
Treasurer . . . . Emory A. Hebard
Auditor of Accounts . . . . Alexander V. Acebo

SUPREME COURT

Franklin S. Billings Jr., Chief Justice
Ernest W. Gibson III
William C. Hill
Louis P. Peck
Wynn Underwood

GENERAL ASSEMBLY

President of the Senate . . . . Peter Smith
President Pro Tem of the Senate
. . . . Robert A. Bloomer
Secretary of the Senate . . . . Robert H. Gibson

Speaker of the House . . . . Stephan A. Morse
Clerk of the House . . . . Robert L. Picher

STATISTICS

Land Area (square miles) 9,273
   Rank in Nation 43rd
Population 511,456
   Rank in Nation 48th
   Density per square mile 55.2
Number of Representatives in Congress 1
Capital City . . . . Montpelier
   Population 8,241
   Rank in State 5th
Largest City . . . . Burlington
   Population 37,712
Number of Places over 10,000 Population 3

Virginia

Nickname . . . . The Old Dominion
Motto . . . . *Sic Semper Tyrannis*
                   (Thus Always to Tyrants)
Flower . . . . Dogwood
Bird . . . . Cardinal
Tree . . . . Dogwood
Song . . . . *Carry Me Back to Old Virginia*
Animal . . . . Foxhound
Shell . . . . Oyster
Entered the Union . . . . June 25, 1788
Capital . . . . Richmond

SELECTED OFFICIALS

Governor . . . . Charles S. Robb
Lieutenant Governor . . . . Richard J. Davis
Secretary of the Commonwealth
. . . . Laurie Naismith
Attorney General . . . . Gerald L. Baliles

SUPREME COURT

Harry Lee Carrico, Chief Justice
George M. Cochran
A. Christian Compton
Alex M. Harman Jr.
Richard H. Poff
Charles S. Russell
Rosco B. Stephenson
John Charles Thomas
(Vacancy)

GENERAL ASSEMBLY

President of the Senate . . . . Richard J. Davis
President Pro Tem of the Senate
. . . . Edward E. Willey
Clerk of the Senate . . . . Jay T. Shropshire

Speaker of the House . . . . A.L. Philpott
Clerk of the House . . . . Joseph H. Holleman Jr.

STATISTICS

Land Area (square miles) 39,704
   Rank in Nation 36th
Population 5,346,818
   Rank in Nation 14th
   Density per square mile 134.7
Number of Representatives in Congress 10
Capital City . . . . Richmond
   Population 219,214
   Rank in State 3rd
Largest City . . . . Norfolk
   Population 266,979
Number of Places over 10,000 Population 33

Washington

Nickname . . . . The Evergreen State
Motto . . . . *Alki* (By and By)
Flower . . . . Western Rhododendron
Bird . . . . Willow Goldfinch
Tree . . . . Western Hemlock
Song . . . . *Washington, My Home*
Dance . . . . Square Dance
Gem . . . . Petrified Wood
Fish . . . . Steelhead Trout
Entered the Union . . . . November 11, 1889
Capital . . . . Olympia

SELECTED OFFICIALS

Governor . . . . John Spellman
Lieutenant Governor . . . . John A. Cherberg
Secretary of State . . . . Ralph Munro
Attorney General . . . . Kenneth O. Eikenberry
Treasurer . . . . Robert S. O'Brien
Auditor . . . . Robert V. Graham
Supt. of Public Instruction . . . . Frank Brouillet
Insurance Commissioner . . . . Richard G. Marquardt
Commissioner of Public Lands . . . . . . Brian J. Boyle

SUPREME COURT

Robert F. Brachtenbach, Chief Justice
Carolyn R. Dimmick   Hugh J. Rosellini
James M. Dolliver   Charles F. Stafford
Fred H. Dore   Robert F. Utter
Vermon R. Pearson   William H. Williams

LEGISLATURE

President of the Senate . . . . John A. Cherberg
President Pro Tem of the Senate . . . . . Barney Goltz
Secretary of the Senate . . . . Sidney R. Snyder

Speaker of the House . . . . Wayne Ehlers
Speaker Pro Tem of the House . . . . John L. O'Brien
Chief Clerk of the House . . . . Dean R. Foster

STATISTICS

Land Area (square miles) 66,511
    Rank in Nation 20th
Population 4,132,156
    Rank in Nation 20th
    Density per square mile 62.1
Number of Representatives in Congress 8
Capital City . . . . Olympia
    Population 27,447
    Rank in State 15th
Largest City . . . . Seattle
    Population 493,846
Number of Places over 10,000 Population 36

West Virginia

Nickname . . . . The Mountain State
Motto . . . . *Montani Semper Liberi*
                    (Mountaineers Are Always Free)
Flower . . . . Big Rhododendron
Bird . . . . Cardinal
Tree . . . . Sugar Maple
Songs . . . . *West Virginia, My Home Sweet Home;*
                    The West Virginia Hills; and
                    This Is My West Virginia
Animal . . . . Black Bear
Fish . . . . Brook Trout
Entered the Union . . . . June 20, 1863
Capital . . . . Charleston

SELECTED OFFICIALS

Governor . . . . John D. Rockefeller IV
Secretary of State . . . . A. James Manchin
Attorney General . . . . Chauncey H. Browning
Treasurer . . . . Larrie Bailey
Auditor . . . . Glen B. Gainer Jr.
Commissioner of Agriculture . . . . . . Gus R. Douglass

SUPREME COURT OF APPEALS

Thomas E. McHugh, Chief Justice
Sam R. Harshbarger
Darrell V. McGraw Jr.
Thomas B. Miller
Richard Neely

LEGISLATURE

President of the Senate . . . . Warren R. McGraw
President Pro Tem of the Senate . . . . James L. Davis
Clerk of the Senate . . . . Todd C. Willis

Speaker of the House . . . . Clyde M. See Jr.
Clerk of the House . . . . Donald L. Kopp

STATISTICS

Land Area (square miles) 24,119
    Rank in Nation 41st
Population 1,949,644
    Rank in Nation 34th
    Density per square mile 80.8
Number of Representatives in Congress 4
Capital City . . . . Charleston
    Population 63,968
    Rank in State 1st
Largest City . . . . Charleston
Number of Places over 10,000 Population 15

Wisconsin

Nickname.....................The Badger State
Motto................................*Forward*
Flower.............................Wood Violet
Bird......................................Robin
Tree............................Sugar Maple
Song...........................*On, Wisconsin!*
Rock.............................Red Granite
Mineral..................................Galena
Animal...................................Badger
Wildlife Animal................White-tailed Deer
Domestic Animal....................Dairy Cow
Fish..............................Muskellunge
Symbol of Peace.................Mourning Dove
Insect..............................Honey Bee
Soil..........................Antigo Silt Loam
Entered the Union..................May 29, 1848
Capital..................................Madison

SELECTED OFFICIALS

Governor.......................Anthony S. Earl
Lieutenant Governor..............James T. Flynn
Secretary of State.............Douglas La Follette
Attorney General..........Bronson C. La Follette
Treasurer......................Charles P. Smith
Supt. of Public Instruction.......Herbert J. Grover

SUPREME COURT

Nathan S. Heffernan, Chief Justice
Shirley S. Abrahamson
William A. Bablitch
William G. Callow
Louis J. Ceci
Roland B. Day
Donald W. Steinmetz

LEGISLATURE

President of the Senate.............Fred A. Risser
Chief Clerk of the Senate......Donald J. Schneider

Speaker of the Assembly.......Thomas A. Loftus
Assembly Speaker Pro Tempore
.....................David E. Clarenbach
Chief Clerk of the Assembly........Joanne Duren

STATISTICS

Land Area (square miles)..................54,426
   Rank in Nation..........................25th
Population............................4,705,767
   Rank in Nation..........................16th
   Density per square mile....................86.5
Number of Representatives in Congress..........9
Capital City............................Madison
   Population..........................170,616
   Rank in State............................2nd
Largest City..........................Milwaukee
   Population..........................636,212
Number of Places over 10,000 Population.......55

Wyoming

Nickname....................The Equality State
Motto.............................*Equal Rights*
Flower.......................Indian Paintbrush
Bird...............................Meadowlark
Tree...............................Cottonwood
Song...............................*Wyoming*
Stone....................................Jade
Entered the Union..................July 10, 1890
Capital...............................Cheyenne

SELECTED OFFICIALS

Governor.........................Ed Herschler
Secretary of State.............Thyra Thomson
Treasurer...........................Stan Smith
Auditor...........................Jim Griffith
Supt. of Public Instruction.........Lynn Simmons

SUPREME COURT

John J. Rooney, Chief Justice
C. Stuart Brown
G. Joseph Cardine
Robert R. Rose Jr.
Richard V. Thomas

LEGISLATURE

President of the Senate.........Edward D. Moore
Vice President of the Senate........John F. Turner
Chief Clerk of the Senate.............Ed Wren Jr.

Speaker of the House...............Russ Donley
Speaker Pro Tem of the House...........Jack Sidi
Chief Clerk of the House.......Herbert D. Pownall

STATISTICS

Land Area (square miles)..................96,989
   Rank in Nation..........................9th
Population............................469,557
   Rank in Nation..........................49th
   Density per square mile....................4.8
Number of Representatives in Congress..........1
Capital City...........................Cheyenne
   Population...........................47,283
   Rank in State............................2nd
Largest City.............................Casper
   Population...........................51,016
Number of Places over 10,000 Population........8

District of Columbia

Motto . . . . *Justitia Omnibus* (Justice for All)
Flower . . . . American Beauty Rose
Bird . . . . Wood Thrush
Tree . . . . Scarlet Oak
Became U.S. Capital . . . . December 1, 1800

OFFICERS

Mayor . . . . Marion S. Barry Jr.
City Administrator . . . . Thomas Downs
Secretary . . . . Dwight Cropp
Corporation Counsel . . . . Inez Reid

U.S. COURT OF APPEALS FOR THE DISTRICT OF COLUMBIA

Chief Judge . . . . J. Skelly Wright

DISTRICT OF COLUMBIA COURT OF APPEALS

Chief Judge . . . . Theodore R. Newman, Jr.

U. S. DISTRICT COURT FOR THE DISTRICT OF COLUMBIA

Chief Judge . . . . William B. Bryant
U.S. Attorney . . . . Joseph E. DiGenova

THE SUPERIOR COURT OF THE DISTRICT OF COLUMBIA

Chief Judge . . . . H. Carl Moultrie

DISTRICT OF COLUMBIA COUNCIL

Chairman . . . . David Clarke
Chairman Pro Tem . . . . Nadine P. Winter

STATISTICS*

Land Area (square miles) 63
Population 638,333
Density per square mile 10,132.3
Delegate to Congress* 1

---

*Committee voting privileges only.

American Samoa

Motto . . . . *Samoa-Muamua le Atua*
(Samoa, God Is First)
Flower . . . . Paogo
Plant . . . . Ava
Song . . . . *Amerika Samoa*
Became a Territory of the United States 1900
Capital . . . . Pago Pago

SELECTED OFFICIALS

Governor . . . . Peter T. Coleman
Lieutenant Governor . . . . Tufele Li'a
Attorney General . . . . Aviata Fa'alevao

HIGH COURT

Robert Garder, Chief Justice
Thomas W. Murphy, Associate Judge
Tauan'u Faisiota, Chief Judge

LEGISLATURE

President of the Senate . . . . Galea'i P. Poumele
President Pro Tem of the Senate
. . . . Mulitauaopele Tamotu
Secretary of the Senate . . . . Mrs. Salilo K. Levi

Speaker of the House . . . . Tuanaitau F. Tuia
Speaker Pro Tem of the House
. . . . Muasau S. Savali
Chief Clerk of the House . . . . Wally Utu

STATISTICS

Land Area (square miles) 76
Population 32,395
Density per square mile 426.3
Capital City . . . . Pago Pago
Population 3,075
Largest City . . . . Pago Pago
Number of Villages 76

Guam

Nickname .... Pearl of the Pacific
Flower .... *Puti Tai Nobio* (Bougainvillea)
Bird .... *Toto* (Fruit Dove)
Tree .... *Ifit* (Intsiabijuga)
Song .... *Stand Ye Guamanians*
Stone .... Latte
Slogan .... Where America's Day Begins
Animal .... Iguana
Ceded to the United States by Spain
.... December 10, 1898
Created a Territory .... August 1, 1950
Capital .... Agana

SELECTED OFFICIALS

Governor .... Ricardo J. Bordallo
Lieutenant Governor .... Eduardo Reyes
Attorney General .... Richard Opper

DISTRICT COURT OF GUAM

Judge .... Cristobal C. Duenas

SUPERIOR COURT OF GUAM

Presiding Judge .... Paul J. Abbate

LEGISLATURE

Speaker .... Carl Gutierrez
Vice Speaker .... Joe T. San Agustin
Legislative Secretary .... Elizabeth P. Arriola

STATISTICS

Land Area (square miles) 209
Population 105,816
Density per square mile 506.3
Delegate to Congress* 1
Capital City .... Agana
Population 896
Largest City .... Tamuning
Population 8,862

Puerto Rico

Nickname .... Island of Enchantment
Motto .... *Joannes Est Nomen Ejus*
(John Is Thy Name)
Song .... *La Borinquena*
Animal .... Coqui
Became a Territory of the United States
.... December 10, 1898
Became a self-governing commonwealth
.... July 25, 1952
Capital .... San Juan

SELECTED OFFICIALS

Governor .... Carlos Romero-Barcelo
Secretary of State .... Carlos S. Quiros
Secretary of Justice .... Nelson Martinez-Acosta

SUPREME COURT

Jose Trias-Monge, Chief Justice
Carlos V. Davila
Jorge Diaz-Cruz
Carlos J. Irizarry-Yunque
Antonio Negron Garcia
Francisco Rebollo-Lopez
Hiram Torres-Rigual

LEGISLATIVE ASSEMBLY

President of the Senate ... Miguel Hernandez-Agosto
Vice President of the Senate ...... Sergio Pena-Clos
Secretary of the Senate .... Hipolito Marcano
Speaker of the House ... Severo E. Colberg-Ramirez
Vice President of the House
.... Presby Santiago-Garcia
Secretary of the House
.... Julio M. Garcia-Passalacqua

STATISTICS

Land Area (square miles) 3,421
Population 3,187,570
Density per square mile 931.8
Delegate to Congress* 1
Capital City .... San Juan
Population 424,600
Largest City .... San Juan
Number of Places over 10,000 Population 31

*Committee voting privileges only.

Virgin Islands

Flower . . . . Yellow Elder or Ginger Thomas
Bird . . . . Yellow Breast or Bananaquit
Song . . . . *Virgin Islands March*
Purchased from Denmark . . . . March 31, 1917
Capital . . . . Charlotte Amalie

SELECTED OFFICIALS

Governor . . . . Juan F. Luis
Lieutenant Governor . . . . Juilo A. Brady
Attorney General (Acting) . . . . . . J'Ada Finch-Sheen

DISTRICT COURT

Chief Judge . . . . Almeric L. Christian
Judge . . . . David O'Brien

LEGISLATURE

President . . . . Hugo Dennis D. Roebuck
Vice President . . . . Bent Lawaetz
Legislative Secretary . . . . Cleone C. Maynard
Executive Secretary . . . . Eric Dawson

STATISTICS

Land Area (square miles) 132
   St. Croix (square miles) 80
   St. John (square miles) 20
   St. Thomas (square miles) 32
Population 95,591
   St. Croix 49,013
   St. John 2,360
   St. Thomas 44,218
   Density per square mile 724.2
Delegate to Congress* 1
Capital City . . . . Charlotte Amalie, St. Thomas
   Population 11,842

---

*Committee voting privileges only.

Northern Mariana Islands

Tree . . . . Flame Tree
Flower . . . . Plumeria
Administered by the United States as a trusteeship
  for the United Nations . . . . July 18, 1947
Voters approved a proposed constitution
  . . . . June 1975
U.S. President signed covenant agreeing to com-
  monwealth status for the islands . . . . . March 1976
Became a self-governing commonwealth
  . . . . January 9, 1978
Capital . . . . Saipan

SELECTED OFFICIALS

Governor . . . . Pedro P. Tenorio
Lieutenant Governor . . . . Pedro A. Tenorio

U.S. DISTRICT COURT

Judge . . . . Alfred Laureta

COMMONWEALTH TRIAL COURT

Robert A. Hefner, Chief Judge
Herbert Sohl
Thomas Moore

LEGISLATURE

President of the Senate . . . . Olympia T. Borja
Vice President of the Senate
  . . . . Benjamin T. Manglona

Speaker of the House . . . . Benigno R. Fitial
Vice Speaker of the House . . . . Francisco T. Cabrera

STATISTICS

Land Area (square miles) 184
Population 16,780
   Density per square mile 91.1
Capital City . . . . Saipan
   Population 14,549
Largest City . . . . Saipan

Federated States of Micronesia

Administered by the United States as a trusteeship
for the United Nations . . . . July 18, 1947
Voters approved a proposed constitution
. . . . July 12, 1978
Effective date of constitution . . . . May 10, 1979
Capital. . . . . Kolonia, Ponape

SELECTED OFFICIALS

President* . . . . Tosiwo Nakayama
Vice President* . . . . Bailey Olter
Attorney General . . . . David Nevitt

CONGRESS

Speaker. . . . . Bethwel Henry
Vice Speaker . . . . Joab Sigrah
Chief Clerk . . . . Nishima Siron

STATISTICS

Land Area (square miles) 271
    Kosrae District 42
    Ponape District 134
    Truk District 49
    Yap District 46
Population 73,160
    Kosrae District 5,491
    Ponape District 22,081
    Truk District. 37,488
    Yap District 8,100
Capital City . . . . Kolonia, Ponape
    Population 5,549
Largest City . . . . Moen, Truk
    Population 10,351

*Selected by the elected unicameral congress from among its own members.

Marshall Islands

Administered by the United States as a trusteeship
for the United Nations . . . . July 18, 1947
Voters approved a proposed constitution
. . . . March 1, 1979
Effective date of constitution . . . . May 1, 1979
Capital . . . . Majuro

SELECTED OFFICIALS

President . . . . Amata Kabua

MARSHALL ISLANDS HIGH COURT

John C. Lanham, Chief Justice

LEGISLATURE
(Nitijela)

Speaker . . . . Atlan Anien
Vice Speaker . . . . Andrew Hisaiah

STATISTICS

Land Area (square miles) 70
Population 31,042
    Density per square mile 443.5
Capital City . . . . Majuro
    Population 8,667
Largest City . . . . Majuro

Republic of Belau

Administered by the United States as a trusteeship
for the United Nations . . . . July 18, 1947
Voters approved a proposed constitution
. . . . July 9, 1980
Effective date of constitution . . . . January 1981

SELECTED OFFICIALS

President . . . . Haruo I. Remeliik
Vice President . . . . Alfonso R. Oiterong

SUPREME COURT

Mamoru Nakamura, Chief Justice

SENATE

President . . . . Kaleb Udui

STATISTICS

Land Area (square miles) 192
Population 12,177
    Density per square mile 63.4
Capital City . . . . Koror
    Population 6,222
Largest City . . . . Koror

INDEX

(Page numbers in parentheses indicate tables.)

Note: Individual states or other jurisdictions are not listed separately by name. There are several hundred references to each in this book. Nearly all the tables present data on 50 states and at least some other jurisdictions.

For a quick, basic reference to state statistics and elected officials, consult Section IX, The State Pages, beginning on p. 506.

The *Subject and Name Index* is cross-referenced, with one or two main entries for a subject. "See" and "see also" entries direct the reader to the main entries.

AUTHOR INDEX

Amico, Lorraine: State Information Management, 253-55
Augenblick, John, Nancy M. Berve and Christian Pipho: Education, 1982-1983, 353-56
Berry, Frances Stokes and R. Douglas Roederer: State Regulation of Occupations and Professions, 420-22
Berve, Nancy M., John Augenblick and Christian Pipho: Education, 1982-1983, 353-56; (with Gordon Van de Water) Postsecondary Education, 359-61
Beyle, Thad L.: The Governors, 1982-83, 39-41; Governors and Legislatures, 42-43; The Executive Branch: Elective Officials and Organization, 44-46; The Executive Branch: Issues, 47-48
Chi, Keon S.: Developments in State Personnel Systems, 288-90
Cole, Leslie: State Forestry Administration and Management, 472-74
Criz, Maurice: State Aid to Local Government, 30-32; Finances of State-Administered Public Employee Retirement Systems, 279-80; State and Local Government Finances in 1981-82, 299-301; State Finances in 1982, 314-16; State Tax Collections, 341-43
Cummings, Glenn R.: Procurement Challenges, 251-52
Farthing-Capowich, Daina: State of the Judiciary, 142-45
Feigenbaum, Edward D.: Corrections, Courts and Criminal Justice, 415-17
Gambill, John: Recent Trends in State Taxation, 327-28
Glade, Edward H. Jr. and Mae Dean Johnson: State Agriculture, 463-64
Grand, Jon: Environmental Management: Emerging Issues, 450-53
Hartwell, Carol H.: Housing and Community Development, 436-38
Johnson, Mae Dean and Edward H. Glade Jr.: State Agriculture, 463-64
Karel, John: State Parks and Outdoor Recreation, 458-59
Kerker, Robert P.: Budgeting in the 1980s, 242-43
Knapp, Elaine Stuart: Trends in State Legislation: 1982-83, 165-66
Lamb, Eugene and Neil Sampson: Soil and Water Conservation, 482-84
McCabe, John: Uniform State Laws, 173-74
May, Janice and Albert L. Sturm: State Constitutions: 1982-83, 211-13; State Constitutional Changes, 214-17; Sources on State Constitutions, 218-20
Nelson, Richard R.: Labor Legislation: 1982-1983, 488-91
Peterson, Kent A.: General Revenue Sharing, 24-25
Pipho, Christian: Elementary-Secondary Education Issues, 357-58; (with Nancy M. Berve and John Augenblick) Education, 1982-1983, 353-56
Pohlmann, Kay T.: State Financial Administration, 231-32
Pound, William T.: The State Legislatures, 79-83
Reinshuttle, Robert J.: State Economic Development, 434-35
Roberts, Jane F.: Federal-State Relations, 18-19; State-Local Relations, 21-23
Roederer, R. Douglas and Frances Stokes Berry: State Regulation of Occupations and Professions, 420-22
Sampson, Neil and Eugene Lamb: Soil and Water Conservation, 482-84
Smolka, Richard G.: Election Legislation, 180-82
Sostowski, R.H.: State Police and Highway Patrols, 424-25
Stenberg, Carl W.: Intergovernmental Relations, 15-17
Stevens, Alan V.: State Government Employment, 271-73
Stoffel, Lester L.: State Library Agencies, 265-66
Sturm, Albert L. and Janice C. May: State Constitutions: 1982-83, 211-13; State Constitutional Changes, 214-17; Sources on State Constitutions, 218-20
Suelflow, James E.: Developments in Public Utility Regulation, 427-29
Van de Water, Gordon and Nancy M. Berve: Postsecondary Education, 359-61
Vorlander, Carl W.: State Information Systems, 261-62

SUBJECT AND NAME INDEX

Accounting, 231-32, (236-37)
Accounting, Natl. Council on Governmental, 231
Administrative officials: elective, 3, 16, 44, (45, 72); cabinets, (65); methods of selection, (74-77); salaries, (66-71); terms, (72-73); see also titles of individual officials; governors and executive branch
Administrative organization, 42, 43; cabinets, (65); interagency commissions, 47; personnel, 47, 48
Advisory Commission on Intergovernmental Relations, U.S. (ACIR), 16, 218
AFSCME et. al. v. The State of Washington et. al., 289
Age of majority, (171)
Aging, 393-94
Agriculture, 463, 471; products transportation and storage, 463; production, 463, 464, (467, 469); farm income, 463, 464, (465, 466); federal policies, 463-64; land values, 463, (466, 471); livestock and poultry, 464, (468); foreign-owned acreage, (470)
Agriculture and Consumer Protection Act of 1973, 464
Agriculture, U.S. Dept. of, 392, 463, 464, 482, 484; Farmers Home Admin. (FmHA), 463; Soil Conservation Service, 464; supplemental food program (WIC), 404
Aid to Families with Dependent Children (AFDC), see public welfare
Aid to local governments, see state-local relations
Air pollution, see environmental protection
Alcoholic beverages: legal purchasing age, 416; see also taxation
Alexander, Lamar, 21
America in Ruins, 21
American Bar Association, 144
American College Testing (ACT), 306
American Federation of State, County and Municipal Employees (AFSCME), 288, 289
American Library Directory, 265
American Telephone & Telegraph (AT&T): break up, 18, 252, 261, 428
Arbitration Assoc., American, 290
Attorneys General, 43, (74); consumer protection, (63); duties, (62, 63, 64); qualifications, (59); rulings, 48; salaries, (66); terms, (72)
Auditing, 81, 232, (238-40); post, 44; internal, 47
Auditors, 81, 232, (238-40); terms, (72-73)
Baker v. Carr, 79
Blanchard, James A., 473

Block grants, see federal funding
Book of the States, 1982-83 The, 212, 214, 219
Bonds, state, 22, 31-32; general obligation, 231, 301, 437; ratings, 231; revenue, 233, 316, 436
Bridges, 376
Broder, David, 19
Budget, federal, 15, 19, 166, 243; cuts, 253, 353; deficits, 15, 18, 299
Budgeting, state, 39, 42, 242-49; agencies, (246-47, 248-49); balancing measures, 243, 300, 314, 343, 353-54; cutbacks, 16, 39, 359; officials, (248-49); practices, (244-45); procedures, 47, 231, (244-45, 246-47)
Budget Officers, National Assoc., 242, 314
Bush, George, 18
Business and industrial development, see industry; econ. development
Cable television, 16, 18, 427
Campaign finance laws, see elections, funding
Capital punishment, see criminal justice
Carnegie Foundation for the Advancement of Teaching, 353
Carter administration, 15
Cash management, 231, (233-35)
Census Bureau (U.S.), 15, 24, 25, 30, 279, 314
Census of Governments (1982), 279
Chadha case, 43, 83
Chemistry and Soils, Bureau of, 482
Chicago Regional Transportation Auth., 377
Chiefs of Police, International Assoc. of, 424
Children: assistance, 393; child support, 391, 464; Child Support Enforcement, 391, (401); health care, 404; labor laws, 466
Cigarettes, see taxation
Cities, see local government
Cities, Natl. League of, 21
Citizen's Forum on Self-Government, 218, 219
Citizen's Guide to the Alaska Constitution, A, 218
Citizen's Guide to the Texas Constitution, A, 218
Civilian Conservation Corps (CCC), 458, 472, 482
Civil Rights Act (1964), 48, 289
Clean Air Act, 465
Clean Water Act, 464
Clearinghouse on Licensure, Enforcement and Regulation (CLEAR), 3, 422
Clinton, William, 21
Coastal Energy Impact Program, 32
Collective bargaining, see labor; personnel systems
College Board (SAT), 359
Columbia University, 218
Commerce, U.S. Dept. of, 252
Community development, 437-39
Compacts, see interstate compacts
Comparable worth, see courts; employment; personnel systems
Competitive bidding, see procurement systems; Supreme Court, U.S.
Comprehensive Employment and Training Act (CETA), 271, 300, 472-73
Computer use, see information systems
Congress, U.S., 15, 16, 216, 359, 473; comparable worth bills, 290; environmental programs, 450, 451, 452; highway safety programs, 424; House committees, 441; legislation, 18, 436, 464; legislative veto, 19, 42, 83; welfare policies, 390, 393
Congressional Information Service (CIS), 218
Connecticut Law Review, 218
Conservation, see soil and water conservation
Conservation Districts, National Assoc. of, 483
Constitutional revision, 211-17, (216); by amendment, 211; by conventions, 211, 212, 213, 214, 216, (226, 229); by legislature, 211, (212, 223-24); commissions, 212, 213, (228); constitutional initiative, 211, (212), 218, (225); methods of initiation, 211
Constitutions, state, 211-17, (221); amendments, 42, 211-17; sources on, 218-20
Constitution (U.S.), 11, 42; separation of powers in, 42; Commerce Clause, 429
Continuing education, (423)
Container Corp. v. California, 440
Cooperative Forestry Asst. Act, 472
Corporate income taxes, see taxation
Corrections, 415-17, (418), (419); departments of, 44; expenditures for, 301; state employees, 271; see also, criminal justice; police and highway patrol
Council of State Governments, The, 1-7, 40, 219, 422, 483; affiliated organizations, 3; governance and funding, 1; officials, 4, 5, 6, 7; publications, 2-3, 218, 252, 261; regional offices, 1, 2
Counties: home rule, 215; see also local government
Court Administrators, Conf. of State, 144, 145

Courts, 142-63; and comparable worth, 243, 289-90; case management, 143-44; judges' terms, compensation and qualifications, (148-49, 150-51, 152-53); judicial redistricting, 215; last resort, (146-47); personnel, 142, 163; removal of judges, (156-62); rulings, 16, 42; selection of judges, (154-55); state financing, 140; use of technology, 142-43
Courts, Natl. Center for State, 143
Crime, 415-16; arrest rates, 415; computer crime, 261-62
Criminal justice: capital punishment, 166, 214, (418); constitutional proposals on, 214; probation and parole, 415, 416; see also corrections; courts
Davis-Bacon Act, 464
Davison, Don, 458
Death penalty, see criminal justice
Debts, state, 301, (303, 304-07), 316, (317, 318-19), 326; general obligation, 301; interest, 300-01, (311, 312), 315, 316
Delaware River Basin Compact, 11
Democrats, 83; in gubernatorial elections, 39, 40
Deregulation, 19; of telephone industry, 18
Development Council, Natl. (NDC), 435
District of Columbia: statehood, 211, 212, 216
Driver's licenses, see motor vehicles
Drunk driving laws, 15, 166, 416, 424
Drunk Driving, Presidential Comm. on, 416
Dukakis, Michael S., 22, 254
Economic development, 21, 22, 44, 336, 434-35, 436-38, 440-41; departments of, 45, 435; enterprise zones, 16, 22, 165, 435, 440, 441; financial assistance to industry, (442-43); programs, 165-434; special services for industrial development, (447-48); tax incentives, (444-46)
Economic Recovery Tax Act of 1981, 341, 342
Education, 32, 165, 353-75; aid per student, 354, (364); boards, 44; enrollments, (363); expenditures, 301, (311, 312), 315-16, (318, 362, 364); reports on, 165, 353, 355-56, 357; revenues, (365); see also teachers
Education, elementary and secondary, 353, 357-58; enrollments, 354; graduation requirements, 21, 165, (367); minimum competency testing, 357-58, (368); per pupil support, 354; reforms, 21, 357; revenue for, (365); see also, teachers
Education, postsecondary, 359-64, 369-75; admission requirements, 357, 360; appropriation for, (370); basic skills requirements, 359; budgets, 353, 359, (370); employment, 272; enrollments, 360-61, (369); institutions, (372); occupational programs, (373); reports on, 353, 355-56; student aid, 359-60, (371); tuition, 300, 306, 315; work-study program, 360; see also teachers
Education Statistics, Natl. Center for, 361
Education, U.S. Dept. of, 353
Elected state officials, see administrative officials, elective; elections, state officials; governors; legislators; and individual titles
Elections, 180-82; absentee balloting, 180, 214; congressional, 353; constitutional proposals on, 213; exit polls, 181-82; funding, (188-91, 192-96, 197-98); gubernatorial, 39, 40, (210); mail ballots, 181; legislation, 180, 182, (183-96); polling hours, (200-01); presidential, 182, 353, (208); primaries, 182, (206-07); state officials, (202-03, 204-05, 206-07); vote fraud, 180-81; voter registration, 180, 181, (199); voter turnout, (208, 209)
Electricity, see public utilities
Employment, 44, 341; comparable worth, 289-90; full-time equivalents, 271-72; occupational equity, 47, 289-90; payrolls and earnings, 15, 272-73, (274, 276, 278); programs, 45; state government, 39, 271-78, (274, 275); state and local government payrolls, 271
Enterprise zones, see economic development
Entitlement programs, 15, 16; see also, Social Security: Medicaid; Medicare; public welfare
Environmental Law Institute, 452
Environmental protection, 166, 416, 450-53, 482-83; air pollution control, 451; hazardous waste, 11, 45, 166, 252, 416, 450, 451, 452, (455-56, 457); state org., (454); Superfund, 451, 452, (457); wastewater treatment, 450-51; water pollution control, 18, 166, 450, 469
Environmental Protection Agency (U.S.), 405, 450, 451, 452, 483
Equal employment opportunity, 165
Executive branch, see governors and the executive branch; administrative officials
Excellence in Education, Natl. Comm. on, 361
Excise taxes, see taxation
Expenditures, see finances, general expenditure
Family Assistance, Office of, 390, 391
Farms, see agriculture
Federal funding, 15-16, 18, (20), 24-25, (26-28), 30, 31, (30, 31, 33), (37), 82, (304-07, 308, 309, 310), 390-94, (395, 396, 397, 398-99, 400, 401, 402), 404, 405, (412-13), 458, 463, 464, (476, 477); block grants, 15, 16, 18, 19, 43, 45, 47, 82, 391, 392-93, 406, 437, 438; education, 354, 359; entitlement programs, 390, (402); grants-in-aid, 30, 351, 369; high-

ways, (382); industrial development bonds, 437; libraries, 265; mass transit, 376; see also revenue sharing; revenue sources

Federal-state relations, 1, 11, 15-17, 18-19, 30, 31, (37); information systems, 254; see also federal funding

Federalism, see intergovernmental relations; federal-state relations; state-local relations

Feinstein, Dianne, 180

Finances, state, 39, 165, 231-40, 243, 314-16; aid to local governments, 30-37, (33, 34, 35, 36, 37); audits, 232; capital expenditures, 300; cash and securities, 301, 316; courts, 142; general expenditure, 300-01, (306-07, 311, 313), 315, 316, (317, 318-19, 322-23, 324-25); per capita expenditures, (312); summary, (304-05, 306-07, 317, 318-19); see also revenue sources; debts, state

Financial administration, 231-40, (248-49); accounting and reporting, 231-32, (236-37); audits, 231-32, (238-40); cash management, 231, (233-35); collection procedures, 231

Financial markets, 243

Fiscal policy, (125-26), 211, 214, 242; constitutional proposals on, 214

Food and Agriculture Act of 1977, 464

Food stamps, see public welfare

Foreign investment in farms, (470)

Forest Incentive Practices (FIP), 473

Forest Resource Planning Act, 473

Forestry, 472-81; fire, insect, disease control, 472, 473, (476, 478); incentive program, (477); management, 473; products, 472, 473; reforestation, 473, 484; resources, 472, 474, (475); state agencies, 479; taxes, 472-73, (480, 481)

Freedom of information, 48

Fringe benefits, see personnel systems, compensation

Fund-Raising Councils, American, 361

Gambling, legalized, (172), 216

Gasoline taxes, see taxation

Gender gap, 47, 48

General Accounting Office (U.S.), 438

Generally Accepted Accounting Principles (GAAP), 231-32

General revenue sharing, see revenue sharing

Governmental Accounting and Financial Reporting Principles, 231

Government reorganization, 44

Governors and executive branch, 39-48, (49-50); appointive power, 47; compensation, (52, 66); conflicts with legislatures, 42, 43, 242-43; executive branch, elective officials and org., 44-46; executive branch issues, 47-48; executive order, (55-56); governors' elections, 39, 44, (74); powers, (53); qualifications for office, (51); salaries, (66-72); succession and transition, (54), 215; team election, 40-41, 44; terms, 39, 44, (72-73), 215; transitions, 54; veto power, 42

Governors' Association, Natl. (NGA), 40, 251, 314

Gross national product (GNP), 299, 341, 437

Harvard Law Review, 218

Hazardous wastes, see environmental protection

Hazardous Waste Coordination Committee, Northeast, 416

Health: expenditures, 166, 301, (311-12), 315, 316, (319), 392, (411, 412-13); federal programs, 392; preventive health services, 403-04; state health agencies (SHAs), 403-04, 405, 406, (407, 408-10)

Highway patrols, see police and highway patrols

Highway Trust Fund (U.S.), 376

Highways, 376; expenditures, 301, (311, 312), 315, 316, (318, 380); federal aid for, 381; mileage, (378); National Maximum Speed Limit, 424; receipts for, (379); state employees, 271

Hinckley, John Jr., 166

Holidays, state, (294-95)

Hospitals: expenditures for, 301, (311, 312), 315, 316, (319)

Housing, 437-39; expenditures for, 301; housing finance agencies, 436, 437, (439); programs, 18, 436-39, 440

Housing and Urban Development, U.S. Dept. of, 19, 437, 438

Human Development Services, Office of, 393, 394

Human services, 390-402; agencies and commissions, 45; programs, 45

Income: per capita, (352)

Income taxes, see taxation

Indebtedness, see debts, state

Index Digest of State Constitutions, 218

Industry: development, 440, (442-43, 444-46); industrial revenue bonds, 440-42; financial incentive programs, (442-43, 444-47); venture capital, 165, 441

Inflation, 18, 229, 231, 392; rate, 359; subsidence, 280

Information systems, 81-82, 253-64, (256-57, 258-59, 260); administration, 261; budgets, 254, 255; computer use, 254, 261-62; confidentiality, 255, 261; data systems, 81, (134-35), 253-54, 255; Electronic Funds Transfer, 261; judicial, 143-44; problems, (263); security, (264); State Occupational Information Coord. Committees, 254; state statistical activities, (256, 57); State Statistical Task Force, 253; see also telecom-

munications; crime, computer crime

Initiative and referendum, 79, 83, (167, 168-69)

Interest rates, 299, 341; prime rates, 299

Intergovernmental relations, 15-17, 18-37; see also federal-state relations; state-local relations; federal funding

Interior, U.S. Dept. of, 482; Soil Conservation Service, 482, 483

Internal Revenue Service, U.S., 437, 441

Interstate compacts, 11-14, (12-14)

Interstate organizations, 8-10

Jefferson Co. Pharmaceutical v. Abbot Laboratories, 252

Job Training Partnership Act, 18, 19, 440, 466

Judiciary, see courts; criminal justice

Justice, U.S. Dept. of, 180, 415

Kean, Thomas, 22

Labor, 165, 377, 488-91; agricultural workers, 488, 490; child labor, 490, (498-501); collective bargaining, 489; job training, 490; legislation, 488-91; occupational safety, (496), 489; prevailing wage, 488; programs, 45; wage garnishment, 488; workers' compensation, 315, 316, 489-90, (492-93, 494-95); see also unions

Labor Statistics, U.S. Bureau of, 361

League of Women Voters, 218

Legislative Clerks and Secretaries, American Society of, 80

Legislative redistricting, 83, 166, 215; see also reapportionment

Legislative procedures, see legislatures

Legislators, 39; banned from boards and commissions, 42, 43; compensation, 79, 80, (92-94, 95-96, 97-98, 100-02); constitutional proposal on, 214; membership, 83, (85, 103); qualifications, (86-87); terms, (85)

Legislatures, 79-83, (84), 140; and budgeting, 80, 81, 82, (122-23, 125-26); conflicts with executive, 42, 43, 80, 82, 83, 242; council movement, 80-81; introductions and enactments, (104-05, 106-07); leadership selection, (88-89, 90-91); power to confirm appointments, 47; procedures, (114-16, 117, 118-19, 120); reform, 79-82; regulatory powers, 42; review powers, 19, 82, 83, (127, 128), 215; sessions, 79, 80, 81, (108-10); staffs, 81, (121,124); veto overrides, 80, (112-13), 243

Library agencies, 265-69, (267, 268-69); functions and responsibilities, 265, (268-69); information networks, 265-66; structure and appropriations, (267)

Library of Congress, 218

Library Services and Construction Act (LSCA), 265

Licensing: evaluation, 421; licensure boards, 420-21; mandatory continuing education, 421-22, (423); occupational, 420-22; professional, 420-22; tax revenue, (350-51)

Lieutenant governors, 40-41; election of, 44, (74); powers and duties, 40, 44, (58); qualifications and terms, (57, 72-73); salaries, (66)

Lobbyists, (136-37, 138-40), 377

Local government, see intergovernmental relations; finances, state; revenue sharing; state-local relations

Majority, age of, see mimimum age laws

Mass transit, 376

Mayors, U.S. Conference of, 21, 290

Medicaid, 16, 45, 166, 392, 393, (400, 405)

Medicare, 390, 393

Merit systems, 48, 288-90, (291, 294-95, 296-97); see also personnel systems

Migrant and Seasonal Agricultural Worker Protection Act, 488

Minimum age laws, (171)

Model acts, 173, (175-78, 179)

Model State Constitution, 218

Motor vehicles: excise tax, 376; laws, (382-83); no-fault insurance, (384-86); operators' licenses, (388-89); registrations, (388-89)

Municipal League, Natl., see Citizens' Forum on Self Government

National Association for State Information Systems (NASIS), 261

National Civic Review, 219

National Governors' Assoc. (NGA), see Governors' Association

Nation at Risk, A, 357

Natural gas, see public utilities

Natural resources: departments of, 40; management, 11; see also environmental protection; agriculture; forestry; soil and water conservation

New Columbia Admissions Act, 212, 216-17

New England Library Network (NELINET), 265

New Federalism, 15-19

New York Metropolitan Transit Authority, 376-77

No-fault motor vehicle insurance, (384-86)

Occupational licensing, see licensing

Occupational Safety and Health Act, 489, (496)

Office of Management and Budget, U.S. (OMB), 18, 19, 253

Old age assistance, 393-94

Older Americans Act, 393-94

Omnibus Budget Reconciliation Act of 1981, 390, 405
On Line Computer Library Center (OCLC), 265
Open meetings laws, 48
Organizations serving state and local officials, 8-10
Paperwork reduction, 251, 254
Paperwork Reduction Act of 1980, 253
Parks, 458-59, (460-61); attendance, 458, (460-61); funding, 458, 459, (460-61)
Personnel Executives, Natl. Assoc. of, 290
Personnel systems, 47-48, 142, 279, 288-97; administration, 288; collective bargaining, 142, 288, 290, (291-92); comparable worth, 47, 289-90; compensation, 288-90, (293, 294-95); evaluation, 288, (296-97); organization, (291-92); see also retirement systems
Police and highway patrols, 424-25; personnel, (426); see also criminal justice
Polling hours, see elections
Pollution control, see environmental protection
Population: elderly, 279; by state, (352)
Poverty, 391, 392
Primary elections, see elections
Prisons: construction and renovation, 415; library services, 265; overcrowding, 415; populations, (419)
Procurement systems, 251; competitive bidding, 251, 252; Model Procurement Code, 251; standardization, 251, 252
Professional licensing, see licensing
Property taxes, see taxation; revenue sources
Proposition 2½, 300
Proposition 13, 15, 215, 300
Public employees, see employment; personnel systems
Public utilities, 427-32; commissions, 44, 215, 428, 429, (430, 431); communications, 428; electricity, 428, (432); natural gas, 428, (432); water, 427
Public Utility Regulatory Policies Act, 429
Public welfare, 16, 390-402, (402); AFDC, 300, 390-91, 392, (395); earning limits, 390; expenditures, 301, (311, 312), 315, 316, (318), 390; food stamps, 16, 391, 392, 393, (396); Supplemental Security Income, 30, 391, 392, 393, (397, 398-99); Work Incentive Program (WIN), 390-91; workfare, 391; see also children; Medicaid; Medicare; health; federal funding; old age assistance
Purchasing, 251-52; officials, 252; professional service 251-52
Purchasing, Natl. Institute of Governmental, 251
Purchasing Officials, Natl. Assoc. of State, 251
Reagan administration, 82, 440; defense emphasis, 39, 47; environmental policies, 451; and grants, 47; and Social Security benefits, 359; welfare policies, 390, 393
Reagan, Ronald, 16, 18, 165, 393, 440
Reapportionment, 79, 80, 81, 242; see also legislative redistricting
Recall of elected officials, 170
Recession, 30, 251, 280, 299, 314, 315, 341, 353, 458
Recreation, 459
Referendum, see initiative and referendum
Regan, Donald, 440
Regulation, see environmental protection; licensing; public utilities
Regulatory Reform, Task Force on, 18
Regulatory Research Institute, Natl., 427, 429
Republicans, 83; in gubernatorial elections, 40
Resource Conservation and Recovery Act, 451-52
Retirement Systems, 279-87, 301, 315; assets, 280, (281, 284, 285); benefits, 279-80, (281, 282-83); coverage, 279; investments, 280, (286-87); receipts, (280, 281, 286-87)
Revenue sharing, 15, 18, 24-29, 31, 315; entitlement periods and amount, 24-25, (24); payments to local governments, (28-29); payments to state governments, (26-27)
Revenue sources, 82, 299-300, (304-05, 308), 314-15, (318, 320-21), 341-52, (345, 346-47), 376-77; general fund, 314, 315; increases, 314, 353-54; interest, 315; intergovernmental, 17, 299, (304-05, 310), 315; per capita, (309); state and local, 299-300, (308, 309, 310, 317)
Reynolds v. Sims, 79
Right to work, 288
Robinson-Patman Act, 252
Roosevelt, Franklin D., 482
Salaries, 289; administrative and elected officials, (66-71); equity, 289-90; judges, (150-51); legislators, (92-94, 95-96, 97-98, 100-02); see also teachers
Sales tax, see taxation
Scholarship and Grant Programs, Natl. Assoc. of, 360
Scholastic Aptitude Test (SAT), 360
Secretaries of state: duties, (60, 61); qualifications, (59); salaries, (66); terms, 72-73
Severance taxes, see taxation

Sexual discrimination, 288, 290
Slater, Courtenay, 253
Snelling, Richard A., 427
Social Security, 279, 390, 393; Administration, 391; benefits for students, 359
Social Security Act, 390-93; Title IV, 390, 391, 393; Title XIX, 392, 405; Title XX, 393, (402)
Soil and water conservation, 464, 482-87; funding, (483); laws, (482-83); programs, (485); soil conservation districts, 482, 483, (486, 487); see also environmental protection
Soil and Water Resources Conservation Act of 1977, 483
Sources and Documents of United States Constitutions, 218
Speed limit, 424
State and Local Government Purchasing, 2nd Ed., 252
State budgets, see budgeting, state
State-federal relations, see federal-state relations
State Health Agencies (SHAs), see health
State-local relations, 15-17, 21-23, 30-37; ACIRs, 22; education, 21, 31, (33, 36); highways, 31, (33, 36); infrastructure, 31; per capita, 30, (33); public welfare, 31, (33, 36); regulatory activities, 22; state aid, 16, 17, 30, (30, 31, 33, 34, 35, 36, 37)
States Information Center (SIC), 1-2
States Services Organization, 2
Statistical reporting, see information systems
Student Financial Assistance, Natl. Commission on, 359
Suggested State Legislation, 261, 483
Sunset legislation, 82, 83, (130-33), 420, 421, 437
Sunshine laws, see freedom of information
Supplemental Security Income, see public welfare
Supreme Courts, state: Alabama, 214; Idaho, 215; New Hampshire, 213
Supreme Court, U.S., 19, 42, 43, 79, 83; antitrust decisions, 18; ruling on competitive bidding, 252; ruling on unitary tax, 440; ruling on wage discrimination, 290
Surface Transportation Assistance Act of 1982, 376
Susquehanna River Basin Compact, 11
Swindler, William F., 218
Tanner, Jack, 289
Tax Administrators, Federation of, 314
Taxation, 165, (304, 306), 327-39, 341-52, (345); administering agencies, (329, 330); alcoholic beverages, 165, 300, 328, (332), 343, (348-49), 400; collections, 341-43; corporate income, 19, 300, 327-28, (339), 341, 342, (344, 346-47), 440; death and gift tax, (344, 346-47), 473, (481); excise rates, (332-33); forestland, 472-73, (480); food and drug exemptions, (331); income, 165, 216, 315, 327, (334), 341, (342, 344, 346-47, 352), 353, 440; increases in, 39, 82, 165, 300, 315, 327, 328, 341, 342, 343, 353; license, (350-51); motor fuels, 165, 300, 328, (332), 343, (348-49), 440; property, 17, 215, 300, (344, 346-47), 354, 463, 472-73; public utilities, 343, (348-49); sales and gross receipts, 300, 327, 328, (332), 341, 343, (344, 348-49), 353, 376; severance, 315, (336-38, 344, 346-47), 353, 473; surtaxes, 327; tobacco products, 165, 300, 328, (332), 343, (348-49), 440; trends, 299, 314, 315; unitary, 440; see also highways; revenue sources
Tax Equity and Fiscal Responsibility Act of 1982 (TEFRA), 341, 440
Tax Reform Act, 440-41
Teachers: career ladders, 165, 354, 368; certification, 358; collective bargaining, 489; competency tests, 21, 165; education programs, 361; merit pay, 21, 165, 354, 358; numbers, (366); qualifications, 357, 358, 360; salaries, 354, 360, 361, (366, 374, 375)
Telecommunications, 18, 252, 261, 428
Tobacco taxes, see taxation
Tourism, 165; depts. of, 45
Transportation, 22, 376-89; agricultural products, 463; fare structures, 377; mass transit, 376; motor carriers, 376, 463; railroads, 463; see also highways
Transportation, U.S. Dept. of, 424, 425
Treasurers: salaries, (66); terms, (72-73); selection, (74)
Treasury Department, U.S., 441
Unemployment, 165, 390, 435, (504); compensation, 18, 165, 300, 315, 316, (494-95); rates, 299, 315, 328, 341, (505)
Uniform Administrative Requirements for Grants in Aid, 251
Uniform Probate Code, 173, 174
Uniform state laws, 173-79; (175-78)
Uniform State Laws, Natl. Conf. of Commissioners of, 173, 174
Unions, 288, 290; see also labor, right to work
Unitary taxation, 440
United States v. American Telephone & Telegraph, 428
Utilities, see public utilities
Veto, see governors; legislatures
Voting Rights Act Amendments of 1982, 181, 183
Voter registration, see elections
Voting, see elections

Wages and hours, see labor
Water pollution, see environmental protection
Water Pollution Control Act, 469
Welfare, see public welfare
Winter, William F., 474
Workers' compensation, see labor
Worldwide Unitary Taxation Working Group, 440